MARINA DELVECCHIO

Dear Jane

Black Rose Writing | Texas

ISBN: 978-1-68433-172-7
PUBLISHED BY BLACK ROSE WRITING
www.blackrosewriting.com

Printed in the United States of America
Suggested Retail Price (SRP) $16.95

Dear Jane is printed in Chaparral Pro

Praise for

Dear Jane

"No subject is off limits for letters to Jane in this soul-stirring epistolary novel by Marina DelVecchio. *Dear Jane* is a book full of wondrous prose and uplifting courage."

–Donna Kaz, author of *UN/MASKED: Memoirs of a Guerrilla Girl On Tour*

"*Dear Jane* is a heart-wrenchingly beautiful exploration of what it means to not only find the pieces of yourself, but to put them back together."

–Sara Lunsford, author of *Sweet Hell on Fire*

"You are a seven-year-old urchin living on the streets of Athens, the child of an unhinged and violent prostitute. You've known few moments of security in a life filled with privation and violence, when you are ripped from this world and put into an ostensibly safer one. But is it? This is what the protagonist in Marina DelVecchio's trenchant and moving autobiographical first book, *Dear Jane*, must navigate."

–Nancy Rommelmann, author of
To the Bridge, a True Story of Motherhood and Murder

For my children, Joseph and Marina, so that you know me in ways I have never known my mothers. Thank you for trusting me with your hearts and for teaching me the ropes of good mothering. I love you both as you are, and I'm so proud to be your mom and your #1 fan.

To Joe, who has traveled this journey with me these past fifteen years, pushing me forward when I wanted to give up and reminding me of the rewards of surrendering to my dream. Without you, I never would have picked up a pen to write my stories, and without you, I never would have heard myself called by my name.

Dear Jane

"I know I should think well of myself; but that is not enough:
if others don't love me, then I would rather die than live –
I cannot bear to be solitary and hated."
JANE EYRE

Dear Jane,

Two years ago, I tried to kill myself. I was thirteen.

I've never told anyone.

I've never even said the words aloud, even to myself. Hearing them would make it too real, too painful. It's a secret that I have held onto since that night, but it's a secret that keeps taunting me with the vengeance of a school bully that gets bigger and badder as she circles her prey. I wish it would let go because I don't feel strong enough not to follow through with my willful thoughts. They burn into me, whispering how safe I would feel, how light, how free.

I'm scared it might be easier this time. After all, I'm fifteen now. More miserable. Stronger. More confident in my desire to leave this place and all the memories I keep twisted into little knots in the marrow of my bones. Brittle bones that look for hard corners and solid walls to smash into. A break might give me the relief I need to feel something other than shame and hate. All this quiet rage that brings me back to that night two years ago when I stood in the bathroom, cold and alone, the sharp tips of my scissors digging into my chest.

I tell you these things because I know you understand them, understand me. And you're safe. I'm safe with you. After all, you're not real. Just a fictional character, a girl Charlotte Brontë created in her imagination. And yet, you come from somewhere real. From her. From her experiences with being a poor, rejected girl. She created you this way, too. It's probably why I am drawn to you. I am you as you are Charlotte, and the two of you are the ones who come close to understanding me, for I am like you, rejected by those who volunteered to love us – and then chose not to. So maybe I can tell you everything. Every black secret, every memory I am forbidden to breathe into the light, the names of every person that I have been forced to bury into the black matter of my thoughts as if they have never existed. Maybe I can write to you about my new mother, the one that adopted me but wants to raise me in silence.

Maybe I can even tell you about that night.

It all started with a fight over Farida Ali. She was my best friend in eighth grade. Half-Indian and half-Irish, she was beautiful and smart, and half the time I wondered why she was friends with me, because I was, and still am, plain and small and awkward as hell.

We had a half-day at school, so I brought her home with me while my mother, Ann, was working in Brooklyn. She's a middle school science teacher. The truth is, I was breaking her rules by bringing Farida to our apartment. She was the one girl I couldn't have over. My mother hated her, or at least she hated Farida's mother, Linda.

"I don't like her mother," she told me whenever I broached the subject of bringing my friend over or going to her apartment in Forest Hills.

"You've never met her mother." I rolled my gaze away from hers.

My mother pursed her lips in that tight and stern way that she does, as if she's drawing a line between us that I cannot cross. But I crossed it anyway because I was not good at making a lot of friends, and Farida was the closest one I had.

"I spoke to her." My mother raised her head so that when she looked at me, it was at a downward scope, through the lenses of her bifocals sitting at the tip of her Greek aquiline nose. She treats me as if I am one of her students when she does that, not her daughter.

"Your friend's mother called me a few weeks ago, and she had the nerve to tell me that I was being too harsh with you." My mother doesn't name people she doesn't like. Farida was my "friend," and Linda was "she" or "her mother." It's as if by not referring to them by name, they don't exist for her.

I didn't say anything. I was reveling in the fact that someone had stood up for me. Knowing it was Linda made it even better. She was the kind of mom I had imagined prior to my adoption. Warm and funny and loving, she was similar to my Aunt Thalia, back in Greece, who had combed lice out of my hair, cleaned the cuts and infections on my skin, and fed my belly with food that I hadn't found in garbage cans.

"You talk about me," my mother interrupted my thoughts.

"Farida's my friend. We talk about everything."

"You talk about me. To her mother, a complete stranger. You tell them that I'm not your real mother."

"You are my mom," I told her softly. "You're the only mom I have."

"That's not true."

I lowered my lashes and remained mute. How could I tell her that yes, I talked to Linda about her, and when Linda heard that my own mother wouldn't hug me, wouldn't let me tell her about my birth mother and father, my siblings, the abuse I still remember, Linda put her arms around me, pushed the dirty blond hair off my wet cheeks, and kissed my forehead.

"I wish I could adopt you," she smiled at me.

"Please do not talk about me. I don't appreciate it," my mother disrupted my thoughts.

With that, she walked away from me, leaving me alone in the kitchen, or in the living room, or in the hallway. I am always left, somewhere, standing alone, watching as she walks away from me.

What she didn't allow me to say to her was that Farida and her mother weren't strangers. Not to me. Farida was my best friend. Her mother gave me a home away from my own home, where mothers and daughters weren't a mystery to each other.

I brought her to my house that afternoon, despite my mother's wishes, because she wouldn't be there and because I wanted my friend to see where I lived. She had never even seen my room, while I had been in hers plenty of times.

My mother's aunt was staying with us. Her name was Maria, and she was from Athens, Greece. As a matter of fact, she had been the one who had taken care of me while my adoption was being finalized. I was seven then. I did not like her one bit, so having her stay at our apartment was not a comfortable experience for me. I was awkward around her and had nothing to say to her, in English or in Greek. Silence was my armor, and it worked. She wanted as little to do with me as I did with her. Bringing Farida with me that afternoon had much to do with our friendship as it had to do with the fact that I did not want to be alone with yiayia Maria.

Yiayia is how I referred to her in Greece. Grandmother, out of respect for her age and the fact that we couldn't figure out what my connection to her would be, given my adoption into the family. She was my mother's aunt, but her age required me to call her my yiayia.

"Your name is Joyce, OK?" I told Farida as I placed the key inside the lock of our main door.

"Why?" Farida giggled.

"Because Joyce is my friend down the block, and my mom is OK with her coming over. Oh, and squint your eyes so you look Chinese," I instructed her.

"I so do not look Chinese." Farida poked me on the shoulder and turned me around to look at her. Farida had golden skin, thick, light brown hair, and these big, chestnut-shaped eyes that rendered mine ordinary.

"That's because I wear make-up," she told me once when I pointed to the difference in our appearance. "Your eyes would be gorgeous if you let me put mascara and liner on them."

"Ugh," I grunted. "I hate make-up. And," I added, "my mom would kill me."

"No, she wouldn't," Farida shook her head. "You need to break some rules, Kit Kat. You'll see how confident it will make you."

Farida and I didn't do much when I broke this one major rule that would get me into trouble. We hung out on the porch that opened from my bedroom, sunned ourselves, and listened to Light FM songs. Our porch overlooked a row of about six houses that extended toward the park, and we could see people entering and exiting the back entrance. When we saw a group of cute boys, we would laugh aloud, just to get their attention, and when we had it, we chatted a bit.

"Why don't you girls come here and hang out?" one of them called to us.

"Why don't you guys come over here?" Farida called out to them. "Ow!" she squealed when I pinched her.

Just then, yiayia Maria came up behind us.

"*Ti fasaria yinetai etho!*" she yelled at us in her high-pitched Greek.

"No trouble at all, yiayia," I responded in English. "We're just telling those boys to get lost."

"Go inside," she ordered us in English with a thick accent, her fingers pointing to the direction of my room. After we walked past her a few feet to the center of my room, she closed the glass doors that led to the porch and locked it. We stayed in my room the rest of the visit, with the door open, as yiayia Maria had instructed, and when she had to leave, I walked Farida to the train station on Queens Boulevard, around the corner from our apartment building.

When my mom came home around 6, I stayed in my room, awaiting the inevitable. She rushed in, with her aunt trailing behind her.

"Who was here?" she ordered.

"Farida." What else could I say? Farida did not look Chinese.

"I told you I did not want her to come to this house. This is my house, and you disobeyed me."

She was yelling at me, which I had not experienced from her before. Whenever she was irritated with me, she was direct, stern, but quiet. Sometimes there was a tear in her eye, as if I had wounded her, but she did not raise her voice or lose control. Which I loved about her. I had come from a place where mothers lost control, and it wasn't an experience I wanted to have again. Ever. But my new mother, who had not shown me anger before, was yelling and crying, and I wasn't sure if this was because her aunt was witness. My mother was the victim; I was the ingrate that disobeyed her, and there was a witness. Someone who was around to see that she wasn't the bad one in our situation. She wasn't a bad mother. She just had a bad child.

OK. I did disobey her. But I was thirteen, and I had a mind of my own, a will of my own, and not liking Farida because of her mother did not make sense to me. Her friendship meant more to me than my loyalty to my new mother, and I was willing to break this rule that would deprive me of my friend.

I write this part with bafflement because in all the years that I have lived with her, she has not shown me this side of her character. I was shocked when she pushed past me, spread out her freckled arm, and wiped it across my dresser. I watched as my jewelry, picture frames, and my most prized possession, a music box with a ballerina that twirled to the sweet tune of "Swan Lake," fell to the floor, most of which broke when they hit the floor, shards of glass and pieces of the ballerina's mirror scattering about my tattered sneakers.

I just stood there, not knowing what to do, while they both stared at me. My room was tiny, and they stood a foot away from me, but the distance between us seemed greater. I felt the room circling around me – a feeling I hadn't experienced since living in Greece – and definitely had not expected to find here, so many years later, when I was safe – if not happy – from the violence I had encountered there. I didn't know what would come next. A slap. A punch. Hands tightening around my throat that would make me shrink and disappear.

None of that. Just words. Heavy words that filled me with nausea, jolting me with more force than the slap I had anticipated.

"If you keep this up," my mother said to me between tears, "you will turn out just like your mother. A whore."

"You're my mother," I retorted.

Are you calling yourself a whore? I wanted to fling at her but pushed that thought down.

"We both know I'm not your real mother." Her voice was hushed, cool.

My jaw must have dropped at that moment. I'm not sure what surprised me more: the fact that she brought up my birth mother, or that she knew my birth mother had been a whore. You see, my adoptive mother never talked about my birth family, and she did not want me to talk about them either, so when this came up, I was experiencing mixed emotions. My mother called me a whore and brought up my birth mother in the same sentence. It was like speaking a secret no one could say aloud. At least I wasn't. But here she was, throwing it in my face, and all I could think about was that I wanted her to say more.

What do you know? I wanted to scream at her. *Does she want me back?*

And then yiayia Maria spoke, in my native tongue, a language I refused to speak as a new American adoptee angry with those who had abandoned me, sending me to this foreign country with this foreign woman I was required to call "Mama."

"It's true. She was a putana. She came looking for you, your mother. I told her to leave you alone. That you had a good family."

Yiayia Maria's words yanked my eyes towards her, and I couldn't look away. I waited for more, more words, hateful or otherwise. I wanted to hear more the way you want to hear your future when you go to a psychic, waiting for someone to see something in you no one else has because she has the magic ball that reveals everything about you.

But she said nothing more. They waited for me to say something.

Like what? I was in shock, without a voice, my heart pounding in my ears so loud that it was deafening. Blackness overcame me. A fuzziness began inside my head and then made its way to the back of my lids, and while I continued to stare at them, I couldn't see them. I had no voice, no sight. I just felt these shudders pass through my body, and I watched as they regarded each other, shook their heads, and then walked out of my room, leaving me behind, pale and mute, my feet surrounded by the shards of my meager possessions, their words still echoing inside my head.

And that's when I began to move without thinking, without taking note of my movements. I stepped over the debris at my feet, into the hallway, past the closed door of my mother's bedroom, past their whisperings behind that door, and into the hallway bathroom a few feet away. I locked the door, opened the drawer, took out the long, sharp scissors my mom used to cut my bangs, sat on the toilet bowl, took a deep breath, grabbed the scissors with both hands, extended my arms, and then brought them back to me with the force and rage I felt boiling inside me.

But nothing happened.

By the time my hands brought the tips of the scissors back to my chest, the power was gone. The anger was lost. The scissor tips barely touched my t-shirt, and I had to twist them into my skin to make the tear. A minuscule drop of blood peeked through, not the bloodbath I had imagined.

So I tried again.

I extended my arms out in front of me, gripped the scissors tightly with my fingers, and rammed them into me again. But once more, the power disappeared as soon as the scissor tips came into contact with my chest. There was a new hole in my shirt, another tiny prick in my skin, and a second drop of blood. I gave up then. I wasn't even crying at this point. I just felt defeated and sad as I let the scissors dangle loosely between my fingertips.

I sat in that spot, on the toilet seat, locked in the bathroom for an hour. And in that time, my mother never knocked on the door, never asked why I was in there for so long, or why I was in there in the first place. When I came out, the lights were turned off in the apartment, and I had to feel the short distance to my room by sliding my body against the wall. It seemed to hold me up, pushing my legs forward and into the solitary space in the apartment where I could be myself.

My mother's bedroom, right next to mine, was already locked, and the lights were out. Both were her way of letting me know that she did not want to talk to me. I locked my door, too, shutting her out in return. I threw myself onto my twin-sized bed, hating the way it squeaked when I moved or turned, no matter how slight the movement, because I knew she could hear me. And I wanted it to be as if I had disappeared.

I must go now, Jane. I'm so tired. My feet feel as if someone has tied weights to my ankles, and when I pick them up to take a step, it's as if I'm stuck in place. I want to fall where I stand and lie there without moving, go to sleep for a spell. Have you ever felt this way before?

Your friend, Kit Kat

"It was as if a martyr, a hero, had passed a slave or victim, and imparted strength in the transit. I mastered the rising hysteria, lifted my head, and took a firm stand on the stool."
JANE EYRE

Dear Jane,

I found you the next day.

I woke up as if nothing had happened and made my way to school, leaning my head against the dirty window pane of the Q60, the Green Line bus that took me to and from Russell Sage Junior High along Queens Boulevard. I roamed the hallways that day, dragging my feet from classroom to classroom in a haze. I sat in my classes but did not actually hear any lectures, and as avid a note taker as I had been, I lacked the strength to pick up my pen. I ate lunch with my friends, but I couldn't utter a word when they asked me what was wrong.

"Is it your mother again?" Farida asked between her peanut butter sandwich bites.

Her voice sounded far away, even though she was sitting beside me, her thick hair touching mine as she bent her head towards me. I nodded because when I tried to speak, nothing would come out.

"Do you want to talk about it?" she asked.

I shook my head. How could I tell her what I had tried to do? She wouldn't have understood.

"It'll be all right," Farida said, drawing soothing circles on my back with the palm of her hand. "You'll see."

When the dismissal bell rang at 3 p.m., I crept towards the bus stop along the congested boulevard, watching as the cars zoomed past me. I wondered how easy it would be to step into the traffic, how instantly I would go away. But my feet refused to move, and I wished for someone to push me. Standing there without volition, I let one bus after the other pass me by. I didn't want to go home, but I had nowhere else to go.

Then I thought about the library in Rego Park. A miniature square of brick walls and glass windows, it was located equidistant between my apartment and school. With a fixed destination in sight, I tightened my grip on my backpack and made my way to the library via the winding streets specked with houses and apartment buildings of varying sizes and shapes. It would become my favorite path to the library after school, and I would favor the hour-long walk instead of the twenty-minute bus or train ride it took me to get my apartment.

Meandering mindlessly along the suburban sidewalks of Rego Park reminded me of the walks I had once taken with my father, when I was seven years old, before he put me up for adoption, before I had even stepped foot on American soil, or met my adoptive mother.

Armed with souvlaki kabobs and Cokes, he and I spent Saturday nights strolling along the neighborhood he called home in Athens, Greece. We didn't speak as I tore the lamb from the skewer with my teeth and looked around me, but I learned to take in the sights that unfolded before me, wondering who lived in the houses we passed, what television shows they were watching, and if all families ended up the way mine had.

Walking beside him, his thin legs matching the slow rhythm of my own, I wasn't sure how to talk to him or what questions to ask. I was too elated to be near him, to smell the cigarette he was puffing on as it wafted from his clothes and skin, and I bumped into him on purpose just to feel the scratchy material of his jacket against my arm, his large hands reaching out to steady me. I stayed silent and let him guide me back to the house he shared with his sister, even though I no longer lived with him. It was enough just to walk beside him and see the world as he did. Quietly and from a distance.

I know you love books, and that's another thing we have in common. When I read about how you hid behind curtains and in dark rooms in Mrs. Reed's house just so you could read, I thought, wow, that's how I am with my books. I don't have Mrs. Reed's library. No way. Books are expensive. But I do go to the library every chance I get.

To tell you the truth, as conflicted as I am about my adoptive mother, she gave me books and libraries, and for this, I will always be grateful to her. In a surprising way, she taught me how to find you, and you taught me that I can find myself in books.

Anyway, when I came to the United States, I did not speak English. Greek was my language, and aside from a few English words such as "yes," "no," and

"Doctor" – a word that made me cringe with fear – I didn't know much else. I barely finished first grade in Greece; I had to repeat it since I got left back while I was living in the orphanage – another story for another time, but it was akin to Lowood School. Dark and lonely. I hated it. And because of this, I crossed my arms against my chest and let everyone know I hated it there. They held me back, and when I went to live with my aunt and uncle, I had to repeat first grade all over again. My point is that in Greece, kids learned English from middle school into high school. My cousins were learning English, and I couldn't wait to be their age so I could learn it, too. English in Greece is the language kids learn in the same way that in the United States, students learn French and Spanish, and you learned Latin and French in your school in England during the 1800s.

When I first came to the United States, they put me in ESL classes, but I moved out of them mid-year, because I was an avid reader. I swear to you, I had never been inside a library before. Imagine my shock when my new mother took me to one in Maspeth, and I found myself surrounded by stacks and stacks of books. It was as if someone put all this candy in front of me and told me to choose. I just couldn't. I didn't even know where to begin, and I had to sit down and just take it all in. The books, the librarians – that was someone's job, to help you pick books from the shelves, to help you find what you were looking for. There were kids there younger than me, chatting up a storm and pulling books off the rounded tables and taking them to their parents, looking at pictures, pointing to words, giggling at something funny they saw and sharing it with their little friends. It made me so happy to see this, and sad, too, because I hadn't known that. This was a different world to me. There must have been libraries in my Athens, but no one had ever taken me there. And here I was, eight years old, reading picture books alongside toddlers, learning the language in the same way that they did: sounding out words one syllable at a time.

The library had a rule: kids could take out eight books during each visit. And you should have seen me. I just piled on the books until I had eight, read them all in a day or two, and then returned for more. I couldn't get enough. I wish I could remember some of my favorite books, but I don't. I think it's because I was just learning English, and I had to master the words before I could understand the stories. Nothing stands out to me right now to share with you. Not the way you shared books with Helen that is. But it's something, and I can at least share how books and libraries make me feel.

Since then, my adoptive mother has given me all kinds of libraries; they have become my playground. While going to graduate school at night, she often left me in university libraries – Queens College, Hunter College, Stony Brook University – with a pile of books in front of me. I read as I waited for her classes to end, and when I tired of reading, I let myself get lost in the maze of bookshelves erected before me, winding from aisle to aisle, from floor to floor. I did not feel lost there, even when I was lost, tracing my way back to my table by instinct.

When I enter a library, this bubble fills my lungs and collects at my throat, and I want to sing, or dance, or laugh hysterically. It's comparable to when you meet someone you haven't seen in a while. Maybe the way my body would react if I ever saw you in front of me so that I could touch you and feel your skin against mine and see your smile instead of imagining it. Or maybe it would be the way I would feel if I ever saw my brothers and sisters again. I have four, but living here, with my new mother, it's as if I never had them, never knew them, and my mother won't let me talk about them. Maybe I can tell you about them some time.

As soon as I walked through the main doors of the Rego Park Library and past the sensor detectors, I realized I had found my escape. Standing there, I felt this enormous weight slip from my shoulders, and I lingered, consuming the place. Non-fiction books were to my left, fiction in front of me, and the children's section was to the right-hand side of me, along with the checkout desk. There were three or four librarians that I could make out and thousands of books on the shelves, all neatly packed together like sardines.

Tossing my schoolbag on top of a nearby desk, I walked to the fiction section, found the A part of the alphabet for authors' last names, and let my finger guide me down the row of titles. That's how I usually found my books – from the titles. I wasn't the kind of kid that asked for recommendations or for help, and I preferred to find my own way to books – and to everything. I must figure things out on my own. It takes me longer – and it's not as easy – but I don't want to rely on people to help me. It's not as if they help me the way I need it anyway. I think people help as much as they want to help and don't go out of their way, past their comfort. At least, this has been my experience. Even with my mother. She helps only when she wants and only what she wants to help me with. When I ask for anything that I need, it's usually no. So why ask? I won't be disappointed if I just rely on myself.

I was surprised when I couldn't find anything with my finger. And then, lo and behold, as my mother often says, I found you. You were on a cart of books to be shelved. You weren't stacked or in alphabetical order. You were just lying there with your title staring out at me.

Jane Eyre.

The front cover of your book was full of you, a girl dressed in a black dress with a thick white collar that revealed your bare throat. You appeared solemn, your lashes lowered as if in deep contemplation after you had read the letter that you held in your hand. The brown hair that was parted in the middle of your head and fell into ringlets down to your shoulder was haloed by a golden light that lit up your face.

You reminded me a little bit of Emily Dickinson, the way she posed for the picture that is in every book I find her work in. I love her poetry about death, but some of her work is beyond me. She was brilliant, and when I was in middle school, just a few years ago, I wanted to contract tuberculosis, and die as she did. Then my mother would find all my poetry and publish them. But my poetry is nowhere near Emily's. She had that kind of deep intelligence I lack, but I still enjoy writing poetry, usually about death and dying. These thoughts consume me often, which is why I feel the need to write to you. I'm hoping you can save me, I suppose. Or I'm hoping that you can teach me to save myself.

She had "the air of a little nonnette; quaint, quiet, grave, and simple," is how Edward Rochester described you when he met you as the new governess that would later save him and capture his heart. It's how I saw you, too.

I couldn't look away. I wondered if your thoughts were anything like mine. I wondered who you were and what made you look so pensive.

But it was the name that got me. I had not heard of it before, but the name rolled off my tongue as I whispered its syllables aloud. *Jane Eyre* by Charlotte Brontë. Even Charlotte was a perfect sounding name, lovely to look at and pretty to sound out. A woman had written a book about a girl. Perhaps the answers would be in there.

I picked up the book and took it to the librarian without reading the back cover; she stamped it with the due date and handed it back to me without a word.

For the next two weeks that I was in possession of your story, it was as if someone had seen me, claimed me. I had a sister, a mother, an aunt, a place in which I was loved and understood and cared for. I was connected to something solid and real, for even if the story wasn't real, a real woman had written it, had understood the pain that comes with being rejected and lonely; the angst that comes with being a girl severed from her roots and family.

It was with relief that I encountered your childhood experiences, Jane, for we were both orphaned, both assigned to a wealthy aunt and uncle whose children loathed and tormented us, and we both ended up in orphanages. We both hungered for affection and a home to call our own, a place in which to plant our tattered roots and live with purpose and happiness, and we both found ourselves dispensed to an eccentric residence with an emotionally distant owner. We both had to salvage our lives when an angry madwoman, a monster, defiled our lives and attempted to ruin our chances for happiness. Yours was Edward Rochester's mad, unchaste wife; mine was my birth mother, whose madness relegated her – and me – to homelessness and prostitution.

But it was your courage, your boldness that spoke to me, even more so than the parallels of loneliness we shared. You were able to use your cheerless childhood to claim a fearlessness that I lack, and by making you a friend, a sister, I am learning to harness that courage and speak up for myself.

When I imagine you in my head, I see you with your hair up in a tight bun against your scalp, your drab, gray dress buttoned up all the way to the neck, the creases of your dress moving in waves as you move, touching the tattered black boots you've inherited from some older girl with each step you take. You move deliberately, for you're always thinking, living inside your thoughts, collecting knowledge from the book that you hold against your chest as you glide down the corridor of Lowood School, girls rushing around you without you noticing them. This is how I want to be, too. Since you were ten, you seem to have known yourself. You know you're good and kind and smart and not the liar Mrs. Reed has labeled you. I want just a tiny dose of that kind of confidence – of the power that comes when you don't allow people to define you or put you down.

I have none – power or confidence. As I walk down the school corridors, or my apartment's hallway, with a book clenched to my chest, it is with my head down and my back hunched. I have the look of a beaten dog, my tail limp between my legs, awaiting the next blow that is sure to come. I want to walk tall and confident, as you do. Then no one would dare strike me, or threaten me, or beat me down.

You taught me that I am a "free human being with an independent will." That, even though I am "poor, obscure, plain, and little," I am not "soulless and heartless," as my adoptive mother often seems to treat me, and as Rochester presumed to treat you when he met you. More importantly, you taught me how to care for myself even when others did not.

I'm weak and a coward, but since I met you, I think less and less about hurting myself. I still nurse the idea, which is why I'm writing to you, taking one day at a time, but I'm not looking at sharp objects and thinking about driving them into me. Not once this past month, not since I started writing to you, now that I think of it. I've thought about what I did, and the shame of it repels me, but the feeling to do it, to stab myself, is not as bold or as ever-present as it used to be.

Although you were ten when you started to tell your story, it's all the same. No one listens to kids. They tell us what to do – parents, teachers, adults – but they don't listen to hear what we're truly thinking, let alone what we're feeling. And we don't even understand half the things we're feeling. I don't believe they know when we're drowning, or else they would give us a hand up, don't you think?

Your own story is dark, too. You talked about being depressed when you were younger. You even considered starving yourself to death, and you wanted to die for the same reasons I wanted to die: for love, for someone to love you as you are, to see you when you're standing there right in front of her, begging for a hug or a kind word. You lived in a place where no one cared for you, and I know this feeling of being unwanted by your relatives, of being cast aside as if you were a mere weed corroding their plush, green lawn.

Finding you saved my life, and your story has rescued me from drowning when I want nothing more than to disappear. When I want to surrender, I feel your hand reaching for me, grabbing my own resistant fingers, my nails bitten down to the bone, and pulling me out of the darkness to save me from myself. So, thank you!

Your grateful friend, Kit Kat.

*"I was conscious that a moment's mutiny had already
rendered me liable to strange penalties, and, like any other rebel slave,
I felt resolved, in my desperation, to go all lengths."*
JANE EYRE

Dear Jane,

This isn't the first time I've written in a journal. When I was eleven, my adoptive mother bought me one to write in.

"This is so you can write about things you don't feel like talking about," she told me in confidence. I wrote a few things in there, mainly about my friend, Joyce. She was Chinese and my best friend in elementary school. She lived two blocks away from us, and on my way to school I would pick her up, and we would walk another three blocks to PS 102. Even though I was supposed to go directly home after school, I went to Joyce's house instead. We did our homework together and then took her bikes out for a spin. I didn't have one of my own, so I used her brother's dirt bike, but I liked it better than the pink banana seat bicycle Joyce rode. It made me feel tougher. We would find a long, steep hill, ride to the top, and then sail down the road without holding onto the handlebars. I had never felt so free, so happy. I laughed all the way down the hill and wished I could feel contentment more than just this once.

This is the kind of stuff I wrote about, warming myself up to write about more complicated things, like my adoptive mother, and even perhaps my biological mother, the one who sold her body for money. Or my Aunt Thalia, who put me up for adoption. Or my father, who left us all to fend for ourselves. Or my brothers and sisters, who live in another country, a country I was born into and forced to abandon.

I wanted to write about my people, just as I want to write to you about them now. But I was afraid. What if my mother read my diary? She didn't want me to talk to her about them. She's called me a liar before, when I tried to tell her about the family I used to live with, the life I led before she became my mother.

I hid the diary under my desk drawer. I placed it in a plastic bag and taped the bag to the bottom of the middle drawer in the desk that she had bought me from a second-hand store to do my homework on.

But one day, after school, I came in to find my mother in my room. She was holding my diary in trembling hands.

"You said you wouldn't read it," I accused her.

"This is my house. I have a right to know what you're writing about."

I was so mad!

When she left my room, her chin thrust up in the air, I ripped out all the pages I had filled with my scratchy handwriting, tore them to pieces, and threw them in the trash can. Then I picked up my diary, and on the inside of the cover, I drew a picture of Jesus Christ that took up the entire page. He had golden yellow hair, a matching goatee, and a halo atop his head.

"Beware!" I wrote in large, bold red ink. "God is watching! This means YOU!"

Then I wrote for about four pages, free-style ranting about my mother and how much I hated her. It was loathsome, what I wrote, and I can't repeat it here, because I don't want you to know the mean parts of me. I felt as you did, though, when you confronted Mrs. Reed about her deceit, right before she sent you off to Lowood School, reneging on her promise to her dead husband to take care of you: "my soul began to expand, to exult, with the strangest sense of freedom, of triumph."

I left it in the middle of my bed the next day and went off to school, knowing quite well that she would read it.

What did she expect? What did I expect?

When I came home, my diary was where I had left it, but the pages I had written about my mother were torn out and missing. She left Jesus Christ behind.

She was grading science exams in her office when I stormed in there.

"You read my diary again!" I accused her, one hand showing her the empty diary, the other hand on my hips.

"I did." She didn't look up from her grading.

"Well, I want my pages back. They belong to me."

"No." Her tone was the usual crisp and cold with which she served her words to me when I disappointed her. Which was quite often.

"They now belong to me." She yanked open the top drawer of her filing cabinet and removed the folder labeled "Kathryn." She is the only one who refers to me as Kathryn. My friends call me Kit Kat. In it she included cards I had created for her since the third grade, when my English was not quite English. Mother's Day cards, birthday cards, Easter cards, and even some poems I had written about spring flowers were tucked in there also, from the early days of my adoption, when we had both been hopeful about our relationship. But now they were tainted with the nasty diary entry I wrote for her greedy curiosity.

"I'm keeping them," she informed me, "so that I can always remember how ungrateful you are." Then she turned her back to me. I stood there for a while, not knowing what to say or do. I could have hugged her, but those days were gone. I could have consoled her, but she didn't console me. The warm feelings I had for her when I was eight, when she first adopted me, were unreachable to me at eleven. With her back to me, I slunk into my room, feeling small and depleted. As you pointed out after your own rebellious response to Mrs. Reed's cruelty, "A child cannot quarrel with its elders – cannot give its furious feelings uncontrolled play...without experiencing afterwards the pang of remorse and the chill of reaction."

I don't argue with my mother a lot, but when I find the courage to do so, I am often left with pangs of guilt, especially when she starts to ignore me. I suppose at the core of my guilt is also fear. Fear that she regrets adopting me. Fear that she will send me back, although no one there wants me either. After all, they gave me to someone they hadn't even met or spoken to, as if I were a bag of old, bedraggled clothes no one wanted to wear anymore.

I am at the point now that I need to write, at least to you, even if she finds my pages again, which I've hidden in another spot I won't reveal here – just in case – hoping she will not discover them. I'm afraid of what will happen if I don't write. There are too many loose and overwhelming feelings inside me, hiding in the marrow of my bones, and I don't know how to take them out, loosen them from this suffocating grip they have on me. They're clamoring and fighting, waiting for something. I don't know what. All I know is that the noises inside me are deafening, shutting me in this place without words.

Do you know what I mean? I hope you do. And I hope I can keep this up, writing to you, I mean. Because you're my only hope. I have no one else to talk to. Just you. A girl I met on the pages of a book. *Jane Eyre*. A book no one my age reads anymore.

I have to go! My mother's coming.

Your friend, Kit Kat

"I was endeavouring in good earnest
to acquire a more sociable and childlike disposition, a more attractive and
sprightly manner, – something lighter, franker, more natural as it were."
JANE EYRE

Dear Jane,

I was just thinking about how similar my mother is to your Mrs. Reed.

They both sit in their chairs with their backs straight, unbending, and this is also how they rule us. There is no warmth to their tone when they speak to us, and when they look at us, we can sense their disappointment, their disdain for the little girl who has done nothing wrong but stands before them, asking them for love and some affection. That is all I want from her, and when I read your story, I know this is all you wanted from your aunt, Mrs. Reed. To treat you with some love, to look at you the way she looked upon her own kids, John, Georgiana, and Eliza.

My mother doesn't have any other kids. I am the one she adopted, and yet I have already failed her. I am not the daughter she expected when she adopted me.

In fact, just a few days ago, she stopped me in our short hallway. I was headed to the kitchen to get something to snack on, and she was headed to her room in the opposite direction, to shut herself in it again.

"I was thinking," she said, stopping before me until we faced each other. "I was thinking of adopting a Chinese girl. What do you think? Would you like a sister?"

My mother has this ability to hit me from nowhere. Her words aren't menacing, but what they say when you string them together shocks me, paralyzes me. Even this phrase, which isn't abusive, hurt me in these deep and silent places I didn't know existed.

I just stood before her, dumb and quiet, unsure what to say to her, but feeling as if she had just kicked me in the face. I was burning inside, and I felt the heat rise to my cheeks.

Am I so horrible that you want to replace me already? I wanted to hurl at her.

"Do whatever you want to do," I responded and abruptly turned from her, heading into the kitchen. I opened the refrigerator door and leaned into the cool air, but I couldn't remember what it was that I wanted. Suddenly, I wasn't hungry anymore.

My adoptive mother is not the mother I had yearned for when my Greek family told me they were giving me to an American woman, although I must admit that my standards are not high to begin with; I will take any kind of mother. Even her. If only she could see me and love me anyway. Despite where I have come from.

You know how Mrs. Reed treated you harshly for no reason at all? Well, that's how my mother is. I mean, she never locked me in the red-room that Mrs. Reed threw you in, the same room where the dead Mr. Reed lay before he was buried, but she has the same kind of coldness. She shuts me out of rooms when she is in them, but she also shuts me out when I don't behave according to her rules.

The other day, she got angry with me for yet another thing – it could have been my tone, or my refusal to practice the violin again – and she rushed into her room and locked the door, leaving me in the hallway. I heard the typewriter ticking, so I went into my own room and closed my door as well. Next thing I know, I hear a knock on my door, and I rush off my bed to open it – thinking we could talk about why she's so angry with me again – but she's not there.

You know what is?

A typed letter scotch-taped to my door. No kidding!

You can imagine what she wrote: just think about Mrs. Reed and how she speaks to you in that formal way she does, with her nose in the air, watching you with cold regard, as if she's talking to a room full of school children, or servants, completely detached. It's so impersonal. And typed! Whoever heard of such a thing? The least she could have done was write it out if she didn't know how to talk to me. It would have seemed warmer to me in her handwriting. The flair I find in her penmanship is nicer to behold than a cold, flat letter typed by a machine. I mean, I'm not the best communicator, but I know that writing a letter to a child is not the best way to communicate with her.

I just tore the letter up and tossed it in the garbage. That's what she gets for her trouble. How did she expect me to address that letter telling me that I am being disrespectful and rude and she won't tolerate it? Did she want me to write her back?

She can't relate to children or show any sympathy for them. Or maybe it's just me she can't get close to. Maybe there is something wrong with me. Maybe I am unlovable. I don't know.

I wish I were more like you. You have strength and integrity, and you stand up for yourself, no matter the consequence. My mother has made me afraid to stand up for myself. Even at fifteen, I shake with fear at being myself, speaking up for myself, all because I don't want to give her another reason to hate me. Or to return me. What if she gives me back? I don't want to go back, Jane. I'd rather die.

You didn't have anywhere to go back to with Mrs. Reed. She had you since birth, since your parents died and your uncle, Mr. Reed, took you in. He sounded nice. I'm sorry that you lost him, Jane. He would have made your years spent with his wife and children more tolerable. Maybe if he had been around, none of them would have treated you as a servant, an outcast. He would have made you belong. Sometimes I wish my mother had a husband, someone to mediate between us, someone to talk to, to stick up for me. She never married.

"I don't need a man to feel complete," she tells me often. But I think she does. She needs love, someone to chase the coldness out of her, kiss her, and hold her accountable for her behavior. And that someone is not me, because she won't let me get close to her at all. A husband would have told her to get over herself before she started typing up a letter to her daughter, don't you think?

But it's bigger than that. I sense she's afraid to let people in and hurt her.

That's what I believe is wrong with Mrs. Reed, too. She lost her husband, and she has three kids and you to take care of. It probably makes her sad and angry to be alone. Not to justify her treatment of you, Jane. She's mean, even cruel when it comes to you. But she's probably hurting inside, and I am learning that when we hurt, our chief go-to place is anger. Anger comes so easily. There's just so much of it. Too much. And I think we're all walking around this place, with all this anger inside us, trying to tamp it down until one of us bumps into the other, and then all hell breaks loose.

OK. I have to finish my math homework, and math and I are not very good friends. Talk to you later.

Your friend, Kit Kat

> *"[I]t is only on condition of perfect submission*
> *and stillness that I shall liberate you then."*
> *JANE EYRE*

Dear Jane,

My mother is a science teacher who owns her own three-floor apartment building in Elmhurst, Queens. We live on the top floor while she rents out the two lower ones to various individuals from whom she also keeps her distance. With three bedrooms, two bathrooms, a living room, dining room, and a large kitchen, it is bigger than any of the places I have ever lived in. The kitchen smells of strong, freshly brewed black coffee, and I have come to know this room as the warmest space in the house. When she initially adopted me, I used to spend many hours watching and helping in the kitchen as my new mother donned her apron, pressed her face close to the pages of her Greek cookbooks, and followed directions with the kind of concentrated precision that she applied to every task she attempted.

In those days, the oven was in constant use, either broiling beef souvlaki with peppers and onions, or freshly baked pita, a Greek Easter bread that took hours to make, and which I devoured in one sitting. The kitchen brought us together while everything else placed great distances between us. It's where she taught me how to cook and bake, interpret measurements, press the buttons on the mixing bowl as she poured flour and sugar, and cracked eggs into it, encouraging me to lick what was left of the mixture after she had poured it in a baking container. She taught me how to braid the sweet dough of the Easter bread and conceal the wax-wrapped nickel inside it that represented a year's worth of good luck for the individual fortunate enough to bite into it.

We sat together at the kitchen table as she carefully laid out filo and instructed me to use the brush and coat the entire surface with hot, melted butter so that it wouldn't dry up. I watched as she placed a spoonful of cheese filling made up of ricotta, feta, and basil onto the part I had buttered, and then folded the *filo* around it into triangular shapes. *Tyropita*, or cheese triangles, were my favorite Greek snacks, and since I had come to her an already picky eater, my mother made them in large quantities so that I would always have some to eat.

An open doorway led from the kitchen to the dining room, which housed a round wooden table and chairs used for special occasions such as Christmas, Easter, and New Year. On those days, she invited guests, mostly teacher friends who had nowhere else to go, and spent the day cooking for them. This was when I loved the smell of the kitchen the most. There was lamb, turkey, or honeyed ham broiling in the oven, lemon potatoes roasting and sizzling atop the stove, and a finely tossed salad with an assortment of dressings to choose from sitting on the table. The smell of cakes, Greek butter cookies, *baklava, revani,* and sometimes *galatobouriko,* sweet custard wrapped in honeyed filo strips, were waiting atop the mobile bar.

On those busy days, my room was clean, I was dressed in whatever dress my mother had chosen for me, my hair was combed back, out of my eyes, and set in place with a wide pink headband. I remember waiting for our guests with great expectancy, looking out the window as my mother prepared the gourmet, cholesterol-free dishes. I watched as they parked their cars and waited until they rang the bell before running down the two flights of stairs in the dress she had made for me to let them into the building.

It was my job to pass out the *mezethes,* making sure our guests' plates were full of Greek olives, crackers and cheese, teriyaki meatballs, *tyropita* straight out of the oven, and of course, drinks. She made sure she had a few bottles of beer or ouzo for the men. Just two men were ever invited: John, her friend Helen's husband, who had a fig tree in his backyard and would hold me up to gather them when they were ripe; and Mike, her cousin. There was no wine in my house, and soda was limited to three cans of Coke for me and anyone else who desired something other than water. When plates were full of appetizers, I placed a chair in front of the sink in the kitchen, climbed on top of it to give me height, and began to wash dishes, bowls, platters, glasses, and utensils in case we needed more for our guests.

When I was younger, those were days filled with joy, and the only time the house vibrated with energy and laughter. Aside from these holidays, our moments together were without noise. Even our meals were hushed, and it was after years of built-up anger and resentment that I became hyperconscious of the clamor that came from inside her: the wet, slushy sounds of beef being masticated, gnawed, and grounded endlessly between her teeth until they were ingestible; the gulping expressions of her throat as the food particles made their way deep inside her. I heard the smacking of her lips when she opened her mouth to take another bite, for one of the earliest lessons I learned from her was not to chew with my mouth open. Quite often I was bombarded with the churning whines of her stomach, desiring to be filled. I was even aware of the cracking, creaking echoes of her limbs whenever she bent down, sat, or rose from her seat.

The silences between us are now immeasurable, but the sounds of her fill every crack, every possible place unoccupied by words.

Your friend, Kit Kat

*"I was a precocious actress in her eyes: she sincerely
looked on me as a compound of virulent passions,
mean spirit, and dangerous duplicity."*
JANE EYRE

Dear Jane,

Just as Mrs. Reed labeled you an ingrate and a liar, my new mother believed the same things about me. The first time she called me a liar, I had to look the word up in my English-Greek dictionary. I didn't understand the accusation she hurled at me like a hard-edged rock that bruised me in places I couldn't name.

I was eight, and she had just adopted me. Had just brought me home a few days earlier.

My chest was knotted with confusion and apprehension that I didn't have enough words in my vernacular – English or Greek – to help me describe, let alone understand, what I was feeling.

I tried to give birth to them in my mother tongue, hoping that my new mother would understand.

My voice was soft, my Greek slow, as I tried to tell her where I had come from and to whom I had belonged. I wondered why she did not ask, but I felt it was important to tell her.

I started at the beginning, my words coming out in a string of rushed phrases that made me lose my breath. My heart raced, my hands shook, and as I unfolded the scenes of my childhood before her, it was as if I had sprinted in a race I couldn't win.

"Baba left us. Mama hit him with her shoe, her red shoe with a pointed heel, and he was bleeding. His eye was full of blood. And he ran away. He went to live with his sister."

I waited. I waited for her to say something. But she didn't say a word as she sat opposite me at the kitchen table. I stared at the top of her head, studying the hair she cut in a short bob sprinkled with intermittent strands of white and black.

She was staring at her hands. Hands I have grown to adore, wishing they would adore me back, caress me in places a mother would know to touch. Her hands remained out of reach for me, while her words beat into me without mercy.

I took a long breath and stumbled headlong into my memories.

"Mama had a man. He was mean. I have two brothers and two sisters. Maria was the oldest, then Nicholas, Stavros, me, and Baby. All of them went to an orphanage, except for me and Baby. Mama kept us. I was in one – an orphanage – for a year, but she took me back."

I paused again. Maybe she couldn't understand my Greek, I thought. Her own Greek was tangled with English, and her accent was odd when she spoke. It didn't possess the loud, staccato, exuberant tones of my native Greek. It was gentler, softer, foreign.

She wasn't looking directly at me, and the thin lines of her lips were smashed against her face, forming a long, straight line that became a sign between us – a warning.

I recalled telling my Aunt Thalia my stories, and perhaps I had expected the same response. My aunt had wrapped her arms around me and kissed my cheeks.

"You have seen terrible things," my aunt had whispered against my short-cropped hair. "You're not with your mother anymore. You're in a safe place now." I had been safe with my aunt. Safer because she had believed me. She had known my mother and all about her life. My new mother did not, so I suppose it was harder for her to accept that my years before her had been anything but ordinary. But the oddest thing for me was that she didn't ask any questions about me. She didn't seem to know a thing about my roots, and when I sat down to tell her, she rejected my recollections.

I kept talking just to see if her reaction would change, soften somehow.

"We lived in the streets, and I took care of my sister. Her name was Baby. We called her that because she wasn't baptized. She's four now, and ..."

"Enough!" My new mother raised her voice. "I am very disappointed in you. These are all lies, and I will not sit here and listen to a liar. Your behavior is unacceptable."

It was just like Mrs. Reed forcing you to face her as she told you similar words: "I abhor artifice, particularly in children."

"I am telling you the truth," I told her, stunned by her reaction.

"Well, your social worker back in Greece told me that you tell stories. These are tall ones, for sure. I won't listen to you if you lie to me, and I won't accept liars under my roof."

"I'm not a liar." I was confused, because my Greek social worker, Mrs. Papas, had handled my adoption, and she had been so nice to me. She had invited me to her house and let me sleep over and play with her son. I even gave him the toy soldier that my new mother had bought me as a Christmas present while she visited me during the adoption process. I had not lied to either of them.

I watched her push her chair back from the table. Afraid she would leave, I pleaded with her, my hand reaching out to stop her.

"Wait, do you mean Mrs. Papas? She told you I lied? But I didn't. I'm telling the truth."

My new mother turned a look on me that made me feel chill and colorless, unseen.

"All they told me about you was that your mother was a putana; that you were in a detaining hall; and that you had marasmus."

I was familiar with the word *putana*; it was Greek. The lowliest thing one could say about a woman. And it was true. But I couldn't understand the other two words she said to me.

"What's marasmus? What's the other thing...detaining...?"

"A detaining hall is where children go before they are put up for adoption," she explained crisply. Then with a softer tone, she defined marasmus for me.

"Marasmus is the wasting of the flesh. You were dying." Her voice was hushed, and the tenderness in her voice made me feel soft, a little bit quaky, and I wanted so much to feel her arms around me, to be held until I was solid again.

"There was no detaining hall," I said to her instead. "It was an orphanage. For girls. Maria, my sister, was there with me..."

"That's it!" Her voice rose again – not quite a yell – for she didn't yell. But it was a bit above her normal pitch and range, and I knew not to go any further.

With that, my new mother rose from the table and walked away from me. It wasn't until I heard the sound of the lock on her door that I realized she had gone into her room and shut herself in there, leaving me out again, by myself.

Looking back, I know that was the moment I lost my voice, and I've been trying to find it ever since.

Your friend, Kit Kat

*"What creature was it, that, masked in an ordinary woman's
face and shape, uttered the voice, now of a mocking demon,
and anon of a carrion-seeking bird of prey?"*
JANE EYRE

Dear Jane,

During the first few years I lived in America, I had this solitary image that singed the edges of my thoughts, and no matter how much I squeezed my lids shut, I couldn't make the image disappear.

A black and white memory, it was the frozen portrait of a woman. Her eyes were vacant, drooping beneath opaque bushy brows; her hair, wild and uncombed, curled like black flames around her face, deep creases etched at the corners of her unsmiling mouth. She seemed old, ancient, wasted, staring back at me as if I couldn't hide the secrets that railed behind my own guarded look. I saw this woman frequently while living with my new mother. Whether my eyes were open or closed, whether I was in school or in bed, whether I was laughing or crying, she was there, lingering, quietly waiting for me to acknowledge her. She was commanding and fierce, and I couldn't erase her image from my thoughts.

Her name was Athanasia Koutros.

She was my mother. The one who gave birth to me.

In Greek, her name means "the immortal one," and I find this quite ironic, because, even though I left her so many years ago, the memory of her crawls back to me, burrowing beneath my skin, cementing itself against my ribs so that I find it hard to breathe. Whenever I think of her, my breath gives way, my chest heaves with force, and words escape me, since I cannot reveal her existence.

Of course, I don't speak to anyone about her, particularly my new mother.

That she was "a whore" was the single thing she knew about my birth mother, the only fact the social worker on my adoption case revealed about my history. But my new mother used this knowledge to scare me, control me, echo the dangerous path she was scared I would take and the shame that would follow.

But I knew other things about the woman who gave birth to me. Things I haven't told anyone, except you, since I know you can relate.

The first memory I have is of her with blood on her hands.

I was four years old, sitting at the kitchen table of our one-floor house. Beside me were my two older brothers. Nicholas was six, tall and thin, his features pained and angular. Stavros was five, short, with wide, bulbous eyes that made him look as if fear had found a home in him and settled deep into the marrow of his bones.

Other than mentioning their names that initial time I told my new mother about them, I've hidden them from her. But they were there, before her, and witnessed the same scene unfold before us, fear rooting us to the chairs that cradled the sinking weight of our bodies while we held onto the edges with white knuckles, helpless to do anything more but watch.

"Bastard!" our mother screamed, spit collecting at the sides of her mouth.

We watched from our places at the table as she ran to their bedroom, her tangled hair chasing her loosely, like wildflowers desperately clinging to their roots. She returned with her right arm in the air, her fingers clutching one of her bright red stilettos, her features as knotted as her hair, with eyes wide and cold, yellowed top teeth grinding against the lower ones, high cheekbones scraped against pale skin, lips twisted with hatred I had not learned about yet.

She grabbed my father by the collar with one hand and struck him with the blade-like heel of her red shoe with the other. She stabbed him with it once upon his trembling, crooked spine, once upon the back of his balding head, and irreversibly, once upon the corner of his left eye.

The impact of her heel as it struck his eye, the frozen moment in which both connected and then separated, and his guttural screams filling the spaces of our house, our ears, made us tremble in our spots.

My gaze followed the loose blood flow from the corner of his bulging eye, spilling freely, and separating into divergent rivulets that streamed down his cheeks to his chin to the folded layers of his golden neck skin, saturating the white lapel of his dress shirt and resting there – a fixed, crimson, immutable scar that kept getting bigger and darker.

"*Malaka*," she cursed him in Greek, backhanding his olive-toned face.

Fourteen years older than her, he had no armor against the dark-haired woman who stood before him without noticing him, a snarling smirk outlining the full frame of her parted lips, her hair forming a messy and unkempt halo around her sunbathed, ovular face.

He didn't fight back. My mother avenged herself on him with boundless rage.

My childhood was infused with recurring images of her scratching his face, ripping his clothes in frenzied attempts to get at his skin, kicking, punching, and spitting into his sockets, already swollen from the beatings. She battered him with an obsession that made it seem as if she were trying to destroy a demon haunting her. Of course, that demon was not our father.

Even as young children, we recognized our father as a docile and simple man. It was this weakness and simplicity perhaps that made him an available target for my mother's cruelty.

A similar portrait of a dark-haired, wild woman accosted you while you lived in Thornfield Hall, falling in love with the brooding and mysterious Edward Rochester: his wife, Bertha Antoinette Mason. Before you ever saw Rochester's hidden wife, her "laugh struck [your] ear. It was a curious laugh – distinct, formal, mirthless…it was very low…a clamorous peal that seemed to wake an echo in every lonely chamber."

No one cared about her because she was a monster, the ghost of a woman, concealed by a man. She wasn't a person, but a thing, a "crime…incarnate in this sequestered mansion [that] could neither be expelled nor subdued." She escaped her room at night, after Grace Poole drank too much and fell asleep, and crept up and down the corridors, breathing, squealing, jeering at the inhabitants who slept while she crept and crept outside their bolted doors, "snarling, snatching…like a dog quarreling."

She attacked her own brother, Richard Mason when he came unexpectedly to see her during one of Rochester's infamous parties. Bertha bit him in two places and then tried to cut him with a knife: "She sucked the blood: she said she'd drain my heart," Mason said of her. Bertha even tried to kill Rochester while he slept, lighting his room on fire, and the only one who saved him was his own angel, Jane, rousing him from his chamber of flames.

When you first saw Bertha, she was in your bedroom the night before your wedding, wearing your bridal veil before taking it off, shredding it, and then trampling on it with her bare feet. Revenge for attempting to marry her husband.

The woman you described was my mother as I remembered her from my childhood:

[T]all and large, with thick and dark hair hanging long down her back...It was a discoloured face – it was a savage face. I wish I could forget the roll of the red eyes and the fearful blackened inflation of the lineaments!...[She was] purple: the lips were swelled and dark; the brow furrowed; the black eyebrows widely raised over the bloodshot eyes...[like a] Vampyre.

A monstrous thing, a demon, a blood-sucking vampire, Bertha wasn't a person worth knowing. The one person who thought kindly of Bertha was her brother. He wept for her, even after she attacked him, pleading with Rochester to care for her: "let her be treated as tenderly as may be."

I care about Bertha Mason, the discarded wife who haunted the spectral corridors of Thornfield Hall while everyone slept and looked the other way. I care about her because she was my mother, my monster, and I came to know her from the shrill of her piercing screams and the sound of her fists pounding against my father's face with the wanton zeal of an Amazon warrior in battle.

Athanasia wasn't pretty or kind. She was fierce, a prevailing tornado of flesh, instinct, and unfettered rage, and she was the mother I had known first. The mother against which I compared my new one. If there was some kind of race or contest between them, my adoptive mother won, despite her cold demeanor.

My birth mother refused to cook or clean the house, and she let us run around the streets in our soiled underwear without tending to our most basic needs. If my siblings and I cried out in hunger, she told us to go out and work for it.

"When I was your age," she barked at us, "I washed rich people's laundry for food. Nothing was given to me for free."

The latter part of her tirade became hushed as she mumbled to herself, her voice and thoughts disappearing into a world full of ghosts and other unknowns. A world we weren't privy to, but a world that invaded ours nonetheless when she rushed out of it and lunged for us with sudden rage.

Your friend, Kit Kat

> *"Women are supposed to be very calm*
> *generally: but women feel just as men feel."*
> *JANE EYRE*

Dear Jane,

When I look in the mirror, I see my father, Ioannis, or John in English. I inspect the angular features of my face, the golden circles that outline my brown eyes, the aquiline nose that the Asian kids at my elementary school made fun of me for having, calling me "big nose" during recess, laughing and pointing at me for not resembling them. I know my features come from him because I remember him. I remember the way he watched me, from beneath hooded lids and quiet smiles, with a puff of smoke from his cigarette suspended between us. When the cloud cleared, I saw me in him, and I knew I was his daughter. That he was my dad. My baba.

Afraid my new mother will take him from me, too, I keep him tucked in my smiles, beneath the blond hairs of my arms and skin, skin that is as gold and tan as his was when he placed his thick fingers on top of my head, twisting my short and dirty blond hair out of place so that loose tendrils escaped from behind my ears and scraped against my cheek. I loved the feel of his fingers on my skin as he brushed my hair back, so he could see my face again, the face that he had given me.

I don't speak his name, tell my new mother where he hides, or share with her who he was. But he is there now just as much as he was there when he held my hand during our evening walks so many years ago.

In all my memories of him, he was mute. Not because he couldn't talk, but because I don't remember him ever talking. Just sitting or standing, smoking, or crouched on the floor, bloodied, his arms shielding his face from his wife's attacks.

My first memory of him is crowded with the memory of my mother stabbing him with the heel of her red stiletto in our kitchen.

My brothers and I weren't looking at each other. We just sat there, waiting for the battle between them to end. Nicholas had his fingers clenched into fists on his thighs. Stavros' lower lip was trembling. I sat between them, my feet barely touching the floor, sliding my hands from the table onto my lap, so they couldn't see them shaking.

A few feet from us, my mother's shrill voice splintered the air we breathed, forcing us to inhale fragmented shards of memories we would rather forget. But this memory has stuck with me in a way that most of my memories have limped on without so much as a farewell. They just burrowed themselves into little holes that my fingertips cannot fit into to pry them out of their dark and hidden spaces. This one is an embedded sliver of broken glass, its sharp edges rooted into my brain matter. If removed, I would hemorrhage and disappear into the folds of my own memories.

Ioannis in Greek means "full of grace," and he was the gentlest part of my childhood. He was the same size as my mother, short and stocky, but she seemed bigger than him. Even her name, Athanasia, was bigger, bolder, full of the virility his name and body lacked. She was a petite woman but the singular force that shattered the lives of all who came from her and lived with her.

God's grace was nowhere to be encountered when my mother grabbed my father by the back of his neck and pulled his limp body towards our kitchen sink. The sound of his skull meeting the aluminum sink was a hollow reminder of my childhood fixed with blood and violence and vomit that had to be wiped off the floor by my brothers and me.

When she was finished, she left him cradling his knees to his chest on the floor, blood dripping from his nose and mouth. In the past, Nicholas would lift his crumpled body off the floor, take him to the bathroom, and clean him up. When the wounds were too severe, Nicholas would call over our Aunt Asimina, who lived next door and would go with them to the hospital. Stavros and I grabbed towels and wiped our father's blood off the floor, the kitchen cabinets, or the sink, and whatever hard object had received him after the blunt force of her fists.

This time was different.

This time, he scrambled to his knees and ran to the door leading to the veranda my mother and her sister, Asimina, shared. I turned my back to him, shaking like a leaf about to break from its tree branch and be set adrift by a hollow gust of wind. Until that day, he had been that solid piece of driftwood that Nicholas, Stavros, and I clung to so as not to be swept away by the force of our mother's rage. He kept us grounded, made sure we were fed and even loved.

"Asimina!" I heard him yell out my aunt's name in rhythm to his fists pounding on her door. "Georgos!" he called out to her husband. "Help me!" I was still sitting in my chair at the kitchen table, my back solidified against the sounds and sights of my childhood when my aunt opened the door and took him in.

"My God," I heard her wail. "What has she done to you, poor man?"

He disappeared into their home. Nicholas followed. The door closed behind them.

My mother laughed and shook her head as she retreated into her bedroom at the back of the house.

Stavros and I avoided each other's gaze.

I didn't have the words to describe to him that this was different. This was going to change our lives.

What do you call this feeling? It's not foreshadowing, because that's a hint you get from the author in a book. For example, when you heard the screeching laughter that came from Rochester's wife, locked up in the attic, or when she set fire to Rochester's bedroom in an attempt to kill the man who had locked her up and fallen in love with you. Or when the storm cracked that tree in half the night before your wedding to the already married Rochester, whose secret of a mad and hidden wife would break your heart and separate you from the man you loved. That was foreshadowing, but I think this feeling I had was different. Maybe it was a premonition, although I doubt I believe in that stuff.

Either way, I had it. I can still feel it now, this light and heady feeling that had me calmly floating above the chaos of my childhood, able to comprehend that this moment – when my mother struck my father, and he ran out of our house – this moment would change everything.

And it did.

Your friend, Kit Kat

*"He has painful thoughts, no doubt,
to harass him, and make his spirits unequal."*
JANE EYRE

Dear Jane,

My father didn't come back. He was gone for good. In the past, he had returned after the beatings. No matter how severe they had been. Even when she ran out and got on the back of some man's motorcycle, my father stayed. He didn't say anything, but he stayed.

There is one man that I remember all too well. He was a fisherman, and Stavros and I met him together.

A year and a half apart, Stavros, whose name means "the cross" in Greek, and I spent a great deal of time together as children. He was my elder brother and my protector. Not yet six, he took care of me, slept beside me, and wet the bed we shared, the yellow stain of his urine moistening our sheets and sticking to our clammy pores, soaking our skin in its rancid odor, his emaciated body turning and twisting beside me.

The day we met the fisherman, he and I were sitting on the steps that led to the veranda my mother shared with her sister. We heard the loud grumbling of the motorcycle and turned our faces to the right, in unison, our eyes squinting in the sunlight and resting on the hulking figure that rode toward us.

He stopped his bike in front of us and waited, deliberately watching us from behind the dark coating of his wide-rimmed sunglasses. His fisherman's sun-dried hands rolled rapidly forwards and backward over the rubber part of his handlebars, revving the engine, again and again, before suddenly cutting off the machine altogether.

It took me a while to shake off the rumbling sound. The fisherman slid off his bike in one swift movement. He patted the top of my head with the same hands that had caught, sliced open and gutted fish, the smell of their violent death wafting up into my nostrils.

He walked past us, up the four or five steps that led him to our house. The door opened from the inside, and my mother's hands, hands that we had known only in violence and hardness, pulling, pushing, shoving, slapping, now drew this man inside with easy affection and laughter. The door closed behind them, and Stavros and I remained outside, not looking at anything in particular, overtaken by the familiar sounds of their sex-making, the crashing tides of their fanatical grunting, tussling, and moaning hurtling into us, drowning us in guilt and shame and loathing.

Sometimes he brought us ice cream cones, at which we scrunched our noses, but ate nonetheless. We licked them until there was no trace left that they had been given to us by the man who slept with our mother when our father was at work, filling our bellies for the single time that day with frozen, milky-sweet bribes that secured our silence.

During the late nights, the fisherman parked his bike in front of our house and dropped our mother off to the family she continually fled. I watched Baba from my sleeping cot in the living room as he watched Mama from behind the lace-covered glass of the porch doors.

He took a deep drag from his cigarette and turned his arched back away from my mother's frame as she made her entry. Not a word was uttered as she undressed, scattered her clothes and shoes onto the floor, and strolled past us without glancing at our faces, without kissing us goodnight, as we pretended to sleep. She made her way through the back door that connected the kitchen to the bedroom and tossed her naked body onto the mattress she shared with her husband.

My father finished his cigarette and then made his way into their room to lay his brittle body beside her vigorous one, listening to the faint sigh that escaped her lips. Each night I imagined my father falling asleep, inhaling the scents of sweat, sex, and fish intermingled that emanated from her pores.

But he said nothing.

And he stayed.

I don't think it was because he loved my mother.

Athanasia wasn't a good mother or wife. I knew this even as young as I was, because my Aunt Asimina, her elder sister, was, and she and her family lived next door to us. My Aunt Asimina seemed happy with Uncle George, and they had three daughters together. Living next door to them, we were the complete opposite, a malignant, festering cancer that corrupted their suburban dream. Just as my baba found refuge in their home and arms the day my mother beat him until he bled, my brothers and I escaped into their home as well. Aside from the streets, it was the one place we could find peace...and food.

Our house was built by my Uncle Dimitri, their younger brother, the one who married Aunt Thalia and took me in when my mother couldn't take care of me. As the only male left in the family, he couldn't marry my aunt until he had taken care of his sisters. So, he built them a conjoined house and used it as dowry to secure a husband for each.

This is what my Aunt Thalia told me, so I don't know if love was what brought my parents together. My father was already in his forties when he married my mother, in her early twenties. That said, Uncle George and Aunt Asimina didn't have the violent troubles my parents had, so you don't know how two people will end up when they marry. Maybe it's all just about chance. It's not very comforting for me, constantly looking for reasons and justifications.

Our conjoined house split down the middle and rested along a quiet and narrow street in a middle-class neighborhood in Peristeri, Athens. Asimina chose the house on the left, and my mother took the right. Each was a single-floor home and an inverted reflection of the other; a carbon copy adobe that was entered from opposite sides. My aunt's side entrance led her to a mahogany door that opened into a spacious living room on the right and a kitchen on the left. My mother's door led her to the living room on the left and the kitchen on the right. To the back of the kitchen was a folding door that led to the toilet, sink, and bath. Both rooms were tiny and crowded. A few inches away another door folded to the side. When opened, it escorted the sisters into the bedrooms they were to share with their husbands. There were no other rooms in the house, and their children, when they had them, slept on a pull-out couch in the living room.

While the interior was split in half and closed off by a thin layer of sheetrock, affording each woman the privacy she would need with her family, the exterior was an open haven where the two families joined each other for gossip and drink. Both living rooms open to the same front courtyard that they shared through twin glass doors covered by white lace curtains. Both doors led the way to a veranda that was shaded by fig trees and a collection of potted flowers.

A round table with four chairs was situated in the middle of the patio, and we often sat there in the mornings, staring down the narrow suburban streets that were crowded with little European cars and motorcycles parked on the sidewalks to make room for traveling vehicles to pass through. In addition, the sisters shared a garden in which they planted tomatoes, eggplants, cucumbers, and dill.

Asimina took care of the plants. My mama wasn't much for cooking and cleaning and taking care of children. She was hardly home, and when we were hungry, we waited for Baba to come and feed us between his shifts as a sanitation worker, or we went next door for our aunt to feed us. Sometimes, neighborly moms would give Stavros and Nicholas loose drachmas to run errands for them, but I couldn't go along. I was too little and weighed my brothers down. But they shared whatever they bought with me, whether it was a chocolate bar or candy.

Similar to my father, I spent every chance I could at Aunt Asimina's house, playing with her daughters, or watching television. We didn't have a television set, so it was such a great distraction. I could watch Simon Templar, *The Saint*, for hours, wasting much of my day that way.

I loved escaping into my aunt's family, and I understood why my baba found solace there as well after my mother beat him.

What I couldn't understand was why he hadn't returned.

Your friend, Kit Kat

"Jane, you offered me your shoulder once before;
let me have it now."
JANE EYRE

Dear Jane,

The days after their last fight were long and trailed into weeks. Weeks that were empty of my father's soothing presence. Resembling your uncle, Mr. Reed, he was the quiet pocket we could slip into when my mother's rages spiraled out of control. He didn't stand up to her. He was too weak for that. But he did stand between her and us, giving us time to run out of the house and avoid her twitchy fingers.

In losing him, we had lost any chance of peace in our home. You know what that's like because, after Mr. Reed's death, Mrs. Reed no longer suffered the pressure to be kind to you, to regard you as one of her own.

One day, my mother decided to get him back.

"*Ela etho!*" she yelled at me to run to her.

I obeyed her, and she pushed me into an already formed line beside my two brothers. She pulled down Nicholas' shirt, slapped spit atop Stavros' wily hair, and rolled my loose and dirty socks up to my knees.

"We're going to get your baba back," she told us, rubbing her fingers in loose circles along the mid-section of her growing belly. Another baby was on the way.

"Are we going to the sanitation site?" Nicholas piped up. His face brightened; the oldest, he loved our father, and the weeks we had spent without him had turned Nicholas into a tired and brooding old man who didn't speak or eat or smile.

"He's not working there anymore," my mother said. "Uncle Dimitri got him a job at a construction site. We're going there."

As we neared my father's work site, I scanned the area for his familiar 5'3" frame. There was a huge truck that obstructed my view of the building, and I bent down, my knees touching the coarse rocks and soil that supported the heavy vehicle.

That was when I caught a glimpse of my father's shoes.

That's how I recognized him – by the dust-encrusted sides of his worn-out black leather loafers.

I pushed against the firm earth with my hands and ran towards the man who had given me comfort and solace. I don't know if my brothers followed or not. I didn't look behind me to see. All I saw was my father. All I wanted was to make my way to him, to take him back. I didn't care about anything else.

It seemed to take my legs forever to reach him, but when they did, I stopped and peered up at him, beaming. There was a white bandage covering his battered eye, the one my mother had stabbed with the blade of her red heel.

I wrapped my skinny arms around my father's legs, my cheek resting against his thigh, overcome with relief.

His fingers trembled as they touched the top of my head. They pulled back. Then I felt him grab my arms, which were still clinging to his legs, and push them down. Looking up at him questioningly, I caught a glimpse of his good eye, the one that was trying so hard not to look down at me. It was bloodshot and watery.

He swiftly looked away from me and opened his mouth to speak. No sound came out. He closed his mouth and tried again.

"You're not mine," he told me. "You're not my daughter." He walked away without looking back.

My eyes followed him as he escaped into the shadows of the building, abandoning me to the dusty gravel that supported my wobbly legs.

Your fatherless friend, Kit Kat

*"What good it would have done me at that time
to have been tossed in the storms of an uncertain struggling life,
and to have been taught by rough and bitter experience
to long for the calm amidst which I now repined."*
JANE EYRE

Dear Jane,

In losing my father, I also lost pretty much everything else.

The next to go were my brothers.

"With your father gone," my mother told us as she threw their few belongings into one tattered suitcase, "I can't take care of you. You two will go to a school for boys. You'll have each other there."

"What about her?" Nicholas pointed to me darkly.

"She's too young. She stays with me."

I didn't know much about the world and how it worked then, but after being in the U.S. for five years and watching television shows, I'd learned a bit about parents and children and the system, and I am not sure that they hadn't been taken from us. I'm not sure if Greece had foster homes in the 70s, but they did have orphanages for kids without families, or kids whose families did not want to take care of them.

I, too, landed in one, but that's a story for another day. I promise.

I don't know if child care services took them from my mother, or if she threw them into the system, but I do know that they were no longer going to live with us.

A few hours later, my mother and I walked Nicholas and Stavros to the main street near our house and put them on a bus that would take them to a school for boys in another city.

I remember that day, that singular moment of standing on the corner of the bus stop, beside my mother, watching my brothers drag their feet and bags onto the bus that would deposit them at the gates of their orphanage. Once seated, they watched us from behind the glass, their somber faces silhouetted by the dust and grime that had collected upon the surface of the window pane.

I looked back in earnest, trying to commit to memory their boyish features, waving goodbye to them as they disappeared around the bend of the road. I waved long after the bus had coughed a fog of dust between us – until I couldn't see them, and they could no longer see me.

A few months later, my little sister took their place. We called her Baby, because she was not baptized. It was now my turn to care for a child the way my brothers had looked out for me.

When it came to us, I assume my mother enjoyed having us inside her, but she denied us once we came out of her body. While my sister lived inside her, my mother placed her hand upon her rounded belly and caressed the idea of her in circles, strolling up and down the streets with a placid smile upon her lips. She seemed proud of her pregnancy.

I recall the day she returned from the hospital after giving birth to my little sister, her last child. She carried the swathed, dark-haired infant, cradling her against full breasts, a smile gleaming from her lips. Her gait was slow and deliberate as she walked towards our house. Our neighbors approached her, wanting to look at the baby, and she paused long enough for them to pet the child before moving to the next cluster of women and mothers.

I had been standing in the corner, watching, and I, too, approached her, but not to look at the baby. While she and the women were engrossed with new life, I faced my mother's stomach, pulled up her shirt, and ran my forefinger along the newly stitched Caesarian scar that zigzagged below her belly button.

Raw and red, the furious string of stitches seemed to scream at me to run.

Your friend, Kit Kat

*"I once had a kind of rude tenderness of heart...
partial to the unfledged, unfostered, and unlucky;
but Fortune has knocked me about since:
she has even kneaded me with her knuckles,
and now I flatter myself I am hard
and tough as an India-rubber ball."*
JANE EYRE

Dear Jane,

I'm not into boys, so I can't relate to your feelings for Mr. Rochester. I adore love stories, and I must admit that lately I have been reading Harlequin Romances, enjoying the way a single kiss between two people makes my stomach all fluttery and bubbly, but the men in those stories do not resemble the boys at my school. Boys are immature, and I can never kiss them or let them touch me the way the women in the romances beg the men to touch them.

I don't even understand how the girls in my school date these boys. They still have pimples on their faces and boyish bodies. They're not men, and yet a few of them are even having sex. Which grosses me out, because sex is a thing for adults, not kids.

Even Nina, my Indonesian friend, just told me a few days ago that Marco – her boyfriend – wants to have sex and will settle for anal sex. You probably don't even know what this is, Jane, as you come from a very safe and innocent world. The entire concept is disgusting, and I cannot even imagine being so close to someone to let him do that to my body. I have had enough filth, and the idea of two kids my age doing that makes me feel so different from everyone else. Sex is out of my radar right now, let alone anal sex.

Despite all this, I'm glad I'm at the school I am in now because I was zoned for a worse one – one in which some kid got stabbed in the head by another kid just last year. Once my mother heard this, she found me another school to attend.

She is using an address from a friend of hers that lives in Forest Hills, so I can attend a predominantly Jewish school in a Jewish neighborhood. It's a mixed school, but now that I have been moved from the regular track to the SP track (I don't know what SP stands for, but it's for the smarties), I am taking classes with mainly Jewish kids. Which I'm fine with, but these kids are cliquish and not embracing my shiksa self. Just found out that means non-Jewish girl. I was more comfortable with my old section, though, and with the friends I had made there. I went to one class, Biology class, and drew the attention of Mrs. Snell, my science teacher, by answering all her questions, and before I realized it, I had been moved up the food chain. She's a funny teacher with a loud, shrill voice, and when anyone seems to fall behind on her lectures or dozes off, she will raise her voice and screech, "Do you understand that?" It never failed to wake us up, nodding out of our foggy thoughts and into her mitosis and meiosis lessons.

It's interesting when you notice someone noticing you for the first time. Like when Mrs. Snell noticed me. I was just a wallflower in my classes, but I saw her eyes take me in when I answered her questions that day. It's as if she woke up to me, and I was seen. Recognized. Appreciated.

I wish my adoptive mother would see me this way. Take notice of me and my special traits and praise me for them...for being me. She tells me I'm a great poet, so that is something, I suppose.

Anyway, back to boys.

I did have a crush on a boy last year. I liked him a lot. He made me feel the way St. John Rivers felt about his beloved Rosamond Oliver, his hands trembling, his heart palpitating, his entire body feverish and out of control whenever he was near her.

Thank God you did not marry him, by the way. He expected you to sacrifice love for God, as he sacrificed Rosamond for his faith. In many ways, he was a tyrant – the way he ignored your existence when you rejected his marriage proposal – and I'm glad you could see that and did not surrender your heart and passion for him. He was so rigid, and he reminds me of Mrs. Reed and my adoptive mother. It's their way or no way at all. Marrying him, you would have been forced to abandon the fire and passion that is an inherent part of your nature. You would not have been free to be yourself, and you understood that marriage to St. John would be the same as being chained to an immovable rock, a force that would restrain your passions and interests and bend you to his will time and time again: "as a man, he would have wished to coerce me into obedience." And this obedience would have rendered you invisible.

"If I were to marry you," you told St. John, "you would kill me. You are killing me now." This is what my adoption is like, you know? I have a family and home, but I can't be myself. It's quite similar to dying. In order to live here, with my new mother – in order to gain her love – I have to give up pieces of myself. That's not love.

It would have been easy for you to marry him, live as a servant to others in India, and have a steady, unchaotic existence. But I don't think living with someone you're not in love with is proper; in a way, you'd be sacrificing yourself, your passions, your potential for love, and he wasn't worth it. Especially after we found out how he behaved when you disagreed with him: an oaf, cruel and unfeeling. That's no life.

I know we are alike in this way. We are stubborn with our love and heart and won't sacrifice either. For anyone. Not even my new mother, because part of the problem between us is that she wants me to forget my past, and I refuse to. I can't. I am who I am, and I can't deny who I am or where I have come from. I can't forget, nor do I want to forget the people who made me. I won't erase that part of myself just to please her. I may as well kill myself.

See how I go back to her? She's at the root of my unhappiness.

Anyway, the boy that I liked. His name was Scott Birmingham, and he had rich, light auburn curls, hazel eyes, and a tall and lanky form. I was quite in love with Scott. When I saw him in the hallways, time froze. Everything stopped, and I was suspended in this haloed haze of soft and soothing light. My insides went all gel-like and gooey, I couldn't move my legs or my arms, and I lost my voice. My heart pounded in my ears, vibrated against my bones, and my entire body trembled. Kids moved hurriedly around me in between bells, cursing me for stopping short in front of them while they rushed to their classes. I was completely dumb, lost in this trance that only Scott seemed to cast on me just by appearing before me, and I couldn't move again until he had disappeared down the hall, into a classroom that I couldn't enter, for he was a senior.

But then, one day, he spoke to me.

For some reason, he came into our lunchroom while we were eating, and one of the guys in my grade saw me staring at Scott.

"Hey, Scott," he laughed aloud. "Kit Kat has a crush on you!"

"Oh, yeah," Scott grinned, looking over at me. I was mortified and tried to hide inside my sweater, pulling the turtleneck up high enough to hide my mouth and nose.

"She just wants my dick."

And that was it for me. With just that one phrase, my feelings for him dissipated in an instant. There was no more haloed light, no more suspension of limbs, no more wild heart thumping in my blood. I found my voice, but it didn't ring with enthrallment or desire.

"What dick?" I retorted, loud enough for his friends to hear, and while they all hollered, I rose from my seat on the bench I shared with other ninth graders, grabbed my tray, and walked towards the exit doors on the opposite side of where he stood.

It was the last time I spoke to him, and I no longer felt the chills in my body that he used to give me when I found myself near him. My body recoils when I see him in the halls now, onstage when he participates in the Drama Club, or outside in the schoolyard. After Scott, I was done with boys. My disappointment in him lifted this veneer that protected boys, letting me see how foolish they seemed...how immature and dangerous they can be to my self-preservation. Their charm is illusory, and I must preserve myself, Jane, to be more like you and less like my own mother. The one who earned money with her body.

He made me understand that physical attraction to another human being is not real, not worth trusting as real, no matter how good it feels, how natural and unscripted it is. So, I don't mind losing myself in Harlequin Romances. They're not real. Real life, real sex is not like it is in these books that I read, hidden in the corners of my favorite library. It's worse, and I have no intention of being cornered into traps with boys that my friends, Nina, and a few others, are being pressured, or seduced, into – giving up their bodies to childish hands that don't know what to do. Or some of the other girls I know who are openly having sex with these juvenile boys, their faces riddled with pimples, high-fiving each other in the hallways when they get laid.

When I came across your beloved Mr. Rochester, I was already done with him, too. I can't understand how you – patient, sweet, sensible Jane – could fall for such a miserable and slimy character. Mr. Rochester reeked of deceit. Everything about him reminds me not of love and passion and my early feelings for Scott Birmingham, but of the real Scott, the one who opened his mouth, with his easy reference to dicks and pubescent sex jokes.

More importantly, Rochester reminds me too much of the threatening and brooding drifter of my own childhood. The man who filled my world with more dicks and lust and debauchery than I could escape.

I'm sorry. I can't think straight right now. My pen is digging into my fingers and ripping the paper I'm writing on. This happens when I remember this man.

Talk to you later.

Yours, Kit Kat

*"He had a dark face, with stern features
and a heavy brow; his eyes and gathered eyebrows
looked ireful and thwarted."*
JANE EYRE

Dear Jane,

I have to get this out of my system, so here it is.

His name was Kristos. In Greek, his name means "Christ," which is so curious to me, as there was nothing Christ-like about him.

Kristos was a gypsy, resembling the gypsy fortune-teller that Mr. Rochester pretended to play to get you to confess your true feelings about him. Except the gypsy I knew was real and rough and scary. He entered our lives with a suddenness that left me tottering for balance. I don't know where my mother found him. Where he came from or how long she had known him. All I know, all I remember, was that he was suddenly there. In front of me. Behind me. All around me. He was a disturbing and inescapable shadow that swallowed me whole. His fingers were strong and tight when they clamped around my throat.

He was a foot taller than my mother and wore a white baseball cap atop his own long, unkempt black and silver coils of greasy dreads. An equally untidy and nappy beard of salt-and-pepper curls covered much of his face. The features that stood out were his hollow eyes, the brown color of his skin, and the crooked nose that fanned out across the width of his face. Before I knew it, this volatile man was part of my family. He became our protector, my mother's pimp, and I was forced to call him baba. Daddy.

You know how my mother used to beat my father? Well, she didn't touch or threaten Kristos. The opposite. He hit her. Punched her. Kicked her. Grabbed her hair. Had sex with her in front of my little sister and me. She didn't hit back the way she used to strike my father. It's as if she had met her match, someone stronger who could control her. I don't understand this dynamic. I don't know how you can stay with someone who hurts you and uses you in this way. Even my father, who was weak compared to my mother and Kristos – even he managed to find enough courage to leave, even while it meant leaving his children behind to fend for themselves.

After Kristos came into our lives, we lost our house. He made my mother rent it out for extra money, and we lived on the streets, like gypsies. Taking nothing more than a few light blankets, we left our house and settled for abandoned buildings without windows, doors, roofs, or walls.

Our first night away from the comforts and security of our home, we found refuge in a building that was under construction. It consisted of nothing but brick walls, ceilings, and floors. I can picture the building from the outside as it rested on the incline of a steep hill by a busy intersection. I can see the flowers that lay by a tree around the sharp bend of the road, paying homage to someone who had died driving around the blind curve.

During the night, Kristos led Baby and me to a room on the first floor of the abandoned building. He sat on the ground in the corner, lit his cigarette, turned on the music to his boom box, and watched me from under hooded lids as I laid out a blanket we had taken from our house.

I remember his boom box. He took it with him wherever he went, balancing it atop his protruding shoulder bone and clasping it firmly against his ear. To this day, I can't hear Roy Orbison's "Pretty Woman" without thinking of him. It was his favorite song, and he played it while showing off my mother on busy intersections of Athens, baiting male customers to pull their cars to the side and haggle with him for her services as she stood behind him, smiling.

I created a little niche for Baby and me on the hard mortar floor on the opposite side of the room. There were no doors or windows, and the chill air blew into our little nest, making Baby whimper with discomfort. I sat down, leaned my weary head against the cool wall, and cradled Baby in my arms, to keep us both warm. I stroked her black hair, black hair none of the Koutros children had, and whispered calming words into her olive-dark stare.

"Come to your baba," Kristos commanded.

"You're not my baba!" I cried out, gritting my teeth against the cold air, wishing I could spit at him, rip out his eyes with my fingernails, choke the force out of the sneering smile that reminded me how powerless I actually was.

Kristos was the kind of man who pushed himself deep inside me and stayed there, leering and laughing at me. He was the mark on my skin that I could not wash off.

I wanted my mother. He left me alone when she was around.

She had gone off to get us dinner, and when she returned a few hours later, with a bag of broiled chicken in her hands and said, "I did it," to Kristos, I knew.

I knew from the look that she gave him, from the way she clutched at her skirts, the way she avoided my stare, that she had not bought the chicken with money, but with her body.

I know it sounds inconceivable that a young girl would know these things. But I did. I knew it the way I knew my life would change when my mother struck my father with her red heel; the way I knew Kristos was a dangerous man I had to steer clear of, training my body to become aware of his presence, his movements, his knowing look boring into me; and the way I knew that if I didn't escape him, he would make me my mother.

I knew it the way I knew, when I found your lovely, somber face on the cover of a book, that your story would save mine. My childhood trained me to look for both signs and quick exits.

It feels so improper talking to you about this. I mean, you're so innocent. My experiences are more comparable to Rochester's in this area than they are to yours. You grew up sheltered, in a home full of females, followed by an orphanage full of girls. You didn't experience this kind of corruption until you met Mr. Rochester, but this is what I cherish about you. Your innocence. I want to drape it all over me and wipe out my memories, so I can be as innocent and uncorrupted as you are. Then maybe I won't have this darkness scratching and clawing to get out of me. Without it, perhaps I wouldn't need to escape so much of it, itching to slip out of my own life in the middle of the night – a life I didn't ask to occupy.

Rochester tried to kill himself, too, once he found out he had been tricked into marrying a crazy, violent woman. He thought of shooting himself when he realized he would never find a woman good enough, pure enough to set him free, to love him despite his darkness, his rages, his mistresses, and the concealed wife in the attic of his mansion that he pretended didn't exist.

Identical to him in this sense, I also feel duplicitous and corrupted, and I drag my feet through life out of obligation, forced to breathe day in and day out, smiling, hanging out with friends, doing homework, pretending at normalcy. No one knows where I have come from. No one knows of the mother I hide in my attic. The one that beat my father, discarded my siblings, had sex with men in front of me, and surrendered me to strangers who passed me on to more strangers until I was nothing more than a stranger myself. She is better off chained to the walls and muzzled into the silent chambers of my memories where no one can see or hear her.

Your devoted friend, Kit Kat

*"Deceit is, indeed, a sad fault in a child...
and all liars will have their portion
in the lake burning with fire and brimstone."*
JANE EYRE

Dear Jane,

I know the exact day my adoptive mother stopped loving me. I know for anyone else it would be hard to imagine choosing not to love a child, but you know this all too well. After all, Mrs. Reed chose not to love you. She cared for you, as my second mother cares for me, but without the love and affection all children should get. But you and I didn't get the kind of love we expected or desired.

A few years ago, my mother took me to PEEC, an environmental center located in the Poconos. PEEC stands for Poconos Environmental Education Center. It used to be a honeymoon resort with outdoor pools and hot tubs that had not been in use for a decade between our cabins. They were not filled with water and plants and weeds grew out of the cracks in the foundation. Kids often lowered themselves into the empty pools until the counselors or their parents yelled at them to climb back out.

Science educators and environmentalists took their families there in the winter and summer, and we stayed in cabins, ate in a buffet-style hall, took day and evening hikes, canoed or kayaked in the summer, and cross-country skied through the woods in the winter. They offered lectures on endangered hawks and eagles, letting us pet them as they sat perched on the environmentalist's shoulders, held arts and crafts sessions for the kids, and offered music festivals and movies for entertainment. This is where I watched *Bambi* and cried all the way back to my cabin and fell asleep, devastated that this was a children's movie. I was about ten years old when we went there, and I loved the feeling of being encircled by a thick blanket of trees and woods. It was most comforting to me; I felt as if I were being swallowed by my surroundings – cocooned, to be more precise.

That summer was my last summer there. I met a friend, a little boy my age who kept asking me about my father.

"Where is he?" he asked. "How come he's not with you?"

A lot of kids asked about my father. In answering them, I was faced with my earliest conundrum. I was supposed to tell them I didn't have one. After all, it was just my mother and me. But how could I tell them I didn't have a father, when I did?

I still remembered my father: his receding hairline, his features concealed from me by his hunched frame and the smoke he blew out of his lips and nose, the scar on his left eye when my mother nailed him with her heel out of rage, his cowering body when it hit the floor after she punched him, the day he told me I was not his daughter. Memories of my father were fresh and raw, and there was a part of me that refused to relinquish those memories or pretend that he never existed. To say he didn't exist – that none of my family did – would imply that I didn't exist either, but I did.

How could I lie about not having a father? I couldn't understand how she forbid me to lie to her but expected me to lie to everyone else about the most honest parts of me.

"I have a dad. He just doesn't live with us," I told the boy whose name I no longer recall.

"Your parents divorced?" he kept prying. We were sitting atop a metal bar that separated the dining hall from the parking spaces surrounding it. He and I met during the morning hike, and now we were holding onto the rail and flipping ourselves over it, going upside down, and then pushing ourselves in an upright position again.

"No," I huffed. "They're not married."

Now that made me a bastard, and I was not a bastard. I even punched Andrew Spiro in the chest, forcing him to fall off his chair during recess last year just for calling me that. He hasn't spoken to me since.

I faced him.

"Look," I said, frustrated. "I'm adopted, OK? I have a dad, another mother, two brothers and two sisters, but they all live in Greece. This woman here, she's my second mother."

"Oh. OK," he muttered. "How come you were adopted when you have a mom and a dad?" he said after a pause.

I looked at him, heaved a long sigh, and then told him a few bits of my story. My heart pounded in doing so because I was doing something wrong. I wasn't supposed to be adopted; I was supposed to be Ann's daughter. But she didn't talk to me about dealing with people's questions, and I did not feel comfortable asking her. I was on my own, testing limits, and falling on my face.

We were called into the dining hall for dinner, and the rest of the evening went by in slow motion for me – a sour note that made the next couple of years with my new mother a cacophonous experience for both of us.

I sat in my seat, a plate full of food placed before me, and watched as my little friend whispered something to his mom; his mom went over to my mother and spoke to her. I saw her lips squeeze into a tight line, and when she came to sit opposite me, she refused to look at me. Her body was stiff and erect, and her jaw locked. My shoulders sank with shame. I was in trouble.

Without saying a word to anyone, we left the dining hall and made our way to our cabin. Once inside, my mother pulled out our luggage and began to pack.

"Get your things together," she said without looking at me. "We're leaving."

We were supposed to stay the night and leave the next afternoon, but I obeyed without asking for an explanation. After all, I had watched the whole scene in the dining room unfold. I knew exactly why we were leaving. I rushed to get my toothbrush and shampoo from the bathroom and threw them into my little traveling bag. Overwrought with uncertainty, I bit my thumbnail and watched her moving her stiff limbs across the cabin with her usual quiet, tightly wound reserve. I waited for her next command.

"Let's go," she said as she opened the door, exited the cabin with our luggage, and tossed them in the trunk of her green '67 Chevy Nova. I climbed into the front seat of the car, buckled my seat belt, and sank into the leather chair, hoping I would not anger her further. She drove up the hill to the main cabin and went in to inform them that we were leaving early. I sank even deeper into my shame, hoping they would not see me, the reason for this early departure. I was to blame. I was to blame for her coldness, for her loneliness, for her humiliation.

We drove in silence for the three-hour ride back to Queens.

I try hard not to talk about any of them. I assume it's why I move from friend to friend with such ease. I don't want to get too close to them in case they start asking questions about my absent father and my much older mother. I don't want to lie to people, to my friends, but I don't want to disappoint my mother either. The Poconos trip was the last time I spoke about my years before her, sweeping the memories of my parents, brothers, and sisters under the carpet as if they were waste. Unwanted in my new life, so am I as long as I keep brushing them back up to the surface for my new mother to see.

I suppose this is why you're such a safe friend for me. You can't repeat anything I say to you, and my mother can't be angry that I am writing to a non-existent friend.

Going now.

Your very existing friend, Kit Kat

> *"[L]ove would have been my best reward…*
> *without it, my heart is broken."*
> *JANE EYRE*

Dear Jane,

My adoptive mother reminds me of puzzles that are too big and complicated for me to put together. I'm excited to receive them and rip open the box, the hundred tiny misshapen pieces of cardboard slipping between my fingers. I try to be patient and match the parts together so that they fit the picture on the box, but my efforts are futile. I get confused, then agitated when I can't make sense of any of it. This is how I feel when I try to piece my mother together so that I can make sense of her. The task of understanding her is consuming, if not altogether impossible.

She is a practical and frugal woman. She works every day and takes off from her job as a teacher when I am sick. Her life revolves around work and raising me; there is nothing else and no one else. In many ways, she is the better mother of the two that have been handed to me. I know the difference between her and Athanasia, and I am thankful that she has replaced my birth mother. I'm not stupid. I am grateful for this second chance that I've been given.

My new mother makes her own skirt and jacket suits, and when I came along, she even sewed my own dresses, refusing to pay for clothing she could make herself using her own black Singer sewing machine; she checks and changes the oil and tires on her Chevrolet Nova; she rewires the light and fan fixtures in the apartment, paints and papers the walls herself, and moves from one apartment to the next, carrying large pieces of furniture on her back without anyone's aid. I help her a little bit, but she does the bulk of the work. She has traveled to the ends of the world by herself and adopted me in the late 70s, at a period when single women had not begun to consider experiencing motherhood without a man by their side.

She is capable of love.

She loves cats and dogs. She loves good food, the opera, musicals, and black and white movies that feature Fred Astaire and Ginger Rogers gliding on the dance floor in perfect unison. She loves traveling, saving her teaching money during the year so she can spend it all on luxurious trips to unique areas like spending two weeks on a boat while hopping the Galápagos Islands. She loved her mother and father with a depth I have not been able to provoke in her. She did everything for them. She bought them a summer house in Stony Brook, gave them money, took care of them when they were sick, lived with them until they both died, and supported them financially, as they were both uneducated immigrants from Greece.

There is love in her; she just can't give it to me. I am a threat in some way, because I am not hers – not from her own body, her DNA. The origins of my roots are uncertain to her, unkempt and unknown. She can't give herself to me in case I humiliate her, shame her. This is why she is so distant and distrustful of me. Why she can't even tell me she loves me.

There is not much that I know about her. Just as there is much that I don't know about my own birth mother except for my meager memories of her. And in those memories, I see the bad, the unmentionable.

In the past seven years that I have lived with her as my mother, she has told me several stories without going into much detail, but they don't paint a complete portrait of her.

When she was a child, she told me, she had lived in Greece, and she had a pet lamb she loved. Her uncle killed it and served it for dinner. She refused to eat, and that night she tried to run away. But her parents wouldn't let her, promising that the lamb had fled on its own, and her uncle had been joking around. She didn't believe any of it.

She loves telling me this story, and it's almost as if it's the only story of her childhood she recalls. I've heard it countless times. Or perhaps it's the story I evoke because the image of her as a child warms me – gives me solace somehow, reminding me that she, too, was once innocent and young and easily hurt by the adults around her. It gives us something in common.

Her mother, Kathryn, she told me, was stern and rough, once throwing a clock at her head out of frustration. Her father, George, was her favorite. He was warm and loving, and she spent much of her time with him. He was a wrestler in his youth, and he raised her like a son, taking her to wrestling matches.

She even told me about a man she had once fallen in love with, which is comparable to receiving a pot of gold in terms of information, since she does not date at all. He was a fashion photographer, and she worked as his set designer. But she was plain in contrast to the models she prepared for his shots, and she watched him fall in love with and date one of her friends, a beautiful model. I often wonder if that was why she withheld love, why it was so difficult to get to know her. Was he the reason she couldn't give her heart to anyone?

I do not ask her. It would require an intimacy that we don't share.

This occurred all before she went into teaching science in New York City's public schools, when she worked in Manhattan and in France as a fashion designer, dressing the models and designing sets. She worked with famous people, lived in Paris for a year, spoke fluent French, and was one of the first women to wear jeans. Or so she claims. She was even enrolled in law school prior to adopting me, taking night classes in maritime law. But she gave it up when she got me, unable to take care of me, work full-time, and go to law school.

"I was the only woman in the program," she brags, and she has a right to brag.

The most interesting confession to me was that she, too, had been adopted. As an infant. Her parents never told her, but her mother's sister, yiayia Maria, blurted it after her parents had died. "It's why I wanted to adopt," she revealed. "To give back what I had received."

Aside from these short anecdotes, she has not disclosed more to me about herself, almost as if she can't trust me with them – with her. Trying to understand her without these stories, I often rely on pictures of her from her childhood to tell me what she can't – or won't.

My favorite is of one in her teens, dressed as a Greek male dancer. A professional shot, she is standing with one foot raised and leaning on a chair beside her. Smiling, almost as if she's mocking Greek men by appropriating their very traditional and masculine garb, she wears the Greek hat, or *fesi*, that men wear, a white shirt with a colorful red vest, the *fustanella*, which is a white kilt that flares at the kneecaps, white stockings, and the fancy dance shoes men put on with a decorative fuzzy ball of fur at the tip.

I love to look at this picture, for there is such a smug expression on her face that reveals her rebellious nature – a nature that I also possess – the one she tries so hard to stamp out in me.

But the picture that speaks the most to me is one with her father, a black and white shot: when I look at it, I almost feel as if I know her. She is about eleven years old and stands next to her beloved father in the park. She is an awkward and lanky little thing with a bow in her short, shapeless brown hair. Sprinkled with a multitude of freckles, her features are as stony as the statue she poses in front of. Her eyes do not sparkle with joy the way most children's eyes tend to shine when they smile for the camera, promising innocent mischief. Her lips are sealed, drawn in a taut straight line, void of laughter or the slightest hint of childishness, while her arms hang limply at the sides of her thin, rigid frame. This portrait of my mother as a little girl is in stark contrast to that of her father's, whose face is lit up by a bright and jovial grin that spreads from one side of his chubby cheeks to the other. He is as light-hearted as my mother is heavy-hearted.

I still have this picture of her, and although it doesn't explain everything, it does help me understand that this is who she was, before and after me. I wasn't the one who cast this dark, looming shadow over her.

I'd like to know more about her, but I don't ask any questions or prod her to give me more information, because I don't know how to speak to her. Invisible walls go up on both sides, for I have learned the art of protecting myself with my own special kind of armor: I become mute, disappearing into rooms, libraries, schoolwork, books, anger, and silence.

Your friend, Kit Kat

"Hiring a mistress is the next worst thing
to buying a slave."
JANE EYRE

Dear Jane,

There are so many things I want to tell her. As my mother, shouldn't she know about me – from me? She adopted me when I was eight years old, but she knows nothing about me. She won't let me tell her about all the secrets that ache inside me, that crawl under my skin, demanding to be told, to be said aloud.

She knows that my mother was a "putana," a whore, but what about how I lived with that whore – what that did to me? Why doesn't she want to know about that? I need these memories to be given a voice, because then I know they will rest and quiet down and stop shrieking in my head, filling me up with this gloom I can't chase away. I want to understand where I came from, the woman I was born to, and I believe my new mother can shed some light. But she won't. Maybe if she did, she would see that I don't miss that life or my birth mother. That I am happy to be living here, with her, a sane, professional woman who works in a kind of job that provides education to children, instilling in them knowledge, not corruption.

I want to tell her how my birth mother often took Baby and me to the local park, and as Baby and I played in the sandbox, she sat on a bench, crossed her legs in a way that revealed the muscled contours of her bare thigh, and propositioned men as they passed her by.

There were so many men looking for her. Many of them didn't look like Kristos – dirty, mangy. They were clean-cut and well-dressed men with thick, gold wedding bands on their fingers and large wads of bills in their pockets.

If my mother knew this about my childhood, maybe she could explain to me why some women do this, sell themselves to men. And why men use women for sex, paying for something they can have for free with women they care about. This kind of sex isn't in my Harlequin Romances, but it was in my childhood, and I didn't understand it then. I don't understand it now either, and the thought of it makes me feel so dirty that not even a forceful scrubbing can obliterate the shame of it.

Even your dear Rochester relied on these loose women for comfort, Jane. It seems that men move towards these women as if they have some sort of unspoken power over men. Is that what sex is? I mean, he even asked you to live with him as his mistress – his whore – at an era when being a mistress was the worst role a woman could adopt. And for you to be his mistress, without marriage, while he was still legally married to Bertha? I couldn't even believe that he asked you to consider this. That he would want to degrade you in this way. And you even considered it. Out of love for him.

Is that what love does?

Makes women lose their strength and the power over their hearts and bodies, just for the love of a man – even one willing to reduce them to whores? Is that why my mother went from being a housewife and mother to a prostitute once she picked up with Kristos? Was she in love with him?

Thankfully, you are a true role model and said no to him. Even though you did consider it, you were smart enough to understand from his confession that although he relied on loose women for the love that he needed, he saw these women as his inferiors, as castaways. He could visit the lower depths of their sex for stolen pleasure, but he didn't want to stay there. He wanted to stay with you, but at any cost to you, too, and that's even more depressing for me because it shows how selfish Rochester was.

Are all men like this? Because he's like this, and you loved him anyway, marrying him in the end. Kristos was like this, believing all women and girls were exchangeable, replaceable, selling my mother for money. My baba wasn't like this. At least I don't believe so. But he did marry a girl he didn't know just to have a family. One that he would walk away from in the end, his children reduced to collateral damage in the wake of his abandonment.

I'm glad you looked out for yourself enough to protect your own integrity, despite his loving words and helplessness. It's why I was able to keep reading when I got to this part of your story. If you had sacrificed yourself, I would have shut the book and shut you out. It would have been too close to my mother's story – my birth mother – and she leaves a bad taste in my mouth.

I don't imagine I will ever consider such a thing, but that's because my mother was a prostitute. I saw what selling her body was like. There was no love, no respect, no affection. It was a business transaction, but the most intimate of sorts, which is so bizarre. The exchange of bodily fluids and the entire naked part of it – I just couldn't do it. It's so personal, and I look at the boys my age, and I can't even see myself getting naked with them or letting them touch me in places I don't touch unless I have to – when I take a shower.

I'd like to tell my new mother about my feelings and see if there's anything wrong with thinking about sex like this – as this dirty thing. I wonder what she would say.

Sex has come up a few instances in our relationship. When I was in elementary school, I came home and asked her what a blow job was, as I had heard the boys talking about it.

"It's something disgusting," she professed, and I had to rely on my school friends to tell me what it was. My nose and mouth wrinkled. My mother was right.

And then a few weeks ago, we were in her car, driving back from the supermarket and a conversation on abortion and teens came at us from the radio.

"What would you do if I got pregnant?" I asked her out of curiosity.

"I would make you get an abortion," she said, looking straight at the road in front of her.

Since I was eleven, she has warned me that if I misbehave, I will become a whore, just like my mother. I suppose it's her greatest fear for me. But if she let me speak to her, if she listened to my memories, she would realize that that is also my greatest fear for me. I detested that part of my childhood and my birth mother, and if I were to become anything, it would be a teacher. If I were to be compared to anyone, it would be my new mother, my second chance, the teacher, the independent woman who used her intelligence, not her body, to make her way into the world. And you, Jane. Sweet, smart, and full of the integrity that my birth mother did not have.

I'd like to tell my new mother about the days my little sister and I followed my mother from a short distance so the men wouldn't realize we were with her. For some reason, the presence of children was a deal-breaker; motherhood fractured the illusion of the whore – the appeal of purchased sex. Her children made her real, a person, a mother. And no one wanted to have paid sex, violent sex, with a mother.

On many occasions, Baby and I hid in the closet of a bedroom, perhaps a hotel room, as my mother and her johns exchanged favors on the bed. We curled into one another for lack of space, my hand clasped loosely over her mouth in case she let out a whimper or a whine. We were surrounded by blackness, listening to sounds that no longer seemed astonishing to us.

There was groaning, grumbling, mumbling, and often there were even sounds of hands or fists as they struck my mother's body, her screams of protest reaching us from behind the closet door.

In one of my memories, Baby or I made a sound. Perhaps it was a giggle or a sigh of frustration. Perhaps Baby cried out with hunger into the palm of my hand as it clamped against her mouth. Whatever it was, the door that contained us in darkness was yanked open. I squinted at the light that struck me and looked up at the man who had discovered us.

Before I could move, he pulled me up off the floor by my throat. His large, angry fingers pushed me against the wall, my head aching as it made contact with the hard surface. Desperately trying to breathe in air, I flailed my legs, kicking wildly against the open space beneath me in hopes that my legs would find contact with his body.

My mother attacked him from behind, punching the muscles of his back, screaming at him until he let me go, my body falling to the ground with an abruptness that left me gasping for air.

What would my new mother say to all these secrets that I tuck to sleep each and every night like a prayer I serve up to God, asking Him to forgive me for the memories that refuse to fade? Would she place more distance between us, or would she hug me and tell me that everything will be OK?

Or would she just call me a liar again?

Your friend, Kit Kat

*"It is a very strange sensation to inexperienced
youth to feel itself quite alone in the world,
cut adrift from every connection, uncertain whether
the port to which it is bound can be reached."*
JANE EYRE

Dear Jane,

The part of your story that gripped me was when Mrs. Reed sent you to Lowood School for Girls. I had never met a kid that had gone to an orphanage before, and Lowood was an orphanage. I clenched the book to me when I got to this part because what no one knows about me is that I, too, had a stint in a school for girls. Girls with families that didn't want them. Like your friend, Helen Burns, whose father remarried and sent her there, so they could move on without her. Like you, who was unwanted by Mrs. Reed. And like me and my siblings, who had a string of aunts and uncles, a mom and a dad, but ended up there anyway. Throwaways.

Penteli was the name of the orphanage that I spent a year in, and it was no different from the Lowood School for Girls. It was as you described it – an orphan's asylum – providing us with both positive and negative experiences that would define us, haunting us long after we had abandoned its corridors.

An orphanage for girls located nine miles from the center of Athens, Penteli stood on a large piece of land and comprised two buildings adjacent to one another: one was for the regularly abandoned waifs of the city; the other was for girls who were disabled and could not or would not be taken care of by their parents. I was placed in the former.

It was funded by the state, run by the strict and barren code of Greek Orthodox nuns, and housed by many undesirables. I was among them. I slept, ate, and played alongside a select group of girls whose families had abandoned and disregarded them like the squalid cats and dogs that exhausted the streets of the city. Some of them found refuge there from poverty, their parents putting them in an orphanage because they were unable to support their young ones, emotionally or financially. Others had been exiled there because of some physical or mental defect their family was unwilling to tolerate.

I was between five and six years old when I came to live at Penteli, but I'm not sure how I ended up there. I *am* sure that someone found me alone, begging, or playing in the sandbox while my mother was working and placed me there.

My mother certainly did not put me there, because she came for me the first night I spent at Penteli. Like the ceaseless storm I had come to know in her, I heard her pound her fists on the large, wooden door, screaming my name against the wind, willing me to run to her.

"Elektra!" I heard her scream the name she had given me at birth through the hallways. "Come here, *kori mou*. Come to me now!" she bellowed, referring to me as *my daughter*.

But I didn't move. I couldn't. I didn't want to.

Instead, I curled my body into a tight ball, brought the blanket over my head, and placed my hands over my ears. I prayed that the nuns had the strength to keep her out, and after a long pause, I heard the door close, followed by a thick coat of silence. It was only then that I could breathe deeply, and I fell sound asleep instantly, unafraid that construction workers or police would wake me up and push me out of yet another site; unafraid that Baby's cries for food would summon me; and unafraid of Kirstos' body touching mine in the dark. My sleep was deep and uninterrupted. I was safe.

It was there that I slept for one whole year in a twin-sized bed on a soiled mattress that creaked against the springs of its fragile frame, amongst multiple rows of sleeping orphans. I burrowed beneath clean, urine-free sheets and blankets that smelled of fresh soap. I was assigned daily chores and responsibilities, made to attend classes to learn the Greek alphabet, to read, to add and subtract, and to sew. Similar to your instruction at Lowood, these were basic skills that would help me, a girl, function well in society once I got out at the age of eighteen. But I didn't stay there that long.

The following weekend was family day, and my mother, with Baby in her arms and Kristos behind her, came to visit me. The four of us sat on a bench outside, and I played with Baby's pudgy fingers as she sat on my lap and peered up at me.

Kristos was looking at me. I hated his oppressive gaze on me. I hated that he was there. I stared back at him, wishing I could make him disappear with one blink.

But my reaction made him toss his head back and laugh. I slammed my fists against the table, but he laughed even harder.

Lighting a cigarette, he dismissed me, glared at my mother, and told her he was in a hurry.

"You have to stay here for a while. They won't let us take you until we can find a place to live. We'll come back for you then," she told me, taking Baby from me and securing the two-year-old onto her extended hip.

I said nothing.

Despite all her shortcomings, her abuse and depravity, she was all I had known. Her nomadic existence had been the framework of my childhood, my playground. It was her way, our way. I didn't fight or cry. I just sat there and let the seams of the life I had known be unfastened by her recklessness.

"Kiss your baba goodbye," she commanded.

"He's not my baba!" I yelled and ran back into Penteli, seeking refuge in the billowing skirts of my new mother-nuns.

After they left, the nuns encouraged me to eat. Obeying them, I ate, crushing the soft peas between my teeth, a bubble of green paste forming and filling the open sores that festered inside my mouth. The effort appeased my watchful protectors, and they smiled approvingly as they retreated to their place at the end of the dinner table, the long, black fabric of their skirts cascading over the edges of their chairs.

But my body rejected the food, and waves of nausea overtook me. I wiped the dregs of vomit from my lips and stared at the regurgitated green mess that lay before me.

To this day, I will not eat peas. My mother watches me as I spend painstaking minutes pushing the green balls to the edges of my plate, not understanding that my aversion to them has nothing to do with how they taste.

How can I tell her the truth? She doesn't want to hear it.

Love, Kit Kat

*"To live, for me, Jane, is to stand
on a crater crust which may crack and spue fire any day."*

JANE EYRE

Dear Jane,

Memories of Penteli come to me in fragments, tearing me open from the inside like shrapnel fixed between my bone and skin. They make me ache in places I can't name or even remember. But they are there nonetheless, following me without relief, reminding me so I don't forget.

They come to me in spurts when I least expect them. I catch a whiff of a specific medicinal odor and the smell catapults me to the days when the nuns chopped off my hair and placed lice treatment on my scalp, a red handkerchief sprinkled with white powder pulled around my head, behind my ears, and tied into a secure knot at the back of my neck.

Whenever I sit at the dentist's chair, my mouth open wide, hands clenched against my hips, I conjure a song that will calm my nerves – any song – as long as I can concentrate on it and shake my leg in rhythm. Closing my lids, I swallow in the black depths of memory that remind me of a moment in the orphanage I sat in a similar room, on a similar chair, pushed back, my mouth open, while the fingers of a cool, unresponsive man scratched and scraped metallic dentistry tools along my teeth, and then...blackness. I went out, and I don't know what happened to me next. I suppose it was so painful that I passed out. Or maybe I was drugged into submission. All I know is that when my new mother took me to an American dentist, I flailed my arms and screamed, kicking and punching anyone who came near me. All they wanted to do was to take X-rays, but I ran out of that office gasping for air, tears streaming down my cheeks.

I had the same reaction when she took me to a regular physician, and he asked me to take off my shirt. Even with my mother in the room, I refused to comply, fearful of dangers I couldn't recall, let alone share with the woman who had become my only parent. Shaking my head, I refused to unclench my fingers from around the buttons of my shirt, pressing them even harder against my chest. Between my mother, who was embarrassed by my antics, and the doctor, I had no choice but to stand before the two of them, my flat chest bared, my skin shivering under the cool touch of his stethoscope. I haven't gotten used to dentists, but they're more tolerable to me than regular physicians, who insist that I stand before them practically naked. I don't think I will ever get used to that. I don't like being uncovered, and I hate male doctors looking at me, or even touching me.

I am surprised at how intolerant I am of people, and I am just fifteen. When I was around eleven, my mother brought home a friend from her job to stay with us for a few weeks, because she was older, had no family, and had just come out of surgery; I scoffed at the woman's helplessness. My mother had to help her from the bed to the bathroom, bathe her, feed her, help her into and out of her clothes daily, and I had no empathy.

"She needs us," my mother said to me, embarrassed by my indifference.

"She's using you," I told her. "She can do all this by herself."

My intolerance for people's weaknesses was just beginning to bare its teeth in me, and I, too, was embarrassed by it. I was generally a good girl, obedient, quiet, and this wasn't me. Confused by my own reaction to this woman, I frowned while a memory surfaced that took me back to Penteli, when I was not yet six and had already lost my compassion for others.

There was a little girl at Penteli, and I sneered in the same way when she fainted. She was about my age, slight and frail, and when she had a chore to do, she fainted. When she was getting reprimanded, she fainted. The nuns rushed to her aid, calling for the smelling salts in panic, placing the vial beneath her nose, cradling her head in their arms, waiting for her to open her weary lids. When she regained consciousness, she was surrounded by a group of girls and a larger group of nuns looking down at her, worry crinkling their brows.

I hated her each time she fainted and each time she awoke. Repulsed by the spectacle, I placed my hands on my hips and shook my head in disbelief.

"Don't you see she's faking it?" I yelled at them, standing outside the circle that enveloped the little girl. I was always outside the circle.

"Hush. She is sick, and we have to care for her," one of the nuns dismissed me.

Who worries for me? I wanted to scream at them, but I didn't, hiding my feelings behind indifference. No one held my head, and I didn't have the luxury of fainting spells to get anyone's attention.

Your unseen friend, Kit Kat

"Your pity, my darling, is the suffering mother of love."
JANE EYRE

Dear Jane,

Like you with Lowood School for Girls, I wasn't happy at Penteli. Initially, it was a break from living with my mother and Kristos, but I came to hate it there. The nuns didn't beat us, but they were harsh and cold, taking care of us without affection.

Between the many stays of blackness in which I don't remember much of my time at Penteli, I find myself sitting at the back of my classroom, my arms clenched against my chest, an angry expression on my features. Unhappy with my situation, I refused to listen in class, to raise my hand, or to do any of my homework. I even failed my rudimentary classes and was left back.

I have to laugh about it now. I love reading, and I do well in school. Of course, there was nothing funny about it then.

Penteli wasn't infested with typhus, and the girls weren't dying of consumption as they did at the Lowood School, but all institutions possess the disease of oppression and abuses executed by the stronger over the weaker, the older over the younger. Even you experienced this, when you showed how that one mean teacher tormented Helen just for being late to class or not being neat and how the stronger and older girls at Lowood stole food and coffee from the younger girls who didn't have the strength to stand up for themselves.

I don't recall being abused at Penteli, but my throat tightens at the thought of the place. I know something happened to me, but I'm not sure what it was. I don't remember everything.

I know that if I had been allowed to talk about my experiences when my mother first adopted me, I would have been able to tell her, but in the years that I have lived with her – in this silence – I have lost many of my experiences. Now they're just feelings. Like the way I don't like to be touched. I can deal with hugs from my closest friends, but I don't want hands or fingers lingering on my skin, where my bones protrude – my knees, elbows, ankles, and my collarbones. What I do remember is fear and helplessness; what I do recall is pretending to be asleep, late at night, forcing my lids to stay shut, holding my breath, and clenching my blanket tightly to my chest while older girls in the orphanage blew breaths against my eyelids to see if I was awake.

I don't know what happened to me when I opened my eyes; I only remember her face, her dark pupils, so close to mine, smiling with a cruelty that made me shudder.

Everything after that went black. Aside from rawness between my legs and spots of blood on my inner thigh the next morning, it all remains black.

My body is the one part of me that remembers, and the way it reacts to a simple touch reminds me that something is not quite right.

What I do know is that I go to bed fully dressed, in layers, pulling the covers over my entire body, my knees tucked under my chin, inviolate.

What I do remember is shame crawling all over my body like a million undetected mites that nibble on infected skin.

I'm ashamed to tell you this next part.

I had sex at Penteli, and I wasn't even seven. I waited until the lights were turned off and the nuns creaked onto their beds. There was a girl. I don't remember if there were any other girls, but I do remember this one. She was small and fair-haired with a ready smile. The one night that I recall with such vividness, I crept out of my bed, my feet touching the cold, hard linoleum floor, and pushed our metal-framed cots together. She and I crawled under the covers and found each other in the dark.

Our hands touched, our fingers probed and caressed, memorizing the thin limbs that willingly received our affections. We embraced and kissed, clinging to each other, pressing our bony thighs together just to get that shivery sensation that came when our private parts met, our sighs mingling with the sounds of our neighboring orphans.

As long as we had each other, we didn't need to twist our sheets into a hard knot and rub the stiff piece of fabric against our genitals when our insides throbbed with need. We role-played, taking turns as husband or wife, and made love, pushing and rubbing our frail, unnourished bodies together. We shared the beautiful untold secrets of love and sex that lacked the ugliness of penetration, aggression, and invasion that I had grown up with. Our love was soft, sweet, gentle, and desperate. Our legs intertwined, we held each other, giggling beneath the covers. We were children, wild and starved and carefree.

A few years later, when I was living with my Aunt Thalia, there was another girl that I met in a camp my aunt had placed me in.

Both her face and name have disappeared into the black sea that has swallowed many of my memories, but everything else about her remains.

She and I disappeared into the isolated hills of the campground, where we were alone and free to do as we pleased. Under my direction, we played house. Assuming the role of her husband and having just arrived home from work, I demanded my dinner, which she placed atop the trunk of a fallen tree.

I was the man, possessive and in control. My earliest lesson as a child was that men had power over women; I wanted to know that power. The girl played my wife. She cleaned and cooked and waited for my return from work, obedient and submissive.

The trees surrounding us became the walls of our house; the grass cushioned us as we lay our bodies on top of it, rolling in it as we embraced and kissed.

I grabbed her, pulled her into my arms, and removed her clothes from her skin. I took off my clothes, and in the open and humid summer air, we kissed and made love on the grass, the blue sky and blazing rays of the sun above us the solitary witnesses to our secret.

I think of her often, turning over the memory in my fingers like a child's snow globe, peering into the image of us, naked, twisting into each other on a bed of grass and weeds, wondering if she had been a willing participant or an infected innocent. Wondering if I had corrupted her the way I had been corrupted.

I don't remember.

The sex I had with these girls was unlike what I had witnessed between my mother and the men who used her, smashing their sweaty bodies against her sagging breasts.

At least that's what I tell myself.

The sex my birth mother taught me was raw and hard, sadistic and scathing; it was violent and dehumanizing. There was the brutal thrashing of bodies, the constant pushing, thrusting, writhing, stabbing, and penetrating of one into the other, the guttural sounds of pain, the frequent hands, and fists that struck my mother's face and breasts, the screams, the profanity, the cursory money exchange. Afterward, her hair and clothing disheveled, her gaze clouded with indifference, my mother counted her sullied money with a calmness that I had not known in her.

This is not a common ground you and I share. This part of my story intersects with the savage veins of Rochester's narrative, who galloped away from his pain on his horse, in the middle of the night, and found comfort, albeit temporary, in the arms of women like my mother. He took them, had sex with them, paid them for the pleasure they gave him, and when he tired of them – because they were dirty, needy, and inferior – he cast them aside, or replaced them, as men did with my mother.

My sex was nothing like my mother's. That's how I want to remember it, and mostly, I'm successful in this – seeing the good parts, the connection to another human being that I needed, to be touched, loved, wanted.

But when I am not successful, when I see it as dirty, when I am reminded that I was just as wicked as my birth mother, as immoral as Rochester, my skin crawls and itches, and I have to shower, letting the soap cleanse me of my sins and shame and the water wash away my memories.

Your sullied friend, Kit Kat

"The more solitary, the more friendless, the more unsustained I am, the more I will respect myself."
JANE EYRE

Dear Jane,

For the longest time, I wanted to be a nun. I think I may still want to be a nun, and not because I love God, or because I want to sacrifice my life to serve others. My desire is much more selfish than that. It's self-serving – the opposite of what it means to be a nun.

I want to be a nun because it's a sheltered existence. With a ring on my finger, I would be left alone, given a roof over my shoulders, three meals a day, and protection from the outside world. I want to be enclosed in a building, maybe even a church, and live a quiet, private, and static life. It sounds so peaceful to me. So wonderful. So uneventful.

Penteli was full of nuns, and they were more maternal to me in the one year I spent with them than my own birth mother had been in all the years I had belonged to her. They replaced her, their shiny, white faces peering out from their habits at me in pity, and it didn't matter to me if their hands were rough and their voices were harsh and commanding. They gave me food and shelter, tolerance, and more security than I had ever known.

There is another reason I want to resemble them – to live as they did in my orphanage. Their vow of chastity stood like a thick, guarded wall between me and my birth mother's prostitution, and all I had was gratitude for them.

In glaring contrast to my mother – who sold her body to men – nuns were covered from head to foot. Their bodies were shielded from the wicked gaze I had encountered when men surveyed my mother. And because they were virgins, celibate, they served no purpose to men.

They were God's daughters and servants – and, even though they wore his ring – they never had to disrobe for him. Pure, their allegiance to God was a symbolic vow. In return for this vow of chastity, the nuns were provided for by the church, protected from the corruption of the outside world. They were untouched by the caresses of men's hands, violent or otherwise.

They were *unsexed* – my favorite word from Shakespeare's *Macbeth*, which we're reading for school right now – and when I surveyed these women, I saw a different kind of power that women can have over men. No one could touch them. No man could harm them. No gaze would linger on them past a dismissive graze.

Nuns get to live in a woman's world, invisible to the outside world that belongs to men, and at the age of six, that is all I wanted: the power that comes with being invisible to the eyes of men.

Still invisible, your friend, Kit Kat

"Well, you too have power over me, and
may injure me; yet I dare not show you where I am
vulnerable, lest...you should transfix me at once."
JANE EYRE

Dear Jane,

I was just thinking about last summer and how I got to spend some more time with nuns when my mother sent me to, what I like to call, a nunnery camp. It was somewhere in Paterson, New Jersey, hidden in a wooded area with a huge lake and a swimming pool. I hadn't seen any nuns since my year at Penteli, so this was a surprise to me.

These nuns were Catholic, not Greek Orthodox, although I'm not sure what the difference is. After this camp, I swear I understood more about Catholicism than I ever knew about my own religion. It seems the same to me. The men are priests, dressed in these long robes, chanting in Latin rather than in Greek, and they worship God, Jesus, Mary, and a slew of saints. Our priests can get married and have families, which sounds saner to me than priests who cannot. But whatever.

Our communion is different, and in this case, the Greek communion is much better. When we wait in line to receive communion, the priest spoon-feeds us. He doles out a spoonful of real bread soaked in wine from the golden chalice clasped in his hand, and this is sweeter than the crisp, round, tasteless wafer Catholics get. I took the Catholic wafer communion during camp, just to see what it was like, and it was nothing compared to my Greek bread and wine...actual bread, actual wine.

My concern was eating from the same spoon everyone else in line ate from. That's a major gross factor that I obsess over – even now when my mother forces me to go to Greek church with her. I'm not sure when this obsession started, but I get anxious when I get in line for communion. I try to stand behind my mother since I know her, and her spit is safer than say the old man whose breath reeks and whose mouth is caked in day-old grimy saliva, his gray mustache hair, caked with his spit, slithering onto the spoon that will soon go into my own mouth.

I'm not tidy or clean. You should see my room. You would chastise me for it. The carpeted floor in my room is hidden from sight because I throw my clothes on it. There are piles of dirty clothes. I leave plates with food on my dresser until maggots grow out of nothingness and I am forced to rush the plates to the kitchen sink, drowning the maggots in an overflow of cold water from the faucet. Dust particles have solidified on my trinkets: jewelry boxes, picture frames, books, etc. The only time my room is cleaned is when we have company, during Thanksgiving or Christmas or New Year's. And even then, I clean it by collecting all my crap and throwing it into the closet or kicking it under my bed. In the past, my mother tried desperately to get me to clean my room, even bribing me with an alarm clock radio, but as soon as I got the radio, the bad habits kicked in again.

When it comes to food, though, I am very picky. If I see blood or veins in my chicken, I won't eat it. If someone chews with their mouth open, and I can see the food being mashed by their teeth, while I'm eating, that's it. I'm done eating. If I hear someone's tongue make that gushy, clucking sound tongues sometimes make while anyone near me is eating, I'm done then, too. The same thing happens to me when I take my communion. Sharing drinks and food with people disgusts me, so imagine how my body reacts when I have to share wine and bread communion from the same spoon a hundred or so other people – strangers – slide their mouths, teeth, and tongues over before it gets into my mouth. It just isn't right.

I make sure to get in line behind children who are much younger than me, mainly girls, because they are cleaner than boys. They're safer than old Greek men with false teeth and rotting saliva, or foul-mouthed teenagers who don't bathe or brush their teeth, or middle-aged women who spit out their phlegm onto the street outside the large, wooden church doors.

These are the differences that I have observed between going to my church on Sundays and this Catholic camp that I went to last summer. The nuns were different, too. In Penteli, they seemed older, more grounded in their religion, and harsh. As if they'd lived tough, poor lives themselves.

They were very similar to the despised Miss Scatcherd at the Lowood School for Girls, the teacher who commanded Helen to bring her a bundle of twigs with which she could strike the girl for daydreaming during her lessons, for being too slow in getting dressed, for mispronouncing a word, and other ridiculous infractions:

> Burns, you are standing on the side of your shoe, turn your toes out immediately...Burns, you poke your chin most unpleasantly; draw it in...Burns, I insist on your holding your head; I will not have you before me in that attitude...You dirty, disagreeable girl! You have never cleaned your nails this morning!

Of course, not one nun comes to mind. Not one nun's face or name has stayed with me in these seven years that I have lived in New York. I didn't like it there. Not at all. Although I hated being sent to a camp for girls for the whole summer in New Jersey years later, I was fond of the nuns there. They were active and loud, and they laughed. They ran relays with us, cheered for us when we swam underwater without using our nose plugs (yes, that one was me), peeled leeches off our legs and arms after swimming in the lake (that was me, too), taught us how to canoe, play baseball, and recite the Hail Mary prayers for each rosary bead lent to me by one of the nuns in the camp.

It was my cabin nun who noticed that I was sick while my cabin group and I were practicing a dance to Corey Hart's "I Wear my Sunglasses at Night" towards the end of the camp, mid-August.

"Kathryn," she called to me, using the formal version of my adoptive name, "why don't you sit down? You appear to be ill."

"I'm fine, Sister Theresa," I called back to her, my head and nose so stuffy I sounded as if I had a pillow pushed against my face. I was sick. I even had a fever, but this was our last week in camp, we were rehearsing as a cabin group for the Talent Show, and the girls in our cabin had asked me to join them, which was significant. I couldn't say no, and I couldn't give in to my sickness.

Sister Theresa was the nun that had witnessed my being shunned from these same girls. She sat with me in my cabin and played cards with me the day all the girls in our cabin had been invited to one of the girls' birthday party. Let's call her Ashley, petite and pretty. Her parents had taken the rest of them to their house to swim and eat cake and sing 'Happy Birthday.' The two kids not invited were me and Janine, the one black girl in our cabin. Her name I remember, because she was like me. Uninvited in the most obvious and painful of ways.

Sister Theresa was also the nun that insisted I wasn't on the list for pick-up two weeks into the camp, the frown lines twisting and intersecting on her forehead.

"Kathryn," she prodded again, "are you sure your mother said she was picking you up today?"

I had all my things packed into my trunk – a trunk we had to buy especially for this camp – and I sat on the edge of my twin-sized bed, ready to run out of there when the announcement from the main office would reach my ears. Two weeks into camp, and I was ready to go. I enjoyed the nuns and the rosary recitations, but I didn't mix well with the girls at the camp. I was too awkward and shy and unbubbly. I couldn't seem to shed the anxiety that came with making new friends, and I never grasped what to say to anyone.

"You're not on the list, honey. Someone in the office would have let me know if you were."

"My mom said she would pick me up in two weeks, and today is two weeks since she dropped me off," I explained to her again.

"Well, why don't you walk to the main office and have them check for you. I'm sure they'll know."

I trudged up the hill to the main office, waited in the short line, and when it was my turn, asked the nun behind the desk if I was on the list to be picked up that day.

I wasn't on the list, she told me.

"I don't understand. She said she would pick me up after two weeks, and it's been two weeks to the day. Can I call her?"

"We'll call her for you, dear. But you're not on the list. As a matter of fact, your mother paid for the entire summer."

"What?"

"Yup. Sorry dear," she said after noticing my disappointment.

I let gravity and the hill drag my feet back down to my cabin where I walked past the silent Sister Theresa and fell flat on my bed, wondering which part of the message I had gotten wrong.

I swore I was right.

There were no phone calls between us the rest of the summer, but I wrote to my mother to bring my violin to camp for the talent show.

She came on a Saturday, when parents could visit. She asked me to get in her green car, and as she drove to the lake down the road, I felt this rising anxiety in the back of my throat.

We sat in the front seat in silence, until I found the courage and the words to confront her.

"Why didn't you pick me up after two weeks, like you said? I was waiting for you. I was packed and waiting for you the whole day."

"I went to Spain," she told me. "With Helen and John." Helen was a good friend of hers, and I had spent much of my childhood going to her house for Thanksgiving and Christmas, as well as on some vacations upstate and to California. Her husband, John, was a nice, pudgy man, and he let me toss salads in his kitchen, guiding my hands when cutting the carrots and cucumbers while instructing me on how much oil and vinegar to pour into the mix. My favorite days with him were spent talking about his fig tree. He would take me out into his backyard, tell me how he had to cover the tree with fabric during the winter, and then he would pick me up, usher me towards the branches of the tree, and let me pick a few figs for us to snack on. Figs reminded me of Greece. I had grown up around them, peeling the purple skin back to encounter the juicy red center that I devoured with a hunger I didn't know was in me. They were both Greek, and when I was younger, when Greek was the only language in which I could communicate, they spoke to me with words that made me feel seen and heard.

"What?" I squeaked. "You never told me."

"No, I didn't. But it was a disaster. Helen was anxious about being out of the country, and John. Well, you know how he is. He didn't help calm her down, he is so aggressive and dismissive. We had to take her to the hospital, and then we returned to NY as soon as she was able to get on a plane. She had a nervous breakdown."

I had to move in my seat to face her. All I could do was stare at her. To not tell me she was going out of the country and to put me in a summer camp all summer – she had not done that before, but I couldn't help thinking about all the planning it had involved and how she hadn't said a word.

"Why didn't you take me with you? You never go away without me." This was true. Since the primary year of my adoption with her, my mother had taken me everywhere she had traveled during her summer breaks: Peru, Guatemala, Ecuador, the Galápagos Islands, Hawaii, and even England. Why had this summer been different?

"Why all the secrecy?" I prodded when she didn't answer me. "Why did you tell me you were coming to get me after two weeks and then leave me here for the whole summer? You even missed my birthday!"

"I wanted you to stay here. I heard something about you from one of the neighbors, and I thought it would be better for you to be here."

"What? What did you hear?"

"Someone told me that you bring boys into the house, while I'm at work."

"What?" I balked.

"Don't deny it. I know it's true."

"I have not brought boys into the house while you were at work or ever. Who told you this?"

"It doesn't matter." She dismissed my question with her right hand, her features not facing mine, but looking out over the water of the lake.

"Fine," she consented. "It's Mrs. Bryce, the woman who lives across the street from us."

I studied her then, my gaze seeking hers, trying to force her to look back at me.

"You mean the one you always complain about? The one who leaves nasty letters in our mailbox every day? The one you have told me is crazy? Her?"

"Yes. Her." She wouldn't look at me.

"So you believe a crazy lady instead of me? When I have done nothing to prove to you that I am untrustworthy?"

"Well, I don't know who to believe." She sighed.

"You believe me," I told her. "You believe your daughter. Not a stranger even you think is nuts."

"Well, that's why I didn't come and get you when I said I would," she confessed.

I didn't know what to say to her, so I said nothing. I just scanned the lake's surface, flat and still, wishing my insides felt the same way.

"It's a long drive back to Queens, so let's get going. What piece will you play for the talent show?" she asked while driving me back the short distance to the cabin. "You play the Minuet in G quite well."

"I don't know," I said. She had this way of making me sink into myself. I felt small and numb.

As I watched the back of her car drive off towards the exit of my campground, I had already decided that I wouldn't play the violin for the talent show. I played the violin for her, to please her, and for this offense, I would refuse to play her favorite instrument as my talent. I hated the violin, and at that moment, I hated her for making me feel so alone and suspect.

Boys! Why would I bring boys over when she wasn't there – or even when she was? I hated boys, too. I hated the whole lot of them.

Yours, Kit Kat

"Such is the sole conjugal embrace I am ever to know –
such are the endearments which are to solace my leisure hours."
JANE EYRE

Dear Jane,

I have always been intrigued by the idea that of all the different kinds of women out there who could have adopted me, it was Ann who plucked me off the decaying limbs of my family tree. Ann, who was virginal and untouched herself. Ann, who lived alone, without a man's protection or love. Resembling the nuns of my childhood, she, too, is unsexed, unmoved by love and desire; her life is barren of both, and yet this gives her power over herself and others. Quite the opposite of my birth mother, Ann seems to be exactly what I need after the corruption I came from.

My adoptive mother is her own master. She doesn't date. Linda, Farida's mother dates, and on television, divorced men and women seem to date. But my mother never brings men over or goes on dates with them. The three men – other than plumbers – who come into our house are Uncle Mike, her second cousin, Nick, his son, and John, her friend Helen's husband. They come with their wives, and they pay me a dollar to hear me play the violin on Thanksgiving or Christmas Day. Outside of that, no man enters our apartment.

It's like living in a nunnery, a woman's home. Despite her cold ways, I find this a blessing that I need. She provides me with a model of womanhood, unlike anything I have known, an antidote to the toxic sexual deviance that highlighted my upbringing. In my new mother, I find a new kind of woman I could emulate without feeling shame, and in many ways, I am still trying to fit into her skin – as unsuccessfully as I attempted to fit into the skin of the daughter she wants me to be.

She is both man and woman to me – father and mother – and I don't feel the absence of a father. Sometimes I wish there was another adult living with us. Someone who would put her in check when she is cold to me or ignores my existence, but other than this, I welcome the fact that men do not exist in our lives.

I find it interesting that your life is also without men. You grew up in a house full of women, with the exception of your cousin John, who is vile and childish; and even when you are ejected from Gateshead Hall and sent to the charity school for girls, you are surrounded by fellow orphans and teachers – all female – specifically after Mr. Brocklehurst – the one male hypocrite associated with the school – has his power over the teachers and girls confiscated after the typhoid illness that spreads and kills many of the girls at the Lowood School because of his greed. Miss Temple takes over, and female teachers and students are governed by her gentle wisdom. Once his power is removed, the next eight years at Lowood are peaceful, full of personal growth and fulfilling feminine friendships that develop outside of the realm of male control.

Although there are men in your story, they are described as hypocritical, violent, controlling, or deceptive. The only men who are portrayed as kind and good are dead: your late, missionary father; Uncle John Reed, who took you in as an infant; and Uncle John Eyre, whose death resulted in an inheritance that allowed you to live comfortably, independent, and without the need of a forced marriage. Even Mr. Rochester, the man with whom you fall in love, is an anti-hero, dark, brooding, and full of secrets that nearly dishonor you. To make him deserve your love, Charlotte must humble him by stripping him of his power, status, and home. Blind, alone, and in need of your strength, only then is he worthy of you. Placing all the power in your hands, Charlotte showed me that a woman can save a man, that she can be stronger and wiser when she relies on herself. That she can control her existence, her future. She doesn't have to be a victim of other people's vices.

Your story depicts a girl's world, a woman's world until you meet Rochester, and if you think about it, he is the one who brings darkness to you. You were an innocent until he tried to marry you and even offered to sully you by making you his mistress. Before him, you lived a quiet and unadulterated existence, and, even though you craved excitement and adventure, I don't think being his mistress is what you had in mind. I know you married him in the end, and he was your adventure, but seriously, I never liked him for you. He's too temperamental and destructive, and he almost destroyed you.

Maybe I'm just jaded. I can't help but see Kristos in him. Will I see Kristos in all men? I hope not. That is such a stark kind of living.

As it is, I can't seem to forget him or leave him behind. He followed me to America, where I thought he couldn't find me. He steals into my dreams, reminding me that I can't escape him or the fear that he has taught me.

I have a recurring dream in which I live in an all-girl school, like Penteli. Like Lowood School for Girls.

It is night-time, and there is a madman on campus; he rapes and then stabs his victims to death.

Pandemonium fills the hallways of the school. Girls are running out of the building in their nightgowns and pajamas, screaming for help, their arms pushing through the layers of fog that blind them. I am among them, running down the steps, escaping inside the maze of high-arching trees and thick shrubbery.

I sense him before he makes himself visible to me. His hands catch me from behind, and I feel him breathing heavily against my cool cheeks.

Stripped of my nightgown, I tremble, cold and terrified. I feel the sharp tip of his jagged dagger touch and penetrate the layers of skin on my breast, on my inner thigh, and then between my legs. He disappears, and I lie there, on the soft ground, the dew-packed grass grazing against my skin, seeped in my blood.

I raise myself slowly, wondering why I am not dead. I touch my wounds and look at the blood that flows from them.

But then I feel him near me again. He pushes me to the ground and crouches above me. He raises the dagger high above his muted face, about to crash down upon me, and I begin to laugh at him.

I shove him from me with my fists and stand before him naked, bleeding, jeering.

"You can't kill me!" I scream at him, showing him the blood on my hands and thighs. "Don't you see? I'm already dead."

All I know right now is that growing up in a world without men is a great relief for me, for men scare me, and the boys my age all seem stupid and insignificant. Kristos made sure of that. Despite all the things I don't get from my adoptive mother, she is able, unknowingly, to provide me with the safety I need far from men. And her rule that I not date until I am eighteen is comforting to me.

I did defy her once. Just out of curiosity, not because I had a crush on the guy.

It was six months ago, and his name was Gus. He was in my Chemistry class, and he asked me out. I told my mother I was going to the movies with my best friend, Alexandra.

Yes, I lied. I'm a liar to her, anyway, so what does it matter if I at long last do tell a lie?

I met Gus down the block from my house, and as soon as I saw him, I regretted my decision. He was tall and thin, with wavy, black hair and an easy smile. He was a huge flirt, and maybe that's why I said yes to him. I was surprised that he asked me out, but I wanted to see what this dating stuff was all about from my own experience, not from my Harlequin Romances or the television shows I watched.

When I reached him, he kissed me on the cheek and gave me a grin.

"I have to pee," he said. "Wait here." Shocked, I watched as he went behind a dumpster by St. John's Hospital. When he was done, he came back to where I was standing and grabbed my hand. I let him hold it and stifled the urge to show my disgust on my face. The fact that he could do that in front of me, on our first date, made him even less attractive to me.

We went to the movies around the corner from my apartment, and I refused to eat popcorn once his hands went into the bucket to grab a handful. He also chewed with his mouth open, and the sounds of his chewing and gurgling and swallowing cornered me into this pocket of loathing that I couldn't climb out of.

When the movie was over, I told him that I had to go home. I had a curfew. This was true. When we arrived at the corner near my house, he bent over to kiss me on the lips, but I moved my head at the last minute so that his lips grazed my cheek.

"I'll see you in school on Monday," I said, smiling to ward off his embarrassment.

"Yeah, no problem," he grinned and walked towards the train station.

On Monday, he waved to me during lunch, but that was it. He was standing by the lunch line with a bunch of his friends, and they all laughed as he said something to them I couldn't hear.

In Math class, Alexandra told me that he was going around telling everyone I had slept with him.

That was the end of it. The end of my curiosity with boys. And I'm OK with not dating guys in high school. No one had triggered emotions out of me the way that Scott did back in middle school when the mere sight of him compelled me to sweat and tremble, but to tell you the truth, I wouldn't trust those feelings now even if some boy did turn them on again. I mean, look what happened with him. Look what happened with Gus. They weren't worth it.

You didn't talk about boys until you met Rochester and St. John, and you were eighteen when you fell in love. Who says I have to get romantically involved with them? I'll wait until I'm eighteen, too. Maybe even later. I have my friends and my books, and honestly, romance is so much better in my books. Love is so much better in them, too. Based on my experiences, though, love doesn't seem real. I think it's better in our imagination.

My world now is full of women, and this is safer. All my mother's friends are females and teachers or social workers. Many are married, but they are all working women and mothers, independent and confident, and none of them is a pushover. Men are scarce in our circle as well and rarely encountered. This is just what I need as a girl who grew up around prostitution, johns, and pimps. I go to sleep every night unafraid. I close my eyes and wander off to dreams that don't attack me with fear. I don't wake up suddenly, afraid of finding Kristos' hands on my body, whispers of threats in my ear.

I am thankful every day for my new mother and my adoption. Whenever I am at my most miserable – now, for instance – I just remind myself that I could be somewhere else. At another orphanage, or worse, being prepped by Kristos to serve the physical needs of men.

"I will teach you to be a woman, just like your mother," Kristos used to warn me when we were left alone during those nights my mother went to sell herself for food. And I believed him. Becoming my birth mother is a fear that paralyzes me even now, and I know that if I had stayed in Greece, I would have ended up just like her.

Your safe friend, Kit Kat

"You think too much of the love of human beings;
you are too impulsive, too vehement."
JANE EYRE

Dear Jane,

One of my favorite parts of your story is when you met Helen Burns. She was to you what you are to me. She was a big sister that saw the world from a bigger, broader perspective when you saw it from your wounded and personal space. It's such an inconsequential space, too, just related to you and your feelings. Helen believed in something bigger than herself and people – God – and her belief in God lightened the load she wrestled with.

When you complained about Mrs. Reed and the love she refused you, you confessed how I felt and how far I would I go for human love: "if others don't love me, I would rather die than live." Isn't that why you tried to starve yourself and I tried to stab myself? Everyone has given me up: my baba, my mama, my aunt and uncle, and even my adoptive mother makes it obvious she doesn't care for me. If there's no one to love me, if I'm so unlovable, then what's the purpose?

Helen offered you, and me, a new perspective, and it woke both of us up.

We are too impulsive, too vehement, too desirous of love that we feel entitled to receive from those who care for us.

Helen was stronger than us. She did not rely on humans for what she needed. Sickly, abandoned, God was her savior, and she lived for him, and only for as long as he let her live. She didn't waste a minute on thoughts of revenge or hatred. When she discussed your feelings of hatred towards Mrs. Reed, she was also speaking to me, asking me why I held onto all the bad things that my new mother has said to me, done to me, all the things she doesn't do for me still:

> She has been unkind to you, no doubt...but how minutely
> you remember all she has done and said to you! ...Would you
> not be happier if you tried to forget her severity, together

with the passionate emotions it excited? Life appears to me too short to be spent in nursing animosity or registering wrongs.

When Helen Burns died, with you sleeping beside her, I cried. I cry whenever I read that passage, because she was the one spark of light in your childhood, and she left it as swiftly as she entered it.

I, too, had a Helen at my orphanage. But her name was Maria, and she was my blood sister.

I was still at Penteli, and she came to me while I was swaying back and forth on the swings between our two buildings.

"I'm Maria," she said to me. "I'm your sister." When she discovered that a girl with the same last name had come to Penteli, Maria told me, she knew it had to be me.

I stood up and looked at her, finding our father's amber flecks in her stare. I smiled and pulled her into a hug that was so good to fill with a person.

"You know about me?" she asked, her voice low with surprise.

"Of course." I squeezed her hand. "Nicholas and Stavros told me all about you."

I would have known even without them telling me. Although she was five years older than me, we looked alike. We resembled each other in the same way we all bore a resemblance to our father. We shared his dirty blond hair, the oval shape of his face, and his almond-shaped eyes. We inherited his petite frame and the olive tone of his skin that gave us a golden tan when we stood beneath the strong Athenian summer sun for too long. We even bore the symmetrical lines of his high cheekbones and the hooked nose that many Greeks possess.

The first-born, Maria, which means "bitterness" in every language (I know, I looked it up), was also the most imperfect, and my mother got rid of her as soon as her imperfections became evident.

When my sister, attached to a bloodied umbilical cord, rushed out to meet our mother, she appeared as if she had struggled to be born. Not only was she the first to learn of our mother's inability to take care of or love her children, but she was also the only one of our siblings to be plagued with physical defects that Athanasia could not accept or forgive.

While pregnant with Maria, Aunt Thalia once told me, my mother had been prescribed thalidomide, a popular drug that promised to alleviate morning sickness. This drug caused severe birth defects among the infants. My sister was one of them.

When Maria was born, the defects were obvious. Her forehead was exceedingly high and wide, and her eyes were stretched abnormally apart. She didn't have the ten fingers and ten toes every parent searches for on their infant. Maria was missing the entire foot of her right leg, and three of her five fingers on her right hand rounded off at the knuckles.

She was the first of my mother's children to disappear from our family, and I don't know if it's because she gave her away or because the state took Maria from her. Maria told me that our mother was glad to be rid of her.

"She tried selling me to the gypsies," she confessed to me many months later.

I peeked at her fingers. They appeared to have been cut in half and reformed into short stubs that rounded midway, missing nail beds and nails. Because of the missing part of her foot, she had to wear special black boots designed to provide a cushion for the absent parts of her. I can recall the way she limped along the fenced-in length of the park that connected our two buildings – the park that we shared as sisters.

When I think of Maria, I think merry-go-rounds, old, tethered swings, and see-saws protruding from the sandy soil that was centered between her building and mine. Because of her physical deficits, she lived in another building, where girls with special needs could get more individualized care. Although I couldn't go into her building and she couldn't come into mine, we met in the playground where all the girls played as equals.

She skipped and hobbled as we ran along the merry-go-round, our hands gripping the bars on opposite sides, pulling it to make it turn faster, and then jumping into it at the count of three, our bodies falling limply onto the wooden base of the hardened surface. Rolling onto our backs, we stretched towards one another. Our fingers intertwined, we fixed our eyes upwards, the tapestry of blue sky and puffy white clouds whirling above us like a kaleidoscope. We held onto each other, spinning out of control with the same kind of intensity our childhood had fostered, but we were laughing, squealing with delight, our father's infectious grin plastered on our smaller faces. We were light and earthy, unburdened, playing as if we had not been cheated out of our innocence.

When Athanasia came to reclaim me, after showing the state that she had secured an apartment for us to live in, she didn't take Maria. I left Penteli without saying goodbye to the one person I had grown to love, being dragged out of the building by my mother's unyielding grip.

I couldn't understand why mama took me, but left Maria back there, all alone, when she had a family to care for her. I never understood how any of us had been placed in orphanages and forced to live as orphans when we had parents and an even larger extended family to care for us. Orphans have no one. We had so many people who could have stepped up to take us.

"I don't have another daughter in there!" Mama yelled at me, pulling me towards the bus that would take me back to the low life she shared with Kristos and my little sister, Baby.

We had a tiny apartment in the city, and I no longer had to live on the streets again, but everything else was still the same. My mother was still a prostitute, and Kristos was still her pimp.

They gave me back to her because she proved she could provide for me, but nothing changed. There was no food in the refrigerator, mangy cats covered our floorboards, and a yellow-stained mattress lay on the floor a few feet from the kitchen. We all slept on it, Baby, me, Kristos, and my mama. Every night, I hugged the edge of it, placing Baby's slight frame between Kristos and me. He and my mother both slept naked beside us.

Your friend, Kit Kat

"I felt an inward power; a sense of influence, which supported me."
JANE EYRE

Dear Jane,

When I was six, I took down my villain.

My mother, my little sister, and I were begging in the streets again, when the police rounded us up and took us to the precinct in Athens.

"We're looking for Kristos," the officer told my mother. "Where is he?"

My mother's lips curled into a smirk, but she remained silent.

This was my chance, Jane. My chance to get rid of that jerk once and for all, and before I knew it, my mouth opened of its own volition and the words erupted out of it.

"I know where he is. I can tell you."

I felt the flat part of my mother's hand come into sharp contact with the right side of my face, and one of the rings on her finger ground against my cheekbone, but I ignored the sting. The officer came to stand between my mother and me, and he bent down to look at me, his broad shoulders concealing my mother's face and hands from me. The fragmented images I could capture from my vantage point were her knees, the way her black skirt covered them, and the tiny, restless feet that belonged to my sister, four years younger than me, as she cooed on my mother's lap, her face concealed from me by the cop's rounded shoulder blades.

"He's at our apartment, sleeping, in Peristeri." I believe the man in the blue uniform understood the light that shone in my look that day, the delirious happiness that jumped out from my pupils as I gave him directions to our place, that dirty, crappy home I spent every morning cleaning while he and my mom slept on the soiled mattress on the floor, completely naked, smoking cigarettes, and laughing at me from behind the veil of smoke they puffed out of their mouths and nostrils.

"Come give your baba a kiss," Kristos commanded in the morning. And every morning, I would remind him: "you're not my baba!"

"I'm the only father you have, remember? Yours left you, and I am the one who takes care of you and watches out for you."

I wanted to punch him. I had nightmares that involved me straddling his chest, squeezing his body between my thighs, and punching him in the face. But when my fists touched his cheek or his nose, there was no power behind it. The power and force and rage that came with every strike faded as soon as my fists got to his face, and by then, I had no power left, no rage. Just like when I tried to stab myself. Exactly like that.

"Come here and give me a kiss," he barked at me again. His tone gave me no choice. I had to, but I glanced at my mother for guidance first. She puffed smoke at me, tilted her chin towards him, and told me, "You know he won't give up until you do as you're told. Just give him a kiss already."

I walked towards him with heavy feet anchoring every step to the rickety floorboards beneath my weight. With dishrag clenched in my fist, I stopped a few inches from him, giving me enough room to run if I had to. He grabbed my short-cropped hair from behind and brought my head to his, planting a loud, wet, open kiss on my lips. I shut my eyes and tried to erase the feel of him from my own mouth. When he at last let me go, he laughed, and the smell of his rancid breath caused my stomach to moan with fear. I stared at him, my mouth pressed shut, not wanting to open it and taste the combination of smoke and rank saliva that he left behind when he kissed me.

I moved away from him so he couldn't catch me with his hands again. I locked my gaze with his, as I often did to let him know how much I hated him, pulled the dishrag up to my face, and thoroughly wiped my mouth clean of him.

His laughter – and hers – chased me out of that apartment – and I tried to figure out a way out of there – from both of them. That day, at the police precinct, I knew my day had come. I did not hesitate to tell them where Kristos was, nor did I care if they found him and locked him away for good.

I did not have a lot of power, but that day, I was triumphant. That is a very good word to describe it. When I feel weak and dispirited with my adoptive mother, I remind myself of that day, because I had the courage to get rid of a man who threatened me and hit me and scared me out of my already brutalized skin. I did good that day, and everything that happened afterward changed the course of my journey, bringing me closer to a life without my prostitute mother and her pimp.

After the policeman called in the location for Kristos, I hoped I would never see him again. I hoped that he was out of my life for good. And he was. I didn't see him again – except in my dreams – but I always woke up from them, and he was nowhere to be found then. I was proud of myself, and nothing has matched this feeling since. I mean, I am fifteen, so who knows. Something could replace it, but that's a huge feat for a girl like me, at that age, getting rid of a monster that my own mother had brought into our lives without any concern for her daughters.

I have come to believe that people enter our lives to bring about change, and hopefully, it's a good change. That's how you are for me; when you came to me, I found someone to talk to, someone who experienced similar troubles and could teach me how to survive people who have hurt me. Even my adoptive mother changed the path I was going down, and without her, I wouldn't be here right now, reading and writing, and finding you in books.

That policeman, whose name I don't know and whose face I cannot even recall – set all the pieces together that brought me here – to my second mother, to America, and even to you.

"What's this?" he asked, grabbing my arms and turning them over and under for, a better look.

"Oh, those are just scratches from the cats. They follow us everywhere and want food. Sometimes they bite my sister and me when we have chicken," I piped up. My arms were riddled with cuts and scratches that intersected beneath my hair. Some of them were healing, and others were fresh and burning red.

"They love chicken," I told him, and he peered at me with a tenderness I felt in the pit of my stomach.

"*Koukla*," he said, calling me a doll, "take your little sister and go wait for me outside the office, OK? I want to talk to your mother."

"OK." I picked up my sister from my mother's lap, avoiding the anger I would find in her stare, and carried her to the waiting room outside his office. I could see them through the glass windows, but after a while, Baby was too heavy for me, and I had to place her on the floor and watch her make sure she didn't pick up anything and put it in her mouth. She was a lot of work. But she was mainly my responsibility when my mother went to her "job." There was no one else to watch her except for me.

After a few minutes, Mama stormed out of the policeman's office, scooped up Baby into her arms, yanked my hand, and pulled me out of there.

"I hope you're satisfied," she huffed in anger. "Not only did you get Kristos in trouble, but now I'm in trouble. If anything happens to you, he'll put me in jail. Now, what am I supposed to do with you? I wish people would mind their own business," she grumbled beneath her breath, yanking me even harder toward our apartment.

When we got there, Kristos was nowhere to be found, and the place was a mess. But that's how it usually was. Kristos and Mama were not clean people. They were lucky to have me because I loved to clean. Well, maybe I didn't love it. I just had to do it. It gave me something to do when I was miserable. This urge built up and expanded inside me like a balloon about to rupture, and the only way to keep it from bursting was to clean, to scrub every cobweb from the corners, remove every stain from the cabinets, extinguish every smell that intruded my nostrils and planted seeds of self-loathing inside me. When every surface was clean – as clean as I could get it – I was able to breathe deeply. My chest no longer ached with this indescribable yearning, and my stomach stopped screaming for the food we didn't have.

Glancing at my work with pride, I couldn't help laughing aloud.

Kristos was gone. My sister and I were safe.

Your fearless friend, Kit Kat

"All said I was wicked, and perhaps I might be so."
JANE EYRE

Dear Jane,

A week after the police station incident, my mother brought me to her brother's construction site. Uncle Dimitri owned a construction business, and my aunt and uncle were well off. I had not known this kind of life that they had: it was secure, normal, consistent. Mine up until that point had been nothing of the sort.

"I can't keep her," Mama told my Uncle Dimitri. "The police will put me in prison if anything happens to her. You have to help me," she pleaded with him. "Please take her. Just for a while."

I smiled at this. I almost laughed out loud, but I knew better. My laughter would earn me a sharp slap across the ear, so I stifled it.

When Mama dropped me off at my Uncle Dimitri's construction site, for good, she told me, elation tingled my pores. I had no love for her. None. I wanted to be gone from her. To abandon her to the same streets on which she forced me to walk and beg, dragging my sister behind me, barefoot, with snot dripping from her nose, crusting at the top of her lip until she licked it off like a cat lapping up milk onto her tongue.

While she was rambling to my aunt and uncle about the police officer and how he would arrest her if I died in her care, I peered down at my little sister, whose fist was doubled over the fabric of my shirt. She was two, and she still had no name.

I had been in charge of her since I was four and she was a baby. I fed her, changed her, and watched over her as if she were my own. We hid in closets and waited in the streets at night while my mother worked, and we pillaged food from garbage cans or begged tourists for money together. We had been inseparable, but I was being sent to my aunt and uncle, and she wasn't.

Knowing what I had to do, I led her from the adults and their adult conversation.

"Hey, Baby," I said to her. "Let's play hide-and-go-seek."

I had taught her this game, and we had played it often as a way of calming our spirits and the pangs of hunger that disturbed our bodies when we couldn't find food.

Taking her little hand for the last time and intertwining her fingers with my own, I told her to cover her eyes with them, and she did, trustingly, obstructing my view of the warm brown irises that resembled my own.

I stood before her for a few deafening seconds and watched her, my beautiful little sister in rags, smiling, waiting for the game to begin.

"Remember, don't open them until I call out to you that I'm ready," I cautioned her.

When I saw that she had locked me out of her sight and would not peek, I stumbled past her, practically sprinting towards my freedom.

I didn't say goodbye to her.

I didn't even look back.

I ran from her, towards the secure path my aunt and uncle promised me. I ran away from her, my own survival coming first. Just like my father.

I see her, my tiny sister, hungry, dirty, tired of roaming the streets aimlessly, trudging along behind me as I fumed at her between gritted teeth to quicken her pace. She stopped to rest her pudgy and wobbly feet, tears streaming down her chubby cheeks, her lower lip quivering out of want of food and comfort.

But I was young, and I had no comfort to give her. I didn't know what comfort was.

I had no food, no love, no patience. I had anger rising from my gut and the burden of taking care of a child a few years younger than me.

I turned around, irate, shaking, my jaw locked in rage. I grabbed her arm and pulled her off the curb. She cried out and pulled back.

I let go, half-smiling, knowing she would lose her balance and fall.

And when she did, I watched as she curled her little body into a fetal ball atop the debris and grime of the city's paved streets, weeping for the things that I could not give her: love, protection, sympathy, patience, food. Her mother.

Watching her weep and scream, I wanted to do the same. My anger bent towards numbness until I didn't feel anything.

Surrendering, I walked towards her, sat beside her on the curb, and waited out her fit.

I waited until she was ready to get back on her feet, walk the streets, and beg for food again.

Not a day goes by that I don't think of her, wonder what has happened to her.

When I was in middle school, I awoke from a dream, trembling, drenched in sweat.

In the dream, I live in a basement of a building with my mother and sister. There are men coming down the stairs. There are three of them, dressed in baggy pants and wearing matching shirts with their company's logo on them. They are large, boisterous, and laughing. Their hands are hairy, their arms bulking as they carry furniture and boxes from our basement, up the stairs, and into the moving truck. I don't trust them, so I leave my place beside my sister and follow two of them up the stairs and outside, the sun beating against my face, forcing me to squint. My little sister has followed me and is standing beside me, rubbing her cheek against my elbow.

One of the men grabs my attention. He's loud, gruff, and he's looking down at my sister, smiling at her. I don't trust his look, how it preys on her, how it consumes her; it's the way men look at my mother before they buy her.

I tell my sister to go back down the stairs, back to our mother. She won't budge, so I push her, yell at her, my heart pounding, my gaze glued to the man, still smiling at her. There's a gleam in there, a leer that makes my stomach churn.

She moves from me and runs down the stairs; his eyes trail after her, and he licks his lips. Then, grinning, he turns towards the stairs and walks to the threshold of the doorway. His body covers the entire entrance, and I can't see past him.

I want to move, to run in the direction of the stairs, to push him out of the way, but my feet are weighed down by a heaviness that is not attached to anything.

I open my mouth to scream, but no sound comes out. All I can do is watch as he descends the stairs, gradually disappearing from my sight one step after the other.

I don't know where she is right now, or who she has become in my mother's care. I left her to save myself, and that makes me no different than the father that left us behind to fend for himself. We were both cowards. Selfish, selfish cowards.

Your friend, Kit Kat

"I was a discord in Gateshead Hall; I was like nobody there."
JANE EYRE

Dear Jane,

I've brought up my Aunt Thalia, but I haven't told you about her. Her name in Greek means "flower in bloom." I miss her so very much, and it just hurts to talk about her, especially when I compare her to my two mothers. If you want to know what she's like, just compare her to your Miss Temple. I was just browsing through my copy of your story, and I underlined this description of her:

> Miss Temple had always something of serenity in her air, of state in her mien, of refined propriety in her language...which chastened the pleasure of those who looked on her, and listened to her, by a controlling sense of awe.

This is how I felt about my aunt. She had lovely blond hair, which is rare for Greek women; they usually have dark features, dark hair, angular noses, and chins that stick out. But my aunt's face was soft, and every part of her face – her nose, her eyes, her chin – was rounded and modest in size. Her daughter, Maria, was just as lovely, just as pretty as her mom, and while I lived with them, I was consumed with regret at my fate – to be born to a woman who was ugly, inside and out, dirty, vile, and mean.

What made me be born to Athanasia and not Thalia? Who decided these things, and why was my cousin Maria so lucky, while I had been so decidedly unlucky?

These are the thoughts that cross my mind when I recall the days I spent with my aunt and uncle and cousins. They're dreadful thoughts, but I feel cheated. I know you understand, having lived with those rude, entitled Reed cousins of yours.

My other cousin's name was John, too – just like your cousin, John Reed. But my cousin didn't hit me as John struck you, smacking you and throwing books at your face, making you bleed. He didn't hunt me down, looking for a fight, or make me fall on my knees before him, bowing to the king of the Reed residence. He mostly ignored me.

I remember the way my cousins sat on the couch in my aunt and uncle's living room the night they brought me to live with them. They were seated next to each other, stiff as stones, and their faces projected that their world was coming apart. I mean, I was just six. How much trouble could I be? But they didn't want me there, and I knew it. I felt as you did, living in the Reeds' home, an "interloper"; that's how you described it. Someone who didn't belong, nipping at their calves like a flea they had to get rid of before it began to breed.

Living with my aunt and uncle was such a different world, like being wrapped up in a huge bubble that kept me floating in mid-air. I could look out at the sordid world and witness its darkness, but nothing touched me, nothing could seep into my bubble and harm me. I loved that feeling of safety, of control. I envied my cousins Maria and John for this, because the security they had, with their parents, was real. It belonged to them in a way that it did not belong to me. They were born into it, without ever having earned it or asked for it.

How lucky is that? To be born into a family of goodness and safekeeping and love you did not have to ask for. I don't know this, and neither did you. We both begged for it after asking for it did us no good, and it was all for nothing. Because we were asking for it from the wrong people: your Mrs. Reed and my adoptive mother. And my Aunt Thalia. And my birth mother.

I don't believe we should have to ask for it. It should be given to us in the same way we give it out to those we care for. The way I used to give it to my adoptive mother before she made me feel wrong about who I was.

I didn't ask for my aunt and uncle to take me into their lives, but they did, and they gave me the kind of home I had not imagined – a lovely and affluent one that resembled the Reeds' Gateshead Hall. There was a television set and food overflowing the dinner plates, the dining table, and the refrigerator. They had a refrigerator that was full of something to eat. They had different bedrooms, and they didn't all sleep on a soiled mattress similar to the one I had been sharing with my mother, her pimp, and my little sister. They were clean – all of them – and they had nice clothes that they washed on a weekly basis. They had machines that washed and dried their clothes and their plates and utensils, and I had never seen anything like it before.

I was in awe, swimming with gratitude when my aunt gave me a bath in a huge tub full of warm water and soapy bubbles. Gentle hands scrubbed my hair and body clean, and I wasn't afraid that those hands would touch me in places my mother's pimp promised to exploit.

I was able to sleep at night without fear that Kristos would graze his naked body against my smaller one, which I had trained to curl into a fetal ball, tight and impenetrable, fully clothed, and taut with alertness. I didn't have to hide in closets while my mother moaned and laughed with johns in seedy hotel rooms or keep an eye on my sister in sandboxes while my mother exchanged bodily fluids with men behind trees and bushes or in the back seat of their cars. I had even just begun not to shrink from the sudden movement of raised hands, fearful that they would punch me in the face, the head, or hit me with objects, Kristos' boom box being smashed against the back of my head.

At my aunt's house, someone asked me how I had slept every morning, how I was doing, and if I needed anything. This was new to me. I had not come from a world where anyone cared enough to ask. I had to fend for myself, and I had been the only one aware of my basic needs – such as eating or sleeping or having to go to the bathroom. Anything else was non-essential.

"You have to eat something, *agapi mou*." She bent over my dinner plate, and I responded to her "my love" phrase by leaning into the waves of her blond hair just to feel them against my cheek, to inhale the smell of a devoted mother.

"But I'm not hungry, *thia*," I told her. I wasn't used to all this food, good, healthy food that I didn't have to dig through garbage cans to find. My stomach didn't recognize it, and it was all suspicious to me.

"If you don't eat, baby, you will get sick. Try and eat something," she coaxed.

My adoptive mother articulated similar comments when she adopted me. The truth is, food grosses me out. I suppose it's because I had to find my food in garbage cans back in Greece. I was so hungry that I had to force myself to eat anything I could find – no matter how chewed up it was by someone else's mouth or that it had come into contact with some other soiled debris. I hate eating in general, and whenever food is placed before me, I need to examine it. For example, if I see veins or blood pockets in my chicken, I won't eat it. Even if my mother cuts them out and shows me there are no veins on it, it's a done deal for me. There's no turning back. I spent almost an entire year hiding my lunch box in the boiler room before she found out. She found out because she saw the box while doing laundry. There were ants crawling all over it.

Fries are good. No veins, no blood, no gross factor. And a layer of salt can hide anything that would gross me out: the fact that someone had touched them, dropped them, or spit on them while talking or laughing. Just the thought of these things occurring to my food makes me lose my appetite.

"I can eat the French fries," I told my Aunt Thalia. She nodded her head, turned up the television set for me, and left me to eat my fries. I put tons of salt on them, and when I tried to eat them, they were disgusting. I took the plate of fries to the sink and ran it under the tap water. I dried the pile of fries with a paper towel and then sat down to watch my television show. They didn't taste good, all watered down, but they were clean, and after a few bites, my stomach was already full.

I was watching a documentary about the Holocaust. It was in black and white, and they showed actual recordings of Nazi soldiers forcing Jewish men and women and children to dig these huge trenches. When the holes were deep and wide, the soldiers ordered the Jews to stand by the edges surrounding the hole, facing the ditch, and then a spray of gunfire exploded into them, and one by one, they fell into their grave.

I don't know if my Aunt Thalia knew I was watching this show, but it left a mark on me. To this day, I have nightmares, and no matter the story that plays out in my dreams, there is always a machine gun, a Nazi soldier, and me hiding in dark corners, in even darker basements.

I was probably a pain for my cousins. Smitten with my cousin Maria, who was about four or five years older than me, I followed her around the house content just to watch her read or play with her friends.

"Leave me alone," she scolded when I begged her to play with me. I had been the older sibling before I sped past my little sister. This time, I was the little sister – at least, the little cousin – and it was nice to follow someone instead of being followed and pulled at and cried at.

I cried in front of her, hoping that my tears would melt her heart enough to play with me – her lowly cousin. But she just complained to her mother, until my aunt asked me to come help her with dinner.

John was no better. A year older than Maria, he was a boy and an aloof one. He kept to himself and didn't even go near me unless he had to.

Going to school with them was the worst. They walked ahead of me to school and ahead of me after school. They rushed me when they wanted to leave the schoolyard and forced me to wait when they wanted more time with their friends. One day, though, I had enough of waiting around for them, pleading with them to love me enough to treat me like family.

I was in the schoolyard at the end of the day, and I was sitting on the curb of the street, waiting for them to lead me home. Instead, they were laughing and chatting with their friends, giving me sideways glances and dismissing me.

I just left. I stood up, pulled my bag over my shoulder, and started walking down the familiar path from school towards our apartment – well, their apartment. I can't say it was ever mine. I was a guest there.

I knew that my aunt would be angry with them and with me for returning alone, but I didn't care. And what she and my adoptive mother never understood is that I had been on my own before. I had walked down the avenues and crossed major intersections by myself since I was four, when Kristos initiated our move out of our house and into the streets, finding shelter at night in construction sites. I knew when to walk and when to run, especially when the crazy *mihanakia* zoomed around blind turns on two wheels, the motorcyclists gunning their engines and beeping their horns for me and cars to get out of their way. Motorcyclists were the worst on the roads; they weaved between cars and other motorcycles with ease, but it was dangerous when you consider that the streets in Athens didn't have definitive lanes to separate their travel. They – cars and motorcycles and taxis – gunned and swerved and stopped on and on, and I was amazed that they didn't crash into each other. But Nea Smirni, where my aunt lived, was not the wild, untamed streets of the main city of Athens; there were hardly any cars in this area of the suburbs, and when you saw them, they drove by slowly, aware of children playing ball and women with shopping bags or pushing strollers and aging folk strolling down the quiet paths of the neighborhood.

Just to be safe – and to mind my aunt, in case she prodded – I asked adults to guide me across the streets, and they did, smiling at my seeming innocence.

When I arrived, my cousins were already there, seated on the couch in the living room, scorn outlining their features. Two pairs of russet irises glared at me with suspicion, and I sat at the kitchen table, my back straight, swallowing my delight with savory gulps.

I wasn't innocent. I had crossed dangerous roads, had fist fights with cats and dogs that bit and snarled at me for scraps of food, and I had taught myself to shrink into shadows and nothingness so that Kristos and my mother's johns didn't see me – even while I stood before them. I had been beaten and leered at and threatened with fists and words alike, and while my cousins' rejection of me hurt my feelings, it was nothing compared to where I had come from. I was between six and seven, but I was worlds older than them. They were the innocent ones, and I didn't need their protection while crossing major intersections, or their friendship. The one person I wanted from their mix was my Aunt Thalia. She was the mother I wanted and hated them for having.

The truth is that – just as Eliza, Georgiana, and John Reed detested you – my cousins didn't appreciate me either. I couldn't blame them. I had invaded their family and adopted their mother as my own. I loved her, and I couldn't hide it. I found myself moved by the golden depths of her eyes when they surveyed me with warmth and humanity. I felt loved and cared for. The last time I had nestled in that kind of devotion was with my baba, before he deserted us.

Your friend, Kit Kat

"Even for me life had its gleams of sunshine."
JANE EYRE

Dear Jane,

A few months later, while living with my Aunt Thalia, I arrived from school to find my father sitting at the kitchen table, talking to my aunt and uncle.

I had waited for this day; I had imagined it; imagined forgiving him for the last memory I had of him – when he had told me I was not his daughter. When he had pulled away from me, my arms still locked around his legs. In my dreams, I ran to him without a word, embraced him, kissed him, and clung to him – as I had that day – so that he could not let me go again.

But this wasn't a dream. He stood before me, unsure and reticent. And I stood before him feeling numb, my heart racing against the soft skin of my throat. I looked at him, lowered my gaze, and walked towards him, propelled by bewilderment.

My aunt and uncle left us alone, and as I sat down opposite him at the table, I saw him clearly: he was shriveled. There was a jagged scar by his eye where my mother's heel had found its mark. He had blue and puffy bruises under his watery eyes. His mouth quivered when he smiled at me.

I folded my hands on my lap, fingers intertwined, the way I had been taught to sit in school, and kept my gaze glued to the surface of the table. I waited for him to speak, not understanding why he was sitting before me, now, when he had been missing these past three years.

"I thought..." He released a slight cough and continued much softer. "I thought that I could pick you up every Saturday from here and take you with me for the weekend. I'm living with my sister Marina and her husband George, you know."

I nodded.

"Well?" he queried, peering at me from his own lowered eyelids. "What do you think about that?" He took a drag from his cigarette, and as I gazed at his rough and worn hands, I noticed they were trembling slightly. He placed them on the table to still them. I detected his discomfort, his hesitation, and that made him more real to me.

"OK, Baba," I said.

For the next few weeks, my father waited for me each Saturday at my aunt and uncle's house. Aunt Thalia handed him a little bag with my pajamas, toothbrush, underwear, and change of clothes. As my father held the bag in one hand and my fingers in the other, he led me to the taxi that would take me to the house he had been living in since he had left us.

I had not forgotten my Aunt Marina. Her house and her arms had often secured a temporary sanctuary for my brothers, my father, and me during those violent days when we had all lived with my mother.

It was a modest house, and my aunt and uncle owned it. Their rooftop was shaded by a trellis coiled with grapevines that blossomed countless sweet-tasting grapes. They also had a little vegetable garden with tomatoes, cucumbers, and eggplants behind the house, and I ran to it to see if it was still there. The gardening and growing of these delights were my Uncle George's pride and joy. His name in Greek means "tiller of the soil." As soon as he saw me, he ushered me up on the roof to show me the grapes and figs he had grown. This is where my love of figs comes from.

My Aunt Marina was flustered when she greeted me. Her name means "of the water," and a hug from her was like returning to the womb – safe, loved. At five feet, she was a round and robust woman who sputtered and choked on her memories of my brothers, my father, my mother, and me. She recalled days that had begun to blur in my mind.

"I knew your mother was no good. I knew she was hurting your father and all of you. He never came out and told me, but I knew," she muttered, her voice rising to a thunderous treble as she continued.

"I hid in the bushes, ready to take my brother with me, cleaning up the blood, patching up the bruises. But still, he wouldn't say a thing about it." Her words clashed with the noise of the pots and pans she was cleaning, clanking and banging against each other as she dried them with force.

She heaved a long sigh and shook her head. She eyed me. "Sometimes, I even took you with me. You were so little. I brought you with me, and you sat there, quietly, just as you're doing now, not saying a word. Just listening. Always watching and listening. That was you."

She wiped at her tears with the dishrag, and then a toothy smile welcomed me back into the warmth of her kitchen and her home.

"I'm sorry I couldn't take you...all of you. I had to care for George, his mother, and then your father. I just couldn't take care of all of you."

"Einai kala, *thia.*" I smiled at my aunt and reached over to pat her thick hand as it rested on the table between us. It's all good, I told her.

She cooked five-course meals for us, the two men she loved and her niece, satiating our most basic needs. Her meats, salad, and French fries were all saturated in oil and filled me from the inside, while her bulky arms and breasts encircled me, filling me from the outside.

Every Saturday night, my father took me with him for long strolls along the suburban streets of the neighborhood. It was dusk, and the cool breeze solidified the grin on my lips.

He took me inside his friend's taverna and introduced me as his daughter. The men smiled at me and took a drink of their ouzo. The man behind the counter gave me lamb souvlaki skewered on a stick, a soft, warm piece of bread staked at the top. My baba paid for it and passed me a bottle of Coca-Cola. He didn't buy anything for himself, and I ate and drank as we strolled down the street, the blue tint from the television sets flashing on and off from window to window, the lights reflecting the warmth and vibrancy I felt.

We walked in silence. He was lost in some memory, some faraway place, and I was too young to engage in a deep conversation with him. To ask him why he sat by the living room bay window for hours, staring out at nothing, smoking one cigarette after another.

But I was his daughter again, and I was content to just walk beside him.

Your "found" friend, Kit Kat

"I can but die...and I believe in God.
Let me try to wait His will in silence."
JANE EYRE

Dear Jane,

One Saturday, my father caught me off guard.

"Do you know what adoption is, *kori mou*?" I didn't, but I liked hearing him call me "my daughter." *MY.* I belonged to him.

"There is a woman in America, in New York. She is Greek and a teacher, and she is looking to adopt a little girl just like you."

I sat mute before him.

"She knows all about you and wants to adopt you, be your mother, give you the opportunities we cannot give you."

I already have a mother, I wanted to say to him. *I have a father. You're my father.*

But I said nothing. Instead, I tried to calm my rapidly beating heart. I could hear it in my ears and feel it pulsing from beneath my skin. It was so loud.

He took a long drag from his cigarette and exhaled sharply, his hand trembling.

"You don't have to say yes," he said.

It was up to me, he murmured. They would all do as I wished.

I glanced at my Aunt Thalia, who was talking to my uncle in the living room a few feet away. She turned and smiled at me, and I realized that this had been her idea. She was trying to give me a home and a family, because hers could not contain me.

I understood that it was because of the discord that existed between my cousins and me. They were making sacrifices for their children's happiness, triggering this hunger in me for someone who would love me enough to make sacrifices for me – not sacrifice me.

I gave them what they wanted, without protest. I did what would please them.

I put on my armored smile and looked up at him.

"OK, Baba."

What else was I supposed to say? *No! Keep me! Don't give me away!* How could I?

They didn't want me. Not my mother, not my aunt and uncle, and now, not even my father.

How can you stay where you're unwanted? How could I? So, I began to believe that they had given me a choice and that I chose to be adopted. But not really. I wanted to stay with my father, not move to a foreign country and call a foreign woman "mama."

You chose to leave Gateshead Hall and Mrs. Reed. You made a choice, used your voice to rid yourself of the Reeds. I wish I had used my voice. I would have compelled them to keep me. But I didn't have one back then.

Your friend, Kit Kat

*"I was the most wicked and abandoned child
ever reared under a roof...I felt, indeed, only bad
feelings surging in my breast."*
JANE EYRE

Dear Jane,

After my fate had been decided, my father stole back into his silent world but kept me beside him to share in that stillness. He continued to pick me up on Saturday afternoons and to deposit me at my aunt's house on Sundays until the moment came for me to leave. He bought me a gold cross with the protruding image of Jesus Christ nailed to the crucifix. He had my name engraved on the back so that I would in no way forget my real identity, where I came from, or what family I had belonged to.

Elektra Koutros.

I was named after a literary character. In the famous Greek tragedy, Elektra was the daughter of King Agamemnon. Upon discovering that her mother and her mother's lover had murdered the King, Elektra orchestrated their deaths, seeking revenge for her father's death. I guess I should have told you earlier, but it's not the name I live by now. I'm Kathryn now.

But Elektra was my birth name, my identity, and I didn't know then that it was possible to lose your name – that someone could take it from you. My father must have known. It's why he gave me the cross with my name on it, so that I wouldn't forget it.

He continued to take me for our walks during the cool nights of Greece and offer me gifts of souvlaki and Coca-Cola. I learned to forgive him.

Then there was his final present for me.

One Sunday he took me to see my siblings. First, we went to visit Stavros and Nicholas at their orphanage. They were to stay there until they turned eighteen, and then they, too, would be cast off into the cold, unfeeling wasteland of the world. It turns out that my father visited them often and had them spend their summer vacations with him at my Aunt Marina's house.

Jealousy stung me, and I had to hide it. All these years, he had gone to see them, spent time with them, but me, I had been stuck with our mother and her pimp. And her johns. And the streets. Why?

I didn't ask him. My words were stuck in my throat, like broken chicken bones, and I was afraid that if I let a word slip out, the bones would shift, the fragments would pierce my insides, and I would cry out in pain.

I didn't want to cry. Instead, I concentrated on my older brothers.

Our first few moments together were awkward. We had not seen each other in three years, and we spoke as if we didn't know each other. It took us a while, but after a few minutes in their playground, the three of us became instant friends. Stavros and I ran to the swings and had a race to see who could swing the highest. He won. He pushed me in the swing for a while, making me go higher than I could go by myself, and Nicholas hung upside down from the monkey rings.

"Look at me," he called out, and I smiled as he showed off how strong he was. Holding onto the rings, he flipped himself repeatedly until I laughed. "Victory" is the Greek definition of Nicholas' name. I just found out that St. Nicholas was a bishop who saved a poor man's daughters from a life of prostitution. How ironic is that?

Finally, our father told them I was leaving for America and that we wouldn't see each other again. We all became somber, recollecting the last instance we had said our farewells. Nicholas became agitated and silent and continued to look at me as if trying to memorize my face. Stavros sat down and wrote me a letter, telling me how much he would miss me. As I read it, I made corrections, instructing him on the editing process. I reread the letter, treasuring each word, each syllable of his illegible handwriting.

The moment came to leave, and we hugged. There were no tears. There were only immeasurable sadness and the beginning of an inexplicable void inside me. My brothers walked us to the main gate of their orphanage and stood behind it, waving to us through the bars as we trailed off towards the bus stop. I glanced back once to compress their faces into one image I would take with me to America. I promised myself I would not forget how they looked, but time and absence proved to be cruel companions, erasing the features of both Stavros and Nicholas from my memory, leaving me with two faceless figures to recollect as my brothers.

The bus ride to Athens was a quiet one. My father buried himself in his world of no voices, and I relived the last few hours spent with my brothers. I shut out my surroundings and silently mouthed the syllables of their names, afraid that I would forget them. Nicholas, Stavros. Nicholas, Stavros. I repeated their names, praying that I would not misplace a syllable, a letter, or the sound each name produced as I uttered them aloud.

The following week, my father took me to see Maria. She was where I had left her, at Penteli. During our visit, she was ill or depressed. I'm not sure which. She lay in her bed, still and silent, along with all the other sick girls in her room. The beds were arranged in rows, the same way the beds in my dorm had been set up when I had lived in the building across from hers.

I didn't climb into her bed as you climbed into Helen's the night she died. I just sat there, next to my father, looking at my sister, a stranger I had a great longing for. Not much was said between us. She stared past us, out the window, and our visit was short-lived. Numbness overtook me as my father and I sat beside her cot, watching her look through us.

"Goodbye, Maria." I hugged her to me but didn't feel her respond.

"*Filakia.*" Little kisses.

Your friend, Kit Kat

"It is hard work to control the workings of inclination
and turn the bent of nature...God has given us...
the power to make our own fate."
JANE EYRE

Dear Jane,

Leaving the earliest part of my childhood behind, with its Greek roots saturated in angst, was a positive moment.

At least, everyone else thought so. It's similar to when you were leaving the Reeds' home and Bessie, the servant, was nice to you. I presume it is guilt. They want us to remember them as being good to us, not as they were: negligent, harsh, thoughtless with our feelings.

They all had me rejoicing in the fact that no one wanted me, and even I began to believe that I would be better off if I lived with a foreigner in a foreign land than with my blood family and the country in which I had been born.

In school, my teacher and classmates treated me like a prized citizen destined for greatness. My teacher brought me to the front of the class and announced to my peers that I was to be leaving for that great country, America. She prepared a lesson out of my future journey. Having taught me a phrase in English, she instructed me to write it out on the board so that the class could translate it. We discussed the cultural differences between Greece and the United States, and she emphasized what a lucky little girl I was to be moving there.

My classmates were awed by my fortune, and finding myself at the center of their envy and admiration, I took advantage of my status. I gathered them under the stairway during recess and taught them an American song. Of course, I did not speak any more English than they did, so the words that sprang from my mouth were gibberish. With a boldness that I lack today, I taught them a song that did not exist, and my little friends mimicked the nonsensical phrases I created with absolute trust.

The most difficult part of leaving was saying goodbye to the woman who had come so close to becoming a mother to me. Aunt Thalia handed me a box with a gold, chain-linked ID bracelet inside. She showed me the engraving of her name and address on the back.

"This is so you don't forget where we live, in case you want to come back and see us. Will you write to me and let me know how you are doing?"

"Of course, *thia mou*," I said and smiled as she gave me one last embrace – tight, long, and fierce. After saying goodbye to my uncle and cousins, I was set to go.

I had my father's cross around my neck with my name on it and a bracelet with my aunt's name and address. I could not lose my way even if I tried. I knew who I was and to whom I truly belonged. I was sure that if anything went wrong, I could come back; the path had been cleared for my return.

I never feared that I would lose both my name and theirs. I never considered that I would not be allowed to find my way back to them.

I left them with a smile and a lazy wave.

Your friend, Kit Kat

"I dared commit no fault: I strove to fulfil every duty;
and I was termed naughty and tiresome, sullen and sneaking,
from morning to noon, and from noon to night."
JANE EYRE

Dear Jane,

On my last day with my aunt and uncle, a woman came to pick me up. Mrs. Papas was the court-appointed social worker assigned to my case, and she took my bag and led me to the taxi that would take me, not to the airport headed for America as we had all expected, but to Nea Smirni, twenty minutes away.

I remember squinting and staring out the window of the cab. The sun was bright, unusually strong, and leaning my head against the cool base of the window, I closed my lids to rest them, to shut out my fears, hoping that the migraine I had developed would disappear. To this day, I recall the intensity of that headache, for many have followed since to torture me, to remind me, to keep me captive of all that I lost.

Mrs. Papas led me to the home of Maria, my new mother's Greek aunt. Because she was much older, in her seventies, I called her yiayia, or grandmother. I told you about her before, about the night I tried to stab myself. That was her.

Yiayia Maria lived in a tall apartment building on a quiet street. When you walk in, there is a long hallway that leads into the living room with a couch and television set, and a table for company to place their drinks on. On the right of the living room, there is a dining room, and a doorway to the right that leads into a pocket-sized kitchen. Through the kitchen, there is another doorway that leads into an even tinier bathroom, followed by yiayia Maria's bedroom. It's like taking a U-turn. I slept on a cot in the living room. Bathrooms are quite funny in Greece. The container of water is above the toilet bowl – not the way it is in America.

My favorite part of living with her was the chocolate store located at the courtyard outside the building. When she wanted me out of the way, or when my adoptive mother came to visit from New York, yiayia Maria would send me down to buy a box of chocolates that had a picture of Mona Lisa on the wrapper. She was beautiful with her dark, lovely hair and somber eyes staring back at me. But inside the wrapper were layers of chocolate with a walnut in the middle. I ate each one the same way: layer by layer, until I got to the walnut.

Not many people visited. Once, a couple had come over. A young one, and I think this was an interview for an apartment she was trying to rent out in the building – which she apparently owned.

"*Kathisai etho me isihia*," she ordered me. And I intended to sit there, unobtrusively. I did. But I was so excited when I saw how clean my schoolbag was that I had to show her. I had been sitting in the foyer, rubbing the bag with some sort of cleaner that turned the gray and dull shades of my schoolbag into bright hues of white and red. It appeared brand new.

"Yiayia, look," I piped up, jumped to my feet, and ran over to the back of the apartment, where she was sitting with the young couple.

"Look how clean it is!" I thrust the bag at her, standing between her and the young man and woman.

Next thing I know, yiayia Maria slapped me out of nowhere. It shook me so hard that I was trembling, and I could see the bag, still in my grasp, move to the rhythm of my shaky hands. I didn't cry. I didn't. I would not let her see me cry. I just went back to my little chair and sat there. I couldn't even look at the bag. It reminded me too much of my Aunt Thalia. She's the one who bought it for me when I lived with her, and she sent me to school. She never hit me. Not once. And she had a right to hit me. She was my aunt. This woman – yiayia Maria – was not family. She was nobody, and she had no business touching me.

I hated her. I really did. I hated the black dresses she used to wear, the tight black bun she collected her hair into and clipped at the back of her head. I hated the creases on her face, the muddy, brown irises that looked at me with such cold disregard, the wrinkled, hard hands that lunged for me with violence when I broke her vase by accident or did not move fast enough when going to the store. I even hated the sight of her false teeth, which she placed in a cup full of water by the bathroom sink. It's the last thing I saw in the evenings when I brushed my own teeth. Sometimes, I just wanted to smash the cup, toss it onto the floor, and stomp on her teeth. What would she do then? How would she meet clients in her living room, toothless?

The sight of that just makes me laugh!

I thought I was done with being hit. I thought my real mother, Athanasia, and her pimp, Kristos, were the hitters, and that once I was taken from them, no one would hit me again. Aunt Thalia did not hit me, or her own children. Her hands touched me with kindness, and I thought everyone would be like that in my adoption. Yiayia Maria disrupted my dream. And for the first time since I found out I would be adopted, I was afraid of what would await me. What if I was hit more? What if I got lost and couldn't find my way back?

It was yiayia Maria who forced me to hide in the bathroom and bid me to keep my mouth shut when my Aunt Thalia knocked on the door, asking to see me.

"What do you want?!" yiayia yelled at the door gruffly, peering at my aunt through the keyhole.

"I want to see my niece. Just to talk to her. I didn't know she was still here. I thought she was taken to America," I heard my aunt pleading.

"Go to the bathroom," yiayia Maria's harsh whisper drilled into me. "Lock the door."

I stood motionless, my feet stuck to the floor. I was torn between fear of this old woman and trying to figure out how to make my way past the solid frame of her body and the door that she pressed herself against, to get to my aunt, who was a few feet away from me.

Yiayia rushed to me, grabbed me, and pushed me into the bathroom, slamming the door shut.

"You stay in there!" she warned me. "Don't you dare come out. She's not your family anymore."

I sat on the toilet, my pulse crashing in waves against my ears, as the old woman told the only family who had come looking for me to leave me alone, to let me go.

"She doesn't belong to you anymore," I heard her telling my aunt without opening the door. "Leave her be."

There was a muffled response from my aunt, but I couldn't understand it.

I wanted to burst through the door and into the arms of the woman who had stirred in me the desire for love, but I remained rooted to my spot – out of fear and obedience – and out of anger, too.

Yiayia Maria, despite her faults, was right.

I didn't belong to my aunt anymore. She had given me away.

People are hard to understand. As a kid, you're powerless. You have to go where they go, do what they say, and feel what they want you to feel. They strike out in anger or shame or fear, but it all looks the same to me. They hit with words and hands, and they don't say sorry afterward. They don't explain or even acknowledge what they do. I'm just a kid. I'm not owed an explanation. I don't deserve an apology.

I guess part of it was that yiayia Maria didn't want me. She was old, her daughters were grown and mothers of their own, and she had lived alone for over a decade. She was just doing this – taking me in – as a favor to her niece. I had to stay somewhere while the adoption papers were being put together and the court case was being resolved, and everyone on my side of the family signed me away legally. Yiayia Maria's apartment was the place that made sense. She was related to my new mother-to-be, and she lived in Greece. For the most part, she sent me down the block to play with her nieces' kids during the day.

I don't remember much about the kids or their parents. I can't tell you what they looked like, or what kind of games we played. I do remember what yiayia Maria's nieces fed me when I did go over to play. They took egg whites, beat them until they were foamy, and then sprinkled sugar into them. That was a delicacy. I loved it, and it was the one thing I looked forward to eating when I went over there. That is all I remember about them – eggs beaten in sugar and how smoothly and sweetly it dripped down my throat, filling every wound in me with a warm, foamy substance I don't even have a name for.

This is what happens to memories when you can't say them out loud. I can't speak them to my new mother, so I lose them. I've lost so many memories, but I hold onto the ones that I need.

Your friend, Kit Kat

> *"After a youth...passed in unutterable misery*
> *and half in dreary solitude...I have found you."*
> *JANE EYRE*

Dear Jane,

My adoptive mother's real name is Evangelia, "of the angels," but everyone calls her Ann. She was forty-eight years old, unmarried and childless when we met. Her parents had died a few years before, and she was left all alone, as I was. There was gray in her hair, and the slightest hint of make-up on her face was the light shade of pink gloss outlining the two wafer-thin lines of her lips. She wore big, tan sunglasses outside, and slim bifocals that rested below the bridge of her nose when reading. She had the hooked Greek nose that most Greeks have, but it was the only big part of her face. The rest of her features were smaller: honey-brown eyes, penciled brows that she drew into wide, arching lines, an equally fine set of lips that widened when she smiled but drew into a frown when something you said was confusing or concerned her.

Everything about her was quiet and orderly. Her attire was neat, and as she sat down in her matching gray, below-the-knees skirt suit, she crossed her stockinged feet, displaying the graceful curvature of her legs. Her demeanor was regal, and she sat with her back straight and her fingers elegantly strewn upon her lap. Unlike the woman who had mothered me, Ann was a figure of moderation and self-control.

The one thing that was grand about her was her jewelry. She wore rings and necklaces crafted out of large gems that she had purchased at gem shows. Not diamonds and emeralds, stones that glittered and shone, but gems of various shades of aqua blue and green, which she had collected throughout her many travels. They were big and gawky upon her delicate fingers, not intended to exhibit or flaunt her wealth, because she was not rich, but rather to display her extensive travels and knowledge, her affinity for rocks and gems, and all things scientific.

She was the opposite of my own mother, the image of her face having already grown faint in my memory. My mother was robust, angry, loud, and crude. This one, Ann, was the complete opposite. Although her Greek had a hint of a foreign accent, her tone when she spoke to me was gentle, soft. There was no violence to her, no out of control rages or stormy ranting. She appeared to be docile – the type of mother I had not known but recognized as someone I hungered for.

When she spoke, there was a serenity in her voice that calmed me and bid me to trust her. And I did. I drove my smile into her, hoping it would take root, sat on her lap, and crossed my arms about her shoulders. I welcomed her into my embrace without judgment or fear and gave myself completely to her. She was my savior, my angel, sent to me by the God that I was loyal to in my nightly prayers. I wanted her and vowed to make her love me so that nothing could force her to return me after she had signed the adoption papers.

Under the spell of my hopeful imaginings, I didn't notice that her arms didn't clasp me closely, evidence of her discomfort with prolonged physical contact. Her kisses, as she laid them upon my cheeks, were not playful, loving, and warm as mine were, but rather rushed and taut with uneasiness, her lips not quite touching the skin on my face, but grazing sideways against it. Nor did I notice that her smiles were watchful and cautious, her words carefully considered, the tone in her voice caked with sternness that reminded me so much of your Mrs. Reed when I came across her in your story. I did not notice any of these characteristics because I had not encountered them before and because I was lost in the moment of this new woman that wanted me without ever having met me. I found her enthralling, intimidating, and kind.

She found me smart, cute, and frail. Wanting to shine in the glow of her approval, I spoke when I had something clever to say and behaved in the manner that would gain her affections. We were two individuals looking to each other to fill a void in our lives, perfectly matched, it seemed.

During those three visits, Ann taught me how to eat with my fork and knife and to drink from a cup with my pinky suspended in the air. She instructed me to keep my elbows off the table while eating, to chew with my lips sealed, and not to speak while there was a morsel of food in my mouth. She explained how to brush my teeth the right way, up and down, and to do it diligently, after every meal.

I showed her how I could pray on my knees and watched her from beneath thick lashes as she listened to my prayers, asking God to watch over my brothers and sisters, and adding her name to the end of the list. She did not ask who the other names belonged to, and I did not volunteer their identities, assuming she had been told.

Ann took it upon herself to stop me from biting my nails. She and her Aunt Maria tried it all. They put salt on my fingertips, but I just licked it off. They directed me to sit on my hands as I watched TV and reminded me not to bite them whenever my fingers found their place of security. Yiayia Maria told me that my nails would grow in my stomach and that they would kill me, piercing me from within. I giggled and continued to nibble.

Their efforts were wasted on me. Biting my nails calmed me; it still does. It had become the one physical act that betrayed the nervous tension and anxiety that lives underneath my placid facade. On the outside I was quiet, a girl of very few words, resisting exposure, but fears, insecurities, and anger were all bottled up and brewing inside my little body. They saw only the habit.

Ann taught me about Santa Claus and the presents he would leave under our tree every Christmas if I was a good little girl. I had not known about Christmas or Saint Nicholas, chimneys or presents before this. It was hard to swallow that a big, fat, jolly man would come down the chimney yiayia Maria didn't have in her apartment just to leave presents under the tree. My introduction to this enigmatic character occurred during one of Ann's required visits. It was Christmas, and as I slept on yiayia Maria's couch in the living room, Santa placed a nutcracker soldier beside me. Of course, I knew it was Ann, and she laughed with delight to discover that I was such a bright and knowing little girl.

Looking back, I must shake my head at her naïveté. She thought she was getting a pure child, an innocent, unmarked little girl. By ignoring the existence of my first eight years, she assumed I was the average eight-year-old. But I wasn't. Magic and fairy tales, Santa Claus and Easter bunnies did not exist for me. The kind of childhood experiences I had left no room for the absurdity of make-believe personalities. The two things I believed in were God and Ann. They stood for promise, hope, and change. They were real, and I had complete faith in them.

During one of her visits, I sat on her lap and wrapped my arms around her freckled neck. I wanted her to want me as much as I wanted her.

"Will you teach me to use the sewing machine?" I asked her in Greek.

"Of course!" she replied in her American-accented Greek. "I will make you dresses, too, just like mine." She pointed to the skirt suit she was wearing. It was a plain gray skirt with a matching jacket. They were both soft with two pockets in the jacket, and she had a habit of placing her hands in whichever pocket was closest, digging for her reading glasses that often sat on top of her graying head.

"You made this yourself?" I asked, fingering the parallel stitches that rounded the lapel of her jacket. I let my fingers slip off the material to touch her neck skin. It was soft, and the freckles that painted her skin were all different shapes and sizes. I'd never seen so many freckles on any one person. I enjoyed being near her then, touching her, feeling her arms around my waist. Aside from Aunt Thalia, I don't recall being touched in a nice way. They had been hard and angry, the touches I had known. Pulling me, shoving me, striking me.

My adoptive mother doesn't touch me anymore. Neither do I. I don't hug her or kiss her as I used to. I forgot how to, it's been so long. And there is an anger inside me that stops me when I feel the urge to move towards her in a loving way. I think that the only way I can touch her the way I want her to touch me is to be forced, and I wish she would force me. I wish she would grab me, pull me to her, and bury her face in my hair. Kiss me. Tell me she loves me. But I know this won't happen. We are strangers again, living in the same house, moving around each other like ghosts without the power to touch or feel, muted from each other and our surroundings.

It hurts, not being hugged and loved and kissed. I know you've felt this way, too, in Mrs. Reed's house with just verbal rebukes to remind you that you are there, that you exist – an angry stain on their fine linen that won't be removed, no matter how hard they scrub at you.

Of course, Mrs. Reed had always been like that to you. Not Ann. There was a stretch when she hugged back, when she planted soft kisses – even though they kissed the air beside my angular cheekbones – on my face, when she held my hand while crossing the streets. I have known her touch, some parts of her that show love and laugh and joke around. They're hard to find nowadays, and I wonder how much this change has to do with me and how much it has to do with who she is and who she is incapable of being.

When I was seven, though, sitting on her lap in yiayia Maria's flat and stringing my skinny arms around her neck, feeling the loose tendrils of her gray-brown hair touch the blond hair on my arms, listening to unheard-of stories of a mysterious Santa Claus that would come through my window and give me presents for being good, being promised to go to the movies for the first time, she was as open to me as I was to her. We hid nothing from each other, for I wanted nothing more than a mother, and she wanted a little girl. What kind of mother I got and what kind of little girl she got was not a consideration then. At least, it wasn't for me. Any kind of mother was better than the one I had been born to. And Ann seemed perfect to me. Almost as perfect as my Aunt Thalia.

While my new mother-to-be was busy acquiring letters of recommendation from the Greek Orthodox priests of her church, her employer, neighbors, and friends, and committing to a trial date set for the finalization of my adoption, I was forced to remain with yiayia Maria.

The old woman sat me down and told me that once the adoption was finalized, I would fly to America on my own, and her niece would pick me up at the airport.

"She is your family, now. No one else," she told me brusquely. "If you talk about them, you will be hurting her, and you don't want to hurt the woman who is giving you a new life, now, do you?"

I shook my head. I understood what she was telling me, and I agreed to comply, not realizing how difficult and harmful keeping that promise would be.

It wasn't until I had lived with my new mother for a while that I realized she also expected this self-denial from me. It became my job to protect her from the truth of my childhood. She required me to give up all of them, and me, to shield her from hurt, from the burden of dealing with them. I had to denounce what I had known and seen and experienced and pretend that I had come from her untried womb; it became my duty to make everyone believe that she had been the only mother I had ever had. And I assumed the responsibility of taking care of her feelings, even though she denied me mine.

But this all occurred after I became her legal daughter, after I was expected to suppress everything that had crafted me into who I had already become.

Before all of this, I was struck with awe and relief by the novelty of this woman that betrayed no similarities to the crazy mother I had come from.

My hand is cramping, Jane, and I'm feeling a bit low right now. I'll write to you tomorrow.

Your friend, Kit Kat

*"[T]he real world was wide, and that a varied field of hopes and fears,
of sensations and excitements, awaited those who had the courage
to go forth into its expanse, to seek real knowledge of life amidst its perils."*
JANE EYRE

Dear Jane,

On a sunny day in October, three months after my eighth birthday, yiayia Maria ushered me into a taxicab with my valise, and sitting beside me, she ordered the driver to take us to Athens International Airport.

The airport is also called Eleftherios Venizelos, named after the revered politician from Xania, Crete, and the former Prime Minister of Greece, which loosely translated, means free (Eleftherios), good (vene), and interesting (zilos). Ironically, my adoption papers, which I found a few weeks ago while going through my adoptive mother's files (without her knowing, of course), used the same language to describe my adoption. The judge wrote that this adoption would "prove to be a good and interesting one for said child."

I wasn't invited to the hearing. The most important decision of my life had been achieved without me present, without my voice.

I was in a taxicab, taking the forty-minute-long ride to the airport, yet another port that would lead me to my freedom, to a new home and family that was already deemed "good and interesting."

The ride to the airport was a silent one.

I was eight, and I would board an airplane destined for New York by myself.

"Come," urged yiayia Maria in her gruff voice. Taking hold of my hand, she guided it into the manicured fingers of the gentle and smiling stewardess who was to take me to my seat on the plane.

"Now don't forget what I told you," she scolded me, wagging her wrinkled and pudgy forefinger in front of my face. "Don't talk about your family to my niece. She is your mother, now, no one else."

The stewardess tugged at my hand and guided me toward the gate from which we were to leave, and I followed.

I glanced back once to see yiayia shuffling down the passageway, her back already to me.

Although my adoptive mother later told me that an older woman, an acquaintance of yiayia Maria's, was supposed to watch out for me on the plane, my eleven-hour flight was spent alone, with me sitting by the window and watching the sky go from blue to white, from light to dark, and then back to light again.

You had a similar journey when you left Mrs. Reed's house for the Lowood School for Girls. Instead of on a plane, though, you were placed on a coach led by four horses, sitting among people you didn't know. It took an entire day, you passed many towns, and you feared being abducted, since you were so young and slight, traveling without a guardian. You were ten.

The only person who spoke to me was the flight attendant that had brought me onto the plane. She checked up on me, asking in Greek if I wanted a drink or something to eat.

As I heard the engines of the plane rumble and begin its ascent, I pressed my nose against the pane of the tiny, oval window and watched all that I was leaving behind.

I felt nothing as the orange rooftops, and the green hills of Athens became distant and imperceptible, and the waters of the Mediterranean Sea danced up to and kissed the shores of my country, my Greece.

I was going home. My new home.

When my gaze began to fill with the white of the clouds, I averted my gaze upward, where I imagined God to be.

I asked Him to watch over the people I was leaving behind.

I prayed for my crazy mother, filled with rage, and my feeble father, who sat in the same seat day in and day out staring at nothing perched beyond his window frame, his features overshadowed by the cigarette smoke he exhaled.

I prayed for Maria who limped past the pains of her life, Nicholas and Stavros, two slight boys isolated and abandoned within the confines of an orphanage, and Baby, the last little sister to be born, who at the age of four had not been given a name.

I prayed that my new mother would be waiting for me when the plane landed, for my greatest fear was being lost and not being found. I tried to devise a plan that would guide me towards my new mother in case she wasn't there when I exited the plane.

I prayed that she, too, would not give me away, for no one knew me in America. I had been given all the second chances anyone was possibly worth.

Exhausted, I curled up in my seat, feet tucked beneath me, pressed my head against the cool surface of the window, and fell asleep, encasing myself in a darkness that drowned out the noises of the plane and the chatter and my fears.

I did not look out the window again until the plane landed on the foreign soil that would become my new country, my new home.

After most of the passengers had disembarked, I remained in my seat, not sure what to do.

The flight attendant who had seated me and had taken care of my needs during the flight came to my seat to lead me off the plane.

I didn't ask her name, and she didn't offer it.

"Are you ready?" she asked me in a version of Greek that resembled Ann's, a combination of Greek and English that I would soon assume myself.

I nodded my head and rose from my seat, feeling light suddenly.

Sensing my hesitation, she leaned towards me; she was so close that I could smell the sweet scent of her perfume.

"Your mom is waiting for you outside by the waiting area. Come on. I'll take you to her."

She held out her hand, thin and bony, and I studied it, trailing my gaze up her arm to her long neck, all the way up into the golden light that peered back at me. She was smiling, and I responded without thinking, giving in to her, passing my clammy and cold hand into her warm one.

Hers was bigger and stronger, more confident as she pulled me up the aisle towards the exit door.

I trailed behind her, tripping over my own feet and my bag, which beat against my thigh, breaking the rhythm I was trying to match to the flight attendant's steady pace. Despite my awkwardness, she didn't let go of my hand but kept leading me past all the empty chairs, the other flight attendants who had already begun to clean up after the passengers, and past the smiling pilots that had begun to disembark.

They were all a blur as I blindly followed the flight attendant who had my hand in hers, my concentration riveted to the light blue patterns of her uniformed shirt. She guided me through the long, moveable bridge, a labyrinth of lights and shadows that led from the plane's door to the airport terminal. She did not loosen her warm and firm grip until she had to release my hand into the delicate grasp that belonged to my new mother.

I sensed her walking away, but I couldn't force any words of gratitude out of my mouth. Instead, I stared at the freckles on my new mother's hands, unable to move or speak.

It was when she squeezed my hand that I let my gaze find hers. There was reassurance there, familiarity, and I was reminded that she wasn't alien to me. I had sat on her lap, kissed her cheeks, and wrapped my arms around her neck months earlier.

I peeked at our hands, my smaller one clasped in her elegant one, intertwined, and I was safe.

She held onto my hand as she led me past terminals, crowded gates, exit doors, swarms of people, parking lots, blinding lights, and congested highways.

She didn't let go until she brought me home.

Your friend, Kit Kat

"How could she really like an interloper, not of her race, and
unconnected with her...? It must have been most irksome to find herself bound...
in the stead of a parent to a strange child she could not love."
JANE EYRE

Dear Jane,

The first night I slept in my new apartment, in my own room, on my own bed, I cried for my baba. Even though he had abandoned us, I realized that he had to leave because of my mother. He was the quietest part of my childhood, and I couldn't understand why he had given me up to a woman he had not met when he could have cared for me. I couldn't understand why he had left without any of us. Why he left all his children behind to weather the storm of our mother even he – an adult – could not contain. Of all the people I could have wept for that night, as the daughter of a stranger in a foreign country with an even more foreign language, it was for him that I cried. It was him I missed and longed for.

"What is the matter?" My new mother came into my room and sat on the edge of my single bed, the weight of her body on the mattress making me shift closer to her.

"I miss my baba," I told her.

"Well," she said after a while, "he's the one who gave you up. I saw him, at the courthouse. He was there, and he signed the papers."

Her words silenced me in the same way my birth mother's violent hands had done in the past. They fashioned me inarticulate, and I would continually become mute around her when she spoke to me in such a matter-of-fact way that left no room for discussion.

She patted my leg that night, rose from my bed, and walked out of my room.

A few days later, I asked her if she knew where my father's cross was. It was missing. So was my Aunt Thalia's name bracelet. The one that had her address on it, so I could find my way back.

"I put them in the bank, in a safe deposit box, where I keep my own jewelry," she told me. "They'll be safe there, and I will give them back to you when you are older."

I want them back now, I wanted to scream at her. But I said nothing instead, concentrating on my heartbeat as it began to race wildly inside me.

"As a matter of fact, I wanted to talk to you about something else." She came over to my bed, sat on the edge, and bid me sit down next to her.

"I'd like to call you Kathryn from now on," she said, pressing her lips into a straight line, a forced smile where the sides didn't rise.

I tried to control my breathing but remained silent.

"Kathryn was my mother's name," she explained. "I want to name you after her."

I stared at her and crinkled my nose.

I already had a name; a name that had been uttered, screamed, whispered, cried, written on paper, and inscribed in gold. A name that means "amber." "Shining." "Incandescent."

Elektra.

God, the Greek Orthodox Church, its patrons, and my family had witnessed the day my name had been given to me. It was that same day that the warm and sanctified oil of Christ touched my head and trickled down my cheeks and throat, evidence that the Lord Himself had blessed my name.

Elektra.

If God had accepted it, she had no reason to deny me what had been assigned to me since birth.

My new mother noted my confusion and dismissed it.

"You'll keep your given name, of course," she continued rather fast. "But Kathryn will be your name, and Elektra will become your middle name."

She smiled, patted the hands that rested limply upon my lap, and walked back to her room, closing the door behind her.

My name is Elektra, I wanted to scream at her retreating back.

But I said nothing.

Feeling helpless, I held back my tongue out of confusion, out of loyalty, out of this terrible desire that had already been born in me to please her, for as young as I was, I understood her.

Unconscious of my own feelings, I became keenly aware of hers. I understood that she needed to make me hers completely and that she couldn't do that with the presence of jewelry, names, and memories reminding her that I had belonged to another life, another family. Perhaps she wasn't trying to make me forget and move on as much as she was trying to make herself and others forget that I hadn't come from her; I don't believe she ever considered what I was thinking or feeling.

Now that I look back, I see that she had not adopted me to save me from my childhood, as I had let myself to believe. She adopted me to save her, to fill the voids that existed in her world. She wanted a child; it didn't matter what child it was, as long as her name was Kathryn and she came with a blank slate.

I couldn't fight her expectations, not at the age of eight.

I resigned to turn my head toward the foreign sound of my new persona whenever she was summoned. Inwardly, I flinched at the fake and hollow echoes of a name that didn't belong to me, had been forced on me, and functioned to negate the eight-year-old identity that had begun the exceptional story of my life. Being Kathryn was living a lie.

Initially, my new mother kept her word and had me down on certain documents as Kathryn Elektra. Eventually, my identity dwindled to Kathryn E. until it diminished to the plain and dull lulls of Kathryn, with Elektra slipping between my fingers like running water. Only I know who she was.

My transition to Kathryn was quiet and unspoken. Except for my stubborn persistence in holding onto my few memories, there is no outward, physical trace to Elektra Koutros. The death of my sister-self remains a solemn and overlooked instance. She is dead and buried deep within the seams of the girl that I had once been, and for years I let her remain undeclared, unexpressed, along with her memories and strength. She died in silence, and no one has grieved her subtle passing but me.

Your friend, Kit Kat

> *"You have no right to preach to me,*
> *you neophyte, that have not passed the porch of*
> *life, and are absolutely unacquainted with its mysteries."*
> JANE EYRE

Dear Jane,

My name is Kathryn and has been for the past seven years. Kathryn means "purity," but I don't feel pure. Nothing from my childhood was pure, and everything I saw and experienced corrupted me. My adoptive mother wants me to be Kathryn, to be pure, but I cannot change who I was and who I continue to be. I can't erase myself or my past, no matter how much she wishes I could. No matter how much I wish I could.

I have tried to become accustomed to her sound, but I ultimately fail in carrying my new and regal self with the comfort and poise she represents. Of course, no one except my mother ever calls me Kathryn. It gives me pleasure when my friends shorten it to Kathy, Kath, Kat, or Kit Kat. In Spanish class, it is Catalina, in Greek, Katerina, but one person ever calls me Kathryn, and whenever she does I recoil as if I have been struck. My jaw clenches, my limbs freeze, and I shake in those obscure places she doesn't know exist.

When someone asks me if I want to be called Kathryn, I say, "not unless you want me to call you *mother*," or "only my mother calls me that." It becomes a running joke for me, and my audience laughs politely, but now I realize that this has been my way of instructing them not to call me by that name.

Kathryn is a quiet girl, but she isn't me. She is this external layer of foreign skin that has been forcibly patched over mine in hopes that the two would mesh into one. Her texture is frail and weak, and she leaves me writhing beneath her full of frustration and anger.

She makes me weak and silent, when all I want to do is scream and fight. Maybe that's who I was attempting to kill the night I tried to stab myself.

There was a time when I had been brave. I had been a hero, and I even had a voice to match. That girl breathed and spit and screamed in me. She had fire in her brain and steam coming out of her nostrils, and she was just six. Her name was Elektra.

"You're not my baba!" she had screamed at Kristos when he commanded she call him her daddy. She talked back to him, even though he was at least four feet taller than her and had mean hands and bloodied knuckles. And when he smashed his radio against her face, her head, she didn't cry or falter; she saw red, clenched her fists, and threw punches at his thighs.

She tossed a spoiled chocolate bar at a store owner who refused to return her money or replace the expired bar in Athens, and ran from him, laughing, with Baby clinging to her hand, running behind her; that chocolate bar was the sole meal she had been able to buy for them that day with money she had collected by begging on the corners of her birth city.

She had fought stray cats – cats that somehow traipsed behind the skirts of her mother – for scraps of chicken. Uneven scars from their sharp fangs and curled claws were visible from beneath the blond hairs that covered her arms. When her mother brought food to any of the construction sites they slept in, there was a scuffle and chicken to be won. Ravenous, she tore at the baked flesh, slinking backward into solid corners lest someone tried to steal it. Cats were kicked and pried off and thrown to the opposite side, hissing as they flew through the air.

And when the police in Athens picked her mother up, with her and her little sister in tow, demanding to know where Kristos could be found, she smiled, knowingly, openly, aware that her knowledge of his whereabouts would set her free; all she had to do was open her mouth, and she would have her revenge. Her voice that day caused Kristos to disappear.

By the age of thirteen, when I had tried to stab myself, this girl had disappeared, and I was left with trace memories of who she was. It is hard for me to imagine that I had been that little, smart, brave girl back in Greece. That girl had a horrible childhood, but she never cowered, never even thought of ending her life. I want her back. I want her courage, her spirit.

I have become the girl that, at the age of eleven, sat upon my seventy-year-old Austrian teacher's lap during my violin lesson and froze when his hands crawled under my shirt to caress the smooth skin of my spine and shoulders.

I sat like a frozen statue atop his bony legs while his freckled and shaky hand slipped under my shirt and caressed me. In the end, he awarded me twenty dollars – the same twenty dollars my mother had paid him for my lesson.

I did it. Sat on his lap and took the money, because I was eleven; because he had been my teacher for two years and I trusted him; because I didn't want him to get into trouble; and because I didn't know what else to do. I thought I had escaped this when I was adopted, but Mr. Schwartz reminded me that any man could be Kristos.

The following Tuesday, the girl that I had become went back, sat on his lap when he grabbed her hand and asked her to, again, took the money again, and didn't say a word again. After both instances, she tore the bills into tiny little pieces and threw them in the garbage, spitting at their remains.

Mr. Schwartz rendered me the whore Kristos had promised to make of me. He made me the whore my adoptive mother told me I would become, just as my birth mother had been. Of course, I couldn't tell her about it, but not wanting to turn into my birth mother was enough to give me my voice back – if only for a while – but it wasn't your voice, Jane, not a hellraiser's voice.

Feeling persecuted by Mrs. Reed, you recoiled like a python and struck her with words that were equally venomous to Mrs. Reed's cold character.

"I am not deceitful," you cried out to your aunt. "If I were, I should say I love you, but I declare I do not love you: I dislike you the worst of anybody in the world except John Reed...People think you a good woman, but you are bad; hard-hearted. *You* are deceitful."

Having not met you yet, I just had Kathryn's voice to guide me out of this mess.

"I think I need a new music teacher," I told my mother in the car after school a few days after the second time Mr. Schwartz paid me to touch my skin. I was afraid that during my next lesson, he would touch more than the skin on my back.

"Why?"

"Mr. Schwartz is nice and all, but he doesn't teach me theory or notes. I know how to sight-read, but I couldn't tell you the name of a note if you pointed it out," I explained to her. "He's a good teacher, but if you want me to be a violinist, it's not going to be with him."

That's all I had to say to her; my education was paramount, and the following week, I was enrolled in Queens College's music program. I never had to hear again what a lovely man, a talented man Mr. Schwartz was. I never again had to feel his hands on me.

But I had sat on his lap. Kathryn had. Elektra would not have done that. She would have laughed in his face, jammed her fingers in his chest, and spit into his black orbs. She would have treated him with the same loathing she had treated Kristos when he smiled and threatened to make a woman out of her.

As Kathryn, I surrendered, not realizing that with each surrender, with each word I swallowed, with each truth that remained unspoken, all the feelings I drowned in silence would erupt into a storm that I would not be able to contain.

By the end of my first year as her daughter, my adoptive mother watched from the threshold of my bedroom doorway as I experienced the kind of fit you had in the red-room that Mrs. Reed confined you to when you misbehaved. I grabbed the sides of my bookcase and pulled and rammed it against the wall with all my might until the books trembled and fell on top of my head and into my face. My screams and sobs were uncontrollable, and they shattered the silences, the secrets, the unvoiced needs that my new mother and I couldn't satisfy for each other or for ourselves.

Like Mrs. Reed did with you during your tantrum in the red-room, my own mother closed the door and left me to the shadowy corners of my room, alone, angry, my hunger hopelessly unnourished.

I surrendered, not knowing at the age of eight what I would come to know at the age of eleven when I looked straight into her and pointed out what she was doing with me.

"You know," I said, "you can't take an older kid and mold her into something else – something that you want. She has a history, she's already somebody. You can mold a baby, but not an older kid like me."

She nodded her head.

"I originally wanted your little sister, because she was younger, but your mother refused to give her up. So, I took you instead."

Your friend, Kit Kat

> *"Many a time, as a little child, I should have been glad*
> *to love you if you would have let me; and I long*
> *earnestly to be reconciled to you now."*
> *JANE EYRE*

Dear Jane,

My adoptive mother is not an emotional woman. Similar to your Mrs. Reed, she keeps things reined in; even her body is one long, rigid line that does not bend or waver. She doesn't yell or scream, rant or rave, as I do when I get angry or feel frustrated. I am all emotion, and I respond to words and actions like a live wire about to burst. Perhaps it's because I hate the controlled, the silenced; it reminds me too much of my life with my second mother, shut up in my room, with no one to talk to, frustrations and words and memories padlocked inside me, against my will.

I can't be myself with her. I must hide my past, the experiences I have known, the pain and rage that wrestle wildly inside me for just one moment of relief. I hide everything that I am because she doesn't believe me; she doesn't want the girl I am. I am "an underhand little thing...with so much cover," as Mrs. Reed thought of you, and no one sees anything more in me.

Not being believed has done something disorienting to me; it has made me disappear. And when she changed my name to Kathryn, although it seemed unnatural to be called by someone else's name, it was good timing.

I put on Kathryn's skin and assumed a new identity – one that would please my new mother. I became the blank slate she desired, and I let her paint different colors on my skin, etch new qualities that would be more palatable to a mother like her: I was obedient, silent, malleable; I became her companion; traveled with her; went to operas and ballets at the Met, and art and history museums all over the country and the world; played the violin when all I wanted was to smash the damn thing against the wall; won awards in English, Math, Spanish, Science, and in writing; moved up to the honors courses in middle school; and I am second in my high school right now with a 97 average. Nancy Rodriguez is leading with a 98. I can't beat her because she's better than me in Math, and Geometry and I are still battling it out.

Every grade I get is for my mother, so when she began to introduce me to everyone as Kathryn, it was as if I were her real daughter – the one she had wanted. It doesn't always work. A good example is when I got an F in PE because I refused to chase balls across the gymnasium. My mother slapped me in front of everyone during the parent/teacher conference for my F. But I try.

Hunched over the pages of your story, I believe you in the way that Mrs. Reed and my mother don't believe us or in us. I believe that you were a good girl, for you were speaking to me and recounting the ways your good behavior was often overlooked and misinterpreted. I know that you would believe me, also, had you been a real girl, listening to my stories, and patting my back with the compassion you showed your dear friend, Helen. We are one in our honesty. To see how a girl like you, a good girl, could be perceived by others, your identity tainted by your family, makes me feel close to someone other than myself.

If you can overcome it, I know I can.

Thanks, Jane.

Your friend, Kit Kat

"When we are struck at without a reason,
we should strike back again very hard...so hard
as to teach the person who struck us never to do it again."
JANE EYRE

Dear Jane,

On the last day of middle school, after I had reconciled to remain in my life because of my inability to kill myself, I was supposed to stay in school, pick up my final report card, and then go home. But I did not.

I knew it was the last time I would see Farida. My mother had arranged for me to go to a high school in Jamaica, near her job, and I had no choice in the matter, so I made the best of it.

During lunch, Farida and I cut school. I'd never done it before, and it was thrilling. We went to her house, and she did my hair and make-up. That was also a first for me. I was not cool or chic or made-up in middle school. I wore the second-hand clothes my mother bought for me at consignment stores in Long Island, and make-up was not something that we ever talked about.

After Farida was done, and I looked in the mirror, I was staring back at a different girl. One with big eyes and defined cheekbones. When I smiled at the girl in the mirror, she seemed happy and confident looking back at me. She was worth the wait, the last day spent with Farida, cutting school, and getting caught. And I did get caught, because when we returned to school, everyone had left, and we couldn't get our report cards. Farida's mom wouldn't care; it was the last day of middle school. My mom would. She would be livid.

But by this point, I didn't care.

Something happens to you when you try to rid yourself of your life, and you realize you can't do it. That you lack the courage. Something dies. It's the one secret you don't tell anyone – not your mother, not your friends, no one. The knowledge of the attempt, the failure, lives inside you, festering, reeking, quietly abiding. I was sleepwalking, trying not to feel anything while living my teen years with my adoptive mother. It was the only way to get through it – to survive her.

Having removed all the make-up from my face, I waited for her in the living room, surrounded by Chinese sculptures of elephants and African masks that hung on our walls, adjusting my weight to alleviate my thighs from sticking to the plastic cover that encased our blue floral couch. It was our formal room, and whenever I was in trouble, that is where we would sit.

When she came home from work and asked for my report card, I looked at her, tilted my head to the left, and told her without any artifice that I did not have it.

"Farida and I went out for lunch, and we didn't get back in time to pick it up."

She did not say a word to me. She just scooped up her purse, retrieved her car keys, and left the apartment. She picked it up for me. To insult her even more, I got an F. In English. How funny is that?

To punish me, she refused to attend my middle school graduation.

When my birth mother or Kristos hit me, I knew I was there, present. I felt their knuckles gnash against my skin, and the sting of it filled me with shame, but I was there. I sensed my feet rooted to the ground, my own fists clenched at my sides, the spit collecting inside my mouth, ready to be catapulted into the eyes of my attackers. They saw me standing there, aimed for me, felt the soft tissue of my skin, the bones sheltered beneath it, when they hurled the punch into my cheek, my head, my chest. They smiled when I went down or lost my footing, when they saw tears streaming down my face against my will. They knew I was there. They needed me to be there. The power they had over me gave them more power when I fell at their feet and covered my head against the more aggressive attacks that would be raining down on me.

My adoptive mother did not fight this way. Her power came from rendering me non-existent. She cut me down with one word, one aloof look veiled behind wide glass frames. She pretended I wasn't there, which told me all I needed to know about myself: I was nothing.

That's how I felt the night I tried to stab myself. But when she refused to attend my graduation, simply because I had spent a day with my friend, Farida, I didn't want to hurt myself again. This time, I thought of you, how bold you were with your Mrs. Reed, and I only experienced anger.

To punish her, I refused to stand in honor of our parents during my graduation. I was the one kid in the auditorium not to stand up, and I was seated in the middle, below the stage, with clarinet in hand, as a member of the school band.

That's how I stood up to her. By not standing up for her in the same way that she refused to stand up for me.

Sitting there, while everyone around me rose, knowing I was at the center and that all could see me rebelling, I felt the way you must have when you stood up to Mrs. Reed: "my soul began to expand, to exult, with the strangest sense of freedom, of triumph...It seemed as if an invisible bond had burst, and that I had struggled out into unhoped-for liberty."

I experienced the power that comes with standing up for myself, and, even though it was short-lived, and my mother wasn't there to see me dishonor her, it gave me the burst of courage I needed to keep moving further in this life that had become mine and had been assigned me against my will: to moving on to a high school I didn't want to go to; to sharing a home with a woman who ignored me; and to not giving up or giving in to my sadness again.

I will not throw away my life for her.

Your friend, Kit Kat

"When our energies seem to demand a sustenance they cannot get –
when our will strains after a path we may not follow –
we need neither starve from inanition nor stand still in despair:
we have but to seek another nourishment."
JANE EYRE

Dear Jane,

Farida was the last true friend I had.

I looked elsewhere for sustenance.

During my freshman year in high school, my attention shifted to Gina and Lorraine, friends who listened to Madonna and mimicked her notorious fashion sense: short, frilly miniskirts over black or white tights; pink, lacy gloves that covered their palms and wrists but left the fingertips bare; long, startling red nails; ripped tank tops and bra straps that peeked from beneath short, loose shirts hanging low and baring the smooth curvature of one shoulder, teasing onlookers with the glow of young, pubescent, unmarred skin; and an array of crosses and Star of David pendants clinging from gold chains and collected at the base of their throats. They each caked their faces with splashes of bright colors that accentuated their lids, lashes, lips, and cheeks.

I didn't fit into their clique with my plain hair hanging limply from my scalp; my simple clothes, mainly jeans and sneakers bought from second-hand stores; and a face that was long and pale, clean of make-up, my big, chestnut eyes peering out from their sunken, opaque sockets. In middle school, I was encircled by pretty girls, their faces painted and their pimples concealed by layers of tinted powder and pink blush. My pimples stood out like bright red globs the size of anthills and no make-up to keep them hidden.

At fifteen, I am surrounded by dolled-up and made-up girls who seem more sophisticated and mature and womanly than I could even comprehend. It is difficult to find my place among them, and even my friendship with Gina and Lorraine was hard to navigate as I didn't have the freedoms they had – going to the movies or the shopping mall without parents, having money to spend on food and clothes, or buying frilly, girly products that helped them achieve a femininity that felt like more lies to me. A girl myself, I don't wear skirts. I hate them. I am comfortable in jeans and sneakers, and dressing up like them – like Madonna – like a girl in the 80s, just didn't feel right to me. It all went against my nature. I was pretending, and I hate to pretend at anything. It takes too much energy, and I don't have much to begin with. Pretending to be Kathryn is already costing me too much.

When my friendship with Gina and Lorraine took a dark turn of two against one, I took my leave and found another circle to belong to, one that included about seven of us, all smart, simple, and non-American: Shilpa was Indian, and when I went to her house, her parents enfolded me in their arms, fed me brown rice with peas, onions, and other ingredients I didn't inquire about but wolfed down with the hunger of a starved child, and took pictures of us dressed in Shilpa's exotic and soft-layered saris; Nina was Indonesian, and she smiled so much that we told her sad stories just to see if she could lose it. She didn't.

We became The Screaming Sisters, after the famous rock group Twisted Sister, and even bought matching shirts that we wore whenever we went to parties. The three of us hung out with a group of boys from Chinese, Korean, and Latino descent, and we all went to the movies together, watched porn together, the girls giggling, the boys crossing their legs while Debbie did Dallas, and attended parties that included dancing and spin the bottle. But we were an innocent group, and I loved this most about my new friends. There was no liquor or sex in our parties, even when the parents were not there. We had soda, chips and dip, and our version of spin the bottle included all of us slow dancing with the person we were matched with to songs by Madonna, Whitney Houston, Peter Gabriel, Cindi Lauper, Lionel Richie, and U2. These are the friends I hang out with today.

Although I love my friends, I hardly feel secure, and it is as easy for me to slip out of friendships as it is to slip into them. I can't quite attach myself to anything, and this is partly because I am not honest with them about who I am. None of the friends I had during my first year in high school truly knew me – my history, where I came from. My friendships were, and still are, superficial, which is why it is so easy to slip away when I get bored, or feel lonely, or misunderstood. No one knows me. Not even my mother. I am an airborne seed, just passing through, never staying long enough to find root.

My mother has already taught me what will happen to me if I speak about myself and the years before my adoption. Our trip to PEEC taught me that, and I don't need another reminder that the consequences for expressing the unutterable will cast me in a place of oppressive silence. There are warnings, of course, for whenever I bring Shilpa or Nina home after school, my adoptive mother watches us, listening to our conversations for clues to my traitorous tongue. After they leave, she penetrates me with a glare that tells me not to bother lying. She knows who I am.

"Did you tell them?" she asks me.

"Tell them what?" I play dumb.

"That you are adopted. About your *real* family."

"Of course not." This is the truth. "We don't talk about you." This is a lie.

I do talk about her. I can't help myself. In talking about her – her overprotectiveness, her cool, reserved nature, her own inability to attach – I tell my friends that I am adopted. I have to. It is the only way I can quiet the questions: *Where's your dad? Why isn't she married? How old is she? Is she your grandmother?*

I discovered that one sentence can answer their questions without forcing me to tell them more, the parts that my mother doesn't want to know herself and which she has forbidden me to give voice to: *I am adopted.* That's all. That's all I need to say, and they are satisfied enough to move on, assuming my adoption occurred at birth.

Of course, I know I am betraying her. She doesn't even want anyone to know about that. I tell them as much as I can without bombarding them with a childhood they cannot fathom, and because of this – because I cannot be wholly honest with them – my friendships are as vulnerable and fragile as a spider's web, easily destroyed by poking a finger into it and prying it apart.

At the heart of my misery is that I am unloved by the one person that should love me: my mother. Her love, her approval, means everything to me, even more than my own life. But when she speaks to me, it is with a distance that I don't have the skills to diminish; her words push me even further, reminding me of my deficiencies: I am a liar, an ingrate, a whore. Staring straight at me, she can't see the girl who longs for her, and I don't know how to show her who I am. I don't even know at this point who I am, but I know that I am not a liar, I am not an ingrate, and I am no more a whore than she is.

Your friend, Kit Kat

"Disasters came thick on me...
I began to see and acknowledge the hand of God in my doom."
JANE EYRE

Dear Jane

The first time I learned about God and Jesus Christ, I was in my first-grade classroom, while I was living with my aunt and uncle in Greece. My little friends and I sat in a circle around our teacher, Mrs. Ganagakis, as she read to us about Christ's struggles from a children's version of the Bible.

"Jesus Christ is the Son of God; He is the flesh and soul of God, our Father. He is God in the flesh, and He is our savior. He died for our sins, He saves our souls, and it is through an open and trusting relationship with Him that we can find our way to God."

"Is He a real person?" one of my little friends asked.

"He was a real person. He traveled and made many friends – even those who were supposed to be His enemies. He spoke to women when no man was supposed to talk to a woman. He saved people from being stoned or shunned for their choices. He even committed miraculous deeds." Her voice was soft, sending a chill up my spine.

"Like what?" I whispered. I was suspicious. Christ bore the same name as the devil of my childhood: Kristos. How could two men who had the same name be completely different from each other? How could someone like Kristos, who had a black heart and no compassion, be given the name of Christ Himself? It didn't make any sense to me.

"Well, for instance, there was a time when He cleansed leprosy, or skin disease, from a man. He touched the man's skin, and all the red marks and open sores disappeared. It is how people began to believe in Him; they saw what He could do and believed that He was our savior."

"Was He a magician?" another one piped up.

"Not a magician," Mrs. Ganagakis corrected him. "He was a healer and a teacher. He healed anyone, even if that person was an evil person or someone society didn't approve of. Through His miracles, He taught us to believe in

Him, but also to love Him and to love one another. He taught us to accept differences in people."

I raised my hand.

"Yes, Elektra." She smiled at me.

"Did He forgive all bad people, no matter what bad things they did?" I asked.

"Yes. He forgave them so that we could learn to forgive them, too."

Would He forgive my mother? I wanted to ask. *Would He forgive me, for abandoning my sister, without even saying goodbye to her? For the things I had done at Penteli?*

I shuddered just thinking about the bad things I had already done, and I wasn't even eight.

Out of all the stories that she told us from the Bible, there was one that stayed with me: Jesus stopping a crowd from stoning a prostitute by asking them simply if they had not also committed any sins.

This was the only time I came across the word *prostitute* and connected the dots of the word to my mother's profession. At last, I had a word that sounded cleaner, nicer than *putana*.

It was my first active experience with religion. I cannot imagine that the nuns at Penteli had not taught us about the ways of Greek Orthodoxy, but for whatever reason, lessons about faith and forgiveness had not resonated with me as they did while living with my aunt and uncle. Having Aunt Thalia in my life, I was full of optimism and the prospect of faith. Because she made me feel loved and wanted, I opened myself up to harmonious philosophies that come with believing beyond ourselves.

I began to pray, and each night I knelt beside my bed, clasped my hands under my chin, and asked God to forgive my mother and father, to watch over Maria, Nicholas, Stavros, and little Baby. I thanked Him for the roof over my head, and the generosity of my aunt and uncle, and hoped that my cousins would learn to like me.

I took this prayer with me when I moved to New York and a new life, adding my new mother to my list of those I wanted to be protected. Each night my prayers were the same, and each night I slept peacefully, knowing that I was being watched over and cared for by a force that did not abandon or sacrifice His beloved as the adults around me had done. It was this faith that taught me that my experiences were seamless and connected to something bigger, as if everything was meant to occur the way it did, horrific or extraordinary.

By the time I was eight years old and headed for the United States, I believed myself to be one of God's well-crafted creatures drawn against a larger-than-life canvas that He especially splashed with vivid colors and nuances. I was comforted by the idea that I had a father – not the mortal kind, with weaknesses that could force him to abandon his children – but an omniscient and all-powerful one that punished and rewarded with might and great vengeance.

As my Father, He had a plan for me.

This was confirmed when my second mother adopted me.

I found God in your story, too, Jane. Your dear friend, Helen, surrendered herself to God's will, and that takes courage, letting Him drive her existence. God was her Maker and Master, the one who would take her out of the sickly and poor world in which she had been born. He was the light and life was the abysmal darkness she wished to abandon. She waited patiently for Him to take her, biding her time as a student at Lowood School for Girls. When she died, it was expected and a relief.

You are different, more like me. You relied on God for strength and power, but you did not bend to Him. You relied on Him when you were weak in body and spirit, when you recognized that temptation was stronger than the religious teachings that came with your schooling. You evoked God's stronghold on you when tempted to live with Rochester as his mistress after finding out that he was already married. Having no family of your own, no one to judge you, I suppose your love and pity for Rochester and his desperation moved you, which threatened to destroy your convictions and your good sense. God was your "conscience, turned tyrant," the voice of reason inside your head that told you to avoid the temptation of Rochester's pleas, as well as the voice that told you no one would help you tear yourself from Rochester; you had to find the courage to do it yourself.

When I called out to God, He gave me Ann.

No matter how dejected I was – at least at the beginning of my adoption – I would remind myself of where I would have ended up if she had not come along, scooped me up, and removed me from the dregs of society to which I had been born. I would have been back with my mother, with Kristos, on the streets, and any kind of life with Ann was better than that.

When she came to me, I felt this great surge of relief wash over me that caused me to stand up straight and tall. Of all the women in the world to assign me as my mother, God chose Ann, a woman who was so unlike my own, the differences so profound that even a child could observe them.

But it wasn't until I saw the beauty marks on her body that I grasped God bringing us together was more than just wishful thinking. I saw them early on, when God and my new mother and being adopted were still romantic notions to me.

Atop her left breast was a perfectly round mole, and when my eyes rested on it, I had to refrain from touching mine, resting in the same exact place. When she lifted her left arm, I located another mole that mirrored mine, right beneath my own armpit. For a child trying to find her place in this world, this was it.

She was my mother, and it was God's doing. He had found us, oceans apart – a girl in need of a mother, a woman in need of a child – and He paired us off. This was physical proof that we were meant to be placed together as mother and child. It went beyond our wills and desires, and we couldn't undo what God and nature had intended, no matter who we had been born to.

It was God who brought you and Rochester together, allowing you to hear each other calling while many miles apart. You had become independent and Rochester, although blind, had found his humanity, his humility, making you both ready to receive each other as equals.

In this way, no matter what happened between my new mother and me, I was where I was supposed to be and everything happened as it should—to make me stronger, to teach me lessons, to get me ready for the next path He would place before me. Every dot in my life – every person I met, every decision I chose, every path I took – was supposed to lead me to the next – to my purpose. Perhaps it was His hand that made it so difficult for me to stab myself two years ago. He pulled the scissors from me as I was pulling them towards me.

This is how I felt about my adoptive mother, how I still feel about her, even after she had the mole on her chest lasered off during a regular visit with her physician. And this is how I felt upon locating you, Jane, in the book and in the girl. My new mother was a way out of a debauched existence I needed to escape, but you're the buoy placed before me so that I could hang onto you when I got too tired of living or too close to drowning.

Starving for my adoptive mother's approval, I almost lost myself in my need for another person – a person who refused me and my affections. You taught yourself to be an independent girl that governed her own place in society – and, although you found love and happiness in the end – you got there after learning to care for yourself first.

You taught me to love myself more than I needed to be loved by someone else – even if that someone else was a parent. You showed me that no matter how hard I try, how much of myself I give up for my adoptive mother, she will never see me, never love me. It was the same for you with Mrs. Reed; this endless cycle of desire and self-sacrifice only to come against rejection was the parallel that helped me understand that my efforts are futile and my needs will not be met – at least, not by my mother.

It isn't in her nature.

Of all the books in the world I could have picked up that day – in a moment of panic and despondency – it wasn't just luck that I found *Jane Eyre*. Of all the books to discover, I came upon the one about a lonely, dejected girl who spent her childhood in an orphanage. Of all the books to find me, this is the one that fell into my hands when I needed saving. It was yet another gift that God brought my way to remind me that He was there, watching me, fathering me, helping me feel connected to something bigger than myself – to Him perhaps.

He led me to you, who advised me when no one else could: "the sovereign Hand that created your frame, and put life into it, has provided you with other resources than your feeble self, or than creatures feeble as you."

Jane Eyre was that resource, and it safeguarded me.

I don't feel alone anymore. Even when it all seems so incomprehensible that I wish the ocean that is life would open and swallow me, I have learned not to give in to that desire, but to take a deep breath and float on my back until the storm breaks, until the next wave nudges me forward, until some special person I hadn't expected teaches me something new about myself, or until another book shows me the way out of my own inherent gloom.

There must be something else, something more, and there is. The next person I am supposed to meet. The next book I am supposed to read. The next lesson I am supposed to acquire. God places them before me just at the right moment, just when I need it most, just as He did when I was thirteen and couldn't find anything to live for. He brought me to you – just as He had once brought me to my adoptive mother – teaching me to take what I need from what is being offered – and to ask for nothing more. It is in our nature to fail each other; people cannot meet all our needs, but I know one thing for sure:

God has not failed me.

People have. People always will.

But He hasn't, and neither have you, Jane.

Your devoted friend, Kit Kat

*"After a youth...passed in unutterable misery and half in dreary solitude...
I have found you. You are my sympathy – my better self – my good angel...
a fervent, a solemn passion is conceived in my heart;
it leans to you, draws you to my centre spring of life,
wraps my existence around you."*
JANE EYRE

Dear Charlotte,

When you and Jane found me in the library so many years ago, I was "a lamp quenched, waiting to be relit...dependent on another for that office." But there was no one in my life willing or able to relight that dimmed lamp. My adoption was nothing as I had hoped it would be. I thought it would provide me with the kind of childhood I had missed out on; instead, I was given to someone who had also anticipated something different from it. I was too young to give my adoptive mother what she required, and she had no idea what I needed; she didn't even know where I had come from.

When I locked myself in the bathroom and attempted to stab myself, no one knew me. Not even her. I was alone, and my memories of Greece were stuck in my chest, jammed down the wrong pipe and trapped there. Everyone had known me as Kathryn, and the stories they learned of me came from my adoptive mother's perspective. The girl who was disobedient. The girl who was willful. The ingrate who didn't appreciate the gifts she had given me.

I *was* disobedient. I *was* willful. I *was* an ingrate. I was all these things because I wanted more than gifts and opportunities; I wanted to be heard, to be seen. I wanted someone to ask me where I had come from, to hold me, to counsel me. I wanted someone to know all of me, to nurture the tangled roots of my childhood and to feed me the love I deserved in spite of them. Simply, I wanted to be loved. I wanted all these things from my mother, from Ann, but she was always an arm's length away from me, and when she looked at me, she didn't see me – the one who stood before her trembling with fear and loss – she saw the daughter she had wanted and had not acquired.

At thirteen, I didn't know how to be that girl – I wasn't Jane, the martyr, the innocent. I wasn't even you, the strong and ambitious writer. It will take me decades to become as strong as you and Jane were. I wasn't even as spirited as you. I was wasted, just as my adoptive mother often described me when she caught me looking at myself in the mirror, my skin pale, except for the shadows that had begun to burrow beneath my eyes like black-blue bags. I was a shell, dragging my feet from obligation to obligation, looking out from a hollow gaze.

When I caught myself in the mirror, I didn't see a vibrant young girl; I didn't see Jane or you. I didn't even see Kathryn, the girl my mother had worked so hard to turn me into. I saw hatred and obscurity.

You and Jane taught me how to be solitary without feeling lonely – how to hang back from the crowd, for safety, for self-regulation, for the power of observation and full understanding. Both of you, the real and the fictitious, were solitary creatures. You navigated life's storms without much guidance from others. However, both of you learned to fend for yourselves amidst innumerable losses and austere conditions.

You helped me calmly navigate through violent seas, sift through the debris to find the clearest, purest parts that I could drink from for the nourishment I needed. I learned how to be part of the crowd without becoming part of the mob, holding onto my own identity, securing my individuality so as not to lose sight of the most important part of growing up: my humanity.

"The more solitary, the more friendless, the more unsustained I am, the more I will respect myself," Jane revealed during the early years, and it was in this phrase I grasped the truth of my situation with my mother: I would never acquire my mother's affections; crying, begging, and asking for them had led to more resistance, so I was better off relying on me for the affection and regard that I sought.

Having found the threads of my own experiences in Jane's narrative, the characters of my own experiences embroiled in catastrophic conflicts within the pages of fiction, I was trying to discover models and heroines to save me. And saved I was.

I am eighteen now. I just finished my first year of college, and because of *Jane Eyre*, I took a Gothic Literature course that brought me back to you and

Jane. I read about your life. I even read a volume of your letters, and I realized how much of you is in Jane, at least in the first part of her story. You, too, lost your mother early, had a dreary and rigid aunt who took care of you and ended up in a school for girls during which you lost two of your sisters to the typhus fever. Your own story is as much about the need to be mothered and overcoming losses as Jane's story and mine are. In this, we are the same, even though we come from different parts of the world and different periods in history. But through Jane, you found me, and I found you, and in finding you, I found myself, my own voice, my own strength, and I haven't thought about suicide since you taught me to stand up for myself to those who had more power than me.

I would love to tell you that my relationship with my adoptive mother has improved, or that I learned to speak to her – that she learned to listen to me. But neither has happened. As a matter of fact, it got worse. But that's the way it goes. It has to get worse before we can pick up our lives and make the changes we need to save ourselves.

About six months ago, I met my best friend, Alexandra, at the bus stop so we could go to our Math tutoring sessions together. We were equally bad at math and aware that we had to get tutoring to pass our class. We were both Greek, both English majors, and had been friends in high school. Since then, we had been inseparable.

She was quiet as we walked to McKinnon Hall side-by-side. I knew something was wrong by the way she kept giving me cautious looks and twirling her already black, curly hair between her fingers.

"What's wrong with you?" I couldn't stand her awkwardness anymore.

"I have something to tell you, but you have to promise not to get mad," she said after another pause, pursing her red lips together and then blurting the words out in a rush.

"OK." I smiled to give her my full attention.

She sighed and then her look met mine full on. Her face was a piece of art. She never left her house in the Greek part of Jamaica without whitening her olive-toned skin with layers of cover-up to conceal pimples; she penciled in long, arched eyebrows with black liner that also outlined the bottom and top parts of her lids; a little bit of blush was pasted onto her round cheeks in perfect circles, and matching red lipstick was drawn on her lips and stuck to her teeth when she talked.

"Your mom called me last night," she said at last.

"What?" My glance tripped from her mouth to her eyes, and I stared at her, it seemed, from a distance.

"Don't get upset," Alexandra pleaded.

"What did she say?"

"She told me not to be your friend. Let me see if I can use her exact words: 'Kathryn is using you. You are a pawn in her game, and she is using you to get what she wants.' That's what she said."

I couldn't find my footing suddenly, so I stopped in my tracks and looked around me. I loved the Queens College campus. It was full of brick buildings, but right smack in the middle was the Quad, a long stretch of green lawn full of students sitting and talking, reading books, playing frisbee, or just lying down. The sight of human movement usually made me feel alive, but at this moment, I was frozen with confusion.

I hadn't had a fight with my adoptive mother in a while, so I couldn't understand where this had come from. The one thing I could come up with is that she felt neglected because I had been spending a lot of my time with Alexandra. So, this was jealousy? How is a parent jealous of a teen's friendship?

"What did you tell her?" I asked Alexandra, wondering if my mother would cost me yet another friend.

"I just hung up on her," she said, resting her chubby fingers on my shoulder. "I don't believe her, Kit-Kat. I know you're not like that."

My eyes moistened, and I managed a smile at her.

"It's all right. Let's just go. We're going to be late."

It wasn't all right. I couldn't understand what my mother had intended to accomplish by saying those things about me. She believed I was a user, and in my mind, I expect it came down to my adoption. She assumed that I used her. That I tricked her into adopting me and that I failed to be what she wanted. In a way, she was telling me that she regretted her decision to adopt me. I was the better for it in many ways, but she gained nothing from it.

When I got home that evening, I didn't tell her about my conversation with Alexandra. That I knew what she had done and said about me. I was too humiliated. Too stunned, still.

I went into the bathroom, the same one that I had tried to kill myself in so many years ago, and I took a hard look at myself. I had the same bangs, the same sunken eyes, and a perm to make my hair curly instead of flat and straight.

"Look at you," I heard my mother's voice next to me. The door was open, and I took hold of her glare through the mirror as she stood in the hallway, facing me through the doorway.

"You look old, and you're only eighteen," she continued. "You're wasting yourself. What are you doing with yourself? If you're not careful, you're going to end up..."

My heart raced and tumbled to my throat, giving me a voice I had never reached for before this moment.

"Fuck you!"

Just as the words rushed out and I turned to face her, my cheek began to burn from the impact of her open hand striking my face.

And then it all happened so fast that I couldn't even stop it. My hand went up to her throat, squeezed it, pulled her into the bathroom, and pushed the back of her head against the mirror. My knees buckled beneath me, but my hand, trembling, kept its grip tight and strong around her neck, and I could feel the beat of her heart struggle against her skin and into my fingers.

I brought my face close to hers and looked straight into the eyes I wish would see the real me, not the one she imagined me to be all these years. I was in college, taking eighteen credits, majoring in English, minoring in Education, and I worked two jobs to pay for my tuition, since she refused to pay for it unless I was home every day by eight o'clock. I wasn't drinking or clubbing or dating. I was just trying to work hard so I could move out and be on my own. But she didn't see any of it. She didn't see me. And I was tired.

"If you ever hit me again," I seethed into her face, "it will come right back at you." I loosened my grip then, rushed into my room, and locked the door. Since being adopted, I began to see the girl I had been so many years ago in Greece, fighting with Kristos, my birth mother's pimp. I found the fire inside me, and no gratitude or guilt would subdue me again.

It was then that I realized I couldn't live there anymore. Not with her. I owed her for adopting me, for giving me a home and a future, but I didn't owe her my life, my self-esteem. I was grateful, but I wouldn't sacrifice myself for her. Not anymore. If she couldn't see me now, she would never see me. The only way to save myself was to move out.

For the next month, I made plans to find a place near the college and moved into a room in an apartment with three other college girls looking for a roommate. I found a full-time job as an office clerk in a pharmaceutical company that paid me more than my two part-time jobs combined, and I cut down on my course load so I could afford rent and college tuition. I was hungry. A lot, often surviving on a large order of McDonald's fries for the entire day, but I was free, and I didn't have someone I wanted to love (and to love me) standing over my shoulder, telling me all the bad things she saw in me when there were so many good parts of me that stayed hidden because of her.

I have not seen her since, but I think of her often. Usually when I am low, and sad, and hungry. But then I turn to the memories I couldn't share, scattering them across my bed like splintered glass, fitting them together from instinct, making them whole enough, solid enough to reflect the full story of my childhood. I turn to my studies, all the literature courses I am taking, and my copy of *Jane Eyre* to remind me why I must stay away, no matter how desperate I still am for my mother's love.

I have learned that I am strong enough to determine my own reactions to her and the emotional desolation I have encountered as her daughter. Moving out and away from her, I don't have to fight anymore. I feel this is all I have ever done. What have I been fighting for all these years? To be loved? Why should anyone have to fight for love? I don't have to fight, or hide myself from her, or surrender my voice to accommodate hers. Those days are over.

But I wasn't alone.

You taught me that as lonely as I felt, I had friends in you and Jane, and you both provided me with the key to my liberation: education. By teaching me to find myself and my lessons in literature, I learned the value of discernment, drawing connections between what I read and what was going on in my everyday existence. If I could make these associations between fiction and life, between literary characters and me, then I could transfer this skill to everything that lay in wait for me outside of my books, where it was scarier for me to live without a guide.

It is in this that you and I are alike, and thanks to *Jane Eyre* – the book and the girl – I veered away from the loathsome feelings that would have turned me into the wicked and self-loathing Rochester or the mad and violent Bertha. I don't want to resemble them – not just because they are volatile and remind me so much of Kristos and Athanasia – but also because they are full of anger and unhappiness. I have had enough of that. You and Jane showed me that girls can be strong and tough and smart, and I want to live as you did.

You have helped me see my adoptive mother not as a parent that can't give me what I need, but as a model of womanhood – a woman unlike my birth mother. In looking at her, I have learned to discriminate, to find things that I need out of the muck, like a scavenger, and there are a lot of treasures waiting for me in the trough of Ann.

She is educated, free, and her will determines the path that she will follow. There is no man, husband, or pimp telling her what to do or second-guessing her choices. In many ways, she is the kind of woman you and Jane endeavored to become, despite the limitations placed on women during the Victorian era. You took those limitations, stretched them, refashioned them to suit your own needs and ambitions: Jane went out in the world on her own, seeking adventure and love, and settling down with her beloved once she was independent and wealthy; and you, Charlotte, became a famous and esteemed writer by assuming the name of a man, Currer Bell. Even after it became known that you and Currer Bell were one and the same, a young woman, your editors continued to publish your work, and your readers, men and women alike, continued to read you.

Because of you, I have determined that what has made my mother so similar to my heroines and a worthy model for a girl like me is her education – an ambition towards independence. This is the treasure that I have scavenged from her, the trait that I have adopted as my own, pursuing my own education above anything else.

I know you hated teaching, but this is what I want to do with the rest of my life. I want to share my love of books with youngsters. In your letters, you describe teaching as a prison, mainly because it was the singular vocation for women during your day, and you were forced to teach to support your family. This is how you saw teaching:

[A]m I to spend all the best part of my life in this wretched bondage, forcibly suppressing my rage at the idleness the apathy and the hyperbolical & most asinine stupidity of these fat-headed oafs and on compulsion assuming an air of kindness, patience, and assiduity? Must I from day to day sit chained to this chair prisoned within these four bare-walls... [while] the time I am losing will never come again?

I don't see teaching this way. I want my students to find value in words and stories and characters, as well as to discover how these are connected to their own lives. You and Jane and I were lost among adults, silenced, and we found ourselves in books and learning, and there are tons of lost kids out there that feel the same way. If I can just reach one of them with a book that helps her find her identity and purpose, then my job is done. I want to save lives with books, just as your book on Jane saved my own.

Guided by you and Jane, I have turned myself into the protagonist of my own narrative, seeking my fortune, my success, for myself. In my story, I have full control over myself, my body, my choices, and no one, not my birth mother or my adoptive mother, is going to define me. As the writer of my narrative, I write my own story, my way. Just like Jane. Just like you.

Thank you, Charlotte. For giving me Jane. For giving me you through Jane. Knowing the two of you has made all the difference. You became my friends and my champions when I did not have any.

You understood me. You saw my longing, my desperation, and you took hold of me with page after page of "I will save you. I am here for you." You wouldn't let me put the book down or surrender to depression or thoughts of self-harm.

"I hate my life. I hate her!" I screamed loud enough for my mother to hear, tearing my hair from my scalp.

"You're not alone," you whispered through Jane.

"You're not alone," you reminded me from your own personal letters:

I abhor myself – I despise myself...I am already an outcast – You cannot imagine how hard rebellious and intractable all my feelings are...don't desert me – don't be horrified at me, you know what I am.

As long as I had that book – as long as I had your voice and Jane's during my teen years – I didn't feel alone. You didn't desert me, and, in turn, I have not deserted myself.

I have not forgotten who I am.

Your loyal friend, Elektra.

Acknowledgments

My gratitude primarily goes to Joe and our children, Joseph and Marina, for making my writing part of our family discussions. Without their participation and support, this book would not have been written. It is for them that I write and endeavor to fulfill my dreams, so they can learn to make their own dreams a reality.

Thank you to Reagan Rothe of *Black Rose Writing* for offering me a generous contract in publishing my book and making the process so easy and flawless.

Many thanks to my MFA peers and teachers from Queens University of Charlotte in North Carolina. Many versions of this book were read and critiqued by my teachers/writers Michael Kobre, Jon Pineda, Emily White, Emily Fox Gordon, Rebecca McClanahan, and Pinckney Benedict. My deepest love and respect for my writing peers, for their patience and guidance in their critiques of my writing, and for being the first readers of my work. Thank you, Donna Brooks, Laurie Hertzel, William Boden, Katy Nelson, Sumanah Khan, Kellie Roblin, Michelle Harris, Nancy Rommelmann, Scott Mason, Tennill Mitchell, and JC Young. Thank you to Fred Leebron and Melissa Bashor for the best time of my life and the best MFA program imaginable.

Thank you to Matt Rance, the "Proofprofessor," at www.proofprofessor.com, for his generous edits and comments on my manuscript.

Thank you also to my students for inspiring me to share with them my love of books and writing, for reminding me why I teach, and for teaching me that it's never too late to begin again, to dream again.

Finally, thank you to my brothers and sisters, for meeting me and loving me as if you had never lost me. Αγάπη και φιλιά ... είσαστε η πρώτη μου αγάπη.

About the Author

Marina DelVecchio is a college professor of literature and women's studies and lives in North Carolina with her family. Her work can be found online at *Ms Magazine, The Huffington Post, The Tishman Review, Her Circle Ezine, BlogHer,* and *The New Agenda.*

Website: www.marinadelvecchio.com
Facebook: www.facebook.com/marinadelvecchio727
Twitter: @marinagraphy
Instagram: https://www.instagram.com/marina.delvecchio

Thank you so much for reading one of our **Young Adult Fiction** novels.
If you enjoyed our book, please check out our recommended title for your
next great read!

What the Valley Knows by Heather Christie

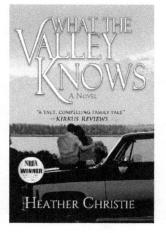

"A taut, compelling family tale." *–KIRKUS REVIEWS*

BLACK ROSE
writing™

CPSIA information can be obtained
at www.ICGtesting.com
Printed in the USA
LVHW011439190319
611157LV00002B/426/P

9 781684 331727

GERMANY

24th Edition

Where to Stay and Eat
for All Budgets

Must-See Sights
and Local Secrets

Ratings You Can Trust

Fodor's Travel Publications   New York, Toronto, London, Sydney, Auckland
www.fodors.com

FODOR'S GERMANY

Editors: Salwa Jabado (lead project editor), Christina Knight
Editorial Contributors: Matthew Lombardi, Jess Moss
Writers: Uli Ehrhardt, Lee A. Evans, Jürgen Scheunemann, Ted Shoemaker, Tim Skelton

Production Editor: Tom Holton
Maps & Illustrations: David Lindroth, Mark Stroud, *cartographers*; Bob Blake, Rebecca Baer, *map editors;* William Wu, *information graphics*
Design: Fabrizio La Rocca, *creative director*; Guido Caroti, Siobhan O'Hare, *art directors*; Tina Malaney, Chie Ushio, Ann McBride, Jessica Walsh, *designers*; Melanie Marin, *senior picture editor*
Cover Photo: (Restaurant window, Luneberg): Ernst Haas/Stone/Getty Images
Production Manager: Amanda Bullock

24th Edition

ISBN 978–1–4000–0708–0

ISSN 1525–5034

SPECIAL SALES
This book is available at special discounts for bulk purchases for sales promotions or premiums. Special editions, including personalized covers, excerpts of existing books, and corporate imprints, can be created in large quantities for special needs. For more information, write to Special Markets/Premium Sales, 1745 Broadway, MD 6-2, New York, New York 10019, or e-mail specialmarkets@randomhouse.com.

AN IMPORTANT TIP & AN INVITATION
Although all prices, opening times, and other details in this book are based on information supplied to us at press time, changes occur all the time in the travel world, and Fodor's cannot accept responsibility for facts that become outdated or for inadvertent errors or omissions. So **always confirm information when it matters,** especially if you're making a detour to visit a specific place. Your experiences—positive and negative—matter to us. If we have missed or misstated something, **please write to us.** We follow up on all suggestions. Contact the Germany editor at editors@fodors.com or c/o Fodor's at 1745 Broadway, New York, NY 10019.

PRINTED IN THE UNITED STATES OF AMERICA

10 9 8 7 6 5 4 3 2 1

Be a Fodor's Correspondent

Your opinion matters. It matters to us. It matters to your fellow Fodor's travelers, too. And we'd like to hear it. In fact, we need to hear it.

When you share your experiences and opinions, you become an active member of the Fodor's community. That means we'll not only use your feedback to make our books better, but we'll publish your names and comments whenever possible. Throughout our guides, look for "Word of Mouth," excerpts of your unvarnished feedback.

Here's how you can help improve Fodor's for all of us.

Tell us when we're right. We rely on local writers to give you an insider's perspective. But our writers and staff editors—who are the best in the business—depend on you. Your positive feedback is a vote to renew our recommendations for the next edition.

Tell us when we're wrong. We're proud that we update most of our guides every year. But we're not perfect. Things change. Hotels cut services. Museums change hours. Charming cafés lose charm. If our writer didn't quite capture the essence of a place, tell us how you'd do it differently. If any of our descriptions are inaccurate or inadequate, we'll incorporate your changes in the next edition and will correct factual errors at fodors.com immediately.

Tell us what to include. You probably have had fantastic travel experiences that aren't yet in Fodor's. Why not share them with a community of like-minded travelers? Maybe you chanced upon a beach or bistro or B&B that you don't want to keep to yourself. Tell us why we should include it. And share your discoveries and experiences with everyone directly at fodors.com. Your input may lead us to add a new listing or highlight a place we cover with a "Highly Recommended" star or with our highest rating, "Fodor's Choice."

Give us your opinion instantly at our feedback center at www.fodors.com/feedback. You may also e-mail editors@fodors.com with the subject line "Germany Editor." Or send your nominations, comments, and complaints by mail to Germany Editor, Fodor's, 1745 Broadway, New York, NY 10019.

You and travelers like you are the heart of the Fodor's community. Make our community richer by sharing your experiences. Be a Fodor's correspondent.

Gute Reise!

Tim Jarrell, Publisher

CONTENTS

CONTENTS

ABOUT THIS BOOK

Our Ratings

Sometimes you find terrific travel experiences and sometimes they just find you. But usually the burden is on you to select the right combination of experiences. That's where our ratings come in.

As travelers we've all discovered a place so wonderful that its worthiness is obvious. And sometimes that place is so experiential that superlatives don't do it justice: you just have to be there to know. These sights, properties, and experiences get our highest rating, **Fodor's Choice**, indicated by orange stars throughout this book.

Black stars highlight sights and properties we deem **Highly Recommended**, places that our writers, editors, and readers praise again and again for consistency and excellence.

By default, there's another category: any place we include in this book is by definition worth your time, unless we say otherwise. And we will.

Disagree with any of our choices? Care to nominate a place or suggest that we rate one more highly? Visit our feedback center at www. fodors.com/feedback.

Budget Well

Hotel and restaurant price categories from ¢ to $$$$ are defined in the opening pages of each chapter. For attractions, we always give standard adult admission fees; reductions are usually available for children, students, and senior citizens. Want to pay with plastic? **AE, D, DC, MC, V** following restaurant and hotel listings indicate whether American Express, Discover, Diners Club, MasterCard, and Visa are accepted.

Restaurants

Unless we state otherwise, restaurants are open for lunch and dinner daily. We mention dress only when there's a specific requirement and reservations only when they're essential or not accepted—it's always best to book ahead.

Hotels

Hotels have private bath, phone, TV, and air-conditioning and operate on the European Plan (a.k.a. EP, meaning without meals), unless we specify that they use the Continental Plan (CP, with a Continental breakfast), Breakfast Plan (BP, with a full breakfast), or Modified American Plan (MAP, with breakfast and dinner), or are all-inclusive (including all meals

and most activities). We always list facilities but not whether you'll be charged an extra fee to use them, so when pricing accommodations, find out what's included.

Many Listings

★	Fodor's Choice
★	Highly recommended
✉	Physical address
✚	Directions
🕮	Mailing address
☎	Telephone
🖷	Fax
⊕	On the Web
✍	E-mail
💷	Admission fee
☉	Open/closed times
Ⓜ	Metro stations
▭	Credit cards

Hotels & Restaurants

🏨	Hotel
🛏	Number of rooms
⚿	Facilities
⦿	Meal plans
✕	Restaurant
🖙	Reservations
✕🏨	Hotel with restaurant that warrants a visit

Other

☾	Family-friendly
⇨	See also
✉	Branch address
☞	Take note

1

Experience Germany

WORD OF MOUTH

"You don't have to stay in Munich to enjoy Oktoberfest. We have stayed in Garmisch-Partenkirchen
and in Pfaffenhofen and taken the train in. The walk
from the U-Bahn to the fest is short. Also many of the
towns around Bavaria have local fests. We did a
fest in Pfaffenhofen the week before Oktoberfest."
— norrisken

WHAT'S WHERE

The following numbers refer to chapter numbers.

2 Munich. If Germany has a second capital, it must be Munich. Munich boasts wonderful opera, theater, museums, and churches, but the main appeal is its laid-back attitude, appreciated best in its parks, cafés, and beer gardens.

3 The Bavarian Alps. Majestic peaks, lush green pastures, and frescoed houses brightened by flowers make for Germany's most photogenic region. Quaint villages like Mittenwald, Garmisch-Partenkirchen, Oberammergau, and Berchtesgaden have preserved their charming historic architecture. Regardless of the season, nature is the prime attraction here, with the country's finest hiking and skiing.

4 The Romantic Road. The Romantische Strasse is more than 355 km (220 mi) of soaring castles, medieval villages, half-timber houses, and imposing churches, all set against a pastoral backdrop. Winding its way from Würzburg to Füssen, it features such top destinations as Rothenburg-ob-der-Tauber and Schloss Neuschwanstein, King Ludwig II's fantastical castle.

5 Franconia & the German Danube. Thanks to the centuries-old success of craftsmanship and trade, Franconia is a proud, independent-minded region in northern Bavaria. Franconia offers plenty of outdoor diversions as well as urban treasures such as Nürnberg's famed Christkindlmarkt in December.

6 The Bodensee. The sunniest region in the country, the Bodensee (Lake Constance) itself is the highlight. The region is surrounded by beautiful mountains and the dense natural surroundings offer an enchanting contrast to the picture-perfect towns and manicured gardens.

7 The Black Forest. Synonymous with cuckoo clocks and primeval woodland that is great for hiking, the Black Forest includes the historic university town of Freiburg—one of the most colorful and hippest student cities in Germany—and proud and mercurial Baden-Baden, with its long tradition of spas and casinos.

8 Heidelberg & the Neckar Valley. This medieval town is quintessential Germany, full of cobblestone alleys, half-timber houses, vineyards, castles, wine pubs, and Germany's oldest university—all of which attract crowds of camera-carrying vacationers. Still, if you're looking for a fairy-tale town, Heidelberg is it.

Münster

NORTH RHIN WESTPHALI

Dortmund

Hagen

Düsseldorf

Cologne/Köln

Aachen

Bonn

Sieg

Rhine

Koblenz

RHINELAND-PALATINATE

Wiesbade

Mainz

Bingen

Mosel

Trier

Worm

SAARLAND

Ludwigshaf

Speye

Saarbrücken

Baden-Baden

0   50 mi
0   50 km

Offenbu

Rhine (Rhein)

7

Bla For

Freiburg

FRANCE

Rheinfelden

SWITZERLAND

WHAT'S WHERE

9 Frankfurt. Nicknamed "Mainhattan" because it is the only German city with appreciable skyscrapers, Frankfurt is Germany's financial center and transportation hub.

10 The Pfalz & Rhine Terrace. Wine reigns supreme here. Bacchanalian festivals pepper the calendar between May and October, and wineries welcome drop-ins for tastings year-round. Three great cathedrals are found in Worms, Speyer, and Mainz.

11 The Rhineland. The region along the mighty Rhine River is one of the most dynamic in all of Europe. Fascinating cities such as Köln (Cologne), steeped in Roman and medieval history, offer stunning symbols of Gothic architecture, such as the Kölner Dom. Visit during Karneval for boisterous celebrations.

12 The Fairy-Tale Road. The Märchenstrasse, stretching 600 km (370 mi) between Hanau and Bremen, is definitely the brothers Grimm country. They nourished their dark and magical imaginations as children in Steinau an der Strasse, a beautiful medieval town in this region of misty woodlands and ancient castles.

13 Hamburg. Hamburg loves to be snobbish, and the Hanseaten can be a little stiff, but the city, dominated by lakes, canals, the river Elbe, and Germany's biggest harbor, is undeniably beautiful. World-class museums of modern art, the Reeperbahn, and a new warehouse quarter make Hamburg worth the visit.

14 Schleswig-Holstein & the Baltic Coast. Off the beaten path, this region is scattered with medieval towns, fishing villages, unspoiled beaches, and summer resorts like Sylt, where Germany's jet set go to get away.

15 Berlin. No trip to Germany is complete without a visit to Berlin—Europe's hippest urban destination. Dirty, noisy, and overcrowded, it has an intensity that makes it a unique laboratory for new trends and ideas. Cutting-edge art exhibits, stage dramas, musicals, and rock bands compete for your attention with two cities' worth of world-class museums and historical sights.

16 Saxony, Saxony-Anhalt & Thuringia. The southeast is a secret treasure trove of German high culture. Friendly, vibrant cities like Dresden, Leipzig, Weimar, and Eisenach are linked to Schiller, Goethe, Bach, Luther, and the like.

Sy

No

East Frisian Islands

Norden

Wilhelmshaven

Emden

Oldenburg

Ems

Osnabrüc

Münster

NORTH RHINE-WESTPHALIA

Essen   Dortmund

Hagen

Düsseldorf

Cologne/Köln

Aachen

Sieg

Bonn

Rhine

11 Koblenz

RHINELAND-PALATINATE

Wiesbad

Mainz

Bingen

Mosel

Trier

10 Worm

Mannheir

SAARLAND   Ludwigshafen

Sylt
Niebüll
Flensburg

DENMARK
Rodbyhavn
Gedser

Husum · **14**

Rügen

Baltic Sea

Kiel

Fehmarn

Stralsund

SCHLESWIG-
HOLSTEIN

Neustadt

Greifswald

Rendsburg

North Sea

Rostock · MECKLENBURG-
VORPOMMERN

Usedom

Cuxhaven

Lübeck · **13**

Wismar

Güstrow

Anklam

Elbe

Schwerin

Teterow

Neubrandenburg

Bremerhaven

HAMBURG

Hamburg

Waren

Ludwigslust

Neustrelitz

Bremen

FORMER BORDER
BETWEEN EAST AND
WEST GERMANY

Elbe

Wittenberge

Oder

BREMEN

LOWER SAXONY

Stendal

Oranienburg

Hanover

Brandenburg

Berlin · **15**
Potsdam

ck

Braunschweig

BRANDENBURG

Frankfurt-
an-der-Oder

12

Magdeburg

Bielefeld

Hildesheim

Halberstadt

Wittenberg

Lübben

Cottbus

Dessau

Göttingen

HARZ
MOUNTAINS

SAXONY-
ANHALT

Saale

16

Nordhausen

Elbe

Kassel

Halle

Leipzig

Meissen

Dresden

Buchenwald

Eisenach
Erfurt

Weimar

SAXONY

egen

Bad Hersfeld

Gera

Chemnitz

Marburg

Alsfeld

Ilmenau

Zwickau

HESSEN

Thüringer
Wald

THURINGIA

Plauen

Bad Homburg
Offenbach

Fulda

Meiningen

Hof

den · **9**

Coburg

Münchberg

Frankfurt-am-Main

Bamberg

Bayreuth

CZECH REPUBLIC

Taunus

Darmstadt

Main

ms

im
n

Würzburg

Fürth · Nuremberg

0 _____ 100 miles
0 _____ 150 km

GERMANY PLANNER

When to Go

A year-round destination, Germany is particularly wonderful in August and September for the long warm days that stretch sightseeing hours and are perfect for relaxing in beer gardens.

In the north, January can be dark and cold, with a constant wind that cuts to the bone. Southern Germany, on the other hand, is a great winter destination, with world-class skiing, spas, and wellness options.

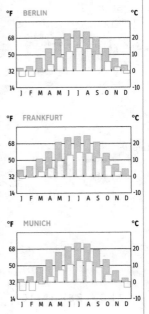

Getting Here

Most flights into Germany arrive at Frankfurt's Flughafen Frankfurt Main (FRA) or Munich's Flughafen München (MUC). Flying time to Frankfurt is 1½ hours from London, 7½ hours from New York, 10 hours from Chicago, and 12 hours from Los Angeles. Some international carriers serve Köln (Cologne), Hamburg, and Berlin. Germany is well connected by train to most European destinations. Cruise ships often call at Rostock and there are ferry services to Harwich from Hamburg.

Getting Around

Once in Germany you can travel by train, car, bus, or air. Keep in mind tickets with flexible schedules cost more.

Travel by train is the most relaxing and often fastest way to go. The Deutsche Bahn (German Railroad) serves most destinations with relative frequency, speed, and comfort. Train stations are usually in the city center, and tickets are always less expensive online or from ticket machines than from ticket agents.

Domestic air travel can be cheaper than the train, especially from Munich to Hamburg or Cologne and Berlin to Munich or Cologne. Air Berlin, GermanWings, and Lufthansa offer very low fares on inter-German routes.

All major car-rental companies are represented in Germany. Gasoline is very expensive (about €5.50 per gallon), and parking in major cities can be difficult. Nevertheless, a car gives you the flexibility to explore on your own, and is one of the best options in the Bavarian Alps. Most cars in Germany have manual transmission.

A few rules of the road to remember: Children under 10 may not ride in the front seat, and seatbelts are required of all passengers. Large German cities like Berlin require all cars to have an environmental inspection before entering the city center—rental cars and foreign visitors are not exempt. Always pay the parking meter and obey speed limits.

Dining: The Basics

Daily specials, or *Tageskarten*, offer regional specialties or seasonal produce.

In most restaurants it is not customary to wait to be seated. Simply walk in and take any unreserved space. When in doubt, ask.

German restaurants do not automatically serve water. If you order water, you will be served mineral water and be expected to pay for it. The concept of free refills or the bottomless cup of coffee is also completely foreign.

Tipping: When you get the check, round up to the next even euro. Add a euro if the total is more than €20. For larger amounts, rounding up and adding 5% is appropriate.

German waitstaff are more than happy to split the check so that everyone can pay individually. Remember to pay the waiter directly; do not place the money on the table and leave.

Credit cards are increasing in popularity, but are not universally accepted. When in doubt, ask.

Lodging: The Basics

The standards of German hotels are very high. The *Gasthöfe* (country inns that serve food and also have rooms) offer a great value. An alternative to hotels are *Fremdenzimmer,* meaning simply "rooms," normally in private houses. Look for the sign reading ZIMMER FREI (room available) or ZU VERMIETEN (to rent) on a green background; a red sign reading BESETZT means there are no vacancies. For a taste of rural life, try an *Urlaub auf dem Bauernhof,* a farm that rents rooms. You can also opt to stay at a winery's *Winzerhof* or at an historic castle (*Schloss*). The country's hundreds of *Jugendherbergen* (youth hostels) are among the most efficient and up-to-date in Europe.

Prices are generally higher in summer, so consider visiting during the off-season (but be aware that some attractions are closed or have shorter hours in winter). Most resorts offer between-season (*Zwischensaison*) and edge-of-season (*Nebensaison*) rates, and tourist offices can provide lists of hotels that offer low-price weekly packages (*Pauschal-angebote*).

It's wise to avoid cities during major trade fairs as rates skyrocket. Consider staying in nearby towns and commuting in.

Social Mores

When addressing someone always use the formal *Sie* until you are begged by them to switch to the informal *du*. When in doubt, shake hands; both as a greeting and at parting.

It's polite to ask if someone speaks English (*Sprechen Sie Englisch?*) before addressing them in English.

It is acceptable in casual conversation to tactfully mention World War II.

Dress & Undress

Casual clothes and jeans can be worn just about anywhere as long as they're neat. When visiting churches, dress conservatively—shorts and halter tops are not appropriate.

Don't be surprised to find nude sunbathers, even in the most public parks. It's also normal to see children running around without clothes on in parks, at swimming pools, or at the beach.

Tipping

■ Tip tour guides €2–€5 per person.

■ Taxi drivers tack on extra fees for additional bags, so round up to the next euro and add one, but no more than €2.

■ Doormen, room-service, and housekeeping staff do not expect gratuities, but €1 is certainly appropriate.

TOP GERMANY ATTRACTIONS

Museumsinsel (Museum Island), Berlin

(A) Germany's capital boasts over 150 museums, but this UNESCO World Heritage site is the absolute must-see. It is in fact a complex of five state museums, the oldest being the Altes Museum, built in 1830, with a permanent collection of Classical Antiquities. The Alte Nationalgalerie houses an outstanding collection of 18th- to early 20th-century paintings and sculptures from the likes of Cézanne, Rodin, Degas, and Germany's own Max Liebermann. The Bode-Museum contains German and Italian sculptures, Byzantine art, and coins. The Pergamonmuseum's highlight is the world-famous Pergamon Altar, a Greek temple dating from 180 BC.

Luther's Country

(B) Eastern Germany was home to Martin Luther and the Protestant Reformation. It was in the little town of Lutherstadt-Wittenberg where the young priest, enraged that the Roman Catholic Church was pardoning sins through the sale of indulgences, nailed his 95 Theses to the Schlosskirche (Castle Church) in 1517. The town is dedicated to preserving his legacy through period re-enactments and the Lutherhaus museum. You can also see where Frederick the Wise hid Luther for almost a year in the incredible Wartburg castle in Eisenach and visit the reformer's home in Eisleben, where he was born and died.

Munich's Oktoberfest

(C) For 12 days at the end of September and into early October, Munich hosts the world's largest beer bonanza. Originally, the festival celebrated the marriage of Theresa von Sachsen to Ludwig I in 1810. It proved to be such a success that it soon morphed into a yearly festival, one that now welcomes over 6 million visitors and serves more than 5 million liters of beer.

Many other cities celebrate Oktoberfest, but it's hard to beat the original.

Neuschwanstein Castle

(D) Look familiar? Walt Disney modeled the castle in *Sleeping Beauty* and later the Disneyland castle itself on Neuschwanstein. Its position at the end of the Romantic Road only adds to its fairy-tale quality. "Mad" King Ludwig II's creation is best admired from the heights of the Marienbrücke, a delicate-looking bridge over a deep, narrow gorge.

Frauenkirche, Dresden

(E) Dresden's Church of Our Lady is a masterpiece of baroque architecture. Completed in 1743, the magnificent domed church was destroyed as a result of Allied bombing in February 1945. The church ruins stood as a war memorial for 50 years until German reunification provided the impetus to rebuild it. Amazingly, the church was largely rebuilt from the original rubble, and entirely through private donations.

Roman Ruins, Trier

(F) Founded in 16 BC as Augusta Treverorum, Trier is Germany's oldest city and home to some of the best Roman architecture on the continent. The remnants of the town's fortifications, especially the Porta Nigra (*Black Gate*); thermal baths; and amphitheater, where you can still see gladiators battle it out, testify to over four centuries of Roman rule.

Bodensee (Lake Constance)

(G) The largest lake in Germany, which shares shores with Switzerland and Austria, is actually not a lake at all but a swelling of the Rhine River. This is one of the warmest and sunniest resort areas in the country, and a great place for water sports, sailing, and biking.

QUINTESSENTIAL GERMANY

Meeting at the Market

The tradition of market shopping still thrives in Germany, especially in cities. On market day, often Saturday, a square or small street is closed to traffic, and vendors—from butchers to beekeepers— set up stands. You'll see fewer grand- mothers and more fashionably dressed thirtysomethings selecting from seven kinds of breads at the baker or organic (Bio) vegetables from the hippie farmer. When it comes to Christmastime, Ger- man markets are world famous. Every- thing you need to celebrate the holiday is sold at the *Weihnachtsmarkt* (Christmas market): handmade wooden ornaments from the Erzgebirge (Erz Mountains), *Stollen* (a breadlike fruitcake) from Dresden, and *Lebkuchen* (gingerbread) from Nürnberg. The cold may come in, but big-store consumerism is out, mak- ing even shopping for Christmas gifts an enjoyable fresh-air experience.

Kaffe und Kuchen

The tradition of afternoon coffee and cake, usually around 3 PM, is a serious matter especially in Bavaria and Saxony. Germans bake over a thousand different kinds of cakes; although every town and region has its own special cake or pas- try, the undisputed king is the famous *Schwarzwälder Kirschtorte* (Black Forest Cake), a chocolate layer cake, soaked in *Kirsch* schnapps, complete with cherries, whipped cream, and chocolate shavings. Two more to try are the *Sachertorte*, a dense chocolate cake made famous by the Sacher hotel in Vienna, and the *Bienen- stich* (bee sting), a layered sponge-cake, filled with cream and topped with a layer of crunchy honey-caramelized almonds. Pistachio marzipan is another do not miss. If you're feeling extra decadent, order your cake *mit Schlagsahne*, with extra whipped cream on the side.

If you want to get a sense of contemporary German culture and indulge in some of its pleasures, start by familiarizing yourself with the rituals of daily life.

Karneval

Every year on November 11, tradition dictates that women plant kisses upon the cheeks or lips of their choice—a fine start to the long Karneval season that ends the night before Ash Wednesday. In Germany, the Rhineland celebrates this Catholic festival, also called Fasching, with the most traditions; and the epicenter of revelry is Köln (Cologne).

The final days of the "fifth season" begin with *Weiberfestnacht*, a day when women doll themselves up and get into all sorts of mischief, including cutting off men's ties. For the next four days and nights business in Köln nearly grinds to a halt, and copious amounts of the local brew, Kölsch, fuel evenings of masked balls and parties, culminating in the main parade on Rosenmontag (the Monday before "Fat Tuesday").

More Beer, Bitte

The ideal beer is simply one enjoyed in the fresh air of a Biergarten. A beer garden, such as the famous Chinese Pavilion in Munich's English Garden, might seat hundreds. Or, it could simply be a café's back garden of gravel and soaring chestnut trees. You can enjoy a liquid lunch, or go to self-serve areas that might offer pastas or lamb in addition to grilled sausages and pretzels. While beer gardens are found all over Germany, the smoky beer hall experience—with dirndls and oompah bands—is unique to Bavaria. One in three of the world's breweries is in Germany, some strongly associated with a city, others available primarily within their state, and many which cross borders. Try the local brews, and discover how different the combination of four key ingredients—malt, hops, yeast, and water—can taste.

IF YOU LIKE

Being Outdoors

Germans have a long-standing love affair with mother nature, and have designated large tracts of land as national recreation areas and urban parks and gardens. Cities have created many miles of bike paths, especially along waterways, and in places such as **Würzburg** you can set off along the river and reach pure countryside within 30 minutes.

The most unusual landscape in the country is 30 km (19 mi) south of Dresden in the **Sächsische Schweiz**, a national park of twisting gorges and sheer cliffs. Rock climbers fascinate those driving up the steep switchbacks to reach bald mesas. At a much higher altitude are the Bavarian Alps, where the Winter Olympics town **Garmisch-Partenkirchen** offers cable cars to ascend Germany's highest mountain. This is one of the country's best spots for skiing in the winter and hiking in the summer.

Lakes such as **Chiemsee** and **Bodensee** dot the area between the Alps and Munich and many hikers and bikers enjoy circling them. Boat rentals are possible, but you'll often need a German-recognized license. On the island of **Rügen**, the turn-of-the-20th-century resort town **Binz** fronts the gentle (and cold) waters of the Baltic Sea. Even on windy days you can warm up on the beach in a sheltered beach chair for two. The Baltic Coast's most dramatic features are Rügen's white chalk cliffs in **Jasmund National Park,** where you can hike, bike, or sign up for nature seminars and tours.

Medieval Towns

The trail of walled towns and half-timber houses known as the **Romantic Road** is a route long marketed by German tourism, and therefore the road more traveled. The towns are lovely, but if you'd prefer fewer tour groups spilling into your photographs, venture into the **Harz Mountains** in the center of Germany.

Goslar, the unofficial capital of the Harz region, is one of Germany's oldest cities, and is renowned for its Romanesque Kaiserpfalz, an imperial palace where emperors held diets. Goslar has been declared a UNESCO World Heritage site, as has the town of **Quedlinburg,** 48 km (30 mi) to the southeast. With 1,600 half-timber houses, Quedlinburg has more of these historic, typically northern German buildings than any other town in the country.

A mighty fortress south of the Harz Mountains is the **Wartburg,** in the ancient, half-timber town of **Eisenach.** Frederick the Wise protected Martin Luther from papal proscription within these stout walls in the 16th century.

Options for exploring closer to Munich include **Regensburg** and **Nürnberg.** The former is a beautiful medieval city, relatively unknown even to Germans, and has a soaring French Gothic cathedral that can hold 6,000 people. Nürnberg dates to 1050, and is among the most historic cities in the country. Not only emperors but artists convened here, including the Renaissance genius Albrecht Dürer.

The Arts

Leipzig is definitely the "new" star in the European art world. The city owns one of the finest collections of art in Germany. The **Museum der Bildenden Künste** (Museum of Fine Arts) is the city's leading gallery, followed closely by the **Grassimuseum** complex. The **Spinnerei** (a former cotton mill) has become Leipzig's prime location for contemporary art, and houses more than 80 artists and galleries, especially those of the New Leipzig School.

If you're interested in buying works by German or international artists, **Köln (Cologne)** has the largest concentration of galleries—though most of the artists are working in affordable studios in **Berlin**.

The capital shows its art in small galleries and major museums like Mies van der Rohe's **New National Gallery**. The **Berlinische Galerie** dedicates itself to art, photography, and architecture created in the city from 1870 to the present. The must-see and -hear music venue in the city is the acoustically exceptional **Berlin Philharmonic**.

In summer many orchestras and opera houses shut down for the season, and outdoor music festivals substitute for arriving tourists. In Bayreuth the **Wagner Festival** is an important indoor exception.

Fans of old master painters must haunt the halls of the **Zwinger** in Dresden, where most works were collected in the first half of the 18th century, and the **Alte Pinakothek** in Munich, which has one of the world's largest collections of Rubens. Throughout the country, opera and concert tickets can be very inexpensive, but you must book tickets far in advance, as Germany is home to many music lovers.

Castles & Palaces

Watching over nearly any town whose name ends in "-burg" is a medieval fortress or Renaissance palace, often now serving the populace as a museum, restaurant, or hotel.

The **Wartburg** in Eisenach is considered "the mother of all castles," and broods over the foothills of the Thuringian Forest. Supple vineyards surround **Schloss Neuenburg**, which dominates the landscape around the sleepy village of Freyburg (Unstrut). The castle ruins overlooking the Rhine River are the result of ceaseless fighting with the French, but even their remains were picturesque enough to inspire 19th-century Romantics. The island fortress of **Pfalzgrafenstein** re-creates sparse, medieval living quarters, while just across the Rhine **Burg Rheinstein** is rich with Gobelin tapestries, stained glass, and frescoes.

Schloss Heidelberg mesmerizes with its Gothic turrets, Renaissance walls, and abandoned gardens. Other fortresses lord over the Burgenstrasse (Castle Road) in the neighboring **Neckar Valley.** You can stay the night (or just enjoy an excellent meal) at the castles of **Hirschhorn** or **Burg Hornberg,** or at any of a number of other castle-hotels in the area.

Louis XIV's Versailles inspired Germany's greatest castle-builder, King Ludwig II, to construct the opulent **Schloss Herrenchiemsee**. One of Ludwig's palaces in turn inspired a latter-day visionary—his **Schloss Neuschwanstein** is the model for Walt Disney's Sleeping Beauty Castle. **Schloss Linderhof**, also in the Bavarian Alps, was Ludwig's favorite retreat, and the only one of the royal residences completed in his lifetime.

GREAT ITINERARIES

GERMAN ABCS: ARCHITECTURE, BEER & CAPITAL CITIES

Day 1: Arrival Munich

Though it is a wealthy city with Wittelsbach palaces, great art collections, and a technology museum holding trains, planes, and even an imitation coal mine, what really distinguishes Munich from other state capitals are its beer halls, beer gardens, and proud identity: even designer-conscious Müncheners wear traditional dirndls and hunter-green jackets for special occasions. Stroll the streets of the Altstadt (Old City), visit the Frauenkirche, choose a museum (the best ones will occupy you for at least three hours), and save the Hofbräuhaus or any other teeming brew house for last. Munich might be touristy, but hordes of German tourists love it as well. ⇨ *See Chapter 2, Munich*

Day 2: Neuschwanstein

From Munich it's an easy day trip to Germany's fairy-tale castle in Schwangau. Though the 19th-century castle's fantastic silhouette has made it famous, this creation of King Ludwig II is more opera set than piece of history—the interior was never even completed. A tour reveals why the romantic king earned the nickname "Mad" King Ludwig. Across the narrow wooded valley from Schloss Neuschwanstein is the ancient castle of the Bavarian Wittelsbach dynasty, Schloss Hohenschwangau, also open for tours. ⇨ *See Chapter 4, The Romantic Road*

Day 3: Munich to Dresden

That Saxony's capital, Dresden, is the pinnacle of European baroque is obvious in its courtyards, newly rebuilt Frauenkirche, and terrace over the Elbe River. The city was largely shaped by Augustus

TRAVEL TIPS

■ It's likely you'll use public transit at least three times a day in Berlin: buy day passes for a better value. If your week ends with an early flight out of Munich on Day 7, take a train from Berlin in the late afternoon on Day 6. The journey takes 5 hours.

the Strong, who in 1730 kindly invited the public to view the works crafted from precious stones in his Green Vault. Many of Dresden's art treasures lie within the Zwinger, a baroque showpiece. Spend the evening at the neo-Renaissance Semper Opera, where Wagner premiered his works, and drink Radeberger Pilsner at intermission. It's the country's oldest pilsner. ⇨ *See Chapter 16, Saxony, Saxony-Anhalt & Thuringia*

Day 4: Dresden & Berlin

Spend the morning touring some of Dresden's rich museums before boarding a train to Berlin. Germany's capital is not only unique for its division between 1949 and 1989, but is unlike any other German city in its physical expanse and diversity. Attractions that don't close until 10 PM or later are Sir Norman Foster's glass dome on the Reichstag, the TV tower at Alexanderplatz, and the Checkpoint Charlie Museum. ⇨ *See chapters 15 and 16, Berlin and Saxony, Saxony-Anhalt & Thuringia*

Days 5 & 6: Berlin

Begin your first Berlin morning on a walk with one of the city's excellent tour companies. They'll connect the broadly spaced dots for you and make the events of Berlin's turbulent 20th century clear. Berlin is a fascinating city in and of itself, so you don't have to feel guilty if you don't get to many museums. Since the mid-1990s, world-renowned architects have changed the city's face. You'll find the best nightlife in residential areas such as Prenzlauer Berg, Kreuzberg, or the northern part of Mitte. Berlin is a surprisingly inexpensive city, so you can treat yourself to more here than in Munich. ⇨See Chapter 15, Berlin

Day 7: Munich

On your last day, have breakfast with the morning shoppers at the open-air Viktualienmarkt. Try to find *Weisswurst* (white sausage), a mild, boiled sausage normally eaten before noon with sweet mustard, a pretzel—and beer! ⇨See Chapter 2, Munich

CASTLES IN WINE COUNTRY

Day 1: Arrival Koblenz/the Rhineland

Start your tour in Koblenz, at the confluence of the rivers Rhine and Mosel. Once you have arrived in the historic downtown area, head straight for the charming little Hotel Zum weissen Schwanen, a half-timber inn and mill since 1693. Explore the city on the west bank of the Rhine River and then head to Europe's biggest fortress, the impressive Festung Ehrenbreitstein on the opposite riverbank. ⇨ See Chapter 11, The Rhineland

Day 2: Koblenz & Surrounding Castles

Get up early and drive along the most spectacular and historic section of "Vater Rhein." Stay on the left riverbank and you'll pass many mysterious landmarks on the way, including Burg Stolzenfels, and later the Loreley rock, a 430-foot slate cliff named after a legendary, beautiful, blonde nymph. Stay the night at St. Goar

---

TRAVEL TIPS

■ St. Goar is on the left riverbank, St. Goarhausen is on the right; a ferry goes back and forth between them. On Day 3, you'll want to be on the right riverbank to continue southeast by car on B–42 to Eltville.

---

or St. Goarshausen, both lovely river villages. ⇨See Chapter 11, The Rhineland

Day 3: Eltville & the Eberbach Monastery

The former Cistercian monastery Kloster Eberbach, in Eltville, is one of Europe's best-preserved medieval cloisters. Parts of the film *The Name of the Rose*, based on Umberto Eco's novel and starring Sean Connery, were filmed here. If you're interested in wine, spend the night at the historic wine estate Schloss Reinhartshausen. This is a great opportunity to sample the fantastic wines of the region. ⇨See Chapter 11, The Rhineland

Day 4: Heidelberg

On Day 4, start driving early so you can spend a full day in Heidelberg (the drive from Eltville takes about an hour). No other city symbolizes German spirit and history better than this meticulously restored, historic town. Do not miss the impressive Schloss, one of Europe's greatest Gothic-Renaissance fortresses. Most of the many pubs and restaurants here are very touristy, overpriced, and of poor quality—so don't waste your time at them. Instead, head for the Romantik Hotel zum Ritter St. Georg, a charming 16th-century inn with a great traditional German restaurant. ⇨See Chapter 8, Heidelberg & the Neckar Valley

GREAT ITINERARIES

Days 5 & 6: The Burgenstrasse & the Neckar Valley
Superb food and wine can be enjoyed in the quaint little villages in the Neckar Valley just east of Heidelberg—the predominant grapes here are Riesling (white) and Spätburgunder (red). Try to sample wines from small, private wineries—they tend to have higher-quality vintages. Sightseeing is equally stunning, with a string of castles and ruins along the famous Burgenstrasse (Castle Road). Since you have two days for this area, take your time and follow B–37 to Eberbach and its romantic Zwingenberg castle, tucked away in the deep forest just outside the village. In the afternoon, continue on to Burg Hornberg at Neckarzimmern, the home to the legendary German knight Götz von Berlichingen. Stay the night here, in the former castle stables.

The next morning, continue farther to Bad Wimpfen, the most charming valley town at the confluence of the Neckar and Jagst rivers. Spend half a day in the historic city center and tour the Staufer Pfalz (royal palace). Soaring high above the city, the palace was built in 1182, and emperor Barbarossa liked to stay here. ⇨ *See Chapter 8, Heidelberg & the Neckar Valley*

Day 7: German Wine Route
Devote your last day to the German Wine Route, which winds its way through one of the most pleasant German landscapes, the gentle slopes and vineyards of the Pfalz. The starting point for the route is Bad Dürkheim, a spa town proud to have the world's largest wine cask, holding 1.7 million liters (450,000 gallons). You can enjoy wine with some lunch in the many Weinstuben here or wait until you reach Neustadt farther south, Germany's largest wine-growing community. Thirty of the vintages grown here can be sampled (and purchased) at the downtown Haus des Weines. If time permits, try to visit one of the three major castles along the route in the afternoon: Burg Trifels near Annweiler is a magnificent Hohenzollern residence, perched dramatically on three sandstone cliffs, the very image of a medieval castle in wine country. ⇨ *See Chapter 10, The Pfalz & the Rhine Terrace*

ON THE CALENDAR

		Germany ranks number one in the world for the number of foreign visitors attending fairs and exhibitions. Oktoberfest in Munich is by far the best-known festival, but there are many others to plan a trip around. For event listings, see the German National Tourist Office's Web site (⊕*www.germany-tourism.de*).
WINTER	December	**Christmas Markets,** outdoor festivals of light, choral and trumpet music, handcrafted gift items, and mulled wine (*Glühwein*), are held in just about every German city. Dresden's and Nürnberg's are the most famous.
		New Year's Eve is a noisy, fireworks-filled event in Berlin.
	January	Ostensibly a 10-day farm show, **Internationale Grüne Woche** (*Green Week* ⊕*www.gruenewoche.com*) draws thousands to Berlin's convention center with its produce and fine edibles.
	February	The Rhineland is Germany's **Karneval** capital, though many other regions celebrate it as well. Festivities always run through February, finishing on Fasching Dienstag (Shrove or Fat Tuesday).
		Frankfurt International Fair is a major consumer-goods trade fair.
		International Filmfestspiele Berlin (⊕*www.berlinale.de*) is one of Europe's leading film festivals.
		The **International Toy Fair** takes place in Nürnberg.
	March	**ITB** (⊕*www.itb-berlin.de*), one of Europe's largest international tourism fairs, takes place in Berlin.
		Strong Beer Season in Munich brings out the bands and merrymaking in all the beer halls.
SPRING	April	**Spargelzeit** begins in late April, with the first white-asparagus harvest. Restaurants and cafés feature special asparagus menus.
		On the night before May Day, towns in the Harz Mountains celebrate **Walpurgis** with spooky, Halloween-like goings-on.
		Celebrate **Tag des Deutschen Bieres** (*German Beer Day*) on April 23: the anniversary of the German Beer Purity Law.

ON THE CALENDAR

May	By downing a huge tankard of wine in one gulp, a 17th-century mayor of Rothenburg-ob-der-Tauber saved the town from sacking. On Pentecost weekend his Meistertrunk is reenacted at a **Medieval Festival.**
	Religious processions are particularly spectacular in Catholic eastern Bavaria during Pentecost weekend. The best ones are at Bogen, Sankt Englmar, and Kötzting.
	With great fanfare, wine from the last year's harvest is introduced in April. Each of Germany's 13 growing regions holds tastings and festivals that culminate in the ubiquitous **Kellerfest** in May.
	May 2, 2009 is **German Sparkling Wine Day** (*Tag des Sektes*).
SUMMER May–September	**Rhine in Flames** (⊕*www.rlp-info.de*) highlights the river with fireworks, floodlighted castles, and a fleet of illuminated boats; it's held around Bonn (May), Rüdesheim (July), Koblenz (August), and St. Goar (September).
June	**Kiel Week** (⊕*www.kieler-woche.de*) is an international sailing regatta and cultural festival in the town of Kiel in Schleswig-Holstein.
June–September	**Castle Illuminations,** with spectacular fireworks, are presented in Heidelberg in June, July, and September.
	The **Schleswig-Holstein Music Festival** (⊕*www.shmf.de*) takes place over six weeks in July and August.
	Several hundred **Wine Festivals,** held throughout the 13 German wine-growing regions, celebrate local wine from early summer until the harvest in late autumn.
	Lutherstadt-Wittenberg celebrates the marriage of Martin Luther to Katharina von Bora the second weekend in June during **Luthers Hochzeit.**
July	**Kinderzeche** is Dinkelsbühl's medieval pageant and festival.
	The **Richard Wagner Festival** unfolds the Wagner operas in Bayreuth in July and August. Reserve well in advance; the waiting list for tickets is epic.
August	Berlin hosts the **International Beer Festival** (⊕*www.bierfestival-berlin.de*) on the first weekend in August, with over 300 breweries from around the globe, eighteen stages and hundreds of food stands.

		Kulmbach Beer Festival takes place in Franconia.
		Most villages and towns celebrate a medieval fair, or **Altstadtfest** in August.
FALL	September	Berlin Festival Weeks (⊕ *www.berlinerfestspiele.de*) feature classical music concerts, exhibits, and many other special events.
		Folk and Beer Festival at Stuttgart/Bad Cannstatt is said to be just as big and raucous as Munich's Oktoberfest.
		Oktoberfest (⊕ *www.muenchen-tourist.de*) in Munich (late September–early October) draws millions of visitors to cavernous beer tents and fairgrounds.
		Wurstmarkt, the world's largest wine festival, is held next to a giant cask in Bad Dürkheim.
	October	**Bremen Freimarkt** is a centuries-old folk festival and procession in Bremen.
		Frankfurt Book Fair is a famous annual literary event and a browser's paradise.
	November	**St. Martin's Festival** includes children's lantern processions and is celebrated throughout the Rhineland and Bavaria.
		Jazz Fest Berlin (⊕ *www.berlinerfestspiele.de*) is an international jazz festival held each autumn.

BEATING THE EURO

Travelers posting in the Travel Talk Forums at Fodors.com recommend the following budget-saving tips.

Food & Drink

"Look for the daily fixed price menus (Tagesmenu) posted outside many cafes or restaurants. Prices are usually under €10, depending on the location." —bettyk

"Munich's beer gardens have a BYO food tradition. You can get a lot of great food there, of course, but you can bring your own sandwiches or snacks and eat them there." —Cowboy1968

"We often ate at Turkish doner stands and cafes. When we did this dinner for two cost between 7 to 9 euros–(and it was always delicious!)" —outwest

Lodging

"In many large cities the main business of hotels isn't tourism but business travel. The times to avoid are trade fairs, when prices double or triple. On weekends many hotels might be nearly empty, and some offer special fares. A good tool is www.hrs.de." —Hans

"The best lodging bargains in Germany are apartments (Ferienwohnungen) and Fremdenzimmer and Privatzimmer at farms in the rural areas. It is still possible to find a single room for less than $25—double rooms and apartments for less than $50. Farm families are some of the friendliest people in Europe." —bavariaben

"We have rented vacation apartments on our last two trips to Germany and have been thrilled with the results. The prices are wonderful; 70 euros a night for two bedrooms. Each apartment had a balcony with wonderful views, a full kitchen and lots of room to relax." —tcreath

Sights

"We found the 3 day "SchauLUST Museen BERLIN" museum pass to be fantastic deal. They now cost €19 and provide for free admission to around 70 museums, including almost all of the major museums and some fine smaller collections. You will run out of time before you run out of good museums to visit." —noe847

"If you're visiting Bavaria and plan to tour through several castles & palaces, I would recommend the Bavarian Castle Pass as a budget tip. They offer a 14-day partner pass for €36. www.schloesser. bayern.de. We ended up saving €60 total." —artstuff

Sports & the Outdoors

"One of the best ways to SKI in Europe is to use the 'Ski Packages' that the Hotels/Pensions offer that usually include 2 meals and lift pass for 4, 5 or 6 days. By also using the shoulder season (before Christmas, and early January-mid February) you will get the best rates for the area." —bmw732002

Transportation

"For taxi rides in Berlin, if you are going under 2 km you can request a short trip (Kurtzstrecke) rate—3 euros as long as the trip is under 2 km. You must hail a moving cab—request the fare before the cabbie activates his meter. It can even be less expensive than public transport." —RufusTFirefly

Travel on the subway and regional trains (S-Bahn and U-Bahn) is really easy in Munich. Even if you do not speak a word of German, the stations are easy to navigate, the trains are easy to identify and maps are easy to find and understand." —kgh8m

Munich

2

WORD OF MOUTH

"I think München is one of the most beautiful European cities, beautifully preserved architecture, lovely residential quarters and friendly people"
—AndrewDavid

"I didn't have high expectations for Munich—we were there because we could get airline tickets using frequent flier miles and figured we would stay a day and head out. Then we started doing some research and decided to stay longer and use Munich as a base for day trips. We ended up liking Munich so much we only did 1 day trip and spent the rest of our time in town. I actually think I was hooked on Munich the first afternoon we were there."
—november_moon

Updated by
Uli Ehrhardt

KNOWN AS THE CITY OF "LAPTOPS AND LEDERHOSEN," Munich traces its history back to the 12th century, when it began as a market town on the "salt road" between mighty Salzburg and Augsburg. For all its business drive and the cosmopolitan style of its millionaires, Munich represents what the rest of the world sees as "typical Germany," embodied in the world-famous Oktoberfest, traditional *lederhosen* (leather pants), busty Bavarian waitresses in *dirndls* (traditional dresses), beer steins, and sausages. There are myriad local brews to say Prost (cheers) with, either in one of the cavernous beer halls or a smaller *Kneipe,* a bar where all types of people get together for meals and some drinks. When the first rays of spring sun begin warming the air, follow the locals to their beloved beer gardens, shaded by massive chestnut trees. Those around you might work at one of Germany's prestigious publishing houses, a top-notch digital postproduction company, or a world-class film studio. The concentration of electronics and computer firms—Siemens, Microsoft, and SAP, for example—makes the area a sort of Silicon Valley of Europe.

Respect for the fine arts is another Munich hallmark. "All-nighter" events throughout the year celebrate museum-going, literature, and musical performances. The city's appreciation of the arts began under the kings and dukes of the Wittelsbach Dynasty, which ruled Bavaria for more than 750 years until 1918. The Wittelsbach legacy is alive and well in the city's fabulous museums, the Opera House, the Philharmonic, and of course, the Residenz, the city's royal palace. Any walk in the city center will take you past ravishing baroque styling and grand 19th-century architecture.

Munich's cleanliness, safety, and Mediterranean pace give it an ever so slightly rustic feeling. The broad sidewalks, endless fashionable boutiques and eateries, views of the Alps, a sizeable river running through town, and a huge green park that easily gives Central Park a run for its money make Munich one of Germany's most enjoyable cities.

ORIENTATION & PLANNING

GETTING ORIENTED

In the relaxed and sunnier southern part of Germany, Munich (München) is the proud capital of the state of Bavaria. Even Germans come here to vacation, mixing the city's pleasures with the nearby natural surroundings—on clear days it's even possible to see the Alps from downtown. The city bills itself *"Die Weltstadt mit Herz"* ("the cosmopolitan city with heart"), but in rare bouts of self-deprecatory humor, friendly Bavarians will remind you that it isn't much more than a country town with a million people. It's the overall feeling of *Gemütlichkeit*—loosely translated as conviviality—that makes the place so special, with open-air markets, numerous parks, the lovely Isar River, and loads of beer halls.

TOP REASONS TO GO

Views from the Frauenkirche: This 14th-century church tower gives you a panorama of downtown Munich that cannot be beat. There are 86 steps in a circular shaft to get to the elevator, but it's worth it.

Deutsches Museum: The museum has a world-renowned collection of science and technology exhibits, and its location on the lovely Isar River is perfect for a relaxing afternoon stroll.

Street food: The Viktualienmarkt is a unique farmers'-market-style culinary shopping experience with fresh produce, Turkish finger food, and Argentine wine. Grab a snack, sit in the beer garden, and watch the world go by.

A lazy afternoon in Gärtnerplatz: Gärtnerplatz, 200 yards from Viktualienmarkt, is a relaxing roundabout with a few cafés where you can sit, have lunch, and enjoy Munich's hippest neighborhood before checking out the numerous trendy boutiques.

Englischer Garten: With expansive greens, picturesque lakes, a handful of beer gardens, and creeks running through it, the English Garden is a great place for a bike ride or a long walk. Enjoy a mug of cold beer at the Chinese Tower, take in the scenery, and snack on some local grub.

The City Center. The Marienplatz, Rathaus, and shopping streets radiating in all directions form a hub for both locals and tourists. Here you'll find the soaring towers of the Frauenkirche, Munich's landmark church. East of the Marienplatz, down towards the Isar River, is the maze of Old Town's smaller streets.

Royal Munich. Münchner, the inhabitants of Munich, will always be sure to inform you that the Residenz, or royal palace, is larger than Buckingham Palace in London. Bordering the Residenz to the north is the Hofgarten, or Palace Garden. Continue a bit farther northeast and you come to the Englischer Garten, where you can walk or ride a bicycle (or even a horse) for miles.

Schwabing & Maxvorstadt. One side of Maxvorstadt is made up of Ludwigstrasse, a wide avenue flanked by impressive buildings such as those of the university, running from the Feldherrnhalle and Odeonsplatz to the Victory Arch. A block farther west are Maxvorstadt's smaller streets, lined with shops and restaurants frequented by students. The big museums lie another two blocks west. Schwabing starts north of the Victory Arch, where Ludwigstrasse becomes Leopoldstrasse, which although not as wide and impressive, is lined with trees and restaurants.

MUNICH PLANNER

WHEN TO GO

Munich is a year-round city, but it is nicer to walk through the Englischer Garten in June and have your beer under a shady chestnut tree in August. But if fate takes you to Munich in winter, there are lots museums and good restaurants to keep you entertained. Theater and opera fans will especially enjoy the winter season, when the tour buses and the camera-toting crowds are gone. Munich comes alive during Fasching, the German Mardi Gras, in the pre-Easter season. The festival of festivals, Oktoberfest, takes place from the end of September to early October.

GETTING HERE & AROUND

BY AIR   Munich's International Airport is 28 km (17 mi) northeast of the city center and has excellent air service from all corners of the world.

An excellent train service links the airport with downtown. The S-1 and S-8 lines operate from a terminal directly beneath the airport's arrival and departure halls. Trains leave every 10 minutes, and the journey takes around 40 minutes. The easiest way is to buy a "Tageskarte" (day card) for €10, which allows you to travel anywhere on the system for the rest of the day till 6 AM the next morning. The bus service is slower than the S-bahn link and more expensive (€9 one-way, €14.50 round-trip). A taxi from the airport costs around €50. During rush hours (7 AM–10 AM and 4 PM–7 PM), allow up to an hour of driving time. If you're driving from the airport to the city yourself, take route A–9 and follow the signs for MÜNCHEN STADTMITTE (downtown). If you're driving from the city center, head north through Schwabing, join the A–9 autobahn at the Frankfurter Ring intersection, and follow the signs for the airport (FLUGHAFEN).

BY BUS   Touring Eurolines buses arrive at and depart from Arnulfstrasse, north of the main train station in the adjoining Starnberger Bahnhof. Check their excellent Web site for trips to Neuschwanstein and the Romantic Road.

BY CAR   From the north (Nürnberg or Frankfurt), leave the autobahn at the Schwabing exit. From Stuttgart and the west, the autobahn ends at Obermenzing, Munich's most westerly suburb. The autobahns from Salzburg and the east, Garmisch and the south, and Lindau and the southwest all join the Mittlerer Ring (city beltway). When leaving any autobahn, follow the signs reading STADTMITTE for downtown Munich.

BY PUBLIC TRANSIT   Munich has an efficient and well-integrated public-transportation system, consisting of the U-bahn (subway), the S-bahn (suburban railway), the Strassenbahn (streetcars), and buses. Marienplatz forms the heart of the U-bahn and S-bahn network, which operates from around 5 AM to 1 AM. The main service counter under the Marienplatz sells tickets and gives out information, also in English.

A basic *Einzelfahrkarte* (one-way ticket) costs €1.10 for a journey of up to four stops, €2.20 for a longer ride in the inner zone. If you're taking a number of trips around the city, save money by buying a *Mehrfahrtenkarte,* or multiple 10-strip ticket for €10.50. On a journey of up to four stops validate one ticket, for the inner zone, two. If you plan to do several trips during one day, buy a "Tageskarte" (day card) for €10, which allows you to travel anywhere until 6 AM the next morning. For a family of up to five (two adults and three children under 15) the "Tageskarte" costs €18. A three-day card costs €12.30 for a single and €21 for the partner version. All tickets must be validated at a time stamping machine at the station or on buses and trams. Spot checks for validated tickets are common, and you'll be fined €40 if you're caught without a valid ticket. All tickets are sold at the blue dispensers at U- and S-bahn stations and at some bus and streetcar stops. Bus drivers have only single tickets (the most expensive kind).

■ TIP➜ **Holders of a EurailPass, a Youth Pass, or an Inter-Rail card can travel free on all suburban railway trains (S-bahn).** Be forwarned: if caught on anything but the S-bahn without a normal public transport ticket, you will be fined €40, with no exceptions.

BY TAXI Munich's cream-color taxis are numerous. Hail them in the street or phone for one (there's an extra charge of €1 if you call). Rates start at €2.90. Expect to pay €8–€10 for a short trip within the city. There's a €0.50 charge for each piece of luggage.

BY TRAIN All long-distance rail services arrive at and depart from the Hauptbahnhof; trains to and from some destinations in Bavaria use the adjoining Starnberger Bahnhof, which is under the same roof. The high-speed InterCity Express (ICE) trains connect Munich, Augsburg, Frankfurt, and Hamburg on one line, Munich, Nürnberg, Würzburg, and Hamburg on another. Regensburg can be reached from Munich on Regio trains. You can purchase tickets by credit card at vending machines. For travel information at the main train station, go to the DB counter at the center of the main departures hall. With more complex questions, go to the EurAide office, which serves English-speaking train travelers.

TOURS

■ TIP➜ **For the cheapest sightseeing tour of the city center on wheels, board Streetcar 19 outside the Hauptbahnhof on Bahnhofplatz and make the 15-minute journey to Max Weber Platz. Explore the streets around the square, part of the old bohemian residential area of Haidhausen (with some of the city's best bars and restaurants, many on the village-like Kirchenstrasse), and then return by a different route on Streetcar 18 to Karlsplatz.**

A novel way of seeing the city is to hop on one of the bike-rickshaws. The bike-powered two-seater cabs operate between Marienplatz and the Chinesischer Turm in the Englischer Garten. Just hail one; the cost is €37 per hour.

The tourist office offers individual guided tours for fees ranging between €100 and €250. Bookings must be made at least 10 days in advance. Taxi tours with specially trained drivers are offered by Isar-Funk Taxizentrale GmbH. These are a good alternative for groups of up to four people. Cost is €68 per trip for the first hour and €18 for each subsequent half hour. ⇨ *See Sports & the Outdoors for information on bike tours.*

BUS TOURS Panorama Tours also has one-hour tours of Munich highlights that depart every 20 minutes and cost €13. Other options include a trip to Bavaria Film Studios, Munich by Night, and an FC Bayern Munich soccer team tour.

Yellow Cab Stadtrundfahrten has a fleet of yellow double-decker buses, in which tours are offered simultaneously in eight languages. They leave hourly between 10 AM and 4 PM from the front of the Elisenhof shopping complex on Bahnhofplatz. Tours cost €9.

WALKING Two-hour tours of the Old City center are given daily in summer
TOURS (March–October) and on Friday and Saturday in winter (November–February). Tours organized by the visitor center start at 10:30 and 1 in the center of Marienplatz. The cost is €8. The theme walks of Radius Tours & Bikes include Munich highlights, Third Reich Munich, Jewish Munich, and the Dachau concentration camp. The cost is €10 (€19 for the Dachau tour). Tours depart daily from the Hauptbahnhof, outside the EurAide office by Track 11, and also meet 15 minutes later at the New Town Hall's glockenspiel on Marienplatz.

VISITOR The Hauptbahnhof tourist office is open Monday–Saturday 9–8 (in
INFORMATION winter 10–6) and Sunday 10–6; the Info-Service in the Rathaus is open weekdays 10–8 and Saturday 10–4.

For information on the Bavarian mountain region south of Munich, contact the Tourismusverband München-Oberbayern.

ESSENTIALS **Airport Information Flughafen München** (☎ *089/97500* ⊕ *www.munich-airport.de*).

Bus Information Touring Eurolines (Administrative offices ✉ *Hirtenstr. 14 Leopoldvorstadt* ☎ *089/ 8898–9513* ⊕ *www.touring.de*).

Taxi Information Taxi (☎ *089/21610 or 089/19410*).

Tour Information IsarFunk Taxizentrale GmbH (☎ *089/450–540*). **Munich Tourist Office** (☎ *089/2333–0234*). **Radius Tours & Bikes** (☎ *089/5502–9374* ⊕ *www.radiusmunich.com*). **Sightseeing Tours** (✉ *Schützenstr. 9, Leopoldvorstadt* ☎ *089/5490–7560*).

Visitor Information Hauptbahnhof (✉ *Bahnhofpl. 2, Leopoldvorstadt* ⊕ *www.munich-tourist.de*). **Info-Service** (✉ *Marienpl., City Center* ☎ *089/2332–8242*). **Tourismusverband München-Oberbayern** (*Upper Bavarian Regional Tourist Office* ✉ *Radolfzeller 15* ☎ *089/829–2180*).

PLANNING YOUR TIME

Set aside at least a whole day for the Old Town, hitting Marienplatz when the glockenspiel plays at 11 AM or noon before a crowd of spectators. The pedestrian zone can get maddeningly full between noon and 2, when everyone in town seems to be taking a quick shopping break. If you've already seen the glockenspiel, try to avoid the area at that time. Avoid the museum crowds in Schwabing and Maxvorstadt by visiting as early in the day as possible. All Munich seems to discover an interest in art on Sunday, when most municipal and state-funded museums are free; you might want to take this day off from culture and have a late breakfast or brunch at the Elisabethmarkt. Some beer gardens and taverns have Sunday-morning jazz concerts. Many Schwabing bars have happy hours between 6 and 8—a relaxing way to end your day.

DISCOUNTS & DEALS

Admission to most municipal and state-funded museums is free on Sunday.

EXPLORING MUNICH

Munich is a wealthy city—and it shows. At times this affluence may come across as conservatism. But what makes Munich so unique is that it's a new city superimposed on the old. Hip neighborhoods are riddled with traditional locales, and flashy materialism thrives together with a love of the outdoors.

THE CITY CENTER

Munich's Old Town has been rebuilt so often over the centuries that it no longer has the homogeneous look of so many other German towns. World War II leveled a good portion of the center, but an amazing job has been done to restore a bit of the fairy-tale feel that once prevailed here.

MAIN ATTRACTIONS

⑰ **Deutsches Museum** *(German Museum)*. Aircraft, vehicles, locomotives,
Fodor'sChoice and machinery fill a monumental building on an island in the Isar
★ River. The immense collection is spread out over 19 km (12 mi) of cor-
☾ ridors, six floors of exhibits, and 30 departments. Children now have their own area, the **Kinderreich,** where they can learn about modern technology and science through numerous interactive displays (parents must accompany their child). The most technically advanced planetarium in Europe has up to six shows daily and includes a Laser Magic display. The Internet café on the third floor is open daily 9–3. ■TIP→ **To arrange for a two-hour tour in English, call at least two weeks in advance.** The **Verkehrszentrum** (Center for Transportation), on the former trade fair grounds at the Theresienhöhe (where Oktoberfest is held), has been completely renovated and houses an amazing collection of the museum's transportation exhibits. It is open until 8 PM on Thursday. ⊠ *Museumsinsel 1, City Center* ☎ *089/21791, 089/217–9252 for tour* ⊕ *www.deutsches-museum.de* ⊠ *Museum €8.50, Center for Transportation €2.50 (€10 with museum plus shuttle)* ☉ *Daily 9–5* Ⓜ *Isartor (S-bahn).*

❺ **Frauenkirche** *(Church of Our Lady)*. Munich's *Dom* (cathedral) is a dis-
★ tinctive late-Gothic brick structure with two towers. Each is more than 300 feet high, and both are capped by onion-shape domes. The towers are an indelible feature of the skyline and a Munich trademark—some say because they look like overflowing beer mugs.

The main body of the cathedral was completed in 20 years (1468–88)—a record time in those days. The onion domes on the towers were added, almost as an afterthought, in 1524–25. Jörg von Halspach, the Frauenkirche's original architect, apparently dropped dead after laying the last brick and is buried here. The building suffered severe dam-

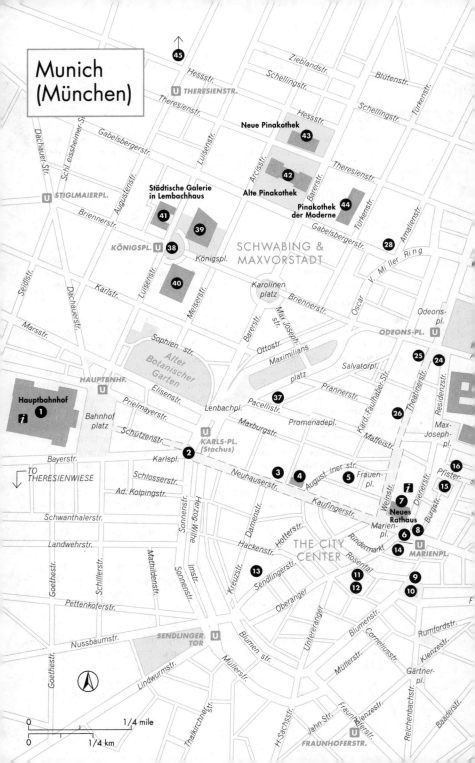

2

age during Allied bombing and was restored between 1947 and 1957. Inside, the church combines most of von Halspach's original features with a stark, clean modernity and simplicity of line, emphasized by slender, white octagonal pillars that sweep up through the nave to the tracery ceiling. As you enter the church, look on the stone floor for the dark imprint of a large foot—the *Teufelstritt* (Devil's Footprint). According to lore, the devil challenged von Halspach to build a nave without windows. The architect accepted the challenge. When he completed the job, he led the devil to the one spot in the bright church from which the 66-foot-high windows could not be seen. The devil stomped his foot in rage and left the Teufelstritt. The cathedral houses an elaborate 15th-century black-marble tomb guarded by four 16th-century armored knights. It's the final resting place of Duke Ludwig IV (1302–47), who became Holy Roman Emperor Ludwig the Bavarian in 1328. The Frauenkirche's great treasure, however, is the collection of 24 wooden busts of the apostles, saints, and prophets above the choir, carved by the 15th-century Munich sculptor Erasmus Grasser.

The observation platform high up in one of the towers offers a splendid view of the city. But beware—you must climb 86 steps to reach the tower elevator. ⊠ *Frauenpl., City Center* ☎ *089/290–0820* ⊠ *Cathedral free, tower €3* ⊙ *Tower elevator Apr.–Oct., Mon.–Sat. 10–5* Ⓜ *Marienplatz (U-bahn and S-bahn).*

❻ **Marienplatz.** Bordered by the Neues Rathaus, shops, and cafés, this
★ square is named after the gilded statue of the Virgin Mary that has watched over it for more than three centuries. It was erected in 1638 at the behest of Elector Maximilian I as an act of thanksgiving for the city's survival of the Thirty Years' War, the cataclysmic religious struggle that devastated vast regions of Germany. When the statue was taken down from its marble column for cleaning in 1960, workmen found a small casket in the base containing a splinter of wood said to be from the cross of Christ. ■ TIP→ **On the fifth floor of a building facing the Neues Rathaus is the Café Glockenspiel. It overlooks the entire Platz and provides a perfect view of the glockenspiel from the front and St. Peter's Church from the back terrace. Entrance is around the back.** ⊠ *Bounded by Kaufingerstr., Rosenstr., Weinstr., and Dienerstr., City Center* Ⓜ *Marienplatz (U-bahn and S-bahn).*

❸ **Michaelskirche** *(St. Michael's Church).* A curious story explains why this sturdy Renaissance church has no tower. Seven years after the start of construction the main tower collapsed. Its patron, pious Duke Wilhelm V, regarded the disaster as a heavenly sign that the church wasn't big enough, so he ordered a change in the plans—this time without a tower. Completed seven years later, the barrel vaulting of Michaelskirche is second in size only to that of St. Peter's in Rome. The duke is buried in the crypt, along with 40 other Wittelsbach family members, including the eccentric King Ludwig II. A severe neoclassical monument in the north transept contains the tomb of Napoléon's stepson, Eugene de Beauharnais, who married one of the daughters of King Maximilian I and died in Munich in 1824. The church is the venue for free performances of church music. A poster to the right of the front portal gives the dates.

✉*Neuhauserstr. 52, City Center* ☎*089/231–7060* 🎫*€2 crypt* 🕐*Daily 8–7, except during services* Ⓜ*Karlsplatz (U-bahn and S-bahn).*

2

❼ **Neues Rathaus** *(New Town Hall).* Munich's present town hall was built between 1867 and 1908 in the fussy, turreted, neo-Gothic style so beloved by King Ludwig II. Architectural historians are divided over its merits, though its dramatic scale and lavish detailing are impressive. Perhaps the most serious criticism is that the Dutch and Flemish styles of the building seem out of place amid the baroque and rococo styles of so much of the rest of the city. The tower's 1904 **glockenspiel** (a chiming clock with mechanical figures) plays daily at 11 AM, noon, and 9 PM, with an additional performance at 5 PM June–October. As chimes peal out over the square, the clock's doors flip open and brightly colored dancers and jousting knights act out two events from Munich's past: a tournament held in Marienplatz in 1568 and the *Schäfflertanz* (Dance of the Coopers), which commemorated the end of the plague of 1517. When Munich was in ruins after World War II, an American soldier contributed some paint to restore the battered figures, and he was rewarded with a ride on one of the jousters' horses, high above the cheering crowds. ∎TIP➜ **You, too, can travel up there, by elevator, to an observation point near the top of one of the towers. On a clear day the view is spectacular.** ✉*Marienpl., City Center* 🎫*Tower €2* 🕐*Nov.– Apr., Mon.–Thurs. 9–4, Fri. 9–1; May–Oct., weekdays 9–7, weekends 10–7* Ⓜ*Marienplatz (U-bahn and S-bahn).*

⓮ **Peterskirche** *(St. Peter's Church).* Munich's oldest and smallest parish church traces its origins to the 11th century and has been restored in various architectural styles. The rich baroque interior has a magnificent late-Gothic high altar and aisle pillars decorated with exquisite 18th-century figures of the apostles. In clear weather it's well worth the long climb up the 300-foot tower—the view includes glimpses of the Alps on a clear day. ✉*Rindermarkt, City Center* ☎*089/260–4828* 🎫*Tower €1.50* 🕐*Mon.–Sat. 9–6, Sun. 10–6* Ⓜ*Marienplatz (U-bahn and S-bahn).*

❾ **Viktualienmarkt** *(Victuals Market).* The city's open-air market really is
★ the beating heart of downtown Munich. It has just about every fresh fruit or vegetable you can imagine, as well as German and international specialties. All kinds of people come here for a quick bite, from well-heeled businesspeople and casual tourists to mortar- and paint-covered workers. It's also the realm of the garrulous, sturdy market women who run the stalls with dictatorial authority. ∎TIP➜ **Whether here, or at a bakery, *do not* try to select your pickings by hand. Ask for it first and let it be served to you.** Try Poseidon's for quality fish treats, Mercado Latino on the south side of the market for an empanada and fine wines from South America, or Freisinger for Mediterranean delights. There's also a great beer garden (open pretty much whenever the sun is shining), where you can enjoy your snacks with some cold local beer. A sign above the counter tells you which beer is on tap. The choice rotates throughout the year among the six major Munich breweries, which are displayed on the May Pole. These are also the only six breweries officially allowed to serve their wares at the Oktoberfest, because they all brew within the city limits. Ⓜ*Marienplatz (U-bahn and S-bahn).*

BEATING THE EURO

Prices for decent accommodation drop substantially when you choose a hotel outside the city center. A small, nice suburban hotel will be clean, quiet, and often allow for free parking either at its own lot or on a side street. To save money on meals, don't go where tourists are expected, but to places where students eat. Take the U-bahn 3 or 6 past Odeonsplatz to Universität.

At the back of the main university building is a solid block bordered by the parallel Amalienstrasse and Türkenstrasse, and Schellingstrasse to the south and Adalbertstrasse to the north. Along them are 38 eateries, restaurants, or bakeries with a few stand-up tables, all catering to the hundreds of students who come out of class at noontime.

ALSO WORTH SEEING

⑮ **Alter Hof** (*Old Palace*). This palace was the original medieval residence of the Wittelsbachs, the ruling dynasty established in 1180. The palace now serves as local government offices. Don't pass through without turning to admire the oriel (bay window) that hides on the south wall, just around the corner as you enter the courtyard. The west wing is home to the **Vinorant Alter Hof**, a fine restaurant and wine cellar with decent prices. ⊠*Burgstr., City Center* Ⓜ*Marienplatz (U-bahn and S-bahn)*.

⑧ **Altes Rathaus** (*Old Town Hall*). Munich's first town hall was built in
☾ 1474. Its great hall—destroyed in 1944 but now fully restored—was the work of architect Jörg von Halspach. It's used for official receptions and is not normally open to the public. The tower provides a fairy-tale-like setting for the **Spielzeugmuseum** (Toy Museum), accessible via a winding staircase. Its toys and dolls are on display, with a collection of Barbies from the United States. ⊠*Marienpl., City Center* ☎*089/294–001* 🕮*Museum €3* ☉*Daily 10–5:30* Ⓜ*Marienplatz (U-bahn and S-bahn)*.

⑬ **Asamkirche** (*Asam Church*). Munich's most unusual church has a suit-
★ ably extraordinary entrance, framed by raw rock foundations. The insignificant door, crammed between its craggy shoulders, gives little idea of the opulence and lavish detailing within the small 18th-century church (there are only 12 rows of pews). Above the doorway St. Nepomuk, a 14th-century Bohemian monk who drowned in the Danube, is being led by angels from a rocky riverbank to heaven. The church's official name is Church of St. Johann Nepomuk, but it's known as the Asamkirche for its architects, the brothers Cosmas Damian and Egid Quirin Asam, who lived next door. The interior of the church is a prime example of true southern German late-baroque architecture. Frescoes by Cosmas Damian Asam and rosy marble cover the walls. The sheer wealth of statues and gilding is stunning—there's even a gilt skeleton at the sanctuary's portal. ⊠*Sendlingerstr., City Center* ☉*Daily 9–5:30* Ⓜ*Sendlingertor (U-bahn)*.

2

❹ **Deutsches Jagd- und Fischereimuseum** *(German Museum of Hunting and Fishing).* This quirky museum contains the world's largest collection of fishhooks, some 500 stuffed animals (including a 6½-foot-tall North American grizzly bear), a 12,000-year-old skeleton of a deer found in Ireland, and a valuable collection of hunting weapons. You'll even find the elusive *Wolpertinger,* the Bavarian equivalent of the jackalope. The museum also sells fine hunting equipment, from knives and rifles to sturdy clothing. ✉*Neuhauser-str. 2, City Center* ☎*089/220–522* 💶*€3.50* ⏱*Daily 9:30–5.* Ⓜ*Karlsplatz (U-bahn and S-bahn).*

> **TOURING TIPS**
>
> **Information:** There are city tourist offices in the Hauptbahnhof and at Marienplatz.
>
> **Scenic Spot:** Ride an elevator to the top of one of the Frauenkirche's trademark towers for a great view of the city.
>
> **Snacks:** Grab some stand-up grub at one of the many stalls around the Viktualienmarkt or take a load off at the beer garden.

OFF THE BEATEN PATH

Franziskanerklosterkirche St. Anna *(Franciscan Monastery Church of St. Anne).* This striking example of the two Asam brothers' work in the Lehel district impresses visitors with its sense of movement and heroic scale. The ceiling fresco by Cosmas Damian Asam glows in all its original glory. The ornate altar was also designed by the Asam brothers. Towering over the delicate little church, on the opposite side of the street, is the neo-Romanesque bulk of the 19th-century church of St. Anne. ✉*St.-Anna-Str. 19, Lehel* ☎*089/212–1820* Ⓜ*Lehel (U-bahn).*

❶ **Hauptbahnhof** *(Central Station).* Obviously not a cultural site, but it is a particularly handy spot. The city tourist office here has maps and helpful information on events around town. On the underground level are all sorts of shops that remain open even on Sunday and holidays. There are also a number of places to get a late-night snack in and around the station. ✉*Bahnhofpl., Hauptbahnhof* ☎*089/2333–0256 or 089/2333–0257* Ⓜ*Hauptbahnhof (U-bahn and S-bahn).*

⓬ **Jewish Center Munich.** The striking new Jewish Center Munich has transformed the formerly sleepy Jakobsplatz into an elegant modern square. The Center includes a museum focusing on Jewish history in Munich, a formidable new synagogue with rough marble slabs, and a community center with kosher restaurant (☎*089/202–400333*) that is open Sunday to Thursday from 11:30 to 11. Free, guided tours of the synagogue are in great demand, so to see it, arrange a time weeks in advance. ✉*St.-Jakobspl. 16, City Center* ☎*089/233–96096, tours 089/202–400 100* 🌐*www.juedisches-museum-muenchen.de* 💶 *Museum €6* ⏱*Museum Tues.–Sun. 10–6; synagogue by prior arrangement* Ⓜ*Marienplatz (U-bahn and S-bahn).*

❷ **Karlsplatz.** In 1755 Eustachius Föderl opened an inn and beer garden here, which became known as the Stachus. The beer garden is long gone, but the name has remained—locals still refer to this busy intersection as the Stachus. One of Munich's most popular fountains is here—it acts as a magnet on hot summer days, when city shoppers and office workers seek a cool place to relax. ■ TIP→ **In winter it makes way for an ice-skating rink.** It's a bustling meeting point. Ⓜ *Karlsplatz (U-bahn and S-bahn).*

⓫ **Münchner Stadtmuseum** *(City Museum).* Wedged in by Oberanger, Rosental, and St.-Jakobsplatz, this museum is as eclectic inside as the architecture is outside. The original building facing St.-Jakobsplatz dates to 1491. Inside are instrument collections, international cultural exhibits, a film museum showing rarely screened movies, notably German silents, a photo and fashion museum, a puppet theater, and a very lively café. ⊠ *St.-Jakobspl. 1, City Center* ☎ *089/2332–2370* ⊕ *www.stadtmuseum-online.de* ⊡ *€4, free Sun.* ⊙ *Tues.–Sun. 10–6* Ⓜ *Marienplatz (U-bahn and S-bahn).*

⓰ **Münze** *(Mint).* Originally royal stables, the Münze was created by court architect Wilhelm Egkl between 1563 and 1567 and now serves as an office building. A stern neoclassical facade emblazoned with gold was added in 1809. The interior courtyard with Renaissance-style arches is worth a look. ⊠ *Pfisterstr. 4, City Center* ⊡ *Free* ⊙ *Mon.–Thurs. 8–4, Fri. 8–2* Ⓜ *Marienplatz (U-bahn and S-bahn).*

⓾ **Schrannenhalle.** On the south side of the Viktualienmarkt, behind the Pschorr tavern, is the Schrannenhalle. A former grain depot from the mid-1850s until just after the turn of the 20th century, the hall now houses numerous shops, bars, and restaurants serving Asian cuisine, sushi, traditional Bavarian food, and more. One vendor even serves champagne with Berlin-style Currywurst (sausage with curry ketchup and curry powder). Events range from swing jazz to rock-and-roll concerts. ■ TIP→ **One unusual and welcome feature of the Schrannenhalle is its opening times: 24 hours a day, seven days a week there is always something open here, be it a coffee shop or the late-night** *Weisswurst* **(Bavarian white sausage) stand.** Ⓜ *Marienplatz (U-bahn and S-bahn).*

ROYAL MUNICH

From the modest palace of the Alter Hof, the Wittelsbachs expanded their quarters northward, away from the jumble of narrow streets in the old quarter. Three splendid avenues radiated outward from their new palace and garden grounds, and fine homes arose along them. One of them—Prinzregentenstrasse—marks the southern edge of Munich's huge public park, the Englischer Garten, which was also created by a Wittelsbach. Lehel, an upmarket residential neighborhood that straddles Prinzregentenstrasse, plays host to one of Munich's most famous museums, the Haus der Kunst, as well as to some lesser-known but architecturally stunning museums.

MAIN ATTRACTIONS

㉛ **Englischer Garten** *(English Garden).* This endless park, which melds into ★ the open countryside at Munich's northern city limits, was designed for the Bavarian prince Karl Theodor by Benjamin Thompson, later Count Rumford, from Massachusetts, who fled America after having taken the wrong side during the War of Independence. Practically speaking, it's 5 km (3 mi) long and 1½ km (about 1 mi) wide, making it Germany's largest city park. The open, informal landscaping—reminiscent of the rolling parklands with which English aristocrats of the 18th century liked to surround their country homes—gave the park its name. It has a boating lake, four beer gardens, and a series of curious decorative and monumental constructions, including the Monopteros, a Greek temple designed by Leo von Klenze for King Ludwig I and built on an artificial hill in the southern section of the park. There are great sunset views of Munich from the Monopteros hill. In the center of the park's most popular beer garden is a Chinese pagoda erected in 1789. It was destroyed during the war and then reconstructed. ■**TIP**➔ **The Chinese Tower beer garden is world famous, but the park has prettier places for sipping a beer: the Aumeister, for example, along the northern perimeter. The Aumeister's restaurant is in an early-19th-century hunting lodge.** At the Seehaus, on the shore of the Kleinhesseloher *See* (lake), choose between a smart restaurant or a cozy *Bierstube* (beer tavern) in addition to the beer garden right on the lake.

TOURING TIPS

Breakfast: Start with a Bavarian breakfast of Weisswurst, pretzels, and Weissbier at the Weisses Bräuhaus on Tal Street between Marienplatz and Isartor or at the Wirtshaus Isarthor just across the road from the Isartor itself.

Scenic Spot: Head to Odeonsplatz and take a peek at the Hofgarten—the former palace grounds.

Snacks: Grab a bite at one of the many laid-back cafés on Schellingstrasse.

The Englischer Garten is a paradise for joggers, cyclists, musicians, soccer players, sunbathers, dog owners, and, in winter, cross-country skiers. The park has designated areas for nude sunbathing—the Germans have a positively pagan attitude toward the sun—so don't be surprised to see naked bodies bordering the flower beds and paths. ✉ *Main entrances at Prinzregentenstr. and Königinstr., Schwabing and Lehel.*

㉔ **Feldherrnhalle** *(Generals' Hall).* This open-sided pavilion was modeled after the 14th-century Loggia dei Lanzi in Florence, and honors three centuries of Bavarian generals. Two huge Bavarian lions are flanked by the larger-than-life statues of Count Johann Tserclaes Tilly, who led Catholic forces in the Thirty Years' War, and Prince Karl Philipp Wrede, hero of the 19th-century Napoleonic Wars. The imposing structure was turned into a militaristic shrine in the 1930s and '40s by the Nazis, who found it significant because it marked the site of Hitler's abortive coup, or putsch, in 1923. All who passed it had to give the Nazi salute. Viscardigasse, a tiny alley behind the Feldherrnhalle linking Residenzstrasse and Theatinerstrasse and now lined with exclusive boutiques, was used by those who wanted to dodge the tedious routine. ✉ *South end of Odeonspl., City Center* Ⓜ *Odeonsplatz (U-bahn).*

㉜ **Haus der Kunst** *(House of Art).* This colonnaded, classical-style building is one of Munich's few remaining examples of Hitler-era architecture, and was officially opened by the Führer himself. In the Hitler years it showed only work deemed to reflect the Nazi aesthetic. One of its most successful postwar exhibitions was devoted to works banned by the Nazis. It hosts exhibitions of art, photography, and sculpture, as well as theatrical and musical happenings. The survival-of-the-chicest disco, P1, is in the building's west wing. ⊠ *Prinzregentenstr. 1, Lehel* ☎ *089/2112–7113* ⊕ *www.hausderkunst.de* ✉ *Varies; generally €7* ⊙ *Daily 10–8* Ⓜ *Odeonsplatz (U-bahn).*

⓲ **Hofbräuhaus.** Duke Wilhelm V founded Munich's most famous brewery in 1589. Hofbräu means "court brewery," and the golden beer is poured in pitcher-sized liter mugs. If the cavernous ground-floor hall is too noisy for you, there is a quieter restaurant upstairs. In this legendary establishment Americans, Australians, and Italians far outnumber Germans, and the brass band that performs here most days adds modern pop and American folk music to the traditional German numbers. ⊠ *Am Platzl 9, City Center* ☎ *089/290–1360* ⊙ *Daily 11–11* Ⓜ *Marienplatz (U-bahn and S-bahn).*

㉓ **Hofgarten** *(Royal Garden).* The formal garden was once part of the royal palace grounds. It's bordered on two sides by arcades designed in the 19th century by court architect Leo von Klenze. On the east side of the garden is the state chancellery, built around the ruins of the 19th-century Army Museum and incorporating the remains of a Renaissance arcade. Its most prominent feature is a large copper dome. Bombed during World War II air raids, the museum stood untouched for almost 40 years as a grim reminder of the war. In front of the chancellery stands one of Europe's most unusual—some say most effective—war memorials. Instead of looking up at a monument, you are led down to a **sunken crypt** covered by a massive granite block. In the crypt lies a German soldier from World War I. The crypt is a stark contrast to the **memorial** that stands unobtrusively in front of the northern wing of the chancellery: a simple cube of black marble bearing facsimiles of handwritten wartime manifestos by anti-Nazi leaders, including the youthful members of the White Rose resistance movement. ⊠ *Hofgartenstr., north of Residenz, City Center* Ⓜ *Odeonsplatz (U-bahn).*

㉒ **Residenz** *(Royal Palace).* One of the city's true treasures, Munich's ★ royal palace began as a small castle in the 14th century. The Wittelsbach dukes moved here when the tenements of an expanding Munich encroached upon their Alter Hof. In succeeding centuries the royal residence developed according to the importance, requirements, and interests of its occupants. It came to include the Königsbau (on Max-Joseph-Platz) and then (clockwise) the Alte Residenz; the Festsaal (Banquet Hall); the newly renovated Altes Residenztheater/Cuvilliés-Theater; the Allerheiligenhofkirche (All Saints' Church), a venue for cultural events; the Residenztheater; and the Nationaltheater.

Building began in 1385 with the **Neuveste** (New Fortress), which comprised the northeast section. Most of it burned to the ground in 1750, but one of its finest rooms survived: the 16th-century **Antiquarium,** which was built for Duke Albrecht V's collection of antique statues (today it's used chiefly for state receptions). The throne room of King Ludwig I, the **Neuer Herkulessaal**, is now a concert hall. The accumulated Wittelsbach treasures are on view in several palace museums. The **Schatzkammer** (*Treasury* ⊠€6, combined ticket with Residenzmuseum €9 ⊘ Apr.–Oct. 15, daily 9–6; Oct. 16–Mar., daily 10–4) has a rather rich centerpiece—a small Renaissance statue of St. George studded with 2,291 diamonds, 209 pearls, and 406 rubies. Paintings, tapestries, furniture, and porcelain are housed in the **Residenzmuseum** (⊠€6 ⊘ Apr.–Oct. 15, daily 9–6; Oct. 16–Mar., daily 10–4). Antique coins glint in the **Staatliche Münzsammlung** (⊠€2, free Sun. ⊘ Wed.–Sun. 10–5). Egyptian works of art make up the **Staatliche Sammlung Ägyptischer Kunst** (⊠ Hofgarten entrance ☎089/298–546 ⊠€5, Sun. €1 ⊘ Tues. 9–5 and 7–9 PM, Wed.–Fri. 9–5, weekends 10–5). ■TIP➔ All the different ent halls and galleries of the Residenz can be visited with a combination ticket that costs €9. In summer, chamber-music concerts take place in the inner courtyard. Also in the center of the complex is the small, rococo **Altes Residenztheater/Cuvilliés-Theater** (⊠ Residenzstr. ⊠€3 ⊘ Closed during rehearsals). It was built by François Cuvilliés between 1751 and 1755, and performances are still held here. The French-born Cuvilliés was a dwarf who was admitted to the Bavarian court as a decorative "bauble." Prince Max Emanuel recognized his innate artistic ability and had him trained as an architect. The prince's eye for talent gave Germany some of its richest rococo treasures. ⊠ Max-Joseph-Pl. 3, entrance through archway at Residenzstr. 1, City Center ☎089/290–671 ⊘ Closed a few days in early Jan. Ⓜ Odeonsplatz (U-bahn).

㉕ Theatinerkirche (*Theatine Church*). This glorious baroque church owes its Italian appearance to its founder, Princess Henriette Adelaide, who commissioned it in gratitude for the birth of her son and heir, Max Emanuel, in 1663. A native of Turin, the princess distrusted Bavarian architects and builders and thus summoned a master builder from Bologna, Agostino Barelli, to construct her church. Barelli worked on the building for 11 years, but was dismissed before the project was completed. It was another 100 years before the building was finished. Its lofty towers frame a restrained facade capped by a massive dome. The superb stuccowork on the inside has a remarkably light feeling owing to its brilliant white color. ■TIP➔ The expansive square before the Feldherrnhalle and Theatinerkirche is often used for outdoor stage events. ⊠ Theatinerstr. 22, City Center Ⓜ Odeonsplatz (U-bahn).

NEED A BREAK? Munich's oldest café, Tambosi (⊠ Odeonspl., Maxvorstadt ☎ 089/224–768), borders the street across from the Theatinerkirche. Watch the hustle and bustle from an outdoor table, or retreat through a gate in the Hofgarten's western wall to the café's tree-shaded beer garden. If the weather is cool or rainy, find a corner in the cozy, eclectically furnished interior.

ALSO WORTH SEEING

㉟ Archäologische Staatssammlung (*State Archaeological Collection*). This is Bavaria's fascinating record of its prehistoric, Roman, and Celtic past. The perfectly preserved body of a ritually sacrificed young girl, recovered from a Bavarian peat moor, is among the more spine-chilling exhibits. Head down to the basement to see the fine Roman mosaic floor. ⊠ *Lerchenfeldstr. 2, Lehel* ☎*089/211–2402* ⊕*www. archaeologie-bayern.de* ⏎*€3, €1 on Sun.* ⊙*Tues.–Sun. 9 :30–5* Ⓜ*Lehel (U-bahn).*

㉝ Bayerisches Nationalmuseum *(Bavarian National Museum).* Although the museum places emphasis on Bavarian cultural history, it has art and artifacts of international importance and regular exhibitions that attract worldwide attention. The museum is a journey through time, from the Middle Ages to the 20th century, with medieval and Renaissance wood carvings, works by the great Renaissance sculptor Tilman Riemenschneider, tapestries, arms and armor, a unique collection of Christmas crèches (the *Krippenschau*), and Bavarian and German folk art. ⊠ *Prinzregentenstr. 3, Lehel* ☎*089/211–2401* ⊕*www.bayerisches-nationalmuseum.de* ⏎*€5 recommended combined ticket for museum and Bollert collection, €1 Sun.* ⊙*Tues.– Sun. 10–5, Thurs. 10–8* Ⓜ*Lehel (U-bahn).*

㉚ GedenkStätte Weisse Rose *(Memorial to the White Rose Resistance Group).* Siblings Hans and Sophie Scholl, fellow students Alexander Schmorell and Christian Probst, and Kurt Huber, professor of philosophy, founded the short-lived resistance movement against the Nazis in 1942–43 known as the Weisse Rose (White Rose). All were executed by guillotine. A small exhibition about their work is in the inner quad of the university, where the Scholls were caught distributing leaflets and denounced by the janitor. ⊠ *Geschwister-Scholl-Pl. 1, Maxvorstadt* ☎*089/2180–3053* ⏎*Free* ⊙*Weekdays–4* Ⓜ*Universität (U-bahn).*

㉖ Kunsthalle der Hypo-Kulturstiftung *(Hall of the Hypobank's Cultural Foundation).* Chagall, Giacometti, Picasso, and Gauguin were among the artists featured in the past at this exhibition hall in the midst of the commercial pedestrian zone, within the upscale **Fünf Höfe shopping mall.** The foundation's success over the years has led to its expansion, designed by the Swiss architect team Herzog and de Meuron, who also designed London's Tate Modern. ⊠ *Theatinerstr. 8, City Center* ☎*089/224–412* ⊕*www.hypo-kunsthalle.de* ⏎*€8* ⊙*Daily 10–8* Ⓜ*Odeonsplatz (U-bahn).*

㉙ Ludwigskirche *(Ludwig's Church).* Planted halfway along the stark, neoclassically styled Ludwigstrasse is this curious neo-Byzantine–early-Renaissance church, built at the behest of Ludwig I to provide his newly completed suburb with a parish church. It's worth a stop to see the fresco of the *Last Judgment* in the choir. At 60 feet by 37 feet, it's one of the world's largest. ⊠ *Ludwigstr. 22, Maxvorstadt* ☎*089/287– 7990* ⊙*Daily 7–7* Ⓜ*Universität (U-bahn).*

⑲ Maximilianstrasse. Munich's sophisticated shopping street was named after King Maximilian II, who wanted to break away from the Greek-influenced classical architecture favored by his father, Ludwig I. He thus created this broad boulevard lined with majestic buildings culminating on a rise above the Isar River at the stately **Maximilianeum,** a lavish 19th-century palace built for Maximilian II and now home to the Bavarian state parliament. Only the terrace can be visited.

36 **Museum Villa Stuck.** This beautiful neoclassical villa is the former home of one of Munich's leading turn-of-the-20th-century artists, Franz von Stuck (1863–1928). His work, at times haunting, at times erotic, and occasionally humorous, covers the walls of the ground-floor rooms. The museum also features the artist's former quarters as well as special exhibits. There are now guided tours in English. ✉ *Prinzregentenstr. 60, Haidhausen* ☎ *089/455–5510* ⊕ *www.villastuck.de* 💳 *€4* ⊙ *Tues.–Sun. 11–6* Ⓜ *Prinzregentenplatz (U-bahn).*

21 **Nationaltheater** *(National Theater).* Built in the late 19th century as a royal opera house with a pillared portico, this large theater was bombed during the war but is now restored to its original splendor and has some of the world's most advanced stage technology. It is home to the Bavarian State Opera Company. ✉ *Max-Joseph-Pl. 2, City Center* ☎ *089/2185–1920 for tickets* Ⓜ *Odeonsplatz (U-bahn).*

34 **Schack-Galerie.** Florid and romantic 19th-century German paintings (some now obscure) make up the collections of the Schack-Galerie, originally the private collection of Count Schack. ✉ *Prinzregentenstr. 9, Lehel* ☎ *089/2380–5224* 💳 *€3, €1 Sun.* ⊙ *Wed.–Sun. 10–5* Ⓜ *Lehel (U-bahn).*

27 **Siegestor** *(Victory Arch).* Marking the beginning of Leopoldstrasse, the Siegestor has Italian origins—it was modeled after the Arch of Constantine in Rome—and was built to honor the achievements of the Bavarian army during the Wars of Liberation (1813–15). The inscription on the side facing the inner city reads: DEDICATED TO VICTORY, DESTROYED BY WAR, ADMONISHING PEACE. ✉ *Leopoldstr., Schwabing* Ⓜ *Universität (U-bahn).*

28 **SiemensForum.** Siemens has been one of Germany's major employers and technological innovators for more than 150 years. This surprisingly entertaining company museum, housed in a spaceship-like building, shows visitors the many areas in which Siemens has been active, from old-fashioned telegraph systems to hypermodern dentist chairs and fuel cells. Hands-on displays such as video telephones spice up the experience. ✉ *Oskar-von-Miller-Ring, Maxvorstadt* ☎ *089/6363–3210* ⊕ *www.siemensforum.de* 💳 *Free* ⊙ *Weekdays 9–4* Ⓜ *Odeonsplatz (U-bahn).*

LUDWIGSTRASSE ARCHITECTURE

The stretch of buildings designed by royal architect Leo von Klenze gives Ludwigstrasse a grandiose air. Klenze swept aside the small dwellings and alleys that once stood here and replaced them with severe neoclassical structures such as the Universität (University) and the peculiarly Byzantine Ludwigskirche. Müncheners tend to either love or hate Klenze's formal buildings, which end at the Siegestor (Victory Arch). Another leading architect, Friedrich von Gärtner, took over from here, adding more delicate structures that are a pleasant backdrop to the busy street life of Schwabing.

2

㉒ Staatliches Museum für Völkerkunde *(State Museum of Ethnology)*. Arts and crafts from around the world are displayed in this extensive museum. There are also regular special exhibits. ✉ *Maximilianstr. 42, Lehel* ☏ *089/2101–3610* ⊕ *www.voelkerkundemuseum-muenchen.de* 💶 *€3.50, €1 Sun.* ⊙ *Tues.–Sun. 9:30–5:30* Ⓜ *Lehel (U-bahn).*

LEOPOLDSTRASSE

Leopoldstrasse throbs with life from spring to fall, with cafés, wine terraces, and the occasional artist stall. Formerly Munich's bohemian quarters, Schwabing has unfortunately become a bit monotonous in its present-day form, but you can explore the side streets of old Schwabing around Wedekindplatz near Münchener Freiheit or enjoy the shops and cafés in the student quarter to the west of Leopoldstrasse.

SCHWABING & MAXVORSTADT: ART MUSEUMS & GALLERIES

Most of the city's leading art galleries are located in lower Schwabing and Maxvorstadt, making this area the primary museum quarter. Schwabing, the former artists' neighborhood, is no longer quite the bohemian area where such diverse residents as Lenin and Kandinsky were once neighbors, but the cultural foundations of Maxvorstadt are immutable. Where the two areas meet, in the streets behind the university, life hums with a creative vibrancy that is difficult to detect elsewhere in Munich. The difficult part is having time to see it all.

MAIN ATTRACTIONS

㊷ Alte Pinakothek *(Old Picture Gallery)*. The long, massive brick Alte Pinakothek was constructed by Leo von Klenze between 1826 and 1836 to exhibit the collection of old masters begun by Duke Wilhelm IV in the 16th century. By all accounts it is one of the world's great picture galleries. Among the European masterpieces here from the 14th to the 18th centuries are paintings by Dürer, Titian, Rembrandt, Rubens (the museum has one of the world's largest collections of works by Rubens), and two celebrated Murillos. Not to be missed. ✉ *Barerstr. 27, Maxvorstadt* ☏ *089/2380–5216* ⊕ *www.alte-pinakothek.de* 💶 *€5.50, €1 Sun.* ⊙ *Tues.–Sun. 10–6* Ⓜ *Königsplatz (U-bahn).*

Fodor'sChoice ★

㊳ Königsplatz *(King's Square)*. Monumental Grecian-style buildings designed by Leo von Klenze line this elegant and expansive square on three sides, giving Munich the nickname Athens on the Isar. The two templelike structures opposite each other are now the Antikensammlungen and the Glyptothek museums. Although a busy road passes through it, the square has maintained the dignified appearance intended by Ludwig I thanks to the broad green lawns in front of the museums. In summertime, concerts and outdoor cinema take place on this grand square. Ⓜ *Königsplatz (U-bahn).*

㊸ Neue Pinakothek *(New Picture Gallery)*. This fabulous museum opened in 1981 to house the royal collection of modern art left homeless and scattered after its building was destroyed in the war. The exterior of the modern building mimics an older one with Italianate influences. The interior offers a magnificent environment for picture gazing, at least

Bavaria: A Country Within a Country

For most visitors, Bavaria, with its traditional Gemütlichkeit, beer gardens, quaint little villages, and culturally rich cities, is often seen as the quintessence of Germany. In fact, nothing could be further from the truth. Of the 16 German Länder, as the German federal states are called, none is more fiercely independent than Bavaria. In fact, it was an autonomous dukedom and later kingdom until 1871, when it was incorporated into the German nation state.

For Bavarians, anything beyond the state's borders remains foreign territory. The state has its own anthem and its own flag, part of which—the blue-and-white lozenges in the center—has virtually become a regional trademark symbolizing quality and tradition. Bavarian politicians discussing the issue of Europe in speeches will often refer to Bavaria almost as if it were a national state. They inevita-

bly call it by its full official name: Freistaat Bayern, or simply der Freistaat, meaning "the Free State." The term was coined by Kurt Eisner, Minister President of the Socialist government that rid the land of the Wittelsbach dynasty in 1918. It is simply a German way of saying republic—a land governed by the people. Bavaria's status as a republic is mentioned in the first line of the separate Bavarian constitution that was signed under the aegis of the American occupation forces in 1946.

Bavaria is not the only Freistaat in Germany, a fact not too many Germans are aware of. Thuringia and Saxony also boast that title. But the Bavarians are the only ones who make such a public point of it. As they say, clocks in Bavaria run differently. Now you know why.

–Marton Radkai

partly owing to the natural light flooding in from skylights. French impressionists—Monet, Degas, Manet—are all well represented. The 19th-century German and Scandinavian paintings—misty landscapes predominate—are only now coming to be recognized as admirable products of their time. Anothermust-see. ⊠ *Barerstr. 29, Maxvorstadt* ☎ *089/2380–5195* ⊕ *www.neue-pinakothek.de* ⊠ *€5.50, €1 Sun.* ⊙ *Wed.–Mon. 10–6* Ⓜ *Königsplatz (U-bahn).*

㊹ Pinakothek der Moderne. Munich's latest cultural addition is also Germany's largest museum for modern art, architecture, and design. The striking glass-and-concrete complex holds four outstanding art and architectural collections, including modern art, industrial and graphic design, the Bavarian State collection of graphic art, and the Technical University's architectural museum. Exhibitions rotate every several months. This one is another must in the museum quarter. ⊠ *Barerstr. 40, Maxvorstadt* ☎ *089/2380–5360* ⊕ *www.pinakothek-der-moderne. de* ⊠ *€9.50, €1 Sun.* ⊙ *Wed.– Mon. 10–6* Ⓜ *Königsplatz (U-bahn).*

NEED A BREAK?   A good spot especially if you are visiting the neighboring Pinakotheks, the ever-popular Brasserie Tresznjewski (⊠ *Theresienstr. 72, at Barerstr., Maxvorstadt* ☎ *089/282–349*) serves a menu with a slight French accent, well into the wee hours.

41 Städtische Galerie im Lenbachhaus *(Municipal Gallery)*. This exquisite late-19th-century Florentine-style villa is the former home and studio of the artist Franz von Lenbach (1836–1904). If for no other reason, this museum is worth a visit for the awe-inspiring assemblage of art from the early-20th-century Der *Blaue Reiter* (Blue Rider) group: Kandinsky, Klee, Jawlensky, Macke, Marc, and Münter. But there are also vivid pieces from

the New Objectivity movement, and a variety of local Munich artists are represented here. Rotating exhibits round off this eclectic and stylish museum. Lenbach's former chambers are on display as well. The adjoining **Kunstbau** (art building), a former subway platform of the Königsplatz station, hosts changing exhibitions of modern art. ⊠ *Luisenstr. 33, Maxvorstadt* ☎ *089/233–32000* ⊕ *www.lenbachhaus.de* ⌨ *€6* ⊘ *Tues.–Sun. 10–6* Ⓜ *Königsplatz (U-bahn).*

ALSO WORTH SEEING

40 Antikensammlungen *(Antiquities Collection).* This museum has a beautiful collection of small sculptures, Etruscan art, Greek vases, gold, and glass. ⊠ *Königspl. 1, Maxvorstadt* ☎ *089/5998–8830* ⊕ *www.antike-am-koenigsplatz.mwn.de* ⌨ *€3.50 €1 Sun.; combined ticket to Antikensammlungen and Glyptothek (valid three days) €5.50* ⊘ *Tues. and Thurs.–Sun. 10–5, Wed. 10–8* Ⓜ *Königsplatz (U-bahn).*

37 Dreifaltigkeitskirche *(Church of the Holy Trinity).* Take a quick look at this fanciful church near Maximiliansplatz. After a local woman prophesied doom for the city unless a new church was erected, its striking baroque exterior was promptly built between 1711 and 1718. It has frescoes by Cosmas Damian Asam depicting various heroic scenes. ⊠ *Pacellistr. 10, City Center* ☎ *089/290–0820* ⊘ *Daily 7–7, except during services* Ⓜ *Karlsplatz (U-bahn and S-bahn).*

45 Elisabethmarkt *(Elisabeth Market).* Schwabing's permanent outdoor market is smaller than the popular Viktualienmarkt, but hardly less colorful. It has a pocket-size beer garden, where a jazz band performs on Saturdays in summer. ⊠ *Arcistr. and Elisabethstr., Schwabing* Ⓜ *Giselastrasse (U-bahn).*

39 Glyptothek. This amazing collection of Greek and Roman sculptures ★ is among the finest exhibits in Munich. ■ TIP→ **The small café that expands into the quiet courtyard is a favorite for visitors, which include budding artists practicing their drawing skills.** ⊠ *Königspl. 3, Maxvorstadt* ☎ *089/286–100* ⊕ *www.antike-am-koenigsplatz.mwn.de* ⌨ *€3.50; €1 Sun.; combined ticket (valid 3 days) to Glyptothek and Antikensammlungen €5.50* ⊘ *Tues., Wed., and Fri.–Sun. 10–5, Thurs. 10–8* Ⓜ *Königsplatz (U-bahn).*

OKTOBERFEST

Not even the wildest Bavarians can be held wholly responsible for the staggering consumption of beer and food at the annual Oktoberfest, which starts at the end of September and ends in early October. On average, around 1,183,000 gallons of beer along with 750,000 roasted chickens and 650,000 sausages are put away by revelers from around the world. To partake, book lodging by April, and if you're traveling with a group, also reserve bench space within one of the 14 tents.

See Munich's Web site, ⊕ *www.muenchen-tourist.de*, for beer-tent contacts. The best time to arrive at the grounds is lunchtime, when it's easier to find a seat—by 4 PM it's packed and they'll close the doors. Take advantage of an hour or two of sobriety to tour the fairground rides, which are an integral part of Oktoberfest. Under no circumstances attempt any rides—all of which claim to be the world's most dangerous—after a couple of beers.

OUTSIDE THE CENTER

MAIN ATTRACTIONS

Oktoberfest Grounds at Theresienwiese. The site of Munich's notorious Oktoberfest and the seasonal Tollwood markets is only a 10-minute walk from the Hauptbahnhof, or one stop on the subway (U-4 or U-5). The enormous exhibition ground is named after Princess Therese von Sachsen-Hildburghausen, who celebrated her marriage to the Bavarian crown prince Ludwig I here in 1810. The fair was such a success that it became an annual event that has now morphed into a 16-day international beer bonanza attracting more than 6 million people each year (it is the *Oktober* fest because it always ends on the first Sunday in October).

Overlooking the Theresienwiese is a 19th-century hall of fame (Ruhmeshalle) featuring busts of numerous popular figures of the time—one of the last works of Ludwig I—and a monumental bronze statue of the maiden **Bavaria,** more than 60 feet high. The statue is hollow, and 130 steps take you up into the braided head for a view of Munich through Bavaria's eyes. €3 ⊙ *Apr.–Nov., daily 9–6* Ⓜ *Theresienhöhe (U-bahn)*.

☺ **Olympiapark** *(Olympic Park)*. On the northern edge of Schwabing, undulating circus-tent-like roofs cover the stadiums built for the 1972 Olympic Games. The roofs are made of translucent tiles that glisten in the sun and act as amplifiers for the rock concerts held here. Tours of the park are conducted on a Disneyland-style train throughout the day. An elevator will speed you up the 960-foot **Olympia Tower** (€4) for a view of the city and the Alps (on a clear day). There's also a revolving restaurant near the top. ☎ *089/3066–8585 restaurant* ⊕ *www.olympiapark-muenchen.de* ☎ *Adventure tour €7, stadium tour €5, tower €4* ⊙ *Tour schedules vary; call ahead for departure times* Ⓜ *Olympiazentrum (U-bahn 3)*.

★ **Schloss Nymphenburg.** This glorious baroque and rococo palace is the largest of its kind in Germany, stretching more than 1 km (½ mi) from one wing to the other. The palace grew in size and scope over a period of more than 200 years, beginning as a summer residence built on land given by Prince Ferdinand Maria to his beloved wife, Henriette Adelaide, on the occasion of the birth of their son and heir, Max Emanuel, in 1663. The princess hired the Italian architect Agostino Barelli to build both the Theatinerkirche and the palace, which was completed in 1675 by his successor, Enrico Zuccalli. Within the original building, now the central axis of the palace complex, is a magnificent hall, the **Steinerner Saal,** extending over two floors and richly decorated with stucco and grandiose frescoes. In summer, chamber-music concerts are given here. One of the surrounding royal chambers houses the famous **Schönheitsgalèrie** (Gallery of Beauties). The walls are hung from floor to ceiling with portraits of women who caught the roving eye of Ludwig I, among them a butcher's daughter and an English duchess. The most famous portrait is of Lola Montez, a sultry beauty and high-class courtesan who, after a time as the mistress of Franz Liszt and later Alexandre Dumas, so enchanted King Ludwig I that he almost bankrupted the state for her sake and was ultimately forced to abdicate.

The palace is in a park laid out in formal French style, with low hedges and gravel walks extending into woodland. Among the ancient tree stands are three fascinating structures. The **Amalienburg** hunting lodge is a rococo gem built by François Cuvilliés. The silver-and-blue stucco of the little Amalienburg creates an atmosphere of courtly high life, making clear that the pleasures of the chase did not always take place outdoors. Of the lodges, only Amalienburg is open in winter. In the lavishly appointed kennels you'll see that even the dogs lived in luxury. The **Pagodenburg** was built for royal tea parties. Its elegant French exterior disguises a suitably Asian interior in which exotic teas from India and China were served. Swimming parties were held in the **Badenburg,** Europe's first post-Roman heated pool.

Nymphenburg contains so much of interest that a day hardly provides enough time. Don't leave without visiting the former royal stables, ☉ now the **Marstallmuseum** (*Museum of Royal Carriages* 🖾€2.50). It houses a fleet of vehicles, including an elaborately decorated sleigh in which King Ludwig II once glided through the Bavarian twilight, postilion torches lighting the way. On the walls hang portraits of the royal horses. Also exhibited are examples of Nymphenburg porcelain, produced here between 1747 and the 1920s. A popular museum in the north wing of the palace has nothing to do with the Wittelsbachs but is one of Nymphenburg's major attractions. The **Museum Mensch und Natur** (*Museum of Man and Nature* ☎089/179–5890 🖾€2.50, €1 Sun. ⊙Tues.–Fri. 9–5, weekends 10–6) concentrates on three areas of interest: the variety of life on Earth, the history of humankind, and our place in the environment. Main exhibits include a huge representation of the human brain and a chunk of Alpine crystal weighing half a ton. Take Tram 17 or Bus 41 from the city center to the Schloss Nymphenburg stop. ✉*Notburgastr. at bridge crossing Nymphen-*

burg Canal, Nymphenburg ☎*089/179–080* ⊕*www.schloesser.bay-ern.de* ✉*Schloss Nymphenburg complex, combined ticket including Marstallmuseum but not Museum Mensch und Natur, €10, €8 in winter, when parts of complex are closed* ⊘*Apr.–Oct. 15, daily 9–6; Oct. 16–Mar., daily 10–4.*

ALSO WORTH SEEING

Bavaria Filmstadt. For real movie buffs, Munich has its own Hollywood-like neighborhood, the Geiselgasteig, on the southern outskirts of the city. Films like *Das Boot* (*The Boat*) and *Die Unendliche Geschichte* (*The Neverending Story*) were made here. There are a number of tours and shows ranging in price from €4.50 to a combined €20 ticket. Check the Web site or call for more information. ✉*Bavaria Filmplatz 7, Geiselgasteig* ☎*089/64990* ⊕*www.filmstadt.de* ⊘*English tour daily at 1 pm.*

BMW Museum. Munich is the home of the famous BMW car company. Its museum, a circular tower that looks as if it served as a set for *Star Wars*, is closed for the time being. Until the reopening, the exhibition has been moved across the street to a building next to the Olympia tower. It contains not only a dazzling collection of BMWs old and new but also items and exhibitions relating to the company's social history and its technical developments. It's a great place to stop in if you're at the Olympia Park already. ✉*Olympia Park 2* ⊕ *www.bmw-museum.de* ✉*€2* ⊘*Daily 10–8* Ⓜ*Petuelring (U-bahn).* The **BMW factory** (✉*Petuelring 130, Milbertshofen* ☎*018/02 11–8822* ⊕*www.bmw-plant-munich.com* ⊘*€6, tours weekdays 6 PM*) is also nearby and can be toured on weekdays. However, registration for plant tours (which last a maximum of 2.5 hours) is only possible in advance using the electronic registration form or via phone. ■TIP➔**Reserve weeks in advance if you want to get a slot during your trip.**

Botanischer Garten *(Botanical Garden).* Located on the eastern edge of Schloss Nymphenburg, this collection of 14,000 plants, including orchids, cacti, cycads, Alpine flowers, and rhododendrons, makes up one of the most extensive botanical gardens in Europe. Take Tram 17 or Bus 41 from the city center. ✉*Menzingerstr. 67, Nymphenburg* ☎*089/1786 1316* ✉*€4* ⊘*Garden Oct.–Mar., daily 9–4:30; Apr., Sept., daily 9–6; May, Aug., daily 9–7. Hothouses close 30 min earlier and during lunch 11:45–1 in summer.*

Deutsches Museum–"Flugwerft Schleissheim." Connoisseurs of airplanes and flying machines will appreciate this magnificent offshoot of the Deutsches Museum, some 20 km (12 mi) north of the city center. It's an ideal complement to a visit to Schloss Schleissheim. ■TIP➔ **There is a combination ticket with the Deutsches Museum, too.** ✉*Effnerstr. 7, Oberschleissheim* ☎*089/315-7140* ⊕*www.deutsches-museum.de* ✉*€5, combined ticket with Deutsches Museum €15* ⊘*Daily 9–5* Ⓜ*Oberschleissheim (S-bahn 1) and 15-min walk or bus 292 (no weekend service).*

Hellabrunn Zoo. Set right down on the Isar a bit upstream from town, this attractive zoo has many parklike enclosures but a minimum of cages. Some of the older buildings are in typical art nouveau style.

Care has been taken to group animals according to their natural and geographical habitats. The **Urwaldhaus** (Rain-Forest House) offers guided tours at night (call ahead of time). The 170 acres include restaurants and children's areas. Take Bus 52 from Marienplatz or U-bahn 3 to Thalkirchen, at the southern edge of the city. ⊠ *Tierparkstr. 30, Thalkirchen* ☎*089/625–080* ⊕*www.tierpark-hellabrunn.de* ⊠*€9* ⊙ *Apr.–Sept., daily 8–6; Oct.–Mar., daily 9–5* Ⓜ*Thalkirchen (U-bahn).*

Schloss Schleissheim *(Schleissheim Palace).* In 1597 Duke Wilhelm V decided to look for a peaceful retreat outside Munich, and found what he wanted at this palace. Prince Max Emanuel later added two more palaces. One, the **Lustheim,** houses Germany's largest collection of Meissen porcelain. Take the S-bahn 1 line to Oberschleissheim station and then walk about 20 minutes or take Bus 292 (no weekend service). ⊠*Maximilianshof 1, Oberschleissheim* ☎*089/315–8720* ⊠*Combined ticket for 3 palaces €6* ⊙*Apr.–Sept., Tues.–Sun. 9–6; Oct. –Mar., Tues.–Sun. 10–4.*

WHERE TO EAT

Munich claims to be Germany's gourmet capital. It certainly has an inordinate number of very fine restaurants, but you won't have trouble finding a vast range of options in both price and style. For connoisseurs, wining and dining at Tantris, widely regarded as Munich's best restaurant, or the Königshof could well turn into the equivalent of a religious experience. Alternatively, the high-quality traditional fare at more modest establishments will get you into the Bavarian swing of things. Either way, epicureans are convinced that one can dine as well in Munich as in any other city on the continent.

Some Munich restaurants serve sophisticated cuisine and expect their patrons to dress for the occasion. Unfortunately, Münchner have a tendency to look down their noses at the sartorially unprepared. Most restaurants, however, will serve you regardless of what you wear.

WHAT IT COSTS IN EUROS					
	¢	$	$$	$$$	$$$$
AT DINNER	under €9	€9–€15	€16–€20	€21–€25	over €25

Restaurant prices are per person for a main course at dinner.

CITY CENTER

$$$–$$$$ ✕**Königshof.** As you cross the threshold of its unremarkable building,
★   you step into a different world. From a window table in this elegant and luxurious restaurant in one of Munich's grand hotels, you can watch the hustle and bustle of Munich's busiest square below. You'll forget the outside world, however, when you taste the outstanding French- and Japanese-influenced dishes created by chef Martin Fauster,

2

former sous-chef at Tantris. Ingredients are fresh and menus change often, but you might see lobster with fennel and candied ginger, lamb with sweetbreads, venison with goose liver and celery, and for dessert, flambéed peach with champagne ice cream. Service is expert and personal; let the sommelier help you choose from the fantastic wine selection. ⊠ *Karlspl. 25, City Center* ☎ *089/5513–6142* ⊕ *www. koenigshof-hotel.de* ⌖ *Reservations essential. Jacket and tie* ⊟ *AE, DC, MC, V* ⊙ *Closed 1st week in Jan., Aug., Sun. and Mon.* Ⓜ *Karlsplatz (U-bahn and S-bahn).*

$$–$$$ ✕ **Halali.** With nearly 100 years of history to its credit, the Halali is an old-style Munich restaurant with polished wood paneling and antlers on the walls, and it is *the* place to try traditional dishes of venison and other game in a quiet and elegant atmosphere. Save room for the homemade vanilla ice cream. Reservations are essential for dinner. ⊠ *Schönfeldstr. 22, City Center* ☎ *089/285–909* ⌖ *Jacket and tie* ⊟ *AE, MC, V* ⊙ *Closed Sun. and public holidays. No lunch Sat.* Ⓜ *Odeonsplatz (U-bahn and S-bahn).*

$$–$$$ ✕ **Seven Fish.** A couple of hundred yards from Viktualienmarkt is the
★ upmarket Seven Fish restaurant. With decor reminiscent of New York, there is a delightful array of seafood dishes which change daily and a nice wine selection. You can either go for a lovely multi-course meal or choose the Japanese-influenced appetizers at the tiny bar. Sit outside if the weather is nice and watch the people go by on Gärtnerplatz. Reservations recommended. ⊠ *Gärtnerpl. 6, City Center* ☎ *089/2300–0219* ⊟ *AE, MC, V* Ⓜ *Marienplatz (U-bahn).*

$$–$$$ ✕ **Spatenhaus an der Oper.** The best seats are the window tables on the second floor. The quiet dining room walls and ceiling are paneled with old hand-painted wood and have a wonderful view of the square and the opera house. Make a reservation if you want to come after a performance. The outdoor tables are a favorite for people-watching. There's no better place for roasted fillet of brook trout, lamb with ratatouille, or duck with apple and red cabbage. Leave room for one of the wonderful desserts featuring fresh fruit. ⊠ *Residenzstr. 12, City Center* ☎ *089/292–7060* ⊟ *AE, MC, V* Ⓜ *Odeonsplatz (U-bahn).*

$$ ✕ **Buffet Kull.** This simple yet comfortable international bistro deliv-
★ ers a high-quality dining experience accompanied by a good variety of wines and friendly service. Dishes range from Bohemian pheasant soup to venison medallions and excellent steaks. The daily specials are creative, portions are generous, and the prices are good value for the quality. Reservations are recommended, or at least get there early (dinner service starts at 6 PM). ⊠ *Marienstr. 4, City Center* ☎ *089/221–509* ⊟ *AE, DC, MC, V* Ⓜ *Marienplatz (U-bahn and S-bahn).*

$$ ✕ **Hundskugel.** This is Munich's oldest tavern, and also one of the city's smallest. You'll be asked to squeeze together and make room for latecomers looking for a spot at one of the few tables clustered in the handkerchief-size dining room. The tavern dates from 1440. It has atmosphere, but it is expensive for the typical German fare served. ⊠ *Hotterstr. 18, City Center* ☎ *089/264–272* ⊟ *AE, D, MC, V* Ⓜ *Marienplatz (U-bahn and S-bahn).*

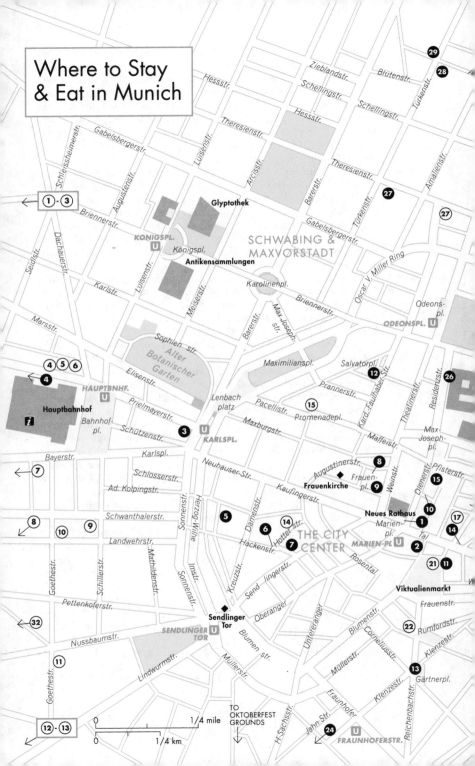

Where to Stay & Eat in Munich

Glyptothek

KÖNIGSPL. Ⓤ

Königspl.

Antikensammlungen

SCHWABING & MAXVORSTADT

Karolinenpl.

ODEONSPL. Ⓤ

Odeons-pl.

Sophien str.

Alter Botanischer Garten

Lenbach platz

Maximilianspl.

Salvatorpl.

HAUPTBNHF. Ⓤ

Hauptbahnhof

Bahnhof-pl.

ⓘ

KARLSPL. Ⓤ

Pacellistr.

Promenadepl.

Max-Joseph-pl.

Frauenkirche

Frauen-pl.

Neues Rathaus

Marien-pl.

MARIEN-PL. Ⓤ

THE CITY CENTER

Viktualienmarkt

SENDLINGER TOR Ⓤ

Sendlinger Tor

TO OKTOBERFEST GROUNDS

FRAUNHOFERSTR. Ⓤ

① · ③

④ ⑤ ⑥
④

③

⑦

⑧ ⑩ ⑨

㉜

⑪

⑫ · ⑬

㉙
㉘

㉗

㉗

㉖

⑫

⑮

⑧
⑨

⑮

⑩

①
②

⑰
⑭

㉑ ⑪

㉒

⑬

㉔

⑤
⑥
⑦

⑭

0   1/4 mile
0   1/4 km

Restaurants ▼	
Andescher am Dom	**8**
Augustiner Keller	**4**
Bier-und Oktoberfest Museum	**20**
Bratwurstherzl	**11**
Buffet Kull	**18**
Cohen's	**27**
Due passi	**16**
Dürnbräu	**19**
Faun	**24**
Gandl	**25**
Gasthaus Isarthor	**21**
Halali	**31**
Hofbräuhaus	**17**
Hundskugel	**6**
Jodlerwirt	**10**
Königshof	**3**
Max-Emanuel-Brauerei	**28**
Nero Pizza & Lounge	**23**
Nürnberger Bratwurst Glöckl am Dom	**9**
Oskar Maria	**12**
Pfälzer Residenz Weinstube	**26**
Prinz Myshkin	**7**
Saf im Zerwirk	**2**
Seven Fish	**13**
Spatenhaus an der Oper	**1**
Tantris	**30**
Vinorant Alter Hof	**15**
Vorstadt Café	**29**
Weinhaus Neuner	**5**
Weisses Bräuhaus	**14**
Wirtshaus in der Au	**22**

Hotels ▼	
Admiral	**19**
Adria	**26**
Advokat	**20**
Bayerischer Hof	**15**
Biederstein	**30**
Brack	**12**
Cortiina	**17**
Creatif Hotel Elephant	**5**
Eden–Hotel Wolff	**4**
Erzgiesserei Europe	**3**
Gästehaus am Englischen Garten	**29**
Hotel Amba	**6**
Hotel am Markt	**21**
Hotel Concorde	**23**
Hotel Mirabell	**10**
Hotel Pension Am Siegestor	**31**
Hotel-Pension Mariandl	**11**
Hotel–Pension Schmellergarten	**13**
Hotel Uhland	**32**
Hotel Vier Jahreszeiten München Kempinski	**24**
Jagdschloss	**7**
Kriemhild	**1**
Kurpfalz	**9**
Mercure	**14**
Oper	**25**
Park-Hotel Theresienhöhe	**8**
Pension Seibel	**22**
Platzl	**16**
Renner Hotels-Carlton	**27**
Rotkreuzplatz	**2**
Torbräu	**18**
The Westin Grand München Arabellapark	**28**

SNACKS

It seems that Munich loves to snack, and a tempting array of food is available almost anytime. The generic term for a snack is *Imbiss*, and thanks to growing internationalism you'll find all types of them, from the generic *Wiener* (hot dogs) to the Turkish *Döner Kebab* sandwich (pressed and roasted lamb, beef, or chicken). Almost all butcher shops and bakeries offer some sort of *Brotzeit* snack, which can range from a modest sandwich to a steaming plate of goulash with potatoes and salad.

Some edibles come with social etiquette attached. The *Weisswurst*, a tender minced-veal sausage—made fresh daily, steamed, and served with sweet mustard and a crisp roll or a pretzel—is a Munich institution, and is served before noon with a *Weissbier* (wheat beer), supposedly to counteract the effects of a hangover. Legend has it that this white sausage was invented in 1857 by a butcher who *had* a hangover and mixed the wrong ingredients. A plaque on a wall on Marienplatz marks where the "mistake" was made. Some people use a knife and fork to remove the edible part from the skin; the rougher crowd might indulge in *auszuzeln*, sucking the sausage out of the Weisswurst.

Another favorite Bavarian specialty is *Leberkäs*—literally "liver cheese," although neither liver nor cheese is among its ingredients. It's a sort of meat loaf baked to a crusty turn each morning and served in succulent slabs throughout the day. A *Leberkäs Semmel*—a wedge of the meat loaf between two halves of a crispy bread roll slathered with a slightly spicy mustard—is the favorite Munich on-the-go snack. For late-night snacks go to the Schrannenhalle next to the Viktualienmarkt.

$$ ✕ **Nürnberger Bratwurst Glöckl am Dom.** Munich's most original beer tavern is dedicated to the delicious *Nürnberger Bratwürste* (finger-size sausages), a specialty from the rival city of Nürnberg. They're served by a busy team of friendly waitresses dressed in Bavarian dirndls who flit between the crowded tables with remarkable agility. There are other options available as well. In summer, tables are placed outside under a large awning and in the shade of the nearby Frauenkirche. In winter the mellow dark-panel dining rooms provide relief from the cold. ■TIP➔ **For a quick beer you can check the side door where, just inside, there is a little window serving fresh Augustiner from a wooden barrel. You can stand there with some of the regulars or enjoy the small courtyard if the weather is nice.** ⊠*Frauenpl. 9, City Center* ☎*089/220–385* ⊟*DC, MC, V* Ⓜ*Marienplatz (U-bahn and S-bahn).*

$$ ✕ **Oskar Maria.** A mixed crowd frequents this stylish gallery, bistro, ★ and restaurant in the Literaturhaus, a converted city mansion. The vaulted high ceiling and plate glass windows make for a light and spacious atmosphere. Fare includes German nouvelle cuisine and Mediterranean flavors, but there's a strong Gallic touch with dishes such as veal marengo and leg of venison. ⊠*Salvatorpl. 1, City Center* ☎ *089/2919–6029* ⊟ *AE, DC, MC, V* Ⓜ*Odeonsplatz (U-bahn).*

$$ ✕**Vinorant Alter Hof.** If you don't make it to Franconia, then you can at least get a taste of the region's food and wine in this simply decorated restaurant nestled in the old vaulted cellar and first floor of Munich's castle. The wine bar in the cellar serves hearty Franconian snacks along with Franconian wines, which can be ordered in small amounts, allowing your taste buds to travel the region's vineyards. ■TIP➜ **It's a nice place to end the evening after a concert at the nearby National Theater or the Residenz.** ⊠*Alter Hof 3, City Center* ☎*089/2424–3733* ▭*AE, DC, V* ☉*Closed Sun.* Ⓜ*Marienplatz (U-bahn and S-bahn).*

$$ ✕**Weinhaus Neuner.** Munich's oldest wine tavern serves good food as well as superior wines in its two nooks: the wood-panel restaurant and the Weinstube. The choice of food is remarkable, from roast duck to fish to traditional Bavarian. ⊠*Herzogspitalstr. 8, City Center* ☎*089/260–3954* ▭*AE, MC, V* ☉*Closed Sun.* Ⓜ*Marienplatz (U-bahn and S-bahn).*

$–$$ ✕**Andechser am Dom.** At this Munich mainstay for both locals and visitors, the vaulted, frescoed ceiling and the old stone floor recall the Andechs monastery. The boldly Bavarian food—blood sausage with potatoes, or roast duck—and fine selection of delectable Andechs beers will quickly put you at ease. The covered terrace with a view of the Frauenkirche is a favorite meeting place, rain or shine, for shoppers, local businesspeople, and even the occasional VIP. ⊠ *Weinstr. 7a, City Center* ☎*089/298–481* ▭*AE, MC, V* Ⓜ*Marienplatz (U-bahn and S-bahn).*

$–$$ ✕**Dürnbräu.** A fountain plays outside this picturesque old Bavarian inn, a true Munich classic. Inside, the central 21-foot table is the favorite and fills up first. Your fellow diners there will range from businesspeople to students. The food is resolutely traditional. ⊠*Dürnbräug. 2, City Center* ☎*089/222–195* ▭*MC* Ⓜ*Marienplatz (U-bahn and S-bahn).*

$–$$ ✕**Jodlerwirt.** This cozy Alpine lodge-styled restaurant in a small street behind the Rathaus is a treat for those craving an old-world tavern, complete with live accordion playing. As its name suggests, yodelers perform most nights, telling jokes and poking fun at their adoring guests in unintelligible Bavarian slang. The food is traditional, including *Käsespätzle* (a hearty German version of macaroni and cheese), goulash, and meal-size salads. The tasty beer is from the Ayinger brewery. The place is small and fills up fast. ⊠*Altenhofstr. 4, City Center* ☎*089/221–249* ▭*No credit cards* ☉*Closed Sun. and Mon. No lunch* Ⓜ*Marienplatz (U-bahn and S-bahn).*

$–$$ ✕**Prinz Myshkin.** Break away from the meaty Bavarian diet at this
★ sophisticated vegetarian restaurant that spices up predictable cuisine by mixing Italian and Asian influences. You have a choice of antipasti, homemade gnocchi, tofu, stir-fried dishes, and excellent wines. The airy room has a high, vaulted ceiling and there's always some art exhibited to feed the eye and mind. ⊠*Hackenstr. 2, City Center* ☎*089/265–596* ▭*MC, V* Ⓜ*Sendlinger Tor (U-bahn).*

$–$$ ✕ **Saf im Zerwirk.** A two flight walk upstairs will land you in a minimalist dining room with hard to find vegetarian entrees. Try the excellent refreshing summer salad or one of the many other vegan dishes, very

A REAL MEAL

Typical, more substantial dishes in Munich include *Tellerfleisch*, boiled beef with freshly grated horseradish and boiled potatoes on the side, served on wooden plates (there is a similar dish called *Tafelspitz*). Among roasts, sauerbraten (beef) and *Schweinebraten* (roast pork) are accompanied by dumplings and sauerkraut. *Hax'n* (ham hocks) are roasted until they're crisp on the outside and juicy on the inside. They are served with sauerkraut and potato puree. Game in season (venison or boar, for instance) and duck are served with potato dumplings and red cabbage.

As for fish, the region has not only excellent trout, served either smoked as an hors d'oeuvre or fried or boiled as an entrée, but also the perch-like *Rencke* from Lake Starnberg.

You'll also find soups, salads, casseroles, hearty stews, and what may well be the greatest variety and the highest quality of baked goods in Europe, including pretzels. And for dessert, indulge in a bowl of Bavarian cream, apple strudel, or *Dampfnudel*, a fluffy leavened-dough dumpling usually served with vanilla sauce.

nicely arranged, served with a smile, and accompanied by an excellent red or white wine. The Hofbräuhaus is not a city block, but light years away. ⊠ *Ledererstr. 3, City Center* ☎ *089/2323–9195* ♨ *Reservations essential* 🖃 *AE, DC, MC, V* ⊗ *Closed Sun. and 4–6.*

$ ✕ **Bier-und Oktoberfest Museum.** In one of the oldest buildings in Munich, dating to 1327, the museum takes an imaginative look at the history of this popular elixir, the monasteries that produced it, the Purity Laws that govern it, and Munich's own long tradition with it. A restaurant consisting of a few heavy wooden tables opens along with the museum at 1 PM and serves hot meals from 6 PM. ■TIP→ **You can visit the restaurant without paying the museum's admission fee and try beer from one of Munich's oldest breweries, the Augustiner Bräu.** ⊠ *Sterneckstr. 2, City Center* ☎ *089/2423–1607* ⊕ *www.bier-und-oktoberfestmuseum.de* 🖃 *€4* ⊗ *Tues.–Sat. 1–5* Ⓜ *Isartor (U-bahn and S-bahn).*

$ ✕ **Bratwurstherzl.** Tucked into a quaint little square off the Viktualienmarkt, this low-key Bratwurst joint cooks up their specialty sausages right in the main room over an open grill. For those looking for a bit less meat, there is also a hearty farmer's salad with turkey strips and tasty oyster mushrooms. They have outdoor seating, perfect for people-watching when the weather is good. ⊠ *Dreifaltigkeitspl. 1, City Center* ☎ *089/295–113* 🖃 *AE, MC, V* ⊗ *Closed Sun. and public holidays* Ⓜ *Marienplatz (U-bahn and S-bahn).*

¢–$ ✕ **Faun.** Not quite City Center, but still central to the action, the beloved ★ Faun is off Klenzestrasse, past Gärtnerplatz. It's a happy combination of Munich tavern and international bistro, with great outdoor seating on a small square where five streets meet and five trees are planted. Their Thai curries are wonderful, and their juicy Schweinebraten will satisfy any meat cravings. The dishes on the daily changing menu are tasty, filling, and easy on your wallet. The beer served is Augustiner, so you can't go wrong there. Build up your appetite by browsing your way through the neighborhood shops and boutiques, or walk off your meal along the river back toward the Isartor. ⊠*Hans-Sachs-Str. 17, Isarvorstadt* ☎*089/263–798* ☰ *No credit cards.*

¢–$ ✕**Hofbräuhaus.** A classic. The pounding oompah band draws the curious into this father of all beer halls, where singing and shouting drinkers contribute to the earsplitting din. This is no place for the fainthearted, although a trip to Munich would be incomplete without at least having a look. Upstairs is a quieter restaurant, but let's face it: the food isn't why you come here. In March, May, and September ask for one of the special, extra-strong seasonal beers (Starkbier, Maibock, Märzen), which complement the traditional Bavarian fare. ⊠*Am Platzl 9, City Center* ☎ *089/290–1360* ⚑*Reservations not accepted* ☰*AE. DC, MC, V* Ⓜ*Marienplatz (U-bahn and S-bahn).*

¢–$ ✕**Pfälzer Residenz Weinstube.** A huge stone-vaulted room, a few smaller rooms on the side, wooden tables, flickering candles, dirndl-clad waitresses, and a long list of wines add up to a storybook image of a timeless Germany. The wines are mostly from the *Pfalz* (Palatinate), as are many of the specialties on the limited menu. Beer drinkers, take note—beer is not served here. ⊠*Residenzstr. 1, City Center* ☎*089/225–628* ⚑*Reservations not accepted* ☰*AE, MC, V* Ⓜ*Odeonsplatz (U-bahn).*

¢–$ ✕**Weisses Bräuhaus.** If you've developed a taste for Weissbier, this institution in downtown Munich is the place to indulge it. The flavorful brew (from Schneider) is served with hearty Bavarian dishes, mostly variations of pork and dumplings or cabbage. The waitresses here are famous in Munich for purposely giving some customers a hard time, but if you're good-natured, the whole thing can be quite funny. The art nouveau styling of the restaurant is beautifully restored, and when the weather is good it's a great place to sit outside. ⊠*Tal 7, City Center* ☎*089/299–875* ☰*No credit cards* Ⓜ*Isartor (S-bahn).*

¢ ✕**Due passi.** This former dairy shop, now an Italian specialty shop, offers Italian meals for a quick, stand-up lunch. There's a small but fine selection of fresh antipasti and pasta. You can eat at the high marble tables and counters or take your food to go. Menus change daily. ⊠*Ledererstr. 11, City Center* ☎*089/224–271* ☰*No credit cards* ☉*Closed Sun. No dinner Sat.* Ⓜ*Isartor (S-bahn).*

¢ ✕**Nero Pizza & Lounge.** The pies are great here: try the Diavolo, with spicy Neopolitan salami. On a side street between Gärtnerplatz and Isartor, Nero's has high ceilings that give it a very open feel; you can sit upstairs in the lounge for a cozier experience. ⊠*Rumfordstr. 34, City Center* ☎*089/2101–9060* ☰*AE, MC, V* ☉ *No lunch* Ⓜ*Marienplatz (U-bahn)*

LEHEL

$–$$ ✕**Gandl.** This Italian specialty shop, where you can buy various staples from vinegar to coffee, doubles as a comfortable, relaxed restaurant. Their extensive Saturday buffet breakfast is popular in the neighborhood. Seating can become a little crowded inside, but the excellent service will make up for it and make you feel right at home. For lunch it's just the place for a quick pastry or excellent antipasto misto before proceeding with the day's adventures. Dinner is more relaxed, with Mediterranean influenced cuisine. ⊠*St.-Anna-Pl. 1, Lehe* ☎*089/2916–2525* 🖃 *No credit cards* ⊘*Closed Sun.* Ⓜ*Lehel (U-bahn).*

¢–$ ✕**Gasthaus Isarthor.** This old-fashioned *Wirtshaus* is one of the few
★ places that serve Augustiner beer exclusively from wooden kegs, freshly
tapped on a daily basis. It simply doesn't get any better than this (the
traditional Bavarian fare is all good, too). All kinds are drawn to the
simple wooden tables of this solid establishment. Antlers and a wild
boar look down on actors, government officials, apprentice craftsper-
sons, journalists, and retirees, all sitting side by side. ⊠*Kanalstr. 2,
Lehel* ☎*089/227–753* 🖃No *credit cards* Ⓜ*Isartor (S-bahn).*

SCHWABING & MAXVORSTADT

$$$$ ✕**Tantris.** Despite the unappealing exterior, this restaurant will spoil
Fodor's Choice you for other food for days. Select the menu of the day and accept the
★ suggestions of the charming and competent sommelier or choose from
the à la carte options and you'll be treated to a feast that may include
langostino with curry bok choy, mushrooms, and spicy coconut cream,
a lightly smoked pigeon breast with goose liver, turbot with artichoke
stock, and carré of lamb. No wonder Chef Hans Haas has kept his
restaurant at the top of the critics' charts in Munich. When the last
course of dessert arrives, you'll hesitate to disturb the inventive creation
put before you. But not for long. ⊠*Johann-Fichte-Str. 7, Schwabing*
☎*089/361–9590* ⌔*Reservations essential. Jacket and tie* 🖃*AE, DC,
MC, V* ⊘*Closed Sun. and Mon.* Ⓜ*Münchener Freiheit (U-bahn).*

$$ ✕**Cohen's.** Reviving the old Jewish Central European tradition of good,
healthy cooking together with hospitality and good cheer seems to be
the underlying principle at Cohen's. Dig into a few hearty latkes, a
steaming plate of Chulend stew, or a standard gefilte fish doused with
excellent Golan wine from Israel. The kitchen is open from 12:30 PM to
about 10:30 PM, and if the atmosphere is good, patrons may hang out
chattering until the wee hours. ■TIP➔ **Klezmer singers perform on some
Friday evenings.** ⊠*Theresienstr. 31, Maxvorstadt* ☎*089/280–9545*
🖃*AE, MC, V* Ⓜ*Theresienstrasse (U-bahn).*

$–$$ ✕ **Vorstadt Café.** Young professionals mix with students at this lively
restaurant on the corner of Adalbert and Türkenstrasse. Thirteen differ-
ent breakfasts are a big draw, especially on weekends. Their daily lunch
specials, served quickly, are good value. The atmosphere at dinner is
relaxed, complete with candlelight. Reservations are advised on weekends. ⊠ *Türkenstr. 83, Maxvorstadt* ☎*089/272–0699* 🖃No *credit
cards* Ⓜ*Universität (U-bahn).*

¢–$ ✕**Max-Emanuel-Brauerei.** This historic old brewery tavern is a great
value, with Bavarian dishes rarely costing more than €10. The best
part about this place, however, is the cozy, secluded little beer garden with huge chestnut trees, tucked in the back amid the apartment
blocks. ⊠*Adalbertstr. 33, Schwabing* ☎*089/271–5158* 🖃*AE, MC*
Ⓜ*Josephsplatz (U-bahn).*

LEOPOLDVORSTADT

¢–$ ✕**Augustiner Keller.** This 19th-century establishment is the flagship beer restaurant of one of Munich's oldest breweries. It is also the location of the absolutely unbeatable Augustiner beer garden, which you have to experience once in your life. The menu changes daily and offers Bavarian specialties, but try to order their "top seller" —¼ duck with a good slab of roast suckling pig, dumpling, and blue cabbage. Follow that with a *Dampfnudel* (yeast dumpling served with custard), and you probably won't feel hungry again for quite a while. ✉*Arnulfstr. 52, Leopoldvorstadt* ☎*089/594–393* ☐*AE, MC* Ⓜ*Hauptbahnhof (U-bahn and S-bahn).*

HAIDHAUSEN

$–$$ ✕**Wirtshaus in der Au.** One of the oldest taverns in Munich, this Wirt-
★ shaus with a yawning vaulted room and beer steins all over the place makes you feel welcome, hungry, and thirsty! It has an excellent combination of fantastic service and outstanding local dishes. It serves everything from *Hofente* (roast duck) to *Schweinsbraten* (roast pork), but the real specialty is *Knödel* (dumplings), which, in addition to traditional *Semmel* (bread) and *Kartoffel* (potato) varieties, come in spinach, cheese, and even red-beet flavors. Weather permitting, you can sit in the small beer garden under, of course, chestnut trees. It's only a three-minute walk from the bridge at the Deutsches Museum. ✉*Lilienstr. 51, Haidhausen* ☎*089/448–1400* ☐*AE, MC* Ⓜ*Isartor (S-bahn and Tram).*

WHERE TO STAY

Though Munich has a vast number of hotels in all price ranges, booking one can be a challenge, as this is a trade-show city as well as a prime tourist destination. If you're visiting during any of the major trade fairs such as the ispo (sports, fashion) in February or the IHM (crafts) in mid-March, or during Oktoberfest at the end of September, try to make reservations at least a few months in advance. It is acceptable practice in Europe to request to see a room before committing to it, so feel free to ask the concierge.

Some of the large, upscale hotels that cater to expense-account business travelers have very attractive weekend discount rates—sometimes as much as 50% below normal prices. Conversely, hotels raise their regular rates by at least 30% during big trade fairs and Oktoberfest. Online booking sites like Hotel Reservation Service (⊕*www.hrs.com*) often have prices well below the hotel's published prices (i.e., price ranges in this book) in slow periods and on short notice. Look for the names we suggest here and search online for potential deals.

■TIP→**Munich's tourist information office has two outlets that can help you with hotel bookings if you haven't reserved in advance. One is at the central station and the other is on Marienplatz, in the Rathaus. Your best bet is to visit in person.**

A technical note: many hotels in Munich have chosen of late to farm out their wireless Internet services to third parties—meaning that you can get online with their Wi-Fi hotspot, but you log in with a credit card and pay with a separate service provider. Convenient, but not very personal.

WHAT IT COSTS IN EUROS					
	¢	$	$$	$$$	$$$$
FOR TWO PEOPLE	under €50	€50–100	€101–€175	€176–€225	over €225

Hotel prices are for two people in a standard double room, including tax and service.

CITY CENTER

$$$$
Fodor'sChoice
★

Bayerischer Hof. This is the address for luxury in Munich, as it has been since 1841, when His Majesty Ludwig I of Bavaria came twice a month to take a "royal bath," as his own residence lacked a bathtub. He probably never imagined that 167 years later guests would enjoy a magnificent view over Munich while swimming in a rooftop pool. Today the guest rooms have everything from fireplaces and whirlpool tubs to antique furniture and flat screen TVs; huge windows frame the fabulous view and some suites have kitchens. In addition to the excellent Bavarian restaurant Palais Keller there are four very different restaurants to choose from in-house. When meeting someone at "the bar," specify which one: there are five, as well as a nightclub. **Pros:** posh public rooms with valuable oil paintings, the roof garden restaurant has an impressive view of the Frauenkirche just two blocks away, impressive amenities and views. **Con:** expensive. ⊠ *Promenadepl. 2–6, City Center,* ☎ *089/21200* ⊕ *www.bayerischerhof.de* 🛏 *313 rooms, 60 suites* ⌂ *In-room: safe, Ethernet, Wi-Fi. In-hotel: 4 restaurants, room service, 6 bars, laundry service, concierge, executive floor, pool, spa, public Internet, public Wi-Fi, parking (fee), no-smoking rooms, some pets allowed (fee)* ⊟ *AE, DC, MC, V* �’◎’*BP* Ⓜ *Karlsplatz (U-bahn and S-bahn) or Marienplatz (U-bahn and S-bahn).*

$$$$
Hotel Vier Jahreszeiten München Kempinski. Its lobby has been called the "most beautiful living room in Munich," and just as the world's wealthy and titled have felt for more than 150 years, you'll feel at home enjoying a drink and a bite in this "lived-in" spacious and luxurious room with glass dome and with dark-wood paneling. Trend and tradition blend throughout the property, especially in the new guest rooms where flat screen TVs hang on the same walls as original oil paintings and Bose stereos rest on antique cupboards. In the Vue Maximilian restaurant your attention may be torn between the excellent food and watching people on Maximilianstrasse, Munich's premier shopping street. **Pros:** great location, occasional special packages that are a good value. **Cons:** no Wi-Fi, Ethernet not always reliable. ⊠ *Maximilianstr. 17, City Center* ☎ *089/21250* ⊕ *www.Kempinski-Vierjahreszeiten.de* 🛏 *303 rooms, 65 suites* ⌂ *In-room: safe, Ethernet. In-hotel: restau-*

rant, room service, bar, pool, gym, concierge, public Internet, parking (fee), no-smoking rooms, some pets allowed (fee) ⊟AE, DC, MC, V ⏏️BP Ⓜ️Tram 19 Kammerspiele (Tram).

$$$–$$$$ 🔲 **Mercure.** This straightforward, comfortable hotel is a great deal for its location. Set just between Marienplatz and Sendlingertor, it is within walking distance of the city center. An extra €13 buys breakfast in the hotel. It's better than many breakfasts you'll get at a restaurant. **Pros:** central location, moderate price. **Cons:** public parking garage is 200 meters away, hotel can become noisy with guests. ✉️Hotterstr. 4, City Center ☎089/232–590 ⊕www.mercure.com ⇗75 rooms ♿In-room: Wi-Fi. In-hotel: public Internet, no-smoking rooms ⊟AE, MC, V ⏏️EP Ⓜ️Marienplatz (U-bahn and S-bahn).

$$$–$$$$ 🔲 **Torbräu.** Munich's oldest hotel, the Torbräu, has been run by the same family for more than a century. It is next to one of the ancient city gates—the 14th-century Isartor—and the location is perfect for this walkable downtown, as it's midway between the Marienplatz and the Deutsches Museum (and around the corner from the Hofbräu-haus). Comfortable rooms are decorated in a plush and ornate Italian style. Its Italian restaurant, La Famiglia, is one of the best in town. **Pros:** nice rooms, central location, good restaurant, very attentive service. **Cons:** underground parking difficult, front rooms noisy. ✉️Tal 41, City Center ☎089/242–340 ⊕www.torbraeu.de ⇗89 rooms, 3 suites ♿In-room: Ethernet, Wi-Fi. In-hotel: restaurant, public Internet, public Wi-Fi, no-smoking rooms, some pets allowed (fee) ⊟AE, MC, V ⏏️BP Ⓜ️Isartor (S-bahn).

$$$ 🔲 **Cortiina.** One of Munich's designer hotels, Cortiina follows the mini-malist gospel. The reception is done in sleek gray stone with a high-tech gas fireplace along one wall. For guests, the emphasis is on subtle luxury—fresh flowers, mattresses made from natural rubber, sheets made of untreated cotton. The rooms are paneled in dark moor oak and come with all the amenities. In the Annex, 50 meters away, are 30 apartments with cooking facilities. **Pros:** welcoming modern reception and bar, nice comfortable rooms, personalized service. **Cons:** Wi-Fi is expensive. ✉️Ledererstr. 8, City Center ☎089/242–2490 ⊕www.cortiina.com ⇗54 rooms ♿In-room: Ethernet, Wi-Fi. In-hotel: bar, public Wi-Fi, parking (fee), no-smoking rooms, some pets allowed ⊟AE, DC, MC, V ⏏️BP Ⓜ️Marienplatz (U-bahn and S-bahn).

$$–$$$ 🔲 **Platzl.** The privately owned Platzl has won awards and wide recogni-tion for its ecologically aware management, which uses heat recyclers in the kitchen, environmentally friendly detergents, recyclable materi-als, waste separation, and other ecofriendly practices. It stands in the historic heart of Munich, near the famous Hofbräuhaus beer hall and a couple of minutes' walk from Marienplatz and many other land-marks. Its Pfistermühle restaurant, with 16th-century vaulting, is one of the area's oldest and most historic establishments. **Pros:** good res-taurant, around the corner from the Hofbräuhaus. **Cons:** rooms facing the Hofbräuhaus get more noise, some rooms are on the small side. ✉️Sparkassenstr. 10, City Center ☎089/237–030, 800/448–8355 in U.S. ⊕www.platzl.de ⇗167 rooms ♿In-room: no a/c (some), Eth-ernet, Wi-Fi (some). In-hotel: restaurant, bar, gym, parking (fee), no-smoking rooms, some pets allowed (fee) ☐AE, DC, MC, V ❘○❘BP Ⓜ Marienplatz (U-bahn and S-bahn).

$$ ☷Hotel am Markt. You can literally stumble out the door of this hotel onto the Viktualienmarkt. Perfect location, fair prices, simple rooms is what you get here. Small meals are served in the café connected with the hotel. Wi-Fi Internet access is available for free in the hotel's public spaces. Pros: excellent location, very friendly helpful service, free Wi-Fi. Cons: rooms are simple, some spots could use fresh paint. ⊠ Heiliggeiststr. 6, City Center ☏089/225–014 ⊕www.hotel-am-markt.eu ❤22 rooms &In-room: no a/c. In-hotel: public Wi-Fi ☐No credit cards ❘○❘CP Ⓜ Marienplatz (U-bahn and S-bahn).

HAUPTBAHNHOF

$$–$$$ ☷Creatif Hotel Elephant. Tucked away on a quiet street near the train station, this hotel appeals to a wide range of travelers, from businesspeople to tourists on a budget. The rooms are simple, clean, and quiet. A bright color scheme in the reception and breakfast room creates a cheery atmosphere. Wi-Fi is free in the building. ∎TIP→Check out the hotel's online booking deals for dramatically reduced rates. Pros: close to main station, free Wi-Fi. Cons: no restaurant. ⊠ Lämmerstr. 6, Leopoldvorstadt ☏089/555–785 ⊕www.creatifelephanthotel.com ❤40 rooms &In-room: no a/c, Wi-Fi. In-hotel: public Wi-Fi, some pets allowed ☐AE, MC, V ❘○❘BP Ⓜ Hauptbahnhof (U-bahn and S-bahn).

$$–$$$ ☷Eden-Hotel Wolff. Beyond a nice, light lobby a spacious bar with dark-wood paneling beckons, contributing to the old-fashioned elegance of this downtown favorite. It's directly across the street from the northern exit of the main train station with U-bahn, S-bahn and trams at your service. The rooms are well furnished with large, comfortable beds, and the colors are relaxing pastels; the back rooms face a quiet street. You can dine on excellent Bavarian specialties in the intimate Zirbelstube restaurant. Pros: great location, all rooms have a/c, free Internet. Cons: windows opening towards the main station will let in the noise. ⊠Arnulfstr. 4, Hauptbahnhof ☏089/551–150 ⊕www.ehw.de ❤209 rooms, 2 suites &In-room: Ethernet, Wi-Fi. In-hotel: restaurant, bar, gym, public Wi-Fi, parking (fee), some pets allowed (fee) ☐AE, DC, MC, V ❘○❘BP Ⓜ Hauptbahnhof (U-bahn and S-bahn).

$$–$$$ ☷Hotel Amba. Right across the street from the main train station, Amba provides clean, bright rooms, good service, no expensive frills, and everything you need to plug and play. The lobby, with a small bar, invites you to relax in a Mediterranean atmosphere of wicker sofas with bright-color upholstery. After a solid breakfast buffet (with sparkling wine) on the second floor overlooking the station, you can hit the nearby sights on foot or use the public transportion options a few meters away. To save money, ask for a room with shared bathroom. There are also occasional special deals on weekends. Pros: convenient to train station and sights. Cons: no restaurant, rooms that face the main street and the station are noisy. ⊠Arnulfstr. 20, Hauptbahnhof ☏089/545–140 ⊕www.hotel-amba.de ❤86 rooms &In-room: no a/c, Wi-Fi. In-hotel: public Wi-Fi, public Internet, no-smoking rooms,

some pets allowed (fee) ☰*AE, DC, MC, V* ⦿|*BP* Ⓜ*Hauptbahnhof (U-bahn and S-bahn).*

\$–\$\$ ⚿**Hotel Mirabell.** This family-run hotel is used to American tourists
★ who appreciate the friendly service, central location (between the main
railway station and the Oktoberfest fairgrounds), and reasonable room
rates. Three apartments are for small groups or families. Rooms are
furnished in modern light woods and bright prints. Breakfast buffet is
included. **Pros:** top location, family run, personalized service. **Cons:**
no restaurant, streets outside the hotel are seedy. ⊠*Landwehrstr. 42,
entrance on Goethestr., Hauptbahnhof* ☎*089/549–1740* ⊕*www.
hotelmirabell.de* ⌨*65 rooms, 3 apartments* ⌂*In-room: no a/c, Wi-Fi.
In-hotel: bar, public Wi-Fi, no-smoking rooms, some pets allowed (fee)*
☰*AE, DC, MC, V* ⦿|*BP* Ⓜ*Hauptbahnhof (U-bahn and S-bahn).*

LEHEL

\$\$\$–\$\$\$\$ ⚿**Opera.** In the quiet residential district of Lehel, the Opera offers
rooms decorated in an elegant style—lots of Empire, some art deco.
Some rooms have glassed-in balconies. There are no minibars, but
guests can order room service round the clock. Enjoy summer breakfast in the back courtyard decorated with orange and lemon trees.
The street it's on is a cul-de-sac accessed through the neo-Renaissance
arcades of the Ethnographic Museum. **Pros:** elegant, pleasant courtyard, quiet location, special service. **Cons:** not enough parking close to
the hotel, no restaurant. ⊠*St.-Anna-Str. 10, Lehel* ☎*089/210–4940*
⊕*www.hotel-opera.de* ⌨*25 rooms* ⌂*In-room: no a/c, Wi-Fi. In-
hotel: bar, public Wi-Fi, no-smoking rooms, some pets allowed* ☰*AE,
MC, V* ⦿|*BP* Ⓜ*Lehel (U-bahn).*

\$\$–\$\$\$ ⚿**Adria.** This modern hotel is located near a number of great museums
and the English Garden. Rooms are large and tastefully decorated. A
breakfast buffet (including a glass of sparkling wine) is included in the
room rate. There's no hotel restaurant, but there's free coffee and tea
in the lobby. Wi-Fi Internet access is free in the lobby, but there is a fee
for it in the rooms. **Pros:** good location, nice lobby. **Cons:** no bar or restaurant, impersonal service. ⊠*Liebigstr. 8a, Lehel,* ☎*089/242–1170*
⊕*www.adria-muenchen.de* ⌨*43 rooms* ⌂*In-room: no a/c, dial-up,
Wi-Fi. In-hotel: public Wi-Fi, no-smoking rooms, some pets allowed
(fee)* ☰*AE, MC, V* ⦿|*BP* Ⓜ*Lehel (U-bahn).*

\$\$ ⚿**Hotel Concorde.** The privately owned Concorde is right in the middle
of Munich and yet very peaceful owing to its location on a narrow side
street. The nearest S-bahn station (Isartor) is only a two-minute walk
away. Rooms in one tract are done in pastel tones and light woods;
in the other tract they tend to be somewhat darker and more rustic.
Fresh flowers and bright prints add a colorful touch. A large breakfast buffet is served in a stylish, mirrored dining room. **Pros:** quiet,
functional, good location. **Cons:** no restaurant or bar. ⊠*Herrnstr. 38,
Lehel* ☎*089/224–515* ⊕*www.concorde-muenchen.de* ⌨*67 rooms, 4
suites* ⌂*In-room: no a/c, Wi-Fi. In-hotel: public Wi-Fi, parking (fee),
no-smoking rooms, some pets allowed (fee)* ☰*AE, DC, MC, V* ⦿|*BP*
Ⓜ*Isartor (S-bahn).*

ISARVORSTADT

$$$

Fodor's Choice
★

Admiral. The small, privately owned Admiral enjoys a quiet side-street location and its own garden, close to the Isar River and Deutsches Museum. A very comfortable bar with comfortable easy chairs is right behind the lobby. Many of the nicely furnished and warmly decorated bedrooms have a balcony overlooking the quiet, secluded garden. The breakfast buffet is a dream, complete with homemade jams, fresh bread, and Italian and French delicacies; two tables are set out in the garden. The use of the minibar is included in the room price and Wi-Fi Internet access is free. **Pros:** quality prints on the wall, attention to detail, excellent service. **Cons:** no restaurant, small lobby. ⊠ *Kohlstr. 9, Isarvorstadt* ☎ *089/216–350* ⊕ *www.hotel-admiral.de* ⬏ *33 rooms* ⚘ *In-room: no a/c, Ethernet, Wi-Fi. In-hotel: bar, public Internet, public Wi-Fi, parking (fee), no-smoking rooms, some pets allowed* ▭ *AE, DC, MC, V* ⦿ *BP* Ⓜ *Isartor (S-bahn).*

$$–$$$

Advokat. If you value the clean lines of modern taste over plush luxury, this is the hotel for you. Breakfast, the use of the minibar, and Wi-Fi are included in the room price. The location is great: the subway is across the street; Isartor is two minutes away on foot, and the Viktualienmarkt seven. **Pros:** modern rooms, spacious lobby. **Cons:** no bar or restaurant, rooms facing the front are noisy. ⊠ *Baaderstr. 1, Isarvorstadt,* ☎ *089/216–310* ⊕ *www.hotel-advokat.de* ⬏ *50 rooms* ⚘ *In-room: no a/c, Ethernet, Wi-Fi. In-hotel: public Internet, public Wi-Fi, parking (fee), no-smoking rooms, some pets allowed* ▭ *AE, DC, MC, V* ⦿ *BP* Ⓜ *Isartor (S-bahn).*

$

Pension Seibel. If you're looking for a very affordable little "pension" just a stone's throw from the Viktualienmarkt, this is the place. You can't get any closer than this for the price. The rooms are simple; there are also three larger rooms for 4 to 6 people. **Pros:** great location at a great price. **Cons:** tiny breakfast room, no elevator. ⊠ *Reichenbachstr. 8, Isarvorstadt* ☎ *089/99520* ⊕ *www.seibel-hotels-munich.de* ⬏ *22 rooms* ⚘ *In-hotel: no elevator* ▭ *AE, MC, V* ⦿ *BP* Ⓜ *Marienplatz (U-bahn and S-bahn).*

MAXVORSTADT

$$

Renner Hotels–Carlton. The Carlton is one of three little hotels—all within a block of each other—that form a privately owned chain in the heart of the museum quarter and a hop-skip from the English Garden and Schwabing. The location is also really close to downtown, just north of City Center. The Carlton has a bit more flair than the other two (Antare and Savoy), but if the Carlton is booked up you have a good chance of getting something at the others. All three are clean and simple, have generous breakfast buffets, and are very fairly priced. **Pros:** centrally located, fairly priced. **Cons:** elevator only goes up to the 4th floor, you have to climb the stairs to go higher, rooms on main street can be noisy, parking is a short walk away. ⊠ *Fürstenstr. 12, Maxvorstadt* ☎ *089/282–061* ⊕ *www.carlton-garni.de* ⬏ *32 rooms* ⚘ *In-room: no a/c, Wi-Fi. In-hotel: public Wi-Fi* ▭ *MC, AE, V* ⦿ *CP* Ⓜ *Between Universität and Odeonsplatz (U-bahn).*

2

$ ⊞ **Hotel Pension Am Siegestor.** Modest but very appealing, this is a great
★   deal in a fairly expensive city. The pension takes up three floors of a fin-
de-siècle mansion between the Siegestor monument, on Leopoldstrasse,
and the university. An ancient elevator with a glass door brings you to
the fourth-floor reception desk. Most of the simply furnished rooms
face the impressive Arts Academy across the street. Rooms on the fifth
floor are particularly cozy, tucked up under the eaves. **Pros:** a delightful
and homey place to stay. **Cons:** if elevators make you nervous, don't
use this old one; no restaurant or bar. ⊠ *Akademiestr. 5, Maxvorstadt*
☎ *089/399–550* ⊕ *www.siegestor.com* 🛏 *20 rooms* ⬩ *In-room: no a/*
c, no phone, no TV (some). In-hotel: public Internet 🖃 *No credit cards*
🍴 *CP* Ⓜ *Universität (U-bahn).*

SCHWABING

$$–$$$ ⊞ **Biederstein.** A modern, block of a building, but covered with gera-
niums in summer, the Biederstein seems to want to fit into its old
Schwabing surroundings at the edge of the English Garden. The many
advantages here: peace and quiet; excellent service; and comfortable,
well-appointed and renovated rooms. Guests are requested to smoke
on the balconies, not inside. The breakfast buffet costs €9.50 extra but
is worth it. **Pros:** wonderfully quiet location, all rooms have balconies,
exemplary service, U-bahn is four blocks away. **Con:** no restaurant.
⊠ *Keferstr. 18, Schwabing* ☎ *089/389–9970* ⊕ *www.hotelbiederstein.*
de 🛏 *34 rooms, 7 suites* ⬩ *In-room: no a/c. In-hotel: bar, bicycles,*
public Internet, parking (no fee), some pets allowed (fee) 🖃 *AE, DC,*
MC, V Ⓜ *Münchner Freiheit (U-bahn).*

$–$$ ⊞ **Gästehaus am Englischen Garten.** Reserve well in advance for a room
★   at this popular converted water mill, more than 300 years old, adjoining the English Garden. The hotel is only a five-minute walk from the
bars, shops, and restaurants of Schwabing. Be sure to ask for one of the
12 nostalgically old-fashioned rooms in the main building, which has a
garden on an island in the old millrace; a modern annex down the road
has 13 apartments, all with cooking facilities. In summer, breakfast is
served on the terrace of the main house. There is free Internet access at
their partner hotel, the Biederstein around the corner. **Pros:** quiet location, ideal for walking or cycling, wonderfully cozy rooms. **Cons:** no
elevator, no restaurant. ⊠ *Liebergesellstr. 8, Schwabing* ☎ *089/383–*
9410 ⊕ *www.hotelenglischergarten.de* 🛏 *12 rooms, 6 with bath or*
shower; 13 apartments ⬩ *In-room: no a/c. In-hotel: bicycles, parking*
(no fee), no elevator, some pets allowed (fee) 🖃 *AE, DC, MC, V* 🍴 *BP*
Ⓜ *Münchner Freiheit (U-bahn).*

LUDWIGVORSTADT

$$ ⊞ **Brack.** A nice, light-filled lobby makes the first good impression
here. Oktoberfest revelers value the Brack's proximity to the beer-fes-
tival grounds, and its location—on a busy, tree-lined thoroughfare just
south of the city center—is handy for city attractions. The rooms are
furnished in light, friendly veneers and are soundproof (a useful feature

during Oktoberfest) and have amenities such as hair dryers. The buffet breakfast, which lasts until noon, will prepare you for the day. **Pros:** good location for accessing Oktoberfest and city; late breakfast. **Con:** noisy front rooms. ⊠*Lindwurmstr. 153, Ludwigvorstadt* ☎*089/747–2550* ⊕*www.hotel-brack.de* 🛏*50 rooms* ⌂*In-room: no a/c, Wi-Fi. In-hotel: public Wi-Fi, parking (no fee), some pets allowed* ⊟*AE, MC, V* ⏀*BP* Ⓜ*Poccistrasse (U-bahn).*

$–$$ 🏨**Hotel-Pension Mariandl.** The American armed forces commandeered this turn-of-the-20th-century neo-Gothic mansion in May 1945 and established Munich's first postwar nightclub, the Femina, on the ground floor. Breakfast is served downstairs in the Café am Beethovenplatz, which also has free Wi-Fi Internet access. Most rooms are mansion-size, with high ceilings and large windows overlooking a leafy avenue. The Oktoberfest grounds and the main railway station are both a 10-minute walk away. Prices during Oktoberfest increase substantially. **Pros:** hotel and café are a charmingly worn and a bit bohemian. **Cons:** hotel and café are charmingly worn and a bit bohemian, no elevator. ⊠*Goethestr. 51, Ludwigvorstadt* ☎*089/534–108* ⊕*www.hotelmariandl.com* 🛏*28 rooms* ⌂*In-room: no a/c, no phone, no TV (some), Wi-Fi (some). In-hotel: restaurant, public Internet, public Wi-Fi, no elevator, some pets allowed* ⊟*AE, DC, MC, V* ⏀*BP* Ⓜ*Hauptbahnhof (U-bahn and S-bahn).*

$–$$

Fodor'sChoice

★

🏨**Hotel Uhland.** This stately villa is a landmark building and is additionally special in that the owner and host was born here and will make you feel at home, too. She and her staff welcome all questions and seem to love answering them. The spacious, inviting breakfast room filled with light and the excellent food will get you ready for the day ahead. Some of the pleasant rooms are quite large and can accommodate three people. **Pros:** a real family atmosphere, care is given to details. **Cons:** no restaurant or bar. ⊠ *Uhlandstr. 1, Ludwigvorstadt* ☎*089/543–350* ⊕*www.hotel-uhland.de* 🛏*27 rooms* ⌂*In-room: no a/c, Wi-Fi (some). In-hotel: public Internet, public Wi-Fi, some pets allowed* ⊟*AE, DC, MC, V*

$ 🏨**Hotel-Pension Schmellergarten.** Popular with young budget travelers, this genuine family business tries to make everyone feel at home. It's a little place on a quiet street off Lindwurmstrasse, a few minutes' walk from the Theresienwiese (Oktoberfest grounds). The Poccistrasse subway station is around the corner to take you into the center of town. Wi-Fi Internet access is free. **Pros:** good location, good price. **Cons:** no elevator, no hotel services. ⊠*Schmellerstr. 20, Ludwigvorstadt* ☎*089/773–157* ✎*milankuhn@web.de* 🛏*14 rooms* ⌂*In-room: no a/c, no TV. In-hotel: no elevator, some pets allowed* ⊟ *MC* ⏀*CP* Ⓜ*Poccistrasse (U-bahn).*

THERESIENHÖHE

$$–$$$

Park-Hotel Theresienhöhe. The Park-Hotel claims that none of its rooms is less than 400 square feet. Suites are larger than many luxury apartments, and some of them come with small kitchens. The sleek, modern rooms are mostly decorated with light woods and pastel-color fabrics and carpeting; larger rooms and suites get a lot of light, thanks to the floor-to-ceiling windows. Families are particularly welcome. There's no in-house restaurant, but you can order in. **Pros:** spacious rooms, good quiet location. **Cons:** no restaurant, modern with little charm. ⊠*Parkstr. 31, Theresienhöhe* ☎*089/519–950* ⊕*www.park hoteltheresienhoehe.de* ⤢*50 rooms* △*In-room: no a/c, Wi-Fi. In-hotel: bar, no-smoking rooms, some pets allowed* ⊟*AE, DC, MC, V* ◯❘*BP* Ⓜ*Theresienwiese (U-bahn).*

$$

Kurpfalz. Visitors have praised the friendly welcome and service they receive at this well-maintained and affordable lodging above the Oktoberfest grounds. Rooms are comfortable, if furnished in a manner only slightly better than functional. There is free Wi-Fi Internet access in the building. **Pros:** good location, good prices. **Cons:** no restaurant, rooms are simple, it's best to confirm your reservation. ⊠*Schwantalerstr. 121, Theresienhöhe* ☎*089/540–9860* ⊕*www.kurpfalz-hotel.de* ⤢*44 rooms* △*In-room: no a/c, Ethernet. In-hotel: public Wi-Fi, bar, no-smoking rooms, some pets allowed* ⊟*AE, MC, V* ◯❘*BP* Ⓜ*Hackerbrücke (S-bahn).*

NYMPHENBURG

$$–$$$

Erzgiesserei Europe. Rooms in this modern hotel are bright, decorated in soft pastels with good reproductions on the walls. The cobblestone garden café is quiet and relaxing. Rates vary greatly, even on their own Web site. The English Cinema is around the corner if you're hankering for a film, and the subway station is a seven-minute walk. **Pros:** relatively quiet location, nice courtyard, a/c in all rooms. **Cons:** charm of a business hotel. ⊠*Erzgiessereistr. 15, Nymphenburg* ☎*089/126–820* ⊕*www.topinternational.com* ⤢*105 rooms, 1 suite* △*In-room: no a/c, Wi-Fi. In-hotel: restaurant, bar, Wi-Fi, parking (fee), no-smoking rooms, some pets allowed (fee)* ⊟*AE, DC, MC, V* ◯❘*BP* Ⓜ*Stiglmaierplatz (U-bahn).*

$–$$

Kriemhild. This welcoming, family-run pension is in a quiet western suburb. If you're traveling with children, you'll appreciate that it's a 10-minute walk from Schloss Nymphenburg and around the corner from the Hirschgarten Park. The tram ride (No. 16 or 17 to Kriemhildenstrasse stop) from the train station is 10 minutes. Wi-Fi Internet access is free in the building. **Pros:** quiet location, family run. **Cons:** far from the city sights, no elevator. ⊠*Guntherstr. 16, Nymphenburg* ☎*089/171–1170* ⊕*www.kriemhild.de* ⤢*18 rooms* △*In-room: no a/c, Wi-Fi. In-hotel: public Wi-Fi, bar, free parking, some pets allowed, no elevator* ⊟*AE, MC, V* ◯❘*BP* Ⓜ*Kriemhildstrasse (Tram-bahn 16/17).*

BOGENHAUSEN

$$$-$$$$ ⚄ **The Westin Grand München Arabellapark.** The building itself with
★ its 22 floors may raise a few eyebrows. It stands on a slight eleva-
tion and is not the shapeliest of the Munich skyline. What goes on
inside, however, is sheer five-star luxury. Guests of the four top floors,
the Tower Rooms and Suites, are greeted with a glass of champagne;
snacks, drinks, and a fantastic view of the city and the Bavarian Alps
are available in the Towers Lounge. Room service is available around
the clock. The excellent restaurant Ente vom Lehel is here as well. And
if you'd like to add a special Bavarian flavor to your stay, book one of
the 60 "Bavarian rooms" on the 15th and the 16th floors with antique
wood furniture and a country feel. **Pros:** luxurious lobby and restau-
rant, rooms facing west toward the city have a fabulous view. **Cons:** it's
not possible to reserve west-facing rooms, hotel is difficult to reach via
public transportation. ⊠ *Arabellastr. 5, Bogenhausen* ☎ *089/92640*
⊕ *www.arabellasheraton.de* ⤳ *629 rooms, 28 suites* ⚭ *In-room: dial-
up, Wi-Fi (some). In-hotel: 2 restaurants, room service, bars, pool,
laundry service, concierge, public Internet, public Wi-Fi, parking (fee),
no-smoking rooms, some pets allowed (fee)* ⊟ *AE, DC, MC, V* ⊺⚮ *BP*
Ⓜ *Arabellapark (U-bahn).*

OUTSIDE THE CENTER

$-$$ ⚄ **Jagdschloss.** This century-old hunting lodge in Munich's leafy Obermenzing suburb is a delightful hotel. The rustic look has been retained,
with lots of original woodwork and white stucco. Many of the comfortable pastel-tone bedrooms have wooden balconies with flower boxes
bursting with color. In the beamed restaurant or sheltered beer garden
you'll be served Bavarian specialties by a staff dressed in traditional
lederhosen (shorts in summer, breeches in winter). **Pros:** peaceful location, beer garden, easy parking. **Cons:** out in the middle of nowhere,
convenient only with a car, no elevator. ⊠ *Alte Allee 21 München-
Obermenzing* ☎ *089/820-820* ⊕ *www.jagd-schloss.com* ⤳ *22 rooms,
1 suite* ⚭ *In-room: no a/c, Ethernet. In-hotel: restaurant, bar, parking
(no fee), some pets allowed, no elevator* ⊟ *MC, V* ⊺⚮ *BP.*

NIGHTLIFE & THE ARTS

THE ARTS

Bavaria's capital has an enviable reputation as an artistic hot spot.
Details of concerts and theater performances are listed in *Vorschau*
and *Monatsprogramm*, booklets available at most hotel reception
desks, newsstands, and tourist offices. The English-language magazine *Munich Found* also has some information. Otherwise, just keep
your eye open for advertising pillars and posters, especially on church
walls. Tickets for performances at the Bavarian State Theater–New
Residence Theater, Nationaltheater, Prinzregententheater, and Staatstheater am Gärtnerplatz are sold at the **central box office** (⊠ *Marstallpl.*

5, City Center ☎089/2185–1920). It's open weekdays 10–7, Saturday 10–7, and one hour before curtain time. One ticket agency, **München Ticket** (☎089/5481–8181 ⊕*www.muenchenticket.de*), has a German-language Web site where tickets for most Munich theaters can be booked. Two **Zentraler Kartenverkauf** (✉*City Center* ☎089/264–620) ticket kiosks are in the underground concourse at Marienplatz.

CONCERTS

Munich and music go together. The city has two world-renowned orchestras. The Philharmonic is now directed by Christian Thielemann, formerly of the Deutsche Oper in Berlin; the Bavarian State Opera Company is managed by Japanese-American director Kent Nagano. The leading choral ensembles are the Munich Bach Choir, the Munich Motettenchor, and Musica Viva, the last specializing in contemporary music. The choirs perform mostly in city churches.

The Bavarian Radio Symphony Orchestra sometimes performs at the **Bayerischer Rundfunk** (✉*Rundfunkpl. 1, Hauptbahnhof* ☎089/558–080 ⊕*www.br-online.de*) and other city venues like Gasteig. The box office is open weekdays 9–4.

Munich's world-class concert hall, the **Gasteig Culture Center** (✉*Rosenheimerstr. 5, Haidhausen* ☎089/480–980 ⊕*www.muenchenticket.de*), is a lavish brick complex standing high above the Isar River, east of downtown. Its Philharmonic Hall is the permanent home of the Munich Philharmonic Orchestra and the largest concert hall in Munich. Gasteig also hosts the occasional English-language work. Ⓜ*Rosenheimerplatz (S-bahn).*

Herkulessaal in der Residenz (✉*Hofgarten, City Center* ☎089/2906–7263) is a leading orchestral and recital venue in the former throne room of King Ludwig I. Free concerts featuring conservatory students are given at the **Hochschule für Musik** (✉*Arcisstr. 12, Maxvorstadt* ☎089/289–27450).

The Bavarian State Orchestra is based at the **Nationaltheater** (aka *Bayerische Staatsoper Opernplatz, City Center* ☎089/2185–1920 ⊕*www.staatsorchester.de*). Munich's major pop-rock concert venue is the **Olympiahalle** (✉*U-3 Olympiazentrum stop, Georg-Brauchle-Ring* ⊕*www.olympiapark-muenchen.de*). The box office, at the ice stadium, is open weekdays 10–6 and Saturday 10–3. You can also book by calling **München Ticket** (☎089/5481–8181). The romantic art nouveau **Staatstheater am Gärtnerplatz** has a variety of performances including operas, ballet, and musicals. (✉*Gärtnerpl. 3, Isarvorstadt* ☎089/2185–1960).

FESTIVALS In early May the **Long Night of Music** (☎089/3061–0041 💶€10) is devoted to live performances through the night by untold numbers of groups, from heavy-metal bands to medieval choirs, at more than 100 locations throughout the city. One ticket covers everything, including transportation on special buses between locations.

Munich's Bavarian State Opera Company and its ballet ensemble perform at the **Nationaltheater** (✉ *Opernpl., City Center* ☎ *089/2185–1920*). The **Staatstheater am Gärtnerplatz** (✉ *Gärtnerpl. 3, Isarvorstadt* ☎ *089/2185–1960* ⊕ *www.staatstheater-am-gaertnerplatz.de*) presents a less ambitious but nevertheless high-quality program of opera, ballet, operetta, and musicals.

THEATER

Munich has scores of theaters and variety-show venues, although most productions will be largely impenetrable if your German is shaky. Listed here are all the better-known theaters, as well as some of the smaller and more progressive spots. Note that most theaters are closed during July and August.

Amerika Haus (*America House* ✉ *Karolinenpl. 3, Maxvorstadt* ☎ *089/552–5370* ⊕ *www.amerikahaus.de*) is the venue for the very active American Drama Group Europe, which presents regular English-language productions.

Bayerisches Staatsschauspiel/Neues Residenztheater (*Bavarian State Theater–New Residence Theater* ✉ *Max-Joseph-Pl., City Center* ☎ *089/218–501* ⊕ *www.bayerischesstaatsschauspiel.de*) is Munich's leading stage for classic playwrights such as Goethe, Schiller, Lessing, Shakespeare, and Chekhov.

Musicals, revues, balls, and big-band shows take place at **Deutsches Theater** (✉ *Schwanthalerstr. 13, Leopoldvorstadt* ☎ *089/5523–4444* ⊕ *www.deutsches-theater.de*). The box office is open weekdays noon–6 and Saturday 10–1:30.

The **English Comedy Club** at the **Substanz Live Club & Bar**, (✉ *Rupertstr. 28, Isarvorstadt* ☎ *089/721–2749* ⊕ *www.englishcomedyclub.de*) has gotten rave reviews. Entry for this evening on the first Monday of each month is €18.

A city-funded rival to the nearby state-backed Staatliches Schauspiel, **Münchner Kammerspiele-Schauspielhaus** (✉ *Maximilianstr. 26, City Center* ☎ *089/233–96600* ⊕ *www.muenchner-kammerspiele.de*) presents the classics as well as new works by contemporary playwrights.

NIGHTLIFE

Munich has a lively nocturnal scene ranging from beer halls to bars to chic, see-and-be-seen clubs. The fun neighborhoods for a night out are City Center, Isarvorstadt (around Gärtnerplatz), and Schwabing around Schellingstrasse and Münchener Freiheit. Regardless of their size or style, many bars, especially around Gärtnerplatz, have DJs spinning either mellow background sounds or funky beats. The city's eclectic taste in music is quite commendable.

In summer, last call at the beer gardens is around 11 PM; ask your table neighbors where they are heading afterward—it's the best way to find out what's happening on the ground. Most of the traditional Bavarian

CLOSE UP

All About German Beer

However many fingers you want to hold up, just remember the easy-to-pronounce *Bier* (beer) *Bit-te* (please) when ordering a beer. The tricky part is, Germans don't just produce *one* beverage called beer; they brew more than 5,000 varieties. Germany has about 1,300 breweries, 40% of the world's total. The hallmark of the country's dedication to beer is the Purity Law, *das Reinheitsgebot,* unchanged since Duke Wilhelm IV introduced it in Bavaria in 1516. The law decrees that only malted barley, hops, yeast, and water may be used to make beer, except for specialty Weiss- or Weizenbier (wheat beers, which are a carbonated, somewhat spicy, and sour brew, often with floating yeast particles).

Most taverns have several drafts in addition to bottled beers. The type available depends upon the region you're in, and perhaps on the time of

year. The alcohol content of German beers also varies. At the weaker end of the scale is the light Munich Helles (a lager, from 3.7% to 4.8% alcohol by volume); stronger brews are the bitter-flavored Pilsner (around 5%) and the dark Doppelbock (more than 7%).

In Munich you'll find the most famous breweries, the largest beer halls and beer gardens, the biggest and most indulgent beer festival, and the widest selection of brews. Even the beer glasses are bigger: a *Mass* is a 1-liter (almost 2-pint) serving; a *Halbe* is half liter and the standard size. The Hofbräuhaus is Munich's best-known beer hall, but its oompah band's selections are geared more to Americans and Australians than to your average Münchener. You'll find locals in one of the English Garden's four beer gardens or in the local *Wirtshaus* (tavern).

–Robert Tilley

joints stay open until 1 AM or so and are great for a couple of hours of wining and dining before heading out on the town. Most bars stay open until at least 3 AM on weekends; some don't close until 5 or 6 AM. The easiest way to find what you like is to just ask people at your table.

Be warned that the bouncers at clubs and discos in Munich can make it frustratingly difficult to get into often not-so-special establishments. They can be rude, and have achieved dubious notoriety throughout Germany. They are in charge of picking who is "in" and who is "out," and there's no use trying to warm up to them.

BARS

CITY CENTER Around the corner from the Hofbräuhaus, **Bar Centrale** (⊠ *Ledererstr. 23, City Center* ☎ *089/223–762*) is very Italian—the waiters don't seem to speak any other language. The coffee is excellent; small fine meals are served as well. They have a retro-looking back room with leather sofas. Also near the Hofbräuhaus is the **Atomic Café** (⊠ *Neutrumstr. 5, City Center* ☎ *089/2283–053*). This club/lounge has excellent DJs nightly, playing everything from '60s Brit pop to '60s/'70s funk and soul. Atomic also has great live acts on a regular basis. Cover charge is typically €7. Just behind the Frauenkirche, **Kilian's Irish Pub and Ned Kelly's Australian Bar** (⊠ *Frauenpl. 11, City Center* ☎ *089/2421–9899*) offers an escape from the German tavern scene. Naturally, they have Guinness and Foster's, but they also serve Munich's lager, Augustiner, and regularly televise international soccer, rugby, and sports in general. At **Schumann's** (⊠*Odeonspl. 6–7, City Center* ☎*089/229–060*) the bartenders are busy shaking cocktails after the curtain comes down at the nearby opera house. Exotic cocktails are the specialty at **Trader Vic's** (⊠*Promenadenpl. 4, City Center* ☎*089/226–192*), a smart cellar bar in the Hotel Bayerischer Hof that's popular among out-of-town visitors. The Bayerischer Hof's **Night Club** (⊠*Promenadepl. 2–6, City Center* ☎*089/212–00*) has live music, from jazz to reggae to hip-hop; a small dance floor; and a very lively bar.

Eisbach (⊠*Marstallplatz 3, City Center* ☎*089/2280–1680*) occupies a corner of the Max Planck Institute building opposite the Bavarian Parliament. The bar is among Munich's biggest and is overlooked by a mezzanine restaurant area where you can choose from a limited but ambitious menu. Outdoor tables nestle in the expansive shade of huge parasols. The nearby Eisbach brook, which gives the bar its name, tinkles away like ice in a glass.

The **Kempinski Vier Jahreszeiten** (⊠*Maximilianstr. 17, City Center* ☎*089/21250*) offers piano music until 9 PM and then dancing to recorded music or a small combo. At the English, nautical-style **Pusser's New York Bar** (⊠*Falkenturmstr. 9, City Center* ☎*089/220–500*), great cocktails and Irish-German black and tans (Guinness and strong German beer) are made to the sounds of live jazz. Try the "Pain Killer," a specialty of the house. The pricey sandwiches are about the only "New York" in Pusser's.

ISARVORSTADT   Around Gärtnerplatz are a number of cool bars and clubs for a somewhat younger, hipper crowd. Take a seat on Grandma's retro couches at **Trachtenvogel** (⊠*Reichenbachstr. 47, Isarvorstadt* ☎*089/215–160*). DJs spin on most weekend nights, playing everything from reggae to hip-hop and soul. Trachtenvogel serves good toasties and Tegernseer beer, a favorite in Munich. For a New York City–corner-bar type experience, check out **Holy Home** (⊠*Reichenbachstr. 21, Isarvorstadt* ☎*089/2014–546*). A hip local crowd frequents this smoky hole-in-the-wall that books great low-key DJs.

If you're looking for a bit more action, check out the **Café am Hochhaus** (⊠*Blumenstr. 29, Isarvorstadt* ☎*089/8905–8152*). The glass-front former coffee shop is now a scene bar with funky DJs playing music to shake a leg to (if it's not too crowded).

SCHWABING   Media types drink Guinness and Kilkenny at the square bar at **Alter Simpl** (⊠*Türkenstr. 57, Schwabing* ☎*089/272–3083*). More than 100 years old, this establishment serves German pub food until 2 AM. Across the street is the **Türkenhof** (⊠*Türkenstr. 78, Schwabing* ☎*089/2800–235*), another solid local joint that serves Augustiner and good food. Up on Schellingstrasse is **Schall und Rauch** (⊠*Schellingstr. 22, Schwabing* ☎*089/2880–9577*). This legendary student hangout, whose name literally means "Noise and Smoke," has great music and food. Another absolute cornerstone in the neighborhood is the **Schelling Salon** (⊠*Schellingstr. 54, Schwabing* ☎*089/2720–788*). On the corner of Barerstrasse, the bar has several pool tables and even a secret Ping-Pong room in the basement with an intercom for placing beer orders. It's closed on Tuesday and Wednesday.

BEER GARDENS

Everybody in Munich has at least one favorite beer garden, so you're usually in good hands if you ask someone to point you in the right direction. You do not need to reserve. No need to phone either: if the weather says yes, then go. Some—but not all—allow you to bring your own food, but if you do, don't defile this hallowed territory with something so foreign as pizza or a burger from McDonald's. Note that Munich has very strict noise laws, so beer gardens tend to close around 11.

CITY CENTER The only true beer garden in the city center, and therefore the easiest to find, is the one at the **Viktualienmarkt** (☎*089/2916–5993*). The beer on tap rotates every six weeks among the six Munich breweries to keep everyone happy throughout the year. The rest of the beer gardens are a bit farther afield and can be reached handily by bike or S- and U-bahn.

AROUND TOWN The famous **Biergarten am Chinesischen Turm** (⊠*Englischer Garten 3* ☎*089/383–8730*) is at the five-story Chinese Tower in the Englischer Garten. Enjoy your beer to the strains of oompah music played by traditionally dressed musicians. The Englischer Garten's smaller beer garden, **Hirschau** (⊠*Gysslingstr. 15* ☎*089/322–1080*) is about 10 minutes north of the Kleinhesselohersee. The **Seehaus im Englischen Garten** (⊠*Kleinhesselohe 3* is on the banks of the artificial lake Kleinhesselohersee, where all of Munich converges on hot summer days (bus line 44, exit at Osterwaldstrasse; you can't miss it).

The **Augustiner Beer Garden** (⊠*Arnulfstr. 52, Hauptbahnhof* ☎*089/594–393*) is one of the more authentic of the beer gardens, with excellent food, beautiful chestnut shade trees, a mixed local crowd, and Munich Augustiner beer. From the north exit of the main train station, go left on Arnulfstrasse and walk about 10 minutes. It's on the right.

Surprisingly large and green for a place so centrally located is the **Hofbräukeller** (⊠*Innere Wiener Str. 19, tramway 18 to Wiener-Pl. or U-bahn 4 or 5 to Max-Weber-Pl., Haidhausen* ☎*089/459–9250*), which serves the same beer as the Hofbräuhaus. It also has a spacious cellar and cheap eats (€5).

Out in the district of Laim is the huge **Königlicher Hirschgarten** (⊠*Hirschgarten 1* ☎*089/1799–9119*), where the crowd is somewhat more blue-collar and foreign. To get there, take any S-bahn toward Pasing, exit at Laim, walk down Wotanstrasse, and take a right on Winifriedstrasse and then a left onto De-la-Paz-Strasse.

The crowd at the **Taxisgarten** (⊠*Taxisstr. 12* ☎*089/156–827*) in the Gern district (U-bahn Gern, Line 1 toward Olympia Einkaufszentrum) is more white-collar and tame, but the food is excellent, and while parents refresh themselves, children exhaust themselves on the playground.

If you want to get out of town either on a bike or with the S-bahn, the **Waldwirtschaft Grosshesselohe** (aka *the "Wawi"* ✉ *Georg-Kalb-Str. 3, Grosshesselohe* ☎ *089/795–088*) is a fantastic beer garden a few miles south of town. It's a superb location—on a cliff overlooking the Isar—and if it's a nice day the excursion is well worth it. They've got a great jazz band. Take the S-bahn 7 to Grosshesselohe. From there it's about a 10-minute walk. Or by bike you can cruise the path along the west side of the Isar until you see a small sign saying Waldwirtschaft pointing up a steep hill. Ask someone if you can't find it.

> ## UNDER THE CHESTNUT TREES
>
> Munich has more than 100 beer gardens, ranging from huge establishments that seat several hundred to small terraces tucked behind neighborhood pubs and taverns. Beer gardens are such an integral part of Munich life that a council proposal to cut down their hours provoked a storm of protest in 1995, culminating in one of the largest mass demonstrations in the city's history. They open whenever the thermometer creeps above 10°C (50°F) and the sun filters through the chestnut trees that are a necessary part of beer-garden scenery.

DANCE CLUBS

There are a few dance clubs in town worth mentioning, but be warned: the larger the venue the more difficult the entry. In general, big nightclubs are giving way to smaller, more laid-back lounge types of places scattered all over town. If you're really hankering for a big club, go to Optimolwerke in the Ostbahnhof section. Otherwise, enjoy the handful of places around the city center.

CITY CENTER, LEHEL & ISARVORSTADT
Bordering the Englischer Garten, **P1** (✉ *Prinzregentenstr., on west side of Haus der Kunst, Lehel* ☎ *089/294–252*) is definitely one of the most popular clubs in town for the see-and-be-seen crowd. It is chockablock with the rich and the wannabe rich and can be fun if you're in the mood. Good luck getting past the bouncer. If you don't get in, head across the street to **Edmoses** at Prinzregentenstrasse 2. **Erste Liga** (✉ *Hochbrückenstr. 3, right near Sendlinger Tor, Isarvorstadt* ☎ *089/1893–2788*) is a popular club with a variety of music styles and the occasional surprise live performance by hip-hop bands or well-known DJs. The neighborhood is also very lively, and has lots of other options if you don't get in.

HAIDHAUSEN/ OSTBAHNHOF
A former factory premises hosts the city's largest late-night party scene: the **Optimolwerke** (✉ *Friedenstr. 10, Ostbahnhof* Ⓜ *Ostbahnhof [S-bahn]*) has no fewer than 13 clubs including a Latin dance club, the (in)famous Temple Bar, and more snack trucks than you can shake a currywurst at. **Muffathalle** (✉ *Rosenheimerstr. 1, behind Müllersches Volksbad near river, Haidhausen* ☎ *089/4587–5010*) usually posts orange-and-purple schedules on advertising pillars. It has a wide range of concerts, and the crowd is refreshingly unpretentious. The café-bar

here has different DJs just about every night of the week and can be really fun.

LAIM The **Backstage** (✉*Friedenheimerbrücke 7, Laim* Ⓜ*Friedenheimerbrücke [S-bahn]* ☎*089/126–6100*) is out past the Hauptbahnhof and is mostly a live-music venue for alternative music of all kinds, but they have a chilled-out club as well with a beer garden.

GAY & LESBIAN BARS

Munich's well-established gay scene stretches between Sendlingertorplatz and Isartorplatz in the Glockenbach neighborhood. For an overview, check ⊕*www.munich-cruising.de.*

The laid-back **Selig** (✉*Hans-Sachs-Str. 3, Isarvorstadt* ☎*089/2388–8878*) has a bit of outdoor seating, diverse cuisine, and good breakfasts. Right across the street from Selig, **Nil** (✉*Hans-Sachs-Str. 2, Isarvorstadt* ☎*089/265–545*) is famous for its decent prices and its schnitzel. The upscale **Morizz** (✉*Klenzestr. 43, Isarvorstadt* ☎*089/201–6776*) fills with a somewhat moneyed crowd.

The **Ochsengarten** (✉*Müllerstr. 47, Isarvorstadt* ☎*089/266–446*) is Munich's leather bar. **Old Mrs. Henderson** (✉*Rumfordstr. 2, Isarvorstadt* ☎*089/263–469*) puts on the city's best transvestite cabaret for a mixed crowd and has various other events. You can dance here too.

JAZZ

Munich has a decent jazz scene, and some beer gardens have even taken to replacing their brass oompah bands with funky combos. Jazz musicians sometimes accompany Sunday brunch, too.

The **Jazzbar Vogler** (✉*Rumfordstr. 17, City Center/Isarvorstadt* ☎*089/294–662*) is a nice bar with jam sessions on Monday nights and regular jazz concerts. At tiny **Alfonso's** (✉*Franzstr. 5, Schwabing* ☎*089/338–835*) the nightly live music redefines the concept of intimacy. The tiny **Mr. B's** (✉*Herzog-Heinrich-Str. 38, Ludwigvorstadt* ☎*089/534–901*) is a treat. It's run by New Yorker Alex Best, who also mixes great cocktails and, unlike so many other barkeeps, usually wears a welcoming smile.

The **Unterfahrt** (✉*Einsteinstr. 42, Haidhausen* ☎*089/448–2794*) is the place for the serious jazzologist, though hip-hop is making heavy inroads into the scene. The **Jazz Cantina** (✉*Steinstr. 83, Haidhausen* is a cozy little place with live music and Mexican food. Outdoor seating in summer.

The **Big Easy** (✉*Frundsbergstr. 46, Nymphenburg* ☎*089/158–90253*) is a classy restaurant with jazz-accompanied Sunday brunch for €17.50, not including drinks. Pricey, but good. Sunday is set aside for jazz at **Waldwirtschaft Grosshesselohe** (aka *the "Wawi"* ✉*Georg-Kalb-Str. 3, Grosshesselohe* ☎*089/795–088; see Beer Gardens section*), a lovely beer garden in a southern suburb. If it's a nice day, the excursion is worth it.

SPORTS & THE OUTDOORS

The **Olympiapark** (Ⓜ*Olympiazentrum [U-bahn]*), built for the 1972 Olympics, is one of the largest sports and recreation centers in Europe. The Olympic-size pool is open for swimming. For general information about sports in and around Munich, contact the sports emporium **Sport Scheck** (✉*Sendlingerstr. 6, City Center* ☎*089/21660*). The big store not only sells every kind of equipment but is very handy with advice.

BICYCLING

A bike is hands-down the best way to experience this flat, pedal-friendly city. There are loads of bike lanes and paths that wind through its parks and along the Isar River. The rental shop will give you maps and tips, or you can get a map at any city tourist office.

Weather permitting, here is a route to try: Go through Isartor to the river and head north to the Englischer Garten. Ride around the park and have lunch at a beer garden. Exit the park and go across Leopoldstrasse into Schwabing, making your way back down toward the museum quarter via the adorable Elisabethmarkt. Check out one or two of the galleries then head back to town passing Königsplatz.

You can also take your bike on the S-bahns (except during rush hours from 6 AM to 9 AM and from 4 PM to 6 PM), which take you out to the many lakes and attractions outside town. Bicycles on public transportation cost either one strip on a multiple ticket or €2.50 for a day ticket, €0.90 for a single ticket.

TOURS **Mike's Bike Tours** (☎*089/2554–3988* ⊕*www.mikesbiketours.com*) is the oldest bike tour operation in Munich. Mike's tours last 3½ hours, with a 45-minute break at a beer garden, and cover approximately four miles. Tours start daily at the Altes Rathaus at the end of Marienplatz at 11:30 and 4 (Apr. 15–Aug. 31) and at 12:30 (Mar. 1–Apr. 15 and Sept. 1–Nov. 10). There are tours at 12:30 on Saturday in November and February if weather permits. The cost is €24, including the bike. No reservations required. Bus Bavaria (part of Mike's Bikes) also offers a more active day trip to Neuschwanstein castle. You travel to the area via coach in high season (€49), via train in the shoulder season (€39).

RENTALS **Mike's Bike Tours** (✉*Bräuhausstr. 10, City Center* ☎*089/2554–3988* ⊕*www.mikesbiketours.com*) also rents bikes, Mike's is around the corner from the rear entrance of the Hofbräuhaus, Day rental is €12 for the first day, €9 for subsequent days. Return time is 8 PM May–August, earlier in other seasons.

Based at the central station, **Radius Bike Rental** (✉*Opposite platform 32, Hauptbahnhof* ☎*089/596–113*) rents bikes. A 3-gear bike costs €15 per day. A 21-gear bike costs €18. Hourly rates are €3 and €4, respectively.

ICE-SKATING

Global warming permitting, there's outdoor skating on the lake in the Englischer Garten and on the Nymphenburger Canal in winter. Watch out for signs reading GEFAHR (danger), warning you of thin ice. In winter the fountain on **Karlsplatz** is turned into a public rink with music and an outdoor bar.

JOGGING

The best place to jog is the **Englischer Garten,** which is 11 km (7 mi) around and has dirt and asphalt paths throughout. The banks of the **Isar River** are a favorite route as well. You can also jog through **Olympiapark** if you're in the area. The 500-acre park of **Schloss Nymphenburg** (⊠ *Tramway 12 to Romanplatz*) is also ideal for running.

SWIMMING

Munich set itself a goal of making the Isar River drinkable by 2005, and nearly did it. Either way, the river is most definitely clean enough to wade in on a hot summer day. Hundreds of people sunbathe on the banks upriver from the Deutsches Museum and take the occasional dip. If you prefer stiller waters, you can try swimming outdoors in the Isar River at the Maria-Einsiedel public pool complex. However, because the water comes from the Alps, it's frigid even in summer. Warmer lakes near Munich are the **Ammersee** and the **Starnbergersee.**

SHOPPING

Munich has three of Germany's most exclusive shopping streets. At the other end of the scale, it has flea markets to rival those of any other European city. In between are department stores, where acute German-style competition assures reasonable prices and often produces outstanding bargains. Artisans and artists bring their wares of beauty and originality to the Christmas markets. Collect their business cards—in summer you're sure to want to order another of those little gold baubles that were on sale in December.

SHOPPING DISTRICTS

Munich has an immense central shopping area, a 2-km (1-mi) *Fussgängerzone* (pedestrian zone) stretching from the train station to Marienplatz and then north to Odeonsplatz. The two main streets here are Neuhauserstrasse and Kaufingerstrasse, the sites of most major department stores. For upscale shopping, Maximilianstrasse, Residenzstrasse, and Theatinerstrasse are unbeatable and contain classy and tempting stores that are some of the best in Europe. Schwabing, north of the university, has more offbeat shopping streets—Schellingstrasse and Hohenzollernstrasse are two to try. ■ TIP→ **The neighborhood around Gärtnerplatz also has a slew of new boutiques to check out.**

DEPARTMENT STORES & MALLS

The main pedestrian area has two mall-type locations. The aptly named **Arcade** (⊠ *Neuhauserstr. 5, City Center*) is where the young find the best designer jeans and accessories. **Kaufinger Tor** (⊠ *Kaufingerstr. 117, City Center*) has several floors of boutiques and cafés packed neatly together under a high glass roof. For a more upscale shopping experience, visit the many stores, boutiques, galleries, and cafés of the **Fünf Höfe,** a modern arcade carved into the block of houses between Theatinerstrasse and Kardinal-Faulhaber-Strasse. The architecture of the passages and courtyards is cool and elegant, in sharp contrast to the facades of the buildings. There's a great Thai restaurant in there as well.

Apartment 20 (✉*Hohenzollernstr. 20, Schwabing* ☎*089/391–519*) is in the midst of a ton of boutiques and sells an assortment of brandname gear and urban styles. For a classic selection of German clothing, including some with a folk touch, and a large collection of hats, try Munich's traditional family-run **Breiter** (✉*Kaufingerstr. 26, City Center* ☎*089/599–8840.*

★   **Karstadt** (✉*Bahnhofpl. 7, City Center* ☎*089/55120–2009*) commanding an entire city block between the train station and Karlsplatz, is the largest and, many claim, the best department store in the city. On the fourth floor is a cafeteria with a great selection of excellent and inexpensive dishes. **Hirmer** (✉*Kaufingerstr. 28, City Center* ☎*089/236–830*) has Munich's most comprehensive collection of German-made men's clothes, with a markedly friendly and knowledgeable staff. **Karstadt** (✉*Neuhauserstr. 18, City Center* ☎*089/290–230* ✉*Schleissheimerstr. 93, Schwabing* ☎*089/13020*), in the 100-year-old Haus Oberpollinger, at the start of the Kaufingerstrasse shopping mall, is another upscale department store, with Bavarian arts and crafts.

Galeria Kaufhof (✉*Karlspl. 21–24, City Center* ☎*089/51250* ✉*Marienpl., City Center* ☎*089/231–851*) offers goods in the middle price range. ■**TIP➔ The end-of-season sales are bargains. Ludwig Beck** (✉*Marienpl. 11, City Center* ☎*089/236–910*) is considered a step above other department stores by Müncheners. It's packed from top to bottom with highly original wares and satisfies even the pickiest of shoppers.

Pool (✉*Maximilianstr. 11, City Center* ☎*089/266–035*) is a hip shop on the upscale Maximilianstrasse, with fashion, music, and accessories for house and home. A shopping experience for the senses. **Slips** (✉*Gärtnerplatz. 2, Isarvorstadt* ☎*089/2022–500*), a beautiful shop on Gärtnerplatz, has a wide range of dresses, jeans, shoes, and accessories. Prices are a bit outrageous, but it's a successful store, so they must be doing something right.

GIFT IDEAS

Munich is a city of beer, and items related to its consumption are obvious choices for souvenirs and gifts. Munich is also the home of the famous Nymphenburg Porcelain factory. Between Karlsplatz and the Viktualienmarkt there are loads of shops for memorabilia and trinkets.

CRAFTS
Bavarian craftspeople have a showplace of their own, the **Bayerischer Kunstgewerbe–Verein** (✉*Pacellistr. 6–8, City Center* ☎*089/290–1470*); here you'll find every kind of handicraft, from glass and pot-

V.A.T. REFUNDS AT MUNICH'S AIRPORT

When departing from Munich for home, you can claim your V.A.T. refund (for purchases made during your stay). If the items are packed in your check-in luggage, tell the check-in agent who will give you a destination sticker for your bags, which you then take to German customs at terminal 1/B. Present your receipts, which will be stamped, and customs will forward your luggage to your flight (it is simpler to pack the items in your carry-on-bag, and follow the same procedure). With your stamped receipts in hand, go to the Global Refund office, 50 meters from the customs office to receive your V.A.T. refund.

tery to textiles. If you've been to the Black Forest and forgot to equip yourself with a clock, or if you need a good Bavarian souvenir, try **Max Krug** (⊠ *Neuhauserstr. 2, City Center* ☎*089/224–501*) in the pedestrian zone.

FOOD & BEER

Dallmayr (⊠ *Dienerstr.14–15, City Center* ☎*089/21350*) is an elegant gourmet food store, with delights ranging from the most exotic fruits to English jams, served by efficient Munich matrons in smart blue-and-white-linen costumes. The store's famous specialty is coffee, with more than 50 varieties to blend as you wish. There's also an enormous number of breads and a temperature-controlled cigar room.

Götterspeise (⊠ *Jahnstr. 30, Isarvorstadt* ☎*089/2388–7374*) is across the street from the restaurant Faun. The name of this delectable chocolate shop means "ambrosia," a fitting name for their gifts, delights, and hot drinks. **Chocolate & More** (⊠ *Westenriederstr. 15, City Center* ☎*089/255–44905*) specializes in all things chocolate.

Ludwig Mory (⊠ *Marienpl. 8, City Center* ☎*089/224–542*) has everything relating to beer, from mugs of all shapes and sizes and in all sorts of materials to warmers for those who don't like their beer too cold.

PORCELAIN

Porzellan Nymphenburg (⊠ *Odeonspl. 1, City Center* ☎*089/282–428*) resembles a drawing room in the Munich palace of the same name and has delicate, expensive porcelain safely locked away in bowfront cabinets. You can buy directly from the factory called Porzellanmanufaktur Nymphenburg (open weekdays 10–5, Saturday 11–4) on the grounds of **Schloss Nymphenburg** (⊠ *Nördliches Schlossrondell 8, Nymphenburg* ☎*089/1791–9710*).

For Dresden and Meissen porcelain wares, go to **Kunstring** (⊠ *Briennerstr. 4, City Center* ☎*089/281–532*) near Odeonsplatz.

MISCELLANEOUS

In an arcade of the Neues Rathaus is tiny **Johanna Daimer Filze aller Art** (✉ *Dienerstr., City Center* ☎ *089/776–984*), a shop selling every kind and color of felt imaginable. **Lehmkuhl** (✉ *Leopoldstr. 45, Schwabing* ☎ *089/3801–5013*), is Munich's oldest and one of its finest bookshops, and also sells beautiful cards.

Check out **Sebastian Wesely** (✉ *Rindermarkt 1, at Peterspl., City Center* ☎ *089/264–519*) for beer-related vessels and schnapps glasses (*Stampferl*), walking sticks, scarves, and napkins with the famous Bavarian blue-and-white lozenges. **Spielwaren Obletters** (✉ *Karlspl. 11–12, City Center* ☎ *089/5508–9510*) has two extensive floors of toys, many of them handmade playthings of great charm and quality.

SPECIALTY STORES

ANTIQUES

A few small shops around the Viktualienmarkt sell Bavarian antiques, though their numbers are dwindling under the pressure of high rents. Also try the area north of the university—Türkenstrasse, Theresienstrasse, and Barerstrasse are all filled with antiques stores.

Strictly for window-shopping—unless you're looking for something really rare and special and money's no object—are the exclusive shops lining Prannerstrasse, at the rear of the Hotel Bayerischer Hof. Interesting and inexpensive antiques and assorted junk from all over Eastern Europe are laid out at the weekend flea markets beneath the Donnersberger railway bridge on Arnulfstrasse (along the northern side of the Hauptbahnhof).

In **Antike Uhren Eder** (✉ *Opposite Hotel Bayerischer Hof, Prannerstr. 4, City Center* ☎ *089/220–305*), the silence is broken only by the ticking of dozens of highly valuable German antique clocks and by discreet negotiation over the high prices. Nautical items and antiquated sports equipment fill the curious **Captain's Saloon** (✉ *Westenriederstr. 31, City Center* ☎ *089/221–015*). For Munich's largest selection of dolls and marionettes, head to **Die Puppenstube** (✉ *Luisenstr. 68, Maxvorstadt* ☎ *089/272–3267*). Antique German silver and porcelain are the specialty of **Roman Odesser** (✉ *Westenriederstr. 21, City Center* ☎ *089/226–388*). Old, beautiful beer steins are the specialty of **Ulrich Schneider** (✉ *Am Radlsteg 2, City Center* ☎ *089/292–477*).

BOOKSTORES

Hugendubel (✉ *Marienpl. 22, 2nd fl., City Center* ☎ *089/23890* ✉ *Karlspl. 3, City Center* ☎ *089/552–2530*) has a good selection of novels in English. The **Internationale Presse** (☎ *089/5511–7170*) in the main train station has magazines and novels. **Lehmkuhl** (✉ *Leopoldstr. 45, Schwabing* ☎ *089/3801–5013*) is Munich's oldest and one of its finest bookshops; it also sells beautiful cards.

FOLK COSTUMES

If you want to deck yourself out in lederhosen or a dirndl, or acquire a green loden coat and little pointed hat with feathers, you have a wide choice in the Bavarian capital. ■TIP➔ **There are a couple of other shops along Tal "street" that have new and used lederhosen and dirndls at very good prices in case you want to spontaneously get into the spirit of the 'Fest.**

Much of the fine loden clothing on sale at **Loden-Frey** (⊠ *Maffeistr. 7, City Center* ☎ *089/210–390*) is made at the company's own factory, on the edge of the Englischer Garten. The tiny **Lederhosen Wagner** (⊠ *Tal 2, City Center* ☎ *089/225–697*), right up against the Heiliggeist Church, carries lederhosen, woolen sweaters called *Walk* (not loden), and children's clothing. For a more affordable option on loden clothing, try the department store **C&A** (⊠ *Kaufingerstr. 13, City Center* ☎ *089/231930*) in the pedestrian zone.

MARKETS

Munich's **Viktualienmarkt** is *the* place to shop and to eat. Just south of Marienplatz, it's home to an array of colorful stands that sell everything from cheese to sausages, from flowers to wine. A visit here is more than just an opportunity to find picnic makings; it's a key part of understanding the Müncheners' easy-come-easy-go nature. If you're in the Schwabing area, the daily market at **Elisabethplatz** is worth a visit— it's much, much smaller than the Viktualienmarkt, but the range and quality of produce are comparable. ■TIP➔ **There are also fruit stands scattered all over the city with prices that mostly beat the grocery stores.**

From the end of November until December 24, the open-air stalls of the **Christkindlmarkt** (⊠ *Marienpl., City Center*) are a great place to find gifts and warm up with mulled wine. Two other perennial Christmas-market favorites are those in Schwabing (Münchner-Freiheit Square) and at the Chinese Tower, in the middle of the Englischer Garten.

SIDE TRIPS FROM MUNICH

Munich's excellent suburban railway network, the S-bahn, brings several quaint towns and attractive rural areas within easy reach for a day's excursion. The two nearest lakes, the Starnbergersee and the Ammersee, are popular year-round. Dachau attracts overseas visitors, mostly because of its concentration-camp memorial site, but it's a picturesque and historic town in its own right. Landshut, north of Munich, is way off the tourist track, but if it were the same distance south of Munich, this jewel of a Bavarian market town would be overrun. All these destinations have a wide selection of restaurants and hotels, and you can bring a bike on any S-bahn train. German Railways, DB, often has weekend specials that allow a family or group of five to travel for as little as €17.50 during certain times. (Inquire at the main train station for the *Wochenendticket,* or Weekend Ticket. Look for a *Tageskarte,* or Day Ticket, in the ticket machines in the subway stations.)

■ TIP→ Keep in mind that there are quite a few options for day trips to the famous castles built by King Ludwig, which are only a couple of hours away. Mike's Bike Tours organizes trips, or ask at your hotel for bus-tour excursions. A train out to Füssen and Schloss Neuschwanstein takes 2½ hours. *For more information on this fairy-tale castle and others, see Chapter 4, The Romantic Road.*

STARNBERGERSEE

20 km (12 mi) southwest of Munich.

The Starnbergersee was one of Europe's first pleasure grounds. Royal coaches were already trundling out from Munich to the lake's wooded shores in the 17th century. In 1663 Elector Ferdinand Maria threw a shipboard party at which 500 guests wined and dined as 100 oarsmen propelled them around the lake. Today pleasure steamers provide a taste of such luxury for the masses. The lake is still lined with the small baroque palaces of Bavaria's aristocracy, but their owners now share the lakeside with public parks, beaches, and boatyards. The Starnbergersee is one of Bavaria's largest lakes—20 km (12 mi) long, 5 km (3 mi) wide, and 406 feet at its deepest point—so there's plenty of room for swimmers, sailors, and windsurfers. The water is of drinking quality (like most Bavarian lakes), a testimony to stringent environmental laws and the very limited number of motorboats allowed.

GETTING HERE & AROUND
Starnberg and the north end of the lake are a 25-minute drive from Munich on the A–95 autobahn. Follow the signs to Garmisch and take the Starnberg exit. Country roads then skirt the west and east shores of the lake, but many are closed to the public.

The S-bahn 6 suburban line runs from Munich's central Marienplatz to Starnberg and three other towns on the lake's west shore: Possenhofen, Feldafing, and Tutzing. The journey from Marienplatz to Starnberg takes 35 minutes. The east shore of the lake can be reached by bus from the town of Wolfratshausen, the end of the S-bahn 7 suburban line. A wonderful way to spend a summer day is to rent bicycles in Munich, take the S-bahn to Starnberg and ride along the eastern shore and back. Another appealing option is to take the train to Tutzing and ride up the western shore back to Starnberg.

The nicest way to visit the Starnbergersee area is by ship. On Saturday evenings the ship *Seeshaupt* has dancing and dinner.

ESSENTIALS
Visitor & Tour Information **Seeshaupt** (☎ *08151/12023* ⊕ *www.seenschiffahrt. de*). **Tourismusverband Starnberger Fünf-Seen-Land** (✉ *Wittelsbacher Str. 2c, Starnberg* ☎ *08151/90600* ⊕ *www.sta5.de*).

EXPLORING
The Starnbergersee is named after its chief resort, **Starnberg**, the largest town on the lake and the nearest to Munich. Pleasure boats set off from the jetty for trips around the lake. The resort has a tree-lined lake-

side promenade and some fine turn-of-the-20th-century villas, some of which are now hotels. There are abundant restaurants, taverns, and chestnut-tree-shaded beer gardens both along the shore and in town.

On the lake's eastern shore, at the village of Berg, you'll find the **König Ludwig II Votivkapelle Berg** *(King Ludwig II Memorial Chapel)*. A well-marked path leads through thick woods to the chapel, built near the point in the lake where the drowned king's body was found on June 13, 1886. He had been confined in nearby Berg Castle after the Bavarian government took action against his withdrawal from reality and his bankrupting castle-building fantasies. A cross in the lake marks the point where his body was recovered.

The castle of **Possenhofen,** home of Ludwig's favorite cousin, Sissi, stands on the western shore, practically opposite Berg. Local lore says they used to send affectionate messages across the lake to each other. Sissi married the Austrian emperor Franz Joseph I, but spent more than 20 summers in the lakeside castle. The inside of the castle cannot be visited, but there is a nice park around it.

The **Buchheim Museum,** on the western shore of the lake, has one of the finest private collections of German expressionist art in the form of paintings, drawings, watercolors, and prints. Among the artists represented are Otto Dix, Max Beckmann, Ernst Ludwig Kirchner, Karl Schmitt-Rotluff, and other painters of the so-called Brücke movement (1905–13). The museum is housed in an impressive modern building on the lakeside. Some areas of the museum are reserved for African cultic items and Bavarian folk art. The nicest way to get to the museum from Starnberg is by ship. ⊠*Am Hirschgarten 1* ☎*08158/99700* ⊕*www.buchheimmuseum.de* ⊠*€8.50* ☉*Apr.– Oct., Tues.–Sun. 10–6; Nov.–Mar., Tues.–Sun. 10–5.*

Just offshore is the tiny **Roseninsel** *(Rose Island)*, where King Maximilian II built a summer villa. You can swim to its tree-fringed shores or sail across in a dinghy or on a Windsurfer (rentals are available at Possenhofen's boatyard and at many other rental points along the lake). There is a little ferry service (☎*0171/722 2266* ⊕*www.faehre-roseninsel.de)* for €4. It runs daily between 11 and 6 from May to the end of September.

WHERE TO STAY & EAT

$–$$ ✕**Seerestaurant Undosa.** This restaurant is a short walk from the Starnberg railroad station. Most tables command a view of the lake, which provides very good fish specials. This is the place to try the mild-tasting *Renke,* a perch-type fish. The Undosa also has jazz evenings and a large café, the Oberdeck, also overlooking the lake. ⊠*Seepromenade 1* ☎*08151/998–930* ⌕*Reservations not accepted* ▱*AE, MC, V* ☉*Closed 2 wks in Feb.*

$$–$$$ ▦ **Hotel Schloss Berg.** King Ludwig II spent his final days in the small castle of Berg, from which this comfortable hotel gets its name. It's on the edge of the castle park where Ludwig liked to walk and a stone's throw from where he drowned. The century-old main hotel building is on the lakeside, and a modern annex overlooks the lake from

the woods—in either, make sure you get a room facing the lake. All rooms are spacious and elegantly furnished. The restaurant ($$–$$$) and waterside beer garden are favorite haunts of locals and weekenders. Schloss Berg is in the village of Berg, along the lake near Starnberg. From Munich, head toward Starnberg on the autobahn, but turn toward Berg at the end of the off ramp. **Pro:** very nice view across the lake. **Cons:** the reception desk is in the annex; you need a car to get here. ⊠*Seestr. 17, Berg* ☎*08151/9630* ⊕*www.hotelschlossberg. de* ⇝*60 rooms* ⌂*In-room: no a/c, Ethernet, Wi-Fi. In-hotel: restaurant, bar, bicycles, public Internet, no elevator in old hotel, some pets allowed (fee)* ▭*AE, MC, V* ⦿*BP.*

$$ ⊞**Forsthaus am See.** The handsome, geranium-covered Forsthaus faces the lake, and so do most of the large, pinewood-furnished rooms. The excellent restaurant ($$–$$$) has a daily changing international menu, with lake fish a specialty. The hotel has its own lake access and boat pier, with a chestnut-shaded beer garden nearby. The hotel is not in Starnberg, but rather in the village of Possenhofen. To reach this village, drive through Starnberg, heading south along the lake; you'll see signs for the hotel after about 10 km (6.2 mi). **Pros:** welcoming, wood-paneled rooms facing the lake, secluded location. **Cons:** in the middle of nowhere, rooms that don't face lake are inferior, need a car to get here. ⊠*Am See 1, Possenhofen* ☎*08157/93010* ⊕*www. forsthaus-am-see.de* ⇝*21 rooms, 1 suite* ⌂*In-room: no a/c, Wi-Fi. In-hotel: restaurant, bar, public Wi-Fi, some pets allowed (fee)* ▭*AE, MC, V* ⦿*BP.*

$$ ⊞**Hotel Seehof.** This small hotel right next to the train station has several rooms with a lake view. Rooms are simply done, with light colors and flower prints on the walls. The Italian restaurant attached, Al Gallo Nero ($–$$), has dishes ranging from pizzas to satisfying and pricey fish dishes. **Pros:** good location and restaurant. **Cons:** rooms facing the street are noisy, some rooms are simply furnished. ⊠*Bahnhofpl. 6, Starnberg* ☎*08151/908–500* ⊕*www.hotel-seehof-starnberg.de* ⇝*38 rooms* ⌂*In-room: no a/c, Wi-Fi. In-hotel: restaurant, public Wi-Fi, some pets allowed (fee)* ▭*AE, DC, MC, V* ⦿*BP.*

AMMERSEE

40 km (25 mi) southwest of Munich.

The Ammersee, or the Peasants' Lake, is the country cousin of the better-known, more cosmopolitan Starnbergersee (the Princes' Lake), and, accordingly, many Bavarians (and tourists, too) like it all the more. Munich cosmopolites of centuries past thought it too distant for an excursion, not to mention too rustic, so the shores remained relatively free of villas and parks. Though some upscale holiday homes claim some stretches of the eastern shore, the Ammersee still offers more open areas for bathing and boating than the larger lake to the east. Bicyclists circle the 19-km-long (12-mi-long) lake (it's nearly 6 km [4 mi] across at its widest point) on a path that rarely loses sight of the water. Hikers can spread out the tour for two or three days, staying overnight in any of the comfortable inns along the way. Dinghy sailors and windsurfers zip across in minutes with the help of the Alpine winds that swoop down from the mountains. A ferry cruises the lake at regular intervals during summer, stopping at several piers. Board it at Herrsching.

Herrsching has a delightful promenade, part of which winds through the resort's park. The 100-year-old villa that sits so comfortably there seems as if it had been built by Ludwig II; such is the romantic and fanciful mixture of medieval turrets and Renaissance-style facades. It was actually built for the artist Ludwig Scheuermann in the late 19th century, and became a favorite meeting place for Munich and Bavarian artists. It's now a municipal cultural center and the setting for chamber-music concerts on some summer weekends.

GETTING HERE & AROUND

Take A–96, follow the signs to Lindau, and 20 km (12 mi) west of Munich take the exit for Herrsching, the lake's principal town.

Herrsching is also the end of the S-bahn 5 suburban line, a 47-minute ride from Munich's Marienplatz. From the Herrsching train station, Bus 952 runs north along the lake, and Bus 951 runs south and continues on to Starnberg in a 40-minute journey.

Getting around by boat is the best way to visit. Each town on the lake has an *Anlegestelle* (pier).

ESSENTIALS

Tour Information Verkehrsbüro (✉ *Bahnhofspl. 2, Herrsching* ☎ *08152/5227* ⊘ *May–Oct., weekdays 9–1 and 2–6, Sat. 9–1; Nov.–Apr., weekdays 10–5*).

EXPLORING

The Benedictine monastery **Andechs,** one of southern Bavaria's most famous pilgrimage sites, lies 5 km (3 mi) south of Herrsching. You can reach it on Bus 951 from the S-bahn station (the bus also connects Ammersee and Starnbergersee). This extraordinary ensemble, surmounted by an octagonal tower and onion dome with a pointed helmet, has a busy history going back more than 1,000 years. The church, originally built in the 15th century, was entirely redone in baroque style in the early 18th century. The **Heilige Kapelle** contains the remains of the old treasure of the Benedictines in Andechs, including Charlemagne's "Victory Cross" and a monstrance containing the three sacred hosts brought back from the crusades by the original rulers of the area, the Counts of Diessen-Andechs. One of the attached chapels contains the remains of composer Carl Orff, and one of the buildings on the grounds has been refurbished as a concert stage for the performance of his works.

Admittedly, however, the crowds of pilgrims are drawn not just by the beauty of the hilltop monastery but primarily by the beer brewed here (600,000 liters [159,000 gallons] annually) and the stunning views. The monastery makes its own cheese as well, and serves organic Bavarian food, an excellent accompaniment to the rich, almost black beer. You can enjoy both at large wooden tables in the monastery tavern or on the terrace outside. ☎*08152/376–167* ⊕*www.andechs. de* ⊘*Daily 7–8.*

The little town of **Diessen** at the southwest corner of the lake has one of the most magnificent religious buildings of the whole region: the **Augustine abbey church of St. Mary.** No lesser figure than the great Munich architect Johann Michael Fischer designed this airy, early rococo structure. François Cuvilliés the Elder, whose work can be seen all over Munich, did the sumptuous gilt-and-marble high altar. Visit in late afternoon, when the light falls sharply on its crisp gray, white, and gold facade, etching the pencil-like tower and spire against the darkening sky over the lake. Don't leave without at least peeping into neighboring St. Stephen's courtyard, its cloisters smothered in wild roses. But Diessen is not all church. It has attracted artists and craftspeople since the early 20th century. Among the most famous who made their home here was the composer Carl Orff, author of numerous works inspired by medieval material, including the famous *Carmina Burana.* His life and work—notably the pedagogical Schulwerk instruments—are exhibited in the **Carl-Orff-Museum** (⊠*Hofmark 3, Diessen* ☎*08807/91981* ⊘ *Weekends 2–5*).

WHERE TO STAY

$$–$$$ 🏨**Ammersee Hotel.** This very comfortable, modern resort hotel is the hotel on the lake. It has views from an unrivaled position on the lakeside promenade. Rooms overlooking the lake are more expensive and in demand. The Artis restaurant ($–$$) has an international menu with an emphasis on fish. You can enjoy a spicy bouillabaisse or catfish from the Danube. **Pros:** prime location (request a room with balcony), good restaurant. **Cons:** rooms facing the street are noisy, limited balcony rooms. ⊠*Summerstr. 32, Herrsching* ☎*08152/96870, 08152/399– 440 restaurant* ⊕*www.ammersee-hotel.de* ➥*40 rooms* ⚘*In-room: no a/c, Ethernet, Wi-Fi. In-hotel: restaurant, gym, public Wi-Fi, public Internet, some pets allowed* ⊟*AE, DC, MC, V* ��*BP.*

DACHAU

20 km (12 mi) northwest of Munich.

Dachau predates Munich, with records going back to the time of Charlemagne. It's a handsome town, too, built on a hilltop with views of Munich and the Alps. A guided tour of the town, including the castle and church, leaves from the Rathaus on Saturday at 10:30, from May through mid-October. Dachau is infamous worldwide as the site of the first Nazi concentration camp, which was built just outside it. Dachau preserves the memory of the camp and the horrors perpetrated there with deep contrition while trying, with commendable discretion, to signal that the town has other points of interest.

GETTING HERE & AROUND

Take the B–12 country road or the Stuttgart autobahn to the Dachau exit from Munich. Dachau is also on the S-bahn 2 suburban line, a 20-minute ride from Munich's Marienplatz.

ESSENTIALS

Visitor Information **Tourist Information Dachau** (✉ *Konrad-Adenauer-Str. 1* ☎ *08131/75286* ⊕ *www.dachau.info).*

EXPLORING

To get a sense of the town's history, visit the **Bezirksmuseum,** the district museum, which displays historical artifacts, furniture, and traditional costumes from Dachau and its surroundings. ✉ *Augsburgerstr. 3* ☎ *08131/567–50* 💰 *€3.50* ⊗ *Tues.–Fri. 11–5, weekends 1–5.*

The site of the infamous camp, now the **KZ-Gedenkstätte Dachau** *(Dachau Concentration Camp Memorial)*, is just outside town. Photographs, contemporary documents, the few remaining cell blocks, and the grim crematorium create a somber and moving picture of the camp, where more than 30,000 of the 200,000-plus prisoners lost their lives. A documentary film in English is shown daily at 11:30 and 3:30. The former camp has become more than just a grisly memorial: it's now a place where people of all nations meet to reflect upon the past and on the present. Several religious shrines and memorials have been built to honor the dead, who came from Germany and all occupied nations. By public transport take the S-2 from Marienplatz or Hauptbahnhof in the direction of Petershausen, and get off at Dachau. From there, take the clearly marked bus from right outside the Dachau S-bahn station (it leaves about every 20 minutes). If you are driving from Munich, take the autobahn toward Stuttgart, get off at Dachau, and follow the signs. ✉ *Alte Römerstr. 75* ☎ *08131/669– 970* ⊕ *www.kz-gedenkstaette-dachau.de* 💰 *Free, 2-hr guided tour €3* ⊗ *Tues.–Sun. 9–5. Tours May–Oct., Tues.–Fri. at 1:30, weekends at noon and 1:30; Nov.–Apr., Thurs. and weekends at 1:30.*

Schloss Dachau, the hilltop castle, dominates the town. What you'll see is the one remaining wing of a palace built by the Munich architect Josef Effner for the Wittelsbach ruler Max Emanuel in 1715. During the Napoleonic Wars the palace served as a field hospital and then was partially destroyed. King Max Joseph lacked the money to rebuild it, so all that's left is a handsome cream-and-white building, with an elegant pillared and lantern-hung café on the ground floor and a former ballroom above. About once a month the grand Renaissance hall, with a richly decorated and carved ceiling, covered with painted panels depicting figures from ancient mythology, is used for chamber concerts. The east terrace affords panoramic views of Munich and, on fine days, the distant Alps. There's also a 250-year-old *Schlossbrauerei* (castle brewery), which hosts the town's beer and music festival each year in the first two weeks of August. ✉ *Schlosspl.* ☎ *08131/87923* 💰 *€2* ⊗ *Apr.–Sept., Tues.–Sun. 9–6; Oct.–Mar., Tues.–Sun. 10–4.*

St. Jacob, Dachau's parish church, was built in the early 16th century in late-Renaissance style on the foundations of a 14th-century Gothic structure. Baroque features and a characteristic onion dome were added in the late 17th century. On the south wall you can admire a very fine 17th-century sundial. ✉ *Konrad-Adenauer-Str. 7* ⊗ *Daily 7–7.*

An artists' colony formed here during the 19th century, and the tradition lives on. Picturesque houses line Hermann-Stockmann-Strasse and part of Münchner Strasse, and many of them are still the homes of successful artists. The **Gemäldegalerie** displays the works of many of the town's 19th-century artists. ⊠ *Konrad-Adenauer-Str. 3* ☎*08131/567–516* 🎟*€3.50* ⊙*Tues.–Fri. 11–5, weekends 1–5.*

WHERE TO STAY

$ 🏨 **Hotel Fischer.** You can see this hotel across the square from the S-bahn station. The family atmosphere is welcoming, the rooms are pleasantly modern, and good traditional Bavarian meals are served in the restaurant. Order the "Weisswurst" special with a drop of Weissbier and you'll get a good laugh at how the "drop" is served. **Pros:** prime location, good restaurant. **Con:** on nice evenings, noise from the patio may filter up to your room. ⊠*Bahnhofstr. 4, Dachau city center* ☎*08131/61220 0* ⊕*www.hotelfischer-dachau.de* 🛏*29 rooms* 🛎*In-room: no a/c, Wi-Fi, In-hotel: restaurant, public Wi-Fi, no-smoking rooms, some pets allowed* ▭*MC, V.*

LANDSHUT

64 km (40 mi) north of Munich.

If fortune had placed Landshut south of Munich, in the protective folds of the Alpine foothills, instead of the same distance north, in the subdued flatlands of Lower Bavaria—of which it is the capital—the historic town would be teeming with tourists. Landshut's geographical misfortune is the discerning visitor's good luck, for the town is never overcrowded, with the possible exception of the three summer weeks when the *Landshuter Hochzeit* (Landshut Wedding) is celebrated (it takes place every four years, the next occasion being in 2009). The festival commemorates the marriage in 1475 of Prince George of Bavaria-Landshut, son of the expressively named Ludwig the Rich, to Princess Hedwig, daughter of the king of Poland. Within its ancient walls the entire town is swept away in a colorful reconstruction of the event. The wedding procession, with the "bride" and "groom" on horseback accompanied by pipes and drums and the hurly-burly of a medieval pageant, is held on three consecutive weekends, while a medieval-style fair fills the central streets throughout the three weeks.

Landshut has two magnificent cobblestone market streets. The one in the **Altstadt** (Old Town) is one of the most beautiful city streets in Germany; the other is in **Neustadt** (New Town). The two streets run parallel to each other, tracing a course between the Isar River and the heights overlooking the town.

GETTING HERE & AROUND

Landshut is a 45-minute drive northwest of Munich on either the A-92 autobahn—follow the signs to Deggendorf—or the B-11 highway. The Plattling–Regensburg–Passau train line brings you from Munich in about 50 minutes. A round-trip costs about €20.

ESSENTIALS

Visitor Information Landshut Tourismus (✉ *Altstadt 315* ☎ *0871/922–050* ⊕ *www.landshut.de*).

EXPLORING

A steep path from the Altstadt takes you up to **Burg Trausnitz.** This castle was begun in 1204, and accommodated the Wittelsbach dukes of Bavaria-Landshut until 1503. ☎ *0871/924–110* ⊕ *www.burgtrausnitz. de* ⛊ *€5, including guided tour* ⊙ *Apr.–Sept., daily 9–6; Oct.–Mar., daily 9–5:30.*

The **Stadtresidenz** in the Altstadt was the first Italian Renaissance build-ing of its kind north of the Alps. It was built from 1536 to 1537, but was given a baroque facade at the end of the 19th century. The Wit-telsbachs lived here during the 16th century. The facade of the palace forms an almost modest part of the architectural splendor and integrity of the Altstadt, where even the ubiquitous McDonald's has to serve its hamburgers behind a baroque facade. The Stadtresidenz includes exhi-bitions on the history of Landshut. ✉ *Altstadt 79* ☎ *0871/25143* ⛊ *€3* ⊙ *Apr.–Sept., Tues.–Sun. 9–6; Oct.–Mar., Tues.–Sun. 10–4).*

The **Rathaus** *(Town Hall)*, which stands opposite the Stadtresidenz, is an elegant, light-color building with a typical neo-Gothic roof design. It was originally a set of 13th-century burghers' houses, taken over by the town in the late 1300s. The famous bride and groom allegedly danced in the grand ceremonial hall during their much-celebrated wedding in 1475. The frescoes here date to 1880, however. The tourist informa-tion bureau is on the ground floor. ✉ *Altstadt 315* ☎ *0871/881–215* ⛊ *Free* ⊙ *Weekdays 2–3, and on official tours.*

The **Martinskirche** *(St. Martin's Church)*, with the tallest brick church tower (436 feet) in the world, soars above the other buildings. The church, which was elevated to the rank of *basilica minor* in 2002, con-tains some magnificent late-Gothic stone and wood carvings, notably a 1518 Madonna by the artist Martin Leinberger. It's surely the only church in the world to contain an image of Hitler, albeit in a devilish pose. The Führer and other Nazi leaders are portrayed as executioners in a 1946 stained-glass window showing the martyrdom of St. Kastu-lus. In the nave of the church is a clear and helpful description of its history and treasures in English. Every first Sunday of the month a tour is conducted between 11:30 and 12:30 that will take you up the tower and to the **Schatzkammer,** the church's treasure chamber. ✉ *Altstadt and Kirchg.* ☎ *0871/922–1780* ⊙ *Apr.–Sept., Tues.–Thurs. and week-ends 7–6:30; Oct.–Mar., Tues.–Thurs. and weekends 7–5.*

Built into a steep slope of the hill crowned by Burg Trausnitz is an unusual art museum, the **Skulpturenmuseum im Hofberg,** containing the entire collection of the Landshut sculptor Fritz Koenig. His own work forms the permanent central section of the labyrinthine gallery. ✉ *Kol-pingstr. 481* ☎ *0871/89021* ⛊ *€3.50* ⊙ *Tues.–Sun. 10:30–1 and 2–5.*

OFF THE BEATEN PATH

Freising. This ancient episcopal seat, 35 km (22 mi) southwest of Landshut, houses a cathedral and old town well worth visiting. The town is also accessible from Munich (at the end of the S-bahn 1 line, a 45-minute ride from central Munich).

WHERE TO STAY

There are several attractive Bavarian-style restaurants in the Altstadt and Neustadt, most of them with beer gardens. Although Landshut brews a fine beer, look for a Gaststätte offering a *Weihenstephaner,* from the world's oldest brewery, in Freising. Helles (light) is the most popular beer variety.

$$$$ **Hotel Goldene Sonne.** The steeply gabled Renaissance exterior of the "Golden Sun" fronts a hotel of great charm and comfort. It stands in the center of town, near all the sights. Its dining options are a paneled, beamed restaurant ($–$$); a vaulted cellar; and a courtyard beer garden, where the service is friendly and helpful. The menu follows the seasons and toes the "quintessential Bavarian" line, with pork roast, steamed or smoked trout with horseradish, white asparagus in the spring (usually accompanied by potatoes and ham), and venison in the fall. **Pros:** spacious reception, comfortable rooms, good restaurant. **Cons:** street-facing rooms are noisy, hotel often booked. ✉ *Neustadt 520* ☎ *0871/92530* 🌐 *www.goldenesonne.de* *60 rooms* *In-room: no a/c, Wi-Fi. In-hotel: restaurant, bar, public Internet, public Wi-Fi, no-smoking rooms, some pets allowed* ▭ *AE, DC, MC, V* *BP.*

$$$$ **Romantik Hotel Fürstenhof.** This handsome Landshut city mansion, located a few minutes on foot from the center of town, had no difficulty qualifying for inclusion in the Romantik group of hotels—it just breathes romance, from its plush gourmet restaurant ($$–$$$), covered in wood paneling, to the cozy bedrooms. A vine-covered terrace shadowed by a chestnut tree adds charm. Price includes breakfast buffet and sauna use. **Pros:** very nice restaurant, pleasant rooms. **Cons:** no elevator, restaurant closed Sunday. ✉ *Stethaimerstr. 3* ☎ *0871/92550* 🌐 *www.romantikhotels.com/landshut* *24 rooms* *In-room: no a/c (some), Wi-Fi. In-hotel: restaurant, public Wi-Fi, no-smoking rooms, no elevator* ▭ *AE, DC, MC, V* ⊗ *Restaurant closed Sun.* *BP.*

$ **Hotel-Gasthof zur Insel.** This "Island Hotel" is right on the river and only a two-minute walk from the center of town. The restaurant serves good Bavarian food. If on summer evenings you hear singing coming from the beer garden under your window, remember the old saying, "If you can't beat 'em, join 'em." **Pros:** nice location, good Bavarian restaurant. **Cons:** no elevator, beer garden can be noisy. ✉ *Badstr. 16* ☎ *0871/923160* 🌐 *www.insel-landshut.de* *20* *In-room: no a/c, In-hotel: restaurant, no-smoking rooms, no elevator* ▭ *AE, D, MC, V* .

The Bavarian Alps

WORD OF MOUTH

"There are so many trails in Berchtesgaden you could just go to heaven. Trails are clean, well marked, well scored for difficulty and offer fantastic view of the Alps. If you remember the opening scene of *The Sound of Music,* it is a good example of the scenery of these great hiking areas."

—EmilyC

"I'm also suggesting Mittenwald as the perfect place for a family to wind-down in. I spent a month in an apartment Dec. 06–Jan. 07 and just fell in love with the area. I didn't have a car and didn't miss it one bit. There is a ton of easy walking to do; I would go on a two-hour walk about three times a week."

—swandav2000

www.fodors.com/forums

Updated by
Lee A. Evans

FIR-CLAD MOUNTAINS, ROCKY PEAKS, LEDERHOSEN, and geranium-covered houses: The Bavarian Alps come closest to what most of us envision as "Germany." Quaint towns full of frescoed half-timber houses covered in snow pop up among the mountain peaks and shimmering hidden lakes, as do the creations of "Mad" King Ludwig II. The entire area has sporting opportunities galore, regardless of the season.

Upper Bavaria (Oberbayern) fans south from Munich to the Austrian border, and as you follow this direction, you'll soon find yourself on a gently rolling plain leading to lakes surrounded by ancient forests. In time the plain merges into foothills, which suddenly give way to jagged Alpine peaks. In places such as Königsee, near Berchtesgaden, snow-capped mountains rise straight up from the gemlike lakes.

Continuing south, you'll encounter cheerful villages with richly painted houses, churches and monasteries filled with the especially sensuous Bavarian baroque and rococo styles, and several spas where you can "take the waters" and tune up your system. Sports possibilities are legion: downhill and cross-country skiing, snowboarding, and ice-skating in winter; tennis, swimming, sailing, golf, and, above all (sometimes literally), hiking, paragliding, and ballooning in summer.

ORIENTATION & PLANNING

GETTING ORIENTED

Ask a Bavarian about the "Bavarian Alps" and he'll probably shake his head in confusion. To Bavarians "the Alps" consist of several adjoining mountain ranges spanning the Ammergau, Wetterstein, and Karwendel Alps in the West to the Chiemgauer and Berchtesgadener Alpen in the East. Each region has its die-hard fans. The constants, however, are the incredible scenery, clean air, and a sense of Bavarian Gemütlichkeit (coziness) omnipresent in every Hütte, Gasthof, and beer garden. The area is an outdoor recreation paradise, and almost completely lacks the high culture institutions that dominate German urban life.

Werdenfelser Land & Wetterstein Mountains. Like a village lost in time, Mittenwald is famous for its half-timber houses covered in Lüftlmalerei frescoes. Another historic jewel is the pleasant town of Garmisch-Partenkirchen, which sits serenely in the shadow of Germany's highest point: the Zugspitze. The Wetterstein Mountains offer fantastic skiing and hiking.

Chiemgau. Bavaria's Lake District is almost undiscovered by Westerners, but has long been a secret destination for Germans. Several fine, hidden lakes dot the area, overlooked by the wonderful castle at Aschau. The Chiemsee dominates the Chiemgau, with one of the most impressive German palaces and great water sports. Residents, or Chiemgauer, especially in Bad Tölz, often wear traditional Trachten, elaborate Lederhosen and Dirndl dresses, as an expression of their proud cultural heritage.

TOP REASONS TO GO

Great nature: Whether it be the crystalline Königsee lake, the grandiose Karwendel Mountains with endless views, the fresh air, Garmisch's powdery snow, the deep caves, or the magical forests, the Bavarian Alps seem to have everything the nature lover needs.

Herrenchiemsee: Take the old steam-driven ferry to the island in Chiemsee to visit the last and most glorious castle of Mad King Ludwig. This imitation of Versailles broke the bank, but it has been attracting tourists for over a century.

Rejuvenation in Reichenhall: The new Rupertus spa in Bad Reichenhall has the applications you need to turn back your body's clock, from saltwater baths to mysterious mudpacks.

Religious brewings: Enjoy the monkish life in Tegernsee, where the garden of the ancient monastery catches the first and last rays of the sun. In the hours between, the worthy institution serves its own full-bodied beer with an assortment of hearty dishes.

Meditating in Ettal Basilica: If it isn't the sheer complexity of the baroque ornamentation and the riot of frescoes, then it might be the fluid sound of the ancient organ that puts you in a deep, relaxing trance.

Berchtesgadener Land. The Berchtesgadener Land is not the highest point in the country, but is certainly one of the most ruggedly beautiful regions. Hundreds of miles of hiking trails with serene Alpine cottages and the odd cow make the area a hiking and mountaineering paradise. Berchtesgaden and Bad Reichenhall are famous for the salt trade, and the salt mines provide the visitor with a unique and entertaining insight into the history and wealth of the region. The Königsee is the most photographed place in the country, and for good reason.

BAVARIAN ALPS PLANNER

WHEN TO GO

This mountainous region is a year-round holiday destination. Snow is promised by most resorts from December through March, although there's year-round skiing on the glacier slopes at the top of the Zugspitze. Spring and autumn are ideal times for leisurely hikes on the many mountain trails. November is a between-seasons time, when many hotels and restaurants close down or attend to renovations. Note, too, that many locals take a vacation after January 6, and businesses may be closed for anywhere up to a month. The area is extremely popular with European visitors, who flood the Alps in July and August.

GETTING HERE & AROUND

BY AIR Munich, 95 km (59 mi) northwest of Garmisch-Partenkirchen, is the gateway to the Bavarian Alps. If you're staying in Berchtesgaden, consider the closer airport in Salzburg, Austria—it has fewer international flights, but it is a budget-airline and charter hub.

BY CAR   The Bavarian Alps are well connected to Munich by train, and an extensive network of busses links even the most remote villages. Since bus schedules can be unreliable and are timed for commuters, the best way to visit the area is by car. Three autobahns reach into the Bavarian Alps: A–7 comes in from the northwest (Frankfurt, Stuttgart, Ulm) and ends near Füssen in the western Bavarian Alps; A–95 runs from Munich to Garmisch-Partenkirchen; take A–8 from Munich for Tegernsee, Schliersee, and Chiemsee and for Berchtesgaden. ⚠**The A–8 is the statistically the most dangerous Autobahn in the country, partially due to it simultaneously being the most heavily traveled highway and the road most in need of repair.** The driving style is fast, and tailgating is common, though it is illegal. The "guideline speed" (Richtgeschwindigkeit) on the A–8 is 110 kmh (68 mph); if an accident occurs at higher speeds, your insurance will not necessarily cover it. It is a good idea to pick a town like Garmisch-Partenkirchen, Bad Tölz, or Berchtesgaden as a base and explore the area from there. The Bavarian Alps are furnished with cable cars, steam trains, and cog railroads that whisk you to the tops of alpine peaks allowing you to see the spectacular views without hours of mountain-climbing.

BY TRAIN   Most Alpine resorts are connected with Munich by regular express and slower service trains. With some careful planning—see ⊕*www. bahn.de* for schedules and to buy tickets—you can visit this region without a car.

ESSENTIALS   **Airport Information Salzburg Airport (SZ6)** (☎ *0662/8580* ⊕ *www.salzburg-airport.com).*

Visitor Information Tourismusverband München Oberbayern (✉ *Bodenseestr. 113 Munich* ☎ *089/829–2180* ⊕ *www.oberbayern-tourismus.de/).*

ABOUT THE RESTAURANTS

Restaurants in Bavaria run the gamut from the casual and gemütlich Gasthof to formal gourmet offerings. More upscale establishments try to maintain a feeling of casual familiarity, but you will probably feel more comfortable at the truly gourmet restaurants if you dress up a bit. Note that many restaurants take a break between 2:30 and 6 PM. If you want to eat during these hours, look for the magic words *Durchgehend warme Küche,* meaning warm food served throughout the day, possibly snacks during the off-hours.

ABOUT THE HOTELS

With few exceptions, a hotel or *Gasthof* in the Bavarian Alps and lower Alpine regions has high standards and is traditional in style, with balconies, pine woodwork, and gently angled roofs upon which the snow sits and insulates. Many in the larger resort towns offer special packages online, so be sure to check them out. Private homes all through the region offer Germany's own version of bed-and-breakfasts, indicated by signs reading ZIMMER FREI (rooms available). Their rates may be less than €25 per person. As a general rule, the farther from the popular and sophisticated Alpine resorts you go, the lower the rates. Note, too, that many places offer a small discount if you stay more than one night. By the same token, some places frown on staying only one night, especially during the high seasons, in summer, at Christmas, and on winter weekends. In spas and many mountain resorts a "spa tax" is added to the hotel bill. It amounts to no more than €3 per person per day and allows free use of spa facilities, entry to local attractions and concerts, and use of local transportation at times.

WHAT IT COSTS IN EUROS					
	¢	$	$$	$$$	$$$$
RESTAURANTS	under €9	€9–€15	€16–€20	€21–€25	over €25
HOTELS	under €50	€50–€100	€101–€175	€176–€225	over €225

Restaurant prices are per person for a main course at dinner. Hotel prices are for two people in a standard double room, including tax and service.

PLANNING YOUR TIME

The Alps are spread along Germany's southern border, but are fairly compact and easy to explore. Choose a central base and fan out from there. Garmisch-Partenkirchen and Berchtesgaden are the largest towns with the most convenient transportation connections.

Although the area is a popular tourist destination, the smaller destinations like Mittenwald, Ettal, or the Schliersee are quieter and make for pleasant overnight stays. For an unforgettable experience, try spending the night in an Alpine hut, feasting on a simple but hearty meal and sleeping in the cool night air.

DISCOUNTS & DEALS

One of the best deals in the area is the German Railroad's Bayern Ticket. The Bayern Ticket allows up to five people to travel on any regional train—and almost all buses in the Alps—for €27, and is valid from 9 AM until 3 AM that night. There is a "single" version for €19. Ticket holders receive discounts on a large number of attractions in the area, including the Zugspitzbahn, a cog railroad and cable car that takes you up to the top of the Zugspitze. The ZugspitzCard (3 days €39) offers discounts in almost every city near the Zugspitze. Visitors to spas or spa towns receive a Kurkarte, an ID that proves payment of the spa tax. The document allows discounts and often free access to sights in the town or area. If you've paid the tax, be sure to show the card everywhere you go.

WERDENFELSER LAND & WETTERSTEIN MOUNTAINS

With Germany's highest peak and picture-perfect Bavarian villages, the Werdenfelser Land offers a splendid mix of natural beauty combined with Bavarian art and culture. The region spreads out around the base of the Zugspitze, where the views from the top reach from Garmisch-Partenkirchen to the frescoed houses of Oberammergau, and to the serene Cloister Ettal.

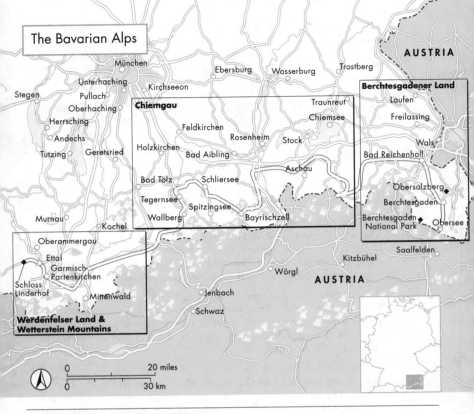

GARMISCH-PARTENKIRCHEN

90 km (55 mi) southwest of Munich.

Garmisch, as it's more commonly known, is a bustling, year-round resort and spa town and is the undisputed capital of Alpine Bavaria. Once two separate communities, Garmisch and Partenkirchen fused in 1936 to accommodate the Winter Olympics. Today, with a population of 28,000, the area is the center of the Werdenfelser Land and large enough to offer every facility expected from a major Alpine resort without being overwhelming. Garmisch is walkable but spread out, and the narrow streets and buildings of smaller Partenkirchen hold snugly together. In both parts of town pastel frescoes of biblical and bucolic scenes decorate facades.

Winter sports rank high on the agenda here. There are more than 99 km (62 mi) of downhill ski runs, 40 ski lifts and cable cars, and 180 km (112 mi) of *Loipen* (cross-country ski trails). One of the principal stops on the international winter-sports circuit, the area hosts a week of races every January. You can usually count on good skiing from December through April (and into May on the Zugspitze).

Maibaum: Bavaria's Maypole

The center of every town in Bavaria is the Maibaum or Maypole. The blue-and-white striped pole is decorated with the symbol of every trade and guild represented in the town, and is designed to help visitors determine what services are available there. The effort and skill required to build one is a source of community pride.

The tradition dates back to the 16th century, and is a governed by a strict set of rules. Great care is taken in selecting and cutting the tree, which must be at least 30 meters (98 feet) long. Once completed, it cannot be erected before May 1. In the meantime, tradition and honor dictate that men from surrounding towns attempt to steal the pole and ransom it for beer and food, so it must be guarded 24 hours a day. Once the pole goes up, with quite a bit of leveraging and manual labor, it cannot be stolen and may only stand for three years.

GETTING HERE & AROUND

Garmisch-Partenkirchen is the cultural and transportation hub of the Werdenfelser Land. The autobahn A–95 links Garmisch directly to Munich. Regional German Rail trains head directly to Munich (90 minutes), Innsbruck (90 minutes), and Mittenwald (20 minutes). German Rail operates buses that connect Garmsich with Oberammergau, Ettal, and the Wieskirche. Garmisch is a walkable city, and you probably won't need to use its frequent city-bus services.

Partenkirchen was founded by the Romans, and you can still follow the Via Claudia they built between Partenkirchen and neighboring Mittenwald, which was part of a major route between Rome and Germany well into the 17th century.

Bus tours to King Ludwig II's castles at Neuschwanstein and Linderhof and to the Ettal Monastery, near Oberammergau, are offered by DER travel agencies. Local agencies in Garmisch also run tours to Neuschwanstein, Linderhof, and Ettal, and into the neighboring Austrian Tyrol.

The Garmisch mountain railway company, the Bayerische Zugspitzbahn, offers special excursions to the top of the Zugspitze, Germany's highest mountain, by cog rail and cable car.

ESSENTIALS

Bus Tours DER (⊠ *Garmisch-Partenkirchen* ☎ *08821/55125*). **Dominikus Kümmerle** (☎ *08821/4955*). **Hans Biersack** (☎ *08821/4920*). **Hilmar Röser** (☎ *08821/2926*). **Weiss-Blau-Reisen** (☎ *08821/3766*).

Railway Tour Bayerische Zugspitzbahn (☎ *08821/7970*).

Visitor Information Garmisch-Partenkirchen (⊠ *Verkehrsamt der Kurverwaltung, Richard-Strauss-Pl. 2* ☎ *08821/180–420* ⊕ *www.garmisch-partenkirchen.de*).

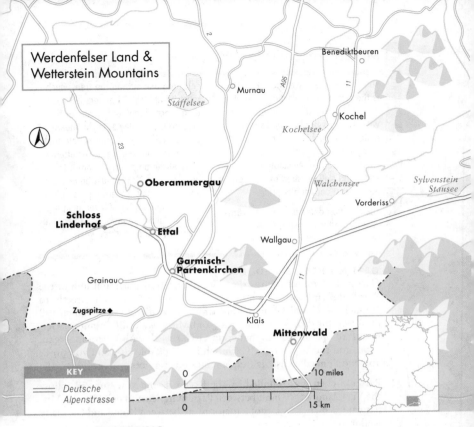

Werdenfelser Land &
Wetterstein Mountains

Benediktbeuren

Murnau

Staffelsee

Kochel

Kochelsee

Oberammergau

Walchensee

Sylvenstein
Stausee

Vorderiss

Schloss
Linderhof

Ettal

Wallgau

Garmisch-
Partenkirchen

Grainau

Zugspitze ◆

Klais

Mittenwald

KEY

Deutsche
Alpenstrasse

0   10 miles

0   15 km

EXPLORING

The number one attraction in Garmisch is the **Zugspitze**, the highest mountain (9,731 feet) in Germany. There are two ways up the mountain: a leisurely 75-minute ride on a cog railway from the train station in the town center, combined with a cable-car ride up the last stretch; or a 10-minute hoist by cable car, which begins its giddy ascent from the Eibsee, 10 km (6 mi) outside town on the road to Austria. There are two restaurants with sunny terraces at the summit and another at the top of the cog railway. ■TIP→ **A round-trip combination ticket allows you to mix your modes of travel up and down the mountain.** Prices are lower in winter than in summer, even though winter rates include use of all the ski lifts on the mountain. You can rent skis at the top.

There are also a number of other peaks in the area with gondolas, but the views from the Zugspitze are the best. A four-seat cable car goes to the top of one of the lesser peaks: the **Wank** or the **Alpspitze**, some 2,000 feet lower than the Zugspitze. You can tackle both mountains on foot, provided you're properly shod and physically fit. ⊠ *Zugspitze: Cog railway leaves from Olympiastr. 27 (approximately 100 meters from the Garmisch train station)* ☎ *08821/7970* ⊕ *www.zugspitze.de* ☎ *Funicular or cable car €45 in summer, €37 in winter, round-trip; parking €3.*

Garmisch-Partenkirchen isn't all sports, however. In Garmisch, beautiful examples of Upper Bavarian houses line Frühlingstrasse, and a pedestrian zone begins at Richard-Strauss-Platz. Off Marienplatz, at one end of the car-free zone, is the 18th-century parish church of **St. Martin**. It contains some significant stuccowork by the Wessobrunn artists Schmutzer, Schmidt, and Bader. The chancel is by another fine 18th-century artist from Austria, Franz Hosp.

Across the Loisach River, on Pfarrerhausweg, stands another **St. Martin** church, dating from 1280, whose Gothic wall paintings include a larger-than-life-size figure of St. Christopher.

Objects and exhibitions on the region's history can be found in the excellent **Werdenfelser Museum,** which is itself housed in a building dating back to around 1200. The museum is spread over five floors, and explores every aspect of life in the Werdenfels region, which was an independent county for more than 700 years (until 1802). ⊠ *Ludwigstr. 47, Partenkirchen* ☎ *08821/2134* ⛁ *€2.50* ☾ *Tues.–Sun. 10–5.*

On the eastern edge of Garmisch, at the end of Zöppritzstrasse, stands the **villa of composer Richard Strauss,** who lived here until his death in 1949. It's the center of activity during the *Richard-Strauss-Tage,* an annual music festival held in mid-June that features concerts and lectures on the town's most famous son. Displays are audiovisual, and each day at 10, 12, 2, and 4 samples of Strauss's works are played in the concert hall.

WHERE TO EAT

$–$$ ✕ **See-Hotel Riessersee.** On the shore of a small, green, tranquil lake—a 3-km (2-mi) walk from town—this café-restaurant is an ideal spot for lunch or afternoon tea (on summer weekends there's live zither music from 3 to 5). House specialties are fresh trout and local game (which fetches the higher prices on the menu). ⊠ *Riess 6* ☎ *08821/95440* ⊟ *AE, MC, V* ☾ *Closed Mon. and Dec. 1–15.*

WHERE TO STAY

For information about accommodation packages with ski passes, call the **Zugspitze** (☎ *08821/7970* ⊕ *www.zugspitze.de*) or get in touch with the tourist office in Garmisch.

$$–$$$ ⊟ **Reindl's Partenkirchner Hof.** Owner Karl Reindl ranks among the
★ world's top hoteliers. His award-winning hotel is a real family affair; his daughter cooks up excellent Bavarian and international dishes, from roasted suckling pig to coq au vin. The light-filled bistro annex ($–$$) serves meals, coffee, and cake in an atmosphere that contrasts sharply with the heavier wood-and-velvet main building. Each guest room has pinewood furniture and a balcony or patio. Some of the double rooms are huge. An infrared sauna and whirlpools soothe tired muscles. If you're planning to stay for several days, ask about specials. **Pros:** ample-size rooms, great views. **Con:** front rooms are on a busy street. ⊠ *Bahnhofstr. 15* ☎ *08821/943–870* ⊕ *www.reindls.de* ⇙ *35 rooms, 17 suites* ⌂ *In-room: no a/c (some), Wi-Fi (some). In-hotel: restaurant, bar, pool, gym, spa, bicycles, no-smoking rooms* ⊟ *AE, DC, MC, V* ⋈ *BP.*

EATING WELL IN THE BAVARIAN ALPS

Bavarian cooking originally fed a farming people, who spent their days out of doors doing heavy manual labor. *Semmelknödel* (dumplings of old bread), pork dishes, sauerkraut, bread, and hearty soups were felt necessary to sustain a person facing the elements. The natural surroundings provided further sustenance, in the form of fresh trout from brooks, *Renke* (pike-perch) from the lakes, venison, and mushrooms. This substantial fare was often washed down with beer, which was nourishment in itself, especially during the Lenten season, when the dark and powerful "Doppelbock" was on the market. Today this regimen will suit sporty types who have spent a day hiking in the mountains, skiing in the bracing air, or swimming or windsurfing in chilly lakes.

Bavaria is not immune to eclectic culinary trends, however: minimalist Asian daubs here, a touch of French sophistication and Italian elegance there, a little Tex-Mex to brighten a winter evening, even some sprinklings of curry. Menus often include large sections devoted to salads, and there are tasty vegetarian dishes even in the most conservative regions. Schnapps, which traditionally ended the meal, has gone from being a step above moonshine to a true delicacy extracted from local fruit by virtuoso distillers. Yes, Bavarian cooking—hearty, homey, and down-to-earth—is actually becoming lighter.

One area remains an exception: desserts. The selection of sinfully creamy cakes in the Konditorei, often enjoyed with whipped-cream-topped hot chocolate, continues to grow. These are irresistible, of course, especially when homemade. A heavenly experience might be a large portion of warm *Apfelstrudel* (apple- and nut-filled pastry) fresh from the oven in some remote mountain refuge.

$$ **Hotel Waxenstein.** It's worth the 7-km (4½-mi) drive eastward to Grainau just to spend a night or a few at the delightful Waxenstein. The Toedts, who run the place, are obviously passionate about their work and their guests. The rooms are generous in size, with luxurious bathrooms. Furnishings combine Bavarian rustic with flights of fancy. The restaurant ($$–$$$) provides a breathtaking view of the Zugspitze, but the excellent food will keep you occupied, from the crispy bread and amuses bouches, to dishes such as gnocchi in ginger-pumpkin sauce, or veal fillet with foie gras. **Pros:** great service, beautiful views of the Zugspitze from the north-facing rooms. **Cons:** rooms somewhat small, no views of the Zugspitze from the south-facing rooms. ⊠ *Höhenrainweg 3* ☎ *08821/9840* ⊕ *www.waxenstein.de* ➪ *35 rooms, 6 suites* ⚏ *In-room: no a/c, dial-up. In-hotel: restaurant, bar, pool, spa some pets allowed* ⊟ *AE, DC, MC, V* ❤ *BP.*

$–$$ **Edelweiss.** Like its namesake, the "nobly white" Alpine flower of *The Sound of Music* fame, this small downtown hotel has plenty of mountain charm. Inlaid with warm pinewood, it has Bavarian furnishings and individually decorated rooms. Breakfast buffet is included in the price. **Pros:** small, comfortable, and homey, great with kids. **Cons:** small hotel lacking in many services. ⊠ *Martinswinkelstr. 15–17* ☎ *08821/2454*

⊕*www.hoteledelweiss.de* ⇦*31 rooms* ⌂*In-room: no a/c. In-hotel: no-smoking rooms, some pets allowed, no elevator* ▭*V* ⑂*BP.*

$ ⊡**Gasthof Fraundorfer.** You can ride to dreamland in this beautiful old Bavarian Gasthof—some of the bed frames are carved like antique automobiles and sleighs. The colorfully painted facade is covered with geraniums most of the year. The tavern-restaurant (¢–$), its walls covered with pictures and other ephemera, presents "Bavarian evenings" of folk entertainment every evening except Tuesdays. There's an Internet café across the street. **Pros:** great location and dining experience. **Cons:** in need of renovation, kitchen smell and noise a problem for the rooms in the back. ✉*Ludwigstr. 24* ☎*08821/9270* ⊕*www.gasthof-fraundorfer.de* ⇦*20 rooms, 7 suites* ⌂*In-room: no a/ c, dial-up. In-hotel: restaurant, some pets allowed* ▭*MC, V* ⊗*Closed late Nov.–early Dec.* ⑂*BP.*

$ ⊡**Hotel-Gasthof Drei Mohren.** All the simple, homey comforts you'd expect can be found in this 150-year-old Bavarian inn tucked into Partenkirchen village. All rooms have mountain views, and most are furnished with farmhouse-style painted beds and cupboards. A free bus to Garmisch and the cable-car stations will pick you up right outside the house. The restaurant ($–$$) serves solid fare, including a series of *Pfanderl,* large portions of meat and potatoes, or delicacies like venison in juniper sauce. **Pro:** perfect setting in a quaint corner of the town center. **Con:** restaurant noise on the first floor. ✉*Ludwigstr. 65* ☎*08821/9130* ⊕*www.dreimohren.de* ⇦*21 rooms, 2 apartments* ⌂*In-room: no a/c. In-hotel: restaurant, bar, public Internet, some pets allowed* ▭*AE, MC, V* ⑂*BP.*

SPORTS & THE OUTDOORS

HIKING & WALKING   There are innumerable spectacular walks on 300 km (186 mi) of marked trails through the lower slopes' pinewoods and upland meadows. If you have the time and good walking shoes, try one of the two trails that lead to striking gorges (called Klammen). The **Höllentalklamm** route starts at the **Zugspitze Mountain railway terminal** (✉*Olympiastr. 27*) in town and ends at the mountaintop (you'll want to turn back before reaching the summit unless you have mountaineering experience). The **Partnachklamm** route is quite challenging, and takes you through a spectacular, tunneled water gorge (entrance fee), past a pretty little mountain lake, and far up the Zugspitze; to do all of it, you'll have to stay overnight in one of the huts along the way. Ride part of the way up in the **Eckbauer cable car** (€8 one-way, €11 round-trip), which sets out from the Skistadion off Mittenwalderstrasse. The second cable car,

---

DER GASTHOF

The Gasthof, or guesthouse, is a typically Bavarian institution that originated as a place where stage-coach travelers could stop, eat, and rest for the night. Today these establishments are a combination of pub, restaurant, and small hotel. Typically, a Gasthof is a dark, half-timber house with a simple wood-paneled dining area. As a hotel, the Gasthof offers an incredible value. The mood at these spots is casual, friendly, and *gemütlich* (cozy). Expect to share a table with strangers: it's a great way to meet the locals.

3

the **Graseckbahn,** takes you right over the dramatic gorges (€3.50 one-way, €6 round-trip). There's a handy inn at the top, where you can gather strength for the hour-long walk back down to the Graseckbahn station. Horse-drawn carriages also cover the first section of the route in summer; in winter you can skim along it in a sleigh. The carriages wait near the Skistadion. Or you can call the local coaching society, the **Lohnkutschevereinigung** (☎08821/942–920), for information.

WORD OF MOUTH

"Hiking the 'klamms' (gorges near Mittenwald or Garmisch) is often fun for kids, or hiking from one alpine 'Sennhütte' to another. These 'huts' often cater food and drinks, and/or sell their own cheese and milk."

—Cowboy1968

Contact Deutscher Alpenverein (*German Alpine Association* ⊠ *Von-Kahr-Str. 2–4 Munich* ☎*089/140–030* ⊕*www.alpenverein.de*) for details on hiking and on staying in mountain huts.

SKIING & SNOWBO Garmisch-Partenkirchen was the site of the 1936 Winter Olympics, and remains Germany's premier winter-sports resort. The upper slopes of the Zugspitze and surrounding mountains challenge the best ski buffs and snowboarders, and there are also plenty of runs for intermediate skiers and families. The area is divided into two basic regions. The **Riffelriss** with the **Zugspitzplatt** is Germany's highest skiing area, with snow guaranteed from November to May. Access is via the **Zugspitzbahn** funicular. Cost for a day pass is €34.50, for a 2½-day pass €75 (valid from noon on the first day). The **CLASSIC-Gebiet,** or classical area, has 17 lifts in the **Alpspitz, Kreuzeck,** and **Hausberg** region. Day passes cost €29.50, a two-day pass €53. The town has a number of ski schools and tour organizers. Skiers looking for instruction can try the **Skischule Alpin** (⊠*Reintalstr. 8, Garmisch* ☎*08821/945–676*). Cross-country skiers should check with the **Erste Skilanglaufschule Garmisch-Partenkirchen** (☎*08821/1516*) at the eastern entrance of the Olympic stadium in Garmisch. For snowboarders, there's the **Snowboardschule Erwin Gruber** (⊠*Mittenwalderstr. 47d, Garmisch* ☎*08821/76490*). Telemark skiing is also popular in these rugged mountains. For information, contact the **Telemark Schule Leismüller** (⊠*Waldeckstr. 7, Garmisch* ☎*08821/752–696*).

The best place for information for all your snow-sports needs is the Alpine office at the tourist information office, **Alpine Auskunftstelle** (⊠*Richard-Strauss-Pl. 2, Garmisch* ☎*08821/180–744* ◷*Mon.–Thurs. 4–6*).

NIGHTLIFE & THE ARTS

In season there's a busy après-ski scene. Many hotels have dance floors, and some have basement discos that pound away until the early hours. Bavarian folk dancing and zither music are regular features of nightlife. In summer there's entertainment every Saturday evening at the **Bayernhalle** (⊠*Brauhausstr. 19*). Wednesday through Monday the cozy tavern-restaurant **Gasthof Fraundorfer** (⊠*Ludwigstr. 24* ☎*08821/9270*) hosts yodeling and folk dancing. The younger, hipper crowd heads to the **Evergreen Lounge** to be heated up by DJs (✉ *Klammstr. 47* ☎ *08821/72– 626* ⊕ *www.disco-evergreen.de* ◷ *Wed.–Sat. 9–5*). Concerts are presented from Saturday to Thursday, mid-May through September, in the park bandstand in Garmisch, and on Friday in the Partenkirchen park. Tickets are available at **Garmisch-Partenkirchen-Ticket** (✉ *Richard-Strauss-Pl. 2* ☎ *08821/752–545* ◷ *Weekdays 9–1 and 2–7, Sat. 9–1*).

The casino, **Spielbank Garmisch** (✉ *Am Kurpark 10* ☎ *08821/95990*), is open daily 3 PM–2 AM and Saturday 3 PM–3 AM, with more than 100 slot machines and roulette, blackjack, and poker tables.

ETTAL

★ *16 km (10 mi) north of Garmisch-Partenkirchen, 85 km (53 mi) south of Munich.*

The village of Ettal is presided over by the massive bulk of Kloster Ettal, a great monastery and centuries-old distillery.

ESSENTIALS

Visitor Information **Ettal** (✉ *Verkehrsamt, Kaiser-Ludwig-Pl.* ☎ *08822/3534*).

The great monastery **Kloster Ettal** was founded in 1330 by Holy Roman Emperor Ludwig the Bavarian for a group of knights and a community of Benedictine monks. This is the largest Benedictine monastery in Germany; approximately 55 monks live here, including one from Compton, Los Angeles. The abbey was replaced with new buildings in the 18th century and now serves as a school. The original 10-sided church was brilliantly redecorated in 1744–53, becoming one of the foremost examples of Bavarian rococo. The church's chief treasure is its enormous dome fresco (83 feet wide), painted by Jacob Zeiller circa 1751–52. The mass of swirling clouds and the pink-and-blue vision of heaven are typical of the rococo fondness for elaborate ceiling painting.

Ettaler liqueurs, made from a centuries-old recipe, are still distilled at the monastery. The monks make seven different liqueurs, some with more than 70 mountain herbs. Originally the liqueurs were made as medicines, and they have legendary health-giving properties. The ad tells it best: "Two monks know how it's made, 2 million Germans know how it tastes." ■TIP➔ **You can visit the distillery right next to the church and buy bottles of the libation from the gift shop and bookstore. The blueberry liqueur is the best.** ☎ *08822/740 for guided tour of church* ✆ *Free* ◷ *Daily 8–6.*

Besides its spirit and spirits, Ettal has made another local industry into an attraction: namely cheese, yogurt, and other milk derivatives. You can see cheese, butter, cream, and other dairy products in the making at the **Schaukäserei** or "public cheese-making plant." There is even a little buffet for a cheesy break. ✉ *Mandlweg 1* ☎ *08822/923–926* ⊕ *www.milch-und-kas.de* ✆ *Free, €2.50 with tour* ◷ *Tues.–Sat. 10–6, Sun. noon–5.*

¢–$ ╳**Edelweiss.** This friendly café and restaurant next to the monastery is an ideal spot for a light lunch or coffee and homemade cakes. ⊠*Kaiser-Ludwig-Pl. 3* ☎*08822/92920* ▭*No credit cards.*

$ ⌂**Hotel Ludwig der Bayer.** Backed by mountains, this fine old hotel is run by the Benedictine order. There's nothing monastic about it, except for the exquisite religious carvings and motifs that adorn the walls. Most come from the monastery's carpentry shop, which also made much of the solid furniture in the comfortable bedrooms. The hotel has two excellent restaurants ($–$$) with rustic, Bavarian atmosphere and a vaulted tavern that serves sturdy fare and beer brewed at the monastery. The extensive wellness area includes a Finnish sauna, herbal steam bath, pool, solarium, a beauty section, and massage. **Pros:** good value, close to Kloster, indoor pool. **Con:** expensive breakfast often not included in price. ⊠*Kaiser-Ludwig-Pl. 10* ☎*08822/9150* ☞*70 rooms, 30 apartments* ⌂*In-room: no a/c. In-hotel: 2 restaurants, bars, tennis court, pool, gym, bicycles, some pets allowed, no elevator* ▭*MC, V* ⦿*BP.*

$ ⌂**Hotel zur Post.** Families are warmly welcomed at this traditional Gasthof in the center of town. There's a playground in the shady garden, and the Bavarian restaurant ($–$$), which has warm wood paneling, offers a children's menu. Breakfast buffet is included in the price. **Pros:** quiet, relaxing, near Kloster. **Cons:** no air-conditioning or in-room telephone. ⊠*Kaiser-Ludwig-Pl. 18* ☎*08822/3596* ⊕*www.posthotel-ettal.de* ☞*21 rooms, 4 apartments* ⌂*In-room: no a/c, no phone, Wi-Fi. In-hotel: restaurant, gym, public Wi-Fi, no-smoking rooms, some pets allowed* ▭*MC, V* ⦿*Closed Oct. 26–Dec. 18* ⦿*BP.*

SCHLOSS LINDERHOF

★ *10 km (6 mi) west of Ettal on B–23, 95 km (59 mi) south of Munich.*

Built between 1870 and 1879 on the spectacular grounds of his father's hunting lodge, Schloss Linderhof was the only one of Ludwig II's royal residences to have been completed during the monarch's short life. It was the smallest of this ill-fated king's castles, but his favorite country retreat among the various palaces at his disposal. Set in sylvan seclusion, between a reflecting pool and the green slopes of a gentle mountain, the charming, French-style, rococo confection is said to have been inspired by the Petit Trianon at Versailles. From an architectural standpoint it's a whimsical combination of conflicting styles, lavish on the outside, somewhat overly decorated on the inside. But the main inspiration came from the Sun King of France, Louis XIV, who is referred to in numerous bas-reliefs, mosaics, paintings, and stucco pieces. Ludwig's bedroom is filled with brilliantly colored and gilded ornaments, the Hall of Mirrors is a shimmering dream world, and the dining room has a clever piece of 19th-century engineering—a table that rises from and descends to the kitchens below.

The formal gardens contain still more whimsical touches. There's a Moorish pavilion—bought wholesale from the 1867 Paris Universal

3

Exposition—and a huge artificial grotto in which Ludwig had scenes from Wagner operas performed, with full lighting effects. It took the BASF chemical company much research to develop the proper glass for the blue lighting Ludwig desired. The gilded Neptune in front of the castle spouts a 100-foot water jet. According to hearsay, while staying at Linderhof the eccentric king would dress up as the legendary knight Lohengrin to be rowed in a swan boat on the grotto pond; in winter he took off on midnight sleigh rides behind six plumed horses and a platoon of outriders holding flaring torches. ⚠ **In winter be prepared for an approach road as snowbound as in Ludwig's day—drive carefully.** ☎ *08822/92030* ⊕ *www.schlosslinderhof.de* ✉ *Summer €7, winter €6; palace grounds only in summer €3* ⏱ *Apr.–Sept., daily 9–6; Oct.–Mar., daily 10–4; pavilion and grotto closed in winter.*

LÜFTLMALEREI

The *Lüftlmalerei* style of fresco-painting is unique to Bavaria and the Tirol where the opulently painted facades were used as a display of wealth. Commonly known as *trompe l'œil*, the detailed frescoes give the illusion of three dimensions. They are painted directly onto fresh plaster, which makes the painting last for centuries.

The term *Lüftlmalerei* originated in Oberammergau after the famous fresco artist Franz Seraph Zwinck painted a fresco on his house, the *Zum Lüftl*. Zwinck became the *Lüftlmaler*, or the painter of the *Lüftl*.

OBERAMMERGAU

20 km (12 mi) northwest of Garmisch-Partenkirchen, 4 km (2½ mi) northwest of Ettal, 90 km (56 mi) south of Munich.

Its location alone, in an Alpine valley beneath a sentinel-like peak, makes this small town a major attraction (allow a half hour for the drive from Garmisch). Its main streets are lined with painted houses (such as the 1784 Pilatushaus on Ludwig-Thoma-Strasse), and in summer the village bursts with color. Many of these lovely houses are occupied by families whose men are highly skilled in the art of wood carving, a craft that has flourished here since the early 12th century.

GETTING HERE & AROUND

The B–23 links Oberammergau to Garmsich-Partenkirchen and to the A–23 to Munich. Frequent bus services connect to Garmisch, Ettal, the Wieskirche, and Füssen. No long-distance trains serve Oberammergau, but a short ride on the Regional-Bahn to Murnau will connect you to the long-distance train network.

ESSENTIALS

Visitor Information Oberammergau (✉ *Verkehrsamt, Eugen-Papst-Str. 9a* ☎ *08822/92310* 🖷 *08822/923–190* ⊕ *www.oberammergau.de*).

EXPLORING

Oberammergau is best known for its **Passion Play,** however, first presented in 1634 as an offering of thanks after the Black Death stopped just short of the village. In faithful accordance with a solemn vow, it will next be performed in the year 2010, as it has every 10 years since 1680. Its 16 acts, which take 5½ hours, depict the final days of Christ, from the Last Supper through the Crucifixion and Resurrection. It's presented daily on a partly open-air stage against a mountain backdrop from late May to late September. The entire village is swept up in the production, with some 1,500 residents directly involved in its preparation and presentation. Men grow beards in the hope of capturing a key role; young women have been known to put off their weddings—the role of Mary went only to unmarried girls until 1990, when, amid much local controversy, a 31-year-old mother of two was given the part.

The immense theater, the **Oberammergau Passionsspielhaus,** in which the Passion Play is performed every 10 years, can be toured. Visitors are given a glimpse of the costumes, the sceneries, the stage, and even the auditorium. ■TIP➜ The Combi-ticket for the Oberammergau Museum, Pilatushaus, and the Passionsmuseum costs €6. ⊠ *Passionstheater, Passionswiese* ☎ *08822/945–8833* ⊉ *€4* ⊙ *Summer daily 10–5, winter irregular.*

You'll find many wood-carvers at work in town, and shop windows are crammed with their creations. From June through October a workshop is open free to the public at the **Pilatushaus** (⊠ *Ludwig-Thoma-Str. 10* ☎ *08822/92310 tourist office*); working potters and painters can also be seen. Pilatushaus was completed in 1775, and the frescoes—considered among the most beautiful in town—were done by Franz Seraph Zwinck, one of the greatest *Lüftlmalerei* painters. The house is named for the fresco over the front door depicting Christ before Pilate. A collection of reverse glass paintings depicting religious and secular scenes has been moved here from the Heimatmuseum. Contact the tourist office to sign up for a weeklong course in wood carving (classes are in German), which costs between €429 and €579, depending on whether you stay in a Gasthof or a hotel.

The **Oberammergau Museum** has historic examples of the wood craftsman's art and an outstanding collection of Christmas crèches, which date from the mid-18th century. Numerous exhibits also document the wax and wax-embossing art, which also flourishes in Oberammergau. ⊠ *Dorfstr. 8* ☎ *08822/94136* ⊉ *€4, includes Pilatushaus* ⊙ *Apr.–Oct., Dec.–Feb., Tues.–Sun. 10–5.*

The 18th-century **St. Peter and St. Paul Church** is regarded as the finest work of rococo architect Josef Schmutzer, and has striking frescoes by Matthäus Günther and Franz Seraph Zwinck (in the organ loft). Schmutzer's son, Franz Xaver Schmutzer, did a lot of the stuccowork. ⊠ *Pfarrpl. 1* ☎ *No phone* ⊙ *Daily 9* AM *–dusk.*

WHERE TO EAT

$$ ✗**Ammergauer Stubn.** A homey restaurant with pink tablecloths and a lot of wood, the Stubn has a comprehensive menu that serves both Bavarian specialties and international dishes. You can expect nice roasts and some Swabian dishes, such as *Maultaschen,* a large, meat-filled ravioli. ⊠ *Wittelsbach Hotel, Dorfstr. 21* ☎*08822/92800* ▤*AE, DC, MC* ⊗*Closed Tues. and Nov.–mid-Dec. No lunch.*

$$ ✗**Doppers.** It looks rustic and Bavarian from the outside, and the small barbecue terrace suggests weighty local foods, but, with the exception of steaks, Doppers specializes in Thai dishes. The curries add to the warming effect of the old green Kachelöfen (enclosed, tiled, wood-burning stoves) in the ground-floor rooms. ⊠ *Ludwig-Thoma-Str. 11* ☎*08822/935–615* ⊗*No lunch.*

$ ✗**Alte Post.** You can enjoy carefully prepared local cuisine at the original pine tables in this 350-year-old inn. There's a special children's menu, and in summer meals are also served in the beer garden. The front terrace of this delightful old building is a great place to watch traffic, both pedestrian and automotive. A part of the café has been reserved for Web surfing. ⊠ *Dorfstr. 19* ☎*08822/9100* ▤*DC, V* ⊗*Closed Nov.–mid-Dec.*

$ ✗**Gasthaus zum Stern.** This is a traditional place (around 500 years old), with coffered ceilings, thick walls, an old Kachelofen that heats the dining room beyond endurance on cold winter days, and smiling waitresses in dirndls. The food is hearty, traditional Bavarian. For a quieter dinner or lunch, reserve a space in the Bäckerstube (Baker's Parlor). ⊠ *Dorfstr. 33* ☎*08822/867* ▤*AE, DC, MC, V* ⊗*Closed Wed.*

WHERE TO STAY

$–$$ ▥**Hotel Landhaus Feldmeier.** This quiet family-run hotel, idyllically set just outside the village, has mostly spacious rooms with modern pine-wood furniture. All have geranium-bedecked balconies, with views of the village and mountains. The rustic restaurant ($$–$$$) is one of the region's best. You can dine on the sunny, covered terrace in summer. Only hotel guests can use credit cards in the restaurant. **Pros:** small and distinguished, quiet. **Con:** outside the city center. ⊠ *Ettalerstr. 29D–82487* ☎*08822/3011* ⊕*www.hotel-feldmeier.de* ⮐*22 rooms, 4 apartments* ⌂*In-room: no a/c. In-hotel: restaurant, gym, public Internet, no-smoking rooms, some pets allowed, no elevator* ▤*MC, V* ⊗*Closed mid-Nov.–mid-Dec.* ¶⊠*BP.*

$–$$ ▥**Hotel Turmwirt.** Rich wood paneling reaches from floor to ceiling in ★ this transformed 18th-century inn, set in the shadow of Oberammergau's mountain, the Kofel. The hotel's own band presents regular folk evenings in the restaurant ($–$$). The *Ammergauer Pfanne,* a combination of meats and sauces, will take care of even industrial-size hunger. Rooms have corner lounge areas, and most come with balconies and sweeping mountain views. Prices are based on length of stay, so you'll pay less if you stay longer. **Pros:** great with children, ask for a room facing the Kofel. **Cons:** expensive Internet, nearby church bells ring every 15 minutes. ⊠ *Ettalerstr. 2D–82487* ☎*08822/92600* ⊕*www. turmwirt.de* ⮐*44 rooms* ⌂*In-room: no a/c. In-hotel: restaurant, pub-*

lic Internet, no-smoking rooms, some pets allowed, no elevator ⊟AE, DC, MC, V ⊘Closed Jan. 7–21 ⊧O⊧BP.

Though the Passion Play theater was traditionally not used for anything other than the Passion Play (next performance, 2010), Oberammergauers decided that using it for opera or other theatrical events during the 10-year pause between the religious performances might be a good idea. The first performances of Verdi's *Nabucco* and Mozart's *Magic Flute* in 2002 established a new tradition. Other passion plays are also performed here. Ticket prices are between €19 and €49. For reservations, call ☎ 08822/923–158.

MITTENWALD

20 km (12 mi) southeast of Garmisch, 105 km (66 mi) south of Munich.

Many regard Mittenwald as the most beautiful town in the Bavarian Alps. It has somehow avoided the architectural sins found in other Alpine villages by maintaining a balance between conservation and the needs of tourism. Its medieval prosperity is reflected on its main street, **Obermarkt,** which has splendid houses with ornately carved gables and brilliantly painted facades. Goethe called it "a picture book come alive," and it still is. The town has even re-created the stream that once flowed through the market square, and the main road was detoured around Mittenwald, markedly raising the quality of life in town.

In the Middle Ages Mittenwald was the staging point for goods shipped from the wealthy city-state of Venice by way of the Brenner Pass and Innsbruck. From Mittenwald, goods were transferred to rafts, which carried them down the Isar River to Munich. In the mid-17th century, however, the international trade route was moved to a different pass, and the fortunes of Mittenwald declined.

In 1684 Matthias Klotz, a farmer's son turned master violin maker, returned from a 20-year stay in Cremona, Italy. There, along with Antonio Stradivari, he had studied under Nicolo Amati, who gave the violin its present form. Klotz taught the art of violin making to his brothers and friends; before long, half the men in the village were crafting the instruments, using woods from neighboring forests. Mittenwald became known as the Village of a Thousand Violins, and stringed instruments—violins, violas, and cellos—were shipped around the world. In the right weather—sunny, dry—you may even catch the odd sight of laundry lines hung with new violins out to receive their natural dark hue. The violin has made Mittenwald a small cultural oasis in the middle of the Alps. Not only is there an annual violin- (and viola-, cello-, and bow-) building contest each year in June, with concerts and lectures, but also an organ festival in the church of St. Peter and St. Paul held from the end of July to the end of September. The town also boasts a violin-making school.

GETTING HERE & AROUND

The B–11 connects Mittenwald with Garmisch. Mittenwald is the end station on the rail line from Munich via Garmisch-Partenkirchen; some trains continue on to Innsbruck.

ESSENTIALS

Visitor Information **Mittenwald** (⊠ *Kurverwaltung, Dammkarstr. 3* ☎ *08823/33981* ⊕ *www.mittenwald.de).*

EXPLORING

The **Geigenbau und Heimatmuseum** *(Violin-Building and Local Museum)* describes in fascinating detail the history of violin making in Mittenwald. Ask the museum curator to direct you to the nearest of several violin-makers—they'll be happy to demonstrate the skills handed down to them. ⊠ *Ballenhausg. 3* ☎ *08823/2511* ⚑ *€4* ⊙ *Mid-May–Oct., Tues.–Sun. 10–5; Nov.–mid-May, 11–4.*

On the back of the altar in the 18th-century **St. Peter and St. Paul Church** (as in Oberammergau, built by Josef Schmutzer and decorated by Matthäus Günther), you'll find Matthias Klotz's name, carved there by the violin-maker himself. ■ TIP➡ Note that on some of the ceiling frescoes, the angels are playing violins, violas da gamba, and lutes. In front of the church, Klotz is memorialized as an artist at work in vivid bronze sculpted by Ferdinand von Miller (1813–79), creator of the mighty Bavaria Monument in Munich. The church, with its elaborate and joyful stuccowork coiling and curling its way around the interior, is one of the most important rococo structures in Bavaria. Note its Gothic choir loft, added in the 18th century. The bold frescoes on its exterior are characteristic of *Lüftlmalerei*, a style that reached its height in Mittenwald. Images, usually religious motifs, were painted on the wet stucco exteriors of houses and churches. On nearby streets you can see other fine examples on the facades of three famous houses: the Goethehaus, the Pilgerhaus, and the Pichlerhaus. Among the artists working here was the great Franz Seraph Zwinck. ⊠ *Ballenhausg., next to Geigenbau und Heimatmuseum.*

WHERE TO EAT

$$ ✕ **Arnspitze.** Get a table at the large picture window and soak in the
★ views of the towering Karwendel mountain range as you ponder a menu that combines the best traditional ingredients with international touches. Chef and owner Herbert Wipfelder looks beyond the edge of his plate all the way to Asia, if need be, to find inspiration. The fish pot-au-feu has a Mediterranean flair; the jugged hare in red wine is truly Bavarian. The restaurant also offers accommodations in a separate house. ⊠ *Innsbrucker Str. 68* ☎ *08823/2425* ▭ *AE* ⊙ *Closed Nov.–mid-Dec. and Tues. and Wed.*

WHERE TO STAY

$–$$ ⊡ **Post.** Stagecoaches carrying travelers and mail across the Alps stopped here as far back as the 17th century. The hotel retains much of its historic charm, though the elegant rooms come in various styles, from modern to art nouveau to Bavarian rustic. The indoor swimming pool has views of the Karwendel peaks, and a small rose garden is an inviting spot for coffee and cake. Excellent Bavarian fare such as roasts and great *Semmelknödel* (bread dumplings) is served in the wine tavern or at the low-beam Postklause ($–$$). **Pro:** Art nouveau rooms in the back! **Cons:** no elevator, street noise in the evening. ⊠*Obermarkt 9* ☎*08823/938–2333* ⊕*www.posthotel-mittenwald.de* ⌂*74 rooms, 7 suites* ⚴*In-room: no a/c, dial-up. In-hotel: 2 restaurants, bar, pool, no-smoking rooms, some pets allowed* ☰*MC, V* ⦿|*BP.*

$ 🏨**Alpenrose.** Once part of a monastery and later given one of the town's most beautiful painted baroque facades, the Alpenrose is one of the area's handsomest hotels. The typical Bavarian bedrooms and public rooms have lots of wood paneling, farmhouse cupboards, and finely woven fabrics. The restaurant ($–$$) devotes the entire month of October to venison dishes, for which it has become renowned. A zither player strums away most evenings in the Josefi wine cellar. **Pros:** great German decor, friendly staff. **Cons:** some rooms are large, some are cramped, warm in the summer. ⊠*Obermarkt 1* ☎*08823/92700* ⊕*www.hotel-alpenrose-mittenwald.de* ⌂*16 rooms, 2 apartments* ⚴*In-room: no a/c. In-hotel: restaurant, bar, public Internet, some pets allowed, no elevator* ☰*AE, DC, MC, V* ⦿|*BP.*

$ 🏨**Bichlerhof.** Carved oak furniture gives the rooms of this Alpine-style hotel a solid German feel. A breakfast buffet is served until 11 AM and will keep the hardiest hiker going all day. Although the restaurant serves only breakfast, there's no shortage of taverns in the area. Most guest rooms have mountain views. **Pros:** amazing views, well-kept spa area. **Con:** built to look typically Bavarian, but is actually only 30 years old. ⊠*Adolf-Baader-Str. 5* ☎*08823/9190* ⊕*www.bichlerhof-mittenwald.de* ⌂*30 rooms* ⚴*In-room: no a/c, dial-up. In-hotel: pool, gym, no-smoking rooms, some pets allowed* ☰*AE, DC, MC, V* ⦿|*BP.*

$ 🏨**Gasthof Stern.** This white house with brilliant blue shutters is right in the middle of Mittenwald. The painted furniture is not antique, but reminiscent of old peasant Bavaria, and the featherbeds are incredibly soft. Locals meet in the dining room (¢–$) for loud conversation, and the beer garden is a pleasant, familial place to while away the hours with a *Bauernschmaus,* a plate of sausage with sauerkraut and homemade liver dumplings. The restaurant is closed on Thursday. More than one night at the inn makes the price cheaper. **Pro:** great beer garden. **Cons:** needs renovation, upper rooms warm in the summer, no credit cards accepted. ⊠*Fritz-Plössl-Pl. 2* ☎*08823/8358* ⊕*www.stern-mittenwald.de* ⌂*5 rooms* ⚴*In-room: no a/c, no phone. In-hotel: restaurant, bar, some pets allowed, no elevator* ☰*No credit cards* ⦿|*BP.*

SPORTS & THE OUTDOORS

Mittenwald lies literally in the shadow of the mighty **Karwendel** Alpine range, which rises to a height of nearly 8,000 feet. ■**TIP→ There are a number of small lakes in the hills surrounding Mittenwald. You can either walk to the closer ones or rent bikes and adventure farther afield. The information center across the street from the train station has maps, and they can help you select a route.**

The **Dammkar** run is nearly 8 km (5 mi) long and offers some of the best free-riding skiing, telemarking, and snowboarding in the German Alps.

A **cable car** (☎08823/8480 ⛧€13 one-way, €21 round-trip, day pass €29 ☉Dec.–Oct., daily 8:30–5) carries hikers and skiers to a height of 7,180 feet, the beginning of numerous trails down, or farther up into the Karwendel range. You can book a guide with **Bergerlebnis und Wanderschule Oberes Isartal** (☎08651/5835). Skiers, cross-country and downhill, and snowboarders can find all they need, including equipment and instruction, at the **Erste Schischule Mittenwald** (✉Bahnhofsparkpl., parking next to train station ☎08823/3582 or 08823/8548).

SHOPPING

It's not the kind of gift every visitor wants to take home, but if you'd like a violin, a cello, or even a double bass, the Alpine resort of Mittenwald can oblige. There are more than 30 craftsmen whose work is coveted by musicians throughout the world. If you're buying or even just feeling curious, call on **Anton Maller** (✉Obermarkt 2 ☎08823/5865). He's been making violins and other stringed instruments for more than 25 years. The **Geigenbau Leonhardt** (✉Mühlenweg 53a ☎08823/8010) is another good place to purchase one of the town's famous stringed instruments. For traditional Bavarian costumes—dirndls, embroidered shirts and blouses, and lederhosen—try **Trachten Werner** (✉Hochstr. 1 ☎08823/3785). Find out where all the milk from the local cows goes with a visit to **Gabriele Schneider's SchokoLaden** (✉Dekan-Karl-Pl. 15 ☎08823/938–939 ⊕www.schokoladen-mittenwald.de), a homemade chocolate shop.

CHIEMGAU

With its rolling hills with serene lakes in the shadow of the Alpine peaks, the Chiemgau is a natural paradise and a good transition to the Alps. The main attraction is, without a doubt, the Chiemsee with the amazing palace on the Herreninsel. The area is dotted with clear blue lakes and, although tourism is fairly well established, you'll feel like you have the Schliersee and Spitzensee all to yourself. Beer lovers flock to the Tegernsee and relax afterward in the iodine spa in Bad Tölz.

BAD TÖLZ

14 km (8 mi) north of Sylvenstein Lake, 48 km (30 mi) south of Munich.

Bad Tölz's new town, dating from the mid-19th century, sprang up with the discovery of iodine-laden springs, which allowed the locals to call their town *Bad* (bath or spa) Tölz. You can take the waters, either by drinking a cupful from the local springs or going all the way with a full course of health treatments at a specially equipped hotel. ■TIP→ **If you can, visit on a Wednesday or a Friday morning—market days—when stalls stretch along the main street to the Isar River and on the Jungmayr-Fritzplatz.**

This town clings to its ancient customs more tightly than any other Bavarian community. It is not uncommon to see people wearing tradi-

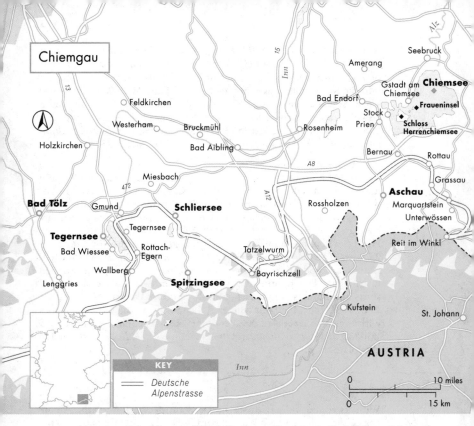

tional clothing as their daily dress. If you're in Bad Tölz on November 6, you'll witness one of the most colorful traditions of the Bavarian Alpine area: the Leonhardiritt equestrian procession, which marks the anniversary of the death in 559 of St. Leonhard, the patron saint of animals, specifically horses. The procession ends north of town at an 18th-century chapel on the Kalvarienberg, above the Isar River.

GETTING HERE & AROUND
Bad Tölz is on the B–472, which connects to the A–8 to Munich. Hourly trains link Bad Tölz with Munich. Bad Tölz is easily walkable and has frequent city-bus services.

ESSENTIALS
Visitor Information **Bad Tölz** (⊠ *Tourist Information, Max-Höfler-Pl. 1* ☎ *08041/78670* ⊕ *www.bad-toelz.de*).

EXPLORING
★ The **Alpamare**, Bad Tölz's very attractive spa complex, pumps spa water into its pools, one of which is disguised as a South Sea beach complete with surf. Its five waterslides include a 1,082-foot-long adventure run. Another—the Alpa-Canyon—has 90-degree drops, and only the hardiest swimmers are advised to try it. A nightmarish dark tunnel is aptly named the Thriller. They have a variety of prices for the

various individual attractions, or combo tickets for more than one. ✉*Ludwigstr. 13* ☎*08041/509–999* ⊕*www.alpamare.de* ✈*4-hr ticket €27; €21 after 5* PM ⊙*Daily 9:30* AM*–10* PM.

The **Stadtmuseum,** in the Altes Rathaus (Old Town Hall), has many fine examples of Bauernmöbel (farmhouse furniture), as well as a fascinating exhibit on the history of the town and its environs. ✉*Marktstr. 48* ☎*08041/504–688* ✈*€2.50* ⊙*Mar.–Jan., Tues.–Sun. 10–4.*

WHERE TO STAY

$$$ ★ 🏨**Hotel Jodquellenhof-Alpamare.** The *Jodquellen* are the iodine springs that have made Bad Tölz wealthy. You can take advantage of these revitalizing waters at this luxurious spa, where the emphasis is on fitness. Vegetarian and low-calorie entrées are served in the restaurant ($$$–$$$$). The imposing 19th-century building, with private access to the Alpamare Lido, contains stylish rooms with granite and marble bathrooms. The room price includes full use of the spa facilities. There are discounts for children. **Pros:** elegant hotel, free access to the spa. **Con:** busy on local school holidays. ✉*Ludwigstr. 13–15* ☎*08041/5090* ⊕*www.jodquellenhof.com* ✈*71 rooms* ⚅*In-room: no a/c, dial-up. In-hotel: restaurant, pool, spa, public Wi-Fi, no elevator* 🞋*AE, DC, MC, V* ⧊*BP.*

$$ 🏨**Hotel Kolbergarten.** Located right near the old town and surrounded by a quiet garden with old trees, this hotel offers comfortable rooms, each carefully done in a particular style such as baroque or Biedermeier. The grand restaurant ($$) in fin-de-siècle style offers a wide range of gourmet dishes created by the Viennese chef Johann Mikschy, from sashimi of yellowfin tuna, to veal boiled with grape leaves. The wine list will take you around the world. **Pros:** large clean rooms, staff is great with children. **Cons:** very popular, often fully booked. ✉*Fröhlichg. 5* ☎*08041/78920* ⊕*www.hotel-kolbergarten.de* ✈*12 rooms, 2 suites* ⚅*In-room: no a/c, dial-up. In-hotel: public Internet, no-smoking rooms, some pets allowed* 🞋*AE, DC, MC, V* ⧊*BP.*

NIGHTLIFE & THE ARTS

Bad Tölz is world-renowned for its outstanding **boys' choir** (☎*08041/78670 for program details from Städtische Kurverwaltung*). When it's not on tour, the choir gives regular concerts in the Kurhaus.

Tom's Bar (✉*Demmeljochstr. 42*) has '60s furnishings with modern music (DJs, theme nights), reasonable prices, and plenty of space.

The **Kult/Advokatenhaus** (✉ *Wachterstr. 16. 42*) has a rather wide range of themes, and it features live music in the terrific setting of an old brewery, with barrel vaults and painted brick walls.

SPORTS & THE OUTDOORS

Bad Tölz's local mountain, the **Blomberg,** 3 km (2 mi) west of town, has moderately difficult ski runs and can also be tackled on a toboggan in winter and in summer. The winter run of 5 km (3 mi) is the longest in Bavaria, although the artificial concrete channel used in summer snakes only 3,938 feet down the mountain. A ski-lift ride to the start of the run and toboggan rental are included in the price. ☎08041/3726 ⊕*www.blombergbahn.de* ➲*€4 per toboggan ride*—3 rides for €11 ☉*Jan.–Oct., daily 9–4; Nov.–Dec., summer toboggan run hrs depend on weather conditions.*

SHOPPING

■**TIP**➜ **Bad Tölz is famous for its painted furniture, particularly farmhouse cupboards and chests.** Several local shops specialize in this type of *Bauernmöbel* (farmhouse furniture, usually hand carved from pine) and will usually handle export formalities. Ask at your hotel or tourist information for a recommendation on where to shop. One to try: **Antiquitäten Schwarzwälder** (✉*Badstr. 2* ☎*08041/41222*).

TEGERNSEE

★ *16 km (10 mi) east of Bad Tölz, 50 km (31 mi) south of Munich.*

The beautiful shores of the Tegernsee are among the most expensive property in all of Germany. The interest in the region shown by King Maximilian I of Bavaria at the beginning of the 19th century attracted VIPs and artists, which led to a boom that has never really faded. Most accommodations and restaurants, however, still have reasonable prices, and there are plenty of activities for everyone. Tegernsee's wooded shores, rising gently to scalable mountain peaks of no more than 6,300 feet, invite hikers, walkers, and picnicking families. The lake itself draws swimmers and yachters. In fall the russet-clad trees provide a colorful contrast to the snowcapped mountains. There are three main towns on the lake: Tegernsee, Rottach-Egern, and Bad Wiessee.

GETTING HERE & AROUND

The best way to reach all three towns is to take the BOB train from Munich to Tegernsee (hourly) and then take a boat ride on one of the eight boats that circle the lake year-round. The boats dock near the Tegernsee train station and make frequent stops, including stops at the Benedictine monastery in Tegernsee, Rottach-Egern, and Bad Wiessee. The monastery is a pleasant half-mile walk from the train station. Busses connect Tegernsee to Bad Tölz.

ESSENTIALS

Visitor Information Bad Wiessee (✉*Tourist-Information, Adrian-Stoop-Str. 20* ☎*08022/86030* ⊕*www.bad-wiessee.de*). **Rottach-Egern/Tegernsee** (✉*Kuramt, Hauptstr. 2* ☎*08022/180–149* ⊕*www.tegernsee.de*).

EXPLORING

★ On the eastern shore of the lake, the laid-back town of Tegernsee is home to a large **Benedictine monastery** (✉ *Schlosspl., Tegernsee*). Founded in the 8th century, this was one of the most productive cultural centers in southern Germany; the Minnesänger (musician and poet) Walther von der Vogelweide (1170–1230) was a welcome guest. Not so welcome were Magyar invaders, who laid waste to the monastery in the 10th century. During the Middle Ages the monastery made a lively business producing stained-glass windows, thanks to a nearby quartz quarry, and in the 16th century it became a major center of printing. The late-Gothic **church** was refurbished in Italian baroque style in the 18th century. The frescoes are by Hans Georg Asam, whose work also graces the Benediktbeuren monastery. Secularization sealed the monastery's fate at the beginning of the 19th century: almost half the buildings were torn down. Maximilian I bought the surviving ones and had Leo von Klenze redo them for use as a summer retreat.

Today there is a high school on the property, and students write their exams beneath inspiring baroque frescoes in what was the monastery. The **Herzogliches Bräustüberl,** a brewery and beer hall, is also on-site. ■TIP→ Try a Mass (a liter-sized mug) of their legendary Tergernseer Helles beer.

The **Olaf Gulbransson Museum** is devoted to the Norwegian painter Olaf Gulbrannson, who went to Munich in 1902 and worked as a caricaturist for the satirical magazine *Simplicissimus*. His poignant caricatures and numerous works of satire depict noisy politicians and snooty social upper-crusters as well as other subjects. The museum is housed in a discreet modern building set back from the main lakeside road of Tegernsee. ✉ *Im Kurgarten, Tegernsee* ☏ *08022/3338* ⊕ *www.olaf-gulbransson-museum.de* ☞ *€5* ◷ *Tues.–Sun. 10–5.*

Maximilian showed off this corner of his kingdom to Czar Alexander I of Russia and Emperor Franz I of Austria during their journey to the Congress of Verona in October 1821. You can follow their steps through the woods to one of the loveliest lookout points in Bavaria, the **Grosses Paraplui.** A plaque marks the spot where they admired the open expanse of the Tegernsee and the mountains beyond. The path starts opposite Schlossplatz in Tegernsee town and is well marked.

Rottach-Egern, the fashionable and upscale resort at the southern end of the lake, has classy shops, chic restaurants, and expensive boutiques. Rottach-Egern's church, **St. Laurentius,** is worth seeing for its baroque influences.

While at the Rottach-Egern tourist office (*Kuramt*), have a look at the collection of horse-drawn vehicles at the adjoining **Kutschen-, Wagen- und Schlittenmuseum.** It contains beautifully restored coaches, sleds, oxcarts, and all the implements of the wagon driver's trade. ✉ *Nördliche Hauptstr. 9 Rottach-Egern* ☏ *08022/671–341* ☞ *€2* ◷ *May–Oct., Tues.–Sun. 2–5.*

WHERE TO EAT

$$–$$$ ✕ **Landhaus Wilhelmy.** Although everything is modern, this inn in Bad Wiessee takes you back to a less-frantic era, and the Ziegelbauers, who restored the buildings, know how to make you feel at home. Classical music accompanies unpretentious yet tasty meals. Try the fish specialties or the light guinea fowl with herb rice and enjoy tea and cake in the little garden. ✉ *Freihausstr. 15Bad Wiessee* ☎ *08022/98680* ▭ *AE, DC, MC, V.*

$$ ✕ **Freihaus Brenner.** Proprietor Josef Brenner has brought a taste of nouvelle cuisine to the Tegernsee. His attractive restaurant commands fine views from high above Bad Wiessee. Try any of his suggested dishes, ranging from roast pheasant in wine sauce to fresh lake fish. There are flexible portion sizes for smaller appetites. ✉ *Freihaushöhe 4 Bad Wiessee* ☎ *08022/82004* 🌐 *www.freihaus-brenner.de* ▭ *MC, V* ⊙ *Closed Tues.*

$–$$ ✕ **Weinhaus Moschner.** Join the locals at a rough wooden table in this dark, old tavern on the edge of ritzy Rottach-Egern. Order a glass of Franconian wine or ale from the monastery brewery. You'll find a wide range of options, from sturdy smoked pork to homemade ravioli filled with grilled salmon, but nobody comes here just to eat. ✉ *Kisslingerstr. 2 Rottach-Egern* ☎ *08022/5522* ▭ *AE, DC, MC, V* ⊙ *Closed Mon. and Tues.*

¢–$ ✕ **Herzogliches Bräustüberl.** Once part of Tegernsee's Benedictine monastery, then a royal retreat, the Bräustüberl is now an immensely popular beer hall and brewery. Only Bavarian snacks (sausages, pretzels, all the way up to steak tartare) are served in this crowded place, but hearty meals can be had in the adjoining **Schlossgaststätte** ($–$$). In summer, quaff your beer beneath the huge chestnut trees and admire the delightful view of the lake and mountains. ✉ *Schlosspl. 1 Tegernsee* ☎ *08022/4141* ✍ *Reservations not accepted* ▭ *No credit cards.*

WHERE TO STAY

$$$ **Hotel Bayern.** The elegant, turreted Bayern and its two spacious annexes sit high above the Tegernsee, backed by the wooded slopes of Neureuth Mountain. Rooms overlooking the lake are in demand despite their relatively high cost, so book early. All guests can enjoy panoramic views of the lake and mountains from the extensive terrace fronting the main building. You can dine in the hotel's stylish little restaurant ($$$–$$$$) or the cozy tavern. The extensive Bayern spa includes a heavenly musical tub and a colored-light and aroma solarium. **Pros:** historical elegance, Czar Nicholas I was a frequent guest, great views, hotel beach on the lake. **Cons:** rooms are sterile and cramped, renovations may not be completed by 2009. ✉ *Neureuthstr. 23 Tegernsee* ☎ *08022/1820* 🌐 *www.hotel-bayern.de* *63 rooms, 10 suites* *In-room: no a/c, dial-up. In-hotel: 2 restaurants, bar, pool, spa, no-smoking rooms, some pets allowed* ▭ *AE, MC, V* *BP.*

$ **Seehotel Zur Post.** The lake views from most rooms are somewhat compromised by the main road outside, but a central location, a winter garden, a terrace, and a little beer garden are pluses. The restaurant (¢–$), with a panoramic view of the mountains and the lake, serves fresh fish and seasonal dishes; the "venison weeks" draw diners from far and wide. **Pros:** great views, friendly service, excellent breakfast. **Con:** the property is past its prime and could stand some renovation. ✉*Seestr. 3 Tegernsee* ☎*08022/66550* ⊕*www.seehotel-zur-post.de* ⇋*43 rooms* ♿*In-room: no a/c. In-hotel: restaurant, no-smoking rooms, public Internet, some pets allowed, no elevator* ⊟*DC, MC, V* ⍐*BP.*

NIGHTLIFE & THE ARTS

Every resort has its **spa orchestra**—in summer they play daily in the music-box-style bandstands that dot the lakeside promenades. A strong Tegernsee tradition is the summer-long program of **festivals,** some set deep in the forest. Tegernsee's lake festival in August, when sailing clubs deck their boats with garlands and lanterns, is an unforgettable experience.

Bad Wiessee has a brand-new **casino** near the entrance of town coming from Gmund (☎*08022/98350*). It is open Sunday–Thursday 3 PM–3 AM and Friday and Saturday 3 PM–4 AM, and is the biggest and liveliest venue in town for the after-dark scene.

The **Bischoff am See** (✉*Schweighoferstr. 53* ☎*08022/3966*), on the lake shore in Tegernsee, has a sensational terrace bar with prices to match one of Bavaria's finest views.

SPORTS & THE OUTDOORS

For the best vista in the area, climb the **Wallberg,** the 5,700-foot mountain at the south end of the Tegernsee. It's a hard four-hour hike or a short 15-minute cable-car ride up (€8 one-way, €13 round-trip). At the summit are a restaurant and sun terrace and several trailheads; in winter the skiing is excellent.

Contact the **tourist office** (☎*08022/180–140* ⊕*www.tegernsee.de*) in the town of Tegernsee for hiking maps.

GOLF Besides swimming, hiking, and skiing, the Tegernsee area has become a fine place for golfing. The **Tegernseer GOLFCLUB e. V** (✉*Bad Wiessee D-83707* ☎*08022/8769*) has an 18-hole course overlooking the lake with a clubhouse and excellent restaurant. It also has fine apartments for rent.

SCHLIERSEE

20 km (12 mi) east of Tegernsee, 55 km (34 mi) southeast of Munich.

Schliersee is smaller, quieter, and less fashionable than Tegernsee but hardly less beautiful. The different histories of the Tegernsee and the Schliersee are made clear in the names local people have long given them: the Tegernsee is *Herrensee* (Masters' Lake), while the Schliersee is *Bauernsee* (Peasants' Lake), although today Schliersee has come up in the world somewhat. There are walking and ski trails on the mountain slopes that ring its placid waters. The lake is shallow and often freezes over in winter, when the tiny island in its center is a favorite hiking destination. The one drawback in town is the heavy and fast traffic; Schliersee is on the road to the skiing areas of Sudelfeld and Spitzingsee.

Schliersee was the site of a monastery built in the 8th century by a group of noblemen. It subsequently became a choral academy, which eventually moved to Munich. Today only the restored 17th-century **Schliersee church,** in the middle of town, recalls this piece of local history. The church has some frescoes and stuccowork by Johann Baptist Zimmermann.

WHERE TO STAY & EAT

¢–$ ✕ **Zum Hofhaus am See.** What better place to enjoy a meal than in a small beer garden on the shore? The Hofhaus radiates friendly intimacy. Down-to-earth food, such as hocks or fresh forest mushrooms in cream with an herbed dumpling, is the order of the day. If the fishburger is on the menu, try it. ■TIP→**Fondue in the winter is a special treat.** ⊠ *Messnerg. 2* ☎ *08026/94499* ▤ *No credit cards.*

$ ⌂ **Gästehaus Franke am See.** Light, clean rooms with simple no-nonsense furniture can be very pleasant as a change from all the heavy dark beams and wood paneling you may have seen on your journey. The house's garden is a few steps from the lake. The Franke is small, giving it a nice family feel. **Pro:** close to the lake. **Con:** spartan rooms. ⊠ *Seestr. 8* ☎ *08026/4097* ⊕ *www.gaestehaus-franke-schliersee.de* ⇔ *7 rooms, 2 suites* ⌂ *In-room: no a/c. In-hotel: some pets allowed, no elevator* ▤ *No credit cards* ⦿*CP.*

SPITZINGSEE

10 km (6 mi) south of Schliersee, 65 km (40 mi) southeast of Munich.

Arguably the most beautiful of this group of Bavarian lakes, the Spitzingsee is cradled 3,500 feet up between the Taubenstein, Rosskopf, and Stumpfling peaks, and the drive here is spectacular. The lake is usually frozen over in winter and almost buried in snow. In summer it's warm enough for a swim. Walking in this area is breathtaking in every season. The skiing is very good, too. The only downside is the town itself; its modern architecture violates almost every rule of aesthetics.

WHERE TO STAY & EAT

¢–$ ✕ **Alte Wurzhütte.** If you can't sit outside on the terrace and enjoy a dreamy view of the lake, then you'll have to make do with the cozy, Bavarian log-cabin atmosphere inside. Dishes here, such as Bavarian duck with red cabbage and a monster potato dumpling, are nice and heavy, and come at excellent prices. Simple and functional rooms are available in the property's two adjacent buildings. ⊠ *Rosskopfweg 1* ☎ *08026/60680* ▤ *No credit cards.*

$$–$$$ ⌂ **Arabella Sheraton Alpenhotel.** For an out-of-the-way break in the mountains, head for this luxurious hotel on the shore of the Spitzingsee—even though its architecture is an eyesore. Rooms meet the high standards of comfort expected from the hotel chain that runs the establishment. If you can't stay overnight, come for a leisurely lunch ($$–$$$) at the **König Ludwig Stuben** or for a fondue night or theme buffet. Try the lake fish or the venison with elderberry sauce and cabbage. For lighter Italian fare, you can enjoy **Osteria L'Oliva,** with a menu of pastas, salads, and dishes from the grill. **Pros:** on the lakeside,

great restaurant and spa. **Cons:** restaurant service a bit spotty, as is the Internet access. ⊠*Seeweg 7* ☎*08026/7980* ⊕*www.arabellasheraton. de* �’*120 rooms, 13 suites* ⌂*In-room: no a/c, dial-up (some). In-hotel: 2 restaurants, bar, tennis courts, pool, gym, public Wi-Fi, some pets allowed, no-smoking rooms* ▤*AE, DC, MC, V* ⦿*BP.*

CHIEMSEE

80 km (50 mi) southeast of Munich, 120 km (75 mi) northeast of Garmisch-Partenkirchen, and 45 km (30 mi) from Spitzingsee.

Chiemsee is north of the Deutsche Alpenstrasse, but it demands a detour, if only to visit King Ludwig's huge palace on one of its idyllic islands. It's the largest Bavarian lake, and although it's surrounded by reedy flatlands, the nearby mountains provide a majestic backdrop. The town of **Prien** is the lake's principal resort. ■ TIP➡ **The tourist offices of Prien and Aschau offer a €19 transportation package covering a boat trip, a round-trip rail ticket between the two resorts, and a round-trip ride by cable car to the top of Kampen Mountain, above Aschau.**

GETTING HERE & AROUND

Prien is the jumping-off point for exploring the Chiemsee. Frequent trains connect Prien with Munich and Salzburg. The Regional trains are met by a narrow-gauge steam train for the short trip to Prien-Stock, the boat dock. The only way to reach the Herreninsel and the Fraueninsel is by boat.

ESSENTIALS

Visitor Information Chiemsee (⊠*Kur- und Tourismusbüro Chiemsee, Alte Rathausstr. 11, Prien* ☎*08051/69050* ⊕*www.chiemsee.de*).

EXPLORING

Fodor'sChoice ★ Despite its distance from Munich, the beautiful Chiemsee drew Bavarian royalty to its shores. Its dreamlike, melancholy air caught the imagination of King Ludwig II, and it was on one of the lake's three islands that he built his third and last castle, sumptuous **Schloss Herrenchiemsee.** The palace was modeled after Louis XIV's Versailles, but this was due to more than simple admiration: Ludwig, whose name was the German equivalent of Louis, was keen to establish that he, too, possessed the absolute authority of his namesake, the Sun King. As with most of Ludwig's projects, the building was never completed, and Ludwig spent only nine days in the castle. Moreover, Herrenchiemsee broke the state coffers and Ludwig's private ones as well. The gold leaf that seems to cover more than half of the rooms is especially thin. Nonetheless, what remains is impressive—and ostentatious. Regular ferries out to the island depart from Stock, Prien's harbor. If you want to make the journey in style, board the original 1887 steam train from Prien to Stock to pick up the ferry. A horse-drawn carriage (€3) takes you to the palace itself.

Most spectacular is the Hall of Mirrors, a dazzling gallery where candlelighted concerts are held in summer. Also of interest are the ornate bedrooms Ludwig planned, the "self-rising" table that ascended from the kitchen quarters, the elaborately painted bathroom with a small pool for a tub, and the formal gardens. The south wing houses a **museum** containing Ludwig's christening robe and death mask, as well as other artifacts of his life. While the palace was being built, Ludwig stayed in a royal suite of apartments in a former monastery building on the island, the Altes Schloss. Germany's postwar constitution was drawn up here in 1948, and this episode of the country's history is the centerpiece of the museum housed in the ancient building, the **Museum im Alten Schloss**. ☎08051/68870 palace ⊕*www.herren-chiemsee.de* ✉*Palace, including Museum im Alten Schloss €7* ⊘*Mid-Mar.–late Oct., daily 9–6; late Oct.–mid-Mar., daily 10–4:15; English-language palace tours daily; once per hr.*

Boats going between Stock and Herrenchiemsee Island also call at the small retreat of **Fraueninsel** *(Ladies' Island)*. The **Benedictine convent** there, founded 1,200 years ago, now serves as a school. One of its earliest abbesses, Irmengard, daughter of King Ludwig der Deutsche, died here in the 9th century. Her grave in the convent chapel was discovered in 1961, the same year that early frescoes there were brought to light. The chapel is open daily from dawn to dusk. Otherwise, the island has just a few private houses, a couple of shops, and a hotel. ■TIP➔**The Benedictine Sisters make delicious fruit liqueurs and marzipan.**

OFF THE BEATEN PATH

Amerang. There are two interesting museums in this town northwest of Chiemsee. In the **Museum für Deutsche Automobilgeschichte** *(Museum of German Automobile History)* the display of 220 automobiles begins with an 1886 Benz and culminates in contemporary models; items on display range from the BMW 250 Isetta—the "rolling egg"—to a 600-hp 935 Porsche. The world's largest small-gauge model-railway panorama is also spread out here over nearly 6,000 square feet. ✉*Wasserburger Str. 38* ☎08075/8141 ⊕*www.efa-automuseum.de* ✉*€8* ⊘*Late Mar.–Oct., Tues.–Sun. 10–6; last entry at 5.* The **Bauernhausmuseum** *(Farmhouse Museum)* consists of four beautiful farmhouses with a bakery, beehives, sawmill, and blacksmith's workshop. It's worth seeing to find out more about everyday life in the Chiemgau over the last several hundred years. The oldest building in the cluster is from 1525. Every Sunday afternoon an 85-year-old roper shows off his craft, as does a lace maker. On alternate Sundays, spinning, felt making, and blacksmithing are demonstrated. You can take in the idyllic surroundings from the beer garden. ✉*Im Hopfgarten* ☎08075/915–090 ⊕*www.bauernhausmuseum-amerang.de* ✉*€3* ⊘*Mid-Mar.–Nov. 5, Tues.–Sun. 9–6; last entry at 5.*

WHERE TO EAT

$$
★
✕Wirth von Amerang. Theme restaurants are an up-and-coming business in Bavaria, and the Wirth is the spearhead. The interior design comes very close to medieval, with brick stoves of handmade bricks, dripping candles, and a floor resembling packed clay. The food is definitely Bavarian, with *Knödel* (dumplings) and pork roast, hocks, and a top-notch potato soup. Reservations are recommended. You may want to purchase the pumpkinseed oil or a homemade schnapps. ✉*Postweg 4, Amerang* ☎08075/185–918 ⊕*www.wirth-von-amerang.de* ⊟*No credit cards* ⊘*No lunch Nov.–Mar.*

WHERE TO STAY

$$ **Inselhotel zur Linde.** Catch a boat to this enchanting inn on the car-free Fraueninsel: but remember, if you miss the last connection to the mainland (at 9 PM), you'll have to stay the night. The island is by and large a credit-card-free zone, so be sure to bring cash. Rooms are simply furnished and decorated with brightly colored fabrics. The Linde is one of Bavaria's oldest hotels, founded in 1396 as a refuge for pilgrims. Artists have favored the inn for years, and one of the tables in the small Fischerstüberl dining room ($–$$) is reserved for them. This is the best place to try fish from the lake. **Pros:** set in lush gardens, nice beer garden. **Con:** the Fraueninsel isn't exactly famous for its nightlife. ⊠*Fraueninsel im Chiemsee 1* ☎*08054/90366* ⊕*www.inselhotel-zurlinde.de* ⟿*14 rooms* ⚲*In-room: no a/c. In-hotel: restaurant, bar, public Internet, no elevator* ▤*MC, V* ⊘*Closed mid-Jan.–mid-Mar.* ⫴◯⫴*BP.*

$–$$ **Hotel Luitpold am See.** Boats to the Chiemsee islands tie up right outside your window at this handsome old Prien hotel, which organizes shipboard disco evenings as part of its entertainment program. Rooms have either traditional pinewood furniture, including carved cupboards and bedsteads, or are modern and sleek (in the new annex). Fish from the lake is served at the pleasant restaurant ($–$$). **Pro:** directly on the lake. **Con:** near a busy boat dock. ⊠*Seestr. 110, Prien am Chiemsee* ☎*08051/609–100* ⊕*www.luitpold-am-see.de* ⟿*79 rooms* ⚲*In-room: no a/c. In-hotel: 2 restaurants, public Internet, some pets allowed, no elevator, no-smoking rooms* ▤*AE, DC, MC, V* ⫴◯⫴*BP.*

$–$$ **Schlosshotel Herrenchiemsee.** This handsome mansion on the island of Herrenchiemsee predates King Ludwig's palace, which is a 15-minute walk through the woods. The rooms aren't palatial but are comfortable. A big plus is the pavilionlike restaurant ($–$$), which serves fresh fish. If you're here just to eat, make sure to catch the last boat to the mainland (9 PM)—otherwise you'll be sleeping on this traffic-free island. **Pros:** quiet and withdrawn, the only hotel on the Herreninsel. **Con:** not all rooms have attached bathrooms. ⊠*Herrenchiemsee* ☎*08051/1509* ⟿*8 rooms, 6 with bath or shower, 1 suite* ⚲*In-room: no a/c, no phone. In-hotel: restaurant, some pets allowed, no elevator* ▤*AE, DC, MC, V* ⊘*Hotel closed Oct.–Easter* ⫴◯⫴*CP.*

SPORTS & THE OUTDOORS

There are boatyards all around the lake and several windsurfing schools. The **Mistral-Windsurfing-Center** (⊠*Waldstr. 20* ☎*08054/909–906*), at Gstadt am Chiemsee, has been in operation for decades. From its boatyard the average windsurfer can make it with ease to the next island. The gentle hills of the region are ideal for golf. **Chiemsee Golf-Club Prien e.V** (☎*08051/62215*), in Prien, has a year-round 9-hole course. **SportLukas** (⊠*Hauptstr. 3 Schlech-*

BOATING & SAILING

All the Bavarian Alpine lakes have sailing schools that rent sailboards as well as various other types of boats. At Tegernsee you can hire motorboats at the pier in front of the Schloss Cafe, in the Tegernsee town center. Chiemsee, with its wide stretch of water whipped by Alpine winds, is a favorite for both sailing enthusiasts and windsurfers. There are boatyards all around the lake and the very good windsurfing school, Surfschule Chiemsee, at Bernau.

ing ☎*08649/243*) provides equipment for any kind of sport imaginable, from skiing to kayaking, climbing to curling, and it organizes tours. For those wanting to learn windsurfing or to extend their skills, the **Surfschule Chiemsee** (✉*Ludwig-Thoma-Str. 15a* ☎*08051/8877*) provides lessons and offers a package deal including board and bike rentals.

ASCHAU

10 km (6 mi) south of Chiemsee, 75 km (46 mi) east of Munich.

Aschau is an enchanting red-roof village nestled in a wide valley of the Chiemgauer Alps.

ESSENTIALS

Visitor Information Aschau (✉*Verkehrsamt, Kampenwandstr. 38* ☎*08052/904–937* ⊕*www.aschau.de*).

Aschau's **Schloss Hohenaschau** is one of the few medieval castles in southern Germany to have been restored in the 17th century in baroque style. After many years of renovation, several rooms were opened to the public for the first time in 2008. These rooms include the spectacular Laubensaal, which was lavishly painted by 17th-century Italian artists. Chamber-music concerts are presented regularly in the Rittersaal (Knights' Hall) during the summer. The **Prientalmuseum** (Museum of the Prien Valley), with historical documents on the region, is in the former deacon's house. Exhibitions by contemporary international artists are also on display. ☎*08052/904–937* ▫*Castle €3* ⊗*May–Sept., Tues.–Fri. tours at 9:30, 10:30, and 11:30; Apr. and Oct., Thurs. at 9:30, 10:30, and 11:30; museum during tour times and Sun. 1:30–5.*

WHERE TO STAY & EAT

$$$–$$$$
Fodor's Choice
★

Residenz Heinz Winkler. Star chef Heinz Winkler has turned a sturdy village inn into one of Germany's most extraordinary hotel-restaurant complexes. Rooms in the main house are noble in proportions and furnishings, and the maisonette-style suites in the annexes are cozy and romantic. All have views of the mountains. The restaurant ($$$$) has kept with ease the awards that Winkler won when in charge of Munich's Tantris. A grand piano and a harp add harmony to this deliciously sophisticated scene. **Pro:** exquisite elite hotel with one of the continent's best restaurants. **Cons:** some staff have a bad attitude, no free Wi-Fi, no air-conditioning. ✉*Kirchpl. 1* ☎*08052/17990* ⊕*www. residenz-heinz-winkler.de* ⬳*32 rooms, 13 suites* ⌂*In-room: no a/c, dial-up. In-hotel: restaurant, bar, pool, spa, some pets allowed* ▭*AE, DC, MC, V* ⊙*BP.*

$ **Hotel Bonnschlössl.** This turreted country palace is set in its own park studded with centuries-old trees. In good weather breakfast is served on the balustraded terrace. The hotel is 6 km (4 mi) north of Aschau and has a similarly enchanting sister property in the nearby village of Bernau, the Gasthof Alter Wirt. Both the Schloss and the Gasthof are protected by preservation orders. Emperor Maximilian I stayed overnight at the Gasthof in 1503 on his way to besiege the castle of Marquartstein. **Pro:** beautifully preserved mansion with reasonable prices. **Cons:**

not directly on the lake, no elevator. ⊠*Kirchpl. 9* ☎*08051/89011* ⊕*www.bonnschloessl.de* ⊶*22 rooms* ⅋*In-room: no a/c. In-hotel: restaurant, bar, spa, some pets allowed, no-smoking rooms* ☰*MC, V* ☽*Closed Mon.* ⑩*BP.*

BERCHTESGADENER LAND

Berchtesgadener Land is the Alps at their most dramatic and most notorious. Although some points are higher, the steep cliffs, hidden mountain lakes, and protected biospheres make the area uniquely beautiful. The salt trade brought medieval Berchtesgaden and Bad Reichenhall incredible wealth, which is still apparent in the large collection of antique houses and quaint streets. Bad Reichenhall is an impressive center of German spa culture. Berchtesgaden's image is a bit tarnished, somewhat unfairly, by its most infamous historical resident, Adolf Hitler. Berchtesgaden National Park is a hiker's dream, and the resounding echo of the trumpet on the Königssee shouldn't be missed.

BAD REICHENHALL

50 km (30 mi) east of Aschau, 20 km (12 mi) west of Salzburg.

Bad Reichenhall is remarkably well located, near the mountains for hiking and skiing, and near Salzburg in Austria for a lively cultural scene. The town shares a remote corner of Bavaria with another prominent resort, Berchtesgaden. Although the latter is more famous, Bad Reichenhall is older, with saline springs that made the town rich. Salt is so much a part of the town that you can practically taste it in the air. Europe's largest source of brine was first tapped here in pre-Christian times; salt mining during the Middle Ages supported the economies of cities as far away as Munich and Passau. The town prospered from a spa in the early 20th century. Lately, it has successfully recycled itself from a somewhat sleepy and stodgy "cure town" to a modern, attractive center of wellness.

GETTING HERE & AROUND

Bad Reichenhall is well connected to Berchtesgaden and Salzburg Hauptbahnhof once every hour. The hourly trains to Munich require a change in Freilassing. To reach the Bürgerbräu and the Predigtstuhl cable car, take Bus 180 and Bus 841 to Königssee.

ESSENTIALS

Visitor Information Bad Reichenhall (⊠ *Kur-und-Verkehrsverein, im Kurgastzentrum, Wittelsbacherstr. 15* ☎ *08651/606–303* ⊕ *www.bad-reichenhall.de*).

EXPLORING

The pride and joy of the Reichenhallers is the steep, craggy mountain appropriately named the **Predigtstuhl** *(Preaching Pulpit)*, which stands at 5,164 feet, southeast of town. A ride to the top offers a splendid view of the area. You can hike, ski in winter, or just enjoy a meal at the **Berghotel Predigtdstuhl** (\$–\$\$). The cable-car ride costs €10 one-way, €17

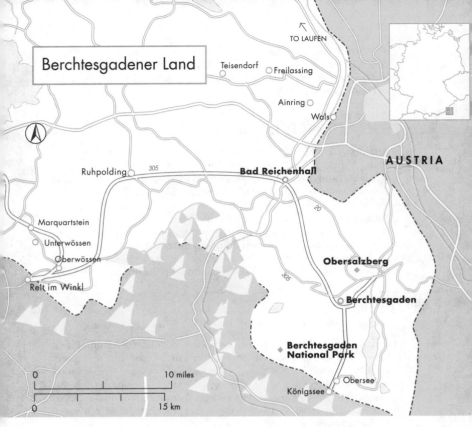

round-trip. Departures begin at 9:30 AM and continue (as needed) until the last person is off the mountain. ⊠*Südtiroler Pl. 1* ☎*08651/2127* ⊕*www.predigtstuhl-bahn.de.*

Hotels here base spa treatments on the health-giving properties of the saline springs and the black mud from the area's waterlogged moors. The waters can also be taken in the elegant, pillared **Wandelhalle** pavilion of the attractive spa gardens throughout the year. Breathing salt-laden air is a remedy for various lung conditions. All you need to do is walk along the 540-foot Gradierwerk, a massive wood-and-concrete construction that produces a fine salty mist by trickling brine down a 40-foot wall of dense blackthorn bundles. ⊠*Salzburgerstr.* ⊘*Mon.– Sat. 8–12:30 and 3–5, Sun. 10–12:30.*

★ Part of Bad Reichenhall's revival included building a new spa facility, the brand new "spa and fitness resort" **Rupertus Therme.** Pools, saunas, and steam rooms are rounded off with a host of special applications using salt, essential oils, mud packs, and massages. ⊠*Friedrich-Ebert-Allee 21* ☎*01805/606–706* ⊕*www.rupertustherme.de* ⊑€ *22, includes sauna area for the day;* €*17 without the sauna* ⊘*Daily 9–10.*

The ancient church **St. Zeno** is dedicated to the patron saint of those imperiled by floods and the dangers of the deep, an ironic note in a town that flourishes on the riches of its underground springs. This 12th-century basilica, the largest in Bavaria, was remodeled in the 16th and 17th centuries, but some of the original Romanesque cloisters remain, although these can be seen only during services and from 11 to noon on Sunday and holidays. ⊠*Kirchpl. 1.*

In the early 19th century King Ludwig I built an elaborate saltworks and spa house—the **Alte Saline und Quellenhaus**—in vaulted, pseudomedieval style. Their pump installations, which still run, are astonishing examples of 19th-century engineering. A "saline" **chapel** is part of the spa's facilities, and was built in exotic Byzantine style. An interesting museum in the same complex looks at the history of the salt trade. ⊠*Salinen Str.* 🕾*08651/7002–146* ⊕*www.alte-saline-bad-reichenhall.de* 🎫*€5.90, combined ticket with Berchtesgaden salt mine €17.50* ⊙*May–Oct., daily 10–11:30 and 2–4; Nov.–Apr., Tues., Fri., and 1st Sat. in the month 2–4.*

> **WHITE GOLD**
>
> Salt, or white gold as it was known in medieval times, has played a key role in the history of both Bad Reichenhall and Berchtesgaden. Organized salt production in the region began around 450 BC, and even included a 30-km (20-mi) wooden pipeline for salt built in the early 1600s. It wasn't until the early 19th century, however, that the town began utilizing its position and geological advantages to attract tourists. The production of salt continues to this day, as does the flow of travelers on the search for the healing saline pools.

WHERE TO STAY & EAT

$ ★ ✕**Bürgerbräu.** Each dining area in this old brewery inn reflects the social class that once met here: politicos, peasants, burghers, and salt miners. Reichenhallers from all walks of life still meet here to enjoy good conversation, hearty local beer, and excellent food. Rooms at the inn are simple, but airy and modern, and centrally located. ⊠*Am Rathauspl.* 🕾*08651/6089* ☐*AE, DC, MC, V* ⦿❘*BP.*

¢–$ ✕**Obermühle.** Tucked away off the main road leading from Bad Reichenhall to the autobahn, this 16th-century mill is a well-kept secret. Fish is the specialty here, though meats (the game in season is noteworthy) are also on the menu. The terrace is an inviting place for a few helpings of excellent homemade cakes. ⊠*Tumpenstr. 11* 🕾*08651/2193* ☐*No credit cards* ⊙*Closed Mon. and Tues.*

$$ 🏨**Parkhotel Luisenbad.** If you fancy spoiling yourself in a typical German fin-de-siècle spa hotel, consider staying here. Although in need of renovation, this fine porticoed and pillared building with an imposing pastel-pink facade promises luxury within. Rooms are large, furnished in deep-cushioned, dark-wood comfort, most with flower-filled balconies or loggias. The elegant restaurant ($–$$) serves international and traditional Bavarian cuisine with an emphasis on seafood (scallops or tuna steak, for example), and a pine-panel tavern, Die Holzstubn'n, pours excellent local brew. **Pros:** quiet, centrally located. **Cons:** in dire need of renovation and staff attitude adjustment. ⊠*Ludwigstr. 33* 🕾*08651/6040* ⊕*www.parkhotel.de* ➥*70 rooms, 8 suites* ⑄*In-*

room: no a/c, Wi-Fi. In-hotel: restaurant, bar, pool, gym, bicycles, public Internet, some pets allowed ☐DC, MC, V ⦶BP.

$-$$ ⊡**Hotel-Pension Erika.** This four-story villa, painted a staid red, has been family-run since 1898, and it shows in the best sense. Everything radiates comfort, from the light-filled dining room to the generous garden. Owner Anton Oberarzbacher occasionally cooks dinner, using herbs from his own garden. The pedestrian zone in town is a minute away. **Pros:** large, spacious rooms, near the pedestrian zone. **Cons:** no elevator or air-conditioning, upper rooms warm in summer. *⊠Adolf-Schmid-Str. 3 ☎08651/95360 ⊕www.hotel-pension-erika.de ⤸32 rooms, 1 suite ⚭In-room: no a/c, dial-up. In-hotel: restaurant, no elevator, some pets allowed ☐AE, MC, V ⊗Closed Nov.–Feb. Restaurant closed Sun.*

$ ⊡**Pension Hubertus.** This delightfully traditional family-run lodging
★   stands on the shore of the tiny Thumsee, 5 km (3 mi) from the town center. The Hubertus's private grounds lead down to the lake, where guests can swim or boat (the water is bracingly cool). Rooms, some with balconies overlooking the lake, are furnished with hand-carved beds and cupboards. Excellent meals or coffee can be taken at the neighboring rustic Madlbauer ($-$$). There are special rates in the off-season (October–April). **Pros:** incredible views, private guests-only sunbathing area. **Cons:** far from city center, no elevator. *⊠Am Thumsee 5 ☎08651/2252 ⊕www.hubertus-thumsee.de ⤸18 rooms ⚭In-room: no a/c, no phone (some). In-hotel: gym, no elevator, some pets allowed, no-smoking rooms ☐AE, DC, MC, V ⦶CP.*

NIGHTLIFE & THE ARTS

Bad Reichenhall is proud of its long musical tradition and of its orchestra, founded more than a century ago. It performs six days a week throughout the year in the chandelier-hung Kurgastzentrum Theater or, when weather permits, in the open-air pavilion, and at a special Mozart Week in March. Call the **Orchesterbüro** (☎08651/8661 🖷08651/710–551) for program details.

As a spa town and winter resort, Bad Reichenhall is a natural for night haunts. The big draw is the elegant **casino** (⊠ *Wittelsbacherstr. 17* ☎08651/95800 ⊠€2.50, free with a Kurkarte; ask for one at your hotel. Jacket and tie), open daily 3 PM–1 or 2 AM depending on business. For some traditional ballroom dancing to live music in the evenings, head for the **Tanzcafe am Kurgarten.** Occasionally they also show soccer games. (⊠*Salzburger Str. 7* ☎08651/1691).

SPORTS & THE OUTDOORS

Though Berchtesgaden definitely has the pull for skiers, Bad Reichenhall is proud of its Predigtstuhl, which towers over the town to the south. Besides fresh air and great views, it offers some skiing, lots of hiking, biking, and even rock climbing. The tourist-information office on Wittelsbacherstrasse, just a couple of hundred yards from the train station, has all the necessary information regarding the numerous sporting activities possible in Bad Reichenhall and its surrounding area.

SHOPPING

Using flowers and herbs grown in the Bavarian Alps, the **Josef Mack Company** (✉ *Ludwigstr. 36* ☎08651/78280) has made medicinal herbal preparations since 1856. **Leuthenmayr** (✉ *Ludwigstr. 27* ☎08651/2869) is a youngster in the business, selling its "cure-all" dwarf-pine oil since 1908. Your sweet tooth will be fully satisfied at the confection emporium of **Paul Reber** (✉ *Ludwigstr. 10–12* ☎08651/60030), makers of the famous chocolate and marzipan *Mozartkugel* and many other dietary bombs. Candle making is a local specialty, and **Kerzenwelt Donabauer** (✉ *Reichenhaller Str. 15, Piding* ☎08651/8143), just outside Bad Reichenhall, has a selection of more than 1,000 decorative items in wax. It also has a free wax museum depicting fairy-tale characters.

BERCHTESGADEN

18 km (11 mi) south of Bad Reichenhall, 20 km (12 mi) south of Salzburg.

Berchtesgaden's reputation is unjustly rooted in its brief association with Adolf Hitler, who dreamed of his "1,000-year Reich" from the mountaintop where millions of tourists before and after him drank in only the superb beauty of the Alpine panorama. The historic old market town and mountain resort has great charm. In winter it's a fine place for skiing and snowboarding; in summer it becomes one of the region's most popular (and crowded) resorts. An ornate palace and working salt mine make up some of the diversions in this heavenly setting.

Salt was once the basis of Berchtesgaden's wealth. In the 12th century Emperor Barbarossa gave mining rights to a Benedictine abbey that had been founded here a century earlier. The abbey was secularized early in the 19th century, when it was taken over by the Wittelsbach rulers. Salt is still important today because of all the local wellness centers. The entire area has been declared a "health resort region" (*Kurgebiet*) and was put on the UNESCO biosphere list.

GETTING HERE & AROUND

The easiest way to reach Berchtesgaden is with the hourly train connection via Bad Reichenhall to Salzburg Hbf. Trains to Munich require a change in Freilassing. Hamburg and Dortmund are both served with one direct train per day. Frequent local bus service makes it easy to explore the town and to reach Berchtesgaden National Park and the Königssee. The Schwaiger bus company runs tours of the area and across the Austrian border as far as Salzburg. An American couple runs Berchtesgaden Mini-bus Tours out of the local tourist office, opposite the railroad station.

ESSENTIALS

Visitor & Tour Information Berchtesgaden (✉ *Kurdirektion* ☎08652/9670 ⊕ *www.berchtesgadener-land.com*). **Berchtesgaden Mini-bus Tours** (☎*08652/64971*). **Schwaiger** (☎*08652/2525*).

The Legend of Edelweiss

Edelweiss (*Leontopodium alpinum*) is the flower most commonly associated with the Alps, thanks to that memorable song from *The Sound of Music*. It usually grows in the inaccessible regions of the Alps and is a protected species (don't pick it). The unique beauty of the white flower is a symbol of purity in Bavaria and a plant shrouded in myth.

As the story goes, high in the Alps lived a hauntingly beautiful queen with a heart of pure ice. The queen's melodious singing lured many forlorn shepherds to her cave. Since her frozen heart was unable to love, she soon tired of them and ordered her loyal gnome slaves to throw the hapless men to their deaths. One day an ordinary shepherd found his way to her cave and the queen fell in love with him. The jealous gnomes, fearing their mistress would marry this mortal and abandon them, threw him into a valley where his heart was crushed. When she learned of the tragedy, her heart melted enough for her to shed one tear. That tear became an Edelweiss.

EXPLORING

At the sleek and classy **Watzmann Therme** you'll find fragrant steam rooms, saunas with infrared cabins for sore muscles, an elegant pool, whirlpools, and more. If you happen to be staying a few days, you might catch a tai chi course, enjoy a bio-release facial massage, or partake in an evening of relaxing underwater exercises. ⊠*Bergwerkstr. 54* ☎*08652/94640* ⊕*www.watzmann-therme.de* ⌨*2 hrs €8.30, 4 hrs €10.80, day pass including sauna €15.30* ☉*Daily 10–10.*

The last royal resident of the Berchtesgaden abbey, Crown Prince Rupprecht (who died here in 1955), furnished it with rare family treasures that now form the basis of a permanent collection—the **Königliches Schloss Berchtesgaden Museum.** Fine Renaissance rooms exhibit the prince's sacred art, which is particularly rich in wood sculptures by such great late-Gothic artists as Tilman Riemenschneider and Veit Stoss. You can also visit the abbey's original, cavernous 13th-century dormitory and cool cloisters. ⊠*Schlosspl. 2* ☎*08652/947–980* ⊕*www.haus-bayern.com* ⌨*€7 with tour* ☉*Mid-May–mid-Oct., Sun.–Fri. 10–noon and 2–4; mid-Oct.–mid-May, weekdays 11–2.*

The **Heimatmuseum,** in the Schloss Adelsheim, displays examples of wood carving and other local crafts. Wood carving in Berchtesgaden dates to long before Oberammergau established itself as the premier wood-carving center of the Alps. ⊠*Schroffenbergallee 6* ☎*08652/4410* ⊕*www.heimatmuseum-berchtesgaden.de* ⌨*€2.50* ☉*Dec.–Oct., Tues.–Sun. 10–4.*

★ The **Salzbergwerk** (*salt mine*) is one of the chief attractions of the region. In the days when the mine was owned by Berchtesgaden's princely rulers, only select guests were allowed to see how the source of the city's wealth was extracted from the earth. Today, during a 90-minute tour, you can sit astride a miniature train that transports you nearly 1 km (½ mi) into the mountain to an enormous chamber where the salt is mined. Included in the tour are rides down the wooden chutes used by miners to get from one level to another and a boat ride on an underground saline lake the size of a football field. Although the tours take about an hour, plan an extra 45–60 minutes for purchasing the tickets and changing into and out of miners clothing. You may wish to partake in the special four-hour **brine dinners** down in the mines (€75). These are very popular, so be sure to book early ⌂ *2 km (1 mi) from center of Berchtesgaden on B–305 Salzburg Rd.* ☏*08652/600–220* ⊕*www. salzzeitreise.de.de* ⌂*€14, combined ticket with Bad Reichenhall's saline museum €17.50* ⊙*May–mid-Oct., daily 9–5; mid-Oct.–Apr., Mon.–Sat. 11:30–3.*

The **Obersalzberg,** site of Hitler's luxurious mountain retreat, is part of the north slope of the Hoher Goll, high above Berchtesgaden. It was a remote mountain community of farmers and foresters before Hitler's deputy, Martin Bormann, selected the site for a complex of Alpine homes for top Nazi leaders. Hitler's chalet, the Berghof, and all the others were destroyed in 1945, with the exception of a hotel that had been taken over by the Nazis, the Hotel zum Türken. Beneath the hotel is a section of the labyrinth of tunnels built as a last retreat for Hitler and his cronies; the macabre, murky **bunkers** (⌂*€3* ⊙*May–Oct., Tues.– Sun. 9–5; Nov.–Apr., daily 10–3)* can be visited. Nearby, the **Dokumentation Obersalzberg** (⌂*Salzbergstr. 41* ☏*08652/947–960* ⊕*www. obersalzberg.de* ⌂*€3* ⊙*Apr.–Oct., Tues.–Sun. 9–5; Nov.–Mar., Tues.– Sun. 10–3)* documents the Third Reich's history by specific themes with rare archival material. Beyond Obersalzberg, the hairpin bends of Germany's highest road come to the base of the 6,000-foot peak on which sits the **Kehlsteinhaus** (☏*08652/2969* ⊕*www.kehlsteinhaus.de*), also known as the Adlerhorst (Eagle's Nest), Hitler's personal retreat and his official guesthouse. It was Martin Bormann's gift to the Führer on Hitler's 50th birthday. The road leading to it, built in 1937–39, climbs more than 2,000 dizzying feet in less than 6 km (4 mi). A tunnel in the mountain will bring you to an elevator that whisks you up to what appears to be the top of the world (you can walk up in about half an hour). There are refreshment rooms and a restaurant. The round-trip from Berchtesgaden's post office by bus and elevator costs €15 per person. The bus runs mid-May through September, daily from 9 to 4:50. By car you can travel only as far as the Obersalzberg bus station. From there the round-trip fare is €14.50. The full round-trip takes one hour. ■ TIP➔**To get the most out of your visit to the Kehlsteinhaus, consider taking one of the informative tours offered by David Harper.** Reserve in advance at ☏*08652/ 64971* or ⊕ *www.eagles-nest-tours.com.* Tours meet across from the train station and cost €45.

WHERE TO STAY

$$ ▦ **Hotel zum Türken.** The view alone is worth the 10-minute journey from Berchtesgaden to this hotel. Confiscated during World War II by the Nazis, the hotel is at the foot of the road to Hitler's mountaintop retreat. Beneath it are remains of Nazi wartime bunkers. The decor, though fittingly rustic, is a bit dated. There's no restaurant, although evening meals can be ordered in advance. **Pros:** location, sense of his-

tory, Frau Schafenberg can cook! **Cons:** not all rooms have attached bathrooms, and some are far away. ✉ *Hintereck 2, Obersalzberg-Berchtesgaden* ☎ *08652/2428* ⊕ *www.hotel-zum-tuerken.de* ⟳ *17 rooms, 12 with bath or shower* ♿ *In-room: no a/c, no phone (some). In-hotel: no elevator, some pets allowed, no-smoking rooms,* 🖃 *AE, DC, MC, V* ⊗ *Closed Nov.–Dec. 20* ❤ *BP.*

$–$$ 🖭 **Stoll's Hotel Alpina.** Set above the Königsee in the delightful little village of Schönau, the Alpina offers rural solitude and easy access to Berchtesgaden. Families are catered to with apartments, a resident doctor, and a playroom. The hotel also has an annex about a half a mile away, the Sporthotel, where rooms are somewhat cheaper. **Pros:** bedrooms are large and comfortable, good for children, great view of the Adlerhorst. **Cons:** service can be brusque. ✉ *Ulmenweg 14, Schönau* ☎ *08652/65090* ⊕ *www.stolls-hotel-alpina.de* ⟳ *52 rooms, 8 apartments* ♿ *In-room: no a/c, dial-up (some). In-hotel: restaurant, pool, no elevator, some pets allowed* 🖃 *AE, DC, MC, V* ⊗ *Closed early Nov.–mid-Dec.* ❤ *BP.*

$ 🖭 **Alpenhotel Denninglehen.** The house was built in 1981 in Alpine style, with lots of wood paneling, heavy beams, and wide balconies with cascades of geraniums in summer. Skiers enjoy the fact that the slopes are about 200 yards away. The restaurant has a large fireplace to warm up winter evenings. The menu ($–$$$) is regional (the usual schnitzels and roasts) with a few items from the French repertoire (a fine steak in pepper sauce, for example). Price includes breakfast buffet and use of the wellness facilities. Nonsmokers appreciate the special dining room set aside just for them in this mountain hotel's restaurant. **Pros:** heated pool with views of the Alps, great hotel for kids. **Con:** narrow and steep access road difficult to find. ✉ *Am Priesterstein 7, Berchtesgaden-Oberau* ☎ *08652/97890* ⊕ *www.denninglehen.de* ♿ *In-room: no a/c. In-hotel: restaurant, pool, some pets allowed, no-smoking rooms* 🖃 *MC* ⊗ *Closed last 2 weeks in Jan.* ❤ *BP.*

$ 🖭 **Hotel Grünberger.** Only a few strides from the train station in the town center, the Grünberger overlooks the River Ache—it even has a private terrace beside the river you can relax on. The cozy rooms have farmhouse-style furnishings and some antiques. The wellness area has in-house acupuncture and traditional Chinese medicine treatments. The hotel restaurant focuses on German fare, with some international dishes to lighten the load. Those who need to check e-mail head to the Internet café nearby. **Pros:** quaintly situated on the river, close to the train station. **Con:** quite far from skiing and outdoor activities. ✉ *Hansererweg 1* ☎ *08652/976–590* ⊕ *www.hotel-gruenberger.de* ⟳ *65 rooms* ♿ *In-room: no a/c, no phone, no TV (some). In-hotel: restaurant, bar, pool, no-smoking rooms* 🖃 *MC, V* ⊗ *Closed Nov.–mid-Dec.* ❤ *BP.*

$ 🖭 **Hotel Wittelsbach.** This is one of the oldest (built in 1892) and most traditional lodgings in the area, so it is wise to reserve well ahead of time. The small rooms have dark pinewood furnishings and deep red and green drapes and carpets. Ask for one with a balcony. The breakfast room has a mountain view. **Pros:** nice, comfortable rooms, with exceptional staff, daily pamphlets show local events and weather.

Cons: horrible parking, slow Internet, street-side rooms can get noisy. ✉*Maximilianstr. 16* ☎*08652/96380* ⊕*www.hotel-wittelsbach.com* ⇌*26 rooms, 3 apartments* ⬧*In-room: no a/c. In-hotel: public Internet, some pets allowed* ⊟*AE, DC, MC, V* ⊙|*BP.*

SPORTS & THE OUTDOORS

Buried as it is in the Alps, Berchtesgaden is a place for the active. The Rossfeld ski area is one of the favorites, thanks to almost guaranteed natural snow. The piste down to Oberau is nearly 6 km (4 mi) long (with bus service at the end to take you back to Berchtesgaden). There is a separate snowboarding piste as well. Berchtesgaden also has many cross-country trails and telemark opportunities. The other popular area is on the slopes of the Götschenkopf, which is used for world cup races. Snow is usually artificial, but the floodlit slopes at night and a lively après-ski scene make up for the lesser quality.

In summer, hikers, power-walkers, and paragliders take over the region. The Obersalzberg even has a summer sledding track. Avid hikers should ask for a map featuring the refuges (Berghütten) in the mountains, where one can spend the night either in a separate room or a bunk. Simple, solid meals are offered. In some of the smaller refuges you will have to bring your own food. For more information, check out ⊕*www.berchtesgaden.de.* And though the Königsee is beautiful to look at, only cold-water swimmers will appreciate its frigid waters.

Germany's highest course, the **Berchtesgaden Golf Club** (✉*Salzbergstr. 33* ☎*08652/2100*), is on a 3,300-foot plateau of the Obersalzberg. Only fit players should attempt the demanding 9-hole course. Seven Berchtesgaden hotels offer their guests a 30% reduction on the €25 greens fee—contact the tourist office or the club for details.

Whatever your mountain-related needs, whether it's climbing and hiking in summer or cross-country tours in winter, you'll find it at the **Erste Bergschule Berchtesgadenerland** (✉*Silbergstr. 25, Strub* ☎*08652/2420 May–Oct., 08652/5371 Nov.–Apr.* 🖶*08652/2420*).

SHOPPING

The **Berchtesgadener Handwerkskunst** (✉*Schlosspl. 1½* ☎*08652/979– 790*) offers handicrafts—such as wooden boxes, woven tablecloths, wood carvings, and Christmas-tree decorations—from Berchtesgaden, the surrounding region, and other parts of Bavaria.

BERCHTESGADEN NATIONAL PARK

5 km (3 mi) south of Berchtesgaden.

The deep, mysterious, and fabled Königsee is the most photographed panorama in Germany. Together with its much smaller sister, the Obersee, it's nestled within the Berchtesgaden National Park, 210 square km (82 square mi) of wild mountain country where flora and fauna have been left to develop as nature intended. No roads penetrate the area, and even the mountain paths are difficult to follow. The park administration organizes guided tours of the area from June through September. *Nationalparkhaus* ✉*Franziskanerpl. 7D–83471 Berchtesgaden* ☎*08652/64343* ⊕*www.nationalpark-berchtesgaden.de.*

One less strenuous way into the Berchtesgaden National Park is by boat. A fleet of 21 excursion boats, electrically driven so that no noise
★ disturbs the peace, operates on the **Königsee** *(King Lake).* Only the skipper of the boat is allowed to shatter the silence—his trumpet fanfare demonstrates a remarkable echo as notes reverberate between the almost vertical cliffs that plunge into the dark green water. A cross on a rocky promontory marks the spot where a boatload of pilgrims hit the cliffs and sank more than 100 years ago. The voyagers were on their way to the tiny, twin-tower baroque chapel of St. Bartholomä, built in the 17th century on a peninsula where an early-Gothic church once stood. The princely rulers of Berchtesgaden built a hunting lodge at the side of the chapel; a tavern and restaurant now occupy its rooms.

Smaller than the Königsee but equally beautiful, the **Obersee** can be reached by a 15-minute walk from the second stop (Salet) on the boat tour. The lake's backdrop of jagged mountains and precipitous cliffs is broken by a waterfall, the Rothbachfall, which plunges more than 1,000 feet to the valley floor.

Boat service (☎*08652/96360* ⊕*www.bayerische-seenschifffahrt.de*) on the Königsee runs year-round, except when the lake freezes. A round-trip to St. Bartholomä and Salet, the landing stage for the Obersee, lasts almost two hours, without stops, and costs €14.80. A round-trip to St. Bartholomä lasts a little over an hour and costs €11.80. In summer the Berchtesgaden tourist office organizes evening cruises on the Königsee, which include a concert in St. Bartholomä Church and a four-course dinner in the neighboring hunting lodge.

The Romantic Road

WORD OF MOUTH

"We stayed two nights in Rothenburg. We enjoyed the town thoroughly. It is crowded during the day but we hiked along the wall and outside the wall to a small town nearby and missed the crowds. We listened to an organ concert in a church there, ate with the English Club, took the Night Watchman's Tour, saw the Crime Museum, shopped, etc."

—kkukura

"After wanting to see for ourselves what all the hype was about, we weren't disappointed [with Rothenburg]. At least not by the cobblestone streets, old half timbered buildings, the walls, towers, etc. What was a disappointment was the scale of commercialism that is Rothenburg."

—pja1

Updated by
Uli Ehrhardt

OF ALL THE TOURIST ROUTES that crisscross Germany, none rivals the aptly named Romantische Strasse, or Romantic Road. The scenery is more pastoral than spectacular, but the route is memorable for the medieval towns, villages, castles, and churches that anchor its 355-km (220-mi) length. Many of these are tucked away beyond low hills, their spires and towers just visible through the greenery.

The Romantic Road concept developed as West Germany rebuilt its tourist industry after World War II. A public-relations wizard coined the catchy title for a historic passage through Bavaria and Baden-Württemberg that could be advertised as a unit. In 1950 the Romantic Road was born. The name itself isn't meant to attract lovebirds, but rather uses the word "romantic" as meaning wonderful, fabulous, and imaginative. And, of course, the Romantic Road started as a road on which the Romans traveled.

Along the way, the road crosses centuries-old battlefields. The most cataclysmic conflict, the Thirty Years' War, destroyed the region's economic base in the 17th century. The depletion of resources prevented improvements that would have modernized the area—thereby assuring the survival of the historic towns' now charmingly quaint infrastructures.

ORIENTATION & PLANNING

GETTING ORIENTED

The Romantic Road is not limited to one area of Germany—it is Germany in a nutshell. From Würzburg, in central Germany, an hour from Frankfurt, it runs right down to Füssen on the Austrian border, crisscrossing between the states of Bavaria and Baden-Württemberg. Along the way, the road passes through the best-preserved medieval town on the continent, Rothenburg-ob-der-Tauber. Farther south it goes through the handsome Renaissance city of Augsburg. The final stop and highlight of the route is King Ludwig II's fantastical castle, Neuschwanstein.

Northern Romantic Road. Wine lovers should plan an extra day for Würzburg, where they can sample very good local wines at reasonable prices. Bad Mergentheim and Creglingen are also worth a look for the home of the Teutonic Knights and the Tilman Riemenschneider altar in the Herrgottskirche.

Central Romantic Road. From the north, the route crosses the rather barren Spessart uplands, before dropping into the lovely Tauber valley. It passes through charming old towns like well-known Rothenburg-ob-der-Tauber, with vineyards visible on the northern slopes of the small valley. After crossing the Danube, the route continues to the affluent city of Augsburg, where the countryside changes again.

Toward the Alps. In this region, vineyards are replaced by alpine meadows and beer beats out wine in the small inns of towns like Landsberg

TOP REASONS TO GO

Würzburg's Baroque Masterpiece: When the prince-bishops decided after 450 years to descend from their lofty hilltop fortress into the city proper, they employed the best artists of their time, including Neumann and Tiepolo, to create the lavishly ostentatious Residenz palace.

An Overnight in a Medieval Town: Dodge the daytrippers by spending the night in Rothenburg-ob-der-Tauber. Patrol the city walls with the night watchman, explore the streets in the morning light (perfect for photos), then get out of town before the tour buses begin to arrive.

768 Steps: That's what it takes to reach the top platform of the highest church steeple in the world, but the incredible view from Ulm's Münster is worth the effort. On a clear day you can see the Austrian, German, and Swiss Alps in the distance, seventy miles away.

A Rococo Jewel: The opposite of Ulm's soaring Gothic cathedral is the Wieskirche, its name meaning "church in the meadow." You get the most stunning views in the late afternoon, when the western sun shines through the high windows, flooding the church with light and highlighting the details.

Neuschwanstein: Walt Disney may have spread the word about this castle, but the sight of the original, rising up against its theatrical backdrop of green mountainside, speaks for itself.

4

and Schongau. The marvelous Wieskirche (Church of the Meadow) is here, just a bit off the Romantic Road, and finally mountains give way to the plain and the fairy-tale Neuschwanstein and Hohenschwangau castles come into view.

THE ROMANTIC ROAD PLANNER

WHEN TO GO

Late summer and early autumn are the best times to travel the Romantic Road, when the grapes ripen on the vines around Würzburg and the geraniums run riot on the medieval walls of towns such as Rothenburg and Dinkelsbühl. You'll also miss the high-season summer crush of tourists. Otherwise, consider visiting the region in the depths of December, when Christmas markets pack the ancient squares of the Romantic Road towns and snow gives turreted Schloss Neuschwanstein a final magic touch.

GETTING HERE & AROUND

BY AIR   The major international airports serving the Romantic Road are Frankfurt and Munich. Regional airports include Nürnberg and Augsburg.

BY BUS   If you prefer not to rent a car, daily bus service covers the northern stretch of the Romantic Road, between Frankfurt and Munich, from April through October. A second bus covers the section of the route between Dinkelsbühl and Füssen. All buses stop at the major sights along the road. Deutsche Touring also operates six more extensive tours along the Romantic Road for which reservations are essential.

BY CAR   The Romantic Road is most easily traveled by car, starting from Würzburg, the northernmost city, and following country highway B–27 south to meet Roads B–290, B–19, B–292, and B–25 along the Wörnitz River. It's on the Frankfurt–Nürnberg autobahn, A–3, and is 115 km (71 mi) from Frankfurt. If you're coming up from the south and using Munich as a gateway, Augsburg is 60 km (37 mi) from Munich via A–8. The roads are busy and have only two lanes, so figure on covering no more than 70 km (40 mi) each hour, particularly in summer. For route maps, with roads and sights highlighted, contact the Touristik-Arbeitsgemeinschaft Romantische Strasse (Central Tourist Information Romantic Road) based in Dinkelsbühl.

BY TRAIN   Infrequent trains link most major towns of the Romantic Road, but both Würzburg and Augsburg are on the InterCity and high-speed InterCity Express routes, and have fast, frequent service to and from Frankfurt, Stuttgart, and Munich.

BIKE TOURS   From April through September, Velotours offers a five-day bike trip from Würzburg to Rothenburg for €350 per person and a five-day trip from Rothenburg to Donauwörth for €350 per person. These two trips can be combined for an eight-day tour for €600. The tour operator Alpenland-Touristik offers several guided six- to eight-day bike tours starting from Landsberg am Lech into the Alpine foothills.

ESSENTIALS   **Airport Contacts Airport Nürnberg** (✉ *Flughafenstr. 100D–90411* ☎ *0911/93700* ⊕ *www.airport-nuernberg.de*). **Augsburg Airport** (✉ *Flughafenstr. 1D–86169* ☎ *0821/270–8111* ⊕ *www.augsburg-airport.de*).

Bike Tours Alpenland–Touristik (✏ *Box 10-13-13, D–86899 Landsberg* ☎ *08191/308–620* 🖶 *08191/4913* ⊕ *www.alpenlandtouristik.de*). **Velotours** (✉ *Ernst-Sachsstr. 1D–78467Konstanz* ☎ *07531/98280* 🖶 *07531/982–898* ⊕ *www.velotours.de*).

Bus Contacts Deutsche Touring (✉ *Am Römerhof 17D–60486 Frankfurt am Main* ☎ *069/790–3501* ⊕ *www.touring-germany.com*).

Visitor Information Touristik-Arbeitsgemeinschaft Romantische Strasse (*Central Tourist Information Romantic Road* ✉ *Segringerstr. 19, Dinkelsbühl* ☎ *09851/551–387* ⊕ *www.romantischestrasse.de*).

ABOUT THE RESTAURANTS

During peak season, restaurants along the Romantic Road tend to be crowded, especially in the larger towns. ■TIP➡ **You may want to plan your mealtimes around visits to smaller villages, where there are fewer people and the restaurants are pleasant.** The food will be more basic Franconian or Swabian, but it will also be generally less expensive than in the well-known towns. You may find that some of the small, family-run restaurants close around 2 PM, or whenever the last lunch guests have left, and open again at 5 or 5:30 PM. Some serve cold cuts or coffee and cake during that time, but no hot food.

ABOUT THE HOTELS

With a few exceptions, the Romantic Road hotels are quiet and rustic, and you'll find high standards of comfort and cleanliness. If you plan to stay in one of the bigger hotels in the off-season, do ask for weekend rates. Make reservations as far in advance as possible if you plan to visit in summer. Hotels in Würzburg, Rothenburg, and Füssen are often full year-round. Augsburg hotels are in great demand during trade fairs in nearby Munich. Tourist-information offices can usually help with accommodations, especially if you arrive early in the day.

WHAT IT COSTS IN EUROS				
	$	$$	$$$	$$$$
RESTAURANTS	under €9	€9–€15	€16–€20	€21–€25	over €25
HOTELS	under €50	€50–€100	€101–€175	€176–€225	over €225

Restaurant prices are per person for a main course at dinner. Hotel prices are for two people in a standard double room, including tax and service.

PLANNING YOUR TIME

The two bigger cities on the Romantic Road, Würzburg and Augsburg, can handle large influxes of visitors at any time. But at the two best-known and therefore most visited places, Rothenburg-ob-der-Tauber and Neuschwanstein, it pays to arrive by night in order to get up early to tour the next morning. You can follow the night watchman in Rothenburg as he makes his rounds, and then see the town in the early morning. Have a late but leisurely breakfast as you watch the bus-tour groups push through the streets around 11. For Neuschwanstein an early start is even more important to beat the crowds.

NORTHERN ROMANTIC ROAD

The northern section of the Romantic Road skirts the wild, open countryside of the Spessart uplands before heading south through the plains of Swabia. It's worth spending a night in Würzburg, but Bad Mergentheim and Creglingen can be quick stops along the road.

WÜRZBURG

115 km (71 mi) east of Frankfurt.

The baroque city of Würzburg, the pearl of the Romantic Road, is a heady example of what happens when great genius teams up with great wealth. Beginning in the 10th century, Würzburg was ruled by powerful (and rich) prince-bishops, who created the city with all the remarkable attributes you see today.

The city is at the junction of two age-old trade routes, in a calm valley backed by vineyard-covered hills. Festung Marienberg, a fortified castle on the steep hill across the Main River, overlooks the town. Con-

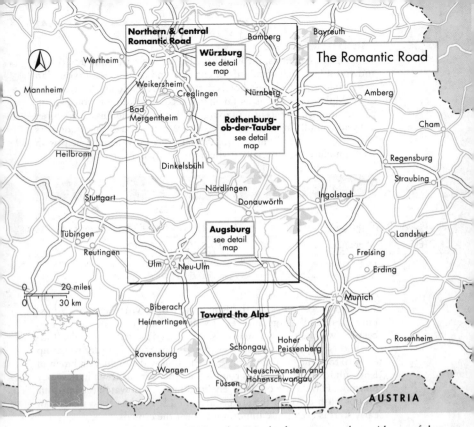

structed between 1200 and 1600, the fortress was the residence of the prince-bishops for 450 years.

Present-day Würzburg is by no means completely original. On March 16, 1945, seven weeks before Germany capitulated, Würzburg was all but obliterated by Allied saturation bombing. The 20-minute raid destroyed 87% of the city and killed at least 4,000 people. Reconstruction has returned most of the city's famous sights to their former splendor. Except for some buildings with modern shops, it remains a largely authentic restoration.

GETTING HERE & AROUND
Würzburg is on a main line of the super-fast ICE Intercity Express trains, a bit more than an hour from Frankfurt and two hours from Munich. Most attractions in the old part of town are easily reached on foot. There is a bus to take you to Marienberg castle up on the hill across the river. A car is the best means of transport if you want to continue your journey past Würzburg, but you can also use regional trains and buses.

One-hour guided strolls (in English) through the old town start at the Haus zum Falken tourist office and take place from mid-June to mid-September, daily at 6:30 PM. Tickets (€5) can be purchased from the guide. If you'd rather guide yourself, pick up a map from the same tourist office and follow the extremely helpful directions marked throughout the city by distinctive signposts.

The Würzburger Personenschiffahrt Kurth & Schiebe operates excursions. A wine tasting (€8) is offered as you glide past the vineyards.

TIMING

You need two days to do full justice to Würzburg. The Residenz alone demands several hours of attention. If time is short, head for the Residenz as the doors open in the morning, before the first crowds assemble, and aim to complete your tour by lunchtime. Then continue to the nearby Juliusspital Weinstuben or one of the many traditional taverns in the area for lunch. In the afternoon, explore central Würzburg. The next morning cross the Main River to visit the Festung Marienberg along with the Mainfränkisches Museum and the Fürstenbaumuseum.

ESSENTIALS

Visitor & Tour Information **Würzburg** (⊠ *Fremdenverkehrsamt, Am Congress-Centrum* ☎ *0931/372–335* ⊕ *www.wuerzburg.de*). **Würzburger Personenschiffahrt Kurth & Schiebe** (⊠ *St.-Norbert-Str. 9 Zell* ☎ *0931/58573*).

EXPLORING

MAIN ATTRACTIONS

⑫ **Alte Mainbrücke** *(Old Main Bridge).* Construction on this ancient structure, which crosses the Main River, began in 1473. Twin rows of infinitely graceful statues of saints line the bridge. They were placed here in 1730, at the height of Würzburg's baroque period. Note the *Patronna Franconiae* (commonly known as the Weeping Madonna). There's a beautiful view of the Marienberg Fortress from the bridge.

⑨ **Dom St. Kilian** *(St. Kilian Basilica).* Würzburg's Romanesque cathedral, the fourth-largest of its kind in Germany, was begun in 1045. Step inside and you'll find yourself in a shimmering rococo treasure house. Prince-Bishop von Schönborn is buried here. His tomb is the work of his architect and builder Balthasar Neumann. Tilman Riemenschneider carved the tombstones of two other bishops buried at the cathedral. ⊠*Paradepl., south end of Schönbornstr.* ☎*0931/321–1830* ☜*Tour €2.50* ☉ *Easter–Oct., daily 8–6; Nov.–Easter, daily 8–noon and 2–6; guided tours May–Oct., daily at 12:20.*

⑭ **Festung Marienberg** *(Marienberg Fortress).* This complex was the original home of the prince-bishops, beginning in the 13th century. The oldest buildings—note especially the **Marienkirche** (Church of the Virgin Mary)—date from around 700, although excavations have disclosed evidence that there was a settlement here in the Iron Age, 3,000 years ago. In addition to the rough-hewn medieval fortifications, there are a number of Renaissance and baroque apartments. ■TIP➔ **To reach the hilltop Marienberg, you can make the fairly stiff climb on foot through vineyards or take bus Number 9, starting at the Residenz, with several stops in the city. It runs about every 40 minutes from April to October.**

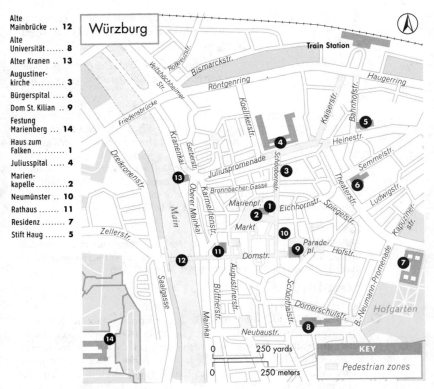

★ The highlight is the remarkable collection of art treasures in the **Main-fränkisches Museum** (*Main-Franconian Museum* ☎*0931/205–940* ⊕*www.mainfraenkisches-museum.de* 🎫*€4* 🕐*Apr.–Oct., Tues.–Sun. 10–5; Nov.–Mar., Tues.–Sun. 10–4*), which traces the city's rich and varied history. Be sure to visit the gallery devoted to Würzburg-born sculptor Tilman Riemenschneider, who lived from the late 15th to the early 16th century. Also on view are paintings by Tiepolo and Cranach the Elder, as well as exhibits of porcelain, firearms, antique toys, and ancient Greek and Roman art. Other exhibits include enormous old winepresses and exhibits about the history of Franconian wine making. From April through October, tours around the fortress are offered for €2 per person, starting from the Scherenberg Tor. The Marienberg collections are so vast that they spill over into another outstanding museum that is part of the fortress, the **Fürstenbaumuseum** *(Princes' Quarters Museum)*, which traces 1,200 years of Würzburg's history. The holdings include breathtaking exhibits of local goldsmiths' art. 🎫*Combined ticket for Mainfränkisches and Fürstenbau museums €5* 🕐*Apr.–Oct., Tues.–Sun. 10–5.*

❹ **Juliusspital.** Founded in 1576 by Prince-Bishop Julius Echter as a home for the poor, the elderly, and the sick, this enormous edifice now houses an impressive restaurant serving wine from the institution's own vineyards. It also sells wineglasses. All profits from the restaurant are used to run the adjacent home for the elderly. ■ TIP→ **A glass of wine is included in a weekly tour of the wine cellars.** ✉*Juliuspromenade 19* ☎*0931/393–1400* ✆*Tour €5* ⊙*Daily 10* AM–*midnight.*

❼ Residenz *(Residence).* The line of Würzburg's prince-bishops lived in this
Fodor'sChoice glorious baroque palace after moving down from the hilltop Festung
★ Marienberg. Construction started in 1719 under the brilliant direction of Balthasar Neumann. Most of the interior decoration was entrusted to the Italian stuccoist Antonio Bossi and the Venetian painter Giovanni Battista Tiepolo. It's the spirit of the pleasure-loving prince-bishop Johann Philipp Franz von Schönborn, however, that infuses the Residenz. Now considered one of Europe's most sumptuous palaces, this dazzling structure is a 10-minute walk from the railway station, along pedestrians-only Kaiserstrasse and then Theaterstrasse.

As you enter the building, the largest baroque staircase in the country, the **Treppenhaus,** greets you. Halfway up, the stairway splits and peels away 180 degrees to the left and to the right. Soaring above on the vaulting is Tiepolo's giant fresco *The Four Continents,* a gorgeous exercise in blue and pink, with allegorical figures at the corners representing the four continents known at the time (take a careful look at the elephant's trunk). Tiepolo immortalized himself and Balthasar Neumann as two of the figures—they're not too difficult to spot. ■ TIP→ **The fresco, which survived a devastating wartime bombing raid, is being restored bit by bit, so don't be surprised to find a small section covered by scaffolding.**

Next, make your way to the **Weissersaal** (White Room) and then beyond to the grandest of the state rooms, the **Kaisersaal** (Throne Room). Tiepolo's frescoes show the 12th-century visit of Emperor Frederick Barbarossa, when he came to Würzburg to claim his bride. If you take part in the guided tour, you'll also see private chambers of the various former residents (guided tours in English are given daily at 11 and 3).

The **Hofkirche** (Court Chapel) demonstrates the prince-bishops' love of ostentation. Among the lavish marble, rich gilding, and delicate stuccowork, note the Tiepolo altarpieces, ethereal visions of *The Fall of the Angels* and *The Assumption of the Virgin.* Finally, tour the **Hofgarten** (Court Gardens); the entrance is next to the chapel. The 18th-century formal garden has stately gushing fountains and trim ankle-high shrubs outlining geometric flower beds and gravel walks. ✉*Residenzpl.* ☎*0931/355–170* ⊕*www.residenz-wuerzburg.de* ✆*€5, including guided tour* ⊙*Apr.–Oct., daily 9–5:30; Nov.–Mar., daily 10–4.*

ALSO WORTH SEEING

❽ Alte Universität *(Old University).* Founded by Prince-Bishop Julius Echter and built in 1582, this rambling institution is one of Würzburg's most interesting Renaissance structures. ✉*Neubaustr. 1–9.*

⓭ Alter Kranen *(Old Crane).* Near the Main River and north of the Old Main Bridge, the crane was erected in 1772–73 by Balthasar Neu-

CLOSE UP

Germany's Master Sculptor

Tilman Riemenschneider, Germany's master of late-Gothic sculpture (1460–1531), lived an extraordinary life. His skill with wood and stone was recognized at an early age, and he soon presided over a major Würzburg workshop. Riemenschneider worked alone, however, on the life-size figures that dominate his sculptures. Details such as the folds of a robe or wrinkles upon a face highlight his grace and harmony of line.

At the height of his career Riemenschneider was appointed city counselor; later he became mayor of Würzburg. In 1523, however, he made the fateful error of siding with the small farmers and guild members in the Peasants' War. He was arrested and held for eight weeks in the dungeons of the Marienberg Fortress, above Würzburg, where he was frequently tortured. Most of his wealth was confiscated, and he returned home a broken man. He died in 1531.

For nearly three centuries he and his sculptures were all but forgotten. Only in 1822, when ditchdiggers uncovered the site of his grave, was Riemenschneider once again included among Germany's greatest artists. Today Riemenschneider is recognized as the giant of German sculpture. The richest collection of his works is in Würzburg, although other masterpieces are on view in churches and museums along the Romantic Road and in other parts of Germany. The renowned *Windsheim Altar of the Twelve Apostles* is in the Palatine Museum in Heidelberg.

---

mann's son, Franz Ignaz Michael. It was used to unload boats; beside it is the old customs building.

③ Augustinerkirche *(Church of St. Augustine).* This baroque church, a work by Balthasar Neumann, was a 13th-century Dominican chapel. Neumann retained the soaring, graceful choir and commissioned Antonio Bossi to add colorful stuccowork to the rest of the church. ✉*Dominikanerpl. 2* ☎*0931/30970* ⊙*Daily 7–7.*

⑥ Bürgerspital *(Almshouse).* Wealthy burghers founded this refuge for the city's poor and needy in 1319; it now sells wine. The arcade courtyard is baroque in style. ■**TIP➜ From mid-March through October there's a weekly tour (Saturday at 2), which includes a small bottle of their wine.** ✉*Theaterstr. 19* ☎*0931/35030* ⊕*www.buergerspital.de* 🎫*Tour €6.*

① Haus zum Falken. The city's most splendid baroque mansion, formerly a humble inn, now houses the city tourist office. Its colorful rococo facade was added in 1751. ✉*Am Marktpl. 9* ☎*0931/372–335* ⊙*Jan.–Mar., weekdays 10–4, Sat. 10–1; Apr.–Dec., weekdays 10–6, Sat. 10–2; May–Oct., Sun. and holidays 10–2.*

② Marienkapelle *(St. Mary's Chapel).* This tranquil Gothic church (1377–1480) tucked modestly away at one end of Würzburg's market square is almost lost amid the historic old facades. Balthasar Neumann lies buried here. ✉*Marktpl.* ☎*0931/321–1830* ⊙*Daily 9–6.*

⑩ Neumünster *(New Minster).* Next to the Dom St. Kilian, this 11th-century Romanesque basilica was completed in 1716. The original church was built above the grave of the early Irish martyr St. Kilian, who brought Christianity to Würzburg and, with two companions, was put to death here in 689. Their missionary zeal bore fruit, however—17 years after their death a church was consecrated in their memory. By 742 Würzburg had become a diocese, and over the following centuries 39 flourishing churches were established throughout the city. ⊠*Schönbornstr.* ☎*0931/321–1830* ☉*Daily 8–5. Closed for reconstruction until 2010.*

⓫ Rathaus. The Gothic town hall, once headquarters of the bishop's administrator, has been the center of municipal government since 1316. A permanent exhibition in the tower documents Würzburg's destruction by Allied bombs, some examples of which are on display. ⊠*Marktpl.* ☎*0931/370* 🏷*Free* ☉*Weekdays 9–5, information only; tours May–Oct., Sat. at 11.*

❺ Stift Haug. Franconia's first baroque church, designed by the Italian architect Antonio Petrini, was built between 1670 and 1691. Its elegant twin spires and central cupola make an impressive exterior. The altarpiece is a 1583 Crucifixion scene by Tintoretto. ⊠*Bahnhofstr. at Heinestr.* ☎*0931/54102* ☉*Daily 8–7.*

WHERE TO EAT

$$–$$$ ✕**Wein- und Speisehaus zum Stachel.** On a warm spring or summer day,
★ have a seat in the ancient courtyard of the Stachel, which is shaded by a canopy of vine leaves and enclosed by tall, ivy-covered walls. The entrées are satisfyingly Franconian, from lightly baked onion cake in season to hearty roast pork, and the atmosphere is satisfyingly unstuffy. ⊠*Gresseng. 1* ☎*0931/52770* ▭*No credit cards.*

$–$$ ✕**Backöfele.** More than 400 years of tradition are sustained by this old
★ tavern. Hidden away behind huge wooden doors in a backstreet, the Backöfele's cavelike interior is a popular meeting and eating place for regulars and newcomers alike. The surprisingly varied menu includes local favorites such as suckling pig and marinated pot roast as well as some good fish. ⊠*Ursulinerg. 2D–97070* ☎*0931/59059* ▭*MC, V.*

$–$$ ✕**Juliusspital Weinstuben.** This tavern serves wine from its own vineyard and good portions of basic Franconian fare. ■TIP➜ **In summer you can enjoy your food and drinks on a quiet terrace in the courtyard.** ⊠*Juliuspromenade 19* ☎*0931/54080* ▭*MC, V.*

$–$$ ✕**Ratskeller.** The vaulted cellars of Würzburg's Rathaus shelter one of the city's most popular restaurants. Beer is served, but Franconian wine is what the regulars drink. The food is staunch Franconian fare. ⊠*Beim Grafeneckart, Langg. 1* ☎*0931/13021* ▭*AE, DC, MC, V.*

WHERE TO STAY

$$–$$$ ▦**Hotel Greifensteiner Hof.** The modern Greifensteiner offers comfort-
★ able, individually furnished rooms in a quiet corner of the city, just off the market square. The slightly more expensive rooms are more spacious. The Fränkische Stuben ($–$$) has excellent cuisine—mostly Franconian specialties. **Pros:** center of town, excellent restaurants, nice bar packed with locals. **Cons:** no spectacular views or grand lobby. ⊠*Dettelbacherg. 2* ☎*0931/35170* ⊕*www.greifensteiner-hof.de* ⮌*49*

rooms ⟨&⟩ *In-room: no a/c (some), safe (some), Wi-Fi. In-hotel: 2 restaurants, bar, public Wi-Fi, parking (fee), some pets allowed, no-smoking rooms* ⊟*AE, DC, MC, V.*

$$ ⌷ **Hotel Walfisch.** Guest rooms are furnished in solid Franconian style with farmhouse cupboards, bright fabrics, and heavy drapes. You'll breakfast in a dining room on the bank of the Main with views of the vineyard-covered Marienberg. For lunch and dinner try the hotel's cozy Walfisch-Stube restaurant ($–$$). They don't serve their namesake (*Walfisch* means "whale"), but they do have excellent fish as well as a good selection of white wines. **Pros:** nice view from front rooms, good restaurant. **Cons:** difficult parking, small improvements needed. ⊠*Am Pleidenturm 5* ☎*0931/35200* ⊕*www.hotel-walfisch.com* ↩*40 rooms* ⟨&⟩ *In-room: safe (some), no a/c (some), Wi-Fi. In-hotel: restaurant, public Wi-Fi, parking (fee), no-smoking rooms* ⊟*AE, DC, MC, V* ⦿*CP.*

$–$$ ⌷ **Ringhotel Wittelsbacher Höh.** Most of the cozy rooms in this historic redbrick mansion offer views of Würzburg and the vineyards. The restaurant's wine list embraces most of the leading local vintages, and Franconian and Italian dishes ($–$$) pack the menu. In summer take a table on the terrace and soak up the view. **Pros:** nice view from rooms and terrace, good food. **Cons:** 2 mi from town, parking difficult. ⊠*Hexenbruchweg 10* ☎*0931/453–040* ⊕*www.wuerzburg-hotel.de* ↩*73 rooms, 1 suite* ⟨&⟩ *In-room: no a/c, Wi-Fi. In-hotel: restaurant, public Wi-Fi, parking, some pets allowed, no-smoking rooms* ⊟*AE, DC, MC, V* ⦿*CP.*

$–$$ ⌷ **Strauss.** Close to the river and the pedestrians-only center, the pink-stucco Strauss has been in the same family for more than 100 years. Rooms are simply furnished in light woods. The beamed restaurant Würtzburg serves Franconian cuisine. **Pros:** close to main station and old town, decent restaurant. **Cons:** small lobby, some rooms need updating. ⊠*Juliuspromenade 5* ☎*0931/30570* ⊕*www.hotel-strauss.de* ↩*75 rooms, 3 suites* ⟨&⟩ *In-room: no a/c, safe (some), Wi-Fi. In-hotel: restaurant, public Wi-Fi, parking (fee), some pets allowed, no-smoking rooms* ⊟*AE, DC, MC, V* ⊙*Restaurant closed Tues., late Dec.–late Jan.*

$ ⌷ **Spehnkuch.** What was once a large apartment with high-ceiling rooms is today a small, spotlessly clean, well-priced pension. It's just opposite the main railway station. **Pros:** welcoming family atmosphere, opposite main station, good value. **Cons:** hotel is on first floor, no elevator, shower and toilet down the hall. ⊠*Röntgenstr. 7* ☎*0931/54752* ↩*7 rooms* ⟨&⟩ *In-room: no a/c, no phone, no TV. In-hotel: no elevator* ⊟*No credit cards* ⊙*Closed 1st wk in Jan.* ⦿*CP.*

FESTIVALS

Würzburg's cultural year starts with the International Film Weekend in January and ends with a Johann Sebastian Bach Festival in November. The annual jazz festival is also in November. Its annual Mozart Festival, **Mozartfest** (⊠*Oeggstr. 2* ☎*0931/372–336* ⊕*www.mozartfest-wuerzburg.de*), between May and June, attracts visitors from all over the world. Most concerts are held in the magnificent setting of the Residenz. The town hosts a series of wine festivals, such as the **Hofkeller Würzburg** (⊠ *Residenzpl. 3* ☎ *0931/305–0931* ⊕ *www. hofkeller.de*), the last week in June. For a list of festivities and more information, contact **Tourismus Würzburg** (⊠ *Am Congress Zentrum* ☎ *0931/372–335* ⊕ *www.wuerzburg.de*). **Mainfranken Theater Würzburg** (⊠ *Theaterstr. 21* ☎ *0931/390–8124* ⊕ *www.theaterwuerzburg. de*) also has information.

SPORTS & THE OUTDOORS

Wine lovers and hikers should visit the **Stein-Wein-Pfad,** a (signposted) trail through the vineyards that rises up from the northwest edge of Würzburg. A two-hour round-trip affords stunning views of the city as well as the chance to try the excellent local wines directly at the source. The starting point for the walk is the vineyard of **Weingut am Stein, Ludwig Knoll** (⊠ *Mittlerer Steinbergweg 5* ☎ *0931/25808* ⊕ *www.weingut-am-stein.de*), 10 minutes on foot from the main railway station.

SHOPPING

Würzburg is the true wine center of the Romantic Road. Visit any of the vineyards that rise from the Main River and choose a *Bocksbeutel,* the distinctive green, flagon-shape wine bottle of Franconia. It's claimed that the shape came about because wine-guzzling monks found it the easiest to hide under their robes. The **Haus des Frankenweins** (*House of Franconian Wine* ⊠ *Kranenkai 1* ☎ *0931/390–110*) has wine tastings for individual visitors. Some 100 Franconian wines and a wide range of wine accessories are sold.

Die Murmel (⊠ *Augustinerstr. 7* ☎ *0931/59349*) is the place to go if you're looking for a special toy. **Ebinger** (⊠ *Karmelitenstr. 23* ☎ *0931/59449*) sells fine antique jewelry, clocks, watches, and silver. At the **Eckhaus** (⊠ *Langg. 8, off Marktpl.* ☎ *0931/12001*) you'll find high-quality gifts. In summer the selection consists mostly of garden and terrace decorations; from October through December the store is filled with delightful Christmas ornaments and candles.

BAD MERGENTHEIM

38 km (23 mi) south of Würzburg.

Between 1525 and 1809 Bad Mergentheim was the home of the Teutonic Knights, one of the most successful medieval orders of chivalry. In 1809 Napoléon expelled them as he marched toward his ultimately disastrous Russian campaign. The expulsion seemed to sound the death knell of the little town, but in 1826 a shepherd discovered mineral springs on the north bank of the river. They proved to be the strongest sodium sulfate and bitter saltwaters in Europe, with health-giving properties that ensured the town's future prosperity.

ESSENTIALS

Visitor Information **Bad Mergentheim** (⊠ *Tourist Information, Marktpl. 3* ☎ *07931/57135* ⊕ *www.bad-mergentheim.de*).

EATING WELL ON THE ROMANTIC ROAD

To sample the authentic food of this area, venture off the beaten track of the official Romantic Road into any small town with a nice-looking Gasthof. Order *Rinderbraten* (roast beef) with *spaetzle* (small boiled ribbons of rolled dough), or try *Maultaschen* (oversized Swabian ravioli), another typical regional dish.

Franconia (including Würzburg) is the sixth-largest wine-producing area of Germany. Franconian wines—half of which are Müller-Thurgau, a blending of Riesling and Sylvaner—are served in distinctive green, flagon-shape wine bottles. Riesling and red wines account for only about 5% of the total production of Franconian wine.

Travel south on the Romantic Road from Würzburg, and you enter beer country. There is a wide range of Franconian and Bavarian brews available from *Räucherbier* (literally, "smoked beer") to the lighter ales of Augsburg. If this is your first time in Germany, beware of the potency of German beer. Even the regular ones are much stronger than the normal American brew. If you want a light beer, in most parts of Germany you ask for "Export"; a small one will be 0.3 liters, a big one 0.5 liters. In most beer tents you will be only served a Stein with one liter.

EXPLORING

The **Deutschordensschloss,** the Teutonic Knights' former castle, at the eastern end of the town, has a museum that follows the history of the order. ✉ *Schloss 16* ☎ *07931/52212* ⊕ *www.deutschordensmuseum. de* 🎫 *€4, guided tour €2* ⊙ *Apr.–Oct., Tues.–Sun. 11–5, tours Thurs. and Sun. at 3; Nov.–Mar., Tues.–Sun. 2–5.*

☺ The **Wildpark Bad Mergentheim,** a few miles outside Bad Mergentheim, is a wildlife park with Europe's largest selection of European species, including wolves and bears. ✉ *B–290* ☎ *07931/41344* ⊕ *www.wildtier park.de* 🎫 *€8* ⊙ *Mid-Mar.–Oct., daily 9–6; Nov.–mid-Mar., weekends 10:30–4.*

WHERE TO STAY & EAT

¢–$ ✗ **Klotzbücher.** You can order 10 different kinds of beer—four from the tap—at the long wooden bar in this renovated Franconian brewery tavern. In the other room, paneled with dark wood, you can have the obligatory bratwurst at heavy wooden tables. In summer, head for the beer garden. ✉ *Boxbergerstr. 6* ☎ *07931/562–928* ⊟ *No credit cards* ⊙ *Closed Wed.*

$$ 🏨 **Hotel Victoria.** An elegant lounge, complete with library and open fireplace, greets you as you enter this hotel. The restaurant Zirbelstube ($$$–$$$$, dinner only) is known as one of the best in the region. In the Vinothek ($–$$), open all day, you can eat at the bar and watch the chefs prepare your next dish behind a huge glass partition. The hotel very conveniently has its own wine shop. **Pros:** Vinothek has very good food with excellent service, guest rooms are spacious. **Cons:** guest rooms are not well ventilated, reception understaffed. ✉ *Poststr. 2–4D– 97980* ☎ *07931/5930* ⊕ *www.victoria-hotel.de* 🛏 *44 rooms, 4 suites*

⌂ *In-room: no a/c, Wi-Fi (some). In-hotel: 2 restaurants, bar, public Wi-Fi, parking (fee), no-smoking rooms* ⊟ *AE, DC, MC, V* ⊘ *Restaurant Zirbelstube closed Jan.–Feb. 15, July 15–Aug., and Sun.* ⦿ *CP.*

CREGLINGEN

20 km (12 mi) east of Weikersheim, 40 km (25 mi) south of Würzburg.

The village of Creglingen has been an important pilgrimage site since the 14th century, when a farmer plowing his field had a vision of a heavenly host.

★ The **Herrgottskirche** *(Chapel of Our Lord)* is in the Herrgottstal (Valley of the Lord), 3 km (2 mi) south of Creglingen; the way there is well signposted. The chapel was built by the counts of Hohenlohe on the exact spot where the farmer had his vision, and in the early 16th century Riemenschneider carved an altarpiece for it. This enormous work, 33 feet high, depicts in minute detail the life and ascension of the Virgin Mary. Riemenschneider entrusted much of the background detail to the craftsmen of his Würzburg workshop, but he allowed no one but himself to attempt its life-size figures. Its intricate detail and attenuated figures are a high point of late-Gothic sculpture. ☎ *07933/508* ⊕ *www.herrgottskirche.de* ✉ *€2* ⊘ *Apr.–Oct., daily 9:15–5:30; Nov., Dec., Feb., and Mar., Tues.–Sun. noon–4.*

The **Fingerhutmuseum** is opposite the Herrgottskirche. *Fingerhut is German for "thimble," and this delightful, privately run museum has thousands of them, some dating from Roman times.* ☎ *07933/370* ⊕ *www. fingerhutmuseum.de* ✉ *€2* ⊘ *Apr.–Oct., daily 10–noon and 2–5; Nov. and Mar., Tues.–Sun. 1–4.*

WHERE TO STAY

¢ ⊡ **Heuhotel Ferienbauernhof.** For a truly off-the-beaten-track experience,
⟳ book a space in the hayloft of the Stahl family's farm in a suburb of Creglingen. Guests bed down in freshly turned hay in the farmhouse granary. Bed linen and blankets are provided. The overnight rate of €18 includes a cold supper and breakfast. You get the same for €35 per person if you swap the granary for one of three double rooms or even an apartment, but you must reserve ahead of time. **Pros:** kids love it, easy on the wallet. **Cons:** in the middle of nowhere on an upland plain, nearly impossible to find without GPS. ⊠ *Frauental-Weidenhof 1* ☎ *07933/378* ⊕ *www.ferienpension-heuhotel.de* ⌂ *In-room: no a/c, no TV. In-hotel: bicycles, no elevator, no-smoking rooms* ⊟ *No credit cards* ⦿ *CP.*

CENTRAL ROMANTIC ROAD

Picturesque Rothenburg-ob-der-Tauber is the highlight of this region, though certainly not the road less traveled. For a more intimate experience check out the medieval towns of Dinkelsbühl or Nördlingen, or

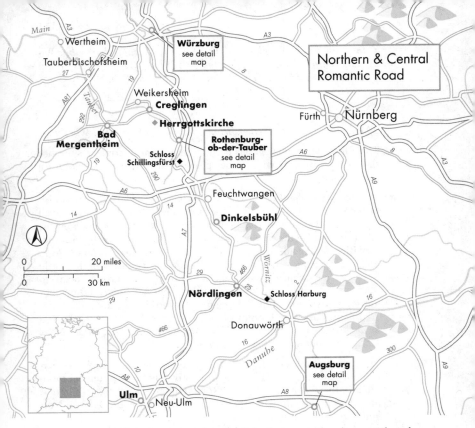

go off the beaten track and off the Romantic Road to see Ulm's famous Münster (church).

ROTHENBURG-OB-DER-TAUBER

Fodor'sChoice
★ *20 km (12 mi) southeast of Creglingen, 75 km (47 mi) west of Nürnberg.*

Rothenburg-ob-der-Tauber (literally, "red castle on the Tauber") is the kind of medieval town that even Walt Disney might have thought too picturesque to be true, with half-timber architecture galore and a wealth of fountains and flowers against a backdrop of towers and turrets. As late as the 17th century it was a small but thriving market town that had grown up around the ruins of two 12th-century churches destroyed by an earthquake. Then it was laid low economically by the havoc of the Thirty Years' War, and with its economic base devastated, the town slumbered until modern tourism rediscovered it. It's undoubtedly something of a tourist trap, but genuine enough for all the hype.

GETTING HERE & AROUND
The easiest way to get here is by car. There are large parking lots just outside the town wall. You can also come by the Romantic Road bus

4

from Frankfurt via Würzburg with a layover day and leave again with the same bus line a day later. By local train it takes about an hour from Würzburg—change trains at Steinach. All attractions within the walled town can easily reached on foot. The costumed night watchman conducts a nightly tour of the town, leading the way with a lantern. From Easter to December a one-hour tour in English begins at 8 PM and costs €6 (a 90-minute daytime tour begins at 2 PM). All tours start at the Marktplatz (Market Square) Private group tours with the night watchman can be arranged through ⊕*www.nightwatchman.de.*

TIMING

Sights are dotted around town, and the streets don't lend themselves to a particular route. Be aware that crowds will affect the pace at which you can tour the town. Early morning is the only time to appreciate the place in relative calm. The best times to see the mechanical figures on the Rathaus wall are in the evening, at 8, 9, or 10.

ESSENTIALS

Visitor Information **Rothenburg-ob-der-Tauber** (⊠ *Tourist-Information, Rathaus, Marktpl. 2* ☎ *09861/404800* ⊕ *www.rothenburg.de*).

EXPLORING

MAIN ATTRACTIONS

② **Herterichbrunnen** *(Herterich Fountain).* A *Schäfertanz* (Shepherds' Dance) was performed around the ornate Renaissance fountain on the central Marktplatz whenever Rothenburg celebrated a major event. The dance is still done, though it's now for the benefit of tourists. It takes place in front of the Rathaus several times a year, chiefly at Easter, on Whitsunday, and in September. ⊠*Marktpl.*

③ **Mittelalterliches Kriminalmuseum** *(Medieval Criminal Museum).* The gruesome medieval implements of torture on display here are not for the fainthearted. The museum, the largest of its kind in Europe, also soberly documents the history of German legal processes in the Middle Ages. ⊠*Burgg. 3* ☎*09861/5359* ⊕*www.kriminalmuseum.rothenburg. de* ⊡*€4* ⊙*Apr.–Oct., daily 9:30–6; Nov., Jan., and Feb., daily 2–4; Dec. and Mar., daily 10–4.*

⑦ **Stadtmauer** *(City Wall).* Rothenburg's city walls are more than 2 km (1 mi) long and provide an excellent way of circumnavigating the town from above. The walls' wooden walkway is covered by eaves. Stairs every 200 or 300 yards provide ready access. There are superb views of the tangle of pointed and tiled red roofs and of the rolling country beyond.

ALSO WORTH SEEING

④ **Puppen und Spielzeugmuseum** *(Doll and Toy Museum).* This complex of medieval and baroque buildings houses more than 1,000 dolls, the oldest dating from 1780, the newest from 1940, as well as a collection of dollhouses, model shops, and theaters guaranteed to charm the kids. ⊠*Hofbronneng. 13* ☎*09861/7330* ⊡*€4* ⊙*Jan. and Feb., daily 11–5; Mar.–Dec., daily 9:30–6.*

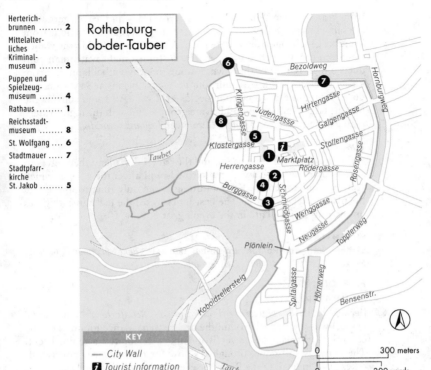

Rothenburg-ob-der-Tauber

KEY

— City Wall
🛈 Tourist information

0   300 meters

0   300 yards

❶ Rathaus. Half of the town hall is Gothic, begun in 1240; the other half is neoclassical, started in 1572. Below the building are the **Historiengewölbe** (*Historic Vaults* 🎫€2 ⊙*Apr.–Oct., daily 9:30–5:30; Christmas market season, daily 1–4*), housing a museum that concentrates on the Thirty Years' War.

Tales of the *Meistertrunk* (Master Drink) and a mighty civil servant are still told in Rothenburg. The story originates from 1631, when the Protestant town was captured by Catholic forces during the Thirty Years' War. During the victory celebrations, the conquering general was embarrassed to find himself unable to drink a great tankard of wine in one go, as his manhood demanded. He volunteered to spare the town further destruction if any of the city councilors could drain the mighty 6-pint draft. The mayor took up the challenge and succeeded, and Rothenburg was preserved. The tankard itself is on display at the Reichsstadtmuseum. On the north side of the main square is a fine clock, placed there 50 years after the mayor's feat. A mechanical figure acts out the epic Master Drink daily on the hour from 11 to 3 and in the evening at 8, 9, and 10. The feat is also celebrated at two annual pageants, when townsfolk parade through the streets in 17th-century garb. ■TIP➜ **The Rathaus tower offers a good view of the town.** ✉*Rathauspl.*

8 **Reichsstadtmuseum** *(Imperial City Museum)*. This city museum is two attractions in one. Its artifacts illustrate Rothenburg and its history. Among them is the great tankard, or *Pokal*, of the Meistertrunk. The setting of the museum is the other attraction; it's in a former Dominican convent, the oldest parts of which date from the 13th century. Tour the building to see the cloisters, the kitchens, and the dormitory; then see the collections. ⊠*Klosterhof 5* ☎*09861/939–043* 🖾*€3.50* ⊙*Apr.–Oct., daily 10–5; Nov.–Mar., daily 1–5.*

6 **St. Wolfgang.** A historic parish church of Gothic origins with a baroque interior, St. Wolfgang's is most notable for the way it blends into the forbidding city wall. ⊠*Klingeng.* 🖾*€1.50* ⊙*Apr.–Sept., daily 10–1 and 2–5.*

5 **Stadtpfarrkirche St. Jakob** *(Parish Church of St. James)*. The church has some notable Riemenschneider sculptures, including the famous *Heiliges Blut* (Holy Blood) altar. Above the altar a crystal capsule is said to contain drops of Christ's blood. There are three 14th- and 15th-century stained-glass windows in the choir, and the Herlin-Altar is famous for its 15th-century painted panels. ⊠*Klosterg. 15* ☎*09861/700–620* 🖾*€2* ⊙*Jan.–Mar. and Nov., daily 10–noon and 2–4; Apr.–Oct., daily 9–5; Dec., daily 10–4. English tour Sat. at 3.*

WHERE TO STAY

$$–$$$ ★ 🏨**Hotel Eisenhut.** It's fitting that the prettiest small town in Germany should have one of the prettiest small hotels. Every one of the 79 rooms is different—each with its own charming color scheme, most with antique furniture. ■TIP➔ **Try for one on the top floor toward the back overlooking the old town and the Tauber River valley.** The restaurant ($$–$$$), one of the region's best, offers impeccable service along with delicious food and a lovely view of the garden. In summer you'll want to eat on the terrace, surrounded by flowers. **Pros:** spacious, elegant lobby, exceptional service, very good food. **Cons:** expensive, caters to elderly guests, nothing for teenage kids. ⊠*Herrng. 3–5* ☎*09861/7050* ⊕*www.eisenhut.com* 🛏*77 rooms, 2 suites* ⚒*In-room: no a/c, Wi-Fi. In-hotel: restaurant, room service, bar, laundry service, public Wi-Fi, parking (fee), no-smoking rooms* ⊟*AE, DC, MC, V*

$$ ★ 🏨**Romantik-Hotel Markusturm.** The Markusturm began as a 13th-century customs house, an integral part of the city defense wall, and has since developed over the centuries into an inn and staging post and finally into a luxurious small hotel. Some rooms are beamed, others have Laura Ashley decor or gaily painted bedsteads, and some have valuable antiques from the Middle Ages. Try to book a reservation for dinner when you arrive, as the beamed, elegant restaurant ($–$$) may fill up. The fish is excellent—you may want to try it as part of their Romantic Gourmet dinner. Besides well-selected wines, you can order three kinds of home-brewed beer. In summer head for the patio. **Pros:** very tastefully decorated hotel and rooms, elegant atmosphere, excellent food, responsive owner. **Cons:** difficult to reach during the day because of the crowds. ⊠*Röderg. 1* ☎*09861/94280* ⊕*www.markusturm.de* 🛏*23 rooms, 2 suites* ⚒*In-room: no a/c, Wi-Fi. In-hotel: restaurant, public Wi-Fi, parking (fee), no-smoking rooms* ⊟*AE, DC, MC, V* ⏐⊙|*CP.*

$–$$ 🏨 **Burg-Hotel.** This exquisite little hotel abuts the town wall and was
Fodor's Choice   once part of a Rothenburg monastery. Most rooms have a view of the
★   Tauber Valley. All have plush furnishings, with antiques or fine repro-
ductions. The Steinway Cellar holds a grand piano. Breakfast is served
in good weather on the terrace on top of the town wall, with an even
more stunning wide-angle view into the Tauber Valley and the hills
beyond. The owner and staff are gracious hosts. **Pros:** no crowds, terrific view from most rooms, nice touches throughout. **Cons:** parking is
difficult for late-comers, no restaurant, too quiet for kids. ⊠*Klosterg.
1–3* 🕿*09861/94890* ⊕*www.burghotel.rothenburg.de* ⏴*17 rooms*
⌂*In-room: no a/c, Wi-Fi. In-hotel: spa, laundry service, public Wi-Fi,
no-smoking rooms* ▤*AE, DC, MC, V* ⁙*CP.*

$–$$ 🏨 **Hotel-Restaurant Burg Colmberg.** East of Rothenburg in Colmberg, this
★   castle turned hotel maintains a high standard of comfort within its
original medieval walls. As you enter the hotel, logs are burning in the
fireplace of the entrance hall, illuminating an original Tin Lizzy from
1917. The restaurant Zur Remise ($–$$) serves venison from the cas-
tle's own hunting grounds. **Pros:** romantic, kids love staying in a real,
historic castle. **Cons:** lonely, once you've arrived there is little else to
explore, quite a few stairs to climb to get to some rooms. ⊠*Burg 1–3,
18 km (11 mi) east of Rothenburg, Colmberg* 🕿*09803/91920* ⊕*www.
burg-colmberg.de* ⏴*24 rooms, 2 suites* ⌂*In-room: no a/c. In-hotel:
restaurant, bar, golf course, bicycles, no-smoking rooms* ▤*AE, MC,
V* ⊗*Closed Feb.* ⁙*CP.*

$–$$ 🏨 **Hotel Reichs-Küchenmeister.** Master chefs in the service of the Holy
Roman Emperor were the inspiration for the name of this historic
hotel-restaurant, one of the oldest trader's houses in Rothenburg. For
five generations it's been run by the same energetic family. Rooms are
furnished in a stylish mixture of old and new; light veneer pieces share
space with heavy oak bedsteads and painted cupboards. **Pros:** in the
middle of town, great for kids to explore the town. **Cons:** small reception
area, restaurant is open to the public. ⊠*Kirchpl. 8–10* 🕿*09861/9700*
⊕*www.reichskuechenmeister.com* ⏴*45 rooms, 2 suites, 5 apartments*
⌂*In-room: no a/c, Wi-Fi. In-hotel: restaurant, bar, public Wi-Fi, no-
smoking rooms* ▤*AE, MC, V* ⁙*CP.*

$ 🏨 **Gasthof Klingentor.** This sturdy old staging post is outside the city
walls but still within a 10-minute walk of Rothenburg's historic center. Rooms are spacious and furnished in the local rustic style. Most
have en-suite facilities. Its inexpensive restaurant serves substantial
Franconian fare. A well-marked path for hiking or biking starts outside the front door. **Pros:** good value, restaurant liked by locals and
guests. **Cons:** front rooms noisy, no elevator. ⊠*Mergentheimerstr. 14*
🕿*09861/3468* ⊕*www.hotel-klingentor.de* ⏴*20 rooms, 16 with bath*
⌂*In-room: no a/c, no TV (some). In-hotel: restaurant, bar, no elevator,
no-smoking rooms* ▤*MC, V* ⁙*CP.*

$ 🏨 **Hotel-Gasthof Post.** This small family-run hotel, two minutes on foot
from the eastern city gate, must be one of the friendliest in town. The
rooms are simple but clean, and all have shower or bath. **Pros:** good
value, friendly family atmosphere. **Cons:** front rooms noisy, no elevator. ⊠*Ansbacherstr. 27* 🕿*09861/938–880* ⊕*www.post-rothenburg.*

com 🛏18 rooms ⚹ *In-room: no a/c. In-hotel: restaurant, no elevator* ▭ *DC, MC, V* 🍽 *CP.*

FESTIVALS

Highlights of Rothenburg's annual calendar are the **Meistertrunk Festival,** over the Whitsun weekend, celebrating the famous wager said to have saved the town from destruction in the Thirty Years' War, and the **Reichsstadt-Festtage,** on the first weekend of September, commemorating Rothenburg's attainment of Free Imperial City status in 1274. Both are spectacular festivals, when thousands of townspeople and local horsemen reenact the events in period costume.

SHOPPING

On the old and atmospheric premises of the **Anneliese Friese** (✉ *Grüner Markt 7–8, near Rathaus* ☎*09861/7166*) you'll find everything from cuckoo clocks and beer tankards to porcelain and glassware. If you are looking specifically for Hummel articles, try **Haus der Tausend Geschenke** (✉*Obere Schmiedeg. 13* ☎*09861/4801*).

Käthe Wohlfahrt (✉*Herrng. 1* ☎*09861/4090*) carries children's toys and seasonal decorations. The Christmas Village part of the store is a wonderland of mostly German-made toys and decorations. **Teddyland** (✉*Herrng. 10* ⊕*www.teddyland.de* ☎*09861/8904*) has Germany's largest teddy-bear population. More than 5,000 of them pack this extraordinary store. ■TIP→ **Children adore the place, but be prepared: these are pedigree teddies, and they don't come cheap. Check out the guided tour on their Web site for photos of bears taking in Rothenburg's sights.**

EN
ROUTE

Schloss Schillingsfürst (✉*Schlosspl. 1* ☎*09868/201* ⊕*www.schloss-schillingsfuerst.de*), a baroque castle of the Princes of Hohenlohe-Schillingsfürst, is 20 km (12 mi) south of Rothenburg-ob-der-Tauber. Standing on an outcrop, it can be seen from miles away. ■TIP→ **If you visit the castle, try to arrive in time for one of the demonstrations of Bavarian falconry, held in the courtyard.** You can watch eagles and falcons, on a single command, shoot down from the sky to catch their prey. The castle can be visited only with a guided tour at 10, noon, 2, or 4. The falconry show is at 11 and 3 (€7 for both tour and show) from March to October.

DINKELSBÜHL

★ *26 km (16 mi) south of Schillingsfürst.*

Within the walls of Dinkelsbühl, a beautifully preserved medieval town, the rush of traffic seems a lifetime away. There's less to see here than in Rothenburg, and the mood is much less tourist-oriented. Like Rothenburg, Dinkelsbühl was caught up in the Thirty Years' War, and it also preserves a fanciful episode from those bloody times. An annual open-air-theater festival takes place from mid-June until mid-August.

GETTING HERE & AROUND

In Dinkelsbühl you can patrol the illuminated old town with the night watchman at 9 PM free of charge, starting from the Münster St. Georg.

ESSENTIALS

Visitor Information **Touristik-Arbeitsgemeinschaft Romantische Strasse (Central Tourist Information Romantic Road)** (⊠ *Segringerstr. 19 Dinkelsbühl* ☎ *09851/551-387* ⊕ *www.romantische strasse.de*). **Dinkelsbühl** (⊠ *Tourist-Information, Marktpl.* ☎ *09851/90240* ⊕ *www.dinkelsbuehl.de*).

EXPLORING

The **Münster St. Georg** *(Minster St. George)* is the standout sight in

town. At 235 feet in length it's large enough to be a cathedral, and it's among the best examples in Bavaria of the late-Gothic style. Note the complex fan vaulting that spreads sinuously across the ceiling. If you can face the climb, head up the 200-foot tower for amazing views over the jumble of rooftops. ⊠ *Marktpl.* ☎ *09851/2245* 🖼 *Tower €1.50* 🕙 *Church daily 9–noon and 2–5; tower May–Sept., weekends 2–6.*

WHERE TO STAY

$$ 🏨 **Hotel Deutsches Haus.** This medieval inn, with a facade of half-timber gables and flower boxes, has many rooms fitted with antique furniture. One of them has a romantic four-poster bed. Dine beneath heavy oak beams in the restaurant ($–$$), where you can try the local specialty, a type of grain called Dinkel. It's very nutritious and often served roasted with potatoes and salmon. **Pros:** genuine antique hotel, modern touches like free Wi-Fi. **Cons:** some rooms noisy, quite expensive. ⊠ *Weinmarkt 3* ☎ *09851/6058* ⊕ *www.deutsches-haus-dkb.de* 🛏 *16 rooms, 2 suites* 🔧 *In-room: no a/c, dial-up (some). In-hotel: restaurant, bar, parking (fee), no-smoking rooms* ⊟ *AE, DC, MC, V* 🕙 *Closed Jan. and Feb.* 🍴 *CP.*

$–$$ 🏨 **Goldene Rose.** Since 1450 the inhabitants of Dinkelsbühl and their guests—among them Queen Victoria in 1891—have enjoyed good food and refreshing drinks in this half-timber house. Dark paneling in the restaurant ($–$$) creates the cozy atmosphere in which you can enjoy good regional cuisine, especially fish and game. Many of the comfortably furnished rooms have half-timber walls. **Pros:** family-friendly atmosphere, good food, hotel has a parking lot. **Cons:** some rooms need renovating, rooms at the front are noisy. ⊠ *Marktpl. 4* ☎ *09851/57750* ⊕ *www.hotel-goldene-rose.com* 🛏 *31 rooms* 🔧 *In-room: no a/c, Wi-Fi. In-hotel: restaurant, bar, public Wi-Fi, parking (fee), some pets allowed* ⊟ *DC, MC, V* 🍴 *CP.*

SHOPPING

Deleika (✉ *Waldeck 33* ☎*09857/97990*) makes barrel organs to order, although it won't deliver the monkey! The firm also has a museum of barrel organs and other mechanical instruments. It's just outside Dinkelsbühl. Call ahead. At **Dinkelsbüler Kunst-Stuben** (✉*Segringerstr. 52* ☎*09851/6750*), the owner, Mr. Appelberg, sells his own drawings, paintings, and etchings of the town.

NÖRDLINGEN

32 km (20 mi) southeast of Dinkelsbühl, 70 km (43 mi) northwest of Augsburg.

In Nördlingen the cry *"So G'sell so"*—"All's well"—still rings out every night across the ancient walls and turrets.

ESSENTIALS

Visitor Information **Nördlingen** (✉ *Tourist-Information, Marktpl. 2* ☎*09081/84116* ⊕ *www.noerdlingen.de*).

EXPLORING

Sentries sound out the traditional *"So G'sell so"* message from the 300-foot tower of the central parish church of **St. Georg** at half-hour intervals between 10 PM and midnight. The tradition goes back to an incident during the Thirty Years' War, when an enemy attempted to slip into the town and was detected by a resident. You can climb the 365 steps up the tower—known locally as the Daniel—for an unsurpassed view of the town and countryside, including, on clear days, 99 villages. The ground plan of the town is two concentric circles. The inner circle of streets, whose central point is St. Georg, marks the earliest medieval boundary. A few hundred yards beyond it is the outer boundary, a wall built to accommodate expansion. Fortified with 11 towers and punctuated by five massive gates, it's one of the best-preserved town walls in Germany. ✉*Marktpl.* ☎*Tower* *€1.50* ☉*Daily 9–dusk.*

Nördlingen lies in the center of a huge, basinlike depression, the **Ries,** that until the beginning of this century was believed to be the remains of an extinct volcano. In 1960 it was proven by two Americans that the 24-km-wide (15-mi-wide) crater was caused by a meteorite at least 1 km (½ mi) in diameter. ■TIP➔ **The compressed rock, or *Suevit,* formed by the explosive impact of the meteorite was used to construct many of the town's buildings, including St. Georg's tower.**

BIKING THE ROMANTIC ROAD

There are three ways to explore the Romantic Road by bicycle and the path (all 420 km [260 mi] of it) is well marked. You can either venture out with as little baggage as possible, finding places to stay along the way. Or, have a tour operator book rooms for you and your group and transport your luggage. Or, you can do day trips. In any town on the Romantic Road you can board the Deutsche Touring bus (with a trailer for bicycles), which travels the length of the Romantic Road daily.

WHERE TO STAY

$–$$ **Kaiserhof-Hotel-Sonne.** The great German poet Goethe stayed here, only one in a long line of distinguished guests starting with Emperor Friedrich III in 1487. The vaulted-cellar wine tavern is a reminder of those days. The three honeymoon suites are furnished in 18th-century style, with hand-painted four-poster beds. The property is right in the center of the city, in the shadow of the big church tower. **Pros:** historic hotel, in the center of town. **Cons:** hotel needs renovating, no Web site. ✉ *Marktpl. 3* ☎ *09081/5067* 📠 *09081/29290* *40 rooms* *In-room: no a/c, Wi-Fi (some). In-hotel: restaurant, bar, parking (no fee), public Wi-Fi, some pets allowed, no-smoking rooms* 💳 *AE, MC, V* ⊙ *Closed Nov. Restaurant closed Jan. and Feb., Sun. dinner, and Wed.* 🍽 *CP.*

$ **Braunes Ross.** This Gasthaus in the central square, directly opposite the city tower, was first mentioned in city archives in 1481 as "a place to eat and drink." The Haubner family bought the house 517 years later, in 1998, and renovated it from top to bottom. It now features modern rooms with cable TV, phones, and private baths, and a cozy, Bavarian-style restaurant. **Pros:** good value, center of town, Bavarian food. **Cons:** some rooms noisy, not enough parking. ✉ *Marktpl. 12* ☎ *09081/290–120* 🌐 *www.hotel-braunes-ross.de* *14 rooms* *In-room: no a/c. In-hotel: restaurant, some pets allowed* 💳 *MC, V* 🍽 *CP.*

$ **Hotel Goldene Rose.** This small, modern hotel is just inside the town wall and is ideal for those who wish to explore Nördlingen on foot. The in-house restaurant serves wholesome, inexpensive dishes. **Pros:** new, small, family-run. **Cons:** Front rooms noisy, restaurant closed on Sunday. ✉ *Baldingerstr. 42* ☎ *09081/86019* 🌐 *www.goldene-rose-noerdlingen.de* *17 rooms, 1 apartment* *In-room: no a/c. In-hotel: restaurant, parking (no fee), no-smoking rooms* 💳 *MC, V* 🍽 *CP.*

SPORTS & THE OUTDOORS

Ever cycled around a huge meteor crater? You can do just that in the **Nördlingen Ries,** the basinlike depression left by a meteor that hit the area in prehistoric times. The **Nördlingen tourist office** (☎ *09081/84116*) has a list of 10 recommended bike routes, including one 47-km (29-mi) trail around the northern part of the meteor crater.

ULM

60 km (40 mi) west of Augsburg.

Ulm isn't considered part of the Romantic Road, but it's definitely worth visiting, if only for one reason: its mighty Münster, which has the world's tallest church tower (536 feet). Ulm grew as a medieval trading city thanks to its location on the Danube River. Today the proximity of the Old Town to the river adds to Ulm's charm. In the Fishermen's and Tanners' quarters the cobblestone alleys and stone-and-wood bridges over the Blau (a small Danube tributary) are especially picturesque. To get to Ulm from Donauwörth, take Highway B–16 west, connecting with B–28. Or, from Augsburg, take a 40-minute ride on one of the superfast ICE (Intercity Express) trains that run to Ulm every hour.

GETTING HERE & AROUND

The tourist office's 90-minute tour includes a visit to the Münster, the Old Town Hall, the Fischerviertel (Fishermen's Quarter), and the Danube riverbank. The departure point is the tourist office (Stadthaus) on Münsterplatz; the cost is €6. From May to mid-October you can view Ulm from aboard the motor cruiser *Ulmer Spatz*. There are 50-minute cruises at 2 and 3 daily (€8). The boats tie up at the Metzgerturm, a two-minute walk from the city hall.

ESSENTIALS

Visitor Information Ulm (⊠ *Tourist-Information, Münsterpl. 50 [Stadthaus]* ☎ *0731/161–2830* ⊕ *www.tourismus.ulm.de*).

EXPLORING

★ Ulm's **Münster,** the largest church in southern Germany, was unscathed by wartime bombing. It stands over the huddled medieval gables of Old Ulm, visible long before you hit the ugly suburbs encroaching on the Swabian countryside. Its single, filigree tower challenges the physically fit to plod 536 feet up the 768 steps of a giddily twisting spiral stone staircase to a spectacular observation point below the spire. On clear days the highest steeple in the world will reward you with views of the Swiss and Bavarian Alps, 160 km (100 mi) to the south. The Münster was begun in the late-Gothic age (1377) and took five centuries to build, with completion in the neo-Gothic years of the late 19th century. It contains some notable treasures, including late-Gothic choir stalls and a Renaissance altar. ■TIP→**The mighty organ can be heard in special recitals every Sunday at 11:15 from Easter until November.** ⊠ *Münsterpl.* ☎ *Tower €3, organ recitals €1.50* ⊗ *Daily 9–5; organ recitals May–Oct., daily at 11:30.*

A reproduction of local tailor Ludwig Berblinger's flying machine hangs inside the elaborately painted **Rathaus.** In 1811 Berblinger, a tailor and local eccentric, cobbled together a pair of wings and made a big splash by trying to fly across the river. He didn't make it, but he grabbed a place in German history books for his efforts. ⊠ *Marktpl. 1.*

German bread is world-renowned, so it's not surprising that a national museum is devoted to bread making. The **Museum der Brotkultur** *(German Bread Museum)* is housed in a former salt warehouse, just north of the Münster. It's by no means as crusty or dry as some might fear, with some often-amusing tableaux illustrating how bread has been baked over the centuries. ⊠ *Salzstadelg. 10* ☎ *0731/69955* ⊕ *www.museum-brotkultur.de* ☎ *€4* ⊗ *Daily 10–5.*

Complete your visit to Ulm with a walk down to the banks of the Danube, where you'll find long sections of the **old city wall** and fortifications intact.

WHERE TO STAY & EAT

$-$$ ✕**Zur Forelle.** For more than 350 years the aptly named Forelle, which
★ means "trout," has stood over the small, clear River Blau, which flows through a large trout basin right under the restaurant. If you're not a trout fan, there are five other fish dishes available, as well as excellent

venison in season. ■TIP→ On a nice summer evening, try to get a table on the small terrace. You'll literally sit over the small river, with a weeping willow on one side, half-timber houses all around you, and the towering cathedral in the background. ⊠*Fischerg. 25, D–89073* ☎*0731/63924* ⊟*DC, MC, V.*

¢–$ ✕**Zunfthaus der Schiffleute.** The sturdy half-timber Zunfthaus (Guildhall) has stood here for more than 500 years, first as a fishermen's pub and now as a charming tavern-restaurant. Ulm's fishermen had their guild headquarters here, and when the nearby Danube flooded, the fish swam right up to the door. Today they land on the menu. One of the "foreign" intruders on the menu is Bavarian white sausage, *Weisswurst*. The local beer is an excellent accompaniment. ⊠*Fischerg. 31* ☎*0731/64411* ⊕*www.zunfthaus-ulm.de* ⊟*AE, MC, V.*

$$–$$$ ▦**Maritim.** Whether you come here to eat or stay, be prepared for incredible views. In the main restaurant ($–$$) on the 16th floor, the international dishes are good but they can't compare with the panorama offered from the huge floor-to-ceiling windows: the Old Town of Ulm with the cathedral, the Danube, and the Swabian Alb, a long plateau, are all visible. The large, luxurious bar, with cozy corners and live piano music every night, has become a favorite with guests. Ask for weekend rates. **Pros:** spacious lobby and rooms, romantic views, nice bar. **Cons:** rooms expensive on weekdays, impersonal atmosphere, chain hotel. ⊠*Basteistr. 40* ☎*0731/9230* ⊕*www.maritim.de* ⤳*287 rooms* ᕓ*In-room: no a/c, dial-up, Wi-Fi (some). In-hotel: 2 restaurants, bar, pool, gym, public Wi-Fi, parking (fee), no-smoking rooms* ⊟*AE, DC, MC, V.*

$ ▦**Hotel am Rathaus/Reblaus.** The owner's love of antique paintings, furniture, and dolls is evident throughout this hotel. Some of the rooms have antique furniture. In the annex, the half-timber Reblaus, most rooms have hand-painted cupboards. If you take a room toward the front, look up from your window and you'll see the cathedral with its huge spire a few hundred feet away. The hotel is behind the old historic Rathaus, on the fringe of the Old City, where you'll find more than a dozen restaurants and taverns. **Pros:** center of the city, artistic touches, good value. **Cons:** no elevator, not enough parking, no breakfast in annex. ⊠*Kroneng. 10* ☎*0731/968–490* ⊕*www.rathausulm. de* ⤳*34 rooms* ᕓ*In-room: no a/c, Wi-Fi. In-hotel: no elevator, public Wi-Fi, parking (no fee), no-smoking rooms* ⊟*AE, DC* ☉*Closed late Dec.–mid-Jan.* ⦿I*CP.*

AUGSBURG

41 km (25 mi) south of Donauwörth, 60 km (37 mi) west of Munich.

Augsburg is Bavaria's third-largest city, after Munich and Nürnberg. It dates to 15 years before the birth of Christ, when a son of the Roman emperor Augustus set up a military camp here on the banks of the Lech River. The settlement that grew up around it was known as Augusta, a name Italian visitors to the city still call it. It was granted city rights in 1156, and 200 years later was first mentioned in municipal records of the Fugger family, who were to Augsburg what the Medici were to Florence.

GETTING HERE & AROUND

Augsburg in on a main line of the super fast ICE trains, which run every hour—about 45 minutes from Munich. The center of town with the main attractions can be visited on foot. To continue on the Romantic Road, there is the romantic Road bus, which leaves from the central marketplace every afternoon in summer to the Wieskirche, Neuschwanstein, and Füssen.

Walking tours (€7) set out from the Rathaus daily at 2. All tours are conducted in German and English.

TIMING

A walking tour of Augsburg is easy, because signs on almost every street corner point the way to the chief sights. The signs are integrated into three-color, charted tours devised by the tourist board. You'll need a complete day to see Augsburg if you linger in any of the museums.

ESSENTIALS

Visitor Information **Augsburg** (⊠ *Tourist-Information, Maximilianstr. 57* ☎ *0821/502–070* ⊕ *www.regio-augsburg.de*).

EXPLORING

MAIN ATTRACTIONS

⑫ **Dom St. Maria** *(Cathedral of St. Mary)*. Augsburg's cathedral, which was built in 9th century, stands out within the city's panorama because of its square Gothic towers, the product of a 14th-century update. A 10th-century Romanesque crypt, built in the time of Bishop Ulrich, also remains from the cathedral's early years. The 11th-century windows on the south side of the nave, depicting the prophets Jonah, Daniel, Hosea, Moses, and David, form the oldest cycle of stained glass in central Europe. Five important paintings by Hans Holbein the Elder adorn the altar.

The cathedral's treasures are on display at the **Diözesan Museum St. Afra** (⊠ *Kornhausg. 3–5* ☎ € 4 ⊙ *Tues.–Sat. 10–5, Sun. noon–6*). A short walk from the cathedral will take you to the quiet courtyards and small raised garden of the former episcopal residence, a series of 18th-century buildings in baroque and rococo styles that now serve as the Swabian regional government offices ⊠ *Dompl.* ⊙ *Daily 9–dusk.*

❹ **Fuggerei.** This neat little settlement is the world's oldest social housing project, established by the Fugger family in 1516 to accommodate the city's deserving poor. The 104 homes still serve the same purpose; the annual rent of "one Rhenish guilder" (€1) hasn't changed, either. Residents must be Augsburg citizens, Catholic, and destitute through no fault of their own—and they must pray daily for their original benefactors, the Fugger family. ⊠ *Jacoberstr.*

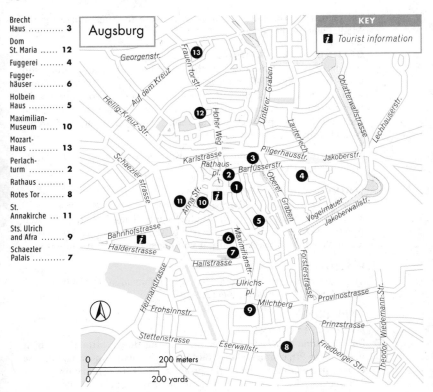

Augsburg

🔟 **Maximilian-Museum.** Augsburg's main museum houses a permanent exhibition of Augsburg arts and crafts in a 16th-century merchant's mansion. ⌧*Philippine-Welser-Str. 24* 🎫*€7* 🕙*Tues.–Sun. 10–5.*

② **Perlachturm** *(Perlach Tower).* This 258-foot-high plastered brick bell tower has foundations dating to the 11th century. Although it's a long climb to the top of the tower, the view over Augsburg and the country-side is worth the effort. ⌧*Rathauspl.* ☎*No phone* 🎫*€2* 🕙*May–mid-Oct., daily 10–6; Dec., weekends noon–7.*

① **Rathaus.** Augsburg's town hall was Germany's largest when it was built in the early 17th century; it's now regarded as the finest Renaissance secular structure north of the Alps. Its **Goldener Saal** (Golden Hall) was given its name because of its rich decoration—a gold-based harmony of wall frescoes, carved pillars, and coffered ceiling. ⌧*Rathauspl.* 🎫*€2* 🕙*10–6 on days when no official functions take place.*

⑨ **Sts. Ulrich and Afra.** Standing at the highest point of the city, this basilica was built on the site of a Roman cemetery where St. Afra was martyred in AD 304. The original structure was begun in the late-Gothic style in 1467; a baroque preaching hall was added in 1710 as the Protestant church of St. Ulrich. St. Afra is buried in the crypt, near the tomb of St. Ulrich, a 10th-century bishop who helped stop a Hungarian army at the gates of Augsburg in the Battle of the Lech River. The remains of a third patron of the church, St. Simpert, are preserved in one of the church's most elaborate side chapels. From the steps of the magnificent altar, look back along the high nave to the finely carved baroque wrought-iron and wood railing that borders the entrance. As you leave, look into the separate but adjacent church of St. Ulrich, the former chapter house that was reconstructed by the Lutherans after the Reformation. ⊠ *Ulrichspl.* ☉ *Daily 9–dusk.*

7 **Schaezler Palais.** This elegant 18th-century city palace was built by the von Liebenhofens, a family of wealthy bankers. Schaezler was the name of a baron who married into the family. Today the palace rooms contain the **Deutsche Barockgalerie** (German Baroque Gallery), a major art collection that features works of the 17th and 18th centuries. The palace adjoins the former church of a Dominican monastery. A steel door behind the banquet hall leads into another world of high-vaulted ceilings, where the **Staatsgalerie Altdeutsche Meister,** a Bavarian state collection, highlights old-master paintings, among them a Dürer portrait of one of the Fuggers. ⊠ *Maximilianstr. 46* 🖅 *€7* ☉ *Tues.–Sun. 10–5.*

ALSO WORTH SEEING

3 **Brecht Haus.** This modest artisan's house was the birthplace of the renowned playwright Bertolt Brecht (1898–1956), author of *Mother Courage* and *The Threepenny Opera.* ⊠ *Auf dem Rain 7* 🖅 *€2* ☉ *Tues.– Sun. 10–5.*

6 **Fuggerhäuser.** The 16th-century former home and business quarters of the Fugger family now houses a restaurant in its cellar and offices on the upper floors. In the ground-floor entrance are busts of two of Augsburg's most industrious Fuggers, Raymund and Anton. Beyond a modern glass door is a quiet courtyard with colonnades, the Damenhof (Ladies' Courtyard), originally reserved for the Fugger women. ⊠ *Maximilianstr. 36–38.*

5 **Holbein Haus.** The rebuilt 16th-century home of painter Hans Holbein the Elder, one of Augsburg's most famous residents, is now a city art gallery, with changing exhibitions. ⊠ *Vorderer Lech 20* 🖅 *Varies* ☉ *May–Oct., Tues., Wed., and Fri.–Sun. 10–5, Thurs. 10–8; Nov.– Apr., Tues., Wed., and Fri.–Sun. 10–4, Thurs. 10–8.*

Maximilianstrasse. This main shopping street was once a medieval wine market. Most of the city's sights are on this thoroughfare or a short walk away. Two monumental and elaborate fountains punctuate the long street. At the north end is the **Merkur,** designed in 1599 by the Dutch master Adrian de Vries (after a Florentine sculpture by Giovanni da Bologna), which shows winged Mercury in his classic pose. Farther up Maximilianstrasse is another de Vries fountain: a bronze **Hercules** struggling to subdue the many-headed Hydra.

13 **Mozart-Haus** *(Mozart House).* Leopold Mozart, the father of Wolfgang Amadeus Mozart, was born in this bourgeois 17th-century residence; he was an accomplished composer and musician in his own right. The house now serves as a Mozart memorial and museum, with some fascinating contemporary documents on the Mozart family. ⊠ *Frauentorstr. 30* ☎ *0821/324–3894* 💶 *€3.50* 🕙 *Tues.–Sun. 10–5.*

❽ Rotes Tor *(Red Gate).* The city's most important medieval gate once straddled the main trading road to Italy. It provides the backdrop to an open-air opera and operetta festival in June and July. ⊠ *Eserwallstr.*

⓫ St. Annakirche *(St. Anna's Church).* This site was formerly part of a Carmelite monastery, where Martin Luther stayed in 1518 during his meetings with Cardinal Cajetanus, the papal legate sent from Rome to persuade the reformer to renounce

> ### TOURING TIPS
>
> **Scenic Spots:** There's an excellent view over the center of the city from the spot where Maximilianstrasse joins Rathausplatz (Town Hall Square).
>
> **Scenic Spots:** Climb the 258 steps of the Perlachturm (beside the town hall) for a spectacular vantage point over the city.
>
> **Snacks:** Recuperate from the climb at the cafés and restaurants on Rathausplatz and Maximilianstrasse.

his heretical views. Luther refused, and the place where he publicly declared his rejection of papal pressure is marked with a plaque on Maximilianstrasse. ■TIP➡ **You can wander through the quiet cloisters, dating from the 14th century, and view the chapel used by the Fugger family until the Reformation.** ⊠ *Anna-Str., west of Rathauspl.* 🕙 *Tues.–Sat. 10–12:30 and 3–6, Sun. noon–6.*

WHERE TO EAT

$$–$$$ ✕**Die Ecke.** Situated on an *Ecke* (corner) of the small square right behind
Fodor'sChoice Augsburg's town hall, the Ecke is valued for the imaginative variety of
★ its cuisine and the scope of its wine list. In season, the venison dishes are among Bavaria's best. The fish, in particular the *Zander* (green pike) or the trout sautéed in butter and lightly dressed with herbs and lemon, is magnificent, and complemented nicely by the Riesling Gimmeldinger Meersspinne, the house wine for 40 years. In summer ask for a table on the patio. ⊠ *Elias-Holl-Pl. 2,* ☎ *0821/510–600* 🍴*Reservations essential* 🟰*AE, DC, MC, V.*

WHERE TO STAY

$$–$$$ 🏨**Steigenberger Drei Mohren Hotel.** Kings and princes, Napoléon, and the Duke of Wellington have all slept here. Except for the modern fourth- and fifth-floor rooms, all the rooms maintain a luxurious, traditional style. Ask for weekend rates. Dining options include the elegant, Mediterranean-style restaurant Maximilian's ($$–$$$) and Bistro 3M ($–$$). The Sunday jazz brunch at Maximilian's has been a town favorite since the late '90s. Bistro 3M is thoroughly French, and the food is excellent. **Pros:** spacious lobby with inviting bar, very good restaurants, cheaper weekend rates. **Cons:** some rooms on top floor are smallish, with only one window, others on lower floors have an '80s feel. ⊠ *Maximilianstr. 40* ☎ *0821/50360* ⊕ *www.augsburg.steigenberger. de* 🛏 *106 rooms, 5 suites* 🔑 *In-room: no a/c (some), Wi-Fi. In-hotel: 2 restaurants, bar, laundry service, public Wi-Fi, some pets allowed, no-smoking rooms* 🟰*AE, DC, MC, V.*

$$ **Privat Hotel Riegele.** The hotel is just opposite the main railway station. The tavern-restaurant ($–$$), the Bräustüble, is a local favorite. The food is good German cooking, and the service is efficient and friendly. Public rooms and some bedrooms have plush armchairs, deep-pile rugs, and heavy drapes. Ask for weekend rates. **Pros:** good restaurant, opposite main railway station. **Cons:** chintzy, several floors and some guest rooms need renovating. ✉ *Viktoriastr. 4* ☎ *0821/509–000* 🌐 *www.hotel-riegele.de* *27 rooms, 1 apartment* *In-room: no a/c, Wi-Fi. In-hotel: restaurant, laundry service, public Wi-Fi, some pets allowed, no-smoking rooms* 💳 *AE, DC, MC, V* ⊙ *No dinner Sun.* 🍽 *CP.*

$–$$ ★ **Dom Hotel.** Just around the corner from Augsburg's cathedral, this snug establishment has personality. **TIP→ Ask for one of the attic rooms, where you'll sleep under beam ceilings and wake to a rooftop view of the city.** Or try for one of the rooms on the top floor that have a small terrace facing the cathedral. A garden terrace borders the old city walls, and in summer you'll have your breakfast in the garden under old chestnut trees. **Pros:** family-run with attention paid to details, free Internet in extended lobby, nice view over the city from top rooms. **Cons:** stairs up to entrance, some rooms can only be reached via stairs, no restaurant or bar. ✉ *Frauentorstr. 8* ☎ *0821/343–930* 🌐 *www.dom-hotel-augsburg.de* *44 rooms, 8 suites* *In-room: no a/c, Wi-Fi. In-hotel: room service, pool, gym, parking (no fee), no-smoking rooms* 💳 *AE, DC, MC, V* ⊙ *Closed late Dec.–mid-Jan.* 🍽 *CP.*

$–$$ ★ **Romantikhotel Augsburger Hof.** A preservation order protects the beautiful Renaissance facade of this charming old Augsburg mansion. Rather than remake an old-world atmosphere inside, the owners opted for a cheerful but classic look with natural wood finishes and flowered curtains. The restaurant ($–$$) serves excellent Swabian specialties and international dishes. In season, try the duck. The cathedral is around the corner; the town center is a five-minute stroll awau. **Pros:** welcoming lobby, rooms with a personal touch, good food. **Cons:** rooms at the front are noisy, must book far in advance. ✉ *Auf dem Kreuz 2* ☎ *0821/343–050* 🌐 *www.augsburger-hof.de* *36 rooms* *In-room: no a/c, Wi-Fi. In-hotel: restaurant, bar, laundry service, public Wi-Fi, parking (fee), some pets allowed, no-smoking rooms* 💳 *AE, DC, MC, V* 🍽 *CP.*

$ **Hotel-Garni Schlössle.** From the main railroad station, a 10-minute ride on tram Number 3 to the end of the line at Stadtbergen brings you to this friendly, family-run hotel. Rooms under the steep eaves are particularly cozy. The location offers fresh country air, walks, and sporting facilities (a golf course is within a good tee-shot's range). **Pros:** good value, friendly, family-run. **Cons:** no restaurant or bar, small rooms. ✉ *Bauernstr. 37, Stadtbergen* ☎ *0821/243–930* 📠 *0821/437–451* *14 rooms* *In-room: no a/c. In-hotel: no-smoking rooms* 💳 *MC, V* 🍽 *CP.*

THE ARTS

Augsburg has chamber and symphony orchestras, as well as ballet and opera companies. The city stages a Mozart Festival of international stature in September. The **Kongresshalle** (✉ *Göggingerstr. 10*

☎*0821/324–2348*) presents music and dance performances from September through July.

Augsburg's annual open-air **opera and operetta** (☎*0821/502–070 city tourist office*) season takes place in June and July. Productions move to the romantic inner courtyard of the **Fugger Palace** for part of July and August. Phone the city tourist office for details.

☺ Children love the city's excellent **Augsburger Puppenkiste** (*Puppet theater* ✉*Spitalg. 15, next to Rotes Tor* ☎*0821/4503–450*).

OFF THE BEATEN PATH

Wieskirche. This church—a glorious example of German rococo architecture—stands in an Alpine meadow just off the Romantic Road. In the village of Steingaden (22 km [14 mi] north of Füssen on the B–17), turn east and follow the signs to Wieskirche. Its yellow-and-white walls and steep red roof are set off by the dark backdrop of the Trauchgauer Mountains. The architect Dominicus Zimmermann, former mayor of Landsberg and creator of much of that town's rococo architecture, built the church in 1745 on the spot where six years earlier a local woman claimed to have seen tears running down the face of a picture of Christ. Although the church was dedicated as the Pilgrimage Church of the Scourged Christ, it's now known simply as the Wieskirche (Church of the Meadow). ■TIP→ **Visit it on a bright day if you can, when light streaming through its high windows displays the full glory of the glittering interior.** A complex oval plan is animated by brilliantly colored stuccowork, statues, and gilt. A luminous ceiling fresco completes the decoration. Concerts are presented in the church from the end of June through the beginning of August. Contact the **Pfarramt Wieskirche** (☎*08862/932–930 Pastor's office* ⊕*www.wieskirche.de*) for details. ☜*Free* ☉*Daily 8–dusk*.

TOWARD THE ALPS

South of Augsburg, the Romantic Road climbs gradually into the foothills of the Bavarian Alps, which burst into view between Landsberg and Schongau. The route ends dramatically at the northern wall of the Alps at Füssen, on the Austrian border. Landsberg was founded by the Bavarian ruler Heinrich der Löwe (Henry the Lion) in the 12th century, and grew wealthy from the salt trade. Solid old houses are packed within its turreted walls; the early-18th-century Rathaus is one of the finest in the region.

Schongau has virtually intact wall fortifications, complete with towers and gates. In medieval and Renaissance times the town was an important trading post on the route from Italy to Augsburg. The steeply gabled 16th-century Ballenhaus was a warehouse before it was elevated to the rank of Rathaus. A popular Märchenwald ("fairy-tale forest") lies 1½ km (1 mi) outside Schongau, suitably set in a clearing in the woods. It comes complete with mechanical models of fairy-tale scenes, deer enclosures, and an old-time miniature railway.

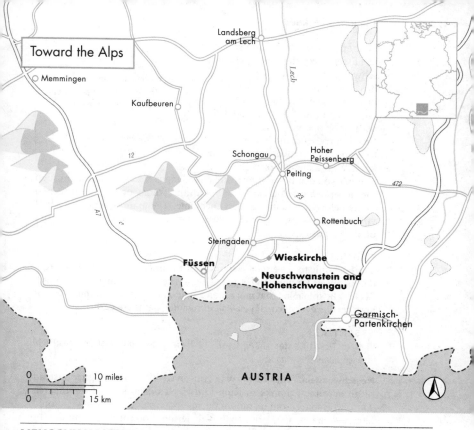

NEUSCHWANSTEIN & HOHENSCHWANGAU

93 km (60 mi) south of Augsburg, 105 km (65 mi) southwest of Munich.

These two famous castles belonging to the Wittelbachs, one historic and the other nearly "make-believe," are 1 km (½ mi) across a valley from each other, near the town of Schwangau. Bavaria's King Ludwig II (1845–86) spent much of his youth at Schloss Hohenschwangau (Hohenschwangau Castle). It's said that its neo-Gothic atmosphere provided the primary influences that shaped his wildly romantic Schloss Neuschwanstein (Neuschwanstein Castle), the fairy-tale castle he built after he became king, which has since become one of Germany's most recognized sights.

GETTING HERE & AROUND

From Schwangau (5 km [3 mi] north of Füssen, 91 km [59 mi] south of Augsburg, 103 km [64 mi] southwest of Munich), follow the road signs marked KÖNIGSCHLÖSSER (King's Castles). After 3 km (2 mi) you come to Hohenschwangau, a small village consisting of a few houses, some good hotels, and five spacious parking lots (parking €4.50). You have to park in one of them and then walk to the ticket center serving both castles. If you are staying in Füssen, take the bus to Hohenschwangau. The clearly marked bus leaves from the train station in Füssen every hour from morning to night, and the cost is €1.60 per person one-way. Tickets are for timed entry, and the average wait to enter Neuschwanstein is one hour. With a deposit or credit-card

number you can book your tickets in advance for either castle through the ticket center. You can change entrance times or cancel up to two hours before the confirmed entrance time. The main street of the small village Hohenschwangau is lined with restaurants and quick eateries of all categories.

TIMING

The best time to see either castle without waiting a long time is a weekday between January and April. The prettiest time, however, is in fall. ■TIP➔ Bear in mind that more than 1 million people pass through one or both castles every year. If you visit in summer, get there early.

ESSENTIALS

Tickets **Ticket Center** (✉Alpseestr. 12 Hohenschwangau ☎08362/930–830 ⊕www.hohenschwangau.de).

Fodor's Choice ★ **Neuschwanstein.** This castle was conceived by a set designer instead of an architect, thanks to King Ludwig II's deep love of the theater. The castle soars from its mountainside like a stage creation—it should hardly come as a surprise that Walt Disney took it as the model for his castle in the movie *Sleeping Beauty* and later for the Disneyland castle itself.

The life of this spectacular castle's king reads like one of the great Gothic mysteries of the 19th century, and the castle symbolizes that life. Yet during the 17 years from the start of Schloss Neuschwanstein's construction until King Ludwig's death, the king spent less than six months in the country residence, and the interior was never finished. The Byzantine-style throne room is without a throne; Ludwig died before one could be installed. However, the walls of the rooms leading to Ludwig's bedroom are painted with murals depicting characters from Wagner's operas—Siegfried and the Nibelungen, Lohengrin, Tristan, and others. Ludwig's bed and its canopy are made of intricately carved oak. A small corridor behind the bedroom was styled as a ghostly grotto, reminiscent of Wagner's *Tannhäuser*. **Castle concerts** (☎08362/81980) are held in September in the gaily decorated minstrels' hall—one room, at least, that was completed as Ludwig conceived it. On the walls outside the castle's gift shop are plans and photos of the castle's construction. There are some spectacular walks around the castle. The delicate **Marienbrücke** (Mary's Bridge) is spun like a medieval maiden's hair across a deep, narrow gorge. From this vantage point there are giddy views of the castle and the great Upper Bavarian Plain beyond.

The Fairy-Tale King

King Ludwig II (1845–86), the enigmatic presence indelibly associated with Bavaria, was one of the last rulers of the Wittelsbach dynasty, which ruled Bavaria from 1180 to 1918. Though his family had created grandiose architecture in Munich, Ludwig II disliked the city and preferred isolation in the countryside, where he constructed monumental edifices born of fanciful imagination, and spent most of the royal purse on his endeavors. Although he was also a great lover of literature, theater, and opera (he was Richard Wagner's great patron), it is his fairy-tale-like castles that are his legacy.

Ludwig II reigned from 1864 to 1886, all the while avoiding political duties whenever possible. By 1878 he had completed his Schloss Linderhof retreat and immediately began Schloss Herrenchiemsee, a tribute to Versailles and Louis XIV (⇨ see Chapter 3). The grandest of his extravagant projects is Neuschwanstein, one of Germany's top attractions and concrete proof of the king's eccentricity. In 1886, before Neuschwanstein was finished, members of the government became convinced that Ludwig had taken leave of his senses. A medical commission declared the king insane and forced him to abdicate. Within two days of incarceration in the Berg Castle, on Starnbergersee (⇨ see Side Trips from Munich in Chapter 2), Ludwig and his doctor were found drowned in the lake's shallow waters. Their deaths are still a mystery.

To reach Neuschwanstein from the ticket center below, take one of the clearly marked paths (about a 40-minute uphill walk) or one of the horse-drawn carriages that leave from Hotel Müller (uphill €5, downhill €2.50). A shuttle bus leaves from the Hotel Lisl (uphill €1.80, downhill €1) and takes you halfway up the hill past an outlook called Aussichtspunkt Jugend to a spot just above the castle. ⚠ **From there it's a steep 10-minute downhill walk to the castle, which is not recommended for the physically handicapped, or a 5-minute uphill walk to the Marienbrücke.** ✉*Neuschwansteinstr. 20* ☎*08362/930–830* ⊕*www. neuschwanstein.de* 🎫*€9, including guided tour; ticket for both castles €17* ☉*Apr.–Sept., daily 8–5; Oct.–Mar., daily 9–3.*

★ **Hohenschwangau.** Built by the knights of Schwangau in the 12th century, this castle was remodeled later by King Ludwig II's father, the Bavarian crown prince (and later king) Maximilian, between 1832 and 1836. Unlike Ludwig's more famous castle across the valley, Neuschwanstein, the somewhat garishly yellow Schloss Hohenschwangau has the feeling of a noble home, where comforts would be valued as much as outward splendor. It was here that the young Ludwig met the composer Richard Wagner. Their friendship shaped and deepened the future king's interest in theater, music, and German mythology—the mythology Wagner drew upon for his *Ring* cycle of operas.

After obtaining your ticket at the ticket center in the village, you can take a 25-minute walk up either of two clearly marked paths to the castle, or board one of the horse-drawn carriages that leave from Hotel Müller (uphill €3.50, downhill €1.50). 🎫*€9, including guided*

tour; ticket for both castles €17
☎ *08362/930–830* ⊕ *www.hohen-*
schwangau.de ⊗ *Apr.–Sept., daily*
8–5; Oct.–Mar., daily 9–3.

WHERE TO STAY

$$ 🏨 **Hotel Müller.** Between the two Schwangau castles, the Müller fits beautifully into the stunning landscape, its creamy Bavarian baroque facade complemented by the green mountain forest. Inside, the baroque influence is everywhere, from the finely furnished bedrooms to the chandelier-hung public rooms and restaurant ($–$$). The mahogany-paneled, glazed veranda (with open fireplace) provides a magnificent view of Hohenschwangau Castle. Round out your day with a local specialty such as the *Allgäuer Lendentopf* (sirloin) served with spaetzle. **Pros:** view of the castles, personalized service, variety of rooms. **Cons:** during the day crowds in and around the hotel, expensive in season. ⊠ *Alpseestr. 16 Hohenschwangau* ☎ *08362/81990* ⊕ *www.hotel-mueller.de* ⬚ *39 rooms, 4 suites* ⬚ *In-room: no a/c. In-hotel: 2 restaurants, bar, public Wi-Fi, parking (no fee), some pets allowed, no-smoking rooms* ⊟ *AE, DC, MC, V* ⊗ *Closed mid–Feb.–late Mar.* ⦿ *CP.*

$$ 🏨 **Schlosshotel Lisl und Jägerhaus.** These jointly run 19th-century properties are across the street from one another, and share views of the nearby castles. The intimate Jägerhaus has five suites and six double rooms, all decorated with floral wallpaper and drapery. The bathrooms have swan-motif golden fixtures. The Lisl's rooms have bright blue carpeting and fabrics. The restaurant, Salon Wittelsbacher ($–$$), provides a view of Neuschwanstein as well as a tasty dish of *Tafelspitz* (boiled beef with horseradish). **Pros:** elegant rooms in the annex Jägerhaus, varied rooms and prices, view of the castles. **Cons:** no breakfast in the Jägerhaus, small lobby. ⊠ *Neuschwansteinstr. 1–3* ☎ *08362/8870* ⊕ *www. lisl.de* ⬚ *42 rooms, 5 suites* ⬚ *In-room: no a/c. In-hotel: 2 restaurants, bar, laundry service, some pets allowed, parking (no fee)* ⊟ *AE, MC, V* ⊗ *Closed Jan.–mid-Feb.*

FÜSSEN

5 km (3 mi) southwest of Schwangau, 110 km (68 mi) south of Munich.

Füssen is beautifully located at the foot of the mountains that separate Bavaria from the Austrian Tyrol. The Lech River, which accompanies much of the final section of the Romantic Road, embraces the town as it rushes northward.

ESSENTIALS

Visitor Information Füssen (⊠ *Tourismus und Marketing, Kaiser-Maximilian-Pl. 1* ☎ *08362/93850* ⊕ *www.fuessen.de*).

EXPLORING

The town's **Hohes Schloss** *(High Castle)* is one of the best-preserved late-Gothic castles in Germany. It was built on the site of the Roman fortress that once guarded this Alpine section of the Via Claudia, the trade route from Rome to the Danube. Evidence of Roman occupation of the area has been uncovered at the foot of the nearby Tegelberg Mountain, and the **excavations** next to the Tegelberg cable-car station are open for visits daily. The Hohes Schloss was the seat of Bavarian rulers before Emperor Heinrich VII mortgaged it and the rest of the town to the bishop of Augsburg for 400 pieces of silver. The mortgage was never redeemed, and Füssen remained the property of the Augsburg episcopate until secularization in the early 19th century. The bishops of Augsburg used the castle as their summer Alpine residence. It has a spectacular 16th-century **Rittersaal** (Knights' Hall) with a carved ceiling, and a princes' chamber with a Gothic tile stove. ⊠ *Magnuspl. 10* ☎ *08362/940–162* ☑ *€2.50* ☉ *Apr.–Oct., Tues.–Sun. 11–4; Nov.– Mar., Tues.–Sun. 2–4.*

The summer presence of the bishops of Augsburg ensured that Füssen received an impressive number of baroque and rococo churches. Füssen's **Rathaus** was once a Benedictine abbey, built in the 9th century at the site of the grave of St. Magnus, who spent most of his life ministering in the area. A Romanesque crypt beneath the baroque abbey church has a partially preserved 10th-century fresco, the oldest in Bavaria. In summer, chamber concerts are held in the high-ceiling baroque splendor of the former abbey's **Fürstensaal** (Princes' Hall). Program details are available from the tourist office. ⊠ *Lechalde 3.*

Füssen's main shopping street, called **Reichenstrasse,** was, like Augsburg's Maximilianstrasse, once part of the Roman Via Claudia. This cobblestone walkway is lined with high-gabled medieval houses and backed by the bulwarks of the castle and the easternmost buttresses of the Allgäu Alps.

WHERE TO STAY & EAT

¢ ✕ **Markthalle.** This is a farmers' market where you can grab a quick bite and drink at very reasonable prices. Try the fish soup. The building started in 1483 as the *Kornhaus* (grain storage) and then became the *Feuerhaus* (fire station). ⊠ *Schrannenpl. 1* ➡ *No credit cards* ☉ *Closed Sun. No dinner Sat.*

$–$$ 🏨 **Hotel Hirsch.** A mother-and-daughter team provides friendly service at this traditional Füssen hotel. Outside the majestic building is its trademark stag (*Hirsch* in German); inside, the decor is Bavarian. You can stay in the King Ludwig room with his pictures on the walls and books about him to read, or stay with King Maximilian or with Spitzweg, a famous German artist who painted in Füssen. Both restaurants ($–$$) serve an interesting variety of seasonal and local specialties. In season, try venison or wild duck with blue cabbage and dumpling. If it's on the menu, the trout is excellent, as it comes fresh from the local rivers. **Pros:** in the center of town, choice of eclectic rooms, good restaurant. **Cons:** front rooms noisy, modern lobby. ⊠*Kaiser-Maximilian-Pl. 7* ☎*08362/93980* ⊕*www.hotelhirsch.de* ⇆*53 rooms* ♿*In-room: no a/c. In-hotel: 2 restaurants, bar, parking (no fee), some pets allowed, no-smoking rooms* ⊟*AE, DC, MC, V* ⊘*Closed Jan.* ⦿CP.

$ 🏨**Altstadthotel Zum Hechten.** Geraniums flower most of the year on this comfortable inn's balconies. It's one of the town's oldest lodgings, and is directly below the castle. In one of the two restaurants (¢–$), which have sturdy, round tables and colorfully frescoed walls, vegetarian meals are served. **Pros:** in the center of town, good value, nice restaurant. **Cons:** no elevator, somewhat difficult stairs, some rooms noisy. ⊠*Ritterstr. 6* ☎*08362/91600* ⊕*www.hotel-hechten.com* ⇆*36 rooms* ♿*In-room: no a/c, Wi-Fi (some). In-hotel: 2 restaurants, public Wi-Fi, parking (no fee), some pets allowed, no smoking rooms* ⊟*AE, MC, V* ⦿*CP.*

Franconia & the German Danube

WORD OF MOUTH

"I've been spending some time lately in Nürnberg and have started to really prefer it to Würzburg or Heidelberg. On my first visit, I wasn't initially impressed with Nürnberg, but we day tripped in on that trip. There are a lot of little nooks and crannies in Nürnberg and each time I find something different to explore. I really like the accessibility from the Altstadt to the Hauptbahnhof which makes connections to FRA very easy. I typically stay at Le Meridien right outside of the Altstadt and across from the Hauptbahnhof."

—LoriS

Updated by
Uli Ehrhardt

ALL THAT IS LEFT OF THE HUGE, ANCIENT KINGDOM of the Franks is the region known today as Franken (Franconia), stretching from the Bohemian Forest on the Czech border to the outskirts of Frankfurt. The Franks were not only tough warriors but also hard workers, sharp tradespeople, and burghers with a good political nose. The name *frank* means bold, wild, and courageous in the old Frankish tongue. It was only in the early 19th century, following Napoléon's conquest of what is now southern Germany, that the area was incorporated into northern Bavaria.

Although many proud Franconians would dispute it, this historic homeland of the Franks, one of the oldest Germanic peoples, is now unmistakably part of Bavaria. Franconian towns such as Bayreuth, Coburg, and Bamberg are practically places of cultural pilgrimage. Rebuilt Nürnberg (Nuremberg in English) is the epitome of German medieval beauty, though its name recalls both the Third Reich's huge rallies at the Zeppelinfeld and its henchmen's trials held in the city between 1945 and 1950.

Franconia is hardly an overrun tourist destination, yet its long and rich history, its landscapes and leisure activities (including skiing, golfing, hiking, and cycling), and its gastronomic specialties place it high on the enjoyment scale.

ORIENTATION & PLANNING

GETTING ORIENTED

Franconia's northern border is marked by the Main River, which is seen as the dividing line between northern and southern Germany. Its southern border is the Danube, where Lower Bavaria (Niederbayern) begins. Despite its extensive geographic spread, however, Franconia is a homogeneous region of rolling agricultural landscapes and thick forests climbing the mountains of the Fichtelgebirge. Nürnberg is a major destination in the area, and the towns of Bayreuth, Coburg, and Bamberg are an easy day trip from one another.

The Danube River passes through the Bavarian Forest on its way from Germany to Austria. West of Regensburg, river cruises and cyclists follow its path.

Northern Franconia. As one of the few towns not destroyed by World War II, Bamberg lives and breathes German history. Wagner fans flock to Bayreuth in July and August for the classical music festival. The beer produced in Kulmbach and Kronach is a major draw.

Nürnberg (Nuremberg). It may not be as well known as Munich, Heidelberg, or Berlin, but when you visit Nuremberg you feel the wealth, power, and sway this city has had through the centuries. Standing on the ramparts of the Kaiserburg *(Imperial Castle)* and looking down on the city, you'll begin to understand why emperors made Nuremberg their home.

TOP REASONS TO GO

A Living Altstadt: This one isn't just for the tourists. Bamberg may be a UNESCO World Heritage Site, but it's also a vibrant town living very much in the present.

The Fortress at Nürnberg: Holy Roman emperors once resided in the vast complex of the Kaiserburg, which has fabulous views over the entire city.

The Bridge in Regensburg: The Golden Gate Bridge may be better known today, but the 12th-century Steinerne Brücke (Stone Bridge) was its match in terms of engineering ingenuity and importance in its day.

"God's Ballroom": Vierzehnheiligen, a church on the Main north of Bamberg, is spectacular both inside and out. Fourteen columns, commemorating a vision of Christ and 14 saints, preside over the scene of swirling rococo decoration and light that earned it the nickname "God's Ballroom."

An Organ Concert in Passau: St. Stephan's Cathedral has the largest church organ in the world: 17,774 pipes all told. You can listen to the mighty sound they create at weekday concerts.

The German Danube. Regensburg and Passau are two relatively forgotten cities tucked away in the southeast corner of Germany in an area bordered by Austria and the Czech Republic. Passau is one of the oldest cities on German soil, built by the Celts and then ruled by the Romans two thousand years ago. Regensburg is a bit younger; about a thousand years ago it was one of the largest and most affluent cities in Germany.

FRANCONIA & THE GERMAN DANUBE PLANNER

WHEN TO GO

Summer is the best time to explore Franconia, though spring and fall are also fine when the weather cooperates. Avoid the cold and wet months from November to March; many hotels and restaurants close, and no matter how pretty, many towns do seem quite dreary. If you're in Nürnberg in December, you're in time for one of Germany's largest and loveliest Christmas markets. Unless you plan on attending the Wagner Festival in Bayreuth, it's best to avoid this city in July and August.

GETTING HERE & AROUND

BY AIR The major international airport serving Franconia and the German Danube is Munich. A regional airport is Nürnberg.

BY CAR Franconia is served by five main autobahns: A–7 from Hamburg, A–3 from Köln and Frankfurt, A–81 from Stuttgart, A–6 from Heilbronn, and A–9 from Munich. Nürnberg is 167 km (104 mi) north of Munich and 222 km (138 mi) southeast of Frankfurt. Regensburg and Passau are reached by way of the A–3 from Nürnberg.

Nürnberg is a stop on the high-speed InterCity Express north–south routes, and there are hourly trains from Munich direct to Nürnberg. Regular InterCity services connect Nürnberg and Regensburg with Frankfurt and other major German cities. Trains run hourly from Frankfurt to Munich, with a stop at Nürnberg. The trip takes about three hours to Munich, two hours to Nürnberg. There are hourly trains from Munich to Regensburg.

Some InterCity trains stop in Bamberg, which is most speedily reached from Munich. Local trains from Nürnberg connect with Bayreuth and areas of southern Franconia. Regensburg and Passau are on the ICE line from Nürnberg to Vienna.

ESSENTIALS

Airport Information Airport Nürnberg (⊠ *Flughafenstr. 100D-90411* ☎ *0911/93700* ⊕ *www.airport-nuernberg.de*).

Visitor Information Franconia Tourist Board (⊠ *Tourismusverband Franken e.V., Wilhelminenstr. 6Nürnberg* ☎ *0911/941–510*).

ABOUT THE RESTAURANTS & HOTELS

Many restaurants in the rural parts of this region serve hot meals only between 11:30 AM and 2 PM, and 6 PM and 9 PM. ■TIP→ ***Durchgehend warme Küche* means that hot meals are also served between lunch and dinner.**

Make reservations well in advance for hotels in all the larger towns and cities if you plan to visit anytime between June and September. During the Nürnberg Toy Fair at the beginning of February, rooms are rare and at a premium. If you're visiting Bayreuth during the annual Wagner Festival in July and August, consider making reservations up to a year in advance. Remember, too, that during the festival prices can be double the normal rates.

WHAT IT COSTS IN EUROS					
	¢	$	$$	$$$	$$$$
RESTAURANTS	under €9	€9–€15	€16–€20	€21–€25	over €25
HOTELS	under €50	€50–€100	€101–€175	€176–€225	over €225

Restaurant prices are per person for a main course at dinner. Hotel prices are for two people in a standard double room, including tax and service.

PLANNING YOUR TIME

Nürnberg warrants at least a day of your time. It's best to base yourself in one city and take day trips to others. Bamberg is the most central of the northern Franconia cities and makes a good base. It is also a good idea to leave your car at your hotel and make the trip downstream to Regensburg or Passau by boat, returning by train.

NORTHERN FRANCONIA

Three major German cultural centers lie within easy reach of one another: Coburg, a town with blood links to royal dynasties throughout Europe; Bamberg, with its own claim to German royal history and an Old Town area designated a UNESCO World Heritage Site; and Bayreuth, where composer Richard Wagner finally settled, making it a place of musical pilgrimage for Wagner fans from all over the world.

COBURG

105 km (65 mi) north of Nürnberg.

Coburg is a surprisingly little-known treasure that was founded in the 11th century and remained in the possession of the dukes of Saxe-Coburg-Gotha until 1918; the present duke still lives here. The remarkable Saxe-Coburg dynasty established itself as something of a royal stud farm, providing a seemingly inexhaustible supply of blue-blood marriage partners to ruling houses the length and breadth of Europe. The most famous of these royal mates was Prince Albert (1819–61), who married the English Queen Victoria, after which she gained special renown in Coburg. Their numerous children, married off to other kings, queens, and emperors, helped to spread the tried-and-tested Saxe-Coburg stock even farther afield. Despite all the history that sweats from each sandstone ashlar, Coburg is a modern and bustling town.

ESSENTIALS

Visitor Information Coburg (✉ *Tourismus Coburg, Herrng. 4* ☎ *09561/74180* ⊕ *www.coburg-tourist.de*).

★ The **Veste Coburg** fortress, one of the largest and most impressive in the country, is Coburg's main attraction. The brooding bulk of the castle guards the town from a 1,484-foot hill. Construction began around 1055, but with progressive rebuilding and remodeling today's predominantly late-Gothic–early-Renaissance edifice bears little resemblance to the original crude fortress. One part of the castle harbors the **Kunstsammlungen,** a grand set of collections including art, with works by Dürer, Cranach, and Hans Holbein, among others; sculpture from the school of the great Tilman Riemenschneider (1460–1531); furniture and textiles; magnificent weapons, armor, and tournament garb spanning four centuries (in the so-called **Herzogin-bau,** or Duchess's Building); carriages and ornate sleighs; and more. The room where Martin Luther lived for six months in 1530 while he observed the goings-on of the Augsburg Diet has an especially dignified atmosphere. The **Jagdintarsien-Zimmer** (Hunting Marquetry Room), an elaborately decorated room that dates back to the early 17th century, has some of the finest woodwork in southern Germany. Finally, there's the **Carl-Eduard-Bau** (Carl-Eduard Building), which contains a valuable antique glass collection, mostly from the baroque age. Inquire at the ticket office for tours and reduced family tick-

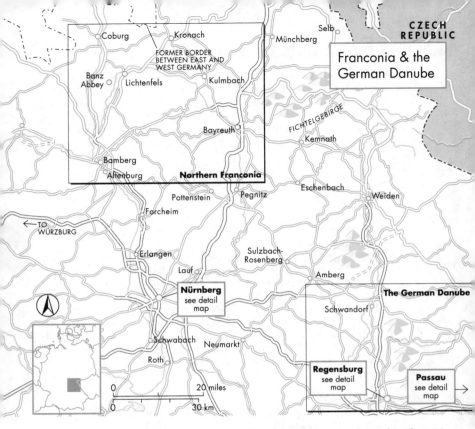

ets. ☎ 09561/8790 ⊕ *www.kunstsammlungen-coburg.de* 🖃 €3.30
⊗ *Museums Apr.–Oct., daily 10–5; Nov.–Mar., Tues.–Sun. 1–4.*

NEED A BREAK?

Relax and soak up centuries of history while sampling a Coburg beer at the Burgschänke (✉ *Veste Coburg* ☎ 09561/80980), Veste Coburg's own tavern. The basic menu has traditional dishes. The tavern is closed Monday and January–mid-February.

Coburg's **Marktplatz** *(Market Square)* has a statue of Prince Albert, Victoria's high-minded consort, standing proudly surrounded by gracious Renaissance and baroque buildings. The **Stadhaus,** former seat of the local dukes, begun in 1500, is the most imposing structure here. A forest of ornate gables and spires projects from its well-proportioned facade. Opposite is the **Rathaus** (Town Hall). ■ TIP→ **Look on the building's tympanum for the statue of the Bratwurstmännla (it's actually St. Mauritius in armor); the staff he carries is said to be the official length against which the town's famous bratwursts are measured.** These tasty sausages, roasted on pinecone fires, are available on the market square.

Prince Albert spent much of his childhood in **Schloss Ehrenburg,** the ducal palace. Built in the mid-16th century, it has been greatly altered over the years, principally following a fire in the early 19th century. Duke

Ernst I invited Karl Friedrich Schinkel from Berlin to redo the palace in the then-popular Gothic style. Some of the original Renaissance features were kept. The rooms of the castle are quite special, especially those upstairs, where the ceilings are heavily decorated with stucco and the floors have wonderful patterns of various woods. The Hall of Giants is named for the larger-than-life caryatids that support the ceiling; the favorite sight downstairs is Queen Victoria's flush toilet, which was the first one installed in Germany. Here, too, the ceiling is worth noting for its playful, gentle stuccowork. The baroque chapel attached to Ehrenburg is often used for weddings. ⊠*Schlosspl.* ☎*09561/80880* ⊕*www.sgvcoburg.de* 🎫*€4* ⊗*Tour Tues.–Sun. 10–3 on the hr.*

Perched on a hill 5 km (3 mi) west of Coburg is **Schloss Callenberg,** until 1231 the main castle of the Knights of Callenberg. In the 16th century it was taken over by the Coburgs. From 1842 on it served as the summer residence of the hereditary Coburg prince and later Duke Ernst II. It holds a number of important collections, including that of the Windsor gallery; arts and crafts from Holland, Germany, and Italy from the Renaissance to the 19th century; precious baroque, Empire, and Biedermeier furniture; table and standing clocks from three centuries; a selection of weapons; and various handicrafts. The best way to reach the castle is by car via Baiersdorf or by Bus 5 from the Marktplatz. ⊠*Callenberg* ☎*09561/55150* ⊕*www.schloss-callenberg.de* 🎫*€4* ⊗*Daily 11–5.*

WHERE TO EAT

¢–$ ✕**Ratskeller.** The local specialties taste better here beneath the old vaults and within earshot of the Coburg marketplace. Try the sauerbraten, along with a glass of crisp Franconian white wine. The prices become a little higher in the evening, and the menu adds a few more dishes. ⊠*Markt 1* ☎*09561/92400* ▤*No credit cards.*

WHERE TO STAY

¢–$ 🏨**Goldene Rose.** One of the region's oldest, this agreeable inn is located about 5 km (3 mi) southeast of Coburg. The interior has simple wooden paneling and floors. On a warm summer evening, however, the beer garden (¢–$) is the best place to enjoy traditional Franconian dishes, or a plate of homemade sausages, and meet some of the locals. Rooms are well appointed and comfortable—the wooden theme is continued, but the style is definitely modern. **Pros:** friendly, family run, very good value, large parking lot behind the hotel. **Cons:** in a small village, front rooms noisy. ⊠*Coburgerstr. 31, Grub am Forst* ☎*09560/92250* ⊕*www.goldene-rose.de* ⇆*14 rooms* ♻*In-room: no a/c, Wi-Fi. In-hotel: restaurant, public Wi-Fi, parking (fee), no-smoking rooms* ▤*MC, V* ⊗*Restaurant closed Mon.* ⦿*BP.*

$$ 🏨**Romantic Hotel Goldene Traube.** The first guests were welcomed to this hotel in 1756. Rooms are individually decorated, and for dining you can choose between the elegant restaurant Meer und Mehr (The Sea and More) or the cozy Weinstüble. After a day of sightseeing, relax in the sauna complex with solarium or with one of the vintages from the small wine boutique just opposite the reception. **Pros:** welcoming spacious lobby, two good restaurants, center of town, nice small wine

shop. **Cons:** traffic noise in front rooms, stairs up to the lobby. ✉*Am Viktoriabrunnen 2* ☎*09561/8760* ⊕*www.goldenetraube.com* ➫*72 rooms, 1 suite* ♿*In-room: no a/c. In-hotel: restaurant, bar, gym, bicycles, public Wi-Fi, parking (fee), some pets allowed, no-smoking rooms* ⊟*AE, DC, MC, V* ⊗*BP.*

$–$$　🏨 **Tulip Inn Coburg.** You can expect modern, clean, well-designed rooms that are airy and functional at the Tulip Inn. This link in the Tulip Inn chain is about 20 minutes, on foot, east of Coburg's center. **Pros:** renovated in 2007, modern 3-star business hotel, easy access, free parking and garage. **Cons:** modern 3-star business hotel, edge of town, surrounded by garages and shopping outlets. ✉*Ketschendorfer Str. 86* ☎*09561/8210* ⊕ *www.goldentulip.com* ➫*123 rooms* ♿*In-room: no a/c, Wi-Fi (some). In-hotel: laundry service, public Wi-Fi, parking (fee), some pets allowed, no-smoking rooms* ⊟*AE, DC, MC, V* ⊗*BP.*

FESTIVALS

Coburg's **Brazilian Samba Festival** is a three-day bacchanal held in mid-July. Check the Coburg tourist office's Web site for this and other events.

SHOPPING

■**TIP**➔ **Coburg is full of culinary delights; its** *Schmätzen* **(gingerbread) and** *Elizenkuchen* **(almond cake) are famous.** You'll find home-baked versions in any of the many excellent **patisseries** or at a Grossman store (there are three in Coburg). Rödental, northeast of Coburg, is the home of the world-famous M. I. Hummel figurines, made by the Göbel porcelain manufacturer. There's a **Hummel Museum** (✉*Coburgerstr. 7, Rödental* ☎*09563/92303* ⊕*www.goebel.de*) devoted to them, and 18th- and 19th-century porcelain from other manufacturers. The museum is open weekdays 9–5 and Saturday 9–noon. Besides the museum's store, there are several retail outlets in the village.

KRONACH

23 km (15 mi) east of Coburg, 120 km (74 mi) north of Nürnberg.

Kronach is a charming little gateway to the natural splendor of the Frankenwald region.

ESSENTIALS

Visitor Information **Kronach**(✉*Tourismus Kronach, Marktpl.* ☎*09261/97236* ⊕*www.kronach.de*).

EXPLORING

In its old medieval section, the **Obere Stadt** *(Upper Town)*, harmonious sandstone houses are surrounded by old walls and surmounted by a majestic fortress. Kronach is best known as the birthplace of Renaissance painter Lucas Cranach the Elder (1472–1553), but there's a running argument as to which house he was born in—Am Marktplatz 1 or in the house called Am Scharfen Eck, at Lucas-Cranach-Strasse 38. The latter was for more than a hundred years a meeting place for locals, where they had their beer and where today you can enjoy a very good, inexpensive Franconian meal. ■**TIP**➔ **On the last weekend in June, Kro-**

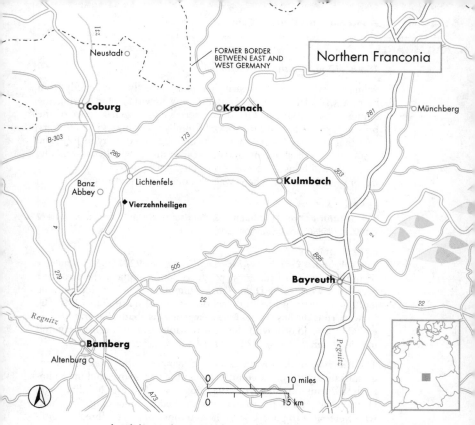

nach celebrates its past with a medieval festival featuring authentic garb, food, and troubadours.

Fodor'sChoice ★ **Festung Rosenberg** *(Rosenberg Fortress)* is a few minutes' walk from the town center. As you stand below its mighty walls it's easy to see why it was never taken by enemy forces. During World War I it served as a POW camp, with no less a figure than Charles de Gaulle as a "guest." Today Rosenberg houses a youth hostel and, more importantly, the **Fränkische Galerie** (the Franconian Gallery), an extension of the Bavarian National Museum in Munich, featuring paintings and sculpted works from the Middle Ages and the Renaissance. Lucas Cranach the Elder and Tilman Riemenschneider are represented, as well as artists from the Dürer School and the Bamberg School. In July and August the central courtyard is an atmospheric backdrop for performances of Goethe's *Faust*. The grounds of the fortress are also used by wood sculptors in the summer. ☎09261/60410 ⊕*www.kronach.de* 💷€3.50 ☉*Fortress Apr.–Oct., Tues.–Sun. 9:30–5:30; Nov.–Mar., Tues.–Sun. 10–2.*

KULMBACH

19 km (12 mi) southeast of Kronach.

A quarter of Kulmbachers earn their living directly or indirectly from beer. A special local brew available only in winter and during the Lenten season is *Eisbock*, a dark beer that is frozen as part of the brewing process to make it stronger. Kulmbach celebrates its beer every year in a nine-day festival that starts on the last Saturday in July. The main festival site, a mammoth tent, is called the *Festspulhaus*—literally, "festival swill house"—a none-too-subtle dig at nearby Bayreuth and its tony *Festspielhaus*, where Wagner's operas are performed.

ESSENTIALS

Visitor Information **Kulmbach** (⊠ *Tourismusservice, Stadthalle, Sutte 2* ☏ *09221/95880* ⊕ *www.kulmbach.de).*

EXPLORING

The **Kulmbacher Brewery** (⊠ *Lichtenfelserstr.* ☏ *09221/7050*), a merger of four Kulmbach breweries, produces among others the strongest beer in the world—the *Doppelbock* Kulminator 28—which takes nine months to brew and has an alcohol content of more than 11%. The brewery runs the **Bayerisches Brauereimuseum Kulmbach** *(Bavarian Brewery Museum)* jointly with the nearby Mönchshof-Bräu brewery and inn. ⊠ *Hoferstr. 20* ☏ *09221/ 80514* ⛁ *€5* ⊘ *Tues.–Sun. 10–5.*

⟳ The **Plassenburg,** the town's castle and symbol, is the most important Renaissance castle in the country. It stands on a rise overlooking Kulmbach, a 20-minute hike from the Old Town. The first building here, begun in the mid-12th century, was torched by marauding Bavarians who were eager to put a stop to the ambitions of Duke Albrecht Alcibiades—a man who spent several years murdering, plundering, and pillaging his way through Franconia. His successors built today's castle, starting in about 1560. Externally, there's little to suggest the graceful Renaissance interior, but as you enter the main courtyard the scene changes abruptly. The tiered space of the courtyard is covered with precisely carved figures, medallions, and other intricate ornaments, the whole comprising one of the most remarkable and delicate architectural ensembles in Europe. Inside, the **Deutsches Zinnfigurenmuseum** (Tin Figures Museum), with more than 300,000 miniature statuettes and tin soldiers, holds the largest collection of its kind in the world. The figures are arranged in scenes from all periods of history. During the day you cannot drive up to the castle. There is a shuttle bus that leaves from the main square every half hour from 9 to 6; cost is €2.20. ☏ *09221/947–505* ⛁ *€4* ⊘ *Apr.–Oct., daily 9–6; Nov.–Mar. 10–4.*

OFF THE BEATEN PATH

Neuenmarkt. In this "railway village" near Kulmbach, more than 25 beautifully preserved gleaming locomotives huff and puff in a living railroad museum. Every now and then a nostalgic train will take you to the Brewery Museum in Kulmbach. Or you can enjoy a round trip to ⟳ Marktschorgast that takes you up the very steep "schiefe Ebene" stretch (literally, slanting level). The museum also has model trains set up in incredibly detailed replicas of landscapes. ⊠ *Birkenstr. 5* ☏ *09227/5700*

⊕ *www.dampflokmuseum.de* ✉ *€5*
🕐 *Tues.–Sun. 10–5.*

WHERE TO STAY

$–$$ 🏨 **Hotel Kronprinz.** This old hotel tucked away in the middle of Kulmbach's Old Town, right in the shadow of Plassenburg Castle, covers all basic needs, though the furnishings are somewhat bland except in the higher-priced rooms. The café serves snacks and cakes. **Pros:** center of town, excellent cakes in café, 3 nice rooms in annex. **Cons:** simple rooms on top of café, no elevator. ✉ *Fischerg. 4–6* ☎ *09221/92180* ⊕ *www.kronprinz-kulmbach.de* 💬 *22 rooms* ⚡ *In-room: no a/c. In-hotel: restaurant, bar, no-smoking rooms* 🕐 *Closed Dec. 24–29* 🍴 *AE, DC, MC, V* 🍽 *BP.*

> ### KULMBACH BREWS
>
> In a country where brewing and beer drinking break all records, Kulmbach produces more beer per capita than anywhere else: 9,000 pints for each man, woman, and child. The locals claim it's the sparkling-clear springwater from the nearby Fichtelgebirge hills that makes their beer so special.

BAYREUTH

24 km (15 mi) south of Kulmbach, 80 km (50 mi) northeast of Nürnberg.

The small town of Bayreuth, pronounced "bye-*roit*," owes its fame to the music giant Richard Wagner (1813–83). The 19th-century composer and musical revolutionary finally settled here after a lifetime of rootless shifting through Europe. Here he built his great theater, the Festspielhaus, as a suitable setting for his grand operas on Germanic mythological themes. The annual Wagner Festival dates to 1876, and brings droves of Wagner fans who push prices sky-high, fill hotels to bursting, and earn themselves much-sought-after social kudos in the process. The festival is held from late July until late August, so unless you plan to visit the town specifically for it, this is the time to stay away.

GETTING HERE & AROUND

To reach Bayreuth, take the Bayreuth exit off the Nürnberg-Berlin autobahn. It is 1½ hours north of Nuremberg. The train trip is an hour from Nürnberg. In town you can reach most points on foot.

Bayreuth offers walking tours beginning at Luitpoldplatz at 10:30 daily from May to October for €5.50.

ESSENTIALS

Visitor Information Bayreuth (✉ *,Kongress- und Tourismuszentrale Luitpoldpl. 9* ☎ *0921/88588* ⊕ *www.bayreuth.de*).

EXPLORING

★ The **Neues Schloss** *(New Palace)* is a glamorous 18th-century palace built by the Margravine Wilhelmine, sister of Frederick the Great of Prussia and a woman of enormous energy and decided tastes. Though Wagner is the man most closely associated with Bayreuth, his choice of this setting is largely due to the work of this woman, who lived 100 years before him. Wilhelmine devoured books, wrote plays and operas (which she directed and, of course, acted in), and had buildings constructed, transforming much of the town and bringing it near bankruptcy. Her distinctive touch is evident at the palace, built when a mysterious fire conveniently destroyed parts of the original one. Anyone with a taste for the wilder flights of rococo decoration will love it. Some rooms have been given over to one of Europe's finest collections of faience. ⊠*Ludwigstr. 21* ☎*0921/759–6921* ☜*€4* ☺*Apr.–Sept., daily 9–6; Oct.–Mar., Tues.–Sun. 10–4.*

Another great architectural legacy of Wilhelmine is the **Markgräfliches Opernhaus** *(Margravial Opera House)*. Built between 1745 and 1748, it is a rococo jewel, sumptuously decorated in red, gold, and blue. Apollo and the nine Muses cavort across the frescoed ceiling. It was this delicate 500-seat theater that originally drew Wagner to Bayreuth; he felt that it might prove a suitable setting for his own operas. It's a wonderful setting for the concerts and operas of Bayreuth's "other" musical festivals, which in fact go on virtually throughout the year. Visitors are treated to a sound-and-light show. ⊠*Opernstr.* ☎*0921/759–6922* ☜*€5* ☺*Apr.–Sept., daily 9–5; Oct.–Mar., daily 10–3. Sound-and-light shows daily in opera house every 45 min starting at 9:15 in summer and 10:15 in winter. Closed during performances and on rehearsal days.*

Near the center of town, in the 1887 Maisel Brewery building, the **Brauerei und Büttnerei-Museum** *(Brewery and Coopers Museum)* reveals the tradition of the brewing trade over the past two centuries with a focus on the Maisel's trade, of course. The brewery operated here until 1981, when its much bigger home was completed next door. ■TIP➔ **After the 60-minute tour you can quaff a cool, freshly tapped beer in the museum's pub, which has traditional Bavarian Weissbier (wheat beer).** ⊠*Kulmbacherstr. 40* ☎*0921/401–234* ⊕*www.maisel.com* ☜*€4* ☺*Tour daily at 2* PM; *individual tours by prior arrangement.*

The **Altes Schloss Eremitage**, 5 km (3 mi) north of Bayreuth on B–85, makes an appealing departure from the sonorous and austere Wagnerian mood of much of the town. It's an early-18th-century palace, built as a summer retreat and remodeled in 1740 by the Margravine Wilhelmine. Although her taste is not much in evidence in the drab exterior, the interior, alive with light and color, displays her guiding hand in every elegant line. The extraordinary **Japanischer Saal** (Japanese Room), filled with Asian treasures and chinoiserie furniture, is the finest room. The park and gardens, partly formal, partly natural, are enjoyable for idle strolling. Fountain displays take place at the two fake grottoes at the top of the hour 10–5 daily. ☎*0921/759–6937* ☜*Schloss €3, park free* ☺*Schloss Apr.–Sept., daily 9–6.*

WAGNER IN BAYREUTH

The **Festspielhaus** *(Festival Theater)* is by no means beautiful. In fact, this high temple of the Wagner cult is surprisingly plain. The spartan look is explained partly by Wagner's desire to achieve perfect acoustics. The wood seats have no upholstering, for example, and the walls are bare.

The stage is enormous, capable of holding the huge casts required for Wagner's largest operas. Performances take place only during the annual Wagner Festival, still masterminded by descendants of the composer. ⊠ *Festspielhügel 1* ☎ *0921/78780* ⊒ *€5* ☉ *Tour Dec.–Oct., Tues.–Sun. at 10, 2, and 3. Closed during rehearsals and afternoons during festival.*

"Wahnfried," built by Wagner in 1874 and the only house he ever owned, is now the **Richard-Wagner-Museum**. It's a simple, austere neoclassical building whose name, "peace from madness," was well earned. Wagner lived here with his wife Cosima, daughter of pianist Franz Liszt, and they were both laid to rest here. King Ludwig II of Bavaria, the young and impressionable "Fairy-Tale King" who gave Wagner so much financial support, is remembered in a bust before the entrance. The exhibits, arranged along a well-marked tour through the house, require a great deal of German-language reading, but it's a must for Wagner fans. The original scores of such masterpieces as *Parsifal, Tristan und Isolde, Lohengrin, Der Fliegende Holländer,* and *Götterdämmerung* are on display. You can also see designs for productions of his operas, as well as his piano and huge library. A multimedia display lets you watch and listen to various productions of his operas. The little house where Franz Liszt lived and died is right next door and can be visited with your Richard-Wagner-Museum ticket, but be sure to express your interest in advance. It, too, is heavy on the paper, but the last rooms—with pictures, photos, and silhouettes of the master, his students, acolytes, and friends—are well worth the detour. ⊠ *Richard-Wagner-Str. 48* ☎ *0921/757–2816* ⊕ *www.wagnermuseum.de* ⊒ *€4, during festival €4.50* ☉ *Apr.–Oct., daily 9–5; Nov.–Mar., daily 10–5.*

WHERE TO EAT

¢–$ ✗**Oskar.** A huge glass ceiling gives the large dining room a light atmosphere even in winter. In summer, try for a table in the beer garden to ★ enjoy fine Franconian specialties and continental dishes. The kitchen uses the freshest produce. The room fills up at night and during Sunday brunch, especially if a jazz band is playing in one of the alcoves. ⊠ *Maximilianstr. 33* ☎ *0921/516–0553* ⊟ *No credit cards.*

¢–$ ✗**Wolffenzacher.** This self-described "nostalgic inn" harks back to the days when the local *Wirtshaus* (inn-pub) was the meeting place for everyone from the mayor's scribes to the local carpenters. Beer and hearty food are shared at wooden tables either in the rustic interior or out in the shady beer garden (in the middle of town), weather permitting. The hearty Franconian specialties are counterbalanced by a few lighter French and Italian dishes. ⊠ *Sternenpl. 5* ☎ *0921/64552* ⊟ *MC, V.*

EATING WELL IN FRANCONIA

Franconia is known for its good and filling food and for its simple and atmospheric *Gasthäuser.* Pork is a staple, served either as *Schweinsbraten* (a plain roast) or with *Knödel* (dumplings made from either bread or potatoes). The specialties in Nürnberg, Coburg, and Regensburg are the Bratwürste—short, spiced sausages. The Nürnberg variety is known all over Germany; they are even on the menu on the ICE trains. You can have them grilled or heated in a stock of onions and wine (*saurer Zipfel*).

On the sweet side, try the *Dampfnudel,* a kind of sweet yeast-dough dumpling that is tasty and filling. Loved all over Germany, especially at Christmas time, is *Nürnberger Lebkuchen,* a sort of gingerbread.

Not to be missed are Franconia's liquid refreshments from both the grape and the grain. Franconian wines, usually white and sold in distinctive flagons called *Bocksbeutel,* are renowned for their special bouquet (Silvaner is the traditional grape). The region has the largest concentration of local breweries in the world (Bamberg alone has 10, Bayreuth 7), producing a wide range of brews, the most distinctive of which is the dark, smoky *Rauchbier* and the even darker and stronger *Schwärzla.* Then of course there is Kulmbach, with the strongest beer in the world—the *Doppelbock Kulminator 28*—which takes nine months to brew and has an alcohol content of more than 11%.

WHERE TO STAY

$$–$$$ ★ **Schlosshotel Thiergarten.** Staying at this 250-year-old former hunting lodge is like being at your favorite aunt's, if she's an elderly millionaire. Rooms are individually furnished and have a plush, lived-in feel. The intimate Kaminhalle, with an ornate fireplace, and the Venezianischer Salon, dominated by a glittering 300-year-old Venetian chandelier, offer regional and international cuisine ($$–$$$). The fabulous setting may outshine the food, but dining here you will feel a bit like royalty yourself. The hotel is 8 km (5 mi) from Bayreuth in the Thiergarten suburb. **Pros:** elegant, historic, set in a park. **Cons:** set in a park, to be reached only by car, restaurant closed Sunday evening and Monday. ✉ *Oberthiergärtenerstr. 36* ☎ *09209/9840* 🌐 *www.schlosshotel-thiergarten.de* *8 rooms, 1 suite* *In-room: no a/c, Wi-Fi. In-hotel: restaurant, bar, pool, public Internet, parking, some pets allowed, no-smoking rooms* *AE, DC, MC, V* *Restaurant closed Sun. evening and Mon.* *BP.*

$–$$ Fodor's Choice ★ **Goldener Anker.** No question about it, this is *the* place to stay in Bayreuth. The hotel is right next to the Markgräfliches Opernhaus and has been entertaining composers, singers, conductors, and instrumentalists for hundreds of years. The establishment has been run by the same family since 1753. Some rooms are small; others have a royal splendor. One huge suite has a spiral staircase leading up to the bedroom. All are individually decorated, and many have antique pieces. The restaurant ($$–$$$) is justly popular. Book your room far in advance during festival times. **Pros:** authentic historic setting with all modern amenities, exemplary service, excellent restaurant. **Cons:** no elevator, some rooms are on the small side, restaurant closed Monday and Tuesday. ⊠*Opernstr. 6* ☎*0921/65051* ⊕*www.anker-bayreuth. de* ⮂*38 rooms, 2 suites* ⚿*In-room: no a/c, Ethernet (some). In-hotel: restaurant, public Wi-Fi, parking (fee), some pets allowed, no-smoking rooms* ☐*AE, DC, MC, V* ☉*Restaurant closed Mon., Tues., and Dec. 20–Jan. 15* ⦿*BP.*

$–$$ ⛺**Hotel Lohmühle.** The old part of this hotel is in Bayreuth's only half-timber house, a former sawmill by a stream. It's just a two-minute walk from the town center. The rooms are rustic, with visible beams; the newer, neighboring building has correspondingly modern rooms. The restaurant offers traditional, hearty cooking ($$), such as Schäufele or carp. **Pros:** nice setting with reasonable prices, good food. **Cons:** stairs between hotel and restaurant, front rooms let in traffic noise, bar is closed. ⊠*Badstr. 37* ☎*0921/53060* ⊕*www.hotel-lohmuehle. de* ⮂*42 rooms* ⚿*In-room: no a/c, Wi-Fi (some). In-hotel: restaurant, public Wi-Fi, some pets allowed, no-smoking rooms* ☐*AE, DC, MC, V* ☉*No dinner Sun.* ⦿*BP.*

NIGHTLIFE & THE ARTS

Opera lovers swear that there are few more intense operatic experiences than the annual **Wagner Festival** in Bayreuth, held July and August. For tickets, write to the **Bayreuther Festspiele Kartenbüro** (✍*Postfach 100262 Bayreuth, D–95402* ☎*0921/78780*), but be warned: the waiting list is years long. You'll do best if you plan your visit a couple of years in advance. Rooms can be nearly impossible to find during the festival, too. If you don't get Wagner tickets, console yourself with visits to the exquisite 18th-century **Markgräfliches Opernhaus** (⊠*Opernstr.* ☎*0921/759–6922*). In May the *Fränkische Festwochen* (Franconian Festival Weeks) take the stage with works of Wagner, of course, but also Paganini and Mozart.

SHOPPING

The **Hofgarten Passage,** off Richard-Wagner-Strasse, is one of the fanciest shopping arcades in the region; it's full of smart boutiques selling everything from German high fashion to simple local craftwork.

BAMBERG

Fodor'sChoice ★

65 km (40 mi) west of Bayreuth, 80 km (50 mi) north of Nürnberg.

Few towns in Germany survived the war with as little damage as Bamberg, which is on the Regnitz River. ■**TIP→ This former residence of one of Germany's most powerful imperial dynasties is on UNESCO's World Heritage Site list.** Bamberg, originally nothing more than a fortress in the hands of the Babenberg dynasty (later contracted to Bamberg), rose to prominence in the 11th century thanks to the political and economic drive of its most famous offspring, Holy Roman Emperor Heinrich II. He transformed the imperial residence into a flourishing episcopal city. His cathedral, consecrated in 1237, still dominates the historic area. For a short period Heinrich II proclaimed Bamberg the capital of the Holy Roman Empire of the German Nation. Moreover, Bamberg earned fame as the second city to introduce book printing, in 1460.

GETTING HERE & AROUND

Traveling to Bamberg by train will take about 45 minutes from Nürnberg; from Munich it takes about two hours. On the A–73 autobahn, Bamberg is two hours from Munich. Everything in town can be reached on foot.

Guided walking tours set out from the tourist information office April–October, daily at 10:30 and 2; November–March, Monday–Saturday at 2 and Sunday at 11. The cost is €5.50.

In Bamberg, Personenschiffahrt Kropf boats leave daily from March through October beginning at 11 AM for short cruises on the Regnitz River and the Main-Donau Canal; the cost is €7.

ESSENTIALS

Boat Tour Personenschiffahrt Kropf (⊠ *Kapuzinerstr. 5, Bamberg* ☎ *0951/26679* ⊕ *www.personenschiffahrt-bamberg.de*) .

Visitor Information Bamberg (⊠ *Tourismus und Congresservice Geyerswörthstr. 3* ☎ *0951/297–6200* ⊕ *www.bamberg.info*).

EXPLORING

Bamberg's historic core, the **Altes Rathaus** *(Old Town Hall)*, is tucked snugly on a small island in the Regnitz. To the west of the river is the so-called Bishops' Town; to the east, Burghers' Town. This rickety, extravagantly decorated building was built in this unusual place so that the burghers of Bamberg could avoid paying real-estate taxes to their bishops and archbishops. The excellent collection of porcelain here is a vast sampling of 18th-century styles, from almost sober Meissens with bucolic Watteau scenes to simple but rare Haguenau pieces from Alsace and faience from Strasbourg. ⊠ *Obere Brücke 1* ☎ *0951/871–871* 💶 *€4* ⊙ *Tues.–Sun. 9:30–4:30.*

NEED A BREAK?
Before heading up the hill to the main sights in the Bishops' Town, take a break with coffee, cake, small meals, or cocktails in the half-timber Rathaus-Schänke (⊠ *Obere Brücke 3* ☎ *0951/208–0890*). It overlooks the river on the Burghers' Town side of the Town Hall.

The **Neue Residenz** *(New Residence)* is a glittering baroque palace that was once the home of the prince-electors. Their plan to extend the immense palace even further is evident at the corner on Obere Karolinenstrasse, where the ashlar bonding was left open to accept another wing. The most memorable room in the palace is the **Kaisersaal** (Throne Room), complete with impressive ceiling frescoes and elaborate stuccowork. The rose garden behind the Neue Residenz provides an aromatic and romantic spot for a stroll with a view of Bamberg's roof landscape.

The palace is also home to the **Staatsbibliothek** (State Library) (⊕ *www.Staatsbibliothek-bamberg.de* ⊙ *Weekdays 9–5, Sat. 9–noon* 💶 *Free*). Among the thousands of books and illuminated manuscripts here are the original prayer books belonging to Heinrich II and his wife, a 5th-century codex of the Roman historian Livy, and manuscripts by the 16th-century painters Dürer and Cranach. You have to take a tour to see the Residenz itself, but you can visit the library free of charge at any time during its open hours. ⊠ *Neue Residenz, Dompl. 8* ☎ *0951/955–030* 🖃 *€4* ⊙ *Neue Residenz by tour only, Apr.–Sept., daily 9–6; Oct.–Mar., daily 10–4.*

★ Bamberg's great **Dom** *(Cathedral)* is one of the country's most important, a building that tells not only the town's story but that of Germany as well. The first building here was begun by Heinrich II in 1003, and it was in this partially completed cathedral that he was crowned Holy Roman Emperor in 1012. In 1237 it was destroyed by fire, and the present late-Romanesque–early-Gothic building was begun. The dominant features are the massive towers at each corner. Heading into the dark interior, you'll find a striking collection of monuments and art treasures. The most famous piece is the **Bamberger Reiter** (Bamberg Rider), an equestrian statue carved—no one knows by whom—around 1230 and thought to be an allegory of chivalrous virtue or a representation of King Stephen of Hungary. Compare it with the mass of carved figures huddled in the tympana above the church portals. In the center of the nave you'll find another masterpiece, the massive tomb of Heinrich and his wife, Kunigunde. It's the work of Tilman Riemenschneider. Pope Clement II is also buried in the cathedral, in an imposing tomb beneath the high altar; he's the only pope to have been buried north of the Alps. ⊠ *Dompl.* ☎ *0951/502–330* ⊙ *Nov.–Mar., daily 10–5; Apr.–Oct., daily 10–6. No visits during services.*

The **Diözesanmuseum** *(Cathedral Museum)*, directly next to the cathedral, contains one of many nails and splinters of wood reputed to be from the cross of Jesus. The "star-spangled" cloak stitched with gold that was given to Emperor Heinrich II by an Italian prince is among the finest items displayed. More macabre exhibits in this rich ecclesiastical collection are the elaborately mounted skulls of Heinrich and Kunigunde. The building itself was designed by Balthasar Neumann (1687–1753), the architect of Vierzehnheiligen, and constructed between 1730 and 1733. ⊠ *Dompl. 5* ☎ *0951/502–325* 🖃 *€3* ⊙ *Tues.–Sun. 10–5; tour in English by prior arrangement.*

Bamberg's wealthy burghers built no fewer than 50 churches. Among the very special ones is the Church of Our Lady, known simply as the **Obere Pfarre** *(Upper Parish)*, whose history goes back to around 1325. It's unusual because it's still entirely Gothic from the outside. Also, the grand choir, which was added at a later period, is lacking windows. And then there's the odd, squarish box perched atop the tower. This watchman's abode served to cut the tower short before it grew taller than those of the neighboring cathedral, thereby avoiding a great scandal. The interior is heavily baroque. Note the slanted floor, which allowed crowds of pilgrims to see the object of their veneration, a 14th-century Madonna. Don't miss the *Ascension of Mary* by Tintoretto at the rear of the church. Around Christmas, the Obere Pfarre is the site

5

of the city's greatest Nativity scene. Avoid the church during services, unless you're worshipping. ⊠*Untere Seelg.* ⊙*Daily 7–7.*

St. Michael, a former Benedictine monastery, has been gazing over Bamberg since about 1015. After being overwhelmed by so much baroque elsewhere, entering this haven of simplicity is quite an experience. The entire choir is intricately carved, but the ceiling is gently decorated with very exact depictions of 578 flowers and healing herbs. The tomb of St. Otto is in a little chapel off the transept, and the stained-glass windows hold symbols of death and transfiguration. The monastery is now used as a home for the aged. One tract, however, was taken over by the **Franconian Brewery Museum,** which exhibits everything that has to do with beer, from the making of malt to recipes. ⊠*Michelsberg 10f* ☎*0951/53016* ▣*Museum €3* ⊙*Apr.–Oct., Wed.–Sun. 1–5.*

NEAR BAMBERG

Fodor's Choice
★

Vierzehnheiligen. On the east side of the Main north of Bamberg is a tall, elegant yellow-sandstone edifice whose interior represents one of the great examples of rococo decoration. The church was built by Balthasar Neumann (architect of the Residenz at Würzburg) between 1743 and 1772 to commemorate a vision of Christ and 14 saints—*vierzehn Heiligen*—that appeared to a shepherd in 1445. The interior, known as "God's ballroom," is supported by 14 columns. In the middle of the church is the Gnadenaltar (Mercy Altar) featuring the 14 saints. Thanks to clever play with light, light colors, and fanciful gold-and-blue trimmings, the interior seems to be in perpetual motion. Guided tours of the church are given on request; a donation is expected. On Saturday afternoon and all day Sunday the road leading to the church is closed and you have to walk the last half mile. ⊠*36 km (22 mi) north of Bamberg via Hwy. 173* ☎*09571/95080* ⊕*www.vierzehnheiligen. de* ⊙*Mar.–Oct., daily 7–6; Nov.–Feb., daily 8–5.*

Kloster Banz *(Banz Abbey).* This abbey, which some call the "holy mountain of Bavaria," proudly crowns the west bank of the Main north of Bamberg. There had been a monastery here since 1069, but the present buildings—now a political-seminar center and think tank—date from the end of the 17th century. The highlight of the complex is the **Klosterkirche** (Abbey Church), the work of architect Leonard Dientzenhofer and his brother, the stuccoist Johann Dientzenhofer (1663–1726). Balthasar Neumann later contributed a good deal of work. Concerts are occasionally held in the church, including some by members of the renowned Bamberger Symphoniker. To get to Banz from Vierzehnheiligen, drive south to Unnersdorf, where you can cross the river. ☎*09573/7311* ⊙*May–Oct., daily 9–5; Nov.–Apr., daily 9–noon; call to request a tour.*

WHERE TO EAT

¢–$ ✕**Bischofsmühle.** It doesn't always have to be beer in Bamberg. The old mill, its grinding wheel providing a sonorous backdrop for patrons, specializes in wines from Franconia and elsewhere. The menu offers Franconian specialties such as the French-derived *Böfflamott,* or beef stew. ⊠*Geyerswörthstr. 4* ☎*0951/27570* ▭*No credit cards* ⊙*Closed Wed.*

¢–$ ✕**Klosterbräu.** This massive old stone-and-half-timber house has been standing since 1533. Regulars nurse their dark, smoky beer called Schwärzla near the big stove. If you like the brew, you can buy a 5-liter bottle as well as other bottled beers and the requisite beer steins at the counter. The cuisine is basic, robust, filling, and tasty, with such items as a bowl of beans with a slab of smoked pork, or marinated pork kidneys with boiled potatoes. ⊠*Obere Mühlbrücke* ☎*0951/52265* ▭*No credit cards.*

WHERE TO STAY

$$ ▦**Hotel-Restaurant St. Nepomuk.** This half-timber house seems to float
Fodor's Choice over the Regnitz. The dining room, with its podium fireplace, discreet
★ lights, and serene atmosphere, has a direct view of the river. The Grüner family makes a special effort to bring not only high-quality food to the restaurant ($$$) but a world of excellent wines as well. The individually decorated rooms are comfortable, and many have quite a view of the water and the Old Town Hall on its island. **Pros:** nice view, very nicely decorated rooms, an elegant dining room with excellent food. **Cons:** cannot be reached by car, public garage 200 meters away, water taxi not yet available. ⊠*Obere Mühlbrücke 9* ☎*0951/98420* ⊕*www. hotel-nepomuk.de* ⬦*47 rooms* ♿*In-room: no a/c, Wi-Fi. In-hotel: restaurant, public Wi-Fi, parking (fee), some pets allowed, no-smoking rooms* ▭*MC, V* ⊙|*BP.*

$$ ▦**Romantik Hotel Weinhaus Messerschmitt.** Willy Messerschmitt of avia-
★ tion fame grew up in this beautiful late-baroque house with a steep-eaved, green-shutter, stucco exterior. The very comfortable hotel has spacious and luxurious rooms, some with exposed beams and many of them lighted by chandeliers. Fifty new rooms were added in 2006. You'll dine under beams and a coffered ceiling in the excellent Messerschmitt restaurant ($$–$$$), one of Bamberg's most popular culinary havens for Franconian specialties. **Pros:** elegant dining room with very good food, choice of different rooms. **Cons:** older property, front rooms are noisy, expensive. ⊠*Langestr. 41* ☎*0951/297–800* ⊕*www. hotel-messerschmitt.de* ⬦*67 rooms* ♿*In-room: no a/c. In-hotel: restaurant, bar, no-smoking rooms* ▭*AE, DC, MC, V* ⊙|*BP.*

THE ARTS

The **Sinfonie an der Regnitz** (⊠*Muss-Str. 1* ☎*0951/964–7200*), a fine riverside concert hall, is home to Bamberg's world-class resident symphony orchestra. The **Hoffmann Theater** (⊠*E.-T.-A.- Hoffmann-Pl.1-* ☎*0951/873030*) has opera and operetta from September through July. The city's first-class choir, **Capella Antiqua Bambergensis,** concentrates on ancient music. Throughout the summer organ concerts are given Saturdays at noon in the **Dom.** For program details and tickets to all cultural events, call ☎*0951/297–6200.*

SHOPPING

■**TIP→** If you happen to be traveling around Christmastime, make sure you keep an eye out for crèches, a Bamberg specialty. Of the many shops in Bamberg, the **AGIL** (⊠*Schranne 4c* ☎*0951/519–0389*) may be the one you'll want to visit for an unusual souvenir.

From Bamberg you can take either the fast autobahn (A–73) south to Nürnberg or the parallel country road (B–4) that follows the Main-Donau Canal (running parallel to the Regnitz River at this point) and joins A–73 just under 25 km (15 mi) later at Forchheim-Nord.

Eighteen kilometers (11 mi) south of Bamberg in the village of Buttenheim is a little blue-and-white half-timber house where Löb Strauss was born—in egregious poverty—in 1826. Take the tape-recorded tour of the **Levi-Strauss Museum** (⊠ *Marktstr. 33* ☎ *09545/442–602* ⊕ *www. levi-strauss-museum.de* ✉ *€2.60* ☉ *Tues. and Thurs. 2–6, weekends 11–5 and by appointment*) and learn how Löb emigrated to the United States, changed his name to Levi, and became the first name in denim. The stone-washed color of the house's beams, by the way, is the original 17th-century color.

NÜRNBERG (NUREMBERG)

Nürnberg (Nuremberg in English) is the principal city of Franconia and the second-largest city in Bavaria. With a recorded history stretching back to 1050, it's among the most historic of Germany's cities; the core of the Old Town, through which the Pegnitz River flows, is still surrounded by its original medieval walls. Nürnberg has always taken a leading role in German affairs. It was here, for example, that the Holy Roman emperors traditionally held the first Diet, or convention of the estates, of their incumbency. And it was here, too, that Hitler staged the most grandiose Nazi rallies; later, this was the site of the Allies' war trials, where top-ranking Nazis were charged with—and almost without exception convicted of—crimes against humanity. The rebuilding of Nürnberg after the war was virtually a miracle, considering the 90% destruction of the Old Town. Nürnberg, in 2001, became the world's first city to receive the UNESCO prize for Human Rights Education.

As a major intersection on the medieval trade routes, Nürnberg became a wealthy town where the arts and sciences flowered. Albrecht Dürer (1471–1528), the first indisputable genius of the Renaissance in Germany, was born here in 1471. He married in 1509 and bought a house in the city where he lived and worked for the rest of his life. Other leading Nürnberg artists of the Renaissance include painter Michael Wolgemut (a teacher of Dürer), stonecutter Adam Kraft, and the brass founder Peter Vischer. The tradition of the Meistersinger also flourished here in the 16th century, thanks to the high standard set by the local cobbler Hans Sachs (1494–1576). The Meistersinger were poets and musicians who turned songwriting into a special craft, with a wealth of rules and regulations. They were celebrated three centuries later by Wagner in his *Meistersinger von Nürnberg.*

The Thirty Years' War and the shift to sea routes for transportation led to the city's long decline, which ended only in the early 19th century when the first railroad opened in Nürnberg. Among a great host of inventions associated with the city, the most significant are the pocket watch, gun casting, the clarinet, and the geographic globe (the first of which was made before Columbus discovered the Americas). Among Nürnberg's famous products are *Lebkuchen* (gingerbread of sorts) and Faber-Castell pencils.

GETTING HERE & AROUND

Nuremberg is centrally located in southern Germany, an hour from Munich and two hours from Frankfurt by train. Five autobahns meet here: A3 Düsseldorf-Passau, A6 Mannheim-Nürnberg, A9 Potzdam-München, A73 Coburg-Feucht, B8 (four lane near Nürnberg) Würzburg-Regensburg. Most places in the Old Town may be reached on foot.

English-language bus tours of the city are conducted April–October and in December, daily at 9:30, starting at the Mauthalle, Hallplatz 2. The 2½-hour tour costs €11. For more information, call ☎*0911/202–290*. An English-language tour on foot through the Old Town is conducted daily May–October at 1; it departs from the tourist-information office on the Hauptmarkt. The tour costs €8 (plus entrance to the Kaiserburg €6). City tours are also conducted in brightly painted trolley buses April–October, daily at one-hour intervals beginning at 10 at the Schöner Brunnen. The cost is €5. For more information call the Nürnberg tourist office.

TIMING

You'll need a full day to walk around Nürnberg's Old Town, two if you wish to take more time at its fascinating museums and churches. Most of the major sights are within a few minutes' walk of each other. The Kaiserburg is a must-visit on any trip to Nürnberg. Plan at least half a day for the Germanisches Nationalmuseum, which is just inside the city walls near the main station.

ESSENTIALS

Visitor Information **Nürnberg** (⊠ *Congress- und Tourismus-Zentrale, Frauentor-graben 3D–90443* ☎*0911/23360* ⊕ *www.nuernberg.de*).

EXPLORING NÜRNBERG'S OLD TOWN

Walls, finished in 1452, surround Nürnberg's Old Town. Year-round floodlighting adds to the brooding romance of their moats, sturdy gateways, and watchtowers.

MAIN ATTRACTIONS

⑩ **Albrecht-Dürer-Haus** *(Albrecht Dürer House).* The great painter Albrecht
★ Dürer lived here from 1509 until his death in 1528. This beautifully preserved late-medieval house is typical of the prosperous merchants' homes that once filled Nürnberg. Dürer, who enriched German art with Italianate elements, was more than a painter. He raised the woodcut, a notoriously difficult medium, to new heights of technical sophistication, combining great skill with a haunting, immensely detailed drawing style and complex, allegorical subject matter, while earning a good living at the same time. A number of original prints adorn the walls, and printing techniques using the old press are demonstrated in the

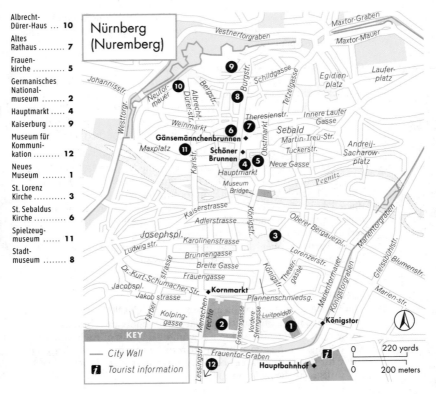

studio. An excellent opportunity to find out about life in the house of Dürer is the Saturday 2 PM tour with a guide role-playing Agnes Dürer, the artist's wife. ✉ *Albrecht-Dürer-Str. 39* ☎ *0911/231–2568* 💶 *€5, with tour €7.50* 🕐 *Tues., Wed., and Fri.–Sun. 10–5, Thurs. 10–8; guided tour in English Sat. at 2.*

② **Germanisches Nationalmuseum** (*German National Museum*). You could

Fodor'sChoice spend days visiting this vast museum, which showcases the country's

★ cultural and scientific achievements, ethnic background, and history. It's the largest of its kind in Germany, and perhaps the best arranged. The museum is in what was once a Carthusian monastery, complete with cloisters and monastic outbuildings. The extensions, however, are modern. The exhibition begins outside, with the tall, sleek pillars of the Strasse der Menschenrechte (Street of Human Rights), designed by Israeli artist Dani Karavan. Thirty columns are inscribed with the articles from the Declaration of Human Rights. There are few aspects of German culture, from the Stone Age to the 19th century, that are not covered by the museum, and quantity and quality are evenly matched. One highlight is the superb collection of Renaissance German paintings (with Dürer, Cranach, and Altdorfer well represented). Others may prefer the exquisite medieval ecclesiastical exhibits—manuscripts, altarpieces, statuary, stained glass, jewel-encrusted reliquaries—the collections of arms and armor, the scientific instruments, or the toys. ⊠*Kartäuserg. 1* ☎*0911/13310* ⊕*www.gnm.de* ☜*€6* ⊗*Tues. and Thurs.–Sun. 10–6, Wed. 10–9.*

Opposite the Germanisches National-museum is Vivere (⊠*Kartäuserg. 12* ☎*0911/244–9774* ⊗*Closed Mon.*). Al dente pasta or meat and fish dishes with excellent wines will revive you after the long hours spent in the museum.

 Kaiserburg *(Imperial Castle).* The city's main attraction is a grand yet playful collection of buildings standing just inside the city walls; it was once the residence of the Holy Roman emperors. The complex comprises three separate groups. The oldest, dating from around 1050, is the **Burggrafenburg** (Castellan's Castle), with a craggy old pentagonal tower and the bailiff's house. It stands in the center of the complex. To the east is the **Kaiserstallung** (Imperial Stables), built in the 15th century as a granary and now serving as a youth hostel. The real interest of this vast complex of ancient buildings, however, centers on the westernmost part of the fortress, which begins at the **Sinwell Turm** (Sinwell Tower). The **Kaiserburg Museum** is here, a subsidiary of the Germanisches Nationalmuseum that displays ancient armors and has exhibits relating to horsemanship in the imperial era and to the history of the fortress. This section of the castle also has a wonderful Roman-esque **Doppelkappelle** (Double Chapel). The upper part—richer, larger, and more ornate than the lower chapel—was where the emperor and his family worshipped. Also visit the **Rittersaal** (Knights' Hall) and the **Kaisersaal** (Throne Room). Their heavy oak beams, painted ceilings, and sparse interiors have changed little since they were built in the 15th century. ⊠*Burgstr.* ☎*0911/24465–9115* ☜*€6* ⊗*Apr.–Sept., daily 9–6; Oct.–Mar., daily 10–4.*

 Neues Museum *(New Museum).* Anything but medieval, this museum is devoted to international design since 1945. The collection, supplemented by changing exhibitions, is in a slick, modern edifice that achieves the perfect synthesis between old and new. It's mostly built of traditional pink-sandstone ashlars, while the facade is a flowing, transparent composition of glass. The interior is a work of art in itself—cool stone, with a ramp that slowly spirals up to the gallery. Extraordinary things await, including a Joseph Beuys installation (*Ausfegen*, or *Sweep-out*) and *Avalanche* by François Morellet, a striking collection of violet, argon-gas-filled fluorescent tubes. The café-restaurant adjoining the museum contains modern art, silver-wrapped can-

5

dies, and video projections. ⊠*Luitpoldstr. 5* ☏*0911/240–200* ☞€4 ⊘*Tues.–Fri. 10–8, weekends 10–6.*

ALSO WORTH SEEING

❼ **Altes Rathaus** *(Old Town Hall).* This ancient building on Rathausplatz abuts the rear of St. Sebaldus Kirche; it was erected in 1332, destroyed in World War II, and subsequently restored. Its intact medieval dungeons, consisting of 12 small rooms and one large torture chamber called the **Lochgefängnis** (or the Chapel, owing to the vaulted ceilings), provide insight into the gruesome applications of medieval law. **Gänsemännchenbrunnen** (Gooseman's Fountain) faces the Altes Rathaus. This lovely Renaissance bronze fountain, cast in 1550, is a work of rare elegance and great technical sophistication. ⊠*Rathauspl. 2* ☏*0911/231–2690* ☞€3, *minimum of 5 people for tours* ⊘*Tues.– Sun. 10–4.*

❺ **Frauenkirche** *(Church of Our Lady).* The fine late-Gothic Frauenkirche was built in 1350, with the approval of Holy Roman Emperor Charles IV, on the site of a synagogue that was burned down during a 1349 pogrom. The modern tabernacle beneath the main altar was designed to look like a Torah scroll as a kind of memorial to that despicable act. The church's real attraction is the **Männleinlaufen,** a clock dating from 1509, which is set in its facade. It's one of those colorful mechanical marvels at which Germans have long excelled. ■TIP➜ **Every day at noon the seven electors of the Holy Roman Empire glide out of the clock to bow to Emperor Charles IV before sliding back under cover. It's worth scheduling your morning to catch the display.** ⊠*Hauptmarkt* ⊘*Mon.–Sat. 9–6, Sun. 12:30–6.*

❹ **Hauptmarkt** *(Main Market).* Nürnberg's central market square was at one time the city's Jewish Quarter. When the people of Nürnberg petitioned their emperor, Charles IV, for a big central market, the emperor was in desperate need of money and, above all, political support. The Jewish Quarter was the preferred site, but as the official protector of the Jewish people, the emperor could not just openly take away their property. Instead, he instigated a pogrom that left the Jewish Quarter in flames and more than 500 dead. He then razed the ruins and resettled the remaining Jews.

Towering over the northwestern corner of the Hauptmarkt, **Schöner Brunnen** (Beautiful Fountain) looks as though it should be on the summit of some lofty cathedral. Carved around the year 1400, the elegant 60-foot-high Gothic fountain is adorned with 40 figures arranged in tiers—prophets, saints, local noblemen, sundry electors of the Holy Roman Empire, and one or two strays such as Julius Caesar and Alexander the Great. ■TIP➜ **A gold ring is set into the railing surrounding the fountain, reportedly placed there by an apprentice carver. Touching it is said to bring good luck.** A market still operates in the Hauptmarkt. Its colorful stands are piled high with produce, fruit, bread, homemade cheeses and sausages, sweets, and anything else you might need for a snack or picnic. It's here that the Christkindlemarkt is held.

Jüdisches Museum Franken. The everyday life of the Jewish community in Franconia and Fürth is examined in this Jewish museum: books, seder plates, coat hangers, old statutes concerning Jews, and children's toys are among the exhibits. Among the most famous members of the Fürth community was Henry Kissinger, born here in 1923. Changing exhibitions relate to contemporary Jewish life in Germany, and in the basement is the mikwe, the ritual bath, which was used by the family who lived here centuries ago. In the museum you will also find a good Jewish bookshop as well as a nice small café. A subsidiary to the museum, which houses special exhibitions, is in the former synagogue in nearby Schnaittach. To get to the museum from Nürnberg, you can take the U1 U-bahn to the Rathaus stop. ⊠*Königstr. 89, 10 km (6 mi) west of Nürnberg, Fürth* ☎*0911/770–577* ⊕*www.juedisches-museum.org* 🖾*€5* ⊗ *Wed.–Sun. 10–5, Tues. 10–8.*

⑫ **Museum für Kommunikation** *(Communication Museum).* Two museums have been amalgamated under a single roof here, the German Railway Museum and the Museum of Communication—in short, museums about how people get in touch. The first train to run in Germany did so on December 7, 1835, from Nürnberg to nearby Fürth. A model of the epochal train is here, along with a series of original 19th- and early-20th-century trains and stagecoaches. Philatelists will want to check out some of the 40,000-odd stamps in the extensive exhibits on the German postal system. You can also find out about the history of sending messages—from old coaches to optical fiber networks. ⊠*Lessingstr. 6* ☎*0911/219–2428* 🖾*€4* ⊗*Tues.–Sun. 10–5.*

❸ **St. Lorenz Kirche** *(St. Laurence Church).* In a city with several striking churches, St. Lorenz is considered by many to be the most beautiful. It was begun around 1250 and completed in about 1477; it later became a Lutheran church. Two towers flank the main entrance of the sizable church, which is covered with a forest of carvings. In the lofty interior, note the works by sculptors Adam Kraft and Veit Stoss: Kraft's great stone tabernacle, to the left of the altar, and Stoss's *Annunciation,* at the east end of the nave, are their finest works. There are many other carvings throughout the building, testimony to the artistic wealth of late-medieval Nürnberg. ⊠*Lorenzer Pl.* ⊗*Mon.–Sat. 9–5, Sun. noon–4.*

❻ **St. Sebaldus Kirche** *(St. Sebaldus Church).* Although St. Sebaldus lacks the quantity of art treasures found in its rival St. Lorenz, its nave and choir are among the purest examples of Gothic ecclesiastical architecture in Germany: elegant, tall, and airy. Veit Stoss carved the crucifixion group at the east end of the nave, while the elaborate bronze shrine containing the remains of St. Sebaldus himself was cast by Peter Vischer and his five sons around 1520. Not to be missed is the **Sebaldus Chörlein,** an ornate Gothic oriel that was added to the Sebaldus parish house in 1361 (the original is in the Germanisches Nationalmuseum). ⊠*Albrecht-Dürer-Pl. 1* ☎*0911/214–2500* ⊗*Daily 10–5.*

⑪ **Spielzeugmuseum** *(Toy Museum).* Young and old are captivated by this playful museum, which has a few exhibits dating from the Renaissance; most, however, are from the 19th century. Simple dolls vie with mechanical toys of extraordinary complexity, such as a wooden Ferris wheel from the Erz Mountains adorned with little colored lights. The top floor displays Barbies and intricate Lego constructions. ⊠*Karlstr. 13–15* ☏*0911/231–3164* ✑*€5* ⊘*Tues.–Sun. 10–5.*

⑧ Stadtmuseum *(City Museum)*. This city history museum is in the Fembohaus, a dignified patrician dwelling completed in 1598. It's one of the finest Renaissance mansions in Nürnberg. Each room explores another aspect of Nürnberg history, from crafts to gastronomy. The 50-minute multivision show provides a comprehensive look at the city's long history. ⊠*Burgstr. 15* ☏*0911/231–2595* ✑*€5* ⊘*Tues.–Sun. 10–5.*

EXPLORING NÜRNBERG'S NAZI SIGHTS

To reach the Documentation Center by public transit, take streetcar Number 9 from the Hauptbahnhof; the Center is the final stop on the line. If you are driving, follow Regensburger Strasse in the direction of Regensburg until you reach Bayernstrasse. Plan for at least an hour to tour the exhibition.

Documentation Centre Nazi Party Rally Grounds. On the eastern outskirts of the city, the **Ausstellung Faszination und Gewalt** (Fascination and Terror Exhibition) documents the political, social, and architectural history of the Nazi Party. The 19-room exhibition is within a horseshoe-shape Congressional Hall that was intended to harbor a crowd of 50,000; the Nazis never completed it. The Nazis did make famous use of the nearby Zeppelin Field, the enormous parade ground where Hitler addressed his largest Nazi rallies. Today it sometimes shakes to the amplified beat of pop concerts. ☏*0911/231–5666* ⊕*www.museen. nuernberg.de* ✑*€5* ⊘*Museum daily 9–6, weekends 10–6.*

The Nürnberg Trials. Nazi leaders and German organizations were put on trial here in 1945 and 1946 during the first international war-crimes trials, conducted by the Allied victors of World War II. The trials were held in the Landgericht (Regional Court) in courtroom No. 600 and resulted in 11 death sentences, among other convictions. The guided tours are in German, but English-language material is available. Take the U1 subway line to Bärenschanze. ∎**TIP➔The building will be closed from July 2008 to the beginning of 2010 for the construction of the Nürnberg Trials Memorial.** ⊠*Bärenschanzstr. 72* ☏*0911/231–8411* ⊕*www. museen.nuernberg.de* ✑*€5* ⊘Closed until 2010.

WHERE TO EAT

$$$–$$$$ ✕**Essigbrätlein.** The oldest restaurant in Nürnberg is also the top res-
Fodor'sChoice taurant in the city and among the best in Germany. Built in 1550, it
★ was originally used as a meeting place for wine merchants. Today its
tiny but elegant period interior caters to the distinguishing gourmet
with a taste for special spice mixes (owner Andrée Köthe's hobby).
The menu changes daily. ⊠ *Weinmarkt 3, D–90403* ☎*0911/225–131*
⌖*Reservations essential* ▤*AE, DC, MC, V* ⊘*Closed Sun., Mon.,*
and late Aug.

$–$$ ✕**Heilig-Geist-Spital.** Heavy wood furnishings and a choice of more
★ than 100 wines make this huge, 650-year-old wine tavern—built as
the refectory of the city hospital—a popular spot. Try for a table in
one of the alcoves, where you can see the river below you as you eat
your fish. The menu also includes grilled pork chops, panfried potatoes,
and other Franconian dishes. ⊠*Spitalg. 16* ☎*0911/221–761* ▤*AE,*
DC, MC, V.

¢–$ ✕**Historische Bratwurst-Küche Zum Gulden Stern.** The city council meets
★ here occasionally to decide upon the official size and weight of the
Nürnberg bratwurst. It's a fitting venue for such a decision, given that
this house, built in 1375, holds the oldest bratwurst restaurant in the
world. The famous Nürnberg bratwursts are always freshly roasted
on a beechwood fire; the boiled variation is prepared in a tasty stock
of Franconian wine and onions. ⊠*Zirkelschmiedg. 26* ☎*0911/205–*
9288 ▤*MC, V.*

WHERE TO STAY

$$$–$$$$ ▦**Le Meridien Grand Hotel.** Across the square from the central railway
★ station is this stately building with the calling card GRAND HOTEL arch-
ing over its entranceway. The spacious and imposing lobby with marble
pillars feels grand and welcoming. Since 1896 kings, politicians, and
celebrities have soaked up the luxury of large rooms and tubs in marble
bathrooms. On Friday and Saturday evenings and on Sunday at noon,
locals arrive for the candlelight dinner or exquisite brunch ($$–$$$) with
live piano music in the restaurant of glittering glass and marble. The
trout is a standout in an impressive list of fish dishes, and the lamb is a
good pick from the meat entrées. Be sure to ask for weekend rates. **Pros:**
luxury property, impressive lobby, excellent food, valet parking. **Cons:**
expensive, for example, €6 just to check e-mail; Germanic efficiency at
reception desk; difficult to reach the hotel with big bags from the main
station as you have to go through an underpass with stairs. ⊠*Bahn-*
hofstr. 1D–90402, ☎*0911/23220* ⊕*www.nuremberg.lemeridien.com*
⤴*186 rooms, 5 suites* ⌖*In-room: Ethernet. In-hotel: restaurant, bar,*
laundry service, concierge, public Internet, public Wi-Fi, parking (fee),
some pets allowed, no-smoking rooms ▤*AE, DC, MC, V.*

$$ ▦**Hotel-Weinhaus Steichele.** An 18th-century bakery has skillfully converted into this hotel, which has been managed by the same family
for four generations. It's close to the main train station, on a quiet
street of the old walled town. The cozy rooms are decorated in rustic Bavarian style. Two wood-paneled, traditionally furnished taverns ($–$$) serve Franconian fare with an excellent fish menu. **Pros:**

5

nice restaurants with good food and service, cozy rooms. **Cons:** small rooms and lobby, walls could use a fresh coat of paint. ⊠*Knorrstr. 2–8* ☎*0911/202–280* ⊕*www.steichele.de* ⌛*56 rooms* ⌂*In-room: no a/c. In-hotel: restaurant, bar, laundry service, some pets allowed* ▤*AE, DC, MC, V* ⦿|*BP.*

$–$$ ▦ **Agneshof.** This comfortable hotel is north of the Old Town between the fortress and St. Sebaldus Church. Interiors are very modern and tastefully done. The hotel also has a small wellness center and even some lounges for sunning in the small garden. **Pros:** warm yet professional welcome, lobby and rooms modern yet tasteful. **Cons:** getting to the hotel and parking are difficult, no restaurant. ⊠*Agnesg. 10* ☎*0911/214–440* ⊕*www.agneshof-nuernberg.de* ⌛*72 rooms* ⌂*In-room: no a/c, safe, Wi-Fi. In-hotel: bar, laundry service, public Wi-Fi, parking (fee), some pets allowed, no-smoking rooms* ▤*AE, DC, MC, V* ⦿|*BP.*

$–$$ ▦ **Burghotel Stammhaus.** The service is familial and friendly at this little family-run hotel where accommodations are small but cozy. If you need more space, ask about the wedding suite. The breakfast room with its balcony overlooking the houses of the Old Town has a charm all its own. **Pros:** family run, comfortable, pool, good value. **Cons:** small rooms, tiny lobby, parking is not easy. ⊠*Schildg. 14* ☎*0911/203–040* ⊕*www.burghotel-stamm.de* ⌛*22 rooms* ⌂*In-room: no a/c, Wi-Fi. In-hotel: pool, public Wi-Fi, parking (fee), some pets allowed, no-smoking rooms* ▤*AE, DC, MC, V* ⦿|*BP.*

$–$$ ▦ **Hotel Drei Raben.** Legends and tales of Nürnberg form the leitmotif
★ running through the designer rooms at this hotel. One room celebrates the local soccer team with a table-soccer game; in another room sandstone friezes recall sights in the city. There are also standard rooms in the lower price category. The reception room, with its pods, is modeled after *2001: A Space Odyssey*, yet doesn't seem overbearingly modern. It's three minutes from the train station, just within the Old Town walls. **Pros:** free drink at the reception desk, designer rooms, valet parking, free Wi-Fi. **Cons:** reception and breakfast room could use updating, no restaurant. ⊠*Königstr. 63* ☎*0911/274–380* ⊕*www.hotel-drei-raben. de* ⌛*25 rooms* ⌂*In-room: no a/c, Wi-Fi. In-hotel: bar, public Wi-Fi, some pets allowed, no-smoking rooms* ▤*AE, DC, MC, V* ⦿|*BP.*

FESTIVALS

Nürnberg is rich in special events and celebrations. By far the most famous is the **Christkindlemarkt** (Christ-Child Market), an enormous pre-Christmas fair that runs from the Friday before Advent to Christmas Eve. One of the highlights is the candle procession, held every second Thursday of the market season, during which thousands of children parade through the city streets.

Nürnberg has an annual summer festival, **Sommer in Nürnberg,** from May through July, with more than 200 events. Its international organ festival in June and July is regarded as Europe's finest. From May through July classical music concerts are given in the Rittersaal of the **Kaiserburg.** For details, call ☎*0911/244–6590.*

SHOPPING

Step into the **Handwerkerhof,** in the tower at the Old Town gate (Am Königstor) opposite the main railway station, and you'll think you're back in the Middle Ages. Craftspeople are busy at work in a "medieval mall," turning out the kind of handiwork that has been produced in Nürnberg for centuries: pewter, glassware, basketwork, wood carvings, and, of course, toys. The Lebkuchen specialist **Lebkuchen-Schmidt** has a shop here as well. The mall is open mid-March–December 24, weekdays 10–6:30, Saturday 10–4. December 1–24 the mall is also open Sunday 10–6:30.

THE GERMAN DANUBE

For many people, the sound of the Danube River (Donau in German) is the melody of *The Blue Danube,* the waltz written by Austrian Johann Strauss. The famous 2,988-km-long (1,800-mi-long) river originates in Germany's Black Forest and flows through ten countries. In Germany it's mostly a rather unremarkable stream as it passes through cities such as Ulm on its southeasterly route. However, that changes at Kelheim, just west of Regensburg, where the Main-Donau Canal (completed in 1992) brings big river barges all the way from the North Sea. The river becomes sizable in Regensburg, where the ancient Steinerne Brücke (Stone Bridge) needs 15 spans of 30 to 48 feet each to bridge the water. Here everything from small pleasure boats to cruise liners joins the commercial traffic. In the university town of Passau, two more rivers join the waters of the Danube before Europe's longest river continues into Austria.

REGENSBURG

85 km (52 mi) southeast of Nürnberg, 120 km (74 mi) northwest of Munich.

Few visitors to Bavaria venture this far off the well-trodden tourist trails, and even Germans are surprised when they discover medieval Regensburg. ■TIP➜ **The town escaped World War II with no major damage, and it is one of the best-preserved medieval cities in Germany.**

Regensburg's story begins with the Celts around 500 BC. In AD 179, as an original marble inscription in the Historisches Museum proclaims, it became a Roman military post called Castra Regina. The Porta Praetoria, or gateway, built by the Romans, remains in the Old Town, and whenever you see huge ashlars incorporated into buildings, you are looking at bits of the old Roman settlement. When Bavarian tribes migrated to the area in the 6th century, they occupied what remained of the Roman town and, apparently on the basis of its Latin name, called it Regensburg. Anglo-Saxon missionaries led by St. Boniface in 739 made the town a bishopric before heading down the Danube to convert the heathen in even more far-flung lands. Charlemagne, first of the Holy Roman emperors, arrived at the end of the 8th century

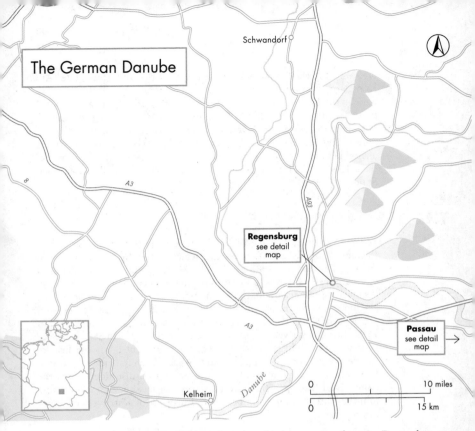

The German Danube

Schwandorf

Regensburg
see detail
map

Passau
see detail
map

Kelheim

Danube

| 0 | | 10 miles |

| 0 | | 15 km |

and incorporated Regensburg into his burgeoning domain. Regensburg benefited from the fact that the Danube wasn't navigable to the west, and thus it was able to control trade as goods traveled between Germany and Central Europe.

By the Middle Ages Regensburg had become a political, economic, and intellectual center. For many centuries it was the most important city in southeast Germany, serving as the seat of the Perpetual Imperial Diet from 1663 until 1806, when Napoléon ordered the dismantling of the Holy Roman Empire.

Today the ancient and hallowed walls of Regensburg continue to buzz with life. Students from the university fill the restaurants and pubs, and locals do their daily shopping and errand running in the inner city, where small shops and stores have managed to keep international consumer chains out.

GETTING HERE & AROUND

Regensburg is at the intersection of the autobahns 3 and 93. It is an hour away from Nürnberg and two hours from Munich by train. Regensburg is compact; its Old Town center is about 1 square mi. All of its attractions lie on the south side of the Danube, so you won't have

Cruising on the Danube

Although Passau is the natural gateway to the cruising destinations of Eastern Europe on the Danube, it is by no means the only starting point. You can board a deluxe river cruise ship in Nürnberg, landlocked but for the very small river Pegnitz, then cruise "overland" through Franconia on the Main-Danube canal across the Continental Divide until you join the Danube at Kehlheim, a few miles west of Regensburg. After Passau you enter Austria, where you come to the city that most people automatically associate with the Blue Danube, Vienna. The next border crossing brings you into Slovakia and to your second capital, Bratislava. Budapest, Hungary is next, and capital number four is Belgrade, Serbia. Some of the Danube cruises begin in Amsterdam, making them five-capital cruises.

Two American and one British company offer most of the long-distance trips on the Danube, which pass through or originate from Regensburg or Passau.

Viking River Cruises has a Grand European Tour from Amsterdam to Budapest. The two-week Eastern European Odyssey starts in Nürnberg and ends at Bucharest. The reverse direction is also available on both cruises.

Amadeus Waterways offers half a dozen cruises through Franconia and the German Danube, including a Christmastime cruise, which stops at the fascinating Christmas markets between Nürnberg and Budapest. The reverse direction is also available.

The British **Blue Water Holidays** has nine cruises starting on the Rhine, some from Basel in Switzerland, which follow the Main-Danube Canal to the Danube and four cruises from Nuremberg or Passau to Vienna or Budapest.

ESSENTIALS

Amadeus Waterways (☎ *800/626-0126* ⊕ *www.amadeuswaterways. com*). **Viking River Cruises, Inc.** (☎*800/304–9616* ⊕ *www.vikingriver cruises.com*). **Blue Water Holidays** (⊕ *www.cruisingholidays.co.uk*).

5

to cross it more than once—and then only to admire the city from the north bank.

English-language guided walking tours are conducted May–September, Wednesday and Saturday at 1:30. They cost €6 and begin at the tourist office.

In Regensburg all boats depart from the Steinerne Brücke. The most popular excursions are boat trips to Ludwig I's imposing Greek-style Doric temple of Walhalla. There are daily sailings to Walhalla from Easter through October. The round-trip costs €8 and takes three hours. Don't bother with the trip upriver from Regensburg to Kehlheim.

TIMING

Although the Old Town is quite small, you can easily spend half a day strolling through its narrow streets. Any serious tour of Regensburg includes an unusually large number of places of worship. If your spirits wilt at the thought of inspecting them all, you should at least see the Dom (cathedral), famous for its Domspatzen (boys' choir—the literal translation is "cathedral sparrows"). You'll need

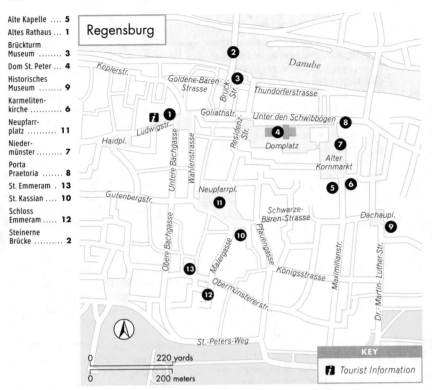

Regensburg

about another two hours or more to explore Schloss Emmeram and St. Emmeram Church.

ESSENTIALS

Boat Tours Personenschiffahrt Klinger (✉ *Thundorfstr. 1D–93047 Regensburg* ☎ *0941/55359* ⊕ *www.schifffahrtklinger.de*).

Visitor Information Regensburg (✉ *Altes Rathaus* ☎ *0941/507–4410* ⊕ *www. regensburg.de*).

MAIN ATTRACTIONS

❶ Altes Rathaus *(Old Town Hall)*. The picture-book complex of medieval half-timber buildings, with windows large and small and flowers in tubs, is one of the best-preserved town halls in the country, as well as one of the most historically important. It was here, in the imposing Gothic **Reichssaal** (Imperial Hall), that the Perpetual Imperial Diet met from 1663 to 1806. This parliament of sorts consisted of the emperor, the electors (seven or eight), the princes (about 50), and the burghers, who assembled to discuss and determine the affairs of the far-reaching German lands. The hall is sumptuously appointed with tapestries, flags, and heraldic designs. Note the wood ceiling, built in 1408, and the different elevations for the various estates. The Reichssaal is occasionally used for concerts. The neighboring **Ratssaal** (Council Room) is where the electors met for their consultations. The cellar holds the city's torture chamber; the **Fragstatt** (Questioning Room); and the execution room, called the **Armesünderstübchen** (Poor Sinners' Room). Any prisoner who withstood three degrees of questioning without confessing was considered innocent and released—which tells you something about medieval notions of justice. ⊠*Rathauspl.* ☎*0941/507–4411* *€7.50* ⊘*Guided tours in English Apr.–Oct., daily at 3.*

NEED A BREAK? Just across the square from the Altes Rathaus is the Prinzess Confiserie Café (⊠*Rathauspl.* 2 ☎*0941/595-310*), Germany's oldest coffeehouse, which first opened its doors to the general public in 1686. The homemade chocolates are highly recommended, as are the rich cakes.

❸ Brückturm Museum *(Bridge Tower Museum)*. With its tiny windows, weathered tiles, and pink plaster, this 17th-century tower stands at the south end of the Steinerne Brücke. The tower displays a host of items relating to the construction and history of the old bridge. It also offers a gorgeous view of the Regensburg roof landscape. The brooding building with a massive roof to the left of the Brückturm is an old salt warehouse. ⊠*Steinerne Brücke* ☎*0941/507–5888* *€2* ⊘*Apr.–Oct., daily 10–5; call ahead to ask about English tours.*

❹ Dom St. Peter *(St. Peter's Cathedral)*. Regensburg's transcendent cathe-★ dral, modeled on the airy, vertical lines of French Gothic architecture, is something of a rarity this far south in Germany. Begun in the 13th century, it stands on the site of a much earlier Carolingian church. Remarkably, the cathedral can hold 6,000 people, three times the population of Regensburg when building began. Construction dragged on for almost 600 years, until Ludwig I of Bavaria, then ruler of Regensburg, finally had the towers built. These had to be replaced in the mid-1950s. Behind the Dom is a little workshop where a team of 15 stonecutters is busy full-time during the summer recutting and restoring parts of the cathedral.

Before heading into the Dom, take time to admire the intricate and frothy carvings of its facade. Inside, the glowing 14th-century stained glass in the choir and the exquisitely detailed statues of the archangel Gabriel and the Virgin in the crossing (the intersection of the nave and the transepts) are among the church's outstanding features. ⊠*Dompl.* ☎*0941/586–5500* *Tour, only in German (for tours in English call ahead), €3* ⊘*Cathedral tour daily at 2.*

Be sure to visit the **Kreuzgang** *(Cloisters)*, reached via the garden. There you'll find a small octagonal chapel, the Allerheiligenkapelle (All Saints' Chapel), a Romanesque building that is all sturdy grace and massive walls, a work by Italian masons from the mid-12th century. You can barely make out the faded remains of stylized 11th-century frescoes on its ancient walls. The equally ancient shell of St. Stephan's Church, the cloisters, the chapel, and the Alter Dom (Old Cathedral), are included in the Cathedral tour. The **Domschatzmuseum** *(Cathedral Museum)* contains valuable treasures going back to the 11th century. Some of the vestments and the monstrances, which are fine examples of eight centuries' worth of the goldsmith's trade, are still used during special services. The entrance is in the nave. ⊠*Dompl.* ☎*0941/ 5972530* 🎫*€2* ⊙*Apr.–Oct., Tues.–Sat. 10–5, Sun. noon–5; Dec.–Mar., Fri. and Sat. 10–4, Sun. noon–4.*

NEED A BREAK?

The restaurant Haus Heuport (⊠*Dompl. 7* ☎*0941/599–9297*), opposite the entrance to the Dom, is in one of the old and grand private ballrooms of the city. The service is excellent, and the tables at the windows have a wonderful view of the Dom. In summer, head for the bistro area in the courtyard for snack fare, such as sandwiches and salads.

❾ ★ Historisches Museum *(Historical Museum)*. The municipal museum vividly relates the cultural history of Regensburg. It's one of the highlights of the city, both for its unusual and beautiful setting—a former Gothic monastery—and for its wide-ranging collections, from Roman artifacts to Renaissance tapestries and remains from Regensburg's 16th-century Jewish ghetto. The most significant exhibits are the paintings by Albrecht Altdorfer (1480–1538), a native of Regensburg and, along with Cranach, Grünewald, and Dürer, one of the leading painters of the German Renaissance. Altdorfer's work has the same sense of heightened reality found in that of his contemporaries, in which the lessons of Italian painting are used to produce an emotional rather than a rational effect. His paintings would not have seemed out of place among those of 19th-century Romantics. Far from seeing the world around him as essentially hostile, or at least alien, he saw it as something intrinsically beautiful, whether wild or domesticated. Altdorfer made two drawings of the old synagogue of Regensburg, priceless documents that are on exhibit here. ⊠*Dachaupl. 2–4* ☎*0941/507–2448* ⊕ *www.museen-Regensburg.de* 🎫*€2.20* ⊙*Tues.–Sun. noon–4.*

⓬ Schloss Emmeram *(Emmeram Palace)*. Formerly a Benedictine monastery, this is the ancestral home of the princely Thurn und Taxis family, which made its fame and fortune after being granted the right to carry official and private mail throughout the empire and Spain by Emperor Maximilian I (1493–1519) and by Philip I, king of Spain, who ruled during the same period. Their business extended over the centuries into the Low Countries (Holland, Belgium, and Luxembourg), Hungary, and Italy. The little horn that still symbolizes the post office in several European countries comes from the Thurn und Taxis coat of arms. For a while Schloss Emmeram was heavily featured in the gossip columns thanks to the wild parties and somewhat extravagant lifestyle of the young dowager Princess Gloria von Thurn und Taxis. After the death of her husband, Prince Johannes, in 1990, she had to auction off belongings in order to pay inheritance taxes. Ultimately a deal was cut, allowing her to keep many of the palace's treasures as long they were put on display.

The **Thurn und Taxis Palace,** with its splendid ballroom and throne room, allows you to witness the setting of courtly life in the 19th century. A visit usually includes the fine **Kreuzgang** (cloister) of the former Benedictine abbey of St. Emmeram. The items in the **Thurn und Taxis Museum,** which is part of the Bavarian National Museum in Munich, have been carefully selected for their fine craftsmanship—be it dueling pistols, a plain marshal's staff, a boudoir, or a snuffbox. The palace's **Marstallmuseum** (former royal stables) holds the family's coaches and carriages as well as related items. ☎*0941/504–8133* ✆*Museum Apr.– Oct., daily 1–5. Tours of palace and cloisters Apr.–Oct., weekdays at 11, 2, 3, and 4, weekends at 10, 11, 1, 2, 3, 4* ✉*Museum €4.50, palace and cloisters €11.50.*

② **Steinerne Brücke** *(Stone Bridge).* This impressive old bridge resting on massive pontoons is Regensburg's most celebrated sight. It was completed in 1146 and was rightfully considered a miraculous piece of engineering at the time. As the only crossing point over the Danube for miles, it effectively cemented Regensburg's control over trade. The significance of the little statue on the bridge is a mystery, but the figure seems to be a witness to the legendary rivalry between the master builders of the bridge and those of the Dom.

FodorsChoice
★

ALSO WORTH SEEING

⑤ **Alte Kapelle** *(Old Chapel).* The Carolingian structure was erected in the 9th century. Its dowdy exterior gives little hint of the joyous rococo treasures within—extravagant concoctions of sinuous gilt stucco, rich marble, and giddy frescoes, the whole illuminated by light pouring in from the upper windows. ✉*Alter Kornmarkt 8* ☎*No phone* ✆*Daily 9–dusk.*

⑥ **Karmelitenkirche** *(Church of the Carmelites).* This lovely church, in the baroque style from crypt to cupola, stands next to the Alte Kapelle. It has a finely decorated facade designed by the 17th-century Italian master Carlo Lurago. ✉*Alter Kornmarkt.*

⑪ **Neupfarrplatz.** This oversize open square was once a Jewish ghetto. Hard economic times and superstition led to their eviction by decree in 1519. While the synagogue was being torn down, one worker survived a very bad fall. A church was promptly built to celebrate the miracle, and before long a pilgrimage began. The **Neupfarrkirche** (New Parish Church) was built as well to accommodate the flow of pilgrims. During the Reformation, the Parish Church was given to the Protestants, hence its bare-bones interior. In the late 1990s, excavation work (for the power company) on the square uncovered well-kept cellars and, to the west of the church, the old synagogue, including the foundations of its Romanesque predecessor. Archaeologists salvaged the few items they could from the old stones (including a stash of 684 gold coins) and, not knowing what to do with the sea of foundations, ultimately carefully reburied them. Recovered items were carefully restored and are on exhibit in the Historisches Museum. Only one small underground area to the south of the church, the **Document**, accommodates viewing of the foundations. In a former cellar, surrounded by the original walls, visitors can watch a short video reconstructing life in the old Jewish ghetto. Over the old synagogue, the Israeli artist Dani Karavan designed a stylized plaza where people can sit and meet. Call the educational institution VHS for a tour of the Document (reservations are requested). For spontaneous visits, tickets are available at Tabak Götz on the western side of the square, at Neupfarrplatz 3. ⊠*Neupfarrpl.* ☎*0941/507–2433 for tours led by VHS* ⊕*www.vhs-regensburg.de* ✉*Document €5* ⊙*Church daily 9–dusk, document tour Thurs.–Sat. at 2:30.*

NEED A BREAK?

A Dampfnudel is a kind of sweet yeast-dough dumpling that is tasty and filling. The best in Bavaria can be had at Dampfnudel Uli (⊠ *Watmarkt 4* ☎*0941/53297* ⊙*Tues.–Fri. 10–6, Sat. 10–4*), a little establishment in a former chapel. The decoration is incredibly eclectic, from Bavarian crafts to a portrait of Ronald Reagan inscribed "To Uli Deutzer, with best wishes, Ronald Reagan."

7 **Niedermünster.** This 12th-century building with a baroque interior was originally the church of a community of nuns, all of them from noble families. ⊠*Alter Kornmarkt 5* ☎*0941/586–5500.*

8 **Porta Praetoria.** The rough-hewn former gate to the old Roman camp, built in AD 179, is one of the most interesting relics of Roman times in Regensburg. Look through the grille on its east side to see a section of the original Roman street, about 10 feet below today's street level. ⊠*North side of Alter Kornmarkt.*

13 **St. Emmeram.** The family church of the princely Thurn und Taxis family stands across from their ancestral palace, the Schloss Emmeram. The foundations of the church date to the 7th and 8th centuries. A richly decorated baroque interior was added in 1730 by the Asam brothers. St. Emmeram contains the graves of the 7th-century martyred Regensburg bishop Emmeram and the 10th-century saint Wolfgang. ⊠*Emmeramspl. 3* ☎*0941/51030* ⊙*Mon.–Thurs. and Sat. 10–4:30, Fri. 1–4:30, Sun. noon–4:30.*

10 **St. Kassian.** Regensburg's oldest church was founded in the 8th century. Don't be fooled by its dour exterior; inside, it's filled with delicate rococo decoration. ⊠*St. Kassianpl. 1* ☎*No phone* ⊙*Daily 9–5:30.*

WHERE TO EAT

¢–$ ✕**Café Felix.** A modern bi-level café and bar, Felix offers everything from sandwiches to steaks, and buzzes with activity from breakfast until the early hours. Light from an arty chandelier and torch-like fixtures bounces off the many large framed mirrors. The crowd tends to be young. ⊠*Fröhliche-Türkenstr. 6* ☎*0941/59059* ▭*No credit cards.*

¢–$ ✗**Leerer Beutel.** Excellent international cuisine—from antipasti to solid pork roast—is served in a pleasant vaulted room supported by massive rough-hewn beams. The restaurant is in a huge warehouse that's also a venue for concerts, exhibitions, and film screenings, making it a good place to start or end an evening. ⊠*Bertoldstr. 9* ☎*0941/58997* ▤*AE, DC, MC, V.*

¢ ✗**Historische Wurstküche.** Succulent Regensburger sausages—the best in town—are prepared right before your eyes on an open beechwood charcoal grill in this tiny kitchen. If you want to eat them inside in the tiny dining room, you'll have to squeeze past the cook to get there. On the walls—outside and in—are plaques recording the levels the river reached in the various floods that have doused the restaurant's kitchen in the past 100 years. ⊠*Thundorferstr. 3, just by stone bridge* ☎*0941/466–210* ▤*No credit cards.*

WHERE TO STAY

$$ ▥**Hotel-Restaurant Bischofshof am Dom.** This is one of Germany's most historic hostelries, a former bishop's palace where you can sleep in an apartment that includes part of a Roman gateway. Other chambers are only slightly less historic, and some have seen emperors and princes as guests. The hotel's restaurant (¢–$) serves regional cuisine (including the famous Regensburger sausages) at reasonable prices. The beer comes from a brewery founded in 1649. **Pros:** historic building, no-smoking rooms only, nice courtyard beer garden. **Cons:** no-smoking rooms only, restaurant not up to hotel's standards. ⊠*Krauterermarkt 3* ☎*0941/58460* ⊕*www.hotel-bischofshof.de* ⤸*55 rooms, 4 suites* ⌂*In-room: no a/c. In-hotel: restaurant, bar, parking (fee), some pets allowed, only no-smoking rooms* ▤*AE, DC, MC, V.*

$–$$ ▥**Hôtel Orphée.** It's difficult to choose from among the very spacious
Fodor's Choice rooms at the three different properties of this establishment—the Hotel
★ Orphée, the Petit Hotel Orphée on the next street; and the Grand Hotel Orphée. A Country Manor Orphée is on the other side of the river about 2 km (1 mi) away. You may decide to take an attic room with large wooden beams or an elegant room with stucco ceilings on the first floor. The French bistro–style restaurant ($$–$$$) prepares a selection of crepes, salads, and tasty meat dishes. **Pros:** in 2006, the hotel was completely and very tastefully renovated, excellent restaurant, center of town. **Cons:** 2 buildings: the Country Manor Orphée on the other side of the river and the Hôtel Orphée; difficult parking, front rooms are noisy. ⊠ *Grand Hôtel Orphee: Untere Bachg. 8, Petit Hotel Orphee: Wahlengasse 1; Country Manor Orphée: Andreasstr. 26* ☎*0941/596–020* ⊕*www.hotel-orphee.de* ⤸ *56 rooms* ⌂*In-room: no a/c, Wi-Fi. In-hotel: restaurant, bar, public Wi-Fi, parking (fee), some pets allowed, no-smoking rooms* ▤*AE, DC, MC, V.*

$–$$ ▥**Kaiserhof am Dom.** Renaissance windows punctuate the green facade of this historic city mansion. The rooms are 20th-century modern. Try for one with a view of the cathedral, which stands directly across the street. Breakfast is served beneath the high-vaulted ceiling of the former 14th-century chapel. **Pros:** front rooms have a terrific view, historic breakfast room. **Cons:** front rooms are noisy, no restaurant or bar. ⊠*Kramg. 10–12* ☎*0941/585–350* ⊕*www.kaiserhof-am-*

dom.de ⟳*30 rooms* 🛇*In-room: no a/c, Wi-Fi. In-hotel: public Wi-Fi, some pets allowed* ⊟*AE, DC, MC, V* ☉*Closed Dec. 21–Jan. 8.*

$ 🏨 **Am Peterstor.** The clean and basic rooms of this popular hotel in the heart of the Old Town are an unbeatable value. The many local eateries, including the excellent Café Felix a few doors away, more than compensate for the lack of an in-house restaurant. **Pros:** unbeatable value, center of town. **Cons:** simple rooms, no restaurant or bar, no phones in rooms, breakfast extra. ✉*Fröhliche-Türken-Str. 12,* ☎*0941/54545* ⊕*www.hotel-am-peterstor.de* ⟳*36 rooms* 🛇*In-room: no a/c, no phone* ⊟*MC, V.*

$ 🏨 **Hotel Münchner Hof.** The original arches of the ancient building are visible in some of the rooms at this little hotel. It is in a block near the Neupfarrkirche. The restaurant is quiet and comfortable, serving Bavarian specialties and good Munich beer. The bottom line: you get top service at a good price, and Regensburg is at your feet. **Pros:** some rooms with historic touch, center of town, nice little lobby. **Cons:** entrance in narrow street, difficult parking. ✉*Tändlerg. 9,* ☎*0941/58440* ⊕*www.muenchner-hof.de* ⟳*53 rooms* 🛇*In-room: no a/c, Wi-Fi. In-hotel: restaurant, public Wi-Fi, some pets allowed, no-smoking rooms* ⊟*AE, DC, MC, V.*

SHOPPING

The winding alleyways of the Altstadt are packed with boutiques, ateliers, jewelers, and other small shops offering a vast array of arts and crafts. You may also want to visit the daily market (Monday through Saturday 9–4) at the Neupfarrplatz, where you can buy regional specialties such as *Radi* (juicy radish roots), which local people love to wash down with a glass of wheat beer.

NIGHTLIFE & THE ARTS

Regensburg offers a range of musical experiences, though none so moving as a choral performance at the cathedral. ■**TIP→ Listening to the Regensburger Domspatzen, the boys' choir at the cathedral, can be a remarkable experience, and it's worth scheduling your visit to the city to hear them. The best sung mass is held on Sunday at 9** AM. If you're around in summer, look out for the Citizens Festival (Bürgerfest) and the Bavarian Jazz Festival (Bayreisches Jazzfest, ⊕*www.bayernjazz.de*) in July, both in the Old Town.

The kind of friendly, mixed nightlife that has become hard to find in some cities is alive and well in this small university city in the many *Kneipen,* bar-cum-pub-cum-bistros or -restaurants, such as the Leerer Beutel. Ask around to discover the latest in spot.

NEAR REGENSBURG

★ **Walhalla.** Walhalla (11 km [7 mi] east of Regensburg) is an excursion from Regensburg you won't want to miss, especially if you have an interest in the wilder expressions of 19th-century German nationalism. Walhalla—a name resonant with Nordic mythology—was where the god Odin received the souls of dead heroes. Ludwig I erected this monumental temple in 1840 to honor important German personages from ages past. In keeping with the neoclassic style then prevailing, the

Greek-style Doric temple is actually a copy of the Parthenon in Athens. The expanses of costly marble are evidence of both the financial resources and the craftsmanship at Ludwig's command. Walhalla may be kitschy, but the fantastic view it affords over the Danube and the wide countryside is definitely worth a look.

A boat ride from the Steinerne Brücke in Regensburg is the best way to go. On the return trip, you can steer the huge boat about half a mile, and, for €5 extra, you can earn an "Honorary Danube Boat Captain" certificate. Kids and grown-ups love it (*see Getting Here & Around, above*). To get to the temple from the river, you'll have to climb 358 marble steps.

To drive to it, take the Danube Valley country road (unnumbered) east from Regensburg 8 km (5 mi) to Donaustauf. The Walhalla temple is 1 km (½ mi) outside the village and well signposted.

Stiftskirche Sts. Georg und Martin *(Abbey Church of Sts. George and Martin)*. In Weltenburg (25 km [15 mi] southwest of Regensburg) you'll find the great Stiftskirche Sts. Georg und Martin, on the bank of the Danube River. The most dramatic approach to the abbey is by boat from Kelheim, 10 km (6 mi) downstream. On the stunning ride the boat winds between towering limestone cliffs that rise straight up from the tree-lined riverbanks. The abbey, constructed between 1716 and 1718, is commonly regarded as the masterpiece of the brothers Cosmas Damian and Egid Quirin Asam, two leading baroque architects and decorators of Bavaria. Their extraordinary composition of painted figures whirling on the ceiling, lavish and brilliantly polished marble, highly wrought statuary, and stucco figures dancing in rhythmic arabesques across the curving walls is the epitome of Bavarian baroque. Note especially the bronze equestrian statue of St. George above the high altar, reaching down imperiously with his flamelike, twisted gilt sword to dispatch the winged dragon at his feet. In Kehlheim there are two boat companies that offer trips to Kloster Weltenburg every 30 minutes in summer. You cannot miss the landing stages and the huge parking lot. ⊙ *Daily 9–dusk.*

EN ROUTE It's about a two-hour drive on the autobahn between Regensburg and Passau. Be forewarned, however, that if your trip coincides with a German holiday, it can be stop-and-go traffic for hours along this stretch. Halfway between Regensburg and Passau, the village of Metten is a worthwhile diversion or break. Stop to refuel at Cafe am Kloster (✉ *Marktplatz 1* ☎ *0991/9989380*). Once you are seated in the beer garden, the quality and the prices may well tempt you to linger longer than you had anticipated.

PASSAU

137 km (86 mi) southeast of Regensburg, 179 km (111 mi) northeast of Munich.

Flanking the borders of Austria and the Czech Republic, Passau dates back more than 2,500 years. Originally settled by the Celts, then by the Romans, Passau later passed into the possession of prince-bishops whose domains stretched into present-day Hungary. At its height, the Passau episcopate was the largest in the entire Holy Roman Empire.

Passau's location is truly unique. Nowhere else in the world do three rivers—the Ilz from the north, the Danube from the west, and the Inn from the south—meet. Wedged between the Inn and the Danube, the Old Town is a maze of narrow cobblestone streets lined with beautifully preserved burgher and patrician houses and riddled with churches. Many streets have been closed to traffic, enhancing the appeal of an Old Town stroll.

GETTING HERE & AROUND

Passau is on the A–3 autobahn from Regensburg to Vienna. It is an hour from Regensburg and about four hours from Vienna by train.

The Passau tourist office leads tours from May through October at 10:30 and 2:30 on weekdays and at 2:30 on Sunday; November through April the tours are held weekdays at noon. Tours start at the entrance to the cathedral and last one hour.

In Passau cruises on the three rivers begin and end at the Danube jetties on Fritz-Schäffer Promenade. Donauschiffahrt Wurm + Köck runs eight ships.

TIMING

Passau can be toured leisurely in the course of one day. Try to visit the Dom at noon to hear a recital on its great organ, the world's largest. Early morning is the best time to catch the light falling from the east on the Old Town walls and the confluence of the three rivers.

ESSENTIALS

Boat Tours **Donauschiffahrt Wurm + Köck** (✉ *D–94032 Passau* ☎ *0851/929292* ⊕ *www.donauschiffahrt.de*).

Visitor Information **Passau** (✉ *Tourist-Information Passau, Rathauspl. 3* ☎ *0851/955–980* ⊕ *www.passau.de*).

EXPLORING

MAIN ATTRACTIONS

❺ **Dom St. Stephan** *(St. Stephan's Cathedral)* rises majestically on the highest point of the earliest-settled part of the city. A baptismal church stood here in the 6th century. Two hundred years later, when Passau became a bishop's seat, the first basilica was built. It was dedicated to St. Stephan and became the original mother church of St. Stephan's Cathedral in Vienna. A fire reduced the medieval basilica to ruins in 1662; it was then rebuilt by Italian master architect Carlo Lurago. What you see today is the largest baroque basilica north of the Alps, complete with an octagonal dome and flanking towers. Little in its marble- and stucco-encrusted interior reminds you of Germany, and much proclaims the exuberance of Rome. Beneath the dome is the largest church organ assembly in the world. Built between 1924 and 1928 and enlarged in 1979–80, it claims no fewer than 17,774 pipes

Fodor'sChoice
★

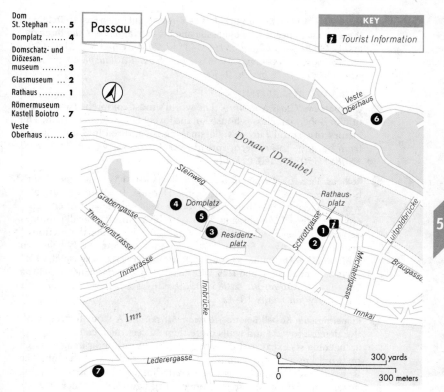

and 233 stops. The church also houses the most powerful bell chimes in southern Germany. ✉ *Dompl.* ☎ *0851/3930* 🎫 *Concerts midday €4, evening €8* ⊙ *Daily 8–11 and 12:30–6; tours May–Oct., weekdays at 12:30; Nov.–Apr., at noon.*

④ Domplatz *(Cathedral Square).* This large square in front of the Dom is bordered by sturdy 17th- and 18th-century buildings, including the **Alte Residenz,** the former bishop's palace and now a courthouse. The fine statue depicts Bavarian king Maximilian Joseph I.

③ Domschatz- und Diözesanmuseum *(Cathedral Treasury and Diocesan Museum).* The cathedral museum houses one of Bavaria's largest collections of religious treasures, the legacy of Passau's rich episcopal history. The museum is part of the **Neue Residenz,** which has a stately baroque entrance opening onto a magnificent staircase—a scintillating study in marble, fresco, and stucco. ✉ *Residenzpl.* 🎫 *€1.50* ⊙ *Apr.–Oct., Mon.–Sat. 10–4.*

⑥ Veste Oberhaus *(Upper House Stronghold).* The powerful fortress and summer castle commissioned by Bishop Ulrich II in 1219 looks over Passau from an impregnable site on the other side of the river, opposite the Rathaus. Today the Veste Oberhaus is Passau's most important museum, containing exhibits that illustrate the city's 2,000-year history. ■TIP➜ From the terrace of its café-restaurant (open Easter–October), there's a magnificent view of Passau and the convergence of the three rivers. ✉ *Oberhaus 125* ☎ *0851/493–3512* 🖼 *Museum €5* ◎ *Mar.–Oct., weekdays 9–5, weekends 10–6* ⌖ *Bus from Rathauspl. to museum Apr.–Nov. every ½ hr 10:30–5 €5.*

ALSO WORTH SEEING

❷ **Glasmuseum** *(Glass Museum).* The world's most comprehensive collection of Bohemian glass is housed in the lovely Hotel Wilder Mann. The history of Central Europe's glassmaking is captured in 30,000 items, from baroque to art deco, spread over 35 rooms. ✉ *Am Rathauspl.* ☎ *0851/35071* 🖼 *€5* ◎ *Daily 1–5.*

❶ **Rathaus.** Passau's 14th-century city hall sits like a Venetian merchant's house on a small square fronting the Danube. It was the home of a wealthy German merchant before being declared the seat of city government after a 1298 uprising. Two assembly rooms have wall paintings depicting scenes from local history and lore, including the (fictional) arrival in the city of Siegfried's fair Kriemhild, from the Nibelungen fable. ■TIP➜ The Rathaus tower has Bavaria's largest glockenspiel, which plays daily at 10:30, 2, and 7:25, with an additional performance at 3:30 on Saturday. ✉ *Rathauspl.* ☎ *0851/3960* 🖼 *€1.50* ◎ *Apr.–Oct. and late Dec.–early Jan., daily 10–4.*

❼ **Römermuseum Kastell Boiotro** *(Roman Museum).* A stout fortress with five defense towers and walls more than 12 feet thick came to light as archaeologists excavated the site of a 17th-century pilgrimage church on a hill known as Mariahilfberg, on the south bank of the Inn. The Roman citadel Boiotro was discovered along with a Roman well, its water still plentiful and fresh. Pottery, lead figures, and other artifacts from the area are housed in this museum at the edge of the site. ✉ *Ledererg. 43* ☎ *0851/34769* 🖼 *€2* ◎ *Mar.–Nov., Tues.–Sun. 10–4.*

WHERE TO EAT

$–$$ ✕ **Gasthaus zur blauen Donau.** Passau's esteemed chef Richard Kerscher turned this old house with thick walls and recessed windows into a simple but stylish restaurant. The first-floor dining room has a commanding view of the Danube. His delicacies are all based on traditional German recipes. ✉ *Höllg. 14* ☎ *0851/490–8660* ▣ *No credit cards.*

¢–$ ✕ **Blauer Bock.** This is one of Passau's oldest houses (first mentioned in city records in 1257), and has been welcoming travelers since 1875. The Danube flows by the tavern windows, and in summer you can watch the river traffic from a beer garden. The food is traditional; you'll find pork and potatoes in every variety. The tavern also offers accommodation in tastefully fitted rooms. ✉ *Höllg. 20* ☎ *0851/34637* ▣ *AE, MC, V.*

¢–$ ✕ **Peschl Terrasse.** The beer you sip on the high, sunny terrace overlooking the Danube is brought fresh from the Old Town brewery below, which, along with this traditional Bavarian restaurant, has been in the same family since 1855. ✉ *Rosstränke 4* ☎ *0851/2489* ▣ *DC, MC, V.*

WHERE TO STAY

$$ Hotel König. Though built in 1984, the König blends successfully with the graceful Italian-style buildings alongside the elegant Danube waterfront. Rooms are large and airy; some have a fine view of the river. **Pros:** some rooms with nice view of the Danube, spacious rooms. **Cons:** no restaurant, some small rooms. ✉ *Untere Donaulände 1D–94032* ☎*0851/3850* ⊕*www.hotel-koenig.de* 🛏*61 rooms* △*In-room: no a/c, Wi-Fi (some). In-hotel: bar, public Wi-Fi, parking (fee), some pets allowed, no-smoking rooms* ▤*AE, DC, MC, V.*

$–$$ Hotel Wilder Mann. Passau's most historic hotel dates from the 11th century and shares prominence with the ancient city hall on the waterfront market square. Empress Elizabeth of Austria and American astronaut Neil Armstrong have been among its guests. On beds of carved oak you'll sleep beneath chandeliers and richly stuccoed ceilings. For sheer indulgence, ask for either the King Ludwig or Sissi (Empress Elisabeth) suite. The esteemed Glasmuseum is within the hotel. **Pros:** historic hotel with some luxurious suites, center of town, some rooms with nice view of the river, others are a good value. **Cons:** historic hotel with some rooms in need of updating, no restaurant or bar. ✉*Am Rathauspl. 1,* ☎*0851/35071* ⊕*www.rotel-tours.de* 🛏*49 rooms, 5 suites* △*In-room: no a/c, Wi-Fi (some). In-hotel: public Wi-Fi, parking (fee), no-smoking rooms* ▤*AE, DC, MC, V.*

$–$$ Schloss Ort. This 13th-century castle's large rooms have views of the Inn River, which flows beneath the hotel's stout walls. The rooms are decorated in a variety of styles, with old-fashioned four-poster beds or modern wrought-iron details. The restaurant is closed in winter and on Monday, but the kitchen will always oblige hungry hotel guests. In summer the garden terrace is a delightful place to eat and watch the river. **Pros:** wonderful view of the river, nice garden, good restaurant. **Cons:** restaurant closed in winter, not in the center of town. ✉*Ort 11,* ☎*0851/34072* ⊕*www.schlosshotel-passau.de* 🛏*18 rooms* △*In-room: no a/c. In-hotel: restaurant, parking (fee), some pets allowed, no-smoking rooms* ▤*AE, DC, MC, V.*

¢ Rotel Inn. "Rotels" are usually hotels on wheels, an idea developed by a local entrepreneur to accommodate tour groups in North Africa and Asia. The first permanent Rotel Inn is on the bank of the Danube in central Passau and resembles an ocean liner. Its rooms are truly shipshape—hardly any wider than the bed inside—but they're clean, decorated in a pop-art style, and amazingly cheap. The building's unique design—a red, white, and blue facade with flowing roof lines—has actually been patented. It's definitely for young travelers, but also fun for families. **Pro:** very easy on the wallet. **Cons:** very, very small rooms; bathrooms down the hall, no restaurant. ✉*Am Hauptbahnhof/Donauufer,* ☎*0851/95160* ⊕*www.rotel-tours.de* 🛏*100 rooms* △*In-room: no a/c* ▤*No credit cards* ☉*Closed Oct.–late Apr.*

SPORTS & THE OUTDOORS

Cyclists can choose between eight long-distance paths along the rivers Danube (as far as Vienna) and Inn (tracing the river to its source in the Swiss Engadine). Bikes are permitted on most Danube boats and local trains for a small fee (usually €2), so you can cover part of the journey by river or rail. **Fahrrad-Laden Passau** (⊠ *Rosstränke 12* ☏ *0851/722–26*) is the best address in Passau for renting and repairing bicycles.

FESTIVALS

Passau is the cultural center of Lower Bavaria. Its **Europäische Wochen** *(European Weeks)* festival—featuring everything from opera to pantomime—is a major event on the European music calendar. Now in its 53rd year, the festival runs from June to July. For program details and reservations, write the **Kartenzentrale der Europäischen Wochen Passau** (⊠ *Dr.-Hans-Kapfinger-Str. 22D–94032 Passau* ☏ *0851/752020* ⊕ *www.europaeische-wochen-passau.de*).

Passau's **Christmas fair**—the Christkindlmarkt—is the biggest and most spectacular of the Bavarian Forest. It's held in and around the Nibelungenhalle from late November until just before Christmas.

The Bodensee

WORD OF MOUTH

"You'll love all the towns around Lake Constance and don't forget to visit Mainau Island, an island filled with so many flowers you'll run out of film. My husband and I enjoyed it so much we are going back next year."

—NancyAnn

"Lake Constance is, despite dense settlement, also an agricultural region famous for its products: Fruit, especially apples to be eaten as fruit or drunk as fruit liquor (Obstler from apples and pears, Williams from pears). Hops to flavour good beers, such as the Rothaus Pils found there or the tasty and refreshing Farny Weizen. Hagnau, Meersburg and Überlingen are also noted wine regions."

—hhildebrandt

www.fodors.com/forums

Updated by
Uli Ehrhardt

LAPPING THE SHORES OF GERMANY, Switzerland, and Austria, the Bodensee (Lake Constance), at 65 km (40 mi) long and 15 km (9 mi) wide, is the largest lake in the German-speaking world. Though called a lake, it's actually a vast swelling of the Rhine, gouged out by a massive glacier in the Ice Age and flooded by the river as the ice receded. The Rhine flows into its southeast corner, where Switzerland and Austria meet, and flows out at its west end. On the German side, the Bodensee is bordered almost entirely by the state of Baden-Württemberg (a small portion of the eastern tip, from Lindau to Nonnenhorn, belongs to Bavaria).

A natural summer playground, the Bodensee is ringed with little towns and busy resorts. It's one of the warmest areas of the country, not just because of its southern latitude but also owing to the warming influence of the water, which gathers heat in the summer and releases it in the winter. The lake itself practically never freezes over—it has done so only once in the last two centuries. The climate is excellent for growing fruit, and along the roads you'll find stands and shops selling apples, peaches, strawberries, jams, juices, wines, and schnapps, much of it homemade.

ORIENTATION & PLANNING

GETTING ORIENTED

This lake is off the beaten path for visitors from overseas and from other parts of Europe. If you venture here, you can be pretty sure you won't meet your countrymen. Even the Swiss and the Austrians, who own part of the shore of the Bodensee, tend to vacation elsewhere. For Germans, however, it is a favorite summer vacation spot, so it is wise to reserve rooms in advance.

The Northern Shore. A dozen charming little villages and towns line the northern shore of the lake. In good weather there is a wonderful view across the 10 mi of water to the Swiss mountains.

The Upper Swabian Baroque Road. Nearly every village has its own baroque treasure, from the small village church to the mighty Basilica Weingarten. The more miles between you and the Bodensee, the easier it is on your wallet, which may be reason enough to venture to this region.

Around the Bodanrück Peninsula. Konstanz is the biggest city on the international lakeshore, situated on the Bodanrück Peninsula and separated from the northern shore by a few miles of water. Konstanz survived WWII unscathed by leaving its lights burning every night, so the allied bomber pilots could not distinguish it from the touching Swiss city of Kreuzlingen. The small towns of the "Untersee"(Lower Lake), as this part of the Bodensee is called, have a more rural atmosphere than those of the northern shore.

TOP REASONS TO GO

Altes Schloss in Meersburg: Explore the oldest continuously inhabited castle in Germany, from the sinister dungeons to the imposing knights' hall with its panoramic view over the lake.

Schloss Salem, near Überlingen: The castle itself has plenty to see, what with furnished rooms, stables, gardens, and museums all on the site; an added bonus is the 8-km (5-mi) walking path that leads cross-country from its grounds to Wallfahrtskirche Birnau.

Wallfahrtskirche Birnau, near Überlingen: A vineyard slopes down from this pilgrimage church to a castle on the lakeshore. The scene inside belies the church's plain exterior: it is a riot of color and embellishment. The *Honigschlecker*

("honey sucker"), a gold-and-white cherub beside the altar, is dedicated to St. Bernard of Clairvaux, "whose words are sweet as honey."

Mainau Island: More than one million tulips and narcissi grace the flower island of Mainau in spring, and they are later followed by rhododendrons and azaleas, roses, and dahlias. A boat trip is the most delightful way to get there, and you'll have the best views of Mainau castle on its small hill.

Zeppelin Museum, Friedrichshafen: Step inside the gracious passenger rooms of the airship, and you may find yourself questioning whether the air transport of today, though undeniably bigger and faster, is a real improvement.

THE BODENSEE PLANNER

WHEN TO GO

The Bodensee's temperate climate makes for pleasant weather from April to October. In spring orchard blossoms explode everywhere, and on Mainau, the "island of flowers," more than a million tulips, hyacinths, and narcissi burst into bloom. Holiday crowds come in summer, and autumn can be warm and mellow. Quite a few hotels and restaurants in the smaller resort towns as well as many tourist attractions close for the winter.

GETTING HERE & AROUND

BY AIR The closest international airport to the Bodensee is in Zürich, Switzerland, 60 km (37 mi) from Konstanz, connected by the autobahn. There are also direct trains from the Zürich airport to Konstanz. There are several flights from Berlin, Düsseldorf, Frankfurt, London, and other destinations to the regional airport at Friedrichshafen.

BY BOAT & ■TIP→Note that the English pronunciation of "ferry" sounds a lot like the
FERRY German word *fähre,* which means car ferry. *Schiffe* is the term used for passenger ferries. Car and passenger ferries have different docking points in the various towns. The car ferries run all year; in summer you may have to wait in line. The passenger routes, especially the small ones, often do not run in winter, from November to March.

The Weisse Flotte line of boats, which is run by the BSB, or Bodensee-Schiffsbetriebe, links most of the larger towns and resorts. One of the nicest trips is from Konstanz to Meersburg and then on to the island of Mainau. At this writing, the round-trip fare was €13; rates are subject to change. Excursions around the lake last from one hour to a full day. Many cross to Austria and Switzerland; some head west along the Rhine to the Schaffhausen and the Rheinfall, the largest waterfall in Europe. Information on lake excursions is available from all local tourist offices and travel agencies.

BY BUS Buses serve most smaller communities that have no train links, but service is infrequent. Along the shore there are buses that run every half-hour during the day from Überlingen to Friedrichshafen, stopping in towns such as Meersburg, Hagnau, and Immenstaad.

BY CAR Construction on the A–96 autobahn that runs from Munich to Lindau is ongoing. For a more scenic route, take B–12 via Landsberg and Kempten. For a scenic but slower route from Frankfurt, take B–311 at Ulm and follow the Oberschwäbische Barockstrasse (Upper Swabian Baroque Road) to Friedrichshafen. Lindau is also a terminus of the Deutsche Alpenstrasse (German Alpine Road). It runs east–west from Salzburg to Lindau.

Lakeside roads in the Bodensee area boast wonderful vistas but experience occasional heavy traffic in summer. Stick to the speed limits in spite of the aggressive tailgaters: speed traps are frequent, especially in built-up areas. Formalities at border-crossing points are few. However, in addition to your passport you'll need insurance and registration papers for your car. For rental cars, check with the rental company to make sure you are allowed to take the car into another country. Car ferries link Romanshorn, in Switzerland, with Friedrichshafen, as well as Konstanz with Meersburg. Taking either ferry saves substantial mileage. The fare depends on the size of the car.

BY TRAIN From Frankfurt to Friedrichshafen and Lindau, take the ICE (InterCity Express) to Ulm and then transfer (total time 3½ hours). There are direct trains to Konstanz from Frankfurt every 2 hours (travel takes 4½ hours), which pass through the beautiful scenery of the Black Forest. From Munich to Lindau, the EC (Europe Express) train takes 2½ hours. From Zürich to Konstanz, the trip lasts 1½ hours. Local trains encircle the Bodensee, stopping at most towns and villages.

TOURS Most of the larger tourist centers have city tours with English-speaking guides, but call ahead to confirm availability. The Bodensee is a paradise for bike travelers, with hundreds of miles of well-signposted paths that keep riders safe from cars. You can go on your own or enjoy the comfort of a customized tour with accommodations and baggage transport around the Bodensee (including a bike, if need be). Wine-tasting tours are available in Überlingen, in the atmospheric Spitalweingut zum Heiligen Geist, as well as in Konstanz and Meersburg. Call the local tourist offices for information. Zeppelin tours operated by the DZR (Deutsche Zeppelin Reederei) are not cheap (sightseeing trips cost €200–€715), but they do offer a special feel and a reminder of the grand old days of flight. The zeppelins depart from the airport in Friedrichshafen.

ESSENTIALS   **Airport Contacts Flughafen Friedrichshafen (FDH)** (☎07541/284-01 ⊕ *www. fly-away.de*). **Zürich Airport (ZRH)** (☎43/816-2211 ⊕ *www.zurich-airport.com*).

Boat & Ferry Contacts Bodensee-Schiffsbetriebe (✉ *Hafenstr. 6 Konstanz* ☎07531/3640–389 ⊕ *www.bsb-online.com*).

Tour Contacts Bodensee-Radweg-Service GmbH (✉ *Mainaustr. 34, Konstanz* ☎07531/819930 ⊕ *www.bodensee-radweg.com*). **velotours** (✉ *Ernst-Sachsstr. 1 , Konstanz* ☎07531/98280 ⊕ *www.velotours.de*).

Visitor Information Internationaler Bodensee Tourismus (✉ *Hafenstr. 6 Konstanz* ☎07531/90940 ⊕ *www.bodensee-tourismus.com*).

ABOUT THE RESTAURANTS & HOTELS

In this area, international dishes are not only on the menu but on the map—you have to drive only a few miles to try the Swiss or Austrian dish you're craving in its own land. *Seeweine* (lake wines) from vineyards in the area include Müller-Thurgau, Spätburgunder, Ruländer, and Kerner.

The towns and resorts around the lake have a wide range of hotels, from venerable wedding-cake-style, fin-de-siècle palaces to more modest *Gasthöfe*. If you're visiting in July and August, make reservations in advance. For lower rates in a more rural atmosphere, consider staying a few miles away from the lake.

WHAT IT COSTS IN EUROS					
	¢	$	$$	$$$	$$$$
RESTAURANTS	under €9	€9–€15	€16–€20	€21–€25	over €25
HOTELS	under €50	€50–€100	€101–€175	€176–€225	over €225

Restaurant prices are per person for a main course at dinner. Hotel prices are for two people in a standard double room, including tax and service.

PLANNING YOUR TIME

Choosing a place to stay in these parts is a question of finance and interest. The closer you stay to the water, the more expensive and lively it becomes. Many visitors to Lake Constance pass by on their way from one country to another, so during the middle of the day the best-known places like Konstanz, Mainau, Meersburg, and Lindau tend to be crowded. Try to visit these places either in the morning or in the late afternoon, and make your day trips to the lesser-known destinations, the Baroque churches in upper Swabia, the Swiss cities along the southern shore, or the nearby mountains in Switzerland and Austria.

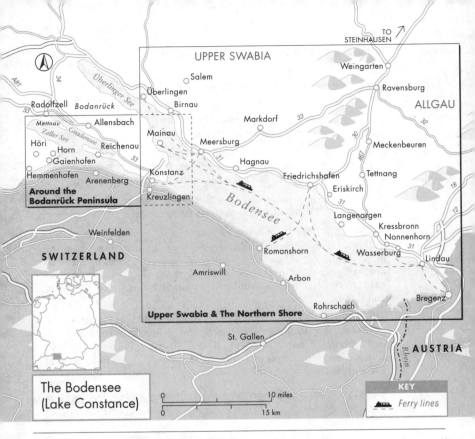

The Bodensee
(Lake Constance)

THE NORTHERN SHORE

There's a feeling here, in the midst of a peaceful Alpine landscape, that the Bodensee is part of Germany and yet separated from it—which is literally the case for towns such as Lindau, which sits in the lake tethered to land by a causeway. At the northwestern finger of the lake, Überlingen, a beautiful resort beached on a small inlet of water, attracts many vacationers and spa goers. Clear days reveal the snowcapped mountains of Switzerland to the south and the peaks of the Austrian Vorarlberg to the east.

LINDAU

180 km (112 mi) southwest of Munich.

By far the best way to get to know this charming old island city is on foot. Walk across the bridge from the mainland and keep going, losing yourself in the maze of small streets and passageways flanked by centuries-old houses. Wander down to the harbor for magnificent views. You automatically look up to the Austrian mountains on your left. At just 13 km (8 mi) away, they are nearer than the Swiss mountains that appear in the distance on your right.

Lindau was made a Free Imperial City within the Holy Roman Empire in 1275. It had developed as a fishing settlement and then spent hundreds of years as a trading center along the route between the rich lands of Swabia and Italy. The Lindauer Bote, an important stagecoach service between Germany and Italy in the 18th and 19th centuries, was based here; Goethe traveled via this service on his first visit to Italy in 1786. The stagecoach was revived a few years ago, and every June it sets off on its 10-day journey to Italy. You can book a seat through the Lindau tourist office.

As the German empire crumbled toward the end of the 18th century, battered by Napoléon's revolutionary armies, Lindau fell victim to competing political groups. It was ruled by the Austrian Empire before passing into Bavarian control in 1805. Lindau's harbor was rebuilt in 1856.

GETTING HERE & AROUND
Lindau is halfway between Munich and Zurich, and about two hours from both on the EC (European Express) train. From Frankfurt it takes about four hours—change from the ICE (Inter City Express) train in Ulm to the IRE (Inter Regio Express) train. You can also reach Lindau by boat: it takes about 25 minutes from Bregenz across the bay. Once in Lindau, you can reach everything on foot.

ESSENTIALS
Visitor Information **Lindau** (✉ *ProLindau Tourismus Stadtpl.* ☎ *08382/260–030* ⊕ *www.lindau.de).*

EXPLORING
Its most striking landmark is a **seated lion**, the proud symbol of Bavaria. Carved from Bavarian marble and standing 20 feet high, the lion stares out across the lake from a massive plinth.

Standing sentinel with the seated lion is the **Neuer Leuchtturm** *(New Lighthouse)*, across the inner harbor's passageway.

At the harbor's edge is the **Alter Leuchtturm** *(Old Lighthouse)*, firmly based on the weathered remains of the 13th-century city walls.

The third tower watching over the harbor is the old **Mangturm**, which was once the seat of the clothiers' guild.

A maze of ancient streets leading from the harbor makes up the **Altstadt**. Half-timber and gable houses line its main street, pedestrians-only Maximilianstrasse.

The **Altes Rathaus** *(Old Town Hall* ✉ *Maximilianstr.)* is the finest of Lindau's handsome historic buildings. It was constructed between 1422 and 1436 in the midst of a vineyard and given a Renaissance face-lift 150 years later, though the original stepped gables remain. Emperor Maximilian I held an imperial diet here in 1496; a fresco on the south facade depicts the scene. The building houses offices and cannot be visited.

The **Barfüsserkirche** (*Church of the Barefoot Pilgrims* ✉*Fischerg.*), built from 1241 to 1270, is now Lindau's principal theater, and the Gothic choir is a memorable setting for concerts.

Ludwigstrasse and Fischergasse lead to a watchtower, once part of the original city walls. Pause in the little park behind it, the **Stadtgarten** *(City Park)*. If it's early evening, you'll see the first gamblers of the night making for the neighboring casino.

The **Peterskirche** (*St. Peter's Church* ✉*Schrannenpl.*) is a solid Romanesque building, constructed in the 10th century and reputedly the oldest church in the Bodensee region. Step inside to see the frescoes by Hans Holbein the Elder (1465–

> ## BREGENZ, AUSTRIA
>
> Bregenz is a mere 13 km (8 mi) from Lindau, on the other side of the bay. It's a 20-minute ride on a pleasure boat to get there, and visiting this Austrian town is a great side trip. Wander around the lakeshore and the lovely, romantic remains of the once-fortified medieval town. An enormous floating stage is the site for performances of grand opera and orchestral works under the stars. Ascend Pfänder Mountain, in Bregenz's backyard, via the cable tramway for views that stretch as far as the Black Forest and the Swiss Alps.

1524) on the northern wall, some of which depict scenes from the life of St. Peter, the patron saint of fishermen. Attached to the church is the old 16th-century bell foundry, now housing a pottery, where you can pick up plates, bowls, candleholders, and other household objects. Also noteworthy is the adjacent Unterer Schrannenplatz, where the bellmakers used to live. A 1989 fountain depicts five of the *Narren* (Fools) that make up the VIPs of the Alemannic Mardi Gras celebrations.

Lindau's **Marktplatz** *(market square)* is an almost austere place. It's lined by a series of sturdy and attractive old buildings. The Gothic **Stephanskirche** (St. Stephen's Church) is simple and sparsely decorated, as befits a Lutheran place of worship. It dates to the late 12th century, but went through numerous transformations. One of its special features is the green-hue stucco ornamentation on the ceiling, which immediately attracts the eye toward the heavens. In contrast, the Catholic **Marienkirche** (St. Mary's Church), which stands right next to the Stephanskirche, is exuberantly baroque.

The **Haus zum Cavazzen** home dates to 1728. It belonged to a wealthy merchant and is now considered one of the most beautiful houses in the Bodensee region, owing to its rich decor of frescoes. Today it serves as a local history museum, with collections of glass and pewter items, paintings, and furniture from the last five centuries. ✉*Am Marktpl. 6* ☎*08382/2775–6514* ✉*€2.50* ⊙*Apr.–Oct., Tues.–Fri. and Sun. 11–5, Sat. 2–5.*

WHERE TO EAT

$$$–$$$$ ✕**Restaurant Hoyerberg Schlössle.** A commanding terrace view across the ★ lake to Bregenz and the Alps combined with excellent nouvelle cuisine makes this one of the best dining experiences in Lindau. The special-

EATING WELL BY THE BODENSEE

On a nice day you could sit on the terrace of a Bodensee restaurant forever, looking across the sparkling waters to the imposing heights of the Alps in the distance. The fish on your plate, caught that very morning in the lake perhaps, is another reason to linger. Fish predominates on the menus of the region; 35 varieties swim in the lake, with *Felchen* (whitefish) the most highly prized. Felchen belongs to the salmon family and is best eaten *blau* (poached in a mixture of water and vinegar with spices called *Essigsud*) or *Müllerin* (baked in almonds). A white *Seewein* (lake wine) from one of the vineyards around the lake goes well with the fish. Sample a German and a Swiss version. Both use the same grape, and yet they produce wines with very different tastes, despite the fact that the vineyards are only a few miles apart. The Swiss like their wines very dry, whereas the Germans like it slightly sweeter.

One of the best-known Swabian dishes is *Maultaschen,* a kind of ravioli, usually served floating in a broth strewn with chives. Another specialty is *Pfannkuchen* (pancakes) generally filled with meat, or chopped into fine strips and scattered in a clear consommé known as *Flädlesuppe.* The Swabian Sunday *Zwiebelrostbraten* (roast beef with lots of fried onions) and *Spätzle* (roughly chopped, golden-color fried egg noodles) is accompanied by a good strong Swabian beer.

ties, which change seasonally, are fish and game, and there are prix-fixe menus of four and six courses (€80); one offers tuna carpaccio, monkfish medallion, and Thai coconut soup with scampi. Brick-trim arched windows, fresh flowers, and elegant high-back chairs complete the experience. ⊠*Hoyerbergstr. 64* ☎*08382/25295* ⚑*Reservations essential* ⊟*AE, DC, MC, V* ☉*Closed Mon. and Feb. No lunch Tues.*

$–$$ ✕**Gasthaus zum Sünfzen.** This ancient inn was serving warm meals to the patricians, officials, merchants, and other good burghers of Lindau back in the 14th century. The current chef insists on using fresh ingredients preferably from the region, such as fish from the lake in season, venison from the mountains, and apples—pressed to juice or distilled to schnapps—from his own orchard. Try the herb-flavored *Maultaschen* (large ravioli), the excellent *Felchen* (whitefish) fillet in wine sauce, or the peppery Schübling sausage. ⊠*Maximilianstr. 1* ☎*08382/5865* ⊟*AE, MC, V* ☉*Closed Feb.*

WHERE TO STAY

$$–$$$ 🏨**Hotel Bayerischer Hof/Hotel Reutemann.** This is *the* address in town, a
★ stately hotel directly on the edge of the lake, its terrace lush with semi-tropical, long-flowering plants, trees, and shrubs. Most of the luxuriously appointed rooms have views of the lake and the Austrian and Swiss mountains beyond. Freshly caught pike perch is a highlight of the extensive menus in the stylish restaurants ($$–$$$). Rooms at the Reutemann are a little cheaper than those at the Bayerischer Hof next door. **Pros:** very pretty lake view from many rooms, elegant dining room with very good food. **Cons:** not all rooms have a lake view, on weekends in summer parking is difficult. ⊠*Seepromenade* ☎*08382/9150*

⊕*www.bayerischerhof-lindau.de* ⟲*97 rooms, 2 suites* ⟶*In-room: no a/c, Wi-Fi (some). In-hotel: 2 restaurants, bar, pool, bicycles, laundry service, public Internet, public Wi-Fi, parking (fee), some pets allowed, no-smoking rooms* ▤*AE, DC, MC, V* ⟦◎⟧*BP.*

$–$$ ▦**Insel-Hotel.** Rooms at this family-run enterprise are perhaps not the most modern, but the atmosphere is friendly. In good weather breakfast can be taken on a street in the pedestrian zone, where you can watch the town come alive. **Pros:** center of town, family run. **Cons:** some rooms need some new furnishing and paint, parking is difficult. ✉*Maximilianstr. 42* ☎*08382/5017* ⊕*www.insel-hotel-lindau.de* ⟲*24 rooms* ⟶*In-room: no a/c, Wi-Fi (some). In-hotel: restaurant, some pets allowed, public Wi-Fi, no-smoking rooms* ▤*AE, MC, V* ⟦◎⟧*BP.*

$ ▦ **Gasthof Engel.** The Engel traces its pedigree back to 1390. Tucked into one of the Old Town's ancient, narrow streets, the property creaks with history. Twisted oak beams are exposed inside and outside the terraced house. The bedrooms are simply furnished but comfortable. The restaurant (¢–$) serves Swabian specialties with a few Swiss potato dishes (*Rösti*) for good measure. **Pros:** quaint rooms, historic building, in the center of town. **Cons:** no elevator, no credit cards accepted. ✉*Schafg. 4* ☎*08382/5240* ⟲*9 rooms, 7 with shower* ⟶*In-room: no a/c, no TV. In-hotel: restaurant, bar, some pets allowed, no elevator, no-smoking rooms* ▤*No credit cards* ⊙*Closed Jan. and Feb.* ⟦◎⟧*CP.*

$ ▦**Hotel garni Brugger.** This small, family-run hotel stands on the site occupied by the city wall in the Middle Ages. It's especially appealing for families, as you can always add another bed to your three-bed room. **Pros:** center of town, family-run atmosphere, good value for families. **Cons:** caters to families, no elevator. ✉*Bei der Heidenmauer 11* ☎*08382/93410* ⊕*www.hotel-garni-brugger.de* ⟲*23 rooms* ⟶*In room: no a/c. In hotel: no elevator, some pets allowed, no-smoking rooms* ▤*MC, V* ⊙*Closed Dec.* ⟦◎⟧*BP.*

$ ▦**Jugendherberge.** This well-run youth hostel is open to travelers up to 26 years old and families with at least one child under 18. Rooms have one to six beds and a shower and toilet. There are also special family rooms. **Pros:** very good value, caters to young people. **Cons:** noisy, young people, not on the island. ✉*Herbergsweg 11* ☎*08382/96710* ⊕*www.lindau.jugendherberge.de* ⟲*65 rooms* ⟶*In-room: no a/c, no phone, no TV. In-hotel: restaurant, laundry facilities* ▤*DC, MC, V* ⊙*Closed Jan.* ⟦◎⟧*CP.*

NIGHTLIFE & THE ARTS

Enjoy opera in an intimate setting at the **Lindauer Marionettenoper,** where puppets do the singing. Tickets are available at the **Stadttheater** (✉*Barfüsserpl. 1a* ☎*08382/944–650* ⊕*www.lindauer-mt.de* ⊙*Mon.–Thurs. 10–1:30 and 3–5).*

A dramatic floating stage supports orchestras and opera stars during the famous **Bregenzer Festspiele** (*Bregenz Music Festival* ✉*Bregenz* ☎*0043/5574–4076* ⊕*www.bregenzerfestspiele.com*) from mid-July to the end of August. Make reservations well in advance. Bregenz is 13 km (8 mi) from Lindau, on the other side of the bay.

SPORTS & THE OUTDOORS

BOATING &
WINDSURFING
■TIP→ **The best way to see Lindau is from the lake.** Take one of the plea-sure boats of the **Weisse Flotte** that leave Lindau's harbor five or six times a day for the 20-minute ride to Bregenz in Austria. These large boats carry up to 800 people on three decks. The round-trip costs €9.

The **Bodensee Yachtschule** (✉*Christoph Eychmüller Schiffswerfte 2* ☎*08382/944–588* ⊕*www.bodensee-yachtschule.de*), in Lindau, char-ters yachts and has one-week camp sessions for children.

You can rent windsurfing boards at **Windsurfschule Kreitmeir** (✉*Strand-bad Eichwald* ☎*08382/23330* ⊕*www.hermanno.de*).

EN
ROUTE
Six kilometers (4 mi) west of Lindau lies **Wasserburg,** whose name means "water castle," an exact description of what this enchanting island town once was—a fortress. It was built by the St. Gallen monas-tery in 924, and the owners, the counts of Montfort zu Tettnang, sold it to the Fugger family of Augsburg. The Fuggers couldn't afford to maintain the drawbridge that connected the castle with the shore and instead built a causeway. In the 18th century the castle passed into the hands of the Habsburgs, and in 1805 the Bavarian government took it over. ■TIP→ **Wasserburg has some of the most photographed sights of the Bodensee: the yellow, stair-gabled presbytery; the fishermen's St. Georg Kirche, with its onion dome; and the little Malhaus museum, with the castle, Schloss Wasserburg, in the background.**

6

FRIEDRICHSHAFEN

24 km (15 mi) west of Lindau.

Named for its founder, King Friedrich I of Württemberg, Friedrich-shafen is a young town (dating to 1811). In an area otherwise given over to resort towns and agriculture, Friedrichshafen played a central role in Germany's aeronautics tradition, which saw the development of the zeppelin airship before World War I and the Dornier seaplanes in the 1920s and '30s. The zeppelins were once launched from a floating hangar on the lake, and the Dornier water planes were tested here. The World War II raids on its factories virtually wiped the city off the map. The current layout of the streets is the same, but the buildings are all new and not necessarily pretty. The atmosphere, however, is good and lively, and occasionally you'll find a plaque with a picture of the old building that stood at the respective spot. The factories are back, too. Friedrichshafen is home to such international firms as EADS (airplanes, rockets, and helicopters) and ZF (gear wheels).

GETTING HERE & AROUND

It takes about one hour from Ulm on the ICE (Inter City Express) train. Most trains stop at Friedrichshafen airport. The car ferry takes you on a forty minute run across the lake to Romanshorn in Switzerland where you have direct express trains to the airport and the city of Zürich. In town you can reach most places on foot.

A fascinating way to view the lake is from a three-passenger Cessna operated by Slansky/Dussmann from Friedrichshafen's airport. They will also take you into the Alps, if you wish.

ESSENTIALS
Airplane Tours Slansky/Dussmann (☎ 07532/808–866 or 08388/1269).

Visitor Information **Friedrichshafen** (✉ Tourist-Information, Bahnhofpl. 2 ☎ 07541/30010 ⊕ www.friedrich shafen.de).

EXPLORING
★ Graf Zeppelin (Ferdinand Graf von Zeppelin) was born across the lake in Konstanz, but Friedrich-

shafen was where, on July 2, 1900, his first "airship"—the LZ 1—was launched. The fascinating story of the zeppelin airships is told in the **Zeppelin Museum**, which holds the world's most significant collection of artifacts pertaining to airship history in its 43,000 square feet of exhibition space. In a wing of the restored Bauhaus **Friedrichshafen Hafenbahnhof** (harbor railway station), the main attraction is the reconstruction of a 108-foot-long section of the legendary *Hindenburg*, the LZ 129 that exploded at its berth in Lakehurst, New Jersey, on May 6, 1937. (The airships were filled with hydrogen, because the United States refused to sell the Germans helium, for political reasons.) Climb aboard the airship via a retractable stairway and stroll past the authentically furnished passenger room, the original lounges, and the dining room. The illusion of traveling in a zeppelin is followed by exhibits on the history and technology of airship aviation: propellers, engines, dining-room menus, and films of the airships traveling or at war. Car fans will appreciate the great Maybach standing on the ground floor; passengers once enjoyed being transported to the zeppelins in it. The museum's restaurant is a good place to take a break and enjoy lunch or dinner. ✉ *Seestr. 22* ☎ *07541/38010* ⊕ *www.zeppelin-museum.de* 🎫 *€7.50* ⊙ *May, June, and Oct., Tues.–Sun. 9–5 (last entry at 4:30); July–Sept., daily 9–5; Nov.–Apr., Tues.–Sun. 10–5.*

The **Deutsche Zeppelin Reederei GmbH** operates zeppelins at the Friedrichshafen airport. You can board the *Zeppelin NT* (New Technology) for an aerial tour, or from May to October you can also take a tour of the zeppelin itself on its mooring mast. ✉ *Allmannsweilerstr. 132* ☎ *07541/59000* ⊕ *www.zeppelinflug.de.*

WHERE TO EAT
$-$$ ✕ **Zeppelin-Museumrestaurant.** The grand view of the harbor and the lake is only one of the attractions of this café and restaurant in the Zeppelin Museum. You can enjoy cakes and drinks or a wide range of Swa-

bian specialties (such as lentils) or more Italianate dishes. ⊠*Seestr. 22* ☎*07541/33306* ⊟*MC, DC, V.*

¢–$ ✕*Lukullum.* Students, businesspeople, and guests from the nearby hotels rub elbows at this lively, novel restaurant. The friendly service keeps up with the pace of the socializing. Partitioned areas named after tourist regions allow privacy for groups or families. Other sitting arrangements are theme oriented: you sit in a beer barrel, in a bedroom, or next to a waterwheel. The dishes are good and basic, with surprising international touches, everything from a Balkan kebab to jambalaya. ⊠*Friedrichstr. 21* ☎*07541/6818* ⊟*AE, DC, MC, V* ⊘*No lunch Mon.*

WHERE TO STAY

$$–$$$ ▦ **Buchhorner Hof.** This traditional hotel near the train station has been run by the same family since it opened in 1870. Hunting trophies on the walls, leather armchairs, and Turkish rugs decorate the public areas; bedrooms are large and comfortable. One floor is reserved for business travelers, with fax machines and extra-large desks in the rooms. The restaurant ($$–$$$) is plush and subdued, with delicately carved chairs and mahogany-panel walls. It offers a choice of menus with dishes such as pork medallions, perch fillet, and lamb chops. **Pros:** business floor, cozy and big lobby, excellent restaurant, many rooms have nice views. **Cons:** many rooms look onto a busy main street, parking is difficult. ⊠*Friedrichstr. 33* ☎*07541/2050* ⊕*www. buchhorn.de* ➟*90 rooms, 4 suites, 2 apartments* △*In-room: no a/c (some), dial-up, Wi-Fi. In-hotel: restaurant, bar, gym, bicycles, laundry service, public Wi-Fi, parking (fee), some pets allowed, no-smoking rooms* ⊟*AE, DC, MC, V* ⊙|*BP.*

$$ ▦ **Ringhotel Krone.** This Bavarian-theme hotel, made up of four build-
★ ings, is in the Schnetzenhausen district's semirural surroundings, 6 km (4 mi) from the center of town. You can roam the area on a bike rented from the hotel. All rooms have balconies. The restaurant ($–$$) specializes in game dishes and fish. **Pros:** great variety of rooms, very good food, lots of parking space. **Cons:** 4 mi from the center of town, a few rooms have street noise. ⊠*Untere Mühlbachstr. 1* ☎*07541/4080* ⊕*www.ringhotel-krone.de* ➟*135 rooms* △*In-room: no a/c (some), Wi-Fi. In-hotel: restaurant, bar, tennis courts, pool, gym, bicycles, public Internet, public Wi-Fi, some pets allowed, parking (no fee), no-smoking rooms* ⊟*AE, DC, MC, V* ⊙|*BP.*

$–$$ ▦ **Flair Hotel Gerbe.** A farm with a tannery in Friedrichshafen Ailingen, about 5 km (3 mi) from the city center, is now a pleasant, spacious hotel. Many of the rooms have balconies looking out onto the garden, the countryside, and, on a clear day, the Swiss mountains on the other side of the lake. In summer you can enjoy the Swabian food on the big terrace that leads into the garden. Even if you don't plan to jump into their indoor pool, take a peek at it and its surprising barrel ceiling, which was constructed by some ingenious brick layers for the tannery more than 400 years ago. **Pros:** new rooms in an old historic building, spacious rooms with good views, ample parking. **Cons:** 3 mi from center of town, some rooms have street noise. ⊠*Hirschlatterstr. 14* ☎*07541/5090* ⊕*www.hotel-gerbe.de* ➟*59 rooms* △*In-room: no* *a/c, Wi-Fi. In-hotel: restaurant, bar, pool, gym, bicycles, laundry service, public Internet, public Wi-Fi, parking (no fee), no-smoking rooms* ▭ *MC, V* ⏐◎⏐*CP.*

NIGHTLIFE & THE ARTS

College students and a mostly young crowd raise their glasses and voices above the din at **Cafebar Belushi** (✉*Montfortstr. 3* ☎*07541/32531*). A more mature crowd meets for music, food, dancing, and drinks at the **Halbhuber** (✉*Flughafen, P2 parking* ☎*07541/953–350*), which is in the airport to the west of town.

Friedrichshafen's **Graf-Zeppelin-Haus** (✉*Olgastr. 20* ☎*07541/2880*) is a modern convention center on the lakeside promenade, a seven-minute walk from the train station. It's also a cultural center, where musicals, light opera, and classical as well as pop-rock concerts take place several times a week. The Graf-Zeppelin-Haus has a good modern restaurant with a big terrace overlooking the harbor.

SHOPPING

The gift shop **Ebe** (✉*Buchhornpl.* ☎*07541/388–430*) sells handmade candles, dolls, and postcards. Excellent chocolates are sold at **Weber & Weiss** (✉*Charlottenstr. 11* ☎*07541/21771*). ◼TIP→ **Look for a specialty candy in the shape of a zeppelin airship.**

MEERSBURG

18 km (11 mi) west of Friedrichshafen.

Meersburg is one of the most romantic old towns on the German shore of the lake. Seen from the water on a summer afternoon with the sun slanting low, the steeply terraced town looks like a stage set, with its bold castles, severe patrician dwellings, and a gaggle of half-timber houses arranged around narrow streets. It's no wonder that cars have been banned from the center: the crowds of people who come to visit the sights on weekends fill up the streets. The town is divided into the Unterstadt (Lower Town) and Obere Stadt (Upper Town), connected by several steep streets and stairs.

ESSENTIALS

Visitor Information **Meersburg** (✉*Gästeinformation , Kirchstr. 4* ☎*07532/440400* ⊕*www.meersburg.de*).

EXPLORING

★ Majestically guarding the town is the **Altes Schloss** *(Old Castle)*, the original Meersburg ("sea castle"). It's Germany's oldest inhabited castle, founded in 628 by Dagobert, king of the Franks. The massive central tower, with walls 10 feet thick, is named after him. The bishops of Konstanz used it as a summer residence until 1526, at which point they moved in permanently. They remained until the mid-18th century, when they built themselves what they felt to be a more suitable residence—the baroque Neues Schloss. Plans to tear down the Altes Schloss in the early 19th century were shelved when it was taken over by Baron Joseph von Lassberg, a man much intrigued by the castle's

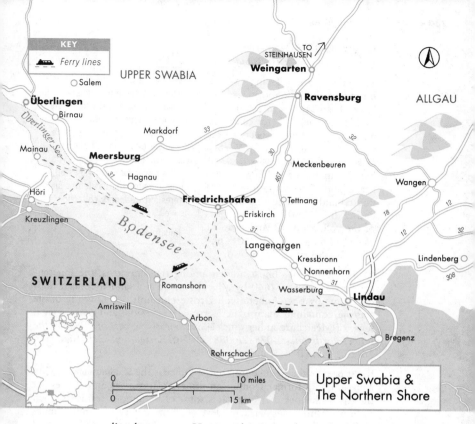

KEY	
⛴ Ferry lines	
○ Salem	

UPPER SWABIA

TO STEINHAUSEN ↗

Weingarten

Ravensburg

ALLGAU

○ **Überlingen**

Birnau

Markdorf

33

Überlinger See

Mainau

Meersburg

Hagnau

Meckenbeuren

30

467

Wangen

Höri

31

Bodensee

Friedrichshafen

Eriskirch

Tettnang

18

12

Kreuzlingen

Langenargen

31

12

32

SWITZERLAND

Romanshorn

Kressbronn

Nonnenhorn

Lindenberg

Wasserburg

31

308

Amriswill

Arbon

Wasserburg

Lindau

Rohrschach

Bregenz

| 0 | | | 10 miles |
| 0 | | | 15 km |

**Upper Swabia &
The Northern Shore**

---

medieval romance. He turned it into a home for like-minded poets and artists, among them the Grimm brothers and his sister-in-law, Annette von Droste-Hülshoff (1797–1848), one of Germany's most famous poets. The Altes Schloss is still private property, but much of it can be visited, including the richly furnished rooms where Droste-Hülshoff lived and the chamber where she died, as well as the imposing knights' hall, the minstrels' gallery, and the sinister dungeons. The **Altes Schloss Museum** (Old Castle Museum) contains a fascinating collection of weapons and armor, including a rare set of medieval jousting equipment. ☎07532/80000 💶€6.50 ⏰Mar.–Oct., daily 9–6; Nov.–Feb., daily 10–5:30.

The spacious and elegant **Neues Schloss** (New Castle) is directly across from its predecessor. Designed by Christoph Gessinger at the beginning of the 18th century, it took nearly 50 years to complete. The grand double staircase, with its intricate grillwork and heroic statues, was the work of Balthasar Neumann. The interior's other standout is the glittering **Spiegelsaal** (Hall of Mirrors). In an unlikely combination of 18th-century grace and 20th-century technology, the first floor of the palace houses the **Dornier Museum**. Three rooms are devoted to Claude Dornier, the pioneer airplane builder, and his flying machines, which are exhibited in model form and pictures. Several videos are shown on

request. ☎07532/440–4900 ☜€4
⊙Apr.–Oct., daily 10–1 and 2–6.

Sunbathed, south-facing Meersburg and the neighboring towns
have been the center of the
Bodensee wine trade for centuries.
You can pay your respects to the
noble profession in the **Weinbau
Museum** *(Vineyard Museum)*. A
barrel capable of holding 50,000
liters (about the same number of
quarts) and an immense winepress
dating from 1607 are highlights
of the collection. ✉*Vorburgg. 11*
☎*07532/440–260* ☜€2 ⊙*Apr.–
Oct., Tues., Fri., and Sun. 2–6.*

An idyllic retreat almost hidden among the vineyards, the Fürsten-
häusle was built in 1640 by a local vintner and later used as a holiday home by poet Annette von Droste-Hülshoff. It's now the **Droste
Museum,** containing many of her personal possessions and giving a vivid
sense of Meersburg in her time. ✉*Stettenerstr. 9, east of Obertor, the
town's north gate* ☎*07532/6088* ☜€5 ⊙*Easter–mid-Oct.,Tues.–Sat.
10–12:30 and 2–6, Sun. 2–6.*

Right next to the Meersburg Tourist Office is the **Stadtmuseum,** or City
Museum, in a former Dominican priory. You can see an overview of
the town's history that celebrates some of its famous residents, such
as Franz Anton Mesmer, who developed the theory of "animal mag-
netism." (His name gave rise to the verb "mesmerize.") ✉*Kirchstr. 4*
☎*07532/440–4801* ☜€2 ⊙*Apr.–Oct., Wed., Thurs., and Sat. 2–6.*

WHERE TO EAT

$–$$ ✕ **Winzerstube zum Becher.** Fresh fish from the lake is a specialty at
★   this traditional restaurant, which has been in the Benz family for
three generations. You can pair the day's catch with white wine from
their own vineyard. A popular meat entrée is *badische Ente* (duck
with bacon and apples in a wine-kirsch sauce). The restaurant is
near the New Castle, and reservations are recommended. ✉*Höllg. 4*
☎*07532/9009* ⊕*www.winzerstube-zum-becher.de* ▬*AE, DC, MC,
V* ⊙*Closed Jan. and Mon.*

WHERE TO STAY

$$–$$$ ▦ **Romantik Hotel Residenz am See.** Most of the elegant rooms at this
★   tastefully modern hotel face the lake, but the quieter ones look out
onto a vineyard. The hotel is across the street from the lake and about
a three-minute walk from the harbor and the old town. The restaurant ($$$$) has earthy, terra-cotta-tone walls and floor-to-ceiling windows. Fish is the specialty—try the pike perch in season. The vegetarian
menu is a pleasant surprise. Any guilt you feel at disturbing the form of
your artfully composed dessert will quickly dissipate once you taste it.
Pros: very good food, creative dishes, pleasant rooms with lake view,

quiet rooms toward the vineyards. **Cons:** not in center of town, only no-smoking rooms. ✉ *Uferpromenade 11* ☎ *07532/80040* 🌐 *www.hotel-residenz-meersburg.com* *23 rooms* *In-room: no a/c, Wi-Fi. In-hotel: restaurant, bar, public Wi-Fi, parking (no fee), no-smoking rooms* ▭ *MC, V* 🍴 *BP.*

$$ ★ **See Hotel Off.** Colors, lots of glass, and a fantastic lakeside location make this a place you will not want to leave. Owner Elisabeth Off has added personal touches to the rooms that make you feel completely at home. Twelve rooms have been designed according to the laws of feng shui. In the restaurant ($–$$) her husband, chef Michael Off, transforms local ingredients into gustatory adventures with a nod to nouvelle cuisine. The wellness area includes all sorts of alternative healing measures, from Reiki to aromatherapy. And you are only a few steps away from the lake if you feel like a swim. **Pros:** close to the lake, personalized rooms, away from center of town. **Cons:** not in center of town, only no-smoking rooms. ✉ *Uferpromenade 51* ☎ *07532/44740* 🌐 *www.hotel.off.mbo.de* *19 rooms* *In-room: no a/c, Wi-Fi. In-hotel: restaurant, bar, spa, public Wi-Fi, parking, some pets allowed, no-smoking rooms* ▭ *MC, V* 🍴 *BP* ⊙ *Closed Jan.*

$–$$ **Löwen.** This centuries-old, ivy-clad tavern on Meersburg's market square is a local landmark. Its welcoming restaurant ($$–$$$), with pine paneling, serves regional and seasonal specialties, notably a tasty stew of local fish. Guest rooms are cozily furnished and have their own sitting corners, and some have genuine Biedermeier furniture. **Pros:** center of town, pleasant rooms, good food in a cozy restaurant. **Cons:** during the day lots of noise from tourists, no elevator. ✉ *Marktpl. 2* ☎ *07532/43040* 🌐 *www.hotel-loewen-meersburg.de* *21 rooms* *In-room: no a/c. In-hotel: restaurant, bar, bicycles, no elevator, some pets allowed, no-smoking rooms* ▭ *AE, DC, MC, V* 🍴 *BP.*

$ **Gästehaus am Hafen.** This family-run, half-timber pension is in the middle of the Old Town, near the harbor. The rooms are small but have room for a child's bed, if needed. There's a place to store bikes as well. **Pros:** close to the harbor, in the center of the Lower Town, good value. **Cons:** small rooms, no credit cards, parking is five minutes away on foot. ✉ *Spitalg. 3* ☎ *07532/7069* 🌐 *www.amhafen.de* *7 rooms* *In-room: no a/c, no phone, refrigerator. In-hotel: restaurant, some pets allowed, no-smoking rooms* ▭ *No credit cards* ⊙ *Restaurant closed Nov.–Mar.* 🍴 *CP.*

$ **Zum Bären.** Built in 1605 and incorporating 13th-century Gothic foundations, the Bären was an important staging point for Germany's first postal service. The ivy-covered facade, with its characteristic steeple, hasn't changed much over the centuries, but interior comforts certainly have. The restaurant ($–$$) is rustic in an uncluttered way; people travel from afar to enjoy the rack of lamb. Some rooms are furnished with Bodensee antiques and brightly painted rustic wardrobes. If you have the chance, book Room 23 or Room 13. Both have semicircular alcoves with two overstuffed armchairs and six windows overlooking the marketplace. **Pros:** center of town, historic building, good value. **Cons:** no elevator, some rooms are small. ✉ *Marktpl. 11* ☎ *07532/43220* 🌐 *www.baeren-meersburg.de* *20 rooms* *In-*

room: no a/c. In-hotel: restaurant, no elevator, parking, no-smoking rooms ☐*No credit cards* ⊘*Closed Dec.–Mar. 15* ⏻I*BP.*

SHOPPING

Just at the entrance to Schlossplatz—the square in front of the Neues Schloss—are a few nice shops. **Ulmer** (☐*Schlosspl. 3* ☎*07532/5788*) has interesting gifts. Its specialty is children's clothes, including charming lederhosen for kids. If you can't find something at the incredible gift shop (toys, enamelware, books, dolls, model cars, and much more) called **Omas Kaufhaus** (☐*Marktpl. at Steigstr. 2* ☎*07532/433–9611* ⊘*Daily 10–6:30*), then at least you should see the exhibition of toy trains and tin boats on the first floor, the latter in a long canal filled with real water.

▌EN
ROUTE

As you proceed northwest along the lake's shore, a settlement of **Pfahlbauten** *("pile dwellings")*—a reconstructed village of Stone Age and Bronze Age dwellings built on stilts—sticks out of the lake. This is how the original lake dwellers lived, surviving off the fish that swam outside their humble huts. Real dwellers in authentic garb give you an accurate picture of prehistoric lifestyles. The nearby **Pfahlbauten Freilichtmuseum** (Open-Air Museum of German Prehistory) contains actual finds excavated in the area. ☐*Strandpromenade 6, Unteruhldingen* ☎*07556/8543* ⊕*www.pfahlbauten.de* ☐*€7 including obligatory tour of 45 min* ⊘*Apr.–Oct., daily 9–7; Nov.–Mar., 2 guided tours daily, check for times.*

ÜBERLINGEN

13 km (8 mi) west of Meersburg, 24 km (15 mi) west of Friedrichshafen.

This Bodensee resort has an attractive waterfront and an almost Mediterranean flair. It's midway along the north shore of the Überlingersee, a narrow finger of the Bodensee that points to the northwest. Überlingen is ancient—it's first mentioned in records dating back to 770. In the 13th century it earned the title of Free Imperial City and was known for its wines. No fewer than seven of its original city gates and towers remain from those grand days, as well as substantial portions of the old city walls. What was once the moat is now a grassy walkway, with the walls of the Old Town towering on one side and the Stadtpark stretching away on the other. The **Stadtgarten** (city garden), which opened in 1875, cultivates exotic plants and has a famous collection of cacti, a fuchsia garden, and a small deer corral. The heart of the city is the Münsterplatz.

ESSENTIALS

Visitor Information **Überlingen** (☐ *Tourist Information Am Landungspl. 14* ☎*07551/947–1522* ⊕*www.ueberlingen.de*).

EXPLORING

★ The huge **Münster St. Nikolaus** *(Church of St. Nicholas)* was built between 1512 and 1563 on the site of at least two previous churches. The interior is all Gothic solemnity and massiveness, with a lofty stone-vaulted ceiling and high, pointed arches lining the nave. The single most remarkable feature is not Gothic at all but opulently Renaissance—the massive high altar, carved by Jörg Zürn from lime wood that almost looks like ivory. The focus of the altar is the Christmas story. ⊠ *Münsterpl.*

Inside the late-Gothic **Altes Rathaus** *(Old Town Hall)* is a high point of Gothic decoration, the **Rathaussaal**, or council chamber, which is still in use today. Its most striking feature amid the riot of carving is the series of figures, created between 1492 and 1494, representing the states of the Holy Roman Empire. There's a naïveté to the figures—their beautifully carved heads are all just a little too large, their legs a little too spindly—that makes them easy to love. ⊠ *Münsterpl.* 🎫 *Free* ⏰ *Apr.–mid-Oct., weekdays 9–noon and 2:30–5, Sat. 9–noon.*

The **Städtisches Museum** *(City Museum)* is in the Reichlin-von-Meldegg house, 1462, one of the earliest Renaissance dwellings in Germany. It displays exhibits tracing Bodensee history and a vast collection of antique dollhouses. ⊠ *Krummebergstr. 30* ☎ *07551/991–079* 💶 *€3* ⏰ *Apr.–Oct., Tues.–Sat. 9–12:30 and 2–5, Sun. 10–3.*

Ⓒ **Schloss Salem** *(Salem Castle)* is in the tiny inland village of Salem (10

Fodor's Choice km [6 mi] north of Überlingen). This huge castle began its existence as
★ a convent and large church. After many architectural permutations, it was transformed into a palace for the Baden princes, though traces of its religious past can still be seen. You can view the royally furnished rooms of the abbots and princes, a library, stables, and the church. The castle also houses an interesting array of museums, workshops, and activities, including a museum of firefighting, a potter, a musical instrument builder, a goldsmith shop, a glassblowing shop, pony farms, a golf driving range, and a fantasy garden for children. There is a great path that leads from the southwestern part of the grounds through woods and meadows to the pilgrimage church of Birnau. The route was created by the monks centuries ago and is still called the Prälatenweg (path of the prelates) today. It's an 8-km (5-mi) walk (no cars permitted). ⊠ *Salem,* ☎ *07553/81437* 🌐 *www.salem.de* 💶 *€7* ⏰ *Apr.–Oct., Mon.–Sat. 9:30–6, Sun. 10:30–6.*

Just northwest of Unteruhldingen, the **Wallfahrtskirche Birnau** *(Pilgrimage Church)* overlooks the lake from a small hill. The church was built by the master architect Peter Thumb between 1746 and 1750. Its simple exterior consists of plain gray-and-white plaster and a tapering clock-tower spire above the main entrance. The interior, by contrast, is overwhelmingly rich, full of movement, light, and color. It's hard to single out highlights from such a profusion of ornament, but seek out the *Honigschlecker* ("honey sucker"), a gold-and-white cherub beside the altar, dedicated to St. Bernard of Clairvaux, "whose words are sweet as honey" (it's the last altar on the right as you face the high altar). The cherub is sucking honey from his finger, which he's just pulled out of a beehive. The fanciful spirit of this dainty play on words is continued in the small squares of glass set into the pink screen that rises high above the main altar; the gilt dripping from the walls; the

6

swaying, swooning statues; and the swooping figures on the ceiling. ⊠*Birnau* ⊙*Daily 7–7.*

OFF THE
BEATEN
PATH

Affenberg *(Monkey Mountain).* On the road between Überlingen and Salem, the Affenberg is a 50-plus-acre park with an old farm that serves as home to more than 200 Barbary apes, as well as aquatic birds, gray herons, coots, and ducks. There's also a gallery with artistic renderings of monkeys. ⊠*On road between Überlingen and Salem* ☎*07553/381* ⊕*www.affenberg-salem.de* ⊡*€7.50* ⊙*Mar. 15–Oct., daily 9–6; last entry at 5:30.*

WHERE TO STAY

$$ 🏨 **Romantik Hotel Johanniter Kreuz.** The setting is a small village 3 km (2 mi) to the north of Überlingen. The old part of the hotel dates from the 17th century and is truly romantic—half-timber, with a huge fireplace in the center of the restaurant ($$). In the modern annex you can relax on your room's balcony. An 18-hole golf course overlooking the lake is just 1½ km (1 mi) away. **Pros:** choice of very different rooms, spacious, modern and yet welcoming lobby, family run, cozy restaurant, quiet surroundings, golf course close by. **Cons:** not in center of town, very long corridors from historic part of hotel to reach elevator in new part of the hotel. ⊠*Johanniterweg 11, Andelshofen* ☎*07551/61091* ⊕*www.johanniter-kreuz.de* ⇄*29 rooms* ♿*In-room: no a/c, Wi-Fi. In-hotel: restaurant, bar, gym, spa, bicycles, public Wi-Fi, parking, some pets allowed, no-smoking rooms* ▭ *DC, MC, V* ⍟*BP.*

$–$$ 🏨 **Bad Hotel mit Villa Seeburg.** This stately hotel has the double advantage of being both on the lake and in the center of town. The spare modern rooms are done in crisp white and cream. Try to get a room looking toward the park and the lake, though it will be a bit more expensive. The restaurant ($–$$) is furnished in the same airy Mediterranean style, and the food is a lighter, healthier version of local Swabian cuisine. **Pros:** on the lake, in the center of town, quiet. **Cons:** rooms in the main building on the busy street can be noisy, parking is 2 minutes away on foot. ⊠*Christophstr. 2* ☎*07551/8370* ⊕*www. bad-hotel-ueberlingen.de* ⇄*65 rooms* ♿*In-room: no a/c, safe (some), Wi-Fi (some). In-hotel: restaurant, bar, public Wi-Fi, parking (fee), no-smoking rooms* ▭*AE, MC, V* ⊙*Restaurant closed Jan.–Mar.* ⍟*BP.*

$–$$ 🏨 **Schäpfle.** The charm of this ivy-covered hotel in the center of town has been preserved and supplemented through time. In the hallways you'll find quaint furniture and even an old Singer sewing machine painted with flowers. The rooms are done with light, wooden Scandinavian farm furniture. Guests and Überlingen residents congregate in the comfortable taproom, where the regional and international dishes are reasonably priced ($). The chef prides himself on his homemade noodles. If you need a lake view, the hotel has a second building a few steps away right on the lake. **Pros:** center of town, local atmosphere in restaurant, annex with lake view. **Cons:** no elevator, no credit cards, no lobby. ⊠*Jakob-Kessenringstr. 14* ☎*07551/63494* ⊕*www.schaepfle.de* ⇄*32 rooms in 2 houses* ♿*In-room: no a/c. In-hotel: restaurant, some pets allowed, no-smoking rooms, no elevator* ▭*No credit cards* ⍟*BP.*

$ 🛏 **Landgasthof zum Adler.** This unpretentious, rustic country inn is in a small village a few miles north of Überlingen. It has a blue-and-white half-timber facade, scrubbed wooden floors, maplewood tables, and thick down comforters on the beds. The Adler also keeps 10 apartments in a separate house for families at very affordable rates. The food ($–$$) is simple and delicious; trout is a specialty, as are several vegetarian dishes, such as potato gratin with fennel. **Pros:** good food in old wooden restaurant, modern rooms in annex. **Cons:** rooms on the street side can be noisy, in a little village miles from Überlingen, no credit cards. ⊠ *Hauptstr. 44, Überlingen-Lippertsreute* ☎ *07553/82550* ⊕ *www.landgasthofadler.de* ➪ *17 rooms* ♿ *In-room: no a/c. In-hotel: restaurant, parking (free), some pets allowed, no-smoking rooms* ⊟ *No credit cards* ⊗ *Closed 2 wks in Nov.* ⏀ *BP.*

SHOPPING

The Bodensee is artists' territory, and shopping means combing the many small galleries for watercolors, engravings, prints, or pottery made by local potters. If you must have Swiss chocolate or a Swiss watch, walk a few feet across the border from Konstanz into Kreuzlingen, the Swiss part of the twin city. Konstanz is the place to look for upscale apparel, cutlery, or exceptional gifts, as the shops cater to the wealthy Swiss from across the border. Across the bay from Lindau is the Austrian city of Bregenz, with some reputable loden shops that carry fashionable Alpine apparel.

6

THE UPPER SWABIAN BAROQUE ROAD

From Friedrichshafen, B–30 leads north along the valley of the little River Schussen and links up with one of Germany's less-known but most attractive scenic routes. The Oberschwäbische Barockstrasse (Upper Swabian Baroque Road) follows a rich series of baroque churches and abbeys, including Germany's largest baroque church, the basilica in Weingarten.

RAVENSBURG

20 km (12 mi) north of Friedrichshafen.

The Free Imperial City of Ravensburg once competed with Augsburg and Nürnberg for economic supremacy in southern Germany. The Thirty Years' War put an end to the city's hopes by reducing it to little more than a medieval backwater. The city's loss proved fortuitous only in that many of its original features have remained much as they were built (in the 19th century, medieval towns usually tore down their medieval walls and towers, which were considered ungainly and constraining). Fourteen of Ravensburg's town gates and towers survive, and the Altstadt is among the best-preserved in Germany.

GETTING HERE & AROUND

Consider taking an official tour of the city, which grants you access to some of the towers for a splendid view of Ravensburg and the surrounding countryside. Tours are available at the tourist office.

ESSENTIALS

Visitor Information Ravensburg (⌧ *Tourist Information, Kirchstr. 16* ☎ *0751/82800* ⊕ *www.ravensburg.de*).

EXPLORING

One of Ravensburg's **defensive towers** is visible from Marienplatz: the **Grüner Turm** (Green Tower), so called for its green tiles, many of which are 14th-century originals. Another stout defense tower is the massive **Obertor** (Upper Tower), the oldest gate in the city walls. One of the city's most curious towers, the **Mehlsack**, or Flour Sack (so called because of its rounded shape and whitewash exterior), stands 170 feet high and sits upon the highest point of the city. ☎ *0751/82800*.

That ecclesiastical and commercial life were never entirely separate in medieval towns is evident in the former **Karmeliterklosterkirche** *(Carmelite Monastery Church)*, once part of a 14th-century monastery. The stairs on the west side of the church's chancel lead to the meeting room of the Ravensburger Gesellschaft (Ravensburg Society), an organization of linen merchants established in 1400. After the Reformation, Catholics and Protestants shared the church, but in 1810 the Protestants were given the entire building. The neo-Gothic stained-glass windows on the west side, depicting important figures of the Reformation such as Martin Luther and Ulrich Zwingli, were sponsored by wealthy burghers.

Many of Ravensburg's monuments that recall the town's wealthy past are concentrated on **Marienplatz.** To the west is the 14th-century **Kornhaus** (Granary); once the corn exchange for all of Upper Swabia, it now houses the public library. The late-Gothic **Rathaus** is a staid, red building with a Renaissance bay window and imposing late-Gothic rooms inside. Next to it stands the 15th-century **Waaghaus** (Weighing House), the town's weigh station and central warehouse. Its tower, the **Blaserturm,** which served as the watchman's abode, was rebuilt in 1556 after a fire and now bears a pretty Renaissance helmet. Finally there's the colorfully frescoed **Lederhaus**, once the headquarters of the city's leather workers, now home to a café. ■TIP→ **On Saturday morning the square comes alive with a large market.**

Ravensburg's true parish church, the **Liebfrauenkirche** *(Church of Our Lady)*, is a 14th-century structure, elegantly simple on the outside but almost entirely rebuilt inside. Among the church's finest treasures are the 15th-century stained-glass windows in the choir and the heavily gilt altar. In a side altar is a copy of a carved Madonna, the *Schutzmantelfrau*; the late-14th-century original is in Berlin's Dahlem Museum. ⌧ *Kirchstr. 18* ⊙ *Daily 7–7.*

Ⓒ Ravensburg is a familiar name to all jigsaw-puzzle fans, because its eponymous Ravensburg publishing house produces the world's largest selection of puzzles, in addition to many other children's games. The company was founded in 1883 by Otto Robert Maier. You can explore its history and have a closer look at its games and puzzles at the **Verlags-museum.** Note the neatly cut-out keyhole on the portal. The museum is being completely restructured and will be reopened some time in 2009. ⊠*Marktstr. 26* ☎*0751/82800*

Just to the west of town in the village of Weissenau stands the **Kirche St. Peter und St. Paul.** It was part of a 12th-century Premonstratensian monastery and now boasts a high baroque facade. The interior is a stupendous baroque masterpiece, with ceiling paintings by Joseph Hafner that create the illusion of cupolas, and vivacious stuccowork by Johannes Schmuzer, one of the famous stucco artists from Wessobrunn. ⊠*Weissenau* ☉*Daily 9–6.*

☼ **Ravensburger Spieleland** is an amusement park designed for small children, located 10 km (6 mi) from Ravensburg, in the direction of Lindau. Entrance is free to children on their birthday. ⊠*Liebenau–Am Hangenwald 1, Meckenbeuren* ☎*07542/4000* ⊕*www.spieleland.de* ☜*€22* ☉*May, and Sept.–mid-Oct., daily 10–5; June–Aug., daily 10–6.*

WHERE TO EAT

$$–$$$
Fodor'sChoice
★
✕**Rebleute.** Follow a small alley off the Marienplatz to this warm, relaxed restaurant set in an old guildhall with a beautiful *Tonnendecke* (barrel ceiling). The restaurant shares a kitchen with the Restaurant Waldhorn; the quality is the same, but the prices at Rebleute are easier on the wallet. Try fish from the Bodensee in season. Reservations are advisable for dinner. ⊠*Schulg. 15* ☎*0751/36120* ⊕*www.waldhorn. de* ▤*AE, MC, V* ☉*Closed Sun.*

¢–$
✕**Café-Restaurant Central.** This popular place, with two floors and a large terrace on Marienplatz, has an international range of dishes, from kebabs and curries to pastas and local specialties. You can also enjoy coffee, cakes, or an aperitif. ⊠*Marienpl. 48* ☎*0751/32533* ▤*MC, V.*

WHERE TO STAY

$$–$$$
★
▥**Romantikhotel Waldhorn.** This historic hostelry has been in the Dressel-Bouley family for more than 150 years. Suites and rooms in the main building overlook the square. Rooms in the annex have views into a quiet street. The menu ($$$$) is prepared by Albert Bouley, fifth-generation proprietor and chef. In the dark-wood-panel dining room you can enjoy the seven-course Waldhorn menu. **Pros:** family-run historic institution, very warm relaxed atmosphere in the restaurant, excellent food, innovative dishes. **Cons:** some wooden floors on the first floor need renovations, main restaurant is very elegant but stuffy. ⊠*Marienpl. 15* ☎*0751/36120* ⊕*www.waldhorn.de* ☜*30 rooms, 3 suites, 7 apartments* ♿*In-room: no a/c, Wi-Fi. In-hotel: 2 restaurants, public Wi-Fi, parking (fee), some pets allowed, no-smoking rooms* ▤*AE, MC, V* ☉*Restaurant closed Sun. and Mon.* ☉❘*BP.*

$
▥**Gasthof Ochsen.** The Ochsen is a typical, family-owned Swabian inn, and the personable Kimpfler family extends a warm welcome. When checking in, reserve a table for dinner, as the wood-paneled restaurant (¢–$) can often book up. This is the place to try Maultaschen

and *Zwiebelrostbraten* (roast beef with lots of onions). **Pros:** warm atmosphere in the cozy restaurant, very good Swabian food. **Cons:** no elevator, rooms simply furnished. ⊠*Eichelstr. 17, just off Marienpl.* ☎*0751/25480* ⊕*www.ochsen-rv.de* ⟳*15 rooms* ⌂*In-room: no a/c, Wi-Fi. In-hotel: restaurant, no elevator, public Wi-Fi, some pets allowed* ▭*AE, MC, V* ⊙|*BP.*

WEINGARTEN

5 km (3 mi) north of Ravensburg.

Weingarten is famous throughout Germany for its huge and hugely impressive basilica, which you can see up on a hill from miles away, long before you get to the town.

ESSENTIALS

Visitor Information Weingarten (⊠*Amt für Kultur- und Tourismus, Münsterpl. 1* ☎*0751/405-125* ⊕ *www.weingarten-online.de*).

EXPLORING

★ At 220 feet high and more than 300 feet long, **Weingarten Basilica** is the largest baroque church in Germany. It was built as the church of one of the oldest and most venerable convents in the country, founded in 1056 by the wife of Guelph IV. The Guelph dynasty ruled large areas of Upper Swabia, and generations of family members lie buried in the church. The majestic edifice was renowned because of its little vial said to contain drops of Christ's blood. First mentioned by Charlemagne, the vial passed to the convent in 1094, entrusted to its safekeeping by the Guelph queen Juditha, sister-in-law of William the Conqueror. At a stroke Weingarten became one of Germany's foremost pilgrimage sites. ▀TIP➔ To this day, on the day after Ascension Thursday, the anniversary of the day the vial of Christ's blood was entrusted to the convent, a huge procession of pilgrims wends its way to the basilica. It's well worth seeing the procession, which is headed by 2,000 horsemen (many local farmers breed horses just for this occasion). The basilica was decorated by leading early-18th-century German and Austrian artists: stuccowork by Franz Schmuzer, ceiling frescoes by Cosmas Damian Asam, and a Donato Frisoni altar—one of the most breathtakingly ornate in Europe, with nearly 80-foot-high towers on either side. The organ, installed by Josef Gabler between 1737 and 1750, is among the largest in the country. ⊙*Daily 8–6.*

If you want to learn about early Germans—residents from the 6th, 7th, and 8th centuries whose graves are just outside town—visit the **Alemannenmuseum** in the Kornhaus, at one time a granary. Archaeologists discovered the hundreds of Alemannic graves in the 1950s. ⊠*Karlstr. 28* ☎*0751/49343.*

OFF THE BEATEN PATH

Hopfenmuseum Tettnang *(Tettnang Hops Museum).* If you're a beer drinker, you've probably already tasted a product of the Tettnang area. Tettnang is the second-largest hops-growing area in Germany, and exports most of its so-called "green gold" to the United States. This museum, dedicated to brewing, is in the tiny village of Siggenweiler, 3 km (2 mi) northwest of Tettnang. In the museum there is a small pub where you can buy a pretzel and of course a beer made of Tettnang hops. ⊠*Siggenweiler* ☎*07542/952–206* 💶€4 ⊕*www.hopfenmuseum-tettnang.de* 🕙*May–Oct., Tues.–Sun. 10:30–6.*

AROUND THE BODANRÜCK PENINSULA

The immense Bodensee owes its name to a small, insignificant town, Bodman, on the Bodanrück Peninsula, at the northwestern edge of the lake. ■TIP➜ **The area's most popular destinations, Konstanz and Mainau, are reachable by ferry from Meersburg, and it's by far the most romantic way to cross the lake.** The other option is to take the road (B–31, then B–34, and finally B–33) that skirts the eastern arm of the Bodensee and ends its German journey at Konstanz.

KONSTANZ

A ½-hr ferry ride from Meersburg.

The university town of Konstanz is the largest on the Bodensee; it straddles the Rhine as it flows out of the lake, placing itself both on the Bodanrück Peninsula and the Swiss side of the lake. The small Swiss town is Kreuzlingen. Konstanz is among the best-preserved medieval towns in Germany; during the war the Allies were unwilling to risk inadvertently bombing neutral Switzerland. On the peninsula side of the town, east of the main bridge connecting Konstanz's two halves, runs **Seestrasse,** a stately promenade of neoclassical mansions with views of the Bodensee. The old town center is a labyrinth of narrow streets lined with restored half-timber houses and dignified merchant dwellings. This is where you'll find eateries, hotels, pubs, and much of the nightlife.

It's claimed that Konstanz was founded in the 3rd century by Emperor Constantine Chlorus, father of Constantine the Great. The story is probably untrue, though it's certain there was a Roman garrison here. In the late 6th century Konstanz was made a bishopric; in 1192 it became a Free Imperial City. What put it on the map was the Council of Constance, held between 1414 and 1418 to settle the Great Schism (1378–1417), the rift in the church caused by two separate lines of popes, one ruling from Rome, the other from Avignon. The Council resolved the problem in 1417 by electing Martin V as the true, and only, pope. The church had also agreed to restore the Holy Roman emperor's (Sigismund's) role in electing the pope, but only if Sigismund silenced the rebel theologian Jan Hus of Bohemia. Even though Sigismund had allowed Hus safe passage to Konstanz for the Council, he won the church's favor by having Hus burned at the stake in July 1415. In a historic satire, French author Honoré de Balzac created a character called Imperia, a courtesan of great beauty and cleverness, who raised the blood pressure of both religious and secular VIPs during the Council. No one visiting the harbor today can miss the 28-foot statue of **Imperia** standing out on the breakwater. Dressed in a reveal-

6

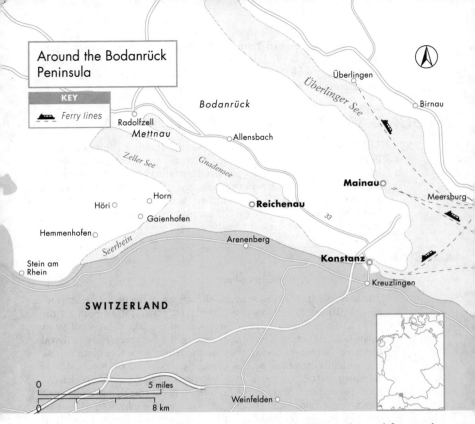

Bodanrück

Überlingen

Birnau

Überlinger See

Radolfzell

Mettnau

Allensbach

Zeller See

Gnadensee

Mainau

Meersburg

Hori

Horn

Reichenau

33

Gaienhofen

Hemmenhofen

Seerhein

Arenenberg

Konstanz

Stein am
Rhein

Kreuzlingen

SWITZERLAND

0   5 miles

0   8 km

Weinfelden

ing and alluring style, in her hands she holds two dejected figures: the emperor and the pope. This hallmark of Konstanz, created by Peter Lenk, caused controversy when it was unveiled in April 1993.

Most people enjoy Konstanz for its worldly pleasures—the elegant Altstadt, trips on the lake, walks along the promenade, the classy shops, the restaurants, the views. The heart of the city is the **Marktstätte** (Marketplace), near the harbor, with the simple bulk of the Konzilgebäude looming behind it. Erected in 1388 as a warehouse, the **Konzilgebäude** (Council Hall) is now a concert hall. Beside the Konzilgebäude are statues of Jan Hus and native son Count Ferdinand von Zeppelin (1838–1917). The Dominican monastery where Hus was held before his execution is still here, doing duty as a luxurious hotel, the Steigenberger Insel-Hotel.

GETTING HERE & AROUND

Konstanz is in many ways the center of the lake area. You can reach Zürich airport by direct train in about an hour and Frankfurt in four and a half hours. Swiss autobahn access to Zürich is about 10 minutes away, and you can reach the autobahn access to Stuttgart in about the same time. To reach the island of Mainau, you can take the bus, but a much more pleasant way to get there is by boat via Meersburg. You can take another boat downriver to Schaffhausen or east to Friedrich-hafen and Lindau and even to Bregenz in Austria. The Old Town is manageable on foot.

ESSENTIALS

Visitor Information **Konstanz** (✉ *Tourist-Information, Konstanz, Fischmarkt 2* ☎ *07531/133–030* ⊕ *www.konstanz.de*).

EXPLORING

The **Altes Rathaus** *(Old Town Hall)* was built during the Renaissance and painted with vivid frescoes—swags of flowers and fruits, shields, and sturdy knights wielding immense swords. Walk into the courtyard to admire its Renaissance restraint.

Within the medieval guildhall of the city's butchers, the **Rosgarten-museum** *(Rose Garden Museum)* has a rich collection of art and arti-facts from the Bodensee region. Highlights include exhibits of the life and work of the people around the Bodensee, from the Bronze Age through the Middle Ages and beyond. There's also a collection of sculp-ture and altar paintings from the Middle Ages. ✉ *Rosgartenstr. 3–5* ☎ *07531/900–246* 🎫 *€3* 🕐 *Tues.–Sun. 10–5.*

Konstanz's cathedral, the **Münster,** was the center of one of Germany's largest bishoprics until 1827, when the seat was moved to Freiburg. Construction on the cathedral continued from the 10th through the 19th centuries, resulting in an interesting coexistence of architectural styles: the twin-tower facade is sturdily Romanesque; the elegant and airy chapels along the aisles are full-blown 15th-century Gothic; the complex nave vaulting is Renaissance; and the choir is severely neoclas-sical. The Mauritius Chapel behind the altar is a 13th-century Gothic structure, 12 feet high, with some of its original vivid coloring and gilding. It's studded with statues of the Apostles and figures depicting the childhood of Jesus. ✉ *Münsterpl.*

The **Niederburg,** the oldest part of Konstanz, is a tangle of twisting streets leading to the Rhine. From the river take a look at the two city towers: the Rheintor (Rhine Tower), the one nearer the lake, and the aptly named Pulverturm (Powder Tower), the former city arsenal.

The huge aquarium **Sealife** has gathered all the fish species that inhabit the Rhine and Lake Constance, from the river's beginnings in the Swiss Alps to its end in Rotterdam and the North Sea. If you're pressed for time, or the aquarium is crowded with schoolchildren, visit the **Bodensee Naturmuseum** at the side entrance, which gives a comprehensive over-view of the geological history of the Bodensee and its fauna and flora right down to the microscopic creatures of the region. ✉ *Hafenstr. 9* ☎ *07531/128–270* ⊕ *www.sealife.de* 🎫 *€13* 🕐 *Daily 10–5.*

WHERE TO EAT

$–$$　✕ **Hafenhalle.** You don't have to cross the Swiss border for Swiss *Rösti*—panfried potatoes and onions mixed with chopped smoked ham—and Bauernbratwurst; you can just take a seat at this warm-weather spot on the harbor. Sit outside on the terrace and watch the busy harbor traffic. The beer garden has a sandbox for children and a screen for watching sports events, and Sunday brunch is served to live Dixieland jazz. ⊠*Hafenstr. 10* ☎*07531/21126* ➠*MC.*

¢–$ ✕**Brauhaus J. Albrecht.** This small brewery with shiny copper cauldrons serves simple dishes as well as regional specialties and vegetarian food on large wooden tables. Tuesday is schnitzel day, with half a dozen varieties on the menu, all of them filling. If you're in a hurry, there are stand-up tables. ⊠*Konradig. 2* ☎*07531/25045* ➠*DC, MC, V.*

WHERE TO STAY

$$$–$$$$ ▦ **Steigenberger Insel-Hotel.** Jan Hus was held prisoner in this former
Fodor's Choice 16th-century monastery, and centuries later Graf Zeppelin was born
★ here. With its original cloisters intact, this is now the most luxurious lodging in town. Bedrooms are spacious and stylish, more like those of a private home than a hotel, and most have lake views. The formal terrace restaurant has superb views of the lake, while the Dominikanerstube is smaller and more intimate. Both restaurants ($$–$$$) feature regional specialties, and there's the clubby, relaxed Zeppelin Bar. **Pros:** wonderful lake views, luxurious, good restaurants. **Cons:** a few rooms look out on railroad tracks, some others need refurnishing. ⊠*Auf der Insel 1* ☎*07531/125–444* ⊕*www.konstanz.steigenberger.com* ➴*100 rooms, 2 suites* ⚫*In-room: no a/c (some), Wi-Fi. In-hotel: 2 restaurants, bar, beachfront, laundry service, public Wi-Fi, parking (fee), some pets allowed, no-smoking rooms* ➠*AE, DC, MC, V* ⌷*BP.*

$$ ▦ **Stadthotel.** It's a five-minute walk to the lake from this friendly hotel. Some rooms are modern and airy with bright colors; try for the rooms on the top floor, which have good views. **Pros:** center of town, quiet location with little traffic. **Cons:** no restaurant, parking garage five minutes away on foot. ⊠*Bruderturmg. 12* ☎*07531/90460* ⊕*www.stadthotel-konstanz.com* ➴*24 rooms* ⚫*In-room: no a/c, Wi-Fi. In-hotel: restaurant, public Wi-Fi, some pets allowed, no-smoking rooms* ➠*AE, DC, MC, V* ⌷*CP.*

$–$$ ▦ **ABC Hotel.** Once upon a time, this sturdy building was a barracks and casino. Rooms here are large, comfortable, and individually furnished. Try for the Turmzimmer (Tower Room). It's about 15 minutes on foot or five minutes by bus from the center of Konstanz. **Pros:** very warm welcome, large airy rooms, quiet location, enough parking space, free Wi-Fi. **Cons:** not in the center of town, no elevator. ⊠*Steinstr. 19* ☎*07531/8900* ⊕*www.abc-hotel.de* ➴*29 rooms* ⚫*In-room: no a/c, Wi-Fi. In-hotel: public Internet, public Wi-Fi, parking, some pets allowed, no-smoking rooms* ➠*AE, DC, MC, V* ⌷*BP.*

$–$$ ▦ **Barbarossa.** This stately old town house has been modernized inside, but historic elements such as the huge wooden support beams are still visible. Some rooms are comfortably furnished, others need redecorating. The stained-glass windows and dark-wood paneling give the restaurant ($–$$) a cozy, warm atmosphere. Fish and game in season are the specialties. **Pros:** historic building, cozy restaurant with wood-paneled walls, stained-glass windows and good food. **Cons:** some rooms simply furnished, no Wi-Fi in rooms. ⊠*Obermarkt 8* ☎*07531/128–990* ⊕*www.barbarossa-hotel.com* ➴*55 rooms* ⚫*In-room: no a/c, dial-up. In-hotel: restaurant, public Internet, some pets allowed, no-smoking rooms* ➠*AE, DC, MC, V* ⌷*BP.*

NIGHTLIFE & THE ARTS

The **Zeltfestival Konstanz** (*Tent Festival* ☎07531/908–844) at the harbor draws international pop stars to Konstanz on weekends throughout the summer, concluding with the **Rock am See** event at the beginning of September. And if you're in Konstanz around August 9, you will experience the one-day city festival Konstanz shares with neighboring Kreuzlingen in Switzerland called **Seenachtfest** *(Lake Night Festival)*, with street events, music, clowns, and magicians, and ending with fireworks over the lake.

The **Stadttheater** (✉*Konzilstr. 11* ☎07531/900–150), Germany's oldest active theater, has staged plays since 1609 and has its own repertory company.

The Bodensee nightlife scene is concentrated in Konstanz. The **casino** (✉*Seestr. 21* ☎07531/81570 ⌨€3) is open 2 PM–2 AM. **K 9** (✉*Obere Laube 71* ☎07531/16713) draws all ages with its dance club, theater, and cabaret in the former Church of St. Paul. Concerts and variously themed DJ nights are held at **Kulturladen** (✉*Joseph Belli Weg 5* ☎07531/52954).

An absolute must is the cozy and crowded **Seekuh** (✉*Konzilstr. 1* ☎07531/27232), which opens at 6 and features the occasional live jazz night. The popular **Theatercafé** (✉*Konzilstr. 3* ☎07531/20243) draws a stylish crowd that's not too hip to dance when the mood strikes.

SHOPPING

It's worthwhile to roam the streets of the old part of town where there are several gold- and silversmiths and jewelers. Elegant **Modehaus Fischer** (✉*Hussenstr. 29* ☎07531/22990) has enough style for a city 10 times the size of Konstanz. The store gets most of its business from wealthy Swiss who come to Konstanz for what they consider bargain prices. Modehaus Fischer deals in well-known names such as Rena Lange and Celine and has some Italian lines such as Cavalli. Accessories from Prada, Armani, and others include handbags and exquisite shoes.

SPORTS & THE OUTDOORS

BIKING Bike rentals generally cost €13 per day. You can book bicycle tours and rent bikes at **velotours** (✉*Ernst Sachs Str. 1* ☎07531/98280 ⊕*www.velotours.de*). **Kultur-Rädle** (✉*Hauptbahnhof* ☎07531/27310 ⊕*www.kultur-raedle.de*) rents bikes at the main train station. The longer you rent the bike, the cheaper the daily rate.

BOATING Sail and motor yachts are available at **Yachtcharter Konstanz** (✉*Hafenstr.*

BIKING THE BODENSEE

From spring through autumn, Germans pack their wheels and head for the scenic bike path that circles the entire lake. You can rent a bike as a guest at many hotels, at some tourist offices, from sports shops, and from bicycle tour operators. You can always save yourself some pumping by cutting across the lake on a ferry. Biking maps are available from newspaper stands, bookshops, and tourist offices, and you can leave your baggage in the long-term storage available at the train stations in Konstanz, Überlingen, Friedrichshafen, and Lindau.

6

8 ☎07531/3633970). Small sailboats can be chartered from **Bodensee Segelschule Konstanz/Wallhausen** (✉*Zum Wittmoosstr. 10, Wallhausen* ☎*07533/4780* ⊕*www.segelschule-konstanz-wallhausen.de*).

MAINAU

7 km (4½ mi) north of Konstanz by road; by ferry, 50 min from Konstanz, 20 min from Meersburg.

★ One of the most unusual sights in Germany, **Mainau** is a tiny island given over to the cultivation of rare plants and splashy displays of more than a million tulips, hyacinths, and narcissi. Rhododendrons and roses bloom from May to July; dahlias dominate the late summer. A greenhouse nurtures palms and tropical plants.

The island was originally the property of the Teutonic Knights, who settled here during the 13th century. In the 19th century Mainau passed to Grand Duke Friedrich I of Baden, a man with a passion for botany. He laid out most of the gardens and introduced many of the island's more exotic specimens. His daughter Victoria, later queen of Sweden, gave the island to her son, Prince Wilhelm, and it has remained Swedish ever since. Today it's owned by the family of Prince Wilhelm's son, Count Lennart Bernadotte. In the former main reception hall in the castle are changing art exhibitions.

Ferries to the island from Meersburg and Konstanz depart from April to October approximately every 1½ hours between 9 and 5. The island is open year-round. There is a small bridge to the island. At night you can use it to drive up to the restaurants.

Beyond the flora, the island's other colorful extravagance is **Das Schmetterlinghaus**, Germany's largest butterfly conservatory. On a circular walk through a semitropical landscape with water cascading through rare vegetation, you'll see hundreds of butterflies flying, feeding, and mating. The exhibition in the foyer explains the butterflies' life cycle, habitats, and ecological connections. Like the park, this oasis is open year-round.

In the island's information center in the Gärtnerturm (Gardener's Tower) in the middle of the island, several films on Mainau and Lake Constance are shown.

ESSENTIALS

Visitor Information **Mainau** ✉*Insel MainauD–78465* ☎*07531/3030* ⊕*www. mainau.de* 🎫*€14* ⊙*Dawn–dusk.*

WHERE TO EAT

There are three restaurants on the island but no lodgings.

$–$$ ✗**Schwedenschenke.** The lunchtime crowd gets what it needs here—fast and good service. At dinnertime

> ### WORD OF MOUTH
>
> "I was just [in Mainau] a few weeks ago. There is a playground, a miniature train, pony rides for the kids and some beautiful gardens to stroll for the adults..."
>
> —gruezi

candlelight adds some extra style. The resident Bernadotte family is Swedish, and so are the specialties of the chef. Have your hotel reserve a table for you. ■ TIP→ **In the evening your reservation will be checked at the gate, and you can drive onto the island without having to pay the admission fee.** ⊠ *Insel Mainau* ☎*07531/3030* ☉*Apr.–Oct. 15* ⚓*Reservations essential* ☰*AE, D, MC, V.*

REICHENAU

10 km (6 mi) northwest of Konstanz, 50 min by ferry from Konstanz.

Reichenau is an island rich in vegetation, but unlike Mainau, it features vegetables, not flowers. In fact, 15% of its area (the island is 5 km [3 mi] long and 1½ km [1 mi] wide) is covered by greenhouses and crops of one kind or another. ■ TIP→ **Though it seems unlikely amid the cabbage, cauliflower, lettuce, and potatoes, Reichenau has three of Europe's most beautiful Romanesque churches. This legacy of Reichenau's past as a monastic center in the early Middle Ages, and its warm microclimate, have earned the island a place on UNESCO's World and Nature Heritage list.** Connected to the Bodanrück Peninsula by just a narrow causeway, Reichenau was secure from marauding tribesmen on its fertile island, and the monastic community blossomed from the 8th through the 12th centuries. Reichenau developed into a major center of learning and the arts. The churches are in each of the island's villages—**Oberzell, Mittelzell,** and **Niederzell,** which are separated by only 1 km (½ mi). Along the shore are pleasant pathways for walking or biking.

ESSENTIALS

Visitor Information Reichenau (⊠ *Tourist Information, Pirminstr. 145* ☎*07534/92070* ⊕ *www.reichenau.de*).

EXPLORING

The **Stiftskirche St. Georg** *(Collegiate Church of St. George)*, in Oberzell, was built around 900; now cabbages grow in ranks up to its rough plaster walls. Small round-head windows, a simple square tower, and massive buttresses signal the church's Romanesque origin from the outside. The interior is covered with frescoes painted by the monks in around 1000. They depict the eight miracles of Christ. Above the entrance is a depiction of the Resurrection.

Begun in 816, the **Münster of St. Maria and St. Markus,** the monastery's church, is the largest and most important of the island's trio of Romanesque churches. Perhaps its most striking architectural feature is the roof, whose beams and ties are open for all to see. The monastery was founded in 725 by St. Pirmin and became one of the most important cultural centers of the Carolingian Empire. It reached its zenith around 1000, when 700 monks lived here. It was then probably the most important center of book illumination in Germany. The building is simple but by no means crude. Visit the **Schatzkammer** (Treasury) to see some of its more important holdings. They include a 5th-century ivory goblet with two carefully incised scenes of Christ's miracles and some priceless stained glass that is almost 1,000 years old. ⊠ *Mün-*

6

sterpl. 3, Mittelzell ☎*07534/92070 for guided tours* ⊙*Apr.–Oct., weekdays 11–noon and 3–4.*

Museum Reichenau, a museum of local history, in the Old Town Hall of Mittelzell lends interesting insights into life on the island over the centuries. ✉*Mittelzell* ☎*07534/92070* 🎫*€3* ⊙*Apr.–Oct., Tues.–Sun. 10:30–4:30.*

The **Stiftskirche St. Peter und St. Paul** *(St. Peter and Paul Parish Church),* at Niederzell, was revamped around 1750. The faded, Romanesque frescoes in the apse are now contrasted with strong rococo paintings on the ceiling and flowery stucco.

WHERE TO STAY

$$–$$$ 🏨**Strandhotel Löchnerhaus.** The Strandhotel (Beach Hotel) stands commandingly on the water's edge and about 80 yards from its own boat pier. Fresh lake fish figures prominently on the menu of the restaurant ($–$$), as do the island's famous vegetables. Most rooms have lake views; those that don't look out over a quiet, shady garden. Ask for one of the recently renovated rooms. **Pros:** very nice location, views over the lake into Switzerland, quiet. **Cons:** not all rooms have been renovated, some rooms expensive. ✉*An der Schifflände 12* ☎*07534/8030* ⊕ *www.loechnerhaus.de* ⟲*41 rooms* &*In-room: no a/c, Wi-Fi. In-hotel: restaurant, gym, beachfront, bicycles, public Internet, public Wi-Fi, parking (fee), no-smoking rooms* ⊟*AE, DC, MC, V* ⊙*Closed Nov. 15–Mar. 15* ❑*BP.*

The Black Forest

7

"Baden Baden is my very favorite city in Germany—
it is a jewel, small but first class and full of charm.
I always...stay at the Brenner's Park Hotel with a
room facing the park.... I love the mountain air
and can never inhale enough of it."

—EuroJen

"If you want to be in the mountains, look into Titisee
(touristy but gorgeous lake setting), Hinterzarten,
Hausach, Triberg. In many of these mountain
towns you get a free pass from your host to ride
trains and buses for free during your stay."

—Russ

Updated by
Tim Skelton

THE NAME CONJURES UP IMAGES of a wild, isolated place where time passes slowly. The dense woodland of the Black Forest—Schwarzwald in German—stretches away to the horizon, but this southwest corner of Baden-Württemberg (in the larger region known as Swabia) is neither inaccessible nor dull. Its distinctive characteristics include the cuckoo clock, the women's native costume with big red or black pom-poms on the hat, and the wild, almost pagan way the Carnival season is celebrated. The first travelers checked in here 19 centuries ago, when the Roman emperor Caracalla and his army rested and soothed their battle wounds in the natural-spring waters at what later became Baden-Baden.

Europe's upper-crust society discovered Baden-Baden when it convened nearby for the Congress of Rastatt from 1797 to 1799, which attempted to end the wars of the French Revolution. In the 19th century kings, queens, emperors, princes, princesses, members of Napoléon's family, and the Russian nobility, along with actors, writers, and composers, flocked to the little spa town. Turgenev, Dostoyevsky, and Tolstoy were among the Russian contingent. Victor Hugo was a frequent visitor. Brahms composed lilting melodies in this calm setting. Queen Victoria spent her vacations here, and Mark Twain waxed poetic on the forest's beauty in his 1880 book *A Tramp Abroad,* putting the Black Forest on the map for Americans.

Today it's a favorite getaway for movie stars and millionaires, and you, too, can "take the waters," as the Romans first did, at thermal resorts large or small. The Black Forest sporting scene caters particularly to the German enthusiasm for hiking. The Schwarzwald-Verein, an outdoors association in the region, maintains no fewer than 30,000 km (18,000 mi) of hiking trails. In winter the terrain is ideally suited for cross-country skiing.

ORIENTATION & PLANNING

GETTING ORIENTED

The southwest corner of Germany divides itself neatly into two distinct geographical regions. The western half borders France and lies in the wide flat plains of the Rhine valley, where all the larger cities are located. To the east tower the rugged hills of the Black Forest itself, crisscrossed by winding mountain roads and dotted with picturesque villages.

The Northern Black Forest. The gem of the northern Black Forest is the genteel spa town of Baden-Baden, full of quiet charm and dripping with elegance.

The Central Black Forest. The central Black Forest typifies the region as a whole. Alpirsbach's half-timbered houses, Triberg's cuckoo clocks, and the nation's highest waterfalls, all nestle among a series of steep-sided valleys.

The Southern Black Forest. In the south, Freiburg is one of the country's most historic cities, and even the hordes of summer visitors can't quell the natural beauty of the Titisee lake.

TOP REASONS TO GO

Healing waters: More than 30 spas with a wide range of treatments await to make visitors feel whole again, but nothing beats the 3½-hour session at the Friedrichsbad in Baden-Baden.

Freiburg Münster: One of the most beautiful sandstone churches in southern Germany, the Cathedral of Freiburg survived the war unscathed. The view from the bell tower is stunning.

Libations at Kaiserstuhl: Enjoy a local wine in the wine-maker's yard or cellar with Black Forest ham and dark bread. It's especially nice when the grapes are being harvested.

Cuisine in Baiersbronn: Put aside all those worries about calories and plunge into the work of creative cooks in the heart of the Black Forest.

Going cuckoo: Look for a cuckoo clock from Triberg (or a nice watch from Pforzheim).

THE BLACK FOREST PLANNER

WHEN TO GO

The Black Forest is one of the most heavily visited mountain regions in Europe, so make reservations well in advance for the better-known spas and hotels. In summer the areas around Schluchsee and Titisee are particularly crowded. In early fall and late spring, the Black Forest is less crowded (except during the Easter holidays) but just as beautiful. Some spa hotels close for the winter.

GETTING HERE & AROUND

Information on the entire Black Forest can be obtained from Schwarzwald Tourismus GmbH.

BY AIR The closest major international airports in Germany are Stuttgart and Frankfurt. Strasbourg, in neighboring French Alsace, and the Swiss border city of Basel, the latter just 70 km (43 mi) from Freiburg, are also reasonably close. An up-and-coming airport is the Baden-Airpark, near Baden-Baden. It is used by European budget carriers including Ryanair (⊕ *www.ryanair.com*) and Air Berlin (⊕ *www.airberlin.com*), serving short-haul international destinations such as London, Dublin, and Barcelona. Note that on Ryanair's Web site Baden-Airpark has been rebranded as "Karlsruhe-Baden."

BY BUS The bus system works closely together with the German Railways to reach every corner of the Black Forest. Bus stations are usually at or near the train station. For more information, contact the Regionalbusverkehr Südwest (Regional Bus Lines) in Karlsruhe.

BY CAR The main autobahns are the A–5 (Frankfurt–Karlsruhe–Basel), which runs through the Rhine Valley along the western length of the Black Forest; A–81 (Stuttgart–Bodensee) in the east; and A–8 (Karlsruhe–Stuttgart), in the north. Good two-lane highways crisscross the entire region. B–3 runs parallel to A–5 and follows the Baden Wine Road. Traffic jams on weekends and holidays are not uncommon. Taking the side roads might not save time, but they are a lot more interesting. The Schwarzwald-Hochstrasse is one of the area's most scenic (but also most trafficked) routes, running from Freudenstadt to Baden-Baden. The region's tourist office has mapped out thematic driving routes: the Valley Road, the Spa Road, the Baden Wine Road, the Asparagus Road, and the Clock Road. Most points along these routes can also be reached by train or bus.

Freiburg, the region's major city, is 275 km (170 mi) south of Frankfurt and 410 km (254 mi) west of Munich.

BY TRAIN   Karlsruhe, Baden-Baden, and Freiburg are served by fast ICE trains zipping between Frankfurt-am-Main and Basel in Switzerland. Regional express trains also link these hubs with many other places locally, including Freudenstadt, Titisee, and, in particular, the spectacular climb from Baden-Baden to Triberg, one of the highest railways in Germany.

Local lines connect most of the smaller towns. Two east–west routes—the Schwarzwaldbahn (Black Forest Railway) and the Höllental Railway—are among the most spectacular in the country. Details are available from Deutsche Bahn.

ESSENTIALS   **Airport Information** **Aeroport International de Strasbourg** (☎ *00333/8864–6767* ⊕ *www.strasbourg.aeroport.fr*). **Baden-Airpark** (☎ *07229/662–000* ⊕ *www.badenairpark.de*). **EuroAirport Basel-Mulhouse-Freiburg** (☎ *00333/8990–3111* ⊕ *www.euroairport.com*). **Flughafen Frankfurt Main** (☎ *01805/372–4636* ⊕ *www.airportcity-frankfurt.de*). **Flughafen Stuttgart** (☎ *01805/948–444* ⊕ *www.flughafen-stuttgart.com*).

Bus Information **Regionalbusverkehr Südwest** (*Regional Bus Lines* ✉ *Karlsruhe* ☎ *0721/84060* ⊕ *www.suedwestbus.de*).

Train Information **Deutsche Bahn** (☎ *0800/150–7090* ⊕ *www.bahn.de*).

Visitor Information **Schwarzwald Tourismus GmbH** (✉ *Ludwigstr. 23 Freiburg* ☎ *0761/896–460* ⊕ *www.schwarzwald-tourist-info.de*).

ABOUT THE RESTAURANTS & HOTELS

Restaurants in the Black Forest range from award-winning dining rooms to simple country inns. Old *Kachelöfen* (tile stoves) are still in use in many area restaurants; try to sit near one if it's cold outside.

Accommodations in the Black Forest are varied and plentiful, from simple rooms in farmhouses to five-star luxury. Some properties have been passed down in the same family for generations. *Gasthöfe* offer low prices and local color.

WHAT IT COSTS IN EUROS					
	¢	$	$$	$$$	$$$$
RESTAURANTS	under €9	€9–€15	€16–€20	€21–€25	over €25
HOTELS	under €50	€50–€100	€101–€175	€176–€225	over €225

Restaurant prices are per person for a main course at dinner. Hotel prices are for two people in a standard double room, including tax and service.

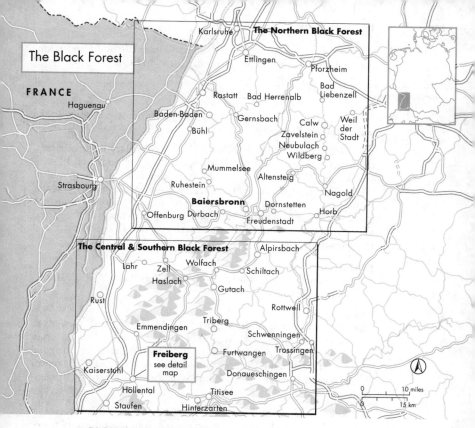

PLANNING YOUR TIME

For those in search of a lively city atmosphere, Freiburg is the obvious base from which to explore the region. Baden-Baden is another charming place with all facilities on tap.

Bear in mind however, that driving times and distances push the farthest points in this chapter out of reach on easy day trips from these cities. The winding and often steep nature of many Black Forest highways can have a dramatic impact on average speeds when you're planning journeys, so you may want to consider adding overnight stays at other locations. Freudenstadt's vast market square lends it a uniquely pleasant atmosphere; Triberg's mountain location is very popular, but it remains picturesque; and Hinterzarten offers sub-Alpine vistas and is a great place for visiting the Titisee once all the day-trippers have left.

THE NORTHERN BLACK FOREST

This region is densely wooded, and dotted with little lakes such as the Mummelsee and the Wildsee. The Black Forest Spa Route (270 km [167 mi]) links many of the spas in the region, from Baden-Baden (the best-known) to Bad Wildbad. Other regional treasures are the lovely

Nagold River; ancient towns such as Bad Herrenalb and Hirsau; and the magnificent abbey at Maulbronn, near Pforzheim.

PFORZHEIM

35 km (22 mi) southeast of Karlsruhe, just off the A–8 autobahn, the main Munich–Karlsruhe route.

The Romans founded Pforzheim at the meeting place of three rivers, the Nagold, the Enz, and the Würm, and it's known today as the "gateway to the Black Forest." The city was almost totally destroyed in World War II, which accounts for its not-so-attractive blocky postwar architectural style. Pforzheim owes its prosperity to its role in Europe's jewelry trade and its wristwatch industry. To get a sense of the "Gold City," explore the jewelry shops on streets around Leopoldplatz and the pedestrian area.

ESSENTIALS

Visitor Information Pforzheim (⊠ *Tourist-Information, Marktpl. 1* ☎ *07231/393–700* ⊕ *www.pforzheim.de*).

EXPLORING

The restored church of **St. Michael** (⊠ *Schlossberg 10* ☉ *Oct.–Apr., weekdays 3–6; May–Sept., Mon. and Wed.–Fri. 3–6*), near the train station, is the final resting place of the Baden princes. The original mixture of 13th- and 15th-century styles has been faithfully reproduced; compare the airy Gothic choir with the church's sturdy Romanesque entrance.

The Reuchlinhaus, the city cultural center, houses the **Schmuckmuseum** *(Jewelry Museum)*. Its collection of jewelry from five millennia is one of the finest in the world. The museum nearly doubled in size in 2006, adding pocket watches and ethnographic jewelry to its collection, plus a shop, a café, and a gem gallery where young designers can exhibit and sell their work. Guided tours are available in English on request. ⊠ *Jahnstr. 42* ☎ *07231/392–126* ⊕ *www.schmuckmuseum-pforzheim. de* ☞ *€3* ☉ *Tues.–Sun. 10–5.*

Pforzheim has long been known as a center of the German clock-making industry. In the **Technisches Museum** *(Technical Museum)*, one of the country's leading museums devoted to the craft, you can see makers of watches and clocks at work; there's also a reconstructed 18th-century clock factory. ⊠ *Bleichstr. 81* ☎ *07231/392–869* ⊕ *www.technisches-museum.de* ☞ *Free* ☉ *Wed. 9–noon and 3–6, 2nd and 4th Sun. of month 10–5.*

★ **Kloster Maulbronn** *(Maulbronn Monastery)*, in the little town of Maulbronn, 18 km (11 mi) northeast of Pforzheim, is the best-preserved medieval monastery north of the Alps, with an entire complex of 30 buildings on UNESCO's World Heritage list. The name Maulbronn (Mule Fountain) derives from a legend. Monks seeking a suitably watered site for their monastery considered it a sign from God when one of their mules discovered and drank at a spring. ■ **TIP→ An audio** guide in English is available. ✉*Off B–35* ☎*07043/926–610* ✆*www. maulbronn.de* ✉*€5.50* ⊙*Mar.–Oct., daily 9–5:30; Nov.–Feb., Tues.– Sun. 9:30–5; guided tour daily at 11:15 and 3.*

WHERE TO EAT

$$$ ✕**Chez Gilbert.** The Alsatian owners of this cozy restaurant serve classic French cuisine. Try the duck with chef Gilbert Noesser's tangy ginger-honey sauce. ✉*Altstädter Kirchenweg 3* ☎*07231/441–159* ▭*AE, DC, MC, V* ⊙*Closed 2 wks in Aug. No lunch Sat. No dinner Sun.*

EN ROUTE

Weil der Stadt, a former imperial city, is in the hills 17 km (10 mi) southeast of Pforzheim. This small, sleepy town of turrets and gables has only its well-preserved city walls and fortifications to remind you of its onetime importance. The astronomer Johannes Kepler, born here in 1571, was the first man to track and accurately explain the orbits of the planets. And, appropriately, the town now has a planetarium to graphically show you what he learned. The little half-timber house in which he was born is now the **Kepler Museum** (✉*Keplerg. 2* ☎*07033/6586* ✆*www.kepler-museum.de* ✉*€2, tour €15* ⊙*Thurs. and Fri. 10–noon and 2–4, Sat. 11–noon and 2–4, Sun. 11–noon and 2–5*) in the town center. It's devoted to his writings and discoveries.

CALW

7

24 km (14 mi) south of Pforzheim on B–463.

Calw, one of the Black Forest's prettiest towns, was the birthplace of Nobel Prize–winning novelist Hermann Hesse (1877–1962). He was born at Marktplatz 6, now a private home. The town's market square, with its two sparkling fountains surrounded by 18th-century half-timber houses whose sharp gables pierce the sky, is an ideal spot for relaxing, picnicking, or people-watching, especially when it's market time.

ESSENTIALS

Visitor Information **Calw** (✉*Stadtinformation Calw, Marktbrücke 1* ☎*07051/968–810* ✆*www.calw.de*).

EXPLORING

The **Hermann Hesse Museum** recounts the life of the Nobel Prize–winning writer, author of *Steppenwolf* and *The Glass Bead Game,* who rebelled against his middle-class German upbringing to become a pacifist and the darling of the Beat Generation. The story of his life is told in personal belongings, photographs, manuscripts, and other documents. (You can rent a recorder with earphones to guide you in English.) ✉*Marktpl. 30* ☎*07051/7522* ✆*www.hermann-hesse.com* ✉*€5* ⊙*Apr.–Oct., Tues.–Sun. 11–5; Nov.–Mar., Tues.–Sun. 2–5.*

Hirsau, 3 km (2 mi) north of Calw, has ruins of a 9th-century monastery, now the setting for the Klosterspiele Hirsau (open-air theater performances) in July and August. Buy advance tickets at the **Calw tourist office** (✉*Marktbrücke 1* ☎*07051/968–810*).

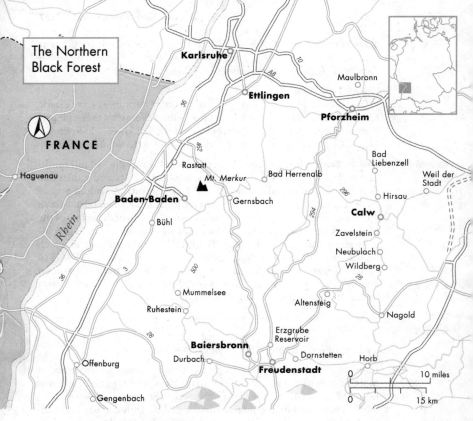

The Northern Black Forest

Karlsruhe

Maulbronn

Ettlingen

Pforzheim

FRANCE

Bad Liebenzell

Haguenau

Rastatt

Mt. Merkur

Bad Herrenalb

Weil der Stadt

Baden-Baden

Gernsbach

Hirsau

Bühl

Calw

Zavelstein

Neubulach

Wildberg

Rhein

Mummelsee

Altensteig

Nagold

Ruhestein

Erzgrube Reservoir

Baiersbronn

Dornstetten

Horb

Offenburg

Durbach

Freudenstadt

Gengenbach

0   10 miles

0   15 km

WHERE TO STAY

$$ 🏨 **Hotel Kloster Hirsau.** This hotel, a model of comfort and gracious hospitality, is in Hirsau, 3 km (2 mi) from Calw. The Klosterschenke restaurant ($–$$) serves such regional specialties as *Flädelsuppe* (containing pieces of a special, very thin pancake) and *Schwäbischer Rostbraten* (panfried beefsteak topped with sautéed onions). **Pros:** quiet location, homey atmosphere. **Con:** a bit out of town. ⊠ *Wildbaderstr. 2 Calw-Hirsau* ☎*07051/96740* ⊕*www.hotel-kloster-hirsau.de* 🛏*42 rooms* 🛆*In-room: no a/c, Ethernet, dial-up, Wi-Fi. In-hotel: restaurant, tennis courts, pool, no elevator, no-smoking rooms, some pets allowed* ⊟*AE, MC, V* ◎|*BP.*

$ 🏨 **Ratsstube.** Most of the original features, including 16th-century beams and brickwork, are preserved at this historic house in the center of Calw. Rooms are small but half-timber like the exterior. The restaurant (¢–$) serves a selection of sturdy German and Greek dishes. A salad buffet will take care of smaller appetites, and lunchtime always has several good-value dishes of the day. There's also an asparagus (Spargel) menu in season. **Pros:** great location on historic square, beautiful old building. **Cons:** parking around the corner, some rooms quite small, historic building means no elevator. ⊠*Marktpl. 12* ☎*07051/92050* ⊕*www.hotel-ratsstube.de* 🛏*13 rooms* 🛆*In-room: no a/c. In-hotel: restaurant, no elevator, some pets allowed* ⊟*MC, V* ◎|*BP.*

FREUDENSTADT

65 km (35 mi) south of Calw, 22 km (14 mi) southwest of Altensteig.

At an altitude of 2,415 feet, Freudenstadt claims to be the sunniest German resort. The town was flattened by the French in April 1945, and it has since been painstakingly rebuilt. It was founded in 1599 to house both silver miners and refugees from religious persecution in what is now the Austrian province of Carinthia (*Freudenstadt* means "city of joy").

The expansive central square, more than 650 feet long and edged with arcaded shops, is Germany's largest marketplace, though it's difficult to admire its vastness. A busy, four-lane street cuts it in two. The square still awaits the palace that was supposed to be built here for the city's founder, Prince Frederick I of Württemberg, who died before work could begin. ■ TIP➜ **When the fountains all spout on this square, it can be quite a sight, and a refreshing one as well.**

BIKING & HIKING

Bicycles can be rented in nearly all towns and many villages, as well as at the Deutsche Bahn train stations. Several regional tourist offices sponsor tours on which the biker's luggage is transported separately from one overnight stop to the next. Six- to 10-day tours are available at reasonable rates, including bed-and-breakfast and bike rental. This region is also ideal for hikers. Similar to the bike tours, tourist offices offer *Wandern ohne Gepäck* (hike without luggage) tours.

GETTING HERE & AROUND

Freudenstadt is served by regular trains from both Karlsruhe and Stuttgart. The huge main square can make the city feel larger than it actually is. The central zone can easily be covered on foot.

ESSENTIALS

Visitor Information Freudenstadt (✉ *Kongresse–Touristik–Kur, Marktpl. 64* ☎ *07441/8640* ⊕ *www.freudenstadt.de*).

EXPLORING

Don't miss Freudenstadt's Protestant **Stadtkirche,** just off the square. Its lofty nave is L-shape, a rare architectural liberty in the early 17th century. It was constructed in this way so the sexes would be separated and unable to see each other during services.

WHERE TO EAT

$$$–$$$$ ✕**Warteck.** The leaded windows with stained glass, vases of flowers, ★ and beautifully upholstered banquettes create a bright setting in the two dining rooms. Chef Werner Glässel uses only natural products and spotlights individual ingredients. Popular dishes include sweetbreads with mushrooms, spinach, and basmati rice. Top off the meal with one of the many varieties of schnapps. ✉ *Stuttgarterstr. 14* ☎ *07441/91920* ▤ *MC, V* ⊗ *Closed Tues.*

¢–$ ✕**Ratskeller.** Though there's a cellar, this restaurant with pine furnishings is more a modern bistro than traditional Ratskeller. Meatless Black Forest dishes, served in frying pans, are huge and filling. Also offered are such Swabian dishes as Zwiebelrostbraten, served with sauerkraut, and pork fillet with mushroom gravy. A special menu for senior citizens has smaller portions. ⊠ *Marktpl. 8* ☎ *07441/952–805* ▭ *AE, MC, V.*

¢–$ ✕ **Turmbräu.** Lots of wood paneling, exposed beams, and a sprinkling of old sleds and hay wagons give this place its rustic atmosphere. So do the large brass kettle and the symphony of pipes that produce the establishment's own beer. Located on Freudenstadt's main square, Turmbräu serves hearty foods, including Bavarian veal sausages, the pizza-like Alsatian *Flammkuchen,* and a kebab of various types of meat marinated in wheat beer. Fondue is offered on Wednesday. Part of the restaurant turns into a disco on weekends. ⊠ *Marktplatz 64* ☎ *07441/905121* ▭ *AE, MC, V.*

EATING WELL IN THE BLACK FOREST

Don't pass up the chance to try *Schwarzwälder Schinken* (pine-cone-smoked ham) and *Schwarzwälder Kirschtorte* (kirsch-soaked layers of chocolate cake with sour cherry and whipped-cream filling). *Kirschwasser,* locally called *Chriesewässerle* (from the French *cerise,* meaning "cherry"), is cherry brandy, the most famous of the region's excellent schnapps varieties. If traveling from April to June, keep an eye out for white asparagus, the "king of vegetables."

WHERE TO STAY

$$–$$$ ⌂ **Bären.** The Montigels have owned this sturdy old hotel and restaurant, just two minutes from the marketplace, since 1878. The family strives to maintain tradition with personal service, comfortable modern hotel rooms, and, especially, a lovely restaurant ($–$$). Local specialties include *Maultaschen,* a dish it is said that the Swabians stole from the Italians. The dish resembles ravioli, but contains a filling of roast meat, spinach, and onions. In the beamed restaurant the wine is served in a *Viertele* glass with a handle and a grape pattern. If you order schnapps, it will come from the family's own distillery. **Pros:** great central location, friendly atmosphere. **Con:** some rooms on the small side. ⊠ *Langestr. 33* ☎ *07441/2729* ⊕ *www.hotel-baeren-freudenstadt.de* ⌐ *33 rooms* ⚇ *In-room: no a/c, dial-up. In-hotel: restaurant, Wi-Fi, no-smoking rooms* ▭ *V* ⊘ *Restaurant closed Fri. No lunch Mon.–Sat.* ⎮○⎮ *BP.*

$–$$ ⌂ **Zum Schwanen.** This bright, white building just a few steps from the main square has a guest room with a waterbed for those with allergies. Many locals come to the restaurant ($) to enjoy fine regional specialties, not to mention pancakes. The pancakes, big as a platter, are topped with everything from salmon and mushrooms to applesauce and plums. Come on Thursday evening, when they are half-price. **Pros:** great location, excellent-value restaurant. **Cons:** no elevator in historic building. ⊠ *Forststr. 6* ☎ *07441/91550* ⊕ *www.schwanen-freudenstadt.de* ⌐ *17 rooms, 1 apartment* ⚇ *In-room: no a/c, Wi-Fi. In-hotel: restaurant, no elevator, Wi-Fi, no-smoking rooms, some pets allowed* ▭ *AE, MC, V* ⎮○⎮ *BP.*

$ ⌂ **Hotel Adler.** This simple hotel sits between the main square and the train station. Some of the very affordable rooms even have balconies, so you can enjoy a view of behind-the-scenes Freudenstadt. The restaurant ($) provides a hearty meal with local dishes. House specialties include *Flammkuchen,* which is similar to a pizza but thinner and with toppings such as sour cream, bacon, and onions. **Pros:** friendly, informal, centrally located. **Cons:** some rooms small, furnishings quite modest. ⊠*Forststr. 15–17* ☎*07441/91520* ⊕*www.adler-fds.de* ⬠*16 rooms* ⬩*In-room: no a/c. In-hotel: restaurant, public Internet, Wi-Fi* ▭*MC, V* ⊗*Restaurant closed Wed.* ⍩*BP.*

SHOPPING

Germans prize Black Forest ham as an aromatic souvenir. You can buy one at any butcher shop in the region, but it's more fun to visit a *Schinkenräucherei* (smokehouse), where the ham is actually cured in a stone chamber. **Hermann Wein** (⊠*Dornstetterstr. 29, Musbach* ☎*07443/2450* ⊕*www.schinken-wein.de*), in the village of Musbach, near Freudenstadt, has one of the leading smokehouses in the area. If you have a group of people, call ahead to find out if the staff can show you around.

BAIERSBRONN

7 km (4½ mi) northwest of Freudenstadt.

The mountain resort of Baiersbronn has an incredible collection of hotels and bed-and-breakfasts providing rest and relaxation in beautiful surroundings. Most people come here to walk, ski, golf, and ride horseback. ■TIP➔ **You may want to walk through the streets to preview the many restaurants.**

ESSENTIALS

Visitor Information Baiersbronn (⊠*Baiersbronn Touristik, Rosenpl. 3* ☎*07442/84140* ⊕*www.baiersbronn.de*).

EXPLORING

Near the town hall and church in the upper part of town is the little **Hauff's Märchenmuseum** *(Fairy-Tale Museum)*, devoted to the crafts and life around Baiersbronn and the fairy-tale author Wilhelm Hauff (1802–27). ⊠*Alte Reichenbacherstr. 1* ☎*07442/84100* ⬛*€1.50* ⊗ *Wed. and weekends 2–5.*

WHERE TO STAY

$$$$ ★ **Bareiss.** This luxury hotel-cum-beauty-and-spa resort commands a hilltop above Baiersbronn. It has no fewer than nine pools, some heated, some with seawater, jet streams, or effervescent water. The fitness program includes saunas, controlled ultraviolet radiation, massages, beauty treatments, hairdressers, and just about anything else well-heeled guests desire. Some rooms have tapestry-papered walls. Suites start at €470; one has its own sauna, solarium, and whirlpool bath. The restaurants include the elegant Bareiss with French cuisine ($$$$), the Kaminstube with European cuisine ($$$–$$$$) and dining near the fireplace, and the Dorfstube ($–$$) with regional specialties. **Pros:** beautiful location, great facilities. **Cons:** far from sights, expensive, credit cards only accepted in the restaurants, not in the hotel. ⊠*Gärtenbühlweg 14 Mitteltal/Baiersbronn* ☎*07442/470* ⊕*www.bareiss.com* ⬠*99 rooms* ⬩*In-room:*

no a/c (some), Wi-Fi. In-hotel: 3 restaurants, bar, tennis court, pool, bicycles, no-smoking rooms, some pets allowed (fee) ▤*AE, DC, MC, V (in restaurants only)* ⏍*MAP.*

$$$$
Fodor'sChoice
★

🏨**Traube Tonbach.** This luxurious hotel has four fine restaurants. If the classic French cuisine of the Schwarzwaldstube ($$$$) is too expensive, try either the international fare of the Köhlerstube ($$–$$$) or the Swabian dishes of the Bauernstube ($–$$). The Silberberg ($$$) serves gourmet classics and is open only to hotel

guests. In the Köhlerstube and Bauernstube you'll dine beneath beamed ceilings at tables bright with fine silver and glassware. The hotel is a harmonious blend of old and new. The Bauernstube dates back to 1778 and is true to the original, yet the rooms, each of which presents a sweeping view of the Black Forest, meet contemporary standards. A small army of extremely helpful and friendly staff nearly outnumbers the guests. **Pros:** beautiful countryside setting, friendly and efficient staff, good choice of dining. **Cons:** expensive, credit cards only accepted in the restaurants, not in the hotel. ✉*Tonbachstr. 237 Tonbach/Baiersbronn* ☎*07442/4920* ⊕*www.traube-tonbach.de* 🛏*135 rooms, 23 apartments, 12 suites* ⌂*In-room: no a/c (some), dial-up. In-hotel: 3 restaurants, bar, tennis court, pool, gym* ▤*AE, DC, MC, V (in restaurants only)* ⏍*BP.*

$$$–$$$$
🏨**Hotel-Café Sackmann.** This imposing cluster of white houses, set in the narrow Murg Valley north of Baiersbronn, has broad appeal. Families can nest here thanks to children's programs, wellness-seekers can take advantage of the spa facilities on the roof, and sightseers can use this as a base for exploring much of the Black Forest. Comfortable guest rooms are in high-end country style, all with generously sized bathrooms. But best of all are the two restaurants under the leadership of one of Germany's finest chefs, Jörg Sackmann. The Anita-Stube ($$–$$$) serves regional specialties, and the Restaurant Schlossberg ($$$) delights diners with stunning creations such as John Dory with grapefruit, marinated bacon, and fresh coriander. **Pros:** good for families, beautiful location. **Cons:** far from the sights. ✉*Murgtalstr. 602 Schwarzenberg/Baiersbronn* ☎*07447/2980* ⊕*www.hotel-sackmann.de* 🛏*65 rooms* ⌂ *In-room: no a/c, dial-up. In-hotel: 2 restaurants, bar, pool, children's programs (ages 7–14)* ▤*AE, DC, MC, V* ⏍*BP.*

$$
🏨**Hotel Lamm.** The steep-roofed exterior of this 200-year-old typical Black Forest building presents a clear picture of the hotel within. Rooms are furnished with heavy oak fittings and some fine antiques. In winter the lounge's fireplace is a welcome sight when you are returning from the slopes (the ski lift is nearby). In its beamed restaurant ($–$$) you can dine on fresh fish, which you may choose to catch yourself from one of the hotel's trout pools. **Pros:** beautiful traditional build-

ing, friendly staff. **Con:** can feel remote in winter. ✉*Ellbacherstr. 4 Mitteltal/Baiersbronn* ☎*07442/4980* ⊕*www.lamm-mitteltal.de* ➘*33 rooms, 13 apartments* ♿*In-room: no a/c. In-hotel: restaurant, pool, some pets allowed* ⊟*AE, DC, MC, V* ⏷*BP.*

BADEN-BADEN

★ *51 km (32 mi) north of Freudenstadt, 24 km (15 mi) north of Mummelsee.*

Baden-Baden, the famous and fashionable spa, is downhill all the way north on B–500 from the Mummelsee. The town rests in a wooded valley and is atop the extensive underground hot springs that gave the city its name. Roman legions of the emperor Caracalla discovered the springs and named the area Aquae. The leisure classes of the 19th century rediscovered the bubbling waters, establishing Baden-Baden as the unofficial summer residence of many European royal families. The town's fortunes also rose and fell with gaming: gambling began in the mid-18th century and was banned between 1872 and 1933. Palatial homes and stately villas grace the tree-lined avenues, and the spa tradition continues at the ornate casino and two thermal baths, one historic and luxurious, the other modern and well used by families.

Though some Germans come here for doctor-prescribed treatments, the spa concept also embraces facilities for those just looking for pampering. Shops line several pedestrian streets that eventually climb up toward the old marketplace. Two theaters present frequent ballet performances, plays, and concerts (by the excellent Southwest German Radio Symphony Orchestra). Furthermore, Baden-Baden is turning into a city of delightful museums. Besides the Frieder Burda Museum, a new museum for art and technology is slated to open in 2008.

GETTING HERE & AROUND

High-speed ICE trains stop at Baden-Baden en route between Frankfurt and Basel. However, the station is some 4 km (2½ mi) northwest of the center. To get downtown, take one of the many buses that leave from outside the station. Once in the center, Baden-Baden is manageable on foot, but there is a range of alternatives available if you get tired, including a tourist train and horse-drawn carriages.

ESSENTIALS

Visitor Information Baden-Baden (✉ *Baden-Baden Kur- und Tourismus GmbH, Solmsstr. 1* ☎ *07221/275–266* ⊕ *www.baden-baden.de*).

SPAS & HEALTH RESORTS

There's an amazing variety of places to have a relaxing soak, from expensive spa towns to rustic places deep in the woods—any town that begins with "Bad" is home to either natural thermal or mineral springs that are pumped into modern spa facilities. Many Germans come here for two- to three-week health treatments; others use the same healing waters as a weekend refresher. Baden-Baden is the most stately and expensive of the spa towns. Hinterzarten also provides opportunities to hike. Many of the spas offer special rates for longer stays.

7

EXPLORING

Bordering the slender Oos River, which runs through town, the **Lichtentaler Allee** is a groomed park with two museums and an extensive rose garden, the **Gönneranlage,** which contains more than 300 types of roses.

Close by, on the corner of Robert Kochstrasse and Lichtentalerstrasse, is the **Russian church** (⊠€1 ⊙ *Feb.–Nov., daily 10–6*), identifiable by its golden onion dome.

The **Museum Frieder Burda** occupies a modern structure by acclaimed New York architect Richard Meier. Construction of this institution contributed greatly to pulling Baden-Baden out of its slumber. The private collection focuses on classic modern and contemporary art. Highlights are works of Picasso, German expressionists, the New York School, and American abstract expressionists. ⊠ *Lichtentaler Allee 8b* ☎ *07221/398–980* ⊕ *www.museum-frieder-burda.de* ⊠ *€9* ⊙ *Tues.– Sun. 11–6.*

The Lichtentaler Allee ends at **Abtei Lichtenthal,** a medieval Cistercian abbey surrounded by defensive walls. The small royal chapel next to the church was built in 1288 and was used from the late 14th century onward as a final resting place for the Baden dynasty princes. Call ahead if your group wants a tour. ⊠ *Hauptstr. 40* ☎ *07221/504–910* ⊕ *www. abtei-lichtenthal.de* ⊠ *Tours €3* ⊙ *Tours Wed. and weekends at 3.*

Baden-Baden is quite proud of its **casino,** Germany's oldest, opened in 1855 after Parisian interior decorators and artists had polished the last chandelier. Its concession to the times is that you may wear your jeans amidst all the frescoes, stucco, and porcelain (but why would you?). Gentlemen must wear a jacket and tie with their jeans, and whatever you do, leave your sneakers at the hotel. It was in 1853 that a Parisian, Jacques Bénazet, persuaded the sleepy little Black Forest spa to build gambling rooms to enliven its evenings. The result was a series of richly decorated gaming rooms in which even an emperor could feel at home—and did. Kaiser Wilhelm I was a regular visitor, as was his chancellor, Bismarck. The Russian novelist Dostoyevsky, the Aga Khan, and Marlene Dietrich all patronized the place. The minimum stake is €2; maximum, €7,000. Passports are necessary as proof of identity. Guided tours (25 minutes) are offered in English, on request. ⊠ *Kaiserallee 1* ☎ *07221/30240* ⊕ *www.casino-baden-baden.de* ⊠ *€3, tour €4* ⊙ *Sun.–Thurs. 2 PM–2 AM, Fri. and Sat. 2 PM–3 AM. Tours Apr.–Sept., daily 9:30–11:30 AM; Oct.–Mar., daily 10–11:30 AM.*

The region's wines, especially the dry Baden whites and delicate reds, are highly valued in Germany. ■ TIP→ **Buy them directly from any vintner on the Baden Wine Road.** At Yburg, outside Baden-Baden, the 400-year-old **Nägelsförster Hof vineyard** (⊠ *Nägelsförsterstr. 1* ☎ *07221/35550*) has a shop where you can buy the product and sample what you buy (weekdays 9–6, Saturday 10–4).

WHERE TO EAT

$$$$ ✗**Der Kleine Prinz.** This gourmet hotel restaurant (⇨ *see the hotel*
★ *review below*) is a local favorite in Baden-Baden. The cheery fireplace,
lit in winter, and candlelit dining, provide an elegant atmosphere that
compliments the finest French-inspired dishes. The extensive wine list
includes some excellent local offerings. As in the hotel, all the decor—
designed by the owner's wife—right down to the dinner plates, reflect
the children's tale from which the restaurant takes its name. ✉*Lich-
tentalerstr. 36* ☎*07221/346–600* ▭*AE, MC, V.*

$$$–$$$$ ✗**Le Jardin de France.** This clean, crisp little French restaurant, whose
owners are actually French, emphasizes elegant, imaginative dining in
a modern setting. The restaurant sits in a quiet courtyard away from
the main street, offering the possibility of al fresco dining in summer.
The duck liver might be roasted with apples and macadamia nuts; the
lobster risotto is served with oysters. It also runs a school for budding
chefs. ✉*Lichtentalerstr. 13* ☎*07221/300–7860* ▭*AE, DC, MC, V*
🕙*Closed Sun. and Mon.*

$–$$ ✗**Klosterschänke.** This rustic restaurant is a 10-minute drive from the
center of Baden-Baden in the neighboring town of Sinzheim, and the
regional and Italian food is well worth the trip, particularly on a summer evening, when you can dine outside on a tree-covered terrace.
You'll probably share a rough oak table with locals; the Baden wine
and locally brewed beer ensure conviviality. The menu is surprisingly
imaginative, and it's the best place for venison when it's in season in
fall and winter. ✉*Landstr. 84, Sinzheim* ☎*07221/25854* ▭*MC, V*
🕙*Closed Mon. and 2 wks in Aug. No lunch Tues.*

$ ✗**Weinstube im Baldreit.** This lively little wine bar enchants you with its
lovely terraces and courtyard. It's nestled in the middle of the old town,
making it the perfect place to meet friends over a dry Riesling. Local
dishes, such as *Maultaschen* (large ravioli) are available to accompany
the libations. ✉*Küferstr. 3* ☎*07221/23136* ▭*MC, V* 🕙*Closed Sun.
No lunch weekdays (Nov.–Mar.)*

WHERE TO STAY

$$$$ ⊡**Brenner's Park Hotel & Spa.** With some justification, this stately hotel
set in a private park claims to be one of the best in the world. Behind it
passes leafy Lichtentaler Allee, where Queen Victoria and Czar Alexander II strolled in their day. Luxury abounds in the hotel, and all rooms
and suites are sumptuously furnished and appointed. An extensive beauty
and fitness program is available. **Pros:** elegant rooms, good location,
quiet. **Con:** professional staff sometimes lack personal touch. ✉*Schillerstr. 6* ☎*07221/9000* ⊕*www.brenners-park.com* ⟿*70 rooms, 30 suites*
⌂*In-room: dial-up. In-hotel: 2 restaurants, bar, pool, gym, public Wi-Fi,
some pets allowed* ▭*AE, DC, MC, V.*

$$$$ ⊡**Schlosshotel Bühlerhöhe.** This "castle-hotel" stands majestically on its
★ own extensive grounds 10 km (6 mi) from Baden-Baden, with spectacular views over the heights of the Black Forest. Walking trails start vir-
tually at the hotel door. Its restaurant, the Imperial ($$$–$$$$; closed
Mon. and Tues. and Jan.–mid-Feb.), features French fare with interna-
tional touches, such as lamb in feta cheese crust with ratatouille and
gnocchi. In the Schlossrestaurant ($$–$$$), overlooking the Rhine Val-

7

ley, regional and international dishes are offered. **Pros:** quiet location, great for hikers. **Con:** a long way from downtown. ⊠*Schwarzwald-hochstr. 1, Bühl* ☎*07226/550* ⊕*www.buehlerhoehe.de* ➳*77 rooms, 13 suites* ♿*In-room: no a/c (some), safe, Wi-Fi. In-hotel: 2 restaurants, bar, tennis court, pool, public Internet, no-smoking rooms, some pets allowed* ▤*AE, DC, MC, V.*

$$$–$$$$
★
🏨**Hotel Belle Epoque.** The sister hotel to Der Kleine Prinz (⇨ *see review below*) is in a building formerly occupied by the army. Large rooms have soaring ceilings, spacious beds, genuine antiques from Louis XV to art deco, and luxurious baths—in some cases cleverly built to comply with strict monument-protection laws. High tea in the salon or the romantic little garden with fountain is a must. Contemporary furnishings distinguish the rooms in the new wing. Six extra rooms will be added some time in 2009. **Pros:** beautiful gardens, room price includes afternoon tea, personal and friendly service. **Con:** only the newer wing has an elevator. ⊠ *Maria-Viktoriastr. 2c* ☎*07221/300–660* ⊕*www.hotel-belle-epoque.de* ➳*28 rooms* ♿*In-room: refrigerator. In-hotel: laundry service, no elevator (some), public Wi-Fi, parking (fee), some pets allowed* ▤*AE, MC, V* ��*BP.*

$$$–$$$$
Fodor'sChoice
★
🏨**Der Kleine Prinz.** Owner Norbert Rademacher, a veteran of New York's Waldorf-Astoria, and his interior-designer wife Edeltraud have skillfully combined two elegant city mansions into a unique, antiques-filled lodging. Antoine de Saint-Exupéry's illustrations for his 1943 French children's classic *Le Petit Prince* charmingly adorn the rooms. The hotel's restaurant (⇨ *see review above*) is worthy of your attention whether you are staying as a guest or not. **Pros:** friendly and welcoming, some rooms have wood-burning fireplaces, most bathrooms have whirlpool tubs. **Cons:** rooms in one of the hotel's two buildings are only accessible via stairs. ⊠*Lichtentalerstr. 36* ☎*07221/346–600* ⊕*www.derkleineprinz.de* ➳*26 rooms, 15 suites* ♿*In-room: refrigerator, dial-up. In-hotel: restaurant, bar, laundry service, public Wi-Fi, parking (fee), some pets allowed* ▤*AE, MC, V* ⓘ*BP.*

$–$$
🏨**Deutscher Kaiser.** This centrally located hotel provides homey and individually styled rooms at prices that are easy on the wallet. Some of the double rooms have balconies on a quiet street. The hotel is just a short walk from the casino. **Pros:** some rooms have balconies; central location. **Cons:** some rooms quite small; down side street so views not great. ⊠*Merkurstr. 9* ☎ *07221/2700* ⊕ *www.deutscher-kaiser-baden-baden.de* ➳*28 rooms* ♿*In-room: no a/c, Wi-Fi. In-hotel: some pets allowed (fee)* ▤*AE, DC, MC, V* ⓘ*BP.*

$–$$
🏨**Merkur.** The Merkur's large, comfortable rooms typify the high standards of German lodgings. A solid breakfast is served in the pleasant breakfast room. In the middle of Baden-Baden, the hotel's setting is quiet. If you stay for at least three days, ask for the special package that includes admission to the casino and the thermal baths, a sumptuous meal, a glass of champagne, and a welcome cocktail at the bar. **Pros:** good deals for stays of three days or more, central location, quiet street. **Con:** down side street so views not great. ⊠*Merkurstr. 8* ☎*07221/3030* ⊕*www.hotel-merkur.com* ➳*34 rooms, 2 suites* ♿*In-*

room: no a/c, dial-up. In-hotel: restaurant, bar, public Wi-Fi, no-smoking rooms ⊟*AE, DC, MC, V* ⍩⏐*BP.*

$ ⬚**Am Markt.** This 250-plus-year-old building houses a modest inn run for more than 50 years by the Bogner family. In the oldest part of town—a traffic-free zone, reached via an uphill climb—it's close to such major attractions as the Roman baths. Ask for a room overlooking the city. **Pros:** quiet location, some rooms have great views. **Con:** a stiff climb up from the main sights. ⊠*Marktpl. 17–18* ☎*07221/27040* ⊕*www.hotel-am-markt-baden.de* ⟳*25 rooms, 17 with bath* ⚃*In-room: no a/c, no TV (some). In-hotel: public Wi-Fi, some pets allowed* ⊟*MC, V* ⍩⏐*BP.*

NIGHTLIFE & THE ARTS

Nightlife revolves around Baden-Baden's elegant **casino,** but there are more cultural attractions as well. Baden-Baden has one of Germany's most beautiful performance halls, the **Theater** (⊠*Goethepl.* ☎*07221/932–700* ⊕*www.theater.baden-baden.de*), a late-baroque jewel built in 1860–62 in the style of the Paris Opéra. It opened with the world premiere of Berlioz's opera *Beatrice et Benedict.* Today the theater presents a regular series of dramas, operas, and ballets.

The **Festspielhaus** (⊠*Beim Alten Bahnhof 2* ☎*07221/301–3101* ⊕*www. festspielhaus.de*) is a state-of-the-art concert hall superbly fitted onto the old train station. The **Kurhaus** (⊠*Kaiserallee 1* ☎*07221/353202* ⊕*www.kurhaus-baden-baden.de*) adjoining the casino hosts concerts year-round.

Baden-Baden attracts a mature crowd, but the deep leather seats of the **Trinkhalle** (⊠*Kaiserallee 3*) make a hip lounge for those under 40. At night this daytime bistro also takes over the portion of the hall where the tourist office has a counter, turning it into a dance floor. The Hotel Merkur has a small nightclub called the **Living Room** (⊠*Merkurstr. 8* ☎*07221/303–366*). For a subdued evening, stop by the **Oleander Bar** (⊠*Schillerstr. 6* ☎*07221/9000*).

SPORTS & THE OUTDOORS

GOLF The 18-hole Baden-Baden course is considered one of Europe's finest. Contact the **Golf Club** (⊠*Fremersbergstr. 127* ☎*07221/23579* ⊕*www. golf-club-baden-baden.de*).

HORSEBACK RIDING The racetrack at nearby **Iffezheim** (☎*07229/1870*) harks back to the days when Baden-Baden was a magnet for royalty and aristocrats. Its tradition originated in 1858; now annual international meets take place in late May, late August, early September, and October. Those wishing to ride can rent horses and get instruction at the **Reitzentrum Balg** (⊠*Buchenweg 42* ☎*07221/55920*).

SWIMMING The **Caracalla Therme** is the most lavish thermal swimming-pool complex in the Black Forest region. Built in the 1980s, it has one indoor and two outdoor pools, six saunas, a solarium, Jacuzzis, and several state-of-the-art fitness areas. ⊠*Römerpl. 1* ☎*07221/275–920* ⊕*www. carasana.de* ⟳*2 hrs €13, 3 hrs €15, 4 hrs €17* ⊙*Daily 8* AM*–10* PM.

The **Friedrichsbad** is a 19th-century bathing paradise of steam baths and thermal pools, to be taken in a particular sequence. The sexes have different entrances but meet in the middle, so to speak, after dipping into various hot (and cold) bathing areas. Visit on Monday or Thursday, or use the Caracalla-Therme if you're not comfortable with the mixed nude bathing on other days. ■TIP→ **Small children aren't allowed in the bath, though babysitting is available.** ✉*Römerpl. 1* ☎*07221/275–920* ⊕*www.carasana.de* ⏱*3 hrs €21* ⊙*Daily 9* AM–10 PM.

ETTLINGEN

19 km (13 mi) north of Rastatt.

Ettlingen is a 1,200-year-old town that is now practically a suburb of its newer and much larger neighbor Karlsruhe, just a streetcar ride away. Bordered by the Alb River, Ettlingen's ancient center is a maze of auto-free cobblestone streets.

If you're here in summer, come for the annual Schlossberg theater and music festival in the beautiful baroque **Schloss.** The palace was built in the mid-18th century, and its striking domed chapel has been converted into a concert hall. Its ornate, swirling ceiling fresco is typical of the heroic, large-scale, illusionistic decoration of the period. ✉*Schlosspl. 3* ☎*07243/101–273* 🎟*Free* ⊙*Wed.–Sun. 10–5; tour weekends at 2.*

WHERE TO STAY & EAT

$$$–$$$$ ✕**Restaurant Erbprinz.** For many people, the real reason for staying at the Hotel Erbprinz (see review below) is to eat in its top-rated restaurant. A two course meal featuring local suckling pig served barbecued and in caraway-thyme sauce will take care of your hunger for at least 24 hours. In summer you can dine in the charming garden. ✉*Rheinstr. 1* ☎*07243/3220* ▭*AE, DC, MC, V* ⊙*No dinner Sun. No lunch Mon.*

$–$$ ✕**Ratsstuben.** Originally used to store salt, these 16th-century cellars by the fast-flowing Alb River now welcome diners who come to enjoy international fare. Flammkuchen, a pizzalike pie from neighboring Alsace, is a local favorite, as are snail dishes. Tables at the back have a river view. ■TIP→ **There's also a pleasant terrace for summer dining.** ✉*Kirchenpl. 1–3* ☎*07243/76130* ▭*AE, MC, V.*

$$$ 🛏**Hotel Erbprinz.** The rooms in this elegant and refined hotel are luxurious and well appointed, and while not the cheapest, they do offer good value for the comforts they provide. The hotel's top-class restaurants, the Restaurant Erbprinz (*see review above*) the Weinstube Sibylla ($$) are also very popular. ■TIP→ **Check out the photographs of the hotel's celebrity guests by the entrance to the Weinstube, and see how many you recognize.** Pros: large rooms, friendly service, good value. Cons: on busy road junction so can be noisy, the maze of corridors can be confusing. ✉*Rheinstr. 1* ☎*07243/3220* ⊕*www.hotel-erbprinz.de* ⇥*72 rooms, 11 suites* ♿*In-room: no a/c (some), refrigerator, Wi-Fi. In-hotel: 2 restaurants, bar, gym, some pets allowed* ▭*AE, DC, MC, V* ⊙*BP* ⊙

KARLSRUHE

10 km (6 mi) north of Ettlingen.

Karlsruhe, founded at the beginning of the 18th century, is a young upstart, but what it lacks in years it makes up for in industrial and administrative importance, sitting as it does astride a vital autobahn and railroad crossroads. It's best known as the seat of Germany's Supreme Court, and has a high concentration of legal practitioners.

ESSENTIALS

Visitor Information Karlsruhe (⊠ *Tourist-Information, Bahnhofpl. 6* ☎ *0721/3720–5383* ⊕ *www.karlsruhe.de*).

EXPLORING

The town quite literally grew up around the former **Schloss** of the Margrave Karl Wilhelm, which was begun in 1715. Thirty-two avenues radiate from the palace, 23 leading into the extensive grounds, and the remaining 9 forming the grid of the Old Town.

The **Badisches Landesmuseum** *(Baden State Museum)*, in the palace, has a large number of Greek and Roman antiquities and trophies that Ludwig the Turk brought back from campaigns in Turkey in the 17th century. Most of the other exhibits are devoted to local history. ⊠*Schloss* ☎*0721/926–6514* ⊕*www.landesmuseum.de* 🎟*€4* ☉*Tues.–Thurs. 10–5, Fri.–Sun. 10–6.*

One of the most important collections of paintings in the Black Forest region hangs in the **Staatliche Kunsthalle** *(State Art Gallery)*. Look for masterpieces by Grünewald, Holbein, Rembrandt, and Monet, and also for work by the Black Forest painter Hans Thoma. In the **Kunsthalle Orangerie**, next door, is work by such modern artists as Braque and Beckmann. ⊠*Hans-Thoma-Str. 2-6* ☎*0721/926–3359* ⊕*www.kunsthalle-karlsruhe.de* 🎟*Both museums €6* ☉*Tues.–Fri. 10–5, weekends 10–6.*

🔄 In a former munitions factory, the vast **Zentrum für Kunst und Medientech-**
★ **nologie** *(Center for Art and Media Technology)*, or simply ZKM, is an all-day adventure consisting of two separate museums. At the **Medi-enmuseum** (Media Museum) you can watch movies, listen to music, try out video games, flirt with a virtual partner, or sit on a real bicycle and pedal through a virtual New York City. The **Museum für Neue Kunst** *(Museum of Modern Art* ☎*0721/81000)* is a top-notch collection of media art in all genres from the end of the 20th century. ▪TIP➜ **Take Tram 6 to ZKM to get here.** ⊠*Lorenzstr. 19* ☎*0721/81000* ⊕*www. zkm.de* 🎟*Either museum €5, combined ticket €8, free after 2 on Fri.* ☉ *Wed.–Fri. 10–6, weekends 11–6.*

WHERE TO STAY & EAT

$$$–$$$$ ✕**Buchmanns.** Elke and Günter Buchmann run a "linen tablecloth and real silver" establishment, with a beer garden and a bar. The various suggested courses are grouped in fancy handwriting on the menu, along with the fancy price of each dish. You can, of course, just order one of the courses, but be prepared for a disapproving look.

The proprietors are Austrian, and the specialties of their country, such as *Tafelspitz* (boiled beef with chive sauce) and *Kaiserschmarrn* (egg pancakes with apples, raisins, cinnamon, and jam), are especially recommended. ✉ *Mathystr. 22–24* ☎ *0721/820–3730* ▤ *AE, V* ⊘ *Closed Sun. No lunch Sat.*

$$ 🏨 **Schlosshotel.** A few steps from the main station and adjacent to the zoo, this hotel looks, and sometimes behaves, like a palace. It's proud of its marble bathrooms, a mirrored elevator dating from 1914, and a menu from 1943, but the guest rooms are similar to those of modern hotels. The restaurant Zum Grossherzog ($$–$$$; closed Sun.) serves international haute cuisine, and the very *gemütlich* Schwarzwaldstube ($$–$$$) has Baden specialties. **Pros:** elegant hotel, friendly service. **Cons:** on a noisy street, modern rooms don't live up to the historic feel of the hotel. ✉ *Bahnhofpl. 2* ☎ *0721/383–20* ⊕ *www.schlosshotel-karlsruhe.de* ⮒ *93 rooms, 3 suites* ⟳ *In-room: no a/c (some), refrigerator, Ethernet. In-hotel: 2 restaurants, bar, gym, public Internet, parking (no fee), some pets allowed, no-smoking rooms* ▤ *AE, DC, MC, V.*

THE ARTS

One of the best opera houses in the region is Karlsruhe's **Badisches Staatstheater** (✉ *Baumeisterstr. 11* ☎ *0721/35570* ⊕ *www.staatstheater. karlsruhe.de*).

THE CENTRAL BLACK FOREST

The Central Black Forest takes in the Simonswald, Elz, and Glotter valleys as well as Triberg and Furtwangen, with their clock museums. The area around the Triberg Falls—the highest falls in Germany—is also renowned for pom-pom hats, thatch-roof farmhouses, and mountain railways. The Schwarzwaldbahn (Black Forest Railway; Offenburg–Villingen line), which passes through Triberg, is one of the most scenic in all of Europe.

ALPIRSBACH

16 km (10 mi) south of Freudenstadt.

The 900-year-old Kloster Alpirsbach, a former monastery, is now the scene of cabarets, concerts, and movies.

ESSENTIALS

Visitor Information Alpirsbach (✉ *Tourist-Information, Hauptstr. 20* ☎ *07444/951–6281* ⊕ *www.alpirsbach.de*).

EXPLORING

The **Brauerei** *(brewery)* was once part of the monastery, and has brewed beer since the Middle Ages. The unusually soft water gives the beer a flavor that is widely acclaimed. There are guided tours of the brewery museum daily at 2:30. ✉ *Marktpl. 1, D–72275* ☎ *07444/67149* ⊕ *www.alpirsbacher-brauwelt.de* ▦ *Tour €6* ⊘ *Mar.–Oct., weekdays 9:30–4:30, weekends 11–3; Nov.–Feb., daily 11–3.*

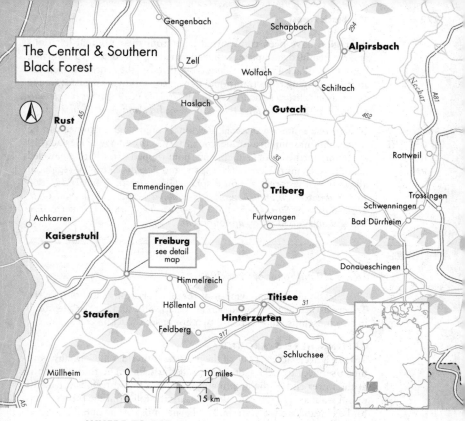

The Central & Southern Black Forest

Gengenbach · Schapbach · Alpirsbach · Zell · Wolfach · Schiltach · Haslach · **Gutach** · Rust · Rottweil · Emmendingen · **Triberg** · Trossingen · Schwenningen · Furtwangen · Bad Dürrheim · Achkarren · **Kaiserstuhl** · Freiburg see detail map · Donaueschingen · Himmelreich · **Titisee** · Höllental · **Hinterzarten** · **Staufen** · Feldberg · Schluchsee · Müllheim

0 — 10 miles
0 — 15 km

WHERE TO EAT

¢–$ ✗**Zwickel & Kaps.** The name is a highly sophisticated brewing term, describing the means by which the brewmaster samples the fermenting product. Sit down at one of the simple beechwood tables and order a satisfying Swabian lentil stew with dumplings and sausages, or something more Mediterranean, such as salmon with pesto. ⊠ *Marktstr. 3* ☎ *07444/51727* ▭ *AE, DC, MC, V* ☾ *Closed Mon.*

GUTACH

17 km (11 mi) north of Triberg.

Gutach lies in Gutachtal, a valley famous for the traditional costume, complete with pom-pom hats, worn by women on feast days and holidays. Married women wear black pom-poms, unmarried women red ones. The village is one of the few places in the Black Forest where you can still see thatch roofs. However, escalating costs caused by a decline in skilled thatchers, and soaring fire-insurance premiums, make for fewer thatch roofs than there were 20 years ago.

Near Gutach is one of the most appealing museums in the Black Forest, the **Schwarzwälder Freilichtmuseum Vogtsbauernhof** *(Black Forest Open-Air Museum).* Farmhouses and other rural buildings from all parts of the region have been transported here from their original locations and reassembled, complete with traditional furniture, to create a living museum of Black Forest building types through the centuries. Demonstrations ranging from traditional dances to woodworking capture life as it was in centuries past. ✉ *B–33* ☎*07831/93560* ⊕*www.vogtsbauernhof.org* ✆*€6* ⊘*Apr.–Oct., daily 9–6; July and Aug. until 7.*

OFF THE
BEATEN
PATH

Schwarzwalder Trachtenmuseum. Regional traditional costumes can be seen at this museum in a former monastery in the village of Haslach, 10 km (6 mi) northwest of Gutach. Pom-pom-topped straw hats, bejeweled headdresses, embroidered velvet vests, and *Fasnet* (Carnival) regalia of all parts of the forest are on display. ✉*Klosterstr. 1* ☎*07832/706–172* ⊕*www.trachtenmuseum-haslach.de.vu* ✆*€2* ⊘*Apr.–mid-Oct., Tues.–Sat. 9–5, Sun. 10–5; mid-Oct.–Dec., Feb., and Mar., Tues.–Fri. 9–noon and 1–5; Jan. by appointment.*

TRIBERG

★ *16 km (10 mi) south of Gutach.*

The cuckoo clock, that symbol of the Black Forest, is at home in the Triberg area. It was invented here, it's made and sold here, it's featured in two museums, and there are two house-sized cuckoo clocks.

GETTING HERE & AROUND

Triberg is accessible via one of the prettiest train rides in Germany, with direct services to Lake Constance and Karlsruhe. The train station is at the lower end of the long main street, and the waterfalls are a stiff uphill walk away. You can take a bus up the hill from the train station to the entrance to the waterfalls, relieving most of the uphill struggle.

ESSENTIALS

Visitor Information **Triberg** (✉ *Tourist-Information, Wahlfahrtstr. 4* ☎ *07722/866–490* ⊕ *www.triberg.de*).

EXPLORING

At the head of the Gutach Valley, the Gutach River plunges more than 500 feet over seven huge granite cascades at Triberg's **waterfall**, Germany's highest. The pleasant 45-minute walk from the center of town is well signposted. A longer walk goes by a small pilgrimage church and the old Mesnerhäuschen, the sacristan's house. ✆ *Waterfall €2.50 Apr.–Oct., €1.50 Nov.–Mar.*

The **Haus der 1000 Uhren** *(House of 1,000 Clocks)* has a shop right at the waterfall. The main store, just off B–33 toward Offenburg in the suburb of Gremmelsbach, boasts another of the town's giant cuckoo clocks. Both stores offer a rich variety of clocks, some costing as much as €3,000. ✉*Hauptstr. 79–81* ☎*07722/96300* ⊕*www.houseof-1000clocks.de* ⊘*Mon.–Sat. 11–5, Sun. 11–4.*

Triberg's famous **Schwarzwaldmuseum** *(Black Forest Museum)* is a treasure trove of the region's traditional arts: wood carving, costumes, handicrafts. The Schwarzwaldbahn is described, with historical displays

CLOSE UP

Cuckoo for Cuckoo Clocks

"In Switzerland they had brotherly love—they had 500 years of democracy and peace, and what did that produce? The cuckoo clock."

So says Harry Lime, played by Orson Welles in the classic 1949 film *The Third Man*. He misspoke in two ways. First, the Swiss are an industrious, technologically advanced people. And second, they didn't invent the cuckoo clock. That was the work of the Germans living in the adjacent Black Forest.

The first cuckoo clock was designed and built in 1750 by Franz Anton Ketterer in Schönwald near Triberg. He cleverly produced the cuckoo sound with a pair of wooden whistles, each attached to a bellows activated by the clock's mechanism.

The making of carved wooden clocks developed rapidly in the Black Forest. The people on the farms needed ways to profitably occupy their time during the long snowbound winters, and the carving of clocks was the answer. Wood was abundant, and the early clocks were entirely of wood, even the works.

Come spring one of the sons would don a traditional smock and hat, mount the family's winter output on a big rack, hoist it to his back, and set off into the world to sell the clocks. In 1808 there were 688 clock makers

and 582 clock peddlers in the districts of Triberg and Neustadt. The *Uhrenträger* (clock carrier) is an important part of the Black Forest tradition. Guides often wear his costume.

The traditional cuckoo clock is made with brown stained wood with a gabled roof and some sort of woodland motif carved into it, such as a deer's head or a cluster of leaves. The works are usually activated by cast-iron weights, in the form of pinecones, on chains.

Today's clocks can be much more elaborate. Dancing couples in traditional dress automatically move to the sound of a music box, a mill wheel turns on the hour, a farmer chops wood on the hour, the Uhrenträger even makes his rounds. The cuckoo itself moves its wings and beak and rocks back and forth when calling.

The day is long past when the clocks were made entirely of wood. The works are of metal and therefore more reliable and accurate. Other parts of the clock, such as the whistles, the face, and the hands, are usually of plastic now, but hand-carved wood is still the rule for the case. The industry is still centered in Triberg. There are two museums in the area with sections dedicated to it, and clocks are sold everywhere, even in kiosks.

7

and a working model. The Black Forest was also a center of mechanical music, and, among many other things, the museum has an "Orchestrion"—a cabinet full of mechanical instruments playing like an orchestra. ✉ *Wallfahrtstr. 4* ☎ *07722/4434* ⊕ *www.schwarzwaldmuseum.de* 🖵€*4.50* ☉ *Daily 10–5.*

You can buy a cuckoo clock, or just about any other souvenir, at the huge **Eble Uhren-Park,** about 3 km (2 mi) from the town center in the district of Schonachbach. It's also the location of one of the house-sized cuckoo clocks. You can enter it for €1.50 and examine the works.

✉ *On Hwy. B–33 between Triberg and Hornberg* ☎ *07722/96220*
⊕ *www.eble-uhren-park.de* ⊘ *Apr.–Oct., Mon.–Sat. 9–6, Sun. 10–6;*
Nov.–Mar., Mon.–Sat. 9–6, Sun. 11–4:30.

Hubert Herr is the only factory that continues to make nearly all of its
own components for its cuckoo clocks. The present proprietors are the
fifth generation from Andreas and Christian Herr, who began making
the clocks more than 150 years ago. The company produces a great variety of clocks, including one that, at 5¼ inches high, is claimed to be "the
world's smallest." ✉ *Hauptstr. 8* ☎ *07722/4268* ⊕ *www.hubertherr.de*
⊘ *Weekdays 9–noon and 1:30–4.*

The Hornberg–Triberg–St. Georgen segment of the **Schwarzwaldbahn**
(Black Forest Railway) is one of Germany's most scenic train rides.
The 149-km (93-mi) Schwarzwaldbahn, built from 1866 to 1873, runs
from Offenburg to Lake Constance via Triberg. It has no fewer than 39
tunnels, and at one point climbs 656 yards in just 11 km (6½ mi). It's
now part of the German Railway, and you can make inquiries at any
station. ☎ *0800/150–7090* ⊕ *www.bahn.de.*

WHERE TO STAY

$$–$$$ 🏨 **Parkhotel Wehrle.** The wisteria-covered facade and steep eaves of
this large mansion dominate the town center. Rooms are individually
furnished in a variety of woods with such pleasant touches as fresh
flowers, and there is a fitness facility. The Ochsenstube ($–$$) serves
duck breast with three types of noodles and a sauce of oranges, pears,
and truffles; the Alte Schmiede ($–$$) tends toward specialties from
Baden, such as trout done a dozen different ways, all delicious. **Pros:**
elegant rooms, friendly service. **Cons:** main street outside can be noisy.
✉ *Gartenstr. 24* ☎ *07722/86020* ⊕ *www.parkhotel-wehrle.de* 🛏 *50
rooms, 1 suite* ⚿ *In-room: no a/c, Ethernet, dial-up, Wi-Fi. In-hotel:
3 restaurants, pool, gym, parking (fee), no-smoking rooms, some pets
allowed* 🖃 *AE, MC, V* ⏐⊙⏐*BP.*

$ 🏨 **Hotel-Restaurant-Pfaff.** Rooms at this restaurant-hotel are very com-
fortable. Some have balconies overlooking the famous waterfall. The
old post-and-beam restaurant ($$–$$$), with its blue-tile Kachelofen,
attracts people of all types with affordable regional specialties. Try the
fresh *Forelle* (trout), either steamed or *Gasthof* (in the pan), garnished
with mushrooms. **Pros:** friendly service, close to waterfall. **Cons:**
some rooms quite small, no elevator. ✉ *Hauptstr. 85* ☎ *07722/4479*
⊕ *www.hotel-pfaff.com* 🛏 *10 rooms* ⚿ *In-room: no a/c. In-hotel: restaurant, no elevator, no-smoking rooms, some pets allowed* 🖃 *AE,
DC, MC, V* ⏐⊙⏐*BP.*

**EN
ROUTE** In the center of Furtwangen, 16 km (10 mi) south of Triberg, drop
in on the **Uhren Museum** *(Clock Museum)*, the largest such museum in
Germany. It charts the development of Black Forest clocks and exhibits all types of timepieces, from cuckoo clocks, church clock mech-
anisms, kinetic wristwatches, and old decorative desktop clocks to
punch clocks and digital blinking objects. The most elaborate piece
is the "art clock" by local artisan August Noll, built from 1880 to
1885 and featuring the time in Calcutta, New York, Melbourne, and

London, among other places. It emits the sound of a crowing rooster in the morning, and other chimes mark yearly events. It's occasionally demonstrated during tours. You can set your own watch to the sundial built into the concrete of the square in front of the museum. This remarkable creation nearly ticks off the seconds. ⊠*Robert-Gerwig-Pl. 1* ☎*07723/920–2800* ⊕*www.deutsches-uhrenmuseum.de* 🎫*€4* 🕑*Apr.–Oct., daily 9–6; Nov.–Mar., daily 10–5.*

THE SOUTHERN BLACK FOREST

In the south you'll find the most spectacular mountain scenery in the area, culminating in the Feldberg—at 4,899 feet the highest mountain in the Black Forest. The region also has two large lakes, the Titisee and the Schluchsee. Freiburg is a romantic university city with vineyards and a superb Gothic cathedral.

TITISEE

37 km (23 mi) south of Furtwangen.

Beautiful Titisee, carved by a glacier in the last ice age, is the most scenic lake in the Black Forest. The landscape is heavily wooded and ideal for long bike tours, which can be organized through the Titisee tourist office. The lake measures 2½ km (1½ mi) long and is invariably crowded in summer. Stop by one of the many lakeside cafés to enjoy some of the region's best Black Forest cherry cake with an unparalleled waterside view.

■TIP→ **Boats and Windsurfers can be rented at several points along the shore.**

ESSENTIALS

Visitor Information **Titisee-Neustadt** (⊠*Tourist-Information, Strandbadstr. 4* ☎*07651/98040* ⊕*www.titisee.de*).

WHERE TO STAY

¢–$ 🏨**Gasthaus Sonnenmatte.** There are countless hotels and restaurants clustered around the lakeshore, but for a quieter time and to escape the crowds in summer, it's worth heading further from the lake. This guesthouse is about 2 km (1 mi) inland, in the middle of a meadow. There's a swimming pool, a barbecue grill, and an outdoor chess set in the garden. Weekly dances are a feature year-round, and in summer the restaurant (¢–$) stages regular grill parties. **Pros:** quiet rural location, friendly service, away from the Titisee crowds. **Cons:** away from the Titisee views, some rooms quite small. ⊠*Spriegelsbach 5 Titisee-Neustadt* ☎*07651/8277* ⊕*www.sonnenmatte.de* 🛏*30 rooms* 🏠*In-room: no a/c, Wi-Fi. In-hotel: restaurant, bar, pool, gym, no-smoking rooms, some pets allowed* ⊟*AE, DC, MC, V* 🍴*BP.*

HINTERZARTEN

5 km (3 mi) west of Titisee, 32 km (20 mi) east of Freiburg.

The lovely 800-year-old town of Hinterzarten is the most important resort in the southern Black Forest. Some buildings date from the 12th century, among them St. Oswaldskirche, a church built in 1146. Hinterzarten's oldest inn, the Weisses Rossle, has been in business since 1347.

ESSENTIALS

Visitor Information **Hinterzarten** (⊠ *Hinterzarten-Breitnau Tourismus GmbH, Freiburgerstr. 1* ☎ *07652/12060* ⊕ *www.hinterzarten-breitnau.de*).

EXPLORING

Hinterzarten is known throughout Germany for its summer ski jump, the **Adlerschanze** (⊠ *Off Winterhaldenweg, to south of town*), which is used for competitions and for training purposes.

The town's small **Schwarzwälder Skimuseum** recounts in photographs, paintings, costumes, and equipment the history of Black Forest skiing, which began in the 1890s on the nearby Feldberg. ⊠ *Im Hugenhof* ☎ *07652/982–192* ⊕ *www.schwarzwaelder-skimuseum.de* ✐ *€3.50* ☉ *Tues., Wed., and Fri. 3–5, weekends noon–5.*

WHERE TO STAY

$$$–$$$$ ★   **Parkhotel Adler.** This 560-year-old hotel, once on the edge of decrepitude, has been turned into an oasis of luxury with a beautiful private park, an extensive fitness facility, and superb service. Many of the rooms have marble baths and balconies overlooking the park. The latest addition is the Diva, a fine café set in a conservatory. The rustic Wirtshuus-Stube ($$$–$$$$), with its wood paneling and tile stove, serves Black Forest specialties. If reserving, mention whether you are tall, since the ceiling is low in most of the dining room. Evenings can be spent in the Leo Lounge enjoying live piano music. **Pros:** luxurious, good service, quiet location. **Con:** low ceilings in dining area. ⊠ *Adlerpl. 3* ☎ *07652/1270* ⊕ *www.parkhoteladler.de* ✐ *46 rooms, 32 suites* ⚭ *In-room: no a/c, dial-up. In-hotel: 2 restaurants, bar, pool, public Wi-Fi, no-smoking rooms, some pets allowed* ⊟ *AE, DC, MC, V* ⏀ *BP.*

$$ **Sassenhof.** Traditional Black Forest style reigns supreme here, from the steep-eaved wood exterior, with window boxes everywhere, to the elegant sitting areas and guest rooms furnished with rustic, brightly painted pieces, many of them decoratively carved. ■ **TIP→ Afternoon tea, like breakfast, is included in the price.** Pros: quiet location, friendly staff. Con: payment by credit card incurs a 4% surcharge. ⊠ *Adlerweg 17* ☎ *07652/918* ⊕ *www.hotel-sassenhof.de* ✐ *17 rooms, 6 suites* ⚭ *In-room: no a/c, Wi-Fi. In-hotel: pool, bicycles* ⊟ *AE, MC, V* ☉ *Closed Nov.* ⏀ *BP.*

SPORTS & THE OUTDOORS

Hinterzarten is at the highest point along the Freiburg–Donaueschingen road; from it a network of far-ranging trails fans out into the forest, making it one of Germany's most popular centers for *Langlauf* (cross-country skiing) in winter and hiking in summer. Cycling is another favorite sport up in these hills and dales. The topography offers something for everyone, gentle excursions or tough mountain-bike expeditions.

The best Alpine skiing in the Black Forest is on the slopes of the Feldberg. The Seebuck, Grafenmatt, and Fahl Alpin areas offer 12 lifts and 25 km (15 mi) of slopes (all accessible with a single lift ticket). For more information, contact **Feldberg Touristik** (⊠ *Kirchg. 1* ☎ *07655/8019* ⊕ *www.feldberg-schwarzwald.de*).

EN ROUTE

To get to Freiburg, the largest city in the southern Black Forest, you have to brave the curves of the winding road through the **Höllental** (Hell Valley). In 1770 Empress Maria Theresa's 15-year-old daughter—the future queen Marie Antoinette—made her way along what was then a coach road on her way from Vienna to Paris. She traveled with an entourage of 250 officials and servants in some 50 horse-drawn carriages. The first stop at the end of the valley is a little village called **Himmelreich**, or Kingdom of Heaven. Railroad engineers are said to have given the village its name in the 19th century, grateful as they were to finally have laid a line through Hell Valley. At the entrance to Höllental is a deep gorge, the **Ravennaschlucht.** It's worth scrambling through to reach the tiny 12th-century chapel of **St. Oswald,** the oldest parish church in the Black Forest (there are parking spots off the road). Look for a bronze statue of a deer high on a roadside cliff, 5 km (3 mi) farther on. It commemorates the legend of a deer that amazed hunters by leaping the deep gorge at this point. Another 16 km (10 mi) will bring you to Freiburg.

FREIBURG

25 km (15 ½ mi) northwest of Hinterzarten.

Freiburg im Breisgau was founded in the 12th century. World War II left extensive damage, but skillful restoration helped re-create the original and compelling medieval atmosphere of one of the loveliest historic towns in Germany. The 16th-century geographer Martin Waldseemüller was born here; in 1507 he was the first to put the name *"America"* on a map.

For an intimate view of Freiburg, wander through the car-free streets around the Münster or follow the main shopping artery of Kaiser-Joseph-Strasse. After you pass the city gate (Martinstor), follow Gerberau off to the left. You'll come to quaint shops along the banks of one

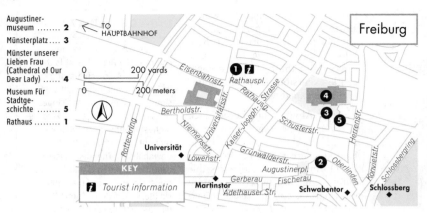

of the city's larger canals, which continues past the former Augustinian cloister to the equally picturesque area around the *Insel* (island). This canal is a larger version of the *Bächle* (brooklets) running through many streets in Freiburg's Old Town. The Bächle, so narrow you can step across them, were created in the 13th century to bring fresh water into the town. Legend has it that if you accidentally step into one of them—and it does happen to travelers looking at the sights—you will marry a person from Freiburg. The tourist office sponsors English walking tours daily at 10:30, with additional tours on Friday and Saturday at 10. The two-hour tour costs €8.

GETTING HERE & AROUND

Freiburg is on the main railway line between Frankfurt and Basel, and regular ICE express trains stop here. The railway station is a short walk from the city center. Although Freiburg is a bustling metropolis, the city center is compact. In fact, since the bulk of the Old Town is closed to traffic, walking is by far the most practical and pleasurable option. The Old Town is ringed with parking garages for those who arrive by car.

ESSENTIALS

Visitor Information Freiburg (⊠ *Tourist-Information, Rathauspl. 2–4* ☎ *0761/388–1880* ⊕ *www.freiburg.de*).

EXPLORING

2 A visit to Freiburg's cathedral is not really complete without also exploring the **Augustinermuseum,** in the former Augustinian cloister. Original sculpture from the cathedral is on display, as well as gold and silver reliquaries. The collection of stained-glass windows, dating from the Middle Ages to today, is one of the most important in Germany. ⊠*Am Augustinerpl.* ☎*0761/201–2531* ⊕*www.museen.freiburg.de* ☑*Free* ⊗*Tues.–Sun. 10–5.*

4 The **Münster unserer Lieben Frau** *(Cathedral of Our Dear Lady)* Freiburg's

 most famous landmark, towers over the medieval streets. The cathedral took three centuries to build, from around 1200 to 1515. You can easily trace the progress of generations of builders through the changing architectural styles, from the fat columns and solid, rounded arches of the Romanesque period to the lofty Gothic windows and airy interior of the choir. The delicately perforated 380-foot spire has been called the finest in Europe. ■ TIP→ **If you can summon the energy, climb the tower. In addition to a magnificent view, you'll get a closer look at the 16 bells, including the 1258 "Hosanna," one of Germany's oldest functioning bells.** ✉ *Münsterpl.* ☎ *0761/388–101* 🎫 *Bell tower €1.50* 🕙 *Mon.– Sat. 9:30–5, Sun. 1–5.*

3 The **Münsterplatz**, the square around Freiburg's cathedral, which once served as a cemetery, holds a market Monday to Saturday. You can stock up on local specialties, from wood-oven-baked bread to hams, wines, vinegars, fruits, and *Kirschwasser* (cherry brandy). The southern side, in front of the Renaissance **Kaufhaus** (Market House), is traditionally used by merchants. On the northern side of the square are farmers with their produce. This is where you can sample some local sausages served with a white roll and heaps of onions. The square is also lined with traditional taverns.

5 The former house of painter, sculptor, and architect Johann Christian Wentzinger (1710–97) houses the **Museum für Stadtgeschichte** *(Museum of City History)*. It contains fascinating exhibits on the history of the city, including the poignant remains of a typewriter recovered from a bombed-out bank. The ceiling fresco in the stairway, painted by Wentzinger himself, is the museum's pride and joy. ✉ *Münsterpl. 30* ☎ *0761/201–2515* ⊕ *www.museen.freiburg.de* 🎫 *€2* 🕙 *Tues.–Sun. 10–5.*

1 Freiburg's famous **Rathaus** is constructed from two 16th-century patrician houses joined together. Among its attractive Renaissance features is an oriel, or bay window, clinging to a corner and bearing a bas-relief of the romantic medieval legend of the Maiden and the Unicorn. ✉ *Rathauspl. 2–4* 🕙 *Mon.–Thurs. 8–5:30, Fri. 8–4.*

WHERE TO EAT

$$–$$$ ✕**Kühler Krug.** Wild game and goose-liver terrine are among the specialties at this elegant yet homey restaurant around 2 km (1½ mi) south of the Old Town. One interesting dish is rabbit in hazelnut sauce with baby vegetables. Those who prefer fish shouldn't despair—there's an imaginative range available, including salmon in saffron foam with a Riesling risotto. ✉ *Torpl. 1, Freiburg-Günterstal* ☎ *0761/29103* 💳 *MC, V* 🕙 *Closed Wed.*

$$–$$$ ✕**Markgräfler Hof.** The creative cuisine in this restaurant and Weinstube ranges from braised tomatoes and artichokes with lukewarm vegetables to fried butterfish with ginger, spring onions, and fried rice balls. Even desserts are imaginative, with elderberry ice cream a favorite. A small but fine wine list complements the menu. ✉ *Gerberau 22* ☎ *0761/32540* 💳 *AE, DC, MC, V* 🕙 *Closed Mon.*

$–$$ ✕**Der Goldene Engel.** Oak beams festooned with plaster casts of cherubs, and angelic paintings on the walls, combine to create a charmingly kitschy atmosphere in "the golden angel". Local dishes are the specialty here, and the Flammkuchen in particular are a good choice.

There's also a good range of pizzas available. ✉ *Münsterpl. 14* ☎*0761/37933* ▤*MC, V.*

WHERE TO STAY

$$$$

Fodor'sChoice

★

⊞ **Colombi.** Freiburg's most luxurious hotel is one of the few where the owners are there to make sure your stay is perfect. Its taste-fully furnished rooms have floor-to-ceiling windows overlooking the romantic old city. Despite its central location, the hotel basks in near-countryside quiet. The Hans Thoma Stube ($$$$, reservations essen-tial) has outfitted itself with venerable tables, chairs, tile stoves, and wood paneling from some older establishments. It has its own bakery, which even makes fancy chocolate creams. The black-tied waiters will also serve you small dishes at merciful prices. **Pros:** friendly service, quiet location, comfortable rooms. **Cons:** business hotel, often fully booked by conference visitors. ✉*Am Colombi Park/Rotteckring 16* ☎*0761/21060* ⊕*www.colombi.de* ⟲*111 rooms, 5 suites* ⚏*In-room: dial-up, Wi-Fi. In-hotel: restaurant, room service, bar, pool, gym, pub-lic Internet, parking (fee), no-smoking rooms, some pets allowed (fee)* ▤*AE, DC, MC, V.*

$$–$$$

⊞ **Best Western Premier Hotel Victoria.** Despite its traditional appearance and comfort, this is a very eco-friendly hotel. Black Forest sawdust has replaced oil for heating, solar panels provide some of the electricity and hot water, windows have thermal panes, bathtubs are ergonomically designed to use less hot water, and everything from the stationery to the toilet tissue is made from recycled paper. None of this detracts from the fact that the hotel, built in 1875 and carefully restored, is totally in line with Black Forest hospitality. **Pros:** eco-friendly, free city bus tickets available to guests. **Con:** outside the medieval center. ✉*Eisenbahn-str. 54* ☎*0761/207–340* ⊕*www.victoria.bestwestern.de* ⟲*63 rooms* ⚏*In-room: no a/c (some), dial-up, Wi-Fi. In-hotel: bar, parking (fee), Wi-Fi, some pets allowed, no-smoking rooms* ▤*AE, DC, MC, V.*

$$

⊞ **Oberkirchs Weinstube.** Across from the cathedral, this wine cellar, res-taurant, and hotel is a bastion of tradition and *Gemütlichkeit* (comfort and conviviality). The proprietor personally bags some of the game that ends up on the menu ($$–$$$). Simple but filling dishes include the fresh trout and the lentils with a sausage called *Saitenwurst*. In sum-mer the dark-oak dining tables spill onto a garden terrace. Approxi-mately 20 Baden wines are served by the glass, many supplied from the restaurant's own vineyards. The charming guest rooms are in the main building and in a neighboring centuries-old house. **Pro:** great central location. **Con:** difficult parking access. ✉*Münsterpl. 22* ☎*0761/202–6868* ⊕*www.hotel-oberkirch.de* ⟲*26 rooms* ⚏*In-room: no a/c, Wi-Fi. In-hotel: restaurant, some pets allowed* ▤*AE, MC, V* ☻*Restaurant closed Sun. and 2 wks in Jan.* ⧖*BP.*

$$

⊞ **Park Hotel Post Meier.** This century-old building near the train sta-tion has a copper dome and stone balconies overlooking a park. You'll be greeted with a drink upon your arrival, find fresh fruit in your room, and can use the phone beside the bed, at the desk, or even in the bathroom. **Pros:** friendly, some rooms have park views. **Con:** outside the medieval center. ✉*Eisenbahnstr. 35–37* ☎*0761/385–480* ⊕*www.park-hotel-post.de* ⟲*43 rooms, 2 apartments* ⚏*In-room: no* *a/c, refrigerator, Wi-Fi. In-hotel: bicycles, no-smoking rooms* ☐*AE, MC, V* ⦿|*BP.*

$$ ☷**Rappen.** This hotel's brightly painted rooms are on the sunny side of the cobblestone cathedral square and marketplace. Three rooms are designated "anti-allergy." At the restaurant ($$–$$$), tables are set out amid the lively chatter of the square in summer. The kitchen serves fresh vegetables, game, and fish, though a simple, filling *Hochzeitssuppe* (marriage soup) with pasta, carrots, spring onions, and other vegetables might be enough. Locals come in for a glass of wine (there are about 40 wines available, German and French). **Pros:** central location, friendly service, clean rooms. **Cons:** difficult to access by car. ☒*Münsterpl. 13* ☎*0761/31353* ⦿*www.hotelrappen.de* ⇆*24 rooms* ⌂*In-room: no a/ c, dial-up, Wi-Fi. In-hotel: restaurant, no-smoking rooms, some pets allowed* ☐*AE, DC, MC, V* ⦿|*BP.*

$$ ☷**Zum Roten Bären.** Like several other hotels, the "Red Bear" claims to
★ be the "oldest in Germany," but this one has authenticated documentation going back 700 years to prove its heritage. The inn dates from 1311 and retains its individual character, with very comfortable lodgings and excellent dining choices. The party preparations are already underway to celebrate the hotel's 700th birthday in 2011.■**TIP→On request, you may tour the two-story wine cellar dating from the 12th century.** **Pros:** dripping with history, great location. **Con:** some rooms quite small. ☒*Oberlinden 12* ☎*0761/387–870* ⦿*www.roter-baeren.de* ⇆*22 rooms, 3 suites* ⌂*In-room: no a/c, dial-up. In-hotel: restaurant, parking (fee), no-smoking rooms, some pets allowed* ☐*AE, DC, MC, V* ⊘*Restaurant closed Sun.* ⦿|*BP.*

$ ☷**Hotel Schwarzwälder Hof.** Part of this hotel occupies a former mint, complete with graceful cast-iron railings on the spiral staircase and, unfortunately, paper-thin walls. It's in the downtown pedestrian zone and is very handy to both a parking garage and public transportation. The Badische Winzerstube ($) provides all you could want in local atmosphere, wine, and food. **Pros:** good central location, clean rooms. **Cons:** parking in public garage around the corner, can be noisy, thin walls, some rooms share bathrooms. ☒*Herrenstr. 43* ☎*0761/38030* ⦿*www.shof.de* ⇆*42 rooms, 3 suites* ⌂*In-room: no a/c, dial-up. In-hotel: restaurant, public Internet, parking (fee), some pets allowed* ☐*MC, V* ⦿|*BP.*

¢–$ ☷**Gasthaus zur Sonne.** The downside: the bathroom is down the hall for some rooms, there are no eggs at breakfast, the bedside lamps may or may not work, and it's a long way from the center of town. The upside: the hotel is spotlessly clean, the food in the restaurant (¢–$) sticks to your ribs, a bus at the door gets you downtown with ease, and you'll find a piece of chocolate on your bedside table each night. Not a bad choice for travelers on a budget. **Pros:** clean, friendly, good value. **Cons:** shared bathrooms, far from the sights. ☒*Hochdorfstr. 1* ☎*07665/2650* ⦿*www.sonne-hochdorf.de* ⇆*15 rooms, 8 with shared bath* ⌂*In-room: no a/c, no phone. In-hotel: restaurant, bar, parking (no fee), some pets allowed* ☐*No credit cards* ⦿|*BP.*

7

NIGHTLIFE & THE ARTS

Nightlife in Freiburg takes place in the city's *Kneipen* (pubs), wine bars, and wine cellars, which are plentiful on the streets around the cathedral. For student pubs, wander around **Stühlinger,** the neighborhood immediately south of the train station. Plenty of people take their nightcap in the Best Western Premier Hotel Victoria at the **Cocktailbar Hemingway** (⊠ *Eisenbahnstr. 54* ☎*0761/207–340*), which stays open until 2 AM on weekends. **Jazzhaus** (⊠*Schnewlinstr. 1* ☎*0761/34973* ⊕*www.jazzhaus.de*) sometimes has live music and draws big acts and serious up-and-coming artists to its brick cellar. A very mixed crowd meets daily and nightly at **Kagan** (⊠*Bismarckallee 9* ☎*0761/767–2766* ⊠*€6*) on the 18th floor of the skyscraper over the train station, with an incomparable view of the Old Town. The club is open Wednesday through Saturday from 10 PM until the wee hours. The café is open Tuesday through Sunday.

STAUFEN

20 km (12 mi) south of Freiburg via B–31.

Once you've braved Hell Valley to get to Freiburg, visit the nearby town of Staufen, where Dr. Faustus is reputed to have made his pact with the devil. The Faustus legend is remembered today chiefly because of Goethe's *Faust* (published in two parts, 1808–32). In this account, Faust sells his soul to the devil in return for eternal youth and knowledge. The historical Faustus was actually an alchemist whose pact was not with the devil but with a local baron who convinced him that he could make his fortune by converting base metal into gold. The explosion leading to his death at Gasthaus zum Löwen produced so much noise and sulfurous stink that the townspeople were convinced the devil had carried him off.

You can visit the ancient **Gasthaus zum Löwen** (⊠*Rathausg. 8* ☎*07633/908–9390* ⊕*www.fauststube-im-loewen.de*), where Faustus lived, allegedly in room No. 5, and died. Guests can stay overnight in the room, which has been decked out in period furniture and had all-modern conveniences removed (including the telephone) to enhance the effect. The inn is right on the central square of Staufen, a town with a visible inclination toward modern art in ancient settings.

WHERE TO STAY

$–$$ ▦**Landgasthaus zur Linde.** Guests have been welcomed here for more than 350 years, but the comforts inside the inn's old walls are contemporary. The kitchen ($$–$$$) creates splendid trout specialties and plays up seasonal dishes, such as asparagus in May and June and mushrooms from the valley in autumn. The terrace is a favorite for hikers passing through, as are the various snacks. **Pros:** friendly, quiet, good restaurant. **Cons:** remote, no elevator. ⊠*Krumlinden 13, 14 km (9 mi) southeast of Staufen Münstertal* ☎*07636/447* ⊕*www.landgasthaus. de* ⇆*11 rooms, 3 suites* ♿*In-room: no a/c. In-hotel: restaurant, no elevator, some pets allowed* ☰*V* ☉*Restaurant closed Mon.* ⏅*BP.*

KAISERSTUHL

20 km (12 mi) northwest of Freiburg on B–31.

One of the unusual sights of the Black Forest is the **Kaiserstuhl** *(Emperor's Chair)*, a volcanic outcrop clothed in vineyards that produce some of Baden's best wines—reds from the Spätburgunder grape and whites that have an uncanny depth. A third of Baden's wines are produced in this single area, which has the warmest climate in Germany. ■TIP➡ The especially dry and warm microclimate has given rise to tropical vegetation, including sequoias and a wide variety of orchids.

The fine little **Weinmuseum** *(Wine Museum)* is in a renovated barn in the village center. A small vineyard out front displays the various types of grapes used to make wine in the Kaiserstuhl region. ⊠*Schlossbergstr., Vogtsburg-Achkarren* ☎*07662/81263* ☑*€2* ⊙*Apr.–Oct., Tues.–Fri. 2–5, weekends 11–5.*

WHERE TO STAY

$ 🏨**Hotel Krone.** You could spend an entire afternoon and evening here even if you don't stay overnight in the comfortable guest rooms. Choose between the terrace or the dining room ($–$$), trying the wines and enjoying, say, a fillet of wild salmon in a horseradish crust, a boar's roast, or some lighter asparagus creation (in season). The house dates to 1561, and the Höfflin-Schüssler family, now in its fourth generation as hoteliers, knows how to make visitors feel welcome. **Pros:** friendly, quiet. **Cons:** can feel remote. ⊠*Schlossbergstr. 15 Vogtsburg-Achkarren* ☎*07662/93130* ⊕*www.Hotel-Krone-Achkarren.de* ⇌*23 rooms* ⌂*In-room: no a/c, dial-up. In-hotel: restaurant, tennis court, some pets allowed* ▭*MC, V* ⊙*Restaurant closed Wed., and Thurs. in winter* ⋈*BP.*

$ 🏨**Posthotel Kreuz-Post.** Set right in the middle of the Kaiserstuhl vineyards, this establishment has been in the hands of the Gehr family since its construction in 1809. The restaurant ($–$$) serves regional and French cuisines with the famous local wines, and the family-owned schnapps distillery can be visited. All rooms are no-smoking. **Pros:** quiet, in the middle of nowhere. **Cons:** quiet, in the middle of nowhere. ⊠*Landstr. 1 Vogtsburg-Burkheim* ☎*07662/90910* ⊕*www.kreuz-post.de* ⇌*35 rooms* ⌂*In-room: no a/c. In-hotel: restaurant, bicycles, no-smoking rooms, some pets allowed* ▭*MC, V* ⋈*BP.*

RUST

35 km (22 mi) north of Freiburg.

The town of Rust, on the Rhine almost halfway from Freiburg to Strasbourg, boasts a castle dating from 1577 and painstakingly restored half-timber houses. But its big claim to fame is Germany's biggest amusement park, with its own autobahn exit.

On an area of 160 acres, **Europa Park** draws more than 3 million visitors a year with its variety of shows, rides, dining, and shops. Among many other things, it has the "Eurosat" to take you on a virtual journey past clusters of meteors and falling stars; the "Silver Star," Europe's highest roller coaster; a Spanish jousting tournament; and even a "4-D" movie in which you might get damp in the rain or be rocked by an earthquake. ⊠*Europa-Park-Str. 2* ☎*01805/776–688* ⊕*www.europapark. de* 🎫*€27* ⊙*Apr.–Oct., daily 9–6.*

WHERE TO STAY

$ 🏨 **Hotel am Park.** This handy hotel, with a waterfall and a statue of a "friendly dragon" in the lobby, is just across the road from the entrance to Europa Park. It's also only 300 yards from a nature preserve and swimming area, and guests can park there free. Knowing that a lot of park visitors will have their kids with them, the restaurant has set up its Casa Nova restaurant (¢–$) with pizza, pasta, and a play area. Its other restaurant, the Am Park, serves German cuisine. **Pros:** friendly, great for kids, convenient for Europa Park. **Cons:** proximity to Europa Park means it can get noisy. ⊠*Austr. 1 Rust* ☎*07822/444–900* 🖷*07822/444–929* ⊕*www.hotels-in-rust.de* 🛏*47 rooms* ⚭*In-room: no a/c, Ethernet. In-hotel: 2 restaurants, some pets allowed* ▤*MC, V* 🍽*BP.*

Heidelberg & the Neckar Valley

WORD OF MOUTH

"Tübingen is a gorgeous city south of Stuttgart. Much smaller but full of cobblestone nooks and crannies, lots of atmosphere, nice places to eat, and a setting on the Neckar River. And just a few miles off the autobahn north to Heidelberg. It's a university town, so livelier than other towns its size. You can't do much better, in my book."

—Russ

"The Neckar Valley from Heidelberg, a gem of a town, to Rothenburg area was dreamy—towns like Bad Wimpfen and others and the valley is really gorgeous and it appears bike routes go along it most of the way."

—PalenQ

Updated by
Uli Ehrhardt

THE NECKAR RIVER UNITES BEAUTY and historic resonance as it flows toward the Rhine through the state of Baden-Württemberg, eventually reaching Heidelberg's graceful baroque towers and the majestic ruins of its red sandstone castle. Much of this route follows the west–east course of the Burgenstrasse (Castle Road), which stretches nearly 1,000 km (621 mi) from Mannheim to Prague, taking in some 70 castles and palaces along the way. Every town or bend in the river seems to have its guardian castle, sometimes in ruins but often revived as a museum or hotel. Off the main road, quiet side valleys and little towns slumber in leafy peace.

ORIENTATION & PLANNING

GETTING ORIENTED

Although not as well known as the Rhine, the Neckar River has a wonderful charm of its own. After Heidelberg it winds its way through a small valley guarded by castles. It then flows on, bordered by vineyards on its northern slopes, passing the interesting and industrious city of Stuttgart, before it climbs towards the Swabian hills. You follow the Neckar until the old half-timbered university town of Tübingen. The river continues toward the eastern slopes of the Black forest, where it originates less than 50 mi from the source of the Danube.

Heidelberg. The natural beauty of Heidelberg is created by the embrace of mountains, forests, vineyards, and the Neckar River—all crowned by the famous ruined castle. The Neckar and the Rhine meet at nearby Mannheim, the biggest train hub for the super-fast ICE (Intercity Express) trains of Germany, a major industrial center and the second-largest river port in Europe.

The Burgenstrasse (Castle Road). If you or your kids like castles, this is the place to go. Of course you can always visit the crowded Heidelberg castle, but the real fun starts when you venture up the Neckar River. There seems to be a castle on every hilltop in the valley. Two of them, Burg Hirschhorn und Burg Hornberg offer lodging and good restaurants.

Swabian Cities. It is said of the Swabians that they live to work—this penchant shows in their affluent and well-cared-for cities. Stuttgart, the state capital, has elegant streets, shops, hotels, and museums, as well as some of Germany's top industries, among them Mercedes and Porsche. Ludwigsburg, with its huge baroque castles and baroque flower gardens, is worth a visit. Heilbronn is known for its surrounding vineyards with nice restaurants. The most charmingly "Swabian" of all these cities is the old half-timber university town of Tübingen.

TOP REASONS TO GO

Heidelberg castle: The architectural highlight of the region's most beautiful castle is the Renaissance courtyard—harmonious, graceful, and ornate.

Neckar Bridge: After a walk under the twin towers that were part of medieval Heidelberg's fortifications, you have the best view of the city and the castle.

Hornberg castle: With its oldest parts dating from the 12th century, this is one of the best of more than a dozen castles between Heidelberg and Stuttgart.

Stuttgart's Mercedes-Benz Museum: The history of the *auto mobil* is illustrated by 160 classic cars, from posh limousines to sleek racing cars.

Tübingen Altstadt: With its half-timber houses, winding alleyways, and hilltop setting overlooking the Neckar, Tübingen is the quintessential German experience.

HEIDELBERG & THE NECKAR VALLEY PLANNER

WHEN TO GO

If you plan to visit Heidelberg in summer, make reservations well in advance and expect to pay top rates. To get away from the crowds, consider staying out of town and driving or taking the bus or train into the city. Hotels and restaurants are much cheaper just a little upriver. A visit in late fall, when the vines turn a faded gold, or early spring, with the first green shoots of the year, can be captivating. In the depths of winter, river mists creep through the narrow streets of Heidelberg's Old Town and awaken the ghosts of a romantic past.

GETTING HERE & AROUND

BY AIR From the Frankfurt and Stuttgart airports, there's fast and easy access, by car and train, to all major centers along the Neckar.

BY BUS & SHUTTLE With advance reservations you can get to Heidelberg from the Frankfurt airport via the shuttle service TLS. The trip takes about an hour and costs €29 per person; with four people, €22.25 each. No reservations are needed for the Lufthansa Airport Bus, which is not restricted to Lufthansa passengers. Service is daily, on the hour, 8–1, 3–7, and 10 or 11 PM. It departs from Frankfurt airport, Terminal One, Hall B, arrivals level. Exit at B–4, close to the *Treffpunkt* (Meeting Point), to reach the bus stop. The trip ends at the Crowne Plaza Hotel in Heidelberg and costs €19 per person.

BY CAR Heidelberg is a 15-minute drive (10 km [6 mi]) on A–656 from Mannheim, a major junction of the autobahn system. Heilbronn is near the east–west A–6 and the north–south A–81. The Burgenstrasse (Route B–37) follows the north bank of the Neckar River from Heidelberg to Mosbach, from which it continues south to Heilbronn as B–27, the road parallel to and predating the autobahn (A–81). B–27 still leads to Stuttgart and Tübingen.

8

BY TRAIN Western Germany's most important rail junction is in nearby Mannheim, with hourly InterCity trains from all major German cities. Heidelberg is equally easy to get to. The super-high-speed InterCity Express service, which reaches 280 kph (174 mph), is Germany's fastest. Travel time between Frankfurt and Stuttgart is less than 1½ hours; between Heidelberg and Stuttgart, 26 minutes. There are express trains to Heilbronn from Heidelberg and Stuttgart and direct trains from Stuttgart to Tübingen. Local services link many of the smaller towns.

ESSENTIALS **Bus Information Lufthansa Airport Bus** (☎ *0180/583–8426 in Heidelberg* ⊕ *www. lufthansa-airportbus.com*).**TLS** (☎ *06221/770–077* ⊕ *www.tls-heidelberg.de*).

Visitor Information State Tourist Board BW (✉ *Esslingerstr. 8D–70182 Stuttgart* ☎ *0711/238580* ⊕ *www.tourismus-bw.de*). **Die Burgenstrasse** (✉ *Allee 28D–74072 Heilbronn* ☎ *07131/564–028* ⊕ *www.burgenstrasse.de*).

ABOUT THE RESTAURANTS

Mittagessen (lunch) in this region is generally served from noon until 2 or 2:30, *Abendessen* (dinner) from 6 until 9:30 or 10. *Durchgehend warme Küche* means that hot meals are also served between lunch and dinner. Slowly but surely, credit cards have gained acceptance, but this is by no means universal, and many restaurants will accept only cash or debit cards issued by a German bank. Casual attire is typically acceptable at restaurants here, and reservations are generally not needed.

ABOUT THE HOTELS

This area is full of castle-hotels and charming country inns that range in comfort from upscale rustic to luxurious. For a riverside view, ask for a *Zimmer* (room) or *Tisch* (table) *mit Neckarblick* (with a view of the Neckar). The Neckar Valley offers idyllic alternatives to the cost and crowds of Heidelberg. Driving or riding the train from Neckargemünd, for example, takes 20 minutes.

WHAT IT COSTS IN EUROS				
¢	$	$$	$$$	$$$$
RESTAURANTS	under €9	€9–€15	€16–€20	€21–25	over €25
HOTELS	under €50	€50–€100	€101–€175	€176–€225	over €225

Restaurant prices are per person for a main course at dinner. Hotel prices are for two people in a standard double room, including tax and service.

PLANNING YOUR TIME

To fully appreciate Heidelberg, try to be up and about before the tour buses arrive. Visit Schwetzingen around midday. After the day-trippers have gone and most shops have closed, the good restaurants and the night spots open up. Visit the castles on the Burgenstrasse at your leisure, maybe even staying overnight. Leaving the valley, you'll drive into wine country. Even if you are not a car enthusiast, the museums of Mercedes and Porsche in Stuttgart are worth a visit. Try to get to Tübingen during the week to avoid the crowds of Swabians coming in for their *Kaffee und Kuchen* (coffee and cake). During the week, try to get a room and spend a leisurely evening in this half-timber university town.

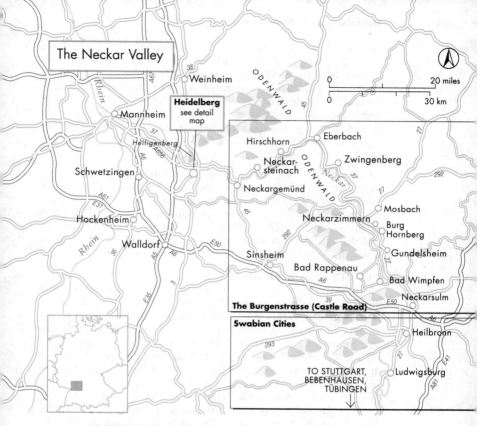

The Neckar Valley

Weinheim

ODENWALD

Heidelberg
see detail
map

0   20 miles

0   30 km

Rhein

Mannheim

Heiligenberg

Hirschhorn   Eberbach

Neckar-   Zwingenberg
steinach   ODENWALD

Schwetzingen

Neckargemünd   Neckar

Hockenheim   Neckarzimmern   Mosbach

Burg
Hornberg

Walldorf   Gundelsheim

Sinsheim   Bad Wimpfen

Bad Rappenau   Neckarsulm

The Burgenstrasse (Castle Road)

Swabian Cities   Heilbronn

TO STUTTGART,   Ludwigsburg
BEBENHAUSEN,
TÜBINGEN

HEIDELBERG

57 km (35 mi) northeast of Karlsruhe.

If any city in Germany encapsulates the spirit of the country, it is Heidelberg. Scores of poets and composers—virtually the entire 19th-century German Romantic movement—have sung its praises. Goethe and Mark Twain both fell in love here: the German writer with a beautiful young woman, the American author with the city itself. Sigmund Romberg set his operetta *The Student Prince* in the city; Carl Maria von Weber wrote his lushly Romantic opera *Der Freischütz* here. Composer Robert Schumann was a student at the university. The campaign these artists waged on behalf of the town has been astoundingly successful. Heidelberg's fame is out of all proportion to its size (population 140,000); more than 3½ million visitors crowd its streets every year.

Heidelberg was the political center of the Rhineland Palatinate. At the end of the Thirty Years' War (1618–48), the elector Carl Ludwig married his daughter to the brother of Louis XIV in the hope of bringing peace to the Rhineland. But when the elector's son died without an heir, Louis XIV used the marriage alliance as an excuse to claim Heidelberg, and in 1689 the town was sacked and laid to waste. Four years later he sacked the town again. From its ashes arose what you see today: a baroque town built on Gothic foundations, with narrow, twisting streets and alleyways.

Above all, Heidelberg is a university town, with students making up a large part of its population. And a youthful spirit is felt in the lively restaurants and pubs of the Altstadt. In 1930 the university was expanded, and its buildings now dot the entire landscape of Heidelberg and its neighboring suburbs. Modern Heidelberg changed as U.S. army barracks and industrial development stretched into the suburbs, but the old heart of the city remains intact, exuding the spirit of romantic Germany.

GETTING HERE & AROUND

Heidelberg is 15 minutes away from Mannheim, where four ICE-trains and five Autobahn routes meet. Everything in town may be reached on foot. A funicular takes you up to the castle and Heidelberg's Königstuhl mountain, and a streetcar takes you from the center of the city to the main station. From April through October there are daily walking tours of Heidelberg in German (Friday and Saturday in English) at 10:30 AM; from November through March, tours are in German only, Saturday at 10:30; the cost is €6. They depart from the Lion's Fountain on Universitätsplatz. Bilingual bus tours run April–October on Thursday and Friday at 2:30 and on Saturday at 10:30 and 2:30. From November through March, bus tours depart Saturday at 2:30. They cost €12 and depart from Universitätsplatz.

DISCOUNTS & DEALS

The HeidelbergCard costs €12 (two days) or €20 (four days), and includes free or reduced admission to most tourist attractions as well as free use of all public transportation (including the Bergbahn to the castle) and other extras, such as free guided walking tours, discounts on bus tours, and a city guidebook. It can be purchased at the Tourist-Information office at the main train station and at many local hotels.

TIMING

Walking the length of Heidelberg's Hauptstrasse (main street) will take an hour—longer if you are easily sidetracked by the shopping opportunities. Strolling through the old town and across the bridge to look at the castle will take you at least another half-hour, not counting the time you spend visiting the sites.

ESSENTIALS

Visitor Information **Heidelberger Convention and Visitors Bureau** (⊠ *Ziegelhäuser, Landstr. 3* ☎ *06221/142–223* ⊕ *www.heidelberg-marketing.de*). **Heidelberg** (⊠ *Tourist-Information am Hauptbahnhof, Willy-Brandt-Pl. 1* ☎ *06221/19433* ⊕ *www.cvb-heidelberg.de*).

EXPLORING HEIDELBERG

MAIN ATTRACTIONS

⑯ Alte Brücke *(Old Bridge).* Framed by two *Spitzhelm* towers (so called for their resemblance to old German helmets), this bridge was part of medieval Heidelberg's fortifications. In the west tower are three dank dungeons that once held common criminals. Above the portcullis you'll see a memorial plaque that pays warm tribute to the Austrian forces who helped Heidelberg beat back a French attempt to capture the bridge in 1799. The bridge itself is one of many to be built on this spot; ice floes and floods destroyed its predecessors. The elector Carl Theodor, who built it in 1786–88, must have been confident that this one would last: he had a statue of himself erected on it, upon a plinth decorated with river gods and goddesses (symbolic of the Neckar, Rhine, Danube, and Mosel rivers). As you enter the bridge from the Old Town, you'll also notice a statue of an animal that appears somewhat catlike. It's actually a monkey holding a mirror. Legend has it that the statue was erected to symbolize the need for both city-dwellers and those who live on the other side of the bridge to take a look over their shoulders as they cross—that neither group is more elite than the other.

⑧ Alte Universität *(Old University).* The three-story baroque structure, officially named Ruprecht-Karl-University, was built between 1712 and 1718 at the behest of the elector Johann Wilhelm. It houses the University Museum, with exhibits that chronicle the history of Germany's oldest university. The present-day Universitätsplatz (University Square) was built over the remains of an Augustinian monastery that was destroyed by the French in 1693. ⊠*Grabeng. 1–3* ☎*06221/542–152* 🖾*€3* ☉*Apr.–Oct., Tues.–Sun. 10–6; Nov.–Mar., Tues.–Sat. 10–4.*

⑮ Friedrich-Ebert-Gedenkstätte *(Friedrich Ebert Memorial).* The humble rooms of a tiny backstreet apartment were the birthplace of Friedrich Ebert, Germany's first democratically elected president (in 1920) and leader of the ill-fated Weimar Republic. Display cases have documents that tell the story of the tailor's son who took charge of a nation accustomed to being ruled by a kaiser. ⊠*Pfaffeng. 18* ☎*06221/91070* ⊕*www.ebert-gedenkstaette.de* 🖾*Free* ☉*Tues., Wed., and Fri.–Sun. 10–6, Thurs. 10–8.*

⑥ Heiliggeistkirche *(Church of the Holy Ghost).* The foundation stone of the building was laid in 1398, but it was not actually finished until 1544. Unlike that of most other Gothic churches, the facade of the Heiliggeistkirche is uniform—you cannot discern the choir or naves from the outside. The gargoyles looking down on the south side (where Hauptstrasse crosses Marktplatz) are remarkable for their sheer ugliness. The church fell victim to the plundering General Tilly, leader of the Catholic League during the Thirty Years' War. Tilly loaded the church's greatest treasure—the Bibliotheca Palatina, at the time the largest library in Germany—onto 500 carts and trundled it off to Rome, where he presented it to the pope. Few volumes found their way back. At the end of the 17th century, French troops plundered the church again, destroying the tombs; only the 15th-century tomb of Elector

Ruprecht III and his wife, Elisabeth von Hohenzollern, remains today. ⊠*Marktpl.* ☎*06221/21117* ⊕*www.heiliggeistkirche.de* ☉*Late Mar.–Oct., Mon.–Sat. 11–5, Sun. 12:30–5; Nov.–mid-Mar., Fri. and Sat. 11–3, Sun. 12:30–3.*

❼ Hotel zum Ritter. The hotel's name refers to the statue of a Roman knight (Ritter) atop one of the many gables. Its French builder, Charles Bélier, had the Latin inscription PERSTA INVICTA VENUS added to the facade in gold letters—"Venus, Remain Unconquerable." It appears this injunction was effective, as this was the city's only Renaissance building to be spared the attentions of the invading French in 1689 and 1693. Between 1695 and 1705 it was used as Heidelberg's town hall; later it became an inn, and it's still a hotel today. ⊠*Hauptstr. 178* ☎*06221/1350.*

❹ Königstuhl *(King's Throne).* The second-highest hill in the Odenwald range—1,700 feet above Heidelberg—is only a hop, skip, and funicular ride from Heidelberg. On a clear day you can see as far as the Black Forest to the south and west to the Vosges Mountains of France. The hill is at the center of a close-knit network of hiking trails. Signs and colored arrows from the top lead hikers through the woods of the Odenwald.

❶ Königstuhl Bergbahn *(funicular).* The funicular hoists visitors to the summit of the Königstuhl in 17 minutes. On the way it stops at the ruined Heidelberg Schloss and Molkenkur. The funicular usually leaves every 10 minutes in summer and every 20 minutes in winter. ⊠*Kornmarkt* ⊕*www.bergbahn-heidelberg.de* ☜*Round-trip to Schloss, Molkenkur, or Königstuhl €3.50.*

❸ Kurpfälzisches Museum *(Palatinate Museum).* This baroque palace was built as a residence for a university professor in 1712. It's a pleasure just to wander around, which is more or less unavoidable, since the museum's layout is so confusing. Among the exhibits are two standouts. One is a replica of the jaw of Heidelberg Man, a key link in the evolutionary chain thought to date from a half-million years ago; the original was unearthed near the city in 1907. The larger attraction is the *Windsheimer Zwölfbotenaltar (Twelve Apostles Altarpiece),* one of the largest and finest works of early Renaissance sculptor Tilman Riemenschneider. Its exquisite detailing and technical sophistication are evident in the simple faith that radiates from the faces of the Apostles. On the top floor of the museum there's a rich range of 19th-century German paintings and drawings, many depicting Heidelberg.
■ TIP → **The restaurant in the museum's quiet, shady courtyard is a good**

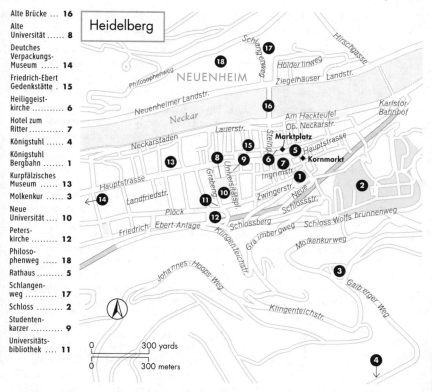

place for a break. ✉*Hauptstr. 97* ☎*06221/583–4020* ⊕*www.museum-heidelberg.de* ☜*€3* ⊗*Tues.–Sun. 10–6.*

Marktplatz *(Market Square).* Heidelberg's main square, with the Rathaus on one side and the Heiliggeistkirche on the other, has been its focal point since the Middle Ages. Public courts of justice were held here in earlier centuries, and people accused of witchcraft and heresy were burned at the stake. The baroque fountain in the middle, the *Herkules-brunnen* (Hercules Fountain), is the work of 18th-century artist H. Charrasky. Until 1740 a rotating, hanging cage stood next to it. For minor crimes, people were imprisoned in it and exposed to the abuse of their fellow citizens. ■TIP→ Today the Marktplatz hosts outdoor markets every Wednesday and Saturday.

❸ **Molkenkur.** The next stop after the castle on the Königstuhl funicular, Molkenkur was the site of Heidelberg's second castle. Lightning struck it in 1527, and it was never rebuilt. Today it's occupied by a restaurant—which bears the creative name Molkenkur Restaurant—with magnificent views of the Odenwald and the Rhine plain.

⓲ **Philosophenweg** *(Philosophers' Path).* You can reach this trail high above the river in one of two ways—either from Neuenheim or by taking the Schlangenweg. Both are steep climbs, but you'll be rewarded with spectacular views of the Old Town and Castle. From Neuenheim, turn right after crossing the bridge and follow signs to a small alleyway.

⑤ Rathaus *(Town Hall)*. Work began on the town hall in 1701, a few years after the French destroyed the city. The massive coat of arms above the balcony is the work of Heinrich Charrasky, who also created the statue of Hercules atop the fountain in the middle of the square. ⊠ *Marktpl.*

⑰ Schlangenweg *(Snake Path)*. This walkway starts just above the Alte Brücke opposite the Old Town and cuts steeply through terraced vineyards until it reaches the woods, where it crosses the Philosophenweg (Philosophers' Path).

② Schloss *(Castle)*. What's most striking is the architectural variety of
Fodor'sChoice this great complex. The oldest parts still standing date from the 15th
★ century, though most of the castle was built in the Renaissance and baroque styles of the 16th and 17th centuries, when the castle was the seat of the Palatinate electors. There's even an "English wing," built in 1612 by the elector Friedrich V for his teenage Scottish bride, Elizabeth Stuart; its plain, square-window facade is positively foreign compared to the castle's more opulent styles. (The enamored Friedrich also had a charming garden laid out for his young bride; its imposing arched entryway, the Elisabethentor, was put up overnight as a surprise for her 19th birthday.) The architectural highlight remains the Renaissance courtyard—harmonious, graceful, and ornate.

The castle includes the **Deutsches Apotheken–Museum** *(German Apothecary Museum* ☎*06221/25880* ☉ *Daily 10–5:30)*. This museum, on the lower floor of the Ottheinrichsbau (Otto Heinrich Building), is filled with ancient flagons and receptacles (each with a carefully painted enamel label), beautifully made scales, little drawers, shelves, a marvelous reconstruction of an 18th-century apothecary shop, dried beetles and toads, and a mummy with a full head of hair. Even if you have to wait, you should make a point of seeing the *Grosses Fass* (Great Cask), an enormous wine barrel in the cellar, made from 130 oak trees and capable of holding 58,500 gallons. It was used to hold wines paid as taxes by wine growers in the Palatinate.

In summer there are fireworks displays from the castle terrace (on the first Saturday in June and September and the second Saturday in July). In July and August the castle hosts a theater festival. Performances of *The Student Prince* often figure prominently. The castle may be reached by taking the Königstuhl Bergbahn. Generations of earlier visitors hiked up to it on the Burgweg, a winding road. ☎*06221/538–431* ⊕*www.heidelberg-schloss.de* ✉*€3; audio tours an additional €4* ☉*Mar.–Nov., daily 9:30–6; Dec.–Feb., daily 10–5; tours in English daily from 11, when demand is sufficient.*

ALSO WORTH SEEING

⑭ Deutsches Verpackungs-Museum *(German Packaging Museum)*. A former church was innovatively converted to house this fascinating documentation of packaging and package design of brand-name products. Representing the years 1800 to the present, historic logos and slogans are a trip down memory lane. The entrance is in a courtyard reached via an alley. ✉ *Hauptstr. 22* ☎ *06221/21361* ⊕ *www.verpackungsmuseum.de* 🎫 *€3.50* ⊘ *Wed.–Fri. 1–6, weekends 11–6.*

Kornmarkt *(Grain Market).* A baroque statue of the Virgin Mary is in the center of this old Heidelberg square, which has a view of the castle ruins.

🔟 **Neue Universität** *(New University).* The plain building on the south side of Universitätsplatz was erected between 1930 and 1932 through funds raised by the U.S. ambassador to Germany, J. G. Schurman, who had been a student at the university. The only decoration on the building's three wings is a statue of Athena, the Greek goddess of wisdom, above the entrance. The inner courtyard contains a medieval tower from 1380, the **Hexenturm** (Witches' Tower). Suspected witches were locked up there in the Middle Ages. It later became a memorial to former students killed in World War I. ✉ *Grabeng.*

OFF THE BEATEN PATH

Neuenheim. To escape the crowds of Heidelberg, walk across the Theodor Heuss Bridge to the suburb of Neuenheim. At the turn of the 20th century this old fishing village developed into a residential area full of posh art nouveau villas. North of the Brückenkopf (bridgehead) you'll find antiques and designer shops, boutiques, and cafés on Brückenstrasse, Bergstrasse (one block east), and Ladenburger Strasse (parallel to the river). To savor the neighborhood spirit, visit the charming farmers' market on Wednesday or Saturday morning at the corner of Ladenburger and Luther streets.

⑫ **Peterskirche** *(St. Peter's Church).* Many famous Heidelberg citizens' tombstones, some more than 500 years old, line the outer walls of the city's oldest parish church (1485–1500). The church is not open for visits. ✉ *Plöck 62.*

⑨ **Studentenkarzer** *(Student Prison).* University officials locked students up here from 1778 to 1914—mostly for minor offenses. They could be held for up to 14 days and were left to subsist on bread and water for the first three days; thereafter, they were allowed to attend lectures, receive guests, and have food brought in from the outside. ■**TIP**➜**There's bravado, even poetic flair, to be deciphered from two centuries of graffiti that cover the walls and ceilings of the narrow cells.** ✉ *Augustinerg.* ☎ *06221/543–554* 🎫 *€3* ⊘ *Apr.–Sept., Tues.–Sun. 10–6; Oct., Tues.–Sun. 10–4; Nov.–Mar., Tues.–Sat. 10–4.*

⑪ **Universitätsbibliothek** *(University Library).* Its 2½ million volumes include the 14th-century *Manesse Codex*, a unique collection of medieval songs and poetry once performed in the courts of Germany by the *Minnesänger* (troubadors). The original is too fragile to be exhibited, so a copy is on display. ✉ *Plöck 107–109* ☎ *06221/542–380* ⊕ *www. ub.uni-heidelberg.de* 🎫 *Free* ⊘ *Mon.–Sat. 10–6.*

WHERE TO EAT

$$$$
★ ✕ **Schlossweinstube.** This spacious baroque dining room specializes in *Ente von Heidelberg* (roast duck), but there's always something new on the seasonal menu. Whatever you order, pair it with a bottle from

8

the extensive selection of international wines. Adjacent to the dining room is the Bistro Backhaus (¢–$), which has rustic furnishings and a nearly 50-foot-high *Backkamin* (baking oven). Light fare as well as coffee and cake are served indoors and on the shaded terrace. You can sample rare wines (Eiswein, Beerenauslese) by the glass in the shared wine cellar, or pick up a bottle with a designer label depicting Heidelberg. Reservations are essential for terrace seating in the summer. ⊠*Schlosshof, on castle grounds* ☎*06221/97970* ☰*AE, DC, MC, V* ⊗*Schlossweinstube closed late-Dec.–Jan. and Wed. No lunch.*

> **LOCAL LEGEND**
>
> During the rule of the elector Carl Philip, the Great Cask in the Schloss was guarded by the court jester, a Tyrolean dwarf called Perkeo. When offered wine, he always answered, "Perche no?" ("Why not?"), hence his nickname. Legend has it that he could consume frighteningly large quantities of wine and that he died when he drank a glass of water by mistake. A statue of Perkeo stands next to the two-story-high barrel.

$$$$
★ ✕**Schwarz Das Restaurant.** Sleek, contemporary furnishings, soft lighting, stunning panoramic views, and Manfred Schwarz's creative cuisine make for unforgettable dining in this 12th-floor restaurant, complete with an apéritif bar and cigar lounge. The five- to seven-course gourmet menu of the month varies from Asiatic to Mediterranean to French. On the menu you may find sautéed goose liver on truffled polenta with raspberry vinegar sauce or gratinéed scallops with chive sauce and caviar. ⊠*Kurfürsten-Anlage 60, opposite train station* ☎*06221/757–030* ☰*AE, DC, MC, V* ⊗*Closed Sun., Mon., and 1st 2 wks of Jan. No lunch.*

$$–$$$
★ ✕**Simplicissimus.** Olive oil and herbs of Provence accentuate many of chef Johann Lummer's culinary delights. Saddle of lamb and sautéed liver in honey-pepper sauce are specialties; the *Dessertteller,* a sweet sampler, is a crowning finish to any meal. The wine list focuses on old-world estates, particularly clarets. The elegant art-nouveau interior is done in shades of red with dark-wood accents. ⊠*Ingrimstr. 16* ☎*06221/183–336* ☰ *MC, V* ⊗*Closed Mon., Feb., and 2 wks in Aug. and Sept. No lunch.*

$–$$
✕**Schnitzelbank.** Little more than a hole in the wall, this former cooper's workshop has been transformed into a candlelit pub. No matter when you go, it seems to be filled with people seated around the wooden tables. If you are interested, ask to look at the old guest books and sign the newest. The menu features specialties from Baden and the Pfalz, such as *Schäufele* (pickled and slightly smoked pork shoulder); or a hearty *Pfälzer Teller,* a platter of bratwurst, *Leberknödel* (liver dumplings), and slices of *Saumagen* (a spicy meat-and-potato mixture encased in a sow's stomach). ⊠*Bauamtsg. 7* ☎*06221/21189* ☰*MC, V* ⊗*No lunch weekdays*

$–$$
✕**Trattoria Toscana.** You can choose from antipasti platters, pasta dishes, pizzas, and special daily offerings, all served in generous portions. If you sit at a table inside the restaurant you can enjoy good Italian food while you watch the crowds push by. ⊠*Marktpl. 1* ☎*06221/28619* ☰*DC, MC, V.*

EATING WELL IN THE NECKAR VALLEY

Fish and *Wild* (game) from the streams and woods lining the Neckar Valley, as well as seasonal favorites—*Spargel* (asparagus), *Pilze* (mushrooms), *Morcheln* (morels), *Pfifferlinge* (chanterelles), and *Steinpilze* (crepes)—are regulars on menus in this area. Pfälzer specialties are also common, but the penchant for potatoes yields to *Knödel* (dumplings) and pasta farther south. The latter includes the Swabian and Baden staples *Maultaschen* (stuffed "pockets" of pasta) and Spätzle (roundish egg noodles), as well as *Schupfnudeln* (finger-size noodles of potato dough), also called *Bube*- or *Buwespitzle*. Look for *Linsen* (lentils) and sauerkraut in soups or as sides. *Schwäbischer Rostbraten* (beefsteak topped with fried onions) and *Schäufele* (pickled and slightly smoked pork shoulder) are popular meat dishes.

Considerable quantities of red wine are produced along the Neckar Valley. Crisp, light Trollinger is often served in the traditional *Viertele*, a round, quarter-liter (8-ounce) glass with a handle. Deeper-color, more substantial reds include Spätburgunder (Pinot Noir) and its mutation Schwarzriesling (Pinot Meunier), Lemberger, and Dornfelder. Riesling, Kerner, and Müller-Thurgau (synonymous with Rivaner), as well as Grauburgunder (Pinot Gris) and Weissburgunder (Pinot Blanc), are the typical white wines. A birch broom or wreath over the doorway of a vintner's home signifies a *Besenwirtschaft* ("broomstick inn"), a rustic pub where you can enjoy wines with snacks and simple fare. Many vintners offer economical B&Bs.

8

$-$$ ✕ **Zur Herrenmühle.** A 17th-century grain mill has been transformed ★ into this romantic restaurant. The old beams add to the warm atmosphere. In summer, try to arrive early to get a table in the idyllic courtyard. Fish, lamb, and homemade pasta are specialties. The prix-fixe menu offers an especially good value. ✉*Hauptstr. 239, near Karlstor* ☎*06221/602–909* 🍽*AE, MC, V* 🕐*Closed Sun. No lunch.*

¢–$ ✕ **Zum Roten Ochsen.** Many of the rough-hewn oak tables here have initials carved into them, a legacy of the thousands who have visited Heidelberg's most famous old tavern. Mark Twain, Marilyn Monroe, and John Wayne may have left their mark—they all ate here. You can wash down simple fare, such as goulash soup and bratwurst, or heartier dishes, such as *Tellerfleisch* (boiled beef) and sauerbraten, with German wines or Heidelberg beer. The "Red Ox" has been run by the Spengel family for 165 years. Come early to get a good seat. ✉*Hauptstr. 217* ☎*06221/20977* 🍽*MC, V* 🕐*Closed Sun. dinner and mid-Dec.–mid-Jan. No lunch Nov.–Mar.*

¢ ✕ **Café Knösel.** Heidelberg's oldest (1863) coffeehouse has always been a popular meeting place for students and professors. It's still producing café founder Fridolin Knösel's *Heidelberger Studentenkuss*. This "student kiss" is a chocolate wrapped in paper showing two sets of touching lips—an acceptable way for 19th-century students to "exchange kisses" in public. ✉*Haspelg. 20* ☎*062217272754* 🍽*MC, V.*

WHERE TO STAY

$$$$ ⊡ **Hotel Die Hirschgasse.** A stunning castle view marks this historic inn
Fodor'sChoice (1472), located across the river opposite Karlstor (15-minute walk to
★ Old Town). Convivial Ernest Kraft and his British wife Allison serve
upscale regional specialties (and wines from the vineyard next door)
in the Mensurstube ($$–$$$), once a tavern where university students
indulged in fencing duels, as mentioned in Mark Twain's *A Tramp
Abroad.* Beamed ceilings, stone walls, and deep red fabrics make for
romantic dining in elegant Le Gourmet ($$$–$$$$). The hotel's decor
is also romantic, filled with floral prints, artwork, and deep shades of
red. The suites are quite large, comfortable, and elegantly appointed.
Pros: terrific view, very elegant suites, very good food in both restau-
rants, only no-smoking rooms. **Cons:** only no-smoking rooms, some-
times not enough parking, expensive. ⊠*Hirschg. 3* ☎*06221/4540*
⊕*www.hirschgasse.de* ⟲*20 suites* ⚒*In-room: no a/c, Wi-Fi. In-hotel:
2 restaurants, bar, laundry service, public Wi-Fi, parking, some pets
allowed, no-smoking rooms* ⊟*AE, DC, MC, V* ⊙*Le Gourmet closed
2 wks in early Jan., 2 wks in early Aug., and Sun. and Mon.; Men-
surstube closed Sun. No lunch at either restaurant.*

$$$–$$$$ ⊡ **Der Europäische Hof–Hotel Europa.** The most luxurious of Heidelberg's
Fodor'sChoice hotels is located on secluded grounds next to the Old Town. Its many
★ public parlors are outfitted with stunning turn-of-the-last-century fur-
nishings, and bedrooms are spacious and tasteful; all suites have whirl-
pool tubs. In the elegant restaurant, the Kurfürstenstube ($$$–$$$$),
rich shades of yellow and blue are offset by the original woodwork of
1865. In summer, meals are served on the fountain-lined terrace. There
are great views of the castle from the two-story, glass-lined fitness and
wellness centers. **Pros:** pure luxury and perfection, warm welcome.
Cons: Kurfürstenstube closed in summer, expensive. ⊠*Friedrich-
Ebert-Anlage 1* ☎*06221/5150* ⊕*www.europaeischerhof.com* ⟲*100
rooms, 15 suites, 3 apartments* ⚒*In-room: no a/c (some), Wi-Fi. In-
hotel: 2 restaurants, bar, pool, gym, laundry service, public Internet,
public Wi-Fi, parking (fee), some pets allowed, no-smoking rooms*
⊟*AE, DC, MC, V* ⭢❘◯❘*BP.*

$$$–$$$$ ⊡ **Romantik Hotel zum Ritter St. Georg.** If this is your first visit to Germany,
★ try to stay here. It's the only Renaissance building in Heidelberg (1592)
and has a top location opposite the market square in the heart of Old
Town. The staff is exceptionally helpful and friendly. Some rooms are
more modern and spacious than others, but all are comfortable. You
can enjoy German and international favorites in the restaurants Belier
($–$$$) and Ritterstube ($–$$). Both are wood paneled and have old-
world charm. **Pros:** charm and elegance, fabulous food and terrific ser-
vice, top location in center of town, nice views, spacious rooms. **Cons:**
expensive, parking garage 5 minutes away on foot. ⊠*Hauptstr. 178*
☎*06221/1350* ⊕*www.ritter-heidelberg.de* ⟲*37 rooms, 1 suite* ⚒*In-
room: no a/c, Wi-Fi. In-hotel: 2 restaurants, laundry service, public
Internet, public Wi-Fi, some pets allowed, no-smoking rooms* ⊟*AE,
DC, MC, V.*

$$$ ⊡ **Crowne Plaza Heidelberg.** Located just a few blocks from the Old
Town, this hotel has an enviable location. Although not quite as luxuri-

ous as some of this well-known hotel chain's properties, it offers very nice accommodations and a full range of amenities. What many do consider luxurious is the indoor swimming pool and spa on the hotel's lower level—it even includes a poolside bar. ■ TIP → On weekends a North American–style brunch buffet is offered at an additional cost of €26. Pros: renovated grand hotel with new spacious lobby, stylish furniture, high ceilings; parking garage behind hotel, pool. Cons: business hotel, restaurant does not serve lunch. ⊠ *Kurfürsten-Anlage 1* ☎ *06221/9170* ⊕ *www. crowneplaza.com* 🛏 *232 rooms, 4 suites* 🔊 *In-room: Wi-Fi (some). In-hotel: restaurant, room service, bar, pool, gym, public Internet, public Wi-Fi, parking (fee), no-smoking rooms* 🖃 *AE, DC, MC, V.*

$$ ▥ **Gasthaus Backmulde.** This traditional tavern in the heart of Heidelberg has a surprising range of items on its menu ($–$$), from delicately marinated fresh vegetables that accompany the excellent meat dishes to imaginative soups that add modern twists to ancient recipes (a Franconian potato broth, for instance, rich with garden herbs). Pros: quiet rooms, good food in a nice restaurant. Cons: very difficult parking, restaurant closed Sunday. ⊠ *Schiffg. 11* ☎ *06221/53660* ⊕ *www. gasthaus-backmulde.de* 🛏 *25 rooms* 🔊 *In-room: no a/c. In-hotel: restaurant, public Internet, parking (fee), some pets allowed* 🖃 *MC, V* ⊗ *Restaurant no lunch Mon.* ⊺⊙⏌*BP.*

$$ ▥ **Holländer Hof.** The pink-and-white-painted facade of this ornate 19th-century building opposite the Alte Brücke stands out in its row fronting the Neckar River. Many of its rooms overlook the busy waterway and the forested hillside of the opposite shore. The rooms are modern and pleasant, and the staff is very friendly. Pros: nice view of river and beyond, comfortable rooms with good value, some rooms are handicap accessible, located beside Old Bridge. Cons: located beside Old Bridge, which means high noise levels at times, no restaurant or bar. ⊠ *Neckarstaden 66* ☎ *06221/60500* ⊕ *www. hollaender-hof.de* 🛏 *38 rooms, 1 suite* 🔊 *In-room: no a/c, Wi-Fi. In-hotel: laundry service, public Internet, public Wi-Fi, no-smoking rooms, some pets allowed* 🖃 *AE, DC, MC, V.*

$$ ▥ **KulturBrauerei Heidelberg.** Rooms with warm, sunny colors and modern decor are brilliantly incorporated into this old malt factory in the heart of Old Town. The restaurant ($–$$; no credit cards) is lively until well past midnight. House-brewed Scheffel's beer is the beverage of choice, although there are some good wines as well. The cellar houses the brewery (tours and tasting possible) and a weekend jazz club; in the courtyard is a huge beer garden. Pros: stylish rooms, lively restaurant, beer garden. Cons: in summer some rooms hear the beer garden noise, difficult parking. ⊠ *Leyerg. 6* ☎ *06221/502–980* ⊕ *www.heidelberger-kulturbrauerei.de* 🛏 *32 rooms, 2 suites* 🔊 *In-room: no a/c, Wi-Fi. In-hotel: restaurant, public Wi-Fi, parking (fee), some pets allowed, no-smoking rooms* 🖃 *MC, V* ⊺⊙⏌*BP.*

$$ ▥ **Schnookeloch.** This lively old tavern ($–$$) dates from 1703 and is inextricably linked with Heidelberg's history and university. Young and old alike crowd around the wooden tables in the wood-panel room, and piano music adds to the din Thursday through Sunday nights. From salads and pasta to hearty roasts and steaks, there's a broad selec-

8

tion of food, including many fish dishes. Upstairs there are modern, pleasantly furnished guest rooms. **Pros:** lively atmosphere in restaurant, good sturdy food. **Cons:** noisy, no elevator, rooms too expensive. ⊠ *Haspelg. 8* ☎ *06221/138–080* ⊕ *www.schnookeloch.de* ☞ *11 rooms* ⟳ *In-room: no a/c. In-hotel: no elevator, restaurant, some pets allowed* ▤ *MC, V* ⊚ *BP.*

$$ 🏨 **Weisser Bock.** Exposed beams and stucco ceilings are part of this hotel's charm. Comfortable rooms are individually decorated with warm wood furnishings. Art deco lovers will be charmed by the decor and pretty table settings of the restaurant ($–$$; no credit cards). Fresh fish is a highlight of the creative cuisine. The homemade smoked salmon and an unusual cream-of-Jerusalem-artichoke soup with crayfish are recommended. The proprietor is a wine fan, and the extensive wine list reflects it. **Pros:** nicely decorated rooms, exceptional food, only no-smoking rooms. **Cons:** only no-smoking rooms, parking difficult. ⊠ *Grosse Mantelg. 24* ☎ *06221/90000* ⊕ *www.weisserbock.de* ☞ *21 rooms, 2 suites* ⟳ *In-room: no a/c, Wi-Fi. In-hotel: restaurant, bar, some pets allowed, no-smoking rooms* ▤ *MC, V.*

$–$$ 🏨 **Nh Heidelberg.** The glass-covered entrance hall is very spacious—not
★ surprising, as it was the courtyard of a former brewery. The hotel is within reasonable walking distance of Heidelberg's major sites, about 1 km (½ mi) from Old Town. You can dine at one of three on-site restaurants, including the Raustubert, which specializes in regional German fare. Rooms are colorful and cozy. As it is mainly a business hotel, you get very good room rates in summer, especially in August. **Pros:** incredibly spacious yet welcoming lobby, good food in two restaurants, good room rates in summer, as it is a business hotel. **Cons:** business hotel, lacks charm, not in center of town. ⊠ *Bergheimerstr. 91* ☎ *06221/13270* ⊕ *www.nh-hotels.com* ☞ *174 rooms* ⟳ *In-room: Wi-Fi. In-hotel: 2 restaurants, room service, bar, gym, laundry service, public Wi-Fi, parking (fee), no smoking rooms* ▤ *AE, DC, MC, V.*

¢ 🏨 **Jugendherberge Tiergartenstrasse.** For youth-hostel cardholders (cards cost €20), these are clean, inexpensive accommodations near miniature golf, a large pool, stables, and the zoo. ■ TIP→ **Check on the curfew and get a key if you plan to stay out late.** To and from the Hauptbahnhof, take Bus 32 (10-minute ride)—ask the reception desk for precise times. Reception is open 7 AM–2 AM. **Pros:** very good prices, young guests. **Cons:** young guests, noisy, away from center of town. ⊠ *Tiergartenstr. 5* ☎ *06221/412–066 or 06221/651–190* ⊕ *www.jugendherberge-heidelberg.de* ☞ *500 beds* ⟳ *In-room: no a/c, no phone, no TV. In-hotel: restaurant, bar, laundry facilities, no-smoking rooms* ▤ *MC, V* ⊚ *BP.*

NIGHTLIFE & THE ARTS

Information on all upcoming events is given in the monthly *Heidelberg aktuell,* free and available from the tourist office or on the Internet (⊕ *www.heidelberg-aktuell.de*). Theater tickets may be purchased at **heidelbergTicket** (⊠ *Theaterstr. 4* ☎ *06221/582–000* ⊕ *www.schlossfestspiele-heidelberg.de*).

THE ARTS   Heidelberg has a thriving theater scene. The **Kulturzentrum Karlstorbahn-hof** (⊠*Am Karlstor 1* ☎*06221/978–911* ⊕*www.karlstorbahnhof.de*) is a 19th-century train station reincarnated as a theater, cinema, and café. The **Theater der Stadt** (⊠*Theaterstr. 8* ☎*06221/583–520* ⊕*www. heidelberg.de*) is the best-known theater in town. Avant-garde productions take place at the **Zimmertheater** (⊠*Hauptstr. 118* ☎*06221/21069* ⊕*www.zimmertheaterhd.de*). Performances are held at the castle during the annual **Schlossfestspiele** (☎*06221/582–000* ⊕*www.schlossfest-spiele-heidelberg.de*).

NIGHTLIFE   Heidelberg nightlife is concentrated in the area around the Heiliggeist-kirche (Church of the Holy Ghost), in the Old Town. Don't miss a visit to one of the old student taverns that have been in business for ages. Mark Twain rubbed elbows with students at **Zum Roten Ochsen** (⊠*Hauptstr. 217* ☎*06221/20977*). **Zum Sepp'l** (⊠*Hauptstr. 213* ☎*06221/23085*) is another traditional, always-packed pub. **Schnookeloch** (⊠*Haspelg. 8* ☎*06221/138–080*) has long been patronized by dueling frats.

Today's students, however, are more likely to hang out in one of the dozen or more bars on **Untere Strasse,** which runs parallel to and between Hauptstrasse and the Neckar River, starting from the market square. **Destille** (⊠*Unterestr. 16* ☎*06221/22808*) has a tree in the middle of the room that is always decorated according to season. The young crowd that packs the place is always having a good time.

The fanciest bars and yuppie cafés are along **Hauptstrasse.** One of these is **Pepper Bar** (⊠*Heug. 1* ☎*06221/168–617*), located on a side street just off the Hauptstrasse. This trendy nightspot, frequented by a young professional crowd, is highly regarded for its tasty cocktails.

Billy Blues (im Ziegler) (⊠*Bergheimer Str. 1b* ☎*06221/25333*) is a restaurant, bar, and disco, with live music Thursday. **Nachtschicht** (⊠*Bergheimer Str. 147* ☎*06221/438–550*), in the Landfried factory, is Heidelberg's biggest disco. The club is open until 4 AM on weekends.

Facing the main train station is the chic, modern **print media lounge** (⊠*Kurfürsten–Anlage 60* ☎*06221/653–949*), where you can dine inexpensively all day or dance all night. It's open Monday–Saturday, with DJs Friday and Saturday. The **Schwimmbad Musik Club** (⊠*Tiergar-tenstr. 13, near the zoo* ☎*06221/470–201*) is a fixture of Heidelberg's club scene. It occupies what was once a swimming pool, hence the name. It's open Thursday to Saturday.

For a nice view of the town, a menu of 120 cocktails, and relaxing music, head for the glass-walled **Turm Lounge** (⊠*Alte Glockengiesserei 9* ☎*06221/434–967*). Choose between the dark-red walls on the seventh floor or the deep-blue shades on the eighth floor. It's worth elbowing your way into **Vetters Alt-Heidelberger Brauhaus** (⊠*Steing. 9* ☎*06221/165–850*) for the brewed-on-the-premises beer.

SHOPPING

Heidelberg's **Hauptstrasse,** or Main Street, is a pedestrian zone lined with shops, sights, and restaurants that stretches more than 1 km (½ mi) through the heart of town. But don't spend your money before

8

exploring the shops on such side streets as **Plöck, Ingrimstrasse,** and **Untere Strasse,** where there are candy stores, bookstores, and antiques shops on the ground floors of baroque buildings. If your budget allows, the city can be a good place to find reasonably priced German antiques, and the Neckar Valley region produces fine glass and crystal. Heidelberg has open-air **farmers' markets** on Wednesday and Saturday mornings on Marktplatz and Tuesday and Friday mornings on Friedrich-Ebert-Platz.

In **Aurum & Argentum** (⊠ *Brücken-str. 22* ☎*06221/473–453*) you'll find a local gold- and silversmith with impeccable craftsmanship. The finely executed pieces start at €150. Its hours are Tuesday through Friday 2:30 to 6:30 and Saturday 10 to 2.

FESTIVALS

The **Schlossfestspiele** occurs on the castle grounds in Schwetzingen (May), Heidelberg (July and August), Zwingenberg (late August), and Ludwigsburg (June to mid-September). Since 1818 thousands have flocked to the Stuttgart suburb of Cannstatt in early October for the annual **Volksfest** (folk festival), which kicks off with a colorful parade of folk-dance groups and horse-drawn brewery wagons. Two wine festivals of particular note are the **Stuttgarter Weindorf,** from late August to early September, and the **Heilbronner Weindorf** in mid-September.

The old glass display cases at **Heidelberger Zuckerladen** (⊠*Plöck 52* ☎*06221/24365*) are full of lollipops and "penny" candy. If you're looking for an unusual gift, the shop fashions colorful, unique items out of sugary ingredients such as marshmallow and sweetened gum. Drop in weekdays noon–7 and Saturday 11–3.

SPORTS & THE OUTDOORS

JOGGING & BICYCLING
The riverside path is an ideal route for walking, jogging, and bicycling, since it's traffic-free and offers excellent views of the area. If you access the paved pathway in the center of town, you can follow it for many kilometers in either direction.

OFF THE BEATEN PATH
A rare pleasure awaits you if you're in **Schwetzingen** in April, May, or June: the town is Germany's asparagus center, and nearly every local restaurant has a *Spargelkarte* (a special menu featuring fresh white asparagus dishes).

THE BURGENSTRASSE (CASTLE ROAD)

Upstream from Heidelberg, the Neckar Valley narrows, presenting a landscape of orchards, vineyards, and wooded hills crowned with castles rising above the gently flowing stream. It's one of the most impressive stretches of the Burgenstrasse. The small valleys along the Neckar Valley road (B–37)—the locals call them *Klingen*—that cut north into the Odenwald are off-the-beaten-track territory. One of the most atmospheric is the Wolfsschlucht, which starts below the castle at Zwingen-

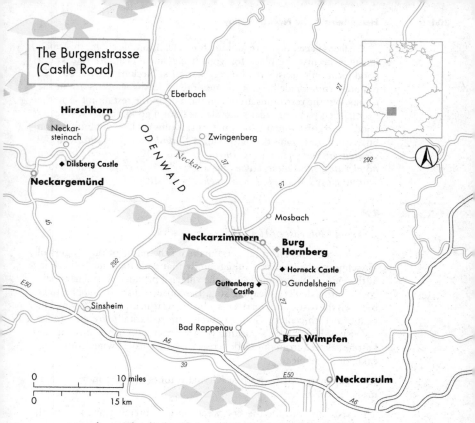

berg. The dank, shadowy little gorge inspired Carl Maria von Weber's opera *Der Freischütz* (The Marksman).

NECKARGEMÜND

11 km (7 mi) upstream from Heidelberg.

The first hamlet on the Burgenstrasse is Neckargemünd, a nice, quiet sort of place, and it can make a good base from which to visit Heidelberg, just 20 minutes by bus or train from the city.

WHERE TO STAY

$ 🏠 **Art Hotel.** Spacious rooms, each individually decorated, make you feel welcome. For small children an extra bed can easily be added to the double room. One junior suite has three beds and another has four, making them perfect for big families. The Stalinger family also runs the Reinbach, a restaurant about a mile from town, and will take you there by shuttle service. **Pros:** rooms decorated with care, good prices. **Cons:** front rooms lead onto busy street, no elevator. ✉ *Hauptstr. 40* 📞 *06223/862–768* 🌐 *www.art-hotel-neckar.de* 🛏 *13 rooms* 🔑 *In-room: no a/c, Wi-Fi. In-hotel: no elevator, public Wi-Fi* 🚮 *AE, DC, MC, V* 🍴 *BP.*

$ ⊞ **Gasthaus Reber.** If you're looking for a clean, simple room, this small inn may be just the place for you. It has an unbeatable rate and a good location opposite the railway station in Neckargemünd, only 20 minutes from Heidelberg. The one drawback: the showers are in the rooms, but the restrooms are down the hall. In the restaurant or in the beer garden you can order a simple meal for a good price. **Pros:** really good prices, opposite the station. **Cons:** rooms to the front look out on busy street, restrooms down the hall. ⊠ *Bahnhofstr. 52* ☎ *06223/8779* ⊕ *www.gasthaus-reber.de* ⌂ *In-room: no a/c, Wi-Fi (some). In-hotel: no elevator, restaurant, some pets allowed* ⊟ *No credit cards* ⊘ *Restaurant closed Wed. No lunch weekdays* ⍵ *BP.*

HIRSCHHORN

23 km (14 mi) east of Heidelberg.

Hirsch (stag) and *Horn* (antlers) make up the name of the knights of Hirschhorn, the medieval ruling family that gave its name to both its 12th-century castle complex and the village it presided over. The town's coat of arms depicts a leaping stag. Ensconced on the hillside halfway between the castle and the river is a former Carmelite monastery and its beautiful 15th-century Gothic church with remarkable frescoes (open for visits). Hirschhorn's position on a hairpin loop of the Neckar can best be savored from the castle terrace, over a glass of wine, coffee and cake, or a fine meal.

June–September there are free (German) tours of Hirschhorn on Saturday at 10.

The past comes to life the first weekend of September at the annual, two-day **Ritterfest,** a colorful "Knights' Festival" complete with a medieval arts-and-crafts market.

ESSENTIALS

Visitor Information Hirschhorn (⊠ *Tourist-Information, Alleeweg 2* ☎ *06272/1742* ⊕ *www.hirschhorn.de*).

WHERE TO STAY

$$ ⊞ **Schlosshotel auf der Burg Hirschhorn.** This very pleasant hotel and res-
★   taurant is set in historic Hirschhorn Castle, perched high over the medieval village. The terrace offers splendid views (ask for Table 30 in the corner). The rooms are modern and well furnished. Eight are in the castle and 17 in the old stables. *Wildschwein* (wild boar), *Hirsch* (venison), and fresh fish are the house specialties ($–$$). The friendly proprietors, the Oberrauners, bake a delicious, warm *Apfelstrudel* based on a recipe from their home in Vienna. A good selection of wines is available. **Pros:** terrific view over the valley, good food in nice setting, good choice of different rooms. **Cons:** winding road to castle, steep path or stairs up to lobby. ⊠ *Auf der BurgHirschhorn/Neckar* ☎ *06272/92090* ⊕ *www.castle-hotel.de* ⇆ *21 rooms, 4 suites* ⌂ *In-room: no a/c, dial-up. In-hotel: restaurant, some pets allowed, no-smoking rooms* ⊟ *AE, MC, V* ⊘ *Closed mid-Dec.–Jan. Restaurant closed Mon.* ⍵ *BP.*

EN
ROUTE
Eight kilometers (5 mi) beyond Eberbach, a castle stands above the village of **Zwingenberg**, its medieval towers thrusting through the dark woodland. Some say it's the most romantic of all the castles along the Neckar (except Heidelberg, of course). The annual **Schlossfestspiele** (☎06263/771 ⊕*www.schlossfestspiele-zwingenberg.de*) take place within its ancient walls in August.

The little town of **Mosbach**, 25 km (16 mi) southeast of Eberbach, is one of the most charming towns on the Neckar. Its main street is pure half-timber, and its ancient market square contains one of Germany's most exquisite half-timber buildings—the early-17th-century **Palm'sches Haus** (Palm House), its upper stories laced with intricate timbering. The **Rathaus,** built 50 years earlier, is a modest affair by comparison.

NECKARZIMMERN

★ *5 km (3 mi) south of Mosbach.*

The massive, circular bulk of **Burg Hornberg** rises above the woods that drop to the riverbank and the town of Neckarzimmern. The road to the castle leads through vineyards that have been providing dry white wines for centuries. Today the castle is part hotel and part museum. In the 16th century it was home to the larger-than-life Götz von Berlichingen (1480–1562). When the knight lost his right arm fighting in a petty squabble, he had a blacksmith fashion an iron replacement. The original designs for this fearsome artificial limb are on view in the castle, as is his suit of armor. For most Germans, the rambunctious knight is best remembered for a remark that was faithfully reproduced in Goethe's play *Götz von Berlichingen.* Responding to an official reprimand, von Berlichingen told his critic, more or less, to "kiss my ass" (the original German is substantially more earthy). To this day the polite version of this insult is known as a *Götz von Berlichingen.* Inquire at the hotel reception about visiting the castle.

WHERE TO STAY

$$ 🏨 **Burg Hornberg.** Your host is the present baron of the castle. From the
★ heights of the terrace and glassed-in restaurant ($–$$)—housed in the former *Marstall,* or royal stables—there are stunning views. Fresh fish and game are specialties, as are the estate-bottled wines. There are good Riesling wines and the rarities Traminer and Muskateller—also sold in the wineshops in the courtyard and at the foot of the hill. The hotel's rooms are comfortable and modern in style. Try for one of the tower rooms overlooking the valley. **Pros:** wonderful historic setting, very nice restaurant, wine shop. **Cons:** no elevator, restaurant can be crowded in season on weekends, not enough parking. ⊠*Marucs Freiherr von Gemmingen* ☎06261/92460 ⊕*www.castle-hotel-hornberg.com* ➪22 *rooms, 2 suites* ♻*In-room: no a/c, dial-up. In-hotel: restaurant, no elevator, no-smoking rooms, some pets allowed* ▤*MC, V* ☒*Closed late Dec.–late Jan.* ⦿*BP.*

EN
ROUTE
One of the best-preserved Neckar castles is the 15th-century **Burg Guttenberg.** Within its stone walls are a museum and a restaurant (closed

January, February, and Monday) with views of the river valley. The castle is also home to Europe's leading center for the study and protection of birds of prey. Demonstration flights are given from the castle walls from April through October, daily at 11 and 3. ⊠ *6 km (4 mi) west of Gundelsheim, Neckarmühlbach* ☏ *07063/950–650* ⊕ *www. burg-guttenberg.de or www. Greifenwarte.de* ✉ *Castle €4, castle and flight demonstration €11* ☉ *Apr.–Oct., daily 10–6.*

BAD WIMPFEN

Fodor's Choice
★

8 km (5 mi) south of Neckarzimmern.

At the confluence of the Neckar and Jagst rivers, Bad Wimpfen is one of the most stunning towns of the Neckar Valley. The Romans built a fortress and a bridge here, on the riverbank site of an ancient Celtic settlement, in the 1st century AD.

GETTING HERE & AROUND

Medieval Bad Wimpfen offers a town walk year-round, Sunday at 2 (€1.80), departing from the visitor center inside the old train station. Private group tours may also be arranged for other days by calling the visitor center in advance.

DISCOUNTS & DEALS

Upon arrival, ask your hotel for a free *Bad Wimpfen à la card* for reduced or free admission to historic sights and museums.

ESSENTIALS

Visitor Information **Bad Wimpfen** (⊠ *Tourist-Information, Bad Wimpfen–Gundelsheim, Carl-Ulrich-Str. 1* ☏ *07063/97200* ⊕ *www.badwimpfen.de*).

EXPLORING

On the hilltop, Wimpfen am Berg, the Staufen emperor Barbarossa built his largest **Pfalz** *(residence)* in 1182. The town not only thrived thereafter but also enjoyed the status of a Free Imperial City from 1300 to 1803.

Wimpfen im Tal (Wimpfen in the Valley), the oldest part of town, is home to the Benedictine monastery Gruessau and its church, **Ritterstiftskirche St. Peter** (⊠ *Lindenpl.*), which dates from the 10th and 13th centuries. The cloisters are delightful, an example of German Gothic at its most uncluttered.

The **Steinhaus**, Germany's largest Romanesque living quarters and once the imperial apartments reserved for women, is now a history museum (closed Monday). Next to the Steinhaus are the remains of the northern facade of the palace, an arcade of superbly carved Romanesque pillars that flanked the imperial hall in its heyday. The imperial chapel, next to the Red Tower, holds a collection of ecclesiastical artworks (closed Monday). ⊠ *Kaiserpfalz.* ☏ *07063/97200* ☉ *Palace tours daily by advance reservation.*

The 13th-century stained glass, wall paintings, medieval altars, and the stone pietà in the Gothic **Stadtkirche** *(city church)* are worth seeing, as are the Crucifixion sculptures (1515) by the Rhenish master Hans Backoffen on Kirchplatz, behind the church. ⊠*Kirchsteige 8* ☎*07131/398338.*

In late August the Old Town's medieval past comes alive during the **Zunftmarkt,** a historical market dedicated to the *Zünfte* (guilds). "Artisans" in period costumes demonstrate the old trades and open the festivities with a colorful parade on horseback.

WHERE TO STAY & EAT

¢–$ ✕**Weinstube Feyerabend.** Here you can have a glass of good Swabian wine with a snack. Or let yourself be tempted by the good-looking cakes from their own bakery. ⊠*Langg. 3* ☎*07063/950–566* ☐*No credit cards* ☉*Closed Mon.*

$–$$ ⊡**Hotel Schloss Heinsheim.** This baroque castle is in a beautiful park. The rooms are individually furnished—some with antiques, others more rustic in style. You can dine on the terrace or in the country-manor-like restaurant. Start with a Swabian *Hochzeitssuppe* (wedding soup), followed by breast of duck with pink peppercorns or Dover sole in champagne sauce. Most wines on the list are French or German. **Pro:** one of few lodging options in the area. **Cons:** rooms a bit shabby, needs updating, restaurants are not reliably open. ⊠*Gundelsheimer Str. 36 Bad Rappenau–Heinsheim* ☎*07264/95030* ⤢*40 rooms, 1 suite* ♿*In-room: no a/c, dial-up (some). In-hotel: restaurant, bar, golf course, pool, bicycles, laundry service, some pets allowed (fee)* ☐*AE, DC, MC, V* ☉*Closed Jan. Restaurant also closed Mon. and Tues.* ℔*BP.*

$ ⊡**Hotel Neckarblick.** You get a good *Neckarblick* (Neckar view) from the terrace, the dining room, and most guest rooms of this pleasant lodging. The furniture is comfortable and modern, like the hotel building. For medieval atmosphere, the heart of Bad Wimpfen is only a few blocks away. **Pros:** terrific view, nice personal family touch. **Cons:** no restaurant or bar, not enough parking space. ⊠*Erich-Sailer-Str. 48* ☎*07063/961–620* ⊕*www.neckarblick.de* ⤢*14 rooms* ♿*In-room: no a/c, Wi-Fi. In-hotel: bicycles, public Wi-Fi, no-smoking rooms, some pets allowed* ☐*AE, MC, V* ℔*BP.*

NECKARSULM

10 km (6 mi) south of Bad Wimpfen.

Motorbike fans won't want to miss the town of Neckarsulm. It's a busy industrial center, home of the German automobile manufacturer Audi and the **Deutsches Zweirad–Museum** *(German Motorcycle Museum).* Among its 300 exhibits are the world's first mass-produced motorcycles (the Hildebrand and Wolfmüller); a number of famous racing machines; and a rare Daimler machine, the first made by that legendary name. All are arranged over five floors in a handsome 400-year-old castle that belonged to the Teutonic Knights until 1806. ⊠ *Urbanstr. 11* ☎ *07132/35271* ⊕ *www.zweirad-museum.de* 🎫 *€4.50* ⊘ *Tues.– Sun. 9–5.*

SWABIAN CITIES

Heilbronn, Ludwigsburg, Stuttgart, and Tübingen are all part of the ancient province of Swabia, a region strongly influenced by Protestantism and Calvinism. The inhabitants speak the Swabian dialect of German. Heilbronn lies on both sides of the Neckar. Ludwigsburg is known for its two splendid castles. Stuttgart, the capital of the state of Baden-Württemberg and one of Germany's leading industrial cities, is surrounded by hills on three sides, with the fourth side opening up toward its river harbor. The medieval town of Tübingen clings to steep slopes and hilltops above the Neckar.

HEILBRONN

6 km (4 mi) south of Neckarsulm, 50 km (31 mi) north of Stuttgart.

The sturdy Rathaus, built in the Gothic style in 1417 and remodeled during the Renaissance, dominates Heilbronn's market square.

GETTING HERE & AROUND

Heilbronn is 50 minutes away from Stuttgart and an hour from Heidelberg by train. In the center of the town you can reach most places on foot, and there is a good tramway system. To get to the nicest places in Heilbronn, namely restaurants in the vineyards, you'll need a car.

Heilbronn's year-round tours are Saturday at 11:30, for €2.10. There's also a tour April–September, Tuesday evening at 6:15 (€4.50), that concludes with a Viertele glass of wine in a Heilbronn wine restaurant.

ESSENTIALS

Visitor Information **Heilbronn** (⊠ *Tourist-Information, Kaiserstr. 17* ☎ *07131/562– 270* ⊕ *www.heilbronn-marketing.de*).

EXPLORING

Set into the Rathaus's clean-lined facade and beneath the steep red roof is a magnificently ornate 16th-century **clock.** The entire elaborate mechanism swings into action at noon. As the hour strikes, an angel at the base of the clock sounds a trumpet; another turns an hourglass and counts the hours with a scepter. Simultaneously, the twin golden rams between them charge each other and lock horns while a cockerel spreads its wings and crows.

Behind the market square is the **Kilianskirche** *(Church of St. Kilian)*, Heilbronn's most famous church, dedicated to the Irish monk who brought Christianity to the Rhineland in the Dark Ages and who lies buried in Würzburg. Its lofty Gothic tower was capped in the early 16th century with a fussy, lanternlike structure that ranks as the first major

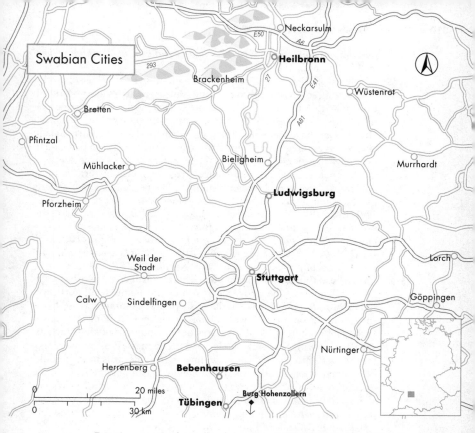

Swabian Cities

Renaissance work north of the Alps. ■TIP→ **Walk around the church to the south side (the side opposite the main entrance) to see the well that gave the city its name.**

WHERE TO EAT

$–$$ ✕**Ratskeller.** Both the handsomely set tables in the vaulted cellar and the seats on the spacious terrace in front of the town hall are pleasant places for tasty food and excellent wines. If they are on the seasonal menu, try the braised rabbit in mustard sauce or a salmon trout fillet in a whipped lemon sauce. ■TIP→ **The** *Tagesessen* **(daily special) is a good value.** ✉*Marktpl. 7* ☎*07131/84628* ▤*AE* ☉*Closed Sun.*

WHERE TO STAY

$$ 🏨**Insel-Hotel.** *Insel* means "island," and that's where this luxurious hotel is—on an island tethered to the city by the busy Friedrich Ebert Bridge. The Mayer family combines a personal touch with polished service and facilities, including 24-hour beverage room service. Enjoy alfresco dining in summer, when chefs fire up the charcoal grill on the terrace of the Schwäbisches Restaurant ($–$$). The roof garden affords great views. **Pros:** nice setting on the river, pleasant rooms, good food, enough parking. **Cons:** business hotel, expensive. ✉*Friedrich-Ebert-Brücke* ☎*07131/6300* ⊕*www.insel-hotel.de* 🛏*122 rooms, 5 suites, 1 apartment* ♿*In-room: no a/c, Wi-Fi. In-hotel: restaurant, bar, pool, gym,*

parking (no fee), public Wi-Fi, some pets allowed, no-smoking rooms ☐*AE, DC, MC, V* ⧫❘*BP.*

$$ ⊡ **Schlosshotel Liebenstein.** Nestled in the hills above the village of Neck-
★ arwestheim, south of Heilbronn, stands one of the area's most beautiful castles. Within the 3-foot-thick, whitewashed castle walls, the peaceful hush of centuries reigns over a setting of comfort and elegance. Guest rooms have views of forests, vineyards, and a golf course. Lazuli ($$$$) serves three- to seven-course menus; Kurfürst ($) offers regional fare—light meals are available in the beer garden. This place is popular, so book rooms well in advance. **Pros:** very nice historic setting, golf course, two very different restaurants. **Cons:** can be reached only by car, often booked solid. ☒*Schloss Liebenstein, Neckarwestheim* ☎*07133/98990* ⊕*www.liebenstein.com* ⌁*22 rooms, 2 suites* ⟁*In-room: no a/c, dial-up. In-hotel: 3 restaurants, bar, golf courses, bicycles, laundry service, public Wi-Fi, no-smoking rooms, some pets allowed* ☐*AE, MC, V* ⊙*Hotel and restaurants closed late Dec.–early Jan. No lunch at Lazuli; no lunch weekdays at Kurfürst* ⧫❘*BP.*

$–$$ ⊡ **Hotel und Gutsgaststätte Rappenhof.** This cheerful country inn is on a hill in the midst of the vineyards of Weinsberg (6 km [4 mi] northeast of Heilbronn). You can take in the fresh air and panoramic views from the terrace or on a scenic walk along the signposted Wine Panorama Path. The restaurant ($–$$) features hearty country cooking, such as sauerbraten with *Semmelknödel* (bread dumplings). **Pros:** modern restaurant with nice view, pleasant rooms, in the vineyards in the middle of nowhere. **Cons:** in the middle of nowhere, can only be reached by car. ☒*Weinsberg,* ☎*07134/5190* ⊕*www.rappenhof.de* ⌁*39 rooms* ⟁*In-room: no a/c, dial-up (some). In-hotel: restaurant, bar, bicycles, public Internet, no-smoking rooms, some pets allowed* ☐*MC, V* ⊙*Closed mid-Dec.–mid-Jan.* ⧫❘*BP.*

NIGHTLIFE & THE ARTS

The Konzert- und Kongresszentrum Harmonie, Theaterschiff, and Stadttheater are the major (but not the only) venues for theater, dance, opera, musicals, and concerts. The city has two resident orchestras: **Württemberg Chamber Orchestra** and **Heilbronn Symphony Orchestra.** The **Heilbronn tourist office** (☎*07131/562–270* ⊕*www.heilbronn.de*) distributes a bimonthly *Veranstaltungskalender* (calendar of events) and also sells tickets to cultural events.

SHOPPING

The city's internationally renowned **Weindorf** wine festival, in mid-September, showcases nearly 300 wines and sparkling wines from the Heilbronn region alone. One of Württemberg's finest producers, the **Staatsweingut Weinsberg** (*State Wine Domain* ☒*Traubenpl. 5, Weinsberg* ☎*07134/504–167*), has an architecturally striking wine shop selling everything made from grapes. It's open weekdays 9 to 5.

LUDWIGSBURG

15 km (9 mi) north of Stuttgart.

Ludwigsburg merits a stop to visit Germany's largest baroque palace, **Residenzschloss Ludwigsburg.** The main palace is also home to the **Keramikmuseum,** a collection of historical treasures from the porcelain manufactories in Meissen, Nymphenburg, Berlin, Vienna, and Ludwigsburg, as well as an exhibit of contemporary ceramics. The **Barockgalerie** is a collection of German and Italian baroque paintings from the 17th and 18th centuries. The **Modemuseum** showcases three centuries of fashion, particularly royal clothing of the 18th century. In another part of the palace you'll find the **Porzellan-Manufaktur Ludwigsburg** (⊕*www.ludwigsburger-porzellan.de*). The castle is surrounded by the fragrant, colorful 74-acre park **Blühendes Barock** *(Blooming Baroque),* filled with thousands and thousands of tulips, huge masses of rhododendrons, and fragrant roses. A Märchengarten (fairy-tale garden) delights visitors of all ages. In the midst of it all, you can take a break in the cafeteria in the Rose Garden. ⊠*Schloss Str. 30* ☎*07141/182–004* ⊕*www.schloesser-und-gaerten.de* ☞*Palace €6, park €7.50, museums €6; combination ticket €15* ☼*Park daily 7:30* AM*–8:30* PM*, palace and museums daily 10–5.*

STUTTGART

50 km (31 mi) south on B–27 from Heilbronn.

Stuttgart is a place of fairly extreme contradictions. It has been called, among other things, "Germany's biggest small town" and "the city where work is a pleasure." For centuries Stuttgart, whose name derives from *Stutengarten,* or "stud farm," remained a pastoral backwater along the Neckar. Then the Industrial Revolution propelled the city into the machine age. Leveled in World War II, Stuttgart has regained its position as one of Germany's top industrial centers.

This is Germany's can-do city, whose natives have turned out Mercedes-Benz and Porsche cars, Bosch electrical equipment, and a host of other products exported worldwide. Yet Stuttgart is also a city of culture and the arts, with world-class museums, opera, and a ballet company. Moreover, it's the domain of fine local wines; the vineyards actually approach the city center in a rim of green hills. Forests, vineyards, meadows, and orchards compose more than half the city, which is enclosed on three sides by woods.

An ideal introduction to the contrasts of Stuttgart is a guided city bus tour. Included is a visit to the needle-nose TV tower, high on a mountaintop above the city, affording stupendous views. Built in 1956, it was the first of its kind in the world. The tourist office also offers superb walking tours. On your own, the best place to begin exploring Stuttgart is the Hauptbahnhof (main train station); from there walk down the pedestrian street Königstrasse to Schillerplatz, a small, charming square named after the 18th-century poet and playwright Friedrich Schiller,

8

who was born in nearby Marbach. It's surrounded by historic buildings, many of them rebuilt after the war.

GETTING HERE & AROUND

Stuttgart is the major hub for the railway system in southwestern Germany, and two autobahns cross here. It is about two and a half hours away from Munich and a bit more than an hour from Frankfurt. The downtown museums and the main shopping streets are doable on foot. For the outlying attractions and to get to the airport, there is a very efficient S-bahn and subway system.

The tourist office is the meeting point for city walking tours in German (year-round, Saturday at 10) for €8. There are daily bilingual walks April–October at 11 am for €18. Bilingual bus tours depart from the bus stop around the corner from the tourist office, in front of Hotel am Schlossgarten (April–October, daily at 1:30; November–March, Friday–Sunday at 1:30) for € 8. All tours last from 1½ to 2½ hours. Stuttgart Tourist Information offers altogether 12 different special-interest tours. Call for details.

DISCOUNTS & DEALS

The visitor-friendly (three-day) Stuttcard Plus (€17) and StuttCard (€11.50), with or without access to free public transportation, are available from the Stuttgart tourist office opposite the main train station.

ESSENTIALS

Visitor Information Stuttgart (✉ *Touristik-Information i-Punkt, Königstr. 1A* ☎ *0711/222–8246* ⊕ *www.stuttgart-tourist.de*).

EXPLORING

Just off Schillerplatz, the **Stiftskirche** (*Collegiate Church of the Holy Cross* ✉ *Stiftstr. 12, Mitte*) is Stuttgart's most familiar sight, with its two oddly matched towers. Built in the 12th century, it was later rebuilt in a late-Gothic style. The choir has a famous series of Renaissance figures of the counts of Württemberg sculpted by Simon Schlör (1576–1608).

A huge area enclosed by royal palaces, **Schlossplatz** *(Palace Square)* has elegant arcades branching off to other stately plazas. The magnificent baroque **Neues Schloss** (New Castle), now occupied by Baden-Württemberg state government offices, dominates the square.

The **Kunstmuseum Stuttgart** *(Stuttgart Art Museum)*, a sleek structure encased in a glass facade, is a work of art in its own right. It features artwork of the 19th and 20th centuries and the world's largest Otto Dix collection (including the *Grossstadt* [*Metropolis*] triptych, which captures the essence of 1920s Germany). ■TIP➔ **The bistro-café on the rooftop terrace affords great views; the foyer houses a café and the museum shop.** ✉ *Kleiner Schlosspl.* ☎ *0711/216–2188* ⊕ *www.kunst museum-stuttgart.de* ⊙ *Tues.–Sun. 10–6.*

Across the street from the Neues Schloss stands the **Altes Schloss** *(Old Castle).* This former residence of the counts and dukes of Württemberg was originally built as a moated castle around 1320. Wings were added in the mid-15th century, creating a Renaissance palace. The palace now houses the **Württembergisches Landesmuseum** (Württemberg State Museum), with imaginative exhibits tracing the development of the area from the Stone Age to modern times. ⊠*Schillerpl. 6, Mitte* ☎*0711/279–3498* ⊕*www.landesmuseum-stuttgart.de* 🎫*€4.50* ⊗*Tues.–Sun. 10–5.*

The **Schlossgarten** *(Palace Garden)* borders the Schlossplatz and extends northeast across Schillerstrasse all the way to Bad Cannstatt on the Neckar River. The park is graced by an exhibition hall, planetarium, lakes, sculptures, and the hot-spring mineral baths Leuze and Berg.

Adjacent to the Schlossgarten is Rosenstein Park, with the city's two natural-history museums and the **Wilhelma** zoological and botanical gardens. ⊠*Neckartalstr., Wilhelma* ☎*0711/54020* ⊕*www.wilhelma. de* 🎫*€11.40; Nov.–Feb. and in summer after 4 PM €8* ⊗*May–Aug., daily 8:15–6; Sept.–Apr., daily 8:15–4.*

FodorsChoice
★ The **Staatsgalerie** *(State Gallery)* displays one of the finest art collections in Germany. The old part of the complex, dating from 1843, has paintings from the Middle Ages through the 19th century, including works by Cranach, Holbein, Hals, Memling, Rubens, Rembrandt, Cézanne, Courbet, and Manet. Connected to the original building is the **Neue Staatsgalerie** (New State Gallery), designed by British architect James Stirling in 1984 as a melding of classical and modern, sometimes jarring, elements (such as chartreuse window mullions). Considered one of the most successful postmodern buildings, it houses works by such 20th-century artists as Braque, Chagall, de Chirico, Dalí, Kandinsky, Klee, Mondrian, and Picasso. ⊠*Konrad-Adenauer-Str. 30–32, Mitte* ☎*0711/470–400* ⊕*www.staatsgalerie.de* 🎫*€4.50, free Wed.* ⊗*Tues., Wed., and Fri.–Sun. 10–6, Thurs. 10–9.*

In late 2002, Stuttgart's "cultural mile" was enriched with yet another postmodern architectural masterpiece by James Stirling, the **Haus der Geschichte Baden-Württemberg** *(Museum of the History of Baden-Württemberg)*. It chronicles the state's history during the 19th and 20th centuries. Theme parks and multimedia presentations enable you to interact with the thousands of fascinating objects on display. ⊠*Konrad-Adenauer-Str. 16, Mitte* ☎*0711/212–3989* ⊕*www.hdgbw.de* 🎫*€3* ⊗*Tues., Wed., and Fri.–Sun. 10–6, Thurs. 10–9.*

★ **Mercedes-Benz Museum.** Less than a year after its opening in 2006, this museum has already become incredibly popular. Most visitors come to see the 160 vehicles on display, but quite a few are interested in the building's stunning futuristic architecture. When you enter, you are taken to the top floor, then wander down following your interests—following the history of automobiles, or looking at how racing cars are developed. The bistro and the café stay open after the museum has closed its doors. ⊠*Mercedesstr. 100, Stuttgart-Untertürkheim* ☎*0711/1730–000* ⊕*www.museum-mercedes-benz.com* 🎫*€8* ⊗*Tues.–Sun. 9–4.30.*

8

Porsche Museum. This Porsche factory in the northern suburb of Zuffenhausen has a small but significant collection of legendary Porsche racing cars. The company plans to open a more extensive museum soon; check the Web site for details. ✉*Porschepl. 1, Stuttgart-Zuffenhausen* ⊕*www.porsche.de.*

WHERE TO EAT

$$$$ ✕**Wielandshöhe.** One of Germany's
★ top chefs, Vincent Klink, and his wife Elisabeth are very down-to-earth, cordial hosts. Her floral arrangements add a baroque touch to the otherwise quiet decor, but your vision—and palate—will ultimately focus on the artfully presented cuisine. To the extent possible, all ingredients are grown locally. House specialties, such as saddle of lamb with a potato gratin and green beans or the Breton lobster with basil potato salad, are recommended. The wine list is exemplary. ✉*Alte Weinsteige 71, Degerloch* ☎*0711/640–8848* ⌑*Reservations essential* ▤*AE, DC, MC, V* ⊗*Closed Sun. and Mon.*

WHERE TO STAY

$$$$ ⌸**Am Schlossgarten.** Stuttgart's top accommodation is a modern struc-
★ ture set in spacious gardens, a stone's throw from many of the top sights and situated opposite the main station. Pretty floral prints and plush chairs add a homey feeling to the elegant rooms. Luxurious baths and business amenities add to the overall comfort. In addition to receiving first-class service, you can wine and dine in the elegant French restaurant Zirbelstube ($$$$); the less-expensive Schlossgarten ($$–$$$); the bistro Vinothek ($$); or the café (¢) overlooking the garden. **Pros:** excellence and elegance, wonderful setting and food, enjoyable rooms with a view into the park, big welcoming lobby, ample parking. **Cons:** not all rooms face the park, expensive: Wi-Fi € 12 for 24 hours, no smaller time slot possible. ✉*Schillerstr. 23, Mitte* ☎*0711/20260* ⊕*www.hotelschlossgarten.com* ⇢*106 rooms, 10 suites* ⌂*In-room: Wi-Fi. In-hotel: 3 restaurants, bar, bicycles, concierge, laundry service, public Internet, public Wi-Fi, no-smoking rooms, some pets allowed* ▤*AE, DC, MC, V* ⊗*Zirbelstube closed 1st 2 wks in Jan., 3 wks Aug., Sun., and Mon. Schlossgarten closed Fri. and Sat. Vinothek closed Sun. and Mon.*

$$$ ⌸**Mövenpick Hotel Stuttgart Airport.** Across the street from Stuttgart airport, the doors of this hotel open leading you into a completely soundproof glass palace. Look up from the spacious and light-filled lobby to find the glass ceiling; the airy guest rooms have wall-to-wall windows, and the suites beckon with all the amenities. There is also an inviting lounge and bar. The new Stuttgart fairgrounds are within walking distance from the hotel, which tends to fill with business travelers—ask for weekend rates. **Pros:** spacious, modern yet welcoming, walking distance to the airport and new fairgrounds. **Cons:** walking distance to

the airport and new fairgrounds so it swells with business travelers. ✉*Flughafenstr. 50, Flughafen* ☎*0711/553 440* ⊕*www.moevenpick-stuttgart-airport.com* ☎*326 rooms, 12 junior suites* ⚐ *In room: safe, Ethernet, Wi-Fi. In hotel: restaurant, room service, bar, gym, spa, laundry service, concierge, executive floor, public Internet, public Wi-Fi, parking(fee), some pets allowed* ☰*AE, D, MC, V*

$$–$$$ 🍴**Der Zauberlehrling.** The "Sorcerer's Apprentice" is aptly named.
★ Many people come for the popular restaurant, Z-Bistro ($$–$$$$; no credit cards), which has entrancing evening entertainment called *Tischzauberei* evenings (which translates as "table magic"). Innovative dishes, a three-course menu of organic products, and regional favorites are all part of the culinary lineup, enhanced by a very good wine list. Enjoy it all on the terrace in summer. But Karen and Axel Heldmann have also conjured up a lovely luxury hotel. Each room's decor is based on a theme (Asian, Mediterranean, country manor). **Pros:** fabulous rooms with lots of surprises, enjoyable restaurant. **Cons:** minuscule lobby, no elevator, new carpet needed on stairs. ✉*Rosenstr. 38, Bohnenviertel* ☎*0711/237-7770* ⊕*www.zauberlehrling.de* ☎*17 rooms* ⚐*In-room: no a/c, Wi-Fi. In-hotel: restaurant, bar, laundry service, public Internet, public Wi-Fi, no-smoking rooms* ☰*AE, MC, V* ⊘*No lunch weekends* ⑪*BP.*

$–$$ 🍴**Wörtz zur Weinsteige.** As you wander through this hotel's small garden you forget that you are in the center of a big city. In summer you can enjoy a glass of well-chosen wine beside the huge pond filled with colorful koi and other fish. Try to get a room in the small annex called the Schlössle (small castle), which is decorated with Italian-style furnishings. **Pros:** welcoming atmosphere, family run, underground garage with elevator to the annex, cozy restaurant with good food and terrific wine list. **Cons:** kitschy gold decorations, older rooms are noisy, no elevator in main building. ✉*Hohenheimerstr. 28* ☎*0711/236-7000* ⊕*www.hotel-woertz.de* ☎*30 rooms* ⚐*In-room: no a/c, Wi-Fi. In-hotel: restaurant, bar, laundry service, parking, public Wi-Fi, no-smoking rooms* ☰*AE, DC, MC, V* ⊘*Restaurant closed Sun. and Mon., 2 wks in Jan., and 2 wks in Aug.* ⑪*BP.*

NIGHTLIFE & THE ARTS

The **i-Punkt tourist office** (✉*Königstr. 1A, Mitte* ☎*0711/22-280* ⊕*www.stuttgart-tourist.de*) keeps a current calendar of events. It sells tickets via phone weekdays 8:30–6; or in the office weekdays 9–8, Saturday 9–6, and Sunday 11–6 (May–October) or 1–6 (November–April).

THE ARTS Stuttgart's internationally renowned ballet company performs in the **Staatstheater** (✉*Oberer Schlossgarten 6, Mitte* ☎*0711/202-090* ⊕*www.staatstheater.stuttgart.de*). The ballet season runs from September through June and alternates with the highly respected State Opera. For program details, contact the Stuttgart tourist office. The box office is open weekdays 10–6, Saturday 10–2.

The **SI-Erlebnis-Centrum** is an entertainment complex (hotels, bars, restaurants, gambling casino, wellness center, cinemas, shops, theaters) built to showcase big-budget musicals such as *42nd Street.* ✉*Plieninger Str. 100, Stuttgart-Möhringen* ⊕*www.si-centrum.de.*

8

NIGHTLIFE   There's no shortage of rustic beer gardens, wine pubs, or sophisticated cocktail bars in and around Stuttgart. Night owls should head for the **Schwabenzentrum** on Eberhardstrasse; the **Bohnenviertel**, or "Bean Quarter" (Charlotten-, Olga-, and Pfarrstrasse); the "party-mile" along **Theodor-Heuss-Strasse; Calwer Strasse;** and **Wilhelmsplatz.**

If you enjoy live music, visit **Café Stella** (✉ *Hauptstätterstr. 57, Mitte* ☎ *0711/640–2583*). It's a trendy restaurant and bar, perfect for an evening of dinner and drinks. To choose from an enormous selection of cocktails, head to **Adulis I** (✉ *Holzstr. 17 City Center* ☎ *0711/243–259*), a popular bar near Charlottenplatz.

SPORTS & THE OUTDOORS

BOAT TRIPS   From the pier opposite the entrance to the zoo, **Neckar-Käpt'n** (☎ *0711/5499–7060* ⊕ *www.neckar-kaeptn.de*) offers a wide range of boat trips, as far north as scenic Besigheim.

HIKING   Stuttgart has a 53-km (33-mi) network of marked hiking trails in the nearby hills; follow the signs with the city's emblem: a horse set in a yellow ring.

SWIMMING &   Bad Cannstatt's mineral springs are more than 2,000 years old and,
SPAS   with a daily output of about 5.8 million gallons, the second most productive (after Budapest) in Europe. The **Mineralbad Cannstatt** (✉ *Sulzerrainstr. 2* ☎ *0711/216–9240*) has indoor and outdoor mineral pools, hot tubs, sauna, steam room, and spa facilities. On the banks of the Neckar near the König-Karl Bridge is the **Mineralbad Leuze** (✉ *Am Leuzebad 2–6* ☎ *0711/216–4210*), with eight pools indoors and out and an open-air mineral-water sauna. **Mineralbad Berg** (✉ *Am Schwanenpl. 9* ☎ *0711/216 7090*) has indoor and outdoor pools and sauna and offers therapeutic water treatments.

SHOPPING

Stuttgart is a shopper's paradise, from the department stores on the Königstrasse to the boutiques in the Old Town's elegant passages and the factory outlet stores. Some of Stuttgart's more unique shops are found in the older **Bohnenviertel** *(Bean Quarter).* A stroll through the neighborhood's smaller streets reveals many tucked-away shops specializing in fashion, jewelry, artwork, and gifts. Calwer Strasse is home to the glitzy chrome-and-glass arcade **Calwer Passage.** Shops here carry everything from local women's fashion (Beate Mössinger) to furniture. Don't miss the beautiful art nouveau **Markthalle** on Dorotheenstrasse. One of Germany's finest market halls, it's an architectural gem brimming with exotic fruits and spices, meats, and flowers.

Günter Krauss (✉ *Kronprinzstr. 21, Mitte* ☎ *0711/297–395*) specializes in designer jewelry. The shop itself—walls of white Italian marble with gilt fixtures and mirrors—has won many design awards. The shop is closed Monday.

Breuninger (✉ *Marktstr. 1–3, Mitte* ☎ *0711/2110*), a leading regional department-store chain, has glass elevators that rise and fall under the dome of the central arcade.

BEBENHAUSEN

6 km (4 mi) north of Tübingen, on west side of B–27/464.

If you blink, you'll miss the turnoff for the little village of Bebenhausen. That would be a shame, because it's really worth a visit.

Fodor'sChoice
★
The **Zisterzienzerkloster** *(Cistercian Monastery)* is a rare example of an almost perfectly preserved medieval monastery dating from the late 12th century. Owing to the secularization of 1806, the abbot's abode was rebuilt as a hunting castle for King Frederick of Württemberg. Expansion and restoration continued as long as the castle and monastery continued to be a royal residence. ☎07071/602–802 ⊕*www.bebenhausen.de* ✉*Monastery €3, castle €3.50* ⊗ *Nov.- Mar., Tues.-Sun. 10–noon and 1–5; Apr.–Oct. 9–6.*

WHERE TO EAT

$$$–$$$$
Fodor'sChoice
★
✕**Waldhorn.** Old favorites such as the *Vorspeisenvariation* (medley of appetizers), are what keep people coming back to this eatery. The wine list features a well-chosen selection of international and top Baden and Württemberg wines. Garden tables have a castle view. A meal here is a perfect start or finale to the concerts held on the monastery-castle grounds in the summer. ✉*Schönbuchstr. 49* ☎07071/61270 ⊕*www.waldhorn-bebenhausen.de* ⚑*Reservations essential* ▭*No credit cards* ⊗*Closed Mon. and Tues and 1 wk after Easter.*

TÜBINGEN

40 km (25 mi) south of Stuttgart on B–27 on the Neckar River.

With its half-timber houses, winding alleyways, and hilltop setting overlooking the Neckar, Tübingen provides the quintessential German experience. The medieval flavor is quite authentic, as the town was untouched by wartime bombings. Dating to the 11th century, Tübingen flourished as a trade center; its weights and measures and currency were the standard through much of the area. The town declined in importance after the 14th century, when it was taken over by the counts of Württemberg. Between the 14th and the 19th centuries, its size hardly changed as it became a university and residential town, its castle the only symbol of ruling power.

Yet Tübingen hasn't been sheltered from the world. It resonates with a youthful air. Even more than Heidelberg, Tübingen is virtually synonymous with its university, a leading center of learning since it was founded in 1477. The best way to see and appreciate Tübingen is simply to stroll around, soaking up its age-old atmosphere of quiet erudition.

GETTING HERE & AROUND

By regional train or by car on the autobahn, Tübingen is an hour south of Stuttgart. In the Old Town you reach everything on foot.

The Tübingen tourist office runs guided city tours year-round, weekends at 2:30. From February through October there are also tours on

8

Wednesday at 10 AM and Tuesday, Thursday, and Friday at 2:30 for €3.10. Tours start at the Rathaus on the market square.

DISCOUNTS & DEALS

Overnight guests receive a free Tourist-Regio-Card from their hotel (ask for it) for reduced admission fees to museums, concerts, theaters, and sports facilities.

TIMING

A leisurely walk around the old part of town will take you about two hours, if you include the castle on the hill and Platanenallee looking at the old town from the other side of the river.

ESSENTIALS

Visitor Information Tübingen (⊠ *Verkehrsverein Tübingen, An der Neckarbrücke* ☎ *07071/91360* ⊕ *www.tuebingen-info.de*).

EXLPORING

Alte Aula *(Old Auditorium).* Erected in 1547, the half-timber university building was significantly altered in 1777, when it acquired an Italian roof, a symmetrical facade, and a balcony decorated with two crossed scepters, symbolizing the town's center of learning. In earlier times grain was stored under the roof as part of the professors' salaries. ⊠ *Münzg.*

Bursa *(Student Dormitory).* The word *bursa* meant "purse" in the Middle Ages and later came to refer to student lodgings such as this former student dormitory. Despite its classical facade, which it acquired in the early 19th century, the building actually dates back to 1477. Medieval students had to master a broad curriculum that included the *septem artes liberales* (seven liberal arts) of Grammar, Dialectic, Rhetoric, Arithmetic, Geometry, Astronomy, and Music. ⊠ *Bursag. 4.*

Hölderlinturm *(Hölderlin's Tower).* Friedrich Hölderlin, a visionary poet who succumbed to madness in his early thirties, lived here until his death in 1843, in the care of the master cabinetmaker Zimmer and his daughter. ⊠ *Bursag. 6* ☎ *07071/22040* ⊕ *www.hoelderlin-gesellschaft. de* ⊠ *€2.50* ⊗ *Tues.–Fri. 10–noon and 3–5.*

OFF THE BEATEN PATH

The **Kunsthalle** *(Art Gallery),* an art gallery north of the Neckar, has become a leading exhibition venue and generates a special kind of "art tourism," making it difficult to find lodging if a popular exhibition is shown. ⊠ *Philosophenweg 76* ☎ *07071/96910* ⊕ *www. kunsthalle-tuebingen.de* ⊠ *€5* ⊗ *Tues.–Sun. 11–6.*

Kornhaus *(Grain House).* During the Middle Ages, townspeople stored and sold grain on the first floor of this structure (built in 1453); social events took place on the second floor. It now houses the City Museum. ⊠ *Kornhausstr. 10* ☎ *07071/204–1711* ⊠ *€2.50* ⊗ *Tues.–Sun. 11–5.*

Marktplatz *(Market Square).* Houses of prominent burghers of centuries gone by surround the square. At the open-air market on Monday, Wednesday, and Friday, you can buy flowers, bread, pastries, poultry, sausage, and cheese.

★ **Rathaus** *(Town Hall).* Begun in 1433, the Rathaus slowly expanded over the next 150 years or so. Its ornate Renaissance facade is bright with colorful murals and a marvelous astronomical clock dating from 1511. The halls and reception rooms are adorned with half-timber and paintings from the late 19th century. ⊠ *Marktpl.*

Schloss Hohentübingen. The original castle of the counts of Tübingen (1078) was significantly enlarged and altered by Duke Ulrich during the 16th century. Particularly noteworthy is the elaborate Renaissance portal patterned after a Roman triumphal arch. The coat of arms of the duchy of Württemberg depicted in the center is framed by the emblems of various orders, including the Order of the Garter. Today the castle's main attraction is its magnificent view over the river and town.

★ **Stiftskirche** *(Collegiate Church).* The late-Gothic church has been well preserved; its original features include the stained-glass windows, the choir stalls, the ornate baptismal font, and the elaborate stone pulpit. The windows are famous for their colors and were much admired by Goethe. The dukes of Württemberg, from the 15th through the 17th centuries, are interred in the choir. ⊠ *Holzmarkt.* 🔔 *Bell tower €1* ⊙ *Daily 9–4.*

Studentenkarzer *(Student Prison).* The oldest surviving university prison in Germany consists of just two small rooms. For more than three centuries (1515–1845) students were locked up here for such offenses as swearing, failing to attend sermons, wearing clothing considered lewd, or playing dice. The figures on the walls are not graffiti but scenes from biblical history that were supposed to contribute to the moral improvement of the incarcerated students. You can enter the prison on a guided tour organized by the Tübingen Tourist Board. ⊠ *Münzg. 20* ☎ *07071/91360* 🎫 *€1* ⊙ *Tour weekends at 2.*

WHERE TO EAT

$–$$ ✕**Forelle.** Beautiful ceilings painted with vine motifs, exposed beams, and an old tile stove make for a *gemütlich* atmosphere. This small restaurant fills up fast, not least because of the Swabian cooking. The chef makes sure the ingredients are from the region, including the inn's namesake, trout. ⊠ *Kronenstr. 8* ☎ *07071/24094* ⊟ *MC, V.*

¢–$ ✕**Wurstküche.** For more than 200 years, all sorts of people have come here. Students, because many of the dishes are filling yet inexpensive. Locals, because the food is the typical Swabian fare their mothers made. And out-of-town visitors, who love the old-fashioned atmosphere. In summer you may get a seat at one of the tables on the sidewalk in front of the restaurant. ⊠ *Am Lustnauer Tor 8* ☎ *07071/92750* ⊟ *No credit cards.*

WHERE TO STAY

$–$$ 🏨**Hotel Am Schloss.** Close to the castle that towers over the town you'll ★ find this charming hotel. In its excellent restaurant ($–$$) you can try a dozen versions of *Maultaschen* (Swabian-style ravioli) and many other regional dishes. In season trout with a white wine from Swabia is especially delicious. In summer, reserve or try for a table on the terrace. From the windows of your room you have a lovely view over the Old Town.

8

The hotel will help you with parking. **Pros:** very nice views, good restaurant with terrace, valet parking. **Cons:** parking difficult, no elevator. ⊠*Burgsteige 18D–72070* ☎*07071/92940* ⊕*www.hotelamschloss.de* ⬅*37 rooms* ♿*In-room: no a/c, Wi-Fi. In-hotel: restaurant, bicycles, laundry service, public Internet, public Wi-Fi, no-smoking rooms, some pets allowed* ⊟*AE, MC, V* ⦿|*BP.*

$–$$ 📖 **Hotel Hospiz.** This modern, family-run hotel provides friendly service, comfortable rooms, and a convenient Altstadt location near the castle. Some of the rooms are on the small side, so see a few before you decide. As parking is difficult, the hotel will help you to park your car, just call ahead. **Pros:** some old beams, convenient location. **Cons:** many stairs in hotel in spite of elevator, rooms simply furnished, no bar or restaurant. ⊠*Neckarhalde 2* ☎*07071/9240* ⊕ *www.hotel-hospiz.de* ⬅*50 rooms* ♿*In-room: no a/c, dial-up. In-hotel: no-smoking rooms, some pets allowed* ⊟*AE, MC, V* ⦿|*BP.*

NIGHTLIFE & THE ARTS

Die Kelter (⊠*Schmiedtorstr. 17* ☎*07071/254–690*) is good for jazz, music, and light fare, and it has a wineshop. In addition to dozens of Old Town student pubs, there's a lively crowd after 9 at the **Jazzkeller** (⊠*Haagg. 15/2* ☎*07071/550–906*). From 9 AM until well past midnight there's action at **Tangente-Jour** (⊠*Münzg. 17* ☎*07071/24572*), a bistro next to the Stiftskirche.

Frankfurt

WORD OF MOUTH

"Well, I have to say that Frankfurt was a wonderful surprise, and we thoroughly enjoyed our one evening there! And, guess what? It was romantic. Perhaps because we had NO expectations, and had planned NOTHING, except the hotel reservation...We took 5 hours, loving walking through gorgeous green parks, full of sculpture, on towards the Opera House (BEAUTIFUL!)...Frankfurt made our trip complete. It was not a wasted 'travel' day stopover. It was a destination of unexpected pleasure and discovery. I loved it."

—4everywhere

Updated
by Ted
Shoemaker

STANDING IN THE CENTER OF THE RÖMERBERG (medieval town square), you'll see the city's striking contrasts at once. Re-creations of neo-Gothic houses and government buildings enfold the square, while just beyond them modern skyscrapers pierce the sky. The city cheekily nicknamed itself "Mainhattan," using the name of the Main River that flows through it to suggest that other famous metropolis across the Atlantic. Although modest in size (fifth among German cities, with a population of 667,000), Frankfurt is Germany's financial powerhouse. Not only is the German Central Bank (Bundesbank) here, but also the European Central Bank (ECB), which manages the euro. Some 300 credit institutions (more than half of them foreign banks) have offices in Frankfurt, including the headquarters of five of Germany's largest banks. You can see how the city acquired its other nickname, "Bankfurt am Main."

According to legend, a deer revealed the ford in the Main River to the Frankish emperor Charlemagne. A stone ridge, now blasted away, made the shallow river a great conduit for trade, and by the early 13th century Frankfurt (*Furt* means "ford") had emerged as a major trading center. The city's stock exchange, one of the half-dozen most important in the world, was established in 1585, and the Rothschild family opened their first bank here in 1798. The long history of trade might help explain the temperament of many Frankfurters—competitive but open-minded. It's also one of the reasons Frankfurt has become Germany's most international city. More than a quarter of its residents are foreign, including a large number of Turks, Italians, Eastern Europeans, and others who relocated here for business.

Because of its commercialism, Frankfurt has a reputation for being crass, cold, and boring. But people who know the city think this characterization is unfair. The district of Sachsenhausen is as *gemütlich* (fun, friendly, and cozy) as you will find anywhere. The city has world-class ballet, opera, theater, and art exhibitions; an important piece of Germany's publishing industry; a large university (35,000 students); and two of the three most important daily newspapers in Germany. There may not be that much here to remind you of the Old World, but there's a great deal that explains the success story of postwar Germany.

ORIENTATION & PLANNING

GETTING ORIENTED

Legend has it that the Frankish Emperor Charlemagne was chasing a deer on the Main's south bank when the animal plunged into the river and, to the emperor's amazement, crossed it with its head always above water. A stone ridge had made the river shallow at that point. That supposedly was the origin of Frankfurt (literally "Frankish Ford") as an important river crossing. Commerce flourished from then on and to this day Frankfurt is an important center of business and finance. This

TOP REASONS TO GO

Sachsenhausen: Frankfurt's "South Bank"—with acres of gourmet restaurants, fast-food joints, live music establishments, and bars—is one big outdoor party in summer.

Paleontology paradise: Beyond a huge dinosaur skeleton, the Senckenberg Natural History Museum has exhibits of many other extinct animals and plants, plus dioramas of animals in their habitat.

Tricycle transportation: The pedal-powered Velotaxi, a three-wheeled vehicle, gets you past traffic jams and to destinations in the pedestrian-only downtown area.

Exotic experience: If you're tired of the humdrum world, go to another at the Frankfurt Zoo's Exotarium. You'll find coral, fish, snakes, alligators, amphibians, insects, and spiders. It's sometimes open at night when the rest of the zoo is closed.

Breathtaking views: The skyline of "Mainhattan," as they call it, is spread before you from the Maintower's restaurant in the clouds.

is surprising since, with a population of 667,000, it is only Germany's fifth largest city.

City Center & Westend. Downtown Frankfurt includes the old city, parts of which have been carefully restored after wartime destruction: the Zeil, allegedly Germany's number one "shop till you drop" mile: the Fressgasse or "Eats Street," and the bank district. The Westend is a mix of the villas of the prewar rich and a skyscraper extension of the business district.

Sachsenhausen. Just across the river from downtown, Sachsenhausen is distinguished by the *Apfelwein* (apple wine) district and the Museumufer (Museum Riverbank). The apple wine district, now with every sort of restaurant and tavern, is one big party, especially in the summer when the tables spill out onto the traffic-free streets. The Museum Riverbank has seven riverbank museums, practically next door to one another.

FRANKFURT PLANNER

WHEN TO GO

The weather in Frankfurt is moderate throughout the year, though rather wet. Summers are mild with the occasional hot day and it rarely gets very cold in winter and hardly ever snows. Watch out for trade fairs during your trip, which can make accommodations scarce and expensive.

GETTING HERE & AROUND

BY AIR There are two airports with the name "Frankfurt": Flughafen Frankfurt Main (FRA), which receives direct flights from many U.S. cities and from all major European cities, and Frankfurt-Hahn (HHN), which is a former U.S. air base 70 mi west of Frankfurt and handles some super-cheap flights, mainly to and from secondary European airports.

AIRPORT
TRANSFERS Flughafen Frankfurt Main is 10 km (6 mi) southwest of the downtown area by the A–5 autobahn and has its own railway station for the high-speed InterCity (IC) and InterCity Express (ICE) trains. Getting into Frankfurt from the airport is easy. S-bahn lines 8 and 9 run from the airport to downtown. Most travelers get off at the Hauptbahnhof (main train station) or at Hauptwache, in the heart of Frankfurt. Trains run at least every 15 minutes, and the trip takes about 15 minutes. The one-way fare is €3.60. A taxi from the airport into the city center normally takes around 20 minutes; allow double that during rush hours. The fare is around €25. If driving a rental car from the airport, take the main road out of the airport and follow the signs reading STADTMITTE (downtown).

Bohr Busreisen offers a regular bus service to and from Frankfurt-Hahn Airport. It leaves hourly, 3 AM to 10 PM, from the south side of the Frankfurt Hauptbahnhof, with a stop 15 minutes later at the Terminal 1 bus station at Flughafen Frankfurt Main. The trip to Flughafen Frankfurt-Hahn takes an hour and 45 minutes, and costs €12.

BY BUS &
SUBWAY
Frankfurt's smooth-running, well-integrated public transportation system (called RMV) consists of the U-bahn (subway), S-bahn (suburban railway), Strassenbahn (streetcars), and buses. Fares for the entire system, which includes a very extensive surrounding area, are uniform, though they are based on a complex zone system. Within the time that your ticket is valid (one hour for most inner-city destinations), you can transfer from one part of the system to another.

Tickets may be purchased from automatic vending machines, which are at all U-bahn and S-bahn stations. Weekly and monthly tickets are sold at central ticket offices and newsstands. A basic one-way ticket for a ride in the inner zone costs €2.20 during the peak hours of 6 AM–9 AM and 4 PM–6:30 PM weekdays (€2.10 the rest of the time). There's also a reduced *Kurzstrecke* ("short stretch") fare of €1.50 the whole day. A day ticket for unlimited travel in the inner zones costs €5.60. If you're caught without a ticket, there's a fine of €40.

Some 100 European cities have bus links with Frankfurt, largely through Deutsche Touring GmbH. Buses arrive at and depart from the south side of the Hauptbahnhof.

BY CAR
Frankfurt is the meeting point of a number of major autobahns. The most important are A–3, running south from Köln and then on east to Würzburg and Nürnberg, and A–5, running south from Giessen and then on toward Heidelberg and Basel.

In Frankfurt speeders are caught with hidden cameras, and tow trucks cruise the streets in search of illegal parkers. There are many reasonably priced parking garages around the downtown area and a well-developed "park and ride" system with the suburban train lines. The transit map shows nearly a hundred outlying stations with a "P" symbol beside them, meaning there is convenient parking there.

BY TAXI
Cabs are not always easy to hail from the sidewalk; some stop, whereas others will pick up only from the city's numerous taxi stands or outside

hotels or the train station. You can always order a cab. Fares start at €2 (€2.50 in the evening) and increase by a per-kilometer (½ mi) charge of €1.60 for the first 3, €1.38 thereafter.

Frankfurt also has Velotaxis, covered tricycles seating two passengers and a driver for sightseeing or getting to places on the traffic-free downtown streets. The basic charge is €1.50, plus €1.50 per kilometer.

BY TRAIN EuroCity, InterCity, and InterCity Express trains connect Frankfurt with all German cities and many major European ones. The InterCity Express line links Frankfurt with Berlin, Hamburg, Munich, and a number of other major hubs. All long-distance trains arrive at and depart from the Hauptbahnhof, and many also stop at the long-distance train station at the airport.

VISITOR INFORMATION For advance information, write to the Tourismus und Congress GmbH Frankfurt–Main. The main tourist office is at Römerberg 27 in the heart of the Old Town. It's open weekdays 9:30–5:30 and weekends 10–4.

The airport's information office is on the first floor of Arrivals Hall B and open daily 6 AM–10 PM. Another information office in the main hall of the railroad station is open weekdays 8 AM–9 PM, weekends 9–6. Both can help you find accommodations.

ESSENTIALS **Airport Contacts Flughafen Frankfurt** (☎ *01805/372–4636* ⊕ *www.airport city-frankfurt.de*)**Flughafen Hahn** (☎ *06543/509–113* ⊕ *www.hahn-airport.de*).

Bus Contacts Bohr Busreisen (☎ *06543/50–190* ⊕ *www.bohr-omnibusse.de*). **Deutsche Touring** (✉ *Mannheimerstr. 15, City Center* ☎ *069/230–735* ⊕ *www. touring.de*). **Verkehrsgesellschaft Frankfurt am Main** (*City Transit Authority* ☎ *069/2132–2425* ⊕ *www.vgf-ffm.de or www.ebbelwei-express.com*).

Taxi Contacts Taxis (☎ *069/250–001, 069/230–001, 069/230–033, or 069/792– 020*). **Velotaxi** (☎ *0700/8356-8294*).

Train Contacts Deutsche Bahn (German Railways ☎ *11861* ⊕ *www.bahn.de*).

Visitor Information Tourismus und Congress GmbH Frankfurt/Main (✉ *Römer- berg 27, Altstadt* ☎ *069/2123–8800* ⊕ *www.frankfurt-tourismus.de*).

DISCOUNTS & DEALS

The Frankfurt tourist office offers a one- or two-day ticket—the Frankfurt Card—allowing unlimited travel on public transportation in the inner zone, and to the airport. It also includes a 50% reduction on admission to 22 museums, the zoo, and the Palmengarten, and a free drink with your meal at many restaurants (€8.70 for one day, €12.50 for two days).

TOURS

APPLE WINE EXPRESS TOUR The one-hour Apple Wine Express (*Ebbelwoi Express*) tram tour is offered hourly Saturday, Sunday, and some holidays. It gives you a quick look at the city's neighborhoods, a bit of Frankfurt history, and a chance to sample Apfelwein (a bottle, along with pretzels, is included in the €6 fare).

9

BOAT TRIPS   Day trips on the Main River and Rhine excursions run from March through October and leave from the Frankfurt Mainkai am Eiserner Steg, just south of the Römer complex. ■**TIP→ The boats are available for private parties, too.**

BUS TOURS   Two-and-a-half-hour city bus tours with English-speaking guides are offered by the Frankfurt Tourist Office throughout the year.

EXCURSION TOURS   Once a month, usually on the last Sunday, the Historische Eisenbahn Frankfurt runs a vintage steam train with a buffet car along the banks of the Main. The train runs from the Eiserner Steg bridge west to Frankfurt-Griesham and east to Frankfurt-Mainkur. The fare is €4.50.

Deutsche Touring buses will take you along the Romantic Road.

WALKING TOURS   The tourist office's walking tours cover a variety of topics, including Goethe, Jewish history, apple wine, architecture, and banking. Tours can also be tailored to your interests. For an English-speaking guide, the group tour cost is €124 for up to two hours.

TOUR ESSENTIALS   **Bicycle Contacts Deutsche Bahn bicycle hotline** (☎ *01805/151–415*).

Boat Tours Frankfurt Personenschiffahrt Primus-Linie (⊠ *Mainkai 36, Altstadt* ☎ *069/133–8370* ⊕ *www.primus-linie.de*).

Tour Contacts Ebbelwoi Express (☎ *069/213–22425* ⊕ *www.ebbelwei-express. com*). **Historische Eisenbahn Frankfurt** (⊠ *Eiserner Steg, Altstadt* ☎ *069/436–093* ⊕ *www.historischeeisenbahnfrankfurt.de*). **Tourismus und Congress GmbH Frankfurt/Main** (☎ *069/2123–8800* ⊕ *www.frankfurt-tourismus.de*).

EXPLORING FRANKFURT

The Hauptbahnhof (main train station) area and adjoining Westend district are mostly devoted to business, as evidenced by the banks towering overhead. You'll find the department stores of the Hauptwache and Zeil a half-mile east of the station, and you'll want to avoid the drug-ridden red-light district southwest of the station. The city's past can be found in the Old Town's restored medieval quarter and in Sachsenhausen, across the river, where pubs and museums greatly outnumber banks.

CITY CENTER & WESTEND

Frankfurt was rebuilt after World War II with little attention paid to the past. Nevertheless, important historical monuments can still be found among the modern architecture. The city is very walkable; its growth hasn't encroached on its parks, gardens, pedestrian arcades, or outdoor cafés. The riverbank paths make for great strolls or bike rides.

MAIN ATTRACTIONS

㉑ Alte Oper (*Old Opera House*). Kaiser Wilhelm I traveled from Berlin for the gala opening of the opera house in 1880. Gutted in World War II, the house remained a hollow shell for 40 years while controversy raged over its reconstruction. The exterior and lobby are faithful to the original, though the remainder of the building is more like a modern multipurpose hall. ⊠ *Opernpl., City Center* ☎ *069/134–0400* ⊕ *www. alte-oper-frankfurt.de* Ⓜ *Alte Oper (U-bahn).*

OFF THE BEATEN PATH

Alter Jüdischer Friedhof *(Old Jewish Cemetery).* The old Jewish quarter is east of Börneplatz, a short walk south of the Konstablerwache, or east of the Römer U-bahn station. Partly vandalized in the Nazi era, the cemetery was in use between the 13th and 19th centuries and is one of the few reminders of pre-war Jewish life in Frankfurt. A newer Jewish cemetery is part of the cemetery at Eckenheimer Landstrasse 238 (about 2½ km [1½ mi] north). ⊠ *Kurt-Schumacher-Str. and Battonstr., City Center* ☎ *069/561–826* 🎟 *Free* 🕙 *Sun.–Fri., 8:30–4:30* Ⓜ *Konstablerwache (U-bahn and S-bahn).*

❷⓪ **Fressgasse** *("Pig-Out Alley").* Grosse Bockenheimer Strasse is the proper name of this pedestrian street, which Frankfurters have given this sobriquet because of its amazing choice of delicatessens, wine merchants, cafés, and restaurants, offering everything from crumbly cheeses and smoked fish to vintage wines and chocolate creams. Ⓜ *Hauptwache (U-bahn and S-bahn), Alte Oper (U-bahn).*

❶❾ ★ **Goethehaus und Goethemuseum** *(Goethe's House and Museum).* The house where Germany's most famous poet was born in 1749 is furnished with many original pieces that belonged to his family, including manuscripts in his own hand. The original house was destroyed by Allied bombing and has been carefully rebuilt and restored in every detail.

Johann Wolfgang von Goethe studied law and became a member of the bar in Frankfurt. He was quickly drawn to writing, however, and in this house he eventually wrote the first version of his masterpiece, *Faust.* The adjoining museum contains works of art that inspired Goethe (he was an amateur painter) and works associated with his literary contemporaries. ⊠ *Grosser Hirschgraben 23–25, Altstadt* ☎ *069/138–800* ⊕ *www.goethehaus-frankfurt.de* 🎟 *€5* 🕙 *Mon.–Sat. 10–6, Sun. 10–5:30* Ⓜ *Hauptwache (U-bahn and S-bahn).*

❹ 🌣 **Historisches Museum** *(Historical Museum).* This fascinating museum encompasses all aspects of the city's history over the past eight centuries. It contains a scale model of historic Frankfurt, complete with every street, house, and church. ⊠ *Saalg. 19, Altstadt* ☎ *069/2123–5599* ⊕ *www.historisches-museum.frankfurt.de* 🎟 *€4* 🕙 *Tues. and Thurs.–Sun. 10–6, Wed. 10–9* Ⓜ *Römer (U-bahn).*

❶❼ **Jüdisches Museum** *(Jewish Museum).* The story of Frankfurt's Jewish quarter is told in the former Rothschild Palais. Prior to the Holocaust, the community was the second-largest in Germany. The museum contains a library of 5,000 books, a large photographic collection, and a documentation center. *Untermainkai 14–15, Altstadt* ☎ *069/2123–5000* ⊕ *www.juedischesmuseum.de* 🎟 *€4* 🕙 *Tues. and Thurs.–Sun. 10–5, Wed. 10–8* Ⓜ *Willy-Brandt-Platz (U-bahn).*

A branch of the Jewish museum, **Museum Judengasse** (⊠ *Kurt-Schumacher-Str. 10, City Center* ☎ *069/297–7419* 🎟 *€2* 🕙 *Tues. and Thurs.–*

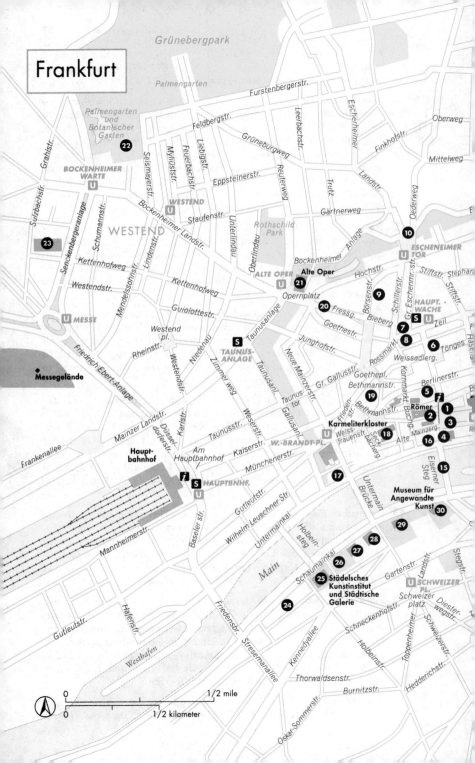

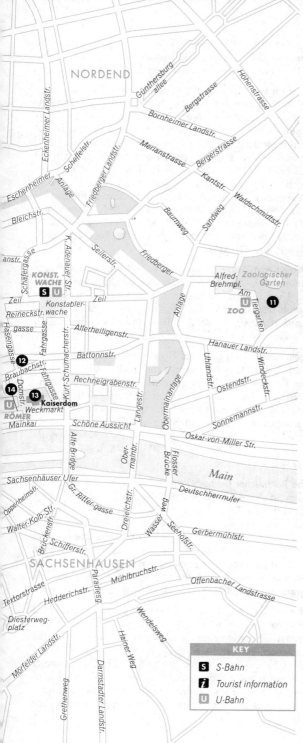

9

KEY

S S-Bahn

i Tourist information

U U-Bahn

Sun. 10–5, Wed. 10–8 Ⓜ*Konstablerwache [U-bahn]*), is built around the foundations of mostly 18th-century buildings, which once made up the Jewish quarter. The branch is also near the Alter Jüdischer Friedhof.

⑬ **Kaiserdom.** Because the Holy Roman emperors were chosen and crowned
★ here from the 16th to the 18th century, the church is known as the Kaiserdom (Imperial Cathedral), even though it isn't the seat of a bishop. Officially the Church of St. Bartholomew, it was built largely between the 13th and 15th centuries and survived World War II with most of its treasures intact. The most impressive exterior feature is the tall, red sandstone tower (almost 300 feet high), which was added between 1415 and 1514. It is anticipated that the public can climb the tower in 2009. The **Dommuseum** (Cathedral Museum) occupies the former Gothic cloister. ✉*Dompl. 1, Altstadt* ☎*069/1337–6184* ⊕*www.domfrankfurt.de* ✉*Dommuseum €3* ☉*Church Mon.–Thurs. and Sat. 9–noon and 2:30–6, Fri. and Sun. 2:30–6. Dommuseum Tues.–Fri. 10–5, weekends 11–5* Ⓜ*Römer (U-bahn)*.

⑫ **Museum für Moderne Kunst** *(Museum of Modern Art)*. Austrian architect Hans Hollein designed this distinctive triangular building, shaped like a wedge of cake. The collection features works by artists such as Andy Warhol and Joseph Beuys. ✉*Domstr. 10, City Center* ☎*069/2123–0447* ⊕*www.mmk-frankfurt.de* ✉*€7* ☉*Tues. and Thurs.–Sun. 10–5, Wed. 10–8* Ⓜ*Römer (U-bahn)*.

㉓ **Naturkundemuseum Senckenberg** *(Natural History Museum)*. An impor-
★ tant collection of fossils, animals, plants, and geological exhibits is
☾ upstaged by the famous diplodocus dinosaur, imported from New York—the only complete specimen of its kind in Europe. ∎**TIP**➜ **Many of the exhibits of prehistoric animals have been designed with children in mind, including a series of dioramas featuring stuffed animals.** ✉*Senckenberganlage 25, Bockenheim* ☎*069/75420* ⊕*www.senckenberg.de* ✉*€6* ☉*Mon., Tues., Thurs., and Fri. 9–5, Wed. 9–8, weekends 9–6* Ⓜ*Bockenheimer Warte (U-bahn)*.

㉒ **Palmengarten und Botanischer Garten** *(Tropical Garden and Botanical*
☾ *Gardens)*. A splendid cluster of tropical and semitropical greenhouses contains a wide variety of flora, including cacti, orchids, and palms. The surrounding park, which can be surveyed from a miniature train, has many recreational facilities, including a small lake where you can rent rowboats, a play area for children, and a wading pool. ∎**TIP**➜ **In summer there's an extensive concert program that takes place in an outdoor pavilion.** ✉*Siesmayerstr. 61, Westend* ☎*069/2123–3939* ⊕*www. palmengarten-frankfurt.de* ✉*€5* ☉*Daily 9–6* Ⓜ*Westend (U-bahn)*.

⑤ **Paulskirche** *(St. Paul's Church)*. The first all-German parliament was held here in 1848. The parliament lasted only a year, having achieved little more than offering the Prussian king the crown of Germany. Today the church, which has been extensively restored, remains a symbol of German democracy and is used mainly for ceremonies. The most striking feature of the interior is a giant, completely circular mural showing an "endless" procession of the people's representatives into the Paulskirche. The work of Johannes Grützke, completed in 1991, it also shows such symbols as a mother and child, a smith to represent the common people and a rejected crown. The plenary chamber upstairs is flanked by the flags of Germany, the 16 states and the city of Frankfurt. ✉*Paulspl., Altstadt* ⏲*Daily 10–5* Ⓜ*Römer (U-bahn).*

> **WORD OF MOUTH**
>
> "You can catch a frequent train from the airport to the Frankfurt Hauptbahnhof, then take a tram or U-bahn right to the Römer and spend your day walking around the heart of Frankfurt. Close to the Römer is the Zeil—one of the great shopping streets of Germany. Cross the Main River and visit some of the great art galleries of the world. Stop by Zum Wagner for the apple wine and the boiled beef with green sauce (a favorite of Goethe)." —Bird

❶ **Römerberg.** This square north of the Main River, lovingly restored after wartime bomb damage, is the historical focal point of the city. The Römer, the Nikolaikirche, and the half-timber Ostzeile houses are all found here. The 16th-century Fountain of Justitia (Justice), which flows with wine on special occasions, stands in the center of the Römerberg. The square is also the site of many public festivals throughout the year, including the Christmas markets in December. ✉*Between Braubachstr. and Main River, Altstadt* Ⓜ*Römer (U-bahn).*

Zeil. The heart of Frankfurt's shopping district is this bustling pedestrian street running east from Hauptwache Square. With mass consumerism in mind, it's lined with department stores, a few smaller boutiques, drugstores, cell-phone franchises, electronics shops, fast-food eateries, restaurants, and more, and there is an outdoor farmers' market every Thursday and Saturday. Ⓜ*Hauptwache, Konstablerwache (U-bahn and S-bahn).*

⓫ ★ **Zoologischer Garten** *(Zoo).* Founded in 1858, this is one of the most important and attractive zoos in Europe. Its remarkable collection includes some 4,500 animals of 500 different species, an exotarium (aquarium plus reptiles), a new large ape house, and an aviary, reputedly the largest in Europe. Nocturnal creatures move about in a special section. ✉*Bernhard-Grzimek-Allee 1, Ostend* ☎*069/2123–3735* 🌐*www.zoo-frankfurt.de* 🎫*€8* ⏲*Nov.–Mar., daily 9–5; Apr.–Oct., daily 9–7* Ⓜ*Zoo (U-bahn).*

ALSO WORTH SEEING

❸ **Alte Nikolaikirche** *(Old St. Nicholas Church).* This small red sandstone church was built in the late 13th century as the court chapel for emperors of the Holy Roman Empire. Try to time your visit to coincide with the chimes of the carillon, which rings three times a day, at 9, noon, and 5. ✉*South side of Römerberg, Altstadt* ☎*069/284–235* ⏲*Oct.–Mar., daily 10–6; Apr.–Sept., daily 10–8* Ⓜ*Römer (U-bahn).*

❾ **Börse** *(Stock Exchange).* This is the center of Germany's stock and money market. The Börse was founded in 1585, but the present domed building dates from the 1870s. These days computerized networks and international telephone systems have removed some of the drama from the dealers' floor, but it's still fun to visit the visitor gallery and watch the hectic activity. You must reserve your visit 24 hours in advance. ✉*Börsepl.,*

City Center 🖀*069/2110* ⊕*www.*
deutsche-boerse.com ✉*Free* ⊙*Visitor gallery weekdays 10–6* Ⓜ*Hauptwache (U-bahn and S-bahn).*

🅕 **Eiserner Steg** *(Iron Bridge).* A pedestrian walkway and the first suspension bridge in Europe, the Eiserner Steg connects the city center with Sachsenhausen. Excursions by boat and an old steam train leave from here.

🅪 **Eschenheimer Turm** *(Eschenheim Tower).* Built in the early 15th century, this tower, a block north

of the Hauptwache, remains the finest example of the city's original 42 towers. It now contains a café. ✉*Eschenheimer Tor, City Center* Ⓜ*Eschenheimer Tor (U-bahn).*

🅐 **Hauptwache.** The attractive baroque building with a steeply sloping roof is the actual Hauptwache (Main Guardhouse), from which the square takes its name. The 1729 building, which had been tastelessly added to over the years, was partly demolished to permit excavation for a vast underground shopping mall. The building was then restored to its original appearance, and now houses a restaurant and café. Ⓜ*Hauptwache (U-bahn and S-bahn).*

🅘 **Karmeliterkloster** *(Carmelite Monastery).* Secularized in 1803, the church and adjacent buildings contain the **Archaeologisches Museum** (Archaeological Museum). The **main cloister** (✉*Free*) displays the largest religious fresco north of the Alps, a 16th-century representation of Christ's birth and death by Jörg Ratgeb. ✉*Karmeliterg. 1, Altstadt* 🖀*069/2123–5896* ⊕*www.archaeologisches-museum.frankfurt.de* ✉*Museum €5, free last Sat. of month* ⊙*Museum and cloister Tues. and Thurs.–Sun. 10–5, Wed. 10–8* Ⓜ*Willy-Brandt-Platz (U-bahn).*

🅑 **Katharinenkirche** *(St. Catherine's Church).* This house of worship, the first independent Protestant church in Gothic style, was originally built between 1678 and 1681. The church it replaced, dating from 1343, was the setting of the first Protestant sermon preached in Frankfurt, in 1522. ✉*An der Hauptwache, City Center* 🖀*069/770–6770* ⊙*Weekdays 2–5* Ⓜ*Hauptwache (U-bahn and S-bahn).*

🅟 **Leonhardskirche** *(St. Leonard's Church).* Begun in the Romanesque style and continued in the late-Gothic style, this beautifully preserved Catholic church has 15th-century stained glass that somehow survived the air raids. Masses are held in English on Saturday at 5 PM and Sunday at 9:30 AM. ✉*Am Leonhardstor and Untermainkai, Altstadt* 🖀*069/2165–9890* ⊙*Apr.–Sept., Tues.–Sun. 10–noon and 3–6; Oct.–Mar., Tues.–Sun. 10–noon and 2–5* Ⓜ*Römer (U-bahn).*

🅖 **Liebfrauenkirche** *(Church of Our Lady).* The peaceful, concealed courtyard of this Catholic church makes it hard to believe you're in the swirl of the shopping district. Dating from the 14th century, the late-Gothic church still has a fine tympanum relief over the south door and ornate rococo wood carvings inside. ✉ *Liebfrauenberg 3, City Center* ☎ *069/297–2960* ⊘ *Daily 5:30 AM–9 PM* Ⓜ *Hauptwache (U-bahn and S-bahn).*

② **Römer** *(City Hall).* Three individual patrician buildings make up the Römer. The mercantile-minded Frankfurt burghers used the complex not only for political and ceremonial purposes but also for trade fairs and other commercial ventures. Its gabled facade with an ornate balcony is widely known as the city's official emblem.

The most important events to take place in the Römer were the festivities celebrating the coronations of the Holy Roman emperors. The first was in 1562 in the glittering **Kaisersaal** (Imperial Hall), which was last used in 1792 to celebrate the election of the emperor Francis II, who would later be forced to abdicate by Napoléon. When no official business is being conducted, you can see the impressive, full-length 19th-century portraits of the 52 emperors of the Holy Roman Empire, which line the walls of the reconstructed banquet hall. ✉ *West side of Römerberg, Altstadt* ☎ *069/2123–4814* 🎫 *€2* ⊘ *Daily 10–1 and 2–5; closed during official functions* Ⓜ *Römer (U-bahn).*

⑭ **Schirn Kunsthalle** *(Schirn Art Gallery).* One of Frankfurt's most modern museums is devoted exclusively to changing exhibits of modern art and photography. The gallery is right beside the Kaiserdom and has a restaurant. ✉ *Am Römerberg 6a, Altstadt* ☎ *069/299–8820* ⊕ *www.schirn-kunsthalle.de* 🎫 *€7* ⊘ *Tues. and Fri.–Sun. 10–7, Wed. and Thurs. 10–10* Ⓜ *Römer (U-bahn).*

☽ **Struwwelpeter Museum** *(Slovenly Peter Museum).* 2009 marks the 200th anniversary of the birth of the Frankfurt physician who created the children's classic *Struwwelpeter,* or Slovenly Peter. Heinrich Hoffmann wrote the poems and drew the rather amateurish pictures in 1844, to warn children of the dire consequences of being naughty. The book has seen several English translations, including one by Mark Twain, which can be purchased at the museum, which is very child-oriented. It has a puppet theater and game room, and is popular for birthday parties. ✉ *Schubertstr. 20, Westend* ☎ *069/747–969* ⊕ *www.struwwelpeter-museum.de* 🎫 *€2, children free* ⊘ *Tues.–Sun. 10–5* Ⓜ *Westend (U-bahn).*

SACHSENHAUSEN

★ The old quarter of Sachsenhausen, on the south bank of the Main River, has been sensitively preserved, and its cobblestone streets, half-timber houses, and beer gardens make it a very popular area to stroll. Sachsenhausen's two big attractions are the **Museumufer** (Museum Riverbank), which has seven museums almost next door to one another, and the famous *Apfelwein* (apple-wine or -cider) taverns around the Rittergasse pedestrian area. You can eat well in these small establishments.

MAIN ATTRACTIONS

28 **Deutsches Filmmuseum** *(German Film Museum)*. Germany's first museum of cinematography has everything from demonstrations of the methods for making animated cartoons to a virtual ride over the city aboard a flying carpet. A theater in the basement has regular evening screenings of every imaginable type of film, historical to avant-garde. There are also showings of films for children in the afternoon. ✉ *Schaumainkai 41, Sachsenhausen* ☎ *069/9612–20220* ⊕ *www.deutschesfilmmuseum.de* 🎫 *€2.50* ⊗ *Tues., Thurs., and Fri. 10–5, Sun. and Wed. 10–7, Sat. 2–7* Ⓜ *SchweizerPlatz (U-bahn).*

NEED A BREAK? Two of Sachsenhausen's liveliest Apfelwein taverns are well removed from the Rittergasse and handy to the Museumufer. You'll find them adjacent to one another if you turn south down Schweizer Strasse, next to the Deutsches Filmmuseum, and walk five minutes. Zum Gemalten Haus (✉ *Schweizerstr. 67, Sachsenhausen* ☎ *069/614–559*) will provide all the hard cider and *Gemütlichkeit* you could want. Zum Wagner (✉ *Schweizerstr. 71, Sachsenhausen* ☎ *069/612–565*) reeks so with "old Sachsenhausen" schmaltz that it's downright corny.

26 **Museum für Kommunikation** *(Museum for Communication)*. This is the place for talking on picture telephones and learning about glass-fiber technology. Exhibitions on historic communication methods include mail coaches, a vast collection of stamps from many countries and eras, and ancient dial telephones with their clunky switching equipment. ✉ *Schaumainkai 53, Sachsenhausen* ☎ *069/60600* ⊕ *www.museums stiftung.de* 🎫 *€2.50* ⊗ *Tues.–Fri. 9–6, weekends 11–7* Ⓜ *Schweizer-Platz (U-bahn).*

25 **Städelsches Kunstinstitut und Städtische Galerie** *(Städel Art Institute and Municipal Gallery)*. You'll find one of Germany's most important art collections at this newly renovated museum, with paintings by Dürer, Vermeer, Rembrandt, Rubens, Monet, Renoir, and other masters. ▮ **TIP➔** The section on German expressionism is particularly strong, with representative works by Frankfurt artist Max Beckmann. ✉ *Schaumainkai 63, Sachsenhausen* ☎ *069/605–0980* ⊕ *www.staedelmuseum.de* 🎫 *€10* ⊗ *Tues. and Fri.–Sun. 10–6, Wed. and Thurs. 10–9* Ⓜ *Schweizer Platz (U-bahn).*

ALSO WORTH SEEING

27 **Deutsches Architekturmuseum** *(German Architecture Museum)*. There are five floors of drawings, models, and audiovisual displays that chart the progress of architecture through the ages. ✉ *Schaumainkai 43, Sachsen-*

hausen ☎069/2123–8844 ⊕www.
dam-online.de ⊠€6 ⊗Tues. and
Thurs.–Sun. 11–6, Wed. 11–8
Ⓜ Schweizer Platz (U-bahn).

㉙ **Museum der Weltkulturen** (*Museum of World Cultures*). The lifestyles and customs of aboriginal societies from around the world are examined through items such as masks, ritual objects, and jewelry. The museum has an extensive exhibition of contemporary Indian, African, Oceanic, and Indonesian art. ⊠Schaumainkai 29–37, Sachsenhausen ☎069/2123–1510 ⊕www.mdw.frankfurt.de ⊠€3.60 ⊗Tues. and Thurs.–Sun. 10–5, Wed. 10–8 Ⓜ Schweizer Platz (U-bahn).

㉚ **Museum für Angewandte Kunst** (*Museum of Applied Arts*). More than 30,000 decorative objects are exhibited in this modern white building set back in grassy grounds. Chairs and furnishings and medieval craftwork are some of the thematic sections you'll find on the same floor. The exhibits come mainly from Europe and Asia. ⊠Schaumainkai 17, Sachsenhausen ☎069/2123–4037 ⊕www.museumfuerangewandtekunst.frankfurt.de ⊠€5, free last Sat. of month ⊗Tues. and Thurs.–Sun. 10–5, Wed. 10–9 Ⓜ Schweizer Platz (U-bahn).

㉔ **Städtische Galerie Liebieghaus** (*Liebieg Municipal Museum of Sculpture*). The sculpture collection in this newly renovated museum, from 5,000 years of civilizations and epochs, is considered one of the most important in Europe. Antiquity, the Middle Ages, the Renaissance, classicism, and the baroque are all represented. There's a café. Some pieces are exhibited in the lovely gardens surrounding the house. ⊠Schaumainkai 71, Sachsenhausen ☎069/650—0490 ⊕www.liebieghaus.de ⊠€7 ⊗Tues. and Thurs.–Sun. 10–5, Wed. 10–8 Ⓜ Schweizer Platz (U-bahn).

WHERE TO EAT

Smoking is now verboten inside Frankfurt's bars and restaurants (and those in much of the rest of Germany, too). It's OK, though, if you puff away out in the beer garden.

WHAT IT COSTS IN EUROS				
	¢	$	$$	$$$	$$$$
AT DINNER	under €9	€9–€15	€16–€20	€21–€25	over €25

Restaurant prices are per person for a main course at dinner.

CITY CENTER

$-$$ ✕**Long Island City Lounge.** From Thursday to Saturday the bar here is just as popular as the restaurant, making this a prime spot for people-watching. The menu has a bit of everything: pasta, salads, seafood, vegetarian dishes, and German fare. ■TIP➜ **Located near the Alte Oper (Old Opera), this is an excellent choice for post-concert dining and business entertaining.** ⊠*Kaiserhofstr. 12, City Center* ☎*069/9139–6146* ▤*AE, DC, MC, V* ⊘*Closed Sun.* Ⓜ*Alte Oper (U-bahn).*

$ ✕**Embassy.** Its location near many of the city's largest banks makes it a venue for business lunches, but it's also a popular spot for socializing. This modern restaurant, bar, and lounge attracts many young professionals for dinner and drinks. The moderately priced menu offers contemporary dishes, including pizzas, pastas, salads, steaks, duck, and a long list of appetizers. ⊠*Zimmerweg 1 (corner of Mainzer Landstr.), City Center* ☎*069/7409–0844* ▤*AE, DC, MC, V* ⊘*Closed weekends* Ⓜ*Taunusanlage (S-bahn).*

$ ✕**Maintower.** Atop the skyscraper that houses the Hessischer Landes-
★   bank, this popular cocktail bar and gourmet restaurant captures an unbeatable view. Through 25-foot floor-to-ceiling windows, you can take in all of "Mainhattan." The cuisine is part global, part regional. It's hard to get a table for supper, though it's less of a problem for afternoon coffee or an evening at the bar. ■TIP➜ **Prices are surprisingly reasonable, though you will have to pay €4.60 per person just to take the elevator up and down.** ⊠*Neue Mainzerstr. 52–58, City Center* ☎*069/3650–4770* ⩫*Reservations essential* ▤*AE, MC, V* Ⓜ*Alte Oper (U-bahn).*

$ ✕**Metropol.** Breakfast is the main attraction at this café near the Römerberg and Dom. The dining room is large, and in the warmer months it's extended to include seating on a garden patio. In addition to the daily selection of tantalizing cakes and pastries, the menu features salads, pastas, and a few traditional German dishes. If you're up late, remember that Metropol is open until 1 AM. ⊠*Weckmarkt 13–15, City Center* ☎*069/288–287* ⊘*Closed Mon.* ▤*No credit cards* Ⓜ*Römer (U-bahn).*

$ ✕**Steinernes Haus.** Diners share long wooden tables beneath traditional clothing mounted on the walls. The house specialty is an uncooked steak brought to the table with a heated rock tablet on which it is prepared. The beef broth is the perfect antidote to cold weather. The menu has other old German standards along with daily specials. If you don't specify a *Kleines,* or small glass of beer, you'll automatically get a liter mug. ⊠*Braubachstr. 35, Altstadt* ☎*069/283–491* ⩫*Reservations essential* ▤*MC, V* Ⓜ*Römer (U-bahn).*

$ ✕**Wiener's.** With the sale in 2007 of the family business known the "Altes Café Schneider," its many loyal regulars hope the new owners will continue rolling out the selection of cakes and goodies of the beloved bakery. And they do seem to be carrying on the traditions. The bakery's output, which still includes chocolate creams, remains impressive, and they roast their own coffee. However, the name Cafe Schneider has largely disappeared from the Frankfurt scene for the first time since 1906. Soups, salads, and mushroom toast are some of

EATING WELL IN FRANKFURT

Many international cuisines are represented in the financial hub of Europe. For vegetarians there's usually at least one meatless dish on a German menu, and substantial salads are popular, too (though often served with bacon). The city's most famous contribution to the world's diet is the *Frankfurter Würstchen*—a thin smoked pork sausage—better known to Americans as the hot dog. (According to one story it was once called a "hot dachshund," being long and thin and from Germany. But, it is said, cartoonist Tad Dorgan didn't know how to spell "dachshund," and gave the sausage its enduring name.) *Grüne Sosse* is a thin cream sauce of herbs served with potatoes and hard-boiled eggs. The oddly named *Handkäs mit Musik* (literally, "hand cheese with music") consists of slices of cheese covered with raw onions, oil, and vinegar, served with bread and butter (an acquired taste for many). There is the *Rippchen* or cured pork chop, served on a mound of sauerkraut, and the *Schlachtplatte*, an assortment of sausages and smoked meats. All these things are served with Frankfurt's distinctive drink, *Apfelwein* (apple wine, or hard cider).

the lunch meals offered. ✉*Kaiserstr. 12, City Center* ☎*069/281–447* 🚪*AE, MC, V* ⊘*No dinner* Ⓜ *Willy-Brandt-Platz (U-bahn).*

$ ✕**Zwölf Apostel.** There are few inner-city restaurants that brew their own beer, and the Twelve Apostles is one of the pleasant exceptions. Enjoy homemade pilsners in the dimly lighted, cavernous cellar, and sample traditional international and Croatian dishes. Servings are large, prices are reasonable, and you can have a small portion at half-price. ✉*Rosenbergerstr. 1, City Center* ☎*069/288–668* 🚪*AE, DC, MC, V* Ⓜ *Konstablerwache (U-bahn and S-bahn).*

¢ ✕**Souper.** Hearty soups seem to be the favorite light lunch in Frankfurt these days. Although the bowls seem small for the price, the best selection can be found in this place near the Hauptwache. The daily selection may include such creations as Thai-style coconut chicken or lentil with sausage. Eat at the counter or take your soup and sandwich to go. ✉*Weissadler. 3, Altstadt* ☎*069/2972–4545* 🚪*No credit cards* ⊘*Closed Sun.* Ⓜ *Hauptwache (U-bahn and S-bahn).*

9

NORDEND/BORNHEIM

$$ ✕**El Pacifico.** Some of Frankfurt's best Mexican cuisine is found in this festive little place. Warm and colorful, this restaurant serves a variety of fruit-flavor margaritas and is well known for its hearty chicken-wings appetizer. The dimly lighted dining room is fairly small; reservations are recommended on weekends. ✉*Sandweg 79, Bornheim* ☎*069/446–988* 🚪*AE* ⊘*No lunch.* Ⓜ*Merianplatz (U-bahn).*

$ ✕**Grössenwahn.** The Nordend is noted for its "scene" establishments, and this corner locale, which is often crowded, is one of the best. The name translates as "megalomania," which says it all. The menu is creative, with German, Greek, Italian, and French elements. ✉*Lenaustr.*

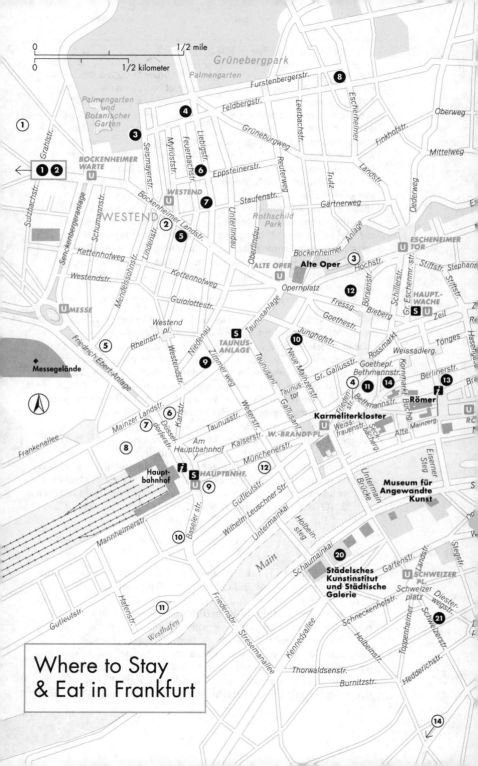

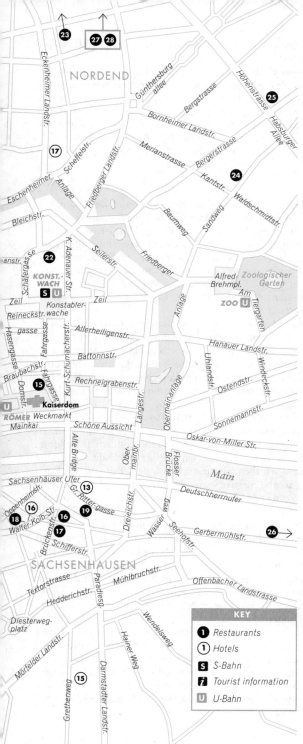

KEY

- ❶ *Restaurants*
- ① *Hotels*
- 🅂 *S-Bahn*
- 🛈 *Tourist information*
- 🆄 *U-Bahn*

9

97, Nordend ☎*069/599–356* ⚑*Reservations essential* ▤*AE, MC, V* Ⓜ*Glauburgstrasse (U-bahn).*

$ ✕**Weisse Lilie.** Come to this Bornheim favorite for the delicious tapas, paella, and other Spanish specialties, not to mention the reasonably priced red wines. The dark interior has wooden tables brightened by fresh-cut flowers and candles, making it a good spot for an intimate dinner. In summer you can dine outside, German style, at long tables. Reservations are essential. ✉*Bergerstr. 275, Bornheim* ☎*069/453–860* ▤*MC, V* ⊗*No lunch* Ⓜ*Bornheim Mitte (U-bahn).*

WESTEND

$$$$ ✕**Erno's Bistro.** This tiny, unpretentious place in a quiet Westend neigh-
★ borhood seems an unlikely candidate for the best restaurant in Germany. Yet that's what one French critic called it. The bistro's specialty, fish, is often flown in from France. It's closed weekends, during the Christmas and Easter seasons, and during much of the summer—in other words, when its patrons, well-heeled business executives, are unlikely to be in town. ✉*Liebigstr. 15, Westend* ☎*069/721–997* ⚑*Reservations essential* ▤*AE, MC, V* ⊗*Closed weekends and July–early Aug.* Ⓜ*Westend (U-bahn).*

$$$$ ✕**Gargantua.** One of Frankfurt's most creative chefs, Klaus Trebes, who
Fodor'sChoice doubles as a food columnist, serves up modern versions of German
★ classics and French-accented dishes. His specialties include angel codfish served with cabbage and a champagne-mustard butter, and stuffed oxtail with mushrooms, onions, and a potato-celery puree. ∎TIP➜ **One corner of the restaurant is reserved for those who only want to sample the outstanding wine list.** ✉*Liebigstr. 47, Westend,* ☎*069/720–718* ▤*AE, MC, V* ⊗*Closed Sun. No lunch Sat.* Ⓜ*Westend (U-bahn).*

$$ ✕**La Boveda.** This quaint but somewhat expensive restaurant is tucked inside the dimly lighted basement of a Westend residential building. (Appropriate, as the name means "wine cellar.") In addition to the smaller plates of tapas, the menu features a long list of entrées. Especially interesting are the creative seafood combinations. And true to its name, La Boveda offers an extensive wine menu. Reservations are recommended on weekends. ✉*Feldbergstr. 10, Westend* ☎*069/723–220* ▤*AE, MC, V* ⊗*No lunch weekends* Ⓜ*Westend (U-bahn).*

$ ✕**Cafe Siesmayer.** Frankfurt's Palmengarten at last has dining facilities worthy of the beloved botanical garden. The newly opened Cafe Siesmayer, accessible either from the garden or from the street, has a terrace where you can enjoy your coffee and cake with a splendid garden view. A full range of main courses is also available, and it is open for breakfast. ✉*Siesmayerstr. 59, Westend* ☎*069/90029–200* ▤ *AE, DC, MC, V* Ⓜ*Westend (U-bahn).*

$ ✕**Omonia.** This cozy cellar serves the city's best Greek cuisine. If you have a big appetite, try the Omonia Platter, with lamb cooked several ways and accompanied by Greek-style pasta. Vegetarians go for the *mestos sestos,* a plate of lightly breaded grilled vegetables served in a rich tomato–feta sauce. This family-owned place is popular, so make a reservation for one of the few tables. ✉*Vogtstr. 43, Westend*

☎069/593–314 ⚑*Reservations essential* ▭*AE, DC, MC, V* ◷*No lunch weekends* Ⓜ*Holzhausenstrasse (U-bahn).*

¢ ✕**Café Laumer.** The ambience of an old-time Viennese café pervades this popular spot, with a lovely summertime garden. It owes its literary tradition to Theodor Adorno, a philosopher and sociologist of the Frankfurt School who dined here frequently. The café is open for breakfast, lunch, and afternoon coffee, but closes at 7 PM. ⊠*Bockenheimer Landstr. 67, Westend* ☎069/727–912 ▭*AE, DC, MC, V* ◷*No dinner* Ⓜ*Westend (U-bahn).*

SACHSENHAUSEN

$$–$$$ ✕**Holbeins.** Portions are not large here, but selections on the international menu are creative. Choose from a variety of pastas, fish, steak, and even a few traditional German dishes. Live piano (and sometimes jazz) is performed every evening. ⊠*Holbeinstr. 1, Sachsenhausen* ☎069/6605–6666 ⚑*Reservations essential* ▭*AE, MC, V* ◷*Closed Mon.* Ⓜ*Schweizer Platz (U-bahn).*

$$–$$$ ✕**Maingau Stuben.** Chef Jörg Döpfner greets you himself and lights your
★ candle at this excellent restaurant. A polished clientele is drawn by the linen tablecloths, subdued lighting, and such nearly forgotten practices as carving the meat at your table. The menu includes asparagus salad with homemade wild-boar ham and braised veal cheek with wild-garlic risotto. The place also has a cellar full of rare German wines. ⊠*Schifferstr. 38–40, Sachsenhausen* ☎069/610–752 ▭*AE, DC, MC, V* ◷*Closed Mon. No lunch Sat., no dinner Sun.* Ⓜ*Schweizer Platz (U-bahn).*

$$ ✕**Lobster.** This small restaurant is a favorite of locals and visitors alike. The menu, dramatically different from those of its neighbors, includes mostly seafood. Fish and shellfish are prepared in a variety of styles, but the strongest influence is French. ■**TIP**➔ **Contrary to the restaurant's name, lobster does not appear on the menu, but is occasionally offered as a special.** Reservations are strongly recommended on weekends. ⊠*Wallstr. 21, Sachsenhausen* ☎069/612–920 ▭*MC, V* ◷*Closed Sun. No lunch* Ⓜ*Schweizer Platz (U-bahn).*

$ ✕**Fichtekränzi.** This is the real thing—a traditional apple-cider tavern in the heart of Sachsenhausen. In summer the courtyard is the place to be; in winter you sit in the noisy tavern at long tables with benches. It's often crowded, so if there isn't room when you arrive, order a glass of apple cider and hang around until someone leaves. Traditional cider-tavern dishes include *Rippchen* (smoked pork). ⊠*Wallstr. 5, Sachsenhausen* ☎069/612–778 ▭*No credit cards* ◷*No lunch* Ⓜ*Lokalbahnhof (S-bahn).*

$ ✕**Zum Wagner.** The kitchen produces the same hearty German dishes as
★ other apple-cider taverns, only better. Try the schnitzel or the *Tafelspitz mit Frankfurter Grüner Sosse* (stewed beef with a sauce of green herbs), or come on Friday for fresh fish. Cider is served in large quantity in the noisy, crowded dining room. This Sachsenhausen classic, with sepia-tone murals of merrymaking, succeeds in being touristy and traditional all at once. Warning: it serves no beer! ⊠*Schweizerstr. 71, Sachsenhausen* ☎069/612–565 ▭*AE, MC, V* Ⓜ*SchweizerPlatz (U-bahn).*

9

CLOSE UP

Apfelwein: Sweet, Sour, or Straight-up?

Apfelwein, sometimes called *ebbelwoi* by locals, is truly unique to Frankfurt and the surrounding state of Hesse. It has great traditions. Taverns serve this special cider from fat-bellied blue stoneware pitchers, called Bembels, and the glasses, usually with a crest, are ribbed to give them "traction." (In the old days, when people used knives and forks less often, this was good for preventing the glass from slipping from greasy hands).

Apfelwein is a part of the life of Frankfurt. On weekends a color-fully painted old streetcar called the Ebbelwoi Express makes the rounds of Frankfurt's tourist sights. A bottle of Apfelwein, a pretzel, and schmaltzy music are included in the price.

To produce Apfelwein, juice from pressed apples is fermented for approximately eight weeks. Some people find it rather sour and mix it with sparkling water (called *sauergespritzt*, or "sour") or with lemonade (called *süssgespritzt*, or "sweet"). You can also get sweet cider, known as *Süsser*.

Locals will be impressed, and may even tell you so, if they see you try it straight. Be careful, though: consuming large quantities of Apfelwein will make most stomachs unhappy.

The largest concentration of Frankfurt Apfelwein establishments is in the old neighborhood of Sachsenhausen. If you want to visit a bar or restaurant that sells its own homemade Apfelwein, look for a pine wreath hanging over the door.

¢ ✕ **Pizza Pasta Factory.** This restaurant started off with a theory: if you offer your food cheaply enough, you can make up the difference by selling a lot of it. So before 4 PM and after 11 PM, this place sells its pizzas and pastas (except lasagna) for only €2.90. The list of toppings for the pizzas includes nearly 30 items, including some unlikely ones like pineapple, corn, and eggs. ⊠ *Paradiesg. 76, Sachsenhausen* ☎ *069/6199– 5004* ⊟ *No credit cards* Ⓜ *Lokalbahnhof (S-bahn).*

OUTER FRANKFURT

$$$$ ✕ **Osteria Enoteca.** You don't have to go to Italy to enjoy the best of *haute cuisine alla italiana.* This place is small, crowded, and some even say stuffy, but it draws well-heeled gourmets from far and wide. The Sicilian chef, Carmelo Greco, has won a galaxy of stars from the critics for his Italian classics. The first dish he created, a Parmesan flan, remains his favorite. The wine cellar and vast choice of cheeses are renowned. ⊠ *Arnoldshainerstr. 2, Rödelheim* ☎ *069/789–2216* ⚑ *Reservations essential* ⊟ *AE, MC, V* Ⓜ *Rödelheim (S-bahn).*

$$$ ✕ **Gerbermühle.** So beautiful that it inspired works by Goethe, Frankfurt's favorite son and a frequent visitor, this beloved destination has come back to life after having closed for a time. Entrepreneurs have restored the 14th-century building and the century-long-plus tradition of hiking or biking to the chestnut-tree-shaded, riverside beer garden has returned. The garden is as nice as ever, and there's an indoor restaurant, hotel rooms, an attractive bar with the original

stone walls, and even a bust of Goethe. An hour eastward down the Main's south bank, the place is so remote it is difficult to reach with public transportation. ✉ *Gerbermühlestr. 105, Oberrad* ☎ *069/689–77790* ▤ *AE, DC, MC, V.*

$$ ✕ **Altes Zollhaus.** Excellent versions of traditional German and international specialties are served in this 230-year-old half-timber house on the edge of town. If you're here in season, try a game dish. In summer you can eat in the beautiful garden. To get here, take Bus 30 from Konstablerwache to Heiligenstock, or drive out on Bundestrasse 521 in the direction of Bad Vilbel. ✉ *Friedberger Landstr. 531, Seckbach* ☎ *069/472–707* ▤ *AE, DC, MC, V* ✆ *Closed Mon. No lunch Tues.–Sat.*

$ ✕ **Arche Nova.** This sunny establishment is a feature of Frankfurt's Öko-haus, which was built according to environmental principles (solar panels, catching rainwater, etc.). It's more or less vegetarian, with such dishes as a vegetable platter with feta cheese or curry soup with grated coconut and banana. Much of what's served, even some of the beer, is organic. ✉ *Kasselerstr. 1a, Bockenheim* ☎ *069/707–5859* ▤ *No credit cards* Ⓜ *Westbahnhof (S-bahn).*

$ ✕ **Zum Rad.** Named for the huge *Rad* (wagon wheel) that serves as a centerpiece, this is one of the few Apfelwein taverns in Frankfurt that makes its own apple wine. It's located in the villagelike district of Seckbach, on the northeastern edge of the city. Outside tables are shaded by chestnut trees in an extensive courtyard. The typically Hessian cuisine, with giant portions, includes such dishes as *Ochsenbrust* (brisket of beef) with the ubiquitous herb sauce. Take the U-4 subway to Seckbacher Landstrasse, then Bus 43 to Draisbornstrasse. ✉ *Leonhardsg. 2, Seckbach* ☎ *069/479–128* ▤ *No credit cards* ✆ *Closed Tues. No lunch.*

WHERE TO STAY

9

Businesspeople descend on Frankfurt year-round, so most hotels in the city are frequently booked up well in advance and are expensive (though many offer significant reductions on weekends). Many hotels add as much as a 50% surcharge during trade fairs (*Messen*), of which there are about 30 a year. The majority of the larger hotels are close to the main train station, fairgrounds, and business district (Bankenviertel). The area around the station has a reputation as a red light district, but is well policed. More atmosphere is found at smaller hotels and pensions in the suburbs; the efficient public transportation network makes them easy to reach.

WHAT IT COSTS IN EUROS				
	¢	$	$$	$$$	$$$$
FOR TWO PEOPLE	under €50	€50–€100	€101–€175	€176–€225	over €225

Hotel prices are for two people in a standard double room, including tax and service.

CITY CENTER, NORDEND & WESTEND

$$$$ **Hessischer Hof.** This is the choice of many businesspeople, not just for its location across from the fairgrounds but also for the air of class that pervades its handsome interior. Many of the public-room furnishings are antiques once owned by the family of the princes of Hesse. The Sèvres Restaurant, so called for the fine display of that porcelain arranged along the walls, features excellent contemporary cuisine. **Pros:** close to the fairgrounds and public transportation; site of Jimmy's, one of the town's cult bars. **Cons:** far from the stores and theaters, lobby can be crowded with businesspeople schmoozing during trade fairs. ⊠*Friedrich-Ebert-Anlage 40, Messe* ☎*069/75400* ⊕*www.hessischer-hof.de* ⤶*106 rooms, 11 suites* ⌂*In-room: refrigerator, dial-up, Wi-Fi. In-hotel: restaurant, room service, bar, parking (fee), some pets allowed, no-smoking rooms* ⊟*AE, DC, MC, V* Ⓜ*Messe (S-bahn).*

$$$$ **Hilton Frankfurt.** This international chain's downtown Frankfurt loca-
★ tion has all the perks the business traveler wants, from fax and modem lines to voice mail and video on command. The Vista Bar & Lounge is just below the hotel's airy and transparent atrium. **Pro:** large terrace overlooking a park. **Cons:** expensive, bathrooms are small for the price. ⊠*Hochstr. 4, City Center* ☎*069/133–8000* ⊕*www.frankfurt. hilton.com* ⤶*360 rooms* ⌂*In-room: safe, refrigerator, Ethernet, Wi-Fi. In-hotel: restaurant, room service, bars, pool, gym, parking (fee), no-smoking rooms, some pets allowed* ⊟*AE, DC, MC, V* Ⓜ*Eschenheimer Tor (U-bahn).*

$$$$ **Steigenberger Hotel Frankfurter Hof.** The neo-Gothic, five-star "Frank-
FodorsChoice furter Hof" is the "first lady" of Frankfurt hotellerie, the first choice
★ of visiting heads of state and business and finance moguls. It fronts on a grand courtyard, and there's little that such guests desire that isn't available: 24-hour room service; suites up to a thousand square feet in dark woods and brass with air conditioning (rare in Germany); marble baths with Jacuzzis, slippers; mirrored, walk-in closets. It's one of the city's oldest hotels, but its modern services earn it kudos. **Pros:** an atmosphere of old fashioned, formal elegance, with burnished wood floors, fresh flowers, and thick carpeting. **Con:** expensive. ⊠*Kaiserpl., City Center* ☎*069/21502* ⊕*www.frankfurter-hof.steigenberger.de* ⤶ *360 rooms, 41 suites* ⌂*In-room: no a/c (some), refrigerator, dial-up, Wi-Fi. In-hotel: 5 restaurants, room service, bar, concierge, public Internet, parking (fee), some pets allowed* ⊟*AE, DC, MC, V* Ⓜ*Willy-Brandt-Platz (U-bahn).*

$$ **Bristol.** You'll notice that great attention is paid to making you comfortable at the Bristol, one of the nicest hotels in the neighborhood around the main train station. The modern hotel features minimalist decor in soothing earth tones. There is a daily breakfast buffet. **Pros:** the bar is open till 5 AM, beautiful garden patio. **Cons:** the neighborhood isn't appealing, small rooms. ⊠*Ludwigstr. 15, City Center* ☎*069/242–390* ⊕*www.bristol-hotel.de* ⤶*145 rooms* ⌂*In-room: no a/c, safe, refrigerator, dial-up, Wi-Fi. In-hotel: restaurant, bar, parking (fee)* ⊟*AE, DC, MC, V* ⅠⓄⅠ*BP* Ⓜ*Hauptbahnhof (U-bahn and S-bahn).*

$$ ⚏**Hotel Nizza.** This beautiful Victorian building, only a five-minute
★ walk from the main train station, is filled with antiques. The proprietor
has added a modern touch in some bathrooms with her own hand-
painted murals. **Pros:** antique furnishings, roof garden with shrubbery
and a view of the skyline. **Con:** right in the unattractive Bahnhof dis-
trict. ✉*Elbestr. 10, City Center* ☎*069/242–5380* ⊕*www.hotelnizza.
de* ⮑*25 rooms* ⌂*In-room: no a/c, Wi-Fi (some). In-hotel: bar, some
pets allowed, no-smoking rooms* ▤*MC, V* ⑩*CP* Ⓜ*Willy-Brandt-
Platz (U-bahn and S-bahn).*

$$ ⚏**Palmenhof.** This luxuriously modern private hotel, in the same family
for three generations, occupies a renovated art-nouveau building dating
from 1890. The high-ceiling rooms retain the elegance of the old building, though the comfort is up-to-date. **Pros:** handy to the city's "green
oasis," the Palmengarten; less expensive than similarly elegant hotels.
Cons: no restaurant, the top floor can get very hot and there is no air
conditioning. ✉*Bockenheimer Landstr. 89–91, Westend* ☎*069/753–
0060* ⊕*www.palmenhof.com* ⮑*46 rooms, 37 apartments, 1 suite*
⌂*In-room: no a/c, dial-up. In-hotel: parking (fee), some pets allowed*
▤*AE, DC, MC, V BP* Ⓜ*Westend (U-bahn).*

$$ ⚏**Villa Orange.** The moderately priced rooms at this bright, charming
hotel include canopy beds and spacious bathrooms. The high-ceiling
lobby and breakfast room are decorated with modern art. Breakfast is
served on a terrace in good weather, hotel staff are friendly and accom-
modating and there is a library with some English-language books.
Pros: centrally located, but tucked away from the bustle on a residen-
tial street. **Con:** hard beds. ✉*Hebelstr. 1, Nordend* ☎*069/405–840*
⊕*www.villa-orange.de* ⮑*38 rooms* ⌂*In-room: dial-up, Wi-Fi. In-
hotel: bar, public Internet, parking (fee), no-smoking rooms* ▤*AE,
DC, MC, V* ⑩*BP* Ⓜ*Musterschule (U-bahn).*

$ ⚏**Ibis Frankfurt Centrum.** The Ibis is a reliable budget hotel offering
simple, clean rooms on a quiet street near the river. Breakfast may
be purchased at an additional cost. **Pro:** short walk from the station
and Sachsenhausen museums. **Cons:** removed from stores and theaters.
✉*Speicherstr. 4, City Center* ☎*069/273–030* ⊕*www.ibishotel.com*
⮑*233 rooms* ⌂*In-room: dial-up, Wi-Fi (some). In-hotel: bar, parking
(fee), no-smoking rooms* ▤*AE, DC, MC, V* Ⓜ*Hauptbahnhof (U-bahn
and S-bahn).*

$ ⚏**InterCity Hotel.** If there ever was a hotel at the vortex of arrivals
★ and departures, it's this centrally located hostelry in an elegant old-
world building across the street from the main train station. Inter-
City hotels were set up by the Steigenberger chain with the business
traveler in mind. The station's underground garage is at your dis-
posal. **Pro:** guests get a pass for unlimited local transportation. **Con:**
overlooks a cargo facility. ✉*Poststr. 8, Bahnhof* ☎*069/273–910*
⊕*www.intercityhotel.com* ⮑*384 rooms, 3 suites* ⌂*In-room: dial-
up, Wi-Fi (some). In-hotel: restaurant, bar, gym, public Internet, some
pets allowed, no-smoking rooms* ▤*AE, DC, MC, V* ⑩*BP* Ⓜ*Haupt-
bahnhof (U-bahn and S-bahn).*

$ ⚏**Leonardo.** Across the street from the main train station, this modern,
sparkling-clean hotel has its own underground garage. The rooms are

some of the least expensive in town. **Pros:** own underground garage, quiet summer garden despite location. **Cons:** on a busy street, in the red-light district. ✉ *Münchenerstr. 59, City Center* ☎ *069/242–320* ⊕ *www.leonardo-hotels.com* 🛏 *107 rooms* ⚒ *In-room: no a/c, Wi-Fi. In-hotel: public Internet, parking (fee)* ☰ *AE, DC, MC, V* 🍴 *BP* Ⓜ *Hauptbahnhof (U-bahn and S-bahn).*

$ 🏨 **Manhattan.** Get to all parts of town quickly from this centrally located hotel. Rooms are fairly spacious, and you can connect to the Internet at one of the terminals in the lobby. There's no restaurant, but the hotel's bar is open around the clock. **Pro:** opposite the main train station. **Cons:** no restaurant, right in the red-light district. ✉ *Düsseldorferstr. 10, City Center* ☎ *069/269–5970* ⊕ *www.manhattan-hotel.com* 🛏 *60 rooms* ⚒ *In-room: no a/c, Wi-Fi. In-hotel: bar, public Wi-Fi, no-smoking rooms* ☰ *AE, DC, MC, V* 🍴 *BP* Ⓜ *Hauptbahnhof (U-bahn and S-bahn).*

$ 🏨 **Pension Aller.** Quiet, solid comforts come with a modest price and friendly welcome at this pension near the river. Frau Kraus, the resident owner, was born in this house and is always eager to share city history and sightseeing recommendations with you. **Pros:** economical, near the station. **Cons:** 10 rooms and often full, need to reserve in advance. ✉ *Gutleutstr. 94, City Center* ☎ *069/252–596* ⊕ *www.pension-aller. de* 🛏 *10 rooms* ⚒ *In-room: no a/c, no phone (some), no TV (some), dial-up (some). In-hotel: no elevator, some pets allowed* ☰ No credit cards 🍴 *BP* Ⓜ *Hauptbahnhof (U-bahn and S-bahn).*

SACHSENHAUSEN

$ 🏨 **Am Berg.** A colorful, romantic inn, the Am Berg is not so much a hotel as a nice guesthouse. Because of its location, hidden away in a residential area near the Südbahnhof (south train station), many locals aren't even aware it exists. Breakfast is an extra €9.50. **Pro:** each room has its own unique decor. **Con:** no elevator. ✉ *Grethenweg 23, Sachsenhausen* ☎ *069/612–021* ⊕ *www.hotelamberg.com* 🛏 *21 rooms* ⚒ *In-room: no a/c. In-hotel: no elevator, parking (no fee), some pets allowed, no-smoking rooms* ☰ *AE, MC, V* Ⓜ *Südbahnhof (U-bahn and S-bahn).*

$ 🏨 **Maingau.** You'll find this pleasant hotel-restaurant in the middle of the lively Sachsenhausen quarter. Rooms are modest but spotless, comfortable, and equipped with TVs; the room rate includes a substantial breakfast buffet. The restaurant, Maingau-Stuben, is one of

BUDGET OPTIONS

Traveling on a budget? Try these hotels and pensions.

■ **Am Berg** (☎ *069/612–021* ⊕ www.hotelamberg.com).

■ **Ibis Frankfurt Centrum** (☎ *069/273–030* ⊕ *www.ibis hotel.com*).

■ **Jugendherberge Frankfurt** (☎ *069/610–0150* ⊕ *www. jugendherberge-frankfurt.de*).

■ **Pension Aller** (☎ *069/252– 596* ⊕ www.pension-aller.de).

■ **Leonardo** (☎ *069/242–320* ⊕ www.hotel-terminus.de).

Frankfurt's best. ⚠ **Caution: Though the hotel is inexpensive, the restaurant is anything but! Pros:** handy to Sachsenhausen nightlife, fantastic restaurant. **Con:** on a busy street. ☒ *Schifferstr. 38–40, Sachsenhausen* ☎ *069/609–140* ⊕ *www.maingau.de* ⇆ *80 rooms* ☖ *In-room: no a/c, refrigerator. In-hotel: restaurant, some pets allowed* ☰ *AE, DC, MC, V* ⎮◯⎮ *BP* Ⓜ *Schweizer Platz (U-bahn).*

¢ 🏨 **Jugendherberge Frankfurt.** This combination youth hostel and family hotel can provide you with a clean, inexpensive, and very central overnight in what is usually a pricey city. It's right on the river in Sachsenhausen, directly across from downtown. A stay in a 10-bed dormitory room will cost you €17 a night (€21.50 if you're over 26), and you can have a private room with bath for a still-reasonable €35.50 (€40 if you're a 27-plus "senior"). That price includes breakfast, and a lunch or dinner buffet is yours for €5. You must be in by 2 AM or get a key. **Pros:** inexpensive, private rooms available, no smoking. **Cons:** no smoking anywhere, without a Youth Hostel card you pay an additional €3.50. ☒ *Deutschherrnufer 12, Sachsenhausen* ☎ *069/610–0150* 🖷 *069/6100–1599* ⇆ *110 rooms* ☖ *In-room: no a/c, no phone, no TV. In-hotel: restaurant* ☰ *MC, V* ⎮◯⎮ *BP* Ⓜ *Lokalbahnhof (S-bahn).*

OUTER FRANKFURT

$$$$ 🏨 **Sheraton Frankfurt.** This huge hotel is connected to one of Frankfurt Airport's terminals. No need to worry about noise, though—the rooms are all soundproofed. In addition to the usual comforts, each room includes an answering machine and a modem, and there is a 24-hour business center. **Pro:** handy to the airport and an autobahn intersection with connections to all of Europe. **Cons:** far from the city center, sometimes a long walk to the elevator, expensive. ☒ *Hugo-Eckener-Ring 15, Flughafen Terminal 1, Airport* ☎ *069/69770* ⊕ *www.sheraton.com/frankfurt* ⇆ *1,008 rooms, 28 suites* ☖ *In-room: dial-up, Wi-Fi. In-hotel: 2 restaurants, bar, gym, concierge, parking (fee), some pets allowed, no-smoking rooms* ☰ *AE, DC, MC, V* ⎮◯⎮ *BP* Ⓜ *Flughafen (S-bahn).*

$$ 🏨 **Falk Hotel.** This hotel is within walking distance of the U-bahn and is a relatively inexpensive alternative for those on a budget. It stands in the heart of Bockenheim, home of numerous cafés, bars, and shops. The room rate includes a full breakfast and discounted rates at a nearby fitness studio. **Pro:** inexpensive. **Cons:** removed from the city center, small rooms. ☒ *Falkstr. 38A, Bockenheim* ☎ *069/7191–8870* ⊕ *www. hotel-falk.de* ⇆ *29 rooms* ☖ *In-room: dial-up, Wi-Fi. In-hotel: no-smoking rooms* ☰ *AE, MC, V* ⎮◯⎮ *BP* Ⓜ *Leipzigerstrasse (U-bahn).*

9

NIGHTLIFE & THE ARTS

THE ARTS

The Städtische Bühnen—municipal theaters, including the city's opera company—are the prime venues for Frankfurt's cultural affairs. The city has what is probably the most lavish theater in the country, the Alte Oper, a magnificently ornate 19th-century opera house. The building is no longer used for opera but as a multipurpose hall for pop and classical concerts and dances.

Theater tickets can be purchased from **Best Tickets GmbH** (⊠ *Zeil 112– 114, City Center* ☎*069/9139–7621* ⊕*www.journal-ticketshop.de*) downtown in the Zeilgalerie.**Frankfurt Ticket GmbH** (⊠ *Hauptwache Passage, City Center* ☎*069/134–0400* ⊕*www.Frankfurt-ticket.de*) sells theater and concert tickets.

BALLET, CONCERTS & OPERA

The most glamorous venue for classical-music concerts is the **Alte Oper** (⊠ *Opernpl., City Center*); tickets to performances can range from €20 to nearly €150.

The **Frankfurt Opera** (⊠ *Städtische Bühnen, Untermainanlage 11, City Center*) has made a name for itself as a company for dramatic artistry.

A slimmed-down version of Frankfurt's once-acclaimed ballet company still performs in the **Bockenheimer Depot** (⊠ *Carlo-Schmidt-Pl. 1, Bockenheim*), a former trolley barn also used for other theatrical performances and music events.

The **Festhalle** (⊠ *Ludwig-Erhard-Anlage 1, Messe*), on the fairgrounds, is the scene of many rock concerts, horse shows, ice shows, sporting events, and other large-scale spectaculars. Tickets are available through Frankfurt Ticket. The city is also the home of the Radio-Sinfonie-Orchester Frankfurt, part of Hessischer Rundfunk. It performs regularly in the 850-seat **Kammermusiksaal** (⊠ *Bertramstr. 8, Dornbusch* ☎*069/155–2000*), part of that broadcasting operation's campuslike facilities.

Telephone ticket sales for the Alte Oper, Frankfurt Opera, and other venues are all handled through **Frankfurt Ticket** (☎*069/134–0400* ⊕*www.frankfurt-ticket.de*).

THEATER

Theatrical productions in Frankfurt are usually in German. For English-language productions, try the **English Theater** (⊠ *Kaiserstr. 34, City Center* ☎*069/2423–1620* ⊕*www.English-theatre.org*), which offers an array of musicals, thrillers, dramas, and comedy with British or American casts. The **Internationales Theater Frankfurt** (⊠ *Hanauer Landstr. 7, Ostend* ☎*069/499–0980* ⊕*www.itf-frankfurt.de*) bills itself as presenting "the art of the world on the Main." It also has regular performances in English, as well as in German, French, Spanish, Italian, Romanian, and Russian. The **Künstlerhaus Mousonturm** (⊠ *Wald-*

schmidtstr. 4, Nordend ☎069/4058–9520 ⊕www.mousonturm.de)
is a cultural center that hosts a regular series of concerts of all kinds,
as well as plays, dance performances, and exhibits. The municipally
owned **Schauspielhaus** (✉ Willy-Brandt-Pl., City Center ☎069/134–
0400 ⊕www.schauspielfrankfurt.de) has a repertoire including works
by Sophocles, Goethe, Shakespeare, Brecht, and Beckett. For a zany
theatrical experience, try **Die Schmiere** (✉Seckbächerg. 2, City Center
☎069/281–066 ⊕www.die-schmiere.de), which offers trenchant satire and also disarmingly calls itself "the worst theater in the world."

NIGHTLIFE

Frankfurt at night is a city of stark contrasts. Old hippies and sharply
dressed bankers, Turkish and Greek workers, people on pensions, chess
players, exhibitionists, and loners all have their piece of the action.
People from the banking world seek different amusements than do
the city's 35,000 students, but their paths cross in such places as the
cider taverns in Sachsenhausen and the gay bars of the Nordend. Sachsenhausen (Frankfurt's "Left Bank") is a good place to start for bars,
clubs, and Apfelwein taverns. The ever-more-fashionable Nordend has
an almost equal number of bars and clubs but fewer tourists. Frankfurt
is one of Europe's leading cities for techno, the computer-generated
music of ultrafast beats that's the anthem of German youth culture.
Most bars close between 2 AM and 4 AM.

BARS & LIVE MUSIC VENUES

The **Balalaika** (✉Schifferstr. 3, Sachsenhausen ☎069/612–226) has
moved to larger quarters, but feels just as intimate, as candles are just
about the only source of light. The proprietor is Anita Honis, an American singer hailing from Harlem. She usually gets out her acoustic guitar
several times during an evening.

In good weather the tables at **Cafe Extrablatt** (✉Eschenheimer Str.
45 ☎069/2199–4899) are scattered around the pleasant plaza that
replaced the once busy street in front of the medieval Eschenheimer
Tower. During Wednesday's "Jumbo Hour," which runs from 7 to midnight, you get a super-sized cocktail when you order an ordinary one.
Cocktails are €3.95 during happy hours, Monday and Thursday after
7, and weekends after 11pm.

Like the rest of the Marriott Hotel, the **Champion's Bar** (✉Hamburger
Allee 2–10, Messe ☎069/7955–2540) is designed to make Americans
feel at home. The wall is lined with team jerseys, autographed helmets, and photographs of professional athletes. The flat-screen TV is
tuned to the American Forces Network, which carries the full range of
American sports. The food leans toward buffalo wings, hamburgers,
and brownies.

The after-work crowd gathers at **EuroDeli** (✉Neue Mainzerstr. 60–66
☎069/2980–1950). Because it's near many of the city's major banks,
its happy hour is on weekdays from 5 to 7. There's a DJ on Tuesday.

9

Frankfurt is teeming with Irish pubs, but there is an occasional English pub, too. A good example is the **Fox and Hound** (⊠ *Niedenau 2, Westend* ☎ *069/9720–2009*). Its patrons, mainly British, come to watch the latest football (soccer to Americans), rugby, and cricket matches. Enjoy the authentic pub grub and the basket of chips.

> ### DANCE THE NIGHT AWAY
>
> Most dance and nightclubs charge entrance fees ranging from €5 to €20. In addition, some trendy nightclubs, such as Living XXL, enforce dress codes—usually no jeans, sneakers, or khaki pants admitted.

★ **Jimmy's Bar** (⊠ *Friedrich-Ebert-Anlage 40, Messe* ☎ *069/6032–9972*) is classy and expensive—like the Hessischer Hof Hotel in which it's located. It's been the meeting place of business executives since 1951. The ladies are more chic; the gentlemen more charming; the pianist, who plays from 10 PM onward, more winning. ■ TIP→ **You must ring the doorbell to get in, although regulars have their own keys.**

Keepers Lounge (⊠ *Schweizerstr. 78, Sachsenhausen* ☎ *069/6060–7210*) is a modern bar that's constantly flooded with young professionals. The cocktail menu looks like a novella.

The place to go for those who are hungry after midnight is **Paolo's Bar & Ristorante** (⊠ *Schweizerstr. 1, Sachsenhausen* ☎ *069/617–146*). It's open until 4 AM, serving highly regarded Italian cuisine.

University students and young professionals frequent the red-walled **d Bar** (⊠ *Abstgässchen 7, Sachsenhausen* ☎ *069/617–116*). You'll find it in a cellar beneath a narrow Sachsenhausen alleyway. DJs usually spin the music, although there are occasional live acts. There's a tiny dance floor if you feel like showing off your moves.

★ The soothing interior attracts many to **Unity** (⊠ *Hanauer Landstr. 2, Ostend* ☎ *069/9434–0555*), a lounge in Frankfurt's East End. Large couches line the walls of this dimly lighted space. A mix of rock, funk, and soul is played by a DJ, except when there is live music on Tuesday.

DANCE & NIGHTCLUBS

One of Germany's most revered DJs, Sven Väth spins regularly at **Cocoon Club** (⊠ *Carl-Benz-Str. 21, Fechenheim* ☎ *069/5069–6948*). This ultramodern nightclub has a spacious dance floor, three bars, and two restaurants serving Asian–European cuisine. Comfort is a priority throughout the expansive club filled with reclining chairs and couches, some of which are built into the walls. Techno is the presiding music genre. ■ TIP→ **A night out here will take a toll on your wallet: a taxi is required to reach its location on the eastern edge of town, cover charges average €15, and cocktails are pricey.** It's open Friday and Saturday only.

Living XXL (⊠ *Kaiserstr. 29, City Center* ☎ *069/242–9370*), one of the biggest restaurant-bars in Germany, is as hyped as the Eurotower, where it happens to be located. The Wednesday after-work parties are popular. The DJ spins hip-hop and soul on Friday and a mix of R&B, soul, and house on Saturday. The spacious, terraced interior has drawn praise from architects.

The type of crowd at **Odeon** (✉*Seilerstr. 34, City Center* ☎*069/285–055*) depends on the night. The large club hosts student nights on Thursday, a "27 Up Club" on Friday (exclusively for guests 27 or older), disco nights on Saturday, as well as "Black Mondays"—a night of soul, hip-hop, and R&B music. It's housed in a beautiful white building that looks like a museum.

JAZZ & TECHNO

Frankfurt was a real pioneer in the German jazz scene, and also has done much for the development of techno music. Jazz musicians make the rounds from smoky backstreet cafés all the way to the Old Opera House, and the local broadcaster Hessischer Rundfunk sponsors the German Jazz Festival in the fall. The Frankfurter Jazzkeller has been the most noted venue for German jazz fans for decades.

The former police headquarters has been transformed into **Praesidium 19/11** (✉*Friedrich-Ebert-Anlage 11, Messe* ☎*069/7474–3978*), a huge nightclub. High ceilings, chandeliers, columns, and a grand staircase fill its stunning interior. The music never stops, as several DJs often perform on a single night. Drinks are reasonably priced—compared to those of other dance clubs. It's open Friday and Saturday only until 5 AM.

There's not much that doesn't take place at Frankfurt's international variety theater, the **Tigerpalast** (✉*Heiligkreuzg. 16–20, City Center* ☎*069/9200–2250*). Guests are entertained by international cabaret performers and the *Palast*'s own variety orchestra. There is an excellent restaurant, and the cozy Palastbar, under the basement arches, looks like an American bar from the 1920s. Shows often sell out, so book tickets as far in advance as possible. It's closed Monday.

JAZZ
The oldest jazz cellar in Germany, **Der Frankfurter Jazzkeller** (✉*Kleine Bockenheimerstr. 18a, City Center* ☎*069/284–927*) was founded by legendary trumpeter Carlo Bohländer. The club has hosted such luminaries as Louis Armstrong. It offers hot, modern jazz, at a cover of €5 to €25, depending on the stature of the performers. There are jam sessions on Wednesday and dancing on Friday. It's closed Monday.

Sinkkasten (✉*Brönnerstr. 5–9, City Center* ☎*069/280–385*), a Frankfurt musical institution, is a class act—a great place for blues, jazz, pop, and rock, with live groups, often up-and-coming ones, frequently replacing the DJ.

SPORTS & THE OUTDOORS

Despite the ever-present smog in summer, Frankfurt is full of parks and other green oases where you can breathe easier. South of the city, the huge, 4,000-acre **Stadtwald** (city forest) makes Frankfurt one of Germany's greenest metropolises. ■ TIP➡ **The forest has innumerable paths and trails, bird sanctuaries, impressive sports stadiums, and a good restaurant.** The Oberschweinstiege stop on streetcar line 14 is right in the middle of the park.

The **Taunus Hills** are also a great getaway for Frankfurters. Take U-bahn 3 to Hohemark. In the Seckbach district, northeast of the city, Frankfurters hike the 590-foot **Lohrberg Hill**. The climb yields a fabulous view of the town and the Taunus, Spessart, and Odenwald hills. Along the way you'll also see the last remaining vineyard within the Frankfurt city limits, the Seckbach Vineyard. Take the U-4 subway to Seckbacher Landstrasse, then Bus 43 to Draisbornstrasse.

BIKING

There are numerous biking paths within the city limits. The Stadtwald in the southern part of the city is crisscrossed with well-tended paths that are nice and flat. The city's riverbanks are, for the most part, lined with paths bikers can use. These are not only on both sides of the Main but also on the banks of the little Nidda River, which flows through Heddernheim, Eschersheim, Hausen, and Rödelheim before joining the Main at Höchst. Some bikers also like the Taunus Hills, but note that word "Hills."

Custom De Luxe (⊠ *Günthersburgallee 6, Nordend* ☎ *069/1381–8313* Ⓜ *Musterschule [U-bahn]*) is something special for Frankfurt: a bicycle café. You can fortify yourself with some coffee and cake, then rent a bike for €3.50 per hour or €16 per day. The staff will handle any repairs you may need and even deliver, and later pick up, a rental bike at your hotel. The café is closed Monday.

JOGGING

The **Anlagenring,** a park following the former city wall, is a popular route. For a vigorous forest run, go to the Stadtwald or the Taunus Hills, though you should think twice about jogging alone in these remote places. The banks of the Main River are a good place to jog, and to avoid retracing your steps you can always cross a bridge and return down the opposite side. In the Westend, **Grüneberg Park** is 2 km (1 mi) around, with a *Trimm Dich* (literally, "get fit") exercise facility in the northeast corner.

SHOPPING

SHOPPING DISTRICTS

Frankfurt, and the rest of Germany, is finally free of the restrictive laws that kept the stores closed evenings and Saturday afternoons—the very times working people might want to shop. Stores now can stay open until 10 PM, though it is still rare for them to be open on Sunday. The tree-shaded pedestrian zone of the **Zeil** is said to be the richest shopping strip in Germany. There's no doubt that the Zeil, between Hauptwache and Konstablerwache, is incredible for its variety of department and specialty stores.

The Zeil is only the centerpiece of the downtown shopping area. The subway station below the Hauptwache also doubles as a vast underground mall, albeit a rather droll one. West of the Hauptwache are two parallel streets highly regarded by shoppers. One is the luxurious **Goethestrasse,** lined with trendy boutiques, art galleries, jewelry stores, and antiques shops. The other is **Grosse Bockenheimer Strasse,** better known as the Fressgasse (Pig-Out Alley). Cafés, restaurants, and pricey food stores line the street.

The **Schillerpassage** (⊠ *Rahmhofstr. 2, City Center*) is strong on men's and women's fashion boutiques.

The moderately priced **Zeilgallerie** (⊠ *Zeil 112–114, City Center*) has 56 shops and an outstanding view from the rooftop terrace.

DEPARTMENT STORES

There are two department stores on the Zeil, offering much in the way of clothing, furnishings, electronics, food, and other items. **Karstadt** (⊠ *Zeil 90, City Center* ☎ *069/929–050*) has a splendid gourmet food department, with plenty of opportunity to try the food and drink on the spot. The **Galeria Kaufhof** (⊠ *Zeil 116–126, City Center* ☎ *069/21910*), with its top-floor Dinea Restaurant, has a striking view of the city.

GIFT IDEAS

The one real gift item that Frankfurt produces is fine porcelain. The **Höchster Porzellan Manufaktur,** (⊠ *Palleskestr. 32, Höchst* ☎ *069/300– 9020*) draws on a tradition dating back 200 years. The hand-made products can be purchased at the workshop.

There are a number of not-so-elegant gift items that you might consider. One thing typical of the city is the Apfelwein (apple wine). You can get a bottle of it at any grocery store, but more enduring souvenirs would be the Bembel pitchers and ribbed glasses that are equally a part of the Apfelwein tradition. Then there is the sausage. You can get the "original hot dog" in cans at any grocery store.

SPECIALTY STORES

CLOTHING STORES

★ **Peek & Cloppenburg** (⊠ *Zeil 71–75, City Center* ☎ *069/298–950*) is a huge clothing store where men and women can find what they need for the office, gym, and nightclub. Clothes range from easily affordable items to pricier designer labels.

Pfüller Modehaus (⊠ *Goethestr. 12, City Center* ☏*069/1337–8070*) offers a wide range of choices on three floors for women, from classic to trendy, from lingerie to overcoats, and from hats to stockings. Ralph Lauren and Hugo Boss are just a few of the many labels sold.

FOOD & DRINK

The pastry shop at **Café Laumer** (⊠ *Bockenheimer Landstr. 67, Westend* ☏*069/727–912*) has local delicacies such as *Bethmännchen und Brenten* (marzipan cookies) and *Frankfurter Kranz* (a kind of creamy cake). All types of sweets and pastries are also found at the **Café Mozart** (⊠ *Töngesg. 23, City Center* ☏*069/291954*).

The **Kleinmarkthalle** (⊠ *Haseng. 5–7, City Center* ☏*069/2123–3696*) is a treasure trove of stands selling spices, herbs, teas, exotic fruits, cut flowers, and live fish flown in from the Atlantic. And it offers all kinds of snacks in case you need a break while shopping.

Weinhandlung Dr. Teufel (⊠ *Kleiner Hirschgraben 4, City Center* ☏*069/283–236*) is as good a place as any for the popular wines, and the best place in town for diversity. There are also chocolate and cigars, a complete line of glasses, carafes, corkscrews and other accessories, and books on all aspects of viticulture.

FLEA MARKET

Sachsenhausen's weekend **flea market** takes place on Saturday from 8 to 2 on the riverbank between Dürerstrasse and the Eiserner Steg. Purveyors of the cheap have taken over, and there's lots of discussion as to whether it is a good use for the elegant, museum-lined riverbank. ■TIP→ **Get there early for the bargains, as the better-quality stuff gets snapped up quickly.** Shopping success or no, the market can be fun for browsing.

SIDE TRIPS FROM FRANKFURT

Destinations reachable by the local transportation system include Höchst and the Taunus Hills, which include Bad Homburg and Kronberg. Just to the northwest and west of Frankfurt, the Taunus Hills are an area of mixed pine and hardwood forest, medieval castles, and photogenic towns that many Frankfurters regard as their own backyard. It's home to Frankfurt's wealthy bankers and business executives, and on weekends you can see them enjoying their playground: hiking through the hills, climbing the Grosse Feldberg, taking the waters at Bad Homburg's health-enhancing mineral springs, or just lazing in elegant stretches of parkland.

BAD HOMBURG

12 km (7 mi) north of Frankfurt.

Emperor Wilhelm II, the infamous "kaiser" of World War I, spent a month each year at Bad Homburg, the principal city of the Taunus

Hills. Another frequent visitor to Bad Homburg was Britain's Prince of Wales, later King Edward VII, who made the name *Homburg* world famous by associating it with a hat.

GETTING HERE & AROUND

Bad Homburg is easily reached by the S-bahn from Hauptwache, the main station, and other points in downtown Frankfurt. S-5 goes to Bad Homburg. There's also a Taunusbahn (from the main station only) that stops in Bad Homburg and then continues into the far Taunus, including the Römerkastell-Saalburg and Wehrheim, with bus connections to Hessenpark. Bad Homburg is about a 30- to 45-minute drive north of Frankfurt on A–5.

The Bad Homburg tourist office is open until 6:30 PM weekdays, 2 PM Saturday, and is closed on Sunday.

ESSENTIALS

Visitor Information Kur- und Kongress GmbH Bad Homburg (✉ *Louisenstr. 58 Bad Homburg* ☎ *06172/1780* ⊕ *www.bad-homburg.de*).

EXPLORING

Bad Homburg's greatest attraction has been the **Kurpark** *(spa)*, in the heart of the Old Town, with more than 31 fountains. Romans first used the springs, which were rediscovered and made famous in the 19th century. In the park you'll find not only the popular, highly saline Elisabethenbrunnen spring but also a Siamese temple and a Russian chapel, mementos left by more royal guests—King Chulalongkorn of Siam and Czar Nicholas II. The Kurpark is a good place to begin a walking tour of the town; Bad Homburg's **tourist office** (✉ *Louisenstr. 58* ☎ *06172/1780*) is in the nearby Kurhaus.

Adjacent to the Kurpark, the **casino** boasts with some justice that it is the "Mother of Monte Carlo." The first casino in Bad Homburg, and one of the first in the world, was established in 1841, but closed down in 1866 because Prussian law forbade gambling. The proprietor, François Blanc, then established the famous Monte Carlo casino on the French Riviera, and the Bad Homburg casino wasn't reopened until 1949. A bus runs between the casino and Frankfurt's Hauptbahnhof (south side). It leaves Frankfurt every hour on the hour between 2 PM and 10 PM and then hourly from 10:25 PM to 1:25 AM. Buses back to Frankfurt run every hour on the hour from 4 PM to 4 AM. The €6 fare will be refunded after the casino's full entry fee has been deducted. You must show a passport or other identification to gain admission. ✉ *Kisseleffstr. 35* ☎ *06172/17010* ✉ *Slot-machine area free, gaming area €2.50* ⊗ *Slot machines noon–4 AM, gaming area 2:30 PM–3 AM.*

The most historically noteworthy sight in Bad Homburg is the 17th-century **Schloss,** where the kaiser stayed when he was in residence. The state apartments are exquisitely furnished, and the Spiegelkabinett (Hall of Mirrors) is especially worthy of a visit. In the surrounding park look for two venerable cedars from Lebanon, both now about 200 years old. ✉ *Herrng.* ☎ *06172/9262–150* ✉ *€4* ⊗ *Tues.–Fri. 10–5, weekends.*

9

Just a short, convenient bus ride from Bad Homburg is the highest mountain in the Taunus, the 2,850-foot, eminently hikable **Grosser Feldberg.**

Only 6½ km (4 mi) from Bad Homburg, and accessible by direct bus service, is the **Römerkastell-Saalburg** *(Saalburg Roman Fort)*. Built in AD 120, the fort could accommodate a cohort (500 men) and was part of the fortifications along the Limes Wall, which ran from the Danube to the Rhine and was meant to protect the Roman Empire from barbarian invasion. The fort was restored more than a century ago. The fort, which includes a museum of Roman artifacts, is north of Bad Homburg on Route 456 in the direction of Usingen. ✉*Saalburg 1* ☎*06175/93740* *€3* *Mar.–Oct., daily 9–6; Nov.–Feb., Tues.–Sun. 9–4.*

About an hour's walk through the woods along a well-marked path from the Römerkastell-Saalburg is an open-air museum at **Hessenpark,** near Neu-Anspach. The museum presents a clear picture of the world in which 18th- and 19th-century Hessians lived, using 135 acres of rebuilt villages with houses, schools, and farms typical of the time. The park, 15 km (9 mi) outside Bad Homburg in the direction of Usingen, can also be reached by public transportation. Take the Taunusbahn from the Frankfurt main station to Wehrheim; then transfer to Bus 514. ✉*Laubwegb 5, Neu-Anspach* ☎*06081/5880* *www.hessenpark.de* *€5* *Mar.–Dec., daily 9–6.*

WHERE TO STAY & EAT

$ ✕ **Kartoffelküche.** This simple restaurant serves traditional dishes accompanied by potatoes cooked every way imaginable. The potato and broccoli gratin and the potato pizza are excellent. For dessert, try potato strudel with vanilla sauce. ✉*Audenstr. 4* ☎*06172/21500* *AE, DC, MC, V.*

$$$ **Maritim Kurhaus Hotel.** The hotel offers large, richly furnished rooms with king-size beds and deep armchairs. Some rooms have balconies. The cozy Bürgerstube ($–$$) serves both solid German cuisine and international dishes. **Pros:** quiet location, near the city center. **Cons:** somewhat removed from the Kurpark. ✉*Ludwigstr. 3* ☎*06172/6600* *www.maritim.de* *148 rooms, 10 suites* *In-room: no a/c, dial-up, Wi-Fi (some). In-hotel: 2 restaurants, bar, no-smoking rooms, some pets allowed* *AE, DC, MC, V* *BP.*

$$$ ★ **Steigenberger Bad Homburg.** Renowned for catering to Europe's royalty in its pre–World War I heyday, this building has been a hotel since 1883. The management knows how to cater to its still well-heeled clientele. Charley's Bistro evokes the spirit of *gaie Paris* with literary dinners and jazz brunches. **Pros:** old world elegance, handy to the Kurpark. **Cons:** expensive, parking is very difficult. ✉*Kaiser-Friedrich-Promenade 69–75* ☎*06172/1810* *www.bad-homburg.steigenberger.de* *152 rooms, 17 suites* *In-room: safe, dial-up, Wi-Fi. In-hotel: restaurant, room service, bar, gym, concierge, laundry service, no-smoking rooms* *AE, DC, MC, V .*

KRONBERG

15 km (9 mi) northeast of Frankfurt.

The Taunus town of Kronberg, 15 km (9 mi) northwest of Frankfurt, has a magnificent castle-hotel originally built by a daughter of Queen Victoria, and an open-air zoo. Kronberg's half-timber houses and crooked, winding streets, all on a steep hillside, were so picturesque that a whole 19th-century art movement, the Kronberger Malerkolonie, was inspired by them.

GETTING HERE & AROUND

Kronberg is easily reached by the S-bahn from Hauptwache, the main station, and other points in downtown Frankfurt. S-4 to Kronberg.

It is about a 30- to 45-minute drive north of Frankfurt on A–66 (Frankfurt–Wiesbaden) to the Eschborn exit, following the signs to Kronberg.

Kronberg's tourist office closes at noon on weekdays and is closed the entire weekend.

ESSENTIALS

Visitor Information **Verkehrs- und Kulturamt Kronberg** (⊠ *Katharinenstr. 7 Kronberg* ☎ *06173/703–1400* ⊕ *www.kronberg.de*).

EXPLORING

★ Established by a wealthy heir of the man who created the Opel automobile, the large **Opel Zoo** has more than 1,400 native and exotic animals, plus a petting zoo and an area where birds fly freely. There's also a playground, a geological garden, and a picnic area with grills. Camel and pony rides are offered in summer. ⊠ *Königsteinerstr. 35* ☎ *06173/79749* ✉ *€9* ⊙ *Apr., May, Sept., and Oct., daily 9–6; June–Aug., daily 9–7; Nov.–Mar., daily 9–5.*

WHERE TO STAY

$$$$ ▦ **Schlosshotel Kronberg.** This magnificent palace was built for Kaiserin Victoria, daughter of the British queen of the same name and mother of Wilhelm II, the infamous kaiser of World War I. It's richly filled with furnishings and works of art and is surrounded by a park with old trees, a grotto, a rose garden, and an 18-hole golf course. It's one of the few hotels left where you can leave your shoes outside your door for cleaning. Jimmy's Bar, with pianist, is a local rendezvous. **Pros:** built for royalty, fit for royalty, shuttle service to the airport. **Cons:** expensive, and you still must pay €21 for breakfast. ⊠ *Hainstr. 25 Kronberg im Taunus* ☎ *06173/70101* ⊕ *www.schlosshotel-kronberg.de* ➽ *51 rooms, 7 suites* ⅏ *In-room: no a/c, refrigerator, Wi-Fi. In-hotel: restaurant, room service, bar, concierge, some pets allowed, no-smoking rooms* ▤ *AE, DC, MC, V* ♭ *BP.*

9

HÖCHST

Take S-1 or S-2 suburban train from Frankfurt's main train station, Hauptwache, or Konstablerwache.

Höchst, a town with a castle and an Altstadt (Old Town) right out of a picture book, was not devastated by wartime bombing, so its castle and the market square, with its half-timber houses, are well preserved. It's a romantic place for outdoor dining and drinking. For a week in July the whole Alstadt is hung with lanterns for the Schlossfest, one of Frankfurt's more popular outdoor festivals.

Höchst was once a porcelain-manufacturing town to rival Dresden and Vienna. Production ceased in the late 18th century, but was revived by an enterprising businessman in 1965. The **Höchster Porzellan Manufaktur** produces exquisite and expensive tableware, but the intriguing part of its output is its accessories. There are replicas of 18th-century items, including vases, cufflinks, and bottle stoppers. You can tour the workshop and shop at the store. ⊠*Palleskestr. 32* ☎*069/300–9020* ⊠*€5* ⊗*Shop weekdays 9:30–6, Sat. 9:30–2., tours Tues. 10 and 3.*

Hochst's most interesting attraction is the **Justiniuskirche** (*Justinius Church*), Frankfurt's oldest building and famous for its organ concerts. Dating from the 7th century, the church is part early Romanesque and part 15th-century Gothic. The view from the top of the hill is well worth the walk. ⊠*Justiniuspl. at Bolongerostr.*

WHERE TO STAY

$ ⛴ **Hotel-Schiff** *Peter Schlott.* The hotel ship is moored on the Main River, close to the Höchst Altstadt. Guest cabins are on the small side, but the river views more than compensate, and there's a common room with a television. ■**TIP➔** It's not for you if you're subject to seasickness, but ideal if you like to be rocked to sleep. Pro: pleasant river view. Cons: very small rooms, narrow, hard-to-navigate stairs. ⊠*Batterie* ☎*069/300–4643* ⊕*www.hotelschiffschlott.de* ⌂*19 rooms* ⊘*In-room: no a/c, no phone. In-hotel: restaurant, some pets allowed* ▤*AE, MC, V* ⦿*BP.*

The Pfalz &
Rhine Terrace

WORD OF MOUTH

"In Mainz (which we now know how to pronounce correctly), we walked to the center of town and toured through the very Romanesque Mainzer Dom. It was early in the morning, and only a few people were in the church, which made it even more haunting and beautiful. ... We arrived at the Gutenberg Museum and immediately went downstairs where they have many different types of printing presses on display, including a reproduction of the original Gutenberg Press. We watched as the docent set the type and pressed a page from the Bible, which he rolled up and gave to me as a souvenir."

—artstuff

Updated by
Tim Skelton

THE ROMANS PLANTED THE FIRST RHINELAND VINEYARDS 2,000 years ago. By the Middle Ages viticulture was flourishing at the hands of the church and the state, and a bustling wine trade had developed. This ancient vineyard area is now the state of Rheinland-Pfalz (Rhineland Palatinate), home to six of Germany's 13 wine-growing regions, including the two largest, Rheinhessen and the Pfalz. Bordered on the east by the Rhine and stretching from the French border north to Mainz, these two regions were the "wine cellar of the Holy Roman Empire." Thriving viticulture and splendid Romanesque cathedrals are the legacies of the bishops and emperors of Speyer, Worms, and Mainz. Two routes parallel to the Rhine link dozens of wine villages. In the Pfalz, follow the Deutsche Weinstrasse (German Wine Road); in the eastern Rheinhessen (Rhine Terrace), the home of the mild wine Liebfraumilch, the Liebfrauenstrasse guides you from Worms to Mainz.

The Pfalz has a mild, sunny climate and an ambience to match. Vines carpet the foothills of the thickly forested Haardt Mountains, an extension of the Alsatian Vosges. The Pfälzerwald (Palatinate Forest) with its pine and chestnut trees is the region's other natural attraction. Hiking and cycling trails lead through the vineyards, the woods, and up to castles on the heights. As the Wine Road winds its way north from the French border, idyllic wine villages beckon with flower-draped facades and courtyards full of palms, oleanders, and fig trees. WEINVERKAUF (wine for sale) and WEINPROBE (wine-tasting) signs are posted everywhere, each one an invitation to stop in to sample the wines.

The border between the Pfalz and Rheinhessen is invisible. Yet a few miles into the hinterland, a profile takes shape. Rheinhessen is a region of gentle, rolling hills and expansive farmland, where grapes are but one of many crops; vineyards are often scattered miles apart. The slopes overlooking the Rhine between Worms and Mainz—the so-called Rhine Terrace—are a notable exception. This is a nearly uninterrupted ribbon of vines culminating with the famous vineyards of Oppenheim, Nierstein, and Nackenheim on the outskirts of Mainz.

ORIENTATION & PLANNING

GETTING ORIENTED

If you're arriving from the dramatic stretch of the Rhine centered around the Lorelei and Koblenz to the north, you'll notice how the landscape here is far gentler. So too is the climate and soil in this region of the Rhine valley, guarded at its northern edge by the medieval city of Mainz and touching the French border at its southern extreme. This helps the land give birth to some of Germany's greatest wines.

The German Wine Road. The picturesque German Wine Road weaves through the valleys and among the lower slopes of the Haardt Mountains. Along its length are a string of pretty half-timbered wine-producing villages, each more inviting than the last.

The Rhine Terrace. Rheinhessen or "Rhine Terrace" is a broad fertile river valley, where grapes are but one of many crops. Here the medieval cities of Mainz, Worms, and Speyer all bear testament to the great

TOP REASONS TO GO

Wine: German Rieslings are the most versatile white wines in the world—on their own or with food. For many, discovering Germany's drier-style wines is a revelation.

Pfälzerwald: The Palatinate Forest is a paradise for hiking and cycling. Even a brief walk under the beautiful pine and chestnut trees is relaxing and refreshing.

Castles: Burg Trifels and Schloss Villa Ludwigshöhe are a contrast in style, inside and out. Both are wonderful settings for concerts.

Cathedrals: The cathedrals in Speyer, Worms, and Mainz are the finest examples of grand-scale Rhenish Romanesque architecture in Germany.

power and wealth brought by the important trading route created by the mighty Rhine itself.

THE PFALZ & RHINE TERRACE PLANNER

WHEN TO GO

The wine-festival season begins in March with the *Mandelblüten* (blossoming of the almond trees) along the Wine Road and continues through October. By May the vines' tender shoots and leaves appear. As the wine harvest progresses in September and October, foliage takes on reddish-golden hues.

GETTING HERE & AROUND

BY AIR Frankfurt is the closest major international airport for the entire Rhineland. International airports in Stuttgart and France's Strasbourg are closer to the southern end of the German Wine Road.

BY BIKE There's no charge for transporting bicycles on local trains throughout Rheinland-Pfalz weekdays after 9 AM and anytime weekends and holidays. For maps, suggested routes, bike-rental locations, and details on *Pauschal-Angebote* (package deals) or *Gepäcktransport* (luggage-forwarding service), contact Pfalz-Touristik or Rheinhessen-Information.

BY CAR It's 162 km (100 mi) between Schweigen-Rechtenbach and Mainz, the southernmost and northernmost points of this itinerary. The main route is the Deutsche Weinstrasse, which is a *Bundesstrasse* (two-lane highway), abbreviated "B," as in B–38, B–48, and B–271. The route from Worms to Mainz is B–9.

BY TRAIN Mainz is on the high-speed ICE (InterCity Express) train route linking Wiesbaden, Frankfurt, and Dresden, and so forms a convenient gateway to the region. An excellent network of public transportation called **Rheinland-Pfalz-Takt** operates throughout the region with well-coordinated **RegioLinie** (buses) and **Nahverkehrszüge** (local trains). Regional trains link Mainz with other towns along the Rhine Terrace, including Worms and Speyer, while local branch lines serve key hubs along the Wine Road such as Neustadt and Bad Dürkheim. Smaller towns and villages connect with these hubs by an excellent network of local buses.

Visitor Information Deutsche Weinstrasse (⊠ *Martin-Luther-Str. 69 Neustadt a.d. Weinstrasse* ☎ *06321/912–333* ⊕ *www.deutsche-weinstrasse.de*). **Pfalz. Touristik** (⊠ *Martin-Luther-Str. 69 Neustadt a.d. Weinstrasse* ☎ *06321/39160* ⊕ *www.pfalz-touristik.de*). **Pfalzwein** (⊠ *Martin-Luther-Str. 69 Neustadt a.d. Weinstrasse* ☎ *06321/912–328* ⊕ *www.pfalzwein.de*). **Rheinhessen-Information** (⊠ *Wilhelm-Leuschner-Str. 44 Ingelheim* ☎ *06132/44170* ⊕ *www.rheinhessen.info*). **Rheinhessenwein** (⊠ *Otto-Lilienthal-Str. 4 Alzey* ☎ *06731/951–0740* ⊕ *www. rheinhessenwein.de*). **Rheinland-Pfalz Tourismus** (⊠ *Löhrstr. 103–105 Koblenz* ☎ *0621/915–200* ⊕ *www.rlp-info.de*). **Südliche Weinstrasse** (⊠ *An der Kreuzmühle 2 Landau* ☎ *06341/940–407* ⊕ *www.suedlicheweinstrasse.de*).

ABOUT THE RESTAURANTS

Lunch in this region is generally served from noon until 2 or 2:30, dinner from 6 until 9:30 or 10. Credit cards have gained a foothold, but many restaurants will accept only cash or debit cards issued by a German bank. Casual attire is typically acceptable at restaurants here, and reservations are generally not needed. Gourmet temples that require reservations and jacket and tie are noted as such in this chapter.

ABOUT THE HOTELS

Accommodations in all price categories are plentiful, but book in advance if your visit coincides with a large festival. Bed-and-breakfasts abound. Look for signs reading FREMDENZIMMER or ZIMMER FREI (rooms available). A *Ferienwohnung* (holiday apartment), abbreviated FeWo in tourist brochures, is an economical alternative if you plan to stay in one location for several nights.

WHAT IT COSTS IN EUROS					
	¢	$	$$	$$$	$$$$
RESTAURANTS	under €9	€9–€15	€16–€20	€21–€25	over €25
HOTELS	under €50	€50–€100	€101–€175	€176–€225	over €225

Restaurant prices are per person for a main course at dinner. Hotel prices are for two people in a standard double room, including tax and service.

PLANNING YOUR TIME

Central hubs such as Bad Dürkheim or Neustadt make good bases for exploring the region, although the cities along the Rhine are livelier, particularly Mainz. Driving the Wine Road takes longer than you might expect, and will probably involve spur of the moment stops, so you may want to consider a stopover in one of the many country inns en route.

When traveling with children, Neustadt or Worms are convenient bases from which to explore nearby Holiday Park.

DISCOUNTS & DEALS

The **Rheinland-Pfalz Card** (€15 for one day, €39 for three days) offers free or reduced admission to museums, castles, and other sights, as well as city tours and boat trips throughout the state. The three-day card also includes admission to the Holiday Park in Hassloch. The **KulturCard** (€5) entitles you to a discount at many cultural events, museums, and sights. The card is sold by mail through the regional broadcaster SWR and at the newspaper *RZ* (RheinZeitung) shops. If you plan to spend more than a few hours in Mainz, consider purchasing a **MainzCard** (€10 for two days). The Wines of Germany office (⇨ *Wine, Beer & Spirits in Travel Smart*) promotes the wines of all the regions.

ESSENTIALS **KulturCard SWR** (⌖ *Stichwort KulturCard, D–55114 Mainz*). *RZ* **shop** (✉ *Grosse Bleiche 17-23, Mainz*).

THE GERMAN WINE ROAD

The Wine Road spans the length of the Pfalz wine region. You can travel from north to south or vice versa. Given its central location, the Pfalz is convenient to visit before or after a trip to the Black Forest, Heidelberg, or the northern Rhineland.

SCHWEIGEN-RECHTENBACH

21 km (13 mi) southwest of Landau on B–38.

The southernmost wine village of the Pfalz lies on the French border. During the economically depressed 1930s, local vintners established a route through the vineyards to promote tourism. The German Wine Road was inaugurated in 1935; a year later the massive stone Deutsches Weintor (German Wine Gate) was erected to add visual impact to the marketing concept. Halfway up the gateway is a platform that offers a fine view of the vineyards—to the south, French, to the north, German. Schweigen's 1-km (½-mi) Weinlehrpfad (educational wine path) wanders through the vineyards and, with signs and exhibits, explains the history of viticulture from Roman times to the present.

10

BAD BERGZABERN

10 km (6 mi) north of Schweigen-Rechtenbach on B–38.

The landmark of this little spa town is the baroque **Schloss** (palace) of the dukes of Zweibrücken. Also on Königstrasse is an impressive Renaissance house (No. 45) with elaborate scrolled gables and decorative oriels. ■ TIP➔ **Visit Café Herzog (Marktstr. 48) for scrumptious, homemade chocolates, cakes, and ice creams made with unexpected ingredients, such as wine, pepper, cardamom, curry, thyme, or *Feigenessig* (fig vinegar). The café is closed Monday and Tuesday.**

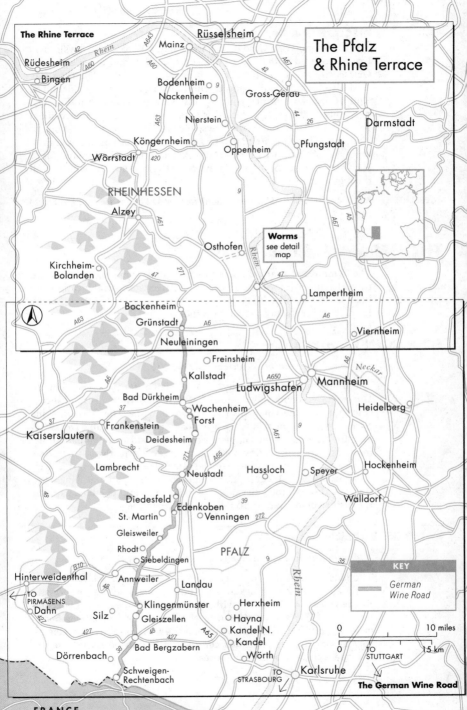

WHERE TO STAY

$$ Fodor's Choice ★ **Hotel–Restaurant Zur Krone.** A simple facade belies an upscale inn, which offers modern facilities, tasteful decor, and, above all, a warm welcome from the Kuntz family. The open fireplace in the lounge is lit in winter. In the hotel's highly rated gourmet restaurant, chef Karl-Emil Kuntz prepares a set menu with French/Mediterranean accents ($$$$, reservations essential). Terrines and parfaits are favorites, as is the homemade goat cheese. The same kitchen team prepares regional specialties at the Pfälzer Stube ($$–$$$). The wine list is excellent. The property is in Hayna, a suburb of Herxheim that lies 20 km (12 mi) east of Bad Bergzabern via B–427. **Pros:** quiet location, friendly atmosphere, great food. **Con:** a big detour off the Wine Road. ✉ *Hauptstr. 62–64 Herxheim-Hayna* ☎ *07276/5080* 🌐 *www.hotelkrone.de* *42 rooms, 7 suites* *In-room: no a/c, Ethernet, Wi-Fi (some). In-hotel: 2 restaurants, bar, tennis courts, pool, bicycles, no elevator, laundry service, public Internet, no-smoking rooms, some pets allowed* *AE, MC, V* *Restaurant Zur Krone closed Mon. and Tues., 1st 2 wks in Jan., and 3 wks in Aug. No lunch* *BP.*

GLEISZELLEN

4 km (2½ mi) north of Bad Bergzabern on B–48.

Gleiszellen's **Winzergasse** (Vintners' Lane) is a little vine-canopied street lined with a beautiful ensemble of half-timber houses. Try a glass of the town's specialty: spicy, aromatic Muskateller wine, a rarity seldom found elsewhere in Germany.

WHERE TO STAY

$ **Gasthof Zum Lam.** Flowers cascade from the windowsills of this half-timber inn in the heart of town. Exposed beams add rustic charm to the airy rooms, while the bright bathrooms are modern. The inviting restaurant ($–$$) has a dome-shape tile stove and natural stone walls. A courtyard and a vine-shaded terrace provide outdoor seating. **Pros:** quiet location, charming courtyard, beautiful old building. **Cons:** access via a narrow street, no elevator. ✉ *Winzerg. 37 Gleiszellen* ☎ *06343/939–212* 🌐 *www.zum-lam.de* *11 rooms, 1 apartment* *In-room: no a/c, Wi-Fi. In-hotel: restaurant, bar, bicycles, no elevator, public Wi-Fi, some pets allowed* *V* *Restaurant closed Wed. No lunch Nov.–Mar.* *BP.*

10

ANNWEILER

15 km (9 mi) northwest of Gleiszellen.

In 1219 Annweiler was declared a Free Imperial City by Emperor Friedrich II. Stroll along Wassergasse, Gerbergasse (Tanners' Lane), and Quodgasse to see the half-timber houses and the waterwheels on the Queich River, which is more like a creek. Annweiler is a gateway to the **Wasgau,** the romantic southern portion of the Palatinate Forest, marked by sandstone cliffs and ancient castles. The forest supported an important timber industry a century ago and is still the source of

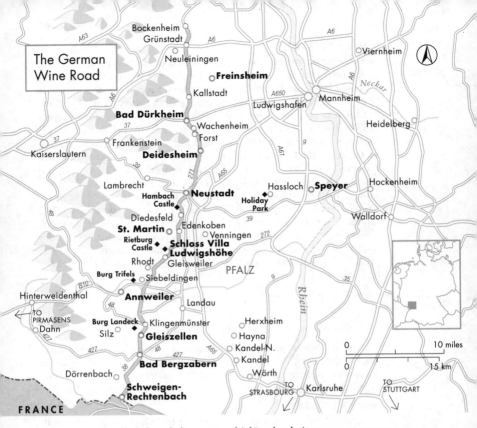

locally beloved chestnuts, which make their way onto restaurant menus in season.

GETTING HERE & AROUND

Annweiler tours are at 10 AM on Wednesday, May through October, free of charge.

ESSENTIALS

Visitor Information Annweiler (✉ *Büro für Tourismus, Messpl. 1* ☎ *06346/2200* ⊕ *www.trifelsland.de).*

EXPLORING

★ **Burg Trifels** perches on the highest of three sandstone bluffs overlooking Annweiler. Celts, Romans, and Salians all had settlements on this site, but it was under the Hohenstaufen emperors (12th and 13th centuries) that Trifels was built on a grand scale. It housed the crown jewels from 1125 to 1274 (replicas are on display today). It was also an imperial prison, perhaps where Richard the Lion-Hearted was held captive in 1193–94.

Although it was never conquered, the fortress was severely damaged by lightning in 1602. Reconstruction began in 1938, shaped by visions of grandeur to create a national shrine of the imperial past. Accordingly,

EATING WELL IN THE PFALZ

The best introduction to regional country cooking is the *Pfälzer Teller,* a platter of bratwurst (grilled sausage), *Leberknödel* (liver dumplings), and slices of *Saumagen* (a spicy meat-and-potato mixture cooked in a sow's stomach), with *Weinkraut* (sauerkraut braised in wine) and *Kartoffelpüree* (mashed potatoes) on the side. Rheinhessen is known for the hearty casseroles *Dippe-Has* (hare and pork baked in red wine) and *Backes Grumbeere* (scalloped potatoes cooked with bacon, sour cream, white wine, and a layer of pork). *Spargel* (asparagus); *Wild* (game); chestnuts; and mushrooms, particularly *Pfifferlinge* (chanterelles), are seasonal favorites. During the grape harvest, from September through November, try *Federweisser* (fermenting grape juice) and *Zwiebelkuchen* (onion quiche)—specialties unique to the wine country.

Savor the local wines. Those from Rheinhessen are often sleeker and less voluminous than their Pfälzer counterparts. Many are sold as *offene Weine* (wines by the glass) and are *trocken* (dry) or *halbtrocken* (semidry). The classic white varieties are Riesling, Silvaner, Müller-Thurgau (also called Rivaner), Grauburgunder (Pinot Gris), and Weissburgunder (Pinot Blanc); Spätburgunder (Pinot Noir), Dornfelder, and Portugieser are the most popular red wines. The word *Weissherbst,* after the grape variety, signals a rosé wine.

the monumental proportions of some parts of today's castle bear no resemblance to those of the original Romanesque structure. The imperial hall is a grand setting for the *Serenaden* (concerts) held in summer. ☎06346/8470 ⊕*www.burgen-rlp.de* ☜€2.60 ☉*Apr.–Sept., daily 9–6; Oct., Nov., and Jan.–Mar., daily 9–5.*

☺ **Museum unterm Trifels,** a historic mill, tanners' houses, and a tannery "beneath Trifels," chronicles the development of Burg Trifels, Annweiler, and the natural surroundings. There's an excellent English translation, and the museum ticket entitles reduced admission at Burg Trifels. ⊠*Am Schipkapass 4* ☎06346/1682 ☜€2.60 ☉*Mid-Mar.–Oct., Tues.–Sun. 10–5; Nov.–mid-Mar., weekends 1–5.*

WHERE TO STAY & EAT

$ ✕**Restaurant s'Reiwerle.** *Schmorbraten vom Weideschaf* (braised lamb) is a specialty at this 300-year-old half-timber house. Look for chestnut-based dishes, such as *Keschtebrieh* (chestnut soup), in autumn. *Reiwerle* (pronounced "*rye*-vair-leh") is dialect for a spigot to tap wine from a cask; two-dozen Pfälzer wines are available by the glass. ⊠*Flitschberg 7* ☎06346/929–362 ⊟*No credit cards ☉Closed 2 wks mid-Jan. and Tues., Jan.–Easter.*

$ ✕**Zur alten Gerberei.** An open fireplace, exposed beams, and sandstone walls give this old *Gerberei* (tannery) a cozy feel. The Queich flows right past the outdoor seats. In addition to Pfälzer specialties and vegetarian dishes, you can try Alsatian *Flammkuchen,* similar to pizza but baked on a wafer-thin crust (¢). There are 20 Pfälzer wines available by the glass. ⊠*Am Prangertshof 11, at Gerberg.* ☎06346/3566 ⊕*www. gerberei.de* ⊟*MC, V ☉Closed Mon. and Jan. No lunch Tues.–Sat.*

10

$ ⊞ **Landgasthaus Sonnenhof.** Matthias Goldberg is the convivial host and creative cook at this Jugendstil villa near the vineyards of Siebeldingen (8 km [5 mi] east of Annweiler). Throughout the house fresh flowers, soft colors, and blond-wood furnishings set the tone. Fresh flowers also adorn the tables on the shady terrace. Light cuisine with Mediterranean and Asian accents is served in the restaurant ($$–$$$). There's no better place to become acquainted with the finest wines of the Südpfalz. **Pros:** romantic location, quiet, friendly. **Cons:** a little off the Wine Road, far from the sights. ⊠ *Mühlweg 2* ☎ *06345/3311* ⊕ *www.soho-siebeldingen.de* ⌑ *14 rooms* ⚒ *In-room: no a/c, dial-up. In-hotel: restaurant, room service, no elevator, public Internet, some pets allowed, no-smoking rooms* ▭ *AE, MC, V* ⊘ *Restaurant closed Thurs.* ⚏ *BP.*

SPORTS & THE OUTDOORS

BIKING & HIKING Dozens of marked trails guide you to the Wasgau's striking geological formations and castles carved into the sandstone cliffs. From Annweiler you can access many of these trails via a circular tour by car (55½ km [35 mi]). Proceed west on B–10 to Hinterweidenthal (16½ km [10 mi]), then south on B–427 to Dahn (7 km [4 mi]), and continue southeast to Erlenbach (9 km [5½ mi]). Return to Annweiler via Vorderweidenthal (1 km [½ mi]) and Silz (7 km [4 mi]). Each town is a good starting point for a scenic ride, climb, or hike.

SCHLOSS VILLA LUDWIGSHÖHE

★   *24 km (15 mi) north of Annweiler, slightly west of Edenkoben on the Wine Rd.*

Bavaria's King Ludwig I built a summer residence on the slopes overlooking Edenkoben, in what he called "the most beautiful square mile of my realm." You can reach the neoclassical **Schloss Villa Ludwigshöhe** by car or bus from Edenkoben or take a scenic 45-minute walk through the vineyards along the Weinlehrpfad. Historical winepresses and vintners' tools are displayed at intervals along the path. It starts at the corner of Landauer Strasse and Villa Strasse in Edenkoben.

The layout and decor—Pompeian-style murals, splendid parquet floors, and Biedermeier and Empire furnishings—of the palace provide quite a contrast to those of medieval castles elsewhere in the Pfalz. An extensive collection of paintings and prints by the leading German impressionist Max Slevogt (1868–1932) is on display. The rooms can only be visited on a guided tour. Tours begin on the hour. ☎ *06323/93016* ⊕ *www.burgen-rlp.de* ⚏ *€2.60* ⊙ *Apr.–Sept., Tues.–Sun. 9–6; Oct., Nov., and Jan.–Mar., Tues.–Sun. 9–5.*

☾ From Schloss Villa Ludwigshöhe you can hike (30 minutes) or ride the Rietburgbahn chairlift (10 minutes) up to the **Rietburg** castle ruins for a sweeping view of the Pfalz. During a festive *Lampionfahrt* in July and August (dates vary each year), the chairlift operates til midnight and the route is lit by dozens of Chinese lanterns. A restaurant, game park, and playground are on the grounds. ☎ *06323/1800* ⚏ *Chairlift*

€5.50 round-trip, €3.50 one-way ⊗ *Mar., Sun. 9–5; Apr.–Oct., week-days 9–5, weekends 9–6.*

WHERE TO STAY

$$ 🏨**Alte Rebschule.** Sonja Schaefer's modern, beautifully appointed hotel on the edge of the forest was once an old *Rebschule* (vine nursery). Fireside seating in the lobby lounge and spacious rooms (all with balcony) make for a pleasant, peaceful stay. The restaurant ($$) serves light, seasonal cuisine with Asian and Mediterranean accents. Sign up for a themed excursion (wine, culture, nature) and ask about health and wellness treatments. Rhodt proper is a 15-minute walk from the hotel. ■**TIP➔** Be sure to take a stroll along Theresienstrasse with its venerable old chestnut trees. It's one of the most picturesque lanes of the Pfalz. Pros: beautiful location, quiet, good restaurant. Cons: remote, far from the sights. ⊠ *3 km (2 mi) west of Schloss Villa Ludwigshöhe, Theresienstr. 200 Rhodt u. Rietburg* ☎*06323/70440* ⊕*www.alte-rebschule.de* 🛏*29 rooms, 1 suite* ⚡ *In-room: no a/c, Ethernet, dial-up. In-hotel: restaurant, room service, bar, spa, laundry service, public Internet, no-smoking rooms* ▤*MC, V* ⊗*No lunch* ❚◎❙*BP.*

ST. MARTIN

★ *26 km (16 mi) north of Annweiler, slightly west of the Wine Road. Turn left at the northern edge of Edenkoben.*

This is one of the most charming wine villages of the Pfalz. The entire **Altstadt** (Old Town) is under historical preservation protection. For 350 years the Knights of Dalberg lived in the castle **Kropsburg,** the romantic ruins of which overlook the town. Renaissance tombstones are among the many artworks in the late-Gothic **Church of St. Martin.**

WHERE TO STAY

$ 🏨**Landhaus Christmann.** This bright, modern house in the midst of the vineyards has stylish rooms decorated with both antiques and modern furnishings. Some rooms have balconies with a view of the Hambacher Schloss. Vintners and distillers, the Christmanns offer 20 wines by the glass in their restaurant, Gutsausschank Kabinett ($), as well as culinary wine tastings. In addition to their wines and spirits, they sell antiques. Pros: excellent value rooms, quiet location, good restaurant. Con: remote. ⊠ *Riedweg 1* ☎*06323/94270* ⊕*www.landhaus-christmann.de* 🛏*6 rooms, 3 apartments* ⚡ *In-room: no a/c, no phone, kitchen (some). In-hotel: restaurant, laundry service, public Internet, public Wi-Fi, no-smoking rooms, some pets allowed* ▤*MC, V* ⊗*Hotel and restaurant closed 4 wks in Jan. and Feb. and 2 wks in July and Aug. Restaurant closed Mon.–Wed. No lunch* ❚◎❙*BP.*

$ 🏨**St. Martiner Castell.** The Mücke family transformed a simple vintner's house into a fine hotel and restaurant, retaining many of the original features, such as exposed beams and an old winepress. Though it's in the heart of town, the hotel is peaceful, particularly the rooms with balconies overlooking the garden. A native of the Loire Valley, Frau Mücke adds French flair to the menu ($$–$$$). The wine list offers a good selection of bottles from a neighboring wine estate. Pros: beauti-

10

ful old home, French restaurant, central location. **Con:** can be noisy. ✉ *Maikammerer Str. 2* ☎ *06323/9510* ⊕ *www.hotelcastell.de* ⇆ *26 rooms* ⭿ *In-room: no a/c, dial-up. In-hotel: restaurant, room service, laundry service, public Internet, public Wi-Fi, no-smoking rooms, some pets allowed* ☰ *MC, V* ☉ *Hotel and restaurant closed Feb. Restaurant closed Tues.* ⁑ *BP.*

THE ARTS

Schloss Villa Ludwigshöhe, Kloster Heilsbruck (a former Cistercian convent near Edenkoben), and **Schloss Edesheim** are backdrops for concerts and theater in summer. For a calendar of events, contact the Südliche Weinstrasse regional tourist office in Landau (☎ 06341/940–407 ⊕ *www. suedlicheweinstrasse.de*).

SHOPPING

Artist Georg Wiedemann is responsible for both content and design of the exquisite products of Germany's premier wine-vinegar estate, **Doktorenhof** (✉ *Raiffeisenstr. 5* ☎ *06323/5505* ⊕ *www.doktorenhof.de*) in Venningen, 2 km (1 mi) east of Edenkoben. Make an appointment for a unique vinegar tasting and tour of the cellars or pick up a gift at his shop. He's open weekdays 8–4, Wednesday until 6, and Saturday 9–2 (no credit cards).

EN ROUTE Leave St. Martin via the Totenkopf-Höhenstrasse, a scenic road through the forest. Turn right at the intersection with Kalmitstrasse and proceed to the vantage point atop the **Kalmit,** the region's highest peak (2,200 feet). The view is second to none.

NEUSTADT

8 km (5 mi) north of St. Martin, 5 km (3 mi) north of Hambach on the Wine Rd.

Neustadt and its nine wine suburbs are at the midpoint of the Wine Road and the edge of the district known as Deutsche Weinstrasse–Mittelhaardt. With around 5,000 acres of vines, they jointly compose Germany's largest wine-growing community.

GETTING HERE & AROUND

Regular trains connect Neustadt with Ludwigshafen (connecting to Worms and Mainz). Coming from Speyer, change in Schifferstadt. Local buses connect Neustadt to other towns along the Wine Road. Once in Neustadt, the best way to get around is on foot. Neustadt tours cost €3 and take place April through October, Wednesday and Saturday at 10:30.

ESSENTIALS

Visitor Information Neustadt-an-der-Weinstrasse (✉ *Tourist-Information, Hetzelpl. 1* ☎ *06321/926–892* ⊕ *www.neustadt.pfalz.com*).

BIKING, HIKING & WALKING

Country roads and traffic-free vineyard paths are a cyclist's paradise. There are also well-marked cycling trails, such as the **Radwanderweg Deutsche Weinstrasse**, which runs parallel to its namesake from the French border to Bockenheim, and the **Radweg** (cycling trail) along the Rhine between Worms and Mainz. The Palatinate Forest, Germany's largest single tract of woods, has more than 10,000 km (6,200 mi) of paths.

The **Wanderweg Deutsche Weinstrasse**, a walking route that traverses vineyards, woods, and wine villages, covers the length of the Pfalz. It connects with many trails in the Palatinate Forest that lead to Celtic and Roman landmarks and dozens of castles dating primarily from the 11th to 13th centuries. In Rheinhessen you can hike along two marked trails parallel to the Rhine: the **Rheinterrassenwanderweg** and the **Rheinhöhenweg** along the heights.

EXPLORING

At the **Haus des Weines** *(House of Wine)*, opposite the town hall, you can sample some 30 of the 100 Neustadt wines sold. The Gothic house from 1276 is bordered by a splendid Renaissance courtyard, the Kuby'scher Hof. ✉ *Rathausstr. 6* ☎ *06321/355–871* ⊕ *www.haus-des-weines.com* ⊘ *Closed Sun. and Mon.*

The **Marktplatz** *(market square)* is the focal point of the Old Town and a beehive of activity on Tuesday, Thursday, and Saturday, when farmers come to sell their wares. The square itself is ringed by baroque and Renaissance buildings (Nos. 1, 4, 8, and 11) and the Gothic **Stiftskirche** (Collegiate Church), built as a burial church for the Palatinate counts. In summer, concerts take place in the church (Saturday 11:30–noon). Afterward, you can ascend the southern tower (187 feet) for a bird's-eye view of the town. The world's largest cast-iron bell—weighing more than 17 tons—hangs in the northern tower. Indoors, see the elaborate tombstones near the choir and the fanciful grotesque figures carved into the baldachins and corbels.

★ The Pfalz is home to the legendary, elusive *Elwetritschen,* part bird and ☺ part human, said to roam the forest and vineyards at night. "Hunting Elwetritschen" is both a sport and an alibi. Local sculptor Gernot Rumpf has immortalized these creatures by depicting them in a **fountain** on Marstallplatz. No two are alike. Near the market square, hunt for the one that "escaped" from its misty home. End a walking tour of the Old Town on the medieval lanes Metzgergasse, Mittelgasse, and Hintergasse to see beautifully restored half-timber houses, many of which are now pubs, cafés, and boutiques.

NEED A BREAK? **For the best "coffee and cake" or handcrafted pralines in town head for Café Sixt** ✉ *Hauptstr. 3* ⊕ *www.cafe-confiserie-sixt.de* ⊘ *Closed Mon.*

The impressionist painter Otto Dill (1884–1957), a native of Neustadt, is known for powerful animal portraits (especially lions, tigers, and

10

horses) and vivid landscapes. The **Otto Dill Museum** displays some 100 oil paintings and 50 drawings and watercolors of the Manfred Vetter collection. ⊠ *Rathausstr. 12, at Bachgängel 8* ☏ *06321/398–321* ⊕ *www. otto-dill-museum.de* ▣ *€2.50* ⊙ *Wed. and Fri. 2–5, weekends 11–5.*

Ⓒ Thirty historic train engines and railway cars are on display at the **Eisenbahn Museum,** behind the main train station. Take a ride through the Palatinate Forest on one of the museum's historic steam trains, the *Kuckucksbähnel* (€14), which departs from Track 5 around 10:30 AM every other Sunday between Easter and mid-October. It takes a good hour to cover the 13-km (8-mi) stretch from Neustadt to Elmstein. ⊠ *Neustadt train station, Schillerstr. entrance* ☏ *06321/30390* ⊕ *www.eisenbahnmuseum-neustadt.de* ▣ *€3* ⊙ *Tues.–Fri. 10–1, weekends 10–4.*

WHERE TO EAT

$$–$$$ ✕ **Brezel.** The gilded *Brezel* (pretzel) hanging in front of the 17th-century half-timber house (once a bakery) is the namesake of Helga and Stefan Braun's classy yet comfortable wine restaurant. White walls, softened by light wooden floors and beams, are hung with paintings by the late impressionist Otto Dill. In the back, dine beneath the vaulted ceiling of a former wine cellar. Fish is the specialty, and the excellent wines are reasonably priced. ⊠ *Rathausstr. 32* ☏ *06321/481–971* ⊕ *www.brezel-restaurant.de* ▤ *MC, V* ⊙ *Closed 1 wk in Feb., 2 wks in mid-June, and Tues. and Wed.*

$–$$ ✕ **Altstadtkeller bei Jürgen.** Tucked behind a wooden portal, this vaulted sandstone "cellar" (it's actually on the ground floor) is a cozy setting. Equally inviting is the terrace, with its citrus, olive, palm, and fig trees. The regular menu includes a number of salads and a good selection of fish and steaks. Owner Jürgen Reis is a wine enthusiast, and his well-chosen list shows it. ⊠ *Kunigundenstr. 2* ☏ *06321/32320* ⊕ *www. altstadtkeller-neustadt.de* ▤ *AE, MC, V* ⊙ *Closed 2 wks in Feb., 2 wks in Nov., and Mon. No dinner Sun.*

$–$$ ✕ **Nett's Restaurant-Weinbar.** Susanne and Daniel Nett operate a chic wine restaurant-bar in a 16th-century vaulted stone cellar at Weingut A. Christmann, a top wine estate. Upscale versions of Pfälzer specialties as well as light cuisine with a Mediterranean touch are offered with about 200 Pfälzer wines and other top German reds and whites. Dining alfresco in the intimate courtyard is a romantic option in summer. ⊠ *Peter-Koch-Str. 43, Neustadt-Gimmeldingen* ☏ *06321/60175* ⊕ *www.nettsrestaurant.de* ▤ *No credit cards* ⊙ *Closed Mon. No lunch except on some holidays.*

WHERE TO STAY

$ ▦ **Mithras-Stuben/Weinstube Kommerzienrat.** Convivial proprietor and
★   wine devotee Bernd Hagedorn rents four spacious apartments with contemporary furnishings, Oriental rugs, and modern baths. Upon request, cell phones are available for the two apartments with no in-room phones. In the restaurant ($–$$), an incredible 300 Pfälzer wines can be sampled by the glass (and 250 imported wines by the bottle). *Rumpsteak* (beef steak), served with tasty *Bratkartoffeln* (home-fried potatoes) or *Rösti* (potato pancakes), and Pfälzer Gyros (a unique meat-and-cheese dish)

are favorites. **Pros:** spacious, perfect for longer stays. **Con:** no elevator. ✉ *Loblocherstr. 34, Neustadt-Gimmeldingen* ☎ *06321/679–0335 or 06321/68200* ⊕ *www.weinstube-kommerzienrat.de* ⇆ *4 apartments* ♿ *In-room: no a/c, no phone (some), kitchen, refrigerator, dial-up (some). In-hotel: restaurant, bar, no elevator, no-smoking rooms, some pets allowed* ⊟ *No credit cards* ⊘ *Hotel and restaurant closed 2 wks late Apr. Restaurant closed Thurs. No lunch.*

$ ⊡ **Rebstöckel/Weinstube Schönhof.** Enjoy vintner's hospitality in Hannelore and Stephan Hafen's 17th-century stone guesthouse at the Weingut Schönhof estate. All rooms have blond-wood furnishings; some have kitchenettes. Try the estate's wines in the Weinstube (¢– $) with a hearty *Schönhof Pfännchen* (ham gratin in a brandy cream sauce). Wine tastings and vineyard hikes can be arranged, and cycling fans can rent bikes at a shop around the corner. Neustadt proper is 5 km (3 mi) north. **Pros:** quiet, friendly, rustic location. **Con:** far from the sights. ✉ *Weinstr. 600, Neustadt-Diedesfeld* ☎ *06321/86198* ⊕ *www. weingut-schoenhof.de* ⇆ *1 room, 4 apartments* ♿ *In-room: no a/c, kitchen (some), refrigerator. In-hotel: restaurant, no elevator, no-smoking rooms* ⊟ *No credit cards* ⊘ *Restaurant closed Wed., Thurs., and Jan. No lunch* ⑩ *BP.*

$ ⊡ **Steinhäuser Hof.** The 14th-century Kuby'scher Hof is an architectural gem in the heart of the Old Town. The former stables have been converted into modern, comfortable rooms and a handsome restaurant ($$–$$$). The half-timber facades lining the courtyard are a lovely backdrop for an outdoor meal. There is a good selection of fish, steaks, and *Wild* (game). Many sauces are flavored with beer, wine, or spirits. For a "flaming finale," try the *Feigen* (figs) in Pernod flambéed tableside. **Pros:** beautiful old building, central location, friendly staff. **Con:** historic building means no elevator. ✉ *Rathausstr. 6 D–67433 Neustadt* ☎ *06321/489–060* ⊕ *www.steinhaeuserhof.homepage.t-online.de* ⇆ *6 rooms* ♿ *In-room: no a/c, no phone, Wi-Fi (some). In-hotel: restaurant, room service, bar, no elevator, public Wi-Fi, some pets allowed* ⊟ *MC, V* ⊘ *Restaurant closed Mon.* ⑩ *BP.*

EN ROUTE The **Holiday Park,** in Hassloch, 10 km (6 mi) east of Neustadt, is one of Europe's largest amusement parks. The admission fee (free on your birthday) covers all attractions, shows including the spectacular Waterski Stuntshow, special events, and the children's world. The free-fall tower, hell barrels, and Thunder River rafting are standing favorites, and *Expedition GeForce* has the steepest drop (82 degrees) of any roller coaster in Europe. For a great panoramic view of the surroundings, whirl through the air on Lighthouse-Tower, Germany's highest carousel in the sky (265 feet). The newest attraction in 2007 was AMACEON, a multimedia voyage through time and space. On Friday and Saturday in summer, the "Summer Nights" spectacular features live music, and the outdoor laser light show "Magic of the Night." ✉ *Holiday Parkstr. 1–6* ☎ *06324/599–3318* ⊕ *www.holidaypark.de* ⊡ *€25.50* ⊘ *Early Apr.–Oct., daily 10–6; in summer, open until midnight Fri. and Sat.*

10

SPEYER

25 km (15 mi) east of Neustadt via B–39, 22 km (14 mi) south of Mannheim via B–9 and B–44.

Speyer was one of the great cities of the Holy Roman Empire, founded in pre-Celtic times, taken over by the Romans, and expanded in the 11th century by the Salian emperors. Between 1294, when it was declared a Free Imperial City, and 1570, no fewer than 50 imperial diets were convened here. The term "Protestant" derives from the diet of 1529, referring to those who protested when the religious freedom granted to evangelicals at the diet of 1526 was revoked and a return to Catholicism was decreed. The neo-Gothic **Gedächtniskirche** on Bartolomäus-Weltz-Platz commemorates those 16th-century Protestants.

GETTING HERE & AROUND
Speyer is served by regular trains from Mannheim and Mainz. Buses ply the main street, but the center is compact enough that getting around on foot is not a problem. Tours (€3.50) are at 11 on weekends from April through October.

ESSENTIALS
Visitor Information **Speyer** (⊠ *Tourist-Information, Maximilianstr. 13* ☎ *06232/142–392* 🖷 *06232/142–332* ⊕ *www.speyer.de*).

EXPLORING
Ascend the **Altpörtel**, the impressive town gate, for a grand view of Maximilianstrasse, the street that led kings and emperors straight to the cathedral. ◲€1 ⊙*Apr.–Oct., weekdays 10–noon and 2–4, weekends 10–5.*

Fodor'sChoice ★ The **Kaiserdom** *(Imperial Cathedral)*, one of the finest Romanesque cathedrals in the world and a UNESCO World Heritage site, conveys the pomp and majesty of the early Holy Roman Emperors. It was built between 1030 and 1061 by the emperors Konrad II, Henry III, and Henry IV. The last replaced the flat ceiling with groin vaults in the late 11th century, an innovative feat in its day. A restoration program in the 1950s returned the building to almost exactly its original condition.

■TIP➜ **There's a fine view of the east end of the structure from the park by the Rhine.** Much of the architectural detail, including the dwarf galleries and ornamental capitals, was inspired and executed by stonemasons from Lombardy, which belonged to the German Empire at the time. The four towers symbolize the four seasons and the idea that the power of the empire extends in all four directions. Look up as you enter the nearly 100-foot-high portal. It's richly carved with mythical creatures. In contrast to Gothic cathedrals, whose walls are supported externally by flying buttresses, allowing for a minimum of masonry and a maximum of light, at Speyer the columns supporting the roof are massive. The **Krypta** (crypt) lies beneath the chancel. It's the largest crypt in Germany and is strikingly beautiful in its simplicity. Four emperors, four kings, and three empresses are buried here. ⊠*Dompl.*

Donation requested ⊘ *Apr.–Oct., daily 9–7; Nov.–Mar., daily 9–5; closed during services.*

★ Opposite the cathedral, the **Historisches Museum der Pfalz** *(Palatinate Historical Museum)* houses the **Domschatz** (Cathedral Treasury). Other collections chronicle the art and cultural history of Speyer and the Pfalz from the Stone Age to modern times. Don't miss the precious "Golden Hat of Schifferstadt," a golden, cone-shape object used for religious purposes during the Bronze Age. The **Wine Museum** exhibits artifacts from Roman times to the present, including the world's oldest bottle of wine, from circa AD 150. The giant 35-foot-long wooden winepress from 1727 is also worth a look. ⊠ *Dompl. 4* 🕾 *06232/13250* ⊕ *www.museum.speyer.de* ✉ *Permanent collection €4, special exhibitions €10, combination ticket with Sea Life €18* ⊘ *Tues.–Sun. 10–6.*

Speyer was an important medieval Jewish cultural center. In the **Jewish quarter,** behind the Palatinate Historical Museum, you can see synagogue remains from 1104 and Germany's oldest (pre-1128) ritual baths, the 33-foot-deep *Mikwe*. Note: although the official address is Judengasse, the entrance is around the corner at Kleine Pfaffengasse 21. ⊠ *Judeng.* j*entrance around the corner at Kleine Pfaffengasse 21* 🕾 *06232/291–971* ✉ *€2* ⊘ *Apr.–Oct., daily 10–5.*

☾ A turn-of-the-20th-century factory hall houses the **Technik-Museum** *(Technology Museum)*, an impressive and vast collection of locomotives, aircraft, old automobiles, and fire engines. Automatic musical instruments, historical dolls and toys, and 19th-century fashion are displayed in the Wilhelmsbau. Highlights of the complex are the 420-ton U-boat (you can go inside) and the massive 3-D IMAX cinemas. There is also an exhibition hall devoted to outer space. ■ **TIP**➔**Allow at least three hours to visit this extensive museum, which covers several large buildings.** ⊠ *Am Technik Museum 1* 🕾 *06232/67080* ⊕ *www.technik-museum.de* ✉ *Museum €13, IMAX €8.50, combined ticket €17* ⊘ *Weekdays 9–6, weekends 9–7.*

☾ **Sea Life,** in Speyer's old harbor, enables you to travel the length of the Rhine from the Alps to the North Sea via a walk through a 33-foot-long tunnel. All types of marine life native to this region glide through 105,600 gallons of water. ⊠ *Im Hafenbecken 5, 15-min walk from large parking lot on Festpl.* 🕾 *06232/69780* ⊕ *www.sealife.de* ✉ *€12.75, combined ticket with historical museum €18* ⊘ *Sept.–June weekdays 10–5, weekends 10–6; July–Aug., daily 10–7.*

WHERE TO EAT

$$$–$$$$ ✕ **Backmulde.** Homemade bread and homegrown produce have long
★ been hallmarks of this upscale wine restaurant. Colorful, aromatic fare is served indoors and amidst palms on the patio. Champagnes and some 850 wines (Pfälzer and international)—spanning decades of vintages—as well as the owners' own wines from the Heiligenstein

vineyard near Speyer await wine lovers. The Backmulde also has three comfortable guest rooms ($) with blond-wood furnishings and hardwood floors. ⊠ *Karmeliterstr. 11–13* ☎ *06232/71577* ⊕ *www. backmulde.de* ▤ *AE, MC, V* ⊙ *Closed Mon.*

$–$$ ✕ **Kutscherhaus.** Charming rustic decor and a profusion of flowers have replaced the *Kutschen* (coaches) in this turn-of-the-20th-century coachman's house. The menu offers Flammkuchen and Pfälzer specialties as well as creative fish, vegetarian, and pasta dishes. In summer you can sit beneath the old plane trees in the beer garden and select from a sumptuous buffet. ⊠ *Fischmarkt 5a* ☎ *06232/70592* ⊕ *www.kutscher-haus-speyer.de* ▤ *AE, MC, V* ⊙ *Closed Wed. (Note: Beer garden open daily all summer)*

$–$$ ✕ **Ratskeller.** Friendly service and Gunter Braun's fresh seasonal dishes make for an enjoyable dining experience in the town hall's vaulted cellar (1578). The frequently changing menu offers creative soups (pretzel soup, Tuscan bread soup) and entrées, such as *Sauerbraten nach Grossmutters Art* (grandma-style marinated pot roast) or *Bachsaibling* (brook char in a red-wine-butter sauce). Wines from the Pfalz predominate, with 18 available by the glass. Small fare and drinks are served in the courtyard May through September. ⊠ *Maximilianstr. 12* ☎ *06232/78612* ▤ *AE, MC, V* ⊙ *Closed 2–3 wks in Feb. and Mon. No dinner Sun.*

$–$$ ✕ **Wirtschaft Zum Alten Engel.** This 200-year-old vaulted brick cellar has rustic wood furnishings and cozy niches. Winter luncheon specials are a good value. Seasonal dishes supplement the large selection of Pfälzer and Alsatian specialties, such as *Ochsenfetzen* (slices of beef in garlic sauce), *Fleeschknepp* (spicy meatball in horseradish sauce), or a hearty *Pfälzer Platte* (a platter of bratwurst, Saumagen, and Leberknödel with sauerkraut and home-fried potatoes). The wine list features about 180 Pfälzer, European, and New World wines. ⊠ *Mühlturmstr. 7* ☎ *06232/70914* ⊕ *www.zumaltenengel.de* ▤ *V* ⊙ *Closed 3 wks in Aug. No lunch May–Aug. or Sun. Sept.–Apr.*

WHERE TO STAY

$ ▦ **Hotel Goldener Engel.** A scant two blocks west of the Altpörtel is the "Golden Angel," a friendly, family-run hotel furnished with antiques and innovative metal-and-wood designer furniture. Paintings by contemporary artists and striking photos of Namibia and the Yukon line the walls—the photos are a tribute to proprietor Paul Schaefer's wanderlust. **Pros:** friendly, good location. **Con:** some rooms are a little

---

THE ALTRHEIN

From April to October, take a brief river cruise to the north or south of Speyer to discover the idyllic landscape of the ancient, forested islands along the *Altrhein* (original course of the Rhine). The islands are home to rare flora, fauna, and many birds. There are grand views of the cathedral from the boat.

Fahrgastschifffahrt Speyer
(⊠ *Dock: opposite Sea Life, in the old harbor* ⊕ *www.ms-sealife.de* ☒ *€8.50*)

Pfälzerland Fahrgastschiff
(⊠ *Dock: Leinpfad (via Rheinallee), on the Rhine riverbank* ☒ *€8*)

small. ✉*Mühlturmstr. 5–7* ☎*06232/13260* ⊕*www.goldener-engel-speyer.de* ⇔*44 rooms, 2 suites* ⚭*In-room: no a/c (some), Ethernet, dial-up. In-hotel: restaurant, laundry service, some pets allowed (fee)* ⊟*AE, DC, MC, V* ⦿❙*BP.*

NIGHTLIFE & THE ARTS

Highlights for music lovers are **Orgelfrühling,** the organ concerts in the Gedächtniskirche (Memorial Church) in spring, the jazz festival in mid-August, and the concerts in the cathedral during September's **Internationale Musiktage.** Call the Speyer tourist office for program details and tickets.

Walk into the town-hall courtyard to enter the **Kulturhof Flachsgasse,** home of the city's art collection and special exhibitions. ✉*Flachsg.* ☎*06232/142–399* ✉*Free* ⊙*Tues.–Sun. 11–6.*

DEIDESHEIM

8 km (5 mi) north of Neustadt via the Wine Rd., now B–271.

Deidesheim is the first of a trio of villages on the Wine Road renowned for their vineyards and the wine estates known as the Three Bs of the Pfalz—Bassermann, Buhl, and Bürklin.

The half-timber houses and historical facades framing Deidesheim's **Marktplatz** form a picturesque group, including the **Church of St. Ulrich,** a Gothic gem inside and out.

GETTING HERE & AROUND

Deidesheim conducts tours May through October on Saturday at 10 (€3).

ESSENTIALS

Visitor Information Deidesheim (✉*Tourist-Information, Bahnhofstr. 5* ☎*06326/96770* 🖶*06326/967–718* ⊕*www.deidesheim.de*).

EXPLORING

The old **Rathaus** *(Town Hall),* whose doorway is crowned by a baldachin and baroque dome, is also on the square. The attractive open staircase leading up to the entrance is the site of the festive *Geissbock-Versteigerung* (billy-goat auction) every Pentecost Tuesday, followed by a parade and folk dancing. The goat is the tribute neighboring Lambrecht has paid Deidesheim since 1404 for grazing rights. Inside, see the richly appointed Ratssaal (council chamber) and the museum of wine culture. ✉*Marktpl.* ✉*Donation requested* ⊙*Mar.–Dec., Wed.–Sun. 3–6.*

Vines, flowers, and *Feigen* (fig trees) cloak the houses behind St. Ulrich on Heumarktstrasse and its extension, Deichelgasse (nicknamed Feigengasse). ■**TIP→ To see the workshops and ateliers of about a dozen local artists and goldsmiths, follow the** *Künstler-Rundweg,* **a signposted trail (black** K **on yellow signs).** The tourist office has a brochure with a map and opening hours. Cross the Wine Road to reach the grounds of **Schloss Deidesheim,** now a wine estate and pub (⊙*Apr.–Oct., closed*

10

Wed.; Nov.–Mar., closed Tues.–Thurs.; no lunch weekdays). The bishops of Speyer built a moated castle on the site in the 13th century. Twice destroyed and rebuilt, the present castle dates from 1817, and the moats have been converted into gardens.

WHERE TO EAT

$$$$ ✕ **Restaurant Freundstück im Ketschauer Hof.** An 18th-century complex in a beautiful park has long been home to the Bassermann-Jordan wine estate. Inside the stunningly elegant restaurant and bistrolike wine bar elements of the original structures harmonize with modern, minimalist decor. Chef Alexander Hess prepares gourmet fare in the restaurant and upscale regional dishes in the wine bar. The excellent wine list includes every vintage of Bassermann-Jordan since 1870. ⊠ *Ketschauerhofstr. 1* ☎ *06326/70000* ⊕ *www.ketschauer-hof.com* ⊟ *AE, MC, V* ⊘ *Closed 3 wks in Jan. Restaurant closed Sun. and Mon. No lunch Sat.*

$$–$$$ ✕ **Restaurant St. Urban.** Named after St. Urban, the vintners' patron saint, this upscale wine restaurant offers excellent regional cuisine and wines in beautiful rooms. Try the *Pfälzer Backhendl* (fried chicken) with potato-and-cucumber salad. The restaurant is part of (and on the front patio of) the Hotel Deidesheimer Hof. ⊠ *Am Marktpl. 1* ☎ *06326/96870* ⊟ *AE, DC, MC, V* ⊘ *Closed 2nd wk of Jan.*

$$–$$$ ✕ **Weinschmecker.** The restaurant and Vinothek of Herbert Nikola, an expert on Pfälzer wines and festivals, is on the eastern edge of town. Italian tiles and whitewashed walls give it a light, airy Mediterranean look—much on the menu reflects the same culture. The focus, however, is on top-quality Pfälzer specialties and wines, 200 of which (from about 40 estates) are featured; 120 are available by the glass. ⊠ *Steing. 2* ☎ *06326/980–460* ⊟ *No credit cards* ⊘ *Closed Sun. and Mon. No lunch.*

WHERE TO STAY

$$–$$$ 🏨 **Hotel Deidesheimer Hof.** Despite the glamour of its clientele—the
Fodor'sChoice names of heads of state, entertainers, and sports stars line the guest
★ book—this hotel retains its country charm and friendly service. Rooms are luxurious, and several have baths with round tubs or whirlpools. The restaurant Schwarzer Hahn ($$$$) is for serious wining and dining. Among the Pfälzer specialties is a sophisticated rendition of the region's famous dish, Saumagen, with foie gras and truffles. More than 600 wines grace the wine list. **Pros:** some rooms have whirlpool baths, friendly staff, good value for the price. **Con:** rates don't include breakfast. ⊠ *Am Marktpl. 1* ☎ *06326/96870* ⊕ *www.deidesheimerhof.de* ➩ *24 rooms, 4 suites* ☖ *In-room: DVD (some), VCR (some), Ethernet, Wi-Fi (some). In-hotel: 2 restaurants, room service, bar, bicycles, laundry service, public Internet, public Wi-Fi, some pets allowed, no-*

SWEET SOUVENIRS

The Biffar family not only runs a first-class **wine estate** but also manufactures very exclusive candied fruits and ginger (delicious souvenirs). The estate is open weekdays 9–noon and 1–5:30, Saturday 10–noon and 1:30–3:30. *Niederkircher Str. 15* ☎ *06326/96760* ⊕ *www.biffar.com.*

smoking rooms ⊟*AE, DC, MC, V* ⊘*Hotel closed 2nd wk of Jan.*
Restaurant closed Sun. and Mon., Jan., and 4 wks in July and Aug.
No lunch.

$$ **Hatterer's Hotel-Restaurant Le Jardin d'Hiver.** Clément Hatterer, the hospitable Alsatian owner and chef, and his son Thomas have anticipated all the comforts you could ask for in this stylish hotel. The first-floor guest rooms have a contemporary look; those on the second floor are more spacious and are outfitted in a country style with wood furniture. Whether you dine in the winter garden, decorated in soothing shades of lilac, or in the sunny courtyard garden filled with exotic plants, the food and wine are exceptional. Like the menu ($$$–$$$$), the wine list features Pfälzer and Alsatian specialties. **Pros:** comfortable, friendly, quiet location. **Cons:** rooms are either "modern" or "rustic"—be clear on your preference when reserving. ⊠ *Weinstr. 12* ☎*06326/6011* ⊕*www.hotel-hatterer.de* ⤳*57 rooms* ♿*In-room: no a/c, refrigerator, Wi-Fi. In-hotel: restaurant, room service, bar, bicycles, laundry service, public WiFi, some pets allowed, no-smoking rooms* ⊟*AE, DC, MC, V* ⊘*Restaurant closed 2 wks in Jan.* ⦿*BP.*

$ **Landhotel Lucashof.** The beautifully decorated, modern guest rooms are named after famous vineyards in Forst, and four have balconies—the room called Pechstein is particularly nice. You can enjoy excellent wines in the tasting room, beneath a shady pergola in the courtyard, or in the privacy of your room (the refrigerator in the breakfast room is stocked for guests). The pubs in Forst's Old Town are a three-minute walk away. **Pros:** quiet location, friendly, good value. **Cons:** far from the sights, difficult to reach without a car. ⊠ *Wiesenweg 1a Forst* ☎*06326/336* ⊕*www.lucashof.de* ⤳*7 rooms* ♿*In-room: no a/c, dial-up. In-hotel: public Internet, some pets allowed, no-smoking rooms* ⊟*No credit cards* ⊘*Closed mid-Dec.–Jan.* ⦿*BP.*

BAD DÜRKHEIM

6 km (4 mi) north of Deidesheim on B–271.

This pretty spa is nestled into the hills at the edge of the Palatinate Forest and ringed by vineyards. The saline springs discovered here in 1338 are the source of today's drinking and bathing cures, and at harvest time there's also a detoxifying *Traubenkur* (grape-juice cure). There's a neoclassical **Kurhaus** with beautiful gardens. The town is also the site of the Dürkheimer Wurstmarkt, the world's largest wine festival, held in mid-September. Legendary quantities of *Weck, Worscht, un Woi* (dialect for rolls, sausage, and wine) are consumed at the fair, including half a million *Schoppen,* the region's traditional pint-size glasses of wine. The festival grounds are the site of the world's largest wine cask, the **Dürkheimer Riesenfass,** with a capacity of 450,000 gallons. Built in 1934 by an ambitious cooper, the cask is now a restaurant that can seat well over 450 people.

GETTING HERE & AROUND
Regional trains link Bad Dürkheim with Freinsheim and Neustadt. Once in town, all the hotels and restaurants are within easy walking

10

FESTIVALS

Attending a wine festival is fun and a memorable part of any vacation in wine country. You can sample local food and wine inexpensively and meet winegrowers without making an appointment. Wine and *Sekt* (sparkling wine) flow freely from March through October at festivals that include parades, fireworks, and rides. The Pfalz is home to the world's largest wine festival, in mid-September, the Dürkheimer Wurstmarkt (Sausage Market, so named because of the 400,000 pounds of sausage consumed during eight days of merrymaking). In Neustadt, the German Wine Queen is crowned during the 10-day Deutsches Weinlesefest (German Wine Harvest Festival) in October. The Mainzer Johannisnacht (in honor of Johannes Gutenberg) in late June, the Wormser Backfischfest (fried-fish festival) in late August, and the Brezelfest (pretzel festival) in Speyer on the second weekend in July are the major wine and folk festivals along this part of the Rhine. See ⊕ *www.germanwines.de* for an events calendar with an up-to-date overview of many smaller, local wine festivals that take place in virtually every village.

distance. Bad Dürkheim has tours (€2) May through October, departing Monday at 10:30 at the sign marked TREFFPUNKT FÜHRUNGEN, near the entrance to the train station.

ESSENTIALS

Visitor Information Bad Dürkheim (⊠ *Tourist-Information, Kurbrunnenstr. 14* ☎ *06322/956–6250* ⊟ *06322/956–6259* ⊕ *www.bad-duerkheim.com*).

EXPLORING

Northwest of town is the **Heidenmauer** *(literally, "heathen wall")* , the remains of an ancient Celtic ring wall more than 2 km (1 mi) in circumference and up to 20 feet thick in parts, and nearby are the rock drawings at **Kriemhildenstuhl,** an old Roman quarry where the legionnaires of Mainz excavated sandstone.

Overlooking the suburb of Grethen are the ruins of **Kloster Limburg** *(Limburg Monastery)*. Emperor Konrad II laid the cornerstone in 1030, supposedly on the same day that he laid the cornerstone of the Kaiserdom in Speyer. The monastery was never completely rebuilt after a fire in 1504, but it's a majestic backdrop for open-air performances in summer. From the tree-shaded terrace of the Klosterschänke restaurant ($–$$), adjacent to the ruins, you can combine good food and wine with a great view (closed Monday).

The massive ruins of 13th-century **Burgruine Hardenburg** *(Hardenburg Fortress)* lie 3 km (2 mi) west (via B–37) of Kloster Limburg. In its heyday it was inhabited by more than 200 people. It succumbed to fire in 1794. ⊠ *B–37* ☎ *€2.10* ⊗ *Apr.–Sept., Tues.–Sun. 9–1 and 1:30–6; Jan.–Mar., Oct., and Nov., Tues.–Sun. 9–1 and 1:30–5.*

WHERE TO EAT

\$\$–\$\$\$ ✕**Philip's Brasserie.** Römerplatz is Bad Dürkheim's culinary hub and the location of this classy restaurant. Paintings by contemporary local artists—including those of your hosts—line the terra-cotta–colored walls. Aromatic and flavorful seasonal cuisine starts with homemade bread and dip. The wine list is a showcase of great wines from the Pfalz, with a selection of international wines as well. ⊠*Römerpl. 3* ☎*06322/68808* ⊕*www.philips-brasserie.de* ➡*No credit cards* ☾*No lunch except Sun. Closed Tues., 1 wk in Jan., and 2 wks in mid-Sept.*

\$–\$\$ ✕**Dürkheimer Riesenfass.** The two-story "giant cask" is divided into various rooms and niches with rustic wood furnishings. Ask to see the impressive *Festsaal mit Empore* (banquet hall with gallery) upstairs. Regional wines, Pfälzer specialties, and international dishes are served year-round. ⊠*St. Michael Allee 1* ☎*06322/2143* ⊕*www.duerkheimer-fass.de* ➡*MC, V.*

\$ ✕**Petersilie.** Römerplatz abounds with cafés and eateries, but behind a group of lush, potted plants and a sign on the pink-and-white house reading BIER- UND WEINSTUBE TENNE is Petersilie, a gem for homemade Pfälzer cuisine and wine. Patio seating is great for people-watching; indoors is warm and cozy, with rustic wooden tables and pillow-lined benches. The weekly changing, three-course Sunday menu (\$) is a great value. ⊠*Römerpl. 12* ☎*06322/4394* ➡*No credit cards* ☾*Closed Mon. and Tues. Oct.–Apr., Feb., and Nov.*

WHERE TO STAY

\$\$ 🏨**Kurparkhotel.** Part of the Kurhaus complex, the Kurparkhotel is the
★ place to be pampered from head to toe. Haus A has the most elegant rooms, several with balconies. Haus B, also modern and comfortable, is less exclusive. This is a typical, elegant spa hotel, with extensive health and beauty facilities, thermal baths, a casino (free admission for hotel guests), and concerts in the garden. The flower-lined terrace at the restaurant Graf zu Leiningen (\$\$–\$\$\$) is a beautiful setting for coffee or tea with delicious homemade pastries in the afternoon or an elegant *Feinschmecker-Menü* (five-course gourmet menu) in the evening. **Pros:** good location, some balconies overlook park. **Con:** for a health spa, the gourmet restaurant may have the opposite effect on your waistline. ⊠*Schlosspl. 1–4* ☎*06322/7970* ⊕*www.kurpark-hotel.de* ➡*113 rooms* ⚿*In-room: no a/c, Ethernet. In-hotel: restaurant, room service, bar, pool, spa, bicycles, laundry service, public Internet, public Wi-Fi, some pets allowed, no-smoking rooms* ➡*AE, DC, MC, V* ⍟*BP.*

10

\$ 🏨**Weingut Fitz-Ritter.** Following his parents' retirement in 2007, Johann Fitz became the 9th-generation owner of the winery, bringing with him the expertise of an economics degree from Berkeley and his oenology studies on his return to Germany. The family has a centuries-old stone cottage that sleeps up to four people on the park-like grounds of their estate, which dates to 1785. You'll have a pool all to yourself, and there are concerts and festivals in the garden, courtyard, and vaulted cellars (request a calendar of events). Tastings and tours of the cellars, vineyards, and garden are possible. The minimum stay is seven nights. **Pros:** quiet location amid the vines, friendly staff. **Cons:** far from the sights. ⊠*Weinstr. Nord 51* ☎*06322/5389* ⊕*www.fitz-ritter.de* ➡*1* *cottage* ♿*In-room: no a/c, kitchen, DVD, VCR, Wi-Fi. In-hotel: pool, no-smoking rooms* 💳*MC, V.*

$ **Weingut und Gästehaus Ernst Karst und Sohn.** This cheerful guesthouse is adjacent to the Karst family's wine estate, in the midst of the vineyards. Rooms are light and airy, furnished mostly in pine; all of them have splendid views of the countryside—which you are invited to explore on the bikes the Karsts loan. Tastings and cellar tours are possible. **Pros:** quiet location amid the vines, friendly staff. **Cons:** far from the sights. ✉*In den Almen 15* ☎*06322/2862* 🌐*www.weingut-karst.de* *3 rooms, 6 apartments* *In-room: no a/c, refrigerator (some), DVD (some), Wi-Fi (some). In-hotel: bar, bicycles, no elevator, public Internet, public Wi-Fi, no-smoking rooms* 💳*No credit cards* ⏲*Closed Nov.–Feb.* 🍽*BP.*

NIGHTLIFE & THE ARTS

The **Spielbank** (*Casino* *€2.50*), in the Kurparkhotel, is a daily diversion after 2 PM; jacket and tie are no longer required, but no sports shoes or T-shirts are allowed. Free introductory tours are offered every other Thursday at 1 PM. Be certain to bring your passport for identification. Minimum age is 18.

Concerts and theater take place at **Kloster Limburg** (Limburg Monastery). Contact the local tourist office for program details.

SHOPPING

Several hundred wines from Bad Dürkheim and vicinity can be sampled and purchased daily (10–6) at the **WEINDOM** next to the "giant cask" on St. Michael Allee. The shop also sells other grape products and accessories. **TIP→ To learn how grapes are cultivated and wines are made, take the Saturday afternoon (4 PM) "Piccolo" tour, which begins at the WEINDOM with a glass of sparkling wine and is followed by a vineyard and cellar tour and tasting at Weingut Fitz-Ritter. Tours last 75 minutes (€6.50).**

FREINSHEIM

7 km (4½ mi) northeast of Bad Dürkheim, via Kallstadt, right turn to Freinsheim is signposted midway through Kallstadt.

The next village on the Wine Road north of Bad Dürkheim is **Kallstadt,** where you can enjoy Saumagen in your glass and on your plate—for this is the home of the excellent **Saumagen Vineyard.** Both its wine and the specialty dish are served with pride everywhere in town.

Off the Wine Road to the east, **Freinsheim's** *Stadtmauer* (town wall), probably built between 1400 and 1540, is one of the best-preserved fortifications in the Pfalz. Walk along it to see the massive town gates (Eisentor and Haintor) and the numerous towers. Many of the town's historical houses are baroque, including the **Rathaus** (1737), with its covered stairway and sandstone balustrade. Next to it is a **Protestant church,** a Gothic structure to which Renaissance and baroque elements were added over the years. No fewer than five large festivals are celebrated here between April and September—quite a showing for a town this small.

Drive 5 km (3 mi) west to Weisenheim am Berg (you'll cross over the Wine Road at Herxheim) and watch for signs toward Bobenheim and Kleinkarlbach. This road, which runs parallel to the Wine Road and along the vineyard heights, affords a wonderful panorama of the expansive vineyards stretching onto the Rhine Plain. Follow the signs to **Neuleiningen,** and then wind your way uphill to reach the romantic Old Town, ringed by a medieval wall. ■TIP→ **The ruins of the 13th-century castle are a good start for a town walk.**

WHERE TO EAT

$–$$ ✕ **Alt Freinsheim.** Chef Axel Steffl's domain is tucked away on a narrow ★ lane between Hauptstrasse and Freinsheim's town wall (northern edge). Old stone walls, exposed beams, and the tiny size of the restaurant make for a cozy dining experience. Whether you opt for his country cooking or a refined entrée with one of his creative sauces (pork fillet tips in bell-pepper and chili sauce), everything is homemade. The good selection of local wines is as reasonably priced as the food. ⊠ *Korng. 5, Freinsheim* ☎ *06353/2582* ⊕ *www.restaurant-alt-freinsheim.de* ⊟ *No credit cards* ◷ *Closed Wed. and 3 wks in July and Aug. No lunch.*

$–$$ ✕ **Weinhaus Henninger.** Walter Henninger numbers among the elite of Pfälzer vintners, but there's nothing pretentious about the atmosphere or cooking at his wood-panel wine pub. It's a jovial place, frequented by locals who come for the delicious, hearty fare and excellent wines. The soups, *Eintopf* dishes (stews), rump steak with sautéed onions, and daily specials are recommended. ⊠ *Weinstr. 93, Kallstadt* ☎ *06322/2277* ⊕ *www.weinhaus-henninger.de* ⊟ *No credit cards* ◷ *No lunch Mon., Jan.–Mar.*

WHERE TO STAY

$–$$ 🏨 **Hotel–Restaurant Alte Pfarrey.** Once a rectory, this hotel-restaurant ★ is on the hilltop above the Old Town of Neuleiningen. The comfortable inn with modern facilities is made up of several Gothic houses. Rooms are distinctive for their antique furnishings. After renovations in 2007, the restaurant is more elegant than ever; there are plans for a few new rooms. Silvio Lange, chef de cuisine and new director, continues the house tradition of personal service and first-rate culinary delights ($$$$). He has a penchant for frothy, flavorful sauces, and the Valrhona chocolate desserts are highly recommended. The wine list is very good, with offerings from the New and Old World. **Pros:** elegant decor, friendly staff, quiet location. **Con:** far from the sights. ⊠ *Unterg. 54 Neuleiningen* ☎ *06359/86066* ⊕ *www.altepfarrey.de* ⤙ *9 rooms* ⌂ *In-room: no a/c, Ethernet, Wi-Fi. In-hotel: restaurant, room service, no elevator, public Internet, public Wi-Fi, some pets allowed, no-smoking rooms* ⊟ *MC, V* ◷ *Hotel and restaurant closed 2 wks in Feb. Restaurant closed Mon. and Tues.*

$–$$ 🏨 **Hotel–Restaurant Luther.** A baroque manor next to Freinsheim's town Fodor'sChoice wall is the setting for this elegant country inn. Modern rooms are comfortable, and there are fresh flowers throughout the house. The handsome table settings and artistic food presentations make dining here ($$$$) a joy for all the senses. One of Germany's leading chefs, Dieter Luther is known for his imaginative combinations, such as lobster with

10

fennel or venison with kumquats. Save room for a chocolate creation or the crème brûlée quintet. Spanish, Bordeaux, and top Pfälzer wines are focal points of the wine list. **Pros:** quiet location, excellent restaurant. **Cons:** restaurant is expensive (although the quality justifies the price). ✉ *Hauptstr. 29 Freinsheim* ☎ *06353/93480* ⊕ *www.luther-freinsheim. de* ⇆ *20 rooms, 1 suite* 🖒 *In-room: no a/c, Wi-Fi. In-hotel: restaurant, no elevator, laundry service, no-smoking rooms* ⊟ *AE, MC, V* ⊗ *Hotel and restaurant closed Jan. and 2 wks in July or Aug. Restaurant closed Sun. No lunch* ⦿| *BP.*

$
★
Hotel–Restaurant Weinkastell Zum Weissen Ross. A wrought-iron sign depicting a *weisser Ross* (white stallion) adorns the cheerful facade of this half-timber house. Rooms have warm colors, solid oak furnishings, and modern baths, and several have romantic alcoves or four-poster beds. Jutta and Norbert Kohnke offer service and cuisine ($$$) that are top-notch. Most of the superb wines come from her brother's wine estate next door, Weingut Koehler-Ruprecht (■ **TIP**➜ **Tours and tastings are possible**), as well as red wines from his affiliated estates in Portugal and South Africa. This is the best place in the Pfalz to sample "Saumagen twice." **Pros:** beautiful old house, good restaurant. **Con:** some rooms on the small side. ✉ *Weinstr. 80–82 Kallstadt* ☎ *06322/5033* ⊕ *www.weinkastell-kohnke.de* ⇆ *13 rooms, 1 apartment* 🖒 *In-room: no a/c, Ethernet. In-hotel: restaurant, bicycles, no elevator, some pets allowed* ⊟ *AE, MC, V* ⊗ *Hotel closed Jan.–mid-Feb. Restaurant closed Mon. and Tues., Jan.–mid-Feb., and 1 wk late July–early Aug.* ⦿| *BP.*

EN ROUTE Neuleiningen is 4 km (2½ mi) west of the Wine Road town Kirchheim. **Bockenheim,** 10 km (6 mi) north, is dominated by an imposing gateway. There's a panoramic view of the Pfalz's "sea of vineyards" from the viewing platform. Like its counterpart in Schweigen-Rechtenbach, the **Haus der Deutschen Weinstrasse** marks the end (or start) of its namesake, the German Wine Road.

THE RHINE TERRACE

Like Speyer, the cities of Worms and Mainz were Free Imperial Cities and major centers of Christian and Jewish culture in the Middle Ages. Germany's first synagogue and Europe's oldest surviving Jewish cemetery, both from the 11th century, are in Worms. The imperial diets of Worms and Speyer in 1521 and 1529 stormed around Martin Luther (1483–1546) and the rise of Protestantism. In 1455 Johannes Gutenberg (1400–68), the inventor of movable type, printed the first Gutenberg Bible in Mainz.

WORMS

15 km (9 mi) east of Bockenheim via B–47 from Monsheim, 45 km (28 mi) south of Mainz on B–9.

Although devastated in World War II, Worms (pronounced *vawrms*) is among the most ancient cities of Germany, with a history going back some 6,000 years. Once settled by the Romans, Worms later became

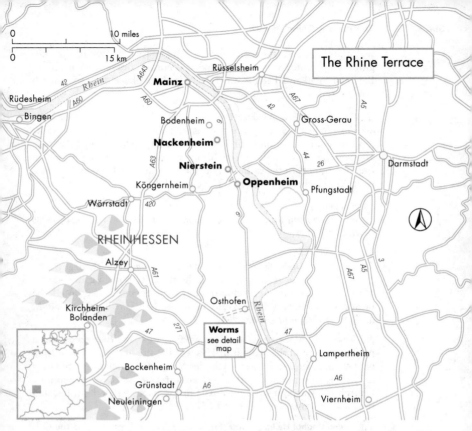

one of the imperial cities of the Holy Roman Empire. More than 100 imperial diets were held here, including the 1521 meeting where Martin Luther pleaded his cause. In addition to having a great Romanesque cathedral, Worms is a center of the wine trade.

Worms developed into an important garrison town under the Romans, but it's better known for its greatest legend, the *Nibelungenlied,* derived from the short-lived kingdom established by Gunther and his Burgundian tribe in the early 5th century. The complex and sprawling story was given its final shape in the 12th century and tells of love, betrayal, greed, war, and death. It ends when Attila the Hun defeats the Nibelungen (Burgundians), who find their court destroyed, their treasure lost, and their heroes dead. One of the most famous incidents tells how Hagen, treacherous and scheming, hurls the court riches into the Rhine. Near the Nibelungen Bridge there's a bronze statue of him caught in the act. The *Nibelungenlied* may be legend, but the story is based on fact. A Queen Brunhilda, for example, is said to have lived here. It's also known that a Burgundian tribe was defeated in 436 by Attila the Hun in what is present-day Hungary.

Not until Charlemagne resettled Worms almost 400 years later, making it one of the major cities of his empire, did the city prosper again. Worms was more than an administrative and commercial center; it was a great ecclesiastical city as well. The first expression of this religious importance was the original cathedral, consecrated in 1018. Between 1130 and 1181 it was rebuilt in three phases into the church you see today.

GETTING HERE & AROUND

Worms can be reached by direct trains from both Mannheim and Mainz (approximately 30 minutes from each). The city center is quite compact and negotiable on foot. Worms begins its tours at the southern portal (main entrance) of the cathedral on Saturday at 10:30 and Sunday at 2 from March through October. The cost is €4.

ESSENTIALS

Visitor Information Worms (⊠ *Tourist-Information, Neumarkt 14* ☎ *06241/25045* ⊕ *www.worms.de*).

EXPLORING

❹ The Lutheran **Dreifaltigkeitskirche** *(Church of the Holy Trinity)* is just across the square from the Heylshofgarten. Remodeling during the 19th and 20th centuries produced today's austere interior, although the facade and tower are still joyfully baroque. ⊠ *Marktpl.* ☉ *Apr.–Sept., daily 9–5; Oct.–Mar., daily 9–4.*

An imperial palace once stood in what is now the **Heylshofgarten**, a park just north of the cathedral. This was the site of the fateful meeting between Luther and Emperor Charles V in April 1521 that ultimately led to the Reformation. Luther refused to recant his theses demanding Church reforms and went into exile in Eisenach, where he translated the New Testament in 1521 and 1522.

❼ The **Judenfriedhof Heiliger Sand** *(Holy Sand Jewish Cemetery)* is the oldest Jewish cemetery in Europe and one of the most atmospheric and picturesque. The oldest of some 2,000 tombstones date from 1076. Entry is via the gate on Willy-Brandt-Ring. ⊠ *Andreasstr. and Willy-Brandt-Ring* ☉ *Daily.*

❸ The **Kunsthaus Heylshof** *(Heylshof ★ Art Gallery)* in the Heylshofgarten is one of the leading art museums of the region. It has an exquisite collection of German, Dutch, and French paintings as well as stained glass, glassware, porcelain, and ceramics from the 15th to the 19th century. ⊠ *Stephansg. 9* ☎ *06241/22000* ⊕ *www.museum-heylshof.de* ☒ *€2.50* ☉ *May–Sept., Tues.–Sun. 11–5; Oct.–Dec. and mid-Feb.–Apr., Tues.–Sat. 2–5, Sun. 11–5.*

> ### TOURING TIPS
>
> **Information:** The tourist office is near the cathedral. Pick up "Two Thousand Years of History," a handy map with suggested walking tours and descriptions of the main sights.
>
> **Scenic Spots:** The Old Town wall between the two towers of the Nibelungen Museum affords a great view of the town.
>
> **Scenic Spots:** From the Holy Sand Jewish Cemetery there is a good view of a portion of the massive Old Town wall, and the cemetery itself is worth exploring.

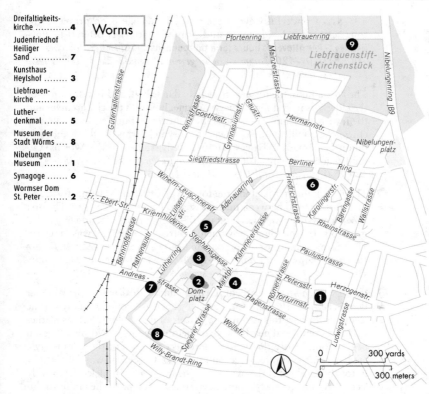

9 On the northern outskirts of Worms, the twin-tower Gothic **Liebfrauen-kirche** *(Church of Our Lady)* is set amid vineyards. ■ TIP→ **The church is the namesake of the mild white wine named Liebfraumilch, literally, the "Milk of Our Lady."** Today this popular wine can be made from grapes grown throughout Rheinhessen, the Pfalz, the Nahe, and the Rheingau wine regions, since the original, small vineyard surrounding the church could not possibly meet demand.

5 The **Lutherdenkmal** *(Luther Monument)* commemorates Luther's appearance at the Diet of Worms. He ended his speech with the words: "Here I stand. I have no choice. God help me. Amen." The 19th-century monument includes a large statue of Luther ringed by other figures from the Reformation. It's set in a small park on the street named Lutherring.

8 To bone up on the history of Worms, visit the **Museum der Stadt Worms** *(Municipal Museum)*, housed in the cloisters of a Romanesque church in the Andreasstift. ✉ *Weckerlingpl. 7* ☎ *06241/946–390* 🖼 *€2* ⊙ *Tues.– Sun. 10–5.*

1 The *Nibelungenlied* comes to life in the **Nibelungen Museum,** a stunning
★ sight-and-sound exhibition cleverly installed in two medieval towers and the portion of the Old Town wall between them. The structure itself is architecturally fascinating inside and out, and the rampart

affords a wonderful view of the town. Language is no problem: the tour script (via headphones and printed matter) is offered in English. ■TIP➔ **Allow 1½ hours for a thorough visit.** ✉*Fischerpförtchen 10* ☎*06241/202–120* ⊕*www.nibelungen-museum.de* 💲*€5.50* ⊙*Tues.–Fri. 10–5, weekends 10–6.*

The **Raschi-Haus,** the former study hall, dance hall, and Jewish home for the elderly, is next door to the synagogue. It houses the city archives and the **Jewish Museum.** The well-written illustrated booklet *Jewish Worms* chronicles a millennium of Jewish history in Worms. Rashi (Rabbi Solomon ben Isaac of Troyes [1040–1105]) studied at the Worms Talmud academy in circa 1060. ✉*Hintere Judeng. 6* ☎*06241/853–4707* 💲*€1.50* ⊙*Tues.–Sun. 10–12:30 and 1:30–5.*

❻ The Jewish quarter is along the town wall between Martinspforte and
★ Friesenspitze and between Judengasse and Hintere Judengasse. The first **Synagoge** *(synagogue)* was built in 1034, rebuilt in 1175, and expanded in 1213 with a building for women. Destroyed in 1938, it was rebuilt in 1961 using as much of the original masonry as had survived. ✉*Hintere Judeng.* ⊙*Apr.–Oct., daily 10–12:30 and 1:30–5; Nov.–Mar., daily 10–noon and 2–4; closed during services.*

❷ If you've seen Speyer Cathedral, you'll quickly realize that the **Wormser**
★ **Dom St. Peter** *(Cathedral of St. Peter),* by contrast, contains many Gothic elements. In part this is simply a matter of chronology. Speyer Cathedral was completed nearly 70 years before the one in Worms was even begun, long before the lighter, more vertical lines of the Gothic style evolved. Furthermore, once built, Speyer Cathedral was left largely untouched, whereas the Worms Cathedral was remodeled frequently as new architectural styles and new values developed. The Gothic influence can be seen both inside and out, from the elaborate tympanum with biblical scenes over the southern portal (today's entrance) to the great rose window in the west choir to the five sculptures in the north aisle recounting the life of Christ. The cathedral was completely gutted by fire in 1689 in the War of the Palatinate Succession. For this reason many of the furnishings are baroque, including the magnificent gilt high altar from 1742, designed by the master architect Balthasar Neumann (1687–1753). The choir stalls are no less decorative. They were built between 1755 and 1759 in rococo style. Walk around the building to see the artistic detail of the exterior. ✉*Dompl.* ☎*06241/6115* 💲*Donation requested* ⊙*Apr.–Oct., daily 9–6; Nov.–Mar., daily 9–5; closed during services.*

WHERE TO EAT

$$$–$$$$ ✕**Rôtisserie Dubs.** A pioneer of the Rheinhessen restaurant scene, Wolf-
★ gang Dubs focused on creative regional cuisine and seasonal specialties long before it was in vogue. Fish, fowl, meat, and game are all expertly prepared and garnished—often with an Asian or Mediterranean accent. ■TIP➔ **For a more casual meal, try his cozy Gasthaus Zum Schiff ($–$$), next door, where the daily specials are a very good value.** A wine enthusiast, Dubs offers his own wines, top German and French estates, and a few New World wines, such as Opus One. Rheindürkheim is 9 km (5½

mi) north of Worms via B–9. The restaurant is near the *Kirche* (church), not far from the riverbank. ⊠*Kirchstr. 6, Worms-Rheindürkheim* ☎*06242/2023* ⊕*www.dubs.de* ⊟*AE, MC, V* ⊗*Closed Tues. and 2 wks in Jan. No lunch Sat.*

¢–$ ✕**Gasthaus Hagenbräu.** Located a little to the west of the center, by the banks of the Rhine, this house brewery serves a good range of classic German dishes and regional specialties such as Saumagen to soak up the beers that are produced on the premises. Service and decor are bright and cheery, and you will be surrounded by copper vats and oak barrels as you dine. The summer terrace by the river is a chance to enjoy a brew with a view. ⊠*Am Rhein 3* ☎*06241/921–100* ⊟*MC, V* ⊗*Closed Mon.*

WHERE TO STAY

$$ ⊡**Dom-Hotel.** The appeal of this hotel with modern, comfortable rooms lies in its friendly staff and its terrific location in the heart of the pedestrian zone (a parking garage is available). **Pro:** centrally located. **Con:** modern building design is somewhat unappealing. ⊠*Obermarkt 10* ☎*06241/9070* ⊕*www.dom-hotel.de* ⤶*54 rooms, 2 suites* ⌂*In-room: no a/c, Ethernet, Wi-Fi (some). In-hotel: room service, laundry service, public Wi-Fi, some pets allowed, no-smoking rooms* ⊟*AE, DC, MC, V* �*BP.*

$ ⊡**Haus Kalisch am Dom.** For more than 30 years the friendly Kalisch family has welcomed guests to its little inn opposite the cathedral. There are no frills, but the rooms are comfortable and have private baths and TVs. **Pro:** central location. **Con:** can be noisy at night. ⊠*Neumarkt 9* ☎*06241/27666* ⤶*13 rooms* ⌂*In-room: no a/c, no phone. In-hotel: no elevator* ⊟*No credit cards* ⊗*Closed 3 wks in Dec. and Jan.* 101*BP.*

$ ⊡**Hotel and Weinstube Römischer Kaiser.** Housed in an 18th-century baroque patrician manor in the center of town, the "Roman Emperor" is a down-to-earth, friendly little hotel and wine pub ($–$$) that quickly fills up with regulars in the evening. Simple, hearty fare is served, such as Flammkuchen, Saumagen, or Wormser *Hackbraten* (meatloaf). The *Fischteller* (fish platter) and grilled meat platter are especially popular. You can also dine on the rooftop terrace and in the vaulted cellar. **Pros:** friendly, central location, good value, popular restaurant. **Cons:** street can be noisy on weekdays, some bathrooms quite small. ⊠*Römerstr. 72* ☎*06241/498–740* ⊕*www.hotel-roemischer-kaiser.eu* ⤶*11 rooms* ⌂*In-room: no a/c, Wi-Fi (some). In-hotel: restaurant, bicycles, no elevator, laundry service, public Wi-Fi, some pets allowed, no-smoking rooms* ⊟*No credit cards* ⊗*Restaurant closed Mon. No lunch Nov.–Mar.* 101*BP.*

$ ⊡**Landhotel Zum Schwanen.** Bärbel Berkes runs this lovingly restored country inn in Osthofen (10 km [6 mi] northwest of Worms). You can linger over a meal or a glass of wine in its pretty courtyard, the hub of the 18th-century estate. Like the rooms, the restaurant ($–$$) is light, airy, and furnished with sleek, contemporary furniture. Regional favorites are served as well as dishes with a Mediterranean touch. The lineup of local wines is exemplary. The beer garden is also inviting. **Pros:** quiet location, friendly staff. **Con:** far from the sights. ⊠*Friedrich-Ebert-*

10

Str. 40, west of B–9 Osthofen ☎06242/9140 🌐www.zum-schwanen-osthofen.de ⇒30 rooms, 4 suites ♁In-room: no a/c, Ethernet (some). In-hotel: restaurant, room service, public Internet, some pets allowed, no-smoking rooms ▭AE, DC, MC, V ⊙Hotel and restaurant closed 2 wks July and Aug. No lunch Sat. No dinner Sun. 🍽BP.

¢–$ **Land- und Winzerhotel Bechtel.** The friendly Bechtel family, winegrowers and proud parents of a former German Wine Queen, offer very pleasant accommodations on the grounds of their wine estate in the suburb of Heppenheim, about 10 km (6 mi) west of Worms (leave Worms on Speyerer Strasse, an extension of Valckenbergstrasse, which runs parallel to the east side of the Dom). The rooms were recently modernized, and all have balconies. You can enjoy country cooking (daily specials) as well as more refined fare with the estate's wines in the restaurant ($–$$). Wine tastings in the vaulted cellars are also possible. **Pros:** quiet location, excellent value for money, rooms have balconies. **Con:** far from the sights. ✉*Pfälzer Waldstr. 100 Worms-Heppenheim ☎06241/36536 🌐www.landhotel-bechtel.de ⇒11 rooms ♁In-room: no a/c, Ethernet. In-hotel: restaurant, room service, bar, gym, bicycles, no elevator, laundry service, public Internet, some pets allowed, no-smoking rooms ▭AE, MC, V 🍽BP.*

NIGHTLIFE & THE ARTS

In 2008, while the **Städtisches Spiel- und Festhaus,** the cultural hub of Worms, is renovated, performances will be held in the **Lincoln Theater** (✉*Obermarkt 10 ☎06241/88385*). Concerts are also held in the Municipal Museum, in the Andreasstift, and at the 19th-century palace Schloss Herrnsheim, in the northern suburb of Herrnsheim.

SHOPPING

For tasteful wine accessories, other products of the grape, and excellent wines, drop by P.J. Valckenberg's wine shop, **Der Weinladen** (✉*Weckerlingpl. 1 ☎06241/911–180 ▭No credit cards ⊙Closed Sun. and Mon.*), near the Municipal Museum and opposite the cathedral. In 2008, "1808 Spätlese," a special bicentennial wine commemorating the purchase of the Liebfrauenstift-Kirchenstuck vineyard surrounding the Liebfrauenkirche, will be offered.

OPPENHEIM

26 km (16 mi) north of Worms, 23 km (16 mi) south of Mainz on B–9.

★ En route to Oppenheim, the vine-covered hills parallel to the Rhine gradually steepen. Then, unexpectedly, the spires of Oppenheim's Gothic **Katharinenkirche** *(St. Katharine's Church)* come into view. The contrast of its pink sandstone facade against a bright blue sky is striking. Built between 1220 and 1439, it's the most important Gothic church between Strasbourg and Köln. The interior affords a rare opportunity to admire original 14th-century stained-glass windows and two magnificent rose windows, the Lily Window and the Rose of Oppenheim. The church houses masterfully carved tombstones, while the chapel behind it has a *Beinhaus* (charnel house) that contains the bones of

20,000 citizens and soldiers from the 15th to 18th century. ⊠*Katharinenstr. at Merianstr., just north of market sq.* ☎*06133/926–685* ⊘*Apr.–Oct., daily 8–6; Nov.–Mar., daily 9–5.*

Oppenheim and its neighbors to the north, Nierstein and Nackenheim, are home to Rheinhessen's best-known, top vineyards. The **Deutsches Weinbaumuseum** *(German Viticultural Museum)* —completely renovated in 2007—has wine-related artifacts that chronicle the region's 2,000-year-old winemaking tradition, not to mention the world's largest collection of mousetraps and more than 2,000 corkscrews. ⊠*Wormser Str. 49* ☎*06133/2544* ⊕*www.dwb-museum.de* ⊠*€3* ⊘*Apr.–Oct., Tues.–Fri. 2–5, weekends 10–5.*

NIGHTLIFE & THE ARTS

Concerts are held in St. Katharine's, and open-air theater takes place in the **Burgruine Landskrone,** the 12th-century imperial fortress ruins a few minutes' walk northwest of the church. ■TIP➔ From here there's a wonderful view of the town and the vineyards, extending all the way to Worms on a clear day.

NIERSTEIN

3 km (2 mi) north of Oppenheim on B–9.

Surrounded by 2,700 acres of vines, Nierstein is the largest wine-growing community on the Rhine and boasts Germany's oldest documented **vineyard** (AD 742), Glöck, surrounding St. Kilian's Church.

You can sample wines at the **Winzergenossenschaft** *(cooperative winery* ⊠*Karolingerstr. 6),* which is the starting point of an easy hike or drive to the vineyard heights and the vantage point at the *Wartturm* (watchtower). Tasting stands are set up along the route, providing delightful wine presentations in the vineyards *am roten Hang* (referring to the steep sites of red soils of slate, clay, and sand) in mid-June.

WHERE TO STAY

$$ ★ **Best Western Wein & Parkhotel.** Quiet elegance and Mediterranean flair mark this country inn. Spacious, light rooms decorated in warm shades of ocher, chic bathrooms, and an inviting lounge and terrace make for comfortable, relaxing quarters. Cuisine at the restaurant Am Heyl'schen Garten($$) ranges from barbecue on the terrace to well-prepared regional specialties and dishes with an Asian touch. Sunday lunch is a generous family buffet ($$$). The Irish pub serves light fare. The staff is exceptionally cheerful and competent. **Pros:** friendly, quiet location. **Cons:** a chain hotel offering few surprises. ⊠*An der Kaiserlinde 1* ☎*06133/5080* ⊕*www.weinhotel.bestwestern.de* ⤸*55 rooms* ⚬*In-room: Ethernet. In-hotel: restaurant, room service, bar, pool, gym, bicycles, public Internet, public Wi-Fi, no-smoking rooms* ⊟AE, MC, V ⍩BP.

$ ★ **Jordan's Untermühle.** The spacious grounds of an old mill are home to two restaurants and a country inn. The upper two stories of the inn have dormer rooms with wooden floors and furnishings. For dining options, choose between the airy Restaurant im Wintergarten,

10

the shady courtyard in summer, or sit beneath exposed beams in the Vinothek. All offer the same menu ($–$$), featuring refined gourmet dishes and heartier country fare; the wine list is a remarkable selection of red and white Rheinhessen wines. **Pros:** beautiful buildings, great value, very quiet. **Cons:** a long way from anywhere, difficult to reach without your own transport. ☒ *Ausserhalb 1 Köngernheim* ✛ *west of B–9, at Nierstein turn left on B–420 (toward Wörrstadt), drive through Köngernheim and turn right toward Selzen* ☎ *06737/71000* ⊕ *www. jordans-untermuehle.de* ☞ *25 rooms, 1 suite* ♿ *In-room: no a/c, Ethernet (some), Wi-Fi (some). In-hotel: 3 restaurants, bicycles, no elevator, laundry service, public Wi-Fi, some pets allowed, no-smoking rooms* ▭ *MC, V* ☽ *No lunch except Sun.* ℺ *BP.*

NACKENHEIM

5 km (3 mi) north of Nierstein on B–9.

This wine village lies slightly to the west of B–9; from the south, turn left and cross the railroad tracks (opposite the tip of the island in the Rhine) to reach the town center, 2 km (1 mi) down the country road. The writer Carl Zuckmayer (1896–1977) was born here, and immortalized the town in his farce *Der fröhliche Weinberg* (*The Merry Vineyard*) in 1925. He described Rheinhessen wine as "the wine of laughter…charming and appealing." You can put his words to the test the last weekend of July, when wine-festival booths are set up between the half-timber town hall on Carl-Zuckmayer-Platz and the baroque **Church of St. Gereon.** The church's scrolled gables, belfry, and elaborate altars are worth seeing.

WHERE TO STAY & EAT

$–$$ ✕ **Zum alten Zollhaus.** Walk through the arched gateway to reach the beautiful garden and entrance to this historic house. Cozy niches, fresh flowers, and handsome antiques provide a pleasant setting for good food and wine. Ilse Hees, the friendly proprietor, offers standards such as *in Dornfelder geschmorte Kalbsbäckchen* (tender veal jowls braised in red wine) or the *Zollhausteller,* a platter of various fillets. The wine list focuses on Rheinhessen wines, and a good number are available by the glass. ☒ *Wormser Str. 7* ☎ *06135/8726* ⊕ *www. zum-alten-zollhaus.de* ▭ *No credit cards* ☽ *Closed Sun. and Mon., 2 wks in Feb. and Mar., and 2 wks in Oct. No lunch.*

$ ▦ **Kartäuser Hof Hotel.** Michaela Schmidt runs this smart little bed-and-breakfast in the wine village of Bodenheim, 9 km (5½ mi) south of Mainz. The historic house has rooms with modern amenities. Drinks are available in the lounge, and if you can find the energy, bicycles can be borrowed. Its location within walking distance of many local vintners' pubs and the personal service offered also make it an attractive overnight option. **Pros:** friendly, good value, quiet. **Con:** rooms are quite small. ☒ *Gaustr. 21 Bodenheim* ☎ *06135/702– 880* ⊕ *www.kartaeuserhof.de* ☞ *11 rooms* ♿ *In-room: no a/c, dial-up, Wi-Fi (some). In-hotel: no elevator, public Internet, some pets allowed, no-smoking rooms* ▭ *MC, V* ℺ *BP.*

$ 🏠 **St. Gereon Restaurant and Landhotel.** The modern rooms in this half-timber country inn have blond-wood floors and light-color furnishings. Stone walls and light pine furniture on terra-cotta tiles give the restaurant ($–$$) a warm, rustic look, too. The food in the restaurant is traditional, and on Friday and Saturday evenings from October to March hearty regional specialties and Flammkuchen are served in the Weinstube (¢–$) in the vaulted cellar. The selection of Rheinhessen and Rheingau wines is small but very good. **Pros:** friendly, quiet, good value restaurant. **Con:** some rooms on the small side. ✉ *Carl-Zuckmayer-Pl. 3* ☎ *06135/704–590* ⊕ *www.landhotel-st-gereon.com* ➪ *15 rooms* ⌂ *In-room: no a/c, Wi-Fi. In-hotel: restaurant, no elevator, laundry service, public Internet, public Wi-Fi, some pets allowed, no-smoking rooms* ▤ *AE, MC, V* ⊘ *No lunch Mon. (restaurant only)* ⏏ *BP.*

SPORTS & THE OUTDOORS

BIKING   The old towpath along the riverbank is an ideal cycling trail to Mainz or Worms, and the vineyard paths are well suited for exploring the countryside.

HIKING   Enjoy the views from the vineyard heights on the **Rheinhöhenweg** trail. Allow three hours to hike the 10-km (6-mi) stretch between Nackenheim, Nierstein, and Oppenheim. Start at the corner of Weinbergstrasse and Johann-Winkler-Strasse. The educational wine path through the St. Alban vineyard is a pleasant walk in Bodenheim (4 km [2½ mi] northwest of Nackenheim).

MAINZ

14 km (9 mi) north of Nackenheim, 45 km (28 mi) north of Worms on B–9, and 42 km (26 mi) west of Frankfurt on A–3.

Mainz is the capital of the state of Rheinland-Pfalz. Today's city was built on the site of a Roman citadel from 38 BC. Given its central location at the confluence of the Main and Rhine rivers, it's not surprising that Mainz has always been an important trading center, rebuilt time and time again in the wake of wars.

GETTING HERE & AROUND

As the regional hub, Mainz is well served by trains, with fast connections to Frankfurt (40 mins) and Cologne (1 hour 40 mins). The station is a short walk west of the center. A comprehensive network of local buses makes getting around the city a breeze (route maps and timetables are posted at bus stops), while the upper areas of town are also served by trams. Although fairly spread out, those with a little energy will find all the sights are quite manageable on foot.

Mainz has year-round tours departing Saturday at 2 (€5) from the Touristik Centrale. The office is one story above street level on the footbridge over Rheinstrasse. There are additional tours from May through October, Wednesday and Friday at 2.

10

DISCOUNTS & DEALS
To see the sights, head for the Touristik Centrale (tourist office) to pick up a *MainzCard,* **a two-day pass, for about €10.** It covers a basic walking tour, unlimited use of public transportation (including travel to and from Frankfurt Airport), and free entry to museums and the casino, as well as a reduction in price on some KD cruises and theater tickets. The card can also be bought from the station, some hotel receptions, and participating museums.

ESSENTIALS
Visitor Information Mainz (⊠ *Touristik Centrale, Brückenturm am Rathaus* ☎ *06131/286–2114* 🖷 *06131/286–2155* ⊕ *www.info-mainz.de/tourist*).

EXPLORING
The **Marktplatz** and *Höfchen* (little courtyard) around the cathedral are the focal points of the town. ■TIP→ **Both are especially colorful on Tuesday, Friday, and Saturday, when farmers set up their stands to sell produce and flowers.**

★ The entrance to the **Dom** *(Cathedral of St. Martin and St. Stephan)* is on the south side of the market square, midway between the eastern and western chancels, which symbolize the worldly empire and the priestly realm, respectively. Emperor Otto II began building the oldest of the Rhineland's trio of grand Romanesque cathedrals in 975, the year in which he named Willigis archbishop and chancellor of the empire. Henry II, the last Saxon emperor of the Holy Roman Empire, was crowned here in 1002, as was his successor, Konrad II, the first Salian emperor, in 1024. In 1009, on the very day of its consecration, the cathedral burned to the ground. It was the first of seven fires the Dom has endured in the course of its millennium. Today's cathedral dates mostly from the 11th to 13th century. During the Gothic period, remodeling diluted the Romanesque identity of the original; an imposing baroque spire was added in the 18th century. Nevertheless, the building remains essentially Romanesque, and its floor plan demonstrates a clear link to the cathedrals in Speyer and Worms. The interior is a virtual sculpture gallery of elaborate monuments and tombstones of archbishops, bishops, and canons, many of which are significant artworks from the 13th to 19th centuries. ⊠ *Domstr. 3 (Markt)* ☎ *06131/253–412* ⊠ *Donations requested* ⊙ *Mar.–Oct., weekdays 9–6:30, Sat. 9–4, Sun. 1–2:45 and 4–6:30; Nov.–Feb., weekdays 9–5, Sat. 9–4, Sun. 1–2:45 and 4–5; closed during services.*

From the Middle Ages until secularization in the early 19th century, the archbishops of Mainz, who numbered among the imperial electors, were extremely influential politicians and property owners. The wealth of religious art treasures they left behind can be viewed in the **Dom und Diözesanmuseum** in the cathedral cloisters. ⊠ *Domstr. 3* ☎ *06131/253–344* ⊕ *www.dommuseum-mainz.de* 🖾 *€3.50, Schatzkammer (treasure chamber) €3, combination ticket €5.* ⊙ *Tues.–Sun. 10–5.*

★ Opposite the east end of the cathedral (closest to the Rhine) is the fascinating **Gutenberg Museum,** devoted to the history of writing and printing from Babylonian and Egyptian times to the present. Exhibits include historical printing presses, incunabula (books printed in Europe before 1501), and medieval manuscripts with illuminated letters, as well as three precious 42-line Gutenberg Bibles printed circa 1455. A replica workshop demonstrates how Gutenberg implemented his invention of movable type. ✉ *Liebfrauenpl. 5* ☎ *06131/122–640* ⊕ *www.gutenberg-museum.de* 🎫 *€5* ⊗ *Tues.– Sat. 9–5, Sun. 11–3.*

★ The Kurfürstliches Schloss (Electoral Palace) houses the **Römisch-Germanisches Zentralmuseum,** a wonderful collection of original artifacts and copies of items that chronicle cultural developments in the area up to the early Middle Ages. One of the highlights is a tiny Celtic glass dog from the 1st or 2nd century BC. The museum entrance is around the back, on the river (east) side of the building. ✉ *Ernst-Ludwig-Pl. on Grosse Bleiche* ☎ *06131/91240* ⊕ *www.rgzm.de* 🎫 *Free* ⊗ *Tues.–Sun. 10–6.*

The remains of five 4th-century wooden Roman warships and two full-size replicas are on display at the **Museum für Antike Schiffahrt** *(Museum of Ancient Navigation)*. These were unearthed in 1981 when the foundation for the Hilton's wing was dug. For more than a decade the wood was injected with a water-and-paraffin mixture to restore hardness. ✉ *Neutorstr. 2b* ☎ *06131/286–630* 🎫 *Free* ⊗ *Tues.–Sun. 10–6.*

The various collections of the **Landesmuseum** *(Museum of the State of Rheinland-Pfalz)* are in the former electors' stables, easily recognized by the statue of a golden stallion over the entrance. Exhibits range from the Middle Ages to the 20th century. Among the highlights are paintings by Dutch masters, artworks from the baroque to art-nouveau period, and collections of porcelain and faience. ✉ *Grosse Bleiche 49– 51* ☎ *06131/28570* ⊕ *www.landesmuseum-mainz.de* 🎫 *€3, free Sat.* ⊗ *Tues. 10–8, Wed.–Sun. 10–5.*

10

Schillerplatz, ringed by beautiful baroque palaces, is the site of the ebullient **Fastnachtsbrunnen** (Carnival Fountain), with 200 figures related to Mainz's "fifth season" of the year.

★ From Schillerplatz it's but a short walk up Gaustrasse to **St. Stephanskirche** *(St. Stephen's Church)*, which affords a hilltop view of the city. In 990 Willigis built a basilica on the site; today's Gothic church dates from the late 13th and early 14th centuries. Postwar restoration included the installation of six vividly blue stained-glass windows depicting scenes from the Bible, designed in the 1970s by the Russian-born painter Marc Chagall. ✉ *Kleine Weissg. 12, via Gaustr.* ☎ *06131/231–640* ⊗ *Mon.–Sat. 10–5, Sun. noon–5.*

CLOSE UP

The Father of Modern Printing

His invention—printing with movable type—transformed the art of communication, yet much about the life and work of Johannes Gutenberg is undocumented, starting with his year of birth. It's estimated that he was born in Mainz circa 1400 into a patrician family that supplied the city mint with metal to be coined. Gutenberg's later accomplishments attest to his own skill in working with metals. Details about his education are unclear, but he probably helped finance his studies by copying manuscripts in a monastic scriptorium. He moved to Strasbourg circa 1434, where he was a goldsmith by day and an inventor by night. It was here that he worked—in great secrecy—to create movable type and develop a press suitable for printing by adapting the conventional screw press used for winemaking. By 1448 Gutenberg

had returned to Mainz. Loans from a wealthy businessman enabled him to set up a printer's workshop and print the famous 42-line Bible. The lines of text are in black ink, yet each of the original 180 Bibles printed from 1452 to 1455 is unique, thanks to the artistry of the handpainted illuminated letters.

Despite its significance, Gutenberg's invention was not a financial success. His quest for perfection rather than profit led to a legal battle during which his creditor was awarded the workshop and the Bible type. Gutenberg's attempts to set up another print shop in Mainz failed, but from 1465 until his death in 1468 he received an allowance for service to the archbishop of Mainz, which spared the "father of modern printing" from dying in poverty.

The hillside **Kupferberg Sektkellerei** *(sparkling wine cellars)* were built in 1850 on a site where the Romans cultivated vines and built cellars. The Kupferberg family expanded the cellars into 60 seven-story-deep vaulted cellars—the deepest in the world. The winery has a splendid collection of glassware; posters from the belle epoque period (1898–1914); richly carved casks from the 18th and 19th centuries; and the **Traubensaal** (Grape Hall), a tremendous example of the art nouveau style. Two-hour tours include a tasting of five sparkling wines; 1½-hour tours include three sparkling wines; 1¼-hour tours include one glass of Sekt. Reservations are required. ⊠ *Kupferbergterrasse 17–19* ☎ *06131/9230* ⊕ *www. kupferbergterrasse.de* 🖃 *2-hr tours €13.50, 1½-hr tours €11.50, 1¼-hr tours €7.50* ⊙ *Shop Mon.–Sat. 10–6* 🖃 *MC, V.*

WHERE TO EAT

$$$ ✗ **Maus im Mollers.** For a fabulous view of Mainz, head for the terrace (fourth floor) or glass-lined restaurant atop the state theater (sixth floor). Use the entrance on the left side of the building. Talented young chef Dirk Maus prepares regional dishes, often with an exotic twist, such as veal fillet and liver with capers, vanilla, and cinnamon. His cooking is very aromatic, colorful, flavorful, and made with the freshest ingredients possible. The wine list is very good, particularly the selection of Rheinhessen wines. ⊠ *Gutenbergpl. 7* ☎ *06131/627–9211* ⊕ *www.mollers.de* 🖃 *AE, MC, V* ⊙ *Closed Mon., Tues., and 4 wks in late July and Aug.*

$$-$$$ ✕**Gebert's Weinstuben.** Gebert's
★ traditional wine restaurant serves refined versions of regional favorites in a very personal atmosphere. The homemade noodles and the *Schweinelendchen unter der Handkäs-Kruste* (pork tenderloin under a cheese crust) are very popular. The *geeister Kaffee* (coffee ice cream and chocolate praline in a cup of coffee) uses delicious, handmade chocolate pralines. German wines (especially Rheinhessen) dominate

the excellent wine list. Summer dining alfresco is possible in the smartly renovated courtyard. ⊠*Frauenlobstr. 94, near Rhine* ☎*06131/611–619* ⊕*www.geberts-weinstuben.de* ▤*AE, DC, MC, V* ⊗*Closed Mon. and 3 wks in July or Aug. No lunch Sat.*

$–$$ ✕**Haus des Deutschen Weines.** Late hours and luncheon specials (€5.50) are among the crowd-pleasers here, and the menu is broad enough to encompass both snacks and full-course meals, both huge salads and game year-round. Mainz specialties include *Spundekäs* (cheese whipped with cream and onions) or *Handkäse mit Musik* (pungent, semihard cheese served with diced onions in vinaigrette). As the name suggests, there's a great selection of German wines. ⊠*Gutenbergpl. 3–5* ☎*06131/221–300* ⊕*www.hdw-mainz.de* ▤*AE, DC, MC, V.*

$–$$ ✕**Heiliggeist.** This lively café-bistro-bar serves breakfast, lunch, and dinner on weekends and dinner until midnight during the week. Modern, minimal decor provides an interesting contrast to the historic vaulted ceilings in this former almshouse and hospital church dating from 1236. In summer the beer garden is always packed. The compact menu includes elaborate salad platters as well as creatively spiced and sauced fish and meat dishes. One house specialty worth trying is the *Croustarte,* an upscale version of pizza. There's an extensive drink list. ⊠*Mailandsg. 11* ☎*06131/225–757* ⊕*www.heiliggeist-mainz.de* ▤*No credit cards* ⊗*No lunch weekdays.*

¢–$ ✕**Eisgrub-Bräu.** It's loud, it's lively, and the beer is brewed in the vaulted cellars on-site. An Eisgrub brew is just the ticket to wash down a hearty plate of *Haxen* (pork hocks) or *Meterwurst* (yard-long, rolled bratwurst), *Bratkartoffeln* (home fries), and sauerkraut. A breakfast buffet (daily) and a buffet lunch (weekdays) are also served. ■TIP→ **Brewery tours are free, but make a reservation in advance.** It's open daily 9 AM–1 AM, weekends until 2 AM. ⊠*Weisslilieng. 1a* ☎*06131/221–104* ⊕*www.eisgrub.de* ▤*MC, V.*

WHERE TO STAY

$$$–$$$$ ▦**Hyatt Regency Mainz.** The blend of contemporary art and architecture with the old stone walls of historical Fort Malakoff on the Rhine is a visually stunning success. From the spacious atrium lobby to the luxurious rooms, everything is sleek, modern, and designed for comfort. The M-Lounge & Bar in the lobby serves light fare, and tables in the garden courtyard are always at a premium in the summer. The

10

boutiques and pubs of the Old Town are a 5- to 10-minute walk away. **Pros:** grand public spaces, friendly, riverside location. **Cons:** top-end rooms expensive. ⊠*Malakoff-Terrasse 1* ☎*06131/731–234* ⊕*www. mainz.regency.hyatt.com* ⇱*265 rooms, 3 suites* ⋌*In-room: DVD, VCR, Ethernet. In-hotel: 2 restaurants, room service, bar, pool, gym, concierge, laundry service, public Internet, no-smoking rooms* ⊟*AE, DC, MC, V.*

$$–$$$ ⬚ **FAVORITE parkhotel.** Mainz's city park is a lush setting for the Barth
★ family's hotel, restaurants, and beer garden with a Rhine view; it's a 10-minute downhill walk through the park to the Old Town. The rooms are quite comfortable, and there are wellness facilities and a rooftop sundeck with a Jacuzzi. The Stadtpark ($$–$$$) serves international cuisine (lobster is a specialty); casual dining is available in the hotel's three other restaurants ($$–$$$). **Pros:** quiet location, friendly staff, good views. **Cons:** a bit from the sights. ⊠*Karl-Weiser-Str. 1* ☎*06131/80150* ⊕*www.favorite-mainz.de* ⇱*115 rooms, 7 suites* ⋌*In-room: no a/c (some), Ethernet, Wi-Fi. In-hotel: 4 restaurants, room service, bar, pool, gym, bicycles, concierge, laundry service, public Internet, public Wi-Fi, some pets allowed, no-smoking rooms* ⊟*AE, MC, V* ☼*Stadtpark closed Sun. evening and Mon.* ⦿*BP.*

$–$$ ⬚ **Hotel Ibis.** Here you'll find modern, functional rooms and a great location on the edge of the Old Town. Ask about the various discount rates that are available (except during trade fairs and major events). **Pros:** central location, good online deals often available. **Cons:** chain hotel lacking in character. ⊠*Holzhofstr. 2, at Rheinstr.* ☎*06131/2470* ⊕*www.ibishotel.com* ⇱*144 rooms* ⋌*In-room: dial-up, Wi-Fi (some). In-hotel: bar, laundry service, public Internet, public Wi-Fi, some pets allowed, no-smoking rooms* ⊟*AE, DC, MC, V* ⦿*BP.*

NIGHTLIFE & THE ARTS

Mainz supports a broad spectrum of cultural events—music (from classical to avant-garde), dance, opera, and theater performances—at many venues throughout the city. Music lovers can attend concerts in venues ranging from the cathedral, the Kurfürstliches Schloss, and the Kupferberg sparkling wine cellars to the Rathaus, market square, and historic churches.

Nightlife is centered in the numerous wine pubs. Rustic and cozy, they're packed with locals who come to enjoy a meal or snack with a glass (or more) of local wine. Most are on the Old Town's main street, **Augustinerstrasse,** and its side streets (Grebenstrasse, Kirschgarten, Kartäuserstrasse, Jakobsbergstrasse), or around the Gutenberg Museum, on Liebfrauenplatz. The wood-panel pub **Wilhelmi** (⊠*Rheinstr. 53* ☎*06131/224–949)* is a favorite with the post-student crowd. **Schreiner** (⊠*Rheinstr. 38* ☎*06131/225–720)* attracts a mixed, jovial clientele and is an old, traditional Mainz favorite.

SHOPPING

The Old Town is full of boutiques, and the major department stores (Karstadt and Kaufhof-Galeria) sell everything imaginable, including gourmet foods in their lower levels. The shopping district lies basically between the Grosse Bleiche and the Old Town and includes the **Am**

Brand Zentrum, an ancient marketplace that is now a pedestrian zone brimming with shops. At the shopping mall **Römerpassage** (Lotharstrasse, near Grosse Bleiche), head for the cellar to see the remains of a Roman temple (AD 1) dedicated to the goddesses Isis and Mater Magna. The discovery was made in 1999 during construction of the mall.

The **Gutenberg-Shop** (⊠ *Markt 17* ⊕ *www.gutenberg-shop.de* ⊘ *Closed Sun.*) on the first floor of the *AZ* (local newspaper) customer center has a better selection of splendid souvenirs and gifts—including pages from the Bible, books, posters, stationery, pens, and games—than the shop in the Gutenberg Museum.

The excellent **Weincabinet am Dom** (⊠ *Leichhofstr. 10, behind the cathedral* ☎ *06131/228–858*) sells an array of the region's best wines and accessories.

The flea market **Krempelmarkt** is on the banks of the Rhine between the Hilton hotel and Kaiserstrasse. It takes place from 7 to 1 the first and third Saturday of the month from April to October and the third Saturday from November to March.

10

The Rhineland

WORD OF MOUTH

"We thought the Mosel River valley the highlight of our trip. And we especially liked Burg Eltz. The area is definitely more scenic and cute than the Romantic Road."

—Cowboy1968

"The Ko, as they call it, is one of the most fashionable streets in Europe, reflecting Dusseldorf's status as a fashion centre competing with the likes of Paris and Milan. The leafy suave street has a canal running down its middle."

—PalenQ

Updated
by Ted
Shoemaker

THE BANKS OF THE Rhine are crowned by magnificent castle after castle and by breathtaking, vine-terraced hills that provide the livelihood for many of the villages hugging the shores. In the words of French poet Victor Hugo, "The Rhine combines everything. The Rhine is swift as the Rhône, wide as the Loire, winding as the Seine…royal as the Danube and covered with fables and phantoms like a river in Asia.…"

The importance of the Rhine can hardly be overestimated. Although not the longest river in Europe (the Danube is more than twice its length), the Rhine has been the main river-trade artery between the heart of the continent and the North Sea (and Atlantic Ocean) throughout recorded history. The Rhine runs 1,320 km (820 mi) from the Bodensee (Lake Constance) west to Basel, then north through Germany, and, finally, west through the Netherlands to Rotterdam.

Vineyards, a legacy of the Romans, are an inherent part of the Rhine landscape from Wiesbaden to Bonn. The Rhine tempers the climate sufficiently for grapes to ripen this far north, and the world's finest Rieslings come from the Rheingau and from the Rhine's its most important tributary, the Mosel. Thanks to the river, these wines were shipped far beyond the borders of Germany, which in turn gave rise to the wine trade that shaped the fortune of many riverside towns. Rüdesheim, Bingen, Koblenz, and Köln (Cologne) remain important commercial wine centers to this day.

The river is steeped in legend and myth. The Loreley, a jutting sheer slate cliff, was once believed to be the home of a beautiful and bewitching maiden who lured boatmen to a watery end in the swift currents. Heinrich Heine's poem *Song of Loreley* (1827), inspired by Clemens Brentano's *Legend of Loreley* (1812) and set to music in 1837 by Friedrich Silcher, has been the theme song of the landmark ever since. The Nibelungen, a Burgundian race said to have lived on the banks of the Rhine, serve as subjects for Wagner's epic opera cycle *Der Ring des Nibelungen* (1852–72).

William Turner captured misty Rhine sunsets on canvas. Famous literary works, such as Goethe's *Sanct Rochus-Fest zu Bingen* (*The Feast of St. Roch*; 1814), Lord Byron's *Childe Harold's Pilgrimage* (1816), and Mark Twain's *A Tramp Abroad* (1880), captured the spirit of Rhine Romanticism on paper, encouraging others to follow in their footsteps.

ORIENTATION & PLANNING

GETTING ORIENTED

The most spectacular stretch of the Rhineland is along the Middle Rhine, between Mainz and Koblenz, which takes in the awesome castles and vineyards of the Rhine Gorge. Highways hug the river on each bank (B–42 on the north and eastern sides, and B–9 on the south and western sides), and car ferries crisscross the Rhine at many points. Cruises depart from many cities and towns, including as far south as

TOP REASONS TO GO

Fastnacht: The Rhineland is a stronghold of Germany's Fastnacht (Carnival festivities), which takes place from 11:11 AM on November 11 to Ash Wednesday, culminating with huge parades, round-the clock music, and dancing in Düsseldorf, Köln, and Mainz the week before Ash Wednesday.

Rhine in Flames: These massive displays of fireworks take place the first Saturday in May in Linz–Bonn; the first Saturday in July in Bingen–Rüdesheim; the second Saturday in August in Koblenz; the second Saturday in September in Oberwesel; and the third Saturday in September in St. Goar.

Drachenfels: This dramatic castle crowns a high hill overlooking the Rhine. In the Nibelungen legend, Siegfried slew a dragon here.

Spectacular Wine: The light white wines of the Rhine and Mosel are distinctive, and a whole culinary tradition has grown up around them.

The Romance of the Rhine: From cruises to Rhine-view rooms, castles to terraced vineyards, the Rhine does not disappoint.

Frankfurt. Trains service all the towns, and the Mainz–Bonn route provides river views all the way.

The Rheingau. Though the course of the Rhine is generally south to north, it bends sharply at Wiesbaden and flows east–west for 19 mi to Rüdesheim. This means that the steep hills on its right bank have a southern exposure, and that vineyards there produce superb wines.

The Mittelrhein. The romance of the Rhine is most apparent in the Middle Rhine, from Bingen to Koblenz. The Rhine Gorge not only has the greatest concentration of castles, but also the storied cliff the Loreley.

The Mosel Valley. Koblenz and Trier aren't very far apart as the crow flies, but the driving distance along the incredible twists and turns of the Mosel River is 125 mi. The journey is worth it, though. The region is unspoiled, the towns gemlike, the scenery a medley of vineyards and forests, and there's a wealth of Roman artifacts, medieval churches, and castle ruins to admire.

Bonn & the Köln (Cologne) Lowlands. North of Koblenz, the Rhine is less picturesque, but it does shoulder the cosmopolitan cities Köln and Düsseldorf, as well as the former capital city of Bonn.

THE RHINELAND PLANNER

WHEN TO GO

The peak season for cultural, food, and wine festivals is March–mid-November, followed by colorful Christmas markets in December. The season for many hotels, restaurants, riverboats, cable cars, and sights is from Easter through October, particularly in smaller towns. Opening hours at many castles, churches, and small museums are shorter in winter. Orchards blossom in March, and the vineyards are verdant from May until late September, when the vines turn a shimmering gold.

GETTING HERE & AROUND

BY AIR The Rhineland is served by three international airports: Frankfurt, Düsseldorf, and Köln-Bonn. Bus and rail lines connect each airport with its respective downtown area and provide rapid access to the rest of the region. There are direct trains from the Frankfurt airport to downtown Köln and Düsseldorf.

No-frills carriers that fly within Europe are based at smaller Frankfurt-Hahn Airport in Lautzenhausen, between the Rhine and Mosel valleys (a one-hour drive from Wiesbaden or Trier; a 1½-hour bus ride from Frankfurt Airport). The Luxembourg Findel International Airport (a 30-minute drive from Trier) is close to the upper Mosel River valley.

BY TRAIN InterCity and EuroCity expresses connect all the cities and towns of the area. Hourly InterCity routes run between Düsseldorf, Köln, Bonn, and Mainz, with most services extending as far south as Munich and as far north as Hamburg. The city transportation networks of Bonn, Köln, and Düsseldorf are linked by S-bahn (for information contact the KVB).

ESSENTIALS Airport Contacts **Flughafen Düsseldorf** (☎ *0211/4210* ⊕ *www.duesseldorf-international.de*). **Flughafen Frankfurt** (☎ *01805/372–4636* ⊕ *www.airportcity-frankfurt. de*). **Flughafen Hahn** (☎ *06543/509–200* ⊕ *www.hahn-airport.de*). **Flughafen Köln/ Bonn** (✉, *Köln* ☎ *02203/404–001* ⊕ *www.koeln-bonn-airport.de*). **Luxembourg Findel International Airport** (☎ *00352/2464–1* ⊕ *www.luxairport.lu*).

Train Contacts **Deutsche Bahn** (☎ *11861* ⊕ *www.bahn.de*). **Kölner Verkehrs-Betriebe** (*KVB* ☎ *0221/547–3333*).

Visitor Information **Rheingau–Taunus Kultur & Tourismus** (✉ *An der Basilika 11a Oestrich–Winkel* ☎ *06723/99550* ⊕ *www.rheingau-taunus-info.de*). **Rheinland-PfalzTourismus** (✉ *Löhrstr. 103–105 Koblenz* ☎ *0261/915–200* 🖷 *0261/915–2040* ⊕ *www.rlp-info.de*).

ABOUT THE RESTAURANTS & HOTELS

Although Düsseldorf, Köln, and Wiesbaden are home to many talented chefs, some of Germany's most creative classic and contemporary cooking is found in smaller towns or country inns.

The most romantic places to lay your head are the old riverside inns and castle hotels. Ask for a *Rheinblick* (Rhine-view) room. Hotels are often booked well in advance, especially for festivals and when there are trade fairs in Köln, Düsseldorf, or Frankfurt, making rooms in Wiesbaden and the Rheingau scarce and expensive. Many hotels close for the winter.

WHAT IT COSTS IN EUROS					
	¢	$	$$	$$$	$$$$
RESTAURANTS	under €9	€9–€15	€16–€20	€21–€25	over €25
HOTELS	under €50	€50–€100	€101–€175	€176–€225	over €225

Restaurant prices are per person for a main course at dinner. Hotel prices are for two people in a standard double room, including tax and service.

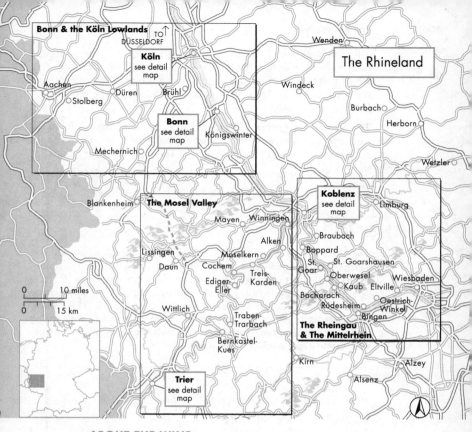

ABOUT THE WINE

The German Wine Institute and Wines of Germany provide background information and brochures about all German wine-growing regions. Tips on wine-related events and package offers are available from regional wine-information offices.

ESSENTIALS **Wine Information German Wine Institute** (⊕ *www.germanwines.de*). **Wines of Germany** (✉ *950 3rd Ave., New York, NY* ☎ *212/994–7523* 🖷 *212/994–7598* ⊕ *www.germanwineusa.org*).

PLANNING YOUR TIME

"Rhine romance" should visit the quaint southern part of it, particularly the Rhine Gorge, with its castles, vineyards, and the Loreley. If nightlife and culture are your preferences, you'll like the cathedral city of Köln and cosmopolitan Düsseldorf; you can still take a day cruise along the Rhine from Köln.

DISCOUNTS & DEALS

The **Rheinland-Pfalz and Saarland Card** (€15 for one day, €39 for two days, €57 for six days) offers free or reduced admission to museums, castles, and other sights, as well as city tours and boat trips throughout the two states. The three-day and six-day cards also include admission to the Holiday Park in Hassloch in the Pfalz. It's available at tourist offices in Rheinland-Pfalz and the Saarland. Many cultural events and museums in the state of Rhineland-Pfalz accept the **KulturCard** (€5), which grants up to 50% discounts. The card is sold by mail through the regional broadcaster SWR and in person at the newspaper *RZ* (RheinZeitung) shops.

The **Mittelrhein Burgen-Ticket**, sold at 10 participating castles in the Mittelrhein area between Rüdesheim and Koblenz, offers a tremendous savings on admission fees to 10 castles. The cost is €19 for adults.

ESSENTIALS   **Discount Card KulturCard** (☐ *SWR, Stichwort KulturCard, D–55114 Mainz*).

Discount Ticket Mittelrhein Burgen-Ticket (⊕ *www.burgen-am-rhein.de*).

THE RHEINGAU

The heart of the region begins in Wiesbaden, where the Rhine makes a sharp bend and flows east to west for some 30 km (19 mi) before resuming its south–north course at Rüdesheim. Wiesbaden is a good starting point for touring any of the well-marked cycling, hiking, and driving routes through the Rheingau's villages and vineyards. ■**TIP➔ Nearly every Rheingau village has an outdoor *Weinprobierstand* (wine-tasting stand), usually near the riverbank. It is staffed and stocked by a different wine estate every weekend in summer.**

WIESBADEN

40 km (25 mi) west of Frankfurt via A–66.

Wiesbaden, the capital of the state of Hesse, is a small city of tree-lined avenues with elegant shops and handsome facades. Its hot mineral springs have been a drawing card since the days when it was known as Aquis Mattiacis ("the waters of the Mattiaci")—the words boldly inscribed on the portal of the Kurhaus—and Wisibada ("the bath in the meadow"). Bilingual walking tours of Wiesbaden depart from the Kurhaus, April–October, Saturday at 10 (November–March, the second and fourth Saturday).

In the first century AD the Romans built thermal baths here, a site then inhabited by a Germanic tribe, the Mattiaci. Modern Wiesbaden dates from the 19th century, when the dukes of Nassau and, later, the Prussian aristocracy commissioned the grand public buildings and parks that shape the city's profile today. Wiesbaden developed into a fashionable spa that attracted the rich and the famous. Their ornate villas on the Neroberg and turn-of-the-20th-century town houses are part of the city's flair.

For a one-hour ride through the city, board the little train **THermine**. The one-day ticket (€6) enables you to get on and off as often as you'd like to explore the sights. From April to October it departs six times daily (10:30–5) from Café Lumen (behind the Marktkirche) and stops at the Rhein-Main-Halle (opposite the museum), Dorint Hotel, Staatstheater, Greek Chapel, and Neroberg railway station.

11

ESSENTIALS

EXPLORING

★ Built in 1907, the neoclassical **Kurhaus** (⊠*Kurhauspl.*) is the cultural center of town. It houses the casino and the Thiersch-Saal, a splendid setting for concerts. The Staatstheater (1894), opulently appointed in baroque and rococo revival styles, and two beautifully landscaped parks flank the Kurhaus.

Today you can "take the waters" in an ambience reminiscent of Roman times in the **Kaiser-Friedrich-Therme** (⊠*Langg. 38–40*), a superb art nouveau bathhouse from 1913.

On Kranzplatz, 15 of Wiesbaden's 26 springs converge at the steaming **Kochbrunnen Fountain**, where the healthful waters are there for the tasting.

Historic buildings ring the Schlossplatz (Palace Square) and the adjoining **Marktplatz** *(Market Square)*, site of the annual wine festival (mid-August) and Christmas market (December). The farmers' market (Wednesday and Saturday) takes place behind the neo-Gothic brick Marktkirche (Market Church).

The **Altstadt** *(Old Town)* is just behind the Schloss (now the seat of parliament, the Hessischer Landtag) on Grabenstrasse, Wagemannstrasse, and Goldgasse.

The **Museum Wiesbaden** is divided into three sections. The art section is known for its collection of expressionist paintings, particularly the works of Russian artist Alexej Jawlensky. The antiquities section has artifacts from the Stone Age, Roman times, and the Middle Ages, while the natural history section exhibits geological and archaeological finds. ⊠*Friedrich-Ebert-Allee 2* ☎*0611/335–2250* ⊕*www.museum-wiesbaden.de* ⊠*€5* ⊙*Tues. 10–8, Wed.–Sun. 10–5.*

WHERE TO EAT

$$$$ ✕**Trüffel.** For years truffle lovers have indulged in the "diamonds of the
★ kitchen" at Cristina and Dr. Manuel Stirn's first-rate restaurant. Personal service and stylish decor make for a very pleasant stay. The place is well worth a visit, but when we stopped by it was offering no truffles. A classy hotel rounds out operations. ⊠*Weberg. 6–8* ☎*0611/990–550* ⊟*AE, DC, MC, V* ⊙*Closed Sun.*

$$$ ✕**Käfer's.** This popular bistro with striking art nouveau decor, a grand piano (live music nightly), and a good-size bar attracts an upscale clientele. Book a table for two in one of the window alcoves (Nos. 7, 12, 25, and 29) for some privacy among the otherwise close-set tables. *Lachstatar* (salmon tartare) and *Bauernente* (farmer's duck) are standard favorites. A few champagnes are available by the glass and bottle. Käfer's also caters the beer garden behind the Kurhaus. ⊠*Kurhauspl. 1* ☎*0611/536–200* ⌂*Reservations essential* ⊟*AE, MC, V.*

$$ ✕**Prinz von Oranien.** Nina and "Fips" Geilfuss run a chic little restaurant near Rheinstrasse and the pedestrian zone. With its sleek, modern

EATING WELL IN THE RHINELAND

The Rhineland's regional cuisine features fresh fish and *Wild* (game), as well as sauces and soups based on the local Riesling and Spätburgunder (Pinot Noir) wines. *Tafelspitz* (boiled beef) and *Rheinischer Sauerbraten* (Rhenish marinated pot roast in a sweet-and-sour raisin gravy) are traditional favorites. The *Kartoffel* (potato) is prominent in soups, *Reibekuchen* and *Rösti* (potato pancakes), and *Dibbe-* or *Dippekuchen* (dialect: *Döppekoche*), a casserole baked in a cast-iron pot and served with apple compote. *Himmel und Erde*, literally "heaven and earth," is a mixture of mashed potatoes and chunky applesauce, topped with panfried slices of blood sausage and onions.

The region is known for its wines: Riesling is the predominant white grape, and Spätburgunder the most important red variety in the Rheingau, Mittelrhein, and Mosel wine regions covered in this chapter. Three abutting wine regions—Rheinhessen and the Nahe, near Bingen, and the Ahr, southwest of Bonn—add to the variety of wines available along the route.

furnishings, fresh flowers, and soft lighting, this dining spot is classy, comfortable, and friendly. The homemade soups, generous salads, and seasonal specialties are recommended, as are traditional favorites, such as breast of duck in a honey-ginger sauce or Charolais steak with potato gratin. ■TIP➡ **The luncheon special (€6) is a great value.** ⊠*Oranienstr. 2* ☎*0611/724–3200* ▭*AE, MC, V* ☺*Closed Sun. No lunch Wed. or Sat.*

$$ ✕**Sherry & Port.** Gerd Royko's friendly neighborhood bistro hosts live music on Friday and Saturday from October through March. During warm months, dine at outdoor tables surrounding a fountain on tree-lined Adolfsallee. In addition to the fantastic number of sherries and ports (60 of them!), there are 18 malt whiskies served by the glass. There is also a good selection of beers (Guinness on tap) and wines to accompany everything from tapas and salads to steaks and popularly priced daily specials (€6.30). ⊠*Adolfsallee 11* ☎*0611/373–632* ▭*No credit cards.*

WHERE TO STAY

$$$$ ⊡**Nassauer Hof.** Wiesbaden's premier address for well over a century,
★   this elegant hotel lies on the site of a Roman fortress that was converted into a spa and, ultimately, a guesthouse. It has luxuriously appointed rooms, top-flight service, and three restaurants. Breakfast is extra and costs 25. **Pro:** nice location opposite the Kurhaus. **Con:** expensive. ⊠*Kaiser-Friedrich-Pl. 3–4* ☎*0611/1330* ⊕*www.nassauer-hof.de* ↪*139 rooms, 30 suites* ♻*In-room: dial-up, Wi-Fi. In-hotel: 3 restaurants, bar, pool, gym, spa, bicycles, concierge, laundry service, public Internet, no-smoking rooms* ▭*AE, DC, MC, V.*

$$ ⊡**Hotel de France.** Behind this 1880 facade is a lovingly restored hotel and a restaurant that's an upscale culinary gem. Both have sleek, modern furnishings and lots of fresh flowers. Rooms in the front overlook a busy street, while those at the back have a view of a lovely Mediter-

ranean garden courtyard. Despite being rather small, the restaurant M ($$$; closed Sun.) is light and spacious. **Pro:** centrally located. **Cons:** on a busy street, small rooms. ⊠*Taunusstr. 49* ☎*0611/959–730* ⊕*www. hoteldefrance.de* ➬*34 rooms, 3 suites* ⟳*In-room: no a/c, refrigerator, Wi-Fi. In-hotel: restaurant, bar, no-smoking rooms, some pets allowed* ⊟*AE, MC, V* ⦺*BP.*

$ ⊞**Ibis.** This modern hotel opposite the Kochbrunnen on Kranzplatz offers excellent value and a location within walking distance of the shop-filled pedestrian zone, the Old Town, and all sights. The well-kept rooms have contemporary furnishings. **Pro:** four handicapped accessible rooms. **Con:** small rooms. ⊠*Georg-August-Zinn-Str. 2* ☎*0611/36140* ⊕*www.ibishotel.com* ➬*131 rooms* ⟳*In-room: dial-up, Wi-Fi. In-hotel: bar, no-smoking rooms, some pets allowed* ⊟*AE, DC, MC, V.*

$ ⊞**Town Hotel.** The Gerbers' modern, new hotel is a five-minute walk
★ from the Kurhaus, Old Town, and shopping district. Terra-cotta and beige tones and parquet floors lend the rooms warmth. Although they are small, they are very cleverly designed for maximum use of space. The staff is particularly friendly and helpful. **Pros:** new and inexpensive. **Con:** often full. ⊠*Spiegelg. 5* ☎*0611/360–160* ⊕*www. townhotel.de* ➬*24 rooms* ⟳*In-room: Ethernet, Wi-Fi (some). In-hotel: bicycles, laundry service, public Internet, no-smoking rooms, some pets allowed* ⊟*AE, MC, V.*

NIGHTLIFE & THE ARTS

In addition to the casino, restaurants, bars, and beer garden at the Kurhaus, nightlife is centered in the many bistros and pubs on Tau-nusstrasse and in the Old Town. The tourist office provides schedules and sells tickets for most venues listed below.

The **Hessisches Staatstheater** (⊠*Chr.-Zais-Str. 3* ☎*0611/132–325* ⊕*www.staatstheater-wiesbaden.de*) presents classical and contemporary opera, theater, ballet, and musicals on three stages: Grosses Haus, Kleines Haus, and Studio. Great classics and avant-garde films are specialties of the **Caligari Filmbühne** (⊠*Marktpl. 9, behind Marktkirche* ☎*0611/313–838*). Smaller dramatic productions and cabaret are performed at the intimate **Pariser Hoftheater** (⊠*Spiegelg. 9* ☎*0611/300–607* ⊕*www.pariserhoftheater.de*). ive concerts (jazz, blues, rock, and pop), often accompanied by theater, are held at the **Walhalla Studio Theater** (⊠*Mauritiusstr. 3a [use entrance of movie theater Bambi Kino]* ☎*0611/910–3743* ⊕*www.walhalla-studio.de*).

The Hessian State Orchestra performs in the **Kurhaus** (⊠*Kurhauspl. 1* ☎*0611/17290*). Concerts and musicals are staged at the **Rhein-Main-Hallen** (⊠*Rheinstr. 20* ☎*0611/1440* ⊕*www.rhein-main-hallen.de*). The sparkling-wine cellars of **Henkell & Söhnlein** (⊠*Biebricher Allee 142* ☎*0611/630*) host a series of concerts in their splendid foyer. Many churches offer concerts, including the free organ concerts Saturday at noon in the **Marktkirche** (⊠*Schlosspl. 4* ☎*0611/900–1611* ⊕*www. marktkirche-wiesbaden.de*).

At the **Spielbank** *(casino)*, the Klassische Spiel (roulette, blackjack) in the Kurhaus is lively from 3 PM to 3 AM, while the Kleines Spiel (slots and poker) in the neighboring Kolonnade is hopping from noon to 3 AM. The former is one of Europe's grand casinos, where jacket and tie are required. (You can be less formal at the Kleines Spiel.) Minimum age is 18 (bring your passport). ⊠ *Kurhauspl. 1* ☎ *0611/536–100* ⊕ *www.spielbank-wiesbaden.de* ☒ *Klassische Spiel €2.50, Kleines Spiel €1.*

THERMAL SPRINGS, SPAS & POOLS

Pamper yourself with the **Kaiser-Friedrich-Therme**'s thermal spring and cold-water pools, various steam baths and saunas, two solaria, and a score of health and wellness treatments in elegant art-nouveau surroundings. Towels and robes can be rented on-site, but come prepared for "textile-free" bathing. Children under 16 are not admitted. On Tuesday the facility is for women only. ⊠ *Langg. 38–40, entrance faces Weberg.* ☎ *0611/172–9660* ☒ *Apr.–Sept. €3.50 an hr, Oct.–Mar. €5* ◐ *Sun.–Thurs. 10–10, Fri. and Sat, 10* AM–*midnight.*

There's year-round swimming indoors and out thanks to the thermal springs (32°C [90°F]) that feed the pools at the **Thermalbad Aukammtal.** The facility includes eight saunas, a whirlpool, massage, and balneological treatments. ⊠ *Leibnizstr. 7, bus No. 18 from Wilhelmstr. to Aukamm Valley* ☎ *0611/172–9880* ☒ *Pools €8.50, saunas €15, combined ticket €20* ◐ *Sun.–Thurs. 8* AM–*10* PM, *Fri. and Sat. 8* AM–*midnight.*

SHOPPING

Broad, tree-lined Wilhelmstrasse, with designer boutiques housed in its fin-de-siècle buildings, is one of Germany's most elegant shopping streets. Wiesbaden is also known as one of the best places in the country to find antiques; Taunusstrasse and Nerostrasse have excellent antiques shops. The Altstadt is full of upscale boutiques; Kirchgasse and its extension, Langgasse, are the heart of the shop-filled pedestrian zone.

ELTVILLE

14 km (9 mi) west of Wiesbaden via A–66 and B–42.

Eltville flourished as a favorite residence of the archbishops of Mainz in the 14th and 15th centuries, and it was during this time that the **Kurfürstliche Burg** *(Electors' Castle)* was built. More than 300 varieties of roses can be admired in the castle's courtyard garden, on the wall, and along the Rhine promenade. During "Rose Days" (the first weekend in June) the flower is celebrated in shops and restaurants (as an ingredient in recipes) throughout town. ⊠ *Burgstr. 1* ☎ *06123/90980* ☒ *Tower €1.50, rose garden free* ◐ *Tower Apr.–mid-Oct., Fri. 2–6 and weekends 11–6; rose garden Easter–mid-Oct., daily 9:30–7, mid-Oct.–Easter, daily 10:30–5.*

The parish church of **Sts. Peter und Paul** has late-Gothic frescoes, Renaissance tombstones, and a carved baptismal by the Rhenish sculptor Hans Backoffen (or his studio).

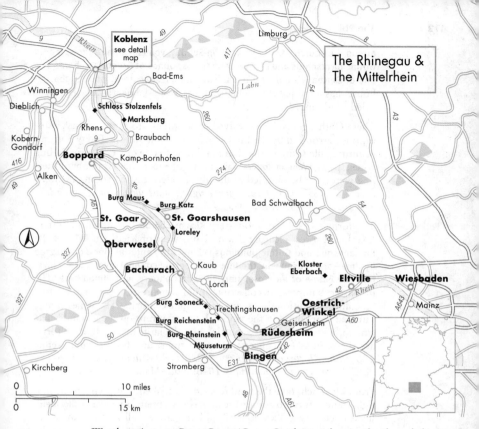

Worth seeing are Burg Crass (Crass Castle) on the riverbank and the half-timber houses and aristocratic **manors** on the lanes between the river and Rheingauer Strasse (B–42), notably the Bechtermünzer Hof (Kirchgasse 6), Stockheimer Hof (Ellenbogengasse 6), and Eltzer Hof (at the Martinstor gateway).

Sekt (sparkling wine) production in the Rheingau is concentrated in Eltville, Wiesbaden, and Rüdesheim. The tree-lined Rhine promenade here hosts the annual Sekt festival during the first weekend of July. The administrative headquarters and main cellars of the **Hessian State Wine Domains**, Germany's largest wine estate, are in town. The estate owns nearly 500 acres of vineyards throughout the Rheingau and in the Hessische Bergstrasse wine region south of Frankfurt. Its shops—in the art nouveau press house built in 1911 and at nearby Kloster Eberbach—offer a comprehensive regional selection. ⊠*Schwalbacher Str. 56–62* ☎*06123/92300* ⊕*www.weingut-kloster-eberbach.de* ⊟*AE, MC, V* ☙ *Weekdays 10–6, Sat. 10–4.*

For a good look at the central Rheingau, make a brief circular tour from Eltville. Drive 3 km (2 mi) north via the Kiedricher Strasse to the Gothic village of **Kiedrich.** In the distance you can see the tower of Scharfenstein Castle (1215) and the spires of **St. Valentine's Church** and St. Michael's Chapel, both from the 15th century. ■TIP→ **If you** attend the church's 9:30 AM mass on Sunday, you can admire the splendid Gothic furnishings and star vaulting to the sounds of Gregorian chants and one of Germany's oldest organs. The chapel next door, once a charnel house, has a unique chandelier sculpted around a nearly life-size, two-sided Madonna.

These Gothic gems have survived intact thanks to 19th-century restorations patronized by the English baronet John Sutton. Today Sutton's beautiful villa south of the church is home to one of Germany's leading wine estates, **Weingut Robert Weil**. Its famed Kiedricher Gräfenberg Riesling wines can be sampled in the ultramodern tasting room. ⊠*Mühlberg 5* ☎*06123/2308* ⊕*www.weingut-robert-weil.com* ⊘ *Weekdays 8–5:30, Sat. 10–5, Sun. 11–5.*

FodorśChoice The former Cistercian monastery **Kloster Eberbach** is idyllically set in
★ a secluded forest clearing 3 km (2 mi) west of Kiedrich. **■TIP➔ Its Romanesque and Gothic buildings (12th–14th centuries) look untouched by time—one reason why the film of Umberto Eco's medieval murder mystery *The Name of the Rose*, starring Sean Connery, was filmed here.** The monastery's impressive collection of old winepresses bears witness to a viticultural tradition that spans nearly nine centuries. The wines can be sampled year-round in the **vinothek** or restaurant on the grounds. The church, with its excellent acoustics, and the large medieval dormitories are the settings for concerts, wine auctions, and festive wine events. ⊠*Stiftung Kloster Eberbach* ☎*06723/91780* ⊕*www.klostereberbach. de* ☎*€3.50* ⊘*Apr.–Oct., daily 10–6; Nov.–Mar., daily 11–5.*

From Eberbach, take the road toward Hattenheim, stopping at the first right-hand turnoff to admire the monastery's premier vineyard, **Steinberg**. It's encircled by a 3-km-long (2-mi-long) stone wall (13th–18th centuries). The vineyard has an **outdoor pub**. ⊘*May–Sept., weekends 11–7.*

The *Brunnen* (springs) beneath the vineyards of Hattenheim and Erbach, both on the Rhine, lend their name to three excellent **vineyards**: Nussbrunnen, Wisselbrunnen, and Marcobrunnen, on the boundary between the two towns. As you return to Eltville (2 km [1 mi] east of Erbach on B–42), you will pass the elegant 19th-century palace Schloss Reinhartshausen (now a hotel and wine estate).

WHERE TO EAT

$$$$ ✕**Kronenschlösschen.** The atmosphere of this stylish art nouveau house
FodorśChoice (1894) is intimate. Chef Patrik Kimpel, vice-president of the German
★ Young Restaurateurs, oversees both the gourmet restaurant Kronenschlösschen and the more casual Bistro. Fish is a house specialty (try the halibut with a lemon-lime crust and a carrot-ginger sauce). You can also dine in the parklike garden. The wine list focuses on the finest Rheingau estates for whites and Old and New World estates for reds. ⊠*Rheinallee Eltville-Hattenheim* ☎*06723/640* ▤*AE, MC, V.*

$$$$ ✕ **Schloss Reinhartshausen.** A palace in every sense of the word, this hotel
★ and wine estate overlooks the Rhine and beautifully landscaped gardens. Antiques and artwork fill the house. You can enjoy breakfast, lunch, and afternoon tea with *Rieslingtorte* in the airy, glass-lined Wintergarten. Upscale dinners are served in the elegant Prinzess von Erbach.

The economical Schloss Schänke, located in the old press house, offers light fare and hearty snacks. The estate's wines are also sold daily in the Vinothek. ⊠ *Hauptstr. 41Eltville-Erbach* ☎ *06123/6760* ⊟ *AE, DC, MC, V.*

$$ ✕ **Zum Krug.** Winegrower Josef Laufer more than lives up to the hospitality promised by the wreath and *Krug* (earthenware pitcher) hanging above the front door. The wood-panel restaurant, with its old tiled stove is cozy. The German fare includes wild duck, goose, game, or sauerbraten served in rich, flavorful gravies. The wine list is legendary for its scope (600 Rheingau wines) and selection of older vintages. ⊠ *Hauptstr. 34 Eltville-Hattenheim* ☎ *06723/99680* ⊟ *MC, V* ⊘ *Closed 2 wks Dec. and Jan. and 2nd half of July.*

$ ✕ **Gutsausschank Baiken.** This restaurant is set on a hilltop amid the famed Rauenthaler Baiken vineyard. The magnificent panorama from the vine-canopied terrace, the fresh country cooking, and superb wines—from the Hessian State Wine Domains—make for a "Rheingau Riesling" experience par excellence. Riesling cream soup and Riesling lasagna (with ground meat and leeks) are house specialties. ⊠ *Wiesweg 86, via Eltville* ☎ *06123/900–345* ⊟ *AE, MC, V* ⊘ *Closed Mon. and Nov.–Apr. No lunch, except Sun.*

$ ✕ **Klosterschänke und Gästehaus Kloster Eberbach.** Beneath the vaulted ceiling of the Klosterschänke you can sample the wines of the Hessian State Wine Domains with regional cuisine. Try the *Weinfleisch* (pork goulash in Riesling sauce) or *Zisterzienser Brot,* which translates to "Cistercian bread" (minced meat in a plum-and-bacon dressing with boiled potatoes). ⊠ *Kloster Eberbach, via Kiedrich or Hattenheim,* ☎ *06723/9930* ⊟ *No credit cards.*

WHERE TO STAY

$ ▦ **Maximilianshof.** For generations the von Oetinger family has shared its home, its wines, and its simple, hearty cooking (¢–$) with guests from near and far. In winter the warm art-nouveau parlor beckons with its plush sofas; in summer tables are set out on the pretty terrace. Across the courtyard there's a cheerful, modern guesthouse with nine rooms, each named after a local vineyard. Honigberg has a private sauna; Hohenrain has a nifty little kitchen and can be booked as a holiday flat for up to five people. **Pros:** art nouveau parlor, terrace. **Con:** removed from Eltville center. ⊠ *Rheinallee 2 Eltville-Erbach* ☎ *06123/92240* ⊕ *www.maximilianshof.de* ⇥ *9 rooms* ⟡ *In-room: no a/c, Ethernet, dial-up. In-hotel: restaurant, laundry service, some pets allowed* ⊟ *AE, MC, V* ❡ *BP*

OESTRICH-WINKEL

21 km (13 mi) west of Wiesbaden, 7 km (4½ mi) west of Eltville on B–42.

Oestrich's vineyard area is the largest in the Rheingau. ■ TIP➔ **Lenchen and Doosberg are the most important vineyards. You can sample the wines at the outdoor wine-tasting stand, opposite the 18th-century crane on the riverbank of Oestrich (nearly opposite Hotel Schwan).**

The village of Winkel (pronounced *vin*-kle) lies west of Oestrich. A Winkeler Hasensprung wine from the fabulous 1811 vintage was Goethe's wine of choice during his stay here with the Brentano family in 1814.

The Goethe Zimmer (Goethe Room) in the Brentanohaus, with mementos and furnishings from Goethe's time, may be visited by appointment only. ⊠*Am Lindenpl. 2* ☎*06723/2068* ⊕*www.brentano.de.*

★ The oldest of Germany's great private wine estates, the 1211 **Schloss Vollrads,** lies 3 km (2 mi) north of town. The moated tower (1330) was the Greiffenclau residence for 350 years until the present palace was built in the 17th century. There is a vinothek, and the period rooms are open during concerts, festivals, and wine tastings. ⊠*North on Schillerstr., turn right on Greiffenclaustr.* ☎*06723/660* ⊕*www. schlossvollrads.com* ⊟*AE, MC, V* ☉*Easter–Oct., weekdays 9–6, weekends 11–7; Nov.–Easter, weekdays 9–5, weekends noon–5.*

★ The origins of the grand wine estate **Schloss Johannisberg** date from 1100, when Benedictine monks built a monastery and planted vines on the slopes below. The palace and remarkable cellars (tours by appointment) were built in the early 18th century. There are tastings at the estate's restaurant. To get here from Winkel's main street, drive north on Schillerstrasse and proceed all the way uphill. After the road curves to the left, watch for the left turn to the castle. ⊠ *Weinbaudomäne Schloss Johannisberg, Geisenheim-Johannisberg* ☎*06722/700–935* ⊕*www.schloss-johannisberg.de* ⊟*AE, MC, V* ☉*Vinothek Mar.–Oct., weekdays 10–1 and 2–6, weekends 11–6; Nov.–Feb., weekdays 10–1 and 2–6, weekends 11–5.*

WHERE TO EAT

\$\$
★ ✕**Gutsausschank Schloss Johannisberg.** The glassed-in terrace affords a spectacular view of the Rhine and the vineyards from which the wine in your glass originated. Rheingau Riesling soup and *Bauernente* (farmer's duck) are house specialties. ⊠*Schloss Johannisberg* ☎*06722/96090* ⊟*AE, MC, V.*

\$\$ ✕**Gutsrestaurant Schloss Vollrads.** Chef Maurice Redelig's seasonal German and light Mediterranean dishes are served with the estate's wines in the cavalier house (1650) or on the flower-lined terrace facing the garden. ⊠*Schloss Vollrads, north of Winkel* ☎*06723/5270* ⊟*AE, MC, V* ☉*Closed Mon. and Tues., Nov.–Mar.*

$ ✗**Die Wirtschaft.** Beate and Florian Kreller provide you with a warm welcome to their historic building on Winkel's Hauptstrasse (main street). Fresh flowers and candles top the tables set in a labyrinth of cozy niches with exposed beams and old stone walls. No less inviting is the pretty courtyard. It's "steak night" some Tuesdays in winter, and there are summer barbecues in the courtyard. Top-quality German specialties, such as *hällisches Landschwein* (Swabian pork), are also served. ⊠*Hauptstr. 70, Winkel* ☎*06723/7426* ⊟*MC, V* ☉*Closed Mon. and 2 wks in July and Aug. No dinner Sun. and Mon.*

WHERE TO STAY

$$ 🏨**Hotel Schwan.** This green-and-white half-timber inn has been in the Fodor'sChoice Wenckstern family since it was built in 1628. All rooms offer modern ★ comforts, though the rooms in the guesthouse are simpler than in the historic main building. Many rooms afford a Rhine view (Rooms 103, 106, 107, and 108 are especially nice), as does the beautiful terrace. The staff is friendly and helpful, and you can sample the family's wines in the cavernous wine cellar and in the restaurant, which has a lovely terrace ($–$$). **Pros:** right at the 18th-century crane and outdoor wine stands. **Cons:** rooms in the guesthouse lack charm. ⊠*Rheinallee 5, in Oestrich Oestrich-Winkel* ☎*06723/8090* ⊕*www.hotel-schwan.de* 🛏*52 rooms, 3 suites* 🍴*In-room: no a/c, dial-up, Wi-Fi (some). In-hotel: restaurant, bar, laundry service, some pets allowed, no-smoking rooms* ⊟*AE, DC, MC, V* 🍴*BP.*

RÜDESHEIM

30 km (19 mi) west of Wiesbaden, 9 km (5½ mi) west of Oestrich-Winkel on B–42.

Tourism and wine are the heart and soul of Rüdesheim.

Visitor Information Rüdesheim (⊠ *Tourist-Information, Geisenheimer Str. 22* ☎ *06722/19433* 🖷 *06722/3485* ⊕ *www.ruedesheim.de*).

Less than 500 feet long, **Drosselgasse** *(Thrush Alley)*, is a narrow, pub-lined lane, which is abuzz with music and merrymaking from noon until well past midnight every day from Easter through October.

Since 1892 the **Asbach Weinbrennerei** has produced one of Germany's most popular brands of *Weinbrand* (wine brandy, the equivalent of cognac). It's a key ingredient in brandy-filled *Pralinen* (chocolates) and in the local version of Irish coffee, Rüdesheimer Kaffee. You can tour the plant and shop for the goodies it produces. ⊠*Asbach Besucher Center, Ingelheimer Str. 4, on eastern edge of town* ☎*06722/497–345* ⊕*www.asbach.de* ☉*Mar.–Dec., Tues.–Sat. 9–5.*

The **Weinmuseum Brömsenburg** *(Brömserburg Wine Museum)*, housed in one of the oldest castles on the Rhine (circa AD 1000), displays wine-related artifacts and drinking vessels dating from Roman times. ■**TIP→** There are great views from the roof and the terrace, where there are occasionally wine tastings (ask at the desk). ⊠*Rheinstr. 2* ☎*06722/2348* ⊕*www.rheingauer-weinmuseum.de* 💶*€5* ☉*Apr.–Oct., daily 10–6.*

High above Rüdesheim and visible for miles stands *Germania,* a colossal female statue crowning the **Niederwald-Denkmal** *(Niederwald Monument).* This tribute to German nationalism was built between 1877 and 1883 to commemorate the rebirth of the German Empire after the Franco-Prussian War (1870–71). Germania faces across the Rhine toward the eternal enemy, France. At her base are the words to a stirring patriotic song: "Dear Fatherland rest peacefully! Fast and true stands the watch, the watch on the Rhine!" There are splendid panoramic views from the monument and from other vantage points on the edge of the forested plateau. You can reach the monument on foot, by car (via Grabenstrasse), or over the vineyards in the *Seilbahn* (cable car). There's also a *Sessellift* (chairlift) to and from Assmannshausen, a red-wine enclave, on the other side of the hill. ⊠ *Oberstr. 37* ☎ *06722/2402* ⊕ *www.seilbahn-ruedesheim.de* 🎟 *One way €4.50, round-trip or combined ticket for cable car and chairlift €6.50* ☉ *Mid-Mar.–Apr. and Oct., daily 9:30–5; May–Sept., daily 9:30–6.*

With the wings of a glider you can silently soar over the Rhine Valley. At the **Luftsport-Club Rheingau** you can catch a 30- to 60-minute *Segelflug* (glider flight) on a glider plane between Rüdesheim and the Loreley; allow 1½ hours for pre- and postflight preparations. ⊠ *3 km (2 mi) north of Niederwald-Denkmal and Landgut Ebenthal* ☎ *06722/2979* ⊕ *www.lsc-rheingau.de* 🎟 *1st 5 min €15, each additional min €0.50; €2 per min in glider with motor* ☉ *Apr.–Oct., weekends 10–7.*

WHERE TO STAY & EAT

$$ ★ ☒ **Breuer's Rüdesheimer Schloss.** Guests at this stylish, historic hotel (note: it was never a castle) are welcomed with a drink from the family's Rheingau wine estate. Marissa Breuer, daughter of gracious hosts Susanne and Heinrich Breuer, was named Rheingau Wine Queen. Most rooms offer a vineyard view. Cellar or vineyard tours and wine tastings can be arranged. If you stay a week you pay only for six days. **Pros:** right off the Drosselgasse. **Cons:** noisy touristic area. ⊠ *Steing. 10* ☎ *06722/90500* ⊕ *www.ruedesheimer-schloss.com* 🛏 *23 rooms, 3 suites* ♿ *In-room: no a/c, refrigerator, dial-up, Wi-Fi. In-hotel: restaurant, bar, bicycles, laundry service, some pets allowed, no-smoking rooms* ☰ *AE, DC, MC, V* ☉ *Closed Christmas–early Jan.* ⦿ *BP.*

$$ Fodor'sChoice ★ ☒ **Hotel Krone Assmannshausen.** From its humble beginnings in 1541 as an inn for sailors and ferrymen, the Krone evolved into an elegant, antiques-filled hotel. Rooms at the back face on busy railroad tracks, but thick glass provides good soundproofing. Two of the suites have their own sauna. The restaurant ($$$$) offers first-class service and fine wining and dining. Classic cuisine prepared by chef Jens Kottke and a superb collection of wines, including the famed Spätburgunder red wines of Assmannshausen, make for very memorable meals indoors or on the terrace overlooking the Rhine. **Pro:** charming views of vineyards and the Rhine. **Con:** right on a main rail line. ⊠ *Rheinuferstr. 10, Rüdesheim-Assmannshausen* ☎ *06722/4030* ⊕ *www.hotel-krone.com* 🛏 *52 rooms, 13 suites, 1 apartment* ♿ *In-room: no a/c, dial-up, Wi-Fi. In-hotel: restaurant, bar, pool, laundry service, no-smoking rooms* ☰ *AE, MC, V*

THE MITTELRHEIN

Bingen, like Rüdesheim, is a gateway to the Mittelrhein. From here to Koblenz lies the greatest concentration of Rhine castles. Most date from the 12th and 13th centuries, but were destroyed after the invention of gunpowder, mainly during invasions by the French. It's primarily thanks to the Prussian royal family and its penchant for historical preservation that numerous Rhine castles were rebuilt or restored in the 19th and early 20th centuries.

Two roads run parallel to the Rhine: B–42 (east side) and B–9 (west side). The spectacular views from the heights can best be enjoyed via the routes known as the Loreley-Burgenstrasse (east side), from Kaub to the Loreley to Kamp-Bornhofen; or the Rheingoldstrasse (west side), from Rheindiebach to Rhens.

BINGEN

35 km (22 mi) west of Wiesbaden via Mainz and A–60; ferry from wharf opposite Rüdesheim's train station.

Bingen overlooks the Nahe-Rhine conflux near a treacherous stretch of shallows and rapids known as the Binger Loch (Bingen Hole). Early on, Bingen developed into an important commercial center, for it was here—as in Rüdesheim on the opposite shore—that goods were moved from ship to shore to circumvent the unnavigable waters. Bingen was also the crossroads of Roman trade routes between Mainz, Koblenz, and Trier. Thanks to this central location, it grew into a major center of the wine trade and remains so today. Wine is celebrated during 11 days of merrymaking in early September at the annual **Winzerfest.**

ESSENTIALS

Visitor Information **Bingen** (✉ *Tourist-Information; Rheinkai 21* ☎ *06721/184–205* 🖶 *06721/184–214* 🌐 *www.bingen.de*).

EXPLORING

Bingen was destroyed repeatedly by wars and fires; thus there are many ancient foundations but few visible architectural remains of the past. Since Celtic times the Kloppberg (Klopp Hill), in the center of town, has been the site of a succession of citadels, all named **Burg Klopp,** since 1282. Here you'll find a museum and a terrace with good views of the Rhine, the Nahe, and the surrounding hills.

Not far from the thousand-year-old Drususbrücke, a stone bridge over the Nahe, is the late-Gothic **Basilika St. Martin.** It was originally built in 793 on the site of a Roman temple. The 11th-century crypt and Gothic and baroque furnishings merit a visit.

★ The **Historisches Museum am Strom** *(History Museum)* is housed in a former power station (1898) on the riverbank. Here you can see an intact set of Roman surgical tools (2nd century), period rooms from the Rhine Romantic era, and displays about Abbess St. Hildegard von Bingen (1098–1179), one of the most remarkable women of the Middle Ages. An outspoken critic of papal and imperial machinations, she was a highly respected scholar, naturopath, and artist whose mystic writings and music are much in vogue today. An excellent illustrated booklet in English on Rhine Romanticism, *The Romantic Rhine*, is sold at the museum shop. ⊠ *Museumsstr. 3* ☎ *06721/990–654 or 06721/991–531* ⊕ *www.bingen.de* ⌦ *€3* ⊙ *Tues.–Sun. 10–5.*

The forested plateau of the Rochusberg (St. Roch Hill) is the pretty setting of the **Rochuskapelle** *(St. Roch Chapel)*. Originally built in 1666 to celebrate the end of the plague, it has been rebuilt twice. On August 16, 1814, Goethe attended the consecration festivities, the forerunner

> **TAKE A HIKE!**
>
> The Rheinhöhenweg (Rhine Heights Path) affords hikers splendid views and descents into the villages en route. These marked trails run between Oppenheim on the Rhine Terrace and Bonn for 240 km (149 mi) and between Wiesbaden and Bonn-Beuel for 272 km (169 mi). The most extensive hiking trail is the Rheinsteig, from Wiesbaden to Bonn on the right side of the Rhine. It comprises 320 km (199 mi) of well-marked paths that offer everything from easy walks to challenging stretches on a par with Alpine routes.

of today's Rochusfest, a weeklong folk festival in mid-August. The chapel (open during Sunday services at 8 and 10) contains an altar dedicated to St. Hildegard and relics and furnishings from the convents she founded on the Ruppertsberg (in the suburb of Bingerbrück) and in Eibingen (east of Rüdesheim). The **Hildegard Forum** (☎ *06721/181–000* ⊕ *www.hildegard-forum.de* ⊙ *Tues.–Sun. 11–6)*, near the chapel, has exhibits related to St. Hildegard, a medieval herb garden, and a restaurant serving tasty, wholesome foods (*Dinkel,* or spelt, is a main ingredient) based on Hildegard's nutritional teachings. The lunch buffets (Tues.–Sat. €9, Sun. €16) are a good value.

WHERE TO EAT

$$$$
Fodor's Choice
★

✕ **Johann Lafer's Stromburg.** It's a pretty 15-minute drive through the Binger Wald (Bingen Forest) to this luxurious castle hotel and restaurant overlooking Stromberg. Johann Lafer is a prolific chef who pioneered cooking shows in Germany. In the elegant Val d'Or the *Variationen* (medley) of foie gras and the *Dessert–Impressionen* are classics. The less formal Turmstube offers tasty regional dishes. The wine list features 200 top Nahe wines and several hundred Old and New World wines, with a particularly fine collection from Bordeaux and Burgundy. ⊠ *Am Schlossberg 1, 12 km (7½ mi) west of Bingerbrück via Weiler and Waldalgesheim Stromberg* ☎ *06724/93100* ⌂ *Reservations essential* ⊟ *AE, DC, MC, V* ⊙ *Le Val d'Or closed Mon. and Tues. No lunch weekdays.*

$
✕ **Weinstube Kruger-Rumpf.** It's well worth the 10-minute drive from Bingen (just across the Nahe River) to enjoy Cornelia Rumpf's refined country cooking with Stefan Rumpf's exquisite Nahe wines (Riesling, Weissburgunder [Pinot Blanc], and Silvaner are especially fine). House specialties are *geschmorte Schweinebacken* (braised pork jowls) with kohlrabi, boiled beef with green herb sauce, and *Winzerschmaus* (casserole of potatoes, sauerkraut, bacon, cheese, and herbs). The

house dates from 1790; the wisteria-draped garden beckons in summer. ⊠ *Rheinstr. 47, 4 km (2½ mi) southwest of Bingen, Münster-Sarmsheim* ☎*06721/43859* ♘ *Reservations essential* ⊟*AE, MC, V* ⊘ *Closed Mon. and 3 wks late Dec.–early Jan. No lunch.*

EN ROUTE

On the 5-km (3-mi) drive on B–9 to Trechtingshausen you will pass by Bingen's landmark, the **Mäuseturm** *(Mice Tower)*, perched on a rocky island near the Binger Loch. The name derives from a gruesome legend. One version tells that during a famine in 969 the miserly Archbishop Hatto hoarded grain and sought refuge in the tower to escape the peasants' pleas for food. The stockpile attracted scads of mice to the tower, where they devoured everything in sight, including Hatto. In fact, the tower was built by the archbishops of Mainz in the 13th and 14th centuries as a *Mautturm* (watch tower and toll station) for their fortress, Ehrenfels, on the opposite shore (now a ruin). It was restored in neo-Gothic style by the king of Prussia in 1855, who also rebuilt Burg Sooneck.

The three castles open for visits near Trechtingshausen (turnoffs are signposted on B–9) will fascinate lovers of history and art. As you enter each castle's gateway, consider what a feat of engineering it was to have built such a massive *Burg* (fortress or castle) on the stony cliffs overlooking the Rhine. They have all lain in ruin once or more during their turbulent histories. Their outer walls and period rooms still evoke memories of Germany's medieval past as well as the 19th-century era of Rhine Romanticism.

FodorsChoice ★

Burg Rheinstein was the home of Rudolf von Habsburg from 1282 to 1286. To establish law and order on the Rhine, he destroyed the neighboring castles of Burg Reichenstein and Burg Sooneck and hanged their notorious robber barons from the oak trees around the Clemens Church, a late-Romanesque basilica near Trechtingshausen. The Gobelin tapestries, 15th-century stained glass, wall and ceiling frescoes, a floor of royal apartments, and antique furniture—including a rare "giraffe spinet" which Kaiser Wilhelm I is said to have played—are well worth seeing. All of this is illuminated by candlelight on some summer Fridays. Rheinstein was the first of many a Rhine ruin to be rebuilt by a royal Prussian family in the 19th century. ☎*06721/6348* ⊕*www.burg-rheinstein.de* ⊠*€4* ⊘ *Mid-Mar.–mid-Nov., daily 9:30–5:30; (weather permitting, call to inquire) mid-Nov.–mid-Mar., weekdays 2–5, weekends 10–5. Terrace café closed Mon. and Tues.*

Burg Reichenstein has collections of decorative cast-iron slabs (from ovens and historical room-heating devices), hunting weapons and armor, period rooms, and paintings. ☎*06721/6117* ⊕*www.burg-reichenstein. de* ⊠*€3.50* ⊘ *Mar.–mid-Nov., Tues.–Sun. 10–6.*

Burg Sooneck, on the edge of the Soon (pronounced *zone*) Forest, houses a valuable collection of Empire, Biedermeier, and neo-Gothic furnishings, medieval weapons, and paintings from the Rhine Romantic era. ⊠*Sooneckstr. 1, Niederheimbach* ☎*06743/6064* ⊕ *ceres.informatik. fh-kl.de/bsa* ⊠*€3* ⊘ *Apr.–Sept., Tues.–Sun. 10–6; Oct., Nov., and Jan.–Mar., Tues.–Sun. 10–5.*

BACHARACH

16 km (10 mi) north of Bingen; ferry 3 km (2 mi) north of town, to Kaub.

Bacharach, a derivative of the Latin *Bacchi ara* (altar of Bacchus), has long been associated with wine. Like Rüdesheim, Bingen, and Kaub, it was a shipping station where barrels would interrupt their Rhine journey for land transport. Riesling wine from the town's most famous vineyard, the Bacharacher Hahn, is served on the KD Rhine steamers, and Riesling ice cream is sold at Eis Café Italia 76 (Oberstrasse 48). In late June you can sample wines at the Weinblütenfest (Vine Blossom Festival) in the side-valley suburb of Steeg and, in late August, at Kulinarische Sommernacht in Bacharach proper.

Park on the riverbank and enter the town through one of its medieval gateways. You can ascend the 14th-century town wall for a walk along the ramparts facing the Rhine, then stroll along the main street (one street but three names: Koblenzer Strasse, Oberstrasse, and Mainzer Strasse) for a look at patrician manors, typically built around a *Hof* (courtyard), and half-timber houses. Haus Sickingen, Posthof, Zollhof, Rathaus (Town Hall), and Altes Haus are fine examples.

ESSENTIALS

Visitor Information Bacharach (⊠ *Tourist-Information, Oberstr. 45* ☎ *06743/919–303* ⊕ *www.rhein-nahe-touristik.de*).

EXPLORING

The massive tower in the center of town belongs to the parish church of **St. Peter.** A good example of the transition from Romanesque to Gothic styles, it has an impressive four-story nave.

From the parish church a set of stone steps (signposted) leads to Bacharach's landmark, the sandstone ruins of the Gothic **Werner Kapelle,** highly admired for its filigree tracery. The chapel's roof succumbed to falling rocks in 1689, when the French blew up Burg Stahleck. Originally a Staufen fortress (11th century), the castle lay dormant until 1925, when a youth hostel was built on the foundations. The sweeping views it affords are worth the 10-minute walk.

WHERE TO EAT

$ ✕ **Gutsausschank Zum Grünen Baum.** The Bastian family runs this cozy tavern in a half-timber house dating from 1421. They are the sole owners of the vineyard Insel Heyles'en Werth, on the island opposite Bacharach. The "wine carousel" is a great way to sample a full range of wine flavors and styles (15 wines). Snacks are served (from 1 PM), including delicious *Wildsülze* (game in aspic) with home fries, sausages, and cheese. ⊠ *Oberstr. 63* ☎ *06743/1208* ⊟ *MC, V* ♥ *Closed Thurs. and Feb.–mid-Mar.*

$ ✕ **Weinhaus Altes Haus.** This charming medieval half-timber house
★ (1390) is a favorite setting for films and photos. The cheerful proprietor, Reni Weber, uses the freshest ingredients possible and buys her meat and game from local butchers and hunters. *Rieslingrahmsuppe* (Riesling cream soup), *Reibekuchen* (potato pancakes), and the hearty

Hunsrücker Tellerfleisch (boiled beef with horseradish sauce) are favorites, in addition to the seasonal specialties. She offers a good selection of local wines. ✉ *Oberstr. 61* ☎ *06743/1209* ▭ *MC, V* ⊗ *Closed Wed. and Dec.–Easter, Apr. and Nov. weekends only.*

WHERE TO STAY

$ **Altkölnischer Hof.** Flowers line the windows of the Scherschlicht family's pretty half-timber hotel near the market square. The rooms are simply but attractively furnished in country style, and some have balconies. Four vacation cabins round out the offerings. **Pro:** half-timber romance. **Cons:** noisy tourist area, far from the station. ✉ *Blücherstr. 2* ☎ *06743/1339* 🌐 *www.altkoelnischer-hof.de* *18 rooms, 2 suites, 4 apartments* *In-room: no a/c, refrigerator, dial-up. In-hotel: restaurant, bar, bicycles, no-smoking rooms* ▭ *AE, MC, V* ⊗ *Closed Nov.–Mar.* *BP.*

¢ **RheinHotel Andreas Stüber.** This friendly, family-run operation is right at the town wall, just a few steps from the town center and beneath a castle. The modern rooms, each named after a vineyard, have Rhine and castle views. The restaurant has an excellent selection of Bacharacher wines to help wash down hearty regional specialties. **Pros:** Rhine and castle views. **Con:** no elevator. ✉ *Langstr. 50, on town wall* ☎ *06743/1243* 📠 *06743/1413* 🌐 *www.rhein-hotel-bacharach.de* *14 rooms, 1 apartment* *In-room: refrigerator, Wi-Fi. In-hotel: restaurant, bar, bicycles, no elevator, laundry service, no-smoking rooms, some pets allowed* ▭ *AE, MC, V* ⊗ *Closed Dec.–Feb.* *BP.*

OBERWESEL

8 km (5 mi) north of Bacharach.

Oberwesel retains its medieval silhouette. Sixteen of the original 21 towers and much of the town wall still stand in the shadow of Schönburg Castle. The "town of towers" is also renowned for its Riesling wines, celebrated at a lively wine festival held the first half of September. Both Gothic churches on opposite ends of town are worth visiting.

The **Liebfrauenkirche** *(Church of Our Lady)*, popularly known as the "red church" because of its brightly colored exterior, has superb sculptures, tombstones and paintings, and one of Germany's oldest altars (1331).

Set on a hill, **St. Martin**—the so-called white church—with a fortresslike tower, has beautifully painted vaulting and a magnificent baroque altar.

WHERE TO STAY & EAT

$$ ✕ **Römerkrug.** Rooms with exposed beams, pretty floral prints, and historic furnishings are tucked behind the half-timber facade (1458) of Elke Matzner's small inn on the market square. Fish (such as fresh trout from the Wisper Valley) and game are house specialties, but Marc Matzner also prepares light cuisine with Asian accents as well as Rhine specialties, such as *Himmel und Erde*. There's a well-chosen selection

of Mittelrhein wines that can be purchased for "take away." ✉ *Markt-tpl. 1* ☎ *06744/7091* ▤ *AE, MC, V* ⊘ *Closed mid-Nov.—mid-Feb.*

$ ✗ **Historische Weinwirtschaft.** Tables in the flower-laden garden in front of this lovingly restored stone house are at a premium in summer, yet seats in the nooks and crannies indoors are just as inviting. Dark beams, exposed stone walls, and antique furniture set the mood on the ground and first floors, and the vaulted cellar houses contemporary-art exhibitions. Ask Iris Marx, the ebullient proprietor, to translate the menu (it's in local dialect). She offers country cooking at its best. The excellent wine list features 32 wines by the glass. ✉ *Liebfrauenstr. 17* ☎ *06744/8186* ▤ *MC, V* ⊘ *Closed Tues. and Jan. No lunch except Sun. May–Sept.*

$$$ 🏨 **Burghotel Auf Schönburg.** Part of the Schönburg Castle complex (12th
Fodor's Choice century) has been lovingly restored as a romantic hotel and restaurant
★ ($$$; closed Mon. except for hotel guests), with terraces in the court-yard and a Rhine view. Antique furnishings and historic rooms (library, chapel, prison tower) make for an unforgettable stay, enhanced by the extraordinarily friendly, personal service of your hosts, the Hüttls, and staff. If you have only a night or two in the area, go for this hotel's first-rate lodging, food, and wine. **Pro:** castle right out of a storybook. **Cons:** lots of climbing, up the hill and up the tower; train tracks nearby. ✉ *Oberwesel* ☎ *06744/93930* ⊕ *www.hotel-schoenburg.com* ⇆ *20 rooms, 2 suites* ⚴ *In-room: no a/c, refrigerator, dial-up, Wi-Fi. In-hotel: restaurant, public Internet, no-smoking rooms* ▤ *MC, V* ⊘ *Closed mid-Jan.–mid-Mar.* ⑩ *BP*

ST. GOAR

7 km (4½ mi) north of Oberwesel; ferry to St. Goarshausen.

St. Goar and St. Goarshausen, its counterpoint on the opposite shore, are named after a Celtic missionary who settled here in the 6th century. He became the patron saint of innkeepers—an auspicious sign for both towns, which now live off tourism and wine. September is especially busy, with Weinforum Mittelrhein (a major wine-and-food presentation in Burg Rheinfels) on the first weekend every other year and the annual wine festivals and the splendid fireworks display "Rhine in Flames" on the third weekend.

St. Goar's tomb once rested in the 15th-century collegiate church, the **Stiftskirche,** built over a Romanesque crypt reminiscent of those of churches in Speyer and Köln. ✉ *Kirchpl.* ⊘ *Apr.–Oct., daily 10–6; Nov.–Mar., daily 11–5.*

☺ The castle ruins of **Burg Rheinfels,** overlooking the town, bear witness to the fact that St. Goar was once the best-fortified town in the Mittelrhein. From its beginnings in 1245, it was repeatedly enlarged by the counts of Katzenelnbogen, a powerful local dynasty, and their successors, the landgraves of Hesse. Although it repelled Louis IV's troops in 1689, Rheinfels was blasted by the French in 1797. Take time for a walk through the impressive ruins and the museum, which has an exquisite model of how the fortress looked in its heyday. To avoid the steep ascent on foot, buy a round-trip ticket (€3) for the Burgexpress, which departs from the bus stop on Heerstrasse, opposite the riverside parking lot for tour buses. ⊠ *Off Schlossberg Str.* ☎ *06741/ 7753* ⊕ *www.burg-rheinfels.com* 🎫 *€4* ⊘ *Mid-Mar.–Oct., daily 9–6; Nov.–mid-Mar., weekends 11–5.*

WHERE TO STAY & EAT

$$ ✕ **Flair Hotel Landsknecht.** Members of the Nickenig family make everyone feel at home in their riverside restaurant ($–$$) and hotel north of St. Goar. Daughter Martina, a former wine queen, and her winemaker husband, Joachim Lorenz, operate the Vinothek, where you can sample his delicious Bopparder Hamm wines. These go well with the restaurant's hearty local dishes, such as Rhine-style sauerbraten or seasonal specialties (asparagus, game). ■ **TIP→** **The hotel is an official Rheinsteig trail partner—perfect for hikers.** ⊠ *Rheinuferstr. (B–9) St. Goar–Fellen* ☎ *06741/2011* 🖷 *06741/7499* 🖹 *AE, DC, MC, V* ⊘ *Closed Jan.*

$$–$$$ 🏨 **Romantikhotel Schloss Rheinfels & Villa Rheinfels.** Directly opposite Burg
★ Rheinfels, this hotel offers modern comfort and expansive views. The rooms are tastefully furnished in country manor style, and the restaurant is noted for game and fish. **Pros:** marvelous views of the Rhine and the town. **Cons:** villa section with one of the suites and all three of the apartments is well removed from the hotel and lacking charm. ⊠ *Schlossberg 47* ☎ *06741/8020* ⊕ *www.schloss-rheinfels.de* ☞ *56 rooms, 3 apartments, 4 suites* ☖ *In-room: no a/c, refrigerator, dial-up (some). In-hotel: 2 restaurants, bar, pool, spa, bicycles, laundry service, public Internet, some pets allowed, no-smoking rooms* 🖹 *AE, DC, MC, V* ❑ *BP.*

ST. GOARSHAUSEN

29 km (18 mi) north of Rüdesheim, ferry from St. Goar.

☺ St. Goarshausen lies at the foot of two 14th-century castles whose names, Katz (Cat) and Maus (Mouse), reflect but one of the many power plays on the Rhine in the Middle Ages. Territorial supremacy and the concomitant privilege of collecting tolls fueled the fires of rivalry. In response to the construction of Burg Rheinfels, the archbishop of Trier erected a small castle north of St. Goarshausen to protect his interests. In turn, the masters of Rheinfels, the counts of Katzenelnbogen, built a bigger castle directly above the town. Its name was shortened to Katz, and its smaller neighbor was scornfully referred to as Maus. Katz is not open to the public. **Maus** has a terrace café with great views and demonstrations featuring eagles and falcons in flight. ☎ *06771/7669* ⊕ *www.burg-maus.de* 🎫 *€8* ⊘ *Mid-Mar.–mid-Oct., Tues.–Sat. at 11 and 2:30, Sun. at 11, 2:30, and 4:30.*

Some 10 km (6 mi) north of the Maus castle, near Kamp-Bornhofen, is a castle duo separated by a "quarrel wall": **Liebenstein and Sterrenberg,** known as the *Feindliche Brüder* (rival brothers). Both impressive ruins have terrace cafés that afford good views.

One of the Rhineland's main attractions lies 4 km (2½ mi) south of St. Goarshausen: the steep (430-foot-high) slate cliff named after the beautiful blond nymph **Loreley.** Here she supposedly sat, singing songs so lovely that sailors and fishermen were lured to the treacherous rapids—and their demise. The rapids really were once treacherous. The Rhine is at its narrowest here, and the current the swiftest. Contrary to popular belief, the Loreley nymph doesn't stem from legend. She was invented in 1812 by author Clemens Brentano, who drew his inspiration from the sirens of Greek legend. Her tale was retold as a ballad by Heinrich Heine and set to music by Friedrich Silcher at the height of Rhine Romanticism in the 19th century. The haunting melody is played on the PA systems of the Rhine boats whenever the Loreley is approached.

OFF THE BEATEN PATH

Besucherzentrum Loreley. The 3-D, 20-minute film and hands-on exhibits at this visitor center are entertaining ways to learn about the region's flora and fauna, geology, wine, shipping, and, above all, the myth of the Loreley. You can stock up on souvenirs in the shop and have a snack at the bistro before heading for the nearby vantage point at the cliff's summit. The center is on the Rheinsteig trail, and other hiking trails are signposted in the landscaped park. There is hourly bus service to and from the KD steamer landing in St. Goarshausen (April to October). ⊠ *Auf der Loreley* ☎ *06771/599–093* ⊕ *www. loreley-besucherzentrum.de* ☑ *€2.50* ⊗ *Mar., daily 10–5; Apr.–Oct., daily 10–6; Nov.–Feb., weekends 11–4.*

BOPPARD

17 km (11 mi) north of St. Goar; ferry to Filsen.

Boppard is a pleasant little resort that evolved from a Celtic settlement into a Roman fortress, Frankish royal court, and Free Imperial City. Boppard's tourist office conducts free walking tours mid-April to mid-October, Saturday at 11, starting at the office on the market square.

ESSENTIALS

Visitor Information **Boppard** (⊠ *Tourist-Information, Altes Rathaus am Marktpl.* ☎ *06742/3888* 🖶 *06742/81402* ⊕ *www.boppard.de*).

EXPLORING

The Roman garrison Bodobrica, established here in the 4th century, was enclosed by a 26-foot-high rectangular wall (1,010 by 505 feet) with 28 defense towers. You can see portions of these in the fascinating open-air **archaeological park** (⊠ *Angertstr. near B–9 and the railroad tracks*).

The **Stadtmuseum** *(town museum)*, housed in the 14th-century Kurfürstliche Burg (elector's castle) built by the archbishop of Trier, has exhibits on Boppard's Roman and medieval past, as well as an extensive collection of bentwood furniture designed by the town's favorite son,

Michael Thonet (1796–1871). ■TIP→ **The cane-bottom Stuhl Nr. 14 (Chair No. 14) is the classic found in coffeehouses around the world since 1859.** ⊠*Burgstr. near ferry dock* ☎*06742/10369* ⊡*Free* ☉*Apr.–Oct., Tues.–Sun. 10–12:30 and 1:30–5.*

Excavations in the 1960s revealed ancient Roman baths beneath the twin-tower, Romanesque **Severuskirche** *(Church of St. Severus; 1236)* on the market square. The large triumphal crucifix over the main altar and a lovely statue of a smiling Madonna date from the 13th century.

Two baroque altars dominate the interior of the Gothic **Karmeliterkirche** *(Carmelite Church)* on Karmeliterstrasse, near the Rhine. It houses intricately carved choir stalls and tombstones and several beautiful Madonnas. Winegrowers still observe the old custom of laying the first-picked *Trauben* (grapes) at the foot of the Traubenmadonna (1330) to ensure a good harvest. The annual wine festival takes place in late September, just before the Riesling harvest.

From the Mühltal station, let the *Sessellift* (chairlift) whisk you 1,300 feet uphill to the **Vierseenblick,** a vantage point from which the Rhine looks like a chain of lakes. ⊠*Round-trip €6.50* ☉*Apr.–Oct., daily 9:30–6:30.*

WHERE TO STAY & EAT

¢ ✕**Weinhaus Heilig Grab.** This wine estate's tavern, Boppard's oldest, is full of smiling faces: the wines are excellent, the fare is simple but hearty, and the welcome is warm. Old chestnut trees shade tables in the courtyard. If you'd like to visit the cellars or vineyards, ask your friendly hosts, Rudolf and Susanne Schoeneberger. ⊠*Zelkesg. 12* ☎*06742/2371* ⊟*06742/81220* ⊟*MC, V* ☉*Closed Tues. and 3 wks late Dec.–early Jan. No lunch*

$$ ⊡**Best Western Hotel Bellevue.** You can enjoy a Rhine view from many of the rooms in this traditional hotel or from the terrace next to the water-front promenade. Afternoon tea, dinner, and Sunday lunch are served in the gourmet restaurant Le Chopin ($$$$). **Pro:** marvelous Rhine view. **Con:** parking is a problem. ⊠*Rheinallee 41* ☎*06742/1020* ⊕*www.bellevue-boppard.de* ⟲*92 rooms, 1 suite* ⌂*In-room: no a/c (some), refrigerator, Wi-Fi. In-hotel: 2 restaurants, bar, pool, gym, spa, laundry service, public Internet, no-smoking rooms, some pets allowed* ⊟*AE, DC, MC, V*

SPORTS & THE OUTDOORS

HIKING The 10-km (6-mi) **Weinwanderweg** *(Wine Hiking Trail)* from Boppard to Spay begins north of town on Peternacher Weg. Many other marked trails in the vicinity are outlined on maps and in brochures available from the tourist office.

KOBLENZ

20 km (12 mi) north of Boppard.

The ancient city of Koblenz is at a geographic nexus known as the **Deutsches Eck** (German Corner) in the heart of the Mittelrhein region.

Rivers and mountains converge here: the Mosel flows into the Rhine on one side; the Lahn flows in on the other a few miles south; and three mountain ridges intersect.

Founded by the Romans in AD 9, the city was first called Castrum ad Confluentes (Fort at the Confluence). It became a powerful city in the Middle Ages, when it controlled trade on both the Rhine and the Mosel. Air raids during World War II destroyed 85% of the city, but extensive restoration has done much to re-create its former atmosphere.

GETTING HERE & AROUND

You can get here speedily by autobahn or via a leisurely scenic drive along the Rhine (or even more mellow, by cruise boat). The Europabus also serves the city. The Koblenz tourist office has guided English-language tours on Saturday at 3 from May to October. Tours are €3 and depart from the Historisches Rathaus on Jesuitenplatz.

ESSENTIALS

Visitor Information Koblenz (✉ *Tourist-Information, Jesuitenpl. 2–4* ☎ *0261/129– 1610* ⊕ *www.koblenz.de*).

EXPLORING

MAIN ATTRACTIONS

❼ The **Deutsches Eck** *(German Corner)* is at the sharp intersection of the Rhine and Mosel, a pointed bit of land jutting into the river like the prow of some early ironclad warship. One of the more effusive manifestations of German nationalism—an 1897 equestrian statue of Kaiser Wilhelm I, first emperor of the newly united Germany—was erected here. It was destroyed at the end of World War II and replaced in 1953 with a ponderous monument to Germany's unity. After German reunification a new statue of Wilhelm was placed atop this monument in 1993. Pieces of the Berlin Wall stand on the Mosel side—a memorial to those who died as a result of the partitioning of the country.

❶ Koblenz is centered on the west bank of the Rhine. On the east bank stands Europe's largest fortress, **Festung Ehrenbreitstein,** offering a commanding view from 400 feet above the river. The earliest buildings date from about 1100, but the bulk of the fortress was constructed in the 16th century. In 1801 it was partially destroyed by Napoléon, and the French occupied Koblenz for the next 18 years. As for the fortress's 16th-century Vogel Greif cannon, the French absconded with it in 1794, the Germans took it back in 1940, and the French commandeered it again in 1945. The 15-ton cannon was peaceably returned by French president François Mitterrand in 1984 and is now part of the exhibit on the history of local technologies, from wine growing to industry, in the fortress's **Landesmuseum** (*State Museum* ☎ *0261/66750* ☑ *€4* ⊙ *Mid-Mar.–mid-Nov., daily 9:30–5*). To reach the fortress on the east bank of the Rhine, take bus No. 9 or 10 from the train station or the **ferry** (☑ *€2.60 round-trip* ⊙ *Apr. and Nov., daily 8:30–6; May– Oct., daily 8–7*) from the Pegelhaus on the Koblenz riverbank (near Rheinstrasse). There is also a direct bus from the station to the fortress Sunday afternoons April–October. Take the **Sesselbahn** (*chairlift*

11

📟 €6.20 round-trip ⊙ Apr. and May, daily 10–4:50; June–Sept., daily 10–5:50) to ascend to the fortress. For an introduction to the fortress and its history, head for the *Besucherdienst* (visitors center) to see the eight-minute English video. English tours are for groups only, but you can often join a group that is registered for a tour. 📞0261/6675–4000 📟*Grounds €1.10, tour €2.10, combined ticket €4* ⊙ *Mid-Mar.–mid-Nov., daily 10–5.*

❽ The **Ludwig Museum** stands just behind the Deutsches Eck, housed in the spic-and-span Deutschherrenhaus, a restored 13th-century building. Industrialist Peter Ludwig, one of Germany's leading contemporary-art collectors, has filled this museum with part of his huge collection. ✉*Danziger Freiheit 1* 📞*0261/304–040* ⊕*www.ludwig museum.org* 📟*€2.50, €3.50 with Mittelrhein Museum* ⊙ *Tues.–Sat. 10:30–5, Sun. 11–6.*

❾ The **St. Kastor Kirche** *(St. Castor Church)* is a sturdy Romanesque basil-★ ica consecrated in 836. It was here in 842 that plans were drawn for the Treaty of Verdun, formalizing the division of Charlemagne's great empire and leading to the creation of Germany and France as separate states. Inside, compare the squat Romanesque columns in the nave with the intricate fan vaulting of the Gothic sections. The **St. Kastor Fountain** outside the church is an intriguing piece of historical one-upmanship. It was built by the occupying French to mark the beginning of Napoléon's ultimately disastrous Russian campaign of 1812. ✉*Kastorhof* ⊙ *Daily 9–6.*

The **Mittelrhein Museum** houses the city's art collection in a lovely 16th-century building near the Old Town's central square, Am Plan. It has an extensive collection of landscapes focusing on the Rhine. It also has a notable collection of secular medieval art and works by regional artists. ✉*Florinsmarkt 15* 📞*0261/129–2520* ⊕*www. mittelrhein-museum.de* 📟*€2.50, €3.50 with Ludwig Museum* ⊙ *Tues.–Sat. 10:30–5, Sun. 11–6.*

ALSO WORTH SEEING

❺ Strolling along the promenade toward town, you'll pass the gracious **Kurfürstliches Schloss**, the prince-elector's palace. It was built in 1786 by Prince-Elector Clemens Wenzeslaus as an elegant escape from the grim Ehrenbreitstein fortress. The palace itself is open to the public the first Sunday in May for *Wein im Schloss*, a large presentation of Lower Mosel, Nahe, Mittelrhein, and Ahr wines. In the garden behind the palace, don't miss the handsome statue of Father Rhine & Mother Mosel.

❿ War damage is evidenced by the blend of old buildings and modern store blocks on and around Am Plan. The **Liebfrauenkirche** *(Church of Our Lady)* stands on Roman foundations at the Old Town's highest point. The bulk of the church is of Romanesque design, but its choir is one of the Rhineland's finest examples of 15th-century Gothic architecture, and the west front is graced with two 17th-century baroque towers. ✉*Am Plan* ⊙ *Mon.–Sat. 8–6, Sun. 9–8.*

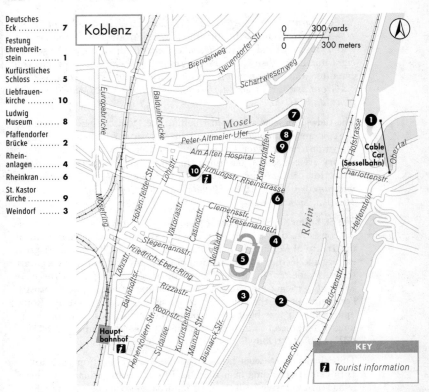

❷ The **Pfaffendorf Brücke** *(Pfaffendorf Bridge)* marks the beginning of the Old Town.

❹ The **Rheinanlagen** *(Rhine Gardens)*, a 10-km (6-mi) promenade, run along the riverbank past the Weindorf.

❻ The squat form of the **Rheinkran** *(Rhine Crane)*, built in 1611, is one of Koblenz's landmarks. Marks on the side of the building indicate the heights reached by floodwaters of bygone years. In the mid-19th century a pontoon bridge consisting of a row of barges spanned the Rhine here; when ships approached, two or three barges were simply towed out of the way to let them through.

❸ Just off the Pfaffendorf Bridge, between the modern blocks of the Rhein-Mosel-Halle and the Hotel Mercure, is the **Weindorf** (⊕*www. weindorf-koblenz.de*), a wine "village" constructed for a mammoth exhibition of German wines in 1925, which is now a restaurant.

WHERE TO EAT

\$\$\$ ✕ **Zum weissen Schwanen.** Guests have found a warm welcome in this
★ half-timber inn and mill since 1693, a tradition carried on by the Kunz family. It's located next to the 13th-century town gateway of Braubach, just below the Marksburg. This is a charming place to overnight or enjoy well-prepared, contemporary German cuisine with regional spe-

cialties. Brasserie Brentano ($) serves lighter fare and Sunday brunch. The hotel is an official Rheinsteig trail partner. ⊠*Brunnenstr. 4, 12 km (7½ mi) south of Koblenz via B–42 Braubach* ☎*02627/9820* ▤ *DC, MC, V*

$$ ✕Da Vinci. Noble and creative are the decor and fare at this smart **★** restaurant in the heart of the Old Town. Da Vinci reproductions, including an original-size rendition of *The Last Supper,* adorn the walls. Leather upholstery, an elegant bar, and soft lighting round out the ambience. Specialties include suckling pig from the Swabian Alb, Charolais and Angus beef, and fresh fish. The wine list focuses on fine Italian wines. There's also a sensational Sunday brunch. ⊠*Firmungstr. 32b* ☎*0261/921–5444* ▤*AE, MC, V.*

$ ✕Café Einstein. Portraits of Einstein line the walls of this lively restaurant. The friendly Tayhus family serves tasty fare daily, from a hearty breakfast buffet (brunch on Sunday—reservations recommended) to late-night finger food. Fish is a specialty in summer. This place fills up quickly on nights with live music—piano music on Wednesday and live bands on Friday and Saturday in the winter. ⊠*Firmungstr. 30* ☎*0261/914–4999* ▤*AE, DC, MC, V.*

$ ✕Palais Restaurant. The atrium of this historic building (once a furniture store) has been turned into a classy yet comfortable meeting point. From early morning until late at night, food and drinks are served amid fabulous art nouveau decor, complete with huge palm trees. The huge terrace on Görres Square is a perfect spot for people-watching and soaking up the sun. On Saturday the lower level turns into a disco. ⊠*Firmungstr. 2, Am Görrespl.* ☎*0261/100–5833* ▤*AE, MC, V.*

$ ✕Weindorf-Koblenz. The Bastian family has upgraded the food and wine selection at this reconstructed "wine village" of half-timber houses grouped around a tree-shaded courtyard. Fresh renditions of traditional Rhine and Mosel specialties, a good selection of local wines, and a fabulous Sunday brunch—wine, beer, and nonalcoholic beverages are included in the price (€24)—make this a popular spot. ⊠*Julius-Wegeler-Str. 2–4* ☎*0261/133–7190* ▤*AE, DC, MC, V* ⊘*No lunch Nov.–Mar.*

$ ✕Weinhaus Hubertus. Hunting scenes and trophies line the wood-panel walls of this cozy wine restaurant named after the patron saint of hunters. Karin and Dieter Spahl serve hearty portions of traditional fare, such as Tafelspitz with horseradish sauce, savoy cabbage, and poatoes. And try their dessert specials, which include a cinnamon-vanilla crepe with port wine, plums, and ice cream. ⊠*Florinsmarkt 6* ☎*0261/31177* ▤*AE, DC, MC, V* ⊘*Closed Tues. Lunch weekends only, May–Oct.*

WHERE TO STAY

$$ ▦Hotel Lorenz Veltins. The Veltins brewery operates this little hotel opposite the tourist-information office in the heart of the Old Town. Guest rooms have hardwood floors and modern furnishings and baths. In the restaurant ($), look for nine types of the Alsatian specialty *Flammkuchen.* **Pros:** near the Deutsches Eck and city center. **Cons:** plain exterior, noisy area. ⊠*Jesuitenpl. 1–3* ☎*0261/133–360* ⊕*www.lorenz-koblenz.de* ⇌*14 rooms* ⚘*In-room: no a/c, Ethernet, dial-up. In-hotel: restaurant, bar, no elevator, some pets allowed* ▤*AE, MC, V* ⓧ*BP.*

NIGHTLIFE & THE ARTS

The **Staatsorchester Rheinische Philharmonie** (*Rhenish Philharmonic Orchestra* ✉*Eltzhoferstr.* 6a ☏*0261/301–2272*) plays regularly in the Rhein-Mosel-Halle. The gracious neoclassic **Theater der Stadt Koblenz** (✉*Clemensstr.* 1–5 ☏*0261/129–2840*), built in 1787, is still in regular use.

Circus Maximus (✉*Stegemannstr.* 30, *at Viktoriastr.* ☏*0261/300–2357*) offers disco sounds, live music, and theme parties practically every evening. **Café Hahn** (✉*Neustr.* 15 ☏*0261/42302*), in the suburb of Güls, features everything from cabaret and stand-up comedians to popular musicians and bands. For Latin American music and good cocktails, head for **Enchilada** (✉*Gerichtsstr.* 2 ☏*0261/100–4666*).

SHOPPING

Koblenz's most pleasant shopping is in the Old City streets around the market square Am Plan. **Löhr Center** (✉*Hohenfelder Str.* at Am Wöllershof), a modern, American-style, windowless mall, has some 130 shops and restaurants.

THE MOSEL VALLEY

The Mosel is one of the most hauntingly beautiful river valleys on earth. Here, as in the Rhine Valley, forests and vines carpet steep hillsides; castles and church spires dot the landscape; and medieval wine hamlets line the riverbanks. The Mosel landscape is no less majestic, but it's less narrow and more peaceful than that of the Rhine Gorge; the river's countless bends and loops slow its pace and lend the region a special charm.

WINNINGEN

11 km (7 mi) southwest of Koblenz on B–416.

Winningen is a gateway to the Terrassenmosel (Terraced Mosel), the portion of the river characterized by steep, terraced vineyards. Winches help winegrowers and their tools make the ascent, but tending and harvesting the vines are all done by hand. ■TIP➔ **For a bird's-eye view of the valley, drive up Fährstrasse to Am Rosenhang, the start of a pleasant walk along the Weinlehrpfad (Educational Wine Path).**

As you head upstream toward Kobern-Gondorf, you'll pass the renowned vineyard site Uhlen. In Kobern the Oberburg (upper castle) and the St. Matthias Kapelle, a 12th-century chapel, are good vantage points. Half-timber houses reflecting the architectural styles of three centuries ring the town's pretty market square.

WHERE TO STAY & EAT

$$ ✕**Alte Mühle Höreth.** At Thomas and Gudrun Höreth's romantic coun-
★ try inn a labyrinth of little rooms and cellars is grouped around oleander-lined courtyards. The menu offers something for every taste, but the absolute hits are the homemade cheeses, terrines, pâtés, and

CLOSE UP

Cruising the Rhine & Mosel Rivers

11

No visit to the Rhineland is complete without at least one river cruise, and there are many options from which to choose. Trips along the Rhine and Mosel range in length from a few hours to days or weeks. **Viking River Cruises** (☎ *0221/25860, 877/668–4546 in the U.S.* ⊕ *www.vikingrivers. com*) offers various multiday cruises on cabin ships.

A major day-trip line is the **Köln-Düsseldorfer Deutsche Rheinschiffahrt** (*KD Rhine Line* ☎ *0221/208–8318* ⊕ *www.k-d.com*). Its fleet travels the Rhine between Köln and Mainz, daily from Easter to late October, and the Mosel from Koblenz to Cochem, daily from June to September. There are many special offers, such as free travel on your birthday; half-price for senior citizens on Monday and Friday; two cyclists for the price of one on Tuesday; and family day on Wednesday.

Many smaller, family-operated boat companies offer daytime trips and, often, nighttime dinner-dance cruises. The Koblenz operator **Rhein- und Moselschiffahrt Hölzenbein** (☎ *0261/37744* ⊕ *www.hoelzenbein. de*) travels between Koblenz and Winningen on the Mosel and between Koblenz and Rüdesheim on the Rhine. From Koblenz, **Personenschiffahrt Merkelbach** (☎ *0261/76810* ⊕ *www. merkelbach.personenschiffe.de*) makes round-trip "castle cruises" to

Schloss Stolzenfels (one hour) or the Marksburg (two hours), passing by six castles en route. The **Hebel-Linie** (☎ *06742/2420* ⊕ *www.hebel-linie. de*) has Loreley Valley trips from Boppard. Two important Mittelrhein specialists traveling from Bingen or Rüdesheim to the Loreley and making brief castle cruises are the **Bingen-Rüdesheimer Fahrgastschiffahrt** (☎ *06721/14140* ⊕ *www. bingen-ruedesheimer.de*) and the **Rösslerlinie** (☎ *06722/2353* ⊕ *www. roesslerlinie.de*). The Frankfurt-based **Primus-Linie** (☎ *069/133–8370* ⊕ *www.primus-linie.de*) cruises between Frankfurt and the Loreley via Wiesbaden and, occasionally, between Wiesbaden and Heidelberg. The spacious, luxurious *Princesse Marie-Astrid* (☎ *00352/758–275* ⊕ *www. moselle-tourist.lu*), headquartered in Grevenmacher, Luxembourg, offers gourmet dining and occasionally evening shows or live music, during Mosel cruises along the German–Luxembourgian border from Trier or Grevenmacher to Schengen. Other lines with Mosel service are **Mosel-Schiffstouristic Hans Michels** of Bernkastel-Kues (☎ *06531/8222* ⊕ *www.mosel-personenschifffahrt.de*), which goes from Bernkastel to Traben-Trarbach, and **Personenschiffahrt Kolb** of Briedern (☎ *02673/1515* ⊕ *www.moselfahrplan.de*), from Cochem to Trier.

Entensülze (goose in aspic), served with the Höreths' own wines. ✉ *Mühlental 17, via B–416 Kobern-Gondorf* ☎ *02607/6474* ☐ *MC, V* ⊗ *No lunch weekdays.*

$$ ✕ **Halferschenke.** This *Schenke* (inn) was once an overnight stop for *Halfer*, who with their horses towed cargo-laden boats upstream. Today the stone inn (1832) is run by a friendly young couple, Thomas and Eva Balmes. In the dining room, light walls, dark-wood, antiques, and lots of candles and flowers are a lovely setting for the artfully prepared food

($$–$$$). An excellent selection of Terrassenmosel wines is available. ⊠*Hauptstr. 63, via B–49, opposite Kobern Dieblich* ☎*02607/1008* 🖃*AE, MC, V* ⊘*Restaurant closed Mon. No lunch Tues.–Sat.*

$ 🏨**Hotel Simonis.** Alexandra de Bruin and Paul Vollmer, a cheerful Dutch couple, have completely renovated this traditional hotel. Rooms are individually decorated with pretty print fabrics, comfortable furnishings, and contemporary art. Two suites are housed in what is allegedly Germany's oldest half-timber house (1321) across the courtyard. Light fare is served in the Weinstube, which has an open fireplace. **Pro:** half-timber setting. **Con:** no elevator. ⊠*Marktpl. 4 Kobern-Gondorf* ☎*02607/203* ⊕*www.hotelsimonis.com* ↩*15 rooms, 2 suites* ⚃*In-room: no a/c (some), refrigerator, Wi-Fi (some). In-hotel: restaurant, bicycles, no elevator, laundry service, public Internet, no-smoking rooms, some pets allowed* 🖃*MC, V* ⊘*Closed Jan.* ⦿*BP.*

ALKEN

22 km (13½ mi) southwest of Koblenz.

The 12th-century castle **Burg Thurant** towers over the village and the Burgberg (castle hill) vineyard. Wine and snacks are served in the courtyard; castle tours take in the chapel, cellar, tower, and a weapons display. Allow a good half hour for the climb from the riverbank. Call ahead in winter to make sure it is open. ☎*02605/2004* ⊕*www.thurant.de* 🎫*€3* ⊘*May–Oct., daily 10–6; Nov.–Feb., weekends 10–4.*

WHERE TO EAT

$$ ✕**Restaurant Burg Thurant.** The Kopowskis' stylish guesthouse sits at the foot of the castle, next to a venerable stone tower on the riverbank. The restaurant serves tasty renditions of *Mosel Aal* (Mosel eel), Mosel perch with wine-sauerkraut, and *Entenbrust an Brombeerjus* (breast of duck in blackberry sauce), accompanied by wines from the region's finest producers. In summer you can dine alfresco on the garden patio. ⊠*Moselstr. 16* ☎*02605/3581* 🖃*MC* ⊘*Closed Thurs. and Feb. No lunch weekdays Nov.–Apr.*

EN ROUTE   **Burg Eltz** *(Eltz Castle)* is one of Germany's most picturesque, genuinely medieval castles (12th–16th centuries), and merits as much attention as King Ludwig's trio of castles in Bavaria. The 40-minute English-language tour, given when enough English-speakers gather, guides you through the period rooms and massive kitchen. There is also a popular treasure vault filled with gold and silver. To get here, exit B–416 at Hatzenport (opposite and southwest of Alken), proceed to Münster-maifeld, and follow signs to the parking lot near the Antoniuskapelle. From here it's a 15-minute walk, or take the shuttle bus (€1.50). Hikers can reach the castle from Moselkern in 40 minutes. ⊠*Burg Eltz/ Münstermaifeld* ☎*02672/950–500* ⊕*www.burg-eltz.de* 🎫*Tour and treasure vault €8* ⊘*Apr.–Oct., daily 9:30–5:30.*

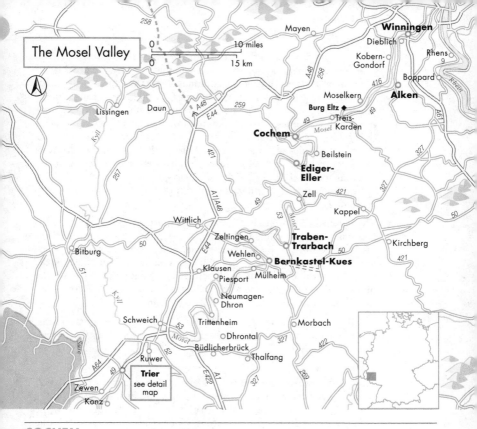

The Mosel Valley

COCHEM

51 km (31½ mi) southwest of Koblenz on B-49, approximately 93 km (58 mi) from Trier.

Cochem is one of the most attractive towns of the Mosel Valley, with a riverside promenade to rival any along the Rhine. It's especially lively during the wine festivals in June and late August. If time permits, savor the landscape from the deck of a boat—many excursions are available, lasting from one hour to an entire day. The tourist office on Endertplatz has an excellent English-language outline for a walking tour of the town. From the **Enderttor** (Endert Town Gate) you can see the entrance to Germany's longest railway tunnel, the Kaiser-Wilhelm, an astonishing example of 19th-century engineering. The 4-km-long (2½-mi-long) tunnel saves travelers a 21-km (13-mi) detour along one of the Mosel's great loops.

ESSENTIALS

Visitor Information Cochem (✉ *Tourist-Information, Endertpl. 1* ☎ *02671/60040* 🌐 *www.cochem.de).*

EXPLORING

The 15-minute walk to the **Reichsburg** *(Imperial Fortress)*, the 1,000-year-old castle overlooking the town, will reward you with great views of the area. ■TIP➔ **Flight demonstrations (eagles and falcons) take place Tuesday through Sunday at 11, 1, 2:30, and 4.** With advance reservations, you can get a taste of the Middle Ages at a medieval banquet, complete with costumes, music, and entertainment. Banquets take place on Friday (7 PM) and Saturday (6 PM) and last four hours; the price (€41.50) includes a castle tour. During the *Burgfest* (castle festival) the first weekend of August, there's a medieval market and colorful tournaments. ☎02671/255 ⊕*www.reichsburg-cochem.de* ☎*€4.50, including 40-min tour; flight demonstration €3.50* ☉*Mid-Mar.–early Nov., daily 9–5.*

The **Historische Senfmühle** is a 200-year-old mustard mill. Wolfgang Steffens conducts daily tours at 11, 2, 3, and 4, showing how he produces his gourmet mustard. Garlic, cayenne, honey, curry, and even Riesling wine are among the types you can sample and purchase in the shop. From the Old Town, walk across the bridge toward Cond. The mill is to the left of the bridgehead. ⊠*Stadionstr. 1* ☎*02671/607–665* ⊕*www.senfmuehle.net* ☎*Tours €2.50* ☉*Daily 10–6.*

A ride on the **chairlift** to the Pinner Kreuz provides great vistas. ⊠*Endertstr.* ☎*02671/989–063* ☎*Round-trip €5.80* ☉*Late Mar.–mid-Nov., daily 10–6.*

WHERE TO EAT

$$$ ✕**Alte Thorschenke.** Next to the Enderttor, this inn dates from 1332. Winding staircases, ancient wooden beams, and historic decor set the mood. Hunting trophies and portraits of prince electors adorn the wood-panel walls of the restaurant. There's also a cozy Weinstube and a patio for alfresco dining. Highly recommended are the *Wildplatte* (game platter), and the Moselmenü. The parent firm, Weingut Freiherr von Landenberg, supplies the excellent Mosel wine and welcomes visitors to tour the estate. ⊠*Brückenstr. 3* ☎*02671/7059* ⊟*AE, DC, MC, V*

$$$ ✕**Lohspeicher–l'Auberge du Vin.** In times past, oak bark for leather tanners was dried and stored in this building (1834). This house near the market square is now a charming inn run by a vivacious young couple, Ingo and Birgit Beth. His delicacies are a pleasure for the palate and the eye. At least one saltwater and one freshwater fish are featured daily. Don't miss the dessert *Variation* (medley). Some 20 French and Italian wines supplement the family's own estate-bottled wines. ⊠*Oberg. 1, at Marktpl.* ☎*02671/3976* ⊟*MC, V* ☉*Closed Wed. and Feb.*

$$ ✕**Moselromantik Hotel Weissmühle.** This lovely inn is set amid the forested hills of the Enderttal (Endert Valley) on the site of a historic mill. Lined with photos and memorabilia from the original mill, it's an oasis from traffic and crowds yet only 2½ km (1½ mi) from Cochem. Beneath the exposed beams and painted ceiling of the restaurant, food from the hotel's own trout farm will grace your table. German and French wines are served. ⊠*Wilde Endert 2, D–56812* ☎*02671/8955* ⊟*MC, V*

EDIGER-ELLER

11

61 km (38 mi) southwest of Koblenz on B–49.

Ediger is another photogenic wine village with well-preserved houses and remnants of a medieval town wall.

The **Martinskirche** (*St. Martin's Church* ✉*Kirchstr.*) is a remarkable amalgamation of art and architectural styles, inside and out. Take a moment to admire the 117 carved bosses in the star-vaulted ceiling of the nave. Among the many fine sculptures throughout the church and the chapel is the town's treasure: a Renaissance stone relief, *Christ in the Wine Press.*

WHERE TO STAY

$ ⌂**Zum Löwen.** This hotel, run by the Saffenreuther family, boasts friendly service and a daughter who was once crowned the Mosel Wine Queen. The rooms have simple decor; some have a balcony facing the Mosel. In addition to wine tastings and hikes in Calmont, Europe's steepest vineyard site, fishing trips can be arranged. **Pro:** fine view of the Mosel. **Con:** on a busy street. ✉*Moselweinstr. 23* ☎*02675/208* ⊕*www.mosel-hotel-loewen.de* ⊷*20 rooms* ⌂*In-room: no a/c, no phone, Wi-Fi. In-hotel: restaurant, laundry service, no-smoking rooms, some pets allowed* ⊟*AE, MC, V* ☉*Hotel and restaurant closed Jan.– mid-Mar. Restaurant closed Tues. and Wed. mid-Mar.–Apr.* ⧖*BP.*

■ EN
ROUTE

As you continue along the winding course of the Mosel, you'll pass Europe's steepest vineyard site, **Calmont**, opposite the romantic ruins of a 12th-century Augustinian convent and before the loop at Bremm.

Zell is a popular village full of pubs and wineshops plying the crowds with Zeller Schwarze Katz, "Black Cat" wine, a commercially successful product and the focal point of a large wine festival in late June. Some 6 million vines hug the slopes around Zell, making it one of Germany's largest wine-growing communities. The area between Zell and Schweich (near Trier), known as the Middle Mosel, is home to some of the world's finest Riesling wines.

TRABEN-TRARBACH

30 km (19 mi) south of Cochem.

The Mosel divides Traben-Trarbach, which has pleasant promenades on both sides of the river. Its wine festivals are held the second and last weekends in July. Traben's art nouveau buildings are worth seeing (Hotel Bellevue, the gateway on the Mosel bridge, the post office, the train station, and town hall).

For a look at fine period rooms and exhibits on the historical development of the area, visit the **Mittelmosel Museum,** in the Haus Böcking (1750). ✉*Casino Str. 2* ☎*06541/9480* ⧉*€2.50* ☉*Mid-Apr.–Oct., Tues.–Sun. 10–5.*

■ EN
ROUTE

During the next 24 km (15 mi) you'll pass by world-famous vineyards, such as Erdener Treppchen, Ürziger Würzgarten, the *Sonnenuhr* (sundial) sites of Zeltingen and Wehlen, and Graacher Himmelreich, before reaching Bernkastel-Kues.

BERNKASTEL-KUES

22 km (14 mi) southwest of Traben-Trarbach, 100 km (62 mi) southwest of Koblenz on B–53.

Bernkastel and Kues straddle the Mosel, on the east and west banks, respectively.

ESSENTIALS

Visitor Information **Bernkastel-Kues** (⊠ *Tourist-Information, Gestade 6* ☎ *06531/4023* 🖷 *06531/7953* ⊕ *www.bernkastel.de*).

EXPLORING

Elaborately carved half-timber houses (16th–17th centuries) and a Renaissance town hall (1608) frame St. Michael's Fountain (1606) on Bernkastel's photogenic **market square.** In early September the square and riverbank are lined with wine stands for one of the region's largest wine festivals, the Weinfest der Mittelmosel.

From the hilltop ruins of the 13th-century castle, **Burg Landshut,** there are splendid views. It was here that Trier's Archbishop Boemund II is said to have recovered from an illness after drinking the local wine. This legendary vineyard, still known as "the Doctor," soars up from Hinterm Graben street near the town gate, Graacher Tor. You can purchase these exquisite wines from Weingut J. Lauerburg at the estate's tasteful wineshop. ⊠ *Am Markt 10* ☎ *06531/3898* 🕑 *Apr.–Oct., weekdays 1–5, Sat. 11–4.*

The philosopher and theologian Nikolaus Cusanus (1401–64) was born in Kues. The **St.-Nikolaus-Hospital** is a charitable *Stiftung* (foundation) he established in 1458, and it still operates a home for the elderly and a wine estate. Within it is the **Mosel-Weinmuseum** (*Wine museum* 🖾 *€2* 🕑 *Mid-Apr.–Oct., daily 10–6; Nov.–mid-Apr., daily 2–5*), as well as a bistro and a wineshop. You can sample more than 100 wines from the entire Mosel-Saar-Ruwer region in the **Vinothek** (🖾 *€15* 🕑 *Mid-Apr.–Oct., daily 10–6; Nov.–mid-Apr., daily 2–5*) in the vaulted cellar. ⊠ *Cusanus-Str. 2* ☎ *06531/2260* 🖾 *Tours €4* 🕑 *Tours Apr.–Oct., Tues. at 10:30, Fri. at 3.*

Some 2,600 wine growers throughout the region deliver their grapes to the **Moselland Winzergenossenschaft** (*Cooperative Winery*), where wines are produced, bottled, and marketed. It's an impressive operation, and the large wineshop is excellent. ⊠ *Bornwiese 6, in industrial park* ☎ *06531/57290* ⊕ *www.moselland.de* 🖾 *Tours, with wine sampling and film €7* 🖃 *MC, V* 🕑 *Tours Tues. and Thurs. at 2. Wineshop Jan.–Mar., weekdays 9–noon and 1–5, Sat. 9–12:30; Apr.–Dec., weekdays 9–noon and 1–6, Sat. 9–12:30.*

WHERE TO EAT

$$$$ ✕**Waldhotel Sonnora.** At their elegant country inn set in the forested
Fodor'sChoice Eifel Hills, Helmut and Ulrike Thieltges offer guests one of Germa-
★ ny's absolute finest dining experiences. Helmut is an extraordinary
chef, renowned for transforming truffles, foie gras, and Persian caviar
into culinary masterpieces. Challans duck in an orange-ginger sauce
is his specialty. The wine list is equally superb. The dining room,
with gilded and white-wood furnishings and plush red carpets, has a
Parisian look. Pretty gardens add to a memorable visit. ⊠ *Auf dem
Eichelfeld, 8 km (5 mi) southwest of Wittlich, which is 18 km (11 mi)
west of Kues via B–50; from A–1, exit Salmtal Dreis* ☎ *06578/98220*
⚑ *Reservations essential* ☰ *AE, MC, V* ☾ *Closed Mon. and Tues.,
Jan. and 1st 2 wks in July.*

$$$ ✕**Weinhotel St. Stephanus.** Rita and Hermann Saxler operate a comfort-
able, modern hotel and upscale restaurant in a 19th-century manor
house on the *Ufer* (riverbank) at Zeltingen. Whether you opt for the
handsome dining room or the terrace overlooking the Mosel, Saxler's
Restaurant is a good destination for fine food. Herr Saxler's personal
favorite is turbot in a passion-fruit and white-wine sauce. The spa
offers vinotherapy—treatments using grape-based products, such as
grapeseed oil. ⊠ *Uferallee 9,Zeltingen-Rachtig* ☎ *06532/680* ☰ *AE,
MC, V* ☾ *No lunch Tues. and Wed.*

WHERE TO STAY

$$ 🏨**Weinromantikhotel Richtershof.** Very comfortable rooms and first-class
★ friendly service gained proprietor Armin Hoeck the title "Host of the
Year 2008" from the hospitality industry magazine Allgemeine Hotel-
und Gastronomie-Zeitung. His 17th-century manor house is set in a
shady park. Relax over a great breakfast or a glass of wine on the garden terrace. Enjoy tasting the Richtershof estate wines during a visit
to the centuries-old vaulted cellars. The spa, reminiscent of Roman
baths, has treatments using grapeseed oil and other products from the
vineyard. **Pros:** garden terrace, 24-hour room service. **Con:** thin walls.
⊠ *Hauptstr. 81–83, 5 km (3 mi) south of Bernkastel via B–53 Mülheim*
☎ *06534/9480* ⊕ *www.weinromantikhotel.de* ↗ *39 rooms, 4 suites*
⚐ *In-room: no a/c, Ethernet, dial-up. In-hotel: restaurant, bar, gym,
spa, bicycles, laundry service, no-smoking rooms, some pets allowed*
☰ *MC, V* ☾ *No lunch Mon.–Sat.* ⏐◎⏐*BP.*

$ 🏨**Gästehaus Erika Prüm.** The traditional wine estate S.A. Prüm has
★ state-of-the-art cellars, a tastefully designed vinothek, and a beautiful guesthouse with an idyllic patio facing the Mosel. The spacious
rooms and baths are individually decorated in a winning mixture of
contemporary and antique furnishings. Erika Prüm is a charming host,
and her husband, Raimund (the redhead), is an excellent winemaker
who offers tastings and cellar tours. **Pros:** spacious rooms and baths.
Con: no elevator. ⊠ *Uferallee 25, north of Kues Bernkastel-Wehlen*
☎ *06531/3110* ⊕ *www.sapruem.com* ↗ *8 rooms* ⚐ *In-room: no
a/c, dial-up. In-hotel: no elevator, some pets allowed* ☰ *AE, MC, V*
☾ *Closed mid-Dec.–Feb.* ⏐◎⏐*BP.*

$ 🏨**Zur Post.** The Rössling family makes you feel welcome at their
comfortable hotel dating from 1827. It's near the riverbank, and the

market square is just around the corner. The wine list at the inviting restaurant is devoted exclusively to Mosel Rieslings. **Pro:** near the market square. **Con:** on a busy street. ⊠ *Gestade 17* ☎ *06531/96700* ⊕ *www.hotel-zur-post-bernkastel.de* ⬚ *42 rooms, 1 suite* ⌂ *In-room: no a/c, refrigerator. In-hotel: restaurant, bar, no-smoking rooms, some pets allowed* ⊟ *DC, MC, V* ⊘ *Closed Jan.* ⦿ *BP.*

EN ROUTE The 55-km (34-mi) drive from Bernkastel to Trier takes in another series of outstanding hillside vineyards, including the Brauneberg, 10 km (6 mi) upstream from Bernkastel. On the opposite side of the river is the Paulinshof (⊠ *Paulinsstr. 14, Kesten* ☎ *06535/544* ⊕ *www. paulinshof.de* ⊘ *Weekdays 8–6, Sat. 9–5*), where Thomas Jefferson was enchanted by a 1783 Brauneberger Kammer Auslese during his visit here in 1788. You can sample contemporary vintages of this wine in the beautiful chapel on the estate grounds.

On a magnificent loop 12 km (7½ mi) southwest of Brauneberg is the famous village of **Piesport,** whose steep, slate cliff is known as the Loreley of the Mosel. The village puts on the *Mosel in Flammen* (Mosel in Flames) fireworks display and festival the first weekend in July. Wines from its 35 vineyards are collectively known as Piesporter Michelsberg; however, the finest individual vineyard site, and one of Germany's very best, is the Goldtröpfchen ("little droplets of gold").

DHRONTAL

25 km (15 mi) from Bernkastel-Kues.

If the heat of the Mosel's slate slopes becomes oppressive in summer, revitalize body and soul with a scenic drive through the cool, fragrant forest of the Dhrontal (Dhron Valley), south of Trittenheim, and make a stop at its oases for food and wine lovers.

WHERE TO EAT

$$$$ ✕ **Rüssels Landhaus St. Urban.** Talented chef Harald Rüssel, his charming
★ wife Ruth, and their friendly staff see to it that guests enjoy excellent food, wine, and service in comfortable surroundings. Aromatic, visually stunning food presentations are served with wines from Germany's leading producers, including the family's Weingut St. Urbans-Hof in Leiwen. The house decor is stylish, and like the food, it reflects Mediterranean flair. ⊠ *Büdlicherbrück 1, 8 km (5 mi) south of Trittenheim, toward Hermeskeil; from A–1, exit MehringNaurath/Wald* ☎ *06509/91400* ⊟ *AE, MC, V* ⊘ *Closed Tues., Wed., 2 wks in Jan.*

$$$$ ✕ **Wein- und Tafelhaus.** For first-class wining and dining in a charming country inn or on its idyllic terrace overlooking the Mosel, this is well worth a detour. Young Austrian couple Daniela and Alexander Oos are friendly, attentive hosts. The homemade soups are delicious, as are his creative renditions of fish and shellfish. Some desserts reflect their Tirolean homeland. Every month there are three new suggestions for a four- or five-course menu—not inexpensive, but good value for a restaurant of this caliber. ⊠ *Moselpromenade 4, Trittenheim* ☎ *06507/702–803*

☐ *No credit cards* ☾ *Closed Mon. and Tues. and 1 wk each in Nov., Jan., and July.*

TRIER

55 km (34 mi) southwest of Bernkastel-Kues via B–53, 150 km (93 mi) southwest of Koblenz; 30 min by car from Luxemburg airport.

By 400 BC a Celtic tribe, the Treveri, had settled the Trier Valley. Eventually Julius Caesar's legions arrived at this strategic point on the river, and Augusta Treverorum (the town of Emperor Augustus in the land of the Treveri) was founded in 16 BC. It was described as a most opulent city, as beautiful as any outside Rome.

Around AD 275 an Alemannic tribe stormed Augusta Treverorum and reduced it to rubble. But it was rebuilt in even grander style and renamed Treveris. Eventually it evolved into one of the leading cities of the empire, and was promoted to "Roma secunda" (a second Rome) north of the Alps. As a powerful administrative capital it was adorned with all the noble civic buildings of a major Roman settlement, as well as public baths, palaces, barracks, an amphitheater, and temples. The Roman emperors Diocletian (who made it one of the four joint capitals of the empire) and Constantine both lived in Trier for years at a time.

Trier survived the collapse of Rome and became an important center of Christianity and, ultimately, one of the most powerful archbishoprics in the Holy Roman Empire. The city thrived throughout the Renaissance and baroque periods, taking full advantage of its location at the meeting point of major east–west and north–south trade routes and growing fat on the commerce that passed through.

GETTING HERE & AROUND
The area is excellent for biking. The train station in Trier rents bikes; call the Deutsche Bahn bicycle hotline to reserve. Cyclists can follow the marked route of the *Radroute Nahe-Hunsrück-Mosel* from Trier to Bingen.

You can circumnavigate the town with the narrated tours of the Römer-Express trolley or a tourist office bus. Both cost €7 and depart from Porta Nigra, near the tourist office. There is also a double-decker "hop on, hop off" bus. A 24-hour ticket on it costs €10.

There are also tours Friday, Saturday, and Sunday April through October, in which actors dressed in Roman costume bring the history of the amphitheater, the Kaiserthermen, and the old town gate to life. Each tour lasts an hour and costs €11. Reservations are essential. If you don't speak German, speak up! The tour guide and/or someone else in the group probably speaks some English and will translate the basic points. The tourist office sells tickets for all tours and also leads various walks. A tour in English (€7) departs Saturday, May through October, at 1:30.

TIMING

To do justice to Trier, consider staying for at least two full days. A walk around Trier will take a good two hours, and you will need extra time to climb the tower of the Porta Nigra, walk through the vast interior of the Dom and its treasury, visit the underground passageways of the Kaiserthermen, and examine the cellars of the Amphitheater. Allow at least another half hour each for the Bischöfliches Museum and Viehmarktthermen, as well as an additional hour for the Rheinisches Landesmuseum.

DISCOUNTS & DEALS

The **Trier Card** entitles the holder to free public transportation and discounts on tours and admission fees to Roman sights, museums, and sports and cultural venues. It costs €9 and is valid for three successive days.

ESSENTIALS

Visitor Information **Trier** (⊠ *Tourist-Information, An der Porta Nigra* ☎ *0651/978–080* ⊕ *www.trier.de/tourismus*).

Tour Information **Deutsche Bahn bicycle hotline** (☎ *01805/151–415*).

EXPLORING

MAIN ATTRACTIONS

⓫ ★ Amphitheater. The sheer size of Trier's oldest Roman structure (circa AD 100) is impressive. In its heyday it seated 20,000 spectators; today it's a stage for the Antiquity Festival. You can climb down to the cellars beneath the arena—animals were kept in cells here before being unleashed to do battle with gladiators. During Brot & Spiele (Bread & Circus) in mid-August, there are live gladiator games in the arena, complete with horses (but not lions). ⊠ *Olewiger Str. 25* ☎ *€2.10, Brot & Spiele €12.50* ☉ *Apr.–Sept., daily 9–6; Oct. and Mar., daily 9–5; Nov.–Feb., daily 9–4.*

❺ Bischöfliches Museum *(Episcopal Museum).* This collection, just behind the Dom, focuses on medieval sacred art, but there are also fascinating models of the cathedral as it looked in Roman times. Look for 15 Roman frescoes, discovered in 1946, that may have adorned the emperor Constantine's palace. ⊠ *Windstr. 6* ☎ *0651/710–5255* ☎ *€3.50; combined ticket with Domschatzkammer €4* ☉ *Apr.–Oct., Mon.–Sat. 9–5, Sun. 1–5; Nov. and Jan.–Mar., Tues.–Sat. 9–5, Sun. 1–5.*

❹ ★ Dom *(Cathedral).* The oldest Christian church north of the Alps, the Dom stands on the site of the Palace of Helen. Constantine tore the palace down in AD 330 and put up a large church in its place. The church burned down in 336, and a second, even larger one was built. Parts of the foundations of this third building can be seen in the east end of the present structure (begun in about 1035). The cathedral you see today is a weighty and sturdy edifice with small round-head windows, rough stonework, and asymmetrical towers, as much a fortress as a church. Inside, Gothic styles predominate—the result of remodeling in the 13th century—although there are also many baroque tombs, altars, and confessionals.

11

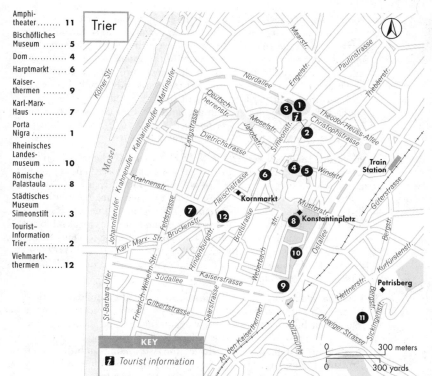

The **Domschatzkammer** (*Cathedral Treasure Chamber* €1.50; combined ticket with Bischöfliches Museum €3 ⏰Apr.–Oct. and Dec., Mon.–Sat. 10–5, Sun. 12:30–5; Nov.–Mar., Mon.–Sat. 11–4, Sun. 2–4) houses many extraordinary objects. The highlight is the 10th-century Andreas Tragaltar (St. Andrew's Portable Altar), constructed of oak and covered with gold leaf, enamel, and ivory by local craftsmen. It's a reliquary for the soles of St. Andrew's sandals, symbolized by the gilded, life-size foot on the top of the altar. ✉Domfreihof 6 ☎0651/979–0790 ⊕www.dominformation.de ✉Tours €3.50 ⏰Apr.–Oct. and Dec., daily 6:30–6; Nov. and Jan.–Mar., daily 6:30–5:30; tours Apr.–Oct., daily at 2 PM.

9 **Kaiserthermen** (*Imperial Baths*). This enormous 4th-century bathing pal-
★ ace once housed cold- and hot-water baths and a sports field. Although only the masonry of the **Calderium** (hot baths) and the vast basements remain, they are enough to give a fair idea of the original splendor and size of the complex. Originally 98 feet high, the walls you see today are just 62 feet high. During Brot & Spiele in mid-August there is a reconstructed Roman village on the sports field, with Roman arts-and-crafts workshops, and a sound-and-light show in the basements. ✉At Weimarer-Allee and Kaiserstr. ☎0651/436–2550 ✉€2.10 ⏰Apr.–Sept., daily 9–6; Oct. and Mar., daily 9–5; Nov.–Feb., daily 9–4.

① **Porta Nigra** *(Black Gate).* The best-preserved Roman structure in Trier
★ was originally a city gate, built in the 2nd century (look for holes left
by the iron clamps that held the structure together). The gate served as
part of Trier's defenses and was proof of the sophistication of Roman
military might and its ruthlessness. Attackers were often lured into the
two innocent-looking arches of the Porta Nigra, only to find themselves
enclosed in a courtyard. In the 11th century the upper stories were
converted into two churches, in use until the 18th century. The tourist office is next door. ⊠ *Porta-Nigra-Pl.* 🖃 *€2.10* 🕙 *Apr.–Sept., daily
9–6; Oct. and Mar., daily 9–5; Nov.–Feb., daily 9–4.*

⑩ **Rheinisches Landesmuseum** *(Rhenish State Museum).* The largest collec-
★ tion of Roman antiquities in Germany is housed here. The highlight
is the 4th-century stone relief of a Roman ship transporting barrels
of wine up the river. This tombstone of a Roman wine merchant was
discovered in 1874, when Constantine's citadel in Neumagen was excavated. Have a look at the 108-square-foot model of the city as it looked
in the 4th century—it provides a sense of perspective to many of the
sights you can still visit today. ⊠ *Weimarer-Allee 1* 🖀 *0651/97740*
⊕ *www.landesmuseum-trier.de* 🖃 *€5* 🕙 *May–Oct., daily 9:30–5;
Nov.–Apr., Tues.–Sun. 9:30–5.*

⑧ **Römische Palastaula** *(Roman Basilica).* An impressive reminder of Trier's
★ Roman past, this edifice is now the city's major Protestant church.
When first built by the emperor Constantine around AD 310, it was
the imperial throne room of the palace. At 239 feet long, 93 feet wide,
and 108 feet high, it demonstrates the astounding ambition of its
Roman builders and the sophistication of their building techniques.
◼TIP→ **The basilica is one of the two largest Roman interiors in existence
(the other is the Pantheon in Rome).** Look up at the deeply coffered ceiling; more than any other part of the building, it conveys the opulence of
the original structure. ⊠ *Konstantinpl.* 🖀 *0651/72468 or 0651/42570*
🕙 *Apr.–Oct., Mon.–Sat. 10–6, Sun. noon–6; Nov.–Mar., Tues.–Sat.
11–noon and 3–4, Sun. noon–1.*

ALSO WORTH SEEING

⑥ **Hauptmarkt.** The main market square of Old Trier—lined with gabled
houses from several ages—is easily reached via Simeonstrasse. The
market cross (958) and richly ornate St. Peter's Fountain (1595), dedicated to the town's patron saint, stand in the square. ◼TIP→ **The farmers' market is open Tuesday and Thursday 8–2.**

⑦ **Karl-Marx-Haus.** Marx was born on May 5, 1818, in this bourgeois house
built in 1727. Visitors with a serious interest in social history will be fas-
cinated by its small museum. A signed first edition of *Das Kapital*, the
study in which Marx sought to prove the inevitable decline of capitalism,
has a place of honor. ⊠ *Brückenstr. 10* 🖀 *0651/970–680* 🖃 *€3* 🕙 *Apr.–
Oct., daily 10–6; Nov.–Mar., Mon. 2–5, Tues.–Sun. 10–1 and 2–5.*

OFF THE
BEATEN
PATH

Roscheider Hof. For a look at 19th- and 20th-century rural life in the
Mosel-Saar area, visit the hilltop open-air Freilichtmuseum near Konz-
Saar (10 km [6 mi] southwest of Trier via B–51). Numerous farm-
houses and typical village buildings in the region were saved from the

wrecking ball by being dismantled and brought to the Roscheider Hof, where they were rebuilt and refurnished as they appeared decades ago. Old schoolrooms, a barbershop and beauty salon, a tavern, a shoemaker's workshop, a pharmacy, a grocery, and a dentist's office have been set up in the rooms of the museum proper, along with period rooms and exhibitions on local trades and household work, such as the history of laundry. In 2005 a large collection of tin figures was added. A Biedermeier rose garden, museum shop, and restaurant with a beer garden (closed Mon., no credit cards) are also on the grounds. ⊠ *Roscheiderhof 1, Konz* ☎ *06501/92710* ⊕ *www.roscheiderhof.de* ⊠ *€4* ⊙ *Apr.–Oct., Tues.–Fri. 9–6, weekends 10–6; Nov.–Mar., Tues.–Fri. 9–5, weekends 10–5.*

❸ **Städtisches Museum Simeonstift** *(Simeon Foundation City Museum)*. Built around the remains of the Romanesque Simeonskirche, this church is now a museum. It was constructed in the 11th century by Archbishop Poppo in honor of the early medieval hermit Simeon, who for seven years shut himself up in the east tower of the Porta Nigra. Collections include art and artifacts produced in Trier from the Middle Ages to the 19th century. ⊠ *Simeonstr. 60* ☎ *0651/718–1454* ⊕ *www.museum-trier. de* ⊠ *€5, free the 1st Sun. of month* ⊙ *Tues.–Sun. 10–6.*

❷ **Tourist-Information Trier.** In addition to dispensing city information, this tourist office sells regional wines and souvenirs, from Trier mouse pads and replicas of Roman artifacts to Porta Nigra pasta. ⊠ *An der Porta Nigra* ☎ *0651/978–080* ⊙ *Jan. and Feb., Mon.–Sat. 10–5, Sun. 10–1; Apr.–Sept., daily 9–6; Oct. and Mar., daily 9–5; Nov.–Feb., daily 9–4; Mar.–Apr. and Nov. and Dec., Mon.–Sat. 9–6, Sun. 10–3; May–Oct., Mon.–Thurs. 9–6, Fri. and Sat. 9–7, Sun. 10–5* ▤ *AE, MC, V.*

⓬ **Viehmarktthermen.** Trier's third Roman bath (early 1st century) was discovered beneath Viehmarktplatz when ground was broken for a parking garage. Finds of the excavations from 1987 to 1994 are now beneath a protective glass structure. You can visit the baths and see the cellar of a baroque Capuchin monastery. ⊠ *Viehmarktpl.* ☎ *0651/994–1057* ⊠ *€2.10* ⊙ *Tues.–Sun. 9–5.*

WHERE TO EAT

$$$$ ⨯ **Becker's Hotel.** This wine estate in the peaceful suburb of Olewig
★ features a gourmet restaurant, a second restaurant serving regional cuisine, and a casual Weinstube. Dining alfresco is a nice option in summer. Bordeaux and Burgundy wines are available in addition to the estate's own wines—and wine tastings, cellar visits, and guided tours on the wine path can be arranged. ⊠ *Olewiger Str. 206 Trier-Olewig* ☎ *0651/938–080* ▤ *AE, MC, V* ⊙ *Gourmet restaurant closed Sun. and Mon.*

$$$$ ⨯ **Pfeffermühle.** For nearly three decades chef Siegbert Walde has offered guests classic cuisine in elegant surroundings. The 18th-century house on the northern edge of town has two stories of cozy niches, with beautiful table settings in shades of pink; the terrace directly overlooks the Mosel. Foie gras is a favorite ingredient, served in a terrine or sautéed and served in *Ahorn-jus* (maple-flavor juices). White wines from

the Mosel's finest producers and top red Bordeaux wines make up the excellent wine list. ⊠*Zurlaubener Ufer 76* ☎*0651/26133* ♨*Reservations essential* ▤*MC, V* ⊘*Closed Sun. No lunch Mon.*

$$$ ✕**Schlemmereule.** The name means "gourmet owl," and, indeed, chef Peter Schmalen caters to gourmets in the 19th-century Palais Walderdorff complex opposite the cathedral. Lots of windows lend a light, airy look, and a replica of one of Michelangelo's Sistine Chapel paintings graces the ceiling. There's courtyard seating in summer. Carpaccio of *Gänsestopfleber* (foie gras) with port-wine vinegar and truffles is a specialty, and the fish is always excellent. Wines from top German estates, particularly from the Mosel, and an extensive selection of red wines are offered. ⊠*Palais Walderdorff, Domfreihof 1B* ☎*0651/73616* ♨*Reservations essential* ▤*AE, DC, MC, V* ⊘*Closed Sun.*

$ ✕**Walderdorff's Vinothek-Café-Club.** This trio has added a lively note to the 19th-century palace opposite Trier cathedral. The café offers salads, pasta, tapas, and steaks. Luncheon specials during the week and Sunday brunch are good value at 12.90. Some 250 local and Old and New World wines are sold in the Vinothek, where tastings are offered. The club offers music and dancing in the baroque cellars. ⊠*Palais Walderdorff, Domfreihof 1A* ☎*0651/9946–9210* ▤*AE, DC, MC, V.*

$ ✕**Zum Domstein.** Whether you dine inside or out, don't miss the collection of Roman artifacts displayed in the cellar. In addition to the German dishes on the regular menu, you can order à la carte or prix-fixe menus based on the recipes of Roman gourmet Marcus Gavius Apicius in the evening. The Gracher family are experts on the subject. ⊠*Am Hauptmarkt 5* ☎*0651/74490* ▤*MC, V.*

¢ ✕**Weinstube Kesselstatt.** The interior has exposed beams and polished wood tables; the shady terrace is popular in summer. Two soups daily, light fare, and fresh, regional cuisine are served with wines from the Reichsgraf von Kesselstatt estate. The *Tagesgericht* (daily special) and *Aktionsmenü* (prix-fixe menu) are always a good bet. ⊠*Liebfrauenstr. 10* ☎*0651/41178* ▤*MC, V* ⊘*Closed Jan.*

WHERE TO STAY

$$ ⬚**Römischer Kaiser.** Centrally located near the Porta Nigra, this handsome patrician manor from 1885 offers well-appointed rooms with handsome baths. Rooms 317 and 318 are quite spacious and have little balconies overlooking flower-filled Porta-Nigra-Platz. While some of Trier's other restaurants offer more flair, the food here is tasty, as is the hearty breakfast buffet. **Pro:** near the Porta Nigra. **Con:** some rooms are dark due to a neighboring building. ⊠*Am Porta-Nigra-Pl. 6* ☎*0651/977–0100* ⊕*www.hotels-trier.de* ⌘*43 rooms* ⬚*In-room: no a/c, refrigerator, dial-up (some), Wi-Fi (some). In-hotel: restaurant, bar, laundry service, some pets allowed, no-smoking rooms* ▤*AE, DC, MC, V* ⦿*BP.*

$ ⬚**Ambiente.** Modern flair marks the style and decor that Markus and Monika Stemper—a passionate cook and a gracious host—offer in their country inn near the Luxembourg border. Their legendary garden (with palms, ponds, and flowers galore), comfortable rooms, and personal service are remarkable. Both Restaurant Jardin ($$$) and Stempers Brasserie ($–$$) serve dishes with Mediterranean accents, enhanced by an extensive wine list. **Pros:** country atmosphere, legendary garden. **Con:** removed from city center. ✉*In der Acht 1–2, 7 km (4½ mi) southwest of Trier via B–49 Trier-Zewen* ☎*0651/827–280* ⊕*www. ambiente-trier.de* ↻*11 rooms* ⬥*In-room: no a/c, refrigerator, Wi-Fi. In-hotel: 2 restaurants, bar, bicycles, no elevator, laundry service, public Internet, no-smoking rooms* ▤*AE, DC, MC, V* ⊘*Restaurants closed Thurs.* ⦉⦊*BP.*

$ ▦**Hotel Petrisberg.** The Pantenburgs' friendly, family-run hotel is high on Petrisberg hill overlooking Trier, not far from the amphitheater. You can walk to the Old Town in 20 minutes. The individually decorated rooms have solid-pine furnishings; all but two have balconies—some with a fabulous view of the city. In the evening, you can enjoy snacks and good local wines in the wine pub. **Pro:** fine view of Trier. **Con:** somewhat removed from the city center. ✉*Sickingenstr. 11–13* ☎*0651/4640* ⊕*www.hotelpetrisberg.de* ↻*31 rooms, 4 apartments* ⬥*In-room: no a/c, dial-up (some), Wi-Fi (some). In-hotel: bar, public Internet, no-smoking rooms* ▤*MC, V* ⦉⦊*BP.*

FESTIVALS

The **Europa-Volksfest** (European Folk Festival), in May or early June, features wine and food specialties from several European countries, in addition to rides and entertainment. In late June the entire Old Town is the scene of the **Altstadtfest.** The amphitheater is an impressive setting for the theatrical performances of the **Antikenfestspiele** (Antiquity Festival) from late June to mid-July. The **Moselfest,** with wine, sparkling wine, beer, and fireworks, takes place in July along the riverbank in Zurlauben, followed by a large **Weinfest** (Wine Festival) in Olewig in early August, and Germany's largest Roman festival, **Brot & Spiele** (Bread & Circus), in mid-August. From late November until December 22, the annual **Weihnachtsmarkt** (Christmas market) takes place on the market square and in front of the cathedral.

NIGHTLIFE & THE ARTS

■**TIP→** For absolutely up-to-the-minute information on performances, concerts, and events all over town, visit the Web site ⊕ *www.trier-today. de*. Pop-up maps show exactly where everything is located.

Theater Trier (✉*Am Augustinerhof* ☎*0651/718–1818*) offers opera, theater, ballet, and concerts.

Concerts, theater, and cultural events are staged at **TUFA–Tuchfabrik** (✉*Wechselstr. 4, at Weberstr.* ☎*0651/718–2412*).

Pubs and cafés are centered on Viehmarktplatz and Stockplatz in the Old Town. **Walderdorff's** (✉*Domfreihof 1A* ☎*0651/9946–9210*) in the Palais Walderdorff has trendy DJ nights, early after-work parties, and occasional live bands.

The discotheque **FORUM** (✉*Hindenburgstr. 4* ☎*0651/170–4363*) features international DJs, theme parties, and live music.

BONN & THE KÖLN (COLOGNE) LOWLANDS

Bonn, the former capital of Germany, is the next major stop after Koblenz on the Rhine. It's close to the legendary Siebengebirge (Seven Hills), a national park and site of Germany's northernmost vineyards. According to German mythology, Siegfried (hero of the Nibelungen saga) killed a dragon here and bathed in its blood to make himself invincible. The lowland, a region of gently rolling hills north of Bonn, lacks the drama of the Rhine Gorge upstream but offers the urban pleasures of Köln (Cologne), an ancient cathedral town, and Düsseldorf, an elegant city of art and fashion. Although not geographically in the Rhineland proper, Aachen is an important side trip for anyone visiting the region. Its stunning cathedral and treasury are the greatest storehouses of Carolingian art and architecture in Europe.

BONN

44 km (27 mi) north of Koblenz, 28 km (17 mi) south of Köln

Bonn was the postwar seat of the federal government and parliament until the capital returned to Berlin in 1999. Aptly described by the title of John le Carré's spy novel *A Small Town in Germany,* the quiet university town was chosen as a stopgap measure to prevent such weightier contenders as Frankfurt from becoming the capital, a move that would have lessened Berlin's chances of regaining its former status. With the exodus of the government from Bonn, the city has lost some of its international flair. Still, other organizations and industries have moved to Bonn to fill the gap, and its status as a U.N. city has been strengthened. The fine museums and other cultural institutions that once served the diplomatic elite are still here to be enjoyed.

GETTING HERE & AROUND

The town center is a car-free zone; an inner ring road circles it with parking garages on the perimeter. A convenient parking lot is just across from the railway station and within 50 yards of the tourist office, which is on Windeckstrasse near the Hauptbahnhof. Or, you can save yourself the walk by taking bus No. 610 or U-bahn 16 to Heussallee.

Bonn has extensive bike paths downtown; these are designated, red-painted or redbrick paths on the edges of roads or sidewalks. ■TIP→ **Pedestrians, beware: anyone walking on a bike path risks getting mowed down.** Bicyclists are expected to follow the same traffic rules as cars. In Bonn the Radstation, at the main train station, will not only rent you a bike and provide maps, but will fill your water bottle and check the pressure in your tires for free.

Bilingual bus and walking tours of Bonn cost €14 and start from the tourist office. They're conducted daily at 2 from April to October, and Saturday only November to March.

DISCOUNTS & DEALS

Bonn's tourism office sells the **Bonn Regio Welcome Card,** which offers an array of reductions, plus free entry into most museums, in combina-

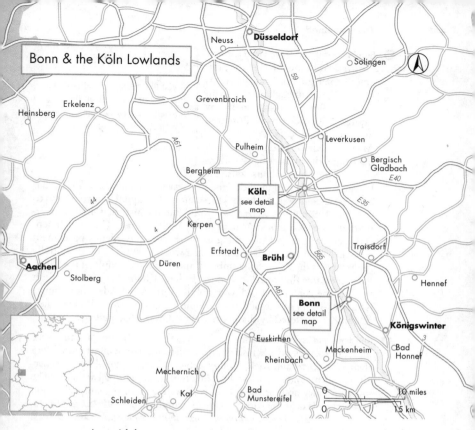

Bonn & the Köln Lowlands

tion with low- or no-cost transportation; the card costs €9 per day, €14 for two days, or €19 for three days.

ESSENTIALS

Visitor Information Bonn (✉ *Bonn Information, Windeckstr. 1* ☎ *0228/775–000* ⊕ *www.bonn.de*).

Bicycle Contact Radstation (✉ *Quantiusstr. 26, Bonn* ☎ *0228/981–4636*).

EXPLORING

MAIN ATTRACTIONS

❷ Beethoven-Haus *(Beethoven House)*. Beethoven was born in Bonn in 1770 and, except for a short stay in Vienna, lived here until the age of 22. You'll find scores, paintings, a grand piano (his last, in fact), and an ear trumpet or two. Thanks to the modern age, there's now an "Interactive Voyage of Discovery" that lets you hear all his works, view his life in text and pictures, make a virtual visit to his last home, and lots more. The attached museum shop carries everything from kitsch to elegant Beethoven memorabilia. ✉ *Bonng. 20* ☎ *0228/981–7525* ⊕ *www.beethoven-haus-bonn.de* 🎫 *€5* ⏰ *Apr.–Oct., Mon.–Sat. 10–6, Sun. 11–6; Nov.–Mar., Mon.–Sat. 10–5, Sun. 11–5.*

7 Bundesviertel *(Federal Government District).* Walking through the amiable former government district is like taking a trip back in time to an era when Bonn was still the sleepy capital of West Germany. Bordered by Adenauerallee, Willy-Brandt-Allee, Friedrich-Ebert-Allee, and the Rhine, the quarter boasts sights such as the **Bundeshaus** with the

WORD OF MOUTH

"If you like hiking, cross the Rhein [from Bonn] and walk up the Drachenfels, a castle ruin on top of a steep hill with great view."

–quokka

Plenarsaal. This building, designed to serve as the new Federal Parliament, was completed only six years before the capital was relocated to Berlin in 1999. A few steps away, you'll find the historic **Villa Hammerschmidt,** the German equivalent of the White House. This stylish neoclassical mansion began serving as the Federal president's permanent residence in 1950, and is still his home when he stays in Bonn. Equally impressive is the **Palais Schaumburg,** another fine example of the Rhein Riveria estates that once housed the Federal Chancellery (1949–76). It became the center of Cold War politics during the Adenauer administration. Tours of the quarter, including a visit to the Villa Hammerschmidt, are offered by the Bonn Tourist Office. ⊠*Adenauerallee.*

8 Kunstmuseum Bonn *(Art Museum).* Devoted to contemporary art, this large museum focuses on Rhenish expressionists and German art since 1945 (Beuys, Baselitz, and Kiefer, for example). Changing exhibits are generally excellent, and help maintain a link to the international art scene. The museum's airy and inexpensive café is preferable to the stuffier version across the plaza at the Kunst- und Ausstellungshalle. ⊠*Friedrich-Ebert-Allee 2* ☎*0228/776–260* ⊕*www.bonn.de/kunstmuseum* ⊠*€5* ☉*Tues. and Thurs.–Sun. 11–6, Wed. 11–9.*

4 Kurfürstliche Residenz *(Prince-Electors' Residence).* Built in the 18th century by the prince-electors of Köln, this grand palace now houses a university. If the weather is good, stroll through the Hofgarten (Palace Gardens). ⊠*Am Hofgarten.*

1 Münster *(Cathedral).* The 900-year-old cathedral is vintage late Romanesque, with a massive octagonal main tower and a soaring spire. It stands on a site where two Roman soldiers were executed in AD 253 for having Christian beliefs. It saw the coronations of two Holy Roman Emperors (in 1314 and 1346) and was one of the Rhineland's most important ecclesiastical centers in the Middle Ages. The 17th-century bronze figure of St. Helen and the ornate rococo pulpit are highlights of the interior. ⊠*Münsterpl.* ☎*0228/985–880* ⊠*Free* ☉*Daily 7–7.*

ALSO WORTH SEEING

3 AltesRathaus *(Town Hall).* Not very austere, this 18th-century rococo town hall looks somewhat like a pink dollhouse. Its elegant steps and perron have seen a great many historic figures, including French president Charles de Gaulle and U.S. president John F. Kennedy. ⊠*Am Markt* ☎*0228/774–288* ⊠*Free* ☉*By tour only, May–Oct., 1st Sat. of month, noon–4.*

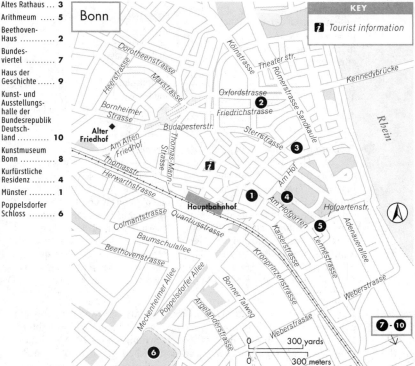

5 **Arithmeum.** Technophiles and technophobes alike enjoy this university-run museum, where even the abstract theme of discrete mathematics is made comprehensible. Its stated aim is to show "the interface of art and technology," and the core of the exhibit is a 1,200-piece collection of historical mechanical-calculating machines, which became obsolete with the advent of computers. The art comes in the form of a collection of constructivist paintings that resemble enlarged, colorful computer-chip designs. ⊠ *Lennéstr. 2* ☎ *0228/738–790* ⊕ *www.arithmeum.uni-bonn.de* ⊠ *€3* ☉ *Tues.–Sun. 11–6.*

9 **Haus der Geschichte** *(House of History).* German history since World War II is the subject of this museum, which begins with "hour zero," as the Germans call the unconditional surrender of 1945. The museum displays an overwhelming amount of documentary material organized on five levels and engages various types of media. It's not all heavy either—temporary exhibits have featured political cartoonists, "Miss Germany" pageants, and an in-depth examination of the song *Lili Marleen,* sung by troops of every nation during World War II. ⊠ *Willy-Brandt-Allee 14* ☎ *0228/91650* ⊕ *www.hdg.de* ⊠ *Free* ☉ *Tues.–Sun. 9–7.*

10 **Kunst- und Ausstellungshalle der Bundesrepublik Deutschland** *(Art and Exhibition Hall of the German Federal Republic).* This is one of the Rhineland's most important venues for major exhibitions about culture and science. Its modern design, by Viennese architect Gustave Peichl, is as interesting as anything on exhibit in the museum. It employs three enormous blue cones situated on a lawnlike rooftop garden. ⊠*Friedrich-Ebert-Allee 4* ☎*0228/917–1200* ⊕*www.bundeskunsthalle.de* ☑*€7.50* ☉*Tues. and Wed. 10–9, Thurs.–Sun. 10–7.*

❻ Poppelsdorfer Schloss *(Poppelsdorf Palace).* This former electors' palace was built in the baroque style between 1715 and 1753, and now houses the university's mineralogical collection. Its botanical gardens exhibit more species, 10,000, than any other garden in Germany. ⊠*Meckenheimer Allee 171* ☎*0228/732–764* ☑*Free* ☉*Apr.–Oct., Sun.–Fri. 9–6; Oct.–Mar., weekdays 9–4.*

CLASSICAL MUSIC

Few regions in Europe rival the quality of classical music performances and venues on the Rhine. Beethoven was born in Bonn, and the city hosts a Beethoven festival every year in mid- to late September. Düsseldorf, once home to Mendelssohn, Schumann, and Brahms, has the finest concert hall in Germany after Berlin's Philharmonie: the Tonhalle, in a former planetarium. Köln also has one of Germany's best concert halls, and its opera company is known for exciting classical and contemporary productions. The cathedrals of Aachen, Köln, and Trier are magnificent settings for concerts and organ recitals.

OFF THE BEATEN PATH

Alter Friedhof *(Old Cemetery).* This ornate, leafy cemetery is the resting place of many of the country's most celebrated sons and daughters. Look for the tomb of composer Robert Schumann (1810–56) and his wife Clara, also a composer and accomplished pianist. To reach the cemetery from the main train station, follow Quantiusstrasse north until it becomes Herwarthstrasse; before the street curves, turning into Endenlicherstrasse, take the underpass below the railroad line. You'll then be on Thomastrasse, which borders the cemetery. ⊠*Bornheimerstr.* ☉*Jan., daily 8–5; Feb., daily 8–6; Mar.–Aug., daily 7:15 AM–8 PM; Sept., daily 8–8; Oct., daily 8–7; Nov. and Dec., daily 8–5.*

WHERE TO EAT

$$ ✕Pirandello. This trattoria with its frescoed brick walls is so cozy that it borders on kitsch. But the decor is redeemed by the quality of chef-owner Fausto Langeu's Italian regional dishes and the wines he chooses to go with them. The seasonally changing menu features pizzas, pastas, fish, and meats. A lunch special offers pasta, salad, and wine for €12. ⊠*Brüderg. 22* ☎*0228/656–606* ☐*MC, V.*

$ ✕Amadeo. The popularity of this neighborhood restaurant is due in part because Germans tend to have an affinity for all things Spanish, but also because its food—40 different tapas, for starters—rarely misses the mark. The kitchen is especially proud of the Spanish cheese platter, featuring the beloved Manchego. ⊠*Mozartstr. 1* ☎*0228/635–534* ☐*No credit cards* ☉*No lunch.*

$ ✕Em Höttche. Beethoven was a regular at this tavern, which has been around since the late 14th century. Today it offers one of the best-value lunches in town. The interior is rustic, the food stout and hearty. ⊠*Markt 4* ☎*0228/690–009* ☐*No credit cards.*

$ ✕**Sassella.** When the Bundestag was still in town, this Bonn institution
★ used to be cited in the press as frequently for its backroom political
dealings as for its Lombardy-influenced food. Locals, prominent and
otherwise, still flock to the restaurant, in an 18th-century house in the
suburb of Kessenich. The style is pure Italian farmhouse, with stone
walls and exposed beams, but the handmade pastas made by Giorgio
and Francesco Tartero often stray from the typical—note the salmon-
filled black-and-white pasta pockets in shrimp sauce. ⊠*Karthäuserpl.*
21 ☏*0228/530–815* ✍*Reservations essential* ▤*AE, MC, V* ⊘*Closed*
Mon. No lunch Sat., no dinner Sun.

WHERE TO STAY

$$$ ⊞**Best Western Premier Domicil.** A group of buildings around a quiet,
central courtyard has been converted into a charming and comfortable
hotel. The rooms are individually furnished and decorated—in styles
ranging from fin-de-siècle romantic to Italian modern. Huge windows
give the public rooms a spacious airiness. **Pros:** quiet courtyard, handy
to the train station. **Cons:** plain exterior. ⊠*Thomas-Mann-Str. 24–26*
☏*0228/729–090* ⊕*www.bestwestern.de* ➥*43 rooms, 1 apartment*
⌂*In-room: no a/c, dial-up, Wi-Fi. In-hotel: restaurant, room service,*
parking (no fee), some pets allowed, no-smoking rooms ▤*AE, DC,*
MC, V ⦿*BP.*

$$ ⊞**Sternhotel.** For solid comfort and a central location in the Old Town,
the Stern is tops. About 80% of the rooms are in a Danish modern
style; the rest are more old-fashioned. Weekend rates are a bargain.
Pros: directly in the old town. **Cons:** some rooms are a bit old-fashioned, noisy marketplace nearby. ⊠*Markt 8* ☏*0228/72670* ⊕*www.*
sternhotel-bonn.de ➥*80 rooms* ⌂*In-room: no a/c, Wi-Fi. In-hotel:*
some pets allowed, no-smoking rooms ▤*DC, MC, V* ⦿*CP.*

$ ⊞**Mozart.** Elegant on the outside and simple on the inside, this small,
attractive hotel is often recommended to friends by Bonn residents.
Part of its appeal is its location amid traditional town houses in the
romantic, residential "musician's quarter," just a four-minute walk
from the main train station and the city center. **Pros:** quiet tree-lined
street, handy to the train station. **Cons:** thin walls. ⊠*Mozartstr. 1*
☏*0228/659–071* ⊕*www.hotel-mozart-bonn.de* ➥*39 rooms, 1 suite*
⌂*In-room: no a/c. In-hotel: parking (fee), no-smoking rooms* ▤*AE,*
DC, MC, V ⦿*BP.*

THE ARTS

MUSIC The Bonn Symphony Orchestra opens its season in grand style every
September with a concert on the market square, in front of city hall.
Otherwise, concerts are held in the **Beethovenhalle** (⊠*Wachsbleiche*
16 ☏*0228/72220*). Indoor and outdoor concerts are held at numerous venues during September's **Beethoven-Festival** (☏*0228/201–030*
⊕*www.beethovenfest-bonn.de*). In the **Beethoven-Haus** (⊠*Bonngasse*
20 ☏*0228/981–750*), intimate recitals are sometimes given on an
18th-century grand piano.

Operas are staged regularly at the **Oper der Stadt Bonn** (⊠*Am Boese-*
lagerhof 1 ☏*0228/778–000* ⊕*www.theater.bonn.de*), popularly
known as La Scala of the Rhineland. The **Pantheontheater** (⊠*Bundes-*

kanzlerpl. 2–10 ☎*0228/212–521*) is a prime venue for all manner of pop concerts and cabaret. Chamber-music concerts are given regularly at the **Schumann**haus(✉*Sebastianstr. 182* ☎*0228/773–656*).

THEATER & Musicals and ballet are performed at the **Oper der Stadt Bonn**. From May
DANCE through September, the **Bonner Sommer** (✉*Tourist office, Windeckstr. 1* ☎*0228/775–000*) festival offers folklore, music, and street theater, much of it outdoors and most of it free. Information is available at the tourist office.

SHOPPING

There are plenty of department stores and boutiques in the pedestrian shopping zone around the Markt and the Münster. Bonn's **Wochenmarkt** *(Weekly Market)* is open daily except Sunday, filling the Markt with vendors of produce and various edibles. Bargain hunters search for secondhand goods and knickknacks at the city's renowned—and huge—**Flohmarkt** *(Flea Market)*, held in Rheinaue park under the Konrad-Adenauer-Brücke on the third Saturday of each month from April through October. **Pützchens Markt**, a huge country fair, takes place in the Bonn area the second weekend of September.

KÖNIGSWINTER

12 km (7 mi) southeast of Bonn.

The town of Königswinter has one of the most-visited castles on the Rhine, the **Drachenfels**. Its ruins crown one of the highest hills in the Siebengebirge, Germany's oldest nature reserve, with a spectacular view of the Rhine. The reserve has more than 100 km (62 mi) of hiking trails. The castle was built in the 12th century by the archbishop of Köln. Its name commemorates a dragon said to have lived in a nearby cave. As legend has it, the dragon was slain by Siegfried, hero of the epic *Nibelungenlied*. You can reach the castle ruins by taking the **Drachenfelsbahn** (✉*Drachenfelsstr. 53* ☎*02223/92090* ⊕*www. drachenfelsbahn-koenigswinter.de*), a steep, narrow-gauge train that makes trips to the summit every hour or occasionally every half hour. The trip costs €9 round-trip. The train runs daily in March and October, from 10 to 6; in April it runs daily from 10 to 7; from May through September, it runs daily from 9 to 7; from November through February, it runs weekdays from noon to 5 and weekends from 11 to 6.

☺ Königswinter's huge **Sea Life Aquarium**, features 3,000 creatures from the sea. The biggest pool has a glass tunnel that enables you to walk on the "bottom of the sea." ✉*Rheinallee 8* ☎*02223/297297* 🎫*€13* ⊙ *Daily 10–6.*

WHERE TO EAT

$$ ✗**Gasthaus Sutorius.** Across from the church of St. Margaretha, this wine tavern serves refined variations on German cuisine with a nice selection of local wines. In summer, food is served outdoors beneath the linden trees. ✉*Oelinghovener Str. 7* ☎*02244/912–240* ▤*MC, V* ⊙*No dinner Sun. or Mon., no lunch Mon.–Sat.*

BRÜHL

20 km (12 mi) southwest of Bonn.

11

In the heart of Brühl you'll discover the Rhineland's most important baroque palace.

Schloss Augustusburg and the magnificent pleasure park that surrounds it were created in the time of Prince Clemens August, between 1725 and 1768. The palace contains one of the most famous achievements of rococo architecture, a staircase by Balthasar Neumann. The castle can be visited only on guided tours, which leave the reception area every hour or so. An English-language recorded tour is available. ⊠*Schlossstr. 6* ☎*02232/44000* ⊕*www.schlossbruehl.de* ☒€*5* ☼*Feb.–Nov., Tues.– Fri. 9–noon and 1:30–4, weekends 10–5.*

The smaller **Jagdschloss Falkenlust,** at the end of an avenue leading straight through Schloss Augustusburg's grounds, was built as a getaway where the prince could indulge his passion for falconry. ⊠*Schlossstr. 6* ☎*02232/12111* ☒€*3* ☼*Feb.–Nov., Tues.–Fri. 9–noon and 1:30–4, weekends 10–5.*

KÖLN (COLOGNE)

28 km (17 mi) north of Bonn, 47 km (29 mi) south of Düsseldorf, 70 km (43 mi) southeast of Aachen.

Köln (Cologne in English) is the largest city on the Rhine (the fourth-largest in Germany) and one of the most interesting. Although not as old as Trier, it has been a dominant power in the Rhineland since Roman times. Known throughout the world for its "scented water," Eau de Cologne (first produced here in 1705 from an Italian formula), Köln is today a major commercial, intellectual, and ecclesiastical center. The city is vibrant and bustling, with a light and jolly flair that is typical of the Rhineland. At its heart is tradition, manifested in the abundance of bars and brew houses serving the local Kölsch beer and old Rhine cuisine. These are good meeting places to start a night on the town. Tradition, however, is mixed with the contemporary, found in a host of elegant shops, sophisticated restaurants, modern bars and dance clubs, and an important contemporary-art scene.

Köln was first settled by the Romans in 38 BC. For nearly a century it grew slowly, in the shadow of imperial Trier, until a locally born noble-woman, Julia Agrippina, daughter of the Roman general Germanicus, married the Roman emperor Claudius. Her hometown was elevated to the rank of a Roman city and given the name Colonia Claudia Ara Agrippinensium (Claudius Colony at the Altar of Agrippina). For the next 300 years Colonia (hence Cologne, or Köln) flourished. Evidence of the Roman city's wealth resides in the Römisch-Germanisches Museum. In the 9th century Charlemagne, the towering figure who united the sprawling German lands (and ruled much of present-day France) as the first Holy Roman Emperor, restored Köln's fortunes and elevated it to its preeminent role in the Rhineland. Charlemagne also appointed the first archbishop of Köln. The city's ecclesiastical heritage is one of its most striking features; it has a full dozen Romanesque churches and one of the world's largest and finest Gothic cathedrals. In the Middle Ages it was a member of the powerful Hanseatic League, occupying a position of greater importance in European commerce than either London or Paris.

Köln was a thriving modern city until World War II, when bombings destroyed 90% of it. Only the cathedral remained relatively unscathed. But like many other German cities that rebounded during the "Economic Miracle" of the 1950s, Köln is a mishmash of old and new, sometimes awkwardly juxtaposed. A good part of the former Old Town along the Hohe Strasse (old Roman High Road) was turned into a remarkably charmless pedestrian shopping mall. The ensemble is framed by six-lane expressways winding along the rim of the city center—barely yards from the cathedral—perfectly illustrating the problems of postwar reconstruction. However, much of the Altstadt (Old Town), ringed by streets that follow the line of the medieval city walls, is closed to traffic. Most major sights are within this area and are easily reached on foot. Here, too, you'll find the best shops.

GETTING HERE & AROUND

City bus tours leave from outside the tourist office, opposite the main entrance to the cathedral, daily at 10, 12, and 2 (also at 4 on Friday and Saturday) from April to October, and at 11 and 2 from November to March. The 90-minute tour costs €15; it's conducted in English and German. A 90-minute Köln walking tour (€9) is available by prior arrangement with the tourist office. Bus trips into the countryside (to the Eifel Hills, the Ahr Valley, and the Westerwald) are organized by several city travel agencies.

In Köln, Rent-a-Bike offers bike rental by the day from April through October as well as three-hour guided bike tours of the city, departing daily at 1:30.

DISCOUNTS & DEALS

Most central hotels sell the Köln Tourismus Card (€9 for one day, €14 for two days, and €19 for three days), which entitles you to discounts on sightseeing tours, admissions to all the city's museums, free city bus and tram travel, and other reductions.

ESSENTIALS

Bicycle Contacts **Rent-a-Bike** (⊠ *Markmannsg. next to the Deutzer Brücke, Köln* ☏ *0171/629–8796* ⊕ *www.koelnerfahrradverleih.de*).

Visitor Information **Köln** (⊠ *Köln Tourismus Office, Unter Fettenhenen 19* ☏ *0221/2213–0400* ⊕ *www.koeln.de*).

EXPLORING

MAIN ATTRACTIONS

❶ **Dom** *(Cathedral).* Köln's landmark embodies one of the purest expressions of the Gothic spirit in Europe. The cathedral, meant to be a tangible expression of God's kingdom on Earth, was conceived with such immense dimensions that construction, begun in 1248, was not completed until 1880, though builders adhered to the original plans. At 515 feet high, the two west towers of the cathedral were by far the tallest structures in the world when they were finished. The cathedral was built to house what are believed to be the relics of the Magi, the three kings who paid homage to the infant Jesus (the trade in holy mementos was big business in the Middle Ages—and not always scrupulous). The size of the building was not simply an example of self-aggrandizement on the part of

> **TOURING TIPS**
>
> **Information:** The tourist office, across from the cathedral, has maps and brochures.
>
> **Sights:** The twin-towered Gothic cathedral is one of the world's great churches. Even if no other cathedral is on your list, you should visit this one.
>
> **Snacks:** The Imhoff-Stollwerck-Museum makes chocolate, tells the history of chocolate, and lets you sample chocolate!

the people of Köln, however; it was a response to the vast numbers of pilgrims who arrived to see the relics. The ambulatory, the passage that curves around the back of the altar, is unusually large, allowing cathedral authorities to funnel large numbers of visitors up to the crossing (where the nave and transepts meet and where the relics were originally displayed), around the back of the altar, and out again.

Today the relics are kept just behind the altar, in the original, enormous gold-and-silver **reliquary.** The other great treasure of the cathedral, in the last chapel on the left as you face the altar, is the **Gero Cross,** a monumental oak crucifix dating from 971. The *Adoration of the Kings* (1440), a triptych by Stephan Lochner, Köln's most famous medieval painter, is to the right. The **Domschatzkammer** (*Cathedral Treasury* ☑€4 ⊙*Daily 10–6*) includes the silver shrine of Archbishop Engelbert, who was stabbed to death in 1225. Other highlights are the stained-glass windows, some dating from the 13th century; the 15th-century altarpiece; and the early-14th-century high altar, with its glistening white figures and intricate choir screens. Climb to the top of the bell tower to get the complete vertical experience. Allow nearly an hour for the whole tour of the interior, treasury, and tower climb. ⊠*Dompl., Altstadt* ☎*0221/9258–4730* ⊕*www.koelner-dom.de* ☑*Tower €2.50, tour of tower and cathedral treasury €5* ⊙*Daily 6 AM–7:30 PM; tower and stairwell Nov.–Feb., daily 9–4; Mar., Apr., and Oct., daily 9–5; May–Sept., daily 9–6; guided tours in English Mon.–Sat. at 10:30 and 2:30, Sun. at 2:30.*

❷ **Museum Ludwig.** This museum is dedicated to art from the beginning of the 20th century to the present day. ■**TIP➜** Its American pop-art collection (including Andy Warhol, Jasper Johns, Robert Rauschenberg, Claes Oldenburg, and Roy Lichtenstein) rivals that of New York's Guggenheim Museum. Within the building and at no extra cost is the **Agfa Foto-Historama** (Agfa Photography Museum), which has one of the world's largest collections of historic photographs and cameras. ⊠*Innenstadt* ☎*0221/2212–6165* ⊕*www.museum-ludwig.de* ☑*€9* ⊙*Tues.–Sun. 10–6; 1st Fri. of every month 10–10. Closed 1 wk mid-Feb.*

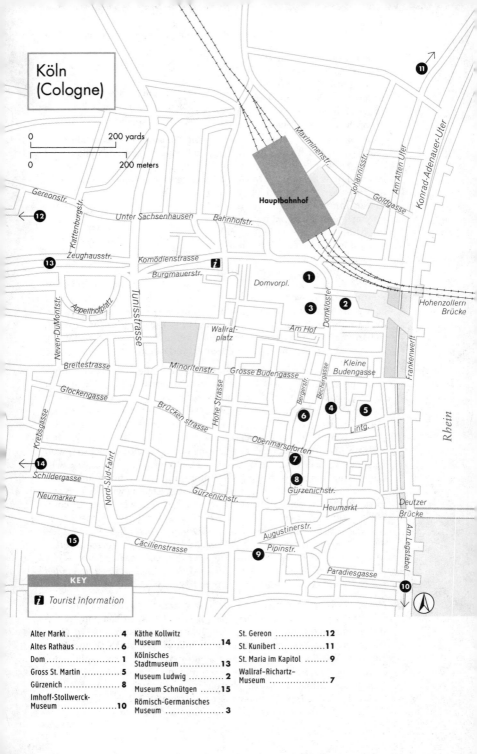

Köln (Cologne)

0 ——— 200 yards

0 ——— 200 meters

Gereonstr.

Unter Sachsenhausen

Bahnhofstr.

Hauptbahnhof

Maximinenstr.

Johannisstr.

Goldgasse

Am Alten Ufer

Konrad-Adenauer-Ufer

Kattenburgstr.

Zeughausstr.

Komödienstrasse

i

Burgmauerstr.

Domvorpl.

1

Domkloster

2

Hohenzollern Brücke

3

Am Hof

Wallraf-platz

Neven-DuMontstr.

Appellhofplatz

Tunisstrasse

Breitestrasse

Minoritenstr.

Grosse Budengasse

Kleine Budengasse

Bergerstr.

Bechergasse

Frankenwerft

Rhein

Glockengasse

Hohe Strasse

Brücken strasse

6

4

5

Krebsgasse

14

Schildergasse

Neumarkt

Nord-Süd-Fahrt

Gürzenichstr.

Obenmarspforten

7

8

Lintg.

Gürzenichstr.

Heumarkt

Deutzer Brücke

15

Cäcilienstrasse

Augustinerstr.

Pipinstr.

9

Paradiesgasse

10

Am Leystapel

11

12

13

KEY

i Tourist information

③ Römisch-Germanisches Museum
★ (Roman-Germanic Museum). This cultural landmark was built in the early 1970s around the famous Dionysius mosaic discovered here during the construction of an air-raid shelter in 1941. The huge mosaic, more than 100 yards square, once formed the dining-room floor of a wealthy Roman trader's villa. Its millions of tiny earthenware and glass tiles depict some of the adventures of Dionysius, the Greek god of wine and, to the Romans, the object of a widespread and sinister religious cult. The pillared 1st-century tomb of Lucius Publicius (a prominent Roman officer), some stone Roman coffins, and everyday objects of Roman life are among the museum's other exhibits. Bordering the museum on the south is a restored 90-yard stretch of the old Roman harbor road. ⊠ *Roncallipl. 4, Altstadt* ☎ *0221/2212–4438* ⊕ *www.museenkoeln.de* 🎫 *€5* ⊙ *Tues.–Sun. 10–5.*

> **KARNEVAL**
>
> Köln puts on Germany's most exciting carnival every February, when the whole city follows the famous motto *Kölle alaaf!* ("Köln is alive") in a four-day revelry with bands, parades, and parties that last all night. People of all ages don costumes, including the customary accent of a clown's red nose. Plenty of drinking goes on, and many museums are closed during Karneval.

⑦ Wallraf-Richartz-Museum. The Wallraf-Richartz-Museum contains paintings spanning the years 1300 to 1900. The Dutch and Flemish schools are particularly well represented, as is the 15th- to 16th-century Köln school of German painting. Its two most famous artists are the Master of the St. Veronica (whose actual name is unknown) and Stefan Lochner, represented by two luminous works, *The Last Judgment* and *The Madonna in the Rose Bower.* Large canvases by Rubens, who spent his youth in Köln, hang prominently on the second floor. There are also outstanding works by Rembrandt, Van Dyck, and Frans Hals. ⊠ *Martinstr. 39, Altstadt* ☎ *0221/2212–119* ⊕ *www.museenkoeln.de* 🎫 *€9* ⊙ *Tues. and Wed., Fri. 10–6, Thurs. 10–10, weekends 11–6.*

ALSO WORTH SEEING

④ Alter Markt *(Old Market).* The square has an eclectic assembly of buildings, most of them postwar; two 16th-century houses survived the war intact—Nos. 20 and 22. The oldest structure dates from 1135. ⊠ *Altstadt.*

⑥ Altes Rathaus *(Old Town Hall).* The Rathaus is worth a look, even from the outside. (Sadly, visitors are no longer permitted inside.) It's the oldest town hall in Germany, erected in the 14th century. The famous bell tower rings its bells daily at noon and 5 PM. Standing on pedestals at one end of the town hall are figures of prophets made in the early 15th century. Ranging along the south wall are nine additional statues, the so-called *Nine Good Heroes,* carved in 1360. Charlemagne and King Arthur are among them. Beneath a small glass pyramid near the south corner of the Rathaus is the **mikwe,** a 12th-century ritual bath from the medieval Jewish quarter. ⊠ *Rathauspl., Altstadt* ☎ *0221/2212–3332.*

⑤ Gross St. Martin *(Great St. Martin).* This remarkable Romanesque parish church was rebuilt after being flattened in World War II. Its massive 13th-century tower, with distinctive corner turrets and an imposing central spire, is another Köln landmark. The church was built on the site of a Roman granary. ✉*An Gross St. Martin 9, Altstadt* ☎*0221/1642–5650* ⊙*Mon. 3–5, Tues.–Fri. 10–noon and 3–5, Sat. 10–12:30 and 1:30–5, Sun. 2–4.*

⑧ Gürzenich. This Gothic structure, located at the south end of Martinsviertel, was all but demolished in World War II, but carefully reconstructed afterward. It's named after a medieval knight from whom the city acquired valuable real estate in 1437. The official reception and festival hall here has played a central role in civic life through the centuries. At one end of the complex are the remains of the 10th-century Gothic church of **St. Alban,** which were left ruined after the war as a memorial. On what's left of the church floor you can see a sculpture of a couple kneeling in prayer, *Mourning Parents,* by Käthe Kollwitz, a fitting memorial to the ravages of war. ✉*Gürzenichstr., Altstadt.*

⑩ Imhoff-Stollwerck-Museum. This riverside museum is a real hit, and so crowded on weekends that it can be unpleasant. It recounts 3,000 years of civilization's production and delectation of chocolate, from the Central American Maya to the colonizing and industrializing Europeans. It's also a real factory, with lava flows of chocolate and a conveyer belt jostling thousands of truffles. The museum shop, with a huge variety of chocolate items, does a brisk business, and the riverside panorama café is very nice. ✉*Am Schockoladenmuseum 1a, Rheinufer* ☎*0221/931–8880* ⊕*www.schokoladenmuseum.de* 🎟*€6.50* ⊙*Tues.–Fri. 10–6, weekends 11–7.*

⑭ Käthe Kollwitz Museum. The works of Käthe Kollwitz (1867–1945), the most important German female artist of the 20th century, focus on social themes like the plight of the poor and the atrocities of war. This is the larger of the country's two Kollwitz collections and comprises all of her woodcuts, as well as paintings, etchings, lithographs, and sculptures. There are also changing exhibits of other modern artists. ✉*Neumarkt 18–24, in Neumarkt Galerie, Innenstadt* ☎*0221/227–2363* ⊕*www.kollwitz.de* 🎟*€3* ⊙*Tues.–Fri. 10–6, weekends 11–6.*

⑬ Kölnisches Stadtmuseum *(Köln City History Museum).* The triumphs and tragedies of Köln's rich past are packed into this museum at the historic *Zeughaus,* the city's former arsenal. Here you'll find an in-depth chronicle of Köln's history—including information about the lives of

---

EAU DE COLOGNE

As Frankfurt was a sausage to many people before it was a city, Cologne was first a fragrance. Eau de Cologne is made from a secret formula and aged in oak barrels. The most famous cologne is 4711, which derives its name from the firm's address at 4711 Glockegasse. The building itself is equipped with a carillon, a museum, and a shop where Eau de Cologne can be purchased. It comes in an elegant bottle with a turquoise and gilt label, and makes a delightful souvenir.

ordinary people and high-profile politicians, the industrial revolution (car manufacturer Henry Ford's influence on the city is also retraced), and the destruction incurred during World War II. For those who've always wanted to be privy to the inside stories surrounding local words such as *Klüngel, Kölsch,* and *Karneval,* the answers are waiting to be discovered within the museum's walls. ✉*Zeughausstr. 1–3, Altstadt* ☎*0221/2212–5790* ⊕*www.museenkoeln.de* ✉€*4.20* ☉*Wed.–Sun. 10–5, Tues. 10–8.*

⑮ Museum Schnütgen. A treasure house of medieval art from the Rhine region, the museum has an ideal setting in a 12th-century basilica. Don't miss the crucifix from the St. Georg Kirche or the original stained-glass windows and carved figures from the Dom. Other exhibits include intricately carved ivory book covers, rock-crystal reliquaries, and illuminated manuscripts. ✉*Cäcilienstr. 29, Innenstadt* ☎*0221/2212–3620* ⊕*www.museenkoeln.de* ✉€*3.20* ☉*Tues.–Fri. 10–5, weekends 11–5.*

NEED A BREAK? Köln's main pedestrian shopping street is practical but utterly uninspiring—some even say ugly. An airy, artsy oasis is Café Stanton, The Fine Art of Leisure (✉*Schilderg. 57, behind Antoniterkirche* ☎*0221/271–0710*), with outdoor terrace seating and a view of the 14th-century Antonite church. The food is international with an emphasis on the Mediterranean; the selection of cakes is divinely German, and there is a jazz dinner every Saturday. Three enormous, surprisingly delicate chandeliers, made entirely of plastic waste, provide lighting.

⑫ St. Gereon. Experts regard St. Gereon as one of the most noteworthy medieval structures in existence. This exquisite Romanesque church stands on the site of an old Roman burial ground six blocks west of the train station. An enormous dome rests on walls that were once clad in gold mosaics. Roman masonry forms part of the structure, which is believed to have been built over the grave of its namesake, the 4th-century martyr and Köln's patron. ✉*Gereonsdriesch 2–4, Altstadt Nord* ☎*0221/134–922* ✉*Free* ☉*Daily 10–6.*

⑪ St. Kunibert. The most lavish of the churches from the late-Romanesque period is by the Rhine, three blocks north of the train station. Its precious stained-glass windows have filtered light for more than 750 years. Consecrated in 1247, the church contains an unusual room, concealed under the altar, which gives access to a pre-Christian well once believed to promote fertility in women. ✉*Kunibertsklosterg. 2, Altstadt-Nord* ☎*0221/121–214* ✉*Free* ☉*Mon.–Sat. 10–1 and 3–6, Sun. 8:30–noon and 3–6.*

⑨ St. Maria im Kapitol. Built in the 11th and 12th centuries on the site of a Roman temple, St. Maria is best known for its two beautifully carved 16-foot-high doors and its enormous crypt, the second-largest in Germany. The powerful organ shakes the building. ✉*Marienpl. 19, Altstadt* ☎*0221/214–615* ✉*Free* ☉*Daily 9:30–6, except during services.*

WHERE TO EAT

$$$$ ✕**Capricorn i Aries.** This hip, fine-dining establishment houses but four
FodorsChoice tables, each covered with crisp, white linens and enhanced by sur-
★ rounding dark wood and sophisticated lighting. You'll be personally
waited on by the owners, Judith Werner (Capricorn) and Klaus Jaque-
mod (Aries), as you indulge in truly heavenly French cuisine with a
Rhineland twist. Just opposite this intimate little restaurant, a new and
very inviting Brasserie serves the staples in French rural cuisine. ✉*Al-
teburger Str. 34, Neustadt Süd* ☎*0221/397–5710 or 0221/323–182*
⌕*Reservations essential* ▭*AE, MC, V* ☺*Closed Sun.*

$$$$ ✕**Fischers Weingenuss und Tafelfreuden.** If someone were to create a shrine
to wine, it would look a lot like this establishment: part vintner, part
caterer, part school, and part restaurant. Run by one of Germany's star
sommeliers (Christina Fischer), the restaurant offers 800 wines, 40 of
which can be sampled by the glass. The dining experience is always
elegant, and an expert staff will help you pick the perfect wine for each
dish. One of the aims is to show how wine and food go together. ✉*Hohenstaufenring 53, Ringe* ☎*0221/310–8470* ⌕*Reservations essential*
▭*MC, V* ☺*Restaurant closed Sun.–Thurs. No lunch*

$$$$ ✕**Le Moissonnier.** Part of the charm of this bistro—arguably one of the
best eateries in the city—is its lack of pretension. The decor radiates
warmth from its mirrors, Tiffany lamps, and painted flowers. Owners
Vincent and Liliane Moissonnier greet their guests in person, seating
them at one of 20 tables. The cuisine is French at its base but inter-
twines an array of global influences. ✉*Krefelder Str. 25, Neustadt-
Nord* ☎*0221/729–479* ⌕*Reservations essential* ▭*MC, V* ☺*Closed
Sun. and Mon.*

$$$ ✕**Casa di Biase.** This romantic eatery serves sophisticated Italian cuisine
★ in a warm, elegant setting. The seasonally changing menu focuses on
fish and game, and the wine list is interesting and extensive—although
sometimes pricey. Just next door is Casa di Biase's smaller and more
casual sister, the Teca di Biasi. This cozy, wood-panel wine bar serves
antipasti, salads, and main dishes for €13 or less. ✉*Eifelpl. 4, Südstadt*
☎*0221/322–433* ▭*AE, MC, V* ☺*Closed Sun. No lunch Sat.*

$$$ ✕**Heising & Adelmann.** A young crowd gathers here to do what people
★ along the Rhine have done for centuries—talk, drink, and enjoy good
company. There's a party every Friday and Saturday with a DJ. Heising
& Adelmann, consistently voted one of the best deals in town, offers
good German beer, tangy cocktails (even a proper Long Island Iced
Tea), and a creative mixture of German and French food. ✉*Friesenstr.
58–60, Neustadt-Nord* ☎*0221/1309–424* ▭*AE, MC, V* ☺*Closed
Sun. No lunch.*

$ ✕**Päffgen.** There's no better *Bräuhaus* in Köln in which to imbibe
Kölsch, the city's home brew. You won't sit long in front of an empty
glass before a blue-aproned waiter sweeps by and places another one
before you. With its worn wooden decor, colorful clientele, and typical German fare (sauerbraten, Hämmchen, and Reibekuchen), Päffgen
sums up tradition—especially when compared to the trendy nightspots
that surround it. ✉*Friesenstr. 64–66, Friesenviertel,* ☎*0221/135–461*
▭*No credit cards.*

¢ ✗**Früh am Dom.** For real down-home cooking, there are few places that compare with this time-honored former brewery. It's often crowded, but the spirit is fantastic. Bold frescoes on the vaulted ceilings establish the mood, and the authentically Teutonic experience is completed by such dishes as *Hämmchen* (pork knuckle). The beer garden is delightful for summer dining. ⊠*Am Hof 12–18, Altstadt* ☎*0221/26130* ▤*No credit cards.*

WHERE TO STAY

The tourist office, across from the cathedral, can make hotel bookings for you for the same night, at a cost of €10 per room. If you plan to be in town for the Karneval, be sure to reserve a room well in advance.

> ### KÖLSCH, BITTE!
>
> It is said that the city's beloved local beer can only be called Kölsch if it is brewed within sight of the cathedral. The light-color beverage is served in traditional *Kölschkneipen*. Your aproned waiter, called a *Köbe*, will replace your empty glass with a full one whether you order another or not. (If you don't want another, leave a swallow in the glass or cover it with a coaster.) This automatic replacement is justified by the fact that the traditional glass, called a *pole*, is quite small. That's because Kölsch doesn't stay fresh for long after it has been poured.

$$$$ ⌖**Excelsior Hotel Ernst.** The Empire-style lobby in this 1863 hotel is striking in sumptuous royal blue, bright yellow, and gold. Old-master paintings (including a Van Dyck) grace the lobby walls; Gobelin tapestries hang in the ballroom of the same name. Breakfast, for an extra charge of €25, is served either in the "petit palais" ballroom or in the two-story atrium; the Taku Restaurant ($$$–$$$$) specializes in Asian cuisine. **Pros:** Van Dyck paintings and Gobelins. **Con:** expensive. ⊠*Trankg. 1, Altstadt* ☎*0221/2701* ⊕*www.excelsiorhotelernst. de* ⤶*142 rooms, 33 suites* ⌂*In-room: no a/c (some), refrigerator, dial-up, Wi-Fi. In-hotel: 2 restaurants, room service, bar, gym, concierge, laundry service, public Internet, parking (fee), some pets allowed, no-smoking rooms* ▤*AE, DC, MC, V* ❙⃝❙*BP.*

$$$$ ⌖**Hotel im Wasserturm.** What used to be Europe's tallest water tower is
★ now an 11-story luxury hotel-in-the-round. The neoclassical look of the brick exterior remains, and few modern architects could create a more unusual setting. The ultramodern interior was the work of the French designer Andrée Putman, known for her minimalist work on Morgans, a stylish hotel in New York City. The menu in the restaurant ($$$$), which changes daily, offers continental haute cuisine. For lighter fare, the hotel runs the oddly named "d/blju" on the ground floor ($$). **Pro:** stunning view of the city from the top floor. **Con:** expensive. ⊠*Kayg. 2, Altstadt* ☎*0221/20080* ⊕*www.hotel-im-wasserturm.de* ⤶*88 rooms, 34 suites* ⌂*In-room: safe, refrigerator, Wi-Fi. In-hotel: 2 restaurants, room service, bar, gym, concierge, laundry service, parking (fee), some pets allowed* ▤*AE, DC, MC, V*

$$ ⌖**Das Kleine Stapelhäuschen.** One of the few houses along the riverbank that survived World War II bombings, this is among the oldest buildings in Köln. You can't beat the location, overlooking the river and right by Gross St. Martin; yet the rooms are reasonably priced, mak-

ing up in age and quaintness for what they lack in luxury. The restaurant is in a slightly higher price bracket and does a respectable enough job with spruced-up versions of German specialties. **Pro:** right on the Rhine. **Con:** furnishings somewhat old and quaint. ⊠ *Fischmarkt 1–3, Altstadt* ☎ *0221/257–7862* ⊕ *www.koeln-altstadt.de/stapelhaeuschen* ⊅ *31 rooms* ♿ *In-room: no a/c, dial-up, Wi-Fi. In-hotel: restaurant, parking (fee), some pets allowed* ⊟ *MC, V* ¶⊙¶ *BP.*

$$ 🏨 **Hopper Hotel et cetera.** The rooms in this former monastery are spare but not spartan, although a startlingly realistic sculpture of a bishop, sitting in the reception area, serves as a constant reminder of the building's ecclesiastic origins. The rooms are decorated with modern works by Köln artists. The courtyard Hopper Restaurant et cetera serves upscale Mediterranean cuisine and has delightful garden seating. **Pro:** chicly renovated. **Con:** not centrally located. ⊠ *Brüsselerstr. 26, Belgisches Viertel* ☎ *0221/924–400* ⊕ *www.hopper.de* ⊅ *48 rooms, 1 suite* ♿ *In-room: no a/c, Wi-Fi. In-hotel: restaurant, gym, public Internet, parking (fee), some pets allowed, no-smoking rooms* ⊟ *DC, MC, V* ¶⊙¶ *BP.*

$ 🏨 **Chelsea.** This designer hotel has a very strong following among artists and art dealers, as well as among the musicians who come to play in the nearby Stadtgarten jazz club. Breakfast is served until noon for these late risers. The best features of the rooms are the luxuriously large bathrooms and bathtubs. It's 20 minutes to the city center on foot, 10 by subway or tram. Breakfast is an extra €9.50 **Pro:** an artsy and artistic clientele. **Con:** somewhat removed from the center. ⊠ *Jülicherstr. 1, Belgisches Viertel* ☎ *0221/207–150* ⊕ *www.hotel-chelsea.de* ⊅ *36 rooms, 2 suites, 1 apartment* ♿ *In-room: no a/c (some), Wi-Fi. In-hotel: restaurant, parking (fee), some pets allowed* ⊟ *AE, DC, MC, V.*

$ 🏨 **Hotel Im Kupferkessel.** The best things about this small, unassuming, family-run hotel are the location (in the shadow of St. Gereon church and a 15-minute walk from the Dom) and the price (single rooms with shared bath can be had for as low as €34). The slightly shabby lobby and breakfast room look as if they might have been decorated by someone's grandmother, circa 1950, but the rooms are nicely renovated and very functional. Be prepared to deal with stairs here, as most of the rooms are on the third and fourth floors. **Pro:** inexpensive. **Con:** no elevator. ⊠ *Probsteig. 6, Alstadt-Nord* ☎ *0221/270–7960* ⊕ *www. im-kupferkessel.de* ⊅ *12 rooms* ♿ *In-room: no a/c, refrigerator, dial-up, Wi-Fi. In-hotel: no elevator, parking (fee)* ⊟ *AE, MC, V* ¶⊙¶ *CP.*

¢ 🏨 **Jugendherberge Köln-Deutz.** This newly built youth hostel provides inexpensive lodging in a very central location. It's just across the Rhine from the Old Town and cathedral. A bed in a four-bed room with shower and bath will cost you €23.30, breakfast included. **Pro:** inexpensive. **Con:** if you don't have a Youth Hostel card, you pay an additional €3.50. ⊠, *Deutz* ☎ *0221/814–711* ⊕ *www.koeln-deutz. jugendherberge.de* ⊅ *157 rooms* ♿ *In-room: no a/c. In-hotel: laundry facilities, public Internet* ⊟ *MC, V* ¶⊙¶ *CP.*

NIGHTLIFE & THE ARTS

Tickets to most arts events can be purchased through **Kölnticket** (☎ *0221/2801* ⊕ *www.koelnticket.de).*

THE ARTS Köln's Westdeutsche Rundfunk Orchestra performs regularly in the city's excellent concert hall, the **Philharmonie** (⊠ *Bischofsgartenstr. 1, Altstadt* ☎ *0221/2801* ⊕ *www.koelnticket.de*). Köln's opera company, the **Oper der Stadt Köln** (⊠ *Offenbachpl., Innenstadt* ☎ *0221/2212–8400* ⊕ *www.buehnenkoeln.de*), is known for exciting classical and contemporary productions. Year-round organ recitals in Köln's cathedral are supplemented from June through August with a summer season of organ music.

Organ recitals and chamber concerts are also presented in many of the Romanesque churches and in the **Antoniterkirche** (⊠ *Schilderg. 57, Innenstadt* ☎ *0221/9258–460*). The Gürzenich Orchestra gives regular concerts in the Philharmonie, but the primary setting for its music is the restored **Gürzenich** (⊠ *Martinstr. 29/37, Altstadt* ☎ *0221/2801*), medieval Köln's official reception mansion. Köln's principal theater is the **Schauspielhaus** (⊠ *Offenbachpl. 1, Innenstadt* ☎ *0221/2212–8400*), home to the 20 or so private theater companies in the city.

NIGHTLIFE Köln's nightlife is centered in three distinct areas: along the river in the Old Town, which seems to be one big party on weekends; on Zulpicherstrasse; and around the Friesenplatz S-bahn station. Many streets off the Hohenzollernring and Hohenstaufenring, particularly Roonstrasse, also provide a broad range of nightlife.

In summer, head straight for the **Stadtgarten** (⊠ *Venloerstr. 40, Ehrenfeld* ☎ *0221/9529–9421*) and sit in the Bier Garten for some good outdoor Gemütlichkeit. At other times of the year it's still worth a visit for its excellent jazz club. ■ TIP→ **In summer the Martinsviertel, a part of the Altstadt around the Gross St. Martin church, which is full of restaurants, brew houses, and** *Kneipen* **(pubs), is a good place to go around sunset.** One particular spot to check out there is **Papa Joe's Biersalon** (⊠ *Alter Markt 50–52, Altstadt* ☎ *0221/258–2132*), which is kind of kitschy but offers oldies from Piaf to Porter. If you prefer live jazz, go to the tiny **Papa Joe's Jazzlokale** (⊠ *Buttermarkt 37, Altstadt* ☎ *0221/257–7931*).

Das Ding (⊠ *Hohenstaufenring 30–32, Ringe* ☎ *0221/246–348*), literally "The Thing," is a student club that is never empty, even on weeknights. For a true disco experience, make for the **Alter Wartesaal** (⊠ *Am Hauptbahnhof, Johannisstr. 11, Altstadt* ☎ *0221/912–8850*) in the Hauptbahnhof on Friday or Saturday night. The old train-station waiting room has been turned into a concert hall and disco, where dancers swivel on ancient polished parquet and check their style in original mahogany-frame mirrors.

SHOPPING

A good shopping loop begins at the **Neumarkt Galerie** (⊠ *Richmodstr. 8, Innenstadt*), a bright, modern indoor shopping arcade with a web of shops and cafés surrounding an airy atrium. From there, head down the charmless but practical pedestrian shopping zone of the Schildergasse. The big department store **Kaufhof** (⊠ *Hohestr. 41–53, Innenstadt* ☎ *0221/2230*) is off the mall and central to city life. Its offerings are rich in quantity and quality.

From Schildergasse, go north on Herzogstrasse to arrive at **Glocken-gasse** (⊠*No. 4711, Innenstadt* ☎*0221/5728–9250*). ■**TIP** **Köln's most celebrated product, Eau de Cologne No. 4711, was first concocted here by the 18th-century Italian chemist Giovanni-Maria Farina.**

On Breite Strasse, another pedestrian shopping street, **Heubel** (⊠*Breite Str. 118, Innenstadt* ☎*0221/257–6013*) carries unusual, beautiful, and often inexpensive imported antiques, housewares, and jewelry. At the end of Breite Strasse is Eherenstrasse, where the young and young-at-heart can shop for hip fashions and trendy housewares. After a poke around here, explore the small boutiques on Benesisstrasse, which will lead you to Mittelstrasse, best known for high-tone German fashions and luxury goods. Follow Mittelstrasse to the end to return to the Neumarkt.

AACHEN

70 km (43 mi) west of Köln.

At the center of Aachen, the characteristic *drei-Fenster* facades, three windows wide, give way to buildings dating from the days when Charlemagne made Aix-la-Chapelle (as it was then called) the great center of the Holy Roman Empire. Thirty-two German emperors were crowned here, gracing Aachen with the proud nickname "Kaiserstadt" (Emperors' City). Roman legions had been drawn here for the healing properties of the sulfur springs emanating from the nearby Eifel Mountains. (The name "Aachen", based on an Old German word for "water", takes note of this.) Charlemagne's father, Pepin the Short, also settled here to enjoy the waters, and to this day the city is also known as Bad Aachen, drawing visitors in search of a cure. One-and-a-half-hour walking tours depart from the tourist office throughout the year at 11 on weekends, as well as at 2 on weekdays from April to October. The Saturday tours are conducted in English as well as German.

ESSENTIALS

Visitor Information **Aachen** (⊠*Aachen Tourist Service, Friedrich-Wilhelm-Pl., Postfach 2007* ☎*0241/180–2960* ⊕*www.aachen-tourist.de).*

EXPLORING

★ Aachen's stunning **Dom** *(Cathedral)*, the "Chapelle" of the town's earlier name, remains the single greatest storehouse of Carolingian architecture in Europe. Though it was built over the course of 1,000 years and reflects architectural styles from the Middle Ages to the 19th century, its commanding image is the magnificent octagonal royal chapel, rising up two arched stories to end in the cap of the dome. It was this section, the heart of the church, that Charlemagne saw completed in AD 800. His bones now lie in the Gothic choir, in a golden shrine surrounded by wonderful carvings of saints. Another treasure is his marble throne. Charlemagne had to journey all the way to Rome for his coronation, but the next 32 Holy Roman emperors were crowned here in Aachen, and each marked the occasion by presenting a lavish gift to the cathedral. In the 12th century Barbarossa donated the great chandelier now hanging in the center of the imperial chapel; his grandson, Friedrich II, donated Charlemagne's shrine. Emperor Karl IV journeyed from Prague in the late 14th century for the sole purpose of commissioning a bust of Charlemagne for the cathedral; now on view in the treasury, the bust incorporates a piece of Charlemagne's skull. ⊠*Münsterpl.* ☎*0241/4770–9142* ☜*Free* ⊕*www.aachendom.de* ☉*Mar.–Oct., daily 7–7; Nov.–Apr., daily 7–6.*

The **Domschatzkammer** *(Cathedral Treasury)* houses sacred art from late antiquity and the Carolingian, Ottonian, and Hohenstaufen eras; highlights include the Cross of Lothair, the Bust of Charlemagne, and the Persephone Sarcophagus. ⊠*Klosterpl. 2* ☎*0241/4770–9127* ☜*€4* ☉*Jan.–Mar., Mon. 10–1, Tues.–Sun. 10–5; Apr.–Dec., Tues and Wed., Fri.–Sun. 10–6, Thurs. 10–9.*

The back of the **Rathaus** *(Town Hall)* is opposite the Dom, across Katschhof Square. It was built in the early 14th century on the site of the *Aula,* or "great hall," of Charlemagne's palace. Its first major official function was the coronation banquet of Emperor Karl IV in 1349, held in the great Gothic hall you can still see today (though this was largely rebuilt after World War II). On the north wall of the building are statues of 50 emperors of the Holy Roman Empire. The greatest of them all, Charlemagne, stands in bronze atop the Kaiserbrunnen (Imperial Fountain) in the center of the market square. ⊠*Marktpl.* ☎*0241/432–7310* ☜*€2* ☉*Daily 10–1 and 2–5.*

The arcaded, neoclassical **Elisenbrunnen** *(Elisa Fountain)*, built in 1822, is south of the cathedral and contains two fountains with thermal drinking water. Experts say that the spa waters here—the hottest north of the Alps—are effective in helping to cure a wide range of ailments. Drinking the sulfurous water in the approved manner can be unpleasant, but as you hold your nose and gulp away, you're emulating the likes of Dürer, Frederick the Great, and Charlemagne.

You can try sitting in the spa waters at **Carolus-Thermen Bad Aachen,** a high-tech spa. In Dürer's time there were regular crackdowns on the orgiastic goings-on at the baths. Today taking the waters is done with a bathing suit on, but be aware—the casual German attitude toward nudity takes over in the sauna area, which is declared a "textile-free zone." ⊠*Passstr. 79* ☎*0241/182–740* ⊕*www.carolus-thermen.de* ☜*€10, €29 with sauna* ☉*Daily 9* AM*–11* PM.

Aachen has a modern side as well—one of the world's most important art collectors, Peter Ludwig, has endowed two museums in his hometown. The **Ludwig Forum für Internationale Kunst** holds a portion of Ludwig's truly enormous collection of contemporary art and hosts traveling exhibits. ⊠*Jülicher Str. 97–109* ☎*0241/180–7104* ⊕*www.*

heimat.de/ludwigsforum ⊠*€5* ⊙*Tues. and Wed., Fri.–Sun. noon–6, Thurs. noon–8.*

The **Suermondt-Ludwig Museum** is devoted to classical painting up to the beginning of the 20th century. ⊠*Wilhelmstr. 18* ☎*0241/479–800* ⊕*www.suermondt-ludwig-museum.de* ⊠*€5* ⊙*Tues., Thurs., and Fri. noon–6, Wed. 11–8, weekends 11–6.*

WHERE TO EAT

$$$$ ✕**La Becasse.** Sophisticated French nouvelle cuisine from Chef Christof Lang is offered in this modern restaurant just outside the Old Town by the Westpark. Try the distinctively light calves' liver. ⊠*Hanbrucherstr. 1* ☎*0241/74444* ⚐*Reservations essential* ▤*DC, MC, V* ⊙*Closed Sun. No lunch Sat. or Mon.*

$ ✕**Am Knipp.** At this Bierstube dating from 1698, run by three genera-tions of the Ramrath family, guests dig into their German dishes at low wooden tables next to the tile stove. Pewter pots and beer mugs hang from the rafters. ⊠*Bergdriesch 3* ☎*0241/33168* ▤*AE, DC, MC, V* ⊙*Closed Tues., Dec. 24–Jan. 2, and 2 wks in Apr. and Oct. No lunch.*

$ ✕**Der Postwagen.** This annex of the more upscale Ratskeller is worth a ★   stop for the building alone, a half-timber medieval edifice at one corner of the old Rathaus. You'll be impressed by the food as well, which also comes from the kitchen of Ratskeller chef Maurice de Boer. Sitting at one of the low wooden tables, surveying the marketplace through the wavy old glass, you can dine very respectably on solid German fare. If you really want to go local, try Himmel und Erde. ⊠*Am Markt 40* ☎*0241/35001* ▤*AE, MC, V.*

$ ✕**Magellan.** With its beer garden set against Aachen's 13th-century city wall, this historic establishment is true to the city's heritage. It bears the name of a celebrated Portuguese explorer, and promises its patrons a culinary voyage of discovery. There is a varied selection of Mediter-ranean cuisine—Greek lamb, Italian scaloppine, Turkish Böregi, plus a Sunday brunch, all under an imposing Greek Orthodox chandelier. Despite the elegant background, the atmosphere is lively and relaxed. ⊠*Pontstr. 78* ☎*0241/401–6440* ▤*DC, MC, V.*

WHERE TO STAY

$$$ 🛏**Pullmann Quellenhof Aachen.** This old-style hostelry is one of Europe's grandes dames. High tea is served in the marvelous fireside hall. Rooms have high ceilings, and there are a great many spa and fitness facilities. Flowers fill the Brasserie Restaurant ($$$$), where light German and French cuisine is served. **Pros:** spacious, elegant, formal. **Cons:** on a busy street, expensive. ⊠*Monheimsallee 52* ☎*0241/91320* ⊕*www. sofitel.com* ⇴*185 rooms, 2 suites* ⚙*In-room: refrigerator, dial-up, Wi-Fi. In-hotel: restaurant, room service, bar, pool, gym, concierge, laundry service, parking (fee), some pets allowed, no-smoking rooms* ▤*AE, DC, MC, V* ⦿*BP.*

$$ 🛏**Hotel Brülls am Dom.** In the historic heart of the city, this family-run hotel offers tradition, convenience, and considerable comfort. It's a short walk from nearly all the major attractions. **Pro:** central location. **Con:** no elevator. ⊠*Hühnermarkt 2–3* ☎*0241/31704* ⇴*12 rooms*

♿*In-room: no a/c. In-hotel: no elevator, parking (fee)* ⊟*No credit cards* ⵙⵔCP.

$ ⛫**Hotel Dura.** This small, family-run hotel, on a noisy street a block from the train station, is one of the few low-budget options in the city. All the same, your reception is warm and friendly. There's no restaurant; breakfast is served in the reception room. **Pros:** inexpensive, close to the train station. **Cons:** on a busy street. ⊠*Lagerhausstr. 5* ☎*0241/403–135* 🖷*0241/401–8450* 🛏*8 rooms* ♿*In-room: no a/c. In-hotel: bar, no elevator, public Wi-Fi* ⊟*MC, V* ⵙⵔCP.

NIGHTLIFE & THE ARTS

Most activity in town is concentrated around the market square and Pontstrasse, a pedestrian street that radiates off the square. Start out at Aachen's most popular bar, the **Dom Keller** (⊠*Hof 1* ☎*0241/34265*), to mingle with locals of all ages at old wooden tables. The Irish pub **Wild Rover** (⊠*Hirschgraben 13* ☎*0241/35453*) serves Murphy's Stout on tap to live music every night starting at 9:30. The municipal orchestra gives regular concerts in the **Kongresszentrum Eurogress** (⊠*Monheimsallee 48* ☎*0241/91310*).

SHOPPING

■**TIP→** Don't leave Aachen without stocking up on the traditional local gingerbread, *Aachener Printen*. Most bakeries in town offer assortments. Some of the best are at the **Alte Aachener Kaffeestuben** (⊠*Büchel 18* ☎*0241/35724*), also known as the *Konditorei van den Daele*. Another tasty Aachen specialty, also available at the Kafeestuben, is Reisfladen, a sort of pancake filled with milk rice and often some fruit — especially pears, apricots, or cherries. The store-café is worth a visit for its atmosphere and tempting aromas, whether or not you intend to buy anything. It also ships goods.

DÜSSELDORF

47 km (29 mi) north of Köln.

Düsseldorf, the state capital of North Rhine–Westphalia, may suffer by comparison to Köln's remarkable skyline, but the elegant city has more than enough charm—and money—to boost its confidence. It has a reputation for being one of the richest cities in Germany, with an extravagant lifestyle that epitomizes the economic success of postwar Germany. Since 80% of Düsseldorf was destroyed in World War II, the city has since been more or less rebuilt from the ground up—in part rebuilding landmarks of long ago and restoring a medieval riverside quarter.

At the confluence of the Rivers Rhine and Düssel, this dynamic city started as a small fishing town. The name means "village on the Düssel," but obviously this Dorf is a village no more. Raised expressways speed traffic past towering glass-and-steel structures; within them, glass-enclosed shopping malls showcase the finest clothes, furs, jewelry, and other goods that money can buy.

GETTING HERE & AROUND

Bus tours of Düsseldorf in the summer leave daily at 11 and 2:30 (in winter only at 2:30 Saturday). Departures are from the corner of Steinstrasse and Königsallee. Tickets (€19 in summer, €16 in winter) can be purchased on the bus, at the information center, or through Adorf Reisebüro.

DISCOUNTS & DEALS

The **Düsseldorf WelcomeCard** costs €9 for one day, €14 for two days, and €19 for three days, and allows free public transportation and reduced admission to museums, theaters, and even boat tours on the Rhine.

ESSENTIALS

Visitor Information **Düsseldorf** (⊠ *Tourismus & Marketing GmbH, Breitestr. 69* ☏ *0211/172–020* ⊕ *www.duesseldorf-tourismus.de*).

EXPLORING

MAIN ATTRACTIONS

The **Königsallee,** the main shopping avenue, is the epitome of Düsseldorf affluence; it's lined with the crème de la crème of designer boutiques and stores. Known as the Kö, this wide, double boulevard is divided by an ornamental waterway that is actually a part of the River Düssel. Rows of chestnut trees line the Kö, shading a string of sidewalk cafés. Beyond the Triton Fountain, at the street's north end, begins a series of parks and gardens. In these patches of green you can sense a joie de vivre hardly expected in a city devoted to big business.

The **Kunstsammlung Nordrhein-Westfalen** *(Art Collection of North Rhine–Westphalia)* will be partly closed in 2009. What remains open, K21, displays international art since about 1980, including the works of Thomas Ruff, Marcel Broodthaers, and Nam June Paik. ⊠ Ständehausstr. 1 ☏ *0211/83810* ⊕ *www.kunstsammlung.de* ⌑ *€10* ⊙ *Tues.–Fri. 10–6, weekends 11–6, 1st Wed. of each month 10–10.*

Neanderthal Museum. Just outside Düsseldorf, the Düssel River forms a valley, called the Neanderthal, where the bones of a Stone Age ancestor of modern man were found. A prize-winning museum, built at the site of discovery in the suburb of Mettmann, includes models of the original discovery, replicas of cave drawings, and life-size models of Neanderthal Man. Many scientists think he was a different species of man; short, stocky, and with a sloping forehead. The bones were found in 1856 by workers quarrying the limestone cliffs to get flux for blast furnaces. ⊠ *Talstr. 300, Mettmann* ☏ *02104/979797* ⊕ *www.neanderthal.de* ⌑ *€7* ⊙ *Tues.–Sun. 10–6.*

The restored **Altstadt** *(Old Town)* is called "the longest bar in the word." Narrow alleys thread their way to some 260 restaurants and taverns offering a wide range of cuisines. All crowd into the 1-square-km (½-square-mi) area between the Rhine and Heine Allee. When the weather cooperates, the area seems like one big sidewalk café.

Traffic is routed away from the river and underneath the **Rhine Promenade,** which is lined by chic shopping arcades and cafés. Joggers, rollerbladers, punks, and folks out for a stroll make much use of the promenade as well.

ALSO WORTH SEEING

The lovely **Hofgarten Park,** once the garden of the elector's palace, is reached by heading north to Corneliusplatz. Laid out in 1770 and completed 30 years later, the Hofgarten is an oasis of greenery at the heart of downtown and a focal point for Düsseldorf culture.

The baroque **Schloss Jägerhof,** at the far-east edge of the Hofgarten, is more a combination town house and country lodge than a castle. It houses the **Goethe Museum,** featuring original manuscripts, first editions, personal correspondence, and other memorabilia of Germany's greatest writer. There's also a museum housing a collection of **Meissen porcelain.** ✉*Jacobistr. 2* ☎*0211/899–6262* ⊕*www.goethe-museum. com* 🖥*€3* ⊙*Tues.–Fri. and Sun. 11–5, Sat. 1–5.*

The **museum kunst palast** *(art museum foundation)* lies at the northern extremity of the Hofgarten, close to the Rhine. The collection of paintings runs the gamut from Rubens, Goya, Tintoretto, and Cranach the Elder to the romantic Düsseldorf school and such modern German expressionists as Beckmann, Kirchner, Nolde, Macke, and Kandinsky. ✉*Ehrenhof 5* ☎*0211/899–2460* ⊕*www.museum-kunst-palast.de* 🖥*€6* ⊙*Tues.–Sun. 11–6.*

The **Heinrich Heine Institute** has a museum and an archive of significant manuscripts. Part of the complex was once the residence of the composer Robert Schumann. ✉*Bilkerstr. 12–14* ☎*0211/899–2902* ⊕*www.duesseldorf.de/heineinstitut* 🖥*€3* ⊙*Tues.–Fri. and Sun. 11–5, Sat. 1–5.*

The stylish **MedienHafen** is an eclectic mixture of late-19th-century warehouses and ultramodern restaurants, bars, and shops. The fashionable and hip neighborhood is one of Europe's masterpieces in urban redevelopment. Surrounding the historic, commercial harbor, now occupied by yachts and leisure boats, many media companies have made this area their home. On the riverbank you'll find Frank Gehry's **Neuer Zollhof,** a particularly striking ensemble of three organic-looking high-rises. The best way to tackle the buzzing architecture is to take a stroll down the promenade.

The traffic-free cobblestone streets of the Old Town lead to **Burgplatz** *(Castle Square).*

The 13th-century **Schlossturm** *(Castle Tower)* is all that remains of the castle built by the de Berg family, which founded Düsseldorf. The tower also houses the **Schifffahrtsmuseum**, which charts 2,000 years of Rhine boatbuilding and navigation. ⊠ *Burgpl. 30* ☎ *0211/899–4195* 🖃 *€3* ☉ *Tues.–Sun. 11–6.*

The Gothic **St. Lambertus** (*St. Lambertus Church* ⊠ *Stiftspl. 7*) is near the castle tower on Burgplatz. Its spire became distorted because unseasoned wood was used in its construction. The Vatican elevated the 14th-century brick church to a basilica minor (small cathedral) in 1974 in recognition of its role in church history. Built in the 13th century, with additions from 1394, St. Lambertus contains the tomb of William the Rich and a graceful late-Gothic tabernacle.

WHERE TO EAT

$$$$ ✕ **Berens am Kai.** This sleek restaurant is the gourmet playground of
★   the young business elite of this affluent city. Set in the once derelict but now modernized Düsseldorf harbor, the glass-and-steel building with its ceiling-to-floor windows looks more like a modern office complex than a restaurant. The steep prices are warranted by the exquisite cuisine by chef Holger Berens, the refined service, and the great setting with magnificent views of the harbor and Düsseldorf, particularly stunning at night. Dishes include creative French recipes, a wine list with vintages from around the world, and tempting desserts—a must-visit if you are tired of old-style German cooking. ⊠ *Kaistr. 16* ☎ *0211/300–6750* ⚓ *Reservations essential* 🖃 *AE, MC, V* ☉ *Closed Sun. No lunch Sat.*

$$$$ ✕ **Im Schiffchen.** Although it's out of the way, a meal at one of Germany's
★   best restaurants makes it worth a trip. This is grande luxe, with cooking, under chef Jean Claude Bourgueil, that's a fine art. The restaurant Jean Claude, on the ground floor, features local specialties created by the same chef but at lower prices. There are 900 wines in the cellar, many available by the glass. ⊠ *Kaiserswerther Markt 9* ☎ *0211/401–050* ⚓ *Reservations essential* 🖃 *AE, DC, MC, V* ☉ *Closed Sun. and Mon. No lunch.*

$$$ ✕ **Malkasten Restaurant.** If artists seem to live in pubs, then the Malkasten ("paint box") shines as a most favored haven. The stylish bar and restaurant, with a park-view terrace, is a designer's dream come true. It serves a mixture of international fare, plus creative regional specialties and a sumptuous brunch on Sunday. ⊠ *Jacobistr. 6* ☎ *0211/173–040* 🖃 *AE, MC, V* ☉ *No lunch Sat.*

$$$ ✕ **Weinhaus Tante Anna.** This charming restaurant, six generations in the same family, is furnished with antiques. The cuisine presents modern versions of German classics, demonstrating that there's a lot more to the country's cooking than wurst and sauerkraut—a specialty is a hearty rump steak baked with mustard and onions. ⊠ *Andreasstr. 2* ☎ *0211/131–163* 🖃 *AE, MC, V* ☉ *Closed Sun. No lunch.*

$ ✕ **Brauerei Zur Uel.** A nontraditional brew house, the Uel is the popular hangout for Düsseldorf's students. The basic menu consists of soups, salads, and pastas; the ingredients are fresh and the portions are generous. Every cultural and political event in the city is advertised in the entry hall. ⊠*Ratingerstr. 16* ☎*0211/325–369* ☒*DC, MC, V.*

¢ ✗**Zum Uerige.** Among beer buffs, Düsseldorf is famous for its *Altbier,* so called because of the old-fashioned brewing method. The mellow and malty copper-color brew is produced by eight breweries in town. This tavern, which brews its own beer, provides the perfect atmosphere for drinking it. The beer is poured straight out of polished oak barrels and served with hearty local food by busy waiters in long blue aprons. The food offered is mainly snacks. ⊠*Bergerstr. 1* ☎*0211/866–990* ☒*No credit cards.*

WHERE TO STAY

$$$–$$$$ ▣**Steigenberger Parkhotel.** Miraculously quiet despite its central location on the edge of the Hofgarten and at the beginning of the Königsallee, this old hotel is anything but stodgy. The soaring ceilings add to the spaciousness of the guest rooms, each individually decorated in a restrained, elegant style. The pampering continues at the breakfast buffet, served in the Menuette restaurant, where champagne and smoked salmon are appropriate starters for a shopping expedition on the Kö. **Pro:** central but quiet. **Con:** expensive. ⊠*Königsallee 1a* ☎*0211/13810* ⊕*www.steigenberger.de* ⌨*119 rooms, 11 suites* ♿*In-room: no a/c (some), safe, refrigerator, dial-up (some), Wi-Fi. In-hotel: restaurant, 2 bars, concierge, laundry service, public Internet, parking (no fee), some pets allowed, no-smoking rooms* ☒*AE, DC, MC, V.*

$$ ▣**Carathotel.** Besides bright, good-size rooms, the true strength of this modern hotel is its location, near the market in the Altstadt. After a generous buffet breakfast you can quickly reach either the Rhine or the Kö with a three-block walk. **Pro:** right in the Altstadt. **Con:** inappropriately modern exterior. ⊠*Benratherstr. 7a* ☎*0211/13050* ⊕*www. carat-hotel.de* ⌨*72 rooms, 1 suite* ♿*In-room: no a/c (some), dial-up, Wi-Fi. In-hotel: public Internet, parking (fee), no-smoking rooms, some pets allowed* ☒*AE, DC, MC, V* ⏐❶*BP.*

NIGHTLIFE & THE ARTS

The **Altstadt** is a landscape of pubs, dance clubs, ancient brewery houses, and jazz clubs in the vicinity of the Marktplatz and along cobblestone streets named Bolker, Kurze, Flinger, and Mühlen. These places may be crowded, but some are very atmospheric. The local favorite for nightlife is the **Hafen** neighborhood. Its restaurants and bars cater to the hip thirtysomething crowd that works and parties there. The most popular dance club is **Sam's West** (⊠*Königsallee 27* ☎*0211/328–171*).

Düsseldorf, once home to Mendelssohn, Schumann, and Brahms, has the finest concert hall in Germany after Berlin's Philharmonie, the **Tonhalle** (⊠*Ehrenhof 1* ☎*0211/899–6123*), a former planetarium on the edge of the Hofgarten. It's the home of the Düsseldorfer Symphoniker, which plays from September to mid-June. **Deutsche Oper am Rhein** (⊠*Heinrich Heine Allee 16a* ☎*0211/892–5211*) showcases the city's highly regarded opera company and ballet troupe. The **Robert Schumann Saal** (⊠*Ehrenhof 4* ☎*0211/899–2450* ⊕*www.museum-kunst-palast. de*) has classical and pop concerts, symposia, film, and international theater. One of Germany's finest variety and artistic shows is presented nightly at the **Roncalli's Apollo Varieté** ($\boxtimes$*Apollopl.* ☎*0211/828–9090* ⊕*www.apollo-variete.com*).

A 30-minute ride outside Düsseldorf by car, train, or S-bahn (from the Hauptbahnhof) will get you to the industrial city of Wuppertal, whose main claim to fame is its transit system of suspended trains, the *Schwebebahn*. It is also home to the **Tanztheater Wuppertal** ($\boxtimes$*Bundesallee 260* ☎*0202/569–4444* ⊕*www.pina-bausch.de*), the dance-theater company of world-famous choreographer Pina Bausch.

SHOPPING

For antiques, go to the area around Hohe Strasse. The east side of the **Königsallee** is lined with some of Germany's trendiest boutiques, grandest jewelers, and most extravagant furriers. The shopping arcade **Kö Center** ($\boxtimes$*Königsallee 30*) features the most famous names in fashion, from Chanel to Louis Vuitton. **Kö Galerie** ($\boxtimes$*Königsallee 60*) has trendy boutiques and includes a Mövenpick restaurant on its luxurious two-story premises. **Schadow Arkaden** ($\boxtimes$*Schadowstr. 11, at end of Kö Galerie*) caters to normal budgets, with such stores as Hennes & Mauritz (H&M) and Habitat.

The Fairy-Tale Road

WORD OF MOUTH

"[The Fairy-Tale Road] starts in Hanau (near Frankfurt) and continues north for about 375 mi and ends in Bremen... Especially noteworthy are Alsfeld, Marburg and Hameln."

—Wolf

"Bremen is an attractive town, lively enough although it's not the first place that comes to mind when looking for nightlife. It's a great base for traveling around this interesting part of Germany, with Lübeck and Muensterland within easy reach. It's an underrated and undervisited region. Near Bremen is the artists and writers town of Worpswede which also has an interesting museum dedicated to Jugendstil."

—BTilke

Updated
by Ted
Shoemaker

IF YOU'RE IN SEARCH OF Sleeping Beauty, the Pied Piper, or Rumpelstiltskin, the Fairy-Tale Road, or Märchenstrasse, is the place to look. One of Germany's designated tour routes, the Märchenstrasse leads deep into the heart of the country through the landscapes that inspired the Brothers Grimm. It's a route perhaps even more in tune with romantics than the Romantic Road. Fairy tales come to life in forgotten villages, ancient castles, and misty valleys where the silence of centuries is broken only by the splash of a ferryman's oar. The meandering, progressive path seems to travel back in time, into the reaches of childhood, imagination, and the German folk consciousness. These old-world settings are steeped in legend and fantasy.

This part of Germany shaped the lives and imaginations of the two most famous chroniclers of German folk history and tradition, the Brothers Grimm. They sought out the region's best storytellers to bring us such unforgettable characters as Cinderella, Hansel and Gretel, Little Red Riding Hood, Rapunzel, Sleeping Beauty, and Snow White.

ORIENTATION & PLANNING

GETTING ORIENTED

The Fairy-Tale Road begins 20 minutes east of Frankfurt in the city of Hanau, and from there wends its way north 600 km (about 370 mi), mainly through the states of Hesse and Lower Saxony, following the Fulda and Weser rivers and traversing a countryside as beguiling as any other in Europe. It doesn't have the glamour of the Romantic Road or the cosmopolitan flair of Germany's great cities, but it also doesn't have the crowds and commercialism. It's a place that inspired fairy tales that are read the world over.

Hesse. With Wiesbaden as its capital, Hesse ranks eighth in area among Germany's 16 states and fifth in population. Its northern part is a place of forests, castles, and inspiration for the tales transcribed by the Grimm brothers.

Lower Saxony. Germany's second-largest state after Bavaria and fourth-most populous, Lower Saxony (Niedersachsen) has a diverse landscape, including the Weser River, which forms a picturesque part of the FairyTale Road, and the Lüneburg Heath. Its capital and largest city is Hannover.

THE FAIRY-TALE ROAD PLANNER

WHEN TO GO
Summer is the ideal time to travel through this varied landscape, although in spring you'll find the river valleys carpeted in the season's first flowers, and in fall the sleepy current of the Weser is often blanketed in mist. Keep in mind that retail stores and shops in the smaller towns in this area often close for two to three hours at lunchtime.

TOP REASONS TO GO

Weser Valley Road: Drive or bike the scenic highway between Hannoversch-Münden and Hameln; a landscape of green hills, Weser Renaissance towns, and inviting riverside taverns.

Marburg: Staircase streets and university students climb the steep hillsides of this half-timber town; snag a seat at an outdoor table on a sunny afternoon and soak up the atmosphere.

Bremen: Browse the shops and galleries lining the picturesque Böttcherstrasse and Schnoorviertel, then savor the city's rich coffee tradition at a café.

Sababurg: The supposed inspiration for Sleeping Beauty's castle is appropriately surrounded by a forest.

12

GETTING HERE & AROUND

BY AIR The closest international airports to this region are in Frankfurt, Hannover, and Hamburg. Frankfurt is less than a half hour from Hanau, and Hamburg is less than an hour from Bremen.

BY BIKE The Fulda and Werra rivers have 190 km (118 mi) of bike paths, and you can cycle the whole length of the Weser River from Hannoversch-Münden to the outskirts of Bremen without making too many detours from the river valley. Five- and seven-day cycle tours of the Fulda and Werra river valleys are possible, including bike rentals, overnight accommodations, and luggage transport between stops.

BY BOAT The eight boats of Flotte Weser operate short summer excursions along a considerable stretch of the Weser River between Bremen and Bad Karlshafen. The trip between Corvey and Bad Karlshafen, for example, takes slightly under three hours and costs €13.50.

Rehbein-Linie Kassel operates a service from Kassel to Bad Karlshafen. It also prides itself on the only "three-river tour" in the area. In a single trip you travel on the Fulda and Werra rivers and also on the river formed when these two meet at the tour's starting point of Hannoversch-Münden, the Weser. One of the company's three boats, the *Deutschland,* has a bowling alley aboard. Personenschifffahrt K. & K. Söllner has two excursion boats plying between Kassel and Hannoversch-Münden.

BY BUS Bremen, Kassel, Göttingen, Fulda, and Hanau are all reachable via Deutsche Touring's Europabus. A local bus serves the scenic Weser Valley Road stretch (B–80 and B–83), between Hannoversch-Münden and Hameln; total mileage is approximately 103 km (64 mi).

Year-round tours of the region are offered by Herter-Reisen.

BY CAR The best way to travel is by car. The autobahn network serves Hanau, Fulda, Kassel, Göttingen, and Bremen directly, but you can't savor the fairy-tale country from this high-speed superhighway. Bremen is 60 km (35 mi) northwest of Hannover and 100 km (60 mi) northwest of Celle.

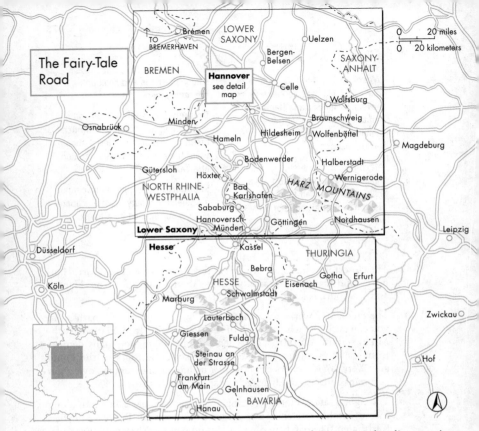

The Fairy-Tale Road incorporates one of Germany's loveliest scenic drives, the Wesertalstrasse, or Weser Vallley Road (B–80 and B–83), between Hannoversch-Münden and Hameln; total mileage is approximately 103 km (64 mi).

BY TRAIN   Hanau, Fulda, Kassel, Göttingen, Hannover, and Bremen are reachable via InterCity Express (ICE) trains from Frankfurt and Hamburg. Rail service, but not ICE service, is available to Hannoversch-Münden, Marburg, Hameln, and Celle.

ESSENTIALS   **Airport Information Langenhagen Airport** (✉ *Petzelstr. 84, Hannover* ☎ *0511/9770*).

Bike Tour Information SRJ GästeService (✉ *Gneisenaustr. 4 Minden* ☎ *0571/889–1900*).

Boat Tour Information Flotte Weser (✉ *Deisterallee 1 Hameln* ☎ *05151/939– 999*). **Personenschifffahrt K. & K. Söllner** (✉ *Die Schlagd Kassel* ☎ *0561/774– 670*). **Rehbein-Linie Kassel** (✉ *Ostpreusenstr. 8 Fuldatal* ☎ *0561/18505*).

Bus Tour Information Herter-Reisen (✉ *Am Klei 26 Coppenbrügge* ☎ *05159/969–244*).

Train information Deutsche Bahn (☎ *0800/150–7090* ⊕ *www.bahn.de*).

Visitor Information **Deutsche Märchenstrasse** (✉ *Kurfürstenstr. 9 Kassel* ☎ *0561/9204–7911* ⊕ *www.deutsche-maerchenstrasse.de*).

ABOUT THE RESTAURANTS & HOTELS

In this largely rural area many restaurants serve hot meals only between 11:30 AM and 2 PM, and 6 PM and 9 PM. You rarely need a reservation here, and casual clothing is generally acceptable.

Make hotel reservations in advance if you plan to visit in summer. Though it's one of the less-traveled tourist routes in Germany, the main destinations on the Fairy-Tale Road are popular. Hannover is particularly busy during trade-fair times.

WHAT IT COSTS IN EUROS					
	¢	$	$$	$$$	$$$$
RESTAURANTS	under €9	€9–€15	€16–€20	€21–€25	over €25
HOTELS	under €50	€50–€100	€101–€175	€176–€225	over €225

Restaurant prices are per person for a main course at dinner. Hotel prices are for two people in a standard double room, including tax and service.

PLANNING YOUR TIME

The Fairy-Tale Road isn't really for the traveler in a hurry. If you only have a day or two to savor it, concentrate on a short stretch of it. A good suggestion is the Weser River route between Hannoversch-Münden and Hameln. The landscape is lovely and the towns are romantic. If you have more time, but not enough to travel the whole route, focus on the southern half of the road. It's more in character with the fairy tales.

DISCOUNTS & DEALS

Free summer weekend performances along the Fairy-Tale Road include Münchausen plays in Bodenwerder, the Dr. Eisenbart reenactments in Hannoversch-Münden, the Town Musicians shows in Bremen, and especially the Pied Piper spectacle at Hameln. Kassel, Hannover, and Bremen also sell visitor cards that let you ride free on public transportation, grant reduced admissions at museums, and give other perks.

HESSE

The first portion of the Fairy-Tale Road, from Hanau to Kassel, lies within the state of Hesse. Since much of the Hessian population is concentrated in the south, in such cities as Frankfurt, Darmstadt, and Wiesbaden, the northern part is quite rural, hilly, forested, and very pretty. Here you'll find Steinau, the almost vertical city of Marburg, and Kassel, all of which have associations with the Grimm brothers.

HANAU

16 km (10 mi) east of Frankfurt.

The Fairy-Tale Road begins in once-upon-a-time fashion at Hanau, the town where the Brothers Grimm were born. Although Grimm fans will want to start their pilgrimage here, Hanau is now a traffic-congested suburb of Frankfurt, with post–World War II buildings that are not particularly attractive.

ESSENTIALS

Visitor Information Hanau (⊠ *Tourist-Information Hanau, Am Markt 14–18* ☎ *06181/295–950* ⊕ *www.hanau.de*).

EXPLORING

Hanau's main attraction can be reached only on foot—the **Nationaldenkmal Brüder Grimm** *(Brothers Grimm Memorial)* in the Marktplatz. The bronze memorial, erected in 1898, is a larger-than-life-size statue of the brothers, one seated, the other leaning on his chair, the two of them pondering an open book. There is also a small Grimm exhibit, featuring clothing, artifacts, and writings, at **Schloss Phillipsruhe** (⊠ *Phillipsruher Allee 45* ☎ *06181/295–564* ⊕ *www.museen-hanau.de*), on the bank of the Main in the suburb of Kesselstadt (Bus 1 will take you there in 10 minutes). ■ TIP→ **Historical Hanau treasures, including a priceless collection of faience, are also on display in the palace museum.**

The solid bulk of Hanau's 18th-century **Rathaus** *(Town Hall)* stands behind the Grimm brothers statue. Every day at 10, noon, 4, and 6 its bells play tribute to another of the city's famous sons, the composer Paul Hindemith (1895–1963), by chiming out one of his canons. ⊠ *Marktpl. 14.*

GELNHAUSEN

20 km (12 mi) northeast of Hanau, 35 km (21 mi) northeast of Frankfurt.

Gelnhausen's picturesque Altstadt (Old Town) offers the first taste of the half-timber architecture and cobblestone streets that await in abundance farther north.

GETTING HERE & AROUND

If you're flying into Frankfurt, Gelnhausen is an ideal spot for your first night on the Fairy-Tale Road. It's smaller and more charming than Hanau, and is still less than an hour's drive from Frankfurt's main airport. April through October, a walking tour leaves from the town hall at 2:30 on Sunday.

ESSENTIALS

Visitor Information Gelnhausen (⊠ *Tourist Information, Obermarkt 7* ☎ *06051/830–300* ⊕ *www.gelnhausen.de*).

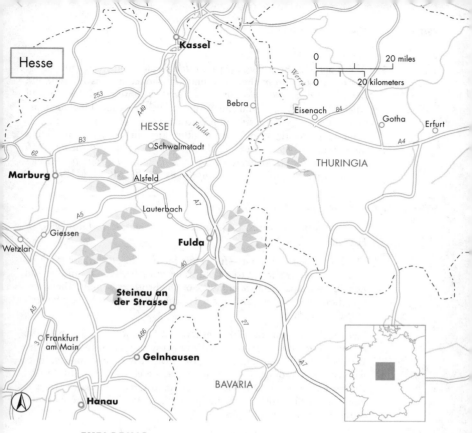

EXPLORING

On an island in the sleepy little Kinzig River you'll find the remains of **the Kaiserpfalz.** Emperor Friedrich I—known as Barbarossa, or Red Beard—built the castle in this idyllic spot in the 12th century; in 1180 it was the scene of the first all-German Imperial Diet, a gathering of princes and ecclesiastical leaders. Today only parts of the russet walls and colonnaded entrance remain. Still, stroll beneath the castle's ruined ramparts on its water site, and you'll get a tangible impression of the medieval importance of the court of Barbarossa. ✉ *Burgstr. 14* ☎ *06051/3805* 💶 *€3.50* 🕐 *Mar.–Oct., Tues.–Sun. 10–5; Nov. and Dec., Tues.–Sun. 10–4.*

The **Hexenturm** *(Witches' Tower)*, a grim prison, remains from the time when Gelnhausen was the center of a paranoiac witch hunt in the late 16th century. Dozens of women were burned at the stake or thrown—bound hand and foot—into the Kinzig River. Suspects were held in the Hexenturm of the town battlements. Today it houses a bloodcurdling collection of medieval torture instruments. Tours of the tower, in German only, are offered on Sunday afternoons from May through October. English-language tours for groups of up to 30 persons can be booked in advance for €60. ✉ *Am Fretzenstein* ☎ *06051/830–300* 🕐 *May–Oct., tour Sun. at 2:30 (except 1st Sun. of month).*

WHERE TO STAY

$$ ⚏ **Romantisches Hotel Burg Mühle.** *Mühle* means "mill," and this hotel, just a few steps from the Kaiserpfalz, was once the castle's mill and sawmill. It delivered flour until 1948. In the restaurant ($–$$) the mill wheel churns away as you eat. Wellness facilities offered include massages, a sauna, and a solarium. **Pros:** large rooms (many with balconies), spotlessly clean. **Con:** furniture and carpeting are showing a little wear. ⊠ *Burgstr. 2* ☎ *06051/82050* ⊕ *www.burgmuehle.de* 🛏 *40 rooms* ⚲ *In-room: no a/c, refrigerator. In-hotel: restaurant, bar, no elevator, public Internet, no-smoking rooms* ▭*DC, MC, V* ��*BP.*

STEINAU AN DER STRASSE

30 km (18 mi) northeast of Gelnhausen, 65 km (40 mi) northeast of Frankfurt.

The little town of Steinau—full name Steinau an der Strasse (Steinau "on the road," referring to an old trade route between Frankfurt and Leipzig)—had a formative influence on the Brothers Grimm. They were preschoolers on arrival and under 12 when they left after their father's untimely death.

Steinau dates from the 13th century, and is typical of villages in the region. Marvelously preserved half-timber houses are set along cobblestone streets; an imposing castle bristles with towers and turrets. In its woodsy surroundings you can well imagine encountering Little Red Riding Hood, Snow White, or Hansel and Gretel. A major street is named after the brothers; the building where they lived is now known as the Brothers Grimm House.

GETTING HERE & AROUND

A city walking tour takes place April to October, the first Sunday of the month, leaving at 2 from the Märchenbrunnen.

ESSENTIALS

Visitor Information Steinau an der Strasse (⊠ *Verkehrsbüro, Brüder-Grimm-Str. 70* ☎ *06663/96310* ⊕ *www.steinau.de*).

EXPLORING

★ **Schloss Steinau** *(Steinau Castle)* is straight out of a Grimm fairy tale. It stands at the top of the town, with a "Fairy-tale Fountain" in front of it. Originally an early-medieval fortress, it was rebuilt in Renaissance style between 1525 and 1558 and first used by the counts of Hanau as their summer residence. Later it was used to guard the increasingly important trade route between Frankfurt and Leipzig. It's not difficult to imagine the young Grimm boys playing in the shadow of its great gray walls or venturing into the encircling dry moat.

The castle houses a **Grimm Museum,** one of two in Steinau, as well as an exhibition of marionettes from the marionette theater. The Grimm Museum exhibits the family's personal effects, including portraits of the Grimm relatives, the family Bible, an original copy of the Grimms' dictionary (the German equivalent of the Oxford English Dictionary),

12

and all sorts of mundane things such as spoons and drinking glasses. Climb the tower for a breathtaking view of Steinau and the countryside. ☎06663/6843 ⌨*Museum €3.50, tower €1, tour of castle and museum €4* ⊘*Mar.–Oct., Tues.–Thurs. and weekends 10–5; Nov.– mid-Dec., Tues.–Thurs. and weekends 10–4.*

The **Steinauer Marionettentheater** *(Steinau Marionette Theater)* is in the castle's former stables and portrays Grimm fairy tales and other children's classics. Performances are held most weekends at 3. ⊠*Am Kumpen 4* ☎06663/245 ⊕*www.die-holzkoeppe.de* ⌨*€6.50.*

The **Museum Steinau and Brüder Grimm Haus,** adjacent to the house where the Grimms lived as children, tells the history of "Steinau on the Road." It displays a coach, old signs from wayside inns, milestones, and a restoration of the marketplace. The Grimm Haus contains books, pictures, and reminders of their work as lexicographers, and in the summer there are fairy-tale plays in the garden. ⊠*Brüder-Grimm-Str. 80* ☎06663/7605 ⊕*www.museum-steinau.de* ⌨*€2 for museum or house, €3 for both* ⊘*Daily 11–5, closed 2 wks in late Dec.*

WHERE TO EAT

$ ✗**Brathähnchenfarm.** This cheery hotel-restaurant is a long, long way from the center of Steinau, uphill all the way. But it's worth it. As your nose will tell you immediately, just about everything on the menu is charcoal-grilled. The name *"Brathähnchenfarm"* (Roast Chicken Farm), sets the theme, though other grilled meats are available. It is, in addition, a place of peace and quiet. ⊠*Im Ohl 1* ☎06663/228 ▭*No credit cards* ⊘*Closed Mon. and mid-Dec.–mid-Feb.*

FULDA

32 km (20 mi) northeast of Steinau an der Strasse, 100 km (62 mi) northeast of Frankfurt.

The episcopal city of Fulda is well worth a detour off the Fairy-Tale Road. There are two distinct parts to its downtown area. One is a stunning display of baroque architecture, replete with cathedral, orangerie, and formal garden, that grew up around the palace. The other is the Old Town, where the incredibly narrow and twisty streets are lined with boutiques, bistros, and a medieval tower. ■TIP→ **You'll find Kanalstrasse and Karlstrasse in the Old Town lined with good but inexpensive cafés and restaurants, ranging from German to Mediterranean.**

GETTING HERE & AROUND

Fulda's walking tours offer a recording with earphones, enabling you to follow the German tours in English. These start at the tourist office on Bonifatiusplatz, April to October, daily at 11:30 and 3; November to March, weekends and holidays at 11:30.

ESSENTIALS

Visitor Information Fulda (⊠*Tourismus- und Kongressmanagement, Bonifatiuspl. 1* ☎*0661/102–1813* ⊕*www.tourismus-fulda.de*).

The Brothers Grimm

The two essential features of a Grimm's fairy tale are generally deep, gloomy forests (*Hansel and Gretel, Snow White*), and castles (*Cinderella, The Sleeping Beauty*) —both of which are in abundance in the region where the stories originated.

This area, mainly in the state of Hesse, was the home region of the brothers Jacob (1785–1863) and Wilhelm (1786–1859) Grimm. They didn't conceive the stories for which they are famous. Their feat was to mine the great folklore tradition that was already deeply ingrained in local culture.

For generations, eager children had been gathering at dusk around the village storyteller to hear wondrous tales of fairies, witches, and gnomes, tales passed down from storytellers who had gone before. The Grimms sought out these storytellers and recorded their tales.

The result was the two volumes of their work *Kinder- und Hausmärchen* (*Children's and Household Tales*), published in 1812 and 1814 and revised and expanded six times during their lifetimes. The last edition, published in 1857, is the basis for the stories we know today. Earlier versions contained more violence and cruelty than was deemed suitable for children.

That is how the world got the stories of Cinderella, Sleeping Beauty, Hansel and Gretel, Little Red Riding Hood, Snow White and the Seven Dwarfs, Rumpelstiltskin, Puss-in-Boots, Mother Holle, Rapunzel, and some 200 others, most of which remain unfamiliar.

Both Jacob and Wilhelm Grimm had distinguished careers as librarians and scholars, and probably would be unhappy to know that they are best remembered for the fairy tales. Among other things, they began what would become the most comprehensive dictionary of the German language and produced an analysis of German grammar.

The brothers were born in Hanau, near Frankfurt, which has a statue memorializing them and a Grimm exhibit at Schloss Phillipsruhe. They spent their childhood in Steinau, 30 km (18 mi) to the north, where their father was magistrate. There are two Grimm museums there, one in their home. On their father's untimely death they moved to their mother's home city of Kassel, which also has an important Grimm museum. They attended the university at Marburg from 1802 to 1805, then worked as librarians in Kassel. It was in the Kassel area that they found the best of their stories. They later worked as librarians and professors in the university town of Göttingen, and spent their last years as academics in Berlin.

EXPLORING

The city's grandest example of baroque design is the immense **Stadtschloss** (*City Palace*), formerly the residence of the prince-bishops. The **Fürstensaal** (Princes' Hall), on the second floor, provides a breathtaking display of baroque decorative artistry, with ceiling paintings by the 18th-century Bavarian artist Melchior Steidl, and fabric-clad walls. The palace also has permanent displays of the faience for which Fulda was once famous, as well as some fine Fulda porcelain.

Also worth seeing is the **Spiegelsaal,** with its many tastefully arranged mirrors. Pause at the windows of the Grünes Zimmer (Green Chamber) to take in the view across the palace park to the **Orangerie,** a large garden with summer-flowering shrubs and plants. ⊠*Schlossstr. 1* ☎*0661/102–1813* 🎫*€3* ⊘*Sat.–Thurs. 10–6, Fri. 2–6.*

The **Dom,** Fulda's 18th-century cathedral with tall twin spires, stands on the other side of the broad boulevard that borders the palace park. The basilica accommodated the ever-growing number of pilgrims who converged on Fulda to pray at the grave of the martyred St. Boniface, the "Apostle of the Germans." A black alabaster bas-relief depicting his death marks the martyr's grave in the crypt. The **Cathedral Museum** (☎*0661/87207* 🎫*€2.10* ⊘*Apr.–Oct., Tues.–Sat. 10–5:30, Sun. 12:30–5:30; Nov., Dec., and mid-Feb.–Mar., Tues.–Sat. 10–12:30 and 1:30–4, Sun. 12:30–4)* contains a document bearing St. Boniface's writing, along with several other treasures, including Lucas Cranach the Elder's fine 16th-century painting Christ and the Adulteress. ⊠*Eduard Schick Pl. 1–3* ⊘*Apr.–Oct., daily 10–6; Nov.–Mar., daily 10–5.*

☺ The **Vonderau Museum** is housed in a former Jesuit seminary. Its exhibits chart the cultural and natural history of Fulda and eastern Hesse. A popular section of the museum is its **planetarium,** with a variety of shows, including one for children. Since it has only 35 seats, an early reservation is advisable. Shows take place Thursday at 7, Friday at 5 and 8, Saturday at 3 and 8, and Sunday at 10:30 and 3. ⊠*Jesuitenpl. 2* ☎*0661/928–350* 🎫*Museum €3 (free Tues.), planetarium €3.50* ⊘*Tues.–Sun. 10–5.*

☺ **Kinder-Akademie-Fulda.** It's called Germany's first children's museum, with interactive objects from science and technology, including a "walk-through heart." ⊠*Mehlerstr. 4* ☎*0661/902–730* ⊕*www.kaf. de* 🎫*€6* ⊘*Weekdays 10–5:30, Sun. 1–5:30.*

WHERE TO EAT

$–$$ ✕**Zum Stiftskämmerer.** This former episcopal treasurer's home, somewhat removed from the center of town, is now a charming tavern-restaurant, its menu packed with local fare prepared with imagination. A four-course menu priced around €30 is an excellent value, although à la carte dishes can be ordered for as little as €7.50. Try the *Schlemmertöpfchen,* a delicious (and very filling) combination of pork, chicken breast, and venison steak. ⊠*Kämmerzeller Str. 10* ☎*0661/52369* ▭*AE, DC, MC, V* ⊘*Closed Tues.*

¢ ✕**La Gondola.** This establishment in the Altstadt pedestrian zone may not be impressive from the outside, but it's cozy, if a bit crowded, and welcoming inside. They serve homemade pasta, pizza (also family-sized), and salad. The health-conscious can even have a whole wheat pizza. ⊠*Karlstr. 29* ☎*0661/71711* ▭*MC, V.*

WHERE TO STAY

$$$ 🏨**Romantik Hotel Goldener Karpfen.** Like many other buildings in Fulda,
★ this hotel dates from the baroque era (circa 1750), though the facade was redone around 1900. Inside, it's been renovated to a high standard of comfort. Afternoon coffee in the tapestry-upholstered chairs at the

EATING WELL ON THE FAIRY-TALE ROAD

A specialty of northern Hesse is sausages with *Beulches*, made from potato balls, leeks, and black pudding. *Weck*, which is local dialect for "heavily spiced pork," appears either as *Musterweck*, served on a roll, or as *Weckewerk*, a frying-pan concoction with white bread. Heading north into Lower Saxony, you'll encounter the ever-popular *Speckkuchen*, a heavy and filling onion tart. Another favorite main course is *Pfefferpothast*, a sort of heavily browned goulash with lots of pepper. Trout and eels are common in the rivers and streams around Hameln, and by the time you reach Bremen, North German cuisine has taken over the menu. *Aalsuppe grün*, eel soup seasoned with dozens of herbs, is a must in summer, and the hearty *Grünkohl mit Pinkel*, a cabbage dish with sausage, bacon, and cured pork, appears in winter. Be sure to try the coffee. Fifty percent of the coffee served in Germany comes from beans roasted in Bremen. The city has been producing the stuff since 1673, and knows just how to serve it in pleasantly cozy or, as locals say, *gemütlich* surroundings.

fireplace of the hotel's lounge is one of Fulda's delights, while dining in the elegant restaurant ($$$), with linen tablecloths, Persian rugs, and subdued lighting, is another. **Pro:** close to the baroque area of town. **Con:** somewhat removed from the downtown. ⊠ *Simpliziusbrunnen 1* ☎ *0661/86800* ⊕ *www.hotel-goldener-karpfen.de* ⌨ *50 rooms* ♿ *In-room: no a/c (some), Ethernet, Wi-Fi. In-hotel: restaurant, bar, some pets allowed, no-smoking rooms* ☰ *AE, DC, MC, V* ❑ *BP*.

$$ ⛺ **Maritim Hotel am Schlossgarten.** This is the luxurious showpiece of the Maritim chain. The large breakfast room and conference rooms are housed in a stunning 18th-century orangerie overlooking Fulda Palace Park. Guest rooms are in a modern wing with a large central atrium. You can dine beneath centuries-old vaulted arches in the basement Dianakeller restaurant ($–$$). **Pros:** large, comfortable rooms; balconies and views of the park. **Con:** no air-conditioning. ⊠ *Paulus-promenade 2* ☎ *0661/2820* ⊕ *www.maritim.de* ⌨ *111 rooms, 1 suite* ♿ *In-room: no a/c, Ethernet. In-hotel: 2 restaurants, bar, pool, some pets allowed (fee)* ☰ *AE, DC, MC, V* ❑ *BP*.

MARBURG

Fodor's Choice
★

60 km (35 mi) northwest of Fulda.

"I think there are more steps in the streets than in the houses." That is how Jacob Grimm described the half-timber hillside town of Marburg, which rises steeply from the Lahn River to the spectacular castle that crowns the hill. Many of the winding, crooked "streets" are indeed stone staircases, and several of the hillside houses have a back door five stories above the front door. The town's famous university and its students are the main influence on its social life, which pulses through the many cafés, restaurants, and student hangouts around the marketplace. The Grimms themselves studied here from 1802 to 1805.

Many of the streets are closed to traffic, and are filled with outdoor tables when the weather cooperates. There is a free elevator near the tourist-information office on Pilgrimstein that can transport you from the level of the river to the old city.

GETTING HERE & AROUND
Take B-254 and then B-62 from Fulda. Fulda has public transport.

ESSENTIALS
Visitor Information Marburg (⊠ *Tourismus und Marketing, Pilgrimstein 26* ☎ *06421/99120* ⊕ *www.marburg.de*).

EXPLORING
Marburg's most important building is the **Elisabethkirche** (*St. Elizabeth Church* ⊠ *Elisabethstr. 3*), which marks the burial site of St. Elizabeth (1207–31), the town's favorite daughter. She was a Hungarian princess, betrothed at 4 and married at age 14 to a member of the nobility, Ludwig IV of Thuringia. In 1228, when her husband fell in one of the Crusades, she gave up all worldly pursuits. She moved to Marburg, founded a hospital, gave her wealth to the poor, and spent the rest of her very short life (she died at the age of 24) in poverty, caring for the sick and the aged. She is largely responsible for what Marburg became. Because of her selflessness she was made a saint only four years after her death. The Teutonic Knights built the Elisabethkirche, which quickly became the goal of pilgrimages, enabling the city to prosper. You can visit the shrine in the sacristy that once contained her bones, a masterpiece of the goldsmith's art. The church is a veritable museum of religious art, full of statues and frescoes. Walking tours of Marburg begin at the church on Saturdays at 10, year-round.

WHERE TO STAY & EAT
¢ ✕ **Cafe Vetter.** This café has the most spectacular view in town—and Marburg is famous for its panoramas. Both an outdoor terrace and a glassed-in terrace take full advantage of the site. The ambience of this institution, four generations in the same family, is "Viennese coffeehouse traditional," but with Internet access. The homemade cakes and chocolate creams are hard to resist. They also have piano music on Saturday and Sunday afternoons and jazz on the occasional Friday evening. ⊠ *Reitg. 4* ☎ *06421/25888* ⊟ *No credit cards* ☾ *No dinner.*

$$ ▦ **Best Western Hotel am Schlossberg.** This rather unconventional hotel is at the river level below the old town. The color scheme is orange, apricot, and yellow, contrasted with fiery-red tables and upholstered furniture. Its Tartagua Restaurant ($), with bar, terrace, and beer cellar, has become a hip meeting place. In addition to the usual rolls, eggs, and sausages, the breakfast buffet includes smoked salmon and champagne. **Pro:** hotel is just across from the elevator to the old city. **Con:** parking is very difficult. ⊠ *Pilgrimstein 29* ☎ *06421/9180* ⊕ *www.schlossberg-marburg. de* ↻ *146 rooms, 3 suites* ♿ *In-room: refrigerator, Ethernet, Wi-Fi. In-hotel: restaurant, bar, parking (fee), some pets allowed, no-smoking rooms* ⊟ *AE, DC, MC, V* ¶◎|*BP.*

KASSEL

100 km (62 mi) northeast of Marburg.

The Brothers Grimm lived in Kassel, their mother's hometown, as teenagers, and also worked there as librarians at the court of the king of Westphalia, Jerome Bonaparte (Napoléon's youngest brother), and for the elector of Kassel. In their researching of stories and legends, their best source was not books but storyteller Dorothea Viehmann, who was born in the Knallhütte tavern, which is still in business in nearby Baunatal.

Much of Kassel was destroyed in World War II, and the city was rebuilt with little regard for its architectural history. The city's museums and the beautiful Schloss Wilhelmshöhe and Schlosspark, however, are well worth a day or two of exploration.

GETTING HERE & AROUND
Travel northeast from Marburg on the B–3 to Borken, then take autobahn A–49 into Kassel.

Guided bus tours of Kassel set off from the Stadttheater on Saturday at 2 from April through October and at 11 in November and December.

DISCOUNTS & DEALS
When you arrive, you may want to purchase a **Kassel Card.** This entitles you to a reduced rate for the city bus tour, free travel on the local transportation system, and reduced admission to the museums and the casino. It's available at the tourist office for €7 for one day and €10 for three days.

ESSENTIALS
Visitor Information Kassel (✉ *Tourist GmbH, Obere Königstr. 15* ☎ *0561/707–707* ⊕ *www.kassel.de*).

EXPLORING
The **Brüder Grimm Museum,** in the center of Kassel, occupies five rooms of the Palais Bellevue, where the brothers once lived and worked. Exhibits include furniture, memorabilia, letters, manuscripts, and editions of their books, as well as paintings, watercolors, etchings, and drawings by Ludwig Emil Grimm, a third brother and a graphic artist of note. ✉*Palais Bellevue, Schöne Aussicht 2* ☎*0561/787–2033* ☜*€1.50* ⊙*Tues. and Thurs.–Mon. 10–5, Wed. 10–8.*

The magnificent grounds of the 18th-century **Schloss und Schlosspark Wilhelmshöhe** *(Wilhelmshöhe Palace and Palace Park)*, at the western edge of Kassel, are said to be Europe's largest hill park. If you have time, plan to spend an entire day here exploring the various gardens, museums, and wooded pathways. Wear good walking shoes and bring some water if you want to hike all the way up to the giant statue of Hercules that crowns the hilltop.

The Wilhelmshöher Park was laid out as a baroque park in the early 18th century, its elegant lawns separating the city from the thick woods of the Habichtswald (Hawk Forest). Schloss Wilhelmshöhe was added between 1786 and 1798. The great palace stands at the end of the 5-km-long (3-mi-long) Wilhelmshöher Allee, an avenue that runs straight as an arrow from one side of the city to the other.

Kassel's leading art gallery and the state art collection lie within Schloss Wilhelmshöhe as part of the **Staatliche Museen.** Its esteemed collection includes 11 Rembrandts, as well as outstanding works by Rubens, Hals, Jordaens, Van Dyck, Dürer, Altdorfer, Cranach, and Baldung Grien. Amid the thick trees of the Wilhelmshöher Park, it comes as something of a surprise to see the turrets of a romantic medieval castle, the **Löwenburg** (*Lion Fortress* ☎*0561/3168–0244 ✉€3.50 including tour ⊘Mar.–Oct., Tues.–Sun. 10–4; Nov.– Feb., Tues.–Sun. 10–3*), breaking the harmony. There are more surprises, for this is no true medieval castle but a fanciful, stylized copy of a Scottish castle, built 70 years after the Hercules statue that towers above it. The Löwenburg contains a collection of medieval armor and weapons, tapestries, and furniture. The giant 18th-century **statue of Hercules** (✉*Schlosspark 3 ☎0561/312–456 ✉€2 ⊘Mar.–Oct., Tues.–Sun. 10–5; Nov.–Feb., Tues.–Sun. 10–3*) that crowns the Wilhelmshöhe heights is an astonishing sight. You can climb the stairs of the statue's castlelike base—and the statue itself—for a rewarding look over the entire city. At 2:30 PM on Sunday and Wednesday from mid-May through September, water gushes from a fountain beneath the statue, rushes down a series of cascades to the foot of the hill, and ends its precipitous journey in a 175-foot-high jet of water. A café lies a short walk from the statue. ✉*Schloss Wilhelmshöhe ☎0561/316–800 ⊕www.museum-kassel.de ✉Schloss €6 ⊘Tues.–Sun. 10–5.*

WHERE TO STAY & EAT

¢ ✗**Autobahnrastätte Knallhütte.** This brewery-cum-inn, established in 1752, was the home of village storyteller Dorothea Viehmann. The Grimms got the best of their stories from her, including "*Little Red Riding Hood,*" "*Hansel and Gretel,*" and "*Rumpelstiltskin.*" To this day "Dorothea" tells her stories here (unfortunately only in German) every Saturday at 5:30. The Knallhütte was once a wayside inn on the road to Frankfurt. That road is now the autobahn, making the tavern a superhighway rest stop. You'll find it on autobahn A–49 between the Baunatal Nord and Baunatal Mitte exits. You can dine at the restaurant at any time. With prior notice, you can tour the brewery and sample the beer and food for €15.90. ✉*Knallhüttestr. 1 Baunatal-Rengershausen ☎0561/492–076 ⊟MC, V.*

$$ ⊡**Hotel Gude.** This modern hotel is 10 minutes by public transporta-
★ tion from the city center. Rooms are spacious and come with marble bathrooms. The Pfeffermühle ($$$) is one of the region's finest restaurants, with an inventive international menu that includes German fare. The hotel, with a pool and sauna, is also noted for its wellness facilities. Massage and physiotherapy can be arranged, and it has its own underground garage. **Pros:** close to the autobahn, easy parking. **Con:** removed from the city center ✉*Frankfurter Str. 299 ☎0561/48050 ⊕www.hotel-gude.de ⊷85 rooms ⌂In-room: no a/c (some), refrigerator, safe, dial-up. In-hotel: restaurant, bar, pool, bicycles, public*

Wi-Fi, parking (no fee), no-smoking rooms, some pets allowed ▤*AE, DC, MC, V* ⦿*BP.*

$$ ⛫ **Schlosshotel Wilhelmshöhe.** This hotel sits right beside the baroque gardens and woodland paths of the hilltop Wilhelmshöhe Park. Secure a window table in the elegant restaurant for a view of the park grounds and the city. **Pros:** tranquil and historic setting. **Con:** contemporary hotel, despite its romantic name. ✉*Am Schlosspark 8* ☏*0561/30880* ⊕*www.schlosshotel-kassel.de* ↝*96 rooms, 5 suites* ⟳*In-room: no a/c. In-hotel: restaurant, bar, some pets allowed, no-smoking rooms* ▤*AE, DC, MC, V.*

LOWER SAXONY

Lower Saxony (Niedersachsen) was formed from an amalgamation of smaller states in 1946. Its picturesque landscape includes one of Germany's most haunting river roads, along the Weser River between Hannoversch-Münden and Hameln. This road, part of the Fairy-Tale Road, follows green banks that hardly show where the water ends and the land begins. Standing sentinal are superb little towns whose half-timber architecture gave rise to the expression "Weser Renaissance." The Lower Saxon landscape also includes the juniper bushes and flowering heather of the Lüneburg Heath.

HANNOVERSCH-MÜNDEN

★ *24 km (15 mi) north of Kassel, 150 km (93 mi) south of Hannover.*

This delightful town, known as Hann. Münden and seemingly untouched by the modern age, shouldn't be missed. You'll have to travel a long way through Germany to find a grouping of half-timber houses (700 of them) as harmonious as these. The town is surrounded by forests and the Fulda and Werra rivers, which join here and flow northward as the Weser River.

Much is made of the fact that the quack doctor to end all quacks died here. Dr. Johann Andreas Eisenbart (1663–1727) would be forgotten today if a ribald 19th-century drinking song (*"Ich bin der Doktor Eisenbart, widda, widda, wit, boom! boom!"*) hadn't had him shooting out aching teeth with a pistol, anesthetizing with a sledgehammer, and removing boulders from the kidneys. He was, as the song has it, a man who could make "the blind walk and the lame see." This is terribly exaggerated, of course, but the town takes advantage of it.

GETTING HERE & AROUND
A walking tour of town takes place April to October, leaving daily at 2 from the town hall.

ESSENTIALS
Visitor Information Hannoversch-Münden (✉*Touristik Naturpark Münden, Lotzestr. 2* ☏*05541/75313* ⊕*www.hann.muenden.de*).

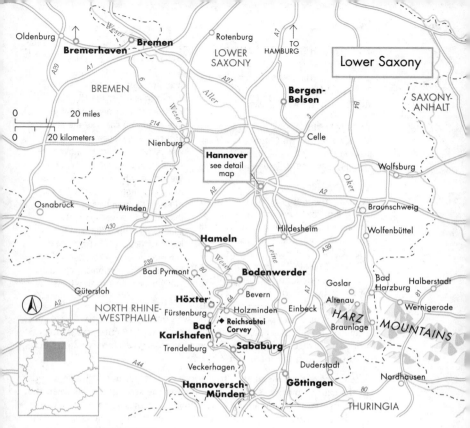

It stages Eisenbart plays 11:15 AM on one Sunday each in May and June and every Sunday in July and August. The doctor also has "office hours" in the city hall at 1:30 on Saturday from mid-May through September; and a glockenspiel on the city hall depicts Eisenbart's feats, to the tune of the Eisenbart song, daily throughout the year at noon, 3 PM, and 5 PM. There's a statue of the doctor in front of his home at Langestrasse 79, and his grave is outside the St. Ägidien Church. For information on the Dr. Eisenbart plays, contact the **City Tourist Office** (☎ *05541/75313* ⊕ *www.hann.muenden.de*).

GÖTTINGEN

30 km (19 mi) northeast of Hannoversch-Münden, 110 km (68 mi) south of Hannover.

Although Göttingen is not strictly on the Fairy-Tale Road, it's closely associated with the Brothers Grimm because they served as professors and librarians at the city's university from 1830 to 1837. Many of the houses bear plaques that link them to a famous student, professor, or Nobel laureate. The university, which dominates life in the town, goes back a long time, but this is a large and modern town.

GETTING HERE & AROUND

Göttingen offers walking tours in English on the first and third Saturdays of the month, April to October at 11 from the Old Town Hall.

ESSENTIALS

Visitor Information **Göttingen** (⊠ *Tourist-Information, Altes Rathaus, Markt 9* ☎ *0551/499–800* ⊕ *www.goettingen.de*).

EXPLORING

Among the delights of Göttingen are the **ancient taverns** where generations of students have lifted their steins. Among the best known are the **Kleiner Ratskeller** (⊠ *Judenstr. 30*) and **Trou** (⊠ *Burgstr. 20*). Don't be shy about stepping into either of these taverns or any of the others that catch your eye; the food and drink are inexpensive, and the welcome is invariably warm and friendly. If the cramped and noisy company of twenty-somethings is not to your taste, try the **cafe Cron und Lanz** (⊠ *Weendert Str. 25*), where tradition and quality come together.

> ### HIKING & WALKING
>
> Two protected nature parks—the Weserergland and the Lüneburg Heath—are in or near the Fairy-Tale Road. You can hike the banks of the Weser, stopping at ancient waterside inns, from Hannoversch-Münden, in the south, to Porta-Westfalica, where the Weser River breaks through the last range of North German hills and into the plain of Lower Saxony. The Lüneburg Heath is flat, and hiking is particularly pleasant in late summer, when the heather is in bloom. The tourist offices can tell you where to find nearby trails.

The statue of **Gänseliesel,** the little Goose Girl of German folklore, stands in the central market square, symbolizing the strong link between the students and their university city. The girl, according to the story, was a princess who was forced to trade places with a peasant, and the statue shows her carrying her geese and smiling shyly into the waters of a fountain. The students of Göttingen gave her a ceremonial role: traditionally, graduates who earn a doctorate bestow a kiss of thanks upon Gänseliesel. Göttingen's citizens say she's the most kissed girl in the world.

WHERE TO EAT

$$ ✕**Gaudi.** The first thing you notice in this Mediterranean restaurant, right in Göttingen's historic Börner Viertel, is the southern flair of its blue and pink color scheme. The professors from the university often dine happily on everything from tapas to fish or pasta, taken from Spanish, Italian, French, and North African recipes. ⊠ *Rote Str. 16* ☎ *0551/531–3001* ◿ *Reservations essential* ⊟ *AE, DC, MC, V*

$ ✕**Historischer Rathskeller.** Dine in the vaulted underground chambers of Göttingen's Altes Rathaus and choose from a traditional menu. If you're tired of cream sauces (which are abundant on menus in this region), try the *Altdeutscher Bauernschmaus*, which includes a small portion of grilled chicken, pork, and sausage—with no cream sauce—as well as fried potatoes and a side salad. ⊠ *Altes Rathaus, Markt 9* ☎ *0551/56433* ⊟ *AE, DC, MC, V.*

$ ✕**Landgasthaus Lockemann.** If you like to walk and hike, consider this half-timber lodge at the edge of the Stadtwald (city forest). Locals descend on the friendly, country-style restaurant for hearty German cooking ($). Take Bus 10 from the Busbahnhof, direction Herbershausen, to the last stop; then walk left on Im Beeke. The trip will take 20 minutes. ⊠ *Im Beeke 1* ☎ *0551/209–020* ▭ *No credit cards*

$ ✕**Zum Schwarzen Bären.** The "Black Bear" is one of Göttingen's oldest
★ tavern-restaurants, a 16th-century half-timber house that breathes history and hospitality. Its specialties are *Bärenpfanne*, a generous mixture of beef, pork, and lamb (but no bear meat), and its wide selection of fried potato dishes. ⊠ *Kurzestr. 12* ☎ *0551/58284* ▭ *AE, MC, V* ⊗ *No lunch Mon.*

WHERE TO STAY

$$$ ▦ **Romantik Hotel Gebhards.** This family-run hotel stands aloof and unflurried on its own grounds, a modernized 18th-century building that's something of a local landmark. Rooms are furnished in dark woods and floral prints highlighted by bowls of fresh flowers. It has a whirlpool and a sauna. **Pro:** across the street from the train station. **Con:** on a busy street. ⊠ *Goethe-Allee 22–23* ☎ *0551/49680* ⊕ *www. romantikhotels.com/goettingen* ↝ *43 rooms, 7 suites* ⚘ *In-room: no a/ c, safe, refrigerator. In-hotel: restaurant, some pets allowed, no-smoking rooms* ▭ *AE, DC, MC, V* ⦿| *BP.*

EN	To pick up the Fairy-Tale Road where it joins the scenic Weser Valley
ROUTE	Road, return to Hannoversch-Münden and head north on B–80. In the
	village of Veckerhagen take a left turn to the signposted Sababurg.

SABABURG

★ *60 km (36 mi) west of Göttingen, 100 km (62 mi) south of Hannover.*

Sababurg is home to the **Dornröschenschloss** *(Sleeping Beauty's Castle).* It stands just as the Grimm fairy tale tells us it did, in the depths of the densely wooded Reinhardswald, still inhabited by deer and wild boar. Today it's a fairly fancy hotel. Even if you don't stay the night, a drive to the castle is scenic. There's a nominal fee to tour the grounds, which include a rose garden and ruins.

☾ The **Tierpark Sababurg** is one of Europe's oldest wildlife refuges. Bison, red deer, wild horses, and all sorts of waterfowl populate the park. There's also a petting zoo for children. ⊠ *Sababurgstr.* ☎ *05671/8001– 2251* ▤ *Mar.–Oct. 5, Nov.–Feb.* €4 ⊗ *Apr.–Sept., daily 8–7; Oct., daily 9–6; Nov.–Feb., daily 10–4; Mar., daily 9–5.*

WHERE TO STAY

$$ ▦ **Dornröschenschloss Sababurg.** The medieval fortress thought to have inspired *"Sleeping Beauty"* is now a small luxury hotel, surrounded by a forest of oaks, a bit to the northeast of Hofgeismar. It's a popular place for weddings, and on request, a "prince" and "princess" will present a version of the Sleeping Beauty story. The restaurant ($$–$$$) serves fine venison in the autumn and fresh trout with a Riesling-based sauce in the spring. **Pro:** incredibly romantic. **Cons:** ordinary hotel rooms that are incompatible with the setting, takes some effort to find

the place. ⊠*Im Reinhardswald Hofgeismar* ☎*05671/8080* ⊕*www. sababurg.deg* ⟿*18 rooms* ⌂*In-room: no a/c. In-hotel: restaurant, bicycles, no elevator, some pets allowed* ⊟*AE, DC, MC, V* ⵏⵔⵉ*BP.*

EN ROUTE A short distance away is another hilltop castle-hotel, **Trendelburg** (⊠*Steinweg 1* ☎*05675/9090*), which also has a fairy-tale association. Legend has it that its tower is the one in which a wicked witch imprisoned Rapunzel. It's near the town of the same name on Route 83 between Hofgeismar and Bad Karlshafen. From Trendelburg follow Route 83 north to Bad Karlshafen.

BAD KARLSHAFEN

42 km (26 mi) north of Hannoversch-Münden, 55 km (34 mi) northwest of Göttingen, 125 km (77 mi) south of Hannover.

Viewed from one of the benches overlooking the inland harbor, there's scarcely a building in the pretty little spa of Bad Karlshafen that's not in the imposing baroque style—grand and starkly white.

ESSENTIALS

Visitor Information Bad Karlshafen (⊠*Kur- und Touristik-Information, Hafenpl. 8* ☎*05672/999–922* ⊕*www.bad-karlshafen.de*).

EXPLORING

The **Rathaus** (⊠*Hafenpl. 8*) is the best example. The town's walking tour leaves from here on Sunday at 3, April to October. Bad Karlshafen stands in surprising contrast to the abundance of half-timber architecture of other riverside towns.

German troops of the state of Waldeck embarked from here to join the English forces in the American War of Independence. Flat barges took the troops down the Weser to Bremen, where they were shipped across the North Sea for the long voyage west.

More recently Bad Karlshafen has been known as a health resort. Its elevation and rural location provide fresh air, and there are salt springs that the Germans think can cure whatever ails you. The Weserberglandtherme is a huge spa facility with whirlpools, sauna and steam baths, heated saltwater pools, and an outdoor pool that it boasts is as salty as the Dead Sea.

WHERE TO STAY

$ ⵏ**Gaststätte-Hotel Weserdampfschiff.** You can step right from the deck of a Weser pleasure boat into the welcoming garden of this popular hotel-tavern. Fish from the river go straight into the tavern's frying pan. The rooms are snug; ask for one with a river view. The restaurant (¢–$$) is closed Monday. **Pros:** fine river view, inexpensive, located near spa facilities. **Cons:** no elevator; busy street. ⊠*Weserstr. 25* ☎*05672/2425* ⟿*14 rooms* ⌂*In-room: no a/c. In-hotel: restaurant, no elevator, some pets allowed* ⊟*No credit cards* ⵏⵔⵉ*BP.*

$ ⵏ**Hessischer Hof.** In the heart of town, this inn started as a tavern for the locals and now includes several comfortably furnished bedrooms, plus an apartment suitable for larger families and the numerous cycling groups that visit. The restaurant (¢–$$) serves good, hearty German fare. Breakfast is included in the room price, or you may request half-pension. **Pro:** centrally located. **Con:** no elevator. ⊠ *Carlstr. 13–15* ☎ *05672/1059* ⊕ *www.hess-hof.de* ⤳ *17 rooms* ☖ *In-room: no a/c, safe. In-hotel: restaurant, bar, no elevator, some pets allowed* ⊟ *AE, DC, MC, V* ⦵ *BP.*

EN ROUTE
12

Germany's second-oldest **porcelain factory** is at Fürstenberg, 8 km (5 mi) south of Höxter, in a baroque castle high above the Weser River. The crowned Gothic letter *F*, which serves as its trademark, is world famous. You'll find Fürstenberg porcelain in Bad Karlshafen and Höxter, but it's more fun to journey to the 18th-century castle where production first began in 1747, and buy directly from the manufacturer. Fürstenberg and most dealers will take care of shipping arrangements and any tax refunds. Tours of the factory in English are possible with advance notice. There's also a sales outlet, museum, and café. ▪ **TIP→ The view from the castle is a pastoral idyll, with the Weser snaking through the immaculately tended fields and woods. You can also spot cyclists on the riverside paths.** ⊠ *Schloss Fürstenberg* ☎ *05271/401–161* ⊕ *www.fuerstenberg-porzellan.com* ⚏ *Museum €5* ⊙ *Museum Apr.– Oct., Tues.–Sun. 10–6; Nov.–Mar., weekends 10–5. Shop Apr.–Nov., Tues.–Sun. 10–5.*

HÖXTER

24 km (14 mi) north of Bad Karlshafen, 100 km (62 mi) south of Hannover.

Stop at Höxter to admire its **Rathaus**, a perfect example of the Weser Renaissance style, combining three half-timber stories with a romantically crooked tower. Though it has no better claim than any other town to the story of Hansel and Gretel, Höxter presents a free performance of the story on the first Saturday of each month, from May to September.

GETTING HERE & AROUND
Between April and October, a town walking tour leaves from the Rathaus at 10 on Wednesday and Saturday.

ESSENTIALS
Visitor Information Höxter (⊠ *Touristik- und Kulturinformation, Historisches Rathaus, Weserstr. 11* ☎ *05271/963–431* ⊕ *www.hoexter.de*).

EXPLORING
The **Reichsabtei Corvey** *(Imperial Abbey of Corvey)*, or Schloss Corvey, is idyllically set between the wooded heights of the Solling region and the Weser River. During its 1,200-year history it has provided lodging for several Holy Roman emperors. Heinrich Hoffmann von Fallersleben (1798–1874), author of the poem "Deutschland, Deutschland über Alles," worked as librarian here in the 1820s. The poem, set to music by Joseph Haydn, became the German national anthem in 1922. A music festival is held in the church and great hall, the Kaisersaal, in May and

June. Corvey, also the name of the village, is reached on an unnumbered road heading east from Höxter (3 km [2 mi]) toward the Weser. There are signposts to "Schloss Corvey." ☎*05271/681–20* ⊕*www.schloss-corvey. de* ✒*€4.20, abbey church €0.60* ⊗*Mar.–Sept., daily 9–6.*

OFF THE
BEATEN
PATH

Einbeck. Bock beer originated in this storybook town 20 km (12 mi) east of Höxter. The good burghers started brewing beer in their houses in 1341; the name *Bockbier* is a corruption of the original Einbecker Bier. The town **tourist office** (✉*Marktstr. 13 Einbeck* ☎*05561/313–1910* 🖷*05561/313–1919* ⊕*www.einbeck.de*) will, with advance notice, organize a visit that includes a welcome by the "Historical Brewmaster," beer tastings, the awarding of a "beer diploma," and a tour of a brewery that still makes the strong stuff.

WHERE TO EAT

$ ✕**Schlossrestaurant.** In summer you can dine under centuries-old trees
★ at the Reichsabtei Corvey's excellent restaurant. ■TIP→ **With advance notice, a** *Fürstenbankett*, **or princely banquet, can be arranged for groups in the vaulted cellars.** ✉*Reichsabtei Corvey* ☎*05271/8323* ▭*MC, V* ⊗*Closed Jan.–Mar. No dinner Apr.–Oct., no lunch Nov. or Dec.*

BODENWERDER

34 km (21 mi) north of Höxter, 70 km (43 mi) south of Hannover.

The charming Weser town of Bodenwerder plays a central role in German popular literature. It's the home of the Lügenbaron (Lying Baron) von Münchhausen (1720–97), who was known as a teller of whoppers. His reputation was not without foundation, but it was mainly created by a book based in part on the baron's stories and published anonymously by an acquaintance. According to one tale, the baron rode a cannonball toward an enemy fortress but then, having second thoughts, returned to where he started by leaping onto a cannonball heading the other way.

ESSENTIALS

Visitor Information **Bodenwerder** (✉*Tourist Information, Münchausenpl. 3* ☎*05533/40542* ⊕ *www.bodenwerder.de*).

EXPLORING

The **Münchhausen-Erinnerungszimmer** *(Münchhausen Memorial Room)*, in the imposing family home in which Baron von Münchhausen grew up (now the Rathaus), is crammed with mementos of his adventurous life, including his cannonball. A fountain in front of the house represents another story. The baron, it seems, was puzzled when his horse kept drinking insatiably at a trough. Investigating, he discovered that the horse had been cut in two by a closing castle gate and that the water ran out as fast as the horse drank. The water in the fountain, of course, flows from the rear of a half-horse. On the first Sunday of the month from May through October, townspeople retell von Münchhausen's life story with performances in front of the Rathaus. ✉*Münchhausenpl. 1* ☎*05533/409–147* ✒*Museum €2* ⊗*Apr.–Oct., daily 10–noon and 2–5.*

WHERE TO STAY & EAT

$ ✕ **Goldener Anker.** The Weser boats tie up outside this half-timber tavern, which prepares hearty German fare and sometimes fresh Weser fish; ■ **TIP→ In summer a beer garden right on the river beckons.** ✉ *Brückenstr. 5* ☎ *05533/400–730* ☰ *AE, MC, V* ⏷⃝ *BP.*

$ ⌕ **Parkhotel Deutsches Haus.** The fine half-timber facade of this comfortable country hotel vies for attention with the nearby home of Baron von Münchhausen, now Bodenwerder's town hall. Original wood beams and oak paneling add to the rural feel inside. The hotel's own extensive grounds adjoin the town park, and the Weser River is a short walk away. The restaurant's terrace (¢–$$) adjoins the Münchhausen house. **Pro:** romantic atmosphere. **Cons:** right on a busy street, narrow elevator. ✉ *Münchhausenpl. 4* ☎ *05533/3925* ⊕ *www.parkhotel-bodenwerder.de* ⤻ *42 rooms* ⏷ *In-room: no a/c (some), Ethernet, Wi-Fi. In-hotel: 2 restaurants, bar, some pets allowed, no-smoking rooms* ☰ *MC, V* ⏷⃝ *BP.*

HAMELN

★ *24 km (15 mi) north of Bodenwerder, 47 km (29 mi) southwest of Hannover.*

Hameln (or Hamelin, in English) is home to the story of the gaudily attired Pied Piper, who rid the town of rats by playing seductive melodies on his flute. The rodents followed him willingly, waltzing their way right into the Weser. When the town defaulted on its contract and refused to pay the piper, he settled the score by playing his merry tune to lead Hameln's children on the same route. As the children reached the river, the Grimms wrote, "they disappeared forever." The tale is included in the Grimms' book *German Legends.* The origin of the story is lost in the mists of time, but the best guess is that it is associated with the forced resettlement of young people to the sparsely populated eastern territories that occurred in the 13th century.

The Pied Piper tale is immortalized in an ultramodern sculpture set above a reflecting pool in the town's pedestrian zone. And there are rat-shape pastries in the windows of Hameln's bakeries.

GETTING HERE & AROUND

Walking tours of Hameln are held year-round, leaving from the tourist office (April to October, Monday to Saturday at 2:30 and Sunday at 10:15 and 2:30; November to March, Saturday at 2:30, Sunday at 10:15).

ESSENTIALS

Visitor Information Hameln (✉ *Hameln Marketing und Tourismus, Deisterallee 1* ☎ *05151/957–823* ⊕ *www.hameln.de*).

EXPLORING

On central Osterstrasse you'll see several beautiful half-timber houses, including the Rattenfängerhaus (Rat-Catcher's House) and the **Hochzeitshaus** *(Wedding House)*, a 17th-century Weser Renaissance building now containing city offices. Between mid-May and mid-September the Hochzeithaus terrace is the scene of two free open-air events commemorating the legend. Local actors and children present a half-hour reenactment each Sunday at noon, and there is now also a 40-minute musical, *Rats*, each Wednesday at 4:30. The carillon of the Hochzeitshaus plays tunes every day at 9:35 and 11:35, and mechanical figures enact the piper story on the west gable of the building at 1:05, 3:35, and 5:35.

WHERE TO STAY & EAT

¢-$ ✕**Rattenfängerhaus.** This brilliant example of Weser Renaissance archi-
★   tecture is Hameln's most famous building, reputedly where the Pied Piper stayed during his rat-extermination assignment (actually, it wasn't built until centuries after his supposed exploits). A plaque in front of it fixes the date of the incident at June 26, 1284. "Rats" are all over the menu, from the "rat-killer liqueur" to a "rat-tail flambé." But don't be put off by the names: the traditional dishes are excellent. ⊠*Osterstr. 28* ☎*05151/3888* ▤*AE, DC, MC, V.*

$-$$ ▧**Hotel zur Krone.** If you fancy a splurge, ask for one of the hotel's
★   elegant suites, with prices starting at €128 a night. It's an expensive but delightful comfort. **Pro:** the building, dating from 1645, is a half-timber marvel. **Cons:** the modern annex lacks charm. ⊠*Osterstr. 30* ☎*05151/9070* ⊕*www.hotelzurkrone.de* ⛱*27 rooms, 5 suites* ⅙*In-room: no a/c, refrigerator, Wi-Fi. In-hotel: restaurant, some pets allowed, no-smoking rooms* ▤*AE, MC, V* ⎮⊚⎮*BP.*

$ ▧**Hotel zur Börse.** This upscale hotel offers comfortable accommodations and friendly service, and its Börsenbistro serves Mediterranean food. **Pro:** right in the pedestrian zone. **Con:** a "modern" look that's inappropriate for the Pied Piper city. ⊠*Osterstr. 41a, entrance on Kopmanshof* ☎*05151/7080* ⊕*www.hotel-zur-boerse.de* ⛱*31 rooms* ⅙*In-room: no a/c, refrigerator. In-hotel: restaurant, bar, some pets allowed* ▤*AE, DC, MC, V* ⎮⊚⎮*BP.*

$ ▧**Pension Ragazzi.** This very reasonable little hostelry, with simple but modern rooms, is pure Fairy-Tale Road, situated in the pedestrian zone in the old part of town. There used to be a pizzeria on the ground floor, but it's now a café. A continental breakfast is included in the rate. **Pros:** inexpensive, central location. **Con:** Italian name is misleading. ⊠*Fischpfortenstr. 25* ☎*05151/21513* ⎙*05151/923–667* ⛱*12 rooms* ⅙*In-room: no a/c. In-hotel: restaurant, no elevator, some pets allowed* ▤*No credit cards* ⎮⊚⎮*BP.*

HANNOVER

47 km (29 mi) northeast of Hameln.

Hannover is somewhat off the Fairy-Tale Road, yet its culture and commerce influence the quieter surrounding towns. As a trade-fair center, where hotel rooms are sometimes hard to come by, Hannover competes with such cities as Munich and Leipzig. It's also an exemplary arts center, with leading museums, an opera house of international repute, and the finest baroque park in the country. Its patronage of the arts is also evident in unexpected places; as part of an international competition, architects and designers created nine unique bus and streetcar stops for the city. Designs include the massive, 60-foot stop with golden domes at the corners at Steintor and the green "roof garden" above the heads of those waiting for a bus at Leinaustrasse.

GETTING HERE & AROUND

Travel northeast from Hameln on autobahn A–33 to Hannover. There is also frequent direct rail service from Hameln. Hannover has an airport, and is served by the InterCity Express (ICE) trains and the Europabus. From May to October, city bus tours of Hannover leave daily at 1:30 from the tourist office.

DISCOUNTS & DEALS

A **Hannover Card** entitles you to free travel on local transportation, reduced admission to six museums, and discounts on certain sightseeing events and performances at the theater and opera. It's available through the tourist office for €9 per day (€15 for three days).

ESSENTIALS

Visitor Information Hannover (⊠ *Hannover Tourismus, Ernst-August-Pl. 8* ☎ *0511/1684–9700* ⊕ *www.hannover.de*).

EXPLORING

MAIN ATTRACTIONS

② Altes Rathaus. It took nearly 100 years, starting in 1410, to build this gabled brick edifice, which once contained a merchants' hall and an apothecary. In 1844 it was restored to the style of about 1500. The facade's fired-clay frieze depicts coats of arms and representations of princes, and a medieval game somewhat comparable to arm wrestling. Inside is a modern interior with boutiques and a restaurant. ⊠ *Köbelingerstr. 2.*

Herrenhausen. The gardens of the former Hannoverian royal summer residence are the city's showpiece (the 17th-century palace was never rebuilt after wartime bombing). The baroque park is unmatched in Germany for its formal precision, with patterned walks, gardens, hedges, and chestnut trees framed by a placid moat. There is a fig garden with a collapsible shelter to protect it in the winter and dining facilities behind a grotto. From Easter until October there are fireworks displays and fountains play for a few hours daily (weekdays 11–noon and 3–5, weekends 11–noon and 2–5). Herrenhausen is outside the city, a short ride on Tramline 4 or 5. ⊠ *Herrenhauserstr. 4* ☎ *0511/1684–7576* ⊕ *www. hannover.de/herrenhausen* ⊠ *€4* ⊙ *Mar.–Apr. and Sept., daily 9–7; May–Aug., daily 9–8; Oct., daily 9–6; Nov.–Feb., daily 9–4:30.*

③ Leineschloss. The former Hannoverian royal palace stands above the River Leine and is now the seat of the Lower Saxony State Parliament. From 1714 to 1837, rulers of the house of Hannover sat on the British throne as Kings George I–IV. The first of them, George I, spoke no English. George III presided over the loss of the American colonies in the Revolutionary War, but sent no Hannoverian troops to help fight,

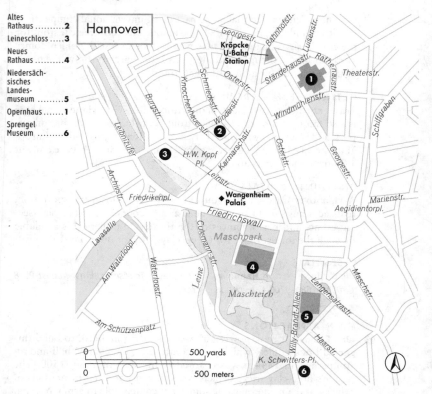

even though he hired troops from other German states for this purpose. The period of joint rule came to an end when Queen Victoria ascended the throne. (Hannover didn't allow female monarchs.) Tours are conducted weekdays. Brochures in English are available. ✉ *Hinrich-Wilhelm-Kopf-Pl. 1* ☎ *0511/3030–2042* 💷 *Free* 🕐 *Tours Mon.–Thurs. at 10 and 1, Fri. at 10.*

5 **Niedersächsisches Landesmuseum** *(Lower Saxony State Museum).* The priceless art collection of this prestigious museum includes works by Tilman Riemenschneider, Veit Stoss, Hans Holbein the Younger, Claude Monet, and Lucas Cranach. There are also historical and natural history sections. ✉ *Willy-Brandt-Allee 5* ☎ *0511/98075* 🌐 *www.nlmh.de* 💷 *€4* 🕐 *Tues., Wed., and Fri.–Sun. 10–5, Thurs. 10–7.*

6 **Sprengel Museum.** An important museum of modern art, the Sprengel holds major works by Max Beckmann, Max Ernst, Paul Klee, Emil Nolde, Oscar Schlemmer. Hans Arp and Pablo Picasso. The street where it's located is named after Kurt Schwitters, a native son and prominent dadaist, whose works are also exhibited. ✉ *Kurt-Schwitters-Pl. 1* ☎ *0511/1684–3875* 🌐 *www.sprengel-museum.de* 💷 *€7* 🕐 *Tues. 10–8, Wed.–Sun. 10–6.*

ALSO WORTH SEEING

4 Neues Rathaus. The massive New Town Hall was built at the start of the 20th century in Wilhelmine style (for Kaiser Wilhelm), at a time when pomp and circumstance were important ingredients of heavy German bureaucracy. Four scale models on the ground floor depict Hannover in various stages of development and destruction: as a medieval walled city, in the years before World War II, imme-

TOURING TIPS

Scenic Spot: The formal park and gardens at Herrenhausen, complete with moat and fountains, are a great photo op.

Red Thread: Hannover's points of interest lie along a tourist trail marked by a red line on the sidewalk. It starts at the tourist office.

12

diately following World War II, and in its present-day form. An elevator rises diagonally to the dome for a splendid view. ⊠ *Trammpl. 2* ☎ *0511/1684–5333* ⌨ *Dome €2.50* ⊗ *Mar.–Oct., daily 9:30–6:30.*

1 Opernhaus. Hannover's neoclassical opera house, completed in 1852, has two large wings and a covered, colonnaded, portico adorned with statues of great composers and poets. The building originally served as the court theater, but now is used almost exclusively for opera. It was gutted by fire in a 1943 air raid and restored in 1948. ■**TIP→ Unless you have tickets to a performance, the only part of the interior you can visit is the foyer with ticket windows.** ⊠ *Opernpl. 1* ☎ *0511/9999–1298.*

WHERE TO EAT

$$$ ✕ **Basil.** Constructed in 1867 as a riding hall for the Royal Prussian military, this hip restaurant's home is as striking as the menu. Cast-iron pillars support the vaulted brick ceiling, and two-story drapes hang in the huge windows. The menu changes every few weeks and includes eclectic dishes from the Mediterranean to Asia. Game and white *Spargel* (asparagus) are served in season. ⊠ *Dragonerstr. 30* ☎ *0511/622–636* ▭ *AE, MC, V* ⊗ *No lunch. Closed Sun.*

$ ✕ **Brauhaus Ernst August.** This brewery has so much artificial greenery that you could imagine yourself in a beer garden. Hannoverian pilsner is brewed on the premises, and regional specialties are the menu's focus. You can collect souvenirs there. Besides beer paraphernalia such as mugs and coasters, you can purchase, empty or full, a huge old-fashioned beer bottle with a wired porcelain stopper. There's live music on weekends and a DJ the other nights. ⊠ *Schmiedstr. 13* ☎ *0511/365– 950* ▭ *AE, MC, V.*

$ ✕ **Grapenkieker.** An ancient pot steams in the aromatic, farmhouse-style kitchen, and simple, hearty fare prevails. Proprietor Karl-Heinz Wolf is locally famous for his culinary prowess and the warm welcome he gives his guests. The half-timber restaurant is 5 km (3 mi) from the city center, in the Isernhagen District, but it's well worth seeking out. ⊠ *Hauptstr. 56* ☎ *05139/88068* ▭ *AE, DC, MC, V* ⊗ *Closed Mon.*

WHERE TO STAY

$$$ ▥ **Kastens Hotel Luisenhof.** Antiques are everywhere in this very traditional hotel, both in appearance and service. Tapestries are on the lobby walls, oil paintings are in the foyer, copper engravings in the bar, and there

is an elegant wardrobe on every floor. There is a newly installed fitness center with sauna on the 6th floor, and the restaurant ($$$$) is international with French touches. **Pro:** near the train station. **Con:** expensive. ⊠ *Luisenstr.1–3* ☎ *0511/30440* ⊕ *www.kastens-hotel-luisenhof. de* ⤳ *148 rooms, 7 suites* ♿ *In-room: no a/c (some), safe, refrigerator, Wi-Fi. In-hotel: restaurant, bar, some pets allowed, no-smoking rooms* ⊟ *AE, DC, MC, V* ⎮◎⎮*BP.*

$$ 🖭 **Hotel Körner.** The modern Körner has an old-fashioned feel, created by the friendly and personal service. Rooms are comfortably furnished in light veneers and pastel shades. The small courtyard terrace has a fountain; breakfast is served here in summer. **Pros:** quiet side street, garage. **Con:** plain exterior. ⊠ *Körnerstr. 24–25* ☎ *0511/16360* ⊕ *www.hotelkoerner.de* ⤳ *77 rooms* ♿ *In-room: no a/c, refrigerator, Ethernet, Wi-Fi. In-hotel: pool, gym* ⊟ *AE, DC, MC, V* ⎮◎⎮*BP.*

NIGHTLIFE & THE ARTS

Hannover's nightlife is centered on the Bahnhof and the Steintor red-light district. The **opera company** (☎ *0511/9999–1298*) of Hannover is internationally known, with productions staged in one of Germany's finest 19th-century classical opera houses. Call for program details and tickets. Hannover's elegant **casino** (⊠ *Osterstr. 40* ☎ *0511/980–660*) is open from 3 PM to 3 AM.

SHOPPING

Hannover is one of northern Germany's most fashionable cities, and its central pedestrian zone has international shops and boutiques, as well as the very best of German-made articles, from stylish clothes to handmade jewelry. In the glassed-over **Galerie Luise** (⊠ *Luisenstr. 5*), directly accessible from an underground garage, you can spend a couple of hours browsing, with a leisurely lunch or afternoon tea at one of the several restaurants and cafés.

EN ROUTE The Fairy-Tale Road continues north of Hannover as far as Bremen, though any connection to the Grimm brothers is faint here. You can reach Bremen in less than an hour by taking autobahn A–7 to the Walsrode interchange and then continuing on autobahn A–27. An alternative is to return to Hameln and follow the Weser as it breaks free of the Wesergebirge uplands at Porta Westfalica. The meandering route runs through the German plains to the sea and Bremen. Another alternative is a quick side trip to the northeast, to the Lüneburg Heath and Bergen-Belsen.

BERGEN-BELSEN

58 km (36 mi) northeast of Hannover.

At the site of the infamous concentration camp on the Lüneburg Heath, the **Gedenkstätte Bergen-Belsen** *(Bergen-Belsen Memorial)* pays tribute to the victims of the Holocaust. Diarist Anne Frank was among the more than 80,000 persons who died here.

Only the gruesome photographs on display will tell what the camp looked like. There's nothing left of it. The British liberators found thousands and thousands of unburied corpses all over the camp, so as a precaution against disease, all structures were burned to the ground. Volunteer youth groups have unearthed the foundations of the barracks.

Those who venture onto the site of the camp may be surprised at its pleasant, parklike appearance. Reminders of the horrors that once happened here include numerous burial mounds, mostly overgrown with heather and with stones with such inscriptions as HERE LIE 1,000 DEAD. Anne Frank probably lies in one of them. The SS officers had hoped to have the dead buried and out of sight before the British forces arrived, but the starving prisoners were too weak for the job. Under the direction of the British, the graves you see were dug and filled by the SS officers themselves. The British tried and executed the camp's SS commandant, Josef Kramer, the "Beast of Belsen."

Monuments and shrines include a Jewish memorial dating to 1946, with a commemorative stone dedicated by the Israeli president in 1987; an obelisk and memorial wall erected by the British; a wooden cross dating from only weeks after the liberation; and a commemorative stone from the German government. The main feature of the memorial is a permanent exhibition on the history of the camp and the Nazi persecution system. It's now located in a splendid new building, opened in 2008, that also houses a library and research facilities.

■TIP➡ **Though all signs are in German, there are supplementary guides in English and eight other languages.** There are also regular showings of a movie on the camp in English, German, and French. Children under 12 are not admitted to the showings, and it's said that one of the British photographers who made the footage couldn't bear to look at his work in later years. ⊠*Just off unnumbered hwy. connecting Bergen and Winsen* ☎*05051/6011* ⊕*www.bergenbelsen.de* ☎*Free* ⊗*Apr.– Sept daily 10–6, Oct.–Mar daily 10–5.*

WHERE TO STAY

$ 🏡**Landhaus Averbeck.** This farm doubling as a bed-and-breakfast proves that the Lüneburg Heath is an ideal place for a farm vacation. Well off the main highway, it's great for children, with ponies to ride, animals to feed, a playground, and a playroom. The farm, which is close to the Bergen-Belsen Memorial and central for day trips to Hamburg and Hannover, also has cattle, with boar and deer in the surrounding forest and meadows. **Pros:** typical heath farm, great with kids. **Con:** far from everything. ⊠*Hassel 3 Bergen* ☎*05054/249* ⊕*www.landhausaverbeck. de* 🛏*12 rooms, 2 apartments* ᓯ*In-room: no a/c, no phone. In-hotel: no elevator, some pets allowed* ⊟*MC, V* ⅉ*BP.*

BREMEN

110 km (68 mi) northwest of Hannover.

Germany's smallest city-state, Bremen, is also Germany's oldest and second-largest port (only Hamburg is larger). Together with Hamburg and Lübeck, Bremen was an early member of the merchant-run Hanseatic League, and its rivalry with the larger port on the Elbe River is still tangible. Though Hamburg may still claim its title as Germany's "door to the world," Bremen likes to boast: "But we have the key." Bremen's symbol is, in fact, a golden key, which you will see displayed on flags and signs throughout the city.

GETTING HERE & AROUND
Bremen offers both bus and walking tours in English. The bus tours depart Sunday through Tuesday at 10:30 from the central bus station on Breiteweg, the walking tours daily at 2 from the Tourist Information Center on Oberstrasse.

ESSENTIALS
Visitor Information **Bremen** (⊠ *Touristik-Zentrale, Findorffstr. 105* ☎ *01805/101– 030* ⊕ *www.bremen-tourism.de*).

DISCOUNTS & DEALS
Bremen has an ErlebnisCARD, which lets you ride free on the public transportation, gets you into museums and other cultural facilities at half price, and gets you a reduction on tours. It costs €7.90 for one day and €9.90 for two days.

EXPLORING
The **Marktplatz** in Bremen's charming Altstadt is an impressive market square. It's bordered by the St. Petri Dom, an imposing 900-year-old Gothic cathedral; an ancient Rathaus; a 16th-century guildhall; and a modern glass-and-steel state parliament building, with gabled town houses finishing the panorama. Alongside the northwest corner of the Rathaus is the famous bronze statue of the four **Bremen Town Musicians,** one atop the other in a sort of pyramid. Their feats are reenacted in a free, open-air play at the Neptune Fountain near the cathedral, at noon each Sunday, from May to October. Another well-known figure on the square is the stone statue of **Roland,** a knight in service to Charlemagne, erected in 1404. Three times larger than life, the statue serves as Bremen's good-luck piece and a symbol of freedom and independence. It is said that as long as Roland stands, Bremen will remain a free and independent state.

Construction of the **St. Petri Dom** (*St. Peter's Cathedral*) began in the mid-11th century. Its two prominent towers, one of which can be climbed, are Gothic, but in the late 1800s the cathedral was restored in the Romanesque style. It served as the seat of an archbishop until the Reformation turned the cathedral Protestant. It has a museum and five functioning organs. ⊠ *Marktpl.* 🖾 *Free* 🕐 *Weekdays 10–5, Sat. 10–2, Sun. 2–5.*

Charlemagne had established a diocese here in the 9th century, and a 15th-century statue of him, together with seven princes, adorns the Gothic **Rathaus,** which acquired a Weser Renaissance facade during the early 17th century. Tours are given in German. ⊠ *Marktpl.* 🖾 *Tour €5* 🕐 *Tours Mon.–Sat. at 11, noon, 3, and 4; Sun. at 11 and noon (unless an official function is in progress).*

Don't leave Bremen's Altstadt without strolling down **Böttcherstrasse** *(Barrel Maker's Street)*, at one time inhabited by coopers. Between 1924 and 1931 their houses were torn down and reconstructed, in a style at once historically sensitive and modern, by Bremen coffee millionaire Ludwig Roselius. (He was the inventor of decaffeinated coffee, and held the patent for many years.) Many of the restored houses are used as galleries for local artists.

At one end of Böttcherstrasse is the **Roselius-Haus,** a 14th-century building that is now a museum, established on the initiative of the coffee

> ## ANIMAL MUSICIANS?
>
> Bremen is central to the fable of the Bremer Stadtmusikanten, or Bremen Town Musicians. A donkey, dog, cat, and rooster ran away because they had become old and their masters were going to dispose of them. In order to support themselves they went to Bremen and tried to hire themselves out as musicians. Their music and singing were so awful that they caused a band of robbers to flee in terror. Statues of this group are in various parts of the city.

baron. It showcases German and Dutch art, notably the paintings of Paula Modersohn-Becker, a noted early expressionist of the Worpswede art colony. Notice also the arch of Meissen bells at the rooftop. ■**TIP→** Except when freezing weather makes them dangerously brittle, these chime daily on the hour from noon to 6 (only at noon, 3, and 6, January–April). ✉*Böttcherstr. 6–10* ☎*0421/336–5077* 💰*€5* ⊘*Tues.–Sun. 11–6.*

★ Also take a walk through the nearby narrow streets of the idyllic **Schnoorviertel** *(Schnoor District)*, a jumble of houses, taverns, and shops once occupied or frequented by fishermen and tradespeople. This is Bremen's oldest district, dating back to the 15th and 16th centuries. The neighborhood is fashionable among artists and craftspeople, who have restored the tiny cottages to serve as galleries and workshops. Other buildings have been converted into popular antiques shops, small cafés, and pubs.

WHERE TO STAY & EAT

$$$–$$$$ ✕**Grashoffs Bistro.** An enthusiastic crowd, willing to put up with incredibly cramped conditions, descends at lunchtime on this gourmet restaurant-cum-deli. The room is so small that there's no room between the square tables; a table has to be pulled out for anyone who has a seat next to the wall. The menu has a French touch, with an emphasis on fresh fish from the Bremerhaven market. The deli has a whole wall of teas, another of cheeses, and a huge assortment of wines. ✉*Contrescarpe 80* ☎*0421/14740* 🍴 *Reservations essential* ▭*AE, DC, MC, V* ⊘*Closed Sun. No dinner.*

$–$$ ✕**Ratskeller.** This cavernous cellar, with a three-story-high vaulted ceiling, is said to be Germany's oldest and most renowned town-hall restaurant—it's been here for 600 years. The waiters and waitresses wear medieval costumes and serve solid, typical North German fare. The walls are lined with wine casks, and there are intimate alcoves with closable doors, once used by merchants as they closed their deals. ■**TIP→** By long tradition only German wines are served here, and the only beer you can get is Beck's from the barrel. ⊠*Am Markt 1* ☏*0421/321–676* ▤*AE, DC, MC, V.*

$$$$
Fodor's Choice
★

🏨 **Park Hotel Bremen.** The waiters wear white ties and the bellhops wear flat caps and brass buttons in this palatial hotel. There is a lake on one side, bordered by a terrace, and an extensive area of park and forest on the other sides. A heated outdoor pool and a fireplace in the lounge tempt you to linger in the public spaces, no matter what the season. The renowned Park Restaurant ($$$$) serves classic French and German dishes in a room of shimmering crystal chandeliers. **Pro:** traditional luxury hotel, right on a lake. **Cons:** expensive, somewhat removed from the city. ⊠*Im Bürgerpark* ☏*0421/340–800* ⊕*www.parkhotel-bremen.de* 🛏*166 rooms, 11 suites* ⚬*In-room: no a/c (some), safe, refrigerator, Wi-Fi. In-hotel: 2 restaurants, bar, pool, bicycles, no-smoking rooms, some pets allowed (fee)* ▤*AE, DC, MC, V* ▧*BP.*

SHOPPING

Bremen's **Schnoorviertel** is the place to go for souvenirs. Its stores are incredibly specialized, selling porcelain dolls, teddy bears, African jewelry, and smoking pipes among many other things.

BREMERHAVEN

66 km (41 mi) north of Bremen.

This busy port city, where the Weser empties into the North Sea, belongs to Bremen, about an hour to the south. You can take in the enormity of the port from a promenade, which runs its length. In addition to being a major port for merchant ships, it is the biggest fishery pier in Europe, which means that the promenade is lined with excellent seafood restaurants. A brand-new hotel and conference center has just opened on the harbor.

GETTING HERE & AROUND

Reederei HaRuFa offers a one-hour trip around the Bremerhaven harbor for €8.50. If you're in a hurry to see the stark, red cliff island of Helgoland, there's a daily round-trip flight for €160 per person with OLT.

ESSENTIALS

Visitor & Tour Information **Bremerhaven** (⊠*Bremerhaven Touristik, H.-H.-Meierstr. 6* ☏*0471/946–4610* ⊕*www.seestadt-bremerhaven.de).* **OLT Airlines** (⊠*Flughafen, Am Luneort 15* ☏*0471/77–188).* **Reederei HaRuFa** (⊠*H.-H.-Meierstr. 4* ☏*0471/415850).*

EXPLORING

The **Deutsches Auswandererhaus** (*German Emigration Center*), declared the 2007 "Museum of the Year" by the European Museum Forum, is made to order for those wanting to trace their German ancestry. The museum's Forum Immigration has a room full of computers at which you can access the museum's own extensive data bank and find links to more than a dozen other relevant Web sites, including an extensive collection of Bremen passenger lists and the large data banks of the

CLOSE UP

Tracing Your German Roots

The opening of the Emigration Museum in Bremerhaven is a reminder that more than 42 million Americans claim German ancestry, and that many have a very strong desire to trace those long-lost roots. The first significant waves of immigration from Germany came after the failed democratic revolutions of 1848, a time period coupled with potato blight in parts of Germany.

The more you can learn about your ancestors before you go, the more fruitful your search will be once you're on German soil. Crucial facts include: the name of your ancestor, his or her date of birth, marriage, or death, town or city of origin in Germany, date of emigration, ship on which he or she emigrated, and where in America he or she settled.

The first place to seek information is directly from members of your family. Even relatives who don't know any family history may have documents stored away that can help with your sleuthing—old letters, wills, diaries, birth and death certificates, and Bibles can be great sources of information.

If family resources aren't leading you anywhere, try turning to the Mormon Church. It has made it its mission to collect mountains of genealogical information, much of which it makes

available free of charge at ⊕ *www. familysearch.org*. The National Archives (⊕ *www.nara.gov*) keeps census records, and anyone can, for a fee, get information from the censuses of 1930 and earlier. U.S. courthouse records, such as court proceedings, deeds, wills, probates, birth records, and death records can also be useful. Community church records, primarily of baptisms and marriages, may add some key details.

The German Embassy in the U.S. lists many resources, including contacts both in the U.S. and Germany, for those wishing to trace their German ancestry. See ⊕ *www.germany. info/relaunch/culture/ger_americans/ ancestors.html* for more information.

Be sure to check out the German National Tourist Office's Web site (⊕ *germanoriginality.com)*, the Family Research Center in BallinStadt, Hamburg (⊕ *www.BallinStadt.de)*, and ⊕ *ComeToGermany.com*, all of which provide further links.

With advance research, you'll know better who to contact once in Germany. And you will, of course, have at your disposal there the computerized facilities of Bremerhaven's German Emigration Center (⊕ *www.dah-bremerhaven.de)*.

Ellis Island Museum and the Mormon church. The museum is right at the spot where 7 million Europeans set sail for the New World. Movie-set makers were called in to build authentic reconstructions of a big, dingy waiting hall and part of a historic steamship. The waiting room is crowded with mannequins in 19th-century costumes and piles of luggage. The "ship" is boarded across a swaying gangway, and once aboard, you can see how miserable life was during the voyage from the cabins and communal sleeping rooms. There is also a theater where visitors can view, in English, a film about six emigrant generations. ✉ *Columbusstr. 65* ☎ *0471/902–200* ⊕ *www.dah-bremerhaven. de* 💶 *€9.50* ⊙ *Mar.–Oct., 10–6; Nov.–Feb., 10–5.*

The country's largest and most fascinating maritime museum, the **Deutsches Schifffahrtsmuseum** *(German Maritime Museum)*, is a fun place to explore. Part of the museum consists of a harbor, open from April through October, with seven old trading ships. ⊠ *Hans-Scharoun-Pl. 1, from Bremen take A–27 to exit for Bremerhaven-Mitte* ☎ *0471/482–070* ⊕ *www.dsm.museum.de* 🎫 *€6* ⊙ *Daily 10–6.*

WHERE TO STAY

$$ ▦ **Hotel Haverkamp.** This centrally located hotel near the new harbor is newly renovated and contains just about all that guests could want. There is the König City Bar, a restaurant with excellent seafood, a sauna, and the only indoor pool in Bremerhaven. **Pros:** central location, indoor pool. **Cons:** somewhat plain exterior, swimming pool is very small. ⊠ *Prager Str. 34* ☎ *0471/48330* ⊕ *www.hotel-haverkamp. de* ⇗ *88 rooms* ⚷ *In-room: no a/c, refrigerator, dial-up, Wi-Fi. In-hotel: restaurant, bar, pool, parking (fee), no-smoking rooms, some pets allowed* ☰ *AE, DC, MC, V*

Hamburg

WORD OF MOUTH

"Hamburg is a comfortable rich city surrounded by waterfront areas. An impressive modern and large waterfront city called 'Hafencity' is being built on areas where the old harbor docks used to be."

—Dax

"We took the boat ride in the harbor and the one along the Altstadt and both were great, particularly along the little canals of the Altstadt."

—skatedancer

"I was in Hamburg last week—our first foray into northern Germany. Loved the city, and the harbor tour was fantastic—an absolute must-see."

—hausfrau

Updated
by Jürgen
Scheunemann

WATER—IN THE FORM OF THE ALSTER LAKES and the Elbe River—is Hamburg's defining feature and the key to the city's success. A harbor city with an international appeal, Hamburg is one of the most open-minded of German cities. The media have made Hamburg their capital by planting some of the leading newspapers, magazines, and television stations here. Add to that the slick world of advertising, show business, and modeling agencies, and you have a populace of worldly and fashionable professionals. Not surprisingly, the city of movers and shakers is also the city with most of Germany's millionaires.

But for most Europeans, the port city invariably triggers thoughts of the gaudy Reeperbahn underworld, that sleazy strip of clip joints, sex shows, and wholesale prostitution that helped earn Hamburg its reputation as "Sin City." Today the infamous red-light district is just as much a hip meeting place for young Hamburgers and tourist crowds, who flirt with the bright lights and chic haunts of the not-so-sinful Reeperbahn, especially on warm summer nights.

Hamburg, or "Hammaburg," was founded in 810 by Charlemagne. For centuries it was a walled city, its gigantic outer fortifications providing a tight little world relatively impervious to outside influences. The city is at the mouth of the Elbe, one of Europe's great rivers and the 97-km (60-mi) umbilical cord that ties the harbor to the North Sea. Its role as a port gained it world renown. It was a powerful member of the Hanseatic League, the medieval union of northern German merchant cities that dominated shipping in the Baltic and North seas.

The Thirty Years' War left Hamburg unscathed, and Napoléon's domination of much of the continent in the early 19th century also failed to affect it. Indeed, it was during the 19th century that Hamburg reached the crest of its power, when the largest shipping fleets on the seas with some of the fastest ships afloat were based here. Its merchants traded with the far corners of the globe. During the four decades leading up to World War I, Hamburg became one of the world's richest cities. Its aura of wealth and power continued right up to the outbreak of World War II. These days, about 15,000 ships sail up the lower Elbe each year, carrying more than 50 million tons of cargo—from petroleum and locomotives to grain and bananas.

What you see today is the "new" Hamburg. The Great Fire of 1842 all but obliterated the original city; a century later World War II bombing raids destroyed port facilities and leveled more than half of the city proper. In spite of the 1940–44 raids, Hamburg now stands as a remarkably faithful replica of that glittering prewar city—a place of enormous style, verve, and elegance, with considerable architectural diversity, including turn-of-the-20th-century art-nouveau buildings.

The distinguishing feature of downtown Hamburg is the Alster (Alster Lakes). Once an insignificant waterway, it was dammed in the 18th century to form an artificial lake. Divided at its south end, it's known as the Binnenalster (Inner Alster) and the Aussenalster (Outer Alster)—the two separated by a pair of graceful bridges, the Lombard Brücke and the John F. Kennedy Brücke. The Inner Alster is lined with stately

TOP REASONS TO GO

Harbor Cruises: Take a bumpy harbor tour through the Hamburger Freihafen, absorb the grand scenery of the city, and gaze at the seafaring steel hulks ready to ply the oceans of the world.

Historic Harbor District: Travel back in time and walk the quaint cobblestone alleys around Deichstrasse and the Kontorhausviertel.

Kunsthalle Hamburg and the Deichtorhallen: Spend an afternoon browsing through the fantastic art collections at two of Germany's leading galleries of modern art.

Retail Therapy: Indulge your inner shopper at the posh shopping arcades Hamburg is famous for; then stroll down elegant Jungfernstieg and end the afternoon at a charming downtown café.

Sin City: Stroll down Reeperbahn, browse in the quirky sex shops, and dive into the bizarre nightlife of Europe's biggest red-light district.

13

hotels, department stores, fine shops, and cafés; the Outer Alster is framed by parks and gardens against a backdrop of private mansions.

ORIENTATION & PLANNING

GETTING ORIENTED

The second-largest city in Germany after Berlin, Hamburg is one of northern Europe's largest ports. Lying along the river Elbe on Northern Germany's fertile lowlands, the city is just 380 feet above sea level. Despite heavy destruction in WW II, Hamburg is surprisingly green and architecturally beautiful. With 1.7 million inhabitants on 755 square km, it is the least densely populated million-person metropolis in the world. Hamburg is spread out around an upscale, historic downtown area of St. Georg, Neustadt, and Rotherbaum, but also contains industrial and younger neighborhoods. New neighborhoods like St. Pauli and Altona, and the shining HafenCity, one of Europe's boldest city development projects, will change the city's face along the Elbe in the years to come.

Downtown Hamburg. Hamburg's downtown area is centered on two long boulevards, the Jungfernstieg and Mönckebergstrasse, which also are the most elegant shopping boulevards in town, pulsating with life.

The Harbor & Historic Hamburg. Hamburg's older sections are a fascinating patchwork of historic periods, where meticulously restored older buildings hold their ground next to sleek high-rises. Along the waterfront, late-medieval and 19th-century warehouses contrast with the modern HafenCity development.

St. Pauli & the Reeperbahn. The Reeperbahn is Hamburg's infamous red-light district, but there is more here than just sex shows; great restaurants and nightlife abound. St. Pauli is defined by its proximity to the Elbe and offers top seafood choices.

HAMBURG PLANNER

WHEN TO GO

Located in the often rainy and windy German north, Hamburg's maritime weather is actually better than its reputation. Summer temperatures can hover around the mid- to high 70°-F from mid-June to mid-August, and sometimes a surprisingly pleasant and warm spring (late April through early June) presents the city with vibrant, blue skies. Summer sees many festivals such as the Sommerdom, or the Alstervergnügen, and is certainly the best time to visit—even if this means solidly booked hotels and restaurants, generally higher prices, and sometimes crowded attractions. September and October are usually good months to visit as well, even though strong winds and rain or sleet will pick up in late October. Despite the many Christmas markets, the occasional winter storm might make a visit during the festive season unpleasant. January, February, and March should be avoided, even though prices will be lower in this off-season, but the often bad weather will prevent you from enjoying a city with many open-air attractions, such as the harbor, the zoo, and the river Elbe.

GETTING HERE & AROUND

BY AIR Hamburg's international airport, Fuhlsbüttel, is 11 km (7 mi) northwest of the city. The Airport-City-Bus (the private Jasper Airport-Shuttle) runs nonstop between the airport and Hamburg's main train station daily at 15- to 30-minute intervals between 5:45 AM and midnight. Tickets are €5 (one-way). The (public) Airport-Express (Bus 110) runs every 10 minutes between the airport and the Ohlsdorf U- and S-bahn stations, a 15-minute ride from the main train station. The fare is €2.50. A taxi to the downtown area will cost about €20. If you're driving a rental car from the airport, follow the signs to STADT-ZENTRUM (downtown).

BY BOAT & HADAG ferries to Altes Land and Lühe depart from the Landungs-
FERRY brücken (⇨ *Tours*) twice daily during the week and four times daily on weekends from April through October. Get off at the stop in Lühe. To reach Neunfelde, take the ferry from Blankenese.

BY BUS & Hamburg's bus station, the Zentral-Omnibus-Bahnhof, is directly
SUBWAY behind the main train station.

The HVV, Hamburg's public transportation system, includes the U-bahn (subway), the S-bahn (suburban train), and buses. As this book was being updated, the city was planning to revamp the ticketing system. At this writing, a one-way fare starts at €1.30; €1.65–€2.60 covers *one* unlimited ride in the Hamburg city area. Tickets are available on all buses and at automatic machines in all stations and at most bus stops. A *Ganztageskarte* (all-day ticket), valid until 6 AM on the next day, costs €6. A *9 Uhr-Tageskarte* for just €5.10 is valid between 9 AM on the day of purchase and 6 AM the next morning. If you're traveling with family or friends, a *Gruppen-* or *Familienkarte* (group or family ticket) is a good value—a group of up to five can travel for the entire day for only €8.60–€21.60 (depending on the number of fare zones the ticket covers).

You must validate your ticket at a machine at the start of your journey. If you are found without a validated ticket, the fine is €40.

In the north of Hamburg, the HVV system connects with the A-bahn (Alsternordbahn), a suburban train system that extends into Schleswig-Holstein. Night buses (Nos. 600–640) serve the downtown area all night, leaving the Rathausmarkt and Hauptbahnhof every hour.

BY CAR Hamburg is easier to handle by car than many other German cities, and traffic is relatively uncongested. During rush hour, however, there can be gridlock. Several autobahns (A–1, A–7, A–23, A–24, and A–250) connect with Hamburg's three beltways, which then easily take you to the downtown area. Follow the STADTZENTRUM signs. To reach Altes Land and Stade from Hamburg, take B–73 west.

BY TAXI Taxi meters start at €2.40, then add €1.68 per km thereafter. You can hail taxis on the street or at stands, or order one by phone.

BY TRAIN There are two principal stations: the central Hauptbahnhof (Main Train Station) and Hamburg-Altona, west of the downtown area. EuroCity and InterCity trains connect Hamburg with all German cities and many major European ones. InterCity Express "supertrain" lines link Hamburg with Berlin, Frankfurt, and Munich. Trains to Stade depart from the Hauptbahnhof.

VISITOR INFORMATION Hamburg has tourist offices around the city. The main office is in the Hauptbahnhof (Main Train Station) and is open Monday to Saturday 8 AM to 9 PM, Sunday 10 AM to 6 PM. At the harbor there's an office at the St. Pauli Landungsbrücken, between Piers 4 and 5, open April to November, daily 8 to 6, and March to October, Monday, Wednesday, and Sunday 10–6; Tuesday, Thursday–Saturday 10–7.

In addition to its comprehensive hotel guide, the tourist office also co-publishes *Hamburger Vorschau,* a free monthly program of events in the city. The free magazine *Hamburg Tips* is issued quarterly and details major seasonal events.

All tourist offices can help with accommodations, and there's a central call-in booking office for hotel and ticket reservations and general information, the Hamburg-Hotline. A €4 fee is charged for every room reserved.

ESSENTIALS **Airport Information Fuhlsbüttel** (☎ 040/50750 ⊕ www.ham.airport.de).

Bus Information Hamburg Passenger Transport Board (*Hamburger Verkehrsverbund* ✉ *Steindamm 94, Altstadt* ☎ 040/325–7750 ⊕ www.hvv.de ⊙ *Daily*). **Zentral-Omnibus-Bahnhof** (*ZOB* ✉ *Adenauerallee 78, St. Georg* ☎ 040/247–576).

Taxi Information Taxi (☎ 040/441–011, 040/686–868, or 040/666–666).

Train Information Hauptbahnhof (✉ *Steintorpl., Altstadt* ☎ 11861).

Visitor Information Hamburg-Hotline (☎ 040/3005–1300 ⊕ www.hamburg-tourism.de). **Hamburg Tourismus GmbH** (✉ *Hauptbahnhof, Altstadt* ☎ 040/3005–1300 ✉ *St. Pauli Landungsbrücken, St. Pauli* ☎ 040/3005–1200 or 040/3005–1203 ✉ *Steinstr. 7, Altstadt* ☎ 040/3005–1144 ⊕ www.hamburg-tourism.de). **Stade**

Tourismus GmbH (✉ *Hansestr. 16Stade* ☎ *04141/40910* 🖶 *04141/409–150* ⊕ *www.stade.de).*

TOURS

BOAT TOURS There are few better ways to get to know the city than by taking a trip around the massive harbor. The HADAG line and other companies organize round-trips in the port, lasting about one hour (€9). Between April and October, excursion boats and barges leave every half hour from the Landungsbrücken—Piers 1, 2, 3, and 7—between 10 AM and 4:30 PM. From early November through March, departures are at 11, 12:30, 2, and 3:30 on weekends. From March through November, an English-language tour leaves at noon daily from Pier 1.

From April through October, Alster Touristik operates boat trips around the Alster Lakes and through the canals. There are two tour options; both leave from the Jungfernstieg promenade in the city center. The Aussenalster 50-minute lake tour (Alster-Rundfahrt) costs €10 and leaves every half-hour, April–October 3, daily 10–6. A two-hour-long *Fleet-Fahrt* costs €15 and explores the canals of the historic Speicherstadt (late March–November, daily at 10:45, 1:45, and 4:45). From late April through October there's also the romantic twilight tour, called Dämmertour, every evening at 8 (€15).

ORIENTATION TOURS Sightseeing bus tours of the city, all with guides who rapidly narrate in both English and German, leave from Kirchenallee by the main train station. A bus tour lasting 1¾ hours sets off at varying times daily and costs €15. For €23, one of the bus tours can be combined with a one-hour boat trip on the Alster Lakes or the harbor. For €30 you can combine a city bus tour, the Alster Lakes, and the harbor boat tour. Departure times for tours vary according to season. City tours aboard the nostalgic *Hummelbahn* (a converted railroad wagon pulled by a tractor) start from the Kirchenallee stop. They run daily April–October. The fare is €13 for 1¾ hours (children under 12 are free).

WALKING TOURS Tours of downtown, the harbor district, and St. Pauli are offered from April through November, weekdays at 2:30 by the Hamburg Tourismus GmbH. All guided walking tours (€7) are conducted in German and start at different locations. Downtown tours by Stattreisen Hamburg are held on Saturday (February–December) and are conducted in German only. Tours of the historic Speicherstadt district are conducted by the Speicherstadtmuseum (Sunday at 11, €7).

TOUR ESSENTIALS **Boat Tour Information Alster Touristik** (☎ *040/357–4240* ⊕ *www.alstertouristik. de).* **Bordparty-Service** (✉ *Landungsbrücken, Pier 9, St. Pauli* ☎ *040/313–687* ⊕ *www.bordparty.de).* **HADAG** (☎ *040/311–7070, 040/313–130, 040/313–959, 040/3178–2231 for English-*

Orientation Tour Information *Hummelbahn* (☎ *040/792–8979* ⊕ *www. hummelbahn.de).*

Walking Tour Information Speicherstadtmuseum (✉ *St. Annenufer 2, Block R, Speicherstadt* ☎ *040/321–191* ⊕ *www.speicherstadtmuseum.de).* **Stattreisen Hamburg** (☎ *040/430–3481* ⊕ *www.stattreisen-hamburg.de).* **Hamburg Tourismus GmbH** (✉ *Steinstr. 7, Altstadt* ☎ *040/3005–1300* ⊕ *www.hamburg-tourism.de).*

PLANNING YOUR TIME

The downtown area features most of Hamburg's must-see attractions, such as the grand, historic churches and most museums. Pride of place goes to the Rathaus, which is a good starting point for exploring the inner city, and the St. Michaeliskirche, while other churches, notably St. Petri, St. Jakobi, and St. Katharinen, are a short 10–15 minutes' walk away from each other. Take a stroll along the two major boulevards in the area, the Jungfernstieg, to take in the Binnenalster, and Mönckeberg-strasse, and venture out to the many side streets and canal-side walks. This can take up several hours, depending on how much of the area you want to explore. Some of the city's most important museums, such as the Kunsthalle with its superb collection of modern art, can be found near the Hauptbahnhof. Any visit to Hamburg should include a walk along the Reeperbahn in St. Pauli, as well as a closer inspection of the Altstadt with its 19th century warehouses and cobblestone alleys. Each of these neighborhoods can easily take up half a day of exploring.

DISCOUNTS & DEALS

Hamburg is one of Germany's most expensive cities, but the tourism board's special deals make attractions more affordable. Available from the city's tourist offices, the **Hamburg Card** allows unlimited travel on all public transportation within Hamburg and admission to state museums. The **Hamburg Card** is valid for 24 hours (beginning at 6 PM through 6 PM the following day) and costs €8 for one adult and up to three children under the age of 14; it costs €18 for three days (valid starting at noon the first day). The **Hamburg Card** *Gruppenkarte* costs €29.30 for any group of five and is valid for three days; a *Gruppenkarte* for just one day is available for €11.80.

EXPLORING HAMBURG

Hamburg's most important attractions stretch between the Alster Lakes to the north and the harbor and Elbe River to the south. This area consists of four distinct quarters. St. Georg is the business district around the Hauptbahnhof (Main Train station). The historic Altstadt (Old City) clusters near the harbor and surrounds the Rathaus (Town Hall). West of the Altstadt is Neustadt (New City). The shabby but thrilling district of St. Pauli includes the Reeperbahn, a strip of sex clubs and bars.

DOWNTOWN HAMBURG

Downtown was heavily bombarded during World War II, so many of the buildings here were constructed after the war, but many red-brick historic 19th-century warehouses, city mansions and historic landmarks have been restored to their old splendor and now house banks, insurance companies, and other big businesses. The city's heart is centered on two long boulevards, the Jungfernstieg and Mönckeberg-strasse. Downtown may not be the most beautiful part of town, but its atmosphere is invigorating.

GETTING HERE & AROUND

The best way to explore the downtown area is to take the U-Bahn to Hamburger Hauptbahnhof. From the main railway station, just follow the shopping boulevard, Mönckebergstrasse, which will lead to you to most of the sights and is a good yardstick for orientation.

TIMING

If you plan two hours for visits to the museums and the Rathaus and two more hours for the delightful boat tour on the Alster Lakes, you'll end up spending more than a full day downtown.

EXPLORING

MAIN ATTRACTIONS

TOURING TIPS

Information: Before you start your walk, stock up on maps and brochures at the tourist office inside the Hauptbahnhof.

Scenic Spot: At Jungfernstieg, walk up to the 1950s style Alsterpavillon, standing on a slightly elevated platform, to enjoy a great view of the Binnen- and Aussenalster lakes.

Snacks: There are many inexpensive eateries in and around the Hauptbahnhof, as well as on Mönckebergstrasse.

② **🌣** **★** **Hagenbecks Tierpark** *(Hagenbecks Zoo).* One of the country's oldest and most popular zoos is family owned. Founded in 1848, it was the world's first city park to let wild animals such as lions, elephants, chimpanzees, and others roam freely in vast, open-air corrals. Weather permitting, you can ride one of the elephants. In the Troparium, an artificial habitat creates a rain forest, an African desert, and a tropical sea. ⊠ *Lokstedter Str. at Hamburg-Stellingen, Niendorf* ☎ *040/540-0010* ⊕ *www.hagenbeck.de* 🎫 *€15* ☉ *Mar.–June, daily 9–6; July and Aug., daily 9–7; Sept. and Oct., daily 9–6; Nov.–Feb., daily 9–4:30; last admission at 3:30* Ⓜ *Hagenbecks Tierpark (U-bahn).*

⑥ **★** **Jungfernstieg.** This wide promenade looking out over the Alster Lakes is the city's premier shopping boulevard. Laid out in 1665, it used to be part of a muddy millrace that channeled water into the Elbe. Hidden from view behind the sedate facade of Jungfernstieg is a network of nine covered arcades that together account for almost a mile of shops selling everything from souvenirs to haute couture. Many of these air-conditioned passages have sprung up in the past two decades, but some have been here since the 19th century; the first glass-covered arcade, called Sillem's Bazaar, was built in 1845. ⊠ *Neustadt* Ⓜ *Jungfernstieg (U-bahn).*

NEED A BREAK?	Hamburg's best-known and oldest café, the Alex im Alsterpavillon (⊠ *Jungfernstieg 54, Neustadt* ☎ *040/350–1870*) is a sleek 1950s retro café with an ideal vantage point from which to observe the constant activity on the Binnenalster.

⑩ **★** **Kunsthalle** *(Art Gallery).* One of the most important art museums in Germany, the Kunsthalle has 3,000 paintings, 400 sculptures, and a coin and medal collection that dates from the 14th century. In the postmodern, cube-shape building designed by Berlin architect O. M. Ungers, the **Galerie der Gegenwart** has housed a collection of international modern art since 1960, including works by Andy Warhol, Joseph Beuys, Georg Baselitz, and David Hockney. Graphic art is well represented, with a special collection of works by Pablo Picasso and the late Hamburg artist Horst Janssen, famous for his satirical worldview. In the old wing, you can view works by local artists dating from the 16th century. The outstanding collection of German Romantic paintings includes pieces by Runge, Friedrich, and Spitzweg. Paintings by Holbein, Rembrandt, Van Dyck, Tiepolo, and Canaletto are also on view, while late-19th-century Impressionism is represented by works by Leibl, Liebermann, Manet, Monet, and Renoir. ⊠ *Glockengiesserwall, Altstadt* ☎ *040/4281–31200* ⊕ *www.hamburger-kunsthalle.de* ☜ *Permanent and special exhibits €8.50, permanent exhibit only €6* ☉ *Tues., Wed., and Fri.–Sun. 10–6, Thurs. 10–9* Ⓜ *Hauptbahnhof (U-bahn).*

> **BEATING THE EURO**
>
> The most expensive boutiques and stores are usually right on Jungfernstieg Street. For more affordable wares, venture into the quiet side streets, where you can find designer clothes for much less in the smaller shops. Fashionable and cheap clothes can also be found in the artsy Schanzen and Katharinenviertel neighborhoods.

8 **Mönckebergstrasse.** This broad, bustling street of shops—Hamburg's major thoroughfare—cuts through both the historic and the new downtown areas. It was laid out in 1908, when this part of the Old Town was redeveloped. ■TIP➔ **The stores and shopping precincts on both sides of the street provide a wide selection of goods at more affordable prices than those on Jungfernstieg.** ⊠ *Altstadt* Ⓜ *Jungfernstieg (U-bahn).*

7 **Rathaus** *(Town Hall).* To most Hamburgers this large building is the symbolic heart of the city. As a city-state—an independent city and simultaneously one of the 16 federal states of Germany—Hamburg has a city council and a state government, both of which have their administrative headquarters in the Rathaus. A pompous neo-Renaissance affair, the building dictates political decorum in the city. To this day, the mayor of Hamburg never welcomes VIPs at the foot of its staircase, but always awaits them at the very top—whether it's a president or the queen of England.

Fodor'sChoice
★

Both the Rathaus and the **Rathausmarkt** (Town Hall Market) lie on marshy land, a fact vividly brought to mind in 1962, when the entire area was severely flooded. The large square, with its surrounding arcades, was laid out after Hamburg's Great Fire of 1842. The architects set out to create a square with the grandeur of Venice's Piazza San Marco. The Rathaus was begun in 1866, when 4,000 piles were sunk into the moist soil to support the structure. It was completed in 1892, the year a cholera epidemic claimed the lives of 8,605 people in 71 days. A fountain and monument to that unhappy chapter in Hamburg's history are in a rear courtyard of the Rathaus.

The immense building, with its 647 rooms (6 more than Buckingham Palace) and imposing central clock tower, is not the most graceful structure in the city, but the sheer opulence of its interior is aston-

13

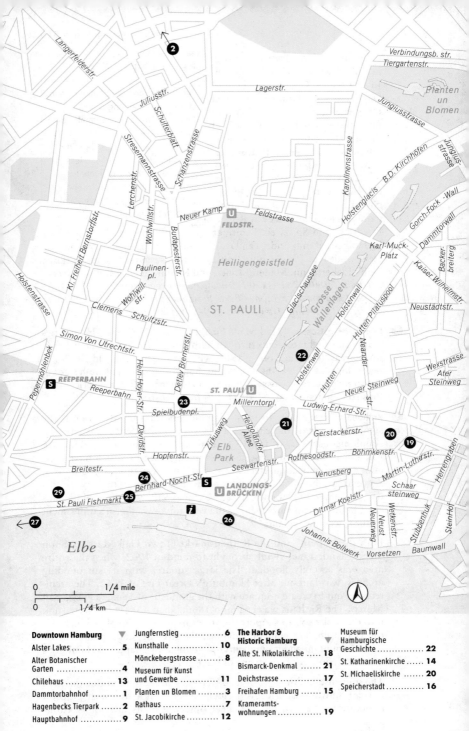

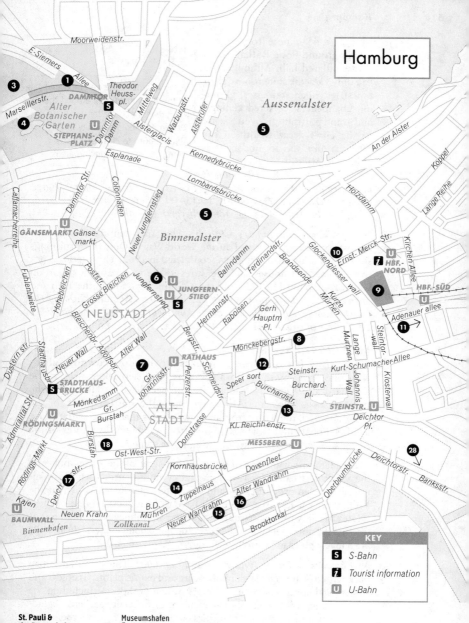

Hamburg

Moorweidenstr.

E.-Siemers Allee

Marseillerstr.

3

1

Theodor Heuss-pl.

DAMMTOR

Alter Botanischer Garten

4

S

U

Dammtor Damm

STEPHANS-PLATZ

Alsterglacis

Mittelweg

Warburgstr.

Alsterufer

Aussenalster

An der Alster

5

Holzdamm

Kirchen Allee

Koppel

Lange Reihe

Esplanade

Kennedybrücke

Lombardsbrücke

Dammtor Str.

Colonnaden

Neuer Jungfernstieg

Binnenalster

5

Ballindamm

Ferdinandstr.

Brandsende

Glockengiesser wall

Ernst-Merck-Str.

i **HBF.-NORD**

U

10

Fuhlentwiete

Callamachererheide

GÄNSEMARKT

Gänse-markt

U

Poststr.

Hohebleichen

Grosse Bleichen

Bleichenbr.

Adolfsbr.

Neuer Wall

NEUSTADT

Jungfernstieg

6

U

S

JUNGFERN-STIEG

Hermannstr.

Raboisen

Gerh Hauptm Pl.

Kurze Mühren

Lange Mühren

Kurt-Schumacher-Allee

9

HBF.-SÜD

Adenauer allee

11

Steintor-wall

Dustern str.

Stadtha usbr.

Alter Wall

Bergstr.

Schmidtstr.

Mönckebergstr.

8

Steinstr.

Johannis Wall

Klosterwall

STADTHAUS-BRÜCKE

S

Mönkedamm

Gr. Johannisstr.

U

7

RATHAUS

Speer sort

12

Burchardstr.

Burchard-pl.

STEINSTR.

U

Deichtor Pl.

RÖDINGSMARKT

U

Gr. Burstah

Pelzerstr.

ALT-STADT

Domstrasse

Kl. Reichh enstr.

13

Rödings-Markt

Burstah

Deich str.

18

Ost-West-Str.

MESSBERG

U

Deichtorstr.

Bankss tr.

28

Oberbaumbrücke

17

Kornhausbrücke

Dovenfleet

Alter Wandrahm

Admiralität str.

BAUMWALL

U

Kajen

Neuen Krahn

BINNENHAFEN

B.D. Mühren

14

Zippelhaus

Neuer Wandrahm

16

15

Brooktorkai

Zollkanal

KEY

S S-Bahn

i Tourist information

U U-Bahn

---

ishing. A 45-minute tour begins in the ground-floor Rathausdiele, a vast pillared hall. Although you can only view the state rooms, their tapestries, huge staircases, glittering chandeliers, coffered ceilings, and grand portraits give you a sense of the city's great wealth in the 19th century and its understandable civic pride. ⊠ *Rathausmarkt, Altstadt* ☎ *040/428–310* ⊕ *www.*

<table>
<tr><td>**INTERNET CAFÉS & HOT SPOTS**</td></tr>
<tr><td>Many Internet cafés can be found in the downtown area around the Hauptbahnhof. An alternative are W-Lan hot spots you may find throughout the city, but mostly along the major shopping areas.</td></tr>
</table>

hamburg.de 🖭 *English-language tour €3* ⊙ *Tours Mon.–Thurs., hourly 10:15–3:15, Fri., hourly 10:15–1:15, Sat., hourly 10:15–5:15, Sun., hourly 10:15–4:15* Ⓜ *Mönckebergstr. (U-bahn).*

⑫ ★ St. Jacobikirche *(St. James's Church)*. This 13th-century church was almost completely destroyed during World War II. Only the furnishings survived, and reconstruction was completed in 1962. The interior is not to be missed—it houses such treasures as the vast baroque organ on which Bach played in 1720 and three Gothic altars from the 15th and 16th centuries. ⊠ *Jacobikirchhof 22, at Steinstr., Altstadt* ☎ *040/303–7370* ⊙ *Daily 10–5. Guided tours: Apr.–Sept., every 2 wks on Wed., 10–5; tour of organ Sun. at 10* Ⓜ *Mönckebergstr. (U-bahn).*

ALSO WORTH SEEING

❺ Alster *(Alster Lakes)*. These twin lakes provide downtown Hamburg with one of its most memorable vistas. The two lakes meet at the Lombard and Kennedy bridges. In summer the boat landing at the Jungfernstieg, below the Alsterpavillon, is the starting point for the *Alsterdampfer,* the flat-bottom passenger boats that traverse the lakes. Small sailboats and rowboats, hired from yards on the shores of the Alster, are very much a part of the summer scene.

Every Hamburger dreams of living within sight of the Alster, but only the wealthiest can afford it. Some lucky millionaires own the magnificent garden properties around the Alster's perimeter, known as the Millionaire's Coast. But you don't have to be a guest on one of these estates to enjoy the waterfront—the Alster shoreline has 6 km (4 mi) of tree-lined public pathways. ■ TIP➡ **Popular among joggers, these trails are a lovely place for a stroll.** Ⓜ *Jungfernstieg (U-bahn).*

❹ Alter Botanischer Garten *(Old Botanical Gardens)*. This green and open park within Wallringpark cultivates rare and exotic plants. Tropical and subtropical species grow under glass in five hothouses, including the large Schaugewächshaus (Show Greenhouse). Specialty gardens, including herbal and medicinal plantings, are clustered around the moat. ⊠ *Stephanspl., Neustadt* ☎ *040/4283–82327* 🖭 *Free* ⊙ *Schaugewächshaus Mar.–Oct., weekdays 9–4:45, weekends 10–5:45; Nov.–Feb., weekdays 9–3:45, weekends 10–3:45* Ⓜ *Stefanspl. (U-bahn).*

⑬ Chilehaus *(Chile House)*. This fantastical 10-story structure, which looks like a vast landlocked ship, is the standout of the **Kontorhausviertel,** a series of imaginative clinker-brick buildings designed in the New Objectivity style of 1920s civic architect Fritz Schumacher. The building was commissioned by businessman Henry Sloman, who traded in saltpeter from Chile, and now houses modern offices. ⊠ *Buchardspl., Altstadt* ⊕ *www.chilehaus.de* Ⓜ *Messberg (U-bahn).*

 Dammtorbahnhof *(Dammtor Train Station).* Built in 1903, this elevated steel-and-glass art nouveau structure is among Hamburg's finest train stations. It's one of many art nouveau buildings you'll see in the city. ■ TIP→ **You can buy a city map at the newsstand in the station.** ⊠ *Ernst-Siemers-Allee, Altstadt* Ⓜ *Dammtor (U-bahn).*

> **BEATING THE EURO**
>
> Hamburg's restaurants can be expensive, but many budget eateries and *Imbisse* (snack bars) can be found in and around the Hauptbahnhof. Many offer Turkish or Middle Eastern food such as kebabs or falafel, others have traditional German and Hamburg fare, such as fish sandwiches or bratwurst. You can easily get a filling snack and soft drink for less than €5.

Deichtorhallen. This complex of warehouses built in 1911–12 is near the Kontorhausviertel and is now one of the country's largest exhibition halls for modern art. Its interior resembles an oversize loft, and its changing exhibits have presented the works of such artists as Andy Warhol, Roy Lichtenstein, and Miró. ⊠ *Deichtorstr. 1–2, Altstadt* ☎ *040/321–030* ⊕ *www.deichtorhallen.de* 🎟 *Varies by exhibit* 🕙 *Tues.–Sun. 11–6* Ⓜ *Steinstr. (U-bahn).*

 Hauptbahnhof *(Main Train Station).* This central train station's cast-iron-and-glass architecture evokes the grandiose self-confidence of imperial Germany. The chief feature of the enormous 394-foot-long structure is its 460-foot-wide glazed roof supported only by pillars at each end. The largest structure of its kind in Europe, it's remarkably spacious and light inside. Though built in 1906 and having gone through many modernizations, it continues to have tremendous architectural impact. Today it sees a heavy volume of international, national, and suburban rail traffic. ⊠ *Steintorpl., St. Georg* Ⓜ *Hauptbahnhof (U-bahn).*

 Museum für Kunst und Gewerbe *(Arts and Crafts Museum).* The museum houses a wide range of exhibits, from 15th- to 18th-century scientific instruments to an art nouveau interior complete with ornaments and furnishings. It was built in 1876 as a combination museum and school. Its founder, Justus Brinckmann, intended it to be a bastion of the applied arts that would counter what he saw as a decline in taste owing to industrial mass production. A keen collector, Brinckmann amassed a wealth of unusual objects, including a collection of ceramics from around the world. ⊠ *Steintorpl. 1, Altstadt* ☎ *040/42813–42732* ⊕ *www.mkg-hamburg.de* 🎟 *€8* 🕙 *Tues., Wed., and Fri.–Sun. 10–6, Thurs. 10–9* Ⓜ *Hauptbahnhof (U-bahn).*

 Planten un Blomen *(Plants and Flowers Park).* Opened in 1935, this huge, tranquil park is renowned in Germany for its well-kept gardens. The park lies within the remains of the 17th-century fortified wall that guarded the city during the Thirty Years' War. If you visit on a summer evening, you'll see the Wasserlichtkonzert, the play of an illuminated fountain set to organ music. ■TIP➔ **Make sure you get to the lake in plenty of time for the nightly show, which begins at 10** PM **from May to August and at 9** PM **in September.** ⊠*Stephanspl., Neustadt* ☎*040/4285–44723* ✉*Free* ⊙*May–Sept., daily 6* AM– *11* PM; *Oct.–Apr., daily 7* AM–*8* PM Ⓜ*Stephanspl. (U-bahn).*

THE HARBOR & HISTORIC HAMBURG

Narrow cobblestone streets with richly decorated mansions lead to churches of various faiths, reflecting the diverse origins of the sailors and merchants drawn to the city. Small museums and old restaurants occupy buildings that once served as sailor taverns. Of note here are Hamburg's Free Port, the Gothic St. Michaeliskirche, the Warehouse district, and the ambitious HafenCity.

GETTING HERE & AROUND

To reach the harbor area from the Messberg U-bahn station, cross the busy Ost-West-Strasse and walk down Dovenfleet, which runs alongside the Zollkanal (Customs Canal). The road, which turns into Bei den Mühren, reaches the Brooksbrück. ■TIP➔ **Bring your passport. When you leave the Free Port over the Brooksbrück, you will pass through a customs control point.**

EXPLORING

MAIN ATTRACTIONS

⑰ ★ Deichstrasse. The oldest residential area in the Old Town of Hamburg, which dates from the 14th century, now consists of lavishly restored houses from the 17th through the 19th centuries. Many of the original houses on Deichstrasse were destroyed in the Great Fire of 1842, which broke out in No. 42 and left approximately 20,000 people homeless; only a few of the early dwellings escaped its ravages. Today Deichstrasse and neighboring **Peterstrasse** (just south of Ost-West-Strasse) are of great historical interest. At No. 39 Peterstrasse, for example, is the baroque facade of the Beylingstift complex, built in 1700. Farther along, No. 27, constructed as a warehouse in 1780, is the oldest of its kind in Hamburg. All the buildings in the area have been painstakingly restored, thanks largely to individual owners. ⊠*Altstadt* Ⓜ*Rödingsmarkt (U-bahn).*

NEED A BREAK? There are two good basement restaurants in this area. The Alt-Hamburger Aalspeicher (⊠*Deichstr. 43, Altstadt* ☎*040/362–990*) serves fresh fish dishes, including Hamburg's famous *Aalsuppe* (eel soup with dried fruits). Das Kontor (⊠*Deichstr. 32, Altstadt* ☎*040/371–471*), an upscale historic

Hamburg tavern, offers some of the city's best fried potatoes and traditional desserts.

⑮ Fodor's Choice ★ ☺ **Freihafen Hamburg.** Hamburg's Free Port, the city's major attraction, dates to the 12th century, when the city was granted special privileges by Holy Roman Emperor Frederick I (Barbarossa). One of these was freedom from paying duties on goods transported on the Elbe River. The original Free Port was

BEATING THE EURO

For a relaxing and inexpensive way to experience the Alster lakes, opt to man your own lakeworthy vessel. Row-, sail-, and pedal-boats can be rented for €10–€20 an hour and usually accommodate up to two adults. Look for boat rentals along the Aussen- and Binnenalster.

13

where the Alster meets the Elbe, near Deichstrasse, but it was moved farther south as Hamburg's trade expanded. When Hamburg joined the German Empire's Customs Union in the late 1800s, the Free Port underwent major restructuring to make way for additional storage facilities. An entire residential area was torn down (including many Renaissance and baroque buildings), and the **Speicherstadt** warehouses, the world's largest block of continuous storage space, came into being between 1885 and 1927. Ⓜ*St. Pauli Landungsbrücken (U-bahn).*

⑳ Fodor's Choice ★ **St. Michaeliskirche** *(St. Michael's Church).* The Michel, as it's called locally, is Hamburg's principal church and northern Germany's finest baroque-style ecclesiastical building. Constructed between 1649 and 1661 (the tower followed in 1669), it was razed after lightning struck almost a century later. It was rebuilt between 1750 and 1786 in the decorative Nordic baroque style, but was gutted by a terrible fire in 1906. The replica, completed in 1912, was demolished during World War II. The present church is a reconstruction.

The distinctive 433-foot brick-and-iron tower bears the largest tower clock in Germany, 26 feet in diameter. Just above the clock is a viewing platform (accessible by elevator or stairs) that affords a magnificent panorama of the city, the Elbe River, and the Alster Lakes. ■TIP→ **Twice a day, at 10 AM and 9 PM (Sunday at noon), a watchman plays a trumpet solo from the tower platform, and during festivals an entire wind ensemble crowds onto the platform to perform.** The **Multivisionsshow** (slide and audio show), located one floor beneath the viewing platform, recounts Hamburg's history on a 16-foot screen. ⊠*St. Michaeliskirche, Altstadt* ☎*040/376–780* ⊕*www.st-michaelis.de* ☎*Tower €2.50; crypt €1.25; tower and show €4; crypt and show €2.75; show, tower, and crypt €4.50* ☉*May–Oct., Mon.–Sat. 9–8, Sun. 12:30–8; Nov.–Apr., Mon.–Sat. 10–6, Sun. 12:30–6; multimedia screening daily on the half hr, 12:30–3:30* Ⓜ*Landungsbrücken, Rödingsmarkt (U-bahn).*

NEED A BREAK?

Just opposite the St. Michaeliskirche is one of Hamburg's most traditional restaurants, the Old Commercial Room (⊠ *Englische Planke 10, Speicherstadt* ☎*040/366–319*). Try one of the local specialties, such as eel soup. If you don't make it to the restaurant, you can buy its dishes (precooked and canned) in department stores in both Hamburg and Berlin.

16 **Speicherstadt** *(Warehouse District)*.
Fodor'sChoice These imposing warehouses in
★ the Freihafen Hamburg reveal
yet another aspect of Hamburg's
extraordinary architectural diversity. A Gothic influence is apparent
here, with a rich overlay of gables,
turrets, and decorative outlines.
These massive rust-brown buildings are still used to store and process every conceivable commodity,
from coffee and spices to raw silks
and hand-woven Oriental carpets.

Although you won't be able to
enter the buildings, the nonstop
comings and goings will give you
a good sense of a port at work. If
you want to learn about the history
and architecture of the old ware-
houses, detour to the **Speicherstadtmuseum**. ⊠*St. Annenufer 2, Block R,
Speicherstadt* ☎*040/321–191* ⊕*www.speicherstadtmuseum.de* 💶*€3*
🕐*Apr.–Oct., Tues.–Fri. 10–5, weekends 10–6; Nov.–Mar., Tues.–Sun.,
10–5* Ⓜ*Messberg (U-bahn)*.

THE SPICE TRADE
Hamburg's proud past as Europe's gateway to the world comes to life at the tiny but fascinating **Spicy's Gewürzmuseum** (⊠*Am Sandtorkai 32* ☎*040/367–989* ⊕*www.spicys.de*) in the Speicherstadt, where you can smell, touch, and feel close to 50 spices. More than 700 objects chronicle five centuries of the once-prosperous spice trade in Hamburg. From November to June the museum is open Tuesday–Sunday 10–5; from July to October it's open daily 10–5. Admission is €3.

Opposite the historic Speicherstadt sits one of Europe's largest urban-
development projects, the **HafenCity**. This new district will have both
business and residential areas spread over 387 acres. Once completed,
the HafenCity will include a cruise-ship terminal, a high-tech symphony hall (the Elbphilharmonie), a maritime art museum, and a science center with an aquarium. You can see a model of the project,
slated for completion in 2025, in the visitor center in Speicherstadt's
old power plant. Take a closer look at the ongoing construction
at a bright red observation platform on Strandkai—the first buildings along the Marco-Polo Terrassen are finally complete. It's a nice
place to watch passing ships. ⊠*Am Sandtorkai 30, Speicherstadt*
☎*040/3690–1799* ⊕*www.hafencity.com* 💶*Free* 🕐*Visitor Center:
Tues.–Sun. 10–6; May–Sept., Tues.–Wed., Fri.–Sun. 10–6, Thurs. 10–8*
Ⓜ*Messberg (U-bahn)*.

ALSO WORTH SEEING

18 **Alte St. Nikolaikirche** *(Old St. Nicholas's Church)*. The tower and outside walls of this 19th-century neo-Gothic church are all that survived
World War II. Today these ruins serve as a monument to those killed
and persecuted during the war. Next to the tower, which offers a magnificent view of the surrounding historic streets, is a center documenting
the history of the church. It's run by a citizens' organization that is also
spearheading private efforts to partially rebuild the church and rede-
sign the surrounding area. ▪TIP→ **A wine cellar is open for browsing and
tasting.** ⊠ *Willy-Brandt-Str. 60, at Hopfenmarkt, Altstadt* ☎*040/371–
125* ⊕*www.mahnmal-st-nikolai.de* 💶*€3* 🕐*Oct.–June, daily 10:30–
5:30; July–Sept., daily 9:30–8:30* Ⓜ*Rödingsmarkt (U-bahn)*.

㉑ Bismarck-Denkmal *(Bismarck Memorial)*. The colossal 111-foot granite monument, erected between 1903 and 1906, is an equestrian statue of Otto von Bismarck, Prussia's Iron Chancellor, who was the force behind the unification of Germany. The plinth features bas-reliefs of various German tribes. Created by sculptor Hugo Lederer, the statue calls to mind Roland, the famous warrior from the Middle Ages, and symbolizes the German Reich's protection of Hamburg's international trade. ⊠*St. Pauli* Ⓜ*St. Pauli (U-bahn)*.

⑲ Krameramtswohnungen *(Shopkeepers' Houses)*. The shopkeepers' guild built this tightly packed group of courtyard houses between 1620 and 1626 for members' widows. The houses became homes for the elderly after 1866. The half-timber, two-story dwellings, with unusual twisted chimneys and decorative brick facades, were restored in the 1970s. ■TIP➔ **The house marked "C" is open to the public.** A visit inside gives you a sense of what life was like in these 17th-century dwellings. ⊠*Historic House C, Krayenkamp 10, Speicherstadt* ☎*040/3750–1988* 🖅*€1, Fri. €.50* 🕙*Tues.–Sun. 10–5* Ⓜ*Rödingsmarkt (U-bahn)*.

㉒ Museum für Hamburgische Geschichte *(Museum of Hamburg History)*. ℃ The museum's vast and comprehensive collection of artifacts gives you an excellent overview of Hamburg's development, from its origins in the 9th century to the present. A new exhibit on German emigration to the United States explains Hamburg's role as one of Europe's most important emigration harbors. It has fascinating background information on five million Germans who emigrated via Hamburg between 1850 and 1934. Pictures and models portray the history of the port and shipping between 1650 and 1860. One exhibit chronicles pirates in the North Sea during the late Middle Ages. ⊠*Holstenwall 24, Neustadt* ☎*040/42813–22380* ⊕*www.hamburgmuseum.de* 🖅*€7.50, Fri. €4* 🕙*Tues.–Sat. 10–5, Sun. 10–6* Ⓜ*St. Pauli (U-bahn)*.

⑭ St. Katharinenkirche *(St. Catherine's Church)*. Completed in 1660, this house of worship was severely damaged during World War II, but has since been carefully reconstructed. Only two 17th-century epitaphs (to Moller and to von der Feehte) remain from the original interior. ⊠*Katharinenkirchhof 1, near Speicherstadt, Altstadt* ☎*040/3037–4730* 🕙 *Weekdays 9–5, weekends 10–6* Ⓜ*Messberg (U-bahn)*.

ST. PAULI & THE REEPERBAHN

The run-down maritime district of St. Pauli is sometimes described as a "Babel of sin," but that's not entirely fair. The Reeperbahn, its major thoroughfare as well as a neighborhood moniker, offers a broad menu of entertainment in addition to the striptease and sex shows. Beyond this strip of pleasures, St. Pauli and Altona are defined by their Elbe waterfront.

GETTING HERE & AROUND

The St. Pauli U-bahn station is at the beginning of the long, neon-lighted street that is the red-light Reeperbahn.

TIMING

This tour can last a full day and a long night, including a very enjoyable boat trip through the harbor and a few hours in the theaters and bars along the Reeperbahn. However, you can walk down the red-light strip and check out the Erotic Art Museum and the Landungsbrücken in less than three hours.

■TIP→ **You have to be either a night owl or an early riser to catch the Fischmarkt on Sunday.**

EXPLORING

MAIN ATTRACTIONS

24 Erotic Art Museum. Sexually provocative art from 1520 to the present—1,800 original works (mostly photographs) in all—is showcased here. The collection is presented with such taste and decorum that it has won the respect of many who doubted the museum's seriousness. ✉ *Bernhard-Nocht-Str. 69, St. Pauli* ☎ *040/3178–4126* ⊕ *www.eroticartmuseum.de* ☞ *Minimum age 16* 🎟 *€8* ⊙ *Sun.–Thurs., noon–10, Fri. and Sat. noon–midnight* Ⓜ *St. Pauli (U-bahn).*

25 Fischmarkt *(Fish Market)*. A trip to the open-air Altona Fischmarkt is worth getting out of bed early for—or staying up all night. The pitch of fervent deal making is unmatched in Germany. Offering real bargains, the market's barkers are famous for their sometimes rude but usually successful bids to shoppers. Sunday fish markets became a tradition in the 18th century, when fishermen sold their catch before church services. Today freshly caught fish are only a part of the scene. You can find almost anything here—from live parrots and palm trees to armloads of flowers and bananas, valuable antiques, and fourth-hand junk. ✉ *Between Grosse Elbestr. and St. Pauli Landungsbrücken, St. Pauli* ⊙ *Apr.–Sept., Sun. 5 AM–9:30 AM; Oct.–Mar., Sun., 7–9:30* Ⓜ *Landungsbrücken (U-bahn).*

26 Landungsbrücken *(Piers)*. A visit to the port is not complete without a tour of one of the most modern and efficient harbors in the world. ■TIP→ **There's usually a breeze, so dress accordingly.** Hamburg is Germany's largest seaport, with 33 individual docks and 500 berths lying within its 78 square km (30 square mi). Barge tours of the harbor leave from the main passenger terminal, along with a whole range of ferries and barges heading to other destinations in the North Sea. *Rickmer Rickmers*, an 1896 sailing ship that once traveled as far as the West Indies, is open to visitors and is docked at Pier 1. ✉ *St. Pauli Landungsbrücken 1, St. Pauli* ☎ *040/319–5959* ⊕ *www.rickmer-rickmers.de* 🚢 *Rickmer Rickmers €3* ⊙ *Daily 10–6* Ⓜ *Landungsbrücken (U-bahn).*

TOURING TIPS

Scenic Spot: A great way to experience harbor life while avoiding the often-choppy waters, is to visit St. Pauli Landungsbrücken, where the arriving and departing cruise boats create an atmosphere buzzing with excitement.

Snacks: If you are an early riser stop by the Fischmarkt for a hearty fish snack. If not, St. Pauli Landungsbrücken has many typical Hamburg snack stands. An alternative is a walk up to the Museumshafen Övelgönne, where you will find many small restaurants.

23 Reeperbahn. The hottest spots in
town are concentrated in the St.
Pauli Harbor area on the Reeperbahn thoroughfare and on a little
side street known as the Grosse
Freiheit (Great Liberty—and that's
putting it mildly). In the early '60s
a then obscure band called the Bea-
tles had their first live acts at the
now demolished Star Club. The
striptease shows are expensive and
explicit, but a walk through this
area is an experience in itself and
costs nothing. Saturday night finds
St. Pauli pulsating with people
determined to have a good time.

> **HARBOR TOURS**
>
> A cruise of Germany's gateway to
> the world is a must. The energy
> from the continuous ebb and
> flow of huge cargo vessels and
> container ships, the harbor's pros-
> perity, and its international flavor
> best symbolize the city's spirit.
> The surrounding older parts of
> town, with their narrow cobble-
> stone streets and late-medieval
> warehouses, testify to Hamburg's
> powerful Hanseatic past.

13

■ TIP➜ It's *not* advisable, however, to venture into the darker side streets
alone in the wee hours of the morning.

Although some of the sex clubs are relatively tame, a good many others
are extremely racy. They all get going around 10 PM, and will accommodate you until the early hours. ■ TIP➜ Order your own drinks rather
than letting the hostess do it, and pay for them as soon as they arrive,
double-checking the price list again before handing over the money.

Among the attractions in the St. Pauli area are theaters, clubs, music
pubs, discos, and all kinds of bizarre shops. Ⓜ *St. Pauli (U-bahn)*.

ALSO WORTH SEEING

27 Blankenese. Blankenese is one of Hamburg's surprises—a suburb west
of the city with the character of a quaint 19th-century fishing village.
Some Germans like to compare it to the French and Italian rivieras;
many consider it the most beautiful part of Hamburg. The most picturesque part of town is the steeply graded hillside, where paths and stairs
barely separate closely placed homes. Weekday ferries to Blankenese
leave from Pier 3 every 10 to 15 minutes and involve two transfers.
☉ *Nonstop HADAG ferries depart from Pier 2 for Blankenese late
Mar.–Oct., weekends at 10:30 and 2:30* Ⓜ *Blankenese (S-bahn)*.

28 Port of Dreams: BallinStadt–Auswandererwelt Hamburg *(Hamburg–City of
Emigrants)*. This new museum and family research center tells the fascinating story of German emigration to the United States and elsewhere
and invites visitors to research their own ancestors' migration history.
The museum is located on a peninsula where in the late 19th century
the HAPAG shipping line—named for the HAPAG General Director
of the time, Albert Ballin—began construction of a departure "city"
("Stadt" in German). Completed in 1907, the city served as a holding
and quarantine area for emigrants leaving Europe; 5 million Germans
made their way to the New World from BallinStadt between 1850 and
1934. The museum includes the historic remains of BallinStadt and
provides a thrilling look at living conditions in the holding facility as
it was 100 years ago. A permanent exhibit focuses on the lives of emi-

grants, their decision to leave Germany, their often arduous journeys, and their lives in America. As compelling as the exhibits are, the main draw is the research booths, where you can search the complete passenger lists of all ships that left the harbor. ■ TIP→**Research assistants are available to help locate and track your ancestors.** From St. Pauli, the museum can be reached by U-bahn or boat at Landungsbrücke No. 10. ⊠ *Veddeler Bogen 2, Veddel* ☎ *040/3197–9160* ⊕ *www.ballinstadt.de* 🖾 *€9.80* ⊙ *Daily 10–6* Ⓜ *Veddel (U-bahn).*

㉙ Museumshafen Övelgönne *(Museum Harbor Övelgönne).* The glorious ⏱ days of *Windjammer,* Hamburg's commercial fleet, come alive in this small harbor museum on the Elbe River. Eighteen antique steam and sailing vessels from the late 19th century can be inspected from the pier, or boarded on weekends if a crew is around. Behind the harbor, along the quay, are charming little cottages with tidy gardens. ⊠ *Anleger Neumühlen, Ottensen* ☎ *040/4191–2761* ⊕ *www.museum shafen-oevelgoenne.de* 🖾 *Free* ⊙ *Daily.*

NEED A BREAK?

No Hanseatic Sunday would be complete without a visit to the Strandperle (⊠ *Am Schulberg, Ottensen* ☎ *040/880–1112*), a small but stylish kiosk on the riverbanks near Övelgönne. Join the Hamburg locals and watch the cargo ships pass while downing your beer with lemonade (an *Alsterwasser*) and munching on a bratwurst.

WHERE TO EAT

Hamburg has plenty of chic restaurants to satisfy the fashion-conscious local professionals, as well as the authentic salty taverns typical of a harbor town.

	WHAT IT COSTS IN EUROS				
	¢	$	$$	$$$	$$$$
AT DINNER	under €9	€9–€15	€16–€20	€21–€25	over €25

Restaurant prices are per person for a main course at dinner.

DOWNTOWN & HISTORIC HAMBURG

$$$
Fodor'sChoice
★
✕ **Die Bank.** In an ironic nod to Wall Street, this restored, late-19th-century bank—complete with steel vault doors—is abuzz with businesspeople and the "it" crowd. Award-winning chef Fritz Schilling dishes out lean, quick international cuisine with a touch of the French brasserie, including fresh oysters. Well-cooked fish, salads, and light meat dishes are the staples, and service is friendly. The bar, under high ceilings, is a great place to "invest" some time. ⊠ *Hohe Bleichen 17, Neustadt* ☎ *040/238–0030* ⊟ *AE, V* ⊙ *Closed Sun.* Ⓜ *Gänsemarkt (U-bahn).*

$$$
★
✕ **Fillet of Soul.** The art of fine dining is celebrated in the open show kitchen of this hip yet casual restaurant right next to the modern art

shows of the Deichtorhallen. Chefs Patrick Gebhardt and Florian Pabst prepare straightforward, light German nouvelle cuisine with an emphasis on fresh fish. The minimalist dining room, highlighted only by a bright-red wall, might not be to everyone's liking, but the buzzing atmosphere, artsy clientele, fragrant food, and great personal attention from the waitstaff make this the top choice. ⊠*Deichtorstr. 2, Speicherstadt* ☎*040/7070–5800* ▭*No credit cards* ⊘*Closed Mon.* Ⓜ*Steinstrasse (U-bahn).*

$$–$$$ ✕**Deichgraf.** This small and elegant fish restaurant in the heart of the old harbor warehouse district is a Hamburg classic. It's one of the best places to get traditional dishes such as *Hamburger Pannfisch* (fried pieces of the day's catch prepared in a wine and mustard sauce) at a very reasonable price. The restaurant is in an old merchant house, and historic oil paintings in the dining room depict the hardships of the fishermen of the late 19th century. Reservations are essential on weekends. ⊠*Deichstr. 23, Altstadt* ☎*040/364–208* ▭*AE, MC, V* ⊘*Closed Sun. No lunch Sat.* Ⓜ*Rödingsmarkt (U-bahn).*

$$ ✕**Das Feuerschiff.** This bright-red lightship served in the English Channel before it retired to the city harbor in 1989 and became a landmark restaurant and pub. Fresh and tasty fish dishes are on the menu, as well as traditional seafood entrées from Scandinavia, Poland, and other seafaring nations. ■**TIP**➜ **On Monday local bands jam, and once a month a cabaret show is staged.** ⊠*Vorsetzen, Hamburg City Sporthafen, Speicherstadt* ☎*040/362–553* ▭*AE, DC, MC, V* Ⓜ*Baumwall (U-bahn).*

$–$$ ✕**Parlament.** Set in what was once the Ratsweinkeller, the town hall's traditional pub, this restaurant is an almost ironic tribute to the basement's former occupant. With an eclectic mix of historic and modern styles, Parlament is an intriguing version of a traditional Hamburg restaurant. On the menu are no-nonsense meat and fish meals with a light touch of German nouvelle cuisine. ⊠*Rathausmarkt 1, Altstadt* ☎*040/7038–3399* ▭*AE, DC, MC, V* ⊘*No dinner Sun.* Ⓜ*Rathaus (U-Bahn).*

ST. PAULI & ALTONA

$$$ ✕**Au Quai.** The Au Quai is still the shining star among the row of romantic restaurants nestled on the harbor's waterfront. The terrace, set directly over the water, makes the elegant, stylishly modern space a summer must. Indulge in French-Asian fusion while watching chugging tugboats, container ships, and sightseeing craft. The staff, dressed in blue-and-white-stripe scoop-neck sailor sweaters, adds to the maritime flair, and the menu offers a tasty selection of fish. ⊠*Grosse Elbstr. 145B-D, Altona* ☎*040/3803–7730* ▭*AE, MC* ⊘*Closed Sun. No lunch Sat.* Ⓜ*Königstrasse (S-bahn).*

$$$ ✕**Tafelhaus.** This airy gourmet restaurant has stunning views of the
★ Hamburg harbor from its bay windows and serves some of the best food in town. Award-winning chef Christian Rach creates innovative German cuisine with Italian and French touches; the menu has light "summer" standards (featured throughout the year, though) and a changing set of imaginative dishes, mostly seafood (pike perch, salmon,

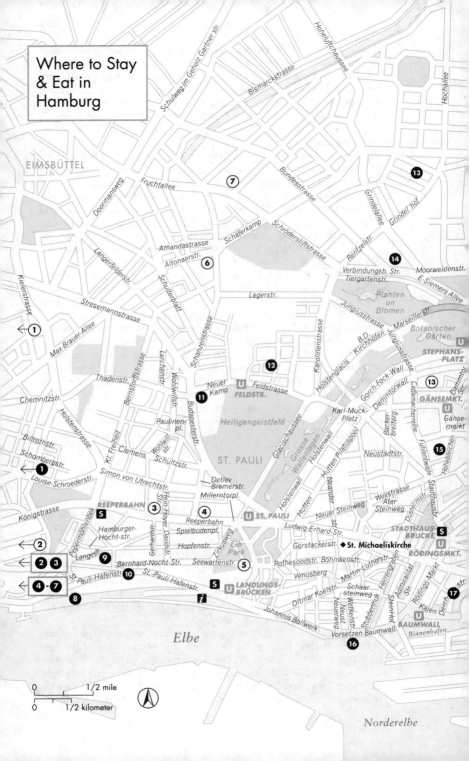

KEY

1 Hotels

1 Restaurants

S S-Bahn

i Tourist information

U U-Bahn

Restaurants ▼

Hotels

oysters) and traditional German meats such as game or pork. ⊠*Neu-mühlen 17, Altona* ☎*040/892–760* ⩠*Reservations essential* ⊟*AE, MC, V* ⊘*Closed Sun. No lunch Sat.* Ⓜ*Altona (U-bahn).*

$$–$$$ ✕ **Fischereihafen-Restaurant Hamburg.** For the best fish in Hamburg, book a table at this sprawling restaurant in Altona, just west of the downtown area. The menu changes daily according to what's available in the fish market that morning. The restaurant and its oyster bar are a favorite with the city's beau monde. ■TIP→ **In summer, try to get a table on the sun terrace for a great view of the Elbe.** ⊠*Grosse Elbstr. 143, Altona* ☎*040/381–816* ⩠*Reservations essential* ⊟*AE, DC, MC, V* Ⓜ*Altona (S-bahn).*

$$–$$$ ✕ **Fischerhaus.** The family-owned fish restaurant may look mediocre, but the food, prepared from family recipes, is outstanding. Most dishes focus on North Sea fish and Hamburg classics such as *Labskaus* (a traditional stew made with pickled meat and potatoes). A favorite is the *Scholle Finkenwerder Art* (panfried flounder with smoked ham and potato salad). When making a reservation, ask for a table upstairs to get a harbor view. ⊠*Fischmarkt 14, St. Pauli* ☎*040/314–053* ⊟*MC, V* Ⓜ*Landungsbrücken (U-Bahn).*

$$–$$$ ✕ **Nil.** Media types—the intellectual and cultural elite of Hamburg—gather at this trendy venue for business dinners and pre-partying on weekends. The Nil is worth a visit for its interior alone: it's in an old 1950s-style, three-floor shoe shop. The kitchen serves seafood and modern German cuisine, including four different three- to six-course menus, offering fare such as *Entenkeule Hamburger Art* (roasted duck joint in spicy sauce) in winter and lighter, Italian-oriented fare in summer. ⊠*Neuer Pferdemarkt 5, St. Pauli* ☎*040/439–7823* ⩠*Reservations essential* ⊟*No credit cards* ⊘*Closed Tues. No lunch* Ⓜ*Feldstrasse (U-bahn).*

$$ ✕ **Rive.** This harborside oyster bar is known for both its German nouvelle cuisine and its classic local dishes. Choose between such dishes as hearty *Matjes mit drei Saucen* (herring with three sauces) or *Dorade in der Salzkruste* (dorado fried in salt crust). Media types come to this shiplike building for the fresh oysters, clams, and spectacular view. ⊠*Van der Smissen Str. 1, Kreuzfahrt-Center, Altona* ☎*040/380–5919* ⩠*Reservations essential* ⊟*AE* Ⓜ*Königstrasse (S-bahn).*

$–$$ ✕ **Abendmahl.** Off the Reeperbahn, the small Abendmahl is a launching point for crowds getting ready for bars and clubs. The fresh dishes on the small menu change daily and focus on French and Italian recipes. But the food plays second fiddle to the inexpensive and inventive drinks and the flirtatious atmosphere. ■TIP→ **The three-course dinner for just €26 is a great deal.** ⊠*Hein-Köllisch-Pl. 6, St. Pauli* ☎*040/312–758* ⊟*No credit cards* ⊘*No lunch* Ⓜ*St. Pauli (U-bahn).*

$–$$ ✕ **River-Kasematten.** There is no other restaurant in town that better
★ embodies Hamburg's international spirit and its lust for style, entertainment, and good seafood. Once a legendary jazz club with performances by Ella Fitzgerald and the like, it now hosts a fascinating mix of hip guests. Sushi, spiced-up regional fish dishes, and exotic soups are the order of the day. The lunch buffet (weekdays noon–3) for just €9.90 is a steal; it's even better on the outside terrace. Nighthawks love

the late-night menu (midnight–4 AM). The ambience—black oak floors, leather seats, and redbrick walls—is elegant yet casual. ✉*Fischmarkt 28–32, St. Pauli* ☎*040/892–760* ♨*Reservations essential* 🖃*AE, DC, MC, V* Ⓜ*Reeperbahn or Landungsbrücken (U-bahn).*

$ ✗**Mess.** This is one of the most popular restaurants in the hip and
Fodor'sChoice upcoming Karolinenviertel (called "Karo-Viertel" by Hamburgers).
★ True to its worldly, young patrons, it dares to offer a wild mixture of old German standards like *Königsberger Klopse* (meatballs in a thick butter-and-caper sauce served with potatoes) along with more exotic fare such as ostrich steak. For lunch, order the three-course menu (€19) or the daily pasta special for just €6. ■TIP→ **In summer, try to get a table in the small garden under the pergola and sample vintages from the restaurant's own specialty wine store.** ✉*Turnerstr. 9, St. Pauli* ☎*040/4325– 0152* 🖃*AE* ⊘*No lunch weekends* Ⓜ*Messehallen (U-bahn).*

ST. GEORG

$$–$$$ ✗**Golden Cut.** This restaurant with its own bar and dance club has
★ become a favorite with the twentysomething crowd that enjoys spending an evening in one hip location. Join them in the funky, retro dining room for fine sushi or fresh Asian-influenced fusion food such as duck on pointed cabbage or coconut soup with tiger prawns. Later, sip cocktails at the tiny bar and dance the night away. ✉*Holzdamm 61, St. Georg* ☎*040/8510–3532* 🖃*AE, MC, V* ⊘*Closed Sun. and Mon.* Ⓜ*Hauptbahnhof (U-bahn and S-Bahn).*

$$ ✗**Cox.** The Cox has been a reliably stylish restaurant for several years. It remains one of the hippest places around, with waitstaff (and patrons, for that matter) who won't give you any attitude. The dishes, mostly German nouvelle cuisine, are known for the careful use of fresh produce and spices from around the globe. The simple and cool interior with red-leather banquettes is reminiscent of a French brasserie. ✉*Lange Reihe 68, at Greifswalder Str. 43, St. Georg* ☎*040/249–422* 🖃*AE* ⊘*No lunch* Ⓜ*Hauptbahnhof (U-bahn and S-Bahn).*

ROTHERBAUM

$$$ ✗**Insel am Alsterufer.** Known for its understated elegance, this complex of
★ two restaurants and a dance club is set in a waterfront villa dating from the Gilded Age. To its hip patrons it's as important for its food as for its status as a place to see and been seen. Serving seafood with a local touch, prepared by award-winning chef Harald Paulus, the second-floor restaurant has great views of the city skyline. The smaller restaurant on the first floor offers lighter (and less expensive) versions of the same food. A bar, a cozy lounge with an open fireplace, and a dance club invite you to party through the night. ✉*Alsterufer 35, Rotherbaum* ☎*040/450– 1850* ♨*Reservations essential* 🖃*AE, DC, MC, V* ⊘*Closed Sun. No lunch Sat.* Ⓜ*Dammtor (U-bahn and S-bahn).*

$ ✗**Balutschi.** A favorite among neighborhood students, Balutschi serves affordable and tasty Pakistani dishes, all prepared with organic products. The richly decorated dining room always seems to be crowded,

EATING WELL IN HAMBURG

Hamburg is undoubtedly one of the best places in the country to enjoy fresh seafood. The flotilla of fishing boats brings a wide variety of fish to the city—to sophisticated upscale restaurants as well as simple harborside taverns. One of the most celebrated dishes among the robust local specialties is *Aalsuppe* (eel soup), a tangy concoction not entirely unlike Marseilles's famous bouillabaisse. A must in summer is *Aalsuppe grün* (eel soup seasoned with dozens of herbs); *Räucheraal* (smoked eel) is equally good. In the fall, try *Bunte oder Gepflückte Finten,* a dish of green and white beans, carrots, and

apples. Available any time of year is *Küken* ragout, a concoction of sweetbreads, spring chicken, tiny veal meatballs, asparagus, clams, and fresh peas cooked in a white sauce. Other northern German specialties include *Stubenküken* (young, male oven-fried chicken); *Vierländer Mastente* (duck stuffed with apples, onions, and raisins); *Birnen, Bohnen, und Speck* (pears, beans, and bacon); and the sailors' favorite, *Labskaus*—a stew made from pickled meat, potatoes, and (sometimes) herring, garnished with a fried egg, sour pickles, and lots of beets.

and the smell of fresh spices and meat dishes, mostly lamb, hangs thick in the air. ■TIP➡ **On weekend nights a reservation is a must.** ✉*Grindelallee 31, Rotherbaum* ☎*040/452–479* ▭*AE, DC, MC, V* Ⓜ*Dammtor (S-bahn).*

OTTENSEN, UHLENHORST & ELSEWHERE

$$$$ ✕**Landhaus Scherrer.** Though this establishment is a 10-minute drive

Fodor'sChoice from downtown, its parklike setting seems worlds away from the high-

★ rise hustle and bustle of the city. Wood-panel walls and soft lighting create a low-key mood in the building, which was originally a brewery. The food fuses sophisticated specialties with more down-to-earth local dishes. The wine list is exceptional. If the restaurant looks too highbrow to you, stick to the small bistro, where you get the same fare at lower prices. ✉*Elbchaussee 130, Ottensen* ☎*040/880–1325* ▭*AE, DC, MC, V* ⊘*Closed Sun.* Ⓜ*Altona (S-bahn).*

$$$$ ✕**Poletto.** Cornelia Poletto is one of Germany's few female chefs to

★ garner a Michelin star. Ranked among the country's best restaurants, Poletto offers straightforward but top-quality Italian cooking. Dishes are prepared without the somewhat affected creativity of other award-winning restaurants but are just as—if not more—tasty. A family-style approach (Mr. Poletto will personally explain the food and wine menus to guests placed around huge round tables) makes the little restaurant even more inviting. ✉*Eppendorfer Landstr. 145, Eppendorf* ☎*040/480–2159* ▭*No credit cards* ⊘*Closed Sun. and Mon. No lunch Sat.* Ⓜ*Lattenkamp (U-bahn).*

$$$$ ✕**Seven Seas.** Süllberg, a small hill in the countryside along the River Elbe, boasts one of northern Germany's most traditional "getaway restaurants." (It also has one of the greatest views of the river you'll find anywhere.) The Seven Seas is run by one of Europe's premier chefs,

Karl-Heinz Hauser, and features international fish specialties served in four- to six-course dinners. ■TIP→ **If you don't want all the frills, try the Bistro dining room.** ⊠*Süllbergsterrasse 12, Blankenese* ☎*040/866– 2520* ▤*AE, MC, V* ⊗*Closed Mon. and Tues. No lunch Wed.–Sat.* Ⓜ*Blankenese (S-bahn).*

$–$$ ✕**Eisenstein.** A longtime neighborhood favorite, Eisenstein serves fantastic food at affordable prices. The bubbly and mostly stylish crowd enjoys the Italian and Mediterranean dishes. The Pizza Helsinki (made with sour cream, onions, and fresh gravlax) is truly delicious. The setting, a 19th-century industrial complex with high ceilings and dark brick walls, is very rustic. ⊠*Friedensallee 9, Ottensen* ☎*040/390– 4606* ♨*Reservations essential* ▤*No credit cards* Ⓜ*Altona (S-bahn).*

$–$$ ✕**Phuket.** Though it has an unimaginative name and dull facade, Phuket ★ is by far the best Thai, or Asian for that matter, restaurant in town. The place is often jammed with locals who come to sample the truly hot fish dishes or the famous chicken in red-wine sauce. ⊠*Adolph-Schönfelder-Str. 33–35, Uhlenhorst* ☎*040/2982–3380* ▤*AE, V* Ⓜ*Hamburger Strasse (U-bahn).*

$–$$ ✕**Shalimar.** The spices and exotic fare the locals have come to know at ★ Freihafen Hamburg are commonplace at Shalimar, *the* Indian restaurant, which has been dazzling Hamburg since 1982. Its refined atmosphere, compliments of the gentle sitar sounds and swift, silent waiters, beguiles its guests as much as its prices. Neither, however, can hold a candle to the food itself. A mixed crowd of students, hipsters, bankers, and Indian businessmen makes for an exciting evening. And be sure to try the mango ice cream—no meal is complete without it. ⊠*ABC-Strasse 46–47, Harvestehude* ☎*040/442–484* ▤*AE, DC, MC, V* ⊗*No lunch* Ⓜ*Hallerstrasse (U-bahn).*

$ ✕**Genno's.** Genno's is far from the downtown district, in Hamburg- ★ Hamm—a run-down residential area where you would hardly expect to find such a gem of high-quality dining. Owner Eugen Albrecht makes you feel at home with warm service and tasty dishes. The cuisine is a mixture of his personal preferences, including dishes such as *Lammfilet mit Senfsauce* (fillet of lamb with mustard sauce). ⊠*Hammer Steindamm 123, Hamm* ☎*040/202–567* ▤*No credit cards* ⊗*Closed Sun. No lunch* Ⓜ*Hasselbrook (S-bahn).*

WHERE TO STAY

Hamburg has a full range of hotels, from five-star, grande-dame luxury enterprises to simple pensions. Nearly year-round conference and convention business keeps most rooms booked well in advance, and the rates are high. But many of the more expensive hotels lower their rates on weekends, when businesspeople have gone home. The tourist office can help with reservations if you arrive with nowhere to stay; ask about the many Happy Hamburg special-accommodation packages.

WHAT IT COSTS IN EUROS				
	¢	$	$$	$$$	$$$$
FOR TWO PEOPLE	under €50	€50–€100	€101–€175	€176–€225	over €225

Hotel prices are for two people in a standard double room, including tax and service.

DOWNTOWN & HISTORIC HAMBURG

$$$$
★
Park Hyatt Hamburg. This elegant hotel, one of the best in northern Germany, is filled with warm, brown colors and furnished with exquisite wooden floors and panels. It sits within the historic walls of the Levantehaus, an old warehouse not far from the train station. Guest rooms have bright and modern furnishings, somewhat minimalist in style. Original artwork by local painters adorns the suites. The Club Olympus pool and fitness area is breathtaking, both for its streamlined design and the variety of activities. The professional, friendly service is outstanding, and the breakfast buffet is undoubtedly the city's tastiest. ■TIP→ **The hotel's back faces busy Mönckebergstrasse, making this the most centrally located five-star property in town—yet it is surprisingly quiet. Pros:** close to shopping on Mönckebergstrasse and Jungfernstieg, maritime, warm interior design, large, quiet rooms with all modern amenities. **Cons:** no outstanding restaurant, formal service, far away from nightlife hot spots. ⊠*Bugenhagenstr. 8, Neustadt* ☎*040/3332–1234* ⊕*www.hamburg.park.hyatt.com* ⇝*252 rooms, 30 apartments* ♿*In-room: refrigerator, Ethernet, dial-up, Wi-Fi. In-hotel: restaurant, room service, bar, pool, gym, concierge, laundry service, public Wi-Fi, parking (fee), no-smoking rooms* ⊟*AE, DC, MC, V* ⫶⊙⫶*BP* Ⓜ*Steinstrasse (U-bahn).*

$$$$
Fodor'sChoice
★
Fairmont Vier Jahreszeiten. Some claim that this 19th-century town house on the edge of the Binnenalster is the best hotel in Germany. Antiques—the hotel has a set of near-priceless Gobelin tapestries—fill the public rooms and accentuate the stylish bedrooms; fresh flowers overflow from massive vases; rare oil paintings adorn the walls; and all rooms are individually decorated with superb taste. ■TIP→ **One of the three restaurants, the Jahreszeiten-Grill, has been restored to its 1920s art deco look with dark woods, making it worth a visit. Pros:** luxury hotel with great view of Alster lakes, close to shopping on Jungfernstieg, charming, large rooms. **Cons:** formal service, high prices even in off-season, far away from nightlife and new city quarters like Schanzen- and Katharinenviertel. ⊠*Neuer Jungfernstieg 9–14, Neustadt* ☎*040/34940* ⊕*www.hvj.de* ⇝*156 rooms, 32 suites* ♿*In-room: safe, refrigerator, Ethernet, dial-up, Wi-Fi. In-hotel: 3 restaurants, room service, bar, gym, concierge, laundry service, public Wi-Fi, parking (fee), no-smoking rooms* ⊟*AE, DC, MC, V* Ⓜ*Jungfernstieg (U-bahn).*

$$$–$$$$
Sofitel Hamburg Alte Wall. This business hotel is one of the city's finest. Behind the facade of Hamburg's 19th-century Postsparkassenamt, the German mail service's customer bank, is a sleek decor dominated by gray, white, and dark-brown hues. All rooms are furnished with time-

lessly stylish furniture, huge beds (by German standards), and even bigger marble bathrooms. **Pros:** centrally located in the historic downtown area, close to upscale shopping, large rooms. **Cons:** modern, somewhat bland design, no real nightlife within walking distance, mostly business travelers. ⊠*Alter Wall 40, Altstadt* ☎*040/369–500* ⊕*www.sofitel. com* ➽*241 rooms, 16 suites* ⟐*In-room: safe, Ethernet, Wi-Fi. In-hotel: restaurant, room service, bar, pool, gym, laundry service, public Wi-Fi, parking (fee), no-smoking rooms, some pets allowed* ⊟*AE, DC, MC, V* ⊺◎⊺*BP* Ⓜ*Rödingsmarkt (U-bahn).*

13

$$ ⊡**Baseler Hof.** It's hard to find a fault in this central hotel near the Binnenalster and the opera house. The service is friendly and efficient, the rooms are neatly furnished, and the prices are quite reasonable for this expensive city. The hotel caters to both individuals and convention groups, so the lounge area can be crowded at times. **Pros:** quiet location near Binnenalster, upscale rooms and service for moderate prices, residential neighborhood. **Cons:** removed from downtown attractions, some rooms with faded elegance, worn furniture. ⊠*Esplanade 11, Neustadt* ☎*040/359–060* ⊕*www.baselerhof.de* ➽*163 rooms, 4 suites* ⟐*In-room: no a/c, Wi-Fi. In-hotel: restaurant, room service, bar, concierge, laundry service, public Wi-Fi, parking (fee), no-smoking rooms* ⊟*AE, DC, MC, V* ⊺◎⊺*CP* Ⓜ*Stephansplatz (U-bahn).*

$$ ⊡**Side.** Deeming itself to be "the luxury hotel of the 21st century," this
★ ultrahip hotel is one of the most architecturally sophisticated places to stay in Germany. Premier Milanese designer Matteo Thun served as the driving force behind the five-star resort in the heart of the city. His vision provided for the stunning lighting arrangement as well as the interior design. Whether soothed by the eggshell-white accents in your room or wowed by the lobby's soaring and stark atrium, you won't ever want to leave. **Pros:** very clean and well-kept hotel, convenient downtown location yet quiet. **Cons:** somewhat sterile, many business travelers, small rooms. ⊠*Drehbahn 49, Altstadt* ☎*040/309–990* ⊕*www. side-hamburg.de* ➽*178 rooms, 10 suites* ⟐*In-room: safe, refrigerator, Ethernet, Wi-Fi. In-hotel: restaurant, room service, bar, gym, spa, laundry service, public Wi-Fi, parking (fee), no-smoking rooms, some pets allowed* ⊟*AE, DC, MC, V* Ⓜ*Gänsemarkt (U-bahn).*

$–$$ ⊡**Hotel Fürst Birmarck Residenz.** Despite its humble location on a busy street opposite the railway station, the Bismarck is a surprisingly attractive hotel, with a homey yet modern flair. Spread throughout two buildings just steps apart, the guest rooms are individually styled, and are comfortable but not overly elegant. **Pros:** centrally located, competitive prices, good and inexpensive breakfast buffet. **Cons:** railway station neighborhood not very appealing, worn and small rooms, cleaning service sometimes spotty. ⊠*Kirchenallee 49, Altstadt* ☎*040/280–1091* ⊜*040/280–1097* ➽*174 rooms* ⟐*In-room: no a/c. In-hotel: no-smoking rooms, some pets allowed* ⊟*AE, DC, MC, V* ⊺◎⊺*CP* Ⓜ*Hauptbahnhof (U-bahn and S-bahn).*

$ ⊡**Hotel Terminus am Hauptbahnhof.** Unlike its famous namesake in Paris, the Hamburg Hotel Terminus is a simple and inexpensive hotel near the central train station. It's popular among British and American budget travelers who appreciate its relaxed atmosphere and reliable service. **Pros:** unbeatable location at Hauptbahnhof, relaxed atmosphere, many affordable eateries nearby. **Cons:** neighborhood unappealing, no hotel restaurant, limited breakfast choices. ✉ *Steindamm 5, Altstadt* ☎ *040/280–3144* ⊕ *www.hotel-terminus-hamburg.de* ⇌ *20 rooms, 1 apartment* ♿ *In-room: no a/c, Wi-Fi* ⊟ *AE, DC, MC, V* ⦿ *CP* Ⓜ *Hauptbahnhof-Süd (U-bahn and S-bahn).*

$ 🏨 **Hotel Village.** Once a thriving brothel nearby the central train sta-
★ tion, this hotel still exudes the hot breath of lasciviousness. Red-and-black carpets and glossy wallpaper in the rooms are a nod to the hotel's past; some rooms even have their old large beds, replete with canopy and revolving mirror. **Pros:** in the heart of downtown, cozy, individually designed rooms, affordable eateries nearby. **Cons:** sometimes casual service, seedy neighborhood not suited for families, some rooms are worn. ✉ *Steindamm 4, Altstadt* ☎ *040/480–6490* ⊕ *www.hotel-village.de* ⇌ *20 rooms* ♿ *In-room: no a/c, Wi-Fi. In-hotel: no elevator, parking (fee), some pets allowed* ⊟ *AE, MC, V* ⦿ *CP* Ⓜ *Hauptbahnhof (U-bahn and S-bahn).*

ST. PAULI & ALTONA

$$ 🏨 **Gastwerk Hotel Hamburg.** Proudly dubbing itself Hamburg's first design hotel, the Gastwerk, in a century-old gas plant, is certainly the most stylish accommodation in town. The simple but incredibly chic furnishings reflect the building's industrial design, but are warmed by the use of natural materials, various woods, and thick carpets. ■ **TIP→** **The loft rooms with large windows, bare walls, and a lot of space are the most exciting accommodations in Hamburg.** **Pros:** large rooms, stunning interior design, large and well-equipped health club. **Cons:** far away from downtown area and any sightseeing, few restaurants nearby, public spaces like breakfast room and bar can get crowded. ✉ *Beim alten Gaswerk 3, at Daimlerstr. 67, Altona* ☎ *040/890–620* ⊕ *www.gastwerk.com* ⇌ *128 rooms, 13 suites* ♿ *In-room: safe, Wi-Fi. In-hotel: restaurant, room service, bar, gym, laundry service, public Wi-Fi, parking (no fee), no-smoking rooms, some pets allowed* ⊟ *AE, DC, MC, V* Ⓜ *Bahrenfeld (S-bahn).*

$$ 🏨 **Hotel Hafen Hamburg.** This harbor landmark, just across from the famous St. Pauli Landungsbrücken, is a good value considering its three-star status. The main part of the hotel has small but nicely reno-vated rooms, while the modern tower annex offers a great view of the harbor. The location makes this hotel a perfect starting point for exploring St. Pauli and the Reeperbahn. **Pros:** top location for harbor and St. Pauli sightseeing, great views, comfortable, fairly large rooms. **Cons:** Altstadt downtown area is far away, no bathroom amenities, poor restaurant selection in neighborhood. ✉ *Seewartenstr. 7–9, St. Pauli* ☎ *040/311–13* ⊕ *www.hotel-hamburg.de* ⇌ *353 rooms* ♿ *In-room: no a/c (some), safe, refrigerator, Wi-Fi. In-hotel: restaurant, bars, laundry service, public Wi-Fi, parking (fee), no-smoking rooms, some pets allowed* ⊟ *AE, MC, V* Ⓜ *Landungsbrücken (U-bahn).*

$ 🏨 **Fritzhotel.** This intimate yet stylish hotel, squeezed into an old city apartment complex, has small but bright designer rooms complete with such amenities as wireless Internet access. The hotel does not offer breakfast, but it shares the relatively quiet street with many bistros and breakfast cafés. **Pros:** very clean rooms at budget prices, both S- and U-bahn nearby, free newspapers, fruits and juices for guests. **Cons:** noisy due to close S-bahn tracks, away from Altstadt and major Hamburg sights, only very limited facilities. ⊠*Schanzenstr. 101–103, St. Pauli* ☏*040/8222–2830* ⊕*www.fritzhotel.com* ⇆*17 rooms* &*In-room: no a/c, refrigerator, Wi-Fi. In-hotel: no elevator, public Wi-Fi* ▤*AE, MC, V* Ⓜ*Sternschanze (U-bahn).*

13

$ 🏨**Hotel Monopol.** This is the only hotel where budget travelers can enjoy a safe and clean stay in the heart of Europe's most bizarre red-light district. The small rooms are mostly old-fashioned, and some look like an odd mixture of 1950s and 1980s designs, but the service is warm and friendly. You might run into an artist performing in a Hamburg musical—or in the live sex shows on Reeperbahn. **Pros:** right in the heart of the Reeperbahn action, U-bahn stations nearby, wide selection of affordable restaurants and pub in walking-distance. **Cons:** in the heart of the Reeperbahn, no a/c, rooms can be stuffy in summer, funky 70s design not to everybody's liking, far away from traditional sightseeing. ⊠*Reeperbahn 48–52, St. Pauli* ☏*040/311–770* ⊕*www.monopol-hamburg.de* ⇆*82 rooms* &*In-room: no a/c, dial-up. In-hotel: restaurant, room service, bar, laundry service, public Wi-Fi, parking (fee), some pets allowed* ▤*AE, MC, V* ⦿*BP* Ⓜ*St. Pauli (U-bahn).*

¢ 🏨**Hotel Stern.** One of the best deals in town, the huge Hotel Stern is in the heart of St. Pauli and primarily attracts students and young backpacker tourists from around the world. The modern rooms are sparsely furnished but well kept. ■TIP➡ **A great plus are the Stern's many partner restaurants, where you can wine and dine for just a few euros.** **Pros:** perfect, central location for exploring Reeperbahn, great variety of affordable eateries nearby, relaxed, young clientele. **Cons:** very simple rooms, sometimes worn furnishings, noisy neighborhood, only basic breakfast serv. ice ⊠*Reeperbahn 154, St. Pauli* ☏*040/3176–9990* ⊕*www.stern-hamburg.de* ⇆*308 rooms* &*In-room: no a/c, dial-up. In-hotel: restaurant, no elevator, parking (fee), some pets allowed* ▤*AE, DC, MC, V* ⦿*BP* Ⓜ*St. Pauli (U-bahn).*

ST. GEORG

$$$$ 🏨**Kempinski Atlantic Hotel Hamburg.** There are few hotels in Germany
★ more sumptuous than this gracious Edwardian palace facing the Aussenalster. The stylish mood is achieved with thick carpets, marble-inlaid floors and walls, sophisticated lighting, and a lobby that is positively grand. Some rooms are traditionally furnished, while others are more modern, but all are typical of Hamburg in their understated luxury. Each room has a spacious sitting area and large bathroom. Guests can lounge in the formal outdoor courtyard, where only the gurgling fountain disturbs the peace. **Pros:** large rooms, great views of lakeside skyline, impeccable service, historic flair. **Cons:** formal service and dress code, some rooms have faded furnishings, few amenities in rooms. ⊠*An der Alster 72–79, St. Georg* ☏*040/28880* ⊕*www.*

kempinski.atlantic.de ⮐*167 rooms, 16 suites* ⚲*In-room: safe, refrigerator, dial-up, Wi-Fi. In-hotel: 2 restaurants, room service, bar, pool, gym, bicycles, concierge, laundry service, public Wi-Fi, parking (fee), no-smoking rooms, some pets allowed* ▭*AE, DC, MC, V* Ⓜ*Hauptbahnhof (U-bahn and S-bahn).*

$$$$ Ⓣ**Le Royal Méridien Hamburg.** This high-tech hostelry, one of the city's
Fodor's Choice over-the-top luxury accommodations, offers grand views of the Alster
★ Lakes. The sleek but unassuming facade and ultramodern interior (with big plasma TVs in every room) might exude a rather cold feel, but the outstanding spa and wellness area (complete with an indoor lap pool) and the impeccable service make guests feel comfortably at ease. ■**TIP**➡ **Don't miss a light French lunch or dinner in the rooftop restaurant Le Ciel: the view of the Alster and the illuminated skyline at night is unforgettable. Pros:** great location with views of the Alster, clean and smartly designed, large rooms, outstanding fitness area. **Cons:** minimalist interior design is very special, public areas can be crowded, high prices even in the off-season. ✉*An der Alster 52–56, St. Georg* ☎*040/21000* ⊕*www.hamburg.lemeridien.de* ⮐*265 rooms, 19 suites* ⚲*In-room: safe, refrigerator, Ethernet, dial-up. In-hotel: restaurant, room service, bars, gym, concierge, laundry service, public Wi-Fi, parking (fee), no-smoking rooms* ▭*AE, DC, MC, V* Ⓜ*Hauptbahnhof (U-bahn and S-bahn).*

$$ Ⓣ**Aussen Alster.** Crisp and contemporary in design, this boutique hotel prides itself on the personal attention it gives its guests. Rooms are compact, with stark white walls and pale carpets that create a bright, fresh ambience. A small bar is open in the evening, and there's a tiny garden for summer cocktails. The restaurant serves Italian fare for lunch and dinner. The Aussenalster, where the hotel keeps a sailboat for guests to use, is at the end of the street. **Pros:** nice little garden, personal, warm service, great location close to downtown sightseeing. **Cons:** good but not outstanding restaurant, somewhat outdated room design, small hotel with limited services. ✉*Schmilinskystr. 11, St. Georg* ☎*040/241–557* ⊕*www.aussenalster.eu* ⮐*27 rooms* ⚲*In-room: no a/c, safe, Wi-Fi. In-hotel: restaurant, room service, bar, bicycles, laundry service, public Wi-Fi, parking (fee), some pets allowed* ▭*AE, DC, MC, V* ⦿*BP* Ⓜ*Hauptbahnhof (U-bahn and S-bahn).*

$$ Ⓣ**Wedina.** Rooms at this small hotel are neat and compact. When you make a reservation, ask for a room in the Italian-style Yellow House or in the minimalist-style Green House. In the main building, the bar and breakfast area face the veranda and a small garden and pool that bring Tuscany to mind. ■**TIP**➡ **All lodgings are a half-block from the Aussenalster and a brisk 10-minute walk from the train station. Pros:** cozy flair and comfortable, quiet rooms, very accommodating, knowledgeable staff, inviting apartments. **Cons:** hotel spread over several buildings, smallish rooms, few restaurants nearby. ✉*Gurlittstr. 23, St. Georg* ☎*040/280–8900* ⊕*www.wedina.de* ⮐*48 rooms, 11 apartments* ⚲*In-room: no a/c, safe, Ethernet, dial-up. In-hotel: bar, bicycles, no elevator, concierge, parking (fee), no-smoking rooms, some pets allowed* ▭*DC, MC, V* ⦿*CP* Ⓜ*Hauptbahnhof (U-bahn and S-bahn).*

$ ⊞**Steen's Hotel.** This small, family-run hotel in a narrow, four-story town house near the central train station provides modest but congenial service. The rooms are spacious and clean but lack atmosphere. Bathrooms are tiny. A great plus are the comfortable beds with reclining head and foot rests. The breakfasts amply make up for the uninspired rooms, and the hotel's garage is a blessing, since there's never a parking space in this neighborhood. **Pros:** highly competitive prices, good breakfast, friendly service. **Cons:** some rooms are worn, few amenities and hotel services, limited restaurant selection nearby. ⊠*Holzdamm 43, St. Georg* ☎*040/244–642* ⊕*www.steens-hotel.com* ⊋*11 rooms* ⌂*In-room: no a/c, refrigerator, Wi-Fi. In-hotel: no elevator, public Wi-Fi, parking (fee)* ▤*AE, DC, MC, V* ⌾|*CP* Ⓜ*Hauptbahnhof (U-bahn and S-bahn).*

13

ELSEWHERE

$$$$ ⊞**Hotel Louis C. Jacob.** Would-be Hanseats frequent this small yet luxurious hotel nestled amid the older wharf dwellings along the banks of
Fodor'sChoice the Elbe. Far from the hustle and bustle of the city, the intimate Louis
★ C. Jacob, named after the French landscape gardener who founded it in 1791, makes a point of meticulously pampering its guests. Artist Max Liebermann stayed here and painted the terrace with its linden trees. One of the classically furnished suites even bears his name. From a river-view room you'll be able to watch passing ships and listen as their foghorns bid Hamburg farewell. **Pros:** outstanding service with attention to personal requests, quiet, serene setting in the city's wealthiest neighborhood, with historic flair, extremely comfortable beds. **Cons:** rooms are surprisingly simple for luxury hotel, away from downtown area and most nightlife, restaurants, and shopping, extra charges for some services. ⊠*Elbchaussee 401–403, Blankenese* ☎*040/822–550* ⊕*www.hotel-jacob.de* ⊋*66 rooms, 19 suites* ⌂*In-room: safe, refrigerator, dial-up, Wi-Fi. In-hotel: 2 restaurants, room service, bar, laundry service, public Wi-Fi, parking (fee), no-smoking rooms, some pets allowed* ▤*AE, DC, MC, V* Ⓜ*Hochkamp (S-bahn).*

$$$–$$$$ ⊞**Hotel Abtei.** On a quiet, tree-lined street about 2 km (1 mi) north of the downtown area, in Harvestehude, this elegant period hotel offers understated luxury and friendly, personal service. If you want a room with a four-poster bed, ask when making a reservation. One of the nicest rooms in the small hotel is No. 7, with its antique 19th-century washing tables. All guest rooms have English antique cherrywood and mahogany furniture. **Pros:** great historic flair, individually designed, upscale rooms, quiet location. **Cons:** very small and personal, away from many major sightseeing spots, very limited restaurant selection nearby. ⊠*Abteistr. 14, Harvestehude* ☎*040/442–905* ⊕*www.abtei-hotel.de* ⊋*6 rooms, 4 suites* ⌂*In-room: no a/c, safe, refrigerator. In-hotel: restaurant, room service, no elevator, laundry service, public Wi-Fi, parking (no fee), some pets allowed* ▤*AE, MC, V* ⌾|*BP* Ⓜ*Klosterstern (U-bahn).*

$$ ⊞**Garden Hotels Hamburg.** The location in posh Pöseldorf, 2 km (1 mi) from the downtown area, may discourage those who want to be

in the thick of things, but this is one of the most appealing hotels in Hamburg, offering outstanding personal service and inviting accommodations in three attractive mansions. **Pros:** very friendly service, inviting, cozy flair, limited but top-quality German breakfast. **Cons:** simple, sometimes outdated rooms, away from many major sights, limited restaurant selection in immediate neighborhood. ⊠ *Magdalenenstr. 60, Pöseldorf* ☎ *040/414–040* ⊕ *www.garden-hotels.de* ⟲ *57 rooms, 3 suites* ⚷ *In-room: no a/c, Wi-Fi. In-hotel: room service, bar, concierge, laundry service, public Wi-Fi, parking (no fee), some pets allowed* ☐ *AE, MC, V* Ⓜ *Hallerstr. (U-bahn).*

$$ 🖭 **Hotel-Garni Mittelweg.** With chintz curtains, flowered wallpaper, old-fashioned dressing tables, and a country-house-style breakfast room, this hotel exudes small-town charm in big-business Hamburg. The converted mansion is in upmarket Pöseldorf, a short walk from the Aussenalster and a quick bus ride from the city center. **Pros:** great location in quiet yet posh neighborhood, good designer shopping nearby, homey atmosphere. **Cons:** away from all major sightseeing, limited restaurant selection, outdated decor in some rooms. ⊠ *Mittelweg 59, Pöseldorf* ☎ *040/414–1010* ⊕ *www.hotel-mittelweg.de* ⟲ *30 rooms, 1 apartment* ⚷ *In-room: no a/c, safe, refrigerator, Ethernet, Wi-Fi. In-hotel: room service, no elevator, public Wi-Fi, parking (fee), no-smoking rooms, some pets allowed* ☐ *AE, DC, MC, V* ⦿ *CP* Ⓜ *Klosterstern (U-bahn).*

$$ 🖭 **Mellingburger Schleuse.** If you prefer off-the-beaten-track lodgings, this member of the Ringhotel-Association is a 20-minute drive from the downtown area, idyllically set in a forest. The Alsterwanderweg hiking trail passes right by the doorstep. The very quiet lodging is more than 200 years old, with a thatch roof, peasant-style furnishings, and a restaurant that serves traditional northern German dishes. **Pros:** set in a green, natural environment, quiet rooms, solid regional cuisine in restaurant. **Cons:** far from downtown and sightseeing, simply furnished rooms, solid but not outstanding breakfast. ⊠ *Mellingburgredder 1, Sasel* ☎ *040/6113–9150* ⊕ *www.mellingburger-schleuse.de* ⟲ *37 rooms, 3 suites* ⚷ *In-room: no a/c, dial-up. In-hotel: 2 restaurants, bar, concierge, no elevator, public Wi-Fi, parking (no fee), no-smoking rooms, some pets allowed* ☐ *AE, DC, MC, V* ⦿ *BP* Ⓜ *Poppenbüttel (U-bahn).*

$$ 🖭 **Nippon Hotel.** You'll be asked to remove your shoes before entering your room at the Nippon. Tatami mats line the floor, futon mattresses are on the beds, and an attentive Japanese staff is at your service. The authenticity might make things a bit *too* spartan and efficient for some, but by cutting some Western-style comforts, the hotel offers a good value in the attractive Uhlenhorst District. The Nippon has a Japanese restaurant and sushi bar. **Pros:** Asian flair; inviting Japanese restaurant, quiet, residential neighborhood. **Cons:** location away from all major sightseeing, very minimalist design, sometimes busy due to business travelers. ⊠ *Hofweg 75, Uhlenhorst* ☎ *040/227–1140* ⊕ *www.nippon-hotel.de* ⟲ *41 rooms, 1 suite* ⚷ *In-room: no a/c, safe, refrigerator, Wi-Fi. In-hotel: restaurant, bicycles, concierge, laundry service, parking (fee), no-smoking rooms* ☐ *AE, DC, MC, V* ⦿ *BP* Ⓜ *Mundsburg (U-bahn).*

$–$$ ★ 🏠**Yoho.** Centrally located between the hip Schanzenviertel and the downtown area, the upscale Yoho is the youth hostel of the 21st century. Housed in an historic, imposing villa with contemporary interior design, it offers simple yet elegant rooms with modern amenities otherwise not found in a hostel. Guests under 27 receive a special rate of €65 for a single or €85 for a double room, including breakfast. Everybody else has to pay €115—still a fair deal considering the great location. **Pros:** located close to hip, artsy neighborhoods, historic flair, very good furnishings at budget prices. **Cons:** limited breakfast, sometimes noisy due to young travelers, away from all major sightseeing. ✉*Moorkamp 5, Eimsbüttel* ☎*040/284–1910* ⊕*www.yoho-hamburg. de* ➪*30 rooms* ⌂*In-room: no a/c, dial-up. In-hotel: restaurant, no elevator, parking (no fee), some pets allowed* ☐*AE, DC, MC, V* ⬚*CP* Ⓜ*Schlump (U-bahn).*

NIGHTLIFE & THE ARTS

THE ARTS

The arts flourish in this cosmopolitan city. Hamburg's ballet company is one of the finest in Europe, and the Ballet Festival in July is a cultural high point. Information on events is available in the magazines *Hamburger Vorschau*—pick it up for free in tourist offices and most hotels—and *Szene Hamburg*, sold at newsstands for €2.50.

■**TIP→** The best way to order tickets for all major Hamburg theaters, musicals, and most cultural events is the central phone **Hamburg-Hotline** (☎*040/3005–1300*). A number of travel agencies also sell tickets for plays, concerts, and the ballet. The tourist office at the **Landungsbrücken** (✉*Between Piers 4 and 5, St. Pauli* ☎*040/3005–1200 or 040/3005–1203*) has a ticket office. One of the large downtown ticket agencies is the **Theaterkasse im Alsterhaus** (✉*Jungfernstieg 16, Neustadt* ☎*040/353–555*). The downtown **Theaterkasse Central** (✉*Gerhart-Hauptmann-Pl. 48, Neustadt* ☎*040/324–312*) is at the Landesbank-Galerie.

BALLET & OPERA
One of the most beautiful theaters in the country, the **Hamburgische Staatsoper** (✉*Grosse Theaterstr. 35, Altstadt* ☎*040/35680 or 040/356–868*) is the leading northern German venue for opera and ballet. The Hamburg Ballet is directed by American John Neumeier.

The **Operettenhaus Hamburg** (✉*Spielbudenpl. 1, St. Pauli* ☎*01805/4444*) stages productions of top musicals.

CONCERTS
Both the Hamburg Philharmonic and the Hamburg Symphony Orchestra appear regularly at the **Laeiszhalle** (✉*Johannes-Brahms-Pl., Neustadt* ☎*040/357–666*). Visiting orchestras from overseas are also presented.

FILM

Independent and mainstream English-language movies are shown at the **Metropolis** (⊠ *Dammtorstr. 30a, Neustadt* ☎ *040/342–353*) and are often subtitled in German. Students often show up at the **Grindel Kino** (⊠ *Grindelberg 7a, Harvestehude* ☎ *040/449–333*) for blockbuster English-language movies.

THEATER

Deutsches Schauspielhaus (⊠ *Kirchenallee 39, St. Georg* ☎ *040/248– 710*), one of Germany's leading drama stages, is lavishly restored to its full 19th-century opulence and is the most important Hamburg venue for classical and modern theater.

English Theater (⊠ *Lerchenfeld 14, Uhlenhorst* ☎ *040/227–7089*) is the city's only theater presenting English-language drama.

Musicaltheater am Hamburger Hafen (⊠ *Norderelbstr. 6, at Hamburger Hafen, follow signs to Schuppen 70, St. Pauli* ☎ *01805–114–113 or 01805/1997*) is staging a German version of the Broadway musical hit *The Lion King.*

Hamburg is by far Germany's capital for musicals, and the **Neue Flora Theater** (⊠ *Stresemannstr. 159a, at Alsenstr., Altona* ☎ *01805–4444 or 040/4316–5133*) offers the best deals.

NIGHTLIFE

THE REEPERBAHN

Whether you think it sordid or sexy, the Reeperbahn, in the St. Pauli District, is as central to the Hamburg scene as the classy shops along Jungfernstieg. A walk down **Herbertstrasse** (men only, no women or children permitted), just two blocks south of the Reeperbahn, can be quite an eye-opener. Here prostitutes sit displayed in windows as they await customers—nevertheless, it's the women choosing their clients, as these are the highest-paid prostitutes in the city. On nearby **Grosse Freiheit** you'll find a number of the better-known sex-show or table-dance clubs: **Colibri,** at No. 34; **Safari,** at No. 24; and **Dollhouse,** at No. 11. They cater to the package-tour trade as well as those on the prowl by themselves. Prices are high. Not much happens here before 10 PM.

The quirky **Schmidts Tivoli** (⊠ *Spielbudenpl. 24–28, St. Pauli* ☎ *040/3177–8899*) has become Germany's most popular variety theater, presenting a classy repertoire of live music, vaudeville, chansons, and cabaret.

BARS

The Hansestadt has a buzzing and upscale bar scene, with many spots that feature live music or DJs and dancing. A nightlife institution still going strong is the fashionable but cozy **Bar Hamburg** (⊠ *Rautenbergstr. 6–8, St. Georg* ☎ *040/2805–4880*). The new **Mandalay** (⊠ *Neuer Pferdemarkt 13, St. Pauli* ☎ *040/4321–4922*) is typical of the new upscale, sleek bars for thirtysomethings in rough St. Pauli. **Christiansen's** (⊠ *Pin-*

nasberg 60, St. Pauli ☎*040/317–2863*), near the Fischmarkt, is said to mix the best cocktails in town.

DANCE CLUBS

One of the most appealing and entertaining clubs in Hamburg, **Stage Club** (✉*Stresenmannstr. 159a, Altona* ☎*040/4316–5460*), on the first floor of the Neue Flora theater, welcomes a mixed crowd to soul, funk, or jazz every night, followed by a DJ. The **China Lounge** (✉*Nobistor 14, St. Pauli* ☎*040/3197–6622*), in a former Chinese restaurant, remains one of Hamburg's coolest lounges, mostly attracting hip and beautiful thirty-somethings. The stylish **Mandarin Kasino** (✉*Reeperbahn 1, St. Pauli* ☎*040/430–4616*), where a young crowd dances to hip-hop, soul, and funk, is the area's premier dance club, bar, and lounge. The more mature business crowd meets at chic after-work clubs such as **La Nuit** (✉*Grosse Elbstrasse 145 b-d, Altona* ☎*040/3803 7731*), at the Au Quai restaurant right on the waterfront.

WHERE TO GO

Here are the hip and happening streets in Hamburg:

■ Reeperbahn, Grosse Freiheit, and the streets around Spielbudenplatz in St. Pauli

■ Elbstrasse in Altona

■ Schanzenviertel in St. Pauli and Rotherbaum

■ Grindelallee and side streets in Rotherbaum

■ Jungfernstieg and streets around Aussen- und Binnenalster in St. Georg

13

JAZZ & LIVE MUSIC CLUBS

Birdland (✉*Gärtnerstr. 122, Hoheluft* ☎*040/405–277*) is one of the leading clubs among Hamburg's more than 100 venues, offering everything from traditional New Orleans sounds to avant-garde electronic noise. The **Cotton Club** (✉*Alter Steinweg 10, Neustadt* ☎*040/343–878*), Hamburg's oldest jazz club, books classic New Orleans jazz as well as swing. **Docks** (✉*Spielbudenpl. 19, St. Pauli* ☎*040/317–8830*) has a stylish bar and is Hamburg's largest venue for live music. It also puts on disco nights.

SPORTS & THE OUTDOORS

BIKING

Most major streets in Hamburg have bicycle lanes. Some of the major hotels will lend their guests bikes. The most central location for renting bikes is at the **Hauptbahnhof** (✉*Entrance on Kirchenallee, St. Georg* ☎*040/3918–50475*). Bikes rent for €8 a day (7 AM–9 PM). A wide selection of bikes, including racing, mountain, and children's bikes, are rented at Mr. Petersen's **Hamburg anders erfahren** (✉*Kleiner Schäferkamp 19, Barmbeck* ☎*040/640–1800*). The bikes cost between €10 and €20 a day. There's a discount on longer rentals. A complete list of bike rentals in Hamburg and the surrounding countryside can be obtained from the **ADFC Hamburg** (✉*Koppel 34–36* ☎*040/390–3955*).

JOGGING

The best places for jogging are the Planten un Blomen and Alter Botanischer Garten parks and along the leafy promenade around the Alster. The latter route is about 6 km (4 mi) long.

SAILING

You can rent rowboats and sailboats on the Alster in summer between 10 AM and 9 PM. Rowboats cost around €10 to 12 an hour, sailboats around €16 an hour (usually accommodating two adults). The largest selection of boats is at the Gurlittinsel pier off An der Alster (on the east bank of the Aussenalster). Another rental outlet is at the very tip of the Alster, at the street Fernsicht.

SHOPPING

SHOPPING DISTRICTS

Hamburg's shopping districts are among the most elegant on the continent, and the city has Europe's largest expanse of covered shopping arcades, most of them packed with small, exclusive boutiques. The streets **Grosse Bleichen** and **Neuer Wall,** which lead off Jungfernstieg, are a big-ticket zone. The Grosse Bleichen leads to six of the city's most important covered (or indoor) malls, many of which are connected. The marble-clad **Galleria** is modeled after London's Burlington Arcade. Daylight streams through the immense glass ceilings of the **Hanse-Viertel,** an otherwise ordinary reddish-brown brick building. The **Kaufmannshaus,** also known as the Commercie, and the **Hamburger Hof** are two of the oldest and most fashionable indoor malls. There are also the historic **Alte Post** with a beautiful, waterfront promenade, the posh **Bleichenhof,** and the stunningly designed, larger **Europa Passage.**

Hamburg's premier shopping street, **Jungfernstieg,** is just about the most expensive in the country. It's lined with jewelers' shops—Wempe, Brahmfeld & Guttruf, and Hintze are the top names—and chic clothing boutiques such as Linette, Ursula Aust, Selbach, Windmöller, and Jäger & Koch.

In the fashionable **Pöseldorf** district north of downtown, take a look at Milchstrasse and Mittelweg. Both are filled with small boutiques, restaurants, and cafés.

Running from the main train station to Gerhard-Hauptmann-Platz, the boulevard **Spitalerstrasse** is a pedestrians-only street lined with stores. ■ TIP➡ Prices here are noticeably lower than those on Jungfernstieg.

DEPARTMENT STORES

Alsterhaus (⊠ *Jungfernstieg 16–20, Neustadt* ☎ *040/359–010*) is Hamburg's most famous department store. A favorite with locals, it's a large and elegant landmark.

Karstadt (⊠ *Mönckebergstr. 16, Altstadt* ☎ *040/30940*) is Germany's leading department-store chain and offers the same goods as the Alsterhaus at similar prices. ■ TIP→ **Hamburg's downtown Karstadt is the city's best place to shop for sports clothing.**

Stilwerk (⊠ *Grosse Elbstr. 66–68, Altona* ☎ *040/3062–1370*), Hamburg's most fashionable shopping mall, resembles a department store, and primarily houses furniture and home-accessory shops.

SPECIALTY STORES

ANTIQUES

Take a look at the shops in the **St. Georg** district behind the train station, especially those between Lange Reihe and Koppel. You'll find a mixture of genuine antiques (*Antiquitäten*) and junk (*Trödel*). You won't find many bargains, however. ABC-Strasse is another happy hunting ground for antiques lovers.

The **Antik-Center** (⊠ *Klosterwall 9–21, Altstadt* ☎ *040/326–285*) is an assortment of 25 shops in the old market hall, close to the main train station. It features a wide variety of antiques from all periods.

FOOD MARKETS

A small but top-class health-food market in the heart of **Blankenese** manages to preserve the charm of a small village and sells only fresh produce from environmentally friendly farms. ⊠ *Bahnhofstr., Blankenese* ⊙ *Wed. 9–1* Ⓜ *Blankenese (S-bahn)*.

Fischmarkt (⇨ *St. Pauli and the Reeperbahn in Exploring Hamburg*).

GIFT IDEAS

Captain's Cabin (⊠ *St. Pauli Landungsbrücken 3, St. Pauli* ☎ *040/316–373*), a Hamburg institution, is an experience not to be missed. It's the best place for all of the city's specialty maritime goods.

Harry's Hafenbasar (⊠ *Erichstr. 56, St. Pauli* ☎ *040/312–482*) is full of dusty goods traders and seamen have brought back from the corners of the globe. This eerie, bazaarlike store is jam-packed and is a bargain-hunter's paradise for anything maritime.

Seifarth and Company (⊠ *Robert-Koch-Str. 19, Norderstedt* ☎ *040/4294–7490*) is one of the best places to buy tea in Hamburg, and Hamburg is one of the

> ### HAUTE HAMBURG
>
> Although not as rich or sumptuous on first sight as Düsseldorf or Munich, Hamburg is nevertheless expensive, and ranks first among Germany's shopping experiences. Chic boutiques sell primarily distinguished and somewhat conservative fashion; understatement is the style here. Some of the country's premier designers, such as Karl Lagerfeld, Jil Sander, and Wolfgang Joop, are native Hamburgers, or at least worked here for quite some time. Hamburg has the greatest number of shopping malls in the country, mostly small but elegant downtown arcades offering entertainment, fashion, and fine food.

best places to buy tea in Europe. Smoked salmon and caviar are terrific buys here as well.

JEWELRY

Wempe (✉ *Jungfernstieg 8, Neustadt* ☎ *040/3344–8824*) is Germany's largest and most exclusive jeweler. This is its flagship store (one of three Hamburg locations); the selection of watches here is particularly outstanding.

MEN'S CLOTHING

The stylish **Doubleeight** (✉ *Jungfernstieg 51, Neustadt* ☎ *040/3571–5510*) carries both designer and less-expensive everyday fashions. The six-story **Thomas I-Punkt** (✉ *Mönckebergstr. 21, Altstadt* ☎ *040/327–172*), a Hamburg classic and a must for the fashion-conscious traveler, sells hip designer clothes and suits of its own label. One of Hamburg's hippest clothing shops is the quirky **feldenkirchen** (✉ *Neue ABC-Strasse 6, Neustadt* ☎ *040/3405–7176*), which has a great selection of top international designer labels. Hamburg's largest store for men's clothes is **Wormland** (✉ *Ballindamm 40, Altstadt* ☎ *040/4689–92700*), which offers both affordable no-name, but very fashionable clothes as well as top designer wear.

WOMEN'S CLOTHING

Anita Hass (✉ *Eppendorfer Landstr. 60, Eppendorf* ☎ *040/465–909*), a Hamburg classic, carries both international brands and several young designers' labels. The historic **Hamburger Hof** (✉ *Jungfernstieg 26–30/ Grosse Bleichen, Neustadt* ☎ *040/350–1680*) is one of the most beautiful, upscale shopping complexes—with a wide variety of designer clothing, jewelry, and gift stores—primarily catering to women. The upscale shopping complex **Kaufrausch** (✉ *Isestr. 74, Eppendorf* ☎ *040/475–718*) has mostly clothing and accessories stores for women. A small but elegant and very personal store, **Linette** (✉ *Eppendorfer Baum 19, Eppendorf* ☎ *040/460–4963*) stocks only top designers.

Schleswig-Holstein & the Baltic Coast

WORD OF MOUTH

"Warnemünde has a pretty nice and picturesque old town, around the old harbor. Plus there are many miles of beaches."

—Cowboy1968

"Wismar has a definite Scandinavian feel—the facades are painted pastel colors in the Altstadt, and the town has an energy which I quite like."

—bellacqui

By Jürgen
Scheunemann

GERMANY'S TRUE NORTH IS A QUIET AND PEACEFUL REGION that belies its past status as one of the most powerful trading centers in Europe. The salty air and lush, green landscape of marshlands, endless beaches, fishing villages, and lakes are the main pleasures here, not sightseeing. On foggy November evenings, or during the hard winter storms that sometimes strand islanders from the mainland, you can well imagine the fairy tales spun by the Vikings who lived here.

In Schleswig-Holstein, Germany's most northern state, the Danish-German heritage is the result of centuries of land disputes between the two nations—you could call this area southern Scandinavia. Since the early 20th century its shores and islands have become popular weekend and summer retreats for the well-to-do from Hamburg. The island of Sylt, in particular, is known throughout Germany for its rich and beautiful sunbathers.

The rest of Schleswig-Holstein, though equally appealing in its green and mostly serene landscape, is far from rich and worldly. Most people farm or fish, and often speak Plattdütsch, or Low German, which is difficult for outsiders to understand. Cities such as Flensburg, Husum, Schleswig, Kiel (the state capital), and even Lübeck all exude a laid-back, small-town charm.

The neighboring state of Mecklenburg-Vorpommern includes the Baltic Coast and is even more rural. On the resort islands of Hiddensee and Usedom, the clock appears to have stopped before World War II. Though it has long been a popular summer destination for families, few foreign tourists venture here.

ORIENTATION & PLANNING

GETTING ORIENTED

The three major areas of interest are the western coastline of Schleswig-Holstein, the lakes inland in Western Mecklenburg, and Vorpommern's secluded, tundralike landscape of sandy heath and dunes. If you only have three days, slow down to the area's pace and focus on one area. In five days you could easily cross the region. Berlin is the natural approach from the east; Hamburg is a launching point from the west.

Schleswig-Holstein. Rural Schleswig-Holstein is accented by laid-back, medieval towns and villages famed for their fresh seafood and great local beers (such as Lübeck), and the bustling island of Sylt, a summer playground for wealthy Hamburgers.

Western Mecklenburg. Lakes, rivers, and seemingly endless fields of wheat and yellow rape characterize this rural landscape. Only a few tourists or day-trippers from nearby Berlin venture here to visit beautiful Schwerin or enjoy the serenity. The area is famous for its many wellness and spa hotels, making it a year-round destination.

TOP REASONS TO GO

Gothic architecture: The historic towns of Lübeck, Wismar, and Stralsund have some of the finest red-brick Gothic architecture in Northern Europe. A walk through medieval Lübeck, in particular, is like a trip into the proud past of the powerful Hanse league.

Sylt: Sylt is a windswept outpost in the rough North Sea. Throughout the year, Sylt is home to Germany's jet set, who come here for the tranquillity, the white beaches, the gourmet dining, and the superb hotels.

Schwerin: Nestled in a romantic landscape of lakes, rivers, forests, and marshland, the Mecklenburg state capital and its grand water palace make a great place to relax.

Rügen: One of the most secluded islands of northern Europe, Rügen is a dreamy Baltic oasis whose endless beaches, soaring chalk cliffs, and quiet pace of life have charmed painters, writers, and artists for centuries.

14

Vorpommern. Remote and sparsely populated, Vorpommern is one Europe's quietest corners. Compared to the coast and islands in the West, sleepy Vorpommern sea resorts like Putbus, Baabe, and the Darss area have preserved a distinct, old-fashioned charm worth exploring.

SCHLESWIG-HOLSTEIN & THE BALTIC COAST PLANNER

WHEN TO GO

The region's climate is at its best when the two states are most crowded with vacationers—in July and August. Winter can be harsh in this area, and even spring and fall are rather windy, chilly, and rainy. ■TIP→ **To avoid the crowds, schedule your trip for June or September. But don't expect tolerable water temperatures or hot days on the beach.**

GETTING HERE & AROUND

BY AIR   The international airport closest to Schleswig-Holstein is in Hamburg. For an eastern approach to the Baltic Coast tour, use Berlin's Tegel Airport.

BY BOAT & FERRY   The Weisse Flotte (White Fleet) line operates ferries linking the Baltic ports, as well as short harbor and coastal cruises. Boats depart from Warnemünde, Zingst (to Hiddensee), Sassnitz, and Stralsund. In addition, ferries run from Stralsund and Sassnitz to destinations in Sweden, Denmark, Poland, and Finland.

Scandlines operates ferries between Sassnitz and the Danish island of Bornholm, as well as Sweden.

BY BUS   Local buses link the main train stations with outlying towns and villages, especially the coastal resorts. Buses operate throughout Sylt, Rügen, and Usedom islands.

BY CAR   The two-lane roads (Bundesstrassen) along the coast can be full of traffic during June, July, and August. The ones leading to Usedom Island can be extremely log-jammed, as the causeway bridges have scheduled closings to let ships pass. Using the Bundesstrassen takes more time, but these often tree-lined roads are by far more scenic than the autobahn.

Sylt island is 196 km (122 mi) from Hamburg via Autobahn A–7 and Bundesstrasse B–199 and is ultimately reached via train. B–199 cuts through some nice countryside, and instead of A–7 or B–76 between Schleswig and Kiel you could take the slow route through the coastal hinterland (B–199, B–203, or B–503). Lübeck, the gateway to Mecklenburg-Vorpommern, is 56 km (35 mi) from Hamburg via A–1. B–105 leads to all sightseeing spots in Mecklenburg-Vorpommern. A faster route is the A–20, connecting Lübeck and Rostock. From Stralsund, Route 96 cuts straight across Rügen Island, a distance of 51 km (32 mi). From Berlin, take A–11 and head toward Prenzlau for B–109 all the way to Usedom Island, a distance of 162 km (100 mi). A causeway connects the mainland town of Anklam to the town of Peenemünde, on Usedom Island; coming from the west, use the causeway at Wolgast.

BY TRAIN   Train travel is much more convenient than bus travel in this area. Sylt, Kiel, Lübeck, Schwerin, and Rostock have InterCity train connections to either Hamburg or Berlin, or both.

A north–south train line links Schwerin and Rostock. An east–west route connects Kiel, Hamburg, Lübeck, and Rostock, and some trains continue through to Stralsund and Sassnitz, on Rügen Island.

ESSENTIALS   **Boat & Ferry Information** **Scandlines** (☎ *01805/116–688* ⊕ *www.scandlines. de*). **Weisse Flotte** (☎ *0180/321–2120 central phone, 03831/519–860 for Warnemünde, 03831/26810 for Stralsund, 0385/557–770 for Schwerin* ⊕ *www. weisseflotteschwerin.de*).

Visitor Information **Tourbu-Zentrale, Landesfremdenverkehrsverband Mecklenburg-Vorpommern** (✉ *Pl. der Freundschaft 1 Rostock* ☎ *0381/403–0500* 🖷 *0381/403–0555* ⊕ *www.tmv.de*).

ABOUT THE RESTAURANTS & HOTELS
Don't count on eating a meal at odd hours in this largely rural area. Many restaurants serve hot meals only between 11:30 AM and 2 PM, and 6 PM and 9 PM. You rarely need a reservation here, and casual clothing is generally acceptable.

In northern Germany you'll find both small *Hotelpensionen* and fully equipped large hotels; along the eastern Baltic Coast, some hotels are renovated high-rises dating from GDR (German Democratic Republic) times. Many of the small hotels and pensions in towns such as Kühlungsborn and Binz have been restored to the romantic, quaint splendor of German *Bäderarchitektur* (spa architecture) from the early 20th century. In high season all accommodations, especially on the islands, are in great demand. ■ TIP➔ **If you can't book well in advance, inquire at the local tourist office, which will also have information on the 150 campsites along the Baltic coast and on the islands.**

WHAT IT COSTS IN EUROS				
¢	$	$$	$$$	$$$$
RESTAURANTS under €9	€9–€15	€16–€20	€21–€25	over €25
HOTELS under €50	€50–€100	€101–€175	€176–€225	over €225

Restaurant prices are per person for a main course at dinner. Hotel prices are for two people in a standard double room, including tax and service.

PLANNING YOUR TIME

The bigger coastal Hanse cities make for a good start before exploring smaller towns. Lübeck is a natural base for exploring Schleswig-Holstein, particularly if you arrive from Hamburg. From here it is easy to venture out into the countryside or explore the coastline and towns such as Kiel, Flensburg, or Husum. The island of Sylt is a one- or two-day trip from Lübeck, though.

If you have more time, you can also travel east from Lübeck into Mecklenburg-Vorpommern: Some of the must-see destinations on an itinerary include Schwerin and the surrounding lakes, the island of Rügen, and the cities Wismar and Rostock.

DISCOUNTS & DEALS

Larger cities such as Kiel, Lübeck, Wismar, Schwerin, and Rostock offer tourism "welcome" cards, which include sometimes considerable discounts and special deals for attractions and tours as well as local public transport. Ask about these at the visitor information bureaus.

SCHLESWIG-HOLSTEIN

This region once thrived, thanks to the Hanseatic League and the Salzstrasse (Salt Route), a merchant route connecting northern Germany's cities. The kings of Denmark warred with the dukes of Schleswig and, later, the German Empire over the prized northern territory of Schleswig-Holstein. The northernmost strip of land surrounding Flensburg became German in 1864. The quiet, contemplative spirit of the region's people, the marshland's special light, and the ever-changing face of the sea are inspiring. Today the world-famous Schleswig-Holstein-Musikfestival ushers in classical concerts to farmhouses, palaces, and churches.

HUSUM

158 km (98 mi) northwest of Hamburg.

The town of Husum is the epitome of northern German lifestyle and culture. Immortalized in a poem as the "gray city upon the sea" by its famous son, Theodor Storm, Husum is actually a popular vacation spot in summer.

The central **Marktplatz** (Market Square) is bordered by 17th- and 18th-century buildings, including the historic Rathaus (Town Hall), which

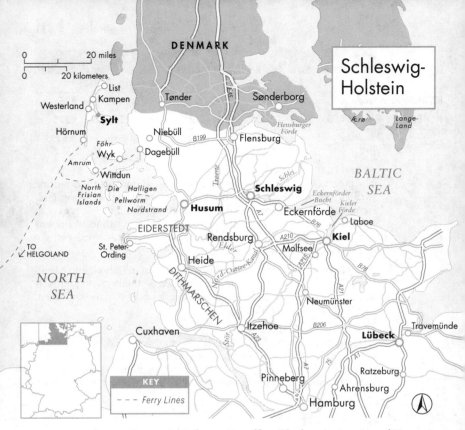

houses the tourist-information office. The best impression of Husum's beginnings in the mid-13th century is found south of the Marktplatz, along **Krämerstrasse**; the **Wasserreihe,** a narrow and tortuous alley; and **Hafenstrasse,** right next to the narrow **Binnenhafen** (city harbor).

ESSENTIALS

Visitor Information Husum (⊠ *Grossstr. 27* ☎ *04841/89870* 🖷 *04841/898–790* 🌐 *www.husum.de*).

EXPLORING

The most famous house on Wasserreihe is the **Theodor-Storm-Haus,** where writer Theodor Storm (1817–88) lived between 1866 and 1880. It's a must if you're interested in German literature or if you want to gain insight into the life of the few well-to-do people in this region during the 19th century. The small museum includes the poet's living room and a small *Poetenstübchen* (poets' parlor), where he wrote many of his novels. ⊠ *Wasserreihe 31* ☎ *04841/803—8630* 🌐 *www.storm-gesell-schaft.de* 💲 *€3* 🕐 *Apr.–Oct., Tues.–Fri. 10–5, Mon. and Sun. 2–5, Sat. 11–5; Nov.–Mar., Tues., Thurs., and Sat. 2–5.*

Despite Husum's remoteness, surrounded by the stormy sea, wide marshes, and dunes, the city used to be a major seaport and administrative center. The **Schloss vor Husum** (*Palace of Husum*), originally built as a Renaissance castle in the late 16th century, was transformed in 1752 by the dukes of Gottorf into a redbrick baroque country palace. ✉ *Professor-Ferdinand-Tönnies-Allee* ☎ *04841/897–3130* 💶 *€3.50* 🕐 *Apr.–Oct., Tues.–Sun. 11–5.*

WHERE TO STAY

$$ 🏨 **Romantik-Hotel Altes Gymnasium.** In a former redbrick high school
Fodor'sChoice behind a pear orchard, you'll find a surprisingly elegant country-style
★ hotel. The rooms are spacious, with wood floors and modern office ame-
nities. The restaurant Eucken ($$) serves game (from its own hunter) and German country cooking such as *Rücken vom Salzwiesenlamm mit Kartoffel-Zucchini-Rösti* (salted lamb back with potato and zuc-
chini hash browns). **Pros:** stylish and quiet setting, a perfect overnight stop on the way to Sylt. **Cons:** far from any other sights, remote area, and not directly on the sea. ✉ *Süderstr. 2–10* ☎ *04841/8330* 🌐 *www. altes-gymnasium.de* 🛏 *66 rooms, 6 suites* 🔧 *In-room: no a/c, safe, Wi-Fi. In-hotel: 2 restaurants, room service, bar, pool, gym, bicycles, no elevator, laundry service, parking (no fee), no-smoking rooms, some pets allowed* 🚪 *AE, DC, MC, V* 🍴 *BP.*

SYLT

Fodor'sChoice *44 km (27 mi) northwest of Husum, 196 km (122 mi) northwest of*
★ *Hamburg.*

Sylt is a long, narrow island (38 km [24 mi] by as little as 220 yards) of unspoiled beaches and marshland off the western coast of Schleswig-Holstein and Denmark. Famous for its clean air and white beaches, Sylt is the hideaway for Germany's jet set.

A popular activity here is *Wattwanderungen* (walking in the Watt, the shoreline tidelands), whether on self-guided or guided tours. The small villages with their thatch-roof houses, the beaches, and the nature conservation areas make Sylt the most enchanting German island.

GETTING HERE & AROUND

Trains are the *only* way to access Sylt (other than flying from Hamburg or Berlin). The island is connected to the mainland via the train cause-
way Hindenburgdamm. Deutsche Bahn will transport you and your car from central train stations at Dortmund, Düsseldorf, Hamburg, Stuttgart, and Frankfurt directly onto the island. In addition, a daily shuttle car train leaves Niebüll roughly every 30 minutes from 5:10 AM to 10:10 PM (Friday and Sunday from 5:10 AM to 9:40 PM). There are no reservations on this train.

ESSENTIALS

Visitor Information Kampen (✉ *Kurverwaltung, Hauptstr. 12* ☎ *04651/46980* 🖨 *04651/469–840* 🌐 *www.kampen.de*). **Westerland** (✉ *Strandstr. 35* ✉ *Stephanstr. 6, Postfach 1260* ☎ *04651/9988* 🖨 *04651/998–6000* 🌐 *www.westerland.de*).

14

EXPLORING

The island's major town is **Wester-land,** which is not quite as expensive as Kampen but more crowded. An ugly assortment of modern hotels lines an undeniably clean and broad beach. Each September windsurfers meet for the Surf Cup competition off the **Brandenburger Strand,** the best surfing spot.

AWAY FROM THE CROWDS

If you're looking for privacy on Sylt, detour to the village of **List,** on the northern tip of the island, or to **Archsum** or **Hörnum.** The last is on the southernmost point of the island and, like List, has a little harbor and lighthouse.

The island's unofficial capital is **Kampen,** which is the main destination for the wealthier crowd and lies 9 km (6 mi) northeast of Westerland. Redbrick buildings and shining white thatch-roof houses spread along the coastline. The real draw—apart from the fancy restaurants and chic nightclubs—is the beaches.

One of the island's best-known features is the **Rotes Kliff** (*Red Cliff*), a dune cliff on the northern end of the Kampen beaches, which turns an eerie dark red when the sun sets.

The **Naturschutzgebiet Kampener Vogelkoje** (*Birds' Nest Nature Conservation Area*) was built in the mid-17th century and once served as a mass trap for wild geese. Today it serves as a nature preserve for wild birds. ⊠ *Lister Str., Kampen* ☎ *04651/871–077* ⌨ *€2.50* ⊗ *May–Oct., daily 10–6.*

For a glimpse of the rugged lives of 19th-century fishermen, visit the small village of **Keitum** to the south, and drop in on the **Altfriesisches Haus** (*Old Frisian House*), which preserves an old-world peacefulness in a lush garden setting. The house also documents a time when most seamen thrived on extensive whale hunting. ⊠ *Am Kliff 13, Keitum* ☎ *04651/31101* ⌨ *€3* ⊗ *Easter–Oct., weekdays 10–5, weekends 11–5; Nov.–Easter, Tues.–Fri. 1–4.*

The 800-year-old church of **St. Severin** was built on the highest elevation in the region. Its tower once served the island's fishermen as a beacon. Strangely enough, the tower also served as a prison until 1806. Today the church is a popular site for weddings. ⊠ *Keitum* ☎ *04651/31713* ⌨ *Free* ⊗ *Apr.–Oct., tour Sun. at 10; Nov.–Mar. at 4.*

The small **Sylter Heimatmuseum** (*Sylt Island Museum*) tells the centuries-long history of the island's seafaring people. It presents traditional costumes, tools, and other gear from fishing boats and tells the stories of islanders who fought for Sylt's independence. ⊠ *Am Kliff 19, Keitum* ☎ *04651/31669* ⌨ *€3* ⊗ *Easter–Oct., weekdays 10–5, weekends 11–5; Nov.–Easter, Tues.–Fri. 1–4.*

WHERE TO EAT

$$$$
Fodor's Choice
★

✕ **Hotelrestaurant Jörg Müller.** Set in an old thatch-roof farmhouse, which doubles as a small hotel, chef and owner Jörg Müller is considered by many to be the island's leading chef, delivering haute cuisine served in a gracious and friendly setting. Of the two restaurants, the Pesel serves

BEACHES

The busiest beaches are at Westerland (Sylt Island), Binz (Rügen Island), Ostseebad Kühlungsborn, and Warnemünde. The most beautiful beaches are at Timmendorf on Poel Island (you can drive there from Wismar or take a White Fleet boat); Kap Arkona (reachable only on foot); and Hiddensee Island, off Rügen. The more remote coves can be found at Kampen on Sylt, at the Ahrenshoop Weststrand, on the Darss Peninsula; at Nienhagen (near Warnemünde); and the Grosser Jasmunder Bodden, on Rügen Island to the west of Lietzow.

Be aware that water temperatures even in August rarely exceed 20°C (65°F). There's a *Kurtaxe* (entrance fee) of €1.50–€5 for most beaches; the fees on Sylt average €3 per entry. Some beaches allow nude bathing. In German it's known as *Freikörperkultur* (literally "free body culture"), or FKK for short. The most popular of these bare-all beaches are on Sylt Island, at Nienhagen, and Prerow (on Darss).

14

local fish dishes, whereas the formal Jörg Müller offers a high-quality blend of international cuisines. Reservations are almost always necessary. ✉*Süderstr. 8 Westerland* ☎*04651/27788* 📠*04651/201–471* 🌐*www.hotel-joerg-mueller.de* ⊟*AE, DC, MC, V.*

$$$
★
✕**Sansibar.** Sansibar is one of the island's most popular restaurants and a long-time favorite for a diverse clientele, who often make it an rambunctious night out by imbibing loads of drinks under the bar's maverick logo, crossed pirates' sabers. The cuisine includes seafood and fondue, served with your choice of more than 800 wines. ■TIP➡ **To get a table even in the afternoon, you must reserve well in advance.** ✉*Strand, Rantum-Süd, Rantum* ☎*04651/964–546* 🍴*Reservations essential* ⊟*AE, MC, V.*

$–$$
✕**Dorfkrug Rotes Kliff.** The Dorfkrug has fed the island's seafaring inhabitants since 1876. Enjoy meals such as *Steinbuttfilet* (halibut fillet) or *Gebratener Zander* (fried perch fillet) in a homey setting where the walls are covered in traditional blue-and-white Frisian tiles. ✉*Braderuper Weg 3, Kampen* ☎*04651/43500* ⊟*AE, MC, V* 🕐*Closed Mon. in Jan.*

WHERE TO STAY

$$$$
Fodor'sChoice
★
🏨**Dorint Söl'ring Hof.** This luxurious resort is set *on* the dunes in a white, thatch-roof country house: the view from most of the rooms is magnificent—with some luck you may even spot frolicking harbor porpoises. The brightly furnished rooms are spacious, covering two floors, and equipped with a fireplace. The real attraction here, however, is the restaurant ($$$), where renowned chef Johannes King creates delicious German-Mediterranean fish dishes. The hotel is in quiet Rantum, at the southeast end of the island. **Pros:** one of the few luxury hotels on the island with perfect service and a top-notch restaurant. **Cons:** remote location, often fully booked. ✉*Am Sandwall 1D–25980 Sylt-Rantum* ☎*04651/836–200* 🌐*www.soelring-hof.de* 🛏*11 rooms, 4 suites* 🗝*In-room: no a/c, safe. In-hotel: restaurant, room service, bar, gym, spa,*

beachfront, no elevator, concierge, laundry service, parking (no fee), no-smoking rooms ▭AE, DC, MC, V ﴾◎﴿BP.

$$–$$$ ⊞**Ulenhof Wenningstedt.** The Ulenhof, one of Sylt's loveliest old thatch-roof apartment houses, is a quiet alternative to the busier main resorts in Kampen and Westerland. The Ulenhof has two buildings 750 yards away from the beach in Wenningstedt. ■TIP➔ **The larger apartments, for up to three persons, are a good deal.** A separate bathing facility offers a huge wellness area with two saunas, a pool, and a *Tecaldarium,* a Roman bathhouse. **Pros:** typical thatch-roof house and a great, but small, spa. **Cons:** off the beaten track and away from the main action in Kampen and Westerland. ⊠*Friesenring 14 Wenningstedt* ☎*04651/94540* ⊕*www.ulenhof.de* ➟*35 apartments* ⌂*In-room: no a/c. In-hotel: pool, gym, no elevator, public Wi-Fi, parking (no fee), no-smoking rooms* ▭*No credit cards* ﴾◎﴿*BP.*

NIGHTLIFE & THE ARTS

The nightspots in Kampen are generally more upscale and more expensive than the pubs and clubs of Westerland. One of the most classic clubs on Sylt is the **Club Rotes Kliff** (⊠*Braderuper Weg 3, Kampen* ☎*04651/43400*), a bar and dance club that attracts a hip crowd of all ages. The **Compass** (⊠*Friedrichstr. 40, Westerland* ☎*04651/23513*) is not as trendy as the typical Sylt nightclub. The mostly young patrons, however, create a cheerful party atmosphere on weekend nights.

SCHLESWIG

82 km (51 mi) southeast of Sylt, 114 km (71 mi) north of Hamburg.

Schleswig-Holstein's oldest city is also one of its best-preserved examples of a typical North German town. Once the seat of the dukes of Schleswig-Holstein, it has not only their palace but also ruins left by the area's first rulers, the Vikings. Those legendary and fierce warriors from Scandinavia brought terror (but also commerce) to northern Germany between 800 and 1100. Under a wide sky, Schleswig lies on the Schlei River in a landscape of freshwater marshland and lakes, making it a good departure point for bike or canoe tours.

The fishing village comes alive along the **Holm,** an old settlement with tiny and colorful houses. The windblown buildings give a good impression of what villages in northern Germany looked like 150 years ago.

The impressive baroque **Schloss Gottorf,** dating from 1703, once housed the ruling family. It has been transformed into the **Schleswig-Holsteinisches Landesmuseum** (State Museum of Schleswig-Holstein) and holds a collection of art and handicrafts of northern Germany from the Middle Ages to the present, including paintings by Lucas Cranach the Elder. ⊠*Schloss Gottorf* ☎*04621/8130* ⊕*www.schloss-gottorf. de* ☝*€6* ♥*Apr.–Oct., daily 10–6; Nov.–Mar., Tues.–Fri. 10–4, weekends 10–5.*

♔ The most thrilling museum in Schleswig, the **Wikinger-Museum Haithabu** *(Haithabu Viking Museum)* is at the site of a Viking settlement. This was the Vikings' most important German port, and the boats, gold

EATING WELL IN SCHLESWIG-HOLSTEIN

The German coastline is known for fresh and superb seafood, particularly in summer. A few of the region's top restaurants can be found on Sylt and in Lübeck. Eating choices along the Baltic Coast tend to be more down-to-earth. However, restaurants in both coastal states serve mostly seafood such as *Scholle* (flounder) or North Sea *Krabben* (shrimp), often with fried potatoes, eggs, and bacon. Meck-

lenburg specialties to look for are *Mecklenburger Griebenroller*, a custardy casserole of grated potatoes, eggs, herbs, and chopped bacon; *Mecklenburger Fischsuppe*, a hearty fish soup with vegetables, tomatoes, and sour cream; *Gefüllte Ente* (duck with bread stuffing); and *Pannfisch* (fish patty). A favorite local nightcap since the 17th century is *Grog*, a strong blend of rum, hot water, and local fruits.

14

jewelry, and graves they left behind are displayed in the museum. ⊠ *Haddeby* 🕾 *04621/813—222* ⊕ *www.schloss-gottorf.de* 🎫 *€4* 🕙 *Apr.–Oct., daily 9–5; Nov.–Mar., Tues.–Sun. 10–4.*

WHERE TO STAY & EAT

$ ✕ **Stadt Flensburg.** This small restaurant in a city mansion dating back to 1699 serves mostly fish from the Schlei River. Fishermen living on the Holm caught your dinner. The food is solid regional fare such as *Zanderfilet* (perch fillets) or *Gebratene Ente* (baked duck). The familial, warm atmosphere and the local dark tap beers more than make up for the simplicity of the setting. Reservations are advised. ⊠ *Lollfuss 102* 🕾 *04621/23984* 🍴 *AE, DC, MC, V* 🕙 *Closed Wed.*

$–$$ 🏨 **Ringhotel Strandhalle Schleswig.** A modern hotel overlooking the small yacht harbor, this establishment has surprisingly low rates. The rooms are furnished in timeless dark furniture. **Pros:** hotel occupies central spot in the heart of Flensburg with great views. **Cons:** lack of flair, rather bland rooms. ⊠ *Strandweg 2* 🕾 *04621/9090* ⊕ *www.hotel-strandhalle.de* 🛏 *25 rooms* 🛎 *In-room: no a/c, safe, refrigerator, Ethernet. In-hotel: restaurant, pool, bicycles, parking (no fee), no-smoking rooms, some pets allowed* 🍴 *AE, MC, V* 🍽 *BP.*

KIEL

53 km (33 mi) southeast of Schleswig, 130 km (81 mi) north of Hamburg.

The state capital, Kiel, is known throughout Europe for its annual Kieler Woche, a regatta that attracts hundreds of boats from around the world. Despite the many wharves and industries concentrated in Kiel, the **Kieler Föhrde** (Bay of Kiel) has remained mostly unspoiled. Unfortunately, this cannot be said about the city itself. Because of Kiel's strategic significance during World War II—it served as the main German submarine base—the historic city, founded more than 750 years ago, was completely destroyed.

ESSENTIALS

Visitor Information **Kiel** (⊠*Andreas-Gayk-Str. 31* ☎*01805/656–700 0.12¢ per minute* 🖷*0431/679–1099* ⊕*www.kiel.de*).

EXPLORING

🌀 At the **Kieler Hafen** *(Kiel Harbor)*, Germany's largest passenger-shipping harbor, you can always catch a glimpse of one of the many ferries leaving for Scandinavia from the **Oslokai** (Oslo Quay).

🌀 The **Schifffahrtsmuseum** *(Maritime Museum)*, housed in a hall of the old fish market, includes two antique fishing boats. ⊠*Wall 65* ☎*0431/901–3428* ⊕*www.kiel.de* 💶*€3* 🕙*Mid-Apr.–mid-Oct., daily 10–6; mid-Oct.–mid-Apr., Tues.–Sun. 10–5.*

WHAT'S NEARBY

Two attractive beach towns close to Kiel, **Laboe** and **Strande,** are crowded with sun-loving Kielers on summer weekends. Both retain their fishing-village appeal, and you can buy fresh fish directly from the boats in the harbor, such as famous *Kieler Sprotten,* a small, salty fish somewhat like a sardine. Though you can get to Laboe and Strande by car, it's more fun to catch a ferry leaving from Kiel.

A grim reminder of a different marine past is exhibited at the **U-Boot-Museum** *(Submarine Museum)* in Kiel-Laboe. The vessels of the much-feared German submarine fleet in World War I were mostly built and stationed in Kiel, before leaving for the Atlantic, where they attacked American and British supply convoys. Today the submarine U995 serves as a public-viewing model of a typical German submarine. The 280-foot-high **Marineehrenmal** (Marine Honor Memorial), in Laboe, was built in 1927–36. You can reach Laboe via ferry from the Kiel harbor or take B–502 north. ⊠*Strandstr. 92, Kiel-Laboe* ☎*04343/42700* 💶*Memorial €4, museum €2.50* 🕙*Apr.– Oct., daily 9:30–7; Nov.–Mar., daily 9:30–5.*

One of northern Germany's best collections of modern art can be found at the **Kunsthalle zu Kiel** *(Kiel Art Gallery)*, which specializes in Russian art of the 19th and early 20th centuries, German expressionism, and contemporary international art. ⊠*Düsternbrooker Weg 1* ☎*0431/880–5756* ⊕*www.kunsthalle-kiel.de* 💶*€6* 🕙*Tues. and Thurs.–Sun. 10–6, Wed. 10–8.*

WHERE TO STAY & EAT

$–$$ ✕**Quam.** Locals aren't looking for old-fashioned fish dishes—that's why there isn't a traditional fish restaurant in town. They prefer preparations of fish from all over the world. The stylish Quam, its yellow walls and dimmed lights paying homage to Tuscany, serves specialties from Germany, Italy, France, and Japan, to a mostly young, very chic crowd. ⊠*Düppelstr. 60* ☎*0431/85195* 🍴*Reservations essential* 🖃*MC, V* 🕙*Closed Sun. No lunch.*

¢–$ ✕**Kieler Brauerei.** The only historic brewery in town has produced beer
★ since the Middle Ages. You can try the *Naturtrübes Kieler* and other North German beers in pitchers. ■TIP→ **You can also order a small barrel for your table and tap it yourself (other patrons will cheer you).** The hearty food—mostly fish, pork, and potato dishes—does not earn

awards, but it certainly helps get down just one more beer. ⊠*Alter Markt 9* ☎*0431/906–290* 🍴*MC, V.*

$$–$$$ 🍴 **Hotel Kieler Yachtclub.** This traditional hotel provides standard yet elegant, newly refurbished rooms in the main building and completely new, bright accommodations in the Villentrakt. The restaurant ($$$) serves mostly fish dishes; in summer try to get a table on the terrace. The club overlooks the Kieler Föhrde. **Pros:** central location in the heart of Kiel, nice views. **Con:** service and attitude can feel a bit too formal at times. ⊠*Hindenburgufer 70* ☎*0431/88130* ⊕*www.hotel-kyc.de* ➡*57 rooms, 4 suites* ⚭*In-room: no a/c, Ethernet. In-hotel: restaurant, room service, bar, laundry service, parking (no fee), no-smoking rooms, some pets allowed* 🍴*AE, DC, MC, V* 🍴*BP.*

NIGHTLIFE & THE ARTS

This city may seem relatively sleepy by day, but that may be due to its thriving nightlife. One of the many chic and hip bars is the **Hemingway** (⊠*Alter Markt 19* ☎*0431/96812*). A college crowd goes to **Traumfabrik** (⊠*Grasweg 19* ☎*0431/544–450*) to eat pizza, watch a movie, or dance (Friday is best for dancing).

LÜBECK

Fodor's Choice
★

60 km (37 mi) southeast of Kiel, 56 km (35 mi) northeast of Hamburg.

The ancient core of Lübeck, dating from the 12th century, was a chief stronghold of the Hanseatic merchant princes. But it was the roving Heinrich der Löwe (King Henry the Lion) who established the town and, in 1173, laid the foundation stone of the redbrick Gothic cathedral. The town's famous landmark gate, the **Holstentor,** built between 1464 and 1478, is flanked by two round, squat towers and serves as a solid symbol of Lübeck's prosperity as a trading center.

GETTING HERE & AROUND

Lübeck is accessible from Hamburg in 45 minutes either by Intercity trains or by car via the A–24 and A–1, which almost takes you from one city center to the other. Lübeck is also well connected by autobahns and train service to Kiel, Flensburg, and the neighboring eastern coastline. The city, however, should be explored on foot or by bike, as the many tiny, medieval alleys in the center cannot be accessed by car. Tours of Old Lübeck depart daily from the tourist offices on the Alter Markt between mid-April and mid-October.

ESSENTIALS

Visitor Information **Lübeck** (⊠*Holstentorpl. 1, D-23552* ☎*01805/882-233* 🖷*0451/409-1992* ⊕*www.luebeck.de*).

EXPLORING

In the **Altstadt** *(Old Town)*, proof of Lübeck's former position as the golden queen of the Hanseatic League is found at every step. ◼**TIP**→ More 13th- to 15th-century buildings stand in Lübeck than in all other large northern German cities combined, which has earned the Altstadt a place on UNESCO's register of the world's greatest cultural and natural treasures.

The **Rathaus,** dating from 1240, is among the buildings lining the arcaded Marktplatz, one of Europe's most striking medieval market squares. ⊠*Breitestr. 64* ☎*0451/122–1005* 🔄*Guided tour in German* €*4* ⊙*Tour weekdays at 11, noon, and 3, and Sat. at 1:30.*

The impressive redbrick Gothic **Marienkirche** *(St. Mary's Church)*, which has the highest brick nave in the world, looms behind the Rathaus. ⊠*Marienkirchhof* ☎*0451/397–700* ⊙*Nov.–Feb., daily 10–4; Mar. and Oct., daily 10–5; Apr.–Sept., daily 10–6.*

The **Buddenbrookhaus–Günter Grass-Haus,** two highly respectable-looking mansions, are devoted to two of Germany's most prominent writers, Thomas Mann (1875–1955) and Günter Grass (born 1927). The older mansion is named after Mann's saga *Buddenbrooks.* Mann's family once lived here, and it's now home to the **Heinrich und Thomas Mann Zentrum,** a museum documenting the brothers' lives. A tour and video in English are offered.

Near the museum is the second mansion, which houses the **Günter Grass-Haus,** devoted to Germany's most famous living writer and winner of the Nobel Prize for Literature (1999). ⊠*Mengstr. 4 and Glockengiesserstr. 21* ☎*0451/122–4190 or 0451/122–4243.* ⊕*www. buddenbrookhaus.de* 🔄*Both museums €7; Grass-Haus €5; Buddenbrookhaus €4* ⊙*Buddenbrockhaus: Apr.–Dec., daily 10–6; Jan.–Mar., daily 11–5. Günter Grass-Haus: Jan.–Mar., Tues.–Sun. 11–5; Apr.–Dec., daily 10–5.*

Take a look inside the entrance hall of the Gothic **Heilig-Geist-Hospital** *(Hospital of the Holy Ghost).* It was built in the 14th century by the town's rich merchants and is still caring for the infirm. ⊠*Am Koberg 11* ☎*0451/7907–841* 🔄*Free* ⊙*Apr.–Sept., Tues.–Sun. 10–5; Oct.–Mar., Tues.–Sun. 10–4.*

Construction of the **Lübecker Dom** *(Lübeck Cathedral)*, the city's oldest building, began in 1173. ⊠*Domkirchhof* ☎*0451/74704* ⊙*Apr.–Oct., daily 10–6; Nov.–Mar., daily 10–4.*

WHERE TO EAT

$$$$ ✕**Wullenwever.** This restaurant has set a new standard of dining sophistication for Lübeck. Committed to the city's maritime heritage, Wullenwever serves fish such as bass, halibut, plaice, pike, and trout, which is fried or sautéed according to local country cooking. It's certainly one of the most attractive establishments in town, with dark furniture, chandeliers, and oil paintings on pale pastel walls. In summer, tables fill a quiet flower-strewn courtyard. ⊠*Beckergrube 71* ☎*0451/704–333* 🔄*Reservations essential* ⊟*AE, DC, V* ⊙*Closed Sun. and Mon. No lunch.*

$–$$
Fodor'sChoice
★
✕**Schiffergesellschaft.** This dark, wood-paneled restaurant dating back to 1535 is the city's old Mariners' Society house, which was off-limits to women until 1870. Today locals and visitors alike enjoy freshly brewed beer and great seafood in church-style pews at long 400-year-old oak tables. Above are a bizarre collection of low-hanging old ship

models. A good meal here is the *Ostseescholle* (plaice), fried with bacon and served with potatoes and cucumber salad. ⊠*Breitestr. 2* ☎*0451/76776* ⊟*AE, V.*

WHERE TO STAY

$$ ⊡**SAS Radisson Senator Hotel Lübeck.** Close to the famous Holstentor, this ultramodern hotel, with its daring architecture, still reveals a North German heritage: the redbrick building, with its oversize windows and generous, open lobby, mimics an old Lübeck warehouse. ■**TIP→ When making a reservation, ask for a (larger) Business Class room, whose price includes a breakfast.** A big plus are the very comfortable beds, which are large by German standards. The Nautilo restaurant ($–$$) serves light Mediterranean cuisine. **Pros:** modern, light luxury hotel in a central location. **Con:** lacks the historic charm typical of medieval Lübeck. ⊠ *Willy-Brandt-Allee 6* ☎*0451/1420* ⊕*www.senatorhotel.de* ⤳*217 rooms, 7 suites* ♿*In-room: Wi-Fi. In-hotel: 2 restaurants, room service, bar, pool, spa, concierge, laundry service, parking (fee), no-smoking rooms, some pets allowed* ⊟*AE, DC, MC, V.*

$–$$ ⊡**Ringhotel Friederikenhof.** A lovely country hotel set in 19th-century, ★ redbrick farmhouses 10 minutes outside of Lübeck, the family-run Friederikenhof is a perfect hideaway with a soothing garden and great view of the city's skyline. Rooms are fairly large and appointed in a slightly modernized, country-house style with all the amenities of a four-star hotel. If you don't want to drive into the city for dinner, try the fresh seafood at their intimate restaurant. **Pros:** charming, old-style farmhouse typical of the region, personal and very friendly service. **Con:** distant location outside Lübeck. ⊠*Langjohrd 15–19* ☎*0451/800–880* ⊕*www.friederikenhof.de* ⤳*30 rooms* ♿*In-room: no a/c, refrigerator, Wi-Fi. In-hotel: restaurant, parking (no fee), some pets allowed* ⊟*AE, MC, V* ❢❘*BP.*

$–$$ ⊡**Ringhotel Jensen.** Only a stone's throw from the Holstentor, this hotel is close to all the main attractions and faces the moat surrounding the Old Town. It's family run and very comfortable, with modern rooms, mostly decorated with bright cherrywood furniture. Though small, the guest rooms are big enough for two twin beds and a coffee table and come with either a shower or a bath. **Pros:** perfect location in the heart of Lübeck's downtown area, major sights are all within walking distance. **Cons:** small pensionlike hotel without many of the amenities of larger hotels, blandly decorated rooms. ⊠*An der Obertrave 4–5* ☎*0451/702–490* ⊕*www.hotel-jensen.de* ⤳*41 rooms, 1 suite* ♿*In-room: no a/c, Wi-Fi. In-hotel: restaurant, no elevator, parking (fee), some pets allowed* ⊟*AE, DC, MC, V* ❢❘*BP.*

$ ⊡**Hotel zur Alten Stadtmauer.** This historic town house in the heart ★ of the city is Lübeck's most charming hotel. Two floors house small, modest, well-kept guest rooms. Comfortable beds, bright birchwood furniture, a quiet setting, and a great (not to mention nutritious) German breakfast buffet make this a perfect choice for budget travelers looking for romance. **Pros:** cozy hotel with personal, friendly service in a great spot. **Cons:** rather simply furnished rooms; if fully booked, the hotel feels cramped. ⊠*An der Mauer 57* ☎*0451/73702* ⊕*www. hotelstadtmauer.de* ⤳*22 rooms, most with bath* ♿*In-room: no a/c,*

14

Wi-Fi. In-hotel: no elevator, parking (fee), no-smoking rooms ▱AE, *DC, MC, V* ❙◎❙*BP.*

SHOPPING

Local legend has it that marzipan was invented in Lübeck during the great medieval famine. According to the story, a local baker ran out of grain for bread and, in his desperation, began experimenting with the only four ingredients he had: almonds, sugar, rose water, and eggs. The result was a sweet almond paste known today as marzipan. The story is more fiction than fact; it is generally agreed that marzipan's true origins lie in the Middle East. ■TIP➔ **Lübecker Marzipan, a designation that has been trademarked, is now considered among the best in the world.** Lübeck's most famous marzipan maker, **Konditorei-Café Niederegger** (⊠*Breitestr. 89* ☎*0451/530–1127*), sells the delicacy molded into a multitude of imaginative forms.

WESTERN MECKLENBURG

This long-forgotten Baltic Coast region, pinned between two sprawling urban areas—the state capital of Schwerin, in the west, and Rostock, in the east—is thriving again. Though the region is close to the sea, it's made up largely of seemingly endless fields of wheat and yellow rape and a dozen or so wonderful lakes. "When the Lord made the Earth, He started with Mecklenburg," wrote native novelist Fritz Reuter.

WISMAR

★ *60 km (37 mi) east of Lübeck on Route 105.*

The old city of Wismar was one of the original three sea-trading towns, along with Lübeck and Rostock, which banded together in 1259 to combat Baltic pirates. From this mutual defense pact grew the great and powerful private-trading bloc, the Hanseatic League, which dominated the Baltic for centuries. The wealth generated by the Hanseatic merchants can still be seen in Wismar's ornate architecture.

ESSENTIALS

Visitor Information Wismar (⊠*Stadthaus, Am Markt 11* ☎*03841/19433* 🖨*03841/251–3090* ⊕*www.wismar.de*).

EXPLORING

★ The **Marktplatz** *(Market Square)*, one of the largest and best preserved in Germany, is framed by patrician gabled houses. Their style ranges from redbrick late Gothic through Dutch Renaissance to 19th-century neoclassical. The square's **Wasserkunst,** the ornate pumping station done in Dutch Renaissance style, was built between 1580 and 1602 by the Dutch master Philipp Brandin.

The ruins of the **Marienkirche** *(St. Mary's Church)* with its 250-foot tower, bombed in World War II, lie just behind the Marktplatz; the church is still undergoing restoration. ■TIP➔ **At noon, 3, and 5, listen for one of 14 hymns played on its carillon.**

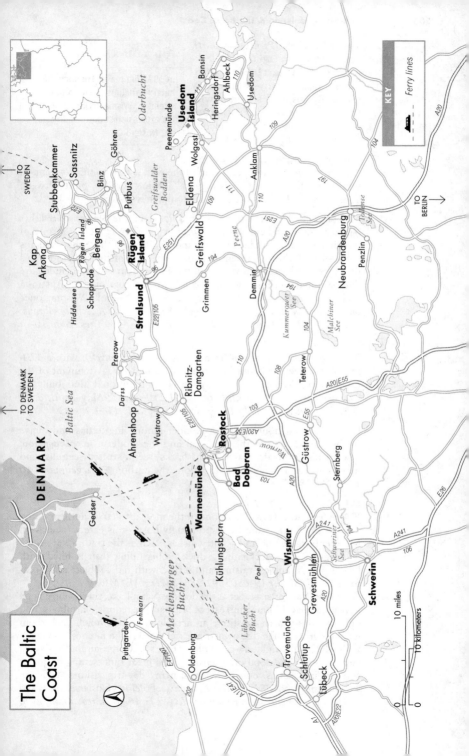

The Baltic Coast

DENMARK

Baltic Sea

Mecklenburger Bucht

Lübecker Bucht

TO DENMARK
TO SWEDEN

TO SWEDEN

TO BERLIN

KEY

- - - Ferry lines

Gedser

Puttgarden

Fehmarn

Oldenburg

Travemünde

Schlütup

Lübeck

Grevesmühlen

Wismar

Poel

Kühlungsborn

Warnemünde

Bad Doberan

Rostock

Schwerin

Sternberg

Güstrow

Schweriner See

Grevesmühlen

Warnow

Wustrow

Ahrenshoop

Darss

Prerow

Ribnitz-Damgarten

Stralsund

Grimmen

Schaprode

Hiddensee

Kap Arkona

Rügen Island

Bergen

Rügen Island

Putbus

Binz

Göhren

Sassnitz

Stubbenkammer

Greifswalder Bodden

Greifswald

Eldena

Wolgast

Peenemünde

Usedom Island

Heringsdorf

Ahlbeck

Bansin

Usedom

Oderbucht

Anklam

Demmin

Peene

Teterow

Kummerower See

Malchiner See

Neubrandenburg

Penzlin

Tollense See

Güstrow

10 miles

10 kilometers

E251

E22/105

E22/105

E251

E55

A20/E55

A20/E55

A20

A20

A20

A24

A24

A1/E47

A1/E22

A20/E22

A1

E26

207

105

194

110

108

109

110

109

111

110

104

104

104

104

103

103

106

106

197

194

108

96

96

90

90

111

192

207

The **Fürstenhof** *(Princes' Court)*, home of the former dukes of Mecklenburg, stands next to the Marienkirche. It's an early-16th-century Italian Renaissance structure with touches of late Gothic. The facade is a series of fussy friezes depicting scenes from the Trojan War.

> **DID YOU KNOW?**
>
> In 1922 filmmaker Friedrich Wilhelm Murnau used the tortuous streets of Wismar's Old Town in his expressionist horror-film classic, *Nosferatu*.

The **St. Georgen zu Wismar** *(St. George's Church)*, another victim of the war, is next to the Fürstenhof. One of northern Germany's biggest Gothic churches, built between 1315 and 1404, it has been almost completely restored.

The city's turbulent history is chronicled at the **Stadtgeschichtliches Museum Wismar Schabbellhaus** *(Museum for City History)*, in one of North Germany's oldest Renaissance buildings, the Schabbellhaus (1569–71). Exhibits present the medieval past of the city and focus on the Swedish occupation during the Thirty Years' War. Included are fine paintings, scrimshaw art, and paintings whose origins (Australia and New Zealand) testify to the extensive trade links Wismar once had. ⊠*Schweinsbrücke 8* ☎*03841/282–350* ⊕*www.schabbellhaus. de* ⊠*€2* ☉*May–Oct., Tues.–Sun. 10–8; Nov.–Apr., Tues.–Sun. 10–5; tours Thurs. at 3.*

The late-Gothic **St. Nikolaikirche** *(St. Nicholas's Church)*, with a 120-foot-high nave, was built between 1381 and 1487. A remnant of the town's long domination by Sweden is the additional altar built for Swedish sailors. ⊠*Marktpl.* ☎*03841/210–143* ☉*May–Sept., daily 8–8; Apr. and Oct., daily 10–6; Nov.–Mar., daily 11–4.*

If you have an hour to spare, wander among the jetties and quays of the port, a mix of the medieval and the modern. **To'n Zägenkrog,** a seamen's haven decorated with sharks' teeth, stuffed seagulls, and maritime gear, is a good pit stop along the harbor. ⊠*Ziegenmarkt 10* ☎*03841/282–716.*

WHERE TO STAY & EAT

$–$$
★
✕**Alter Schwede.** Regarded as one of the most attractive, authentic taverns on the Baltic—and correspondingly busy—this eatery focuses on Mecklenburg's game and poultry dishes, such as the traditional *Mecklenburger Ente* (Mecklenburg duck). This filling dish is filled with baked plums, apples, raisins, and served with red cabbage and potatoes. ⊠*Am Markt 19* ☎*03841/283–552* ⊟*AE, MC, V.*

$$–$$$
▦**Seehotel Neuklostersee.** Set at the dreamy Naun Lake, this country hotel is a hidden gem 15 km (9 mi) east of Wismar. The redbrick farmhouse and old thatch-roof barn constitute an upscale yet casual hotel. Each room has a different design (the owners are acclaimed Berlin interior designers), with white walls and terra-cotta tiles. There's a fine restaurant ($) serving German-Italian seafood on a terrace. **Pros:** great rural setting in quaint surroundings. **Cons:** outside Wismar, many day-trip visitors. ⊠*Seestr. 1 Nakenstorf* ☎*038422/4570* ⊕*www.seehotel-neuklostersee.de* ⇨*10 suites, 3 apartments* ♿*In-room: no a/c, Wi-Fi. In-hotel: restaurant, gym,*

beachfront, bicycles, no elevator, parking (no fee), no-smoking rooms, some pets allowed ▤MC ⋔◎⎮BP.

$$ ⊡**Citypartner Hotel Alter Speicher.** This small and very personal family-owned hotel is behind the facade of an old merchant house in the downtown area. Some of the rooms may be tiny, but their size contributes to the warm and cozy atmosphere. The lobby and restaurants are decorated with wooden beams and panels. The main restaurant ($$–$$$$) primarily serves game, but it also prepares regional dishes. **Pros:** good location, as medieval parts of Wismar are within easy walking-distance. **Cons:** rooms have outdated furnishings and ambience. ✉*Bohrstr. 12–12a* ☎*03841/211–746* ⊕*www.hotel-alter-speicher.de* ⤙*70 rooms, 3 suites, 2 apartments* ♿*In-room: no a/c, safe, refrigerator, Wi-Fi. In-hotel: restaurant, bar, gym, parking (fee), no-smoking rooms, some pets allowed* ▤DC, MC, V ⋔◎⎮BP.

$$ ⊡**Steigenberger–Hotel Stadt Hamburg.** This first-class hotel hides behind a rigid gray facade dating back to the early 19th century. The interior is surprisingly open and airy, with skylights and a posh lobby. The rooms have elegant cherrywood art deco–style furnishings. Downstairs, the Bierkeller, a cavernous 17th-century room with vaulted ceilings, is a trendy nightspot. **Pros:** the only upscale hotel in town, with an appealing interior design, great package deals available. **Cons:** lacks atmosphere and personal touches. ✉*Am Markt 24* ☎*03841/2390* ⊕*www. wismar.steigenberger.de* ⤙*102 rooms, 2 suites* ♿*In-room: no a/c, refrigerator, Wi-Fi. In-hotel: restaurant, no-smoking rooms, some pets allowed (fee)* ▤AE, DC, MC, V ⋔◎⎮BP.

SCHWERIN

★ *32 km (20 mi) south of Wismar on Route 106.*

Schwerin, the second-largest town in the region after Rostock and the capital of the state of Mecklenburg-Vorpommern, is worth a trip just to visit its giant island palace.

ESSENTIALS

Visitor Information Schwerin (✉*Am Markt 14* ☎*0385/592–5212* ⊕*www. schwerin.de*).

EXPLORING

On the edge of Lake Schwerin, the meticulously restored **Schweriner Schloss** once housed the Mecklenburg royal family. The original palace dates from 1018, but was enlarged by Henry the Lion when he founded Schwerin in 1160. Portions of it were later modeled on Chambord, in the Loire Valley. As it stands now, the palace is surmounted by 15 turrets, large and small, and is reminiscent of a French château. The portions that are neo-Renaissance in style are its many ducal staterooms, which date from between 1845 and 1857.

North of the main tower is the **Neue Lange Haus** (New Long House), built between 1553 and 1555 and now used as the **Schlossmuseum.** The Communist government restored and maintained the fantastic opulence of this rambling, 80-room reminder of an absolutist monarchy—

and then used it to board kindergarten teachers in training. Antique furniture, objets d'art, silk tapestries, and paintings are sprinkled throughout the salons (the throne room is particularly extravagant), but of special interest are the ornately patterned and highly burnished inlaid wooden floors and wall panels. ⊠*Lennéstr. 1* ☎*0385/525–2920* ⊕*www.schloss-schwerin.de* ☒€*4* ☉*Mid-Apr.–mid-Oct., daily 10–6; mid-Oct.–mid-Apr., Tues.–Sun. 10–5.*

The **Alter Garten** *(Old Garden)*, the town's showpiece square, was the setting of military parades during the years of Communist rule. It's dominated by two buildings: the ornate neo-Renaissance state theater, constructed in 1883–86; and the **Staatliches Museum** (State Museum), which houses an interesting collection of paintings by Max Liebermann and Lovis Corinth. ⊠*Alter Garten 3* ☎*0385/5958–119* ⊕*www. schloss-schwerin.de* ☒€*3* ☉*Mid-Apr.–mid-Oct., Tues.–Sun. 10–6; mid-Oct.–mid-Apr., Tues.–Sun. 10–5.*

The **Dom**, a Gothic cathedral, is the oldest building (built 1222–48) in the city. The bronze baptismal font is from the 14th century; the altar was built in 1440. Religious scenes painted on its walls date from the Middle Ages. Sweeping views of the Old Town and lake await those with the energy to climb the 219 steps to the top of the 320-foot-high cathedral tower. ⊠*Am Dom 4* ☎*0385/565–014* ☉*Tower and nave May–Oct., Mon.–Sat. 10–5, Sun. noon–5; Nov.–Apr., weekdays 11–4, Sat. 11–4, Sun. noon–4.*

The quintessential experience in Schwerin is one of the **Weisse Flotte** boat tours of the lakes—there are seven in the area. A trip to the island of Kaninchenwerder, a small sanctuary for more than 100 species of waterbirds, is an unforgettable experience. Boats for this 1½-hour standard tour depart from the pier adjacent to the Schweriner Schloss. ⊠*Anlegestelle Schlosspier* ☎*0385/557–770* ⊕*www.weisseflotteschwerin.de* ☒€*9.50* ☉*Apr.–Oct., daily 10–5:30.*

WHERE TO EAT

$–$$ ✕ **Alt-Schweriner Schankstuben.** A small family-owned restaurant and hotel with 16 guest rooms, the Schankstuben emphasizes Mecklenburg tradition. Its inviting restaurant is perfect for sampling local recipes such as *Matjes* (salted fish) or *Maisscholle* (corn-fed plaice). ⊠*Schlachtermarkt 9–13* ☎*0385/592–530* ⊕ *www.alt-schweriner-schankstuben. de* ▭*AE, DC, MC, V*

$–$$ ✕**Weinhaus Krömer.** One of the most traditional and popular eateries
★ in Schwerin, this recently revamped restaurant has a long history of serving good wines and dates back to 1740. The *Weinbistro* offers primarily German wine tasting and a small menu (mostly cheese plates or soups such as lobster cream soup). Regional and international specialties are served in the modern restaurant, while in summer the Weingarten courtyard is one of the city's most secluded spots to enjoy a good glass of wine. ⊠*Schusterstr. 13–15* ☎*0385/562–956* ▭*AE, MC, V.*

WHERE TO STAY

$–$$ ⚏ **Hotel Niederländischer Hof.** The city's most elegant hotel has a 4½-star rating in view of its luxurious interior, decorated in a classic style; its romantic, airy rooms; the impeccable service; and, of course, the fine nouvelle cuisine à la Mecklenburg (mostly seafood dishes). All this is tucked inside a late-19th-century historic mansion located on old Schwerin's Pfaffenteich. **Pros:** interesting packages include tours, dinner, and more, great location right off a lake and within walking distance of the Schloss and downtown museums. **Con:** formal atmosphere. ✉ *Alexandrinnenstr. 12–13* ☎ *0385/591–100* ⊕ *www.niederlaendischer-hof.de* ⟲ *27 rooms, 6 suites ⚭ In-room: no a/c, safe. In-hotel: restaurant, room service, laundry service, public Wi-Fi, parking (no fee), no-smoking rooms, some pets allowed* ☰ *AE, MC, V* ⊙| *BP.*

$–$$ ⚏ **Sorat-Hotel Speicher am Ziegelsee.** Towering seven stories above the old harbor, the Speicher am Ziegelsee was once a wheat warehouse. The 1939 building's rooms and spacious apartments are decorated with natural materials and earthy tones and have all the amenities of a modern, first-class hotel. A choice spot for sitting is the wooden terrace bordering the lake. **Pros:** unbeatable location on a lovely lake and lakeside dining, very friendly and professional service. **Cons:** old-style warehouse building, whose rooms may seem cramped for some travelers. ✉ *Speicherstr. 11* ☎ *0385/50030* ⊕ *www.speicher-hotel.com* ⟲ *59 rooms, 20 apartments ⚭ In-room: no a/c, kitchen. In-hotel: restaurant, room service, bar, laundry service, public Wi-Fi, parking (no fee), no-smoking rooms, some pets allowed* ☰ *AE, DC, MC, V* ⊙| *BP.*

NIGHTLIFE & THE ARTS

The **Mecklenburgisches Staatstheater** (✉ *Am Alten Garten* ☎ *0385/53000*) stages German drama and opera. In June, check out the **Schlossfestspiele** for open-air drama or comedy performances.

The **Mexxclub** (✉ *Klöresgang 2* ☎ *No phone*) is the city's hottest dance club, featuring house and soul DJs who attract a stylish young crowd every Saturday night.

SHOPPING

■ TIP→ **Antiques and bric-a-brac that have languished in cellars and attics since World War II are still surfacing throughout eastern Germany, and the occasional bargain can be found.** The best places to look in Schwerin are on and around **Schmiedestrasse, Schlossstrasse,** and **Mecklenburgstrasse.**

BAD DOBERAN

60 km (37 mi) east of Wismar on Route 105, 90 km (56 mi) northeast of Schwerin.

Bad Doberan, mostly famous for its cathedral, is a quaint town with Germany's oldest sea resort, Heiligendamm. The city is a popular weekend and summer getaway for people from Rostock and Berlin, but has managed to maintain its laid-back charm.

14

ESSENTIALS

Visitor Information Bad Doberan (⊠*Alexandrinenpl. 2* ☎*038203/62154* ⊕*www.bad-doberan.de*).

EXPLORING

★ Bad Doberan is home to the meticulously restored redbrick **Doberaner Münster** *(monastery church)*, one of the finest of its kind in Germany. It was built by Cistercian monks between 1294 and 1368 in the northern German Gothic style, with a central nave and transept. The main altar dates from the early 14th century. ⊠*Klosterstr. 2* ☎*038203/62716* ⊕*www.doberanermuenster.de* 🎫*€2* ⊗*May–Sept., Mon.–Sat. 9–6, Sun. 11–6; Mar., Apr., and Oct., Mon.–Sat. 10–5, Sun. 11–5; Nov.–Feb., Mon.–Sat. 10–4, Sun. 11–4. Tours May–Oct., Mon.–Sat. at noon and 3; Nov.–Apr., Mon.–Sat. at 11 and 1.*

☺ No visit to this part of the country would be complete without a ride on **Molli,** a steam train that has been chugging up and down a 16-km (10-mi) narrow-gauge track between Bad Doberan and the nearby beach resorts of **Heiligendamm** and **Kühlungsborn** since 1886. The train was nicknamed after a little local dog that barked its approval every time the smoking iron horse passed by. In summer *Molli* runs 13 times daily between Bad Doberan and Kühlungsborn. ⊠*Mecklenburgische Bäderbahn Molli, Küstenbus GmbH* ☎*038203/4150* ⊕*www.molli-bahn. de* 🎫*Same-day round-trip €6–€10* ⊗*From Bad Doberan: May–Sept., daily 8:35–6:45; Oct.–Apr., daily 8:35–4:40.*

WHERE TO STAY & EAT

¢–$ ✕**Weisser Pavillon.** Here's a mixed setting for you: a 19th-century Chinese-pagoda-type structure in an English-style park. Come for lunch or high tea; regional specialties are featured. In summer the café stays open until 10 PM. ⊠*Auf dem Kamp* ☎*038203/62326* 🚫*No credit cards.*

$$$–$$$$ 🏨**Kempinski Grand Hotel.** The small beach resort of Heiligendamm has
Fodor'sChoice regained its prewar reputation as a getaway for Berlin's up-and-coming
★ crowd. Nestled in five meticulously restored, gleaming white structures on a secluded beach, the Kempinski displays an almost Californian Bel Air charm and offers timelessly furnished rooms decorated in soft colors. There are endless activities offered, and the spa area is breathtaking. **Pros:** the only real first-class hotel on the Baltic Coast, with a wide range of sports and activities. **Cons:** very large hotel spread out in somewhat long distances, service is formal and stiff at times, books up quickly in high season. ⊠*Grand Hotel at Heiligendamm, Prof.-Dr.-Vogel-Str. 16–18 Heiligendamm* ☎*038203/7400* ⊕*www.kempinski-heiligendamm.com* 🛏*118 rooms, 107 suites* ♿*In-room: safe, Ethernet, Wi-Fi. In-hotel: restaurant, room service, bar, pool, gym, spa, beachfront, concierge, laundry service, public Internet, parking (fee), no-smoking rooms, some pets allowed* 🚫*AE, DC, MC, V* ⊗*BP.*

$–$$ 🏨**Hotel Friedrich-Franz-Palais.** Built in 1793 for a Mecklenburg duke,
★ this whitewashed hotel has accommodated guests for more than 200 years. Completely restored, each room exudes old-world elegance with modern comforts. The small restaurant ($–$$$) serves mostly fresh fish and game in a setting ideal for a candlelight dinner. **Pros:**

beautiful interior design, perfect, central location, very good package deals during the high season. **Con:** wellness area is small. ⊠*Am Kamp* ☏*038203/63036* ⊕*www.friedrich-franz-palais.de* ⮐*50 rooms, 2 suites, 2 apartments* ⅊ *In-room: no a/c, refrigerator. In-hotel: restaurant, room service, bicycles, public Internet, public Wi-Fi, parking (no fee), no-smoking rooms, some pets allowed* ▤*AE, DC, MC, V* ⦿|*BP.*

ROSTOCK

14 km (9 mi) east of Bad Doberan on Route 105.

Rostock, the biggest port and shipbuilding center of the former East Germany, was founded around 1200. Of all the Hanseatic cities, the once-thriving Rostock suffered the most from the dissolution of the League in 1669. The GDR (German Democratic Republic) reestablished Rostock as a major port, but port work has been cut in half since reunification, and though ferries come from Gedser (Denmark) and Trelleborg (Sweden), there's little traffic. ■TIP➡ **The biggest local annual attraction is Hanse Sail, a week of yacht racing held in August.**

14

ESSENTIALS

Visitor Information Rostock–Warnemünde (⊠*Am Strom 59* ☏*0381/548–000* ⎙*0381/548–0014* ⊕*www.rostock.de*).

EXPLORING

The main street, the pedestrians-only **Kröpelinerstrasse,** begins at the old western gate, the Kröpeliner Tor. Here you'll find the finest examples of late-Gothic and Renaissance houses of rich Hanse merchants.

The triangular **Universitätsplatz** *(University Square)*, commemorating the founding of northern Europe's first university here in 1419, is home to Rostock University's Italian Renaissance–style main building, finished in 1867.

At the **Neuer Markt** *(Town Square)* you'll immediately notice the architectural potpourri of the **Rathaus.** Basically 13th-century Gothic with a baroque facade, the town hall spouts seven slender, decorative towers that look like candles on a peculiar birthday cake. Historic gabled houses surround the rest of the square.

Four-century-old **St. Marienkirche** *(St. Mary's Church)*, the Gothic architectural prize of Rostock, boasts a bronze baptismal font from 1290 and some interesting baroque features, notably the oak altar (1720) and organ (1770). Unique is the huge astronomical clock dating from 1472; it has a calendar extending to the year 2017. ⊠*Am Ziegenmarkt 4* ☏*0381/492–3396* ⊙*Oct.–Apr., Mon.–Sat. 10–12:15 and 2–4, Sun. 11–12:15; May–Sept., Mon.–Sat. 10–6, Sun. 11:15–5.*

☾ The **Schifffahrtsmuseum** *(Maritime Museum)* traces the history of shipping on the Baltic and displays models of ships, which especially intrigue children. It's just beyond the city wall, at the old city gateway, Steintor. ⊠*August-Bebel-Str. 1* ☏*0381/4922–697* ⛫*€3* ⊙*Tues.–Sun. 11–6.*

The **Zoologischer Garten** *(Zoological Garden)* has one of the largest collections of exotic animals and birds in northern Germany. This zoo is particularly noted for its polar bears, some of which were bred in Rostock. If you're traveling with children, a visit is a must. ⊠*Rennbahnallee 21* ☎*0381/20820* ⊕*www.zoo-rostock.de* 🎫*€11* ⊗*Nov.–Mar., daily 9–5; Apr.–Oct., daily 9–7.*

WHERE TO EAT

$–$$ ✕**Restaurant & Bar Silo 4.** Rostock's latest culinary venture is proof that eastern Germany can do sleek and modern. At the top of a waterfront office tower, this innovative restaurant offers spectacular views of the river and a fun and interesting approach to Asian-fusion cuisine. The menu consists of a list of ingredients and seasonings. Guests choose what they like and then leave it to the experts in the show kitchen to work their magic. ⊠*Am Strande 3d* ☎*0381/458–5800* ⊕*www.silo4. de* ▤*AE, DC, MC, V* ⊗*Closed Mon. No lunch.*

$ ✕**Petrikeller.** Once you've crossed the threshold of the Petrikeller, you'll find yourself in the medieval world of Hanseatic merchants, seamen, and wild pirates such as Klaus Störtebecker. The restaurant's motto, "*Wer nicht liebt Wein, Weib und Gesang bleibt ein Narr sein Leben lang*" (He who doth not love wine, woman and song will be a fool his whole life long), a quote from reformer Martin Luther no less, sets the right tone. ⊠*Harte Str. 27* ☎*0381/455–855* ⊕*www.petrikeller.de* ▤*No credit cards* ⊗*Closed Mon. No lunch.*

$ ✕**Zur Kogge.** Looking like the cabin of some ancient sailing vessel, ★ the oldest sailors' beer tavern in town serves mostly fish. Order the *Mecklenburger Fischsuppe* (fish soup) if it's on the menu. The *Grosser Fischteller,* consisting of three kinds of fish—depending on the day's catch—served with vegetables, lobster and shrimp sauce, and potatoes, is also a popular choice. ⊠*Wokrenterstr. 27* ☎*0381/493–4493* ⌂*Reservations essential* ▤*DC, MC, V.*

WHERE TO STAY

$$–$$$ 🏨**Steigenberger–Hotel zur Sonne Rostock.** With more than 200 years of ★ history behind it, the "Sun," located within the Old Town, is one of the nicest hotels in Rostock. Guests here relax and enjoy the Hanseatic mansion's maritime atmosphere, the inviting wine bar, very friendly service, and large, modern rooms. ◼TIP➔ **Ask for a top-floor room, cozily fitted under the eaves. Pros:** nice view and near many sights, good restaurants, cafés, and bars nearby. **Cons:** rooms get direct sunlight in summer, and therefore are very warm, open setting of bed in the middle of the room may be unsettling for some. ⊠*Neuer Markt 2* ☎*0381/49730* ⊕*www.rostock.steigenberger.de* ⌁*90 rooms, 21 suites* ⌂*In-room: no a/c, Wi-Fi. In-hotel: restaurant, bar, parking (fee), no-smoking rooms, some pets allowed* ▤*AE, DC, MC, V* ⋉❙*BP.*

$$ 🏨**Pental Hotel.** A 19th-century mansion, this hotel is a genuine part of Rostock's historic Old Town. It provides smooth service, and the modern rooms are tastefully decorated. Despite its downtown location, it's a quiet place to stay. **Pros:** good location, very quiet backstreet. **Cons:** restaurant not very good, bland room design. ⊠*Schwaansche Str. 6* ☎*0381/49700* ⊕*www.pentahotels.com* ⌁*150 rooms, 2 suites*

⚉*In-room: no a/c, Wi-Fi. In-hotel: restaurant, room service, bar, gym, laundry service, parking (fee), no-smoking rooms, some pets allowed* □*AE, DC, MC, V* 🀤*BP.*

WARNEMÜNDE

14 km (9 mi) north of Rostock on Route 103.

Warnemünde is a quaint seaside resort town with the best hotels and restaurants in the area, as well as 20 km (12 mi) of beautiful white-sand beach. It's been a popular summer getaway for families in eastern Germany for years.

GETTING HERE & AROUND

Thanks to its close location to Rostock and the A–20, Warnemünde is easily accessible from any major city in the region. Traffic between the seaside district of Rostock and the downtown area can be heavy on summer weekends. The best way to explore the city is by riding a bike or walking.

EXPLORING

Children enjoy climbing to the top of the town landmark, a 115-foot-high **Leuchtturm** *(lighthouse)*, dating from 1898; on clear days it offers views of the coast and Rostock Harbor.

Inland from the lighthouse is the yacht marina known as **Alter Strom** *(Old Stream)*. Once the entry into the port of Warnemünde, it now has bars and shops.

WHERE TO STAY & EAT

¢–$ ✕**Fischerklause.** Sailors have stopped in at this restaurant's bar since the turn of the 20th century. The smoked fish sampler, served on a lazy Susan, is delicious, and the house specialty of fish soup is best washed down with some Rostocker Doppel-Kümmel schnapps. An accordionist entertains the crowd on weekends. ✉*Am Strom 123* ☎*0381/52516* ⚉*Reservations essential* □*AE, DC, MC, V.*

$$$$ 🏨**Yachthafenresidenz Hohe Düne.** The new star on the Baltic Coast is ★ this huge, modern resort comfortably residing on a peninsula between the yacht harbor, a sandy beach, and the port entrance. Setting a new standard of luxury in the region, the smartly designed Hohe Düne offers maritime-theme rooms and suites with names reminiscent of ship quarters, such as "Boatman's Cabin" or "Captain's Suite." A real catch is the spa, taking up a full three floors with a pool, several saunas, and plenty of massage rooms. **Pros:** very well-run, stylish hotel with a great ambience and all the amenities, impressive wellness and spa area. **Cons:** outside Rostock and not along the central promenade, only a few attractions and restaurants in walking distance. ✉*Hohe Düne, Am Yachthafen 1–8* ☎*0381/5040* ⊕*www.yhd.de* ↩*345 rooms, 23 suites* ⚉*In-room: safe. In-hotel: 6 restaurants, room service, bar, pool, gym, spa, beachfront, concierge, laundry service, public Wi-Fi, parking (fee), no-smoking rooms, some pets allowed* □*AE, DC, MC, V* 🀤*BP.*

$ 🏨**Landhotel Ostseetraum.** This family-owned hotel, in a thatch-roof farmhouse outside Warnemünde, blends contemporary style with rural architecture. The refurbished apartments all feature a kitchenette and separate sitting or living areas. The standard rooms are smaller—some have a maritime flair with dark, heavy furniture and large beds; others, which are even smaller, have a country feel with bright pinewood furnishings. The hotel is 500 yards from the beach. **Pros:** quiet, green setting not far away from the sea, friendly and personalized service, very private apartments. **Cons:** old-fashioned interior design in need of updating in some rooms and public areas. ✉ *Stolteraerweg 34bD–18119 Warnemünde-Diedrichshagen* ☎ *0381/519–1848* ⊕ *www. Ostseetraum.de* ⟳*18 rooms* ⌂ *In-room: no a/c. In-hotel: restaurant, no elevator, parking (no fee), some pets allowed* ⊟*AE, MC, V* ⦿|*BP.*

NIGHTLIFE

The pubs in the marina **Alter Strom** are fun gathering places. The **Skybar** (✉*Seestr. 19, 19th fl. of Neptun Hotel* ☎*0381/7770*) is open Friday and Saturday until 3 AM. ▪TIP➔ **Roof access gives you the chance to sit under the stars and watch ship lights twinkle on the sea.**

VORPOMMERN

The best description of this region is found in its name, which simply means "before Pomerania." This area, indeed, seems trapped between Mecklenburg and the authentic, old Pomerania farther east, now part of Poland. Its remoteness ensures an unforgettable view of unspoiled nature, primarily attracting families and younger travelers.

STRALSUND

68 km (42 mi) east of Rostock on Route 105.

This jewel of the Baltic has retained its historic city center and parts of its 13th-century defensive wall. The wall was built following an attack by the Lübeck fleet in 1249. In 1815 the Congress of Vienna awarded the city, which had been under Swedish control, to the Prussians.

GETTING HERE & AROUND

Stralsund is well linked to both Rostock and Berlin by A–20 and A–19. The city is an ideal base for exploring the coast via the well-developed network of Bundesstrassen around it. Inside the city, walking or biking are better options, though, as the dense, historic downtown area makes it difficult to drive.

ESSENTIALS

Visitor Information **Stralsund** (✉*Alter Markt 9* ☎*03831/24690* ⊕*www. stralsund.de*).

EXPLORING

The **Alter Markt** *(Old Market Square)* has the best local architecture, ranging from Gothic to Renaissance to baroque. Most buildings were rich merchants' homes, notably the late-Gothic **Wulflamhaus**, with 17 ornate, steeply stepped gables. Stralsund's architectural masterpiece, however, is the 14th-century **Rathaus,** considered by many to be the finest secular example of redbrick Gothic.

The treasures of the 13th-century Gothic **St. Nikolaikirche** *(St. Nicholas's Church)* include a 15-foot-high crucifix from the 14th century, an astronomical clock from 1394, and a famous baroque altar. ⊠*Alter Markt* ☎*03831/297–199* ☉*Apr.–Sept., Mon.–Sat. 10–6, Sun. 11–noon and 2–4; Oct.–Mar., Mon.–Sat. 10–noon and 2–4, Sun. 11–noon and 2–4.*

The **Katherinenkloster** *(St. Catherine's Monastery)* is a former cloister; 40 of its rooms now house two museums: the famed Deutsches Meeresmuseum, and the Kulturhistorisches Museum.

The **Kulturhistorisches Museum** *(Cultural History Museum)* exhibits diverse artifacts from more than 10,000 years of this coastal region's history. Highlights include a toy collection and 10th-century Viking gold jewelry found on Hiddensee. You'll reach the museums by walking along Ossenreyerstrasse through the Apollonienmarkt on Mönchstrasse. ⊠*Kulturhistorisches Museum, Mönchstr. 25–27* ☎*03831/28790* ☞*€4* ☉*Daily 10–5.*

14

☺ The Stralsund aquarium of Baltic Sea life is part of the three-floor **Deutsches Meeresmuseum** *(German Sea Museum),* which also displays the skeletons of a giant whale and a hammerhead shark, and a 25-foot-high chunk of coral. ⊠*Katharinenberg 14–20, entrance on Mönchstr.* ☎*03831/265–021* ⊕*www.meeresmuseum.de* ☞*€7.50* ☉*Oct.–May, daily 10–5; June–Sept., daily 10–6.*

The enormous **St. Marienkirche** *(St. Mary's Church)* is the largest of Stralsund's three redbrick Gothic churches. With 4,000 pipes and intricate decorative figures, the magnificent 17th-century Stellwagen organ (played only during Sunday services) is a delight to see and hear. The view from the church tower of Stralsund's old city center is well worth climbing 349 steps. ⊠*Neuer Markt, entrance at Bleistr.* ☎*03831/293–529* ☞*Tour of church tower €4* ☉*May–Oct., weekdays 9–6, weekends 10–noon; Nov.–Apr., weekdays 10–noon and 2–6, weekends 10–noon.*

WHERE TO STAY & EAT

$ ✕**Wulflamstuben.** This restaurant is on the ground floor of the Wulflamhaus, a 14th-century gabled house on the old market square. Steaks and fish are the specialties; in late spring or early summer, get the light and tasty *Ostseescholle* (grilled plaice), fresh from the Baltic Sea. In winter the hearty *Stralsunder Aalsuppe* (Stralsund eel soup) is a must. ⊠*Alter Markt 5* ☎*03831/291–533* ⚒*Reservations essential* ⊟*AE, MC, V.*

$ ✕**Zum Alten Fritz.** It's worth the trip here just to see the rustic interior and copper brewing equipment. Good old German beer and ale of all shades are the main focus. In summer the beer garden gets somewhat rambunctious. ⊠*Greifswalder Chaussee 84–85, at B–96a* ☎*03831/25550* ⊟*MC, V.*

$$ ▦**Hotel zur Post.** This redbrick hotel is a great deal for travelers looking for a homey yet first-class ambience. It's on the market square near the

Old Town. The hotel's interior is a thoughtful mix of traditional North German furnishings and modern design. **Pros:** very good location in the heart of the historic downtown area. **Cons:** very small rooms with too much furniture, some in need of updating. ⊠*Am Neuen Markt, Tribseerstr. 22* ☏*03831/200–500* ⊕*www.hotel-zur-post-stralsund.de* ⇨*104 rooms, 2 suites, 8 apartments* ⌂*In-room: no a/c, safe, Wi-Fi. In-hotel: restaurant, room service, bar, laundry service, parking (fee), no-smoking rooms, some pets allowed* ⊟*AE, MC, V* ⎮⎰⎮*BP.*

$–$$ 🏨 **Dorint im HanseDom.** This hotel, part of a German chain, is a modern
★   property with winning amenities and great hospitality at an unbeatable price. The high-rise hotel doesn't look appealing at first glance, but the spacious rooms (featuring many extras such as a baby bed, satellite TV, and a work desk) are furnished in bright colors and ensure a most pleasant stay. The biggest attraction, the hotel's Vital Spa, is a huge wellness facility. **Pros:** top spa, popular with locals as well, solid and reliable services and amenities, long breakfast service (until 11 AM). **Cons:** for Stralsund, this is a large, busy hotel, far away from city center (15 minutes). ⊠*Grünhofer Bogen 18–20* ☏*03831/37730* ⊕*www.dorint.de* ⇨*109 rooms, 5 suites* ⌂*In-room: safe, Wi-Fi. In-hotel: restaurant, room service, bar, pool, spa, laundry service, public Internet, parking (fee), no-smoking rooms, some pets allowed* ⊟*AE, DC, MC, V* ⎮⎰⎮*BP.*

SHOPPING

Buddelschiffe (ships in a bottle) are a symbol of the magnificent sailing history of this region. They look easy to build, but they aren't, and they're quite delicate. Expect to pay more than €70 for a 1-liter bottle. Also look for *Fischerteppiche* (fisherman's carpets). Eleven square feet of these traditional carpets take 150 hours to create, which explains why they're meant only to be hung on the wall—and why they cost from €260 to €1,200. They're decorated with traditional symbols of the region, such as the mythical griffin.

RÜGEN ISLAND

Fodor'sChoice   *4 km (2½ mi) northeast of Stralsund on Route 96.*
★
Rügen's diverse and breathtaking landscapes have inspired poets and painters for more than a century. Railways in the mid-19th century brought the first vacationers, and many of the grand mansions and villas on the island date from this period. The island's main route runs between the **Grosser Jasmunder Bodden** (Big Jasmund Inlet), a giant sea inlet, and a smaller expanse of water, the **Kleiner Jasmunder Bodden** (Little Jasmund Inlet Lake), to the port of Sassnitz. You're best off staying at any of the island's four main vacation centers—Sassnitz, Binz, Sellin, and Göhren.

GETTING HERE & AROUND

Rügen is an easy two-hour drive from Rostock and a 15-minute drive from Stralsund via the B–96. As there is only one bridge connecting the island to the mainland, the road can get clogged occasionally in summer. On the island, a car is highly recommended to reach the more remote beaches.

ESSENTIALS

Visitor Information Rügen Island (✉ *Tourismusverband Rügen, Bahnhofstr. 15Bergen* ☎ *03838/80770* 🖷 *03838/254–440* ⊕ *www.ruegen.de*). **Sassnitz** (✉ *Hauptstr. 18* ☎ *038392/5160* 🖷 *038392/51616* ⊕ *www.sassnitz.de*).

EXPLORING

The small town of **Bergen,** the island's administrative capital, was founded as a Slavic settlement some 900 years ago. The **Marienkirche** (St. Mary's Church) has geometric murals dating back to the late 1100s and painted brick octagonal pillars. The pulpit and altar are baroque. Outside the front door and built into the church facade is a gravestone from the 1200s.

14

OFF THE
BEATEN
PATH

Hiddensee. Off the northwest corner of Rügen is a smaller island called Hiddensee. The undisturbed solitude of this sticklike island has attracted such visitors as Albert Einstein, Thomas Mann, Rainer Maria Rilke, and Sigmund Freud. As Hiddensee is an auto-free zone, leave your car in Schaprode, 21 km (13 mi) west of Bergen, and take a ferry. Vacation cottages and restaurants are on the island.

Marking the northernmost point in eastern Germany is the lighthouse at **Kap Arkona,** a nature lover's paradise filled with blustery sand dunes. The redbrick lighthouse was designed by Karl Friedrich Schinkel, the architect responsible for so many of today's landmarks in Berlin.

The small fishing town of **Sassnitz** is the island's harbor for ferries to Sweden. Sassnitz is surrounded by some of the most pristine nature to be found along the Baltic Coast. From Sassnitz, walk to **Jasmund Nationalpark** (⊕ *www.nationalpark-jasmund.de*) to explore the marshes, lush pine forests, and towering chalk cliffs. Ten kilometers (6 mi) north of Sassnitz are the twin chalk cliffs of Rügen's main attraction, the **Stubbenkammer** headland. From here you can best see the much-photographed white-chalk cliffs called the **Königstuhl,** rising 350 feet from the sea. A steep trail leads down to a beach.

South of Sassnitz, **Binz** is the largest resort town on Rügen's east coast, with white villas and a beach promenade. Standing on the highest point of East Rügen is the **Jagdschloss Granitz,** a hunting lodge built in 1836. It offers a splendid view in all directions from its lookout tower and has an excellent hunting exhibit. ✉ *2 km (1 mi) south of Binz* ☎ *038393/663–814* 🎫 *€3* 🕙 *May–Sept., daily 9–6; Oct.–Apr., Tues.–Sun. 10–4.* Four kilometers (2½ mi) north of Binz are five concrete quarters of **Bad Prora,** where the Nazis once planned to provide vacation quarters for up to 20,000 German workers. The complex was never used, except by the East German army. Museums and galleries here today include one that documents the history of the site.

The heart of the town **Putbus,** 28 km (17 mi) southwest of Binz, is the Circus, a round central plaza dating back to the early 19th century. The immaculate white buildings surrounding the Circus give the city its nickname, "Weisse Stadt" (White City). In summer the blooming roses in front of the houses (once a requirement by the ruling noble family of Putbus) are truly spectacular.

From Putbus you can take a ride on the 90-year-old miniature steam train, the **Rasender Roland** *(Racing Roland)*, which runs 24 km (16 mi) to Göhren, at the southeast corner of Rügen. Trains leave hourly (every two hours in winter); the ride takes 70 minutes one way. ✉*Binzer Str. 12* ☎*038301/8010* ⊕*www.rasenderroland.de* 💶*€8* ⊙*Apr.–Oct., daily 7:48 AM–7:46 PM with hourly departures from Putbus. Nov.–Mar., daily 7:48 AM–5:44 PM, with departures every 2 hrs.*

SHOPPING

At the end of the 19th century, 16 pieces of 10th-century Viking jewelry were discovered on the Baltic coastline (presently housed in the Kulturhistorisches Museum in Stralsund). Gold and silver replicas of the **Hiddensee Golden Jewelry** are a great souvenir, and their distinctive patterns are found in shops on Rügen Island and on Hiddensee Island.

WHERE TO EAT

$-$$ ✗**Panoramahotel Lohme.** Dinner at this restaurant dubbed "Rügen's bal-
★ cony" offers some of the most beautiful views on the island. While enjoying fresh fish from local waters, prepared with a light Italian touch, you can watch the sunset over the cliffs of Kap Arkona. Chef Marcus Uhlich uses fresh produce from local farmers, and the superb vintages are from small private wineries. ■TIP➡ Make a reservation, and insist on a table in the *Fontane-Veranda* (in winter) or the *Arkonablick-Terrasse* (in summer). ✉*An der Steilküste 8, Lohme* ☎*038302/9110* 🖃*No credit cards.*

WHERE TO STAY

$$ 🏨**Travel Charme Hotel Kurhaus Binz.** The grand old lady of the Baltic
★ Sea, the neoclassical 19th-century Kurhaus Binz is reviving the splendor of times past, when Binz was called the Nice of the North. The four-star Kurhaus is right on the beach, with a breathtaking sea view from most of the spacious and elegantly furnished rooms. The huge Egyptian-theme spa and wellness area is a real treat. Of the two restaurants, the Kurhaus-Restaurant ($$–$$$) is the better choice—it serves traditional seafood but adds exotic touches with special fusion-cuisine. **Pros:** great breakfast buffet, extremely clean rooms and public areas, highly trained and friendly personnel, all the amenities. **Cons:** lacks the feel of a typical Rügen hotel, not very personal or intimate. ✉*Strandpromenade 27D–18609 Binz-Rügen* ☎*038393/6650* ⊕*www.travelcharme.com* 🛏*106 rooms, 20 suites* ⚭*In-room: refrigerator. In-hotel: 2 restaurants, room service, bar, pool, gym, spa, beachfront, concierge, laundry service, public Wi-Fi, parking (fee), no-smoking rooms, some pets allowed* 🖃*AE, DC, MC, V* ⏐⊙⏐*BP.*

$-$$ 🏨**Hotel Godewind.** This small hotel offers food and lodging at very reasonable prices. In addition, the hotel rents small cottages and apartments around the island, which are a good value if you intend to stay for more than a few days. ■TIP➡ **Godewind's restaurant ($) is known on the island for its regional dishes.** **Pros:** quiet setting and very cozy rooms with nice furniture. **Cons:** almost no amenities and services offered. ✉*Süderende 53D–18565 Vitte-Hiddensee* ☎*038300/6600* 🖷*038300/660–222* 🌐*www.hotelgodewind.de* 🛏*23 rooms, 19 cottages* ⚐*In-room: no a/c. In-hotel: restaurant, some pets allowed* 🚫*No credit cards* ❖❘*BP.*

$–$$
★
🏨**Vier Jahreszeiten.** This first-class beach resort in Binz is a sophisticated blend of historic seaside architecture and modern elegance. Behind the ornamental white facade the hotel boasts spacious rooms decorated with 19th-century reproduction furniture, as well as more-secluded apartments. A great plus is the nearly 6,000-square-foot spa and wellness center, one of the best in Mecklenburg-Pomerania. **Pros:** one of the area's few four-star hotels, varied cultural and entertainment programs, stylish spa with great massages. **Cons:** small rooms and bathrooms, many rooms with worn-out mattresses. ✉*Zeppelinstr. 8D–18609 Binz-Rügen* ☎*038393/500* 🌐*www.vier-jahreszeiten.de* 🛏*69 rooms, 7 suites, 50 apartments* ⚐*In-room: dial-up. In-hotel: 3 restaurants, room service, bar, pool, gym, spa, concierge, laundry service, public Wi-Fi, parking (fee), no-smoking rooms, some pets allowed* 🚫*AE, MC, V* ❖❘*BP.*

$
★
🏨**Hotel Villa Granitz.** The little town of Baabe claims to have Rügen's most beautiful beach. This mostly wooden mansion is a small and quiet retreat for those who want to avoid the masses. All rooms are spacious and have a large terrace or balcony; pastel colors (a soft white and yellow) add to the tidy, fairy-tale look of the building. The apartments have small kitchenettes. **Pros:** cozy hotel in the traditional architectural style of the area, very competitive prices for the size and comfort of rooms. **Cons:** off-the-beaten-track at the outskirts of the city, 900 yards from the beach. ✉*Birkenallee 17D–18586 Baabe* ☎*038303/1410* 🌐*www.villa-granitz.de* 🛏*44 rooms, 6 suites, 8 apartments* ⚐*In-room: no a/c, refrigerator. In-hotel: no elevator, laundry service, parking (no fee), no-smoking rooms, some pets allowed* 🚫*No credit cards* ❖❘*BP.*

14

USEDOM ISLAND

Fodor'sChoice
★
67 km (42 mi) to Wolgast bridge from Stralsund.

Usedom Island has almost 32 km (20 mi) of sandy shoreline and a string of resorts. Much of the island's untouched landscape is a nature preserve that provides refuge for a number of rare birds, including the giant sea eagle, which has a wingspan of up to 8 feet. Even in summer this island is more or less deserted, and is ready to be explored by bicycle.

GETTING HERE & AROUND

From the west, Usedom is accessed via the causeway at **Wolgast.** The bridge closes to traffic at times to allow boats to pass through. From the south, the B–110, leads from Anklam to Usedom. In summer, particularly before and after weekends, traffic can be very heavy on both roads.

ESSENTIALS

Visitor Information **Usedom Island** (⊠ *Tourismusverband Insel Usedom e.V., Waldstr. 1Seebad Ückeritz* ☎ *038378/47710* 🖳 *038378/477–1290* ⊕ *www. usedom.de*).

EXPLORING

At the northwest tip of Usedom, 16 km (10 mi) from land-side Wolgast, is **Peenemünde,** the launch site of the world's first jet rockets, the V1 and V2, developed by Germany toward the end of World War II. You can view these rockets as well as models of early airplanes and ships at the extensive **Historisch-Technisches informationszentrum** *(Historical-Technical Information Center)*, housed in a former army power plant. One exhibit covers the secret underground plants where most of the rocket parts were assembled and where thousands of slave laborers died. Explanation of the exhibits in English is available. ⊠ *Im Kraftwerk* ☎ *038371/5050* 🖃 *€6* 🕑 *Apr.–Sept., daily 10–6; Oct.–Mar., daily 10–4; Nov.–Mar., Tues.–Sun. 10–4.*

Ahlbeck, the island's main town, is also one of its best resorts. The tidy and elegant resort is one of the three Kaiserbäder (the two others are Heringsdorf and Bansin) where the Emperor Wilhelm II liked to spend his summers in the early 20th century. Noble families and rich citizens followed the Emperor, turning Ahlbeck into one of the prettiest villas on the Baltic Coast. Ahlbeck's landmark is the 19th-century wooden pier with four towers. Stroll the beach to the right of the pier and you'll arrive at the Polish border.

WHERE TO STAY

$$–$$$ 🏨 **Romantik Seehotel Ahlbecker Hof.** The first lady of Ahlbeck, this
★ four-star hotel calls to mind the island's past as a getaway for Prussian nobility in the 19th century. The restored building sits rights on the beach, just a few steps from the pier. It offers spacious, elegantly appointed rooms overlooking the water. **Pros:** has one of the area's best spas, two gourmet restaurants, near beach. **Con:** no elevator. ⊠ *Dünenstr. 47 Seebad Ahlbeck* ☎ *038378/620* ⊕ *www.seetel.de* 🛏 *70 rooms* ⚷ *In-room: safe, refrigerator. In-hotel: 2 restaurants, room service, bar, pool, gym, spa, beachfront, concierge, laundry service, public Wi-Fi, parking (fee), no-smoking rooms, some pets allowed* 🖃 *AE, DC, MC, V* 🍴 *BP.*

Berlin

WORD OF MOUTH

"If you are interested in modern architecture, ancient and modern art collections, a vibrant city scene and music, Berlin is the place to go."

—JudyC

"I loved Berlin!! To me the city felt smaller than what it really is. Maybe this is because there is more room to walk about and it's not cramped like London or Rome...The area around Brandenburg Gate is beautiful. There is so much history there and throughout the city, it still amazes me. I would highly recommend Berlin to anyone."

—Genabee6

www.fodors.com/forums

Updated
by Jürgen
Scheunemann

SINCE THE FALL OF THE Iron Curtain, no city in Europe has seen more development and change. Two Berlins that had been separated for almost 30 years struggled to meld into one, and in the scar of barren borderland between them sprang government and commercial centers that have become the glossy spreads of travel guides and architecture journals. After successfully uniting its own east and west, Berlin, as the German capital and one of the continent's great cities, now plays a pivotal role in a European Union that has undertaken the same task.

But even as the capital thinks and moves forward, history is always tugging at its sleeve. Between the wealth of neoclassical and 21st-century buildings there are constant reminders, both subtle and stark, of the events of the 20th century. For every new embassy and relocated corporate headquarters, a church stands half-ruined, a synagogue is under 24-hour guard, and an empty lot remains where a building either crumbled in World War II or went up in dynamite as East Germany cleared a path for its Wall. In the chillier months, the scent of coal wafts through the trendy neighborhoods of Prenzlauer Berg and Fried-richshain, where young residents who fuel the cultural scene heat their unmodernized apartments with coal stoves.

Compared to other German cities, Berlin is quite young and, ironically, began as two separate entities in 1237. The Spree River divided the slightly older Cölln on Museum Island from the fishing village Berlin. By the 1300s Berlin was prospering, thanks to its location at the intersection of important trade routes. After the ravages of the Thirty Years' War, Berlin rose to power as the seat of the Hohenzollern dynasty. The Great Elector Friedrich Wilhelm, in the almost 50 years of his reign (1640–88), touched off a renaissance by supporting such institutions as the Academy of Arts and the Academy of Sciences. Later, Frederick the Great (1712–86) made Berlin and Potsdam his glorious centers of the enlightened yet autocratic Prussian monarchy.

In 1871 Prussia, ruled by the "Iron Chancellor" Count Otto von Bismarck, unified the many independent German states into the German Empire. Berlin maintained its status as capital for the duration of that Second Reich (1871–1918), through the post–World War I Weimar Republic (1919–33), and also through Hitler's so-called Third Reich (1933–45). The city's golden years were the Roaring '20s, when Berlin, the energetic, modern, and sinful counterpart to Paris, became a center for the cultural avant-garde. World-famous writers, painters, and artists met here while the impoverished bulk of its 4 million inhabitants lived in heavily overpopulated quarters. This "dance on the volcano," as those years of political and economic upheaval have been called, came to a grisly and bloody end after January 1933, when Adolf Hitler became chancellor. The Nazis made Berlin their capital but ultimately failed to remodel the city into a silent monument to their power. By World War II's end, 70% of the city lay in ruins, with more rubble than in all other German cities combined.

Along with the division of Germany after World War II, Berlin was partitioned into American, British, and French zones in the west and

TOP REASONS TO GO

Museum Island: The architectural monuments and art treasures here will take you from an ancient Greek altar to a Roman market town to 18th-century Berlin and back in a day. Rest up and recover on the lawns of the Lustgarten.

The Reichstag's Cupola: Read up on the parliament's dramatic history at the base of the spectacular glass cupola, and then spiral up to enjoy great views of central Berlin and the leafy Tiergarten.

Trace History's Path: The division of Berlin was an anomaly in urban history. Follow the cobblestone markers that remember the Wall's path from where it bordered the Reichstag and Spree River, past the Holocaust Memorial and rebuilt Potsdamer Platz, and along the street where

the Gestapo was headquartered, to end at the famous border crossing, Checkpoint Charlie.

Affordability: Of western and northern Europe's capitals, Berlin is by far the best bargain. Most museum prices remain under €10, hotel rooms are expansive in comparison, and one night on the town won't rule out a second one.

Long, Creative Nights: Berlin is the only European city without official closing hours, so you can stretch your drinks until the wee hours of the morning without fear of a last call. Young artists and bohemians from the world over keep coming up with installations, performance events, and unusual impromptu venues for parties and bars.

15

a Soviet zone in the east. By 1947 Berlin had become one of the Cold War's first testing grounds. The three western-occupied zones gradually merged, becoming West Berlin, while the Soviet-controlled eastern zone defiantly remained separate. Peace conferences repeatedly failed to resolve the question of Germany's division, and in 1949 the Soviet Union established East Berlin as the capital of its new puppet state, the German Democratic Republic (GDR). The division of the city was cruelly finalized in concrete in August 1961, when the East German government erected the Berlin Wall, the only border fortification in history built to keep people from leaving rather than to protect them.

For nearly 30 years Berlin suffered under one of the greatest geographic and political anomalies of all time, a city split in two by a concrete wall—its larger western half an island of capitalist democracy surrounded by an East Germany run by hard-line Communists. With the Wall relegated to the pile of history (most of it was recycled as street gravel), visitors can now appreciate the qualities that mark the city as a whole. Its particular charm has always lain in its spaciousness, its trees and greenery, and its anything-goes atmosphere. Moreover, the really stunning parts of the prewar capital are in the historic eastern part of town, which has grand avenues, monumental architecture, and museums that house world treasures.

The new Berlin embraces a culturally promising but financially uncertain future. "Poor, but sexy," a line coined by Klaus Wowereit, the flamboyant Governing Mayor, is the city's current state of mind. While unresolved problems such as high unemployment rates and over-stretched city budgets are still worrying many, the city embraces its future as an international center for avant-garde fashion, culture, art, and media, with a zeal rarely found in better-off cities

ORIENTATION & PLANNING

GETTING ORIENTED

Located in eastern Germany, almost halfway between Paris and Moscow, Berlin is laid out on an epic scale and, with 3.5 million residents, is Germany's largest city. When the city-state of Berlin was incorporated in 1920, it swallowed towns and villages far beyond the downtown area around the two main rivers, the Spree and the Havel. Each of its boroughs has distinctive characteristics. Charlottenburg, Schöneberg, and Kreuzberg are popular areas in the west, and to the east, Prenlzauer Berg and Friedrichshain are favored residential and nightlife neighborhoods. Modern urban commercial centers such as Potsdamer Platz and Leipziger Platz still feel like odd insertions between the historically developed quarters surrounding them.

Kurfürstendamm & Western Downtown Berlin. For many locals, Berlin's true heart still beats along Kurfürstendamm, or "Ku'damm"—the easy-to-pronounce nickname for this boulevard that stretches for 3 km (2 mi) through the heart of the western downtown. The area developed in the late 19th century as wealthy Berliners moved out to the "New West," where Ku'damm was modeled after Paris's Champs Élysées. The stately mansions in the posh side streets now house elegant boutiques, restaurants, bars, and galleries. Downtown's center is vibrant Breitscheidplatz, where the somber ruin of the Kaiser-Wilhelm-Gedächtniskirche stands.

Potsdamer Platz & Kreuzberg. Potsdamer Platz and the adjoining Leipziger Platz, the busiest squares in prewar Europe, are the new, yet artificial heart of reunited Berlin. Once a no-man's-land in the shadow of the Wall, Potsdamer Platz reemerged as a shopping, office and entertainment center in the 1990s, offering some of most spectacular modern architecture in Berlin. Hugging the square's backside is the Kulturforum, one of two world-class museum ensembles in the city. The alternative culture of neighboring Kreuzberg makes it one of the most colorful districts in Berlin. A largely Turkish population shares the residential streets with a variegated assortment of political radicals and bohemians of all nationalities. There are few traditional attractions here, but it's a great place to people-watch.

Mitte: Unter Den Linden to Alexanderplatz. Mitte, specifically Museum Island, is the birthplace of the two first settlements—Berlin and Cölln—that later merged to become the proud Prussian and then German capital. Cutting through the historic core of Mitte, all the way from the Brandenburg Gate to Alexanderplatz, is the elegant, grand boulevard Unter den Linden. It will take you past stately government buildings, museums, a university campus, and churches. This area of Mitte includes the elegant shops along Friedrichstrasse. Mitte is a fascinating mix of high-life and high culture.

Mitte's Scheunenviertel & Prenzlauer Berg. Fashion, art, and trends are born in northern Mitte around the hip Hackescher Markt and the Spandauer Vorstadt (the former Jewish Quarter), as well as in the Scheunenviertel (Barn Quarter). Former tenement houses and a few remaining late-18th-century buildings house shops, galleries, and stores. The area certainly rewards an aimless walk with vibrant street life. Northeast of Mitte, the old working-class district of Prenzlauer Berg used to be one of the poorest sections of Berlin. Since the fall of the Wall, affluent West German families, yuppies, and couples have all but replaced the former local population. Both areas are great for people-watching and nightlife.

BERLIN PLANNER

15

WHEN TO GO

Berlin has a moderate, continental climate. However, due to its unprotected location in the northeastern lowlands of Germany, easterly winds often bring surprisingly harsh weather and storms in fall and winter. The perfect time to visit is May to early September, when temperatures usually hover around 70° to 80° F. Late July and early August, however, can be sizzling hot. Many open-air events are staged in summer, when the surprisingly green city is at its most beautiful. October and November can be very overcast and rainy, but the city still sees its fair share of crisp blue autumn skies. Avoid the long winter months: despite the many cultural events, perpetually gray skies are marked by sleet, icy rain, strong winds, and freezing temperatures.

GETTING HERE & AROUND

BY AIR Major airlines will continue to serve western Berlin's Tegel Airport (TXL) after a first stop at a major European hub (such as Frankfurt) until 2011, when eastern Berlin's Schönefeld Airport, about 24 km (15 mi) outside the center, will have been expanded into BBI, the international airport of the capital region. Schönefeld is now used principally by charter and low-budget airlines. Massive Tempelhof Airport, an example of fascist architecture, closed in late 2008. The two Berlin airports share a central phone number.

BY BUS BerlinLinien Bus is the only intra-Germany company serving Berlin. Gullivers Reisen serves foreign destinations. Make reservations ZOB-Reisebüro, or buy your ticket at its office at the central bus terminal, the Omnibusbahnhof. Public buses are the best way to reach the bus terminal, served by the lines X34, X49, 104, 139, 218, and 349. A more central place to buy bus tickets is Mitfahrzentrale, a tiny, busy office that also arranges car-ride shares. Only EC credit cards and cash are accepted.

BY CAR Rush hour is relatively mild in Berlin, but the public transit system is so efficient here that it's best to leave your car at the hotel altogether. As of 2008 cars entering downtown Berlin inside the S-Bahn ring need to have an environmental certificate. Most German rental cars will have these—if in doubt, ask the rental-car agent, as without one you can be fined €40. Daily parking fees at hotels can run up to €18 per day. Vending machines in the city center dispense timed tickets to display on your dashboard. Thirty minutes cost €0.50.

BY PUBLIC TRANSIT
The city has one of the most efficient public-transportation systems in Europe, a smoothly integrated network of subway (U-bahn) and suburban (S-bahn) train lines, buses, and trams (in eastern Berlin only). Get a map from any information booth. ■TIP➔ **Don't be afraid to try buses and trams—in addition to being well marked, they often cut the most direct path to your destination.**

From Sunday through Thursday, U-bahn trains stop around 12:45 AM and S-bahn trains stop by 1:30 AM. All-night bus and tram service operates seven nights a week (indicated by the letter N next to route numbers). On Friday and Saturday nights some S-bahn and all U-bahn lines except U4 run all night. Buses and trams marked with an M mostly serve destinations without S-bahn or U-bahn link.

Most visitor destinations are in the broad reach of the fare zones A and B. At this writing, both the €2.10 ticket (fare zones A and B) and the €2.70 ticket (fare zones A, B, and C) allow you to make a one-way trip with an unlimited number of changes between trains, buses, and trams. There are reduced rates for children ages 6–13. Rates are likely to be higher in the near future.

Buy a Kurzstreckentarif ticket (€1.20) for short rides of up to six bus or tram stops or three U-bahn or S-bahn stops. The best deal if you plan to travel around the city extensively is the Tageskarte (day card for zones A and B), for €6.10, good on all transportation until 3 AM. (It's €6.30 for A, B, and C zones.) A 7-Tage-Karte (seven-day ticket) costs €25.40 and allows unlimited travel for fare zones A and B; €31.30 buys all three fare zones.

The **Berlin WelcomeCard** (sold by EurAid, BVG offices, the tourist office, and some hotels) entitles one adult and three children under age 14 to either two or three days of unlimited travel in the ABC zones for €18 or €24.50 respectively, and includes admission and tour discounts detailed in a booklet. The **CityTourCard**, good for two or three days of unlimited travel in the AB zones, costs €16.50 and €21.50, respectively, and details 50 discounts on a leaflet; up to three children under 6 can accompany an adult.

Tickets are available from vending machines at U-bahn and S-bahn stations. After you purchase a ticket, you are responsible for validating it when you board the train or bus. If you're caught without a ticket or with an unvalidated one, the fine is €60.

DISABILITIES & ACCESSIBILITY
All major S-bahn and U-bahn stations have elevators, and most buses have hydraulic lifts. Check the public transportation maps or call the Berliner Verkehrsbetriebe. The Deutscher Service-Ring-Berlin e.V. runs a special bus service for travelers with physical disabilities, and is a

good information source on all travel necessities, that is, wheelchair rental and other issues.

BY TAXI The base rate is €3, after which prices vary according to a complex tariff system. Figure on paying around €8 for a ride the length of the Ku'damm. ■TIP→ If you've hailed a cab on the street and are taking a short ride of up to 2 km (1 mi), ask the driver as soon as you start off for a special fare (€3.50) called *Kurzstreckentarif*. You can also get cabs at taxi stands or order one by calling; there's no additional fee if you call a cab by phone. U-bahn employees will call a taxi for passengers after 8 PM.

Velotaxis, rickshaw-like bicycle taxis, pedal along Kurfürstendamm, Friedrichstrasse, and Unter den Linden, and in Tiergarten. Just hail one of the cabs on the street or look for the VELOTAXI-STAND signs along the boulevards mentioned. The fare is €5 for up to 1 km (½ mi) and €2 for each additional kilometer, and €22.50 to €30 for longer tours. Velotaxis operate April–October, daily 1–8. ■TIP→ Despite these fixed prices, make sure to negotiate the fare before starting the tour.

BY TRAIN All long-distance trains stop at the huge and modern central station, Hauptbahnhof–Lehrter Bahnhof, which lies at the north edge of the government district in former West Berlin. Regional trains also stop at the two former "main" stations of the past years: Bahnhof Zoo (in the West) and Ostbahnhof (in the East). Regional trains also stop at the central eastern stations Friedrichstrasse and Alexanderplatz.

ESSENTIALS **Accessibility Information Berliner Verkehrsbetriebe** (☎ *030/19449* ⊕ *www. bvg.de*). **Deutscher Service-Ring-Berlin e.V** (☎ *030/859–4010*).

Airport Information Central airport service (☎ *0180/500–0186* ⊕ *www. berlin-airport.de*).

Bus Information Mitfahrzentrale (⊠ *Joachimsthaler Str. 14, Western Downtown* ☎ *030/19444* ⊙ *Weekdays 9–8, weekends 10–6* ⊕ *www.mf24.de*). **ZOB-Reisebüro** (⊠ *Zentrale Omnibusbahnhof, Masurenallee 4–6, at Messedamm, Charlottenburg* ☎ *030/301–0380 for reservations* ⊕ *www.berlinlinienbus.de* ⊙ *Weekdays 6* AM*–9* PM*, weekends 6* AM*–3* PM).

Public Transit Information Berliner Verkehrsbetriebe (☎ *030/19449* ⊕ *www. bvg.de*). **S-Bahn Berlin GmbH** (☎ *030/2974–3333* ⊕ *www.s-bahn-berlin.de*). **VBB** (⊠ *Hardenbergpl. 2, Western Downtown* ☎ *030/2541–4141 or 030/2541–4145* ⊕ *www.vbbonline.de*).

Visitor Information Berlin Infostore (⊠ *Kurfürstendamm 21, Neues Kranzler Eck, Western Downtown* ☎ *030/250–025* ⊙ *Mon.–Thurs. 9:30–8, Fri. and Sat. 9:30–9, Sun. 9:30–6* ⊕ *www.berlin-tourist-information.de*). **MD Infoline** (☎ *030/2474–9888* ⊙ *Weekdays 9–4, weekends 9–1*). **Staatliche Museen zu Berlin** (☎ *030/266–2951 operator* ⊕ *www.smb.museum*). **Tourist Information Center in Prenzlauer Berg** (⊠ *Kuturbrauerei entrances on Schönhauser Allee 36–39, Knaackstr. 97, Sredzkistr. 1* ☎ *030/4435–2170* ⊕ *www.tic-berlin.de*).

Taxi Information Taxis (☎ *030/210–101, 030/210–202, 030/443–322, or 030/260–26*).

TOURS

BOAT TOURS Tours of central Berlin's Spree and Landwehr canals give you up-close and unusual views of sights such as Charlottenburg Palace, the Reichstag, and the Berliner Dom. Tours usually depart twice a day from several bridges and piers in Berlin, such as Schlossbrücke in Charlottenburg; Hansabrücke and Haus der Kulturen der Welt in Tiergarten; Friedrichstrasse, Museum Island, and Nikolaiviertel in Mitte; and near the Jannowitzbrücke S-bahn and U-bahn station. Drinks, snacks, and wursts are available during the narrated trips. Reederei Riedel offers three inner-city trips that range from €6 to €14.

A tour of the Havel Lakes (which include Tegeler See and Wannsee) begins at the Wannsee, where you can sail on either the whale-shape vessel *Moby Dick* or the *Havel Queen*, a Mississippi-style boat, and cruise 28 km (17 mi) through the lakes and past forests (Stern- und Kreisschiffahrt). Tours can last from one to seven hours, and cost between €8 and €14. There are 20 operators.

BUS TOURS Four companies (Berliner Bären, Berolina Berlin-Service, Bus Verkehr Berlin, and Severin & Kühn) jointly offer city tours on yellow, double-decker City Circle buses, which run every 15 or 30 minutes, depending on the season. The full circuit takes two hours, as does the recorded narration listened to through headphones. For €18 you can jump on and off at the 14 stops. The bus driver sells tickets. During the warmer months, the last circuit leaves at 4 PM from the corner of Rankestrasse and Kurfürstendamm. Most companies have tours to Potsdam. Severin & Kühn also runs all-day tours to Dresden and Meissen.

The Stadtrundfahrtbüro Berlin offers a 2½-hour tour (€15) and 1¾-hour tour (€12) at 11, 2, and 3:45. A guide narrates in both German and English. The bus departs from Kurfürstendamm 236, at the corner of Rankestrasse.

WALKING & Getting oriented through a walking tour is a great way to start a Berlin
BIKE TOURS visit. In addition to daily city highlight tours, companies have theme tours such as Third Reich Berlin, Potsdam, and pub crawls. Berlin Walks offers a Monday "Jewish Life" tour, a Potsdam tour on Sunday, and visits to the Sachsenhausen concentration camp. Insider Tours has a "Red Star" Berlin tour about the Soviet era and a bike tour as well. Brit Terry Brewer's firsthand accounts of divided and reunified Berlin are a highlight of the all-day "Brewer's Best of Berlin" tour. Tours cost from €9 to €15. Printable discount coupons may be available on the tour operators' Web sites; some companies grant discounts to WelcomeCard holders. Fat Tire Bike Tours rides through Berlin daily early March–November and has a Berlin Wall tour. The 4½-hour city tour costs €20, bike rental included.

TOUR Boat Tour Information **Reederei Bruno Winkler** (☎ *030/349–9595*). **Reederei**
ESSENTIALS **Riedel** (☎ *030/693–4646*). **Stern- und Kreisschiffahrt** (☎ *030/536–3600* ⊕ *www.sternundkreis.de*).

Bus Tour Information **Berliner Bären Stadtrundfahrten** (*BBS* ✉ *Seeburgerstr. 19b, Charlottenburg* ☎ *030/3519–5270* ⊕ *www.sightseeing.de*). **Berolina Berlin-**

Service (✉ *Kurfürstendamm 220, at Meinekestr., Western Downtown* ☏ *030/8856–8030* ⊕ *www.berolina-berlin.com*). **Bus Verkehr Berlin** (*BVB* ✉ *Kurfürstendamm 225, Western Downtown* ☏ *030/683–8910* ⊕ *www.bvb.net*). **Severin & Kühn** (✉ *Kurfürstendamm 216, Western Downtown* ☏ *030/880–4190* ⊕ *www.severin-kuehn-berlin.de*). **Stadtrundfahrtbüro Berlin** (✉ *Kurfürstendamm 236, Western Downtown* ☏ *030/2612–001* ⊕ *www.stadtrundfahrtbuero-berlin.de*).

Walking & Bike Tour Information Berlin Walks (☏ *030/301–9194* ⊕ *www.berlinwalks.com*). **"Brewer's Best of Berlin"** (☏ *9177/388—1537* ⊕ *www.brewersberlintours.com*). **Insider Tours** (☏ *030/692–3149* ⊕ *www.insidertour.com*). **Fat Tire Bike Tours Berlin** (✉ *Panoramastr. 1a, base of TV tower* ☏ *030/2404–7991* ⊕ *www.fattirebiketoursberlin.com*).

PLANNING YOUR TIME

As one of Europe's biggest cities and certainly one of the world's top capitals, with very distinctive individual neighborhoods and sights, Berlin is difficult to tackle in just one or two days. Any visit should include a walk on the Kurfürstendamm, the city's premier shopping boulevard. For culture buffs, great antique, medieval, Renaissance, and modern art can be found at the Kulturforum in the Tiergarten, and on Museum Island in Mitte—both cultural centers are a must, and either will occupy at least a half-day. Most of the historic sights of German and Prussian history line the city's other grand boulevard, Unter den Linden, in eastern Berlin, which can be strolled in a leisurely two hours, with stops. Avail yourself of the efficient transportation options, and you'll see more. Note that shops are closed on Sunday.

DISCOUNTS & DEALS

Berlin is still one of the cheapest central European destinations. The **Berlin WelcomeCard** (sold by EurAid, BVG offices, the tourist office, and some hotels) entitles one adult and three children under the age of 14 to either two or three days of unlimited travel in the ABC zones for €18 or €24.50 respectively, and includes admission and tour discounts detailed in a booklet. The CityTourCard, good for two or three days of unlimited travel in the AB zones costs €16.50 and €21.50, respectively, and details 50 discounts on a leaflet; up to three children under 6 can accompany an adult.

Many of the 17 Staatliche Museen zu Berlin (state museums of Berlin) are world-renowned, and offer several ticket options (children under 17 are welcomed free of charge). A single ticket ranges €4–€8. A three-day pass (*Tageskarte or ShauLust Museen Ticket*) to all state museums costs €19. This ticket allows entrance to all state museums plus many others for three consecutive days. State museums tend to cluster near one another, and usually a single entrance ticket grants admission to all museums in that area. These areas include Charlottenburg (€6), Dahlem (€6), the Kulturforum in Tiergarten, the out-of-the-way Hamburger Bahnhof in Moabit (€8), and Museum Island (€8) in Mitte. All these entrance tickets are for the permanent exhibitions and include an audio guide; special exhibits cost extra.

15

EXPLORING BERLIN

Berlin is a large city with several downtown centers that evolved during the 30 years of separation. Of Berlin's 12 boroughs, the 5 of most interest to visitors are Charlottenburg-Wilmersdorf in the west; Tiergarten (a district of the Mitte borough) and Kreuzberg-Friedrichhain in the center; Mitte, the historic core of the city in the eastern part of town; and Prenzlauer Berg in the northeast. Southwest Berlin has lovely escapes in the secluded forests and lakes of the Grunewald area.

KURFÜRSTENDAMM & WESTERN DOWNTOWN BERLIN

Shoppers are the life force of the boulevard Kurfürstendamm (Ku'damm), with enough energy and euros to support the local boutiques on the quieter side streets, too. Out-of-towners take it easy at Ku'damm's sidewalk tables as Berliners bustle by with a purpose.

MAIN ATTRACTIONS

❸ **Kaiser-Wilhelm-Gedächtnis-Kirche** *(Kaiser Wilhelm Memorial Church).* A dramatic reminder of World War II's destruction, the ruined bell tower is all that remains of the once massive church, which was completed in 1895 and dedicated to the emperor, Kaiser Wilhelm I. The Hohenzollern dynasty is depicted inside in a gilded mosaic, whose damage, like that of the building, will not be repaired. The exhibition revisits World War II's devastation throughout Europe. On the hour, the tower chimes out a melody composed by the last emperor's great-grandson, the late Prince Louis Ferdinand von Hohenzollern.

In stark contrast to the old bell tower (dubbed the "Hollow Tooth"), which is in sore need of a restoration now, are the adjoining Memorial Church and Tower, designed by the noted German architect Egon Eiermann in 1959–61. These ultramodern octagonal structures, with their myriad honeycomb windows, have nicknames as well: "the Lipstick" and the "Powder Box." Brilliant, blue stained glass from Chartres dominates the interiors. Church music and organ concerts are presented in the church regularly. ⊠ *Breitscheidpl., Western Downtown* ☎ *030/218–5023* ⊕ *www.gedaechtniskirche.de* ☜ *Free* ☉ *Old Tower Mon.–Sat. 10–6:30, Memorial Church daily 9–7* Ⓜ *Zoologischer Garten (U-bahn and S-bahn).*

Kaufhaus des Westens. *(Department Store of the West).* The completely refurbished and modernized KaDeWe, which celebrated its 100th annniversary in 2007, isn't just Berlin's classiest department store; it's also continental Europe's largest, a grand-scale emporium in modern guise and for decades a historic landmark of Western capitalism behind the Iron Curtain. Its seven floors hold an enormous selection, but it's best known for its two top floors' food and delicatessen counters, restaurants, champagne bars, and beer bars, and for its crowning rooftop winter garden. ⊠ *Tauentzienstr. 21–24, Western Downtown* ☎ *030/21210* ⊕ *www.kadewe-berlin.de* ☉ *Mon.–Thurs. 10–8, Fri. 10–9, Sat. 9:30–8* Ⓜ *Wittenbergplatz (U-bahn).*

NEED A BREAK?

Forget the fast-food options at Zoo Station. Instead, follow the train tracks to the back of the taxi and bus queues, where you'll enter Tiergarten and within 100 yards come upon the best hideaway in the area: Schleusenkrug (⊠ *Tiergarten, Western Downtown* ☎ *030/313–9909*). In warmer weather you can order at the window and sit in the beer garden or on the back patio, watching pleasure ships go through the lock. Inside is a casual restaurant with a changing daily menu. Between October and mid-March the Krug closes at 6 PM.

❶ Kurfürstendamm. This busy thoroughfare began as a riding path in the 16th century. The elector Joachim II of Brandenburg used it to travel between his palace on the Spree River and his hunting lodge in the Grunewald. The Kurfürstendamm (Elector's Causeway) was transformed into a major route in the late 19th century, thanks to the initiative of Bismarck, Prussia's Iron Chancellor.

15

Even in the 1920s, the Ku'damm was still relatively new and by no means elegant; it was fairly far removed from the old heart of the city, which was Unter den Linden in Mitte. The Ku'damm's prewar fame was due mainly to its rowdy bars and dance halls, as well as the cafés where the cultural avant-garde of Europe gathered. Almost half of its 245 late-19th-century buildings were completely destroyed in the 1940s, and the remaining buildings were damaged in varying degrees. As in most of western Berlin, what you see today is either restored or newly constructed. Many of the 1950s buildings have been replaced by high-rises, in particular at the corner of Kurfürstendamm and Joachimstaler Strasse.

❺ Zoologischer Garten *(Zoological Gardens).* Polar bear Knut, one of the
★ few of this endangered species to be born in captivity and now a rowdy
 teenager, is a star attraction at Germany's oldest zoo. Home to more than 14,000 animals belonging to 1,500 different species (more than any other zoo in Europe), the zoo has been successful at breeding rare and endangered species. New arrivals in the past years include Ivo (a popular male gorilla), roadrunners, and a pair of Barbary lions. ■ TIP ➡ **Check the feeding times posted to watch creatures such as seals, apes, hippos, crocodiles, and pelicans during their favorite time of day.** The animals' enclosures are designed to resemble their natural habitats, though some structures are ornate, such as the 1910 Arabian-style Zebra house. Pythons, frogs, turtles, invertebrates, and Komodo dragons are part of the three-floor aquarium. ⊠ *Hardenbergpl. 8 and Budapester Str. 34, Western Downtown* ☎ *030/254–010* ⊕ *www.zoo-berlin.de* 🎟 *Zoo or aquarium €12, combined ticket €18.50* 🕐 *Zoo Nov.–mid-Mar., daily 9–5; mid-Mar.-mid-Oct., daily 9–6:30. Aquarium daily 9–6* Ⓜ *Zoologischer Garten (U-bahn and S-bahn).*

ALSO WORTH SEEING

❻ Museum für Fotografie–Helmut Newton Stiftung. Native son Helmut Newton (1920–2004) pledged this collection of 1,000 photographs to Berlin months before his unexpected death. The man who defined fashion photography in the 1960s through 1980s was an apprentice to Yva,

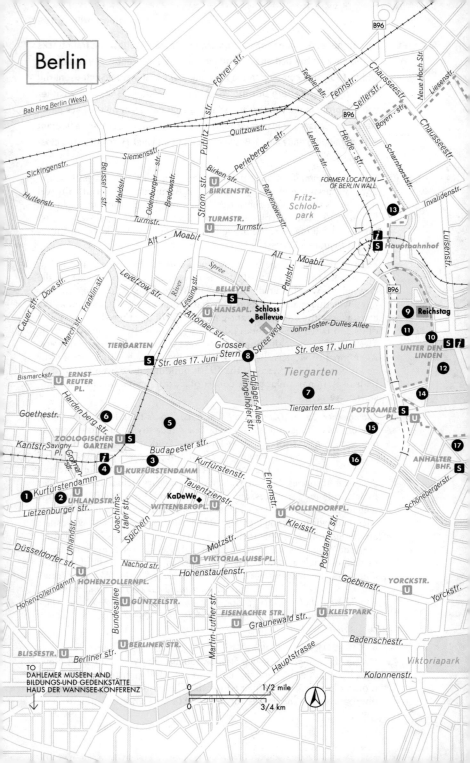

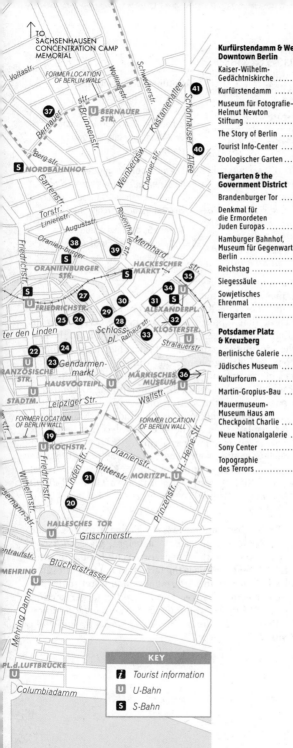

15

a Jewish fashion photographer in Berlin in the 1930s. Newton fled Berlin with his family in 1938, and his mentor was killed in a concentration camp. The photographs, now part of the state museum collection, are shown on a rotating basis in the huge Wilhelmine building behind the train station Zoologischer Garten. You'll see anything from racy portraits of models to serene landscapes. ⊠ *Jebenstr. 2, Western Downtown* ☎ *030/3186–4856* ⊕ *www.smb.museum* 🎫 *€8* ⊙ *Tues., Wed., and Fri.–Sun. 10–6, Thurs. 10–10* Ⓜ *Zoologischer Garten (U-bahn and S-bahn).*

> **TOURING TIPS**

Getting Here: Many bus lines serve the boulevard Kurfürstendamm, and the U-bahn stations Kurfürstendamm or Wittenbergplatz are good starting points.

Scenic Spot: To get the unique Ku'damm buzz, stop at the corner of Joachimsthaler Strasse and survey the modern architecture.

Scenic Spot: Take a ride to the 20th floor of the Europa-Center on Breitscheidplatz for a panoramic view of western downtown.

② **The Story of Berlin.** You can't miss ☾ this multimedia museum for the airplane wing exhibited outside. It was once part of a "Raisin bomber," a U.S. Air Force DC-3 that supplied Berlin during the Berlin Airlift in 1948 and 1949. Eight hundred years of the city's history, from the first settlers casting their fishing lines to Berliners heaving sledgehammers at the Wall, are conveyed through hands-on exhibits, film footage, and multimedia devices in this unusual venue. The sound of footsteps over broken glass follows your path through the exhibit on the *Kristallnacht* pogrom, and to pass through the section on the Nazis' book-burning on Bebelplatz, you must walk over book bindings. Many original artifacts are on display, such as the stretch Volvo that served as Erich Honnecker's state carriage in East Germany. ■TIP➜ **The eeriest relic is the 1974 nuclear shelter, which you can visit by guided tour on the hour.** Museum placards are also in English. ⊠ *Ku'damm Karree, Kurfürstendamm 207–208, Western Downtown* ☎ *030/8872–0100* ⊕ *www.story-of-berlin.de* 🎫 *€9.80* ⊙ *Daily 10–8; last entry at 6* Ⓜ *Uhlandstrasse (U-bahn).*

④ **Tourist Info-Center.** Berlin Tourismus Marketing's main tourist office is hidden inside the Neues Kranzler-Eck, a bright, glass-and-steel high-rise business complex at the busy corner of Ku'damm and Joachimsthaler Strasse. ■TIP➜ **This is the largest of the four Info-Centers, and staff can book tickets to performances and hotel rooms for you.** There's a large selection of free leaflets and a larger section of souvenirs to buy. ⊠ *Kurfürstendamm 21, Western Downtown* ☎ *030/250–025* ⊕ *www.visitberlin.de* ⊙ *Mon.–Sat. 10–8, Sun. 10–6* Ⓜ *Kurfürstendamm (U-bahn).*

TIERGARTEN & THE GOVERNMENT DISTRICT

The Tiergarten, a bucolic 630-acre park with lakes, meadows, and wide paths, is the "green lung" of Berlin. In the 17th century it served as the hunting grounds of the Great Elector. Now it's the Berliners' backyard for sunbathing and barbecuing. Berlin's most fertile grounds for modern architecture—the government district, Potsdamer Platz, and the embassy district—ring the park from its eastern to southern edges. Many of the embassies have exhibitions open to the public, and Germany's parliament convenes beneath one of the city's most popular attractions: the glass dome of the Reichstag. Bordering Tiergarten and the government district is the meticulously restored Brandenburger Tor, the unofficial symbol of the city, and the Memorial to the Murdered Jews of Europe, whose design and scope engendered many debates.

> ### REMINDERS OF THE WALL
>
> The short walk from the Reichstag to the Brandenburger Tor passes a simple fence hung with white, wooden crosses. These are in memory of East Germans who were killed while trying to cross the Wall. The cobblestones embedded in the roadway mark the Wall's path.

15

TIMING

A leisurely walk from Zoo Station through the Tiergarten to the Brandenburger Tor and the Reichstag will take at least 90 minutes, two to three hours if you want to spend more time photographing and visiting the Holocaust Memorial. The line to visit the dome of the Reichstag varies in length with tourist seasons and school vacations. If the line covers the Reichstag's steps and bends around its driveway, expect a 45-minute wait. The Hamburger Bahnhof, Museum für Gegenwart–Berlin isn't ideally located, but Bus 248 does reach it quickly from the Holocaust Memorial or the Reichstag.

MAIN ATTRACTIONS

⑩ **Brandenburger Tor** *(Brandenburg Gate)*. Once the pride of Prussian Berlin and the city's premier landmark, the Brandenburger Tor was left in a desolate no-man's-land when the Wall was built. Since the Wall's dismantling, the sandstone gateway has become the scene of the city's Unification Day and New Year's Eve parties. This is the sole remaining gate of 14 built by Carl Langhans in 1788–91, designed as a triumphal arch for King Frederick Wilhelm II. Its virile classical style pays tribute to Athens's Acropolis. The quadriga, a chariot drawn by four horses and driven by the Goddess of Victory, was added in 1794. Troops paraded through the gate after successful campaigns—the last time in 1945, when victorious Red Army troops took Berlin. The upper part of the gate, together with its chariot and Goddess of Victory, was destroyed in the war. In 1957 the original molds were discovered in West Berlin, and a new quadriga was cast in copper and presented as a gift to the people of East Berlin. A tourist-information center is in the south part of the gate.

Fodor'sChoice ★

The gate faces one of Europe's most famous historic squares, **Pariser Platz**, a classicist piazza with bank headquarters, the ultra-modern French embassy, as well as offices of the federal parliament. On the southern side, Berlin's sleek Academy of Arts, integrating the ruins of its historic predecessor, and the DZ Bank, designed by star architect Frank Gehry, are cheek-by-jowl with the new American embassy, opened on July 4, 2008, built on its prewar location. ⊠ *Pariser Pl., Mitte* Ⓜ *Unter den Linden (S-bahn).*

> ### BEATING THE EURO
>
> On both sides of the Brandenburg Gate, walking tour operators offer free tours of the Platz and the surrounding area in various languages. While most of these are fairly entertaining and really free, be aware that some will end with a sales pitch for paid tours and request tips.

⑫ **Denkmal für die Ermordeten Juden Europas** *(Memorial to the Murdered Jews of Europe).* An expansive and unusual memorial dedicated to the 6 million Jews who were killed in the Holocaust, the monument was designed by American architect Peter Eisenman. The stunning place of remembrance consists of a grid of more than 2,700 concrete stelae, planted into undulating ground. The abstract memorial can be entered from all sides and offers no prescribed path. ∎ TIP→ **It's requested that you do not stand or sit on any of the stelae.** An information center that goes into specifics about the Holocaust lies underground at the southeast corner. ⊠ *Cora-Berliner-Str. 1, Mitte* ☎ *030/2639–4336* ⊕ *www.holocaust-mahnmal.de* ⊠ *Free* ⊙ *Daily 24 hrs; Information Center: Nov.–Feb., Tues.–Sun. 10–7; Mar.–Oct., Tues.–Sun. 10–8* Ⓜ *Unter den Linden (S-bahn).*

⑨ **Reichstag** *(Parliament Building).* After last meeting here in 1933, the
★ Bundestag, Germany's federal parliament, returned to its traditional seat in the spring of 1999. British architect Sir Norman Foster lightened up the gray monolith with a glass dome, which quickly became one of the city's main attractions: you can circle up a gently rising ramp while taking in the rooftops of Berlin and the parliamentary chamber below. At the base of the dome is an exhibit on the Reichstag's history, in German and English. ∎ TIP→ **The best way to visit the Reichstag dome without waiting in line is to arrive at 8** AM, **or to make a reservation for the pricey rooftop Käfer restaurant (** ☎ *030/2262–9933*). **Those with reservations can use the doorway to the right of the Reichstag's main staircase.** Completed in 1894, the Reichstag housed the imperial German parliament and later served a similar function during the ill-fated Weimar Republic. On the night of February 27, 1933, the Reichstag burned down in an act of arson, a pivotal event in Third Reich history. The fire led to state protection laws that gave the Nazis a pretext to arrest their political opponents. The Reichstag was rebuilt but again badly damaged in 1945. The graffiti of the victorious Russian soldiers can still be seen on some of the walls in the hallways. Tours of the interior are only given to groups who have applied in advance by letter or fax. The building is surrounded by ultramodern new federal government offices,

such as the boxy, concrete **Bundes-kanzleramt** (German Federal Chancellery). Built by Axel Schultes, it's one of the few new buildings in the government district by a Berlin architect. Participating in a guided tour of the Chancellery is possible if you apply in writing several weeks prior to a visit. A riverwalk with great views of the government

buildings begins behind the Reichstag. ✉ *Pl. der Republik 1, Tiergarten* ☎ *030/2273–2152, 030/2273–5908 Reichstag* 🖷 *030/2273–0027 Reichstag, 030/4000–1881 Bundeskanzleramt* ⊕ *www.bundestag.de* ✍ *Free* ☉ *Daily 8* AM*–midnight; last admission 10* PM*. Reichstag dome closes for 1 wk 4 times a yr* Ⓜ *Unter den Linden (S-bahn).*

OFF THE BEATEN PATH

The Kennedys. John F. Kennedy, whose historic 1963 speech in West Berlin secured his fame throughout Germany, is honored in the small but intriguing new museum opposite the American embassy on Pariser Platz. Presenting photographs, personal memorabilia, documents, and films, the collection traces the fascination JFK and the Kennedy clan evoked in Berlin and elsewhere. ✉ *Pariser Pl. 4a, Mitte* ☎ *030/2065–3570* ⊕ *www.thekennedys.de* ✍ *€7* ☉ *Daily 10–6* Ⓜ *Unter den Linden (S-bahn).*

❼ **Tiergarten** *(Animal Garden).* The quiet greenery of the 630-acre Tiergarten is a beloved oasis, with some 23 km (14 mi) of footpaths, meadows, and two beer gardens. The inner park's 6½ acres of lakes and ponds were landscaped by garden architect Joseph Peter Lenné in the mid-1800s. On the shore of the lake in the southwest part, you can relax at the **Café am Neuen See** (✉ *Lichtensteinallee 2*), a café and beer garden. Off the Spree River and bordering the Kanzleramt (Chancellery) is the **Haus der Kulturen der Welt** (✉ *House of the World Cultures, John-Foster-Dulles Allee 10* ☎ *030/397–870* ⊕ *www.hkw.de*), referred to as the "pregnant oyster" for its design. Thematic exhibits and festivals take place here, and it's also a boarding point for Spree River cruises.

ALSO WORTH SEEING

⑬ **Hamburger Bahnhof, Museum für Gegenwart–Berlin** *(Museum of Contemporary Art).* This light-filled, remodeled train station is home to a rich survey of post-1960 Western art. In 2003 the museum doubled its exhibition space to accommodate the Flick Collection, the largest and most valuable collection of contemporary art in the world. The 2,000 works rotate, but you're bound to see some by Bruce Naumann, Rodney Graham, and Pipilotti Rist. The permanent collection includes installations by German artists Joseph Beuys and Anselm Kiefer, as well as paintings by Andy Warhol, Cy Twombly, Robert Rauschenberg, and Robert Morris. Works of Marcel Duchamp and Marcel Broodthaers are exhibited on the second floor. ✉ *Invalidenstr. 50–51, Tiergarten* ☎ *030/266–2604* ⊕ *www.smb.museum* ✍ *€8* ☉ *Tues.–Fri. 10–6, Sat. 11–8, Sun. 11–6* Ⓜ *Zinnowitzer Strasse (U-bahn), Hauptbahnhof-Lehrter Bahnhof (S-bahn).*

⑧ Siegessäule *(Victory Column)*. The 227-foot granite, sandstone, and bronze column is topped by a winged, golden goddess and has a splendid view of Berlin. It was erected in front of the Reichstag in 1873 to commemorate Prussia's military successes and then moved to the Tiergarten in 1938–39. You have to climb 285 steps up through the column to reach the observation platform, but the view is rewarding. The gold-tipped cannons striping the column are those the Prussians captured from the French in the Franco-Prussian War. ⊠ *Am Grossen Stern, Tiergarten* ☎ *030/391–2961* 🎫 *€2.20* ⊙ *Nov.–Mar., weekdays 10–5, weekends 10–5:30; Apr.–Oct., weekdays 9:30–6:30, weekends 9:30–7; last admission ½ hr before closing* Ⓜ *Tiergarten (S-bahn), Bellevue (S-bahn)*.

⑪ Sowjetisches Ehrenmal *(Soviet Memorial)*. Built immediately after World War II, this monument stands as a reminder of the Soviet victory over the shattered German army in Berlin in May 1945. The Battle of Berlin was one of the deadliest on the European front. A hulking bronze statue of a soldier stands atop a marble plinth taken from Hitler's former Reichkanzlei (headquarters). The memorial is flanked by what are said to be the first two T-34 tanks to have fought their way into the city. ⊠ *Str. des 17. Juni, Tiergarten* Ⓜ *Unter den Linden (S-bahn)*.

POTSDAMER PLATZ & KREUZBERG

The once-divided capital is rejoined on Potsdamer Platz, which was Berlin's inner-city center and Europe's busiest plaza before World War II. Bombings and the wall system left this area a sprawling, desolate lot, where tourists in West Berlin could climb a wooden platform to peek into East Berlin's death strip. After the Wall fell, Sony, Daimler, Asea Brown Boveri, and other companies made a rush to build their headquarters on this prime real estate. In the mid-1990s Potsdamer Platz became Europe's largest construction site. Today's modern complexes of red sandstone, terra-cotta tiles, steel, and glass have made it a city within a city. The subtle reminder that this was an empty plot for nearly 50 years is a line of cobblestones that traces the path of the Wall on the west side of Stresemannstrasse.

A few narrow streets cut between the hulking modern architecture, which includes two high-rise office towers owned by Daimler, one of which was designed by star architect Renzo Piano. The round atrium of the Sony Center comes closest to rendering a traditional square used as a public meeting point. Farther down Potsdamer Strasse are the state museums and cultural institutes of the Kulturforum.

Kreuzberg held the American side of the border-crossing Checkpoint Charlie, and is one of the liveliest districts in Berlin. A largely Turkish population shares the residential streets with a variegated assortment of political radicals and bohemians of all nationalities. There are few traditional attractions here, but it's a great place to people-watch.

TIMING

The sights on this tour are close to one another until you set off for the Jüdisches Museum. In 30 minutes you can take in the architecture at Potsdamer Platz and reach the Kulturforum complex for a look from the outside. To retrace your steps and reach the Topographie des Terrors will take 20 minutes. Owing to its small size and popularity, you may experience a wait or slow line at the Checkpoint Charlie Museum. Monday is a popular day for both it and the Jüdisches Museum, since the state museums are closed that day.

MAIN ATTRACTIONS

⑮ ★ **Kulturforum** (*Cultural Forum*). This unique ensemble of museums, galleries, and the Philharmonic Hall

> **TOURING TIPS**
>
> **Getting Here:** The Potsdamer Platz U- and S-bahn stations drop you right in the center of the action.
>
> **Scenic Spot:** The Daimler building's rooftop Panorama deck at Potsdamer Platz 1 has one of the best bird's-eye views in all of Berlin.
>
> **Snacks:** On Potsdamer Platz, the best choices for inexpensive snacks are found underground: in the U- and S-bahn station's maze and on the lower level of the Potsdamer Platz Arkaden shopping mall.
>
> **Snacks:** Stop by at any of the cheap Turkish Döner kebab stands in Kreuzberg,

15

was long in the making. The first designs were submitted in the 1960s and the last building completed in 1998. The **Gemäldegalerie** (*Picture Gallery*) reunites formerly separated collections from East and West Berlin. It's one of Germany's finest art galleries, and has an extensive selection of European paintings from the 13th to 18th centuries. Seven rooms are reserved for paintings by German masters, among them Dürer, Cranach the Elder, and Holbein. A special collection has works of the Italian masters—Botticelli, Titian, Giotto, Lippi, and Raphael— as well as paintings by Dutch and Flemish masters of the 15th and 16th centuries: Van Eyck, Bosch, Brueghel the Elder, and van der Weyden. The museum also holds the world's second-largest Rembrandt collection. ⊠ *Matthäikirchpl. 4, Tiergarten* ☎ *030/266–2951* ⊕ *www. smb.museum* 🖾 *€8* ⏱ *Tues., Wed., and Fri.–Sun. 10–6, Thurs. 10–10* Ⓜ *Potsdamer Platz (U-bahn and S-bahn).* Steps away from the Gemäldegalerie are two examples of ultramodern architecture. The **Kunstbibliothek** (*Art Library* ⊠ *Matthäikirchpl. 4, Tiergarten* ☎ *030/266–2951* ⊕ *www.smb.museum* 🖾 *€8* ⏱ *Tues.–Fri. 10–6, weekends 11–6; reading room Mon. 9–8, Tues.–Fri. 9–4*) contains art posters, a costume library, ornamental engravings, and a commercial-art collection. The **Kupferstichkabinett** (*Drawings and Prints Collection* ⊠ *Matthäikirchpl. 4, Tiergarten* ☎ *030/266–2951* ⊕ *www.smb.museum* 🖾 *€8* ⏱ *Tues., Wed., and Fri. 10–6, Thurs. 10–10, weekends 11–6*) has occasional exhibits, which include European woodcuts, engravings, and illustrated books from the 15th century to the present (highlights of its holdings are pen-and-ink drawings by Dürer and drawings by Rembrandt). You can request to see one or two drawings in the study room. Another building displays paintings dating from the late Middle Ages to 1800. Inside the **Kunstgewerbemuseum** (*Museum of Decorative Arts*) are European arts and crafts from the Middle Ages to the present.

Symbols & Shifts in East & West

The year 2009 marks the 20th anniversary of the fall of the infamous Berlin Wall, and pivotal spots that made history in November 1989 will be highlighted with small exhibits and information centers. Art projects such as larger-than-life dominos set up throughout the city will be knocked over—creating a ripple of falling "stones" throughout East and West—and a pop concert at the Brandenburg Gate on the evening of November 9th will recall an event that shaped world history. Many of today's Berliners, both from East and West, are *Einheitskinder*, children of German reunification, and have no recollection of the troubled days of division. After two decades, normalcy had descended upon "Ossis" and "Wessies," blurring all differences but in some slang, income, and the general outlook on life.

Berlin is still a city that protects the character of each *Kiez*, or neighborhood, which has more to do with social reasons than East vs. West. In many areas, such as Prenzlauer Berg and northern Mitte, two proud Eastern districts, the former population has all but vanished: first affluent West Berlin families moved in, and now, even richer West German or foreign "invaders" are taking over leases. At the same time, new niche districts with a low-budget, but artsy, young scene are emerging; Friedrichshain is hotter than ever, and some gurus even talk of Neukölln or Lichtenberg as being the next it place to be.

The days of *Ostalgie* (nostalgia for the East) have long passed, and East Germany's iconography is trendy only for out-of-towners. Nevertheless, many East Berlin designs have crept into the daily life of all Berliners, such as the figure that appears on the crosswalk traffic lights. The stocky East Berlin *Ampelmann* ("street-light man") wears a wide-brim hat and walks with an animated gait, and is now used for every crosswalk in Berlin—he also adorns coffee cups and T-shirts, and there's even candy made in his image. Entire gift shops are dedicated to him, such as in the Hackesche Höfe in Mitte and the Arkaden mall at Potsdamer Platz.

The 18th-century Prussian Brandenburg Gate may be the city symbol for Berlin tourism, but the East German soaring television tower, the Berliner Fernsehturm, is an enormously popular silhouette for Berlin-based companies' logos, nightclubs' flyers, and advertisements of all sorts. Emblematic icons of the Cold War and Berlin's division, such as the old central railway station Bahnhof Zoo in West Berlin, the Tempelhof Airport, and the former Palast der Republik, have lost their function, have been closed, or even torn down. The passing of these symbols confirms that the East-West discourse is no longer a real issue, and that Berlin is ready to move on.

Among the notable exhibits are the Welfenschatz (Welfen Treasure), a collection of 16th-century gold and silver plates from Nürnberg, as well as ceramics and porcelains. ⊠ *Herbert-von-Karajan-Str. 10, Tiergarten* ☎ *030/266–2902* ⊕ *www.smb.museum* ☎ *€8* ☉ *Tues.–Fri. 10–6, weekends 11–6.* The mustard-yellow complex that resembles a great tent belongs to the **Philharmonie** (☎ *030/254–880*), home to the renowned Berlin Philharmonic Orchestra since 1963. Despite a fire in 2008, the now renovated concert hall hasn't lost its heavenly, unique sound. The Philharmonie and the smaller Chamber Music Hall adjoining it were designed by Hans Scharoun. ■TIP→ **There's a free tour of the Philharmonie daily at 1** PM. Across the parking lot from the Philharmonie, the **Musikinstrumenten-Museum** *(Musical Instruments Museum)* has a fascinating collection of keyboard, string, wind, and percussion instruments. ■TIP→ **These are demonstrated during an 11** AM **tour on Saturday, which closes with a 20-minute Wurlitzer organ concert.** *Museum* ⌧*Ben-Gurion-Str. 1, Tiergarten* ☎*030/2548–1129* ⌨*€4* ⊙*Tues., Wed., and Fri. 9– 5, Thurs. 9* AM*–10* PM*, weekends 10–5.* The **Staatsbibliothek** (*National Library* ⌧*Postdamer Str. 33* ☎*030/2660* ⌨*€10* ⊙*Weekdays 9–9, Sat. 9–7*) is one of the largest libraries in Europe, and was one of the Berlin settings in Wim Wender's 1987 film *Wings of Desire.*

> ## CHECKPOINT CHARLIE
>
> One of the most famous hot spots of the Cold War, this border crossing for non-Germans was manned by the Soviet military in East Berlin's Mitte district and, several yards south, by the U.S. military in West Berlin's Kreuzberg district. Tension between the superpowers in October 1961 led to an uneasy stand-off between Soviet and American tanks. Today the much-touristed intersection consists of a replica American guardhouse and signage, plus the cobblestones that mark the old border.

15

⑲ ★ **Mauermuseum-Museum Haus am Checkpoint Charlie.** Just steps from the famous crossing point between the two Berlins, the Wall Museum—House at Checkpoint Charlie tells the story of the Wall and, even more riveting, the stories of those who escaped through, under, and over it. The homespun museum reviews the events leading up to the Wall's construction and, with original tools and devices, plus recordings and photographs, shows how East Germans escaped to the West (one of the most ingenious contraptions was a miniature submarine). Exhibits about human rights and paintings interpreting the Wall round out the experience. ■TIP→ **Come early or late in the day to avoid the multitudes dropped off by tour buses.** Monday can be particularly crowded. ⌧*Friedrichstr. 43–45, Kreuzberg* ☎*030/253–7250* ⊕*www.mauer museum.com* ⌨*€9.50* ⊙*Daily 9* AM*–10* PM Ⓜ*Kochstrasse (U-bahn).*

NEED A BREAK? Try your best to conjure up an image of the Wall from a window seat at Café Adler (⌧*Friedrichstr. 206, Kreuzberg* ☎*030/251–8965*), which once bumped right up against it. The quality fare is inexpensive and the soups are particularly delicious. Breakfast is served until 5 PM.

⑯ ★ **Neue Nationalgalerie** *(New National Gallery).* Bauhaus member Mies van der Rohe originally designed this glass-box structure for Bacardi Rum in Cuba, but Berlin became the site of its realization in 1968. The main exhibits are below ground. Highlights of thecollection of 20th-century paintings, sculptures, and drawings include works by expressionists Otto Dix, Ernst Ludwig Kirchner, and Georg Grosz. Special exhibits often take precedence over the permanent collection however. ⌧*Potsdamer Str. 50, Tiergarten* ☎*030/266–2951* ⊕*www.smb.*

museum ≊€8 ⊙ *Tues., Wed., and Fri. 10–6, Thurs. 10–10, weekends 11–6* Ⓜ *Potsdamer Platz (U-bahn and S-bahn).*

⑭ **Sony Center.** This glass-and-steel construction wraps around a spectacular circular forum. Topping it off is a tentlike structure meant to emulate Mount Fuji. The architectural jewel, designed by German-American architect Helmut Jahn, is one of the most stunning public spaces of Berlin's new center, filled with restaurants, cafés, movie theaters, and apartments. A faint reminder of glorious days gone by is the old **Kaisersaal** (Emperor's Hall), held within a very modern glass enclosure, and today a pricey restaurant. The hall originally stood 50 yards away in the Grand Hotel Esplanade (built in 1907) but was moved here lock, stock, and barrel. Red-carpet glamour returns every February with the Berlinale Film Festival, which has screenings at the commercial cinema within the center.

Within the center the **Filmmuseum Berlin** (⊠ *Potsdamer Str. 2, Tiergarten* ☎ *030/300–9030* ⊕ *www.filmmuseum-berlin.de* ≊€6 ⊙ *Tues., Wed., and Fri.–Sun. 10–6, Thurs. 10–8*) presents the groundbreaking history of German moviemaking with eye-catching displays. The texts are also in English, and there's an audio guide as well. Memorabilia includes personal belongings of Marlene Dietrich and plans and costumes for fantasy and science-fiction films.

⚲ A must-see when traveling with children is the **Legoland Discovery Center** (⊠ *Potsdamer Str. 4, Tiergarten* ☎ *030/301–0400* ⊕ *www.legoland. de* ≊€14.50 ⊙ *Daily 10–5*), the Danish toy company's only indoor park. Children can build their very own towers while their parents live out their urban development dreams, even testing if the miniature construction would survive an earthquake. In a special section, Berlin's landmarks are presented in a breathtaking miniature world made up of thousands of tiny Lego bricks.

ALSO WORTH SEEING

㉑ **Berlinische Galerie.** Talk about site-specific art: all the modern art, photography, and architecture models and plans here, created between 1870 and the present, were made in Berlin (or in the case of architecture competition models, intended for the city). Russians, secessionists, Dadaists, and expressionists all had their day in Berlin, and individual works by Otto Dix, George Grosz, and Georg Baselitz, as well as artists' archives such as the Dadaist Hannah Höch's, are highlights. ■TIP➡ Bus M29 to Lindenstrasse is the closest transportation stop. ⊠*Alte Jakobstr. 124–128* ☎*030/7890–2800* ⊕*www.berlinischegalerie.de* 🎫*€6* ⊙*Wed.–Mon. 10–6* Ⓜ*Kochstrasse (U-bahn)*.

㉗ Jüdisches Museum *(Jewish Museum)*. The history of Germany's Jews from the Middle Ages through today is chronicled here, from prominent historical figures to the evolution of laws regarding Jews' participation in civil society. An attraction in itself is the highly conceptual building, which was designed by Daniel Libeskind. Various physical "voids" represent the loss German society faces because of the Holocaust, and a portion of the exhibits documents the Holocaust itself. ■TIP➡ Reserve at least three hours for the museum, and devote more time to the second floor if you're already familiar with basic aspects of Judaica, which are the focus of the third floor. ⊠*Lindenstr. 9–14, Kreuzberg* ☎*030/2599–3300* ⊕*www.juedisches-museum-berlin.de* 🎫*€5* ⊙*Mon. 10–10, Tues.–Sun. 10–8* Ⓜ*Hallesches Tor (U-bahn)*.

⑰ Martin-Gropius-Bau. This magnificent palazzolike exhibition hall dates back to 1877, and once housed Berlin's Arts and Crafts Museum. Its architect, Martin Gropius, was the uncle of Walter Gropius, the Bauhaus architect who also worked in Berlin. The international, changing exhibits on art and culture here have included Atzec sculptures, Henri Cartier-Bresson's photographs, and the set designs of Ken Adams for Stanley Kubrick's films. ⊠*Niederkirchnerstr. 7, Kreuzberg* ☎*030/2548–6112* ⊕*www.gropiusbau.de* 🎫*Varies with exhibit* ⊙*Wed.–Mon. 10–8* Ⓜ*Kochstrasse (U-bahn), Potsdamer Platz (U-bahn and S-bahn)*.

⑱ Topographie des Terrors *(Topography of Terror)*. Within the cellar remains
★ of the Nazis' Reich Security Main Office (which was composed of the SS, SD, and Gestapo), photos and documents explain the secret state police and intelligence organizations that planned and executed Nazi crimes against humanity. The fates of both perpetrators and victims are included in the free, open-air exhibit. Within a makeshift complex (a new documentation center is scheduled to be completed by 2009), you can leaf through books and copies of official documents. Pick up a free audio guide here before viewing the exhibit. ⊠*Niederkirchnerstr. 8, Kreuzberg* ☎*030/2548–6703* ⊕*www.topographie.de* 🎫*Free* ⊙*Oct.–Apr., daily 10–6; May–Sept., daily 10–8*.

MITTE: UNTER DEN LINDEN TO ALEXANDERPLATZ

The Mitte (Middle) district is where Berlin first began as two fishing villages separated by the Spree River. Throughout its 772-year-plus history it has served as a seat of government for Prussian kings, German emperors, the Weimar Republic, Hitler's Third Reich, the communist German Democratic Republic, and, since 1999, reunited Germany. Treasures once split between East and West Berlin museums are also reunited on Museum Island, a UNESCO World Heritage Site.

The historic boulevard Unter den Linden proudly rolls out Prussian architecture and world-class museums. Its major cross-street is Fried-

15

richstrasse, which was revitalized in
the mid-1990s with car showrooms
(including Bentley, Bugatti, and
Volkswagen) and upscale malls. At
its eastern end, Unter den Linden
turns into Karl-Liebknecht-Strasse,
which leads to vast Alexanderplatz,
where eastern Berlin's handful of
skyscrapers are dwarfed beneath

the city's most visible landmark, the Berlin TV tower.

TIMING

If you don't look closely at any museums or highlights, you could ram-
ble this route in two hours. To speed your way down Unter den Linden, you can hop one of the three bus lines that make stops between
Wilhelmstrasse and Alexanderplatz. A few state museums in this area
are closed on Monday.

MAIN ATTRACTIONS

㉔ Bebelplatz. After he became ruler in 1740, Frederick the Great personally planned the buildings surrounding this square (which has a
huge parking garage cleverly hidden beneath the pavement). The area
received the nickname "*Forum Fridericianum,*" or Frederick's Forum.
On May 10, 1933, Joseph Goebbels, the Nazi minister for propa-
ganda and "public enlightenment," organized one of the nationwide
book-burnings here. The books, thrown on a pyre by Nazi officials
and students, included works by Jews, pacifists, and Communists. In
the center of Bebelplatz, a modern and subtle memorial marks where
20,000 books went up in flames.

A music lover, Frederick the Great had as his first priority the **Staatsoper Unter den Linden** *(State Opera)*. Berlin's lavish opera house was
completed in 1743 by the same architect who built Sanssouci in Potsdam, Georg Wenzeslaus von Knobelsdorff. Daniel Barenboim is maestro of the house, which will undergo a complete makeover starting in
mid-2010, when the historic interior is replaced with a modern design.
⊠ *Unter den Linden 7, Mitte* ☎ *030/203–50* ⊕ *www.staatsoper-berlin.
de* ☉ *Box office weekdays 11–9, weekends 2–9; last hr for tickets to that
night's performance only; reservations by phone Mon.–Sat. 10–8, Sun.
2–8* Ⓜ *Französische Strasse (U-bahn)*. The green-patina dome belongs
to **St. Hedwigskathedrale** *(St. Hedwig's Cathedral)*. Begun in 1747, it was
modeled after the Pantheon in Rome, and was the first Catholic church
built in resolutely Protestant Berlin since the 16th-century Reformation. It was Frederick the Great's effort to appease Prussia's Catholic
population after his invasion of Catholic Silesia (then Poland). A treasury lies inside. ⊠ *Bebelpl., Mitte* ☎ *030/203–4810* ⊕ *www.hedwigs-
kathedrale.de* ☎ *Free* ☉ *Weekdays 10–5, Sun. 1–5* ☞ *Tours (€1.50)
available in English, call ahead* Ⓜ *Französische Strasse (U-bahn)*. Running the length of the west side of Bebelplatz, the former royal library is
now part of **Humboldt-Universität** (⊠ *Unter den Linden 6, Mitte*), whose
main campus is across the street on Unter den Linden. The university
building was built in 1766 as a palace for Prince Heinrich, the brother

of Frederick the Great. With its founding in 1810, the university moved in. The fairy-tale-collecting Grimm brothers taught here, as did political philosophers Karl Marx and Friedrich Engels. Albert Einstein taught physics from 1914 to 1932, when he left Berlin for the United States. Unfortunately, the university has lost its reputation as an elite institution to the Free University Berlin, in the west.

NEED A BREAK?

The Opernpalais (⊠ *Unter den Linden 5, Mitte* ☎ *030/202–683* ⊕ *www. opernpalais.de*), next to the opera house and within the former Crown Princesses' Palace, is home to a café famous for its selection of 40 cakes and pies, plus other sweet treats.

㉙ Berliner Dom *(Berlin Cathedral)*. A church has stood here since 1536, but this enormous version dates from 1905, making it the largest 20th-century Protestant church in Germany. The royal Hohenzollerns worshiped here until 1918, when Kaiser Wilhelm II abdicated and left Berlin for Holland. The massive dome wasn't restored from World War II damage until 1982; the interior was completed in 1993. The climb to the dome's outer balcony is made easier by a wide stairwell, plenty of landings with historic photos and models, and even a couple of chairs. The more than 80 sarcophagi of Prussian royals in the crypt are significant, but to less-trained eyes can seem uniformly dull. All morning services include communion. ⊠ *Am Lustgarten 1, Mitte* ☎ *030/2026–9136* ⊕ *www.berliner-dom.de* ☞€8 ☉ *Mon.–Sat. 9–8, Sun. noon–8* Ⓜ *Hackescher Markt (S-bahn)*.

㉞ Berliner Fernsehturm *(Berlin TV Tower)*. Finding Alexanderplatz is no problem: just head toward the 1,198-foot-high tower piercing the sky. It was completed in 1969 and is not accidentally 710 feet higher than western Berlin's broadcasting tower and 98 feet higher than the Eiffel Tower. You can get the best view of Berlin from within the tower's disco ball-like observation level; on a clear day you can see for 40 km (25 mi). One floor above, the city's highest restaurant rotates for your panoramic pleasure. ■TIP→ Make reservations in advance and stick to the German dishes. ⊠ *Panoramastr. 1a, Mitte* ☎ *030/242–3333* ⊕ *www. berlinerfernsehturm.de* ☞€9.50 ☉ *Nov.–Feb., daily 10* AM*–midnight; Mar.–Oct., daily 9* AM*–midnight; last admission ½ hr before closing* Ⓜ *Alexanderplatz (U-bahn and S-bahn)*.

㉖ Deutsches Historisches Museum *(German History Museum)*. The museum is composed of two buildings. The magnificent pink, baroque Prussian arsenal (Zeughaus) was constructed between 1695 and 1730, and is the oldest building on Unter den Linden. The new permanent exhibits, reopened after much debate in mid-2006, offer a modern and fascinating view of German history since the early Middle Ages. Behind the arsenal, the granite-and-glass Pei-Bau building by I. M. Pei holds often stunning and politically controversial changing exhibits. ⊠ *Unter den Linden 2, Mitte* ☎ *030/203–040* ⊕ *www.dhm.de* ☞€5 ☉ *Daily 10–6*.

㉒ Friedrichstrasse. The once-bustling street of cafés and theaters of prewar Berlin has risen from the rubble of war and Communist neglect to reclaim the crowds with shopping emporiums.

15

Heading south from the train station Friedrichstrasse, you'll pass hotels, bookstores, and, south of Unter den Linden, the car showrooms of the **Lindencorso** and several upscale clothing stores. Standing at the corner of Französische Strasse (meaning "French Street" for the nearby French

Huguenot cathedral) is the French department store **Galeries Lafayette** (⊠ *Friedrichstr. 76–78* ☎ *030/209–480*). French architect Jean Nouvel included an impressive steel-and-glass funnel at its center, which is surrounded by four floors of expensive clothing and luxuries as well as a food department with counters offering French cuisine.

North of the train station you will see the now rejuvenated heart of the entertainment center of Berlin's Roaring Twenties. The ugly **Friedrichstadtpalast,** Europe's largest variety theater, may be just a poor modern copy of its former glamorous past. A few steps away, the meticulously restored **Admiralspalast** (⊠ *Friedrichstr. 101* ☎ *030/4799–7499*), on the other hand, is the successful rebirth of a glittering Jazz Age entertainment temple. Reopened with a hotly debated production of Brecht's *Threepenny Opera,* it now houses two stages, a club, an upscale Italian restaurant, and a spa right above a natural hot spring.

㉓ **Gendarmenmarkt.** Anchoring this large square are the beautifully reconstructed 1818 **Konzerthaus** and the **Deutscher Dom** and **Französischer Dom** (German and French cathedrals). The Französischer Dom contains the **Hugenottenmuseum** (⊠ *Gendarmenmarkt 5, Mitte* ☎ *030/229–1760* 🎟 *€2* ☉ *Tues.–Sat. noon–5, Sun. 11–5*), with exhibits charting the history and art of the French Protestant refugees who settled in Berlin. These Huguenots were expelled from France at the end of the 17th century by King Louis XIV. Their energy and commercial expertise did much to help boost Berlin during the 18th century. The **Deutscher Dom** (⊠ *Gendarmenmarkt 1, Mitte* ☎ *030/2273–0431* ⊕ *www.bundestag. de/deutscher-dom* 🎟 *Free* ☉ *Oct.–Apr., Tues.–Sun. 10–6; May–Sept., Tues.–Sun. 10–7*) holds an extensive exhibition on the emergence of the democratic parliamentary system in Germany since the late 1800s. The free museum is sponsored by the German parliament. Leadership and opposition in East Germany are also documented. ■TIP➔ **An English-language audio guide covers a portion of the exhibits on the first three floors.** Floors four and five have temporary exhibitions with no English text or audio.

㉗ **Museumsinsel** *(Museum Island).* On the site of one of Berlin's two original settlements, this unique complex of four state museums, a UNESCO World Heritage Site, is an absolute must.

Fodor's Choice
★

The **Alte Nationalgalerie** (Old National Gallery, entrance on Bodestrasse) houses an outstanding collection of 18th-, 19th-, and early-20th-century paintings and sculptures. Works by Cézanne, Rodin, Degas, and one of Germany's most famous portrait artists, Max Liebermann, are part of the permanent exhibition. Its Galerie der Romantik (Gallery of Romanticism) collection has masterpieces from such 19th-century German painters as Karl Friedrich Schinkel and Caspar David Friedrich, the leading members of the German Romantic school. The **Altes Museum** (Old Museum), a red-marble, neoclassical building abutting the green Lustgarten, was Prussia's first building purpose-built to serve as a museum. Designed by Karl Friedrich Schinkel, it was completed in 1830. Until fall 2009, when the collection will relocate to the then completely restored Neues Museum, it serves as home to the Egyptian collection, which traces Egypt's history from 4000 BC and whose prize piece is the exquisite 3,300-year-old bust of Queen Nefertiti. The permanent collection of the Altes Museum consists of everyday utensils from ancient Greece as well as vases and sculptures from the 6th to 4th centuries BC. Etruscan art is its highlight, and there are a few examples of Roman art. Antique sculptures, clay figurines, and bronze art of the Antikensammlung (Antiquities Collection) are also housed here; the other part of the collection is in the Pergamonmuseum. At the northern tip of Museum Island is the **Bode-Museum,** a somber-looking gray edifice graced with elegant columns. Reopened in 2006, it now presents the state museums' stunning collection of German and Italian sculptures since the Middle Ages, the Museum of Byzantine Art, and a huge coin collection. Even if you think you aren't interested in the ancient world, make an exception for the **Pergamonmuseum** (entrance on Am Kupfergraben), one of the world's greatest museums. The museum's name is derived from its principal display, the Pergamon Altar, a monumental Greek temple discovered in what is now Turkey and dating from 180 BC. The altar was shipped to Berlin in the late 19th century. Equally impressive are the gateway to the Roman town of Miletus and the Babylonian processional way. Art and culture buffs who want to enjoy as many Berlin museums as possible should consider the Three-Day pass for €19, which allows unlimited access to all of Berlin's state museums. If you get tired of antiques and paintings, drop by any of the museums' cafés. ✉*Entrance to Museumsinsel: Am Kupfergraben, Mitte* ☎*030/–2661 or 030/2090–5577* ⊕*www.smb.museum* 🎫*All Museum Island museums €8, but may be higher during special exhibits.* ⊙*Pergamonmuseum Fri.–Wed. 10–6, Thurs. 10–10. Alte Nationalgalerie Tues., Wed., and Fri.–Sun. 10–6, Thurs. 10–10. Altes Museum Fri.–Wed. 10–6, Thurs. 10–10. Bode-Museum Fri.–Wed. 10–6, Thurs. 10–10* Ⓜ*Hackescher Markt (S-bahn).*

㉝ **Nikolaiviertel** *(Nicholas Quarter).* Renovated in the 1980s and a tad concrete-heavy, this tiny quarter grew up around Berlin's oldest parish church, the medieval, twin-spire **St. Nikolaikirche** (St. Nicholas's Church), dating from 1230. The adjacent Fischerinsel (Fisherman's Island) area was the heart of Berlin 765 years ago, and retains a bit of its medieval character. At Breite Strasse you'll find two of Berlin's oldest buildings: No. 35 is the **Ribbeckhaus,** the city's only surviving Renaissance structure, dating from 1624, and No. 36 is the early baroque **Marstall,** built by Michael Matthais between 1666 and 1669. The area feels rather artificial, but draws tourists to its gift stores, cafés, and restaurants. ✉*Church: Nikolaikirchpl., Mitte* ☎*030/240–020* ⊕*www.*

stadtmuseum.de ✉*Free* ⊙*Tues. and Thurs.–Sun. 10–6, Wed. noon–8* Ⓜ*Alexanderplatz (U-bahn and S-bahn).*

Unter den Linden. The name of this historic Berlin thoroughfare, between the Brandenburg Gate and Schlossplatz, means "under the linden trees"—and as Marlene Dietrich once sang, "As long as the old linden trees still bloom, Berlin is still Berlin." Imagine Berliners' shock when Hitler decided to fell the trees in order to make Unter den Linden more parade-friendly. The grand boulevard began as a riding path that the royals used to get from their palace to their hunting grounds (now Tiergarten). Lining it now are linden trees planted after World War II.

ALSO WORTH SEEING

㉟ Alexanderplatz. This bleak square, bordered by the train station, the Galeria Kaufhof department store, and the 40-story Park Inn Berlin-Alexanderplatz hotel, once formed the hub of East Berlin and was originally named in 1805 for czar Alexander I. German writer Alfred Döblin dubbed it the "heart of a world metropolis" (text from his 1929 novel *Berlin Alexanderplatz* is written on a building across the northeastern side of the square). Today it's a basic center of commerce and the occasional demonstration. The unattractive modern buildings are a reminder not just of the results of Allied bombing but also of the ruthlessness practiced by East Germans when they demolished what remained. A famous meeting point in the south corner is the World Time Clock (1969), which even keeps tabs on Tijuana.

㉚ AquaDom & Sea Life Berlin. The Sea Life group has aquariums Europewide, each with a focus on local marine life. In Berlin the tanks begin with the Spree River, move on to Berlin's lakes, and then take you on a course from fresh- to saltwater. Waterfront city scenes are part of the decor, which gradually gives way to starfish-petting beds, overhead tanks, and a submarinelike room. The last darkened environment emulating a rocky coastline gets dramatic when rains come down and thunder and lightning crash. Don't come looking for sharks or colorful tropical fish: the most exotic creatures here are perhaps the tiny sea horses and spotted rays. The aquarium's finale is a state-of-the-art glass elevator that brings you through a silo-shape fish tank to the exit. Young children love this place, but the timed wait for the elevator can be frustrating for all ages. Be prepared for a line at the entrance, too. ✉*Spandauer Str. 3, Mitte* ☎*030/992–800* ⊕*www.sealife.de* ✉*€19.95* ⊙*Daily 10–7; last admission at 6* Ⓜ*Hackescher Markt (S-bahn).*

㉜ Berliner Rathaus *(Berlin Town Hall).* Nicknamed the *"Rotes Rathaus"* (Red Town Hall) for its redbrick design, the town hall was completed in 1869. Its most distinguishing features are its neo-Renaissance clock tower and frieze that depicts Berlin's history up to 1879 in 36 terracotta plaques, each 6 meters long. Climb the grand stairwell to view the coat-of-arms hall and a few exhibits. ■TIP➔ **The Rathaus has a very inexpensive, cafeteria-style canteen offering budget lunches. The entrance is inside the inner courtyard.** ✉*Jüdenstr. 1, at Rathausstr. 15, Mitte* ☎*030/90260* ✉*Free* ⊙*Weekdays 9–6* Ⓜ*Alexanderplatz (U-bahn and S-bahn).*

**OFF THE
BEATEN
PATH**

East Side Gallery. This 1-km (½-mi) stretch of concrete went from guarded border to open-air gallery within three months. East Berliners breached the wall on November 9, 1989, and between February and June of 1990, 118 artists from around the globe created unique works of art on the longest-remaining section of the Berlin Wall. Much of the paint is now peeling, and many panels have been vandalized with graffiti, despite on-going restoration efforts. One of the best-known works, by Russian artist Dmitri Vrubel, depicts Brezhnev and Honnecker (the former East German leader) kissing, with the caption "My God. Help me survive this deadly love." The stretch along the Spree Canal runs between the Warschauer Strasse S- and U-bahn station and Ostbahnhof. The redbrick Oberbaumbrücke (an 1896 bridge) at Warschauer Strasse makes that end more scenic. Just past the bridge there's also a manmade beach with a bar, restaurant, and club popular with the after work crowd, called **Strandgut** (⊕ *www.strandgut-berlin.com*). ⊠ *Mühlenstr., Friedrichshain* Ⓜ *Warschauer Strasse (U-bahn and S-bahn), Ostbahnhof (S-bahn).*

❸❻ **Märkisches Museum** *(Brandenburg Museum).* This redbrick attic includes exhibits on the city's theatrical past, its guilds, its newspapers, and the March 1848 revolution. Paintings capture the look of the city before it crumbled in World War II. ■ TIP➡ **The fascinating collection of mechanical musical instruments is demonstrated on Sunday at 3** PM. ⊠ *Am Köllnischen Park 5, Mitte* ☎ *030/3086—6215* ⊕ *www.stadtmuseum.de* 🎟 *€6, instrument demonstration €3* ☽ *Tues., Thurs., Sun. 10–6, Wed. noon–8, Fri. and Sat. 2–10* Ⓜ *Märkisches Museum (U-bahn).*

❷❺ **Neue Wache** *(New Guardhouse).* One of many Berlin projects by the early-19th-century architect Karl Friedrich Schinkel, this building served as both the Royal Prussian War Memorial (honoring the dead of the Napoleonic Wars) and the royal guardhouse until the Kaiser abdicated in 1918. In 1931 it became a memorial to those who fell in World War I. Badly damaged in World War II, it was restored in 1960 by the East German state and rededicated as a memorial for the victims of militarism and fascism. After unification it regained its Weimar Republic appearance and was inaugurated as Germany's central war memorial. Inside is a copy of Berlin sculptor Käthe Kollwitz's *Pietà,* showing a mother mourning over her dead son. The inscription in front of it reads, TO THE VICTIMS OF WAR AND TYRANNY. ⊠ *Unter den Linden, Mitte* ☽ *Daily 10–6.*

❸❶ **St. Marienkirche** *(St. Mary's Church).* This medieval church, one of the finest in Berlin, is best known for its late-Gothic, macabre fresco *Der Totentanz* (*Dance of Death*), which is in need of restoration. Tours on Monday and Tuesday at 1 PM highlight the fresco. ⊠ *Karl-Liebknecht-Str. 8, Mitte* ☎ *030/242–4467* 🎟 *Free* ☽ *Apr.–Oct., daily 10–9; Nov.–Mar., daily 10–6. Organ recital Sun. at 10* Ⓜ *Alexanderplatz (U-bahn and S-bahn), Hackescher Markt (S-bahn).*

❷❽ **Schlossplatz** *(Palace Square).* One of the biggest cultural debates in Berlin in recent years swirled around whether to rebuild a portion of the 1,200-room Hohenzollern palace that stood here from the 15th century (which was destroyed in WW II and then blown up by the East German government in 1950) or not, thereby saving the country and city millions of euros. The construction of a modern museum, art, and library complex is now certain. The project is called Humboldt-Forum, and it will integrate some historic palace elements, including a rebuilt palace cupola. Construction will begin in the near future, and the project is slated for completion in 2013. Within the square, a temporary art project, the **White Cube Berlin**, presents international, contemporary art until 2010 in a cube building that seems to float. ⊠*Schlossplatz, Mitte* ☎*030/2576–2040* ⊕*www.white-cube-berlin.org* ✉*Varies with exhibit* Ⓜ*Alexandeprlatz (S-bahn).*

At Schlossplatz's south end is the brick-and-glass **Staatsrat** (State Senate), where East German dictator Eric Honnecker worked. The stone portal to this building was one of the few parts of the palace that the East German government preserved. It's believed that it was from this portal that Karl Liebknecht attempted to declare a Soviet-style republic after the Kaiser abdicated in November 1918. Irony upon irony, this former Communist building is home to a private business university. ⊠*Unter den Linden, Mitte* Ⓜ*Hackescher Markt (S-bahn).*

MITTE'S SCHEUNENVIERTEL & PRENZLAUER BERG

The hip scene of Mitte, the historic core of Berlin, is best experienced in the narrow streets and courtyard mazes of the Scheunenviertel (Barn Quarter), which also encompasses the former Spandauer Vorstadt (Jewish Quarter)—the streets around Oranienburger Strasse. Some streets are lined with edgy shops, bars, and eateries, while others look empty and forlorn. During the second half of the 17th century, artisans, small-business men, and Jews moved into this area at the encouragement of the Great Elector, who sought to improve his financial situation through their skills. As industrialization intensified, the quarter became poorer, and in the 1880s many East European Jews escaping pogroms settled here.

Northeast of Mitte, the old working-class district of Prenzlauer Berg used to be one of the poorest sections of Berlin. In socialist East Germany, the old (and mostly run-down) tenement houses attracted the artistic avant-garde, who transformed the area into a refuge for alternative lifestyles (think punk singer Nina Hagen, step-daughter of a folk singer expelled by the East German government). The renovated 19th-century buildings with balconies and stuccowork tend to feature unwanted graffiti, but Prenzlauer Berg is now a trendy area full of young couples with baby in tow.

Though not full of sightseeing attractions, the two areas are great for wandering, shopping, and eating and drinking. Mitte's Scheunenviertel is popular with tourists, and you'll find a denser concentration of locals in Prenzlauer Berg.

MAIN ATTRACTIONS

39 ★ **Hackesche Höfe** *(Hacke Warehouses).* Built in 1905–07, this series of eight connected courtyards is the finest example of art nouveau industrial architecture in Berlin. Most buildings are covered with glazed white tiles, and additional Moorish mosaic designs decorate the main courtyard off Rosenthaler Strasse. Shops (including one dedicated to Berlin's beloved street-crossing signal, the "Ampelmann"), restaurants, the variety theater Chamäleon Varieté, a klezmer-music venue, and a movie theater populate the spaces

15

once occupied by ballrooms, a poets' society, and a Jewish girls' club. ⊠*Rosenthaler Str. 40–41 and Sophienstr. 6, Mitte* ☎*030/2809–8010* ⊕*www.hackesche-hoefe.com* Ⓜ*Hackescher Markt (S-bahn).*

NEED A BREAK? Within the first courtyard of Hackesche Höfe Anatre Feinkost (⊠*Rosenthaler Str. 40–41, Mitte* ☎*030/2838–9915*) uses top-quality ingredients for its Mediterranean sandwiches and pastas. You can also just sit with a coffee or glass of wine.

38 **Neue Synagoge** *(New Synagogue).* This meticulously restored landmark, built between 1859 and 1866, is an exotic amalgam of styles, the whole faintly Middle Eastern. Its bulbous, gilded cupola stands out in the skyline. When its doors opened, it was the largest synagogue in Europe, with 3,200 seats. The synagogue was damaged on November 9, 1938 (*Kristallnacht*—Night of the Broken Glass), when Nazi looters rampaged across Germany, burning synagogues and smashing the few Jewish shops and homes left in the country. It was destroyed by Allied bombing in 1943, and it wasn't until the mid-1980s that the East German government restored it. The effective exhibit on the history of the building and its congregants includes fragments of the original architecture and furnishings. ■TIP➜ **Sabbath services are held in a modern addition.** ⊠*Oranienburger Str. 28–30, Mitte* ☎*030/8802–8316* ⊕*www.cjudaicum.de* 🎟*€3, €4.60 including special exhibits; tour €1.50, German only* ⊗*Sept.–Apr., Sun.–Thurs. 10–6, Fri. 10–2; May–Aug., Sun. and Mon. 10–8, Tues.–Thurs. 10–6, Fri. 10–5. Tours Wed. at 4, Sun. at 2 and 4. Cupola Mar.–Oct.* Ⓜ*Oranienburger Strasse (U-bahn), Oranienburger Tor (S-bahn).*

ALSO WORTH SEEING

37 **Gedenkstätte Berliner Mauer** *(Berlin Wall Memorial Site).* This site combines memorials and a museum and research center on the Berlin Wall. The division of Berlin was particularly heart-wrenching on Bernauer Strasse, where neighbors and families on opposite sides of the street were separated overnight. The Reconciliation Chapel, completed in

Berlin's Art Scene

Berlin has always been a liberal city, embracing new art movements and young talent. During the Cold War, West Berlin evolved as a laboratory for art, music, and literature. At the same time, the tough Socialist regime in East Berlin pushed artists underground where they created important political art. Today Berlin is attracting artists and gallery owners from around the world—thanks to its inexpensive rents, ample space, and cultural subsidizing programs for young newcomers.

More than 400 galleries showcase works by artists who seem to account for half the entries of world-class art shows such as the documenta in Kassel or the Biennale in Venice. In addition, Berlin's own art fair, the **Art Forum Berlin** (⊕ *www.art-forum-berlin.de*), is staged annually in October. Longtime galleries present classic modern German and European art along Kurfürstendamm's side streets, between Leibnizstrasse and Uhlandstrasse. Equally established institutions are in Tiergarten (Lützowplatz) and Schöneberg, while Kreuzberg plays host to galleries whose alternative days are behind them.

The real buzz is happening in Mitte, specifically in the Scheunenviertel,

where Auguststrasse has emerged as an informal art alley. Typical for Berlin, new galleries and shops open and close all the time; makeshift, temporary locations are a thrill to discover. Berlin is also known for its large-scale sound and art installations and shows in old, empty houses.

Attracting international jetsetters are the top collections in the city, such as the **Flick Collection** at the Hamburger Bahnhof (⊕ *www.friedrich christianflick-collection.com*), the body of modern works owned by Daimler and presented in the **Weinhaus Huth** (⊕ *www.sammlung.daimlerchrysler. com*), or the shows at the **Deutsche Guggenheim** (⊕ *www.deutsche-guggenheim.de*) on Unter den Linden. Privately owned spaces such as **KW Institute for Contemporary Art** (⊕ *www.kw-berlin.de*) located in an abandoned margarine factory in Mitte, or the **Sammlung Hoffmann** (⊕ *www.sammlung-hoffmann.de*) add special appeal. As hard as it is to keep track of a scene constantly on the move, various resources like the city magazines *tip Berlin* (⊕ *www. tip-berlin.de*) and *zitty Berlin* (⊕ *www. zitty.de*), as well as the gallery guide *artery Berlin* (⊕ *www.artery-berlin.de*), will help you find your very own piece of Berlin art.

2000, replaced the community church dynamited by the Communists in 1985. The church had been walled into the "death strip," and was seen as a hindrance to patrolling it. A portion of the Wall remains on Bernauer Strasse, and an installation meant to serve as a memorial unfortunately only confuses those wondering what the border once looked like. For a wealth of images and information, head into the museum, where German-speakers can even hear radio broadcasts from the time the Wall was erected. ⊠ *Bernauer Str. 111, Wedding* ☎ *030/464–1030* ⊕ *www.berliner-mauer-gedenkstaette.de* ✉ *Free; tours €3* ☉ *Apr.–Oct., Tues.–Sun. 10–6; Nov.–Mar., Tues.–Sun. 10–5* Ⓜ *Bernauer Strasse (U-bahn), Nordbahnhof (S-bahn).*

40 **Jüdischer Friedhof** *(Jewish Cemetery)*. Walking across this quaint cemetery in the shadows of old chestnut trees is like a journey through Jewish culture and tradition in Berlin. Founded in 1827 and officially closed for burials in 1976, the cemetery holds 22,800 graves and 750 prominent grave sites. Among the famous Jewish Berliners at rest here are the baroque composer Giacomo Meyerbeer (1791–1864), the painter Max Liebermann (1847–1935), and one of Europe's most important historical publishing figures, Leopold Ullstein (1829–99). Of the many elaborate marble mausoleums, that for banker Julius Leopold Schwabach is the most beautiful. ⊠ *Schönhauser Allee 23–25, Prenzlauer Berg* ☎ *030/441–9824* ⊙ *May–Sept., Sun.–Thurs. 8–5, Fri. 8–3; Oct.–Apr., Sun.–Thurs. 8–4, Fri. 8–3* Ⓜ *Senefelder Platz (U-bahn).*

> ## THE HUB OF JEWISH LIFE
>
> Grosse Hamburger Strasse was once the hub of life in Jewish Berlin. In 1941–42 at the home at Nos. 25–26, Nazis assembled Berlin's last 50,000 Jews to be transported to concentration camps. Of the oldest Jewish cemetery in the city, which dated to 1672, only a green lawn and a few gravestones mark what the Nazis destroyed. In the early 1700s the Jewish community donated part of the cemetery grounds so that the Protestant Sophienkirche (1712) could be built next door.

15

41 **Kulturbrauerei** *(Culture Brewery)*. The redbrick buildings of the old Schultheiss brewery are typical of late-19th-century industrial architecture. Parts of the brewery were built in 1842, and at the turn of the 20th century the complex expanded to include the main brewery of Berlin's famous Schultheiss beer, then the world's largest brewery. Today, the multicinema, pubs, clubs, and a concert venue that occupy it make up a fringe-arts and entertainment nexus (sadly, without a brewery). Pick up information at the Prezlauer Berg tourist office here, and come Christmastime, visit the market, which includes children's rides. ⊠ *Schönhauser Allee 36–39 and Knaackstr. 97, Prenzlauer Berg* ☎ *030/4431–5152* ⊕ *www.kulturbrauerei-berlin.de* Ⓜ *Eberswalder Strasse (U-bahn).*

◼ **NEED A BREAK?** For coffee and cake or Berliner Kindl, Potsdamer Rex, or Paulaner Hefeweizen on tap, stop by Restauration 1900 (⊠ *Husemannstr. 1, Prenzlauer Berg* ☎ *030/442-2494*).

PALACES, MUSEUMS & NATURE IN OUTER BERLIN

The city's outlying areas abound with palaces, lakes, and museums set in lush greenery. Central to the former West Berlin but now a western district of the united city, Charlottenburg was once an independent and wealthy city that became part of Berlin only in 1920. It holds the baroque Charlottenburg Palace and, across the street, a collection of Picassos in the Museum Berggruen. The southwest part of Berlin holds the vast Grunewald (forest), which borders the Havel River and lake Wannsee. In good weather Berliners come out in force, swimming, sailing their boats, tramping through the woods, and riding horseback. A starting point for cruises plying the water is opposite the Wannsee stop on the S-bahn. The Wannsee station is also the transfer point for buses to the Wannsee beach to the north; Bus 216 to Pfaueninsel (Peacock Island); and Bus 114 to the lakeside villa where the Holocaust was first planned. From Wannsee, Potsdam, the city of summer palaces, is just another three stops on the S-bahn.

MAIN ATTRACTIONS

Bildungs- und Gedenkstätte Haus der Wannsee-Konferenz *(Wannsee Conference Memorial Site)*. The lovely lakeside setting of this Berlin villa belies the unimaginable Holocaust atrocities planned here. This elegant edifice hosted the fateful conference held on January 20, 1942, at which Nazi leaders and German bureaucrats, under SS leader Reinhard Heydrich, planned the systematic deportation and mass extinction of Europe's Jewish population. Today this so-called *Endlösung der Judenfrage* ("final solution of the Jewish question") is illustrated with a chilling exhibition that documents the conference and, more extensively, the escalation of persecution against Jews and the Holocaust itself. A reference library offers source materials in English. ■TIP➔ Allow at least two hours for a visit. ⊠*Am Grossen Wannsee 56–58, from the Wannsee S-bahn station, take Bus 114, Zehlendorf* ☎*030/805–0010* ⊕*www.ghwk.de* ☜*Free, tour €2* ☉*Daily 10–6; library weekdays* Ⓜ *Wannsee (S-bahn).*

★ **Museum Berggruen.** This small modern-art museum holds works by Matisse, Klee, Giacometti, and Picasso, who is particularly well represented with more than 100 works. Heinz Berggruen (1914–2007), a businessman who left Berlin in the 1930s, collected the excellent paintings. He narrates portions of the free audio guide, sharing anecdotes about how he came to acquire pieces directly from the artists, as well as his opinions of the women portrayed in Picasso's portraits. ⊠*Schlossstr. 1, Charlottenburg* ☎*030/3269–5815* ⊕*www.smb. museum* ☜*€6* ☉*Tues.–Sun. 10–6* Ⓜ*Sophie-Charlotte-Platz (U-bahn), Richard-Wagner-Platz (U-bahn).*

★ **Sachsenhausen Gedenkstätte** *(Sachsenhausen Memorial)*. This concentration camp near the Third Reich capital was established in 1936. It held prisoners from every nation in Europe, including British officers, Joseph Stalin's son, and 12,000 Soviet prisoners of war who were systematically murdered. The work camp held approximately 200,000 prisoners, and it's estimated that 50,000 died here. Between 1945 and 1950 the Soviets used the site as a prison, where malnutrition and disease claimed the lives of 20% of the inmates. The East German government made the site a concentration camp memorial in April 1961. A few original facilities remain; the barracks, which hold exhibits, are reconstructions. To reach Sachsenhausen, take the S-bahn 1 to Oranienburg, the last stop. The ride from the Friedrichstrasse station will take 50 minutes. Alternatively, take the Regional 5 train, direction north, from one of Berlin's main stations. From the Oranienburg station it's a 25-minute walk (follow signs), or you can take a taxi or Bus 804 (a 7-minute ride, but with infrequent service) in the direction of

Malz. ■TIP➙ An ABC zone ticket will suffice for any type of train travel and bus transfer. Allow three hours at the memorial, whose exhibits and sites are spread apart. Oranienburg is 35 km (22 mi) north of Berlin. ✉*Str. der Nationen 22, Oranienburg* ☎*03301/200–200* ⊕*www.stiftung-bg.de* ✉*Free, audio guide €3* ⊙*Mid-Mar.–mid-Oct., Tues.–Sun. 8:30–6; mid-Oct.–mid-Mar., Tues.–Sun. 8:30–4:30; last admission ½ hr before closing* Ⓜ*Oranienburg (S-bahn).*

Schloss Charlottenburg *(Charlottenburg Palace).* A grand reminder of imperial days, this showplace served as a city residence for the Prussian rulers. The gorgeous palace started as a modest royal summer residence in 1695, built on the orders of King Friedrich I for his wife, Sophie-Charlotte. In the 18th century Frederick the Great made a number of additions, such as the dome and several wings designed in the rococo style. By 1790 the complex had evolved into a massive royal domain that could take a whole day to explore. Behind heavy iron gates, the Court of Honor—the front courtyard—is dominated by a baroque statue of the Great Elector on horseback. ✉*Luisenpl., Charlottenburg* ☎*030/320–911* ⊕*www.spsg.de* ✉*A Tageskarte (day card) for €12 covers admission for all bldgs., excluding tour of Altes Schloss baroque apartments* Ⓜ*Richard-Wagner-Platz, Sophie-Charlotten-Platz (U-Bahn).*

The **Altes Schloss** *(Nering-Eosander-Bau* ☎*030/320—91* ✉*€10 with tour; €2 for upper floor only* ⊙*Apr.–Oct., Tues.–Sun. 10–6; Nov.–Mar., Tues.–Sun. 10–5)* is the main building, with the ground-floor suites of Friedrich I and Sophie-Charlotte. Paintings include royal portraits by Antoine Pesne, a noted court painter of the 18th century. A guided tour visits the Oak Gallery, the early-18th-century palace chapel, and the suites of Friedrich Wilhelm II and Friedrich Wilhelm III, furnished in the Biedermeier style. Tours leave every hour on the hour from 9 to 5. The upper floor has the apartments of Friedrich Wilhelm IV, a silver treasury, and Berlin and Meissen porcelain. It can be seen on its own. The **Neuer Flügel** *(New Wing* ☎*030/3209–1454* ✉*€6* ⊙*Nov.–Mar., Wed.–Mon. 10–5; Apr.–Oct., Wed.–Mon. 10–6)*, where Frederick the Great once lived, was designed by Knobbelsdorff, who also built Sanssouci. The 138-foot-long Goldene Galerie (Golden Gallery) was the palace's ballroom. West of the staircase are Frederick's rooms, in which parts of his extravagant collection of works by Watteau, Chardin, and Pesne are displayed. An audio guide is included in the admission. The park behind the palace was laid out in the French baroque style beginning in 1697, and was transformed into an English garden in the early 19th century. In it stand the Neuer Pavillon by Karl Friedrich Schinkel and Carl Langhan's **Belvedere teahouse** *(*☎*030/3209–145* ✉*€2* ⊙*Late Mar.–Oct., Tues.–Fri. 10–6, weekends 10–5; Nov.–late Mar., Tues.–Sun. noon–5)*, which overlooks the lake and the Spree River and holds a collection of Berlin porcelain. The **Museum für Vor- und Frühgeschichte** *(Museum of Pre- and Early History* ☎*030/326–7480* ✉*€3. A combination ticket for €6 is valid for this museum, the Museum Berggruen, and the Newton Collection.* ⊙*Tues.–Fri. 9–5, weekends 10–5)* traces the evolution of mankind from 1 million BC to AD 1,000. It's opposite Klausener Platz (to the left as you face the palace).

WHERE TO EAT

Neighborhood stalwarts serve residents from morning to night with a mix of German and international cuisine. Berlin is known for curt or slow service, except at very high-end restaurants. Note that many of the top restaurants are closed on Sunday.

The most common food for meals on the go are *Wursts* (sausages). *Currywurst,* a pork sausage served with a mildly curried ketchup, is local to Berlin. Even more popular are Turkish *Döner* shops that sell pressed lamb or chicken in flat-bread pockets.

WHAT IT COSTS IN EUROS					
	¢	$	$$	$$$	$$$$
AT DINNER	under €9	€9–€15	€16–€20	€21–€25	over €25

Restaurant prices are per person for a main course at dinner.

CHARLOTTENBURG & WESTERN DOWNTOWN

$$–$$$ ✕**Dressler.** Both in its cuisine and in its service, Dressler is a mixture of French brasserie culture and German down-to-earth reliability. Accordingly, the dishes are conceived for a range of palates: oysters on the half-shell, duck with red cabbage, or cod with Pommery-mustard sauce, for example. The menu changes with the seasons. Of the two (very similar) Dressler establishments, this one on Ku'damm has the more genuine French atmosphere. ⊠*Kurfürstendamm 207–208, Charlottenburg* ☎*030/883–3530* ⊠*Unter den Linden 39, Mitte* ☎*030/204–4422* ⊟*AE, DC, MC, V.*

$$–$$$ ✕**Francucci's.** This upscale restaurant on the far western end of
★ Kurfürstendamm is one of the best-kept Italian secrets in Berlin. You won't find any tourists here: the posh neighborhood's residents pack the cheerful, rustic dining room. The high-quality, straightforward cooking yields incredibly fresh salads and appetizers (the bruschetta, for example, undoubtedly has the juiciest tomatoes in town), home-made breads, and exquisite pasta recipes. More refined Tuscan and Umbrian creations might utilize wild boar, but also encompass Mediterranean fish classics such as grilled loup de mer or dorade. ■TIP➔ **In warm weather, reserve a sidewalk table on Ku'damm to watch people at Francucci's and on the boulevard.** ⊠*Kurfürstendamm 90, Wilmersdorf* ☎*030/323–3318* ⊟*AE, MC, V* Ⓜ*Adenauerplatz (U-bahn).*

$$ ✕**Florian.** The handwritten menu is just one page, but there's always a changing variety of fish, fowl, and meat dishes in this well-established restaurant in the heart of the buzzing nightlife scene around Savignyplatz. *Steinbeisser,* a white, flaky fish, might be served with an exciting salsa of rhubarb, chili, coriander, and ginger, or you can opt for some

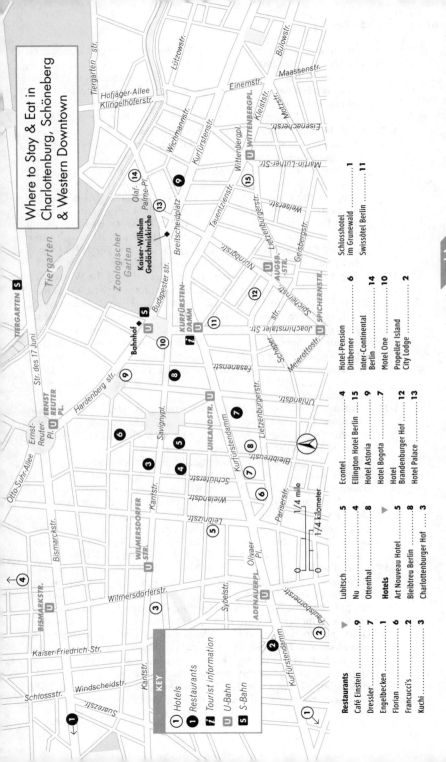

Where to Stay & Eat in Charlottenburg, Schöneberg & Western Downtown

15

Franconian comfort cuisine such as *Kirchweihbraten* (marinated pork with baked apples and plums) or their legendary *Nürnberger Rostbratwurst* (small pork sausages) served as late-night snacks. ■TIP→**The kitchen is open until 1** AM, **and smaller dishes are available until 2** AM. Reservations are advised. ⊠*Grolmanstr. 52, Western Downtown* ☎*030/313–9184* ▤*MC, V* ⊘*No lunch* Ⓜ*Savignyplatz (S-bahn).*

$–$$ ✕**Café Einstein.** The Einstein is a Berlin landmark and one of the lead-
★   ing coffeehouses in town. Set in the historic grand villa of silent movie star Henny Porten, it charmingly recalls the elegant days of the Austrian-Hungarian empire, complete with slightly snobbish waiters gliding across squeaking parquet floors. The Einstein's very own roasting facility produces some of Germany's best coffee, and the cakes are fabulous, particularly the fresh strawberry cake best enjoyed in the shady garden behind the villa in summer. The café also excels in preparing solid Austrian fare such as schnitzel or goulash for an artsy, high-brow clientele. ⊠*Kurfürstenstr. 58, Western Downtown* ☎*030/261–5096* ▤*AE, DC, MC, V* Ⓜ *Kurfürstenstrasse (U-bahn).*

$–$$ ✕**Engelbecken.** The beer coasters are trading cards of the Wittelsbach
★   dynasty in this relaxed but high-quality restaurant serving dishes from Bavaria and the Alps. Classics like Wiener schnitzel, goulash, and grilled saddle steak are made of "bio" meat and vegetable products, meaning that even the veal, lamb, and beef are the tasty results of organic and humane upbringing. ■TIP→**In warm weather, reserve a sidewalk table.** With its corner position facing a park bordering Lake Lietzensee, Engelbecken is a lovely open-air dining spot. ⊠ *Witzlebenstr. 31, Charlottenburg* ☎*030/615–2810* ▤*MC, V* ⊘*No lunch Mon.–Sat.* Ⓜ*Sophie-Charlotte-Platz (U-bahn).*

$–$$ ✕**Lubitsch.** One of the few traditional, artsy restaurants left in bohemian
★   Charlottenburg, the Lubitsch—named after the famous Berlin film director Ernst Lubitsch and exuding a similar air of faded elegance—serves hearty Berlin and German food hard to find these days. Reminiscent of good old home cooking, dishes like Königsberger Klopse (cooked dumplings in a creamy caper sauce) or Kasseler Nacken mit Sauerkraut (salted, boiled pork knuckle) are devoured mostly by locals, who don't mind the dingy seating or good-humored, but sometimes cheeky service. In summer the outdoor tables make for some great people-watching in one of Berlin's most beautiful streets. Enjoy a three-course lunch for just €10 or €12. ⊠*Bleibtreustr. 47, Western Downtown* ☎*030/882–3756* ▤*AE, MC, V* Ⓜ*Savignypl. (S-Bahn).*

$–$$ ✕**Nu.** The Asian-fusion restaurant Nu is a successful and very friendly restaurant cum bar and lounge, one of the few places like this in Berlin without an attitude. Set in the chic but touristy neighborhood of Savignyplatz, the Nu mostly sees well-to-do locals and, particularly at noon, is a modern version of a classic power lunch place. The delicious, spicy food draws on recipes from Southeast Asia, including Singapore, Vietnam, Thailand, and Malaysia, with some Japanese sushi and sashimi platters thrown in. The exotic cocktails are equally top-class, and are just €4.50. DJs play soft house and electro pop music on weekend nights. ⊠*Schlüterstr. 55, Western Downtown* ☎*030/8870–9811* ◬*Reservations essential* ▤*AE, DC, MC, V* Ⓜ*Savignyplatz (S-bahn).*

EATING WELL IN BERLIN

Top-end restaurants can easily import fresh ingredients from other European countries, but some rely on farmers close to home. Surrounding this city is the rural state of Brandenburg, whose name often comes before *Ente* (duck) on a menu. In spring, *Spargel*, white asparagus from Beelitz, is all the rage, showing up in soups and side dishes. Berlin's most traditional four-part meal is *Eisbein* (pork knuckle), always served with sauerkraut, pureed peas, and boiled potatoes. Other old-fashioned

Berlin dishes include *Rouladen* (rolled stuffed beef), *Spanferkel* (suckling pig), *Berliner Schüssel-sülze* (potted meat in aspic) and *Hackepeter* (ground beef). Stands near subway stations sell spicy *Currywurst*, a chubby frankfurter served with tomato sauce made with curry and pepper. Turkish food is an integral part of the Berlin diet. On almost every street you'll find narrow storefronts selling *Döner kebab* (grilled lamb or chicken served with salad in a flat-bread pocket).

15

$–$$ ✕**Ottenthal.** This intimate restaurant with white tablecloths is the city cousin of the Austrian village of Ottenthal, which delivers up the wines, pumpkin-seed oil, and organic ingredients on the menu. Curious combinations might include pike perch with lobster sauce and pepper-pine-nut risotto, or venison medallions with vegetable-potato-strudel, red cabbage, and rowanberry sauce. The huge Wiener schnitzel extends past the plate's rim, and the pastas and strudel are homemade. ■TIP➡ **Offering one of the best meals for your money in Berlin, Ottenthal is a particularly good choice on Sunday evening, when many of Berlin's finer restaurants are closed.** It's just around the corner from both the Zoo and the Ku'damm. ✉*Kantstr. 153, Western Downtown* ☎*030/313–3162* ▤*AE, MC, V* ⊙*No lunch* Ⓜ*Zoologischer Garten (U-bahn and S-bahn).*

$ ✕**Kuchi.** Japanese sushi, sashimi, yakitori, and dunburi dishes along
★ with some Thai, Chinese, and Korean recipes are served in this groovy landmark restaurant, one of the finest sushi places in town. Chefs work with an almost religious devotion to quality and imagination (they even wear shirts saying SUSHI WARRIOR), and the knowledgeable Asian-German staff makes you feel at home. The spicy, fresh, and healthy ingredients and the laid-back vibe pack the restaurant in the evening, so reservations are a must. ■TIP➡ **Try to get a seat at the sushi bar or at one of the three more private tables at the window.** ✉*Kantstr. 30, Western Downtown* ☎*030/3150–7815* ⚑*Reservations essential* ▤*AE, MC, V* Ⓜ*Zoologischer Garten (U-bahn and S-bahn).*

MITTE

$$$$ ✕**Ma Tim Raue.** The shooting star of the new Hotel Adlon luxury annex,
★ the Ma is run by one of Germany's top chefs, Tim Raue, who provides a modern and skilled interpretation of traditional Chinese cuisine. With its use of fresh produce, ingenious compositions, intricate presentation, service, and minimalist, Asian-infused interior design, the Ma easily takes on any other stylish gourmet restaurant in the world. An instant

hit, the Ma is yet another powerhouse for the rich and beautiful, where deals are cut over dinner. The Japanese uma restaurant, the shochu bar, and the Krug Room Berlin, all under the direction of Tim Raue, are inviting nearby alternatives in case the Ma is fully booked. ⊠*Behrenstr. 72, Mitte* ☎*030/3011–17333* ⚖*Reservations essential* ☰*AE, DC, MC, V* ⊘*Closed Sun. No lunch* Ⓜ*Unter den Linden (S-bahn).*

$$$$ ✕**VAU.** Trendsetter VAU defined hip in the Mitte district years ago and remains a favorite even as it ages. The excellent German fish and game dishes prepared by chef Kolja Kleeberg have earned him endless praise and awards. Daring combinations include *Ente mit gezupftem Rotkohl, Quitten, und Maronen* (duck with selected red cabbage, quinces, and sweet chestnuts) and *Steinbutt mit Kalbbries auf Rotweinschalotten* (turbot with veal sweetbread on shallots in red wine). A four-course menu costs €85; a six-course, €115. A lunch entrée is a bargain at €14. The cool interior was designed by one of Germany's leading industrial architects. ⊠*Jägerstr. 54/55, Mitte* ☎*030/202–9730* ⚖*Reservations essential* ☰*AE, DC, MC, V* ⊘*Closed Sun.* Ⓜ*Französische Strasse (U-bahn), Stadtmitte (U-bahn).*

$$$–$$$$ ✕**Borchardt.** The menu changes daily at this fashionable celebrity
   ★   meeting place. The high ceiling, plush maroon benches, art-nouveau mosaic (discovered during renovations), and marble columns create the impression of a 1920s café. The cuisine is high-quality French-German, including several dishes with fresh fish, veal, and some of Berlin's best (and most tender) beef classics. ⊠*Französische Str. 47, Mitte* ☎*030/8188–6262* ⚖*Reservations essential* ☰*AE, MC, V* Ⓜ*Französische Strasse (U-bahn).*

$$–$$$ ✕**Bocca di Bacco.** Hip Bocca di Bacco is the talk of the town, primar-
   ★   ily because of its blend of down-to-earth atmosphere and high-quality cuisine. Homemade pasta dishes, surprisingly hearty Tuscan classics (with an emphasis on wild game and fish), and an equally delectable assortment of desserts make for authentic Italian cooking—perhaps even Berlin's finest. The three-course prix-fixe lunch is €19.50. ⊠*Friedrichstr. 167–168, Mitte* ☎*030/2067–2828* ⚖*Reservations essential* ☰*AE, MC, V* ⊘*No lunch Sun.*

$$–$$$ ✕**Lutter & Wegner.** One of the city's oldest vintners (*Sekt,* German
   ★   champagne, was first conceived here in 1811 by actor Ludwig Devrient), Lutter & Wegner has returned to its historic location across from the Konzerthaus and Gendarmenmarkt. The dark wood-panel walls, parquet floor, and multitude of rooms take you back to 19th-century Vienna. The cuisine is mostly Austrian, with superb game dishes in winter and, of course, a Wiener schnitzel with lukewarm potato salad. The sauerbraten (marinated pot roast) with red cabbage has been a national prizewinner. ■TIP→ **In the Weinstube, meat and cheese plates are served until 3** AM. ⊠*Charlottenstr. 56, Mitte* ☎*030/2029–5417* ☰*AE, MC, V* Ⓜ*Französische Strasse and Stadtmitte (U-Bahn).*

$$–$$$ ✕**Shiro i Shiro.** This new spot with an Asian touch is as daring in its eclectic interior design as it is in the fusion creations on the menu. Living up to its name ("white palace"), the Shiro i Shiro has the city buzzing about its minimalist, dreamy, all-white ambience, accentuated with colorful furniture and art. The food is a wild mixture of European

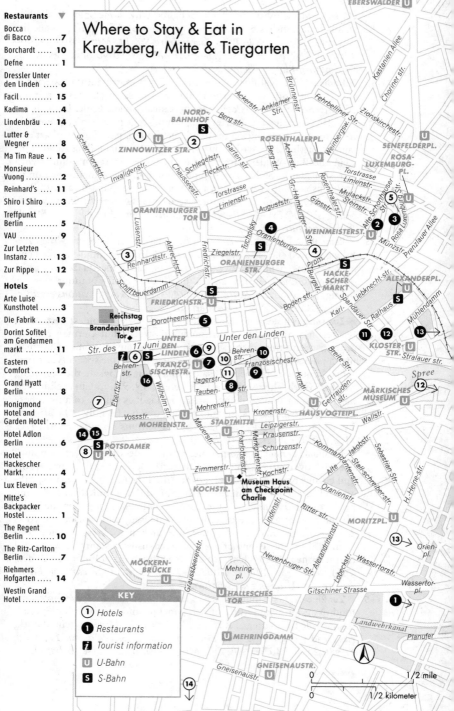

Where to Stay & Eat in Kreuzberg, Mitte & Tiergarten

KEY

① Hotels

● Restaurants

🛈 Tourist information

Ⓤ U-Bahn

Ⓢ S-Bahn

classics with a twist and Asian delights, with some spicy (grilled or steamed) fish dishes being the best creations of them all. The wine list is seemingly endless. ⊠ *Rosa-Luxemburg-Str. 11, Mitte* ☎*030/9700–4790* ⌕*Reservations essential* ⊟*AE, MC, V* ⊗*No lunch* Ⓜ *Rosa-Luxemburg-Platz (U-bahn).*

$-$$ ✕**Kadima.** The Kadima is the city's only top restaurant offering a superb, authentic combination of Jewish-Russian classics and modern interpretations of Israeli, Mediterranean-style cuisine. In the heart of Berlin's old Jewish quarter, it is reminiscent of urban coffeehouses from the 1920s. It showcases two huge modern paintings, and art collages depicting 22 Jewish figures from the '20s—including Albert Einstein and Billy Wilder—are inlaid in the tables. Start your dinner with a fresh Israeli sampler, the Kadima-Runde for two, then move on to grilled fish or one of the hearty meat dishes. Finish your meal with Russian Uswer fruit compote or poppyseed cake. ⊠ *Oranienburger Str. 28, Mitte* ☎*030/2759–4251* ⌕*Reservations essential* ⊟*AE, DC, MC, V* Ⓜ *Oranienburger Strasse (S-bahn).*

$-$$ ✕**Reinhard's.** Friends meet here in the Nikolaiviertel to enjoy the carefully prepared entrées and to sample spirits from the amply stocked bar, all served by friendly, tie-wearing waiters. The honey-glazed breast of duck, *Adlon,* is one of its specialties. There's a nice outdoor area for dining. ⊠ *Poststr. 28, Mitte* ☎*030/242–5295* ⌕*Reservations essential* ⊟*AE, DC, MC, V* Ⓜ *Alexanderplatz (U-Bahn).*

$ ✕**Zur Letzten Instanz.** Established in 1621, Berlin's oldest restaurant resides in a forgotten nest of medieval streets, but German tourists do find it and then disperse among the warren of rooms. The small menu points to Berlin's most traditional dish and the specialty: *Eisbein* (pork knuckle). Napoléon is said to have sat alongside the tile stove, Mikhail Gorbachev sipped a beer here in 1989, and Chancellor Gerhard Schröder treated French president Jacques Chirac to a meal here in 2003. Service can be erratic, though always friendly. ⊠ *Waisenstr. 14–16, Mitte* ☎*030/242–5528* ⌕*Reservations essential* ⊟*AE, DC, MC, V* Ⓜ *Klosterstrasse (U-bahn).*

¢–$ ✕**Treffpunkt Berlin.** This sometimes smoky, side-street "meeting point" is easily overlooked, but down-to-earth Berliners fill its bar stools and cluster of tables. The servers are gracious to non–German speakers and can coach you in eating the *Sol Ei* (hard-boiled egg), a dying breed of Berlin snack, in the correct manner: scoop out the yolk, fill the crevice with the condiments delivered, and replace the yolk. Aside from the Berlin specialties, the kitchen cooks up a spicy goulash. ■**TIP**➔ **This is one of the few inexpensive restaurants with local character near Friedrichstrasse and the attractions of Unter den Linden.** ⊠ *Mittelstr. 55, Mitte* ☎*030/204–1819* ⊟*No credit cards* Ⓜ *Friedrichstrasse (U-bahn and S-bahn).*

¢–$ ✕**Zur Rippe.** This popular place in the Nikolaiviertel serves wholesome food in an intimate setting of oak paneling and ceramic tiles. Specialties include the platter of *Kasseler, Ribbchen, und Eisbein* (cured pork, ribs, and pig knuckle) and a herring casserole. ⊠ *Poststr. 17, Mitte* ☎*030/2250–9302* ⊟*AE, DC, MC, V* Ⓜ *Klosterstrasse (U-bahn).*

¢ ✕**Monsieur Vuong.** Filling this hip eatery are people who share a love for Vietnamese cuisine from Saigon and the Mekong Delta. It's also a convenient place to meet before hitting Mitte's nightlife or for slipping in just a few calories before wiggling into the wares of neighboring boutiques. Inevitably, the same steamy dishes and soups, such as *goi bo* (spicy beef salad), land on each low table, as there are only five items and two specials on offer. The menu changes every two days, but you can always finish with an artichoke or jasmine tea. ⊠ *Alte Schönhauser Str. 46, Mitte* ☎ *030/3087–2643* ⌕ *Reservations not accepted* ⊟ *No credit cards* Ⓜ *Rosenthaler Strasse (U-bahn).*

> **TURKISH MARKET & CAFES**
>
> On Tuesday and Friday from noon to 6:30 you can find the country's best selection of Arab and Turkish foods on the Maybachufer lining the southern bank of the Landwehrkanal. The quirky student bar and café on the Kottbusser bridge, Ankerklause, or those on Paul-Lincke-Ufer, the opposite bank, are great places for a late breakfast, coffee break, and local color. The closest U-bahn stations are Kottbusser Tor and Schönlein Strasse. For Turkish fast food (a chicken or lamb kebab, or falafel), walk up Adalbertstrasse from Kottbusser Tor.

15

TIERGARTEN

$$$$ ✕**Facil.** One of Germany's top restaurants, Facil is also the most afford-
Fodor's Choice able and relaxed one of its class. The elegant, minimalist setting—com-
★ plete with green marble walls, exquisite wall panels, and a Giallo Reale patinato floor, all set under a glass roof (opened in summer, yet no view of the city)—and the impeccable, personal service make the six-course dinners a highlight in any gourmet's life. The food is a careful combination of French and regionally inspired first-class cuisine. Don't hesitate to ask sommelier Felix Voges for advice, as he certainly ranks among the most knowledgeable in his art. ⊠ *Potsdamer Str. 3, at the Mandala Hotel, Tiergarten* ☎ *030/5900–51234* ⊟ *AE, DC, MC, V* ⊙ *Closed weekends* Ⓜ *Potsdamer Platz (U-bahn and S-bahn).*

¢–$ ✕**Lindenbräu.** It's hardly a typical Bavarian brewhouse, but its rooftop and outdoor seating within the quasi-open-air Sony Center provides a place to gape at the glass-and-steel construction. This restaurant, mostly visited by tour groups and out-of-towners, is also the only spot in Berlin where you can get wheat beer brewed on the premises. The long tables with high stools are often occupied with businesspeople enjoying the social part of their Berlin trip. The Bavarian meals are really secondary to the setting and beer. ⊠ *Sony Center, Bellvuestr. 3–5, Tiergarten* ☎ *030/2575–1280* ⊟ *AE, MC, V* Ⓜ *Potsdamer Platz (U-bahn and S-bahn).*

KREUZBERG

$ ✕**Defne.** Among the myriad Turkish restaurants in the city, Defne stands out for its exquisitely prepared food, the friendly service, and the minimalist yet tasteful setting. Beyond simple kebabs, the fresh and healthy menu here includes a great selection of hard-to-find fish dishes from the Bosphorus, such as *acili ahtapot* (spicy octopus served with mushrooms, olives, onions, garlic, and bell pepper in a white wine and tomato sauce). The Defne is near the Maybachufer and its Turkish market in the heart of Kreuzberg 61, and is just a few minutes' walk from the nearest subway station. ⊠ *Planufer 92c, Kreuzberg* ☎ *030/8179–7111* 🍴 *No credit cards* ☯ *No lunch Mon.–Sat.* Ⓜ *Kottbusser Tor (U-bahn).*

WHERE TO STAY

Tourism is on the upswing in Berlin. Though prices in mid-range to luxury hotels have increased, Berlin's first-class hotels still tend to be cheaper than their counterparts in Paris, London, or Rome. And compared to other European cities, most hotel rooms in Berlin are large, though many are part of chains that allow for less individual character. Dorint and Mercure are reliable European chains with several central locations.

Internet services like Expedia can sometimes book a room at a five-star hotel in Berlin for half the normal price, even in summer. Hotels listed here as $$$$ often come down to a $$ level on weekends or when there is low demand. You often have the option to decline the inclusion of breakfast, which can save you anywhere from €8 to €30 per person per day.

■ TIP→ **The least expensive accommodations are in pensions, mostly in western districts such as Charlottenburg, Schöneberg, and Wilmersdorf; hostels with attractive double rooms, mostly in Mitte and Friedrichshain; or those available through private room agencies.** German and European travelers often use rooming agents, and Americans on a budget should consider this as well (apartments start at €300 per month). In Berlin, double rooms with shared bathrooms in private apartments begin around €33. **Wohn-Agentur Freiraum** (⊠ *Wiener Str., Kreuzberg* ☎ *030/618–2008* 🖷 *030/618–2006* ⊕ *www.freiraum-berlin.com*) is an English-speaking agency that has its own guesthouse with rooms and apartments. All of its private-room listings are in the Kreuzberg district.

WHAT IT COSTS IN EUROS					
	¢	$	$$	$$$	$$$$
FOR TWO PEOPLE	under €50	€50–€100	€101–€175	€176–€225	over €225

Hotel prices are for two people in a standard double room, including tax and service.

CHARLOTTENBURG

$$$$ 🏨 **Schlosshotel im Grunewald.** In the beautiful, verdant setting of residential Grunewald, the small but palatial hotel is full of classic style and lavish decor. You might be reminded of a late-19th-century chateau. The interior was designed by Chanel's Karl Lagerfeld, whose personal suite is available to guests if the master himself is not in town. The service is amazingly personal but never intrusive. Arrange for a car, as this location is not convenient for seeing the central sights. **Pros:** quiet and green setting with lovely garden, large rooms in classic style, impeccable service. **Cons:** far away from any sights, sometimes stiff atmosphere, not for families. ⊠ *Brahmsstr. 10, Zehlendorf* ☎ *030/895–840* ⊕ *www.schlosshotelberlin.com* 🛏 *54 rooms* ⌂ *In-room: Wi-Fi. In-hotel: restaurant, room service, bar, pool, gym, concierge, laundry service, parking (fee), no-smoking rooms* ▤ *AE, DC, MC, V* Ⓜ *Grunewald (S-bahn).*

$$ 🏨 **Art Nouveau Hotel.** The owners' discerning taste in antiques, color
★ combinations, and even televisions (designed by Philippe Starck) makes this B&B-like pension a pleasure to live in. Each room has a prize piece, such as a hand-carved 18th-century Chinese dresser or a chandelier from the Komische Oper's set of *Don Carlos*. Several rooms are hung with a large black-and-white photo by Sabine Kačunko. The apartment building shows its age only in the antique wood elevator, high stucco ceilings, and an occasionally creaky floor. You can serve yourself tea or coffee in the breakfast room throughout the day and mix your own drinks at the honor bar. Your English-speaking hosts are Mr. and Mrs. Schlenzka. **Pros:** stylish ambience, friendly and personal service, great B&B feeling, despite being a hotel. **Cons:** can be noisy due to heavy traffic on Leibnizstrasse, few amenties for a hotel of this price category, downtown location, yet longer walks to all major sights in the area. ⊠ *Leibnizstr. 59, Charlottenburg* ☎ *030/327–7440* ⊕ *www. hotelartnouveau.de* 🛏 *19 rooms, 3 suites* ⌂ *In-room: no a/c, Wi-Fi. In-hotel: bar, laundry service, no-smoking rooms* ▤ *AE, MC, V* ⊚ *CP* Ⓜ *Adenauerplatz (U-bahn).*

$–$$ 🏨 **Charlottenburger Hof.** No-fuss travelers will find great value in this low-key hotel. The variety of rooms, all brightened by sunlight and primary-color schemes with prints by Kandinsky, Miró, and Mondrian, can accommodate travelers whether they be friends, couples, or families. All rooms have computers with free Internet access, and amenities include hair dryers; try to avoid the three tiny "King Size" rooms, which are rented as doubles or singles. The 24-hour restaurant serves healthy dishes and draws locals, too. The Ku'damm is a 10-minute walk, and the bus to and from Tegel Airport stops on the next block. **Pros:** budget hotel in great location, solid restaurant, quiet setting. **Cons:** rooms in need of update, few amenities, direct neighborhood may be seedy for some travelers and not suited for children. ⊠ *Stuttgarter Pl. 14, Charlottenburg* ☎ *030/329–070* ⊕ *www. charlottenburger-hof.de* 🛏 *46 rooms* ⌂ *In-room: no a/c, safe, Ethernet. In-hotel: restaurant, bar, laundry facilities, laundry service, parking (fee), no-smoking rooms, some pets allowed, no elevator* ▤ *AE, MC, V* Ⓜ *Charlottenburg (S-bahn).*

15

$–$$ 🏨 **Econtel.** Within walking distance of the Spree River and Charlottenburg Palace, the hotel is also just two stops on Bus X9 from Zoo Station. Families fit in well, most imaginatively in the Hits for Kids rooms with bunk beds. A crib and children's toilet are available free of charge. Those in the business and comfort rooms have Wi-Fi. All rooms are spotless and have a homey feel. The 70-foot breakfast buffet spread (€13) could delay your sightseeing. ■**TIP**➔ **Keep an eye on the Web site for special two- and three-night rates. Pros:** very affordable and great value, familiy-oriented, very quiet setting. **Cons:** most attractions even in western downtown are far away, some rooms in need of update, no special flair or atmosphere. ⊠*Sömmeringstr. 24, Charlottenburg* 🕿*030/346–810* ⊕*www.econtel.de* 🛏*205 rooms* ♿*In-room: no a/c, safe, Wi-Fi (some). In-hotel: restaurant, bar, laundry service, parking (fee), no-smoking rooms, some pets allowed* ▭*AE, MC, V* Ⓜ*Mierendorffplatz (U-bahn).*

$–$$ 🏨 **Propeller Island City Lodge.** Make like Alice and fall down the rabbit hole, but in this wildly eccentric accommodation you can choose from 32 Wonderlands (read the Web site carefully before picking which pill to pop). Multitalented artist Lars Stroschen is responsible for each one-of-a-kind, handcrafted furnishing. Theatrical settings such as the Upside Down and Flying Bed rooms predominate, but there are tamer abodes, like the monastic Orange and Temple rooms. Only children get to inhabit the Gnome Room, which keeps out anyone over 4 feet, 8 inches. ■**TIP**➔ **This creative getaway serves breakfast (€7), but is not service oriented; reception is open 8 AM–noon only.** The location is near the far western end of Ku'damm, but the subway station is only a short walk away. **Pros:** individually designed rooms, personal and friendly atmosphere, quiet location on Ku'damm side street. **Cons:** designer art rooms can be overwhelming, few amenities, slow service. ⊠*Albrecht-Achilles-Str. 58, Charlottenburg* 🕿*030/891–9016 8 AM–noon, 0163/256–5909 noon–8 PM* ⊕*www.propeller-island.de* 🛏*30 rooms, 26 with bath, 1 suite* ♿*In-room: no a/c, no phone, kitchen (some), no TV (some), Wi-Fi. In-hotel: no-smoking rooms, some pets allowed* ▭*MC, V* Ⓜ*Adenauerplatz (U-bahn).*

WESTERN DOWNTOWN

$$$$ 🏨 **Hotel Brandenburger Hof.** The foyer of this turn-of-the-20th-century
★ mansion is breathtaking, with soaring white Doric columns, but once past these you'll find luxurious minimalism. You can breakfast and sip afternoon tea at the sun-soaked tables in the atrium courtyard or, in the evening, sit and listen to piano music. Between courses of French cuisine in the restaurant Quadriga, diners lean back in cherrywood chairs by Frank Lloyd Wright. Guest-room furnishings include pieces by Le Corbusier and Mies van der Rohe. Complementing the timeless Bauhaus style are ikebana floral arrangements. The spa features Asian silk cosmetic treatments. The location on a very residential street makes this a quiet hideaway, but the Tauentzien and KaDeWe are just a short walk away. **Pros:** great mansion, quiet location only steps away from the Ku'damm, large rooms. **Cons:** gourmet restaurant lacks edge.

⊠*Eislebener Str. 14, Western Downtown* ☎*030/214–050* ⊕*www. brandenburger-hof.com* ⬙*58 rooms, 14 suites* ⚿*In-room: no a/c (some), Ethernet, Wi-Fi. In-hotel: restaurant, bar, spa, public Internet, parking (fee), no-smoking rooms* ⊟*AE, DC, MC, V* Ⓜ*Augsburger Strasse (U-bahn).*

$$$$ 🏨**Hotel Palace.** This is the only privately owned first-class hotel in the heart of western downtown, and its First Floor restaurant with a view over the zoo's greenery has made the hotel a favorite of gourmands. Rooms are spacious, and junior suites have Bang & Olufsen TVs and stereos. The exercise room is one of the larger ones in Berlin, and swimmers can flip a switch in the pool to swim against a current. The extensive spa includes an ice grotto and Finnish sauna. **Pros:** large rooms, quiet, central location, impeccable service. **Cons:** interior design outdated in some areas, nearby area of Europe-Center and Breitscheidplatz may be uninviting for some travelers. ⊠*Europa-Center, Budapester Str. 45, Western Downtown* ☎*030/25020* ⊕*www.palace.de* ⬙*250 rooms, 32 suites* ⚿*In-room: safe, Wi-Fi. In-hotel: restaurant, room service, bars, pool, spa, concierge, laundry service, parking (fee), no-smoking rooms, some pets allowed* ⊟*AE, DC, MC, V* Ⓜ*Zoologsicher Garten (U-bahn and S-bahn).*

$$$–$$$$ 🏨**InterContinental Berlin.** From the heavily trafficked street, the huge "Inter-Conti," the epitome of old West Berlin, manages to recall the Louvre with its glass pyramid entranceway. More interesting than its conservative west wing are the east-wing rooms, where the sobriety of gray, black, and beige furnishings is offset by a rotating wall unit that allows you to watch TV while soaking in a tub. The walk-in closet is attached to the bathroom. The Club rooms on the seventh and eighth floors come with their own lounge, meeting rooms, and many extra amenities. The modern spa with several sauna facilities and the 13th-floor award-winning restaurant, Hugo's, are worth staying in for. **Pros:** large rooms with great views, friendly and impeccable service, one of Berlin's best spa areas. **Cons:** street is not very inviting, huge hotel lacks atmosphere and feels very businesslike, room design somewhat bland. ⊠*Budapester Str. 2, Western Downtown* ☎*030/26020* ⊕*www.berlin. interconti.com* ⬙*584 rooms, 50 suites* ⚿*In-room: Ethernet, Wi-Fi. In-hotel: 2 restaurants, room service, bar, pool, gym, spa, concierge, laundry service, parking (fee), no-smoking rooms, some pets allowed* ⊟*AE, DC, MC, V* Ⓜ*Zoologsicher Garten (U-bahn and S-bahn).*

$$–$$$ 🏨**Bleibtreu Berlin.** Opened in 1995, Berlin's first design hotel still feels
★   fresh and light. Rooms are simple and serene, with untreated oak, polished stone, and neutral shades. The eye candy lies in the terra-cotta-tile courtyard, which is secreted from the street but still in front of the hotel. You can sip drinks at its 23-foot-long table, which is covered in shiny blue ceramic shards and rests on a bed of glass pebbles. A tall chestnut tree lends shade. To reinvigorate after shopping at the nearby Ku'damm boutiques, help yourself to the free items in your mini-refrigerator or slip into the herbal steam bath. **Pros:** warm, welcoming service, top location on one of Ku'damm's most beautiful side streets, international clientele. **Cons:** design somewhat dated, rooms not overly comfortable for price, few amenities. ⊠*Bleibtreustr. 31, Western Downtown*

15

☎030/884–740 ⊕*www.bleibtreu.com* 📟*60 rooms* △*In-room: no a/ c, safe, Wi-Fi. In-hotel: room service, bar, laundry service, no-smoking rooms* ▤*AE, DC, MC, V* Ⓜ*Uhlandstrasse (U-bahn).*

$$–$$$ 🏨**Ellington Hotel Berlin.** This new designer hotel is tucked away behind
★ the beautiful, historic facade of a grand Bauhaus-style office building, just around the corner from KaDeWe and Kurfürstendamm. Rooms may be small, but all face the street and are smartly designed in a minimalist style, accentuated with modern art. The quiet courtyard and the restaurant and bar, complete with an open show kitchen, offer a welcome respite from sightseeing in the western downtown. **Pros:** stylish interior design with alluring 1930s touches, perfect location off Tauentzien and great for shopping sprees, nice bar and great, green courtyard. **Cons:** very small rooms, no facilities. ⊠*Nürnberger Str. 50–55, Western Downtown* ☎*030/683–150* ⊕*www.ellington-hotel. com* 📟*285 rooms* △*In-room: Ethernet. In-hotel: restaurant, bar, Wi-Fi, parking (fee), no-smoking rooms* ▤*AE, DC, MC, V* Ⓜ*Wittenberg-platz (U-bahn).*

$$–$$$ 🏨**Swissôtel Berlin.** At the bustling corner of Ku'damm and Joachim-sthaler Strasse, this hotel excels with its reputable Swiss hospitality— from accompanying guests to their floor after check-in to equipping each room with an iron, an umbrella, and a Lavazza espresso machine that preheats the cups. Beds are specially designed to avoid allergens and provide maximum comfort. After using the Wi-Fi, you can store and recharge your laptop in the room safe (the safe also charges cell phones). The unusual, rounded building has a sleek interior with original artwork by Marcus Lüpertz and a respected restaurant. Your room's soundproof windows give you a fantastic view of the area. **Pros:** large, quiet rooms, unobtrusive yet perfect service, great location on western Berlin's busiest street crossings. **Cons:** on top of shopping mall with lobby on higher floor, noisy when room windows are open, mostly for business travelers. ⊠*Augsburger Str. 44, Western Downtown* ☎*030/220–100* ⊕*www.swissotel.com* 📟*291 rooms, 25 suites* △*In-room: safe, dial-up, Wi-Fi. In-hotel: restaurant, room service, bar, gym, concierge, laundry service, public Internet, parking (fee), no-smoking rooms, some pets allowed* ▤*AE, DC, MC, V* Ⓜ*Kurfürstendamm (U-bahn).*

$$ 🏨**Hotel Astoria.** Each simple room in this small building dating to 1898 is different, and the family owners are diligent about making renovations every year. When making a reservation, state whether you'd like a bathtub or shower and ask about weekend specials or package deals for longer stays. The fifth- and sixth-floor rooms have air-conditioning for an extra charge. Two terraces allow you to sun yourself, and a stroll down the charming street leads to the shops along Ku'damm. Internet use at a PC station in the lobby is free; Wi-Fi services in the lobby and in your room are subject to a fee. **Pros:** some rooms are individually designed with old-world style, warm and very personal service, quiet location in central Ku'damm side street. **Cons:** furniture and rooms need update, many rooms on the smaller side, many rooms without a/c. ⊠*Fasanenstr. 2, Western Downtown* ☎*030/312–4067* ⊕*www. hotelastoria.de* 📟*31 rooms, 1 suite* △*In-room: no a/c (some), safe,*

Wi-Fi. In-hotel: room service, bar, laundry service, public Wi-Fi, public Internet, parking (fee), some pets allowed ⊟*AE, DC, MC, V* Ⓜ*Uhlandstrasse (U-bahn), Zoologsicher Garten (U-bahn and S-bahn).*

$–$$ 🏠**Hotel-Pension Dittberner.** For traditional Berlin accommodations, this
★   third-floor pension (with wooden elevator) run by Frau Lange since 1958 is the place to go. Close to Olivaer Platz and next to Ku'damm, the turn-of-the-20th-century house shows its age, but the huge rooms are wonderfully furnished with antiques, plush stuffed sofas, and artwork selected by Frau Lange's husband, a gallery owner. The high ceilings have stuccowork, and some rooms have balconies. Wi-Fi Internet access is available in the foyer. **Pros:** personal touch and feel of a B&B, unusally large rooms, good location on quiet Ku'damm side street. **Cons:** disappointing breakfast, some rooms and furniture in need of update, staff sometimes not up to task. ⊠ *Wielandstr. 26, Western Downtown* ☎*030/884–6950* ⊕*www.hotel-dittberner. de* ⊅*21 rooms, 1 suite* 🔑*In-room: no a/c. In-hotel: concierge, laundry service, some pets allowed, public Wi-Fi* ⊟*AE, MC, V* ⦿*CP* Ⓜ*Adenauerplatz (U-bahn).*

15

$ 🏠**Hotel Bogota.** Fashion photography and hall lamps remind guests of the artists and designers who lived in this apartment house on an elegant Ku'damm side street beginning in 1911. Each basic room is different, but they all share dated elements such as olive rotary phones or sherbet combinations of bright-red carpeting and mango-color walls. Triples and quads can be set up in these mostly high-ceiling rooms, children stay for free, and a warm breakfast is included. Doubles that have a shower but share a toilet with a second room range from €64 to €84. ▮**TIP**→ **Ask for a fourth-floor room.** Special offers may be available in winter and for stays beginning on a Sunday night. **Pros:** historic ambience; on one of Ku'damm's most beautiful side streets; large, comfortable rooms. **Cons:** thin walls; some rooms with 1950s feeling; breakfast is nothing special. ⊠*Schlüterstr. 45, Western Downtown* ☎*030/881– 5001* ⊕*www.bogota.de* ⊅*130 rooms, 60 with bath* 🔑*In-room: no a/c, no TV (some), Wi-Fi. In-hotel: bar, no-smoking rooms* ⊟*AE, DC, MC, V* ⦿*BP* Ⓜ*Uhlandstrasse (U-bahn).*

$ 🏠**Motel One.** The new Motel Ones opening throughout Germany are worlds apart from their North American counterparts. The Motel One at the Bahnhof Zoo is a stylish budget hotel in a prime location; breakfast is served in the loungelike lobby, where guests also enjoy free Wi-Fi. All rooms have comfortable beds, flat-screen TV sets, DVD player, air-conditioning, and a rainforest shower. **Pros:** stylish accommodation at budget prices; central location between Bahnhof Zoo and Theater des Westens; good for families. **Cons:** noise from nearby railway station can be felt and heard; immediate surroundings may appear seedy to some travelers; no real restaurant on-site. ⊠*Kantstr. 7–11a, Western Downtown* ☎*030/3151–7360* ⊕*www.motel-one.de* ⊅*250 rooms* 🔑 *In-hotel: Wi-Fi, parking (fee), no-smoking rooms* ⊟*AE, DC, MC, V* Ⓜ*Bahnhof Zoo (S- and U-bahn).*

MITTE

$$$$ ★ 🔲 **Dorint Sofitel am Gendarmenmarkt.** Built before the Wall came tumbling down, this luxurious lodging has maximized that era's minimalist look. In the formerly austere conference room the designers added an illuminated glass floor that made it a masterpiece. The spa tucked under the mansard roof is suffused with light, thanks to the new, angled windows. Request a room facing Gendarmenmarkt, one of the city's most impressive squares. Decorative motifs are inspired by plant photographer Karl Blossfeldt, whose models inspired wrought-iron craftsmen. Toylike bedside pull chains set off a short tinkling tune to send you off to sleep. **Pros:** great location off one of the city's most beautiful squares, sumptuous breakfast buffet, great Austrian restaurant, Aigner. **Cons:** only top floor has a good view, limited facilities for a luxury hotel, smallish rooms. ⊠ *Charlottenstr. 50–52, Mitte* ☎ *030/203–750* ⊕ *www.sofitel.com* 🖙 *70 rooms, 22 suites* ⚭ *In-room: safe, dial-up, Wi-Fi. In-hotel: restaurant, room service, gym, spa, laundry service, no-smoking rooms* ⊟ *AE, DC, MC, V* Ⓜ *Französische Strasse (U-bahn).*

$$$$ ★ 🔲 **Grand Hyatt Berlin.** Europe's first Grand Hyatt is *the* address for entourages attending the Berlinale Film Festival in February. Stylish guests feel at home with a minimalist, feng shui–approved design that combines Japanese and Bauhaus elements. The large rooms (they start at 406 square feet) have cherrywood furniture and bathrooms that include tubs from which water can safely overflow onto the marble floor. The Premiere channel on your TV allows you to pick free movies, and Wi-Fi is available in public areas. You'll get a wonderful view of Potsdamer Platz from the top-floor pool. The restaurant and bar, Vox, whets guests' appetites for its international and Asian cuisine with a "show kitchen"; there's live jazz Monday–Saturday. **Pros:** large and nicely appointed rooms, plus the city's best service, large, stylish spa and pool area. **Cons:** location can be very busy, architecture may be too minimalist for some travelers, not a hotel for families. ⊠ *Marlene-Dietrich-Pl. 2, Mitte* ☎ *030/2553–1234* ⊕ *www.berlin.grand.hyatt. com* 🖙 *326 rooms, 16 suites* ⚭ *In-room: safe, Ethernet. In-hotel: 2 restaurants, room service, bar, pool, gym, spa, concierge, public Wi-Fi, laundry service, parking (fee), no-smoking rooms* ⊟ *AE, DC, MC, V* Ⓜ *Potsdamer Platz (U-bahn and S-bahn).*

$$$$ ★ 🔲 **Hotel Adlon Berlin.** Aside from its prime setting on Pariser Platz, the allure of the government's unofficial guesthouse is its almost mythical predecessor. Until its destruction during the war, the Hotel Adlon was considered Europe's ultimate luxury resort. Rebuilt in 1997, the hotel's elegant rooms are furnished in 1920s style with cherrywood trim, myrtle-wood furnishings, and brocade silk bedspreads. The large bathrooms are done in black marble. Book a suite for a Brandenburger Tor view. Sipping coffee in the lobby of creamy marble and limestone makes for good people-watching. The new Adlon spa made a huge splash in the city, as did the annex of fine restaurants, under the supervision of Germany's top chef, Tim Rause. **Pros:** top-notch luxury hotel, surprisingly large rooms, excellent in-house restaurants. **Cons:** sometimes stiff service with an attitude, rooms off the Linden are noisy with the windows open, inviting lobby often crowded. ⊠ *Unter den*

Linden 77, Mitte ☎*030/22610* ⊕*www.hotel-adlon.de* ☎*304 rooms, 78 suites* ♻*In-room: safe, Wi-Fi. In-hotel: 3 restaurants, room service, bar, pool, gym, spa, concierge, laundry service, parking (fee), no-smoking rooms, some pets allowed* ▤*AE, DC, MC, V* Ⓜ*Unter den Linden (S-bahn).*

$$$$ 🏨**The Ritz-Carlton Berlin.** Soaring high above Potsdamer Platz in a gray, Rockefeller Center look-a-like high-rise, the hotel is a luxurious, flamboyant love affair with 19th century grandezza. The lobby, complete with gold leaf and heavy marble columns, is a glitzy riot, while the quaint "Curtain Club" bar is a subdued and stylish lounge. Rooms are nicely appointed with exquisite furniture, marble bathrooms, and great views of bustling Potsdamer Platz and the Tiergarten. The hotel's spa is exceptional, and there are two restaurants. The historic French brasserie Desbrosses (brought here from southern France lock, stock, and barrel) serves great steak frites and seafood. **Pros:** stylish and luxurious interior design, great views, elegant setting yet informal service. **Cons:** rooms surprisingly small for a newly-built hotel, not for families. ✉*Potsdamer Pl. 3, Mitte* ☎*030/337–777* ⊕*www.ritzcarlton.com* ☎*263 rooms, 39 suites* ♻*In-room: safe, Wi-Fi. In-hotel: 2 restaurants, room service, bar, pool, gym, spa, concierge, laundry service, parking (fee), no-smoking rooms* ▤*AE, DC, MC, V* Ⓜ*Potsdamer Platz (U-bahn and S-bahn).*

$$$–$$$$ 🏨**The Regent Berlin.** One of Germany's most esteemed hotels, the Regent pairs the opulence of gilt furniture, thick carpets, marble floors, tasseled settees, and crystal chandeliers with such modern conveniences as cell-phone rentals and flat-screen TVs. You'll be escorted to your large guest room, where you'll find first-class amenities, such as a DVD player. Twice-daily housekeeping, overnight dry cleaning, and valet parking are other services. The intimate feel of the property is a sign of its exclusiveness, and the privacy of the often famous Hollywood guests is well guarded. **Pros:** Berlin's most hushed 5-star hotel, unobtrusive service, very large rooms and top location off Gendarmenmarkt. **Cons:** some public areas in need of update, the only hotel restaurant specializes in fish only. ✉*Charlottenstr. 49, Mitte* ☎*030/20338* ⊕*www.theregentberlin.com* ☎*156 rooms, 39 suites* ♻*In-room: Ethernet, Wi-Fi. In-hotel: restaurant, room service, bar, gym, concierge, laundry service, parking (fee), no-smoking rooms, some pets allowed* ▤*AE, DC, MC, V.*

$$$–$$$$ 🏨**Westin Grand Hotel.** This large, recently renovated hotel has a great location at the corner of Friedrichstrasse and Unter den Linden. Rooms have mustard-color floral wallpaper, easy chairs, and the trademark Heavenly Bed found at all Westin hotels. The inner courtyard view is of an attractive garden area with an unusual Dragon House conference pagoda. Soundproof bay windows make for a good night's sleep in any room. The marble-and-brass lobby is light-filled and enlivened with a piano player and guests taking a coffee break at the sofas. **Pros:** impressive lobby, recently updated rooms, perfect location for historic sights and shopping. **Cons:** service often not on 5-star level, no great views, may feel street vibrations in lower rooms off Friedrichstrasse. ✉*Friedrichstr. 158–164, Mitte* ☎*030/20270* ⊕*www.westin-grand.*

15

com ⌐323 *rooms, 35 suites* ⌂*In-room: safe, Ethernet, Wi-Fi. In-hotel: 2 restaurants, room service, bar, pool, concierge, laundry service, parking (fee), no-smoking rooms, some pets allowed* ⊟*AE, DC, MC, V* Ⓜ*Friedrichstrasse (S-bahn and U-bahn).*

$$–$$$ 🏨 **Hotel Hackescher Markt.** Amid the nightlife around the Hackescher Markt, this hotel provides discreet and inexpensive top services. Unlike those of many older hotels in eastern Berlin, rooms here are spacious and light and furnished with wicker chairs and floral patterns in an English cottage style. In winter you'll appreciate the under-floor heating in your bathroom, and in summer you can enjoy a coffee in the small courtyard. The staff is friendly and attentive. Guests can use the gym of the Alexander Plaza hotel nearby. Wi-Fi is available in the bar area. **Pros:** great location for shops, restaurants, and nightlife, large rooms. **Cons:** some rooms may be noisy due to tram stop, no air-conditioning. ✉*Grosse Präsidentenstr. 8, Mitte* ☎*030/280–030* ⊕*www.look-hotels.com* ⌐*28 rooms, 3 suites* ⌂*In-room: no a/c, safe, Wi-Fi. In-hotel: room service, bar, laundry service, parking (fee), public Wi-Fi, no-smoking rooms, some pets allowed* ⊟*DC, MC, V* Ⓜ*Hackescher Markt (S-bahn).*

$$ 🏨 **Arte Luise Kunsthotel.** This hotel's name suggests a bohemian com-
★ mune, but all the residents are paying guests. The Luise is one of Berlin's most original boutique hotels, with each fantastically creative room in the 1825 house or new wing—facing the Reichstag—styled by a different artist. Memorable furnishings range from a suspended bed and airplane seats to a gigantic sleigh bed and a freestanding, podlike shower with multiple nozzles. A lavish breakfast buffet in the neighboring restaurant costs €9. The hotel is a stretch from the Friedrichstrasse train station, but a convenient bus line stops just outside. **Pros:** quiet location, historic flair, individually designed rooms. **Cons:** simple rooms with limited amenities and hotel facilities, some rooms with no noise reduction but still next to railways tracks, no elevator. ✉*Luisenstr. 19, Mitte* ☎*030/284–480* ⊕*www.luise-berlin.com* ⌐*50 rooms, 40 with bath; 3 apartments* ⌂*In-room: no a/c (some), no TV (some), Wi-Fi. In-hotel: restaurant, laundry service, no-smoking rooms, some pets allowed, no elevator in historic part* ⊟*MC, V* Ⓜ*Friedrichstrasse (U-bahn and S-bahn).*

$$ 🏨 **Lux Eleven.** This hidden gem of a designer apartment hotel is coveted
★ for its dicreet service and great minimalist design in white. Among the devoted fans of Lux Eleven are Hollywood celebrities wishing to remain anonymous and young, international, design-oriented travelers. All apartments come with a fully equipped kitchenette, satellite TV with DVD players, and even a washer and dryer in the bathroom. Rooms seem to be taken directly from a Miami Beach hotel and are decorated either in off-white or subdued browns. The "in" restaurant Shiro i Shiro, a stylish Ulf Haines designer fashion store, and a hair salon are also on the premises. **Pros:** great location in northern Mitte, extremely stylish yet comfortable rooms, friendly, knowledgeable service. **Cons:** immediate neighborhood may be noisy, not suitable for families. ✉*Rosa-Luxemburg-Str. 9–13, Mitte* ☎*030/936–2800* ⊕*www.lux-eleven.com* ⌐*72 apartments* ⌂*In-room: no a/c (some),*

Wi-Fi. *In-hotel: restaurant, laundry service, no-smoking rooms* ▤AE, *DC, MC, V* Ⓜ*Rosa-Luxemburg-Pl. (U-bahn.*

$–$$★ 🏨**Honigmond Hotel and Garden Hotel.** These two hotels are charming, quaint oases only a few steps away from the buzzing neighborhoods in Mitte. The former tenement houses, typical of late 19th century Berlin, have been meticulously restored, with wooden floor planks and selected, historic furniture. A small restaurant in the main hotel, looking back on a proud history as a meeting point for political opponents of the East German regime, serves a variety of German standards to a younger, international clientele. The Garden Hotel (set in an older house dating back to 1845) is grouped around a surprisingly green courtyard, and it offers cheaper rooms with or without private baths. **Pros:** individually designed rooms, warm, welcoming service, quiet courtyard rooms. **Cons:** front rooms can be noisy due to busy street, immediate neighborhood not very appealing, restaurant is expensive relative to the area's budget choices. ✉*Tieckstr. 12 and Invalidenstr. 122, Mitte* ☎*030/284–4550* ⊕*www.honigmond-berlin.de* 🛏*30 rooms* ♿*In-room: Wi-Fi. In-hotel: restaurant, parking (fee), no-smoking rooms* ▤*MC, V* Ⓜ*Hauptbahnhof (S-bahn).*

$ 🏨**Mitte's Backpacker Hostel.** Accommodations are simple but creative in this orange-painted hostel, and service goes the extra mile, with cheap bike rentals, free city maps, ticket services, and ride-sharing arrangements. Rooms—from doubles to girls-only sleepaways—are individually decorated. The location is convenient for both sightseeing and nightlife—in the evening you can stay in for happy hour or a film. **Pros:** great, friendly staff, rooms painted in different colors, giving them a happy flair, clientele is mostly young, international and easy to connect with. **Cons:** showers in need of update, very basic rooms and beds, location can be noisy. ✉*Chausseestr. 102, Mitte* ☎*030/2839–0965* ⊕*www.baxpax.de* 🛏*4 double rooms, 2 with bath; 2 singles, 4 quads, 1 triple, 9 dorm rooms* ♿*In-room: no a/c, no phone, kitchen, no TV. In-hotel: bar, bicycles, laundry facilities, public Internet, no elevator* ▤*AE, MC, V.*

KREUZBERG

$$ 🏨**Riehmers Hofgarten.** The appeal of this late-19th-century apartment house with a leafy courtyard is its location in a lively neighborhood marked by the streets Mehringdamm and Bergmannstrasse. The richly decorated facade hints that 100 years ago the aristocratic officers of Germany's imperial army lived here. Rooms with low-lying beds are spartanly modern, quiet, and functional. Downstairs is a light-filled lounge and restaurant. In less than five minutes you can reach the subway that speeds you to Mitte and the Friedrichstrasse train station. **Pros:** good location for exploring Kreuzberg, typical Berlin, high-ceiling, historic rooms, great on-site restaurant, E.T.A. Hoffmann. **Cons:** street-side rooms very noisy, no air-conditioning even in rooms exposed to direct, strong sunlight in summer, breakfast not very special. ✉*Yorckstr. 83, Kreuzberg* ☎*030/7809–8800* ⊕*www.hotel-riehmers-hofgarten.de* 🛏*21 rooms, 1 suite* ♿*In-room: no a/c, Eth-*

15

ernet, Wi-Fi. In-hotel: restaurant, room service, bar, laundry service, parking (fee), no-smoking rooms, some pets allowed, no elevator ⊟*AE, MC, V* ⏻⏐*CP* Ⓜ*Mehringdamm (U-bahn).*

$ 🏨 **Die Fabrik.** Near Kreuzberg's and Friedrichshain's alternative nightlife scene and a five-minute walk from the subway, this former factory building—solar powered—is perfect for those who place a priority on mixing with the local scene. Though this is a backpacker stop, basic double rooms and suites with carpeting and metal lockers are also available. To connect to the Internet, insert a euro into the computer at reception. There are no private bathrooms; seven doubles have a sink, and prices for double rooms drop between November and February. **Pros:** more expensive rooms are very good budget accommodation, small courtyard with plants, decent café. **Cons:** sometimes rude and not very forthcoming staff, hostel can be noisy due to partying guests, beds very simple. ✉*Schlesische Str. 18, Kreuzberg* ☎*030/611–7116* ⊕*www.diefabrik.com* ⛵*50 rooms without bath* 🛏*In-room: no a/c, no phone, no TV. In-hotel: restaurant, public Internet, no elevator* ⊟*No credit cards* Ⓜ*Schlesisches Tor (U-bahn).*

$ 🏨 **Eastern Comfort.** The Spree River is one of Berlin's best assets, and you'll wake up on it in this moored, three-level ship with simple cabins. First-class cabins for one or two people are on the middle deck, and the lower-deck rooms can accommodate one to four guests; some cabins have a private bath. Your view is of either the river or the stretch of the Berlin Wall called the East Side Gallery. Within sight of the wraparound deck is the turreted Oberbaum bridge. The setting is great for watching the sunset and is close to plenty of nightlife. The crew minds the reception desk 24 hours. **Pros:** unique accommodation on boat, friendly staff, perfect location for nightclubbing in Kreuzberg and Friedrichshain. **Cons:** mosquitos, moths, and spiders may be bothersome in summer, smallish rooms not pleasant in rainy or stormy weather, lack of privacy. ✉*Mühlenstr. 73–77, Kreuzberg* ☎*030/6676–3806* ⊕*www.eastern-comfort.com* ⛵*24 cabins* 🛏*In-room: no a/c, no phone, no TV (some). In-hotel: restaurant, bar, bicycles, laundry service, public Internet, no-smoking rooms, no elevator* ⊟*MC, V* Ⓜ*Warschauer Strasse (U-bahn and S-bahn).*

> ### BEATING THE EURO
>
> When staying in or near Kreuzberg, take advantage of the many cheap *Doener imbisse* (*kebab*) stores around Hallesches Tor and Kottbusser Tor. These dingy Turkish outlets often also sell food you would find in any grocery store—only they are less expensive here.

NIGHTLIFE & THE ARTS

THE ARTS

Today's Berlin has a tough time living up to the reputation it gained from the film *Cabaret*. In the 1920s it was said that in Berlin, if you wanted to make a scandal in the theater, you had to have a mother committing incest with *two* sons; one wasn't enough. Political gaffes are now the prime comic material for Berlin's cabarets. Even if nightlife has toned down since the 1920s and '30s, the arts and the avant-garde still flourish. Detailed information about events is covered in the *Berlin Programm,* a monthly tourist guide to Berlin arts, museums, and theaters. The magazines *Tip* and *Zitty,* which appear every two weeks, provide full arts listings (in German), while the free *(030)* is the best source for club and music events. For listings in English, consult the monthly *Ex-Berliner.*

If your hotel can't book a seat for you or you can't make it to a box office directly, go to a ticket agency. Surcharges are 18%–23% of the ticket price. **Showtime Konzert- und Theaterkassen** (⊠ *KaDeWe, Tauentzienstr. 21, Western Downtown* ☎ *030/217–7754* ⊠ *Wertheim, Kurfürstendamm 231, Western Downtown* ☎ *030/882–2500*) has offices within the major department stores. The **Theaterkasse Centrum** (⊠ *Meinekestr. 25, Western Downtown* ☎ *030/882–7611*) is a small agency but employs a very informed and helpful staff. The **Hekticket offices** (⊠ *Karl-Liebknecht-Str. 12, off Alexanderpl., Mitte* ☎ *030/2431–2431* ⊠ *Next to Zoo-Palast, Hardenbergstr. 29d, Western Downtown* ☎ *030/230–9930*) offers discounted and last-minute tickets.

BERLIN FESTIVAL WEEKS

The **Berlin Festival Weeks** (*Kartenbüro* ⊠ *Schaperstr. 24 Berlin* ☎ *030/254–890* ⊕ *www.berlinerfestspiele.de*), held annually from late August through September or early October, include concerts, operas, ballet, theater, and art exhibitions. For information and reservations, write **Berliner Festspiele.**

CONCERTS

Among the major symphony orchestras and orchestral ensembles in Berlin is one of the world's best, the Berlin Philharmonic Orchestra, which resides at the **Philharmonie mit Kammermusiksaal** (⊠ *Herbert-von-Karajan-Str. 1, Tiergarten* ☎ *030/2548–8132* ⊕ *www.berliner-philharmoniker.de*). The Kammermusiksaal is dedicated to chamber music. Tickets sell out in advance for the nights when Sir Simon Rattle or other star maestros conduct the Berlin Philharmonic, but other orchestras and artists appear here as well. Free guided tours take place daily at 1 PM.

The beautifully restored hall at **Konzerthaus Berlin** (⊠ *Gendarmenmarkt, Mitte* ☎ *030/2030–92101 or 030/2030–92102*) is a prime venue for classical music concerts. Its box office is open from noon to curtain time.

DANCE, MUSICALS & OPERA

Berlin's three opera houses also host guest productions and companies from around the world. Vladimir Malakhov, a principal guest dancer with New York's American Ballet Theatre, is a principal in the Staatsballett Berlin as well as its director. The company jetés its classic and modern productions between the Deutsche Oper in the west and the Staatsoper in the east. Of the 17 composers represented in the repertoire of **Deutsche Oper Berlin** (⊠ *Bismarckstr. 35, Charlottenburg*

☎*030/343–8401* ⊕*www.deutscheoperberlin.de*), Verdi and Wagner are the most frequently presented. Most of the operas are sung in German at the **Komische Oper** (✉*Behrenstr. 55–57, Mitte* ☎*030/4799–7400 or 01805/304–168* ⊕*www.komische-oper-berlin.de*). On the day of the performance, discount tickets are sold at the box office on Unter den Linden 41.

Though renovated twice after bombings, the **Staatsoper Unter den Linden** (✉*Unter den Linden 7, Mitte* ☎*030/2035–4555* ⊕*www.staatsoper-berlin.de*) dates to 1743, when Frederick the Great oversaw productions. Maestro Daniel Barenboim oversees a diverse repertoire. Tickets can be as inexpensive as €7.

Sasha Waltz (born 1963) is the heir apparent to the still cutting-edge dance-theater choreographer Pina Bausch. Waltz's modern-dance troupe performs on the enormous stage of the **Schaubühne am Lehniner Platz** (✉*Kurfürstendamm 153, Western Downtown* ☎*030/890–023* ⊕*www.schaubuehne.de*).

Musicals and dance extravaganzas are occasionally staged at the **Schiller-Theater** (✉*Bismarckstr. 110, Charlottenburg* ☎*0800/3111–3000–9842*). The late-19th-century **Theater des Westens** (✉*Kantstr. 12, Western Downtown* ☎*01805–4444* ⊕*www.stage-entertainment.de*), one of Germany's oldest musical theaters, features musicals such as *Dance of the Vampires*.

The white, tentlike **Tempodrom** (✉*Askanischer Pl. 4, Kreuzberg* ☎*030/6953–3885* ⊕*www.tempodrom.de*), beyond the ruined facade of Anhalter Bahnhof, features international music, pop, and rock stars.

The **Tanzfabrik** (✉*Möckernstr. 68, Kreuzberg* ☎*030/786–5861*) is still Berlin's best venue for young dance talents and the latest from Europe's avant-garde. **Hebbeltheater am Ufer** (✉*Stresemann Str. 29, Kreuzberg* ☎*030/2590–0427* ⊕*www.hebbel-am-ufer.de*) consists of three houses (Haus 1, 2, 3) within a five-minute walk of one another. Fringe theater, international modern dance, and solo performers share its stages.

FILM

International and German movies are shown in the big theaters on Potsdamer Platz and around the Ku'damm. If a film isn't marked "OF" or "OV" (*Originalfassung,* or original version) or "OmU" (original with subtitles), it's dubbed. ■TIP→ Previews and commercials often run for 25 minutes, so don't worry if you're late. In February, numerous cinemas host the prestigious **Internationale Filmfestspiele** (⊕*www.berlinale.de*), or Berlinale, a 10-day international festival at which the Golden Bear award is bestowed on the best films, directors, and actors. Individual tickets are first sold three days prior to a film's screening. ■TIP→ Film buffs should purchase the season pass, act quickly when ticket contigents are sold online, or accept shut-outs and third-choice films after hour-long waits at ticket outlets.

On a hard-to-find, dead-end street, **Babylon** (✉*Dresdnerstr. 126, Kreuzberg* ☎*030/6160–9693*) shows English-language films with

German subtitles. You can reach Babylon by cutting through a building overpass off Adalbertstrasse, near the Kottbusser Tor U-bahn station. Mainstream U.S. and British productions are screened in their original versions at the sleek **CineStar im Sony Center** (⊠ *Potsdamer Str. 4, Tiergarten* ☎ *030/2606–6400*). Tuesday and Thursday are discount evenings.

Documentary films, international films in their original language, and German art-house films are shown at **Hackesche Höfe** (⊠ *Rosenthaler Str. 40–41, Mitte* ☎ *030/283–4603*). There's no elevator to this top-floor movie house, but you can recover on the wide banquettes in the lounge.

THEATER

Theater in Berlin is outstanding, but performances are usually in German. The exceptions are operettas and the (nonliterary) cabarets. The theater most renowned for both its modern and classical productions is the **Deutsches Theater** (⊠ *Schumannstr. 13a, Mitte* ☎ *030/2844–1225* ⊕ *www.deutschestheater.de*).

The rebellious actors at the **Schaubühne am Lehniner Platz** (⊠ *Kurfürstendamm 153, Western Downtown* ☎ *030/890–023* ⊕ *www.schaubuehne.de*), once the city's most experimental stage, have somewhat mellowed but are still up to great performances.

The excellent **Berliner Ensemble** (⊠ *Bertolt Brecht-Pl. 1, off Friedrichstr., just north of train station, Mitte* ☎ *030/2840–8155* ⊕ *www.berliner-ensemble.de*) is dedicated to Brecht and works of other international playwrights. The **Hebbel Theater** (⊠ *Stresemannstr. 29, Kreuzberg* ☎ *030/2590–0427* ⊕ *www.hebbel-am-ufer.de*) showcases international theater and modern-dance troupes in three venues (HAU 1, 2, and 3).

The **Volksbühne am Rosa-Luxemburg-Platz** (⊠ *Rosa-Luxemburg-Pl., Mitte* ☎ *030/247–6772 or 030/2476–5777* ⊕ *www.volksbuehne-berlin.de*) is unsurpassed for its aggressively experimental style, and Berliners often fill its 750 seats. The unusual building was reconstructed in the 1950s using the original 1914 plans.

For children's theater, head for the world-famous **Grips Theater** (⊠ *Altonaer Str. 22, Tiergarten* ☎ *030/3974–7477*), whose musical hit *Linie 1,* about life in Berlin viewed through the subway, is just as appealing for adults.

In a black-box theater, the **English Theatre Berlin** (⊠ *Fidicinstr. 40, Kreuzberg* ☎ *030/691–1211* ⊕ *www.etberlin.de*) presents dramas and comedies in English. Three Tall Women by Edward Albee is on the program for March 2009.

VARIETY SHOWS, COMEDY & CABARET

Berlin's variety shows can include magicians, circus performers, musicians, and classic cabaret stand-ups. A popular Berlin comedian and singer is American Gayle Tufts, famous for mixing English and German. Be aware that in order to understand and enjoy traditional cabaret, which involves a lot of political humor, your German has to be up

15

to snuff. The intimate **Bar Jeder Vernunft** (✉*Schaperstr. 24, Wilmers-dorf* ☎*030/883–1582* ⊕*www.bar-jeder-vernunft.de*) is housed within a glamorous tent and features solo entertainers. Within the Hacke-sche Höfe, the **Chamäleon Varieté** (✉*Rosenthaler Str. 40–41, Mitte* ☎*030/400–5930* ⊕*www.chamaeleonberlin.com*) is the most afford-able and offbeat variety venue in town. German isn't required to enjoy most of the productions. Europe's largest variety show takes place at the **Friedrichstadtpalast** (✉*Friedrichstr. 107, Mitte* ☎*030/2326–2326* ⊕*www.friedrichstadtpalast.de*), a glossy showcase for revues, famous for its leggy female dancers. Most of the guests seem to arrive via bus tours and package hotel deals. The completely restored 1920s entertainment emporium **Admiralspalast** (✉*Friedrichstr. 101, Mitte* ☎*030/4799–7499* ⊕*www.admiralspalast.de*) draws on its glitzy Jazz Age glamour, and houses several stages, a restaurant, and a club. The main theater features everything from large-scale shows to theater, comedy, and concerts. **Tipi das Zelt** (✉*Grosse Querallee, Tiergarten* ☎*0180/327–9358* ⊕*www.tipi-das-zelt.de*) is a tent venue between the Kanzleramt (Chancellor's Office) and Haus der Kulturen der Welt. Art-ists featured (such as American Gayle Tufts) are well suited for an inter-national audience, and you can opt to dine here before the show. Even the back-row seats are good. The **Wintergarten Varieté** (✉*Potsdamer Str. 96, Tiergarten* ☎*030/2500–8888* ⊕*www.wintergarten-variete. de*) pays romantic homage to the old days of Berlin's original variety theater in the 1920s.

Social and political satire has a long tradition in cabaret theaters. The **BKA–Berliner Kabarett Anstalt** (✉*Mehringdamm 34, Kreuzberg* ☎*030/202–2007* ⊕*www.bka-luftschloss.de*) features not only guest performances by Germany's leading young comedy talents but also chanson vocalists.

NIGHTLIFE

Berlin's nightspots are open to the wee hours of the morning, but if you stay out after 12:45 Monday–Thursday or Sunday, you'll have to find a night bus line or the last S-bahn to get you home. On Friday and Saturday nights all subway lines (except U4) run every 15 to 20 minutes throughout the night. Clubs often switch the music they play nightly, so their crowds and popularity can vary widely. Though club nights are driven by the DJ name, the music genres are written in English in listing magazines.

Clubs and bars in downtown western Berlin as well as in Mitte tend to be dressier and more conservative; the scene in Kreuzberg, Prenzlauer Berg, the Scheunenviertel, and Friedrichshain is laid-back, alternative, and grungy. For the latest information on Berlin's house, electro, and hip-hop club scene, pick up *(030)*, a free weekly. Dance clubs don't get going until about 12:30 AM, but parties labeled "after-work" start as early as 8 PM for professionals looking to socialize during the week.

BARS & LOUNGES

In Germany the term *Kneipen* is used for down-to-earth bars that are comparable to English pubs. These places are pretty simple and laid-back; you probably shouldn't try to order a three-ingredient cocktail at one unless you spot a lengthy drink menu.

The most elegant bars and lounges are in western downtown Berlin, and though not frequented by Berliners, Berlin's five-star hotels provide stylish, seductive settings. The cocktail menu is the size of a small guidebook at **Bar am Lützowplatz** (⊠*Am Lützowpl. 7, Tiergarten* ☏*030/262—6807*), where an attractive, professional crowd lines the long blond-wood bar. The subdued and elegant **Victoria Bar** (⊠*Potsdamer Str. 102, Tiergarten* ☏*030/2575—9977*) is an ironic homage to the '60s and '70s jet-set age, and ultimately stylish. It usually attracts a middle-age, affluent, and artsy crowd. Old-world **E. & M. Leydicke** (⊠*Mansteinstr. 4, Schöneberg* ☏*030/216–2973*) is a must for out-of-towners. The proprietors operate their own distillery and have a superb selection of sweet wines and liqueurs. Shabby **Kumpelnest 3000** (⊠*Lützowstr. 23, Tiergarten* ☏*030/261–6918*) has a reputation as wild as its carpeted walls. It's the traditional last stop of the evening.

A mature crowd that wants to concentrate on conversing and appreciating outstanding cocktails heads to **Green Door** (⊠*Winterfeldstr. 50, Schöneberg* ☏*030/215–2515*), a Schöneberg classic with touches of 1960s retro style that lighten the mood. Now the oldest posh bar in Mitte, marble-lined **Newton** (⊠*Charlottenstr. 57, Mitte* ☏*030/2029–5421*) flaunts Helmut Newton's larger-than-life photos of nude women across its walls. The laid-back, loungelike **Solar** (⊠*Stresemannstr. 76, Kreuzberg*) is the playground for the city's younger party crowd.

The "see and be seen" set of successful thirty- and fortysomethings has created a whole new genre of lounge, often an odd mix of club, bar, restaurant, and event location. The uncrowned king among these is the **Bangaluu** (⊠*Invalidenstr. 30, Mitte* ☏*030/8096–93077*), a stylish dinner and dance club notorious for its strict door policy. The equally chic but more relaxed **40 seconds** (⊠*Potsdamer Str. 58, Schöneberg* ☏*030/8906–4241*) offers a fantastic panorama view of the night-lit skyline as well as the sight of the city's jet set dancing the night away.

Groups of friends fill the tables, battle at foosball tables, and dance in the small back room at **August Fengler** (⊠*Lychner Str. 11, Prenzlauer*

WHERE TO GO

The happening streets and squares are:

- Savignyplatz in Charlottenburg
- Ludwigkirchplatz in Wilmersdorf
- Nollendorfplatz and Winterfeldplatz in Schöneberg
- Oranienstrasse and Wiener Strasse in Kreuzberg
- Hackescher Markt and Oranienburgerstrasse in Mitte-Scheunenviertel
- Kastanienalle, Kollwitzplatz, and Helmholzplatz in Prenzlauer Berg
- Boxhagenerplatz in Friedrichshain

15

For a Gay Time in Berlin

The area around Nollendorfplatz is the heart and soul of gay Berlin, even though areas like Schönhauser Alle in Prenzlauer Berg, Schlesische Straße in Kreuzberg, and various clubs in the Mitte-Scheunenviertel area are more popular with the younger crowd. However, in a city that historically has been a center of gay culture and one that has an openly gay mayor, Klaus Wowereit, the gay scene is not limited to these areas. Typical for Berlin is the integration of homosexuals of all walks of life throughout the city—from the politician and manager to the bus driver and waiter. The general attitude of most Berliners towards gays is very tolerant and open-minded; however, openly gay couples should avoid areas such as Lichtenberg or the state of Brandenburg. These areas are exceptions in a city that has an estimated 300,000 gays and lesbians in residence.

Large festivals such as the annual Christopher Street Day bring together hundreds of thousands of gays and lesbians each summer. Gay travelers are embraced by the city's tourist office: up-to-date information is provided in special brochures, such as "Out in Berlin" at the tourist infostores. Detailed information on gay-friendly hotels and the clubbing and bar scene are provided by the city's largest gay community center, the Mann-o-Meter e.V. (⊠ *Bülowstr. 106, Schöneberg* ☎ *030/216–8008* ⊕ *www.mann-o-meter.de*). Talks are held in the café, which has a variety of books and magazines. It's open weekdays 3–11, Saturday 3–10.

Berg ☎*030/4435–6640*). On weekends the place is packed. ■TIP➔ **If there's no room, head farther up the street to the bars around Helmholtzplatz.** Sitting canal-side on a deck chair at **Freischwimmer** (⊠ *Vor dem Schlesischen Tor 2a, Kreuzberg* ☎*030/6107–4309*) is perfect for warm nights, but heat lamps and an enclosed section make a cozy setting on cool ones, too. To get here, walk five minutes south of the Schlesisches Tor subway station and turn left down a path after the 1920s gas station.

CLUBS

More like a lounge and party venue than a club, **Week12end** (⊠ *Alexanderpl. 5, Mitte* ☎*030/2363–1676*) not only offers great views of East Berlin's skyline, but some of the most stylish dance floors, welcoming a young, hip crowd. Berlin's mixed, multiculti crowd frequents the **Havanna Club** (⊠ *Hauptstr. 30, Schöneberg* ☎*030/784–8565*), where you can dance to soul, R&B, or hip-hop on four different dance floors. The week's highlights are the wild salsa and merengue nights (Wednesday, Friday, and Saturday, starting at 9 PM). If your Latin steps are weak, come an hour early for a lesson.

Thursday through Saturday, the docked boat **Hoppetosse** (⊠ *Eichenstr. 4, Treptow* ☎*030/5332–0340*) rocks steady to reggae and dancehall, house, techno, or hip-hop. Just south of Kreuzberg, it's a bit out of the way, but you get a fantastic Spree Canal view from either the lower-level dance floor or the top deck.

The ultrahip and leading club in town is the over-the-top **Felix** (✉*Behrenstr. 72 [behind Hotel Adlon], Mitte*). Hollywood stars drop by when shooting in town, and you have to be good-looking, rich, or—even better—both to get in. **Sage-Club** (✉*Köpenicker Str. 78, Mitte* ☎*030/278–9830*) is the most popular of Berlin's venues for young professionals who dance to house and some techno music. On some nights it can be tough getting past the man with the "by invitation only" list.

GAY & LESBIAN BARS

Berlin is unmistakably Germany's gay capital, and many Europeans come to partake in the diverse scene, which is concentrated in Schöneberg (around Nollendorfplatz) and Kreuzberg. Check out the magazines *Siegessäule, (030),* and *blu.*

Close to Wittenbergplatz, the dance club **Connection** (✉*Fuggerstr. 33, Schöneberg* ☎*030/218–1432*) provides heavy house music and lots of dark corners. The decor and the energetic crowd at **Hafen** (✉*Motzstr. 19, Schöneberg* ☎*030/211–4118*) makes it ceaselessly popular and a favorite singles mixer. At 4 AM people move next door to Tom's Bar, open until 6 AM. If you don't bump up against any eye candy at tiny **Roses** (✉*Oranienstr. 187, Kreuzberg* ☎*030/615–6570*) there are always the furry red walls and kitschy paraphernalia to admire. It opens at 10 PM. **Schwuz** (✉*Mehringdamm 61, Kreuzberg* ☎*030/629–0880*) consists of two dance floors underneath the laid-back café Melitta Sundström. Eighties music and house are the normal fare.

JAZZ CLUBS

A-Trane Jazzclub (✉*Bleibtreustr. 1, Charlottenburg* ☎*030/313–2550* ⊕*www.a-trane.de*), on the corner of Pestalozzistrasse, also has nights for electronic jazz, Afro-Cuban music, and "the art of duo." With no columns to obstruct your view, you can see young German artists almost every night at **B-Flat** (✉*Rosenthaler Str. 13, Mitte* ☎*030/283–3123*). The Wednesday jam sessions focus on free and experimental jazz. On Sunday, dancers come for tango night. Snacks are available. **Quasimodo** (✉*Kantstr. 12a, Charlottenburg* ☎*030/312–8086* ⊕*www.quasimodo.de*), the most established and popular jazz venue in the city, has a college-town pub feel in its basement. Seats are few.

SPORTS & THE OUTDOORS

Berlin's famous sports attraction is the 1936 **Olympic Stadium,** which received a thorough modernization in 2004. American sprinter Jesse Owens won his stunning four gold medals in 1936; these days, the Berlin Thunder, a mixed nationality team playing American football in the European league, and the local soccer team Hertha BSC are the stars in the arena. In July 2006 the stadium hosted the World Cup soccer final match and will serve as a spectacular backdrop to the Athletics World Championship in 2009. Different theme tours are offered throughout the year; one option is touring on your own with an audio guide (€6), but only a guided tour will show you the nonpublic areas. ✉*Olympischer Pl. 3, Charlottenburg* ☎*030/2500–2322* 🎟*€4, tours*

€6–€10 ⊗ *Daily general tour at 11, 1, 3, and 5, but open times vary on days before and after major sports events, so call ahead* ⊕*www. olympiastadion-berlin.de* Ⓜ*Olympiastadion (U-bahn).*

BIKING

Bike paths are generally marked by red pavement or white markings on the sidewalks. Be careful when walking on bike paths or crossing them. Many stores that rent or sell bikes carry the Berlin biker's atlas. **Fahrradstation** (⊠*Dorotheenstr. 30, Mitte* ☎*030/2045–4500* ⊕*www. fahrradstation.de*) rents bikes for €15 per day (12 hours) or €35 for three days. Bring ID and call for its other locations. **Fahrrad Vermietung Berlin** (⊠*Kurfürstendamm 236, Western Downtown* ☎*030/261–2094*) rents black bikes with baskets that it keeps in front of the Marmorhaus movie theater, opposite the Gedächtniskirche. Rates are €10 a day, and you must leave either a €50 deposit or ID as security.

JOGGING

The Tiergarten is the best place for jogging in the downtown area. Run down the paths parallel to Strasse des 17. Juni and back, and you'll have covered 8 km (5 mi). Joggers can also take advantage of the grounds of Charlottenburg Palace, 3 km (2 mi) around. For longer runs, make for the Grunewald.

SOCCER

Tickets for the home games of Berlin's premier soccer team, **Hertha BSC** (⊠*Olympic Stadium, Olympischer Pl. 3, Charlottenburg* ☎*01805/189–200* ⊕*www.herthabsc.de* Ⓜ*Olympiastadion [U-bahn]*), held at the Olympic Stadium, can be booked via phone or online.

SWIMMING

The lakes Wannsee, Halensee, Müggelsee, and Plötzensee all have beaches. The huge **Strandbad Wannsee** (⊠ *Wannseebad-weg 25, Zehlendorf* ☎*030/7071–3833*) attracts as many as 40,000 Berliners to its fine, sandy beach on summer weekends.

In summer, a trip to the **Arena Badeschiff** (⊠*Eichenstr. 4, Kreuzberg/ Treptow* ☎*030/5332–030* Ⓜ*Schlesische Strasse [U-bahn]*) is a must. The outdoor pool is set on a boat anchored on the river Spree, offering great views of the Kreuzberg skyline. It's open April to late August, daily 8–midnight. In winter (September–March) the pool is transformed into an indoor sauna.

SHOPPING

What's fashionable in Berlin is creative, bohemian style, so designer labels have less appeal here than in Hamburg, Düsseldorf, or Munich. Young people seem to spend more money on cell-phone cards than clothing.

SHOPPING DISTRICTS

CHARLOTTENBURG

Although Ku'damm is still touted as the shopping mile of Berlin, many shops are ho-hum retailers. The best stretch for exclusive fashions, such as Bruno Magli, Hermès, and Jil Sander, are the three blocks between Leibnizstrasse and Bleibtreustrasse. For home furnishings, gift items, and unusual clothing boutiques, follow this route off Ku'damm: Leibnizstrasse to Mommsenstrasse to Bleibtreustrasse, then on to the ring around Savignyplatz. Fasanenstrasse, Knesebeckstrasse, Schlüterstrasse, and Uhlandstrasse are also fun places to browse.

Ku'damm ends at Breitscheidplatz, but the door-to-door shopping continues along Tauentzienstrasse, which, in addition to international retail stores, offers continental Europe's largest department store, the upscale Kaufhaus des Westens, or KaDeWe.

MITTE

The finest shops in historic Berlin are along Friedrichstrasse, including the French department store Galeries Lafayette. Nearby, Unter den Linden has just a few souvenir shops and a Meissen ceramic showroom. Smaller clothing and specialty stores populate the Scheunenviertel. The area between Hackescher Markt, Weinmeister Strasse, and Rosa-Luxemburg-Platz alternates pricey independent designers with groovy secondhand shops, and a string of ultra-hip flagship stores by the big sports and fashion designer brands. Neue Schönhauser Strasse curves into Alte Schönhauser Strasse, and both streets are full of stylish casual wear. Galleries along Gipsstrasse and Sophienstrasse round out the mix.

DEPARTMENT STORES

The smallest and most luxurious department store in town, **Department Store Quartier 206** (✉ *Friedrichstr. 71, Mitte* ☎ *030/2094–6240*) offers primarily French women's and men's designer clothes, perfumes, and home accessories. Intimate and elegant, **Galeries Lafayette** (✉ *Friedrichstr. 76–78, Mitte* ☎ *030/209–480*) carries almost exclusively French products, including designer clothes, perfume, and all the produce you might need for preparing haute cuisine at home. Anchoring Alexanderplatz, **Galeria Kaufhof** (✉ *Alexanderpl. 9, Mitte* ☎ *030/247–430* ⊕ *www.kaufhof.de*) is the most successful branch of the German chain, though the wares are fairly basic.

The largest department store in continental Europe, classy **Kaufhaus des Westens** (*KaDeWe* ✉ *Tauentzienstr. 21, Western Downtown* ☎ *030/21210* ⊕ *www.kadewe.de*) has a grand selection of goods on seven floors, as well as food and deli counters, champagne bars, beer bars, and a winter garden on its two upper floors. Its wealth of services includes fixing umbrellas and repairing leather and furs.

15

GIFT IDEAS

★ All the books, maps, and souvenirs focus on the city at **Berlin Story** (⊠ *Unter den Linden 26, Mitte* ☎ *030/2045–3842*), which is even open on Sunday. Fashionable **Berlinomat** (⊠ *Frankfurter Allee 89, at Waldeyer Str., Friedrichshain* ☎ *030/4208–1445*) carries the clothes, jewelry, furniture, household goods, and gift items of designers who live and work in Berlin. In a show of civic pride, hip items often feature a city symbol. In a similar vein to Berlinomat, **s.wert** (⊠ *Brunnenstr. 191, Mitte* ☎ *030/4005–66555*) crafts products inspired by Berlin's facades (pillows), grafitti (scratched glasses), and civic symbols (on polo shirts). It opens at noon Monday through Saturday.

Fine porcelain is still produced by **Königliche Porzellan Manufaktur** (⊠ *Wegelystr. 1, Tiergarten* ☎ *030/390–090* ⊠ *Unter den Linden 35, Mitte* ☎ *030/206–4150* ⊠ *Kurfürstendamm 27, Western Downtown* ☎ *030/8862–7961*), the former Royal Prussian Porcelain Factory, also called KPM. You can buy this delicate handmade, hand-painted china at KPM's two stores, but it may be more fun to visit the factory salesroom, which also sells seconds at reduced prices.

Puppenstube im Nikolaiviertel (⊠ *Propststr. 4, Mitte* ☎ *030/242–3967*) is the ultimate shop for any kind of (mostly handmade) dolls, including designer models as well as old-fashioned German dolls. It's for collectors, not kids. Tucked under the elevated train tracks, **Scenario** (⊠ *Savignyplatz 1, Western Downtown* ☎ *030/312–9199*) sells stationery articles, gifts of any kind, and a lot of leather wares and jewelry. The designs here are modern. In the homey setting of **Wohnart Berlin** (⊠ *Uhlandstr. 179–180, Western Downtown* ☎ *030/882–5252*) you can imagine how the stylish European furnishings, lamps, housewares, or stationery items might suit your own pad.

SPECIALTY STORES

ANTIQUES

Not far from Wittenbergplatz lies Keithstrasse, a street full of antiques stores. Eisenacher Strasse, Fuggerstrasse, Kalckreuthstrasse, Motzstrasse, and Nollendorfstrasse—all close to Nollendorfplatz—have many antiques stores of varying quality. Another good street for antiques is Suarezstrasse, between Kantstrasse and Bismarckstrasse. Other antiques stores are found under the tracks from Friedrichstrasse station east to Universitätsstrasse, open Monday and Wednesday–Sunday 11–6.

On weekends from 10 to 5 the lively **Berliner Trödelmarkt und Kunstmarkt** *(Berlin Flea and Art Market)* on Strasse des 17. Juni swings into action. The flea-market stands are nearer the Tiergarten S-bahn station; the handicrafts begin past the Charlottenburg gates.

JEWELRY

Bucherer (⊠ *Kurfürstendamm 45, Western Downtown* ☎ *030/880–4030* ⊕ *www.bucherer.com*) carries fine handcrafted jewelry, watches, and other stylish designer accessories. German designers featured at **Klaus Kaufhold** (⊠ *Kurfürstendamm 197, Western Downtown* ☎ *030/8847–1790*) share a philosophy of sleek minimalism. Rubber and diamond rings and matte platinum and diamond pieces are conscious understatements.

MEN'S CLOTHING

For guys who envy the diversity of wares offered to gals, **Boyz 'R' Us** (⊠ *Maassenstr. 8, Schöneberg* ☎ *030/2363–0639*) is your chance to grab a pink-gingham shirt or spangled turquoise top. Patterned jeans and loud tartan pants make this store a magnet for gay and straight clubbers. The most sought-after German label here is Kresse Hamburg. Handmade and timeless shoes and brogues, mostly from England, Austria, and Hungary, are sold at **Budapester Schuhe** (⊠ *Kurfürstendamm 199, Western Downtown* ☎ *030/881–1707* ⊠ *Friedrichstr. 81, Mitte* ☎ *030/2038–8110*). The gentlemen's outfitter **Mientus** (⊠ *Wilmersdorfer Str. 73, Western Downtown* ☎ *030/323–9077* ⊠ *Kurfürstendamm 52, Western Downtown* ☎ *030/323–9077*) stocks Armani, Versace Classic, and Boss and has an in-house tailor. The Wilmersdorfer Strasse location offers free parking for customers.

WOMEN'S CLOTHING

The designs of **Anette Petermann** (⊠ *Bleibtreustr. 49, Western Downtown* ☎ *030/323–2556*) are a delight of Berlin haute couture. Roses are her trademark; you'll find fabric buds sewn into pinstripe jackets or taffeta stoles. Crushed organza evening wear and functional wool and fur are popular with local celebrities. The creations of Berlin's top avant-garde designer, **Claudia Skoda** (⊠ *Alte Schönhauser Str. 35, Mitte* ☎ *030/280–7211*), are mostly for women, but there's also men's knitwear. The flagship store of German designer **Jil Sander** (⊠ *Kurfürstendamm 185, Western Downtown* ☎ *030/886–7020*) carries her complete line of understated clothing. **Peek und Cloppenburg** (⊠ *Tauentzienstr. 19, Western Downtown* ☎ *030/212–900*), or "P & C," stocks women's, men's, and children's clothes on five floors. Don't miss the designer shop-in-shop areas on the second and third floors and the international, young designer department in the basement.

SIDE TRIP TO POTSDAM

A trip to Berlin wouldn't be complete without paying a visit to Potsdam and its park, which surrounds the important Prussian palaces Neues Palais and Sanssouci. This separate city, the state capital of Brandenburg (the state surrounding Berlin), can be reached within a half-hour from Berlin's Zoo Station.

Potsdam still retains the imperial character it earned during the many years it served as a royal residence and garrison quarters. The Alter Markt and Neuer Markt show off stately Prussian architecture, and both are easily reached from the main train station by any tram heading into the town center. The **Alter Markt** was once dominated by the city's baroque palace, heavily destroyed by Allied bombing in WW II and then blown up by the East German regime in 1960. Reminiscent

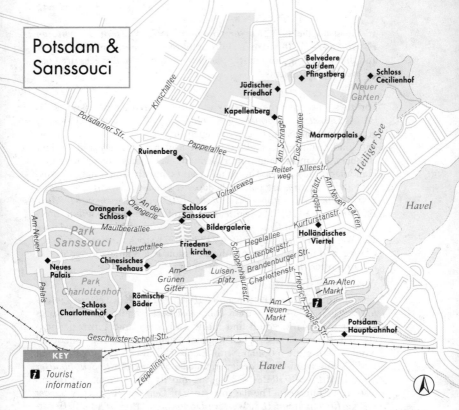

Potsdam & Sanssouci

KEY

🛈 Tourist information

of a similar debate in Berlin, Potsdam, too, has decided to rebuild its palace; the reconstructed structure will house the state parliment, and work is scheduled to begin in 2008. Thanks to private donors, the first element, a magnificent replica of the **Fortunaportal,** now stands proudly on the square.

GETTING HERE & AROUND

Potsdam is 20 km (12 mi) southwest of Berlin's center and a half-hour journey by car or bus. From Zoo Station to Potsdam's main train station, the regional train RE 1 takes 17 minutes, and the S-7 line of the S-bahn takes about 30 minutes; use an ABC zone ticket for either service. City traffic is heavy, so a train journey is recommended. Several Berlin tour operators have Potsdam trips.

There are several tours that include Potsdam (most are two or six hours). They leave from the landing across from Berlin's Wannsee S-bahn station between late March and early October. Depending on the various tours on offer, a round-trip ticket costs €7.50–€23.

ESSENTIALS

Boat Information Stern- und Kreisschiffahrt (☎ 030/536–3600 ⊕ www. sternundkreis.de).

Visitor Information Potsdam Tourist Office (✉ *Touristenzentrum Potsdam, Brandenburger Str. 3, at Brandenburger Tor Potsdam Potsdam* ☎ *0331/275–580* 🖷 *0331/275–5829* ⊕ *www.potsdamtourismus.de*).

EXPLORING

Karl Friedrich Schinkel designed the Alter Markt's domed **Nikolaikirche.** In front of it stands an Egyptian obelisk erected by Schloss Sanssouci architect von Knobelsdorff.

A gilded figure of Atlas tops the tower of the old **Rathaus,** built in 1755.

The region's history museum, the **Haus der Brandenburg-Preussischen Geschichte,** is in the royal stables in the square opposite the Nikolaikirche. ✉ *Am Neuen Markt 9* ☎ *0331/620–8550* ⊕ *www.hbpg.de* 🖷 *€4.50* ⊙ *Tues.–Fri. 10–5, weekends 10–6.*

The center of the small **Holländisches Viertel** *(Dutch Quarter)* is an easy walk north along Friedrich-Ebert-Strasse to Mittelstrasse. Friedrich Wilhelm I built the settlement in 1732 to entice Dutch artisans who could support the city's rapid growth. Few Dutch came, and the gabled, mansard-roof brick houses were largely used to house staff. Stores and restaurants inhabit the buildings now, and the area is Potsdam's most-visited.

15

NEED A BREAK? Fine coffee blends and rich cakes are offered at the Wiener Restaurant-Café (✉ *Luisenpl. 4* ☎ *0331/967–8314*), an old-style European coffeehouse on the way to the Grünes Gitter entrance to Sanssouci. A favorite cake here is the *Sanssouci-Torte.*

Prussia's most famous king, Friedrich II—Frederick the Great—spent more time at his summer residence, **Schloss Sanssouci,** than in the capital of Berlin. Its name means "without a care" in French, the language Frederick cultivated in his own private circle and within the court. Some experts believe tha Frederick actually named the palace "Sans, Souci," which they translate as "with and without a care," a more apt name; its construction caused him a lot of trouble and expense, and sparked furious rows with his master builder, Georg Wenzeslaus von Knobelsdorff. His creation nevertheless became one of Germany's greatest tourist attractions. The palace lies on the edge of Park Sanssouci, which includes various buildings and palaces with separate admissions and hours. ∎TIP➡ **Be advised that during peak tourism times, timed tickets for Schloss Sanssouci tours can sell out before noon.**

Executed according to Frederick's impeccable French-influenced taste, the palace, built between 1745 and 1747, is extravagantly rococo, with scarcely a patch of wall left unadorned. Leading up to the building is an unusual formal terrace where wine was once cultivated. To the west of the palace are the **Neue Kammern** (*New Chambers* ☎ *0331/969–4206* 🖷 *€3, guided tour €4* ⊙ *Late Mar.–Apr., weekends 10–6; Apr.–Oct., Tues.–Sun. 10–6*), which housed guests of the king's family after its beginnings as a greenhouse. Just east of Sanssouci Palace is the **Bildergalerie** (*Picture Gallery* ☎ *0331/969–4181* 🖷 *€3* ⊙ *Apr.–mid-*

Oct., Tues.–Sun. 10–6), with expensive marble from Siena in the main cupola. The gallery displays Frederick's collection of 17th-century Italian and Dutch paintings, including works by Caravaggio, Rubens, and Van Dyck. ⊠*Park Sanssouci* ☎*0331/969–4202* ⊕*www.spsg.de* 🎫*Guided tour €12, or €8 Nov.–Mar.; premium day card for all Berlin-area palaces (including Sanssouci) €15 (available only here), €2 voluntary fee for park entrance only at any of the buildings or visitor center* ☉ *Apr.–Oct., Tues.–Sun. 10–6; Nov.–Mar., Tues.–Sun. 10–5.*

The **Neues Palais** *(New Palace)*, a much larger and grander palace than Sanssouci, stands at the end of the long avenue that runs through Sanssouci Park. It was built after the Seven Years' War (1756–63), when Frederick loosened the purse strings. It's said he wanted to demonstrate that the state coffers hadn't been depleted too severely by the long conflict. Interiors that impress include the Grotto Hall with walls and columns set with shells, coral, and other aquatic decor. The royals' upper apartments have paintings by 17th-century Italian masters. Even if the tour is German, you can borrow a good English guide to follow along with. You can opt to tour the palace yourself only on weekends between late April and mid-May. ⊠*Str. am Neuen Palais, Sanssouci* ☎*0331/969–4361* ⊕*www.spsg.de* 🎫*Apr.–Oct., €5, €6 with tour; Nov.–Apr., €5 with tour* ☉*Apr.–Oct., Wed.–Mon. 10–5:30; Nov.–Mar., Wed.–Mon. 10–4:30.*

Schloss Charlottenhof (☎*0331/969–4228* 🎫*€4 with tour* ☉*Easter week and May–Oct., daily 10–5:30*) is in the southern part of Sanssouci Park. After Frederick the Great died in 1786, the ambitious Sanssouci building program ground to a halt, and the park fell into neglect. It was 50 years before another Prussian king, Friedrich Wilhelm IV, restored Sanssouci's earlier glory. He engaged the great Berlin architect Karl Friedrich Schinkel to build this small palace for the crown prince. Schinkel's demure interiors are preserved, and the most fanciful room is the bedroom, decorated like a Roman tent, with its walls and ceiling draped in striped canvas.

Between the Sanssouci palaces are later additions to the park. In 1836 Friedrich Wilhelm IV built the **Römische Bäder** *(Roman Baths* 🎫*€3 with exhibit* ☉ *May–Oct., Tues.–Sun. 10–5:30*). The **Orangerieschloss und Turm** (🎫*Guided tour €4, tower only €2* ☉*Palace and tower mid-May–mid-Oct., Tues.–Sun. 10–5; tower only Apr. weekends 10–5*) was completed in 1860; its two massive towers linked by a colonnade evoke an Italian Renaissance palace. Today it houses 47 copies of paintings by Raphael. The **Chinesisches Teehaus** *(Chinese Teahouse* 🎫*€2* ☉ *May–Oct., Tues.–Sun. 10–5:30*) was erected in 1757 in the Chinese style, which was all the rage at the time, and houses porcelain from Meissen and Asia. Completed in 1848, the Italianate **Friedenskirche** *(Peace Church* ☎*0331/969–4228* 🎫*Free* ☉*Late Mar.–Apr. and 1st 2 wks in Oct., Mon.–Sat. 11–5, Sun. noon–5; May–Sept., Mon.–Sat. 10–6, Sun. noon–6*) houses a 12th-century Byzantine mosaic taken from an island near Venice.

<table>
<tr><td>NEED A
BREAK?</td><td>Halfway up the park's Drachenberg Hill, above the Orangerie, stands the curious Drachenhaus *(Dragon House)*, modeled in 1770 after the Pagoda at London's Kew Gardens and named for the gargoyles ornamenting the roof corners. It now houses a popular café.</td></tr>
</table>

Resembling a rambling, Tudor manor house, **Schloss Cecilienhof** *(Cecilienhof Palace)* was built for Crown Prince Wilhelm in 1913, on a newly laid-out stretch of park called the New Garden, which borders the Heiliger See. It was in this last palace built by the Hohenzollerns that the Allied leaders Truman, Attlee, and Stalin hammered out the fate of postwar Germany at the 1945 Potsdam Conference. ■TIP→ From Potsdam's main train station, take a tram to Reiterweg/Alleestrasse, and then transfer to Bus 692 to Am Neuer Garten. ☏*0331/969–4244* ⊕*www. spsg.de* ✉*€5, €6 with tour (Nov.–Mar. tour is mandatory); tour of prince's private rooms €3* ⊙ *Tues.–Sun. 10–6. Tours of prince's rooms at 11, 1, and 3.*

On a hill near Schloss Cecilienhof, the colonnaded **Belvedere auf dem Pfingstberg** was a lofty observation platform for the royals. Farther down the hill is the simple **Pomonatempel** (⊙*Apr.–Oct., weekends 3–6)*, the first building built by Karl Friedrich Schinkel (1801). ✉*Am Pfingstberg* ☏*0331/2701972* ⊕*www.pfingstberg.de* ✉*€3.50* ⊙*Apr., May, and Sept., daily 10–6; June–Aug., daily 10–8; Oct., daily 10–4; Mar. and Nov., weekends 10–4.*

15

WHERE TO STAY & EAT

$$–$$$ ✕**Juliette.** In a city proud of its past French influences, the highly praised French cuisine here is delivered to your table by French waiters, no less. The intimate restaurant at the edge of the Dutch Quarter has old-fashioned brick walls and a fireplace. The menu offers small portions of dishes such as rack of lamb, wild-hare pie with hot peppered cherries, and a starter plate of four foie-gras preparations. Its wine list of 120 French vintages is unique in the Berlin area. Potsdam's proximity to the Babelsberg film studios ensures regular appearances by those shooting there. ✉*Jägerstr. 39* ☏*0331/270–1791* ▤*AE, DC, MC, V.*

$$ ▦**Hotel am Luisenplatz.** Behind a somber-looking facade, this intimate hotel conceals a warm, upscale elegance and friendly, personal service. The large rooms are decorated in dark blue, red, or turquoise—and all have bathtubs. There's free Internet use for those who don't have a laptop, and a spa area with sauna and solarium invites guests to relax. The biggest draw, however, is the hotel's location, which offers a spectacular view of historic Luisenplatz and its restored Prussian city mansions. **Pros:** great central location near pedestrian zones of downtown Potsdam, personal flair, great views. **Cons:** tour busses stop for meals, restaurant crowded during these visits, no air-conditioning, sometimes busy Luisenplatz right in front of rooms. ✉*Luisenpl. 5* ☏*0331/971–900* ⊕*www.hotel-luisenplatz.de* ⇆*35 rooms, 3 suites* ⚹*In-room: no a/c, safe. In-hotel: restaurant, spa, laundry service, Wi-Fi, parking (fee), no-smoking rooms, some pets allowed* ▤*AE, MC, V* �'⊙'*CP.*

$$ 🏨 **Steigenberger Hotel Sanssouci.** The terrace of this fine hotel overlooks the palace and park of Sanssouci. Spacious movie-theme rooms (complete with Hollywood and Babelsberg vintage photos and memorabilia) have terra-cotta floors and rattan furniture. A nice plus is the free transportation card for Berlin and Potsdam for the duration of your stay. The hotel restaurant serves international dishes, including those of the Brandenburg region. **Pros:** great location, 10-minute walk away from Sanssouci park, quiet rooms, very good breakfast buffet. **Cons:** restaurant offers only moderate quality, interior design and bathrooms dated in some rooms, impersonal service. ✉ *Allee nach Sanssouci 1* ☎ *0331/90910* ⊕ *www.potsdam.steigenberger.de* 🛏 *133 rooms, 4 suites* 🛎 *In-room: no a/c, Wi-Fi. In-hotel: restaurant, bar, bicycles, laundry service, parking (fee), no-smoking rooms, some pets allowed* 🖃 *AE, DC, MC, V.*

Saxony, Saxony-Anhalt & Thuringia

WORD OF MOUTH

"Leipzig at dusk looks incredible as the old town is lit by the streetlights and the glitzy reflection from the polished cobblestones. The restaurant row at Barfuesschengasse comes alive, but only at night."
—DAX

"Erfurt is a hidden gem hardly anybody knows. Erfurt Full of Towers—the old nickname of the city is still valid. There is hardly a street corner in the center where you won't see at least 2 or 3 steeples. A mix of great history and modern life, cute small shops."

—Quokka

Updated by
Lee A. Evans

GERMANY'S TRADITIONAL CHARM IS MOST EVIDENT in the eastern states of Saxony, Saxony-Anhalt, and Thuringia. The area, one of Europe's best-kept secrets, hides some cultural gems. A comfortable "German" state of mind survives here, the like of which you will never find in West Germany. Communism never penetrated the culture here as deeply as the American influence did in West Germany. The German Democratic Republic (GDR, commonly referred to by its German acronym—DDR) resolutely clung to its German heritage, proudly preserving connections with such national heroes as Luther, Goethe, Schiller, Bach, Handel, Wagner, and the Hungarian-born Liszt. Towns in the regions of the Thüringer Wald (Thuringian Forest) or the Harz Mountains—long considered the haunt of witches—are drenched in history and medieval legend. The area hides a fantastic collection of rural villages and castles unparalleled in other parts of the country.

Many cities, such as Erfurt, escaped World War II relatively unscathed, and the East Germans extensively rebuilt those towns that were bomb-damaged. The historical centers have been restored to their past splendor; however, you will also see eyesores of industrialization and stupendously bland housing projects. Famous palaces and cultural wonders—the Zwinger and Semperoper in Dresden, the Wartburg at Eisenach, the Schiller and Goethe houses in Weimar, Luther's Wittenberg, as well as the wonderfully preserved city of Görlitz—await the traveler here.

ORIENTATION & PLANNING

GETTING ORIENTED

The three states cover the southeastern part of the former East Germany. You will still see old, dirty, and depressing industrial towns that recall the Communist past. However, some of Germany's most historic cities are here, too, and reconstruction programs are slowly restoring them. Dresden is promoting its reputation as "the Florence on the Elbe," and just downstream Meissen has undergone an impressive face-lift. Weimar, one of the continent's old cultural centers, and Leipzig, in particular, have washed off their grime and almost completely restored their historic city centers. Görlitz, Germany's easternmost city, benefited from an infusion of cash and is consistently lauded as one of the country's 10 most beautiful cities.

Saxony. Saxony is the pearl of East Germany: the countryside is dotted with beautifully renovated castles and fortresses, and the people are charming and full of energy. (They also speak in an almost incomprehensible local dialect.) Dresden and Leipzig are cosmopolitan centers that combine the energy of the avant-garde with a distinct respect for tradition.

Saxony-Anhalt. Although long ignored by travelers, Saxony-Anhalt has more UNESCO World Heritage sites than any other region in Europe.

TOP REASONS TO GO

Frauenkirche in Dresden: Rising like a majestic baroque phoenix, the church is a worthy symbol of a city destroyed and rebuilt from its ashes. In the words of one Dresdener, "It feels as if a scar on my soul were healed."

Weimar: The history of Germany seems to revolve around this small town, whose past residents are a veritable who's who of the last 400 years.

Görlitz: Balanced on the border between Germany and Poland, this architectural gem is relatively undiscovered; you'll feel like you have the whole town to yourself.

Coffee and Cake in Leipzig: Take some time off from exploring the city to enjoy a Leipzig institution.

Following Martin Luther: Trace the path of the ultimate medieval rebel. Visiting Wittenberg, Eisenach, and the Wartburg not only exposes you to the rich cultural heritage of the area but also gives valuable insight into the mind and culture of a person whose ideas helped change the world.

Wine Tasting in the Salle-Unstrut: Europe's northernmost wine region is often called "the Tuscany of the North." The castle-topped, rolling hills covered in terraced vineyards are perfect for biking, hiking, and horseback riding. Most of the vineyards are family-run operations with long histories.

16

The city of Naumburg is famed for its cathedral and for the wines produced in the surrounding vineyards.

Thuringia. Of all the East German states, Thuringia had the best tourist infrastructure. Western visitors to the classical jewel of Weimar and those intersted in outdoor sports in the lush Thuringian Forest were vital sources of hard currency. This still holds true today: Thuringia offers unparalleled natural sights as well as classical culture at reasonable prices.

SAXONY, SAXONY-ANHALT & THURINGIA PLANNER

WHEN TO GO

Winters in this part of Germany can be cold, wet, and dismal, so unless you plan to ski in the Harz Mountains or the Thüringer Wald, visit in late spring, summer, or early autumn. Avoid Leipzig at trade-fair times, particularly in March and April. In the summer every city, town, and village has a festival, with streets blocked and local culture spilling out into every open space.

GETTING HERE & AROUND

BY AIR It's easiest, and usually cheapest, to fly into Berlin or Frankfurt and rent a car from there. Desden and Leipzig both have international airports that primarily serve European destinations. Dresden Flughafen is about 10 km (6 mi) north of Dresden, and Leipzig's Flughafen Leipzig-Halle is 12 km (8 mi) northwest of the city.

BY BUS   Long-distance buses travel to Dresden and Leipzig. Bus service within the area is infrequent and mainly connects with rail lines. Check schedules carefully at central train stations or call the service phone number of Deutsche Bahn at local railway stations.

BY CAR   Expressways connect Berlin with Dresden (A–13) and Leipzig (A–9). Both journeys take about two hours. A–4 stretches east–west across the southern portion of Thuringia and Saxony.

A road-construction program in eastern Germany is ongoing, and you should expect traffic delays on any journey of more than 300 km (186 mi). The Bundesstrassen throughout eastern Germany are narrow, tree-lined country roads, often jammed with traffic. Roads in the western part of the Harz Mountains are better and wider.

Cars can be rented at the Dresden and Leipzig airports, at train stations, and through all major hotels. Be aware that you are not allowed to take rentals into Poland or the Czech Republic.

BY TRAIN   The fastest and most inexpensive way to explore the region is by train. The rail infrastructure of Eastern Germany is exceptional; trains serve even the most remote destinations with astonishing frequency. Slower S, RB, and RE trains link smaller towns, while Leipzig, Dresden, Weimar, Erfurt, Naumburg, and Witttenberg are all on major ICE lines. Some cities—Dresden and Meissen, for example—are linked by commuter trains.

From Dresden a round-trip ticket to Leipzig costs about €36.60 (a 1½-hour journey one-way); to Görlitz, €32.20 (a 1½-hour ride). Trains connect Leipzig with Halle (a 30-minute ride, €10), Erfurt (a 1-hour ride, €25), and Eisenach (a 1½-hour journey, €33). The train ride between Dresden and Eisenach (2½ hours) costs €49 one way.

■ TIP➜ **Consider using the Sachsen Ticket, Sachsen-Anhalt Ticket, or Thüringen Ticket, a €27 offer from the German Railroad.**

ESSENTIALS   **Airport Contacts Dresden Flughafen** (☎*0351/881–3360* ⊕*www.dresden-airport.de*). **Flughafen Leipzig-Halle** (☎*0341/224–1155* ⊕*www.leipzig-halle-airport.de*).

ABOUT THE RESTAURANTS

Enterprising young managers and chefs have established themselves in the East, so look for new, usually small restaurants along the way. People in the region are extremely particular about their traditional food (rumor has it that one can be deported for roasting Mützbraten over anything other than birch), but some new chefs have successfully blended nouvelle German with international influences. Medieval-themed restaurants and "experience dining," complete with entertainment, are all the rage in the East ,and warrant at least one try. Brewpubs have sprouted up everywhere, and are a good bet for meeting locals.

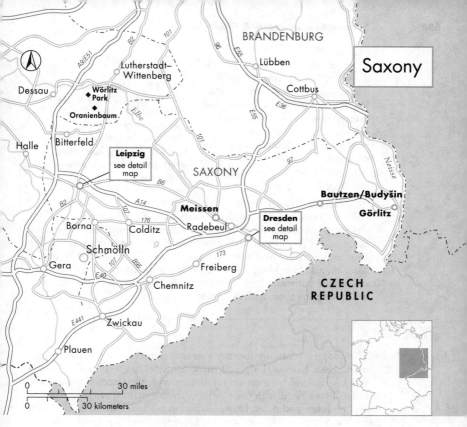

ABOUT THE HOTELS

After Germany's reunification, major hotel chains swooped in and absorbed the old Interhotel infrastructure. The result: in the East it is quite normal to have a major international hotel in a 1,000 year-old house or restored mansion. Smaller and family-run hotels are more charming local options, and often include a good restaurant. Most big hotels offer special weekend or activity-oriented packages that aren't found in the western part of the country.

During the trade fairs and shows of the **Leipziger Messe,** particularly in March and April, most Leipzig hotels increase their prices.

WHAT IT COSTS IN EUROS					
	¢	$	$$	$$$	$$$$
RESTAURANTS	under €9	€9–€15	€16–€20	€21–€25	over €25
HOTELS	under €50	€50–€100	€101–€175	€176–€225	over €225

Restaurant prices are per person for a main course at dinner. Hotel prices are for two people in a standard double room, including tax and service.

DISCOUNTS & DEALS

Most of the region's larger cities offer special tourist exploring cards, such as the **Dresdencard, Hallecard, Leipzigcard,** and **Weimarcard,** which include discounts at museums, concerts, hotels, and restaurants or special sightseeing packages for up to three days. For details, call the cities' tourist-information offices.

> **THE FIVE KS**
>
> A long-standing joke is that the priorities of the people of Saxony, Saxony-Anhalt, and Thuringia can be summed up in five Ks: Kaffee, Kuchen, Klösse, Kartoffeln, and Kirche (coffee, cake, dumplings, potatoes, and church)—in that order.

PLANNING YOUR TIME

Eastern Germany is a small, well-connected region that's well suited for day trips. Dresden and Leipzig are the largest cities with the most facilities, making them good bases from which to explore the surrounding countryside, either by car or train. Both are well connected with Berlin, Munich, and Frankfurt. Any of the smaller towns offer a quieter, possibly more authentic look at the area. A trip into the Salle-Unstrut is well worth the time, with Naumburg as a base.

SAXONY

The people of Saxony identify themselves more as Saxon than German. Their hardworking and rustic attitudes, as well as their somewhat peripheral location on the border with the Czech Republic and Poland, combined with their incomprensible dialect, are the targets of endless jokes and puns. However, Saxon pride is rebuilding three cities magnificently: Dresden and Leipzig—the showcase cities of eastern Germany—and the smaller town of Görlitz, on the Neisse River.

LEIPZIG

184 km (114 mi) southwest of Berlin.

Leipzig is, in a word, cool—but not so cool as to be pretentious. With its world-renowned links to Bach, Schubert, Mendelssohn, Luther, Goethe, Schiller, and the fantastic Neue-Leipziger-Schule art movement, Leipzig is one of the great German cultural centers. It has impressive art nouveau architecture, an incredibly clean city center, meandering back alleys, and the temptations of coffee and cake on every corner. In *Faust*, Goethe describes Leipzig as "a little Paris"; in reality it's more reminiscent of Vienna, while remaining a distinctly energetic Saxon town.

Johann Sebastian Bach (1685–1750) was organist and choir director at the Thomaskirche, and the 19th-century composer Richard Wagner was born here in 1813. Today's Leipzig maintains this tradition with extraordinary offerings of music, theater, and opera, not to mention a fantastic nightlife.

Wartime bombs destroyed much of Leipzig's city center, but reconstruction efforts have uncovered one of Europe's most vibrant cities.

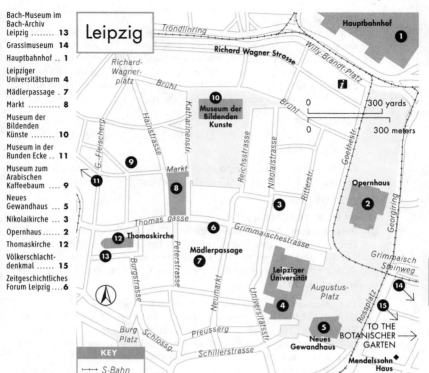

Leipzig's art nouveau flair is best discovered by exploring countless alleys, covered courtyards, and passageways. Many unattractive buildings from the postwar period remain, but only reinforce Leipzig's position on the line between modernity and antiquity.

With a population of about 500,000, Leipzig is the second-largest city in eastern Germany (after Berlin), and has long been a center of printing and bookselling. Astride major trade routes, it was an important market town in the Middle Ages, and it continues to be a trading center, thanks to the *Leipziger Messe* (trade and fair shows) throughout the year that bring together buyers from East and West.

GETTING HERE & AROUND

Leipzig is an hour from Berlin by train. Leipzig-Halle airport serves many European destinations, but no North American ones.

Leipzig Erleben operates several Leipzig bus tours (in English and German), with daily departures at 10:30 and 3:30 (and more frequent and varied schedules in summer). Tours leave from opposite the tourist-information office at Richard-Wagner-Strasse 1. A walking tour of Leipzig (in English) sets off from the tourist office May–September, daily at 1:30; October–April, Saturday at 1:30 and Sunday at 10:30.

TIMING

Leipzig can easily be explored in one day; it's possible to walk around the downtown area in just about three hours. The churches can be inspected in less than 20 minutes each. But if you're interested in German history and art, plan for two full days, so you can spend a whole day just visiting the museums and go to the symphony. The Völkerschlachtdenkmal is perfect for a half-day side trip.

ESSENTIALS

Tour Information **Leipzig Erleben** (⊕ *www.leipzig-erleben.com* ☎ *0351/7104230*).

Visitor Information (⊠ *Leipzig Tourist Service e.V., Richard-Wagner-Str. 1,* ☎ *0341/710–4260* 🖷 *0341/710–4301* ⊕ *www.leipzig.de*).

EXPLORING

MAIN ATTRACTIONS

🕙 **Grassimuseum.** British star architect David Chipperfield restored and modernized this fine example of German art deco in 2003–05. The building, dating to 1925–29, houses three important museums. ⚠ **Due to ongoing renovations, sections of the museums may close briefly until 2010.**

The **Museum für Angewandte Kunst** (*Museum of Applied Art* ☎ *0341/2229–100* ⊕ *www.grassimuseum.de* 🎟 *€5* ⊙ *Tues. and Thurs.–Sun. 10–6, Wed. 10–8*) showcases works from Leipzig's and eastern Germany's proud tradition of handicrafts, such as exquisite porcelain, fine tapestry art, and modern Bauhaus design. The **Museum für Völkerkunde** (*Ethnological Museum* ☎ *0341/9731–300* ⊕ *www. grassimuseum.de* 🎟 *€4* ⊙ *Tues.–Fri. 10–6, weekends 10–5*) presents arts and crafts from all continents and various eras, including a thrilling collection of Southeast Asian antique art. The **Musikinstrumentenmuseum** (*Musical Instruments Museum* ☎ *0341/973–0750* ⊕ *www. uni-leipzig.de/museum/musik* 🎟 *€4* ⊙ *Tues.–Sun. 11–5*) showcases musical instruments, mostly from the Renaissance, including the world's oldest clavichord, constructed in 1543 in Italy. There are also spinets, flutes, and lutes. Sample sounds of these instruments can be heard while looking at them. ⊠ *Johannispl. 5–11.*

🕖 **Mädlerpassage** (*Mädler Mall*). The ghost of Goethe's Faust lurks in every marble corner of Leipzig's finest shopping arcade. Goethe set one of the scenes in *Faust* in the famous Auerbachs Keller restaurant, at No. 2. A bronze group of characters from the play, sculpted in 1913, beckons you down the stone staircase to the restaurant. ■ TIP➔ **Touching the statues' feet brings good luck.** A few yards away is a delightful art-nouveau bar called Mephisto, done in devilish reds and blacks. ⊠ *Grimmaische Str.*

🕗 **Markt.** Leipzig's showpiece is its huge, old market square. One side is occupied completely by the Renaissance town hall, the **Altes Rathaus**, which houses the **Stadtgeschichtliches Museum,** where Leipzig's past is well documented. ⊠ *Markt 1* ☎ *0341/965–130* 🎟 *€3* ⊙ *Tues.–Sun. 10–6.*

Museum der Bildenden Künste (*Museum of Fine Arts*). The city's leading art gallery is set in a new, ultramodern, cubelike complex at the exact location of the original, historic museum, which was destroyed by Allied bombing. The museum has more than 2,700 paintings representing everything from the German Middle Ages to the modern Neue Leipziger Schule. One of its finest collections focuses on Lucas Cranach the Elder. ⊠*Katharinenstr. 10* ☎*0341/216–990* ⊕*www.mdbk.de* ☑*€5, free 2nd Wed. of month* ⊙*Tues. and Thurs.–Sun. 10–6, Wed. noon–8.*

Nikolaikirche (*St. Nicholas Church*). This church with its undistinguished facade was center stage during the demonstrations that helped bring down the Communist regime. Every Monday for months before the government collapsed, thousands of citizens gathered in front of the church chanting "*Wir sind das Volk*" ("We are the people"). Inside are a soaring Gothic choir and nave. Note the unusual patterned ceiling supported by classical pillars that end in palm-tree-like flourishes. Luther is said to have preached from the ornate 16th-century pulpit. ■TIP→ **The prayers for peace that began the revolution in 1989 are still held on Monday at 5** PM. ⊠*Nikolaikirchhof* ☎*0341/960–5270* ☑*Free* ⊙*Mon.–Sat. 10–6; Sun. services at 9:30, 11:15, and 5.*

16

Thomaskirche (*St. Thomas's Church*). Bach was choirmaster at this Gothic church for 27 years, and Martin Luther preached here on Whitsunday 1539, signaling the arrival of Protestantism in Leipzig. Originally the center of a 13th-century monastery, the tall church (rebuilt in the 15th century) now stands by itself. Bach wrote most of his cantatas for the church's famous boys' choir, the Thomanerchor, which was founded in the 13th century; the church continues as the choir's home as well as a center of Bach tradition.

Fodor's Choice

The great music Bach wrote during his Leipzig years commanded little attention in his lifetime, and when he died he was given a simple grave, without a headstone, in the city's Johannisfriedhof (St. John Cemetery). It wasn't until 1894 that an effort was made to find where the great composer lay buried, and after a thorough, macabre search, his coffin was removed to the Johanniskirche. That church was destroyed by Allied bombs in December 1943, and Bach subsequently found his final resting place in the church he would have selected: the Thomaskirche. ■TIP→ **You can listen to the famous boys' choir during the** *Motette,* **a service with a special emphasis on choral music.**

Bach's 12 children and the infant Richard Wagner were baptized in the early-17th-century font; Karl Marx and Friedrich Engels also stood before this same font, godfathers to Karl Liebknecht, who grew up to be a revolutionary as well. ⊠*Thomaskirchhof, off Grimmaische Str.* ☎*0341/2222 24 200* ⊕*www.thomaskirche.org* 💳*Free, Motette €2* ☉*Daily 9–6; Motette Fri. at 6* PM, *Sat. at 3.*

ALSO WORTH SEEING

⑬ **Bach-Museum im Bach-Archiv Leipzig** (*Bach Museum at the Bach Archives Leipzig*). The Bach family home, the old Bosehaus, stands opposite the Thomaskirche, and is now a museum devoted to the composer's life and work ⚠ **The museum is undergoing renovation (due to be competed in 2010), and the interim museum is a fairly small one-room affair.** ⊠*Thomaskirchhof 16* ☎*0341/9137–200* 💳*€3, €4.50 with guided tour Daily 10–5.*

❶ **Hauptbahnhof.** With 26 platforms, Leipzig's main train station is Europe's largest railhead. It was built in 1915 and is now a protected monument, but modern commerce rules in its bi-level shopping mall (the Promenaden). ■**TIP**→ **Many of the shops and restaurants stay open until 10** PM **and are open on Sunday.** ⊠*Willy-Brandt-Pl.* ☎*0341/141–270 for mall, 0341/9968–3275 for train station.*

❹ **Leipziger Universitätsturm** (*Leipzig University Tower*). Towering over Leipzig's city center is this 470-foot-high structure, which houses administrative offices and lecture rooms. Dubbed the "Jagged Tooth" by some University of Leipzig students, it supposedly represents an open book. Students were also largely responsible for changing the university's name, replacing its postwar title, Karl Marx University, with the original one. The **Augustusplatz** spreads out below the university tower like a space-age campus.

Mendelssohn Haus (*Mendelssohn House*). The only surviving residence of the composer Felix Mendelssohn-Bartholdy is now Germany's only museum dedicated to him. Mendelssohn's last residence and the place of his death has been preserved in its original 19th-century state. Concerts are held every Sunday at 11. ■**TIP**→ **2009 marks Mendelssohn's 200th birthday. Check with the museum for special events, concerts, and celebrations.** ⊠*Goldschmidtstr. 12* ☎*0341/127–0294* ⊕*www.mendelssohn-stiftung.de* 💳*€3* ☉*Daily 10–6.*

⑪ **Museum in der Runden Ecke** (*Museum in the Round Corner*). This building once served as the headquarters of the city's secret police, the dreaded *Staatssicherheitsdienst.* The exhibition *Stasi—Macht und Banalität* (Stasi—Power and Banality) not only presents the offices and surveillance work of the Stasi but also shows hundreds of documents revealing the magnitude of its interests in citizens' private lives. The material is written in German, but the items and the atmosphere still give an impression of what life under such a regime might have been like. ⊠*Dittrichring 24* ☎*0341/961–2443* ⊕*www.runde-ecke-leipzig.de* 💳*Free, €3 with tour in English, by appointment only* ☉*Daily 10–6.*

❾ **Museum zum Arabischen Kaffeebaum** (*Arabic Coffee Tree Museum*). This museum and café-restaurant tells the fascinating history of coffee culture in Europe, particularly in Saxony. The café is one of the oldest on the continent, and once proudly served coffee to such luminaries as Lessing, Schumann, Goethe, and Liszt. The museum features many paintings, Arabian coffee vessels, and coffeehouse games. It also explains the basic principles of roasting coffee. The café is divided into traditional Viennese, French, and Arabian coffee houses, but no coffee is served in the Arabian section, as it is only a display. ■TIP→ **The cake is better and the seating more comfortable in the Viennese part.** ⊠ *Kleine Fleischerg. 4* ☎ *0341/9602–632* ⊡ *Free* ☉ *Tues.–Sun. 11–5.*

⑤ Neues Gewandhaus *(New Orchestra Hall).* In the shadow of the Leipziger Universitätsturm is the glass-and-concrete home of the city orchestra, one of Germany's greatest. Kurt Masur is a former director, and Herbert Blomstedt is currently at the helm. Owing to the world-renowned acoustics of the concert hall, a tone resonates here for a full two seconds. ⊠ *Augustuspl. 8* ☎ *0341/127–0280.*

② Opernhaus *(Opera House).* Leipzig's stage for operas was the first postwar theater to be built in Communist East Germany. Its solid, boxy style is the subject of ongoing local controversy. ⊠ *Opposite Gewandhaus, on north side of Augustuspl.*

⑮ Völkerschlachtdenkmal *(Memorial to the Battle of the Nations).* On the city's outskirts, Prussian, Austrian, Russian, and Swedish forces stood ground against Napoléon's troops in the Battle of the Nations of 1813, a prelude to the French general's defeat two years later at Waterloo. An enormous, 300-foot-high monument erected on the site in 1913 commemorates the battle. Despite its ugliness, the site is well worth a visit, if only to wonder at the lengths—and heights—to which the Prussians went to celebrate their military victories, and to take in the view from a windy platform (provided you can climb the 500 steps to get there). The Prussians did make one concession to Napoléon in designing the monument: a stone marks the spot where he stood during the three-day battle. An exhibition hall explains the history of the memorial. The memorial can be reached via Streetcar 15 or 21 (leave the tram at the Probstheida station). ⊠ *Prager Str.* ☎ *0341/878–0471* ⊡ *€5* ☉ *Nov.–Apr., daily 10–4; May–Oct., daily 10–6; tour daily at 10:30, 1:30, and 2:30.*

⑥ Zeitgeschichtliches Forum Leipzig *(Museum of Contemporary History Leipzig).* This is one of the best museums of postwar German history. It focuses on issues surrounding the division and reunification of Germany after World War II. ⊠ *Grimmaische Str. 6* ☎ *0341/2250–500* ⊡ *Free* ☉ *Tues.–Sun. 10–6.*

WHERE TO EAT

$$$$ ✕ **Kaiser Maximilian.** Leipzig's best Mediterranean restaurant serves
★ inventive Italian and French dishes in a setting dominated by high, undecorated walls and black leather seats. The Maximilian is known for its pasta and fish dishes, such as *Schwarze Lachstortelloni im Safransud* (black salmon tortelloni cooked in saffron juice). The gourmet set menu is the reason to visit the Kaiser: three courses for €46, five courses for €60. ⊠ *Neumarkt 9–19* ☎ *0341/3553–3333* ⚄ *Reservations essential* ⊟ *AE, MC, V.*

16

$$ ✕**Auerbachs Keller.** The most famous
Fodor's Choice   of Leipzig's restaurants consists of
★   an upscale, international gourmet
restaurant and another restaurant
specializing in hearty Saxon fare.
■TIP➔ **It has been around since
1530 (making it one of the oldest con-
tinually running restaurants on the
continent), and Goethe immortalized
one of the several vaulted historic
rooms in his _Faust_.** Bach was also
a regular here because of the loca-
tion halfway between the Thom-
askirche and the Nikolaikirche.
The menu features regional dishes
from Saxony, mostly hearty, roasted
meat recipes. There's also a good
wine list. ⊠*Mädlerpassage, Grim-
maische Str. 2–4* ☏*0341/216–100*
⌂*Reservations essential* ⊟*AE, DC, MC, V* ☾*Closed Mon.*

> ### LEIPZIGER LERCHE
>
> As far back as the 18th century,
> Leipzig was known for a bizarre
> culinary specialty: roast meadow-
> lark in crust. The dish was so pop-
> ular that Leipzig consumed more
> than 400,000 meadowlarks every
> month. When the king of Saxony
> banned lark hunting in 1876,
> Leipzig's industrious bakers came
> up with a substitute: a baked
> short-crust pastry filled with
> almonds, nuts, and strawberries.
> Today, the substitute Meadowlark,
> when prepared correctly, is a deli-
> cious treat–but only in Leipzig.

$$ ✕**Barthels Hof.** The English-language menu at this restaurant explains
not only the cuisine but the history of Leipzig as well. Waitresses wear
traditional _Trachten_ dresses, but the rooms are quite modern. With a
prominent location directly on the Markt, the restaurant is popular
with locals, especially for the incredible breakfast buffet. ⊠*Hainstr. 1*
☏*800/165651218* ⊟*AE, DC, MC, V.*

$ ✕**Gasthaus & Gosebrauerei Bayrischer Bahnhof.** Hidden on the far south-
★   east edge of the city center, the Bayrischer Bahnhof was the terminus of
the first rail link between Saxony and Bavaria. The brewery here is the
heart of a cultural renaissance, and is the only place currently brewing
Gose in Leipzig. The restaurant is well worth a visit for its solid Saxon
and German cuisine. Brewery accents surface in dishes such as rump
steak with black-beer sauce. Groups of four or more can try dinner prepared in a _Römertopf_ (a terra-cotta baking dish; the first was brought
to Germany by the Romans, centuries ago). ■TIP➔ **In summer the beer
garden is a pleasant place to get away from the bustle of the city center.**
⊠*Bayrischer Pl. 1* ☏*0341/1245–760* ⊟*No credit cards.*

$ ✕**Thüringer Hof.** One of Germany's oldest restaurants and pubs (dating
back to 1454) served its hearty Thuringian and Saxon fare to Martin Luther and the like—who certainly had more than a mere pint
of the beers on tap here. The menu in the reconstructed, cavernous,
and always buzzing dining hall doesn't exactly offer gourmet cuisine,
rather an impressively enormous variety of game, fish, and bratwurst
dishes. The Thuringian sausages (served with either sauerkraut and
potatoes or onions and mashed potatoes) and the famous Thuringian
sauerbraten (beef marinated in a sour essence) are musts. ⊠*Burgstr.
19* ☏*0341/994–4999* ⊟*AE, MC, V.*

$ ✕**Zill's Tunnel.** The "tunnel" refers to the barrel-ceiling ground-floor
restaurant, where foaming glasses of excellent local beer are served
with a smile. The friendly staff will also help you decipher the Old

EATING WELL IN SAXONY

The cuisine of the region is hearty and seasonal, and almost every town has a unique specialty unavailable outside the immediate area. Look for *Gebratene Kalbsbrust* (roast veal breast), spicy *Thüringer Bratwurst* (sausage), *Schlesische Himmelreich* (ham and pork roast smothered in baked fruit and white sauce with dumplings), *Teichlmauke* (mashed potato in broth), *Blauer Karpfe* (blue carp, marinated in vinegar), and *Raacher Maad* (grated and boiled potatoes fried in butter and served with blueberries). Venison and wild boar are standards in forested and mountainous areas, and lamb from Saxony-Anhalt is particularly good. In Thuringia, *Klösse* (potato dumplings) are a religion.

Eastern Germany is experiencing a Renaissance in the art of northern German brewing. The first stop for any beer lover should be the Bayrische Bahnhof in Leipzig, to give Gose a try. Dresden's Brauhaus Watzke, Quedlinburg's Lüddebräu, and even the Lansdkron brewery in Görlitz are bringing craft brewing back to a region inundated with mass-produced brew.

Saxony has cultivated vineyards for more than 800 years, and is known for its dry red and white wines, among them Müller-Thurgau, Weissburgunder, Ruländer, and the spicy Traminer. The Sächsische Weinstrasse (Saxon Wine Route) follows the course of the Elbe River from Diesbar-Seusslitz (north of Meissen) to Pirna (southeast of Dresden). Meissen, Radebeul, and Dresden have upscale wine restaurants, and wherever you see a green seal with the letter *S* and grapes depicted, good local wine is being served. One of the best-kept secrets in German wine making is the Salle-Unstrut region, which produces incredibly spicy Silvaner and Rieslings. Give them a try in Thuringia and Saxony-Anhalt.

Saxon descriptions of the menu's traditional dishes. Upstairs there's a larger wine restaurant with an open fireplace. ⊠ *Barfussgässchen 9* ☎ *0341/960–2078* ⊟ *AE, DC, MC, V.*

¢–$ ╳**Apels Garten.** This elegant little restaurant in the city center pays homage to nature with landscape paintings on the wall, floral arrangements on the tables, and fresh produce on the imaginative menu. In winter the wild-duck soup with homemade noodles is an obligatory starter; in summer try the *Räucherfischsuppe* (smoked fish soup)—you won't find another soup like it in Leipzig. ⊠ *Kolonnadenstr. 2* ☎ *0341/960–7777* ⊟ *AE, MC, V* ⊗ *No dinner Sun.*

¢ ╳**Kaffeehaus Riquet.** ■**TIP**➔ **Afternoon coffee and cake are one of Leipzig's special pleasures (in a country with an obsession for coffee and cake), and Riquet is the best place in the city to satisfy the urge.** The restored art nouveau house dates from 1908. Riquet is a company that has had dealings in the coffee trade in Africa and East Asia since 1745, as is indicated by the large elephant heads adorning the facade of the building. The upstairs section houses a pleasant Viennese-style coffeehouse, while downstairs is noisier and more active. ⊠ *Schulmachergässchen 1* ☎ *0341/961–0000* ⊟ *No credit cards* ⊗ *Closed Mon.*

WHERE TO STAY

$$$$
Fodor'sChoice
★

Hotel Fürstenhof Leipzig. The city's grandest hotel is inside the renowned Löhr-Haus, a revered old mansion 500 meters from the main train station on the ring road surrounding the city center. The stunning banquet section is the epitome of 19th-century grandeur, with red wallpaper and black serpentine stone; the bar is a lofty meeting area under a bright glass cupola. Rooms are spacious and decorated with cherrywood designer furniture. **Pros:** an elegant full service hotel with stunning rooms. **Cons:** the ring road can be noisy at night, expecially on Friday and Saturday. ⊠ *Tröndlinring 8D–04105* ☎ *0341/140–370* ⊕ *www.luxurycollection.com* ⤸ *80 rooms, 12 suites* ⚐ *In-room: refrigerator, safe, dial-up, Wi-Fi (some). In-hotel: restaurant, room service, bar, pool, gym, spa, concierge, public Wi-Fi, laundry service, parking (fee), no-smoking rooms, some pets allowed* ☰ *AE, DC, MC, V.*

$

Renaissance Leipzig Hotel. One of the largest hotels in the city, the Renaissance Leipzig is popular with business travelers because of its quiet atmosphere. It has large, elegant rooms—with fashionable bathrooms in dark marble. The hotel's restaurant serves light nouvelle German cuisine. Although the Renaissance is outside the ring road (it's behind the opera house), it is nonetheless a good spot from which to explore the city on foot. **Pros:** the Club Floor gives you access to nice lounge for about €12 a day. **Cons:** caters primarily to business travelers. ⊠ *Grosser Brockhaus 3D–04103* ☎ *0341/12920* ⊕ *www.renaissancehotels.com* ⤸ *295 rooms, 61 suites* ⚐ *In-room: dial-up, Wi-Fi. In-hotel: restaurant, room service, bar, pool, gym, concierge, laundry service, parking (fee), no-smoking rooms, some pets allowed* ☰ *AE, DC, MC, V* ⌑*BP.*

$

Ringhotel Adagio Leipzig. The quiet Adagio, tucked away behind the facade of a 19th-century city mansion, is centrally located between the Grassimuseum and the Neues Gewandhaus. All rooms are individually furnished; when making a reservation, ask for a "1920s room," which features the style of the Roaring '20s and bathtubs almost as large as a whirlpool. **Pros:** large rooms with luxurious bathrooms, breakfast served at all hours. **Cons:** room decor is slightly bland, hotel not built to accommodate disabled guests. ⊠ *Seeburgstr. 96D–04103* ☎ *0341/216–690* ⊕ *www.hotel-adagio.de* ⤸ *30 rooms, 2 suites, 1 apartment* ⚐ *In-room: no a/c, dial-up. In-hotel: laundry service, parking (fee), no-smoking rooms, some pets allowed* ☰ *AE, DC, MC, V* ⌑*CP.*

NIGHTLIFE & THE ARTS

With a vast assortment of restaurants, cafés, and clubs to match the city's exceptional musical and literary offerings, Leipzig is a fun city at night. The *Kneipenszene* (pub scene) is centered on the **Drallewatsch** (a Saxon slang word for "going out"), the small streets and alleys around Grosse and Kleine Fleischergasse, and the Barfüsschengasse. A magnet for young people is the **Moritzbastei** (⊠ *Universitätsstr. 9* ☎ *0341/702–590*), reputedly Europe's largest student club, with bars, a disco, a café, a theater, and a cinema. Nonstudents are welcome. One of the city's top dance clubs is the hip **Spizz Keller** (⊠ *Markt 9* ☎ *0341/960–8043*). The **Tanzpalast** (⊠ *Dittrichring* ☎ *0341/960–0596*), in the august setting of the *Schauspielhaus* (city theater), attracts a thirtysomething crowd. The upscale bar, pub, and restaurant **Weinstock** (✉ *Markt 7* ☎ *0341/1406–0606*) is in a Renaissance building and offers a huge selection of good wines. A favorite hangout among the city's business elite is the **Schauhaus** (✉ *Bosestr. 1* ☎ *0341/960–0596*), a stylish bar serving great cocktails.

The **Neues Gewandhaus** (✉ *Augustuspl. 8D–04109* ☎ *0341/127–0280* ⊕ *www.gewandhaus.de*), a controversial piece of architecture, is home to an undeniably splendid orchestra. Tickets to concerts are very difficult to obtain unless you reserve well in advance and in writing only. Sometimes spare tickets are available at the box office a half-hour before the evening performance. Leipzig's annual music festival, **Music Days,** is in June.

> ## GOSE
>
> Bismark once remarked that "Gose isn't a beer, it is a way of viewing the world." Gose, which originated in Goslar, is an obscure, top-fermented wheat beer flavored by adding coriander and salt to the wort. Gose came to Leipzig in 1738, and was so popular that by the end of the 1800s it was considered the local brewing style. Gose is extremely difficult to make, and after beer production stopped during the war (due to grain shortages), the tradition seemed lost. Today, through the efforts of Lothar Goldhahn at the Bayrischer Bahnhof, Gose production has returned to Leipzig.

One of Germany's most famous cabarets, the **Leipziger Pfeffermühle** (✉ *Thomaskirchhof 16* ☎ *0341/960–3196*), has a lively bar off a courtyard opposite the Thomaskirche. On pleasant evenings the courtyard fills with benches and tables, and the scene rivals the indoor performance for entertainment. The variety theater **Krystallpalast** (✉ *Magazing. 4* ☎ *0341/140–660* ⊕ *www.krystallpalast.de*) features a blend of circus, vaudeville, and comedy not to be missed.

The **Gohliser Schlösschen** (✉ *Menckestr. 23* ☎ *0341/589–690*), a small rococo palace outside Leipzig's center, frequently holds concerts. It's easily reached by public transportation: take Streetcar 20 or 24 and then walk left up Poetenweg; or take Streetcar 6 to Menckestrasse. Daytime tours can be arranged for groups.

SHOPPING

Small streets leading off the Markt attest to Leipzig's rich trading past. Tucked in among them are glass-roof arcades of surprising beauty and elegance, including the wonderfully restored **Specks Hof, Barthels Hof, Jägerhof,** and the **Passage zum Sachsenplatz.** Invent a headache and step into the *Apotheke* (pharmacy) at Hainstrasse 9—it is spectacularly art nouveau, with finely etched and stained glass and rich mahogany. For more glimpses into the past, check out the antiquarian bookstores of the nearby **Neumarkt Passage.**

The **Hauptbahnhof** (✉ *Willy-Brandt-Pl.*) offers more than 150 shops, restaurants, and cafés. All shops are open Monday through Saturday 9:30 AM–10 PM, and many are also open on Sunday, with the same hours. Thanks to the historic backdrop, it's one of the most beautiful and fun shopping experiences in eastern Germany.

DRESDEN

25 km (16 mi) southeast of Meissen, 140 km (87 mi) southeast of Leipzig, 193 km (120 mi) south of Berlin.

Saxony's capital city sits in baroque splendor on a wide sweep of the Elbe River, and its proponents are working with German thoroughness to recapture the city's old reputation as "the Florence on the Elbe." Its yellow and pale-green facades are enormously appealing, and their mere presence is even more overwhelming when you compare what you see today with photographs of Dresden from February 1945, after an Allied bombing raid destroyed the city overnight. Dresden was the capital of Saxony as early as the 15th century, although most of its architectural masterpieces date from the 18th century and the reigns of Augustus the Strong and his son, Frederick Augustus II.

Though some parts of the city center still look as if they're stuck halfway between demolition and construction, the present city is an enormous tribute to the Dresdeners' skills and dedication. The resemblance of today's riverside to Dresden cityscapes painted by Canaletto in the mid-1700s is remarkable. Unfortunately, the war-inflicted gaps in the urban landscape in other parts of the city are too big to be closed anytime soon.

GETTING HERE & AROUND

Dresden is two hours from Berlin on the Hamburg-Berlin-Prague-Vienna train line. Dresden's international airport serves mostly European destinations with budget airlines. The newly completed Norman Foster train station is a short walk, along the Prager Strasse, from the city center. The city's streetcars are cheap and efficient.

Dresden bus tours (in German and English, run by the Dresdner Verkehrsbetriebe) leave from Postplatz daily at 10, 11:30, and 3; the Stadtrundfahrt Dresden bus tours (also in German and English) leave from Theaterplatz/Augustusbrücke (April–October, daily 9:30–5 every 30 minutes; November–March, daily 10–3, every hour) and stop at most sights.

TIMING

A full day is sufficient for a quick tour of historic Dresden, but if you plan to explore any of the museums, such as the Zwinger, or take a guided tour of the Semperoper, you'll need more than a day.

ESSENTIALS

Tour Information **Dresdner Verkehrsbetriebe AG** (☎ 0351/857–2201 ⊕ www.dvbag.de). **Stadtrundfahrt Dresden** (☎ 0351/899–5650 ⊕ www. stadtrundfahrt.com).

Visitor Information (✉ Dresden Werbung und Tourismus GmbH, Ostraallee 11, ☎ 0351/491–920 🖷 0351/4919–2244 ⊕ www.dresden-tourist.de).

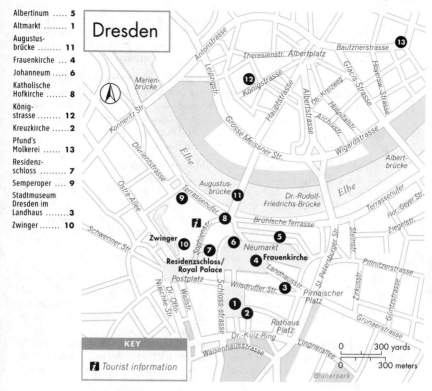

Dresden

KEY

i *Tourist information*

0 ___ 300 yards

0 ___ 300 meters

16

EXPLORING

MAIN ATTRACTIONS

4

Fodor'sChoice

★

Frauenkirche *(Church of Our Lady).* Dresden's Church of Our Lady, completed in 1743, was one of the masterpieces of baroque church architecture. The huge dome set on a smaller square base, known as the Stone Bell, was the inspiration of George Bähr, who designed the church to be built "as if it was a single stone from the base to the top." On February 15, 1945, two days after the bombing of Dresden, the burned-out shell of the magnificent Stone Bell collapsed. For the following five decades the remains of the church, a pile of rubble, remained a gripping memorial to the horrors of war. In a move shocking to the East German authorities, who organized all public demonstrations, a group of young people spontaneously met here on February 13, 1982, for a candlelight vigil for peace.

Although the will to rebuild the church was strong, the political and economic situation in the GDR prevented it. It wasn't until the reunification of Germany that Dresden began to seriously consider reconstruction. In the early 1990s a citizens' initiative, joined by the Lutheran Church of Saxony and the city of Dresden, decided to rebuild the church using the original stones. The goal of completing the church by 2006, Dresden's 800th anniversary, seemed insurmountable. Money soon started started pouring in from around the globe, however, and work began. The rubble was cleared away, and the size and shape of each stone were catalogued. Computer-imaging technology helped place each recovered stone in its original location.

During construction, guided tours and Frauenkirche concerts brought in donations. The biggest supporter of the project in the United Kingdom, the Dresden Trust, is centered in the city of Coventry, itself bombed mercilessly by the German *Luftwaffe* during the war. The Dresden Trust raised more than €600,000, and donated the gold pinnacle cross that now graces the church dome.

On Sunday, October 30, 2005 (almost a year ahead of schedule), Dresden's skyline became a little more complete with the consecration of the Frauenkirche. Leading the service was the Bishop of Coventry. Although the church is usually open to all, it closes frequently for concerts and other events. Check the English-language schedule next to entrance D. ⊠ *An der Frauenkirche* ☎ *0351/498–1131* ⊕ *www.frauenkirche-dresden.org* 🗺 *Free. Cupola and tower €8. Audio guides in English €2.50* ⊙ *Weekdays 10–noon and 1–6. Cupola and tower daily 10–6.*

❼ Residenzschloss *(Royal Palace).* Restoration work is still under way behind the Renaissance facade of this former royal palace, much of which was built between 1709 and 1722. Some of the finished rooms in the **Georgenbau** hold historical exhibits, among them an excellent one on the reconstruction of the palace itself. The palace's main gateway, the Georgentor, has an enormous statue of the fully armed Saxon count George. ■ TIP→ **From April through October, the palace's old Hausmannsturm (Hausmann Tower) offers a wonderful view of the city and the Elbe River.**

But the main attraction is the world-famous **Grünes Gewölbe** (Green Vault). Named after a green room in the palace of Augustus the Strong, the collection is divided into two sections.

The **Neues Grünes Gewölbe** *(New Green Vault)* contains an exquisite collection of unique objets d'art fashioned from gold, silver, ivory, amber, and other precious and semiprecious materials. Among the crown jewels are the world's largest "green" diamond, 41 carats in weight, and a dazzling group of tiny gem-studded figures called *Hofstaat zu Delhi am Geburtstag des Grossmoguls Aureng-Zeb* (the Court at Delhi during the Birthday of the Great Mogul Aureng-Zeb). The unwieldy name gives a false idea of the size of the work, dating from 1708; some parts of the tableau are so small they can be admired only through a magnifying glass. Somewhat larger and less delicate is the drinking bowl of Ivan the Terrible, perhaps the most sensational artifact in this extraordinary museum. The **Historisches Grünes Gewölbe** *(Historic Green Vault* ☎ *0351/4919–2285 for tours* ⊕ *www.skd-dresden.de* 🗺 *€11.50* ⊙ *By appointment only)* is the section of the castle most reflective of Augustus the Strong's obsession with art as a symbol of power. The intricately restored baroque interior is not only a display that highlights the objects in the collection but also an integral part of the presentation itself. The last section of the museum houses the Jewel Room, displaying the ceremonial crown jewels of Augustus the Strong and his son. Access to the Historic Green Vault is limited to 100 visitors per hour and is by appointment only. Tickets can be reserved by phone or online. The palace also houses the **Münzkabinett** (Coin Museum) and the **Kupferstichkabinett** (Museum of Prints and Drawings), with more than 500,000 pieces of art spanning several centuries. Changing exhibits at the Kupferstichkabinett present masterworks by Albrecht Dürer, Peter Paul Rubens, and Jan van Eyck, but also 20th-century art by Otto Dix, Edvard Munch, and Ernst Ludwig Kirchner as well as East European art and some Southeast Asian prints. ✉ *Schlosspl.* ☎ *0351/491–4619* 🖃 *All museums and collections at palace (except Historic Green Vault) €6. Historic Green Vault €11.50* ⏰ *Wed.–Mon. 10–6; Historic Green Vault by appointment only.*

> ### GETTING INTO THE GREEN VAULT
>
> No one should leave Dresden without seeing the Historic Green Vault, but tickets are hard to come by and are often sold out months in advance. Seventy-five percent of the tickets are available for advance purchase, while 25% are held for sale at the door. Even if the advance tickets for the date of your visit are sold out, you should keep checking right up until you get to the city, because it's common for reservations to be canceled. According to the museum, persistence is often rewarded.

16

🔟 **Zwinger** *(Bailey).* Dresden's magnificent baroque showpiece is entered by
Fodor's Choice way of the mighty Kronentor (Crown Gate), off Ostra-Allee. Augustus
★ the Strong hired a small army of artists and artisans to create a "pleasure ground" worthy of the Saxon court on the site of the former bailey, part of the city fortifications. The artisans worked under the direction of the architect Matthäus Daniel Pöppelmann, who came reluctantly out of retirement to design what would be his greatest work, begun in 1707 and completed in 1728. Completely enclosing a central courtyard filled with lawns, pools, and fountains, the complex is made up of six linked pavilions, one of which boasts a carillon of Meissen bells, hence its name: Glockenspielpavillon.

The Zwinger is quite a scene—a riot of garlands, nymphs, and other baroque ornamentation and sculpture. Wide staircases beckon to galleried walks and to the romantic Nymphenbad, a coyly hidden courtyard where statues of nude women perch in alcoves to protect them from a fountain that spits unexpectedly. The Zwinger once had an open view of the riverbank, but the Semper Opera House now closes in that side. Stand in the center of this quiet oasis, where the city's roar is kept at bay by the outer wings of the structure, and imagine the court festivities held here.

The **Gemäldegalerie Alte Meister** *(Gallery of Old Masters* ☎ *0351/491–4679* 🖃 *€6* ⏰ *Tues.–Sun. 10–6),* in the northwestern corner of the complex, was built to house portions of the royal art collections. Among the priceless paintings are works by Dürer, Holbein, Jan van Eyck, Rembrandt, Rubens, van Dyck, Hals, Vermeer, Raphael (*The Sistine Madonna*), Titian, Giorgione, Veronese, Velázquez, Murillo,

Canaletto, and Watteau. On the wall of the entrance archway you'll see an inscription in Russian, one of the few amusing reminders of World War II in Dresden. It reads, in rhyme: MUSEUM CHECKED. NO MINES. CHANUTIN DID THE CHECKING. Chanutin, presumably, was the Russian soldier responsible for checking one of Germany's greatest art galleries for anything more explosive than a Rubens nude. The Zwinger's **Porzellansammlung** (*Porcelain Collection* ☎0351/491–4619 ⊡€5 ⊙ *Tues.–Sun. 10–6*), stretching from the curved gallery that adjoins the Glockenspielpavillon to the long gallery on the east side, is considered one of the best of its kind in the world. The focus, naturally, is on Dresden and Meissen china, but there are also outstanding examples of Japanese, Chinese, and Korean porcelain. The **Rüstkammer** (*Armory* ☎0351/491–4619 ⊡€3 ⊙ *Tues.–Sun. 10–6*) holds medieval and Renaissance suits of armor and weapons ⊠*Zwinger entrance, Ostra–Allee* ⊕*www.skd-dresden.de.*

❾ ★ Semperoper *(Semper Opera House).* One of Germany's best-known and most popular theaters, this magnificent opera house saw the premieres of Richard Wagner's *Rienzi, Der Fliegende Holländer,* and *Tannhäuser* and Richard Strauss's *Salome, Elektra,* and *Der Rosenkavalier.* The Dresden architect Gottfried Semper built the house in 1838–41 in Italian Renaissance style, then saw his work destroyed in a fire caused by a careless lamplighter. Semper had to flee Dresden after participating in a democratic uprising, so his son Manfred rebuilt the theater in the neo-Renaissance style you see today. Even Manfred Semper's version had to be rebuilt after the devastating bombing raid of February 1945. On the 40th anniversary of that raid—February 13, 1985—the Semperoper reopened with a performance of *Der Freischütz,* by Carl Maria von Weber, another artist who did much to make Dresden a leading center of German music and culture. Check the Web site for the performance schedule. Even if you're no opera buff, the Semper's lavish interior can't fail to impress. Velvet, brocade, and well-crafted imitation marble create an atmosphere of intimate luxury (it seats 1,323). Guided tours of the building are offered throughout the day, depending on the opera's rehearsal schedule. Tours begin at the entrance to your right as you face the Elbe River. ⊠*Theaterpl. 2* ☎0351/491–1496 ⊡*Tour €7* ⊙ *Tours usually weekdays at 1:30, 2, and 3; weekends at 10.*

ALSO WORTH SEEING

❺ Albertinum. The Albertinum is named after Saxony's King Albert, who between 1884 and 1887 converted a royal arsenal into a suitable setting for the treasures he and his forebears had collected. This massive, imperial-style building usually houses Dresden's leading art museum, one of the world's great galleries. ⚠ **The Albertinium will be closed for renovation until spring 2010. The art collections will be in storage or lent to other museums until then.** ⊠*Am Neumarkt, Brühlsche Terrasse* ⊕*www.skd-dresden.de.*

❶ Altmarkt *(Old Market Square).* Although dominated by the nearby unappealing Kulturpalast (Palace of Culture), a concrete leftover from the 1970s, the broad square and its surrounding streets are the true center of Dresden. The square's colonnaded beauty (from the Stalin-ist-era architecture of the early 1950s) survived the disfiguring efforts of city planners to turn it into a huge outdoor parking lot. The rebuilt **Rathaus** (Town Hall) is here, as well as the yellow-stucco, 18th-century Landhaus, which contains the Stadtmuseum Dresden im Landhaus.

⓫ Augustusbrücke *(Augustus Bridge)*. This bridge, which spans the river in front of the Katholische Hofkirche, is the reconstruction of a 17th-century baroque bridge blown up by the SS shortly before the end of World War II. The bridge was restored and renamed for Georgi Dimitroff, the Bulgarian Communist accused by the Nazis of instigating the Reichstag fire; after the fall of Communism the original name, honoring Augustus the Strong, was reinstated.

**OFF THE
BEATEN
PATH**

Deutsches Hygiene-Museum Dresden. This unique (even in a country with a national tendency for excessive cleanliness) and unfortunately named museum relates the history of public health and science. The permanent exhibit offers lots of hands-on activities. The building itself housed the Nazi eugenics program, and the special exhibit on this period is not recommended for children under 12. ⊠ *Lingnerpl. 1* ☎ *0351/48460* ⊕ *www.dhmd.de* 💶 *€6* ☾ *Tues.–Sun. 10–6.*

16

❻ Johanneum. At one time the royal stables, this 16th-century building now houses the **Verkehrsmuseum** (Transportation Museum), a collection of historic conveyances, including vintage automobiles and engines. The former **stable exercise yard,** behind the Johanneum and enclosed by elegant Renaissance arcades, was used during the 16th century as an open-air festival ground. A ramp leading up from the courtyard made it possible for royalty to reach the upper story to view the jousting below without having to dismount. More popular even than jousting in those days was *Ringelstechen,* a risky pursuit in which riders at full gallop had to catch small rings on their lances. Horses and riders often came to grief in the narrow confines of the stable yard.

■ TIP→ On the outside wall of the Johanneum is a remarkable example of Meissen porcelain art: a Meissen tile mural of a royal procession, 336 feet long. More than 100 members of the royal Saxon house of Wettin, half of them on horseback, are represented on the giant mosaic of 25,000 porcelain tiles, painted in 1904–07 after a design by Wilhelm Walther. The Johanneum is reached by steps leading down from the Brühlsche Terrasse. ⊠ *Am Neumarkt at Augustusstr. 1* ☎ *0351/86440* ⊕ *www. verkehrsmuseum.sachsen.de* 💶 *€3* ☾ *Tues.–Sun. 10–5.*

❽ Katholische Hofkirche *(Catholic Court Church)*. The largest church in Saxony is also known as the Cathedral of St. Trinitatis. Frederick Augustus II (who reigned 1733–63) brought architects and builders from Italy to construct a Catholic church in a city that had been the first large center of Lutheran Protestantism (like his father, Frederick Augustus II had to convert to Catholicism to be eligible to wear the Polish crown). Inside, the treasures include a beautiful stone pulpit by the royal sculptor Balthasar Permoser and a painstakingly restored 250-year-old organ said to be one of the finest ever to come from the mountain workshops of the famous Silbermann family. In the cathedral's crypt are the tombs of 49 Saxon rulers and a reliquary containing the heart of Augustus the Strong. Owing to restoration work, the cathedral's opening hours may vary. ⊠*Schlosspl.* ☏*0351/484–4712* 🎫*Free* ⊙*Mon.–Thurs. 9–5, Fri. 1–5, Sat. 10–5, Sun. noon–4:30.*

⑫ Königstrasse *(King Street).* The grand estates lining this historic boulevard attest to Dresden's bygone wealth. The street itself was once an important thoroughfare of a residential quarter founded by Augustus the Strong in the early18th century. Some of the meticulously restored buildings house restaurants, shops, and art galleries in their lovely open courtyards. ⊠*Between Grosse Meissner Str. and Albertpl.*

❷ Kreuzkirche *(Cross Church).* Soaring high above the Altmarkt, the richly decorated tower of the baroque Kreuzkirche dates back to 1792. The city's main Protestant church is still undergoing postwar restoration, but the tower and church hall are open to the public. A famous boys' choir, the Kreuzchor, performs here regularly (check Web site or call for scheduled concerts). ⊠*Altmarkt* ☏*0351/439– 390* ⊕*www.dresdner-kreuzkirche.de* 🎫*Tower €1.50* ⊙*Nov.–Mar., weekdays 10–4, Sun. 11–4; Apr.–Oct., daily 10–6.*

⑬ Pfund's Molkerei *(Pfund's Dairy Shop).* This decorative 19th-century shop has been a Dresden institution since 1880, and offers a wide assortment of cheese and other goods. The shop is renowned for its intricate tile mosaics on the floor and walls. Pfund's is also famous for introducing pasteurized milk to the industry; it invented milk soap and specially treated milk for infants as early as 1900. ⊠*Bautzener Str. 79* ☏*0351/808–080* ⊕*www.pfunds.de* ⊙*Mon.–Sat. 10–6, Sun. 10–3.*

OFF THE
BEATEN
PATH
Panometer Dresden. You can step back in time and get a sense of how Dresden looked in 1756 by viewing this 360-degree panorama portrait of the city. Artist Yadegar Asisi's monumental 105 x 27 m painting locates the viewer on the tower of the Stadtschloss, with extremely detailed vistas in all directions. The painting is located in an old natural-gas store. To get here from Dresden Main Station, take S1 or S2 to the station Dresden-Reick (5 minutes). From the Altmarkt take Tram 1 or 2 to the Liebstädterstrasse stop (15 minutes). ⊠*Gasanstaltstr. 8b,* ☏*0351/ 860–3940* ⊕*www.panometer.de* 🎫*€9* ⊙*Tues.–Fri. 9–7, weekends 10–8.*

❸ Stadtmuseum Dresden im Landhaus *(Dresden City Museum at the Landhaus).* The city's small but fascinating municipal museum tells the ups and downs of Dresden's turbulent past—from the dark Middle Ages to the bombing of Dresden in February 1945. There are many peculiar exhibits on display, such as an American 250-kg bomb and a stove made from an Allied bomb casing. ⊠*Wilsdruffer Str. 2* ☏*0351/656– 480* ⊕*www.stmd.de* 🎫*€3* ⊙*Tues.–Sun. 10–6 (Fri. until 8).*

WHERE TO EAT

$
★
✕ Alte Meister. Set in the historic mansion of the architect who rebuilt the Zwinger and named after the school of medieval painters that includes Dürer, Holbein, and Rembrandt, the Alte Meister has a sophisticated old-world flair that charms locals and tourists alike. The food, however, is very current, and the light German nouvelle cuisine with careful touches

of Asian spices and ingredients has earned chef Dirk Wende critical praise. In summer this is one of the city's premier dining spots, offering a grand view of the Semperoper from a shaded terrace. ⊠ *Braun'sches Atelier Theaterpl. 1a* ☎ *0351/481–0426* ▤ *AE, MC, V.*

¢–$ ✕ **Ball und Brauhaus Watzke.** One of the city's oldest microbreweries, the Ballhaus Watzke offers a great reprieve from Dresden's mass-produced Radeberger. Several different homemade beers are on tap (you can even help brew one). Tours of the brewery cost €5 with a tasting or €12.50 with a meal, and you can get your beer to go in a one- or two-liter jug called a *Siphon*. The food is hearty, contemporary Saxon. There is a fantastic panorama view of Dresden and a beer garden. ⊠ *Koetzschenbroderstr. 1* ☎ *0351/852–920* ▤ *AE, MC, V.*

WHERE TO STAY

$$$$ ☷ **Hotel Bülow-Residenz.** One of the most intimate first-class hotels in eastern Germany, the Bülow-Residenz is in a baroque palace built in 1730 by a wealthy Dresden city official. Each spacious room has thick carpets and mostly dark, warm cherrywood furniture as well as individual accents and modern amenities. In summer the verdant courtyard is a romantic setting for dinner. The Caroussel restaurant serves a large variety of sophisticated fish and game dishes. **Pros:** extremely helpful staff. **Cons:** air-conditioning can be noisy, 10 minute walk to the city. ⊠ *Rähnitzg. 19D–01097* ☎ *0351/80030* ⊕ *www.buelow-residenz.de* ⇆ *25 rooms, 5 suites* ⚹ *In-room: no a/c (some), safe, Wi-Fi. In-hotel: restaurant, room service, bar, concierge, laundry service, parking (fee), no-smoking rooms, some pets allowed* ▤ *AE, DC, MC, V.*

$$$ ☷ **Kempinski Hotel Taschenbergpalais Dresden.** Destroyed in wartime
★ bombing but now rebuilt, the historic Taschenberg Palace—the work of the Zwinger architect Matthäus Daniel Pöppelmann—is Dresden's premier address and the last word in luxury, as befits the former residence of the Saxon crown princes. Rooms are as big as city apartments, and suites earn the adjective "palatial"; they are all furnished with bright elm-wood furniture. **Pros:** concierge knows absolutely everything about Dresden. **Cons:** quite expensive extra charges for breakfast and Internet access. ⊠ *Taschenberg 3D–01067* ☎ *0351/49120* ⊕ *www.kempinski-dresden.de* ⇆ *188 rooms, 25 suites* ⚹ *In-room: safe, Ethernet, Wi-Fi. In-hotel: 4 restaurants, room service, bar, pool, concierge, laundry service, parking (fee), no-smoking rooms, some pets allowed* ▤ *AE, DC, MC, V.*

$$ ☷ **artotel Dresden.** The artotel keeps the promise of its rather unusual name. It's all modern, designed by Italian interior architect Denis Santachiara and decorated with more than 600 works of art by Dresden-born painter and sculptor A. R. Penck. It's definitely a place for the artsy crowd; you might find the heavily styled rooms a bit much. The Kunsthalle Dresden and its exhibits of modern art are right next door. Apart from offering art, the hotel's rooms and service have genuine first-class appeal at reasonable prices. **Pros:** art elements make the hotel fun. **Cons:** bathrooms have unusual clear/opaque window, decor is not for everyone. ⊠ *Ostra-Allee 33D–01067* ☎ *0351/49220* ⊕ *www.artotels. de* ⇆ *155 rooms, 19 suites* ⚹ *In-room: dial-up. In-hotel: 2 restaurants,*

16

room service, bar, gym, concierge, laundry service, parking (fee), no-smoking rooms, some pets allowed ⊟*AE, DC, MC, V* ⦿*BP*.

$–$$ 🏨**Rothenburger Hof.** One of Dresden's smallest and oldest luxury hotels, the historic Rothenburger Hof opened in 1865, and is only a few steps away from the city's sightseeing spots. A highlight is the dining room, which gives you some insight as to how Dresden's wealthy wined and dined 150 years ago. The rooms are not very large, but they're comfortable and nicely decorated with furniture that looks antique but, in fact, is reproduction. **Pros:** nice garden and indoor pool. **Cons:** located in Neustadt, about 20 minutes from the city center, street can be noisy in the summer. ✉*Rothenburger Str. 15–17D–01099* ☎*0351/81260* ⊕*www.dresden-hotel.de* ➫*26 rooms, 13 apartments* ♨*In-room: no a/c, Ethernet. In-hotel: room service, public Wi-Fi, bar, pool, gym, laundry service, parking (fee), no-smoking rooms* ⊟*AE, MC, V* ⦿*BP*.

$ 🏨**Hotel Elbflorenz.** This centrally located hotel bears Dresden's somewhat presumptuous nickname *Elbflorenz*, or "Florence on the Elbe." The Italian-designed rooms are bathed in red and yellow tones and sit alongside a garden courtyard. There's a fine sauna and relaxation area, and the hotel's restaurant, Quattro Cani della Citta, serves delicious Italian seafood and other specialties. **Pros:** extrordinary breakfast buffet. **Cons:** in need of renovation, located at edge of city center. ✉*Rosenstr. 36,* ☎*0351/86400* ⊕*www.hotel-elbflorenz.de* ➫*212 rooms, 15 suites* ♨*In-room: safe, dial-up. In-hotel: restaurant, bar, gym, concierge, children's programs (ages infant–14), parking (fee), no-smoking rooms, some pets allowed* ⊟*AE, DC, MC, V* ⦿*BP*.

NIGHTLIFE & THE ARTS

Dresdeners are known for their industriousness and very efficient way of doing business, but they also know how to spend a night out. Most of Dresden's pubs, bars, and *Kneipen* are in the **Äussere Neustadt** district and along the buzzing **Münzgasse** (between the Frauenkirche and the Brühlsche Terrasse).

Folk and rock music are regularly featured at **Bärenzwinger** (✉*Brühlscher Garten* ☎*0351/495–1409*). One of the best bars in town is the groovy and hip **Aqualounge** (✉*Louisenstr. 56* ☎*0351/810–6116*). The name of the **Planwirtschaft** (✉*Louisenstr. 20* ☎*0351/801–3187*) ironically refers to the socialist economic system and attracts an alternative crowd. The hip dance club **Dance Factory** (✉*Bautzner Str. 118* ☎*0351/802–0066*) is in an old Stasi garrison. The **Motown Club** (✉*St. Petersburger Str. 9* ☎*0351/487–4150*) attracts a young and stylish crowd.

The opera in Dresden holds an international reputation largely due to the **Semper Opera House** (*Sächsische Staatsoper Dresden* ✉*Theaterpl.* ⊕*www.semperoper.de* ✉*Evening box office (Abendkasse), left of main entrance* ☎*0351/491–1705*). Destroyed during the war, the building has been meticulously rebuilt and renovated. Tickets are reasonably priced but also hard to come by; they're often included in package tours. ■TIP➡ **Try your luck at reserving tickets at the Web site or stop by the evening box office about a half-hour before the performance.** If that doesn't work, take one of the opera-house tours.

Dresden's fine **Philharmonie Dresden** (*Philharmonic Orchestra Dresden* ✉*Kulturpalast am Altmarkt* ☎*0351/486–6286*) takes center stage in the city's annual music festival, from mid-May to early June. In addition to the annual film festival in April, open-air **Filmnächte am Elbufer** (*Elbe Riverside Film Nights* ✉*Am Königsufer, next to State Ministry of Finance* ☎*0351/899–320*) take place on the bank of the Elbe from late June to late August.

May brings an annual international Dixieland-style **jazz** festival, and the Jazz Autumn festival follows in October. Jazz musicians perform most nights of the week at the friendly, laid-back **Tonne Jazz Club** (✉*Waldschlösschen, Am Brauhaus 3* ☎*0351/802–6017*).

MEISSEN

25 km (15 mi) northwest of Dresden

This romantic city on the Elbe River is known the world over for its porcelain, bearing the trademark crossed blue swords. The first European porcelain was made in this area in 1708, and in 1710 the Royal Porcelain Workshop was established in Meissen, close to the local raw materials.

16

The story of how porcelain came to be produced in Meissen reads like a German fairy tale: the Saxon elector Augustus the Strong, who ruled from 1694 to 1733, urged his court alchemists to find the secret of making gold, something he badly needed to refill a state treasury depleted by his extravagant lifestyle. The alchemists failed to produce gold, but one of them, Johann Friedrich Böttger, discovered a method for making something almost as precious: fine hard-paste porcelain. Already a rapacious collector of Oriental porcelains, Prince August put Böttger and a team of craftsmen up in a hilltop castle—Albrechtsburg—and set them to work.

GETTING HERE & AROUND
Meissen is an easy 45-minute train ride from Dresden. On arrival, exit the station and walk to the left; as you turn the corner expect a beautiful view of Meissen across the river. Trains leave every 30 minutes.

ESSENTIALS
Visitor Information **Tourist-Information Meissen** (✉*Markt 3D–01662* ☎*03521/41940* 🖷*03521/419–419* 🌐*www.touristinfo-meissen.de*).

EXPLORING
The **Albrechtsburg,** where the story of Meissen porcelain began, sits high above Old Meissen, towering over the Elbe River far below. The 15th-century castle is Germany's first truly residential one, a complete break with the earlier style of fortified bastions. In the central *Schutzhof,* a typical Gothic courtyard protected on three sides by high rough-stone walls, is an exterior spiral staircase, the **Wendelstein,** a masterpiece of early masonry hewn in 1525 from a single massive stone block. The ceilings of the castle halls are richly decorated, although many date only from a restoration in 1870. Adjacent to the castle is

an early Gothic cathedral. It's a bit of a climb up Burgstrasse and Amtsstrasse to the castle, but a bus runs regularly up the hill from the Marktplatz. ☎*03521/47070* ⊕*www.albrechtsburg-meissen.de* 🎟*€4, €6 with tour* ⊙*Mar.–Oct., daily 10–6; Nov.–Feb., daily 10–5.*

A set of porcelain bells at the late-Gothic **Frauenkirche** *(Church of Our Lady)*, on the central Marktplatz, was the first of its kind anywhere when installed in 1929.

Near the Frauenkirche is the **Alte Brauerei** *(Old Brewery)*, which dates to 1569 and is graced by a Renaissance gable. It now houses city offices.

The city's medieval past is recounted in the museum of the **Franzis-kanerkirche** *(St. Francis Church)*, a former monastery. ✉*Heinrichspl. 3* ☎*03521/458–857* 🎟*€3* ⊙*Daily 11–5.*

The **Staatliche Porzellan–Manufaktur Meissen** *(Meissen Porcelain Works)* outgrew its castle workshop in the mid-19th century, and today is on the southern outskirts of town. One of its buildings has a demonstration workshop and a museum whose Meissen collection rivals that of the Porcelain Museum in Dresden. ✉*Talstr. 9* ☎*03521/468–208* ⊕*www.meissen.de* 🎟*Museum €8.50; workshop and museum add €3 for guided tour (recommended)* ⊙*May–Oct., daily 9–6; Nov.–Apr., daily 9–5.*

Near the porcelain works is the **Nikolaikirche** *(St. Nicholas Church* ✉*Neumarkt 29)*, which holds the largest set of porcelain figures ever crafted (8¼ feet tall) and also has remains of early Gothic frescoes.

WHERE TO STAY & EAT

$–$$ ✕**Restaurant Vincenz Richter.** Tucked away in a yellow wooden-beam
★ house, this historic restaurant has been painstakingly maintained by the Richter family since 1873. The dining room is adorned with rare antiques, documents, and medieval weapons, as well as copper and tin tableware. Guests can savor the exquisite dishes on the Saxon-German menu while sampling the restaurant's own personally produced white wine; a bottle of the Riesling is a real pleasure. Try the delicious wild rabbit with bacon-wrapped plums, paired with a glass of Kerner *Meissener Kapitelberg*. ✉*An der Frauenkirche 12* ☎*03521/453–285* 💳*AE, DC, MC, V* ⊙*Closed Mon. No dinner Sun.*

¢–$ ✕**Domkeller.** Part of the centuries-old complex of buildings ringing the town castle, this ancient and popular hostelry is a great place to enjoy fine wines and hearty German dishes. It's also worth a visit for the sensational view of the Elbe River valley from its large dining room and tree-shaded terrace. ⊠*Dompl. 9* ☎*03521/457–676* ☰*AE, DC, MC, V.*

$$ ⌐**Mercure Parkhotel Meissen.** This art nouveau villa on the bank of the Elbe sits across from the hilltop castle. Although most of the luxuriously furnished and appointed rooms are in the newly built annexes, try for one in the villa—and for an unforgettable experience book the *Hochzeitssuite* (wedding suite) on the top floor (€203 a night), for its stunning view. The restaurant ($$) serves nouvelle cuisine in a dining room with original stained glass and elegantly framed doors. **Pros:** gorgeous views, elegant rooms, fine dining. **Cons:** villa rooms are not as newly furnished, international chain hotel. ⊠*Hafenstr. 27–31D–01662* ☎*03521/72250* ⊕*www.mercure.de* ⌐*92 rooms, 5 suites* ⌂*In-room: no a/c, Ethernet, dial-up. In-hotel: restaurant, room service, bar, gym, public Wi-Fi, laundry service, parking (fee), no-smoking rooms, some pets allowed* ☰*AE, DC, MC, V* ⌐|*BP.*

THE ARTS
Meissen's cathedral, the **Dom** (⊠*Dompl. 7* ☎*03521/452–490*), has a yearlong music program, with organ and choral concerts every Saturday during the summer. Regular **concerts** (☎*03521/47070*) are held at the Albrechtsburg castle, and in early September the *Burgfestspiele*—open-air evening performances—are staged in the castle's romantic courtyard.

SHOPPING
Meissen porcelain can be bought directly from the **Staatliche Porzellan–Manufaktur Meissen** (⊠*Talstr. 9* ☎*03521/468–700*) and in every china and gift shop in town. To wine connoisseurs, the name "Meissen" is associated with vineyards producing top-quality wines much in demand throughout Germany—try a bottle of Müller-Thurgau, Weissburgunder, or Goldriesling. They can be bought from the producer, **Sächsische Winzergenossenschaft Meissen** (⊠*Bennoweg 9* ☎*03521/780–970*).

BAUTZEN/BUDYŠIN

53 km (33 mi) east of Dresden.

Bautzen has perched high above a deep granite valley formed by the river Spree for more than 1,000 years. Its almost-intact city walls hide a remarkably well-preserved city with wandering back alleyways and fountained squares. Bautzen is definitely a German city, but it is also the administrative center of Germany's only indigenous ethnic minority, the Sorbs.

In the area, the Sorb language enjoys equal standing with German in government and education. Sorbs are known for their colorful folk traditions. As in all Slavic cultures, Easter Sunday is the highlight of the calendar, when ornately decorated eggs are hung from trees and when the traditional *Osterreiten,* a procession of Catholic men on horseback who carry religious symbols and sing Sorbian hymns, takes place.

GETTING HERE & AROUND

Bautzen is exactly halfway between Dresden and Görlitz. Trains leave both cities once every hour; travel time is about an hour.

ESSENTIALS

Visitor Information **Bautzen** (✉ *Tourist-Information Bautzen-Budyšin, Hauptmarkt 1* ☎ *03591/42016* 🖷 *03591/327–629* ⊕ *www.bautzen.de*).

EXPLORING

Bautzen's main market square is actually two squares—the **Hauptmarkt** (Main Market) and the **Fleischmarkt** (Meat Market) are separated by the yellow, baroque **Rathaus** *(City Hall)*. The current City Hall dates from 1705, but there has been a city hall in this location since 1213. Bautzen's friendly tourist information is next door: stop here to pick up a great Bautzen-in-two-hours walking-tour map. ✉ *Fleischmarkt 1.*

Behind the Rathaus is one of Bautzen's most interesting sights. **Dom St. Petri** *(St. Peter's Cathedral)* is Germany's only *Simultankirche,* or simultaneous church. In order to avoid the violence that often occurred during the Reformation, St. Peter's has a Protestant side and a Roman-Catholic side within the same church. A short fence, which once reached a height of 13 feet, separates the two congregations. The church was built in 1213 on the sight of a Milzener (the forerunners of the Sorbs) parish church. ✉ *An der Petrikirche 6* ☎ *03591/31180* ⊕ *www.dompfarrei-bautzen.de* 🖷 *Free* ⊗ *May–Oct., Mon.–Sat. 10–3, Sun. 1–4; Nov.–Apr., daily 11–noon.*

Bautzen's city walls have a number of gates and towers. The most impressive tower is the **Reichenturm** *(Rich Tower),* at the end of Reichenstrasse. Although the tower base dates from 1490, it was damaged in four city fires (in 1620, 1639, 1686, and 1747) and rebuilt, hence its baroque cupola. The reconstruction caused the tower to lean, however, and its foundation was further damaged in 1837. The "Leaning Tower of Bautzen" currently sits about 5 feet off center. ■TIP➡ **The view from the top is a spectacular vista of Bautzen and the surrounding countryside.** ✉ *Reichenstr. 1* ☎ *03591/460431* 🖷 *€1.20* ⊗ *Daily 10–5.*

Erected in 1558, the **Alte Wasserkunst** *(Old Waterworks)* served as part of the town's defensive fortifications, but its true purpose was to pump water from the Spree into 86 cisterns spread throughout the city. It proved so efficient that it provided the city's water supply until 1965. It is now a technical museum. ✉ *Wendischer Kirchhof 7* ☎ *03591/41588* 🖷 *€1.50* ⊗ *Daily 10–5.*

Below the water works and outside the walls, look for three reddish houses. The **Hexenhäuser** *(Witches' Houses)* were the only structures to survive all the city's fires—leading Bautzeners to conclude that they could only be occupied by witches.

WHERE TO STAY & EAT

$$ ✕ **Wjelbik.** The name of Bautzen's best Sorbian restaurant means "pantry." Very popular on Sorb holidays, Wjelbik uses exclusively regional produce in such offerings as the *Sorbisches Hochzeitsmenu* (Sorb wedding feast)—a vegetable and meatball soup followed by beef in creamed horseradish. The restaurant is in a 600-year-old building near the cathedral. ✉ *Kornstr. 7* ☎ *03591/42060* ▤ *MC, V.*

$ 🗹 **Hotel Goldener Adler.** This pleasant hotel occupies a 450-year-old building on the main market square. Great effort has been made to incorporate traditional building elements into the modern and spacious rooms. The restaurant, Bautzen's oldest, serves regional Saxon cuisine. Fondue by candlelight in the wine cellar is highly recommended but must be booked in advance. **Pros:** the best hotel in town, yummy fondue. **Cons:** only worthwhile option in town. ✉ *Hauptmarkt 4* ☎ *03591/48660* ⊕ *www.goldeneradler.de* ⟿ *30 rooms* 🖧 *In-hotel: 2 restaurants, bar, concierge, parking (fee), no-smoking rooms, some pets allowed* ▤ *AE, DC, MC, V.*

GÖRLITZ

48 km (30 mi) east of Bautzen, 60 km (38 mi) northeast of Dresden.

Tucked away on the country's easternmost corner, Görlitz's quiet, narrow cobblestone alleys and exquisite architecture make it one of Germany's most beautiful cities. It was almost completely untouched by the destruction of the Second World War, and as a result it has more than 4,000 historic houses in styles including Gothic, Renaissance, baroque, rococo, Wilhelminian, and art nouveau. Although the city has impressive museums, theater, and music, it's the ambience created by the casual dignity of these buildings, in their jumble of styles, that makes Görlitz so attractive. Notably absent are the typical socialist eyesores and the glass-and-steel modernism found in many eastern German towns.

GETTING HERE & AROUND

Görlitz is the easternmost town in Germany. It's reached by hourly trains from Dresden (1.5 hours) and from Berlin (3 hours, with a change in Cottbus). Görlitz's train station (a wonderful neoclassical building with an art-nouveau interior) is a short tram ride outside of town.

ESSENTIALS

Visitor Information Görlitz (✉ *Tourist-Information, Bruderstr. 1,* ☎ *03581/47570* 🖷 *03581/475–727* ⊕ *www.goerlitz.de*).

16

EXPLORING

The **Karstadt,** dating 1912–13, is Germany's only original art nouveau department store. Its main hall has a colorful glass cupola and several stunning freestanding staircases. The store dominates the Marienplatz, a small square outside the city center that serves as Görlitz's transportation hub. Next to Karstadt is the 15th-century Frauenkirche, the parish church for the nearby hospital and the poor condemned to live outside the city walls. ☒*An der Frauenkirche 5–7* ☎*03581/4600.*

The Dicker Turm (Fat Tower) guards the entrance to the city. The Gothic tower is the oldest in Görlitz, and its walls are 5 m thick.

GÖRLITZ'S SECRET ADMIRER

After German unification, Görlitz was a rundown border town, but renovations costing upward of €400 million returned the city to much of its former splendor. In 1995 it got an additional boost when an anonymous philanthropist pledged to the city a yearly sum of 1 million marks. Every March, Görlitz celebrates the arrival in its cofers of the mysterious Altstadt-Million (albeit, with the change in currency, now €511,000).

The richly decorated Renaissance homes and warehouses on the **Obermarkt** *(Upper Market)* are a vivid legacy of the city's wealthy past. During the late Middle Ages the most common merchandise here was cloth, which was bought and sold from covered wagons and the ground floors of many buildings. Napoleon addressed his troops from the balcony of the house at no. 29.

On the southeast side of the market lies the **Dreifaltigkeitskirche** *(Church of the Holy Trinity)*, a pleasant Romanesque church with a Gothic interior, built in 1245. The interior of the church houses an impressive Gothic triptych altarpiece. The clock on the thin tower is set seven minutes fast in remembrance of a trick played by the city guards on the leaders of a rebellion. In 1527 the city's disenfranchised cloth makers secretly met to plan a rebellion against the city council and the powerful guilds. Their plans were uncovered, and by setting the clock ahead the guards fooled the rebels into thinking it was safe to sneak into the city. As a result they were caught and hanged. On **Verrätergasse** *(Traitors' Alley)*, across the square, is the **Peter-Liebig-Haus,** where the initials of the first four words of the rebels' meeting place, *Der verräterischen Rotte Tor* (the treacherous gang's gate), are inscribed above the door. The Obermarkt is dominated by the **Reichenbach Turm,** a tower was built in the 13th century, with additions in 1485 and 1782. Until 1904 the tower housed the city watchmen and their families. The apartments and armory are now a museum. There are great views of the city from the tiny windows at the top. The massive **Kaisertrutz** (Emperor's Fortress) once protected the western city gates, and now houses late-Gothic and Renaissance art from the area around Görlitz, as well as some impressive historical models of the city. Both buildings are part of the Kulturhistorisches Museum . ☒*Kaisertrutz and Reichenbacher Turm, Platz des 17. Junis* ☎*03581/671–355* ☜*€3.50, tickets valid* *on day of purchase and following day* ⊘ *Tues.–Thurs. and weekends 10–5; Kaisertrutz closed Nov.–Apr.*

The **Untermarkt** *(Lower Market)* is one of Europe's most impressive squares, and a testament to the prosperity brought by the cloth trade. The market is built up in the middle, and the most important building is no. 14, which formerly housed the city scales. The duty of the city scale masters, whose busts adorn the Renaissance facade of the Gothic building, was to weigh every ounce of merchandise entering the city and to determine the taxes due.

The square's most prominent building is the Rathaus. Its winding staircase is as peculiar as its statue of the goddess of justice, whose eyes—contrary to European tradition—are not covered. The corner house on the square, the Alte Ratsapotheke (Old Council Pharmacy), has two intricate sundials on the facade (painted in 1550).

The **Schlesisches Museum** *(Silesian Museum)* explores 900 years of Silesian culture, and is a meeting place for Silesians from Germany, Poland, and the Czech Republic. The museum is housed in the magnificent Schönhof building, one of Germany's oldest Renaissance *Patrizierhäuser* (grand mansions of the city's ruling business and political elite).. ⊠ *Brüderstrasse 8* ☏ *03581/87910* ⊕ *www.schlesisches-museum.de* ☑ *€3* ⊘ *Tues.–Sun. 10–5.*

The **Biblical House** is interesting for its Renaissance facade decorated with sandstone reliefs depicting biblical stories. The Catholic Church banned religious depictions on secular buildings, but by the time the house was rebuilt after a fire in 1526, the Reformation had Görlitz firmly in its grip. ⊠ *Neissestr. 29*

Perched high above the river is the **Kirche St. Peter und Paul** *(St. Peter and Paul Church)*, one of Saxony's largest late-Gothic churches, dating to 1423. The real draw of the church is its famous one-of-a-kind organ, built in 1703 by Eugenio Casparini. The Sun Organ gets its name from the circularly arranged pipes and not from the golden sun at the center. Its full and deep sound, as well as its birdcalls, can be heard on Sunday and Wednesday afternoons. ⊠ *Bei der Peterkirche 5* ☏ *03581/409–590* ☑ *Free* ⊘ *Mon.–Sat. 10:30–4, Sun. 11:30–4; guided tours Thurs. and Sun. at noon.*

OFF THE BEATEN PATH

The Landskron Brewery is Germany's easternmost Brauhaus and one of the few breweries left that give tours. Founded in 1869, Landskron isn't very old by German standards, but it's unique in that it hasn't been gobbled up by a huge brewing conglomerate. Görlitzer are understandably proud of their own Premium Pilsner, but the brewery also produces good dark, Silesian, and winter beers. Landskron Hefeweizen is one of the best in the country. ⊠ *An der Landskronbrauerei* ☏ *03581/465–121* ⊕ *www.landskron.de* ☑ *Tours €6.50–€9.50 by arrangement only* ⊘ *Sun.–Thurs.*

16

$ ✕ **Die Destille.** This small family-run establishment overlooks the Niko-laiturm. The restaurant offers good solid Silesian fare and absolutely the best *Schlesischer Himmelreich* in town. There are also eight inex-pensive, spartan guest rooms where you can stay the night. ⊠*Niko-laistr. 6* ☎*03581/405–302* ⊟*No credit cards* ☉*Sometimes closed in Sept.*

$$ ⊞ **Romantik-Hotel Tuchmacher.** The city's best hotel is also its most mod-★ ern accommodation in antique disguise. In a mansion dating to 1528, guest rooms with wooden floors and thick ceiling beams are sparsely furnished with modern, dark cherrywood furniture. The colorful ceil-ings may remind you of Jackson Pollock paintings, but they are original ornaments from the Renaissance. The Schneider-Stube serves tradi-tional Saxon dishes. **Pro:** luxury hotel in the heart of Görlitz pedestrian zone. **Cons:** limited parking near the hotel, lovers of church bells will be happy. ⊠*Peterstr. 8D–02826* ☎*03581/47310* ⊕*www.tuchmacher.de* ⤶*42 rooms, 1 suite* ⚐*In-room: no a/c, dial-up. In-hotel: restaurant, room service, bar, gym, laundry service, parking (no fee), no-smoking rooms, some pets allowed* ⊟*AE, DC, MC, V* ⵌ*BP.*

$ ⊞ **Hotel Bon-Apart.** The name says it all: this hotel is an homage to Napoléon, whose troops occupied Görlitz, and a splendid departure from a "normal" hotel. Located slightly behind the Marienplatz, the Bon-Apart real draw is the antique-meets-modern interior design. **Pros:** large rooms with kitchens and artistically decorated bathrooms, huge breakfast buffet. **Cons:** eclectic design may not appeal to everyone, neighboring market can be noisy in the morning, no elevator. ⊠*Elis-abethstr. 41D–02826* ☎*03581/48080* ⊕*www.bon-apart.de* ⤶*20 rooms* ⚐*In-room: no a/c, kitchen. In-hotel: restaurant, bar, parking (no fee), no-smoking rooms, some pets allowed, no elevator* ⊟*AE, DC, MC, V.*

SAXONY-ANHALT

The central state of Saxony-Anhalt is a region rich in natural attrac-tions. In the Altmark, on the edge of the Harz Mountains, fields of grain and sugar beets stretch to the horizon. In the mountains them-selves are the deep gorge of the Bode River and the stalactite-filled caves of Rubeland. The songbirds of the Harz are renowned, and though pollution has taken its toll, both the flora and the fauna of the Harz National Park (which encompasses much of the region) are coming back. Atop the Brocken, the Harz's highest point, legend has it that witches convene on Walpurgis Night (the night between April 30 and May 1).

LUTHERSTADT-WITTENBERG

107 km (62 mi) southwest of Berlin, 67 km (40 mi) north of Leipzig.

Protestantism was born in the little town of Wittenberg (officially called Lutherstadt-Wittenberg). In 1508 the fervent, idealistic young

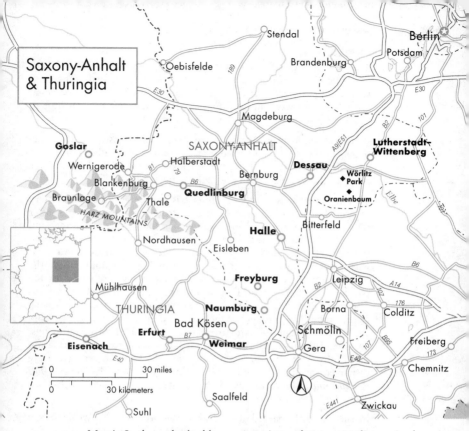

Saxony-Anhalt & Thuringia

Martin Luther, who had become a priest only a year earlier, arrived to study and teach at the new university founded by Elector Frederick the Wise. Nine years later, enraged that the Roman Catholic Church was pardoning sins through the sale of indulgences, Luther posted his 95 Theses attacking the policy on the door of the Castle Church.

Martin Luther is still the center of attention in Wittenberg, and sites associated with him are marked with plaques and signs. You can see virtually all of historic Wittenberg on a 2-km (1-mi) stretch of Collegienstrasse and Schlossstrasse that begins at the railroad tracks and ends at the Schlosskirche (Castle Church).

GETTING HERE & AROUND
Lutherstadt-Wittenberg is approximately halfway between Berlin and Leipzig, and is served by regional and ICE trains. The station is slightly outside the city center, a pleasant walking distance away.

ESSENTIALS
Visitor Information **Wittenberg** (✉ Tourist-Information, Schlosspl. 2 ☎ 03491/498–610 🖷 03491/498–611 ⊕ www.wittenberg.de). **Wittenberg District Rural Information Office** (✉ Neustr. 13 ☎ 03491/402–610 🖷 03491/405–857).

EXPLORING

The best time to visit Wittenberg is during **Luthers Hochzeit** (*Luther's Wedding* ⊕*www.lutherhochzeit.de*), the city festival that commemorates (and reenacts) Martin Luther's marriage to Katharina von Bora. On the second weekend in June the city center goes back in time to 1525, with period costumes and entertainment.

In a small park where Weserstrasse meets Collegienstrasse, the **Luthereiche** *(Luther Oak)* marks the spot where in 1520 Luther burned the papal bull excommunicating him for his criticism of the Church. The present oak was planted in the 19th century.

Fodor'sChoice ★ Within **Lutherhhaus** *(Luther's House)* is the Augustinian monastery where Martin Luther lived both as a teacher-monk and later, after the monastery was dissolved, as a married man. Today it's a museum dedicated to Luther and the Reformation. Visitors enter Lutherhaus through a garden and an elegant door with a carved stone frame; it was a gift to Luther from his wife, Katharina von Bora. Inside the much-restored structure is the monks' refectory, where works by the painter Lucas Cranach the Elder, Luther's contemporary, are displayed. The room that remains closest to the original is the dark, wood-panel Lutherstube. The Luthers and their six children used it as a living room, study, and meeting place for friends and students. Prints, engravings, paintings, manuscripts, coins, and medals relating to the Reformation and Luther's translation of the Bible into the German vernacular are displayed throughout the house. ⊠*Collegienstr. 54* ☎*03491/42030* ⊕*www.martinluther.de* ⌖*€5* ⏺*Apr.–Oct., daily 9–6; Nov.–Mar., Tues.–Sun. 10–5.*

In the elegantly gabled Renaissance **Melanchthonhaus** *(Melanchthon House)*, the humanist teacher and scholar Philipp Melanchthon corrected Luther's translation of the New Testament from Greek into German. Luther was hiding in the Wartburg in Eisenach at the time, and as each section of his manuscript was completed it was sent to Melanchthon for approval. (Melanchthon is a Greek translation of the man's real name, Schwarzerdt, which means "black earth"; humanists routinely adopted such classical pseudonyms.) The second-floor furnishings have been painstakingly re-created after period etchings. ⊠*Collegienstr. 60* ☎*03491/403–279* ⊕*www.martinluther.de* ⌖*€2.50* ⏺*Apr.–Oct., daily 10–6; Nov.–Mar., Tues.–Sun. 10–5.*

From 1514 until his death in 1546, Martin Luther preached two sermons a week in the twin-tower **Stadtkirche St. Marien** *(Parish Church of St. Mary)*. He and Katharina von Bora were married here (Luther broke with monasticism in 1525 and married the former nun). The altar triptych by Lucas Cranach the Elder includes a self-portrait, as well as portraits of Luther wearing the knight's disguise he adopted when hidden away at the Wartburg; Luther preaching; Luther's wife and one of his sons; Melanchthon; and Lucas Cranach the Younger. Also notable is the 1457 bronze baptismal font by Herman Vischer the Elder. On the church's southeast corner you'll find a discomforting juxtaposition of two Jewish-related **monuments**: a 1304 mocking caricature called the Jewish Pig, erected at the time of the expulsion of the town's Jews, and, on the cobblestone pavement, a contemporary memorial to the Jews who died at Auschwitz. ⊠*Kirchpl.* ☎*03491/404–415* 💶*€1.50, including tour* ⊙*May–Oct., daily 10–5; Nov.–Apr., daily 10–4.*

Two statues are the centerpiece of the **Marktplatz** *(market square)*: an 1821 statue of Luther by Johann Gottfried Schadow, designer of the quadriga and Victory atop Berlin's Brandenburg Gate, and an 1866 statue of Melanchthon by Frederick Drake. Their backdrop is the handsome, white High Renaissance **Rathaus** *(Town Hall* ⊠*Markt 26* ☎*03491/421–720* 💶*€3* ⊙*Daily 10–5)*. Gabled Renaissance houses containing shops line part of the square.

The **Cranachhaus** is believed to have been the first home, in town, of Lucas Cranach the Elder, the court painter, printer, mayor, pharmacist, and friend of Luther's. His son, the painter Lucas Cranach the Younger, was born here. Some of the interior has been restored to its 17th-century condition. It's now a gallery with exhibits about Cranach's life and work. ⊠*Markt 4* ☎*03491/420–190* 💶*€3* ⊙*Mon.–Sat. 10–5, Sun. 1–5.*

Renaissance-man Lucas Cranach the Elder, probably the wealthiest man in Wittenberg in his day, lived in two different houses during his years in town. In a second **Cranachhaus,** near the Schlosskirche (Castle Church), he not only lived and painted but also operated a print shop, which has been restored, and an apothecary. The courtyard, where it's thought he did much of his painting, remains much as it was in his day. Children attend the **Malschule** (drawing school) here. ⊠*Schlossstr. 1* ☎*03491/410–912* 💶*Free* ⊙*Mon.–Thurs. 8–4, Fri. 8–3.*

In 1517 the indignant Martin Luther affixed to the doors of the **Schlosskirche** *(Castle Church)* his 95 Theses attacking the Roman Catholic Church's policy of selling indulgences. Written in Latin, the theses might have gone unnoticed had not someone—without Luther's knowledge—translated them into German and distributed them. In 1521 the Holy Roman Emperor Charles V summoned Luther to Worms when Luther refused to retract his position. It was on the way home from his confrontation with the emperor that Luther was "captured" by his protector, Elector Frederick the Wise, and hidden from papal authorities in Eisenach for the better part of a year. Luther's 95 Theses are hung on the original door in bronze. Inside the church, simple bronze plaques mark the burial places of Luther and Melanchthon. ⊠*Schlosspl.* ☎*03491/402–585* 💶*Free, tower € 2* ⊙*May–Oct., Mon.–Sat. 10–5, Sun. 11:30–5; Nov.–Apr., Mon.–Sat. 10–4, Sun. 11:30–4.*

The museum **Haus der Geschichte** is a valiant attempt to evaluate the history of the GDR. The museum provides a fascinating insight into the day-to-day culture of East Germans through the display of over 20,000 objects, ranging from detergent packaging to kitchen appliances. There is a special section dealing with Germans and Russians in the Wittenberg region. ⊠*Schlossstr. 6* ☎*03491/ 409-004* ⊕*www.pflug-ev.de* 💶*€5* ⊙*weekdays 10–5, weekends 11–6.*

16

In 1975 the city erected a typical East German prefab building to house the **Luther Melanchthon Gymnasium** *(Luther Melanchthon High School)*. In the early 1990s, art students contacted Friedensreich Hundertwasser, the famous Austrian architect and avant-garde artist who designed the Hundertwasserhaus in Vienna. Hundertwasser, who argued that there are no universal straight lines or completely flat surfaces in nature, agreed to transform the school, and renovations were completed in 1998. The school is one of three Hundertwasser buildings in eastern Germany and an interesting contrast to the medieval architecture in the rest of the city. Although the building is a school, the students operate a small information office. ⊠*Str. der Völkerfreundschaft 130* 🕾*03491/881–131* ⊕*www.hundertwasserschule.de* 💶*€2* ⊙*Apr.– Oct., Tues.–Fri. 11:30–5, weekends 10–5; Nov.–Mar., Tues.–Fri. 1:30– 4, weekends 10–4.*

The **Wittenberg English Ministry** offers English-speaking visitors the opportunity to worship in the churches where Martin Luther conducted his ministry. During the summer months the ministry brings English-speaking pastors from the United States and provides Lutheran worship services in the Castle Church and in the Parish Church. The services follow German Protestant tradition (albeit in English) and conclude with singing Luther's "A Mighty Fortress Is Our God," accompanied on the organ. The Ministry also offers tours of Wittenberg and other Luther sites. ⊠*Schlosspl. 2* 🕾*03491/498–610* ⊕*www.wittenberg-english-ministry.com* ⊙*May–Oct., Sat. 6:30 at Schlosskirche or Stadtkirche St. Marien, Fri. 11:30 and Wed. 4:30 at Corpus Christi Chapel. Other times by request.*

WHERE TO EAT

$ ✕ **Brauhaus Wittenberg.** This historic brewery-cum-restaurant is the per-
★ fect stop for a cold beer after a long day of sightseeing. ■**TIP→ Set in the Old Town's magnificent Beyerhof, the Brauhaus still produces local beer such as Wittenberger Kuckucksbier.** In the medieval restaurant with its huge beer kettles, you can sample local and South German cuisine; a specialty is the smoked fish, such as eel, trout, and halibut, from the Brauhaus smokery. In summer, try to get a table in the nice and cool courtyard. ⊠*Markt 6* 🕾*03491/433–130* ▭*AE, MC, V.*

$ ✕ **Schlosskeller.** At the back of the Schlosskirche, this restaurant's four dining rooms are tucked away in a basement with 16th-century stone walls and barrel-vaulted ceilings. The kitchen specializes in German dishes, such as *Kümmelfleisch mit Senfgurken* (caraway beef with mustard and pickles). ⊠*Schlosspl. 1* 🕾*03491/480–805* ▭*AE, MC, V.*

DESSAU

35 km (22 mi) southwest of Wittenberg.

The name "Dessau" is known to every student of modern architecture. In 1925–26 architect Walter Gropius set up his highly influential Bauhaus school of design here. Gropius hoped to replace the dark and inhumane tenement architecture of the 1800s with standardized yet spacious and bright apartments. His ideas and methods were used in building 316 villas in the city's Törten section in the 1920s. ■ TIP→ 2009 is international Bauhaus year, so look for special events at any place associated with Bauhaus.

ESSENTIALS

Visitor Information Dessau (✉ *Tourist-Information Dessau, Zerbster Str. 2c* ☎ *0340/204–1442* 🖷 *0340/220–3003* ⊕ *www.dessau.de*).

EXPLORING

★ Architectural styles that would influence the appearance of such cities as New York, Chicago, and San Francisco were conceived in the **Bauhaus Building.** The architecture school is still operating, and the building can be visited. Other structures designed by Gropius and the Bauhaus architects, among them the Meisterhäuser, are open for inspection off Ebertallee and Elballee. ✉ *Gropiusallee 38* ☎ *0340/650–8251* ⊕ *www. bauhaus-dessau.de* 🎟 *€4* ⊙ *Daily 10–6. Meisterhäuser Nov.–mid-Feb., Tues.–Sun. 10–5; mid-Feb.–Oct., Tues.–Sun. 10–6* 🎟 *€5.*

The Bauhaus isn't the only show in town. Professor Hugo Junkers was one of the most famous engineers-cum-inventors of the 20th century, and his factories were at the forefront of innovation in aircraft and industrial design until they were expropriated by the Nazis in 1933. The star of the **Technikmuseum Hugo Junkers** (*Hugo Junkers Technical Museum*) is a completely restored JU-52/3—the ubiquitous German passenger airplane transformed into military transport. The museum also houses a fascinating collection of industrial equipment, machinery, engines, and the original Junkers wind tunnel. ✉ *Kühnauerstr. 161a* ☎ *0340/661–1982* ⊕ *www.technikmuseum-dessau.de* 🎟 *€2.50* ⊙ *Daily 10–5.*

For a contrast to the no-nonsense Bauhaus architecture, look at downtown Dessau's older buildings, including the Dutch-baroque **Georgkirche** (*St. George's Church* ✉ *Georgenstr. 15*), built in 1712.

HALLE

52 km (32 mi) south of Dessau.

Halle is a city that deserves a second look. The first impression given by the ever-under-construction train station and dismal tram ride into town doesn't do justice to this 1,000-year-old city built on the salt trade. It straddles the river Saale, whose name is derived from the German word for salt, and the name Halle comes from the Celtic word for salt. The city has suffered from the shortfalls of Communist urban planning, yet the Old City has an unusual beauty, particularly in its spacious central marketplace, the **Markt,** with its five distinctive sharp-steepled towers.

GETTING HERE & AROUND

Frequent S-bahn trains connect Halle with Leipzig (30 minutes) and with Naumburg (20 minutes).

16

ESSENTIALS

Visitor Information **Halle** (✉ *Stadtmarketing Halle, Grosse Ullrichstr. 60* ☎ *0345/472–330* 🖶 *0345/472–3363* ⊕ *www.halle-tourist.de*).

EXPLORING

Of the four towers belonging to the late-Gothic **Marienkirche** *(St. Mary's Church)*, two are connected by a vertiginous catwalk bridge. Martin Luther preached in the church, and George Frideric Handel (Händel in German), born in Halle in 1685, was baptized at its font. He went on to learn to play the organ beneath its high, vaulted ceiling.

The Markt's fifth tower is Halle's celebrated **Roter Turm** *(Red Tower* ✉ *Markt)*, built between 1418 and 1506 as an expression of the city's power and wealth. The carillon inside is played on special occasions.

The **Marktschlösschen** *(Market Palace)*, a late-Renaissance structure just off the market square, has an interesting collection of historical musical instruments, some of which could have been played by Handel and his contemporaries. ✉ *Marktpl. 13* ☎ *0345/202–9141* 🎟 *Free* 🕑 *Tues.– Fri. 10–7, weekends 10–6.*

Handel's birthplace, the **Händelhaus,** is now a museum devoted to the composer. The entrance hall displays glass harmonicas and curious musical instruments perfected by Benjamin Franklin in the 1760s. ■TIP→ Be sure to look for the small courtyard where Handel played as a child. ✉ *Grosse Nikolaistr. 5* ☎ *0345/500–900* 🎟 *Free* 🕑 *Tues., Wed., and Fri.–Sun. 9:30–5:30, Thurs. 9:30–7.*

The **Moritzburg** *(Moritz Castle)* was built in the late 15th century by the archbishop of Magdeburg after he claimed the city for his archdiocese. The typical late-Gothic fortress, with a dry moat and a sturdy round tower at each of its four corners, was a testament to Halle's early might, which vanished with the Thirty Years' War. Prior to World War II the castle contained a leading gallery of German expressionist paintings, which were ripped from the walls by the Nazis and condemned as "degenerate." Some of the works are back in place at the **Staatliche Galerie Moritzburg,** together with some outstanding late-19th- and early-20th-century art. ■TIP→ You'll find Rodin's famous sculpture *The Kiss* here. ✉ *Friedemann-Bach-Pl. 5* ☎ *0345/212–590* ⊕ *www.moritzburg.halle. de* 🎟 *€4* 🕑 *Tues. 11–8:30, Wed.–Sun. 10–6.*

Halle's only early-Gothic church, the **Dom** *(cathedral),* stands about 200 yards southeast of the Moritzburg. Its nave and side aisles are of equal height, a common characteristic of Gothic church design in this part of Germany. ✉ *Dompl. 3* ☎ *0345/202–1379* 🎟 *Free* 🕑 *June–Oct., Mon.–Sat. 2–4.*

The former archbishop's home, the 16th-century **Neue Residenz** *(New Residence)*, houses the **Geiseltalmuseum** and its world-famous collection of fossils dug from brown coal deposits in the Geisel Valley near Halle. ✉ *Dornstr. 5* ☎ *0345/552–6135* 🎟 *Free* 🕑 *Weekdays 9–noon and 1–5; every 2nd and 4th weekend 9–1.*

Ⓒ The salt trade on which Halle built its prosperity is documented in the **Technisches Halloren- und Salinemuseum** *(Technical Saline Extraction*

Museum). A replica brine mill shows the salt-extraction process, and the exquisite silver-goblet collection of the Salt Workers' Guild (the Halloren) is on display. The old method of evaporating brine from local springs is sometimes demonstrated. The museum is on the south side of the Saale River (cross the Schiefer Bridge to get there). ☒ *Mansfelderstr. 52* ☎ *0345/202–5034* ☒ *€2.10* ☉ *Tues.–Sun. 10–5.*

> ### SALT & CHOCOLATE
>
> In Halle the salt trade was controlled by the *Halloren* (members of the brotherhood of salt workers), who cooked brine into salt on the banks of the Saale river. All that remains of the once incredibly powerful Halloren are the tasty *Halloren-Kügel,* a praline made by the Halloren Schokoladenfabrik, Germany's oldest chocolate factory. The candy is modeled after the silver buttons worn by the Halloren. Very popular in eastern Germany, the chocolates can be purchased just about anywhere—there is an outlet store in the train station.

OFF THE BEATEN PATH

The Halloren Schokoladenfabrik, Germany's oldest chocolate factory, was founded in 1804 and has changed hands several times (including a brief period manufacturing airplane wings during the war). Its Schokoladenmuseum explores 200 years of chocolate production and is unique for a 27-square-meter room made entirely from chocolate. Entrance to the museum also allows you entrance to the glass-enclosed production line, where you can watch almost all aspects of chocolate making. ■ TIP➡ **The factory is on the other side of the train station from the main town. To get here, take Tram 7 to Fiete-Schultze-Strasse and walk back 200 meters.** ☒ *Delitzscherstrasse 70* ☎ *0345/5642–192* ⊕ *www.halloren.de* ☒ *€7* ☉ *Mon.–Sat. 9–4.*

WHERE TO STAY & EAT

Halle's café scene spreads out along the Kleine Ullrichstrasse. It's a good area for searching out an affordable meal and lively conversation.

$–$$ ✕ **Restaurant Mönchshof.** Hearty German fare in heartier portions is served in high-ceiling, dark-wood surroundings. Lamb from Saxony-Anhalt's Wettin region and venison are specialties in season, but there are always fish and crisp roast pork on the menu. The wine list is extensive, with international vintages. The restaurant is popular with locals, and the staff are particularly accommodating with children. ☒ *Talamtstr. 6* ☎ *0345/202–1726* ▭ *AE, MC, V.*

$ ✕ **Hallesches Brauhaus Kühler Brunnen.** Halle's first and best brew-pub serves traditional brewery fare in huge portions at reasonable prices. The Brauhaus is most famous for its large selection of Flammkuchen, a kind of thin-crust pizza originated in the Alsace region of France. The best beer is the brewery's own Hallsch, an amber top-fermented ale served in funky glasses. ☒ *Grosse Nikolaistrasse 2* ☎ *0345/212–570* ▭ No credit cards.

$$ ▦ **Ankerhof Hotel.** The Ankerhof, in an old warehouse, is a unique reflection on Halle's salt-strewn past. All rooms are decorated individually, and most have wooden beams under the ceiling, naked stone walls, and heavy furniture made from exquisite wood. The

16

hotel's Saalkahn restaurant ($–$$) serves both regional and international dishes based on fresh fish and game. The *Geschmorte Hirschkeule "Dubener Heide"* (braised venison shank) is particularly tasty. **Pros:** casual elegance worked into a traditional setting. **Cons:** building creaks and groans when it is windy and can be cold in winter. ⊠ *Ankerstr. 2aD–06108* ☎ *0345/232–3200* ⊕ *www.anker hofhotel.de* ◄🛏 *49 rooms, 1 suite* ⚐ *In-room: no a/c, safe, Ethernet. In-hotel: restaurant, gym, parking (no fee), no-smoking rooms, some pets allowed* ▤ *AE, DC, MC, V* 🍽 *BP.*

THE ARTS

The city of Handel's birth is of course an important music center. Halle is famous for its opera productions, its orchestral concerts, and particularly its choirs. For schedules, prices, and reservations of opera performances staged at the city's renowned **Opernhaus,** call ☎ 0345/5110–0355. The city's main orchestra, the **Philharmonisches Staatsorchester Halle** (*State Philharmonic Orchestra* ⊠ *Grosse Gosenstr. 12* ☎ *0345/523–3141 for concert information and tickets*), performs at the Konzerthalle. The annual **Handel Festival** (☎ *0345/5009–0222*) takes place in the first half of June, and two youth-choir festivals occur in May and October.

> ### SALLE-UNSTRUT: WINE COUNTRY
>
> The Salle-Unstrut is Europe's northernmost wine-growing region, and with more than 30 different grape varieties one of the most diverse. The region stretches from Halle to Eisleben, and has more than 700 vintners operating on a mere 1,600 acres. Grapes are grown on the terraced slopes of rolling hills, guarded by numerous castles and fortresses. The area is easy to explore by the regional train that meanders through the Unstrut Valley once every hour or the bicycle path that stretches along the banks of both rivers.

NAUMBURG

60 km (65 mi) south of Halle

Once a powerful trading and ecclesiastical city, 1,000-year-old Naumburg is the cultural center of the Salle-Unstrut. Although the city is most famous for its Romanesque/Gothic cathedral, it hides a well-preserved collection of patrician houses, winding back alleys, and a marketplace so distinctive that it warrants the appellation "Naumburger Renaissance."

GETTING HERE & AROUND

From the train station the fun way to get into the city is to take the Naumburger Historical Tram, which runs every 30 minutes. A single ride on Europe's smallest tramway, in antique streetcars, costs €1.50.

ESSENTIALS

Visitor Information Naumburg (⊠ *Tourist und Tagungsservice Naumburg, Markt 12* ☎ *03445/273125* 🖨 *03445/273128* ⊕ *www.naumburg-tourismus.deg.de*).

EXPLORING

Perched high above the city and dominating the skyline stands the symbol of Naumburg: the **Dom St. Peter und Paul** *(St. Peter and Paul Cathedral)*. For the most part, the cathedral was constructed during the latter half of the 13th century, and it's considered one of the masterpieces of the late Romanesque period. What makes the cathedral unique, however, is the addition of a second choir in the Gothic style less than 100 years later. The Gothic choir is decorated with statues of the cathedral's benefactors from the workshop of the Naumburger Meister. The most famous statues are of Uta and Ekkehard, the city's most powerful patrons. Uta's tranquil face is everywhere, from postcards to city maps. ⊠*Dompl. 16* ☎*03445/23010* 🎫*€4* ☉*Mon.–Sat. 10–4, Sun. noon–4; guided tours by appointment.*

Naumburg's historic **Marktplatz** lies strategically at the intersection of two medieval trade routes. Although the market burned in 1517, it was painstakingly rebuilt in Renaissance and baroque styles. The Renaissance buildings are so unusual that they are often referred to as being "Naumburger Renaissance." Naumburg's **Rathaus** *(City hall* ⊠*Markt 1)* was rebuilt in 1523, incorporating the remnants of the building destroyed by fire. The **Kaysersches Haus** *(Imperial House* ⊠ *Markt 10)* is supported by seven Gothic gables, and has a carved oak doorway from the Renaissance. The **Schlösschen** *(Little Castle* ⊠*Markt 2)* houses the offices of Naumburg's first and only Protestant bishop, Nikolaus von Amsdorf, who was consecrated by Martin Luther in 1542.

The southern end of the Markt is dominated by the parish church of **St. Wenceslas**. A church has stood on this spot since 1218, but the current incarnation dates from 1426, with interior renovations in 1726. The church is most famous for its huge Hildebrandt Organ, which was tested and tuned by J. S. Bach in 1746. Fans of Lucas Cranach the Elder get their due with two of his paintings, *Suffer the Little Children Come Unto Me* and the *Adoration of the Three*. The 73-meters tall tower belongs to the city, *not* the church, and was used as a watchtower for the city guards, who lived there until 1994. ⊠Topfmarkt ☎03445/208-401 🎫Free, tower €1.50 ☉Mon.–Sat. 10–noon and 2–5, tower daily 10–5.

Naumburg was once ringed by a defensive city wall with five gates. The only remaining gate, the **Marientor**, is a rare surviving example of a dual-portal gate from the 14th century. The museum inside the gate provides a brief history of the city's defenses. ■TIP→**A pleasant walk along the remaining city walls from Marienplatz to the Weingarten is the easiest way to explore the last intact section of Naumburg's wall, moat, and defensive battlements.** ⊠*Marienpl.* ⊕*www.naumburgmuseum.de* 🎫*€0.50* ☉*Daily 10–4:30.*

The philosopher Friedrich Nietzsche's family lived in Naumburg from 1858 to 1897, in a small classical house in the Weingarten. The **Nietzsche Haus Museum** documents the life and times of one of Naumburg's most controversial residents. The exhibition does not delve into Nietzsche's philosophy, but focuses a great deal on his bizarre relationship with his sister and her manipulation of his manuscripts. ✉ *Weingarten 18* ☎ *03445/703–503* ⊕ *www.naumburgmuseum.de* 💲 *€2* ⊗ *Tues.–Fri. 2–5, weekends 10–4*

The **Naumburger Wein und Sekt Manufaktur** produces fine still and sparkling wines on the bank of the Salle River. The 200-year-old monastery is a pleasant 2-km walk or bike ride from Naumburg's city center. Tours of the production rooms and the vaulted cellar, with wine tastings, take place whenever a group forms and last about an hour. The wine garden is a pleasant place to relax on the bank of the river and the restaurant serves small snacks. Larger appetites find relief across the street at the Gasthaus Henne. ✉ *Blütengrund 35* ☎ *03445/202042* ⊕ *www. naumburger.com* 💲 *Tours €5* ⊗ *Daily 11–6, tours given Apr.–Oct.*

WHERE TO STAY & EAT

$ ✗ **Alt-Naumburg.** Enjoy simple but tasty regional specialties directly in front of the Marientor. The Alt-Naumburg beer garden is good place to relax away from the action of the city center. The three-room pension is often booked far in advance. ✉ *Marienpl. 13* ☎ *03445/234–425* 💳 *No credit cards.*

$–$$ 🏨 **Hotel Stadt Aachen.** At this pleasant hotel in a medieval house many of the simply decorated rooms overlook the central market. The staff gladly arranges wine tasting in its own Ottonenkeller. The restaurant Carolus Magnus serves decent regional cuisine with a good selection of local wine. **Pros:** helpful staff. **Cons:** location by the market is sometimes noisy. ✉ *Markt 11 06618* ☎ *03445/2470* ⊕ *www.hotel-stadt-aachen.de* 🛏 *38 rooms* ⚭ *In-hotel: restaurant, parking (fee), no-smoking rooms, some pets allowed* 💳 *AE, DC, MC, V.*

FREYBURG

10 km (6 mi) north of Naumburg.

Stepping off the train in the sleepy town of Freyburg, it is not difficult to see why locals call the area "the Tuscany of the North." With clean, wandering streets, whitewashed buildings, and a huge castle perched on a vine-terraced hill, Freyburg is a little out of place. The town owes its existence to Schloss Neuenburg, which was built by the same Thuringian count who built the Wartburg. Although most visitors head straight for the wine, the historic Old Town and castle certainly warrant a visit.

Freyburg is surrounded by a 1,200-meter-long almost completely intact city wall. The **Ekstädter Tor** was the most important gate into the city, and dates from the 14th century. The gate is dominated by one of the few remaining barbicans in central Germany

ESSENTIALS

Visitor Information **Freyburg** (✉ *Freyburger Fremdenverkehrsverein, Markt 2* ☎ *034464/27260* 🖷 *034464/273760* ⊕ *wwwfreyburg-info.de*).

EXPLORING

In 1225 the Thuringian count Ludwig IV erected **St. Marien Kirche** as a triple-naved basilica and the only church within the city walls. The coquina limestone building, which resembles the cathedral in Naumburg, was renovated in the 15th century into its current form as a single-hall structure. The great carved altarpiece also dates from the 15th century and the baptistery from 1592. ⊠ Markt 2 🎫 Free.

Neuenburg Castle has looked over Freyburg since its foundation was laid in 1090 by the Thuringian Ludwig I. The spacious residential area and huge towers date from the 13th century, when Neuenburg was a part of Thuringia's eastern defenses. The spartan Gothic double-vaulted chapel from 1190 is one of the few rooms that evokes an early medieval past, since most of the castle was renovated in the 15th century. ⊠ *Schloss 1* 🕿 *34464/35530* 🎫 *€6* ⊘ *Tues.–Sun. 10–5.*

The best place to try Salle-Unstrut wine is at the **Winzervereinigung-Freyburg** (Freyburg Vintner's Association). Its 500 members produce some of Germany's finest wines, both white and red, mostly pure varietals, with some limited blends. (A wonderful light red from a hybrid of the Blauer Zweigelt and St. James grape, called Andre, may change how you think about German red wine.) Tastings and tours can be arranged in advance, or you can simply show up. Options range from the simple tour of one of Germany's largest barrel cellars (daily at 1, €3) to the grand tasting (by arrangement, €10.20). The association goes out of its way to cater to the tastes of its guests, and bread, cheese, and water are always in plentiful supply. ⊠ *Querfurter Str. 10* 🕿 *034464/30623* ⊕ *www.winzervereinigung-freyburg.de* ⊘ *Mon.–Sat. 10–6, Sun. 10–4.*

Freyburg is the home of one of Europe's largest producers of sparkling wine, **Rotkäppchen Sektkellerei** *(Little Red Riding Hood Sparkling Wine)*, a rarity in eastern Germany with significant market share in the West. Hour-long tours of the production facility, including the world's largest wooden wine barrel, take place daily at 11 and 2, with additional tours on Saturday and Sunday at 12:30 and 3:30. ⊠ *Sektkellereistr. 5* 🕿 *034464/340* ⊕ *www.rotkaeppchen.de* 🎫 *€5* ⊘ *Daily 10–6.*

WHERE TO EAT

$ ✕ **The Küchenmeisterey.** Where better than a castle serenely overlooking the village of Freyburg for a medieval restaurant? Everything is prepared according to historical recipes with ingredients from the region. Try the roast chicken with honey or any of the grilled meats. Most menu items are available in the spacious beer garden. ⊠ *Schloss 1* 🕿 *034464/ 66200* 🚬 *AE, DC, MC, V* ⊘ *Closed in Jan. No dinner Sun. and Mon.*

QUEDLINBURG

79 km (49 mi) northwest of Halle.

This medieval Harz town has more half-timber houses than any other town in Germany: more than 1,600 of them line the narrow cobblestone streets and squares. The town escaped World War II unscathed, and was treasured in GDR days, though not very well preserved. Today the nicely restored town is a UNESCO World Heritage Site.

For nearly 200 years Quedlinburg was a favorite imperial residence and site of imperial diets, beginning with the election in 919 of Henry the Fowler (Henry I) as the first Saxon king of Germany. It became a major trading city and a member of the Hanseatic League, equal in stature to Köln.

ESSENTIALS

Visitor Information Quedlinburg (⊠ *Tourismus-Marketing GmbH, Markt 2* ☎ *03946/905–624* 🖷 *03946/905–629* ⊕ *www.quedlinburg.de*).

EXPLORING

The Altstadt (Old Town) is full of richly decorated half-timber houses, particularly along Mühlgraben, Schuhof, the Hölle, Breitestrasse, and Schmalstrasse. Notable on the **Marktplatz** are the Renaissance **Rathaus** (Town Hall), with a 14th-century statue of Roland signifying the town's independence, and the baroque 1701 Haus Grünhagen. Street and hiking maps and guidebooks (almost all in German) are available in the information office at the Rathaus. ⊠ *Markt 2* ☎ *03946/90550* 💲 *Free* 🕙 *Mon.–Sat. 9–3.*

The oldest half-timber house in Quedlinburg, built about 1310, is the **Ständerbau Fachwerkmuseum,** now a museum of half-timber construction. ⊠ *Wordg. 3* ☎ *03946/3828* 💲 *€2.50* 🕙 *Nov.–Mar., Fri.–Wed. 10–4; Apr.–Oct., Fri.–Wed. 10–5.*

Placed behind half-timber houses so as not to affect the town's medieval feel is the sophisticated, modern **Lyonel Feininger Gallery.** When the art of American-born painter Lyonel Feininger, a Bauhaus teacher in both Weimar and Dessau, was declared "decadent" by the Hitler regime in 1938, the artist returned to America. Left behind with a friend were engravings, lithographs, etchings, and paintings. The most comprehensive Feininger print collection in the world is displayed here. ⊠ *Finkenherd 5a* ☎ *03946/2238* ⊕ *www.feininger-galerie.de* 💲 *€6* 🕙 *Apr.–Oct., Tues.–Sun. 10–6; Nov.–Mar., Tues.–Sun. 10–5.*

Quedlinburg's largely Renaissance castle buildings perch on top of the Schlossberg (Castle Hill), with a terrace overlooking woods and valley. The grounds include the **Schlossmuseum** *(Castle Museum)*, which has exhibits on the history of the town and castle, artifacts of the Bronze Age, and the wooden cage in which a captured 14th-century robber baron was put on public view. Restored 17th- and 18th-century rooms give an impression of castle life at that time. ⊠ *Schlossberg 1* ☎ *03946/2730* 💲 *€3.50* 🕙 *Mar.–Oct., daily 10–6; Nov.–Feb., Sat.–Thurs. 10–4.*

The simple, graceful **Stiftskirche St. Servatius** *(Collegiate Church of St. Servatius)* is one of the most important and best-preserved 12th-century Romanesque structures in Germany. Henry I and his wife Mathilde are buried in its crypt. The renowned Quedlinburg Treasure of 10th-, 11th-, and 12th-century gold and silver and bejeweled manuscripts is also kept here (what's left of it). In Nazi days SS leader Heinrich Himmler made the church into a shrine dedicated to the SS, insisting that it was only appropriate, since Henry I was the founder of the first German Reich. ✉ *Schlossberg 1* ☎ *03946/709–900* 🔲 *€4* ⊙ *May–Oct., Tues.–Fri. 10–6, Sat. 10–5, Sun. noon–6; Nov.–Apr., Tues.–Sat. 10–4, Sun. noon–4.*

WHERE TO STAY & EAT

$ ✕ **Lüdde Bräu.** Brewing *Braunbier* (a hoppy, bottom-fermented beer)
★ has been a Quedlinburg tradition for several centuries. The Lüdde brewery traces its history back to 1807, when Braunbier breweries dotted the Harz Mountains, and it was the last surviving brewery when it closed its doors in 1966. After German reunification, Georg Lüdde's niece reopened the business, and it remains the only Braunbier brewery in Quedlinburg. Sampling the reemergence of an almost lost German tradition as well as some incredible beer-based game dishes, makes the restaurant well worth a visit—the Braunbier is called *Pubarschknall*. ✉ *Carl-Ritter-Str. 1* ☎ *03946/901–481* ⊕ *www.hotel-brauhaus-luedde.de* 🖃 *MC, V.*

$ 🏨 **Hotel Zum Brauhaus.** The hotel is located in a beautifully restored
★ half-timber house. Many of the rooms have pleasant views of the castle and incorporate the bare load-bearing timbers. Excellent breakfast is served in a huge dining room. **Pros:** friendly staff, location next to Lüdde brewery. **Cons:** a little lacking in the traditional amenities, upper rooms get hot in summer. ✉ *Carl-Ritter-Str. 1D–06484* ☎ *03946/901–481* ⊕ *www.hotel-brauhaus-luedde.de* 🛏 *50 rooms, 1 suite* ⚭ *In-room: no a/c. In-hotel: restaurant, parking (no fee), some pets allowed* 🖃 *MC, V* ⦿ *BP.*

$ 🏨 **Hotel Zur Goldenen Sonne.** Rooms in this baroque half-timber inn
★ are furnished in a pleasing, rustic fashion. The cozy restaurant ($–$$) offers such Harz fare as venison stew with plum sauce and potato dumplings, and smoked ham in apricot sauce. **Pros:** beautiful half-timber house with modern conveniences, reasonable rates. **Cons:** the clock on the square strikes every 15 minutes. ✉ *Steinweg 11D–06484* ☎ *03946/96250* ⊕ *www.hotelzurgoldenensonne.de* 🛏 *27 rooms* ⚭ *In-room: no a/c. In-hotel: restaurant, parking (no fee), no-smoking rooms, some pets allowed* 🖃 *AE, MC, V* ⦿ *BP.*

GOSLAR

48 km (30 mi) northwest of Quedlinburg.

Goslar, the lovely, unofficial capital of the Harz region, is one of Germany's oldest cities and is known for the medieval glamour expressed in the fine Romanesque architecture of the Kaiserpfalz, an imperial palace of the German Empire. Thanks to the deposits of ore close to the town, Goslar was one of the country's wealthiest hubs of trade during the Middle Ages. In this town of 46,000, time seems to have stood still among the hundreds of well-preserved (mostly typical northern German half-timber) houses built over the course of seven centuries. The town has been declared a UNESCO World Heritage Site.

16

Despite Goslar's rapid decline after the breakup of the medieval German empire, the city—thanks to its ore deposits—maintained all the luxury and worldliness born of economic success.

GETTING HERE & AROUND

Hourly trains whisk travelers from Hanover to Goslar in about an hour.

ESSENTIALS

Visitor Information **Goslar** (✉Tourist-Information, Markt 7 ☎05321/78060 🖷05321/780–644 ⊕www.goslarinfo.de).

EXPLORING

The **Rathaus** with its magnificent **Huldigungssaal** (Hall of Honor) dates to 1450 and testifies to the wealth of Goslar's merchants. ✉Markt 7 ☎05321/78060 🗺€3.50 ☉Daily 11–3.

★ The impressive **Kaiserpfalz,** set high above the historic downtown area, dates to the early Middle Ages. It once was the center of German imperial glory, when emperors held their regular diets here. Among the rulers who frequented Goslar were Heinrich III (1039–56) and his successor, Heinrich IV (1056–1106), who was also born in Goslar. You can visit an exhibit about the German medieval kaisers who stayed here, inspect the small chapel where the heart of Heinrich III is buried (the body is in Speyer), and view the beautiful ceiling murals in the Reichssaal (Imperial Hall). ✉Kaiserbleek 6 ☎05321/311–9693 🗺€4.50 ☉Apr.–Oct., daily 10–5; Nov.–Mar., daily 10–4.

The source of the town's riches is outside the city in the **Erzbergwerk Rammelsberg,** the world's only silver mine that was in continuous operation for more than 1,000 years. It stopped operating in 1988, but you can inspect the many tunnels and shafts of the old mine. ✉Bergtal 19 ☎05321/7500 ⊕www.rammelsberg.de 🗺€11, including tour ☉Daily 9–6; tours given as needed 9:30–4:30.

WHERE TO STAY

$$ 🏨 **Kaiserworth-Hotel und Restaurant.** Hidden behind the reddish-brown walls of a 500-year-old house, the seat of medieval tailors and merchants, this hotel offers small but bright, pleasantly furnished rooms. The front rooms have windows on the medieval city market. The restaurant offers reliable German food. ✉Markt 3, ☎05321/7090 ⊕www.kaiserworth.de ⮑66 rooms ⌂In-room: no a/c, dial-up. In-hotel: restaurant, room service, laundry service, parking (fee), no-smoking rooms, some pets allowed ▤AE, DC, MC, V ꭺBP.

THURINGIA

Unlike other eastern states, unassuming Thuringia was not taken from the Slavs by wandering Germanic tribes but has been German since before the Middle Ages. The hilly countryside is mostly rural and forested, and it preserves a rich cultural past in countless small villages, medieval cities, and country palaces. In the 14th century traders used the 168-km (104-mi) Rennsteig ("fast trail") through the dark depths of the Thuringian Forest, and cities such as Erfurt and Eisenach evolved as major commercial hubs. Today the forests and the Erzgebirge mountains are a remote paradise for hiking and fishing. The city of Weimar is one of Europe's old cultural centers, and the short-lived German democracy, the Weimar Republic, was established here in 1918. Thuringia is the land of Goethe and Schiller, but it is also tempered by the ominous presence of one of the Third Reich's most notorious concentration camps, at Buchenwald.

EISENACH

160 km (100 mi) south of Goslar, 95 km (59 mi) northeast of Fulda.

When you stand in Eisenach's ancient market square it's difficult to imagine this half-timber town as an important center of the East German automobile industry. Yet this is where Wartburgs (very tiny, noisy, and cheaply produced cars, which are now collector's items) were made. The cars were named after the Wartburg, the famous castle that broods over Eisenach from atop one of the foothills of the Thuringian Forest. Today West German automaker Opel is continuing the automobile tradition. The GM company built one of Europe's most modern car-assembly lines on the outskirts of Eisenach.

16

GETTING HERE & AROUND

Hourly trains connect Eisenach with Leipzig (2 hours) and Dresden (3 hours). There are frequent connections to Weimar and Erfurt.

ESSENTIALS

Visitor Information **Eisenach** (✉ *Eisenach-Information, Markt 2* ☎ *03691/79230* 🖃 *03691/792–320* ⊕ *www.eisenach-tourist.de*).

EXPLORING

Fodor'sChoice ★ Begun in 1067 (and expanded through the centuries), the mighty **Wartburg Castle** has hosted a parade of German celebrities. Hermann I (1156–1217), count of Thuringia and count palatine of Saxony, was a patron of the poets Walther von der Vogelweide (1170–1230) and Wolfram von Eschenbach (1170–1220). Legend has it that this is where Walther von der Vogelweide, the greatest lyric poet of medieval Germany, prevailed in the celebrated *Minnesängerstreit* (minnesinger contest), which is featured in Richard Wagner's *Tannhäuser.*

Within the castle's stout walls, Frederick the Wise (1486–1525) shielded Martin Luther from papal proscription from May 1521 until March 1522, even though Frederick did not share the reformer's beliefs. Luther completed the first translation of the New Testament from Greek into German while in hiding, an act that paved the way for the Protestant Reformation. You can peek into the simple study in which Luther worked. ■TIP→ **Be sure to check out the place where Luther saw the devil and threw an inkwell at him. Pilgrims have picked away at the spot for centuries, forcing the curators to "reapply" the ink.**

Frederick was also a patron of the arts. Lucas Cranach the Elder's portraits of Luther and his wife are on view in the castle, as is a very moving sculpture, the *Leuchterengelpaar* (Candlestick Angel Group), by the great 15th-century artist Tilman Riemenschneider. The 13th-century great hall is breathtaking; it's here that the minstrels sang for courtly favors. ■ TIP→ **Don't leave without climbing the belvedere for a panoramic view of the Harz Mountains and the Thuringian Forest.** ☎ 03691/2500 ⊕ *www.wartburg-eisenach.de* ✉ *€7, including guided tour* ⊙ *Nov.–Feb., daily 9–3:30; Mar.–Oct., daily 8:30–5.*

The **Lutherhaus,** in downtown Eisenach, has many fascinating exhibits illustrating the life of Luther, who lived here as a student. ⊠ *Lutherpl. 8* ☎ *03691/29830* ⊕ *www.lutherhaus-eisenach.de* ✉ *€3.50* ⊙ *Daily 10–5.*

Johann Sebastian Bach was born in Eisenach in 1685. The **Bachhaus** has exhibits devoted to the entire lineage of the musical Bach family and includes a collection of historical musical instruments. It is the largest collection of Bach memorabilia in the world, and includes a bust of the composer built using forensic science from a cast of his skull. ⊠ *Frauenplan 21* ☎ *03691/79340* ⊕ *www.bachhaus.de* ✉ *€6* ⊙ *Daily 10–6.*

Composer Richard Wagner gets his due at the **Reuter-Wagner-Museum,** which has the most comprehensive exhibition on Wagner's life and work outside Bayreuth. Monthly concerts take place in the old **Teezimmer** (tearoom), a hall with wonderfully restored French wallpaper. The Erard piano, dating from the late 19th century, is occasionally rolled out. ⊠ *Reuterweg 2* ☎ *03691/743–293* ✉ *€3* ⊙ *Tues., Wed., and Fri.–Sun. 11–5, Thurs. 3–8.*

At Johannesplatz 9, look for what is said to be the **narrowest house** in eastern Germany, built in 1890; its width is just over 6 feet, 8 inches; its height, 24½ feet; and its depth, 34 feet.

WHERE TO STAY

$$$–$$$$
★
🏨 **Hotel auf der Wartburg.** In this castle hotel, where Martin Luther, Johann Sebastian Bach, and Richard Wagner were guests, you'll get a splendid view over the town and the countryside. The standard of comfort is above average, and antiques and Oriental rugs mix with modern furnishings. The hotel runs a shuttle bus to the rail station and parking lot of the Wartburg. **Pros:** medieval music and fireplaces in the lobby. **Cons:** it's a hike to and from the city center. ⊠ *Wartburg* ☎ *03691/7970* ⊕ *www.wartburghotel.de* ⇄ *35 rooms* ᗊ *In-room: no a/c, safe, Wi-Fi. In-hotel: 2 restaurants, room service, laundry service, parking (no fee), no-smoking rooms, some pets allowed* ⊟ *AE, DC, MC, V* ⊙I*BP.*

$
🏨 **Hotel Glockenhof.** At the base of Wartburg Castle, this former church-run hostel has blossomed into a handsome hotel, cleverly incorporating the original half-timber city mansion into a modern extension. The excellent restaurant ($–$$) has been joined by a brasserie. The hotel offers many packages that include cultural attractions and city tours. **Pros:** out of the hustle and bustle of the downtown, plenty of park-

ing, an incredible breakfast buffet. **Cons:** uphill walk from the station is strenuous, location is a bit far from the city center. ✉*Grimmelg. 4D–99817* ☎*03691/2340* ⊕*www.glockenhof.de* ⟳*38 rooms, 2 suites* ⚅*In-room: no a/c, dial-up. In-hotel: 2 restaurants, room service, parking (fee), no-smoking rooms, some pets allowed* ▤*AE, DC, MC, V* ⦿|*BP.*

ERFURT

55 km (34 mi) east of Eisenach.

The city of Erfurt emerged from World War II relatively unscathed, with most of its innumerable towers intact. Of all the cities in the region, Erfurt is the most evocative of its prewar self. The city's highly decorative and colorful facades are easy to admire on a walking tour. ■**TIP→** Downtown Erfurt is a photographer's delight, with narrow, busy ancient streets dominated by a magnificent 14th-century Gothic cathedral, the **Mariendom**. The **Domplatz** *(Cathedral Square)* is bordered by houses dating from the 16th century. The pedestrian-zone **Anger** is also lined with restored Renaissance houses. The **Bartholomäusturm** (Bartholomew Tower), the base of a 12th-century tower, holds a 60-bell carillon.

16

ESSENTIALS

Visitor Information **Erfurt** (✉*Tourist-Information, Benediktspl. 1* ☎*0361/66400* ⊞*0361/664–0290* ⊕*www.erfurt-tourist-info.de*).

EXPLORING

On weekends you can take an old-fashioned horse-drawn open-carriage **tour** of Erfurt's Old Town center. Tours leave from the tourist-information office. ✉*Tourist-Information, Benediktspl. 1* ◷*Apr.–Dec., weekdays at 1, weekends at 11 and 1; Jan.–Mar., weekends at 11 and 1.*

★ The **Mariendom** *(St. Mary's Cathedral)* is reached by way of a broad staircase from the expansive Cathedral Square. Its Romanesque origins (foundations can be seen in the crypt) are best preserved in the choir's glorious stained-glass windows and beautifully carved stalls. The cathedral's biggest bell, the Gloriosa, is the largest free-swinging bell in the world. Cast in 1497, it took three years to install in the tallest of the three sharply pointed towers, painstakingly lifted inch by inch with wooden wedges. No chances are taken with this 2-ton treasure; its deep boom resonates only on special occasions, such as Christmas and New Year's. ✉*Dompl.* ☎*0361/646–1265* 🎫*Tour €2.50* ◷*May–Oct., Mon.–Sat. 9–5, Sun. 1–4; Nov.–Apr., Mon.–Sat. 10–11:30 and 12:30–4, Sun. 1–4.*

The Gothic church of **St. Severus** has an extraordinary font, a masterpiece of intricately carved sandstone that reaches practically to the ceiling. It's linked to the cathedral by a 70-step open staircase.

★ Behind the predominantly neo-Gothic Rathaus you'll find Erfurt's most outstanding attraction spanning the Gera River, the **Krämerbrücke** *(Merchant's Bridge)*. This Renaissance bridge, similar to the Ponte Vecchio in Florence, is the longest of its kind in Europe and the only one north of the Alps. Built in 1325 and restored in 1967–73, the bridge served for centuries as an important trading center. Today antiques shops fill the majority of the timber-frame houses built into the bridge, some dating from the 16th century. The bridge comes alive on the third weekend of June for the Krämerbrückenfest.

The area around the bridge, crisscrossed with old streets lined with picturesque and often crumbling homes, is known as **Klein Venedig** *(Little Venice)* because of the recurrent flooding it endures.

Erfurt's main transportation hub and pedestrian zone, **the Anger,** developed as a result of urban expansion due to the growth of the railroad in Thuringia in the early 19th century. With some exceptions, the houses are all architecturally historicized making them look much older than they really are. Look for the **Hauptpostgebäude,** which was erected in 1892 in a mock Gothic style.

The young Martin Luther studied the liberal arts as well as law and theology at Erfurt University from 1501 to 1505. After a personal revelation, Luther asked to become a monk in the **St. Augustin Kloster** *(St. Augustine Monastery)* on July 17, 1505. He became an ordained priest here in 1507, and remained at the Kloster until 1511. Today the Kloster is a seminary and retreat hotel. ⊠ *Augustinerstr. 10* ☎ *0361/ 576–600* ⊕ *www.augustinerkloster.de* ⊙ *Mon.–Sat. 10–noon and 2–4, irregular Sun. hrs.*

Erfurt's interesting local-history museum is in a late-Renaissance house **Zum Stockfisch.** ⊠ *Johannesstr. 169* ☎ *0361/655–5644* 🎫 *Museum €3* ⊙ *Tues.–Sun. 10–6.*

WHERE TO EAT

$$$$ ✕ **Alboth's.** This restaurant in the historic, elegant Kaisersaal edifice is
★   the star in Erfurt's small gourmet sky. Chef Claus Alboth has worked in various top restaurants in Berlin, and now develops his own style and vision of a gourmet restaurant: a cozy, service-oriented oasis in which to enjoy delicious international dishes with a Thuringian accent. If it's offered, order the *Thüringenmenü,* a set four-course dinner with local specialties such as ravioli filled with Thuringian blood sausage. The wine list is one of the best in eastern Germany, offering more than 300 vintages from around the world. ⊠ *Futterstr. 1, 15–16* ⊕ *www. alboths.de* ☎ *0361/568–8207* ⊟ *AE, MC, V* ⊙ *Closed Sun. and Mon. No lunch. Usually closed in Jan. and/or Feb.*

$ ✕ **Faustus Restaurant.** In the heart of historic Erfurt the stylish Faustus defines fine Thuringian dining. This restaurant is in an old mansion, with both an inviting summer terrace and a bright, airy dining room. An after-dinner drink at the superb bar is an absolute must. ⊠ *Wenigermarkt 5* ☎ *0361/540–0954* ⊟ *No credit cards.*

$ ✕ **Luther Keller.** Head down the straw-covered stairs in front of Alboth's restaurant, and you'll find yourself transported to the Middle Ages. The Luther Keller offers simple but tasty medieval cuisine in a candlelit vaulted cellar. Magicians, minnesingers, jugglers, and other players round out the enjoyable experience. Sure, it's pure kitsch, but it is entertaining, and the roast wild boar is delicious. ✉ *Futterstr. 15* ☎ *0361/5688–205* 🍴 *AE, DC, MC, V* ⊘ *Closed Mon.–Sun. No lunch.*

$ ✕ **Zum Goldenen Schwan.** Beer lovers rejoice: in addition to the Braugold brewery, Erfurt has six brewpubs, among which this is by far the best. The house beer is a pleasant unfiltered Kellerbier, and other beers are brewed according to the season. The constantly changing seasonal menu is a step above normal brewpub fare, with the lamb fillet in rosemary–red wine reduction taking the prize. ✉ *Michaelisstr. 9* ☎ *0361/ 262–3742* 🍴 *AE, MC, V* ⊘ *Daily 11* AM–1 AM.

WHERE TO STAY

$$ 🏨 **Radisson SAS Hotel Erfurt.** Since the SAS group gave the ugly high-rise Kosmos a face-lift, the socialist-realist look of the GDR years no longer intrudes on Hotel Erfurt. The hotel underwent several renovations, and the rooms now have bright, modern colors and fabrics (including leather-upholstered furniture). The Classico restaurant ($–$$) serves mostly local dishes and is one of Erfurt's best. **Pros:** a safe, clean option in the city center, fine restaurant. **Cons:** a fairly characterless business hotel. ✉ *Juri-Gagarin-Ring 127D–99084* ☎ *0361/55100* ⊕ *www. radissonsas.com* ⇄ *282 rooms, 3 suites* ⚬ *In-room: Wi-Fi. In-hotel: restaurant, room service, bar, gym, spa, laundry service, parking (fee), no-smoking rooms, some pets allowed* 🍴 *AE, DC, MC, V* ⵙ| *BP.*

OFF THE BEATEN PATH

On the A-4 between Dresden and Erfurt lies the picture-perfect, lost-in-time Thuringian village of **Schmölln.** The town became famous at the end of the 19th as the center of Europe's button trade. Schmölln's industrial ambitions ended with the confiscation of the button industry as war reparations by the Red Army. The **Regional and Button Museum** explores Schmölln's history and culture, while providing a charming insight to the history of the button. ✉ *Sprotter/Ronneburger Strasse* ☎ *034491/7692* ⊕ *www.schmoelln.de* 🎟 *€3* ⊘ *Wed. and Fri. 10–5, weekends 12:30–6.*

Schmölln's medieval Marketplace, which burned in 1772, is the largest in Central Germany and a protected monument.

Schmölln is also famous for *Schmöllner Mutzbraten*, a fist-sized piece of marinated pork-shoulder, spiced with marjoram and spit-roasted over birch. The best place to sample this delicacy is in the beer garden of the **Hotel Reussischer Hof.** (✉ *Gössnitzer Strasse 14* ☎ *034491/231 08* 🍴 *No credit cards)* which is also a good place to spend the night.

Climb the 30 meter high **Ernst-Agnes-Turm,** the Eiffel Tower of East Thuringia, for incredible views of the rolling hills surrounding the Sprotte Valley

WEIMAR

21 km (13 mi) east of Erfurt.

Sitting prettily in the geographical center of Thuringia, Weimar occupies a place in German political and cultural history completely dispro-

16

portionate to its size (population 63,000). It's not even particularly old by German standards, with a civic history that started as late as 1410. Yet by the early 19th century the city had become one of Europe's most important cultural centers, where poets Goethe and Schiller wrote, Johann Sebastian Bach played the organ for his Saxon patrons, Carl Maria von Weber composed some of his best music, and Franz Liszt was director of music, presenting the first performance of *Lohengrin* here. In 1919 Walter Gropius founded his Staatliches Bauhaus here, and behind the classical pillars of the National Theater the German National Assembly drew up the constitution of the Weimar Republic, the first German democracy. After the collapse of the Weimar government, Hitler chose the little city as the site for the first national congress of his Nazi party. On the outskirts of Weimar the Nazis built—or forced prisoners to build for them—the infamous Buchenwald concentration camp.

GETTING HERE & AROUND
Weimar is on the ICE line between Dresden/Leipzig and Frankfurt. IC trains link the city with Berlin. Weimar has an efficient bus system, but most sights are within walking distance in the compact city center.

ESSENTIALS
Visitor Information Weimar (✉ *Tourist-Information Weimar, Markt 10* ☎ *03643/7450* 📠 *03643/745–420* ⊕ *www.weimar.de*).

EXPLORING
Much of Weimar's greatness is owed to its patron, the widowed countess Anna Amalia, whose home, the **Wittumspalais** *(Wittum Mansion)*, is surprisingly modest. In the late 18th century the countess went talent hunting for cultural figures to decorate the glittering court her Saxon forebears had established. Goethe was one of her finds, and he served the countess as a counselor, advising her on financial matters and town design. Schiller followed, and he and Goethe became valued visitors to the countess's home. Within this exquisite baroque house you can see the drawing room in which she held soirées, complete with the original cherrywood table at which the company sat. The east wing of the house contains a small museum that's a fascinating memorial to those cultural gatherings. ✉ *Am Theaterpl.* ☎ *03643/545–377* 💶 *€4* ⊗ *Nov.–Mar., Tues.–Sun. 10–4; Apr.–Oct., Tues.–Sun. 9–6.*

A statue on **Theaterplatz**, in front of the National Theater, shows Goethe placing a paternal hand on the shoulder of the younger Schiller.

Fodor'sChoice
★

Goethe spent 57 years in Weimar, 47 of them in a house two blocks south of Theaterplatz that has since become a shrine attracting millions of visitors. The **Goethe Nationalmuseum** *(Goethe National Museum)* consists of several houses, including the **Goethehaus**, where Goethe lived. It shows an exhibit about life in Weimar around 1750 and contains writings that illustrate not only the great man's literary might but also his interest in the sciences, particularly medicine, and his administrative skills (and frustrations) as minister of state and Weimar's exchequer. You'll see the desk at which Goethe stood to write (he liked to work standing up) and the modest bed in which he died. The rooms are dark and often cramped, but an almost palpable intellectual intensity seems to illuminate them. ⊠*Frauenplan 1* ☎*03643/545–320* ⊕*www.weimar-klassik.de/english* 🎫*€6.50* ⊙*Nov.–Mar., Tues.–Fri. and Sun. 9–4, Sat. 9–7; Apr.–Oct., Tues.–Sun. 9–6.*

The **Schillerhaus,** a green-shuttered residence and part of the Goethe National Museum, is on a tree-shaded square not far from Goethe's house. Schiller and his family spent a happy, all-too-brief three years here (he died here in 1805). Schiller's study is tucked underneath the mansard roof, a cozy room dominated by his desk, where he probably completed *Wilhelm Tell.* Much of the remaining furniture and the collection of books were added later, although they all date from around Schiller's time. ⊠*Schillerstr. 17* ☎*03643/545–350* ⊕*www.klassik-stiftung.de* 🎫*€4* ⊙*Nov.–Mar., Wed.–Mon. 9–4; Apr.–Oct., Wed.–Mon. 9–6.*

Goethe's beloved **Gartenhaus** *(Garden House)* is a modest country cottage where he spent many happy hours, wrote much poetry, and began his masterly classical drama *Iphigenie.* The house is set amid meadowlike parkland on the bank of the River Ilm. Goethe is said to have felt very close to nature here, and you can soak up the same rural atmosphere on footpaths along the peaceful little river. ⊠*Goethepark* ☎*03643/545–375* ⊕*www.weimar-klassik.de/english* 🎫*Cottage €3.50* ⊙*Nov.–Mar., daily 10–4; Apr.–Oct., daily 9–6.*

Goethe and Schiller are buried in the **Historischer Friedhof** *(Historic Cemetery),* a leafy cemetery where virtually every gravestone commemorates a famous citizen of Weimar. Their tombs are in the vault of the classical-style chapel. The cemetery is a short walk past Goethehaus and Wieland Platz. 🎫*Goethe-Schiller vault €2.50* ⊙*Nov.–Mar., Wed.–Mon. 10–1 and 2–4; Apr.–Oct., Wed.–Mon. 9–1 and 2–6.*

On the central town square, at the **Herderkirche** (two blocks east of Theaterplatz), you'll find the home of Lucas Cranach the Elder. Cranach lived here during his last years, 1552–53. Its wide, imposing facade is richly decorated and bears the coat of arms of the Cranach family. It now houses a modern art gallery. The Marktplatz's late-Gothic **Herderkirche** (Herder Church) has a large winged altar started by Lucas Cranach the Elder and finished by his son in 1555.

★ Weimar's 16th-century **Stadtschloss** *(City Castle)* is around the corner from the Herderkirche. It has a finely restored classical staircase, a festival hall, and a falcon gallery. The tower on the southwest projection dates from the Middle Ages, but received its baroque overlay circa 1730. The **Kunstsammlung** (art collection) here includes several works by Cranach the Elder and many early-20th-century pieces by such artists as Böcklin, Liebermann, and Beckmann. ⊠*Burgpl. 4* ☎*03643/545–930* ⊕*www.kunstfreunde-weimar.de* 🎫*€4.50* ⊙*Apr.–Oct., Tues.–Sun. 10–6; Nov.–Mar., Tues.–Sun. 10–4.*

The city is proud of the **Neues Museum Weimar** *(New Museum Weimar),* eastern Germany's first museum exclusively devoted to contemporary art. The building, dating from 1869, was carefully restored and con-

16

verted to hold collections of American minimalist and conceptual art and works by German installation-artist Anselm Kiefer and American painter Keith Haring. In addition, it regularly presents international modern-art exhibitions. ⊠ *Weimarpl. 5* ☎ *03643/545–930* ⊕ *www. kunstsammlungen-weimar.de* ⊠ *€3* ⊙ *Apr.–Oct., Tues.–Sun. 11–6; Nov.–Mar., Tues.–Sun. 11–4.*

Walter Gropius founded the Bauhaus design school in Weimar in 1919. Although the school moved to Dessau in 1925, Weimar's **Bauhaus Museum** is a modest, yet superb collection of the works of Gropius, Johannes Itten, and Henry van de Velde. ⊠ *Theaterpl.* ☎ *03643/545– 961* ⊕ *www.klassik-stiftung.de* ⊠ *€4* ⊙ *Nov.–Mar., Tues.–Sun. 10–4; Apr.–Oct., Tues.–Sun. 10–6.*

OFF THE BEATEN PATH

Gedenkstätte Buchenwald. Just north of Weimar, amid the natural beauty of the Ettersberg hills that once served as Goethe's inspiration, sits the blight of Buchenwald, one of the most infamous Nazi concentration camps. Sixty-five thousand men, women, and children from 35 countries met their deaths here through forced labor, starvation, disease, and gruesome medical experiments. Each is commemorated by a small stone placed on the outlines of the barracks, which have long since disappeared from the site, and by a massive memorial tower. In an especially cruel twist of fate, many liberated inmates returned to the camp as political prisoners of the Soviet occupation; they are remembered in the exhibit Soviet Special Camp #2. Besides exhibits, tours are available. To reach Buchenwald by public transportation, take Bus 6 (in the direction of Buchenwald, not Ettersburg), which leaves every 10 minutes from Goetheplatz in downtown Weimar. The one-way fare is €1.25. ☎ *03643/4300* ⊕ *www.buchenwald.de* ⊠ *Free* ⊙ *May–Sept., Tues.–Sun. 10–5:30; Oct.–Apr., Tues.–Sun. 9–4:30.*

WHERE TO EAT

$ ✕ **Ratskeller.** This is one of the region's most authentic town hall-cellar restaurants. Its whitewashed, barrel-vaulted ceiling has witnessed centuries of tradition. At the side is a cozy bar, where you can enjoy a preprandial drink beneath a spectacular art-nouveau skylight. The delicious sauerbraten and the famous bratwurst (with sauerkraut and mashed potatoes) are the highlights of the Thuringian menu. If venison is in season, try it—likewise the wild duck or wild boar in red-wine sauce. ⊠ *Am Markt 10* ☎ *03643/850–573* ▤ *MC, V.*

¢–$ ✕ **Scharfe Ecke.** If Klösse are a religion, this restaurant is its cathedral. ⟳ Thuringia's traditional *Klösse* (dumplings) are at their best here, but be patient—they're made to order and can take 20 minutes. The Klösse come with just about every dish, from roast pork to venison stew, and the wait is well worth it. The ideal accompaniment to anything on the menu is one of the three locally brewed beers on tap or the fine selection of Salle-Unstrut wines. ⊠ *Eisfeld 2* ☎ *03643/202–430* ▤ *No credit cards* ⊙ *Closed Mon.*

¢–$ ✕ **Sommer's Weinstuben und Restaurant.** The city's oldest pub and restaurant, a 130-year-old landmark in the center of Weimar, is still going strong. The authentic Thuringian specialties and huge *Kartoffelpfannen* (potato pans) with fried potatoes and various kinds of meat are prepared by the fifth generation of the Sommer family, and are as tasty as ever. Add to that the superb wine list with some rare vintages from local vineyards and the romantic courtyard, and your Weimar experience will be perfect. ⊠*Humboldtstr. 2* ☎*03643/400–691* ▤*No credit cards* ⊘*Closed Sun. No lunch.*

¢ ✕**Felsenkeller.** When Ludwig Deinhard purchased the Weimar Stadtbrauerei in 1875, Felsenkeller was already 100 years old. Beer as been brewed here in small batches ever since. Although the brewpub is a outside the city center, it's worth a trip to sample the standard brews and the inventive seasonal selections. The pub serves standard fare at reasonable prices. ⊠*Humboldtstrasse 37* ☎*03643/414–741* ▤*No credit cards* ⊘*Closed Mon.*

WHERE TO STAY

$$ ⛫**Grand Hotel Russischer Hof.** This historic, classical hotel, once the haunt of European nobility and intellectual society, continues to be a luxurious gem in the heart of Weimar—it's one of eastern Germany's finest hotels. Tolstoy, Liszt, Schumann, Turgenev, and others once stayed at this former Russian city palace, whose (partly historic) rooms are decorated today with antique French tapestries, linens, and furniture. The service is impeccable, and the atmosphere is casual yet serene and elegant. The restaurant Anastasia serves fine Austrian-Thuringian cuisine. **Pros:** A quiet hotel in the city center. **Cons:** rooms are on the small side, with thin walls; some overlook an unsightly back courtyard. ⊠*Goethepl. 2* ☎*03643/7740* ⊕*www.russischerhof.com* ⌑*119 rooms, 6 suites* ⌂*In-room: safe, dial-up. In-hotel: restaurant, room service, bar, concierge, laundry service, parking (fee), public Wi-Fi, no-smoking rooms, some pets allowed* ▤*AE, DC, MC, V.*

FodorsChoice ★

$$ ⛫**Hotel Elephant.** The historic Elephant, dating from 1696, is famous for its charm—even through the Communist years. Book here (well in advance), and you'll follow the choice of Goethe, Schiller, Herder, Liszt (after whom the hotel bar is named)—and Hitler—all of whom were guests. Behind the sparkling white facade are comfortable modern rooms decorated in beige, white, and yellow in a timeless blend of art deco and Bauhaus styles. A sense of the past is ever-present. **Pros:** a beautiful historical building right in the city center. **Cons:** no a/c, and the rooms in the front are sometimes bothered by the town clock if windows are open. ⊠*Markt 19D–99423* ☎*03643/8020* ⊕*www.luxurycollection.com* ⌑*94 rooms, 5 suites* ⌂*In-room: no a/c, safe, Ethernet, Wi-Fi (some). In-hotel: 2 restaurants, room service, bar, laundry service, parking (fee), no-smoking rooms, some pets allowed* ▤*AE, DC, MC, V* ⦿*BP.*

FodorsChoice ★

$ ⛫**Amalienhof VCH Hotel.** Book far ahead to secure a room at this friendly little hotel central to Weimar's attractions. The building opened in 1826 as a church hostel. Double rooms are furnished with first-rate antique reproductions; public rooms have the real thing. **Pros:** surprisingly good value, often rooms are upgraded to the highest available category at check-in. **Cons:** street noise can be bothersome ⊠*Amalienstr. 2D–99423* ☎*03643/5490* ⊕*www.vch.de* ⌑*23 rooms, 9 apartments* ⌂*In-room: no a/c. In-hotel: parking (no fee), no-smoking rooms, some pets allowed* ▤*AE, MC, V* ⦿*CP.*

16

UNDERSTANDING GERMANY

GERMANY AT A GLANCE

FAST FACTS

Name in local language: Deutschland
Capital: Berlin
National anthem: *Das Lied der Deutschen (The Song of the Germans)*
Type of government: Federal republic
Administrative divisions: 16 states
Independence: January 18, 1871 (German Empire unification); U.K., U.S., U.S.S.R., and France formally relinquished rights to post–World War II zones on March 15, 1991
Constitution: October 3, 1990
Legal system: Civil law system with indigenous concepts; judicial review of legislative acts in the Federal Constitutional Court
Suffrage: 18 years of age; universal
Legislature: Bicameral parliament consists of the Federal Assembly (603 seats; elected by popular vote under a system combining direct and proportional representation; a party must win 5% of the national vote or three direct mandates to gain representation; members serve four-year terms) and the Federal Council (69 votes; state governments are directly represented by votes; each has 3 to 6 votes depending on population and required to vote as a block)
Population: 82.4 million
Population density: 611 people per square mi
Median age: Female 43.9, male 41.3
Life expectancy: Female 82, male 75.8
Infant mortality rate: 4.1 deaths per 1,000 live births
Literacy: 99%
Language: German (official)
Ethnic groups: German 91.5%; other 6.1%; Turkish 2.4%
Religion: Protestant 34%; Roman Catholic 34%; unaffiliated and other 28.3%; Muslim 3.7%
Discoveries & inventions: Printing press with moveable type, aka "Gutenberg Press" (1440), globe (1492), Bunsen burner (1855), contact lenses (1887), diesel engine (1892), X-ray (1895), Geiger counter (1912), electron microscope (1931), ballistic missile (1944)

German diligence is actually endurance.
—Franz Grillparzer

GEOGRAPHY & ENVIRONMENT

Land area: 349,223 square km (134,836 square mi), slightly smaller than Montana
Coastline: 2,389 km (1,484 mi) along North Sea, Baltic Sea
Terrain: Lowlands in north, uplands in center, Bavarian Alps in south; highest point: Zugspitze 9,721 feet
Natural resources: Arable land, coal, copper, iron ore, lignite, natural gas, nickel, potash, salt, timber, uranium
Natural hazards: Flooding
Environmental issues: Emissions from coal-burning utilities and industries contribute to air pollution; acid rain, resulting from sulfur-dioxide emissions, is damaging forests; pollution in the Baltic Sea from raw sewage and industrial effluents from rivers in eastern Germany; hazardous waste disposal

ECONOMY

Currency: Euro
Exchange rate: €0.69 = $1
GDP: €1.81 trillion ($2.83 trillion)
Per capita income: €20,416 ($31,900)
Inflation: 2.2%
Unemployment: 10.8%
Work force: 43.32 million; services 63.8%; industry 33.4%; agriculture 2.8%
Major industries: Cement, chemicals, coal, electronics, food and beverages, iron, machine tools, machinery, shipbuilding, steel, textiles, vehicles
Agricultural products: Barley, cattle, cabbages, fruit, pigs, potatoes, poultry, sugar beets, wheat

Exports: €866 million ($1.36 trillion)
Major export products: Chemicals, foodstuffs, machinery, metals, textiles, vehicles
Export partners: France 10.3%, U.S. 8.8%, U.K. 8.3%, Italy 7.2%, Netherlands 6.2%, Belgium 5.6%, Austria 5.4%, Spain 5%
Imports: €715 million ($1.121 trillion)
Major import products: Chemicals, foodstuffs, machinery, metals, textiles, vehicles
Import partners: France 9%, Netherlands 8.3%, U.S. 7%, Italy 6.1%, U.K. 5.9%, China 5.6%, Belgium 4.9%, Austria 4.2% (2004)

POLITICAL CLIMATE

Germany's entrance into the European Union was not smooth, leaving political fallout that has been difficult to overcome. Unemployment rose to its highest postwar levels and cutbacks in benefits, which were necessary to meet requirements for the euro, were met with strikes and protests. In 2001 Chancellor Gerhard Schröder's support for the U. S. invasion of Afghanistan strained his coalition. Schröder opposed the U.S.-led war in Iraq in 2003, but disagreement between the Social Democrats and the Greens continued to slow the political agenda. In 2005 federal elections were held after Chancellor Schroeder asked for a Bundestag, or vote of confidence on the SPD-Greens coalition. The July 1, 2005 confidence motion failed, and President Koehler called for elections to be held on September 18, 2005, a year earlier than planned. The results of the main parties of the 2005 Bundestag elections are as follows: CDU 35.2%, SPD 34.2%. After several weeks of negotiations, the CDU/CSU and SPD agreed to form a "grand coalition" under the leadership of Chancellor Angela Merkel. She and the new cabinet were sworn in on November 22, 2005.

DID YOU KNOW?

■ Germany is the world's largest recycler of paper. Almost 80% gets reused, compared to about 35% in the United States.
■ Germany routinely submits more patent applications than any other European country.
■ Between the world wars Germany's inflation was so high that $1 equaled more than 4,000,000,000,000 German Marks.
■ There are 13 breeds of dogs that people are not allowed to breed or sell in Germany because they are labeled "attack dogs." Twenty-nine other breeds are considered potential attack dogs and must be muzzled when walked.
■ German citizens are required to pay special taxes on their dogs.
■ In 1916, Germany became the first country to institute Daylight Savings Time.
■ Munich's Oktoberfest was officially named the world's largest beer festival in 1999, when 7 million people consumed a record 1.5 million gallons of beer in 11 beer tents standing on a site as large as 50 football fields.
■ Many holiday customs originated in Germany, including the Christmas Tree and the Easter Bunny.

CHRONOLOGY

ca. 5000 BC Indo-Germanic tribes settle in the Rhine and Danube valleys

ca. 2000–800 BC Distinctive German Bronze Age culture emerges, with settlements ranging from coastal farms to lakeside villages

ca. 450–50 BC Salzkammergut people, whose prosperity is based on abundant salt deposits (in the area of upper Austria), trade with Greeks and Etruscans; Salzkammerguts spread as far as Belgium and have first contact with the Romans

9 BC–AD 9 Roman attempts to conquer the "Germans"—the tribes of the Cibri, the Franks, the Goths, and the Vandals—and are only partly successful; the Rhine becomes the northeastern border of the Roman Empire (and remains so for 300 years)

212 Roman citizenship is granted to all free inhabitants of the empire

ca. 400 Pressed forward by Huns from Asia, such German tribes as the Franks, the Vandals, and the Lombards migrate to Gaul (France), Spain, Italy, and North Africa, scattering the empire's populace and eventually leading to the disintegration of central Roman authority

486 The Frankish kingdom is founded by Clovis; his court is in Paris

497 The Franks convert to Christianity

EARLY MIDDLE AGES

776 Charlemagne becomes king of the Franks

800 Charlemagne is declared Holy Roman Emperor; he makes Aachen capital of his realm, which stretches from the Bay of Biscay to the Adriatic and from the Mediterranean to the Baltic. Under his enlightened patronage there is an upsurge in art and architecture—the Carolingian renaissance

843 The Treaty of Verdun divides Charlemagne's empire among his three sons: West Francia becomes France; Lotharingia becomes Lorraine (territory to be disputed by France and Germany into the 20th century); and East Francia takes on, roughly, the shape of modern Germany

911 Five powerful German dukes (of Bavaria, Lorraine, Franconia, Saxony, and Swabia) establish the first German monarchy by electing King Conrad I; Henry I (the Fowler) succeeds Conrad in 919

962 Otto I is crowned Holy Roman Emperor by the pope; he establishes Austria—the East Mark. The Ottonian renaissance is marked especially by the development of Romanesque architecture

MIDDLE AGES

1024–1125 The Salian dynasty is characterized by a struggle between emperors and the Church that leaves the empire weak and disorganized; the great Romanesque cathedrals of Speyer, Trier, and Mainz are built

1138–1254 Frederick Barbarossa leads the Hohenstaufen dynasty; there is temporary recentralization of power, underpinned by strong trade and Church relations

1158 Munich, capital of Bavaria, is founded by Duke Henry the Lion; Henry is deposed by Emperor Barbarossa, and Munich is presented to the House of Wittelsbach, which rules it until 1918

1241 The Hanseatic League is founded to protect trade; Bremen, Hamburg, Köln, and Lübeck are early members. Agencies are soon established in London, Antwerp, Venice, and along the Baltic and North seas; a complex banking and finance system results

mid-1200s The Gothic style, exemplified by the grand Köln Cathedral, flourishes

1349 The Black Death plague kills one-quarter of the German population

RENAISSANCE & REFORMATION

1456 Johannes Gutenberg (1400–68) prints the first book in Europe

1471–1553 Renaissance flowers under influence of painter and engraver Albrecht Dürer (1471–1528); Dutch-born philosopher and scholar Erasmus (1466–1536); Lucas Cranach the Elder (1472–1553), who originates Protestant religious painting; portrait and historical painter Hans Holbein the Younger (1497–1543); and landscape-painting pioneer Albrecht Altdorfer (1480–1538). Increasing wealth among the merchant classes leads to strong patronage of the revived arts

1517 The Protestant Reformation begins in Germany when Martin Luther (1483–1546) nails his 95 Theses to a church door in Wittenberg, contending that the Roman Church has forfeited divine authority through its corrupt sale of indulgences. Luther is outlawed, and his revolutionary doctrine splits the Church; much of north Germany embraces Protestantism

1524–30 The (Catholic) Habsburgs rise to power; their empire spreads throughout Europe (and as far as North Africa, the Americas, and the Philippines). Erasmus breaks with Luther and supports reform within the Roman Catholic Church. In 1530 Charles V (a Habsburg) is crowned Holy Roman Emperor; he brutally crushes the Peasants' War, one in a series of populist uprisings in Europe

1545 The Council of Trent marks the beginning of the Counter-Reformation. Through diplomacy and coercion, most Austrians, Bavarians, and Bohemians are won back to Catholicism, but the majority of Germans remain Lutheran; persecution of religious minorities grows

THIRTY YEARS' WAR

1618–48   Germany is the main theater for the Thirty Years' War. The powerful Catholic Habsburgs are defeated by Protestant forces, swelled by disgruntled Habsburg subjects and the armies of King Gustav Adolphus of Sweden. The bloody conflict ends with the Peace of Westphalia (1648); Habsburg and papal authority are severely diminished

ABSOLUTISM & ENLIGHTENMENT

1689   Louis XIV of France invades the Rhineland Palatinate and sacks Heidelberg. At the end of the 17th century, Germany consolidates its role as a center of scientific thought

1708   Johann Sebastian Bach (1685–1750) becomes court organist at Weimar and launches his career; he and Georg Friederic Handel (1685–1759) fortify the great tradition of German music. Baroque and, later, rococo art and architecture flourish

1740–86   Reign of Frederick the Great of Prussia; his rule sees both the expansion of Prussia (it becomes the dominant military force in Germany) and the spread of Enlightenment thought

ca. 1790   The great age of European orchestral music is raised to new heights with the works of Joseph Haydn (1732–1809), Wolfgang Amadeus Mozart (1756–91), and Ludwig van Beethoven (1770–1827)

early 1800s   Johann Wolfgang von Goethe (1749–1832) is part of the Sturm und Drang movement, which leads to Romanticism. Painter Caspar David Friedrich (1774–1840) leads early German Romanticism. Other luminary cultural figures include writers Friedrich Schiller (1759–1805) and Heinrich von Kleist (1777–1811); and composers Robert Schumann (1810–56), Hungarian-born Franz Liszt (1811–86), Richard Wagner (1813–83), and Johannes Brahms (1833–97). In architecture, the severe lines of neoclassicism become popular

ROAD TO NATIONHOOD

1806   Napoléon's armies invade Prussia; it briefly becomes part of the French Empire

1807   The Prussian prime minister Baron vom und zum Stein frees the serfs, creating a new spirit of patriotism; the Prussian army is rebuilt

1813   The Prussians defeat Napoléon at Leipzig

1815   Britain and Prussia defeat Napoléon at Waterloo. At the Congress of Vienna the German Confederation is created as a loose union of 39 independent states, reduced from more than 300 principalities. The Bundestag (national assembly) is established at Frankfurt. Already powerful Prussia increases its territory, gaining the Rhineland, Westphalia, and most of Saxony

1848   The "Year of the Revolutions" is marked by uprisings across the fragmented German Confederation; Prussia expands. A national parliament is elected, taking the power of the Bundestag to prepare a constitution for a united Germany

1862   Otto von Bismarck (1815–98) becomes prime minister of Prussia; he is determined to wrest German-populated provinces from Austro-Hungarian (Habsburg) control

1866   Austria-Hungary is defeated by the Prussians at Sadowa; Bismarck sets up the Northern German Confederation in 1867. A key figure in Bismarck's plans is Ludwig II of Bavaria. Ludwig—a political simpleton—lacks successors, making it easy for Prussia to seize his lands

1867   Karl Marx (1818–83) publishes *Das Kapital*

1870–71 The Franco-Prussian War: Prussia lays siege to Paris. Victorious Prussia seizes Alsace-Lorraine but eventually withdraws from all other occupied French territories

1871   The four South German states agree to join the Northern Confederation; Wilhelm I is proclaimed first kaiser of the united Empire

MODERNISM

1882   The Triple Alliance is forged between Germany, Austria-Hungary, and Italy. Germany's industrial revolution blossoms, enabling it to catch up with the other great powers of Europe. Germany establishes colonies in Africa and the Pacific

ca. 1885 Daimler and Benz pioneer the automobile

1890   Kaiser Wilhelm II (rules 1888–1918) dismisses Bismarck and begins a new, more aggressive course of foreign policy; he oversees the expansion of the navy

1890s   A new school of writers, including Rainer Maria Rilke (1875–1926), emerges. Rilke's *Sonnets to Orpheus* give German poetry new lyricism

1905   Albert Einstein (1879–1955) announces his theory of relativity

1906   Painter Ernst Ludwig Kirchner (1880–1938) helps organize *Die Brücke,* a group of artists who, along with *Der Blaue Reiter,* create the avant-garde art movement expressionism

1907   Great Britain, Russia, and France form the Triple Entente, which, set against the Triple Alliance, divides Europe into two armed camps

1914–18 Austrian archduke Franz-Ferdinand is assassinated in Sarajevo. The attempted German invasion of France sparks World War I; Italy and Russia join the Allies, and four years of pitched battle ensue. By 1918 the Central Powers are encircled and must capitulate

WEIMAR REPUBLIC

1918 Germany is compelled by the Versailles Treaty to give up its overseas colonies and much European territory (including Alsace-Lorraine to France) and to pay huge reparations to the Allies; Kaiser Wilhelm II repudiates the throne and goes into exile in Holland. The tough terms leave the new democracy (the Weimar Republic) shaky

1919 The Bauhaus school of art and design, the brainchild of Walter Gropius (1883–1969), is born. Thomas Mann (1875–1955) and Hermann Hesse (1877–1962) forge a new style of visionary intellectual writing

1923 Germany suffers runaway inflation. Adolf Hitler's Beer Hall Putsch, a rightist revolt, fails; leftist revolts are frequent

1925 Hitler publishes *Mein Kampf* (My Struggle)

1932 The Nazi party gains the majority in the Reichstag (parliament)

1933 Hitler becomes chancellor; the Nazi "revolution" begins. In Berlin, Nazi students stage the burning of more than 25,000 books by Jewish and other politically undesirable authors

NAZI GERMANY

1934 President Paul von Hindenburg dies; Hitler declares himself Führer (leader) of the Third Reich. Nazification of all German social institutions begins, spreading a policy that is virulently racist and anticommunist. Germany recovers industrial might and rearms

1936 Germany signs anticommunist agreements with Italy and Japan, forming the Axis; Hitler reoccupies the Rhineland

1938 The *Anschluss* (annexation): Hitler occupies Austria. Germany occupies the Sudetenland in Czechoslovakia. *Kristallnacht* (Night of Broken Glass), in November, marks the Nazis' first open and direct terrorism against German Jews. Synagogues and Jewish-owned businesses are burned, looted, and destroyed in a night of violence

1939–40 In August Hitler signs a pact with the Soviet Union; in September he invades Poland; war is declared by the Allies. Over the next three years there are Nazi invasions of Denmark, Norway, the Low Countries, France, Yugoslavia, and Greece. Alliances form between Germany and the Baltic states

1941–45 Hitler launches his anticommunist crusade against the Soviet Union, reaching Leningrad in the north and Stalingrad and the Caucasus in the south. In 1944 the Allies land in France; their combined might brings the Axis to its knees. In addition to the millions killed in the fighting, more than 6 million Jews and other victims die in Hitler's concentration camps. Germany is again in ruins. Hitler kills himself in April 1945. East Berlin and what becomes East Germany are occupied by the Soviet Union

THE COLD WAR

1945 At the Yalta Conference, France, the United States, Britain, and the Soviet Union divide Germany into four zones; each country occupies a sector of Berlin. The Potsdam Agreement expresses the determination to rebuild Germany as a democracy

1946 East Germany's Social Democratic Party merges with the Communist Party, forming the SED, which would rule East Germany for the next 40 years

1948 The Soviet Union tears up the Potsdam Agreement and attempts, by blockade, to exclude the three other Allies from their agreed zones in Berlin. Stalin is frustrated by a massive airlift of supplies to West Berlin

1949 The three Western zones are combined to form the Federal Republic of Germany; the new West German parliament elects Konrad Adenauer as chancellor (a post he held until his retirement in 1963). Soviet-held East Germany becomes the Communist German Democratic Republic (GDR)

1950s West Germany, aided by the financial impetus provided by the Marshall Plan, rebuilds its devastated cities and economy—the *Wirtschaftswunder* (economic miracle) gathers speed. The writers Heinrich Böll, Wolfgang Koeppen, and Günter Grass emerge

1957 The Treaty of Rome heralds the formation of the European Economic Community (EEC); West Germany is a founding member

1961 Communists build the Berlin Wall to stem the outward tide of refugees

1969–74 The vigorous chancellorship of Willy Brandt pursues *Ostpolitik,* improving relations with Eastern Europe and the Soviet Union and acknowledging East Germany's sovereignty

mid-1980s The powerful German Green Party emerges as the leading environmentalist voice in Europe

REUNIFICATION

1989 Discontent in East Germany leads to a flood of refugees westward and to mass demonstrations; Communist power collapses across Eastern Europe; the Berlin Wall falls

1990 In March the first free elections in East Germany bring a center-right government to power. The Communists, faced with corruption scandals, suffer a big defeat but are represented (as Democratic Socialists) in the new, democratic parliament. The World War II victors hold talks with the two German governments, and the Soviet Union gives its support for reunification. Economic union takes place on July 1, with full political unity on October 3. In December, in the first democratic national German elections in 58 years, Chancellor Helmut Kohl's three-party coalition is reelected

1991   Nine months of emotional debate end on June 20, when parliamentary representatives vote to move the capital from Bonn—seat of the West German government since 1949—to Berlin, the capital of Germany until the end of World War II

1998   Helmut Kohl's record 16-year-long chancellorship of Germany ends with the election of Gerhard Schröder. Schröder's Social Democratic Party (SPD) pursues a coalition with the Greens in order to replace the three-party coalition of the Christian Democratic Union, Christian Social Union, and Free Democratic Party

1999   The Bundestag, the German parliament, returns to the restored Reichstag in Berlin on April 19. The German federal government also leaves Bonn for Berlin, making Berlin capital of Germany again

1999–2003   For the first time since 1945, the German army (the Bundeswehr) is deployed in combat missions in the former Yugoslavia and Afghanistan

2000   Hannover hosts Germany's first world's exposition, EXPO 2000, the largest ever staged in the 150-year history of the event

2005   Chancellor Schröder asks for a vote of confidence in parliament and fails. After a new election in September, Angela Merkel (CDU) becomes the new chancellor with a "grand coalition" of CDU/CSU and SPD

2006   Germany hosts the 2006 FIFA World Cup, the world's soccer championship

2007   Angela Merkel as German Chancellor and also in her role as the then President of the Council of the European Union hosts the G-8 summit in Heiligendamm, Germany

GERMAN VOCABULARY

	ENGLISH	GERMAN	PRONUNCIATION
BASICS			
	Yes/no	Ja/nein	yah/nine
	Please	Bitte	**bit**-uh
	Thank you (very much)	Danke (vielen Dank)	**dahn**-kuh (**fee**-lun- dahnk)
	Excuse me	Entschuldigen Sie	ent-**shool**-de-gen zee
	I'm sorry.	Es tut mir leid.	es toot meer lite
	Good day	Guten Tag	**goo**-ten tahk
	Good bye	Auf Wiedersehen	auf **vee**-der-zane
	Mr./Mrs.	Herr/Frau	hair/frau
	Miss	Fräulein	**froy**-line
NUMBERS			
	1	ein(s)	eint(s)
	2	zwei	tsvai
	3	drei	dry
	4	vier	fear
	5	fünf	fumph
	6	sechs	zex
	7	sieben	**zee**-ben
	8	acht	ahkt
	9	neun	noyn
	10	zehn	tsane
DAYS OF THE WEEK			
	Sunday	Sonntag	**zone**- tahk
	Monday	Montag	**moan**-tahk
	Tuesday	Dienstag	**deens**- tahk
	Wednesday	Mittwoch	**mit**-voah
	Thursday	Donnerstag	**doe**-ners-tahk
	Friday	Freitag	**fry**-tahk
	Saturday	Sámstag/ Sonnabend	**zahm**-stakh/**zonn**-a-bent

ENGLISH	GERMAN	PRONUNCIATION

USEFUL PHRASES

ENGLISH	GERMAN	PRONUNCIATION
Do you speak	Sprechen Sie	**shprek**-hun zee
English?	Englisch?	**eng**-glish?
I don't speak	Ich spreche kein	ich **shprek**-uh kine
German.	Deutsch.	doych
Please speak	Bitte sprechen Sie	**bit**-uh **shprek**-en-
slowly.	langsam.	zee **lahng**-zahm
I am	Ich bin	ich bin
American/	Amerikaner(in)/	a-mer-i-**kahn**-er(in)/
British	Engländer(in)	**eng**-glan-der(in)
My name is . . .	Ich heiße . . .	ich **hi**-suh
Where are the	Wo ist die	vo ist dee
restrooms?	Toilette?	twah-**let**-uh
Left/right	links/rechts	links/rechts
Open/closed	offen/geschlossen	O-fen/geh-**shloss**-en
Where is . . .	Wo ist . . .	**vo** ist
the train station?	der Bahnhof?	**dare bahn-hof**
the bus stop?	die Bushaltestelle?	**dee booss-hahlt-uh-shtel-uh**
the subway	die U-Bahn-	dee oo-bahn-**staht-**
station?	Station?	sion
the airport?	der Flugplatz?	dare **floog**-plats
the post office?	die Post?	dee **post**
the bank?	die Bank?	dee **banhk**
the police station?	die Polizeistation?	dee po-lee-tsai- **staht**-sion
the Hospital?	das Krankenhaus?	dahs **krahnk**-en-house
the telephone	das Telefon	**dahs te-le-fone**
I'd like . . .	Ich hätte gerne . . .	ich **het**-uh gairn . . .
A room	ein Zimmer	ein **tsim**-er
the key	den Schlüssel	den **shluh**-sul
A map	eine Stadtplan	**I**-nuh **staht**-plahn

ENGLISH	GERMAN	PRONUNCIATION
A ticket	eine Karte	I-nuh cart-uh
How much is it?	Wieviel kostet das?	**vee-feel cost**-et dahs?
I am ill/sick	Ich bin krank	ich bin krahnk
I need . . .	Ich brauche . . .	ich **brow**-khuh
A doctor	einen Arzt	**I-nen** artst
the police	die Polizei	dee po-li-**tsai**
help	Hilfe	**hilf-uh**
Stop!	Halt!	hahlt
Fire!	Feuer!	**foy**-er
Look out/Caution!	Achtung!/Vorsicht!	**ahk**-tung/**for**-zicht

DINING OUT

A bottle of . . .	eine Flasche . . .	I-nuh **flash**-uh
A cup of . . .	eine Tasse . . .	I-nuh **tahs**-uh
A glass of . . .	ein Glas . . .	ein glahss
Ashtray	der Aschenbecher	dare **Ahsh**-en-bekh-er
Bill/check	die Rechnung	dee **rekh**-nung
Do you have . . .?	Haben Sie . . .?	**hah**-ben zee
I am a vegetarian.	Ich bin Vegetarier(in)	ich bin ve-guh-**tah**- re-er
I'd like to order . . .	Ich möchte . . . bestellen	ich **mohr**-shtuh . . . buh-**shtel**-en
Menu	die Speisekarte	dee **shpie**-zeh-car-tuh
Napkin	die Serviette	dee zair-vee-**eh**-tuh

MENU GUIDE

ENGLISH	GERMAN

GENERAL DINING

Side dishes	Beilagen
Extra charge	Extraaufschlag
When available	Falls verfügbar
Entrées	Hauptspeisen
(not) included	. . .(nicht) inbegriffen
Depending on the season	je nach Saison
Lunch menu	Mittagskarte
Desserts	Nachspeisen
at your choice	. . . nach Wahl
at your request	. . . nach Wunsch
Prices are . . .	Preise sind . . .
Service included	inklusive Bedienung
Value added tax included	inklusive Mehrwertsteuer (Mwst.)
Specialty of the house	Spezialität des Hauses
Soup of the day	Tagessuppe
Appetizers	Vorspeisen
Is served from ... to...	Wird von...bis... serviert

BREAKFAST

Bread	Brot
Roll(s)	Brötchen
Eggs	Eier
Hot	heiß
Cold	kalt
Jam	Konfitüre
Milk	Milch
Orange juice	Orangensaft
Scrambled eggs	Rührei
Bacon	Speck

ENGLISH	GERMAN
Fried eggs	Spiegeleier
Lemon	Zitrone
Sugar	Zucker

SOUPS

Stew	Eintopf
Chicken soup	Hühnersuppe
Potato soup	Kartoffelsuppe
Liver dumpling soup	Leberknödelsuppe
Onion soup	Zwiebelsuppe

METHODS OF PREPARATION

Blue (boiled in salt and vinegar)	Blau
Baked	Gebacken
Fried	Gebraten
Steamed	Gedämpft
Grilled (broiled)	Gegrillt
Boiled	Gekocht
Sauteed	In Butter geschwenkt
Breaded	Paniert
Raw	Roh

When ordering steak, the English words "rare, medium, (well) done" are used and understood in German.

GAME AND POULTRY

Duck	Ente
Pheasant	Fasan
Chicken	Hähnchen (Huhn)
Deer	Hirsch
Rabbit	Kaninchen
Venison	Reh
Pigeon	Taube
Turkey	Truthahn
Quail	Wachtel

	ENGLISH	GERMAN
FISH AND SEAFOOD		
	Eel	Aal
	Oysters	Austern
	Trout	Forelle
	Flounder	Flunder
	Prawns	Garnelen
	Halibut	Heilbutt
	Herring	Hering
	Lobster	Hummer
	Scallops	Jakobsmuscheln
	Cod	Kabeljau
	Crab	Krabbe
	Salmon	Lachs
	Mackerel	Makrele
	Mussels	Muscheln
	Squid	Tintenfisch
	Tuna	Thunfisch
MEATS		
	Veal	Kalb(s)
	Lamb	Lamm
	Beef	Rind(er)
	Pork	Schwein(e)
CUTS OF MEAT		
	Example: For "Lammkeule" see "Lamm" (above) + ". . . keule" (below)	
	breast	. . . brust
	leg	. . . keule
	liver	. . . leber
	tenderloin	. . . lende
	kidney	. . . niere
	rib	. . . rippe
	Meat patty	Frikadelle

ENGLISH	GERMAN
Meat loaf	Hackbraten
Ham	Schinken

VEGETABLES

Eggplant	Aubergine
Cauliflower	Blumenkohl
Beans	Bohnen
green	grüne
white	weiße
Peas	Erbsen
Cucumber	Gurke
Cabbage	Kohl
Lettuce	Kopfsalat
Asparagus, peas and carrots	Leipziger Allerlei
Corn	Mais
Carrots	Mohrrüben
Peppers	Paprika
Mushrooms	Pilze
Celery	Sellerie
Asparagus (tips)	Spargel(spitzen)
Tomatoes	Tomaten
Onions	Zwiebeln

CONDIMENTS

Vinegar	Essig
Garlic	Knoblauch
Horseradish	Meerettich
Oil	Öl
Mustard	Senf
Artificial sweetener	Süßstoff
Cinnamon	Zimt
Sugar	Zucker
Salt	Salz

	ENGLISH	GERMAN
CHEESE		
	Mild	Allgäuer Käse, Altenburger (goat cheese), Appenzeller, Greyerzer, Hüttenkäse (cottage cheese), Quark, Räucherkäse (smoked cheese), Sahnekäse (creamy), Tilsiter, Ziegekäse (goat cheese).
	Sharp	Handkäse, Harzer Käse, Limburger.
	curd	frisch
	hard	hart
	mild	mild
FRUITS		
	Apple	Apfel
	Orange	Apfelsine
	Apricot	Aprikose
	Blueberry	Blaubeere
	Strawberry	Erdbeere
	Raspberry	Himbeere
	Cherry	Kirsche
	Grapefruit	Pampelmuse
	Raisin	Rosine
	Grape	Weintraube
	Banana	Banane
	Pear	Birne
DRINKS		
	with/without ice	mit/ohne Eis
	with/without water	mit/ohne Wasser
	straight	pur
	brandy	. . . geist
	liqueur	. . . likör
	Mulled claret	Glühwein
	Caraway-flavored liquor	Kümmel
	Fruit brandy	Obstler

When ordering a Martini, you have to specify "gin (vodka) and vermouth," otherwise you will be given a vermouth (Martini & Rossi).

Travel Smart Germany

GETTING HERE & AROUND

Germany's transportation infrastructure is extremely well developed, so all areas of the country are well connected to each other by road, rail, and air. The autobahns are an efficient system of highways, although they can get crowded during holidays. In winter you may have to contend with closed passes in the Alps or difficult driving on smaller roads in the Black Forest and the Saarland region. High-speed trains are perhaps the most comfortable way of traveling. Munich to Hamburg, for example, a trip of around 966 km (600 mi), takes at most six hours. Many airlines offer extremely cheap last-minute flights, but you have to be fairly flexible.

▌ BY AIR

The least-expensive airfares to Germany are often priced for round-trip travel and usually must be purchased in advance. Airlines generally allow you to change your return date for a fee; most low-fare tickets, however, are nonrefundable. Fares between the British Isles and Germany on "no-frills" airlines such as Air Berlin, EasyJet, and Ryanair can range from €15 to €70. ▌TIP➔ **Although a budget airfare may not be refundable, new EU regulations insist that all other supplemental fees and taxes are. That means that when the €1 fare from Berlin to Munich turns out to cost €70 with fuel surcharges and the like, you only lose €1. Refund procedures vary between airlines.**

Flying time to Frankfurt is 1½ hours from London, 7½ hours from New York, 10 hours from Chicago, and 12 hours from Los Angeles.

Lufthansa is Germany's leading carrier, and has shared mileage plans and flights with Air Canada and United, as well as other airlines.

Germany's internal air network is excellent, with flights linking all major cities in little more than an hour. A handful of smaller airlines—Air Berlin, Germanwings, and TUIfly—compete with low-fare flights within Germany and to other European cities. These companies are reliable, do most of their business over the Internet, and often beat the German rail fares. The earlier you book, the cheaper the fare.

Major Airlines **Air Canada** (☎888/247–2262). **Lufthansa** (☎800/645–3880 ⊕www.lufthansa.com). **United Airlines** (☎800/864–8331 for U.S. reservations, 800/538–2929 for international reservations ⊕www.united.com).

Airlines Within Germany **Air Berlin** (☎01805/737–800, 0870/738–8880 in U.K. ⊕www.airberlin.com). **Germanwings** (☎0900/191–9100 ⊕www.germanwings.com). **TUIfly** (☎01805/757–510 ⊕www.TUIfly.com). **Lufthansa** (☎0180/380–3803 or 0180/5838–42672 ⊕www.lufthansa.com).

AIRPORTS

Frankfurt is Germany's air hub. The large airport has the convenience of its own long-distance train station, but if you're transferring between flights, don't dawdle or you could miss your connection. Munich is Germany's second air hub, with many services to North America and Asia. Delta and Continental have nonstop service between New York and Tegel, the largest of the three airports in Berlin. Continental also has nonstop service between New York and Hamburg. There are a few nonstop services from North America to Düsseldorf. Stuttgart is convenient to the Black Forest. Also convenient to the Black Forest is the EuroAirport Freiburg-Basel-Mulhouse, which is used by many airlines for European destinations and as a stopover.

Airlines & Airports **Airline and Airport Links.com** (⊕www.airlineandairportlinks.com).

Airline Security Issues Transportation
Security Administration (⊕www.tsa.gov).

Airport Information Berlin: **Schönefeld** (SXF
☎01805/000–186 €0.12 per minute ⊕www.
berlin-airport.de). **Tegel** (TXL ☎01805/000–
186 €0.12 per minute ⊕www.berlin-airport.
de). Düsseldorf: **Flughafen Düsseldorf** (DUS
☎0211/4210 ⊕www.duesseldorf-interna-
tional.de). Frankfurt: **Flughafen Frankfurt
Main** (FRA ☎01805/372–4636, 069/6900
from outside Germany ⊕www.airportcity-
frankfur.de). Freiburg: **EuroAirport Freiburg-
Basel-Mulhouse** (MLH ☎0761/1200–3111,
0033/3899–03111 from outside Germany
⊕www.euroairport.com). Hamburg: **Hamburg
International Airport** (HAM ☎040/50750
⊕www.ham.airport.de). Köln: **Flughafen
Köln/Bonn** (CGN ☎02203/404–001 ⊕www.
airport-cgn.de). Munich: **Flughafen München**
(MUC ☎089/97500 ⊕www.munich-airport.
de). Stuttgart: **Flughafen Stuttgart** (STR
☎0711/9480 ⊕www.stuttgart-airport.de).

▌ BY BOAT

Eurailpasses and German Rail Passes
are honored by KD Rhine Line on the
Rhine River and on the Mosel River
between Trier and Koblenz (if you use
the fast hydrofoil, a supplementary fee is
required). The rail lines follow the Rhine
and Mosel rivers most of their length,
meaning you can go one way by ship and
return by train. Cruises generally operate between April and October. If you
are planning to visit Denmark or Sweden
after Germany, the ferries of the TT, TR,
and Scandlines offer discounts for Eurailpass owners.

The MS *Duchess of Scandinavia* carries
passengers and cars three times a week
for the 19½-hour run between Cuxhaven,
Germany, and Harwich, England.

Information **KD Rhine Line** (☎0221/208–
8318 ⊕www.k-d.com). **MS Duchess of Scandinavia** (☎08705/333–111 DFDS Seaways in
U.K., 040/389–0371 in Germany ⊕www.
dfdsseaways.co.uk). **Scandlines**
(☎0381/54350 ⊕www.scandlines.de).

▌ BY BUS

Germany has decent local bus service,
but no nationwide network other than
to the few cities served by BerlinLinien
Bus. Deutsche Touring, a subsidiary of
the Deutsche Bahn, has offices and agents
countrywide, and travels from Germany
to other European cities. You can check
its bilingual German-English Web site for
schedules. It offers one-day tours along
the Castle Road and the Romantic Road.
The Romantic Road route is between
Würzburg (with connections to and from
Frankfurt) and Füssen (with connections
to and from Munich, Augsburg, and
Garmisch-Partenkirchen). With a regular
Deutsche Bahn rail ticket, Eurailpass, or
German Rail Pass you get a 60% discount
on this route. Buses, with an attendant on
board, travel in each direction between
April and October.

All towns of any size have local buses,
which often link up with trams (streetcars) and electric railway (S-bahn) and
subway (U-bahn) services. Fares sometimes vary according to distance, but a
ticket usually allows you to transfer freely
between the various forms of transportation. Most cities issue day tickets at special rates.

Bus Information **BerlinLinien Bus**
(☎030/861–9331 ⊕www.berlinlinienbus.de).
Deutsche Touring (☎069/790–350 ⊕www.
deutsche-touring.de).

▌ BY CAR

Entry formalities for motorists are few: all
you need is proof of insurance, an international car-registration document, and a
U.S., Canadian, Australian, or New Zealand driver's license. If you or your car is
from an EU country, Norway, or Switzerland, all you need is your domestic license
and proof of insurance. *All* foreign cars
must have a country sticker. There are no
toll roads in Germany, except for a few
Alpine mountain passes.

GASOLINE

Gasoline costs are around €1.39 per liter—which is higher than in the United States. Some cars use diesel fuel, which is about €0.15 cheaper, so if you're renting a car, find out which fuel the car takes. German filling stations are highly competitive, and bargains are often available if you shop around, but *not* at autobahn filling stations. Self-service, or *SB-Tanken,* stations are cheapest. Pumps marked *Bleifrei* contain unleaded gas.

PARKING

Daytime parking in cities and small, historic towns is difficult to find. Restrictions are not always clearly marked and can be hard to understand when they are. Rental cars come with a "time wheel," which you can leave on your dashboard when parking signs indicate free, limited-time allowances. Larger parking lots have parking meters (*Parkautomaten*). After depositing enough change in a meter, you will be issued a timed ticket to display on your dashboard. Parking-meter spaces are free at night. In German garages you must pay immediately on returning to retrieve your car, not when driving out. Put the ticket you got on arrival into the machine and pay the amount displayed. Retrieve the ticket, and upon exiting the garage, insert the ticket in a slot to raise the barrier. ■ TIP➔ **You must lock your car when it is parked. Failure to do so risks a €25 fine and liability for anything that happens if the car is stolen.**

RENTAL CARS

If you are going to rent a car in Germany, you will need an International Driving Permit (IDP); it's available from the American Automobile Association and the National Automobile Club. These international permits are universally recognized, and having one in your wallet may save you problems with the local authorities. In Germany you usually must be 21 to rent a car. Nearly all agencies allow you to drive into Germany's neighboring countries. It's frequently possible to return the car in another West European country, but not in Poland or the Czech Republic, for example.

Rates with the major car-rental companies begin at about €55 per day and €300 per week for an economy car with a manual transmission and unlimited mileage. Most rentals are manual, so if you want an automatic, be sure to request one in advance. If you're traveling with children, don't forget to ask for a car seat when you reserve. Note that in some major cities, even automobile-producing Stuttgart, rental firms are prohibited from placing signs at major pickup and drop-off locations, such as the main train station. If dropping a car off in an unfamiliar city, you might have to guess your way to the station's underground parking garage; once there, look for a generic sign such as *Mietwagen* (rental cars). The German railway system, Deutsche Bahn, offers discounts on rental cars.

Depending on what you would like to see, you may or may not need a car for all or part of your stay. Since most parts of Germany are connected by reliable rail service, it might be a better plan to take a train to the region you plan to visit and rent a car only for side trips to out-of-the-way destinations.

ROAD CONDITIONS

Roads are generally excellent. *Bundesstrassen* are two-lane highways, abbreviated "B," as in B–38. Autobahns are high-speed thruways abbreviated with "A," as in A–7. If the autobahn should be blocked for any reason, you can take an exit and follow little signs bearing a "U" followed by a number. These are official detours.

ROADSIDE EMERGENCIES

The German automobile clubs ADAC and AvD operate tow trucks on all autobahns. NOTRUF signs every 2 km (1 mi) on autobahns (and country roads) indicate emergency telephones. By picking up the phone, you'll be connected to an operator who can determine your exact location and get you the services you need. Help is free (with the exception of materials).

Emergency Services Roadside assistance (☎01802/222–222).

ROAD MAPS

The best-known road maps of Germany are put out by the automobile club ADAC, by Shell, and by the Falk Verlag. They're available at gas stations and bookstores.

RULES OF THE ROAD

In Germany, road signs give distances in kilometers. There *are* posted speed limits on autobahns, and they advise drivers to keep below 130 kph (80 mph) or 110 kph (65 mph). A sign saying *Richtgeschwindigkeit* and the speed indicates this. Speed limits on country roads vary from 70 kph to 100 kph (43 mph to 62 mph) and are usually 50 kph (30 mph) through small towns.

Don't enter a street with a signpost bearing a red circle with a white horizontal stripe—it's a one-way street. Blue EIN-BAHNSTRASSE signs indicate you're headed the correct way down a one-way street. The blood-alcohol limit for driving in Germany is very low (.05%). Note that seat belts must be worn at all times by front- *and* back-seat passengers.

German drivers tend to drive fast and aggressively. If you wish to drive comfortably on the autobahn, stay in the right lane. Speeds under 80 kph (50 mph) are not permitted. Though prohibited, tailgating is a favorite sport on German roads. Do not react by braking for no reason: this is equally prohibited. You may not use a hand-held mobile phone while driving.

SCENIC ROUTES

Germany has many specially designated tourist roads that serve as promotional tools for towns along their routes. The longest is the Deutsche Ferienstrasse, the German Holiday Road, which runs from the Baltic Sea to the Alps, a distance of around 1,720 km (1,070 mi). The most famous, however, is the Romantische Strasse *(Romantic Road;* ⇨ *Chapter 4)*, which runs from Würzburg to Füssen in the Alps, covering around 355 km (220 mi).

Among other notable touring routes are the Strasse der Kaiser und Könige (Route of Emperors and Kings), running from Frankfurt to Passau (and on to Vienna and Budapest); the Burgenstrasse (Castle Road), running from Mannheim to Bayreuth; the Deutsche Weinstrasse *(German Wine Road;* ⇨ *Chapter 10)*, running through the Palatinate wine country; and the Deutsche Alpenstrasse, running the length of the country's Alpine southern border from near Berchtesgaden to the Bodensee. Less well-known routes are the Märchenstrasse *(Fairy-Tale Road;* ⇨ *Chapter 12)*, the Weser Renaissance Strasse, and the Deutsche Fachwerkstrasse (German Half-Timber Road).

▮ BY CRUISE SHIP

The American-owned Viking River Cruises company tours the Rhine, Main, Elbe, and Danube rivers, with four- to eight-day itineraries that include walking tours at ports of call. The longer cruises (up to 18 days) on the Danube (Donau, in German), which go to the Black Sea and back, are in great demand, so reserve six months in advance. The company normally books American passengers on ships that cater exclusively to Americans. If you prefer to travel on a European ship, specify so when booking. Köln–Düsseldorfer Deutsche Rheinschiffahrt (KD Rhine Line) offers trips of one day or less on the Rhine and Mosel. Between Easter and October there's Rhine service between Köln and Mainz, and between May and October, Mosel service between Koblenz and Cochem. Check the Web site for special winter tours. You'll get a free trip on your birthday if you bring a document verifying your date of birth.

Cruise Lines **KD Rhine Line** (☎0221/208–8318 ⊕www.k-d.com). **Viking River Cruises** (☎0800/258–4666, 0221/258–209 in Germany, 01372/742033 in U.K. ⊕www.vikingrivercruises.com).

▌ BY TRAIN

Deutsche Bahn (DB—German Rail) is a very efficient, semi-privatized railway. Its high-speed InterCity Express (ICE), InterCity (IC), and EuroCity (EC) trains make journeys between the centers of many cities—Munich–Frankfurt, for example—faster by rail than by air. All InterCity and InterCity Express trains have restaurant cars and trolley service. RE, RB, and IRE trains are regional trains. It's also possible to sleep on the train and save a day of your trip. CityNightLine (CNL) trains serving domestic destinations and neighboring countries have sleepers, couches, and recliners.

Once on your platform (*Gleis*), you can check the notice boards that give details of the layout of trains arriving on that track, showing the locations of first- and second-class cars and the restaurant car, as well as where they will stop along the platform. Large railroad stations have English-speaking staff handling information inquiries.

Fare and schedule information on the Deutsche Bahn information line connects you to a live operator; you may have to wait a few moments before someone can help you in English. The automated number is toll-free and gives schedule information. On the DB Web site, click on "English." A timetable mask will open up. To calculate the fare, enter your departure and arrival points, any town you wish to pass through, and indicate whether you have a bike.

If you would like to work out an itinerary beforehand, Deutsche Bahn has an excellent Web site in English (⊕*www.bahn.de*). It'll even tell you which type of train you'll be riding on—which could be important if you suffer from motion sickness. The ICE, the French TGV, the Swiss ICN, and the Italian Cisalpino all use "tilt technology" for a less jerky ride. One side effect, however, is that some passengers might feel queasy, especially if the track is curvy. An over-the-counter drug for motion sickness should help.

BAGGAGE

Most major train stations have luggage lockers (in four sizes). By inserting exact change into a storage unit, you release the unit's key. Prices range from €1 for a small locker to €3 for a "jumbo" one. Smaller towns' train stations may not have any storage options.

Throughout Germany, Deutsche Bahn can deliver your baggage from a private residence or hotel to another or even to one of six airports: Berlin, Frankfurt, Leipzig-Halle, Munich, Hamburg, or Hannover. You must have a valid rail ticket. Buy a *Kuriergepäck* ticket at any DB ticket counter, at which time you must schedule a pickup three workdays before your flight. The service costs €14.90 for each of the first two suitcases and €15.80 for each suitcase thereafter.

DISCOUNTS

Deutsche Bahn offers many discount options with specific conditions, so do your homework on its Web site or ask about options at the counter before paying for a full-price ticket. For round-trip travel you can save 25% if you book at least three days in advance, 50% if you stay over a Saturday night and book at least three to seven days in advance. However, there's a limited number of seats sold at any of these discount prices, so book as early as possible, at least a week in advance, to get the savings. A discounted rate is called a *Sparpreis*. If you change your travel plans after booking, you will have to pay a fee. The surcharge for tickets bought on board is 10% of the ticket cost, or a minimum of €5.

The good news for families is that children under 15 travel free when accompanied by a parent or relative on normal, discounted, and some, but not all, special-fare tickets. However, you must indicate the number of children traveling with you when you purchase the ticket; to ride free, the child (or children) must be listed on the ticket. If you have a ticket with 25% or 50% off, a *Mitfahrer-Rabatt* allows a second person to travel with you for a 50% discount (minimum of €15 for a second-class ticket). The *Schönes Wochenend Ticket* (Happy Weekend Ticket) provides unlimited travel on regional trains on Saturday or Sunday for up to five persons for €37 (€35 if purchased online or at vending machine). Groups of six or more should inquire about *Gruppen & Spar* (group) savings. Each German state, or *Land*, has its own *Länder-Ticket,* which lets up to five people travel from 9 AM to 3 AM for around €25.

If you plan to travel by train within a day after your flight arrives, purchase a heavily discounted "Rail and Fly" ticket for DB trains at the same time you book your flight. Trains connect with 14 German airports and two airports outside Germany, Basel and Amsterdam.

FARES

A first-class seat is approximately 55% more than a second-class seat. For this premium you get a bit more legroom and the convenience of having meals (not included) delivered directly to your seat. Most people find second class entirely adequate. ICs and the later-generation ICE trains are equipped with electrical outlets for laptops and other gadgets.

Tickets purchased through Deutsche Bahn's Web site can be retrieved from station vending machines. Always check that your ticket is valid for the type of train you are planning to take, not just for the destination served. If you have the wrong type of ticket, you will have to pay the difference on the train, in cash or by credit card.

The ReisePacket service is for travelers who are inexperienced, elderly, disabled, or just appreciative of extra help. It costs €11 and provides, among other things, help boarding, disembarking, and transferring on certain selected trains that serve the major cities and vacation areas. It also includes a seat reservation and a voucher for an on-board snack. Purchase the service at least one day before travel.

PASSES

If Germany is your only destination in Europe, consider purchasing a German Rail Pass, which allows 4 to 10 days of unlimited first- or second-class travel within a one-month period on any DB train, up to and including the ICE. A Twin Pass saves two people traveling together 50% off one person's fare. A Youth Pass, sold to those 12–25, is also much the same but for second-class travel only. You can also use these passes aboard KD Rhine Line *(⇨By Cruise Ship)* along certain sections of the Rhine and Mosel rivers. Prices begin at €169 per person in second class. Twin Passes begin at €125 per person in second class, and Youth Passes begin at €139. Additional days may be added to either pass.

Rail 'n Drive combines train travel and car rental. For instance, two people pay $214 each for two rail-travel days and two car-rental days within a month. You can add up to three more rail days ($66 each), and each additional car-rental day is $45.

Germany is one of 20 countries in which you can use Eurail Passes, which provide unlimited first-class rail travel in all participating countries for the duration of the pass. Two adults traveling together can pay either €426 each for 15 consecutive days of travel or €554 each for 21 days of travel within one month. The Youth fare is €327 for 15 consecutive days and €387 for 10 days within one month. Eurail Passes are available from most travel agents and directly from ⊕*www. eurail.com.*

Eurail Passes and some of the German Rail passes should be purchased before you leave for Europe. You can purchase a Eurail Pass and 5- or 10-day German Rail passes at the Frankfurt airport and at some major German train stations, but the cost will be higher (a youth ticket for 5 days of travel is just under €149). When you buy your pass, consider purchasing Railpass insurance in case you lose it during your travels.

In order to comply with the strict rules about validating tickets before you begin travel, read the instructions carefully. Some tickets require that a train official validate your pass, while others require you to write in the first date of travel.

Many travelers assume that rail passes guarantee them seats on the trains they wish to ride. Not so. You need to book seats ahead even if you are using a rail pass; seat reservations are required on some European trains, particularly high-speed trains, and are a good idea during summer, national holidays, and on popular routes. If you board the train without a reserved seat, you risk having to stand. You'll also need a reservation if you purchase sleeping accommodations. Reservations are free if you make them online at the Deutsche Bahn Web site or at the time of ticket purchase at a vending machine. Otherwise, seat reservations on InterRegioExpress and InterCity trains cost €4, and a reservation is absolutely necessary for the ICE-Sprinter trains (€10 for second class). There are no reservations on regional trains.

TRAVEL FROM GREAT BRITAIN

There are several ways to reach Germany from London on British Rail. Travelers coming from the United Kingdom should take the Channel Tunnel to save time, the ferry to save money. Fastest and most expensive is the route via the Channel Tunnel on Eurostar trains. They leave at two-hour intervals from St. Pancras International and require a change of trains in Brussels, from which ICE trains reach

Köln in 2½ hours and Frankfurt in 3½ hours. Prices for one-way tickets from London to Köln begin at €100–€129. Cheapest and slowest are the 8 to 10 departures daily from Victoria using the Ramsgate–Ostend ferry, jetfoil, or SeaCat catamaran service.

Channel Tunnel Car Transport **Eurotunnel** (☎0870/535–3535 in U.K., 070/223210 in Belgium, 03–21–00–61–00 in France ⊕www. eurotunnel.com). **French Motorail/Rail Europe** (☎0870/241–5415 ⊕www.rail europe.co.uk/frenchmotorail).

Channel Tunnel Passenger Service **Eurostar** (☎0870/518–6186, in U.K. ⊕www.euro star.co.uk). **Rail Europe** (☎888/382–7245 in U.S., 0870/584–8848 in U.K. inquiries and credit-card bookings ⊕www.raileurope.com).

Train Information **Deutsche Bahn** (German Rail ☎0800/150–7090 for automated schedule information, 11861 for 24-hr hotline €0.39 per minute, 491805/996–633 from outside Germany €0.12 per minute ⊕www. bahn.de). **Eurail** (⊕www.eurail.com). **Eurostar** (☎0870/518–6186).

ESSENTIALS

▌ACCOMMODATIONS

The standards of German hotels, down to the humblest inn, are very high. You can nearly always expect courteous and polite service and clean and comfortable rooms. In addition to hotels proper, the country has numerous *Gasthöfe* or *Gasthäuser* (country inns that serve food and also have rooms). At the lowest end of the scale are *Fremdenzimmer,* meaning simply "rooms," normally in private houses. Look for the sign reading ZIMMER FREI (room available) or ZU VERMIETEN (to rent) on a green background; a red sign reading BESETZT means there are no vacancies.

If you are looking for a very down-to-earth experience, try an *Urlaub auf dem Bauernhof,* a farm that has rooms for travelers. This can be especially exciting for children. You can also opt to stay at a winery's *Winzerhof.*

CATEGORY	COST
¢	under €50
$	€50–€100
$$	€101–€175
$$$	€176–€225
$$$$	over €225

Hotel prices are for two people in a standard double room, including tax and service.

Room rates are by no means inflexible and depend very much on supply and demand. You can save money by inquiring about deals: many resort hotels offer substantial discounts in winter, for example. Likewise, many $$$$ and $$$ hotels in cities cut their prices dramatically on weekends and when business is quiet. Major events like Munich's Oktoberfest and the Frankfurt Book Fair will drive prices through the ceiling.

Tourist offices will make bookings for a nominal fee, but they may have difficulty doing so after 4 PM in high season and on weekends, so don't wait until too late in the day to begin looking for your accommodations. If you do get stuck, ask someone—like a mail carrier, police officer, or waiter, for example—for directions to a house renting a Fremdenzimmer or to a Gasthof.

Most hotels and other lodgings require you to give your credit-card details before they will confirm your reservation. If you don't feel comfortable e-mailing this information, ask if you can fax it (some places even prefer faxes). However you book, get confirmation in writing and have a copy of it handy when you check in.

Be sure you understand the hotel's cancellation policy. Some places allow you to cancel without any kind of penalty—even if you prepaid to secure a discounted rate—if you cancel at least 24 hours in advance. Others require you to cancel a week in advance or penalize you the cost of one night. Small inns and B&Bs are most likely to require you to cancel far in advance. Most hotels allow children under a certain age to stay in their parents' room at no extra charge, but others charge for them as extra adults; find out the cutoff age for discounts.

▌TIP→ Assume that hotels operate on the European Plan (EP, no meals) unless we specify that they use the Breakfast Plan (BP, with full breakfast), Continental Plan (CP, continental breakfast), Full American Plan (FAP, all meals), or Modified American Plan (MAP, breakfast and dinner), or are all-inclusive (AI, all meals and most activities).

APARTMENT & HOUSE RENTALS

If you are staying in one region, renting an apartment is an affordable alternative to a hotel or B&B. *Ferienwohnungen,* or vacation apartments, are especially popular in more rural areas. They range from simple rooms with just the basics to luxury apartments with all the trimmings. Some even include breakfast. The best way to find an apartment is through the local tourist office or the Web site of the town or village where you would like to stay.

BED & BREAKFASTS

B&Bs remain one of the most popular options for traveling in Germany. They are often inexpensive, although the price depends on the amenities. For breakfast, expect some muesli, cheese, cold cuts, jam, butter, and hard-boiled eggs at the very least. Some B&Bs also supply lunch baskets if you intend to go hiking, or arrange an evening meal for a very affordable price.

Reservation Services **Bed & Breakfast.com** (☎512/322–2710 or 800/462–2632 ⊕www. bedandbreakfast.com) also sends out an online newsletter. **Bed & Breakfast Inns Online** (☎615/868–1946 or 800/215–7365 ⊕www. bbonline.com). **BnB Finder.com** (☎212/432–7693 or 888/547–8226 ⊕www.bnbfinder.com).

CASTLE-HOTELS

Staying in an historic castle, or *Schloss*, is a great experience. The simpler ones may lack character, but most combine four-star luxury with antique furnishings, four-poster beds, and a baronial atmosphere. Some offer all the facilities of a resort. Euro-Connection can advise you on castle-hotel packages, including four- to six-night tours.

Contacts **Euro-Connection** (☎800/645–3876 ⊕www.euro-connection.com).

FARM VACATIONS

Almost every regional tourist office has a brochure listing farms that offer bed-and-breakfasts, apartments, and entire farmhouses to rent (*Ferienhöfe*). The German Agricultural Association provides an illustrated brochure, *Urlaub auf dem Bauernhof* (Vacation Down on the Farm), that covers more than 2,000 inspected and graded farms, from the Alps to the

North Sea. It costs €9.90 and is also sold in bookstores.

German Agricultural Association **DLG Reisedienst, Agratour** (German Agricultural Association ☎069/247–880 ⊕www.land tourismus.de).

HOME EXCHANGES

With a direct home exchange you stay in someone else's home while they stay in yours. Some outfits also deal with vacation homes, so you're not actually staying in someone's full-time residence, just their vacant weekend place.

Exchange Clubs **Home Exchange.com** (☎800/877–8723 ⊕www.homeexchange. com); $59.95 for a 1-year online listing. **HomeLink International** (☎800/638–3841 ⊕www.homelink.org); $80 yearly for Web-only membership; $125 includes Web access and two catalogs. **Intervac U.S.** (☎800/756–4663 ⊕www.intervacus.com); $78.88 for Web-only membership; $126 includes Web access and a catalog.

HOSTELS

Germany's more than 600 *Jugendherbergen* (youth hostels) are among the most efficient and up-to-date in Europe. The DJH Service GmbH provides a complete list of hostels it represents, but remember that there are also scores of independent hostels. Hostels must be reserved well in advance for midsummer, especially in eastern Germany. Note that weekends and holidays can mean full houses and noisy nights. Either bring earplugs or choose more expensive, but quieter, accommodations.

Many hostels are affiliated with Hostelling International (HI), an umbrella group of hostel associations with some 4,500 member properties in more than 70 countries. Membership in any HI association, open to travelers of all ages, allows you to stay in HI-affiliated hostels at member rates. One-year membership is about $28 for adults; hostels charge about $10–$30 per night. Members have priority if the hostel is full; they're also eligible for discounts around the world, even on rail and bus travel in some countries.

Information DJH Service GmbH
(☎05231/74010 ⊕www.jugendherberge.de). **Hostelling International—USA** (☎301/495–1240 ⊕www.hiusa.org).

HOTELS

Most hotels in Germany do not have air-conditioning, nor do they need it, given the climate and the German style of building construction that uses thick walls and recessed windows to help keep the heat out. Smaller hotels do not provide much in terms of bathroom amenities. Except in four- and five-star hotels, you won't find a washcloth. Hotels often have no-smoking rooms or even no-smoking floors, so it's always worth asking for one when you reserve. Beds in double rooms often consist of two twin mattresses placed side by side within a frame. When you arrive, if you don't like the room you're offered, ask to see another.

Among the most delightful places to stay—and eat—in Germany are the aptly named Romantik Hotels and Restaurants. The Romantik group has 98 members in Germany. All are in atmospheric and historic buildings—a condition for membership—and are run by the owners with the emphasis on excellent amenities and service. Prices vary considerably, but in general they are a good value.

Contacts Romantik Hotels and Restaurants (☎800/650–8018, 817/678–0038 from the U.S., 069/661–2340 in Germany ⊕www. romantikhotels.com).

SPAS

Taking the waters in Germany, whether for curing the body or merely pampering it, has been popular since Roman times. More than 300 health resorts, mostly equipped for thermal or mineral-water, mud, or brine treatments, are set within pleasant country areas or historic communities. The word *Bad* before or within the name of a town means it's a spa destination, where many patients reside in

WORD OF MOUTH

Did the resort look as good in real life as it did in the photos? Did you sleep like a baby, or were the walls paper thin? Did you get your money's worth? Rate hotels and write your own reviews in Travel Ratings or start a discussion about your favorite places in Travel Talk on www.fodors. com. Your comments might even appear in our books. Yes, you, too, can be a correspondent!

health clinics for two to three weeks of doctor-prescribed treatments.

Saunas, steam baths, and other hot-room facilities are often used "without textiles" in Germany—in other words, naked. Wearing a bathing suit is sometimes even prohibited in saunas, but sitting on a towel is always required (you may need to bring your own towels). The Deutsche Heilbäderverband has information in German only.

Contacts Deutsche Heilbäderverband (German Health Resort and Spa Association ☎0228/201–200 ⊕www.deutscher-heilbaederverband.de).

▌ COMMUNICATIONS

INTERNET

Nearly all hotels have in-room data ports, but you may have to purchase, or borrow from the front desk, a cable with an end that matches German phone jacks. If you're plugging into a phone line, you'll need a local access number for a connection. Wireless Internet (called WLAN in Germany) is more and more common in even the most average hotel. The service is not always free, however. Sometimes you must purchase blocks of time from the front desk or online using a credit card. The cost is fairly high, however, usually around €4 for 30 minutes.

There are alternatives. Some hotels have an Internet room for guests needing to check their e-mail. Otherwise, Internet cafés are common, and many bars and restaurants let you surf the Web. Cybercafes.com lists more than 4,000 Internet cafés worldwide.

Contacts **Cybercafes** (⊕ www.cybercafes.com).

PHONES

The good news is that you can now make a direct-dial telephone call from virtually any point on earth. The bad news? You can't always do so cheaply. Calling from a hotel is almost always the most expensive option; hotels usually add huge surcharges to all calls, particularly international ones. In some countries you can phone from call centers or even the post office. Calling cards usually keep costs to a minimum, but only if you purchase them locally. And then there are mobile phones (⇨ below), which are sometimes more prevalent—particularly in the developing world—than land lines; as expensive as mobile phone calls can be, they are still usually a much cheaper option than calling from your hotel.

The country code for Germany is 49. When dialing a German number from abroad, drop the initial "0" from the local area code.

Many companies have service lines beginning with 0180. The cost of these calls averages €0.12 per minute. Numbers that begin with 0190 can cost €1.85 per minute and more.

CALLING WITHIN GERMANY

The German telephone system is very efficient, so it's unlikely you'll have to use an operator unless you're seeking information. For information in English, dial 11837 for numbers within Germany and 11834 for numbers elsewhere. But first look for the number in the phone book or online (⊕ www.teleauskunft. de), because directory assistance is costly. Calls to 11837 and 11834 cost at least €0.50, more if the call lasts more than 30 seconds.

A local call from a telephone booth costs €0.10 per minute. Dial the "0" before the area code when making a long-distance call within Germany. When dialing within a local area code, drop the "0" and the area code.

Telephone booths are not a common feature on the streets, so be prepared to walk out of your way to find one (most post offices have one). Phone booths have instructions in English as well as German. Most telephone booths in Germany are card-operated, so buy a phone card. Coin-operated phones, which take €0.10, €0.20, €0.50, €1, and €2 coins, don't make change.

CALLING OUTSIDE GERMANY

International calls can be made from any telephone booth in Germany. It costs only €0.13 per minute to call the United States, day or night, no matter how long the call lasts. Use a phone card. If you don't have a good deal with a calling card, there are many stores that offer international calls at rates well below what you will pay from a phone booth. At a hotel, rates will be at least double the regular charge.

Access Codes **AT&T Direct** (☎ 0800/225–5288). **Sprint International Access** (☎ 0800/888–0013). **MCI WorldPhone** (☎ 0800/888–8000).

CALLING CARDS

Post offices, newsstands, and exchange places sell cards with €5, €10, or €20 worth of credit to use at public pay phones. An advantage of a card: it charges only what the call costs. A €5 card with a good rate for calls to the United States, United Kingdom, and Canada is Go Bananas!

MOBILE PHONES

If you have a multiband phone (some countries use different frequencies than what's used in the United States) and your service provider uses the world-standard GSM network (as do T-Mobile, Cingular, and Verizon), you can probably use your phone abroad. Roaming fees can be steep, however: 99¢ a minute is considered reasonable. And overseas you normally pay the toll charges for incoming calls. It's almost always cheaper to send a text message than to make a call, since text messages have a very low set fee (often less than 5¢).

If you just want to make local calls, consider buying a new SIM card (note that your provider may have to unlock your phone for you to use a different SIM card) and a prepaid service plan in the destination. You'll then have a local number and can make local calls at local rates. If your trip is extensive, you could also simply buy a new cell phone in your destination, as the initial cost will be offset over time.

Cellular Abroad rents and sells GMS phones and sells SIM cards that work in many countries. Mobal rents mobiles and sells GSM phones (starting at $49) that will operate in 140 countries. Planet Fone rents cell phones, but the per-minute rates are expensive.

■TIP→ **If you travel internationally frequently, save one of your old mobile phones or buy a cheap one on the Internet; ask your cell phone company to unlock it for you, and take it with you as a travel phone, buying a new SIM card with pay-as-you-go service in each destination.**

Contacts **Cellular Abroad** (☎800/287–5072 ⊕www.cellularabroad.com). **Mobal** (☎888/888–9162 ⊕www.mobalrental.com). **Planet Fone** (☎888/988–4777 ⊕www.planetfone.com).

▌ CUSTOMS & DUTIES

You're always allowed to bring goods of a certain value back home without having to pay any duty or import tax. But there's a limit on the amount of tobacco and liquor you can bring back duty-free, and some countries have separate limits for perfumes; for exact figures, check

with your customs department. The values of so-called "duty-free" goods are included in these amounts. When you shop abroad, save all your receipts, as customs inspectors may ask to see them as well as the items you purchased. If the total value of your goods is more than the duty-free limit, you'll have to pay a tax (most often a flat percentage) on the value of everything beyond that limit.

For anyone entering Germany from outside the EU, the following limitations apply: (1) 200 cigarettes or 100 cigarillos or 50 cigars or 250 grams of tobacco; (2) 2 liters of still table wine; (3) 1 liter of spirits over 22% volume or 2 liters of spirits under 22% volume (fortified and sparkling wines) or 2 more liters of table wine; (4) 50 grams of perfume and 250 milliliters of eau de toilette; (5) 500 grams of roasted coffee or 200 grams of instant coffee; (6) other goods to the value of €175.

If you have questions regarding customs or bringing a pet into the country, contact the Zoll-Infocenter, preferably by mail or e-mail.

Information in Germany **Zoll-Infocenter** (☎069/4699–7600 ⊕www.zoll.de).

U.S. Information **U.S. Customs and Border Protection** (⊕www.cbp.gov).

▌ EATING OUT

Almost every street in Germany has its *Gaststätte,* a sort of combination restaurant and pub, and every village its *Gasthof,* or inn. The emphasis in either is on simple food at reasonable prices. A *Bierstube* (pub) or *Weinstube* (wine cellar) may also serve light snacks or meals.

Service can be slow, but you'll never be rushed out of your seat. Something else that may seem jarring at first: people can, and do, join other parties at a table in a casual restaurant if seating is tight. It's common courtesy to ask first, though.

BUDGET EATING TIPS

Imbiss (snack) stands can be found in almost every busy shopping street, in parking lots, train stations, and near markets. They serve *Würste* (sausages), grilled, roasted, or boiled, and rolls filled with cheese, cold meat, or fish. Many stands sell Turkish-style wraps called *Döner*. Prices range from €1.50 to €2.50 per portion. It's acceptable to bring sandwich fixings to a beer garden so long as you order a beer there, just be sure not to sit at a table with a tablecloth.

Butcher shops, known as *Metzgereien,* often serve warm snacks or very good sandwiches. Try *Warmer Leberkäs mit Kartoffelsalat,* a typical Bavarian specialty, which is a sort of baked meat loaf with mustard and potato salad. In northern Germany try *Bouletten,* small meatballs, or *Currywurst,* sausages in a piquant curry sauce. Thuringia has a reputation for its bratwurst, which is usually broken in two and packed into a roll with mustard. Up north, the specialty snack is a fish sandwich with onions.

Restaurants in department stores are especially recommended for appetizing and inexpensive lunches. Kaufhof, Karstadt, Wertheim, and Horton are names to note. Germany's vast numbers of Turkish, Italian, Greek, Chinese, and Balkan restaurants are often inexpensive.

MEALS & MEALTIMES

Most hotels serve a buffet-style breakfast (*Frühstück*) of rolls, cheese, cold cuts, eggs, cereals, yogurt, and spreads, which is often included in the price of a room. Cafés, especially the more trendy ones, offer breakfast menus sometimes including pancakes, omelets, muesli, or even Thai rice soup. By American standards, a cup (*Tasse*) of coffee in Germany is very petite, and you don't get free refills. Order a *Pot* or *Kännchen* if you want a larger portion.

For lunch (*Mittagessen*), you can get sandwiches from most cafés and bakeries, and many fine restaurants have special lunch menus that make the gourmet experience much more affordable. Dinner (*Abendessen*) is usually accompanied by a potato or spätzle side dish. A salad sometimes comes with the main dish.

Gaststätten normally serve hot meals from 11:30 AM to 9 PM; many places stop serving hot meals between 2 PM and 6 PM, although you can still order cold dishes. If you feel like a hot meal, look for a restaurant advertising *durchgehend geöffnet,* or look for a pizza parlor.

Once most restaurants have closed, your options are limited. Take-out pizza parlors and Turkish eateries often stay open later. Failing that, your best option is a train station or a gas station with a convenience store. Many bars serve snacks.

Unless otherwise noted, the restaurants listed in this guide are open daily for lunch and dinner.

PAYING

Credit cards are generally accepted only in moderate to expensive restaurants, so check before sitting down. You will need to ask for the bill in order to get it from the waiter, the idea being that the table is yours for the evening. Round up the bill 5% to 10% and pay the waiter directly rather than leaving any money or tip on the table.

Meals are subject to 19% tax (abbreviated as MWST on your bill).

For guidelines on tipping see Tipping below.

CATEGORY	COST
¢	under €9
$	€9–€15
$$	€16–€20
$$$	€21–€25
$$$$	over €25

Restaurant prices are per person for a main course at dinner.

RESERVATIONS & DRESS

Regardless of where you are, it's a good idea to make a reservation if you can. In some places (Hong Kong, for example), it's expected. We only mention them specifically when reservations are essential (there's no other way you'll ever get a table) or when they are not accepted. For popular restaurants, book as far ahead as you can (often 30 days), and reconfirm as soon as you arrive. (Large parties should always call ahead to check the reservations policy.) We mention dress only when men are required to wear a jacket or a jacket and tie.

Note that even when Germans dress casually, their look is generally crisp and neat.

SMOKING

For such an otherwise health-conscious nation, Germans smoke a lot. New anti-smoking laws came into effect in 2008, effectively banning smoking in all restaurants and many pubs. Many hotels have no-smoking rooms and even no-smoking floors. However, a smoker will find it intrusive if you request him or her to refrain.

WINES, BEER & SPIRITS

"Wines of Germany" promotes the wines of all 13 German wine regions and can supply you with information on wine-festivals and visitor-friendly wineries. It also arranges six-day guided winery tours in spring and fall in conjunction with the German Wine Academy.

Germany holds its brewers to a "purity law" that dates back to 1516. It's legal to drink beer from open containers in public (even in the passenger seat of a car), and having a beer at one's midday break is nothing to raise an eyebrow at. Bavaria is not the only place to try beer. While Munich's beers have achieved world fame—Löwenbräu and Paulaner, for example—beer connoisseurs will really want to travel to places further north like Bamberg, Erfurt, Cologne, or Görlitz,

> ### WORD OF MOUTH
>
> Was the service stellar or not up to snuff? Did the food give you shivers of delight or leave you cold? Did the prices and portions make you happy or sad? Rate restaurants and write your own reviews in Travel Ratings or start a discussion about your favorite places in Travel Talk on www.fodors.com. Your comments might even appear in our books. Yes, you, too, can be a correspondent!

where smaller breweries produce top-notch brews.

Wine Information German Wine Academy (☎ 06131/282–942 ⊕ www.germanwines.de). **Wines of Germany** (☎ 212/994–7523 ⊕ www.germanwineusa.org).

▌ ELECTRICITY

The electrical current in Germany is 220 volts, 50 cycles alternating current (AC); wall outlets take Continental-type plugs, with two round prongs.

Consider making a small investment in a universal adapter, which has several types of plugs in one lightweight, compact unit. Most laptops and mobile phone chargers are dual voltage (i.e., they operate equally well on 110 and 220 volts), so require only an adapter. These days the same is true of small appliances such as hair dryers. Always check labels and manufacturer instructions to be sure. Don't use 110-volt outlets marked FOR SHAVERS ONLY for high-wattage appliances such as hair-dryers.

Steve Kropla's Help for World Travelers has information on electrical and telephone plugs around the world. Walkabout Travel Gear has a good coverage of electricity under "adapters."

Contacts Steve Kropla's Help for World Travelers (⊕ www.kropla.com). **Walkabout Travel Gear** (⊕ www.walkabouttravelgear.com).

■ EMERGENCIES

Throughout Germany call ☎110 for police, ☎112 for an ambulance or the fire department.

Foreign Embassies **U.S. Embassy** (✉Neustädtische Kirchstr. 4–5, Berlin ✉Clayallee 170 [consular section] ☎030/83050, 030/832–9233 for American citizens ⊕www.usembassy.de).

■ ETIQUETTE

CUSTOMS OF THE COUNTRY
Being on time for appointments, even casual social ones, is very important. Germans are more formal in addressing each other than Americans. Always address acquaintances as Herr (Mr.) or Frau (Mrs.) plus their last name; do not call them by their first name unless invited to do so. The German language has an informal and formal pronoun for "you": formal is *"Sie,"* and informal is *"du."* Even if adults are on a first-name basis with one another, they may still keep to the *Sie* form.

Germans are less formal when it comes to nudity: a sign that reads FREIKÖRPER or FKK indicates a park or beach that allows nude sunbathing. If enjoying a sauna or steam bath, you will often be asked to remove all clothing.

GREETINGS
The standard *"Guten Tag"* is the way to greet people throughout the country. When you depart, say *"Auf Wiedersehen."* *"Hallo"* is also used frequently, as is *"Hi"* among the younger crowd. A less formal leave-taking is *"Tschüss"* or *"ciao."* You will also hear regional differences in greetings.

LANGUAGE
English is spoken in most hotels, restaurants, airports, museums, and other places of interest. However, English is not widely spoken in rural areas or by people over 40; this is especially true of the eastern part of Germany. Learning the basics before going is always a good idea, especially bitte (please) and danke (thank you). Apologizing for your poor German before asking a question in English will make locals feel respected and begins all communication on the right foot.

A phrase book and language-tape set can help get you started. *Fodor's German for Travelers* (available at bookstores everywhere) is excellent.

⚠ Under no circumstances use profanity or pejoratives. Germans take these very seriously, and a slip of the tongue can result in expensive criminal and civil penalties. Calling a police office a "Nazi" or using vulgar finger gestures can cost you up €10,000 and two years in jail.

■ HEALTH

Warm winters have recently caused an explosion in the summertime tick population, which often causes outbreaks of Lyme disease. If you intend to do a lot of hiking, especially in the southern half of the country, be aware of the danger of ticks spreading Lyme disease. There is no vaccination against them, so prevention is important. Wear high shoes or boots, long pants, and light-color clothing. Use a good insect repellent, and check yourself for ticks after outdoor activities, especially if you've walked through high grass.

SHOTS & MEDICATIONS
Germany is by and large a healthy place. There are occasional outbreaks of measles—including one in North Rhine–Westfalia—so be sure you have been vaccinated.

■ HOURS OF OPERATION

Business hours are inconsistent throughout the country and vary from state to state and even from city to city. Banks are generally open weekdays from 8:30 or 9 AM to 3 or 4 PM (5 or 6 PM on Thursday), sometimes with a lunch break of about an hour at smaller branches. Some banks close by 2:30 on Friday afternoon. Banks at airports and main train stations open as early as 6:30 AM and close as late as 10:30 PM.

Most museums are open from Tuesday to Sunday 10–6. Some close for an hour or more at lunch. Many stay open until 8 PM or later one day a week, usually Thursday. In smaller towns or in rural areas, museums may be open only on weekends or just a few hours a day.

Most pharmacies are open 9–6 weekdays and 9–1 on Saturday. Those in more prominent locations often open an hour earlier and/or close an hour later. A list of pharmacies in the vicinity that are open late or on Sunday is posted on the door under the sign *Apotheken-Bereitschafts-dienst*. When you find the pharmacy, it will have a bell you must ring.

All stores are closed on Sunday, with the exception of those in or near train stations. Larger stores are generally open from 9:30 or 10 AM to 8 or 9 PM on weekdays and close between 6 and 8 PM on Saturday. Smaller shops and some department stores in smaller towns close at 6 or 6:30 on weekdays and as early as 4 on Saturday. German shop owners take their closing times seriously. If you come in five minutes before closing, you may not be treated like royalty. Apologizing profusely and making a speedy purchase will help.

Along the autobahn and major highways, as well as in larger cities, gas stations and their small convenience shops are often open late, if not around the clock.

HOLIDAYS

The following national holidays are observed in Germany: January 1; January 6 (Epiphany—Bavaria, Saxony-Anhalt, and Baden-Württemberg only); Good Friday; Easter Monday; May 1 (Workers' Day); Ascension; Pentecost Monday; Corpus Christi (southern Germany only); Assumption Day (Bavaria and Saarland only); October 3 (German Unity Day); November 1 (All Saints' Day—Baden-Württemberg, Bavaria, North Rhine-Westphalia, Rhineland-Pfalz, and Saarland); December 24–26 (Christmas).

Pre-Lenten celebrations in Cologne and the Rhineland are known as Carnival, and for several days before Ash Wednesday work grinds to a halt as people celebrate with parades, banquets, and general debauchery. Farther south, in the state of Baden-Württenburg, the festivities are called Fasching, and tend to be more traditional. In either area, expect businesses to be closed both before and after "Fat Tuesday."

▌ MAIL

A post office in Germany (*Postamt*) is recognizable by the postal symbol, a black bugle on a yellow background. In some villages you will find one in the local supermarket. Stamps (*Briefmarken*) can also be bought at some news agencies and souvenir shops. Post offices are generally open weekdays 8–6, Saturday 8–noon.

Airmail letters to the United States, Canada, Australia, and New Zealand cost €1.70; postcards, €1. All letters to the United Kingdom and within Europe cost €0.55; postcards, €0.45. These rates apply to standard-size envelopes. Letters take approximately 3–4 days to reach the United Kingdom, 5–7 days to the United States, and 7–10 days to Australia and New Zealand.

You can arrange to have mail (letters only) sent to you in care of any German post office; have the envelope marked "Postlagernd." This service is free, and the mail will be held for seven days. Or you can have mail sent to any American Express office in Germany. There's no charge to cardholders, holders of American Express traveler's checks, or anyone who has booked a vacation with American Express.

SHIPPING PACKAGES

Most major stores that cater to tourists will also ship your purchases home. You should check your insurance for coverage of possible damage.

The Deutsche Post has an express international service that will deliver your letter or package the next day to countries within the EU, within one to two days to the United States, and slightly longer to Australia. A letter or package to the United States weighing less than 200 grams costs €48.57. You can drop off your mail at any post office, or it can be picked up for an extra fee. Deutsche Post works in cooperation with DHL. International carriers tend to be slightly cheaper (€35–€45 for the same letter) and provide more services.

Express Services Deutsche Post Express International (☎08105/345–2255 ⊕www. deutschepost.de). DHL (☎0800/225–5345 ⊕www.dhl.de). FedEx (☎0800/123–0800 ⊕www.fedex.com). UPS (☎0800/882–6630 ⊕www.ups.com).

▌MONEY

Credit cards are welcomed by most businesses, so you probably won't have to use cash for payment in high-end hotels and restaurants. Many businesses on the other end of the spectrum don't accept them, however. It's a good idea to check in advance if you're staying in a budget lodging or eating in a simple country inn. When you get large bills in euros, either from an exchange service or out of an ATM, it's a good idea to break them immediately so that you have smaller bills for unexpected expenses, such as paying restroom attendants.

Prices throughout this guide are given for adults. Substantially reduced fees are almost always available for children, students, and senior citizens.

▌TIP➜ Banks never have every foreign currency on hand, and it may take as long as a week to order. If you're planning to exchange funds before leaving home, don't wait till the last minute.

ATMS & BANKS

Twenty-four-hour ATMs (*Geldautomaten*) can be accessed with Plus or Cirrus credit and banking cards. Your own bank will probably charge a fee for using ATMs abroad, and some German banks exact €3–€5 fees for use of their ATMs. Nevertheless, you'll usually get a better rate of exchange via an ATM than you will at a currency-exchange office or even when changing money in a bank. And extracting funds as you need them is a safer option than carrying around a large amount of cash. Since some ATM keypads show no letters, know the numeric equivalent of your password.▌TIP➜ PIN numbers with more than four digits are not recognized at ATMs in many countries. If yours has five or more, remember to change it before you leave.

CREDIT CARDS

All major U.S. credit cards are accepted in Germany. The most frequently used are MasterCard and Visa. American Express is used less frequently, and Diner's Club even less. Since the credit-card companies demand fairly substantial fees, some businesses will not accept credit cards for small purchases. Cheaper restaurants and lodgings often do not accept credit cards. It's always a good idea to ask beforehand.

Throughout this guide, the following abbreviations are used: **AE**, American Express; **DC**, Diners Club; **MC**, MasterCard; and **V**, Visa.

It's a good idea to inform your credit-card company before you travel, especially if you're going abroad and don't travel internationally very often. Otherwise, the credit-card company might put a hold on your card owing to unusual activity—not a good thing halfway through your trip. Record all your credit-card numbers—as well as the phone numbers to call if your cards are lost or stolen—in a safe place, so you're prepared should something go wrong. Both MasterCard and Visa have general numbers you can call (collect if you're abroad) if your card is lost, but you're better off calling the number of your issuing bank, since MasterCard and Visa usually just transfer you to your bank; your bank's number is usually printed on your card.

If you plan to use your credit card for cash advances, you'll need to apply for a PIN at least two weeks before your trip. Although it's usually cheaper (and safer) to use a credit card abroad for large purchases (so you can cancel payments or be reimbursed if there's a problem), note that some credit-card companies *and* the banks that issue them add substantial percentages to all foreign transactions, whether they're in a foreign currency or not. Check on these fees before leaving home, so there won't be any surprises when you get the bill.

■TIP→ **Before you charge something, ask the merchant whether or not he or she plans to do a dynamic currency conversion (DCC). In such a transaction the credit-card** *processor* **(shop, restaurant, or hotel, not Visa or MasterCard) converts the currency and charges you in dollars. In most cases you'll pay the merchant a 3% fee for this service in addition to any credit-card company and issuing-bank foreign-transaction surcharges.**

Dynamic currency conversion programs are becoming increasingly widespread. Merchants who participate in them are supposed to ask whether you want to be charged in dollars or the local currency, but they don't always do so. And even if they do offer you a choice, they may well avoid mentioning the additional surcharges. The good news is that you *do* have a choice. And if this practice really gets your goat, you can avoid it entirely thanks to American Express; with its cards, DCC simply isn't an option.

Reporting Lost Cards American Express (☎800/992–3404 in U.S., 336/393–1111 collect from abroad ⊕www.americanexpress. com). **Diners Club** (☎800/234–6377 in U.S., 303/799–1504 collect from abroad ⊕www. dinersclub.com). **MasterCard** (☎800/622–7747 in U.S., 636/722–7111 collect from abroad ⊕www.mastercard.com). **Visa** (☎800/847–2911 in U.S., 410/581–9994 collect from abroad ⊕www.visa.com).

CURRENCY & EXCHANGE

Germany shares a common currency, the euro (€), with 15 other countries: Austria, Belgium, Cyprus, Finland, France, Greece, Ireland, Italy, Luxembourg, Malta, the Netherlands, Portugal, Slovenia, and Spain. The euro is divided into 100 cents. There are bills of 5, 10, 20, 50, 100, and 500 euros and coins of €1 and €2, and 1, 2, 5, 10, 20, and 50 cents.

You should have no problem exchanging currency. The large number of banks and exchange services means that you can shop around for the best rate, if you're so inclined. But the cheapest and easiest way to go is using your ATM card.

At this writing time, the exchange rate was €0.63 for a U.S. dollar. But the exchange rate changes daily. There are a number of handy Web sites that can help you find out how much your money is worth. Google does currency conversion; just type in the amount and how you want it converted (e.g., "100 dollars in euros"), and then voilà. Onada allows you to print out a handy table with the current day's conversion rates. XE also does currency conversion.

■TIP→ **Even if a currency-exchange booth has a sign promising no commission, rest assured that there's some kind of huge, hidden fee. (Oh…that's right. The sign didn't say no** *fee***.) And as for rates, you're almost always better off getting foreign currency at an ATM or exchanging money at a bank.**

Currency Conversion Google (⊕www. google.com). **Oanda.com** (⊕www.oanda.

com). **XE.com** (⊕ www.xe.com) is a good currency conversion Web site.

∎ PACKING

For visits to German cities, pack as you would for an American city: dressy outfits for formal restaurants and nightclubs, casual clothes elsewhere. Jeans are as popular in Germany as anywhere else, and are perfectly acceptable for sightseeing and informal dining. In the evening, men will probably feel more comfortable wearing a jacket in more expensive restaurants, although it's almost never required. Many German women wear stylish outfits to restaurants and the theater, especially in the larger cities.

Winters can be bitterly cold; summers are warm but with days that suddenly turn cool and rainy. In summer, take a warm jacket or heavy sweater if you are visiting the Bavarian Alps or the Black Forest, where the nights can be chilly even after hot days. Germans rarely wear shorts other than when engaging in sports, particularly in cities.

To discourage purse snatchers and pickpockets, carry a handbag with long straps that you can sling across your body bandolier style and with a zippered compartment for money and other valuables.

For stays in budget hotels, take your own soap. Many provide no soap at all or only a small bar.

∎ RESTROOMS

Public restrooms are found in large cities, although you are not guaranteed to find one in an emergency. If you are in need, there are several options. You can enter the next café or restaurant and ask very politely to use the facilities. You can find a department store and look for the "WC" sign. Museums are also a good place to find facilities.

Train stations are increasingly turning to McClean, a privately run enterprise that demands €0.60 to €1.10 for admission to its restrooms. These facilities, staffed by attendants who clean almost constantly, sparkle. You won't find them in smaller stations, however. Their restrooms are usually adequate.

On the highways, the vast majority of gas stations have public restrooms, though you may have to ask for a key—we won't vouch for their cleanliness. You might want to wait until you see a sign for a restaurant.

It's customary to leave a €0.20–€0.30 gratuity if a restroom has an attendant.

To read up on restrooms in advance of your trip, the Bathroom Diaries is flush with unsanitized info on restrooms the world over—each one located, reviewed, and rated.

Find a Loo The Bathroom Diaries (⊕ www. thebathroomdiaries.com).

∎ SAFETY

Germany has one of the lowest crime rates in Europe. There are some areas, such as the neighborhoods around train stations and the streets surrounding red-light districts, where you should keep an eye out for potential dangers. The best advice is to take the usual precautions. Secure your valuables in the hotel safe. Don't wear flashy jewelry, and keep expensive electronics out of sight when you are not using them. Carry shoulder bags or purses so that they can't be easily snatched, and never leave them hanging on the back of a chair at a café or restaurant. Avoid walking alone at night, even in relatively safe neighborhoods.

When withdrawing cash, don't use an ATM in a deserted area. Make sure that no one is looking over your shoulder when you enter your PIN code. And never use a machine that appears to have been tampered with.

■TIP➔ Distribute your cash, credit cards, IDs, and other valuables between a deep front pocket, an inside jacket or vest pocket, and a hidden money pouch. Don't reach for the money pouch once you're in public.

Contact **Transportation Security Administration** (TSA ⊕ www.tsa.gov).

■ TAXES

Most prices you see on items already include Germany's 19% value-added tax (V.A.T.). Some goods, such as books and antiquities, carry a 7% V.A.T. as a percentage of the purchase price. An item must cost at least €25 to qualify for a V.A.T. refund.

When making a purchase, ask for a V.A.T. refund form and find out whether the merchant gives refunds—not all stores do, nor are they required to. Have the form stamped like any customs form by customs officials when you leave the country or, if you're visiting several European Union countries, when you leave the EU. After you're through passport control, take the form to a refund-service counter for an on-the-spot refund (which is usually the quickest and easiest option), or mail it to the address on the form (or the envelope with it) after you arrive home. You receive the total refund stated on the form, but the processing time can be long, especially if you request a credit-card adjustment.

Global Refund is a Europe-wide service with 225,000 affiliated stores and more than 700 refund counters at major airports and border crossings. Its refund form, called a Tax Free Check, is the most common across the European continent. The service issues refunds in the form of cash, check, or credit-card adjustment.

V.A.T. REFUNDS AT THE AIRPORT

If you're departing from Terminal 1 at Frankfurt Airport, where you bring your purchases to claim your tax back depends on how you've packed the goods. If the

FODORS.COM CONNECTION

Before your trip, be sure to check out what other travelers are saying in Talk on ⊕ *www.fodors.com.*

items are in your checked luggage, check in as normal, but let the ticket counter know you have to claim your tax still. They will give you your luggage back to bring to the customs office in departure hall B, Level 2. For goods you are carrying on the plane with you, go to the customs office on the way to your gate. After you pass through passport control, there is a Global Refund office.

If you're departing from Terminal 2, bring goods in luggage to be checked to the customs office in Hall D, Level 2 (opposite the Delta Airlines check-in counters). For goods you are carrying on the plane with you, see the customs office in Hall E, Level 3 (near security control).

At Munich's airport, the Terminal 2 customs area is on the same level as check-in. If your V.A.T. refund items are in your luggage, check in first, and then bring your bags to the customs office on Level 04. From here your bags will be sent to your flight, and you can go to the Global Refund counter around the corner. If your refund items are in your carry-on, go to the Global Refund office in the customs area on Level 05 south. Terminal 1 has customs areas in modules C and D, Level 04.

V.A.T. Refunds **Global Refund** (☎ 800/566–9828 ⊕ www.globalrefund.com).

■ TIME

Germany is on Central European Time, which is six hours ahead of Eastern Standard Time and nine hours ahead of Pacific Standard Time. Daylight savings time begins on the last Sunday in October and ends on the last Sunday in March.

Timeanddate.com can help you figure out the correct time anywhere.

Germans use the 24-hour clock, or military time (1 PM is indicated as 13:00) and write the date before the month, so October 3 will appear as 03.10.

Time Zones **Timeanddate.com** (⊕ www.timeanddate.com/worldclock).

▌TIPPING

Tipping is done at your own discretion. Theater ushers and tour guides do not necessarily expect a tip, while waiters, bartenders, and taxi drivers do. Rounding off bills to the next highest sum is customary for bills under €10. Above that sum you should add a little more.

Service charges are included in all restaurant checks (listed as *Bedienung*), as is tax (listed as *MWST*). Nonetheless, it is customary to round up the bill to the nearest euro or to leave about 5%–10%. Give it to the waitstaff as you pay the bill; don't leave it on the table, as that's considered rude.

TIPPING GUIDELINES FOR GERMANY	
Bartender	Round up the bill for small purchases. For rounds of drinks, around 10% is appropriate.
Bellhop	€1 per item.
Hotel Concierge	€3–€5 if the concierge performs a special service for you.
Hotel Doorman	€1–€2 if he helps you get a cab.
Hotel Maid	€1 per day.
Hotel Room-Service Waiter	€1 per delivery.
Taxi Driver	Round up the fare if the ride is short. For longer trips, about €1 is appropriate.
Tour Guide	€1–€2, or a bit more if the tour was especially good.

TIPPING GUIDELINES FOR GERMANY	
Valet Parking Attendant	€1–€2, but only when you retrieve your car.
Waiter	Round off the bill, giving 5% to 10% for very good service.
Restroom Attendant	€0.20–€0.30 is fine for most places, but about €1 is expected in high-end establishments.

▌VISITOR INFORMATION

Local tourist offices are listed in the individual chapters. Staff at the smaller offices might not speak English. Many offices keep shorter hours than normal businesses, and you can expect some to close during weekday lunch hours and as early as noon on Friday. Almost all German cities and towns have an Internet presence under www.cityname.de, for example, ⊕ *www.naumburg.de*. The Internet portal Deutschland.de has lots of information about the country's best-known sights, as well as those that are often overlooked.

Contacts **German National Tourist Office** (☎ 212/661-7200 or 800/651-7010 ⊕ www. cometogermany.com). **Deutschland.de** (⊕ www.deutschland.de).

INDEX

NOTES

NOTES

NOTES

NOTES

NOTES

NOTES

ABOUT OUR WRITERS

Uli Ehrhardt, a native German, has had a long career in the travel and tourism fields. He began as an interpreter and travel consultant in the United States. He then worked for several years in Switzerland and Paris in the same capacity. Uli covered Munich, where he currently makes his home, and the Bodensee (Lake Constance), where he was director of the State Tourist Board and a teacher in the State College of Tourism for over 20 years. He also updated The Romantic Road, Franconia & the German Danube, and Heidelberg & the Neckar Valley chapters in this edition.

Lee A. Evans is originally from northeast Washington, but he calls his favorite city, Berlin, home. As the manager of the German Railroad's Eurail Aid Office, he has helped thousands of weary travelers discover Eastern Germany's hidden secrets. He is a contributing editor to *New Berlin Magazine* and a closet currywurst aficionado.

Jürgen Scheunemann grew up in Hamburg and fell in love with Berlin 21 years ago. He has written, published, and translated several history and travel books on U.S. and German cities, including *Fodor's Berlin*, and has been an editor at Berlin's leading daily, *Der Tagesspiegel*, and an associate producer for BBC Television. Today his award-winning articles are also published in U.S. magazines such as *Hemispheres*.

Ted Shoemaker was first sent to Germany as a U.S. Army officer. He met and married a German girl there, and they settled in Frankfurt after he left the service. For many years he has been active as a journalist there, editing three English-language magazines and acting as a correspondent for many American publications. He updated the Frankfurt, Rhineland, and Fairy-Tale Road chapters in this edition.

Tim Skelton was born in England, but has lived in the Netherlands since 1994, working as a freelance writer and editor. Whenever possible he likes to travel to nearby Cologne, to climb the Dom tower and to reward himself with a glass or two of the local *Kölsch*. For this edition Tim updated the Black Forest and Pfalz & Rhine Terrace chapters. He has also contributed to *Fodor's Amsterdam & the Netherlands* and *Fodor's Belgium*, and is the author of Bradt Travel Guide's *Luxembourg*.